Guide to Gale Literary Criticism Series

For criticism on	Consult these Gale series
Authors now living or who died after December 31, 1999	*CONTEMPORARY LITERARY CRITICISM (CLC)*
Authors who died between 1900 and 1999	*TWENTIETH-CENTURY LITERARY CRITICISM (TCLC)*
Authors who died between 1800 and 1899	*NINETEENTH-CENTURY LITERATURE CRITICISM (NCLC)*
Authors who died between 1400 and 1799	*LITERATURE CRITICISM FROM 1400 TO 1800 (LC)* *SHAKESPEAREAN CRITICISM (SC)*
Authors who died before 1400	*CLASSICAL AND MEDIEVAL LITERATURE CRITICISM (CMLC)*
Authors of books for children and young adults	*CHILDREN'S LITERATURE REVIEW (CLR)*
Dramatists	*DRAMA CRITICISM (DC)*
Poets	*POETRY CRITICISM (PC)*
Short story writers	*SHORT STORY CRITICISM (SSC)*
Literary topics and movements	*HARLEM RENAISSANCE: A GALE CRITICAL COMPANION (HR)* *THE BEAT GENERATION: A GALE CRITICAL COMPANION (BG)*
Asian American writers of the last two hundred years	*ASIAN AMERICAN LITERATURE (AAL)*
Black writers of the past two hundred years	*BLACK LITERATURE CRITICISM (BLC)* *BLACK LITERATURE CRITICISM SUPPLEMENT (BLCS)*
Hispanic writers of the late nineteenth and twentieth centuries	*HISPANIC LITERATURE CRITICISM (HLC)* *HISPANIC LITERATURE CRITICISM SUPPLEMENT (HLCS)*
Native North American writers and orators of the eighteenth, nineteenth, and twentieth centuries	*NATIVE NORTH AMERICAN LITERATURE (NNAL)*
Major authors from the Renaissance to the present	*WORLD LITERATURE CRITICISM, 1500 TO THE PRESENT (WLC)* *WORLD LITERATURE CRITICISM SUPPLEMENT (WLCS)*

Twentieth-Centu
Literary Criticis

ISSN 0276-8178

Volume 157

Twentieth-Century Literary Criticism

**Criticism of the
Works of Novelists, Poets, Playwrights,
Short Story Writers, and Other Creative Writers
Who Lived between 1900 and 1999,
from the First Published Critical
Appraisals to Current Evaluations**

Linda Pavlovski
Project Editor

THOMSON

GALE

Detroit • New York • San Francisco • San Diego • New Haven, Conn. • Waterville, Maine • London • Munich

Twentieth-Century Literary Criticism, Vol. 157

Project Editor
Linda Pavlovski

Editorial
Jessica Bomarito, Kathy D. Darrow, Jeffrey W. Hunter, Jelena O. Krstović, Michelle Lee, Ellen McGeagh, Joseph Palmisano, Thomas J. Schoenberg, Lawrence J. Trudeau, Russel Whitaker

Data Capture
Francis Monroe, Gwen Tucker

Indexing Services
Laurie Andriot

Rights and Acquisitions
Peg Ashlevitz, Edna Hedblad, Sue Rudolph

Imaging and Multimedia
Dean Dauphinais, Robert Duncan, Leitha Etheridge-Sims, Mary Grimes, Lezlie Light, Michael Logusz, Dan Newell, Kelly A. Quin, Denay Wilding

Composition and Electronic Capture
Kathy Sauer

Manufacturing
Rhonda Williams

Product Manager
Janet Witalec

LIBRARY OF CONGRESS CATALOG CARD NUMBER 76-46132

ISBN 0-7876-8911-4
ISSN 0276-8178

Printed in the United States of America
10 9 8 7 6 5 4 3 2 1

Contents

Preface vii

Acknowledgments xi

Literary Criticism Series Advisory Board xiii

Preface

Since its inception more than fifteen years ago, *Twentieth-Century Literary Criticism* (*TCLC*) has been purchased and used by nearly 10,000 school, public, and college or university libraries. *TCLC* has covered more than 500 authors, representing 58 nationalities and over 25,000 titles. No other reference source has surveyed the critical response to twentieth-century authors and literature as thoroughly as *TCLC*. In the words of one reviewer, "there is nothing comparable available." *TCLC* "is a gold mine of information—dates, pseudonyms, biographical information, and criticism from books and periodicals—which many librarians would have difficulty assembling on their own."

Scope of the Series

TCLC is designed to serve as an introduction to authors who died between 1900 and 1999 and to the most significant interpretations of these author's works. Volumes published from 1978 through 1999 included authors who died between 1900 and 1960. The great poets, novelists, short story writers, playwrights, and philosophers of the period are frequently studied in high school and college literature courses. In organizing and reprinting the vast amount of critical material written on these authors, *TCLC* helps students develop valuable insight into literary history, promotes a better understanding of the texts, and sparks ideas for papers and assignments. Each entry in *TCLC* presents a comprehensive survey on an author's career or an individual work of literature and provides the user with a multiplicity of interpretations and assessments. Such variety allows students to pursue their own interests; furthermore, it fosters an awareness that literature is dynamic and responsive to many different opinions.

Every fourth volume of *TCLC* is devoted to literary topics. These topics widen the focus of the series from the individual authors to such broader subjects as literary movements, prominent themes in twentieth-century literature, literary reaction to political and historical events, significant eras in literary history, prominent literary anniversaries, and the literatures of cultures that are often overlooked by English-speaking readers.

TCLC is designed as a companion series to Thomson Gale's *Contemporary Literary Criticism,* (*CLC*) which reprints commentary on authors who died after 1999. Because of the different time periods under consideration, there is no duplication of material between *CLC* and *TCLC*.

Organization of the Book

A *TCLC* entry consists of the following elements:

- The **Author Heading** cites the name under which the author most commonly wrote, followed by birth and death dates. Also located here are any name variations under which an author wrote, including transliterated forms for authors whose native languages use nonroman alphabets. If the author wrote consistently under a pseudonym, the pseudonym will be listed in the author heading and the author's actual name given in parenthesis on the first line of the biographical and critical information. Uncertain birth or death dates are indicated by question marks. Single-work entries are preceded by a heading that consists of the most common form of the title in English translation (if applicable) and the original date of composition.

- A **Portrait of the Author** is included when available.

- The **Introduction** contains background information that introduces the reader to the author, work, or topic that is the subject of the entry.

- The list of **Principal Works** is ordered chronologically by date of first publication and lists the most important works by the author. The genre and publication date of each work is given. In the case of foreign authors whose works have been translated into English, the English-language version of the title follows in brackets. Unless otherwise indicated, dramas are dated by first performance, not first publication.

- Reprinted **Criticism** is arranged chronologically in each entry to provide a useful perspective on changes in critical evaluation over time. The critic's name and the date of composition or publication of the critical work are given at the beginning of each piece of criticism. Unsigned criticism is preceded by the title of the source in which it appeared. All titles by the author featured in the text are printed in boldface type. Footnotes are reprinted at the end of each essay or excerpt. In the case of excerpted criticism, only those footnotes that pertain to the excerpted texts are included.

- A complete **Bibliographical Citation** of the original essay or book precedes each piece of criticism. Source citations in the Literary Criticism Series follow University of Chicago Press style, as outlined in *The Chicago Manual of Style,* 14th ed. (Chicago: The University of Chicago Press, 1993).

- Critical essays are prefaced by brief **Annotations** explicating each piece.

- An annotated bibliography of **Further Reading** appears at the end of each entry and suggests resources for additional study. In some cases, significant essays for which the editors could not obtain reprint rights are included here. Boxed material following the further reading list provides references to other biographical and critical sources on the author in series published by Thomson Gale.

Indexes

A **Cumulative Author Index** lists all of the authors that appear in a wide variety of reference sources published by Thomson Gale, including *TCLC.* A complete list of these sources is found facing the first page of the Author Index. The index also includes birth and death dates and cross references between pseudonyms and actual names.

A **Cumulative Nationality Index** lists all authors featured in *TCLC* by nationality, followed by the number of the *TCLC* volume in which their entry appears.

A **Cumulative Topic Index** lists the literary themes and topics treated in the series as well as in *Classical and Medieval Literature Criticism, Literature Criticism from 1400 to 1800, Nineteenth-Century Literature Criticism,* and the *Contemporary Literary Criticism* Yearbook, which was discontinued in 1998.

An alphabetical **Title Index** accompanies each volume of *TCLC.* Listings of titles by authors covered in the given volume are followed by the author's name and the corresponding page numbers where the titles are discussed. English translations of foreign titles and variations of titles are cross-referenced to the title under which a work was originally published. Titles of novels, dramas, nonfiction books, and poetry, short story, or essay collections are printed in italics, while individual poems, short stories, and essays are printed in roman type within quotation marks.

In response to numerous suggestions from librarians, Thomson Gale also produces a paperbound edition of the *TCLC* cumulative title index. This annual cumulation, which alphabetically lists all titles reviewed in the series, is available to all customers. Additional copies of this index are available upon request. Librarians and patrons will welcome this separate index; it saves shelf space, is easy to use, and is recyclable upon receipt of the next edition.

Citing *Twentieth-Century Literary Criticism*

When citing criticism reprinted in the Literary Criticism Series, students should provide complete bibliographic information so that the cited essay can be located in the original print or electronic source. Students who quote directly from reprinted criticism may use any accepted bibliographic format, such as University of Chicago Press style or Modern Language Association (MLA) style. Both the MLA and the University of Chicago formats are acceptable and recognized as being the current standards for citations. It is important, however, to choose one format for all citations; do not mix the two formats within a list of citations.

The examples below follow recommendations for preparing a bibliography set forth in *The Chicago Manual of Style,* 14th ed. (Chicago: The University of Chicago Press, (1993); the first example pertains to material drawn from periodicals, the second to material reprinted from books:

Morrison, Jago. "Narration and Unease in Ian McEwan's Later Fiction." *Critique* 42, no. 3 (spring 2001): 253-68. Reprinted in *Twentieth-Century Literary Criticism.* Vol. 127, edited by Janet Witalec, 212-20. Detroit: Gale, 2003.

Brossard, Nicole. "Poetic Politics." In *The Politics of Poetic Form: Poetry and Public Policy,* edited by Charles Bernstein, 73-82. New York: Roof Books, 1990. Reprinted in *Twentieth-Century Literary Criticism.* Vol. 127, edited by Janet Witalec, 3-8. Detroit: Gale, 2003.

The examples below follow recommendations for preparing a works cited list set forth in the *MLA Handbook for Writers of Research Papers,* 5th ed. (New York: The Modern Language Association of America, 1999); the first example pertains to material drawn from periodicals, the second to material reprinted from books:

Morrison, Jago. "Narration and Unease in Ian McEwan's Later Fiction." *Critique* 42.3 (spring 2001): 253-68. Reprinted in *Twentieth-Century Literary Criticism.* Ed. Janet Witalec. Vol. 127. Detroit: Gale, 2003. 212-20.

Brossard, Nicole. "Poetic Politics." *The Politics of Poetic Form: Poetry and Public Policy.* Ed. Charles Bernstein. New York: Roof Books, 1990. 73-82. Reprinted in *Twentieth-Century Literary Criticism.* Ed. Janet Witalec. Vol. 127. Detroit: Gale, 2003. 3-8.

Suggestions are Welcome

Readers who wish to suggest new features, topics, or authors to appear in future volumes, or who have other suggestions or comments are cordially invited to call, write, or fax the Product Manager:

Product Manager, Literary Criticism Series
Thomson Gale
27500 Drake Road
Farmington Hills, MI 48331-3535
1-800-347-4253 (GALE)
Fax: 248-699-8054

Acknowledgments

The editors wish to thank the copyright holders of the criticism included in this volume and the permissions managers of many book and magazine publishing companies for assisting us in securing reproduction rights. We are also grateful to the staffs of the Detroit Public Library, the Library of Congress, the University of Detroit Mercy Library, Wayne State University Purdy/Kresge Library Complex, and the University of Michigan Libraries for making their resources available to us. Following is a list of the copyright holders who have granted us permission to reproduce material in this volume of *TCLC*. Every effort has been made to trace copyright, but if omissions have been made, please let us know.

COPYRIGHTED MATERIAL IN *TCLC*, VOLUME 157, WAS REPRODUCED FROM THE FOLLOWING PERIODICALS:

American Literary History, v. 12, fall, 2000 for "Jazz Fractures: F. Scott Fitzgerald and Epochal Representation" by Mitchell Breitwieser. Copyright © 2000 Oxford University Press. Reproduced by permission of the publisher and the author.—*American Studies,* v. 40, spring, 1999. Copyright © Mid-America American Studies Association, 1999. Reprinted by permission of the publisher.—*Critical Quarterly,* v. 18, spring, 1976. Reproduced by permission of Blackwell Publishers.—*English Language Notes,* v. 25, December, 1987. Copyright © 1987, Regents of the University of Colorado. Reproduced by permission.—*The Explicator,* v. 59, fall, 2000; v. 60, fall, 2001. Copyright © 2000, 2001 by Helen Dwight Reid Educational Foundation. Both reproduced with permission of the Helen Dwight Reid Educational Foundation, published by Heldref Publications, 1319 18th Street, NW, Washington, DC 20036-1802.—*Gurdjieff International Review,* v. 2, spring, 1999. Copyright © 1969 Traditional Studies Press. Copyright © 1999 Gurdjieff Electronic Publishing. Reproduced by permission.—*Journal of American Studies,* v. 32, December, 1998. Copyright © Cambridge University Press 1998. Reprinted with the permission of Cambridge University Press.—*Journal of Dramatic Theory and Criticism,* v. 11, spring, 1997 for "Ortonesque/Carnivalesque: The Grotesque Realism of Joe Orton" by Grant Stirling; v. 15, spring, 2001 for "Joe Orton: A High Comedy of Bad Manners" by Joel Greenberg. Copyright © 1997, 2001 by the Joyce and Elizabeth Hall Center for the Humanities and the Department of Theatre and Film at the University of Kansas, Lawrence, Kansas 66045, U.S.A. Both reproduced by permission of the respective authors.—*Journal of Modern Literature,* v. 24, fall, 2000. Copyright © Indiana University Press, 2001. Reproduced by permission.—*Lambda Book Report,* v. 8, December 1999 for "Ruining Civilization" by Richard Helfer. Reproduced by permission of the author.—*Modern Austrian Literature,* v. 25, 1992. Copyright © International Arthur Schnitzler Research Association, 1992. Reproduced by permission.—*Modern Fiction Studies,* v. 38, autumn, 1992; v. 46, winter, 2000. Copyright © 1992, 2000 by Purdue Research Foundation, West Lafayette, IN 47907. All rights reserved. Both reproduced by permission of The Johns Hopkins University.—*Neophilologus,* v. 76, January, 1992 for "Georges Kien and the 'Diagnosis of Delusion' in Elias Canetti's *Die Blendung*" by Peter Morgan. Reproduced by permission of the author.—*The New Republic,* v. 200, April, 1989. Copyright © 1989 by *The New Republic,* Inc. Reproduced by permission of *The New Republic.*—*New Theatre Quarterly,* v. 4, November 1988 for "Entertaining Mr. Loney: An Early Interview with Joe Orton" by Glenn Loney. Reproduced by permission of the author.—*New York,* v. 22, December 18, 1989. Copyright © 1989 PRIMEDIA Magazine Corporation. All rights reserved. Reproduced with the permission of *New York* Magazine.—*The New York Review of Books,* v. 34, September 1987. Copyright © 1987 by NYREV, Inc. Reproduced with permission from *The New York Review of Books.*—*Orbis Litterarum,* v. 48, 1993; v. 54, 1999. Copyright © 1993, 1999 Munksgaard International Publishers, Ltd. All rights reserved. Both reproduced by permission of Blackwell Publishers Ltd.—*Paideuma,* v. 17, spring, 1988 for "'A Profounder Didacticism': Ruskin, Orage and Pound's Perception of Social Credit" by Michael Coyle. Copyright © 1988 by the National Poetry Foundation, Inc. Reproduced by permission of the author.—*Papers on Language & Literature,* v. 20, spring, 1984. Copyright © 1984 by The Board of Trustees, Southern Illinois University at Edwardsville. Reproduced by permission.—*Partisan Review,* v. LXVII, fall, 2000 for "The Power of Elias Canetti" by Eugene Goodheart. Copyright © 2000 by *Partisan Review,* Inc. Reproduced by permission of the author.—*Publications of the Arkansas Philological Association,* v. 10, fall, 1984. Reproduced by permission.—*Publishers Weekly,* v. 231, June, 1987. Copyright © 1987 by Reed Publishing USA. Reproduced from *Publishers Weekly,* published by the Bowker Magazine Group of Cahners Publishing Co., a division of Reed Publishing USA., by permission.—*The Sewanee Review,* v. 105, summer, 1997. Copyright © 1997 by Jeffrey Hart. Reproduced with the permission of the editor and the author.—*The Spectator,* v. 281, November 7, 1998. Copyright © 1998 by *The Spectator.* Reproduced by permission of *The Spectator.*—*Studies in the Novel,* v. 29, winter, 1997. Copyright © 1997 by North Texas State University. Reproduced by permission.—*Texas Studies in Literature and Language,* v. 31, winter, 1989 for "'Uncommunicable Forever': Nick's Dilemma in *The Great Gatsby*" by Caren J. Town. Copyright © 1989 by the University of Texas Press. All rights reserved. Reproduced by permission of the publisher and the author.—*Textual Practice,* v. 4, summer, 1990. Reproduced

COPYRIGHTED MATERIAL IN *TCLC,* VOLUME 157, WAS REPRODUCED FROM THE FOLLOWING BOOKS:

PHOTOGRAPHS AND ILLUSTRATIONS APPEARING IN *TCLC,* VOLUME 157, WERE RECEIVED FROM THE FOLLOWING SOURCES:

Thomson Gale Literature Product Advisory Board

The members of the Thomson Gale Literature Product Advisory Board—reference librarians from public and academic library systems—represent a cross-section of our customer base and offer a variety of informed perspectives on both the presentation and content of our literature products. Advisory board members assess and define such quality issues as the relevance, currency, and usefulness of the author coverage, critical content, and literary topics included in our series; evaluate the layout, presentation, and general quality of our printed volumes; provide feedback on the criteria used for selecting authors and topics covered in our series; provide suggestions for potential enhancements to our series; identify any gaps in our coverage of authors or literary topics, recommending authors or topics for inclusion; analyze the appropriateness of our content and presentation for various user audiences, such as high school students, undergraduates, graduate students, librarians, and educators; and offer feedback on any proposed changes/enhancements to our series. We wish to thank the following advisors for their advice throughout the year.

Elias Canetti
1905-1994

Bulgarian-born Swiss novelist, aphorist, autobiographer, and nonfiction writer.

The following entry provides criticism on Canetti's works from 1962 through 2001. For criticism prior to 1962, see *CLC*, Volumes 3, 14, 25, 75; and for an obituary entry on Canetti, see *CLC*, Volume 86.

INTRODUCTION

The recipient of the 1981 Nobel Prize for literature, Canetti is best known for his novel *Die Blendung* (1935-36; *Auto-da-Fé*) and his treatise on mass behavior, *Masse und Macht* (1960; *Crowds and Power*). Both of these works probe the ways in which individuals are affected by participation in a group. More recent critical attention has focused on Canetti's plays and his three-volume autobiography. While often criticized for the unscientific methods and subjective conclusions presented in his writings, Canetti is recognized for his insightful analysis of crowd psychology and vivid depictions of crowd phenomena as well as for his portrait, in his autobiography, of twentieth-century European intellectual life.

BIOGRAPHICAL INFORMATION

Canetti was born on July 25, 1905, in Rutschuk (now Ruse), Bulgaria, to parents who were descendants of the Sephardic Jews of Spain. Because of this heritage, he was exposed to numerous languages early in his life, namely Bulgarian, Hebrew, and Ladino, a fifteenth-century patois of Spanish and Hebrew spoken in his family's home and in the Sephardic community. Canetti's parents were ardent students of German literature and spoke to each other in German when they did not want their children to understand their conversations; remembering his fascination with the air of mystery that he perceived in these discussions, Canetti later adopted German as the language of his intellectual and literary pursuits. In 1911 the Canetti family moved to London. When his father died suddenly in 1912, his mother moved the family first to Vienna and then to other cities in the German-speaking countries of Europe. Fearing that he would become "soft" without the guidance of a father, Canetti's mother taught him German and pressured him to study chemistry, deriding his

growing interest in literature and writing. During the 1920s he immersed himself in the cultural life of Berlin and Vienna, where he met such figures as satirist Karl Kraus, artist George Grosz, and novelists Robert Musil, Hermann Broch, and Thomas Mann. In 1922 Canetti joined a demonstration in reaction to the murder of the German-Jewish industrialist Walter Rathenau, and in 1927 he was part of a crowd that burned down the Vienna Palace of Justice while protesting the acquittal of men indicted for killing workers in the Austrian province of Burgenland. These events confirmed in him the desire to make a life's work of the study of mass psychology. After receiving his doctorate in chemistry from the University of Vienna in 1929, Canetti produced his first and only novel, *Auto-da-Fé*. During the 1930s he translated the writings of Upton Sinclair into German and completed one play, *Die Hochzeit* (1965; *The Wedding*), before fleeing to England after the annexation of Austria by Germany and the anti-Semitic violence of Krystallnacht. Canetti continued to write in German during his wartime exile in England, devoting his time to works such as *Crowds and Power*. In ensuing decades, Canetti divided his time between Hampstead, England, and Zurich, and published essays, aphorisms, and three volumes of autobiography. When he was awarded the Nobel Prize for literature, Bulgaria, England, and Austria all claimed him as their own. Canetti died in Zurich on August 14, 1994, and is buried there next to the grave of Irish modernist novelist James Joyce.

MAJOR WORKS

Canetti's only novel, which he intended to be the first installment of an eight-volume novel series entitled "The Human Comedy of Madmen," *Auto-da-Fé* details the ruination of Peter Kien, a world-renowned sinologist whose life revolves around his 25,000-volume library. Kien is obsessed with his books, which he regards as companions. The other major characters in the novel also exhibit obsessions that dominate their lives: Kien's housekeeper, Therese Krumbholz, is preoccupied with satisfying her appetites for money and sex; Benedikt Pfaff, the manager of Kien's apartment house, with seizing money and power; and the dwarf Fischerle with becoming a wealthy and famous chess champion. *Auto-da-Fé* satirizes the greed, cruelty, and intolerance of each of these individuals, who all readily join in the persecution of one another and at the same time are themselves victimized.

Crowds and Power, which Canetti worked on for thirty years, draws on the resources of his erudition in numerous fields, including literature, anthropology, and science, in an attempt to explain the origins, behavior, and significance of crowds as forces in society. Organized as a large volume of brief, aphoristic essays explaining various aspects and examples of mass psychology, the book scrutinizes crowds and crowd phenomena found in nature, mythology, and history. In an effort to take a fresh look at his subject, Canetti created his own terminology for discussing mass phenomena, disregarded modern scientific study of crowds, and ignored important contemporary examples of crowd behavior and manipulators, most notably nazism and Adolf Hitler. However, because Canetti avoided scientific techniques and language, his study is highly original in its approach and accessible to most readers.

Although Canetti's plays are generally considered difficult, if not impossible, to produce on stage, they have begun to receive more critical attention in recent years. Throughout his career, Canetti considered himself first and foremost a dramatist. In his plays—*The Wedding, Die Befristeten* (1956; *The Numbered*), and *Die Komödie der Eitelkeit* (1965; *The Comedy of Vanity*)—Canetti extended his interest in character type to types of social life. This connected his plays with his anthropological pursuits. But whereas in *Crowds and Power* he had intended an inventory of the human condition, in his dramas he was engaged in the exploration of unrealized possibilities of human existence.

Collections of Canetti's essays, sketches, and aphorisms, as well as his autobiographical trilogy, have garnered more significant attention of late, particularly his connections to and observations of Friedrich Nietzsche and Franz Kafka.

CRITICAL RECEPTION

Critics have by turns praised and scorned Canetti's examination of the psychology of crowds because its scholarship is unscientific and it draws conclusions without the support of arguments or empirical proof. Furthermore, some contend that *Auto-da-Fé* is little more than a biting satire of dementia. Nevertheless, many commentators praise the book for its treatment of the dual nature of human beings as both individuals and members of a group. Critical examination of Canetti's works also focuses on the question of Canetti's interpretation of such figures as the anti-Semitic, misogynist Otto Weininger, Nietzsche, and Kafka.

PRINCIPAL WORKS

Die Blendung [*Auto-da-Fé*] (novel) 1935-36
Fritz Wotruba (criticism) 1955

Die Befristeten [*The Numbered*] (play) 1956; also published as *Life-Terms*, 1983
Masse und Macht [*Crowds and Power*] (nonfiction) 1960
Dramen (plays) 1964
Aufzeichnungen 1942-1948 (aphorisms) 1965
Die Hochzeit [*The Wedding*] (play) 1965
Die Komödie der Eitelkeit [*The Comedy of Vanity*] (play) 1965
Die Stimmen von Marrakesch: Aufzeichnungen nach einer Reise [*The Voices of Marrakesh: A Record of a Visit*] (travel essay) 1967
Der andere Prozeß: Kafkas Briefe an Felice [*Kafka's Other Trial: The Letters to Felice*] (criticism) 1969
Alle vergeudete Verehrung: Aufzeichnungen 1949-1960 (aphorisms) 1970
Die gespaltene Zukunft: Aufsätze und Gespräche (essays) 1972
Macht und Überleben: Drei Essays (essays) 1972
Die Provinz des Menschen: Aufzeichnungen 1942-1972 [*The Human Province*] (aphorisms) 1973
Der Ohrenzeuge: Fünfzig: Charaktere [*Earwitness: Fifty Characters*] (sketches) 1974
Das Gewissen der Worte [*The Conscience of Words*] (essays) 1975
Die gerettete Zunge: Geschichte einer Jugend [*The Tongue Set Free: Remembrance of a European Childhood*] (autobiography) 1977
Die Fackel im Ohr: Lebensgeschichte 1921-1931 [*The Torch in My Ear*] (autobiography) 1980
Das Augenspiel: Lebensgeschichte 1931-1937 [*The Play of the Eyes*] (autobiography) 1985
Das Geheimherz der Uhr: Aufzeichnungen 1973-1985 [*The Secret Heart of the Clock: Notes, Aphorisms, Fragments 1973-1985*] (aphorisms) 1987
Die Fliegenpein [*The Agony of Flies*] (sketches, notes, and aphorisms) 1992
Nachtage aus Hampstead: Aus den Aufzeichnungen, 1954-1971 [*Notes from Hampstead: The Writer's Notes*] (notebook) 1994
Aufzeichnungen 1992-1993 (aphorisms) 1996
The Memoirs of Elias Canetti (memoirs) 1999

CRITICISM

Theodor Adorno and Elias Canetti (interview date 1962)

SOURCE: Adorno, Theodor, and Elias Canetti. "Elias Canetti: Discussion with Theodor W. Adorno." *Thesis Eleven*, no. 45 (1996): 1-15.

[*In the following interview, originally conducted in 1962, Canetti and Adorno discuss psychoanalysis and crowd psychology.*]

[Adorno]: *I know that in many respects you differ strongly from Freud and are very critical toward him. In one methodological respect, however, you are surely in agreement with what he often emphasized, above all when psychoanalysis was still in its formative stage and had not yet become something completely reified, that he had no intention of rejecting or disputing the results of other established sciences but wanted to add what they had neglected. This neglect and its causes he considered extremely essential, since it possesses a crucial character for human life together, just as is the case for you. You could, I believe, elucidate this best through the central importance that the question of death plays in your work, as it does also for many, in the widest sense, anthropological works today. Precisely in relation to this death complex—if I can speak in such a pompous way of this most elementary fact—you could give our listeners an idea, a model of what this neglected dimension actually is, and what aspects in the experience of death for instance have special value for you, so that we can gain insight into the fruitfulness of your method and recognize that it is not only a question of things which are scarcely reflected but of the dangers of their self-evident acceptance, which you want to bring to consciousness and defuse in the spirit of enlightenment.*

[Canetti]: It is, I think, completely correct that the consideration of death plays a major role in my investigation. If I am to give an example of what you referred to, then it would be the question of survival, which in my opinion has been far too little considered. The moment in which a human being survives another is a *concrete* moment, and I believe that the experience of this moment has very grave consequences. I think that this experience is covered up by convention, by what one *should* be feeling when the death of another human being is experienced, but behind this a certain feeling of satisfaction lies hidden and from this feeling of satisfaction, which can even be triumph—as in the case of a combat—something very dangerous can come, if it occurs more frequently and accumulates. This dangerously accumulated experience of the death of another human being is, I believe, a very essential germ of power. I give this example only abruptly and without going into it more closely. As you speak of Freud—I am the first to admit that the innovative way in which Freud approached things, without allowing himself to be distracted or frightened, made a deep impression on me in my formative period. It is certainly the case that I am now no longer convinced of some of his results and must oppose some of his special theories. But for the way he tackled things, I still have the deepest respect.

Precisely at this point which you just raised, I would like to register that there is a very strong contact between us. In the Dialectic of Enlightenment *Horkheimer and I analyzed the problem of self-preservation, of self-preserving reason and discovered in the process that this principle of self-preservation which finds its first classic formulation in the philosophy of Spinoza, and which you call in your terminology the moment of survival, that is, the situation of survival in the exact sense that this motif of self-preservation, when it becomes as it were "wild", when it loses any relation to others, is transformed into a destructive force. You did not know our work and we did not know yours. I believe that our agreement here is not by chance but points to what has become acute in the crisis of the contemporary situation, which is after all the very crisis of a wild self-preservation, a wild survival.*

I am pleased to hear that your own thinking has led to similar results and that the fact of our independence adds to their cogency.

I think so too. On the other hand, however, there is a methodological problem which is important for our intention of determining the place of your thinking. For a thinker like myself, whether he calls himself a philosopher or a sociologist, what strikes me first of all about your book, and what is—if I may say so openly—something of a scandal, is what I would call the subjectivity of your approach. By subjectivity I do not mean the subjectivity of thought, the subjectivity of the author—on the contrary: precisely the freedom of a subjectivity, which does not tie thinking in advance to the approved rules of the sciences and does not respect the boundaries imposed by the division of labour, is enormously sympathetic to me—but I mean by subjectivity the point of departure from the subjects under investigation, put more sharply, the point of departure from forms of representation (Vorstellungsweisen). I am very conscious that you derive, moreover, not so very differently from Freud, the basic concepts you employ—crowds and power—ultimately from real conditions, just as I would, that is, from real crowds and real powers, from experiences of the real. Nevertheless, the reader cannot quite shake off the feeling that in the development of your book the imagination—the representation of these concepts or facts, the two go together—is in fact of a greater significance than they are themselves: for instance, the concept of invisible crowds, which plays a major role for you, points to this. And I would like to put the really simple question to you to give our listeners a clearer idea of what is actually involved—how do [you] evaluate the real significance of crowds and of power or the bearers of power in relation to the inner representation, in relation to the images, analysis would say, the imagines *of the crowd and power, with which you are concerned?*

I would like to take some time to answer this question. You refer to my concept of invisible crowds. Here I would like to say that invisible crowds only appear in the short chapter 14 of my book, which is preceded by 13 other chapters, in which I deal with the real crowd very intensively. The concept of the book is, I believe, as real as it can be. I begin with what I call the fear of being touched. I think that the individual human being feels threatened by others and has for this reason an anxiety about being touched by something unknown, and that he seeks to protect himself by all means from being touched by the unknown by creating distances around himself, by striving not to come into too close contact with other human beings. All human beings have experienced this, that you try not to jostle against others, that you do not like being jostled by others. In spite of all preventative measures human beings never lose completely their fear of being touched. What is remarkable is that this fear disappears completely in the crowd. It is a really important paradox. Human beings only lose their fear of being touched when they stand closely packed together in a crowd, when they are surrounded on all sides by other human beings, so that they no longer know who is pressing against them. At this moment the individual no longer fears contact with others. His fear of being touched reverses into the opposite; I believe that one of the reasons why people like to become a crowd, like to become part of the crowd, is the relief they feel at this reversal of the fear of being touched. I think this is a very concrete approach; it starts from a concrete experience which everybody knows from the crowd. Now, in the following chapters I examine other aspects of the real crowd. I speak of open and closed crowds. I stress that crowds always want to grow, that this compulsion to grow is decisive for them. I talk about the feeling of equality within the crowd and many other things which I do not want to mention now. Then in chapter 14 I come to the concept of invisible crowds, about which I would perhaps like to say something briefly: for anyone who has occupied himself with religions, and especially with primitive religions, it is very striking the extent to which these religions are peopled by crowds, which human beings cannot actually see. We need only think of the spirits which play such a role in primitive religions. There are countless examples of the human belief that the whole air is filled by these spirits, that these spirits occur in massed forms—this carries over into our universal religion. We know the role that the idea of the devil, of angels played in Christendom. There are very many testimonies in the Middle Ages. Devils are thought to occur in endless crowds. A medieval Cistercian abbot, Richelin, stated that when he closed his eyes he sensed devils around him as thick as dust. These invisible crowds play a major role in religions and in the conceptions of believers. I would not for this reason regard them as unreal, since these people do in fact believe in these crowds, for them they are something wholly real. In order to understand this fully, we need only recall that in the modern world we also know such invisible crowds. They are no longer devils, but they are perhaps just as dangerous and aggressive and are feared by us just as much. After

all we all believe in the existence of bacilli. Only very few people have looked in a microscope and actually seen them but we all assume that we are threatened by millions of bacilli, which are always there, which can be everywhere, and our representation of them plays an important role.

These would be invisible crowds, which in a certain sense I would call real; I believe that you would concede that we can speak here of a kind of reality of these invisible crowds.

Please excuse the pedantry of an epistemologist in my reply. First of all, there is a difference between primitive consciousness, which does not yet distinguish so strictly between reality and representation, and the developed Western consciousness which rests in fact on this separation. The fact that in archaic thinking, in primitive thinking no distinction is yet made between the imagination of such djinns, or whatever spirits it may be, and their real existence does not mean that they have become objectively real. We cannot jump over our own shadow, which tells us in God's name that the world is not peopled by spirits. And for that reason I would say, according to what you have said so far, that a certain primacy of the imaginative, of the transposition into the world of representation is dominant with you in relation to drastic unmediated reality, since I do not believe—this is perhaps not unimportant for clarifying your intentions—I do not believe that you espouse the position represented by Klages on the one hand and by Oskar Goldberg at the other extreme, namely that these images, these imagines *possess as collective entities a direct reality, comparable for example with the reality of the masses in modern mass society.*

No, I certainly would not say that. Nevertheless, I have arrived at the establishment of a concept, which seems important to me: the concept of crowd symbols. By crowd symbols I understand collective units, which admittedly do not consist of human beings but which are nevertheless felt as crowds. To these units belong representations like fire, the ocean, the forest, wheat, the treasure, heaps of many kinds,—for example, heaps of the harvested. Now these are surely units which actually exist; they are used in the mind of the individual as crowd symbols. It is necessary to explore these individual symbols and show why they have this function and what significance they acquire in this function. In order to give a practical example, I would say that these crowd symbols had decisive importance for the formation of national consciousness.

Absolutely!

When human beings who identify themselves with a nation at an acute moment of national existence, let us say, define themselves as English or French or German at the beginning of a war, then they think of a crowd or a crowd symbol as that to which they relate. And this has an extremely powerful effect in their minds and is of the greatest importance for their actions. You would, I think, perhaps go this far with me in seeing the undeniable effectivity of such crowd symbols, present in the individual.

Here I agree with you completely. I think that with your discovery of the forest, for example, as an imago, *as a crowd symbol you have hit on something really essential. I consider these things eminently fruitful. Compared with the somewhat bare archaic symbols we find in Freud and on the other hand the somewhat arbitrary archetypes of Jung, it seems to me that such categories represent a real advance. But may I also say: even after this explanation, in which the concept of the symbol is not by chance central, it still remains the case that your interest is directed to categories which have already been internalized, already transposed into the imagination. What I would like to ask you is something very simple and straightforward—a question also to be put analogously to psychoanalytically oriented social theory—namely whether you believe that these symbols are really crucial for the problematic of contemporary society, which is your primary concern no less than mine. Or are the real, the actual masses, that is, simply the enormous pressure exerted by the gigantic numbers of human beings (even though the organization of society simultaneously supports and hinders the preservation of life)—is not the pressure of these real masses on political decision-making more important for contemporary society than these imaginary, in a wider sense social-psychological, matters to which you refer? Let us not forget that it turned out that even movements, which were apparently extreme dictatorships without any democratic consideration for popular opinion, such as Fascism and National Socialism, always latently possessed what the sociologist Arkadi Gurland has called a compromise character, that is to say, even in these forms of domination and tyrannization of the masses consideration of the real interest of the masses and of their real existence always asserted itself, even if in a hidden way. What really concerns me—to which you could perhaps reply—is this: how do you actually evaluate, in your conception of society and the crowd, the weight, this real weight of the masses in relation to the whole realm of the symbolic?*

Yes, I would of course say that the value, the significance of the real masses is incomparably greater. I would not hesitate for a moment, I would in fact go as far as to say that the dictatorships we have experienced are made up entirely of crowds, that without the growth of crowds, which is especially important, and without the deliberate artificial excitation of ever larger crowds, the power of dictatorships would be completely unthinkable. This fact is the starting point of my whole investigation. A contemporary of the events of the last 50 years since the outbreak of World War One, who has experienced first wars, then revolutions, inflations and then fascist dictatorship, cannot help feeling the necessity under the pressure of these events of trying to come to terms with the question of crowds. I would be very disappointed if the fact, that in the course of a investigation over many years I had arrived at other aspects of the crowd, should lead anyone to think that the real meaning of crowds is not decisive and above all important for me.

This seems to me of fundamental importance for a proper understanding of your intention. If I may make a theoretical point, it would be that a kind of mediation, not in the sense of compromise but of the Hegelian concept of mediation, should be assumed: precisely the real pressure, as you quite rightly recognize, of the deeply entwined categories, crowds and power, has increased to such an extent that the resistance, the self-assertion of the individual has become infinitely difficult. The symbolic significance of these categories has thus also increased, such that human beings retreat as it were back into archaic phases of their psychic world, where these internalized categories acquire a bodily meaning and are completely identified with. It is presumably only through the growth of these two correlative categories that human beings have come to resign themselves to their own disempowerment, by giving them meaning as something numinous, perhaps even irrational and therefore holy. To this extent I think there exists a connection between the growing symbolic significance of these things and their reality. However, I would like to stress a nuance: and that is, what then returns under pressure, namely the symbolic and the irrational, is not directly what it once was, but is now, I would say, a kind of result, made up of the real situation of human beings and of the world of images, to which they recur or even regress. It seems to me that the fatal, deadly threatening colouring which concepts like leader or crowd so readily take on today, especially when they are short-circuited, comes from the fact that we are no longer dealing with the original circumstances in which they were effective; now they are invoked as it were, and what is invoked from a distant past no longer possesses any truth but is transformed into a kind of poison through its untruth in the present.

There is much that needs to be said here about the details, where I would correct you in terms of my position. But by and large I would agree with you. I would say perhaps that one of the essential points—a point which always recurs when we consider crowds today—are the archaic elements we find in them. I do not know whether you agree with me that one must pay special attention to these archaic elements as something particularly important. It is not possible to investigate the crowd only as it appears today, even though it appears clearly enough and in multiple form. I believe it is also important to derive it from what has long been there and has often appeared in different forms.

I would of course agree with you. The archaism, which emerges in crowd formation, has been repeatedly recognized in the tradition of modern social psychology—first of all by Gustave Le Bon in his Psychology of Crowds, *where he described precisely these archaic, irrational modes of behaviour in crowds and then derived them from the somewhat problematic and vague category of suggestion, and then by Freud, who in his, in my opinion, very significant short work* Group Psychology and Analysis of the Ego *set out to underpin Le Bon's description of crowds with a genetic-psychological derivation. Since you stand in dispute with this after all very considerable tradition of social thought—to which the American sociologist McDougall also belongs—it would be good, in the interest of a topological determination of your thinking, if you could indicate the specific differences of your own theory to these authors.*

First of all I would like to go back to the question of the form which the crowd takes in primitive societies, as it is quite clear that primitive societies, which consist of only very few persons, cannot lead to the crowd formations which we know today.

I have been wanting to raise this very question: can we even speak of crowds in primitive societies, where there were precious few persons? I am glad that you brought this up.

Here, I think, we need to introduce a new concept. I speak of the pack, and by the pack I mean a small group of human beings in a special state of excitement, which is closely related to the state of excitement of our modern crowds but which is different in that it is limited as opposed to the unlimited growth of our crowds. Packs occur in societies which consist of small groups, some of only 10, 20, 30 human beings, who wander in search of food. The famous models in the ethnological literature for such small groups are the bands of the Australian aborigines. What is striking is that out of these bands, under certain conditions of life, small excited groups form, which have a powerful goal and seek this goal with great energy and in extreme excitement. One kind of these bands is for example the hunting pack. There is a very large animal which individuals cannot master; several must come together in order to hunt down this animal, or the appearance of a large number of animals is involved. They want to hunt down as many as possible, they do not want them to escape, they could disappear again or a time of drought could return and there would be very few animals. For this reason they come together and set out to hunt the one or many animals. The concept of the hunting pack is so

evident that we do not need to say much about it. The second pack—which is also obvious—is the one directed against another pack, and this brings us to the war pack. Where there are two packs which threaten each other, then something emerges which we know now from war in sharply increased, indeed enormous dimensions. This situation, however, is already there in early societies: when one pack fights against another. The third form, which is not so evident, is what I have called, perhaps for the first time, a lamenting pack. When a small group loses a member, when a member is torn from them through death, then the group usually comes together to take cognizance in some way of this death. At first they try to hold back, to keep the dying person in the group; when he has died they will turn to some rite, which removes him from the group, which reconciles him with his fate, which prevents him from becoming a dangerous enemy of the group. There are innumerable very important ceremonies and there is scarcely a people on earth which does not know them. All these connected phenomena I term lamenting packs. Now we come to the fourth form of the pack, which is perhaps the most interesting for us: human beings, who existed in very small numbers, always wanted to be more. If they were more, they could hunt more. If they were more, they could maintain themselves better against another group attacking them. There are innumerable rites and ceremonies which serve increase. Increase does not only mean increase of human beings but also the increase of the animals and plants from which they live. Everything connected with this I term increase packs.

These four forms of the pack seem to me to be firmly established. I think they can be demonstrated in many ways, and it also seems to me that their effect reaches into our time, but it must be added that the first three have a kind of archaic effect. The hunting pack has become the lynch mob in our modern world. We know cases of lynchings, when people suddenly attack a person

a pogrom pack!

That naturally goes back to the early example of the hunting pack. We know war, it is all too familiar. We know lament, perhaps more from religions than from the very mild form which it now takes socially. It plays an enormous role in Christendom and in other religions. The increase pack, however, has transformed itself. It was of course completely dependent on changes in the relations of production, and when one speaks of the importance of the relations of production, then I believe we think above all of everything which relates to the increase pack. It is not only an archaic form but has undergone qualitative changes, to such an extent that we do not recognize it in our society, where it appears as production. I believe it is important—I do not know how far you would agree—to distinguish sharply the forms of the pack, which have a purely archaic character, from those which have entered modern life and have become a really contemporary part of our life.

Let me try to express the core of what you said. There is something essential here: for you the concept of the crowd is not a purely quantitative concept, as is often the case today, but determined by a series of qualitative aspects because it is related to the model concept of the pack, such as hunting, war—which is a somewhat more rational, intensified and higher developed stage of hunting—lament and what you call increase. I think it is important to stress this, as it shows how superficial the current phrases about the age of the masses and so on are, as if it were only a matter of numbers. As Stefan George put it in a well known poem: your number is itself sacrilege, whereas the sacrilege does not lie in the number but in these qualitative aspects which you have emphasized. Of these categories of the pack the first three are very clear, although you would surely agree with me that they cannot be statically separated from each other so simply, but that there is an interdependence between them. Hunting pack and war pack merge with each other, even though the more organized war pack, compared with what we could call the spontaneous hunting pack, represents the negation of the latter's immediacy.

If I may interject, briefly: I am convinced that the war pack emerged originally from the hunting pack.

emerged, yes!

It was a question of exacting revenge on a person who had perhaps committed a murder, and so a group formed, set off in order to revenge this murder. If the group, to which the murderer belonged, defended itself, a second pack was formed and we already have the model of the war pack.

Exactly! This is, I think, the general opinion of ethnology on this point. To be honest, I have a certain difficulty with the concept of the increase pack, as the whole will to increase seems to me a bit problematic. We have to consider that the commandment to increase, which we have in the great religions, above all Judaism and Catholicism, that this commandment occurs precisely in those religions which are distinguished from the mythical or magical natural religions. One has to assume that in primitive stages of the development of humanity—I am thinking for instance of the construction of a stage of hetaerism—the question of human increase was given no value. I would rather be inclined to say that this commandment to increase is of historical origin and is tied to the category of property, of property which can be handed down. Only when there is something like property, that must be preserved, that is fetishized, in-

herited—only at this point can it become a commandment to create heirs, who will take over this property. As a result this urge to increase appears as secondary not as primary.

It would be interesting if you could first say something about this. I would then like to say something about what I see as very fruitful in this category of increase.

Of the great number of examples, which I have collected, I would like to present two: In the Shi-King, the classical songbook of the Chinese, there is a poem about locusts, which equates the number of descendants with the number of locusts as something to be wished. This poem is short. I would like to read it to you: The wings of the locusts say: join, join. O, may your sons and nephews follow in endless line. The wings of the locusts say: unite, unite. O, may your sons and nephews be for ever one. We have here the large number, the continuity of the descendents, unity, that is, three wishes for the descendents. That the locusts are used here as a symbol for the descendents is particularly remarkable, because locusts were of course feared. Nevertheless, the enormity of their number is exactly what one wishes for one's descendents.

But isn't this a very late stage of an already organized, institutionalized society, of a state and an organized religion as compared with natural conditions?

This could perhaps be said. The Shi-King is very old, but . . .

All the same, it presumes a highly developed and indeed developed hierarchical society.

That is perhaps true. And that is why I would like to give you another example. This is especially interesting because it concerns totemic myths, which were published only some 15 years ago. The younger Strehlow recorded them among the Aranda. I want to tell one of them. It is about the origin of the bandicoot totem and it says: the ancestor of the bandicoot totem, old Korora, is represented lying at the bottom of a pond in eternal sleep, he has been sleeping for an eternity. One day an enormous number of bandicoots come out of his navel and armpits and he is completely surrounded by them. But he is still asleep. The sun rises. He sits up, gets up, feels hungry, notices that he is surrounded by an enormous number of bandicoots, he grabs in all directions, seizes one of these bandicoots, cooks it in the fierce sun and eats it—eats, that is, one of the creatures which has originated from him. He lies down to sleep and that night a bull roarer falls from his armpit, changes shape and becomes a human being. It is his first son, who grows and is recognized by him as his son the following morning. In the following night more of these sons fall from his armpits. And so it continues every night.

Finally 50 sons emerge together from his armpits, and he sends his sons to find bandicoots, which they catch, cook and live from.

We have here a kind of double increase: first he is the ancestor of the bandicoots, which are suddenly generated in gigantic masses, then later a large number of sons are generated from him, the father. One could call him a crowd mother, since he is composed, one could say, of bandicoots and of sons. The relation between these bandicoots and his sons is very interesting. The one feeds on the other. Thus he produced food and also his own sons. He is the ancestral father of the bandicoot totem, and this totem signifies that bandicoots and human beings, who belong to this totem, are related in the closest fashion. The human beings, his human sons, are so to speak the younger brothers of these bandicoots. Many similar traditions could be added to this myth. I believe that we can speak here of a very strong urge to increase.

I would say here that we are dealing with something very ambivalent—it would take us far afield and I don't think we can discuss this fully here. There is certainly an archaic element which pulls in the direction of the manifold, the amorphous multiplicity of forms. But there is also the opposed element, and it seems to me hardly possible any more to separate the primary and the secondary; and in general it doesn't really help in these questions to ask what is primary and derived. Today at any rate it appears to be the case that the idea of increase—which has of course clear and familiar civilizational and economic grounds—is both desired and feared. This applies to single individuals and families as well as peoples and humanity as a whole, which senses the danger to its survival in the present forms of organization and beyond that is plagued by the doubt, in part surely imaginary, whether our old earth will be able to feed the measureless increase of humankind.

If I may add something: this idea of an overfilled earth is also very old and mythical. It already occurs with the ancient Persians and it is also to be found among peoples with a strong tendency to increase, who always emphasized this desire for increase.

In this ambivalence there is certainly the deep consciousness, on the one hand that all possible life has the right to exist, but on the other hand, given the forms, the institutions in which humanity lived and still lives, that every additional human being on the horizon is at the same time a threat to the survival of the rest. This ambivalence has not only psychological but equally real grounds, however distant. But I would like to broach an issue in your theory of increase which appears very fruitful. You show in one part of your book that production, that is, the increase of goods, has become a kind of self-purpose today or as I would say, it

has become fetishized. Now with an economic theory of society one can give rational or pseudo-rational grounds why this has happened, that under present conditions the apparatus of production, and thereby the whole relations of production, can only keep itself going by creating ever new circles of purchasers for its products—a remarkable reversal of the primary and the secondary, with the result that human beings, for whom supposedly this is all there, are in reality dragged along by the machine, which is their own product.

Your theory fills a very good function here. We probably could not understand why this culture of production for the sake of production flourishes everywhere on earth, independent of the different political systems, if it did not appeal so strongly to something in human subjectivity, in the whole unconscious, archaic inheritance we have.

Otherwise how could the simple objection fail to be raised: why should we produce more and more when what is produced in reality has long been sufficient to satisfy our needs. That this question is not asked, seems to me to indicate that this apparatus of production can mobilize enormous libidinal energies in the masses, which it can use for its own constant and ultimately very problematic expansion. That is why I consider your viewpoint altogether productive, even if, like me, one is inclined not to place this urge or will to increase at the beginning, as you do.

May I come back to the question which I put to you earlier and to which you have not as yet responded, that is, the question of the difference between our approach and your theories about the crowd and those of Le Bon and Freud, which are after all well known. In general the fruitfulness of a theory lies to a large extent in the minute differences which separate it from related theories.

Perhaps you will permit me to stress more the differences between Freud's theory and mine, as I find . . .

Le Bon is not actually a theory, rather a description. A description of a relatively narrow phenomenon. The crowds he describes are really the crowds which arise only in quite specific situations such as conflagrations, theatre fires and similar occasions and which are not prototypical for the concept of the crowd as such. I agree that it would be better to discuss Freud rather than Le Bon.

In relation to Freud, there are some observations to be made: Freud speaks of two concrete crowds, one is the church and the other the army. That he selects two hierarchically structured—let us call them groups—in order to explain his crowd theory, seems to me very characteristic for him. I do not regard the crowd as hierarchically structured. An army is not a crowd for me. An army is a collection of human beings, who are held together by a specific structure of command in such a way that they *cannot* become a crowd. It is extremely important in an army that five persons can be split off by a command; 300 can be deployed as a unit somewhere else. An army can be split at any time. Sometimes, at certain moments, in the moment of flight or perhaps of a very violent attack, it can become a crowd, but in principle an army is not at all in my sense a crowd. It is thus quite significant that Freud exemplifies his theory through the army. Another aspect, which I would emphasize as an important difference, is that Freud actually only speaks of crowds which have a leader. He always sees a single individual, to whom the crowd relates.

That of course is connected with the theory of the primal father, the father of the horde.

There are, however, and here I think you will agree with me, also crowds of quite a different kind: for instance, a flight crowd. People in one place are suddenly threatened by . . .

This he conceives as the decomposition of the crowd, quite consistently from his standpoint.

No, here I think we must distinguish between a flight crowd and a panic crowd. The flight crowd is still in a crowd state, like a fleeing herd, when they all flee together. Panic is a breaking apart of the crowd when each individual simply wants to save his own life. The flight crowd, which is not yet panic and is still a unity, has no leader. It has a direction. The direction is: away from danger! All the same, it shows quite explicit crowd phenomena, which can be individually explained and which are very important. I believe that the lynching crowd does not always have a leader. You will rightly object that lynching crowds are incited by demagogues . . .

Above all in history it has always been the case that precisely lynching crowds were not spontaneous but manipulated. This was already the case during the pogroms of the Crusades.

That is certainly correct. Nevertheless, I believe there is a lynching crowd before and beyond these directed, leader-related crowds. There are other examples. You will recall that I also presented the feast crowd. This is an example which has nothing to do with a leader. It is a question of a gathering of people and of a great amount of harvest produce, which they want to enjoy together in a state of joy and excitement. Everything is in commotion; one can't even talk of a direction, let alone a leader. Freud's concept of the crowd is, I believe, too dependent on Le Bon's.

He worked from it. It is actually a commentary or an interpretation, a genetic interpretation of Le Bon's phenomenology of the crowd.

I would also say: even if we take this restricted case of the crowd, which Freud sought to explain according to Le Bon's description, there are still further objections. There is above all the question of the concept of identification. I consider this concept to be insufficiently reflected, too imprecise, not really clear. Freud says at many places in his work when talking of identification that it is the question of an exemplary model, of the child for example identifying with his father and wanting to be like his father. The father is the model. Now this is certainly right. But what really happens in this relation to the model has never been shown exactly. You were surely rather surprised that such a large part of my book is devoted to the problems of metamorphosis. The second volume will contain much more on metamorphosis. I have really made it my task to investigate all aspects of metamorphosis completely afresh, in order to be able to determine what a model actually is, and what really occurs between a model and the person who follows a model. Only then perhaps will we be able to have clearer ideas about identification. As long as this is not the case I am inclined to avoid the whole concept of identification. You won't find it in my whole presentation of the crowd. I try to do without identification. I have mentioned only a few points, there are others.

Your critique seems to me to be extremely fruitful and correct in many points, for the very reason that Freud's basic tendency to replace the theory of society by individual psychology extended to the collectivity, leads him time and again to the invariant fundamental quanta of the unconscious, neglecting essential historical modifications. As a result his social psychology remains somewhat abstract. I fully agree that army and church cannot simply be subsumed under the concept of the crowd, rather they are reactions, reactive formations, in which the archaic crowd aspect, which Freud had in mind is also present, but essentially negated and contained by hierarchy and a certain kind of rationality. And if we take this further, then we can see that precisely so-called crowd phenomena cannot be conceived simply as primary manifestations of the archaic crowd, as Freud thought during the First World War, but consist of reactive formations, that is, regressions to social stages which are actually no longer compatible with the present.

As far as the feast is concerned, it is certainly quite right that we cannot speak of leadership here. May I draw your attention to a very significant work on the feast by the French cultural anthropologist Roger Caillois, in which he attributes the feast to a reactive formation, to a reversal of hierarchically strict rites within very rigid, barbaric societies. They can only assure their own institutional survival by reversing their rules and by allowing in certain exceptional situations, even making a duty of precisely what is otherwise forbidden. In this sense what you would call the feast crowds would also be an historically dynamic and not a primary phenomenon. If I may say something else, what made the greatest impression on me in your book is something which belongs less to the theory of the crowd than to the theory of power, which is of course the inseparable corollary of the crowd theory, namely your theory of the command, which seems to me to be so eminently enlightening and essential because you spell out—and here I would like to recall our Dialectic of Enlightenment—*what otherwise largely disappears behind the facade of society. I mean that behind all socially approved and expected forms of behaviour there stands, however distantly, immediate physical violence, the threat of annihilation. I think that only when we are clearly aware that society, and thus the self-preservation of human beings itself, has as part of its substance the threat of death, can we fully grasp the frightful interlocking of survival, as you call it, and of death, in the way that you have formulated it. It would be good if in conclusion if you could say a few words about your theory of the command.*

Willingly, although it can't be condensed to a few words: I derive the command—biologically—from the flight command. I believe that the threat from an animal, which feeds on other animals, leads to their flight. A lion in search of prey announcing itself through its roar causes other animals to flee. This seems to me to be the germ of the command, as it developed later and became a very important institution for us. It is originally a flight command. This is very important, since this model has been employed and has become intrinsic to our society. Commands are conveyed without human beings perhaps being aware that they are also receiving a death threat. However commands are given, the threat of death stands behind them. And through the execution of death sentences, common to most societies, the command always regains its frightfulness. The warning is given, if you do not do what is demanded of you, then what is happening in this execution will happen to you.

Every execution is directed to those who are not executed.

And then, to mention a further point, examination of the command led me to see that the command can be divided into what constitutes its propelling force, its motor energy, which leads to its execution, and another part, which I call the sting of command. This sting has exactly the form of the command, its content, and it remains in the person who carries it out. A person who carries out a command is not happy about it. Perhaps he doesn't know it; perhaps he doesn't think about it. How-

ever, the sting of this command remains in him and this sting is completely unchanging. That is particularly important. Human beings can store up stings and these may come from commands which they received 20 or 30 years ago. They are all there in them and they all want to come to light again through a kind of reversal. Human beings want to free themselves from these stings, they feel oppressed by these stings, and they often seek situations, which represent an exact reversal of the original situation of command, in order to be able to get rid of their stings. It is obvious to what consequences that leads. It is simply a fact that every human being who lives in society is full of stings of whatever kind. They can amount to so many that the individual is driven to quite monstrous deeds, because he is suffocating from his stings of command.

This is something extraordinarily thought-provoking, above all because it expresses in a very original and unconventional way that the threat of direct violence lives on in all mediations. Every attempt to extract oneself from this sphere is caught in the spell of this mythical cycle, to do again what has been done to one. Nietzsche's wonderful idea, that human beings must be redeemed from revenge, refers exactly to the state of affairs of which you speak. By naming it, by naming this spell in your book, your book is striving—if I have understood you correctly—to serve this purpose, by naming as it were the magic charm of this spell which has bewitched human beings, so that it might one day be possible to escape from this spell.

Peter Morgan (essay date January 1992)

SOURCE: Morgan, Peter. "Georges Kien and the 'Diagnosis of Delusion' in Elias Canetti's *Die Blendung*.'" *Neophilologus* 76, no. 1 (January 1992): 77-89.

[*In the following essay, Morgan examines the roles of irony and "narrative self-reflexion" in* Die Blendung.]

Since the republication of Elias Canetti's **Die Blendung** in the early 1960s, interpreters have asked whether a resolution is posited between the extremes of "Kopf" and "Welt," or at least whether it is possible to find a perspective in the novel on Peter Kien's crisis. The figure of Georges Kien, Peter's brother, the psychiatrist, who in the last section of the novel saves Peter from his humiliation at the hands of Therese and Pfaff, has become central to this question in the critical literature on **Die Blendung**. Georges dominates the third part of the novel and appears to represent—and restores sanity and order in an otherwise grotesque and senseless world. While Raymond Williams sounded an early note of warning about the extent to which the ending can be seen as a "diagnosis of delusion,"[2] many critics have viewed Georges as a positive counterpart to his brother. More recent criticisms have focused on negative aspects of the characterization of Georges. In the critical discussion of Peter and Georges Kien however, little attention has been paid to aspects of irony and narrative self-reflexion in Canetti's text.

Peter Kien is the world's leading sinologist, whose life work lies in the reconstruction of ancient Asian texts (14). In books and scholarly work he finds his only point of reference to the world.

The novel opens comically, with an incident in Kien's daily walk. A young boy gains Kien's attention by interposing himself between Kien and the display window of a bookshop. After a brief conversation, the boy elicits from Kien a promise to see Kien's personal library. That Kien allows the boy to interfere with his thoughts at all is uncharacteristic. He justifies his behaviour on the basis that the boy's interest in Chinese heralds a future as a leading scholar. But later on he realises to his horror that he both wasted his time talking to a child and promised to display his precious books. Kien tries to justify the unaccustomed intrusion of everyday reality into his life, but even this justification of his behaviour shows the extent to which he is afraid of the outside world disrupting his scholarly life.

This meeting indirectly sets the story into motion: it is Therese's refusal to allow the boy into the flat which wins Kien's admiration, and indirectly leads to his proposal of marriage. Kien marries Therese in order to gain extra protection for his books and himself. The opening incident of the story indicates that Kien's defenses against the "world" are breaking down under pressure from inside as well as from outside.

While Kien has a religious respect for scholarly books, his attitude to novels is one of contempt. In gratitude at Therese's fulfilment of her duties (i.e. dusting his books and protecting him from disturbances), and in the belief that she has a genuine, if primitive, interest in learning, he promises to select a book from his library for her:

> Für sie kam bloß ein Roman in Betracht. Nur wird von Romanen kein Geist fett. Den Genuß, den sie vielleicht bieten, überzahlt man sehr: sie zersetzen den besten Charakter. Man lernt sich in allerlei Menschen einfühlen. Am vielen Hin und Her gewann man Geschmack. Man löst sich in die Figuren auf, die einem gefallen. Jeder Standpunkt wird begreiflich. Willig überläßt man sich fremden Zielen und verliert für länger die eigenen aus dem Auge. Romane sind Keile, die ein schreibender Schauspieler in die geschlossene Person seiner Leser treibt. Je besser er Keil und Widerstand berechnet, um so gespaltener läßt er die Person zurück. Romane müßten von Staats wegen verboten sein.
>
> (35)

For Peter Kien novels are a threat: in encouraging sympathy or identification with fictive characters, they penetrate the wall which he has built up around himself, breaking down his intellectual single-mindedness. For him character and learning cannot manifest themselves in understanding, sympathy or vicarious identification with the fictive characters of a novel. In seeing others' aims or desires in life, one weakens or distorts the focus of the intellect. The image of the "Keil," the wedge driven by the "writing actor" into the "closed person" of the reader moreover, expresses Kien's fear of the subversive power of the text. The novelist undermines morals and the sense of duty, dissolves the sense of self, and fragments identity.[3]

This image of the novel as "wedge" relates back to the dream Kien had immediately before he awoke and remembered his promise to Therese. In the dream a sacrificial victim is attacked by two jaguars, which are Mexican priests in disguise. Finally one of the priests drives a stone wedge ("Keil") into the victim's heart. Peter Kien, the onlooker, closes his eyes, expecting a gush of blood, but opening them again sees, to his horror, not blood, but books springing from the man's gaping chest. The blood dripping from the hammer used to drive in the wedge sets the books alight as they fall from the man's body, and Kien commands him to close his chest. The victim frees his hands and tears his chest wide open, releasing a stream of books into the fire about his feet. As Kien tries to save the books he is hindered by people clinging to his body: "Ein unbrauchbarer Mensch, wo es drauf ankommt, versagt er." (33) This however is not the end of the dream. The voice of God proclaims from above: "Hier gibt es keine Bücher. Alles ist eitel." (34) Realizing the truth, Kien leaps free of the burning bodies, saved and calm amidst the stink of burning flesh and twitching limbs, now that no books are in danger. Suddenly however this recognition is belied by the transformation of the burning people into books and he again plunges into the flames to rescue them. Again God's voice releases him, and again he plunges into the fire, thinking that the people have become books. This happens four times, until God maliciously and derisively tells him "Jetzt sind es Bücher!" (34). upon which he awakens.

Peter Kien's dual role as onlooker and actor suggests a conflict between the desire to act and the fear of being dragged down into a world of unreason. The image of the orgy of clinging bodies has sexual connotations ("Da hat sich ihm schon einer an den Mund geworfen und hält sich an den zusammengepreßten Lippen fest," 33). Peter Kien fears the irruption of feelings and desires as incompatible with knowledge, enlightenment or reason.

The dream indicates the psychological dimension of Kien's repression of feelings for the sake of knowledge. Knowledge has become laden with repressed feeling—

and vice versa, feeling is laden with the guilt of squandered knowledge. In manifesting the ambivalence of "Kopf" and "Welt" in the image of books and people (the transformation from the one to the other), the dream reveals Kien's deep fear of losing his ability to distinguish between the two—i.e. his ability to maintain the purity of knowledge. Hence the imagery of eyesight and blindness ("Blendung") in the dream. "Blendung" is not simply "blinding," it is also "bedazzlement," the result of too much light, or bright images superimposed over one another. It is an image of the inability to see, distinguish and define clearly. Peter Kien's fear of blindness throughout the novel, his fear of no longer having access to books, masks the deeper fear of "Blendung," of no longer being able to distinguish between books and people, knowledge and life. As a result of this fear, he attempts to reinforce the barriers against the "world" first by marrying Therese, and then by bribing the brutal concierge, Pfaff. However these strategies undermine rather than reinforce his security. The dream at the beginning of the novel preempts the "auto da fé" of the end.

Through the image of the wedge ("Keil") driven into the victim's heart, Kien's dream is linked to his contempt for the novel which cleaves and fragments the identity of the reader. Novels split the reader, forcing open his closed identity, leading to the situation where he can no longer distinguish between knowledge (the books of the dream) and feelings (the people clinging to his mouth and limbs); and the writer has become a cynical God revealing not one, but several contradictory and confusing truths.

On the morning after his dream, in response to Therese's reminder, Kien selects for her his oldest, grimiest, most battered book, Willibald Alexis' *Die Hosen des Herrn von Bredow*. However her solicitous reverence for even this miserable volume incites surprise and then guilt and gratitude in Kien, leading to his proposal of marriage, and ultimately to the expulsion from his library-paradise and his wanderings in the underworld of part two of the novel.

Returning to his library after the marriage ceremony, and wondering what would follow, Peter Kien wishes for the help of brother Georges. Georges is a gynaecologist turned psychiatrist, who moved to Paris and became famous and wealthy as a doctor and socialite (43). At the end of part two of the novel, after Peter has been hounded from his home by Therese and Pfaff, Georges is called to Vienna by the dwarf, Fischerle, in a telegram in the name of Peter Kien. After Peter's wanderings in the grotesque, nightmarish and brutal underworld of Vienna, the arrival of Georges seems to promise the restoration of order.

Georges Kien has been seen mostly positively as an antithesis to Peter. Manfred Durzak interprets the third part of the novel as a resolution through synthesis of the alienated values of the first two parts, of "Kopf" and "Welt" respectively. For Durzak, Georges Kien is an authorial figure, an alter-ego of Canetti himself, who thereby brings the other characters of the novel into perspective.[4] Likewise, Auer, Dissinger, Suchy and others see Georges and/or his psychiatric patients positively in comparison to Peter Kien and the "world" of the novel.[5] David Roberts however rejects this interpretation. While he interprets Georges as an antithetical character to Peter, he sees the final section, "Welt im Kopf," as a "negative dialectic." Georges, the embodiment of "Welt" in contrast to Peter, stands outside—and provides a perspective on—the world of *Die Blendung,* in the theoretical recognition of "die Macht der Masse im Menschen." Although he recognizes the negative aspects of Georges, Roberts nevertheless gives him a privileged position of authorial approval in terms of the theories Canetti later expounded in *Masse und Macht.*[6] Barnouw in 1977, summing up interpretative attitudes to Georges, regards Roberts' interpretation as a turning point from unquestioningly positive, to more critical approaches.[7] Certainly, with the exception of Krumme most recently,[8] interpretations of Georges since Roberts' study have been more and more negative, with Meili in 1985 condemning him as manipulative, power-hungry and protofascist.[9]

After a chance meeting with the Gorilla, a madman in gorilla-costume, Georges rejected his life as socialite, womanizer and gynaecologist, to become a psychiatrist. This meeting provides a key to Georges' role in the novel. Roberts considers it:

> . . . eine Begegnung von existentieller Bedeutung: die Erfahrung, die der Gorilla vermittelt, nachdem er sich leidenschaftlich auf den Boden geworfen hat, erschüttert Georges im Innersten seines Wesens . . . Die Schuppen fallen ihm von den Augen: sein Leben mit seinem Erfolg, seiner Eleganz, Geschliffenheit, Feinfühligkeit, wird in all seinem Ungenügen als das eines 'Halbmenschen' . . . Das erstickende Gefängnis von Konvention und Sicherheit zerbricht unter dem Eindruck dieser neuen Dimension des Seins.[10]

The Gorilla is the brother of a wealthy banker, who keeps him sequestered in his villa. The Gorilla answers the door, and greets Georges in a strange language:

> Ein angek leideter Gorilla trat vor, streckte die langen Arme aus, legte sie auf die Schultern des Arztes und begrüßte ihn in einer fremden Sprache. . . . An einem runden Tisch hieß er sie Platz nehmen. Seine Gebärden waren roh, aber verständlich und einladend. Über die Sprache zerbrach sich der Arzt den Kopf. Am ehesten erinnerte sie ihn noch an einen Negerdialekt.

(355)

The narration of this section is highly ironic, playing off Georges' refinement against the Gorilla's primitive behaviour. The juxtaposition of the polite tone and the crude happenings is grotesquely comic in the style of Kafka and other central European novelists[11]: "Der Gorilla hielt den männlichen Besuch fest, er hatte ihm wohl viel zu erklären." The genteel expression, "männlichen Besuch," contrasts ironically with both the Gorilla's appearance, and Georges' racist assumption that he is speaking a "Negerdialekt."

The Gorilla's behaviour toward his female companion moreover mirrors Georges' carefully disguised contempt for women:

> Unwillkürlich ging er (Georges) mit den Damen um, als liebte er sie. Jede gab seinem Geschmack recht und zog die Konsequenzen daraus. Bei den Äffchen verbreitete sich die Sitte des Krankseins.
>
> (354)

It is ironically appropriate that the francophile Georges, who refers to his French women patients as "Äffchen" (354), should become obsessed by a Gorilla, who hates the French language.

> Er (der Gorilla) sprach stärker, mehr aus der Tiefe, hinter seinen Lauten lauerten Affekte. Sie (die "Sekretärin") warf manchmal ein französisches Wort hin, vielleicht um anzudeuten, was gemeint sei. 'Sprechen Sie nicht Französisch?' fragte Georges. 'Aber natürlich . . . Ich bin Pariserin!' Sie überschüttete ihn mit einem eiligen Schwall von Worten, die schlecht ausgesprochen und noch schlechter zusammengefügt waren, wie wenn sie die Sprache halb verlernt hätte. Der gorilla brüllte sie an, sofort schwieg sie. . . . 'Er haßt die französische Sprache,' flüsterte sie zum Besuch. 'Er arbeitet schon seit Jahren an einer eigenen. Er ist noch nicht ganz fertig.'
>
> (355-6)

Georges becomes captivated by the Gorilla's self-created language of primitive emotions. Durzak views this admiration positively as a sign of Georges' breaking out of a life of superficiality and convention.[12] However Georges' fascination is a measure of his intellectual and emotional alienation, and lack of sense of purpose, rather than proof of the naive genius of the Gorilla. It is described as intellectual mystification, not enlightened understanding:

> In wenigen gewaltigen Worten, die wie abgeschnittene lebende Baumstämme ins Zimmer geschleudert wurden, vernahm Georges ein mythisches Liebesabenteuer, das ihn bis zum tiefsten Zweifel an sich selbst erschütterte. Er sah sich als Wanze neben einem Menschen. . . . Welche Anmaßung, mit einem solchen Geschöpf an einem Tisch zu sitzen, gesittet, gönnerhaft, an allen Poren der Seele von Fett und täglich frischem Fett verstopft, ein Halbmensch für den praktischen Gebrauch, ohne den Mut zum Sein, weil Sein in unserer Welt ein Anders-Sein bedeutet, eine Schablone für sich, eine aufgezogene Schneiderreklame, durch einen gnädigen Zufall in Bewegung oder in Ruhestand versetzt,

je nach dem Zufall eben, ohne den leisesten Einfluß, ohne einen Funken Macht, immer dieselben leeren Sätze leiernd, immer aus gleicher Entfernung verstanden.

> (356-7)

This mixture of cultural pessimism, primitivism and vitalism parodies the types of philosophical-mystical constructs of popular thinkers such as Spengler and Weininger, which were influential between the wars in Europe.

The women with whom Georges used to associate are now considered the pathetic, painted dolls of an over-refined civilisation, whereas the secretary has become something of an "Übermensch" under the influence of the Gorilla's will:

> Die Frauen, die Georges mit Liebe bestürmen und ihm zuliebe ihr Leben hergäben, besonders wenn er sie gerade umarmt, sind . . . glattgepflegte Hauttierchen, mit Kosmetik oder Männern beschäftigt. Diese Sekretärin aber, von Haus aus ein gewöhnliches Weib, nicht anders als andere, ist unter dem mächtigen Willen des Gorillas zu einem eigenartigen Wesen geworden: stärker, erregter, hingebender.
>
> (357)

Georges rejects his earlier life of empty relationships and "Höflichkeit"—the world of the French novels he used to read—for a re-education in terms of primitive emotions:

> Mit unendlicher Mühe erlernte er seine (i.e. the Gorilla's) Sprache. . . . Hier waren die Beziehungen das Ursprüngliche, beide Zimmer und was sie enthielten lösten sich in ein Kraftfeld von Affekten auf.
>
> (357)

And the Gorilla has become a romantic messiah:

> Er bevölkerte zwei Zimmer mit einer ganzen Welt. Er schuf, was er brauchte, und fand sich nach seinen sechs Tagen am siebenten darin zurecht. Statt zu ruhen, schenkte er der Schöpfung eine Sprache.
>
> (358)

The Gorilla in his two rooms with their dirt-covered floors and his scantily-clad "secretary" is a reverse image of Peter in his immaculate library with his housekeeper-wife, Therese, encased in her blue skirt. However the Gorilla's vitalism is not posited as an alternative to Peter's crisis of reason. On the contrary, the Gorilla episode parodies the types of irrationalism which have been used since Rousseau as defence against what is seen as an all-encompassing, dehumanising rationalism.

Through his contact with the Gorilla, Georges returns to his childhood and learns a language of emotions, denied to him as a child. This process of relearning of language amounts to the rejection of his past, which is so dominated by his older brother Peter, and of the ideals of civilisation and enlightenment ("eine überwundene, blasse Zeit," 358) for a primitivist philosophy.

George's fascination with the Gorilla is the result of his inability to come to terms with reason and emotion ("Kopf" and "Welt"). Through his apprenticeship to the Gorilla and rejection of the traditional psychiatry of his predecessor, he tries to reform his past and Peter's influence, by opting for an ideology of loss of "self" and release of primal instincts:

> Von der viel tieferen und eigentlichsten Triebkraft der Geschichte, dem Drang der Menschen, in eine höhere Tiergattung, die Masse, aufzugehen und sich darin so vollkommen zu verlieren, als hätte es nie einen Menschen gegeben, ahnten sie nichts. Denn sie waren gebildet und Bildung ist ein Festungsgürtel des Individuums gegen die Masse in sich selbst.
>
> (365)

Georges soon makes use of his discovery. As a disciple of the Gorilla he becomes a prophet to the common people.

> Georges war Gelehrter genug, um eine Abhandlung über die Sprache dieses Irren zu veröffentlichen. . . . (Er) ging zur Psychiatrie über, aus Bewunderung für die Großartigkeit der Irren, . . . mit dem festen Vorsatz, von ihnen zu lernen und keinen zu heilen. Von der schönen Literatur hatte er genug.
>
> (358)

Given his adulation of the Gorilla, it is not surprising that Georges takes an immediate liking to Pfaff when he arrives in Vienna. The brutal and sadistic Pfaff suggests an alternative possibility for the realization of the teachings of the Gorilla in the world.

Georges' utopian vision of the future "allgemeine Weltrepublik" of the insane and of his own role as "Volkskommissar für Irre" (367) finds symbolic expression in his vision of the termites' nest, an image of organic community and individual subservience and sacrifice which has clear similarities to fascist ideologies of the period. Half fascinated, half horrified, Georges later suggests to Peter the possibility of a human collective freed from the burden of individual sexual drives, finding release in mass-executions/suicides for the sake of the group:

> Im Schwarm, bei dem Tausende und Abertausende von Tieren scheinbar sinnlos zugrunde gehen, sehe ich eine Befreiung von der gespeicherten Geschlechtlichkeit des Stockes. Sie opfern einen kleinen Teil ihrer Masse, um den größeren von Liebeswirrungen freizuhalten. Der Stock würde an Liebe, wäre sie einmal erlaubt, zugrunde gehen. Ich weiß keine großartigere Vorstellung als die einer Orgie im Termitenstock. Die Tiere

> vergessen . . . was sie sind, blinde Zellen eines fanatischen Ganzen. . . . Eine plötzliche Verkehrung des Sinnreichsten ins Sinnloseste.
>
> (384-5)

Georges links this image of the loss of individual identity to the situation of Peter setting fire to his books. He later regrets having made the comparison, but by then it is too late. The image will be realized in Peter's suicide.

At the time of the action, Georges has been director of an asylum for two years and is married to the wife of the previous director. Even before this however, Georges had effectively run the asylum and had been "der gute Engel eines teuflischen Vorgesetzten" (351). His predecessor was close in type to Peter Kien. As a traditional and conservative psychiatrist he had represented "die offizielle Psychiatrie mit der Hartnäckigkeit eines Irren" (351):

> Er hielt es für seine eigentliche Lebensaufgabe, das riesige Material, über welches er verfügte, als Stütze für gangbare Bezeichnungen zu verwenden. . . . Er hing an der Fertigkeit des Systems und haßte Zweifler. Menschen, besonders Geisteskranke und Verbrecher, waren ihm gleichgültig.
>
> (351)

His refusal to modify theory on the basis of psychiatric practice aligns him with Peter Kien as a closed character, a "Kopf ohne Welt," who, like Peter Kien also, in the end is despatched by his wife in favour of a young, handsome lover. After the meeting with the Gorilla, and in reaction against the orthodox and autocratic attitude of the previous director, Georges rejects traditional psychiatry:

> In der harten Schule seines Vorgängers hatte er sich rasch zu dessen genauem Gegenteil entwickelt. Die Kranken behandelte er als wären sie Menschen. Geduldig ließ er sich Geschichten erzählen, die er schon tausendmal gehört hatte, und zeigte über die ältesten Gefahren und Ängste immer neue Überraschung.
>
> (352)

He treats his mentally ill patients "as though they were people," and seeks to penetrate their minds in a way in which his predecessor could not. The subjunctive verb "wären" betrays the exploitative and functional aspects of Georges' new methods of treatment. Roberts writes of Georges' discovery of psychiatry:

> . . . auf der Suche nach der 'zackigen, schmerzlichen, beißenden Vielgestalt des Lebens' läßt er auch die Leere seiner erfolgreichen Karriere hinter sich, eine Karriere, wie sie zu einem Romanhelden paßt. Er gibt diese erfolgreiche Vergangenheit für jene Dimension der Wirklichkeit und Erfahrung der *Welt* auf, die vom Roman versteckt, ihm den Verrückten aber enthüllt wird. Er ist die einzige Gestalt, die sich öffnen und verlieren

kann. Er anerkennt die persönlichen Welten seiner Patienten und strebt so danach, die Blindheit der Sprache, den Widerspruch zwischen Verständigung und Individuation zu überwinden, der in ihren verrückten Systemen zum Äußersten getrieben wird. . . . Dies ist *sein* Weg zur Erkenntnis.[13]

However Georges' procedures are described as aggressive, insidious and even sinister acts:

Ein blitzschneller Blick genügte. Wo er eine leise Veränderung, einen Riß, die Möglichkeit, in die fremde Seele zu schlüpfen, gewahrte, griff er rasch zu und nahm den Betreffenden in seine Privatwohnung mit. . . . Da erwarb er, wenn er es noch nicht hatte, spielend das Vertrauen von Menschen, die sich jedem andern gegenüber hinter ihre Wahngebilde versteckten. . . . Er wurde ihr einziger Vertrauter, den sie, vom Augenblick ihrer Anerkennung ab, über die Veränderungen ihrer eigenen Bereiche auf dem laufenden hielten und um Rat angingen.

(352)

He develops into a talented actor, ("Mit der Zeit entwickelte er sich zu einem großen Schauspieler," 352) and can even respond to the fragmented and contradictory personalities of paranoiacs and schizophrenics (352-3).

While the results of his method are astounding however, he simultaneously worships the mental illness of those whom he is "healing":

Er lernte von ihnen mehr, als er ihnen gab. Sie bereicherten ihn um ihre einmaligen Erlebnisse: er vereinfachte sie nur, indem er sie gesund machte. Wieviel Geist und Schärfe fand er bei manchen! Sie waren die einzigen wirklichen Persönlichkeiten, von vollendeter Einseitigkeit, wahre Charaktere, von einer Geradheit und Macht des Willens, um die sie Napoleon beneidet hätte.

(353)

The question of language and identity is central to Georges' discovery of the worlds of the Gorilla and the insane. He must renounce his adopted language (French), and even the broken French of the Gorilla's secretary, in order to learn the Gorilla's language. Later, in the asylum he adopts the individual "languages" of the insane in order to penetrate their personalities. His desire to penetrate and comprehend his patients borders on the wish for self-fulfillment through their fantasies and ruptured personalities, and suggests self-abasement and weakness of character, concealed behind the charisma and patronising superiority of the professional psychiatrist. Although capable of curing the Gorilla, he refuses to do so out of admiration for his character, and on meeting patients whom he has cured, he is frustrated and disappointed to find that they have become "normal" (359).

Through his contact with the Gorilla and the insane Georges finds a means of escape from his own intellectual and emotional insecurity, which the relationship with his older brother has instilled in him since childhood. Indeed his move to Paris and name-change from "Georg" to "Georges" may be seen as an attempt to escape the past which is so dominated by Peter. The infatuation with the vitalism of the Gorilla and the worlds of the insane, that is, may be the latest in a series of attempts at establishing an identity capable of standing up to the annihilating contempt Peter shows for him (cf. pp. 380-1; 406-7). Georges' discovery of passion and, in the asylum, extremes of personality and emotion, does not represent a fulfilment and extension of his personality, but rather another attempt to free himself from his deep-seated sense of inferiority to Peter.[14] In this respect he does not stand outside the novel, but is characterized in terms of the relationship with his brother.

In the train on the way to Vienna Georges meets a blind man who reminds him of Peter. This meeting triggers a childhood memory of a time when he and Peter were sick with measles, and Peter was suffering temporary blindness (369 f.). On the basis of this memory, Georges assumes that Peter fears blindness and therefore has sent him the telegram calling for his help. The blind man on the train becomes an image of the Peter he hopes to find in Vienna. Georges, that is, diagnoses the fear of blindness in accordance with his fantasy of subduing Peter. By the end of the journey he is fully convinced that he will be able to establish himself as the stronger partner in the relationship, after having reduced Peter to the level of the thankful patient and raised himself to that of physician and saviour. He thereby hopes to rewrite the history of his childhood— and lifelong—subservience to Peter.

From the end of his daydream until the end of the novel, however, "Georges" becomes "Georg," and the old relationships are re-established. Peter, despite his weakened and humiliated state in Pfaff's room, reverts to his old self ("der alte Peter," 376) on recognising his brother. Georges uses his new skills as actor-psychiatrist to play the old Georg, denying everything that he has come to admire in the Gorilla and his patients, in order to find his way into Peter's mind:

Heile ich die Leute nicht, so verbleiben sie in ihrem barbarischen Zustand. Um ihnen den Weg zur Bildung, wenn auch einer späten, zu eröffnen, muß ich sie gesund machen.

(383)

Georges' diagnosis of Peter's problem is wrong, he makes false judgements about Therese and Pfaff, and the fantasy of coming as "deus ex machina"[15] to rescue a blinded, humbled Peter crumbles as he realizes his failure, and Peter, although verging on insanity, sees through Georges' pretence to re-establish his authority:

Georg begann sich unsicher zu fühlen. Nicht ein Zehntel der besprochenen Bücher war ihm bekannt. Er verachtete dieses Wissen, das ihn erdrückte. Peters Arbeitslust regte sich gewaltig. Sie weckte in Georg die Sehnsucht nach dem Ort, wo er ein ebenso absoluter Herrscher war, wie Peter in seiner Bibliothek.

(406)

Georges' attempt at healing both himself and his brother fails—and with it his hope of overcoming his sense of inferiority to Peter. He tries to bring about a restoration of the status quo. He returns Peter's life to the state before Therese entered it: the pawned books are bought back, both Therese and Pfaff are bribed to leave the house, Peter is returned to his library, and "Georg" leaves for the asylum where he can become the "absolute ruler," "Georges," again. At the end of the novel, he has not only failed to save Peter, but has also failed to come to terms with the duality of "Kopf" and "Welt" in himself.

As with Peter Kien earlier, Georges' character is linked to his attitude to the novel as a literary form.[16] Ever since he "discovered" madness and the insane, Georges has given up the reading of novels:

Seit er zu ihnen und ganz in ihre Gebilde aufging, verzichtete er auf schöngeistige Lektüre. In Romanen stand immer dasselbe. Früher hatte er mit Leidenschaft gelesen und an neuen Wendungen alter Sätze, die er schon für unveränderlich, farblos, abgegriffen und nichtssagend hielt, großes Vergnügen gefunden . . . die besten Romane waren die, in denen die Menschen am gewähltesten sprachen. Wer sich so ausdrücken konnte wie alle anderen Schreiber vor ihm, galt als ihr legitimer Nachfolger. Eines solchen Aufgabe bestand darin, die zackige, schmerzliche, beißende Vielgestalt des Lebens, das einen umgab, auf eine glatte Papierebene zu bringen, über die es sich rasch und angenehm hinweglas.

(353-4)

The literary form of the novel reduces the diversity of life to artful, trite verbal formulations. Roberts sees Georges' rejection of the novel in terms of his rejection of the superficialities and conventions of life, after having found "seinen Weg in die Wildheit" through the contact with the insane.[17] Georges rejects the novel for the opposite reason to Peter. Where Peter Kien feared the novel as a form which fragments identity and shows the diversity of truth, Georges Kien sees only formalistic clichés, the reduction of diversity to uniformity:

Lesen als Streicheln, eine andere Form der Liebe, für Damen und Damenärzte, zu deren Berut feines Verständnis für die intime Lektüre der Dame gehörte. Keine verwirrenden Wendungen, keine fremden Worte, je öfter ein Geleise befahren war, um so differenzierter die Lust, die man ihm abgewann. Die gesamte Romanliteratur ein einziges Lehrbuch der Höflichkeit. Belesene Menschen wurden zwangsweise artig. Ihre Teilnahme am Leben der anderen erschöpfte sich in Gratulation und Kondolation.

(354)

Georges' perception of the function of the novel as the reduction of the jagged edges of life into the smooth literary formulation contrasts with Canetti's implicit understanding and use of novelistic form in *Die Blendung*. Precisely the function of the novel is to express the "zackige . . . Vielgestalt des Lebens" on the "glatte Papierebene," *without* thereby losing the sense of individual experience or reducing life to a "handbook" of courteous and empty phrases. Georges' view of reading as "stroking" knows nothing of irony, distance, critical perspective or cutting "against the grain." This aspect of the characterization of Georges—like that of Peter Kien analysed above—brings a critical, ironic perspective on him in this novel. The author of *Die Blendung* implicitly rejects both Peter's and Georges' negative, non-ironic conceptions of the novel as a form. Neither Peter nor Georges reads the novel as the novelist Canetti implies an ideal reader would. The critical attempt to view Georges as a figure outside the world of the novel, runs against Canetti's implied reading of the novel as a form which does not reduce the multi-facetted and contradictory nature of reality to a single truth. Raymond Williams' fear that Canetti, through the character of Georges in the final part of the novel, attempts to comprehend or "answer" the crisis of Austrian society in the inter-war period, is not supported by the text. Georges belongs within the world of the novel, historically as a pre-fascist intellectual, and psychologically in terms of his relationship to his brother Peter.

The scholar and intellectual, Peter Kien, cannot maintain his existence of "Kopf ohne Welt," and his self-immolation is a parody of the synthesis of "Kopf" and "Welt" which is implied as a necessity for human survival, but is nowhere realized in the novel.

Peter Kien's suicide mirrors the image of the burning Theresianum—an image of Austria—outside his library. Georges Kien too, far from offering a resolution of the themes of "Kopf" and "Welt," is a problematic character: an intellectual who turns his back on reason for a proto-fascist, primitivist mythology. Georges' life has been a series of attempts to escape the overshadowing figure of his brother. His adulation of the Gorilla reflects his sense of inferiority and subservience to Peter, and as an intellectual he rejects critical, distanced objectivity for an ethos of self-dissolution and redemption through a mythology of organic unity and individual self-sacrifice. Just as Peter's fetishization of books and knowledge finds a mirror-image in Therese's attitudes toward money and sex, so too Georges' primitivist mythology finds an ironic mirror-image in the everyday brutality of the proto-Nazi, Pfaff. Georges is an alienated intellectual who, in despair at finding any form of synthesis, submerges himself in—rather than closing himself off from—the outside world. In the context of the 1930s, he must be seen in the light of the intellectuals who succumbed to the promise of redemption through proto-fascist ideologies. There is no synthesis of the symbolic opposites of "Kopf" and "Welt." Georges' intellectualization of the "world," the "Welt im Kopf" of the final part is not a resolution, but a renunciation of critical intellect.

Peter Kien's dream and Georges Kien's meeting with the Gorilla are two important junctures in the novel, in which the crisis of reason, the alienation of knowledge from humanity, is reflected upon, through reference to the novel as a form of communication.

Canetti's response to this crisis lies in his implicit demand for the ironic reader: the reader who can maintain an ironic, critical distance from the characters and the novel as a whole, the reader who consistently refuses to fall into the trap of mistaking the intellectual construct for the human whole. Peter Kien's single-minded adoption of Confucius' and Kant's philosophies of "Pflicht um der Pflicht willen" (380) leads directly to catastrophe, but Georges' inability to achieve critical distance from the mythologies of the Gorilla's charismatic vitalism and the collectivity of the termite-nest is also portrayed negatively. In the motif of the reader and the novel, occurring at two important points in the novel, Canetti implies the necessity of a dynamic relationship between the reader and the text, where the reader is a critical, thinking subject, and the text a self-reflexive world. Canetti's implied reader, unlike the two readers of the novel, Peter and Georges, can be "open" even where the fictional figures remain "closed." Thus a central theme of the work is the novelist's task of enlightenment, of "opening" the reader to the danger of "closed" structures of understanding, while still maintaining coherence. Through the implied call for critical dialogue with the reader of this novel, Canetti maintains the role of enlightened intellectual which both Peter and Georges Kien have abandoned.

The fire in the Theresianum—an image of the burning of the "Justizpalast" on July 15, 1927[18]—is reflected in the burning of the library. The fire as symbol of political upheaval is negative: the potentially revolutionary image is destructive in a society without a tradition of democratic thought and responsible—as opposed to charismatic—political leadership. It is associated with madness, the end of enlightenment (i.e. book-burning) and the irruption of unreason as the dominant force of society.

The final image of the novel is closed. The fires in the library ("Kopf") and the Theresianum ("Welt") reflect each other. Only the literary form of the novel itself remains as a statement of the possibility of enlightenment, of the re-establishment of meaning as a social category through the critical dialogue between author and reader.

Notes

1. Page references in brackets following quotations are to Elias Canetti, *Die Blendung* (Frankfurt: Fischer, 1979).

2. Raymond Williams, "Fiction and Delusion. A note on 'Auto-da-Fé,'" *New Left Review* 15 (1962): 106.

3. "Peter fürchtet die Spaltung, die Auflösung der Persönlichkeit, die Kluft, die ihn der Verteidigung beraubt." David Roberts, *Kopf und Welt. Elias Canettis Roman 'Die Blendung'* (München: Hanser, 1975) 100.

4. Manfred Durzak, "Versuch über Elias Canetti," *Akzente* 17 (1970) 174.

5. Karl Markus Michel, "Der Intellektuelle und die Masse. Zu zwei Büchern von Elias Canetti," *Die Neue Rundschau* 75 (1964) 311; Annemarie Auer, "Ein Genie und sein Sonderling—Elias Canetti und die Blendung," *Interpretationen zu Elias Canetti,* ed. Manfred Durzak (Stuttgart: Klett, 1983) 51; Dieter Dissinger, *Vereinzelung und Massenwahn. Elias Canettis Roman 'Die Blendung,'* Studien zur Germanistik, Anglistik und Komparistik, vol. 11 (Bonn: Bouvier, 1971) 114 f.; Edward A. Thomson, "Elias Canetti's *Die Blendung* and the Changing Image of Madness," *German Life and Letters* 26 (1972) 44; Viktor Suchy, "Exil in Permanenz. Elias Canetti und der unbedingte Primat des Lebens," *Die deutsche Exilliteratur 1933-1945,* ed. Manfred Durzak (Stuttgart: Reclam, 1973) 288; Walter H. Sokel, "The Ambiguity of Madness: Elias Canetti's Novel *Die Blendung,*" *Views and Reviews of Modern German Literature.* Festschrift for Adolf D. Klarmann, ed. Karl S. Weimar (München: Delp, 1974) 182-83; Roman Karst, "Elias Canetti's *Die Blendung:* A Study in Insanity," *Modern Austrian Literature* 16 (1983) 133; Detlef Krumme, *Lesemodelle. Elias Canetti, Günter Grass, Walter Höllerer* (München: Carl Hanser, 1983) 82 f.

6. In answering the question whether Georges represents an alternative to Peter, Roberts is unclear. On the one hand Georges stands "tatsächlich außerhalb der Welt der 'Blendung,' theoretisch in seiner Anerkennung der Macht der Masse im Menschen, praktisch in seiner Fähigkeit zu Mitgefühl und seinem Hunger nach den Verwandlungen des Augenblicks." On the other hand, however, he is caught in the double-bind of having the knowledge to cure his patients, but at the same time regretting what this cure brings about—i.e. normality. Roberts uses the rather difficult term, "negativer Dialektik" to characterize the relationship of the brothers. Roberts 108.

7. Dagmar Barnouw, *Elias Canetti,* Sammlung Metzler 180, (Stuttgart: Metzler, 1979) 25, 29.

8. Krumme 82 f.

9. Cf. Martin Bollacher, "Elias Canetti, *Die Blendung* (1935/36)," *Deutsche Romane des 20. Jahrhunderts. Neue Interpretationen,* ed. Paul Michael Lützeler (Königstein: Athenäum, 1983) 243; Friedbert Aspetsberger, "Weltmeister der Verachtung. Zur *Blendung," Blendung als Lebensform. Elias Canetti,* eds. Friedbert Aspetsberger and Gerald Stieg (Königstein/Ts.: Athenäum, 1985) 118-19; Barbara Meili, *Erinnerung und Vision. Der lebensgeschichtliche Hintergrund von Elias Canettis Roman 'Die Blendung,'* Stud. z. Germanistik, Anglistik und Komparatistik, vol. 115 (Bonn: Bouvier, 1985) 166 (Georges as "ethisch fragwürdig"), 177 (as power hungry), 180 (as fascist) and 194 (as "Anklage gegen die zeitgenössische Intelligenz").

10. Roberts 86-87.

11. Cf. Pavel Petr, "Marxist Theories of the Comic," *Comic Relations. Studies in the Comic, Satire and Parody,* eds. Pavel Petr, David Roberts, Philip Thomson (Frankfurt: Peter Lang, 1985) 57-66.

12. See in particular Durzak, "Versuch" 173.

13. Roberts 101-2.

14. On the train to Vienna Georges dreams "von zwei Hähnen," the larger of which, "rot und schwach" is Peter, and the smaller, "gepflegt und verschlagen," himself. They are fighting cocks ("Kampfhähne"), and their "Kampf zog sich lange hin." The end of this fight is ambiguous. The smaller (Georges himself) "gab sich zufrieden. Er hatte gesiegt . . ." However the larger (Peter) grows in size and strength of colour until Georges awakens and sees the rising sun through his window. (372) The ambiguity of the role relationships in the dream foreshadows the ambiguity of Georges' "victory" over Peter. Cf. Dissinger, *Vereinzelung und Massenwahn* 68.

15. Roberts 85.

16. Critics have tended to see Peter's and Georg's views of the novel in terms of their attitudes to each other. Dissinger sees the two brothers as incorporating polarized aspects of the artistic consciousness: "Peter Kien weiß um die Form, sie ist ihm bereits Inhalt. Georg kennt Inhalte, ohne ihnen gültige Form zu geben. Die ungleichen Brüder vertreten zwei Extreme, die nur zusammen den Dichter ermöglichen." Dieter Dissinger, "Der Roman *Die Blendung," Text und Kritik* 28 (1973) 37. Roberts sees the attitudes of the two brothers as reflecting the differences in their personalities:
"Beide Brüder sind dem Roman gegenüber negativ eingestellt: dem einen ist der Roman zu bedrohlich, dem anderen ist er zu zahm." Roberts 101. For Meili, both characters' rejection of the novel is indicative of their inability to cope with reality. Meili 188.

17. Roberts 101.

18. Cf. Gerald Stieg, "Früchte des Feuers. Der 15. Juli 1927 in der *Blendung* und in den *Dämonen,"* Aspetsberger and Stieg, *Blendung als Lebensform* 143-75; and Bollacher 240-41.

David Darby (essay date 1992)

SOURCE: Darby, David. "A Literary Life: The Textuality of Elias Canetti's Autobiography." *Modern Austrian Literature* 25, no. 2 (1992): 37-49.

[In the following essay, Darby examines Canetti's apparent awareness in the narrative of his autobiography of the difficulty of writing an autobiographical work.]

I propose a reading of Elias Canetti's three volumes of autobiography against the grain.[1] Unlike the author's other extended prose narrative, ***Die Blendung,*** which exploits overtly complex narrative strategies to disrupt the ease of the reader's task, these texts have generally been received as works of a reassuring structural order and simplicity. This essay offers a study of the inconsistencies of the narrative and thereby an exploration of one aspect of the formal artifice which characterizes the narration of Canetti's literary life. By reading "against the grain," I mean that I will focus my attention on the frequent passages in the text which reveal in the narration an awareness of the problems inherent in writing a literary life. These are points where the mimetic illusion enunciated by the discreet third-person past-tense narrator is suspended as a result of an interruption by a present-tense consciousness in the narration. My reading will not approach Canetti's autobiography as a document of an age and a world gone by, in the sense that I will not emphasize its historical truth-function over aspects of its textuality. Neither do I intend to participate in a debate concerned with the veracity or fictionality of the story it tells.[2] Rather, I will concentrate on the tension evident in these texts between the mimetic, retrospective function of autobiography and the self-conscious, present-tense reference which is essential to the teleological project of these texts.

The most thorough and incisive structural examination of these three volumes is presented in the second chapter of Friederike Eigler's 1988 monograph on Canetti's autobiographical writings.[3] My observations are to a considerable extent complementary to Eigler's view of the autobiography as a consciously constructed narrative text. My reading differs from hers in that I see the tensions of the relationship between the respective fictional (?) intelligences of narrating subject and narrated subject as imposing an essentially disruptive intrusion into a generally discreetly or harmoniously structured text. I propose to continue Eigler's general project of reading the life of Canetti as a textual construct, and so to participate in that kind of reading of the autobiography which moves beyond a vision of the easy seduction of the reader through the apparent formal and stylistic naivety of the narration of an indisputably fascinating life-story.

The difference between narrating and narrated subject is logically essential to any narrative text, although Lejeune's famous "pacte autobiographique" involves a stabilization and at least a partial, apparent deproblematization of this relationship as it pertains to autobiography in terms of the "*identité de nom* entre l'auteur . . . le narrateur et le personnage dont on parle."[4] In Canetti's autobiography this nominal identity is established early and clearly. Nevertheless, it is logically indisputable that this pact, along with its referential implications, is a conventional textual strategy identifying beings living in entirely separate ontological spheres of existence. Their true relationship is more than simply temporal: it is determined essentially by a potentially very complex act of conscious and deliberate reconstruction.

The process of remembering is explicitly emphasized as a central concern in Canetti's texts, as it is of course in any traditional autobiographical narrative, and its thematization is to some degree both conventional and necessary to the organization of the narrative-communicative situation of such texts. However, where Canetti's autobiography becomes especially interesting in this respect is in its foregrounding of the inconsistencies and failures in the narrator's capacity to remember. On the one hand there is the precision, intensity, and authority with which the narrating Canetti recalls, for example, his earliest visual memory at the beginning of *Die gerettete Zunge* in order patently to consolidate the terms of the "pacte autobiographique"; similar statements of the power of his audile memory are frequent, especially in the first volume, such as his comment on an accusation made by his maternal grandfather: "'Fálsu!'—'Falscher!' . . . ich habe es im Ohr, als wäre ich gestern bei ihm zu Besuch gewesen" (*GZ* [*Die gerettete Zunge*] 31). On the other hand, and in distinct contrast to such authenticating claims, stand passages which throw into doubt the traditional idea of the narrator, autobiographical or otherwise, as what Patrick O'Neill calls the "*gnarus,* a knowing one . . . master of the communicative situation . . . an authority who narrates what he knows."[5]

Very early in the autobiography the narrator emphasizes the structuring function of memory, as historical circumstances are thrown into question, here concerning the comet he sees as a child: "Vielleicht hat er sich in meiner Erinnerung verlängert, vielleicht nahm er nicht den halben, sondern einen kleineren Teil des Himmels ein" (*GZ* 34). This kind of uncertainty of proportion appears, on a first reading, to be a natural and innocent characteristic of one's recollections of childhood; the point is, however, that in textual terms the comet has been stretched from a brief sighting to the length of half a chapter of narrative, and thus the present-tense utterance reveals itself as a self-referential strategy whereby the text explicitly discusses the compromising of its own mimetic, representational axis. The admission of an analogous distortion of spatial-temporal relationships is found in *Die Fackel im Ohr* with regard to the chapter devoted to Isak Babel: "Einen großen Raum in meiner Erinnerung an die Berliner Zeit nimmt Isaak Babel ein. . . . Ich denke, er war gegen Ende September da und blieb in Wirklichkeit nicht länger als zwei Wochen" (*FO* [*Die Fackel im Ohr*] 317-318).

A marked, literally traductive effect of the process of remembering is foregrounded in another passage early in the Rustschuk section of the autobiography: "Alle Ereignisse jener ersten Jahre spielten sich auf spanisch oder bulgarisch ab. Sie haben sich mir später zum größten Teil ins Deutsche übersetzt. . . . [D]as meiste, und ganz besonders alles Bulgarische . . . trage ich deutsch im Kopf" (*GZ* 18-19). Again, this traduction—"diese geheimnisvolle Übertragung" (*GZ* 18)—is perhaps a necessary event in a life whose critical developmental phases have been experienced in a series of different languages of which Ladino, Bulgarian and German represent only a small number. But such a statement is, for all that, no less of an indication of a severe strain in the relationship of identity between the various textual subjects essential to autobiography. By foregrounding the problematic function of memory in these terms several pages into the text, the narrator calls into question the literal veracity of memories—recounted in German and including direct-speech quotations in German—for whose literal precision he has previously vouched. This is not, however, the only possible reading of Canetti's confession of the mediated condition of his recollections: taking an alternative perspective, one can reasonably view this commentary on the traductive aspect of memory and writing as a narrative strategy of damage control. By conceding the questionable status of the textual manifestations of only a limited quantity of early experience, the narrative proceeds to consolidate the illusion of the unmediated authenticity of the whole of the remaining body of experience whose translation into a linear narrative text is implicit, silent, and—where the narrator insists on the absolute immediacy of the events recounted—even denied.

During the narration of the childhood years, the narrating voice points at intervals to holes in its knowledge and authority. These lacunae are sometimes filled by the report of data obtained from other sources (for example: "Alles was von diesem Augenblick an geschah, ist mir nur aus Erzählungen bekannt" [*GZ* 49]), in which case the character of the narrative is determined by a surrender of the authority of memory and by a superimposition of other informational sources. Other gaps are left open, with statements of the narrative impotence of the *gnarus* Canetti: "Ich kann mich nicht erinnern . . ." (*GZ* 70); "Ich habe kaum eine Erinnerung ans erste Wiener Jahr . . ." (*GZ* 116); "An die letzten Tage in Wien kann ich mich nicht erinnern. Ich weiß nicht mehr. . . . Ich habe auch keine Erinnerung an die Reise. Ich sehe uns erst in Reichenhall wieder" (*GZ* 177); "Ich habe nur drei Zimmer in Erinnerung, in denen wir uns bewegten; aber es muß auch ein schmäleres, viertes Zimmer gegeben haben . . ." (*GZ* 197).

These quotations are all drawn from the first volume of the autobiography, *Die gerettete Zunge,* which covers the first sixteen years of Canetti's life. Given that fact, it is perhaps not surprising that such lacunae are to be found in an account published by a mature author sixty or so years after the events narrated. However, such narrative phenomena are not restricted solely to this volume. Indeed, their occurrence in the subsequent volumes is no less frequent. In *Die Fackel im Ohr,* covering the next ten years, the narrating Canetti is at various points unable to remember events clearly: "Ich kann mich . . . nicht erinnern. Ich weiß nicht . . . Ich *sehe* mich nicht gut an diesem Tag . . ." (*FO* 277). Names are often forgotten (*FO* 200, 209, 336, 357) as well as the details of incidents and conversations; for example: "Keinen Satz, keine Silbe dieser Wortgeplätscher könnte ich wiederholen . . ." (*FO* 164, cf. 321). In the third volume, *Das Augenspiel,* there are further instances of the forgetting of conversations, but here another, non-audible mode of memory becomes dominant: "Ich weiß nicht, was dann gesagt wurde. Ich habe mich bemüht, die ersten Worte, ihre wie meine, wiederzufinden. Sie sind untergegangen. . . . Ich habe die erste Begegnung mit ihr [Anna Mahler] bewahrt, indem ich sie von allen Worten befreit habe . . ." (*A* [*Das Augenspiel*] 81); and similarly with *Fritz Wotruba:* "[V]on diesem ersten Gespräch habe ich nur den einen Satz, mit dem es begann, in Erinnerung behalten. Wohl aber sehe ich ihn vor mir. . . . Vielleicht habe ich darum das Gespräch vergessen" (*A* 103-105). Further lapses of audile memory are found in connection with Dr. Sonne (*A* 148) and Robert Musil (*A* 183, 211).

Once again, these forgotten details may be seen to function as a trope of psychological realism in the composition of the identity of the narrating Canetti as the subject of the enunciation, and may be read as contributing to a function of verisimilitude. So far, this function is entirely consistent with Lejeune's "pacte référentiel," which, as it applies to autobiography, legitimizes a com-

promised version of absolute biographical or historical truth. Lejeune discusses this pact as "une preuve supplémentaire d'honnêteté," a restriction of the autobiographical project "au *possible* (la vérité telle qu'elle m'apparaît, dans la mesure où je puis la connaître, etc., faisant la part des inévitables oublis, erreurs, déformations involontaires, etc.)."[6] What must be borne in mind is the lack of hesitation with which Canetti is prepared—elsewhere in the autobiography—to abandon this problematic of psychological verisimilitude and thereby irretrievably to compromise Lejeune's "pacte référentiel." This happens most notably in the reproduction, allegedly word for word, of dialogues recollected after a period of over fifty years, whose citing, almost completely uninterrupted by the narrator's commentary, stretches over several pages elsewhere in the text (for example, *GZ* 366-371). There is nothing new or surprising in pointing out that memory is selective. The point here, however, is that the narrative is tacitly suggesting the deliberateness (or, at least, the consciousness) of the act of selection. An even less innocent conception of other acts of forgetting is suggested by Gerhard Melzer's discussion of Canetti's "Rhetorik der Entwertung," as part of which "das Vergessen . . . das *Schweigen* bzw. *Verschweigen* und das *Wegsehen*" all function as strategies of power, suppression, and survival.[7] Waltraud Wiethölter similarly writes of "der völlig ungebrochene Herrschaftsgestus, mit dem Canetti das autobiographische Material verwaltet."[8]

A more visual mode of remembering becomes dominant in the later sections, and the lacunae frequently become quite sense-specific. In the earlier sections a quasi-cinematographic technique is exploited in order to resume interrupted narrative sequences with expressions such as "Ich sehe uns erst in Reichenhall wieder" (*GZ* 177). Later, the visual sequences, such as those cited above which refer to Anna Mahler and Fritz Wotruba, are so durable that they cannot, the text states, be interrupted by the ostensibly unwanted lacunae caused by failures of audile memory.

However, as Eigler indicates, it is not inevitable that the overt manifestations of a polytropic narrator's operations will have the effect of suspending or, at the very least, distracting from the texts' mimetic function; rather, they may serve conversely to emphasize the density of textual organization and the logic of the story told.[9] The frequency of analeptic and proleptic reference to points both within and beyond the narrated time-frame of these three volumes (1905-1937) serves to give the sense of a conscious teleological structure and self-understanding to the narrative. This autobiography reads as a kind of *Entwicklungsroman,* a constructed portrait of the author of a very specific group of works as a young man. Of these works, the development of the writer toward the authorship of *Masse und Macht* (published in 1960, twenty-three years after the end of the period covered in the autobiography) is especially stressed. In fact, the anticipation of that book is a principal focus of the second and third volumes, *Die Fackel im Ohr* and *Das Augenspiel,* and eclipses even the attention paid to those other texts—*Die Blendung, Hochzeit,* and the *Komödie der Eitelkeit*—whose writing falls within the narrated time-scale of the autobiography. (My perception of the teleological focus of the autobiography differs here in detail from that of Gerald Stieg's categorization of the first two volumes of Canetti's autobiography "als Prähistorie, als Archäologie der *Blendung,*" a view accepted by Sigurd Paul Scheichl.[10] While the composition of the novel represents the obvious climax of *Die Fackel im Ohr,* my argument is based both on the repeated references throughout the three extant volumes to Canetti's work on *Masse und Macht,* and to the overall subordination in the autobiography of *Die Blendung* to the later theoretical work.)

Another specific kind of prolepsis which is found throughout all three volumes of Canetti's autobiography both interrupts the mimetic axis of the text and offers further evidence of the careful artifice characteristic of the construction of the writer's own life. This concerns the author's gaining in later years of a mature understanding of his own youthful experiences. These reflexive references to the process of narrative structuration (distributed evenly through the three volumes, and by no means more common with respect to childhood events) make the narrating subject explicit in two distinct ways: the understanding may be stated to have been gained either at the point of narration or at some intermediate point in the years separating the narrated world from the act of narration. The differentiation of perspectives is a characteristic feature of these texts, and its interpretative function stands in conflict with the sense of unmediated memory toward which most critical readings have tended. Such distinctions are generally made in the form of a variety of narrative tags, of which the following list represents only a small selection: "Als Kind hatte ich keinen Überblick . . ." (*GZ* 10); "Ich wußte damals noch nicht . . ." (*GZ* 90); "Wenn ich es heute bedenke . . ." (*GZ* 95); "Erst später begriff ich . . ." (*GZ* 102); "Erst jetzt, da ich diese Dinge ein wenig bedenke, begreife ich . . ." (*GZ* 301); "Ich wußte damals nichts . . ." (*FO* 20); "Ich begriff erst viel später . . ." (*FO* 166); "erst heute, nach 50 Jahren, erkenne ich an ihr wie an mir alle Zeichen der Verliebtheit . . ." (*FO* 212); "Es war, so sehe ich es heute, ein guter Instinkt . . ." (*FO* 284); "Sein Schweigen fiel mir erst später mehr und mehr auf . . ." (*A* 41); "aber das denke ich mir erst heute . . ." (*A* 90); "das wird mir jetzt erst klar . . ." (*A* 110); "das habe ich aber erst später erkannt . . ." (*A* 250); "Jahre danach, im Krieg, ich war in England, fiel es mir wie Schuppen von den Augen . . ." (*A* 322).

These points are of interest since they represent one of the most explicit manifestations of the disparity between subjects on different ontological levels in the narration. It is in them that the tense equilibrium between the two axes essential to autobiographical—and, in general, to all realistic—narrative is exposed. The first of these is the mimetic, that is, the illusion of a natural, authentic, and verisimilar representation of a series of reconstituted earlier experiences; the second axis is the artificial activity of narration, in which the earlier experiences are organized in a teleologically determined pattern, and thereby structured into a linear narrative. *Die gerettete Zunge, Die Fackel im Ohr,* and *Das Augenspiel* all foreground this latter function by means of the several modes of present-tense reference already discussed: the thematization of memory, personal or gnomic commentaries, analeptic or proleptic reference, differentiation between present and past knowledge or comprehension, accreditation of sources of knowledge other than the personal-empirical, intertextual reference in terms either of discreet structural parallels to individual texts (Robert Gould, for example, sees *Dichtung und Wahrheit* here as an applicable intertext)[11] or of overtly explanatory comparisons in the text of the autobiography to a vast range of both verbal and visual texts, or with various mythic traditions. Obviously, the more explicitly these texts emphasize this aspect of their construction, the more radically they compromise the transparency of their mimetic function.

It is in moments either where memory fails (partially or completely) or where memory is superceded—or, at least, supplemented—by other sources of textual data that the relationship of these two axes is shown to be a complex and delicate balancing act. The illusion of the teleologically structured literary life is maintained exclusively by virtue of the organizational activities of the narrating textual intelligence, and conversely by virtue also of that intelligence's willingness to conceal the narrative strategies it exploits in order to produce and discourse a realistic story. These points where the narrating voice indicates the unreliability or inadequacy of memory make unmistakably clear even to the most determinedly mimesis-oriented reader that the story the reader is receiving is not (and could not possibly be) the same as that experienced by the young Canetti. By exposing the illusory nature of Philippe Lejeune's "*identité de nom,*" they necessarily disrupt the terms of the pact deliberately established at the opening of *Die gerettete Zunge.*

Noteworthy on the subject of this identity of name linking intelligences on two ontologically distinct planes is the differentiation between, on the one hand, references to Canetti's younger brother Georg in the autobiography and, on the other, the paratextual dedication of the first volume to Georges Canetti (the name assumed by the adult Georg Canetti following his emigration to

Paris). In this case the text uses different nominal signifiers to distinguish between the brother of the narrated Canetti and the brother of the narrating Canetti. By doing so it moves the relationship of these two subjects beyond the merely temporal. The importance of this is that by inverse analogy this logically exposes the shifting quality of reference essential to—but at first glance invisible in—pronominal signifiers as characterized by the autobiographer's "ich."

A further kind of informational lacuna is made explicit, which, while by no means threatening the implicit identification of the narrating Canetti with the narrated Canetti, does not sit very comfortably with the picture of the former as the teleologically conscious, structuring *gnarus* of these three volumes. This concerns the extraordinary frequency of expressions of uncertainty and ignorance of the motivations of various narrated-world figures throughout all three volumes. Canetti's autobiography is riddled with instances of such confessions, the starkly simple and confessional words "vielleicht" and "ich weiß nicht" occurring with a quite remarkable regularity in such contexts. This in some ways reinforces the "pacte autobiographique," since these uncertainties and areas of negligence are apparently not acquired in the time span between experience and narration but rather preserved intact as informational gaps from narrated youth to narrating maturity. However, it is obviously not customary in realist, readerly narratives for the narrator to draw attention to things of which he or she is ignorant, and certainly not with the frequency evident in these texts. By mentioning them, the narrating Canetti on the one hand lends a sense of modest naivety to his activity, and on the other he conversely throws into doubt his implicit authority to determine and organize the events of the story he is discoursing in such a way that they make sense of the life of the author.

The present-time reference of the narration, as I suggested above, is most explicit at points in the text where the immediacy—and (the text implies) therefore the veracity—of memories is being stressed, or where authoritative narrative commentary on earlier events is evident in the text. There are two types of present-tense usage in this autobiography: one I will refer to as the personal present, the other as the gnomic present.

The personal present tense is found in two distinct contexts. These are: firstly, in expressions of judgment with reference to the narrative present, such as: "Ich wundere mich nicht, daß es zur Katastrophe kam" (*GZ* 45); "dieses Buch . . . das mir vom ersten Wort an widerstrebte und das mir heute, 55 Jahre danach, nicht weniger widerstrebt . . ." (*FO* 168); "[ein] Hochgefühl, wie ich es seither nie wieder gekannt habe" (*FO* 402); and secondly, in reflexive, metanarrative commentaries which arrest the mimetic illusion of the autobiography:

"Ich kann es—sehr unzulänglich—nur ein Leben der Besessenheit nennen" (*GZ* 362); "Ich will nicht sagen, daß es ein Vergnügen war" (*FO* 57); "ich habe seither nie von ihm gesprochen und es fällt mir schwer, ihn zu schildern" (*FO* 155); "Nicht leichten Herzens befasse ich mich mit Broch, denn ich weiß nicht, wie ich ihm gerecht werden soll" (*A* 28).

The gnomic present is noticeably less common in these texts, but the instances of its deployment in the narrative are of considerable interest, since they usually involve the inception of an explicitly self-referential focus in the writing. The first such passage occurs two hundred pages into *Die gerettete Zunge,* with reference to Canetti's schooling in Zürich. The passage is over one page long, and one part of it proposes a typology of teachers as a frame for the structural ordering and reading of a life: "Es wäre nicht schwierig und vielleicht auch reizvoll, ein späteres Leben danach zu durchforschen, welchen und wievielen dieser Lehrer man unter anderen Namen wiederbegegnet ist . . ." (*GZ* 211). While this suggestion is not actively pursued in Canetti's autobiography, the goal it implies—a unified principle for writing a life—is of course of central importance in both biography and autobiography. In *Die Fackel im Ohr,* the narrating voice notes, again in the gnomic mode: "Es ist nichts unwiderstehlicher als die Lockung, den inneren Raum eines Menschen zu betreten" (*FO* 184). Here the narrator is providing at least the illusion of such a temptation, but this gnomic commentary serves the double function of inviting the reader's complicity in the mimetic project of the autobiography, while conversely pointing directly toward the very self-consciousness of narrating which highlights the constructed textuality of the figure whose inner space is under exploration.

The third volume shows considerably more evidence of such gnomic reflexive commentary, in part because of its discussion of other writings by Canetti, firstly of *Die Blendung,* and in part because of its breadth of focus on the lives and works of a range of writers and artists in Vienna in the 1930s. One comment in particular is of interest: over eight hundred pages into his autobiography, and twenty-six years into his narrated life, and with—at that stage—the hindsight of another fifty-four years which have not (or, perhaps, not yet) been included in the autobiographical project, one reads: "Es ist überwältigend zu erleben, *wieviel* man über sich zu sagen hat" (*A* 36). Given the comprehensive humorlessness—indeed even pomposity—of Canetti's autobiography, it is extremely difficult to read this comment as ironic. The implication, that to avoid being overwhelmed by the experiences of which one wishes to tell a degree of selection and structure is necessary, is reinforced by a subsequent passage of gnomic present tense. Here, the dangers of unstructured knowledge are discussed in terms of the "amorphe Sucht der Vielwisserei, des Ausgreifens in diese und jene Richtung, des Wieder-erfahrenlassens eines erst Berührten, kaum noch Ergriffenen . . . diese Neugier, die gewiß mehr als Neugier ist, denn sie hat keine Absicht und endet in nichts . . . dieses Zucken und Ziehen nach allen Seiten . . ." (*A* 149). The self-referentiality of this commentary is readily apparent: the passage stands persuasively as a statement of Canetti's rationale for his careful teleological structuring of his own literary life. The problem is how to reconcile this kind of commentary with such personal present-tense confessions as that found near the end of *Die gerettete Zunge,* where Canetti cites Conrad Ferdinand Meyer's couplet: "Ich bin kein ausgeklügelt Buch, ich bin ein Mensch mit seinem Widerspruch" (*GZ* 340). He then goes on to reflect on his creative situation: "Heute, da ich gestaltete Geschichte nicht mehr ertrage, da ich nur die Quellen selbst, naive Berichte oder harte Gedanken zu ihnen suche . . ." (*GZ* 341). The narrating Canetti wants, it seems, to have his teleological cake and eat it too, to insist on the immediacy, vibrancy, and veracity of his narrated world—and his narrated subject—while presenting that world as an ordered (and therefore necessarily mediated) narrative structure.

There are, then, several consciousnesses in play in these texts: that of the young narrated-world actant Canetti, that of the Canetti of the years between the end of the story of the autobiography in 1937 and the present time of the autobiographer, and that of the narrating Canetti. I propose that none of these alone represents the single, indivisible subject of the three volumes of this autobiography. In a passage in *Die Fackel im Ohr* discussing the textual transformation of "der amorphe Knäuel"[12] of his experiences in Berlin during the summer of 1928 into the fictional world of the novel *Die Blendung,* Canetti states: "Nun wäre es gar kein Unglück gewesen, daß nichts von den Berliner Wochen versickert war, daß man alles bewahrt hatte. Es hätte sich aufschreiben lassen und es wäre ein farbiger und vielleicht gar nicht uninteressanter Bericht geworden. Es ließe sich heute noch schreiben, so lange hat es sich erhalten. Aber ein Bericht hätte das Wesentliche daran nie erfaßt. . . . Denn der eine, einheitliche Mensch, der es aufgefaßt hatte und nun scheinbar alles in sich enthielt, war ein Truggebilde" (*FO* 350).

In terms of fiction, a structural model has been developed which differentiates such a fictional textual subject from both the empirical author and the narrator. It is obviously quite impossible to achieve the complete and integrated reconstruction of a human life and consciousness—fictional or otherwise—in linear, narrative form, even in a retrospective, autobiographical context. However, a reconstruction of this "Truggebilde" as an implicit authorial presence as part of the textual communication act—that is, an authority whose identity can be deduced exclusively from textual data—is clearly fea-

sible as a task for a reader. This kind of model is equally appropriate to the analysis of traditional autobiographical texts, since the teleological intention of such texts projects a clearly ordered, ideal picture. Since, as Friederike Eigler's study of the autobiography indicates, the reader has no objective yardstick for establishing the precise degree of historical authenticity, the ideal picture assumes its illusion of historical and biographical authenticity by default once Lejeune's pact of nominal identity is sealed. The empirical author remains hidden behind the blind of the image he constructs of himself. The principle which finally distinguishes autobiographical texts from others is that the very act of authorial concealment flaunts itself deceitfully in the guise of a generous and sensitive act of personal confession.

In conclusion, however, one must acknowledge that the mimetic illusion of the teleological project has proved in *Die gerettete Zunge, Die Fackel im Ohr,* and *Das Augenspiel* extremely durable. These volumes have found—apparently on account of the persuasiveness of this illusion—remarkably broad critical and popular approval, according to which the tale has generally been taken to be more compelling than an analysis of its telling. The concentration on the truth-function of the texts, which has been characteristic of such readings, is seen to represent a failure to heed the narrative small-print incorporated in these texts. This is even openly suggested at one point in *Die Fakkel im Ohr* where Canetti offers what to all intents and purposes appears to be a disclaimer of authorial responsibility for factual truthfulness. He is at pains to absolve the act of story-telling from the possible accusation of bad faith. The position which he takes pleads for a certain amorality in the recounting of a life-story, and it radically contradicts Lejeune's definition of autobiographies as primarily referential texts whose aim "n'est pas la simple vraisemblance, mais la ressemblance au vrai. Non 'l'effet du réel,' mais l'image du réel."[13] Concerning his Odysseus-like activity as a young man of inventing fictional women in his life with the aim of distracting his mother from her ferocious verbal attacks on his future wife Veza, Canetti offers both a reflexive commentary on his own story-telling as a whole, and an argument which can be read as an explicit warning against a naive reading focusing exclusively on the mimetic—and even documentary—axis of the three volumes of his autobiography: "Was man gut erfand," states the narrating Canetti's observation, "war eine Geschichte, keine Lüge . . ." (*FO* 252).

Notes

1. Elias Canetti, *Die gerettete Zunge: Geschichte einer Jugend* (München: Hanser, 1977); *Die Fackel im Ohr: Lebensgeschichte 1921-1931* (München: Hanser, 1980); and *Das Augenspiel: Lebensgeschichte 1931-1937* (München: Hanser,

1985). References to these texts will be given in parentheses, the respective volumes being identified as *GZ, FO,* and *A.*

2. See for example: Bernd Witte, "Der Erzähler als Tod-Feind: Zu Elias Canettis Autobiographie" in: *Text und Kritik,* Heft 28, third edition (September, 1982), 68-70; Gerald Stieg, "Betrachtungen zu Elias Canettis Autobiographie" in: *Zu Elias Canetti,* ed. Manfred Durzak (Stuttgart: Klett, 1983), p. 158; and Madeleine Salzmann, *Die Kommunikationsstruktur der Autobiographie: Mit kommunikationsorientierten Analysen der Autobiographien von Max Frisch, Helga M. Novak und Elias Canetti* (Bern: Lang, 1988), especially pp. 30-41.

3. Friederike Eigler, *Das autobiographische Werk von Elias Canetti: Identität—Verwandlung—Machtausübung* (Tübingen: Stauffenburg, 1988), pp. 30-77.

4. Philippe Lejeune, *Le pacte autobiographique* (Paris: Seuil, 1975), pp. 23-24.

5. Patrick O'Neill, *The Comedy of Entropy: Humour, Narrative, Reading* (Toronto: University of Toronto Press, 1990), p. 204.

6. Lejeune, p. 36.

7. Gerhard Melzer, "Der einzige Satz und sein Eigentümer: Versuch über den symbolischen Machthaber Elias Canetti" in: *Experte der Macht: Elias Canetti,* ed. Kurt Bartsch and Gerhard Melzer (Graz: Droschl, 1985), p. 66.

8. Waltraud Wiethölter, "Sprechen—Lesen—Schreiben: Zur Funktion von Sprache und Schrift in Canettis Autobiographie" in: *Deutsche Vierteljahresschrift für Literaturwissenschaft und Geistesgeschichte,* 64 (1990), 150.

9. Eigler, p. 58.

10. Gerald Stieg, "Elias Canetti und Karl Kraus: Ein Versuch" in: *Modern Austrian Literature,* 16/3-4 (1983), 200; Sigurd Paul Scheichl, "Hörenlernen: Zur teleologischen Struktur der autobiographischen Bücher Canettis" in: *Elias Canetti: Blendung als Lebensform,* ed. Friedbert Aspetsberger and Gerald Stieg (Königstein/Taunus: Athenäum, 1985), pp. 73, 77.

11. Robert Gould, "*Die gerettete Zunge* and *Dichtung und Wahrheit:* Hypertextuality in Autobiography and its Implications" in: *Seminar,* 21 (1985), 79-107; see also Witte, p. 66.

12. Elias Canetti, "Das erste Buch: *Die Blendung*" in: *Das Gewissen der Worte: Essays* (München: Hanser, 1975), p. 229.

13. Lejeune, p. 36.

Sigurd Paul Scheichl (essay date 1992)

SOURCE: Scheichl, Sigurd Paul. "Is Peter Kien a Jew? A Reading of Elias Canetti's *Auto-da-fé* in its Historical Context.'" In *The Jewish Self-Portrait in European and American Literature,* edited by Hans Jürgen Schrader, Elliott M. Simon, and Charlotte Wardi, pp. 159-70. Tübingen, Germany: Max Niemeyer Verlag, 1996.

[*In the following essay, originally read at the universities of Poznan and Coimbra in 1992, Scheichl examines historical events in Canetti's lifetime that appear, literally or representatively, in* Auto da fé.]

The English title of Elias Canetti's only novel, **Auto-da-fé** (1935, finished in 1931)[2] refers to the end of the book, when the protagonist burns himself and his library. The German title, **Die Blendung,** "The Blinding", refers to something quite different: to the loss of the central character's ability to see reality, but also to the Biblical tale of Samson and Delilah (Judges, ch. 13-16), to Samson's loss of force and the destruction of his eyesight.

The relation to the Bible can be corroborated by textual signs: the protagonist, Peter Kien, is described as being very tall, reminding us of Samson, whom we imagine as a very big man: "Already at dawn his long legs were in motion" (p. 167). ("In aller Frühe war er schon auf den langen Beinen;" **Bl** [**Die Blendung**], p. 178). This quotation seems important also by the fact that the German original uses an idiom ('auf den Beinen sein') but modifies it in a way which is not correct grammatically, a device frequently used in satire. While the source and secret of Samson's force is his hair, Kien's strength depends on his books. As soon as they, his allies, are taken away by his wife, Therese, he—who has always been physically feeble (p. 113; **Bl,** p. 118)—loses his force and becomes extremely weak and vulnerable.[3] Another parallel to the tale of Samson is the scene in which Kien is bound to his bed by Therese (cf. Judges, ch. 16; p. 108; **Bl,** p. 113). The end of the novel, the destruction of the library by Kien/Samson, who has found again his books/his force, recalls once more the Biblical text—although it is his allies that die with him, while he is survived by the Philistines.

The Biblical allusion is all the more likely because Canetti has been enormously impressed by Rembrandt's painting *Die Blendung Simsons* in the Frankfurt museum;[4] in fact, it is certainly to the painting and not directly to the Bible that Canetti's novel refers.[5] The writer also takes care to mention this canvas in his second autobiographical book, **Die Fackel im Ohr,**[6] which may be regarded as a justification of his literary work,[7] and, in the end of this book, explains the title of his novel as a reminiscence of Samson's blinding, an "Erinnerung an Simsons Blendung."[8] It may well be that no painting elucidates Canetti's work better than this Rembrandt canvas.[9] There are also significant correspondences in details: the man who blinds Samson is called a "Kriegsknecht" in the autobiography,[10] while Pfaff in *Auto-da-fé* is a *landsknecht* for Kien (p. 114; *Bl,* p. 119); Therese's frock has the same colour as Delilah's dress; etc.[11] The Biblical tale of Samson is, moreover, at about the same time an important motif in Canetti's play *The Wedding.*

This intertextual relation to the Bible—incidentally, there are several Biblical allusions in the text of the novel[12]—enables us to read the conflict between the protagonist and his wife, Therese Krumbholz, with her main ally, the janitor Benedikt Pfaff, as the conflict between Jews and Philistines (although the word *Philister,* still often used for anti-intellectual *petit bourgeois* attitudes in the German language of the first half of the century, is apparently not to be found in the novel). It seems possible to interpret the basic structure of the book as that of a conflict not only between the intellectual and his environment, but perhaps equally so between the Jew and the gentile world around him.[13] We must also bear in mind that the procurer and chess player Fischerle, Kien's only ally, even if he is a fake ally, is explicitly introduced as a Jew.[14]

Another indicator for the possibility of such a political reading of Canetti's rather enigmatic *opus magnum* is its involvement in Austrian politics of the twenties, pointed out in a major study by Gerald Stieg,[15] who has shown that the burning of the *Justizpalast,* the Court of Justice, in Vienna in 1927 has had a seminal function for the writing of *Auto-da-fé.* The revolutionary attack of the Viennese workers against the symbol of *bourgeois* justice was the most spectacular event in a long history of frequently very violent political conflicts that opposed Social Democrats and Christian conservatives, then led by chancellor Ignaz Seipel, a priest, called the 'prelate without pity' because of his attitude in 1927.

Now, Jew-baiting was one of the main features of that unhappy First Republic of Austria,[16] and antisemitism opposed basically the same groups that fought against each other in July 1927: the large majority of the Austrian Jews were supporters of the Social Democratic party, whose major politicians were Otto Bauer and Robert Danneberg, both from Jewish families, while the Christian Socials and their political allies, pre-Nazi groups, had an antisemitic program.

The representative of violence in Canetti's novel bears the name Benedikt Pfaff, a manifest allusion to the dominant political group in Austria. (*Pfaff* is a very depreciatory word for a Catholic priest, frequently used in the radicalized political language of the First Republic of Austria; the first name Benedikt has an evident Catholic ring, too.) The name of Kien's wife, Therese

Krumbholz, particularly her Christian name, seems to be typical for somebody coming from the Catholic Austrian countryside; the family name (approximately 'crooked wood') is also a telling name, accentuating Therese's ugliness (which, incidentally, makes it difficult to push the parallel between the novel and the Bible too far, because we cannot possibly imagine Samson falling in love with a Delilah resembling Therese). Finally, when the novel talks about the attitudes of the Jew Fischerle, antisemitism is explicitly mentioned: "You never can tell. The world is crawling with antisemites. A Jew always has to be on guard against deadly enemies" (p. 180) ("Kann man wissen? Die Welt wimmelt von Antisemiten. Ein Jude ist immer auf der Hut vor Todfeinden;" *Bl,* p. 194).

Jewish themes are rate in Canetti's work[17] (as in the work of many authors of Jewish origin writing in German), but Fischerle need not be the only exception to this rule.[18] It, therefore, should be interesting to find out what becomes of *Auto-da-fé* when we extend the parallel between Kien and Samson to identifying the protagonist of Canetti's novel as a Jew.

One major argument for understanding Kien as a Jew are the autobiographical elements, which Barbara Meili has shown to be very important in this novel.[19] Even if she does not pay particular attention to Canetti, the Jew, it is very likely that the traces of his life that are integrated into *Auto-da-fé* and into the character of Kien also reflect the author's Jewish origin. Peter Kien is in a way a self-portrait or rather a self-caricature of Elias Canetti, particularly of his fanatic love of books, of which he talks in his autobiography.[20] Motifs like the brother and some traits that Therese has in common with Canetti's mother[21] point into the same direction.

A further hint at such an understanding of Kien is his name. Canetti could not possibly have known the artist and writer Peter Kien, born in Czechoslovakia only in 1919 and murdered in Auschwitz in 1944,[22] but the existence of this man proves that Kien can be a Jewish name. Moreover, Kien resembles Kohn, perhaps the most stereotyped of all Jewish names. Since we know how much thought the author has given to the choice of his main character's name,[23] it is hard to believe that he should not have been conscious of its possible Jewish associations. Kien is certainly not a name frequent among Austrian gentiles.

A short description of Kien's face insists on the ugliness of his nose, also a feature reminding the reader of antisemitic clichées (p. 173; *Bl,* p. 185). This description of his exterior makes appear a certain similarity between the protagonist and Fischerle, whom we see through Kien's eyes (p. 174f.; *Bl,* p. 187), just as Kien observes himself in a mirror.

A slightly humorous element pointing to the Jewishness of Kien is his securing the help of a matchmaker (p. 36;

Bl, p. 34), a very illustrious one in this case. Match-makers were important in Jewish life, in the East any-way, but apparently still for a long time also among as-similated Jews in the West. If the motif can be read as a Jewish motif at all, it certainly has a satirical slant.

Kien's social status also corresponds to a position frequently forced upon Jewish scholars. In Austria and Germany they were often refused a normal career in the predominantly antisemitic universities, thus being reduced to the situation of *Privatgelehrte,* as the Jean Paul editor Eduard Berend.[24] Literary precursors and parallels are Bernhard Ehrenthal in Freytag's *Soll und Haben* (*Debit and Credit*)[25] and Chaim Breisacher in Thomas Mann's *Doctor Faustus.* Certainly, Kien himself refuses university positions that he is offered (p. 18; *Bl,* p. 16), but in the end his status is identical to that of a Jew on the margin of the academic world.

Kien is, furthermore, introduced as being fairly rich; he doesn't have to work for a living but spends his inherited fortune, the interests of which would have assured him a comfortable income; he prefers, however, to use this money, his *Kapital*—this word is a leitmotif of the novel—, for his library so that an end to his easy life seems to be imminent (p. 47; *Bl,* p. 46). Despite his intellectual activities, Kien is depicted by Canetti as somebody very much interested in money, and this image of the character converges with the public stereotype of the greedy Jew; Kien's fascination with the number of his books or of books to be bought must also be mentioned here. One example: when he believes to hear Therese talking about a dowry he begins to think of money. "The legacy of capitalism, favoured and practised by his family for centuries, awoke in him with colossal strength, as though in a struggle of twenty-five years it had not been always the loser" (p. 138) ("Das Erbteil des Kapitalismus, in seiner Familie jahrhundertelang beliebt und geübt, erwachte mit ungeheurer Kraft, als hätte es in einem Kampf von fünfundzwanzig Jahren nicht längst den kürzeren gezogen;" *Bl,* p. 146). Kien also speaks quite frequently about the funds he has invested in his books (e.g. p. 45; *Bl,* p. 45) and about their value. This is also important as an autobiographical allusion: Canetti himself on the one hand totally refused the capitalist attitudes prevalent in his family[26], on the other hand he was well aware of the fact that he could not totally escape from this tradition. Nevertheless, Kien's enemies are no less interested in money than himself, they, Therese, Pfaff, are just as greedy as he and the hunchback Jew Fischerle.

While Kien's wealth and his interest in money are after all features to be found everywhere in the bourgeoisie,[27] another trait of his character, his fascination with books, with everything written, his philological enthusiasm reminds us directly of Jewish, in particular of Jewish religious traditions. Although the manuscripts Kien deals with are Chinese or Japanese, he studies them as zealously as if they were the Holy Scriptures (and many of them seem to be, by the way, religious texts). He cannot live without books, books are the main source of his strength. Kien is thus presented as a typical intellectual, which is another feature that could be understood as Jewish. The reader is reminded of Nahum Fischelson, the main character in I. B. Singer's short story *The Spinoza of Market Street* (around 1962),[28] whose contents bear some surprising similarities to Canetti's novel.

As such an intellectual, Kien is totally isolated from his surroundings; his only contacts with other people (his house-keeper, the janitor, people in the hotels) are based on money. He hardly ever speaks to anybody, and it is not by chance that Canetti has the novel start with a scene that shows precisely this incapability of communication with others, with so-called ordinary people; later on, we learn that Kien's contacts with the scholarly community are also limited to exchanges of letters (p. 17ff.; *Bl,* pp. 16ff.). This isolation is an isolation from reality, too, which Kien seems totally unaware of. Canetti's insisting on the motifs of the eye and of blindness is highly ironical, because his main character, right from the beginning of the book, does not 'see' anything.

Although we may tend to admire Kien as a scholar and may even pity him in the course of events, we must admit that this character is basically a caricature of intellectual man, a satire on people who are not ready to face reality and rather prefer to hide behind books; as already mentioned, it is possible that this satire contains autobiographical features and thence some self-criticism of the author.[29] Elfriede Pöder has shown that the character of Kien alludes to Weininger, and that it may be read as a radical satire on Weininger's concept of "M", the philosopher's idealistic construct of the typical male.[30]

Kien, then, is not at all a positive character, and if we are ready to accept him as the portrait of a Jew, we must admit that Canetti here stands in the tradition of Jewish self-criticism quite frequent in the Vienna of his days. Weininger has already been mentioned, who, as we know from Canetti's autobiography, was frequently discussed among young (Jewish) intellectuals in the twenties.[31] Karl Kraus, whom the author of *Auto-da-fé* never ceased to admire, is another example of this attitude among Jews, but even staunch supporters of the cause of the assimilated Jews such as Hugo Bettauer insist in a generalising manner on negative traits among Jews.[32] If Kien is a Jew, Canetti's self-portrait of the Jew is fairly close to the image of the Jew in the *Kulturkritik* of the period: Kien is some kind of a 'rootless intellectual' turned too much towards money. The echoes of Weininger in *Auto-da-fé* have so far been discussed mainly in regard to the image of 'Man' and 'Woman', but it can by no means be excluded that the (pseudo-)philosopher's unfortunate chapter on the Jewish character has also left its traces in Canetti's novel.

Another argument for a possible Jewish background of Kien is the place given to Jews in a list of cultural traditions that appear in a dream of the protagonist: "Mexican pictorial writings", Eratosthenes of Alexandria, Michelangelo; and: "A certain medieval woodcut, whose ingenuousness always made him smile, depicted about thirty Jews on a burning pyre flaming to heaven yet obstinately screeching their prayers." (p. 41f.). ("Auf einem mittelalterlichen Holzschnitt, über dessen Naivität er immer lachte, waren einige dreißig Juden verzeichnet, die lichterloh brannten und verstockt noch auf dem Scheiterhaufen ihre Gebete schrien." *Bl,* p. 41).

Of course, Fischerle must be briefly discussed in this paper, as the only character who is explicitly described as a Jew and who even talks in the manner of half-assimilated Leopoldstadt Jews. His language is what Canetti calls an *akustische Maske,* an acoustic mask, which is the author's principal device of characterising personages; a marked accent in German and a particular syntax, which were considered as typical of badly assimilated Jews, are important features in the portrayal of this Jewish figure, reminiscent of stock jokes on and by Jews. Fischerle thus thinks in questions such as "Kann man wissen?" (insufficiently translated as "You never can tell." p. 180; *Bl,* p. 194). (Yiddish words, however, hardly occur in Fischerle's speech.) Kien thinks of him, in the rather colloquial style made possible by the use of free indirect speech, as of the "harmloseste Jud von der Welt" ("the most harmless little Jew in the world") (p. 176f.; *Bl,* p. 189), while the narrative voice uses the correct form "Jude" (p. 180; *Bl,* p. 194).[33]

Among Fischerle's 'Jewish' traits[34] is his greed, which he has, however, in common with Therese and other non-Jewish enemies of Kien (and, in a way, with Kien himself). His fascination with chess does at least not exclude an allusion to many famous chess champions of Jewish origin (e. g. Rudolf Spielmann, born in 1884). This remnant of intellectuality in very obtuse surroundings may suggest a typically Jewish quality as well as Fischerle's ambitions, which can be read as ambitions both at a social career and at assimilation (an ambition also shown by the typical first name "Siegfried"). But on the other hand Fischerle lives in a milieu that has nothing to do with the well-to-do bourgeoisie which one would normally identify with the Jewish minority of Vienna. Canetti here shows his thorough knowledge of the margins of Vienna society, of all types of *Nachtcafé* where he liked to listen to people talking.[35] No doubt that Fischerle is to some extent a satirical figure and that we have to take into account a certain pleasure of the author in characterising the comic features of a

lower-class Jew. (We must not forget that Canetti as a Sephardic Jew, who, moreover, has learnt German as a foreign language, has himself always been very far from using this type of language.) These passages are close to the critical or rather the self-ridiculing image of the Jew that was frequent in several types of Jewish comedy and *Kabarett* in Vienna, as, e.g., with Heinrich Eisenbach and Armin Berg, although they rather insist on comic than on negative features of their Jewish contemporaries.[36]

There are important correspondences between Fischerle, the procurer and petty criminal, and the great scholar Kien. I have already pointed to the slight physical similarities between the protagonist and his friend. Then, Fischerle is described as a genius of chess, which may also be an ironic reference to Weininger,[37] who does not accept the idea of specialized but only that of universal genius; the imagined genius of Kien is limited to Chinese philology and is, thus, not less specialized than Fischerle's. Both Kien and Fischerle are interested in numbers and quantities, which may concern money or books; this is a feature they share with the majority of characters in the novel. The overpowering ambitions of both characters must also be mentioned here. The relations of the two men to women, to Therese and to the "the Capitalist" ("Pensionistin," p. 177; *Bl,* p. 190), and the two women themselves also show some parallels; the bad observer Kien once in a while even identifies the two. And we should not forget that as Kien recognizes Fischerle as a Jew, Fischerle takes his rich friend for one. A final major parallel—final in the full sense of the word—between the two marginalized characters is the end of their lives; although Fischerle is murdered and Kien commits suicide, both die because of their inability to adapt to hostile surroundings and of their blindness, Kien much more so than Fischerle, towards the true intentions and the whole amount of brutality of their enemies. Canetti does not, however, see this blindness, which is much more accentuated with Kien than with Fischerle, as an excuse but rather as guilt.

Their awful way of dying is perhaps the most important element the two figures have in common. As Samson falls a victim of the Philistines, the enemies, Fischerle is betrayed by his Delilah and killed by a brutal and certainly non-Jewish customer of his wife; if we take his hump as a symbol of his non-assimilation,[38] his dreams of assimilation become true in a very cynical way, because it is cut off by his murderer. Kien, though on the whole closer to the Biblical hero and to the Rembrandt painting, is not killed by the Philistines but destroys himself and his books as soon as he regains his library, which means his strength. But in spite of these differences both characters are presented as dying in a conflict with the majority of ordinary people.

Certainly, the procurer is more rused than his victim and he has, as an apparent ally and real enemy of Kien, some traits in common with Therese. The main differences between Kien and Fischerle are the milieu they come from and the different languages of these milieus; within their respective environments, however, their positions are quite comparable: within the Viennese underworld, Fischerle is just as isolated as Kien is in more regular surroundings. Their marginal positions are accentuated by physical particularities: while Fischerle is a dwarf and a hunchback, Kien is described as an awkward and ugly giant. (This physical contrast is of course also one of several intertextual references to Don Quixote and Sancho Panza.) Both characters have to be seen as negative, although we may tend to pity them as victims.

The key to finding something like a Jewish self-portrait in this novel is exactly its end. The conflict between the isolated intellectual, who does not find the contact either to reality or to the masses, can be read as the conflict between the isolated Jew and the gentile majority around him into which he wants to be integrated but which brutally refuses this integration. Gerald Stieg has already mentioned the possibility of reading Canetti's labyrinthic book as a parable on the theme of assimilation.[39] This problem is more easily traced in the story of Fischerle than in the fate of Kien, who does not strive for but rather refuses integration (which would be the equivalent of assimilation), but it is at the heart of both 'biographies'.

The importance of this aspect of the novel becomes quite apparent when we have a look at Kien's and Fischerle's enemies, who are much closer to the image of antisemites than Kien is to the image of a Jew. The name of the janitor Benedikt Pfaff has again to be mentioned since it recalls the Christian, in Austria: the Catholic roots of the hatred of Jews. This function of his name is made more likely by the fact that the character of Pfaff is a political allusion anyway: Canetti makes him a former police-man, because the events of July 15th, 1927 were marked by an extreme brutality of the Viennese police, who killed about 90 people.[40] Pfaff's violence against Kien could also remind the contemporary reader of everyday antisemitic violence mainly against Jewish students in the Vienna of the twenties. Although such outrages against Jews were mainly an affair of the pre-Nazi groups in Vienna, Canetti's chosing of a 'Catholic' name for the janitor seems justified not only because of Seipel, but also because of the fact that the Christian Social movement represented something like a respectable form of antisemitism in Austria in the 1920s. This element of brutality, completely absent in Fischerle and Kien, is also to be found in Therese and particularly in Fischerle's murderer, Schwer.[41]

Canetti's critical attitude towards intellectuals proud of their isolation and refusing contact with other people, with the mass, is manifest in this novel, but his position

towards Therese's and Pfaff's hatred of intellect is quite as negative. Therese, Pfaff and the "Capitalist" are depicted as people hardly able to formulate a thought, maybe even unable to think; they are close to an animal existence. This again takes up well-known historical circumstances: Austrian antisemitism has always had a strong anti-intellectual component, and in spite of large groups of antisemitic students the mass basis of this movement were people like Therese and Pfaff, people without education and with hardly any chance to improve their social status. The janitor (*Hausmeister*) had been considered a typical representative of the Christian Socials in the time of Lueger, before 1914. Canetti's insisting on the greed of these characters may also be read as a satire[42] on antisemitism, Jews and antisemites sharing the same pre-occupation with money. It is not untypical that the end of poor Fischerle is more brutal than the death of Kien: historical antisemitism in Vienna also turned most brutally against the economically weak segment of the city's Jewish population.

There are, however, two main obstacles against this reading of *Auto-da-fé* and particularly of the character of Kien as a Jewish self-portrait of the early thirties—even if we do not take into account, as a third such argument, that the non-Jew Schreber may have been a model for some traits of Kien.

One main argument against my interpretation is to be derived from the (scarce) contemporary reception of the novel, which seems hardly to have discussed this aspect of the book.[43] From the fact that readers in the thirties did not remark the topicality suggested in this paper we may conclude that the book does not contain the political allusions I have tried to show here. But on the other hand, the critics, in 1935, eight years after 1927, were so much appalled by the terrible events told in this book and by those happening in reality that it took them quite a while to grasp its satirical character, although many elements of the book, even in the microstructure of sentences, support such an understanding.[44] So the contemporary reception may not completely invalidate the reading of *Auto-da-fé* I propose here.

But one sentence in *Auto-da-fé* seems to do just that. When Fischerle explains that "stipendium" "means exactly the same as capital does in Jewish!" (p. 180) ("Dieses Wort [. . .] heißt dasselbe wie das jüdische Kapital!" *Bl*, p. 193), the dwarf wonders about the reaction of Kien, who might be an antisemite (of whom Fischerle would, of course, be afraid), and takes from Kien's surprise at this remark that the new guest is a Jew himself. In this passage, which seems to be the only one where antisemitism is explicitly mentioned, Canetti writes, in one of the few comments that it is not free indirect speech so abundantly used in this novel but can be attributed directly to the narrative voice: "[Fischerle] from that moment decided that Kien must be a Jew, which he certainly was not." (p. 180) ("[. . .] und hielt von diesem Augenblick an Kien, der nichts weniger war, für einen Juden." *Bl*, p. 194). Another passage (p. 159; *Bl*, p. 169) even suggests that Kien is a Christian, who "had long forgotten how to pray."

The house of cards of my hypothesis does not, however, collapse because of this sentence; on the contrary, one could understand this comment, precisely because it comes from the narrative voice, as a proof of my interpretation. This sentence may have seemed necessary to the author, because, being conscious of the Jewish features of his protagonist but not wanting him to appear (only) as a Jew at the expense of more general levels of meaning in his great novel, he had to exclude a possible reduction of Kien to a Jewish identity. In saying that Kien is not a Jew, Canetti admits that he could be taken as such. Kien, thus, would be a parallel case to Broch's Esch, who also can be understood as an explicity non-Jewish figure representing Jewish problems.

Of course, the more general levels of meaning are very important in *Auto-da-fé,* and I am far from believing that the novel should or could be reduced to the theme of the conflict between Jews and antisemites.[45] It is a book about many other problems of modern man, and the criticism of the intellectual who refuses social contacts as he refuses social responsibility is not a criticism directed particularly against Jewish intellectuals. But a reading particularly of the end of the novel also in terms of the conflict between the modern assimilated Jews and the modern Philistines, who not only refuse the integration of the Jewish minority but want to annihilate it, has historical relevance.

The portrait of the Jew in this novel is very negative; but the book does not have any positive characters anyway. Since the intellectuals are, however, the victims of their brutal enemies, we cannot read a book like this after 1945 without pity for these victims, even if they deserve their fate in the terms of the novel.

In an early passage Kien interprets one of his dreams by remembering a medieval wood-cut showing Jews burning at the stake (p. 42; *Bl*, p. 41). This wood-cut is the representation of an historical *auto-da-fé*, which makes it likely that the Sephardic Jew Canetti, in authorising the English title, may have consciously alluded to the fate of the Spanish and Portuguese Jews at the hands of the Inquisition. Thus, both the German and the English title would refer to the history of the European Jews.[46]

As far as the structure of Canetti's book is concerned, this wood-cut is an anticipation of the terrible end of *Auto-da-fé*. But the novel itself, on one of its many levels, also seems to be an anticipation, an anticipation of an even more terrible catastrophe. Maybe this was not the author's intention in 1931, but history has given a new significance to this text. It may not have been a book on the fate of the Jews in Austria and on their blindness in face of the brutality of their enemies but, unfortunately, it has become such a book.[47]

Notes

1. This paper has also been read, in German, at the universities of Poznan (1992) and Coimbra (1996). An abridged German version will be published in 1996/1997 by RUNA, the Portuguese review of German studies.

2. Elias Canetti: *Auto-da-fé*. Translated from the German under the personal supervision of the author by C. V. Wedgwood (1947). New York: Noonday Press 1984. (The first American edition appeared under the title *The Tower of Bable*.) Page references are to this edition, followed by *Bl* and the page of the quotation in: Elias Canetti: Die Blendung. Frankfurt 1982 (Fischer Taschenbuch 696). (Unfortunately, there are at least three different editions of the German paperback—with the same volume number—, which may make page references puzzling.)

3. Cf., also for interesting details, Detlef Krumme: Die Bestrafung der Unkeuschheit. Elias Canettis Romanheld Peter Kien als moderner Simson. In: Sprache im technischen Zeitalter 1985, pp. 148-154. Krumme is the first and so far only one to stress the allusions to Samson in *Auto-da-fé*. Bernhard Greiner: Das Bild und die Schriften der "Blendung": Über den biblischen Grund von Canettis Schreiben. In: Franz Link (ed.): Paradeigmata. Literarische Typologie des Alten Testaments. 2. Teil: 20. Jahrhundert. Berlin (W): Duncker & Humblot 1989, pp. 543-562 (Schriften zur Literaturwissenschaft 5/2), is not very helpful for the argument of this paper, if it is helpful at all.

4. On this painting cf. the leaflet by Paul Eich: Rembrandt van Rijn. Die Blendung Simsons, 1636. Frankfurt: Städel 1982 (Kleine Werkmonographie 28). Canetti saw the painting before its recent restoration, which entailed major changes.

5. Cf. Piet van Meeuwen: Elias Canetti und die bildende Kunst von Bruegel bis Goya. Bern: Lang 1988, p. 50 (Europäische Hochschulschriften I, 1041).

6. Elias Canetti: Die Fackel im Ohr. Lebensgeschichte 1921-1931. München: Hanser 1980, pp. 133ff. Since it is rather difficult to get hold of English translations of Canetti in this country, I quote the autobiography from the German. (The English title is *The Torch in my Ear*.)

7. Cf. the quotations in Sigurd Paul Scheichl: Hörenlernen. Zur teleologischen Struktur der autobiographischen Bücher Canettis. In: Friedbert Aspets-

berger, Gerald Stieg (eds.): Elias Canetti. Blendung als Lebensform. Kronberg/Ts.: Athenäum 1985, pp. 73-79; p. 73.

8. *Die Fackel im Ohr* (note 6), p. 408.

9. Van Meeuwen (note 5), p. 43.

10. *Die Fackel im Ohr* (note 6), p. 134.

11. For a comprehensive list of parallels between *Auto-da-fé* and both Rembrandt and the Bible see van Meeuwen (note 5), pp. 42-53.

12. E.g. p. 40 (*Bl*, p. 39), p. 94 (*Bl*, p. 98), p. 40 (*Bl*, p. 39), p. 158 (*Bl*, p. 168), p. 165 (*Bl*, p. 176), etc. I list only allusions to the Old Testament.

13. The first Canetti scholar to hint at the possibility of such a reading is Gerald Stieg: Frucht des Feuers. Canetti, Doderer, Kraus und der Justizpalastbrand. Wien: Edition Falter im Österreichischen Bundesverlag 1990, p. 127.

14. This aspect of the conflict between Jews and Philistines is not mentioned by van Meeuwen (note 5).

15. Stieg (note 13).

16. Cf. e.g. Bruce F. Pauley: From Prejudice to Persecution: A History of Austrian Anti-Semitism. Chapel Hill: University of North Carolina Press 1992.

17. Paolo Consigli: Ebraicitá in Canetti e caos del reale. In: Annali. Studi Tedeschi 25. 1982, pp. 167-187; p. 172. Consigli's study deals with Jewish aspects in Canetti's work without paying particular attention to *Auto-da-fé,* except for the character of Fischerle.

18. Ibid.

19. Barbara Meili: Erinnerung und Vision. Der lebensgeschichtliche Hintergrund von Elias Canettis Roman "Die Blendung". Bonn 1985 (Studien zur Germanistik, Anglistik und Komparatistik 115).

20. Ibid., p. 11.

21. Cf. ibid., p. 79.

22. Cf. Jürgen Serke: Böhmische Dörfer. Wanderungen durch eine verlassene literarische Landschaft. Wien: Zsolnay 1987, pp. 447-450.

23. Elias Canetti: Das erste Buch: Die Blendung (1973). In: EC: Das Gewissen der Worte. Essays. Frankfurt 1981, pp. 241-253; pp. 241, 244, 251.

24. Cf. Hanne Knickmann: "Was ich davon denke, brauche ich Ihnen wohl nicht zu sagen." Zu den gescheiterten Habilitationsversuchen des Jean Paul-Forschers Eduard Berend (1883-1973). In: Marbacher Arbeitskreis für Geschichte der Germanistik. Mitteilungen. Nr. 7/8. 1994, pp. 45-50.

25. On Ehrenthal cf. Mark H. Gelber: An Alternative Reading of the Role of the Jewish Scholar in Gustav Freytag's *Soll und Haben.* In: Germanic Review 58. 1983, pp. 83-88.

26. Cf. *Die Fackel im Ohr* (note 6), p. 155ff.

27. Cf. Consigli (note 17), p. 169: Kien is the symbol of the bourgeois I.

28. Isaac Bashevis Singer: The Spinoza of Market Street. In: IBS: The Spinoza of Market Street. Harmondsworth 1981, pp. 7-25 (Penguin Books).

29. Meili (note 19), p. 33. Meili here also shows the political topicality of Kien's blindness.

30. Elfriede Pöder: Spurensicherung. Otto Weininger in der "Blendung". In: Aspetsberger, Stieg (note 7), pp. 57-72; pp. 59ff. I was unable to consult Claudia Zerkowitz: Geist versus Geschlechtlichkeit: Otto Weiningers Mann-Frau-Dichotomie in Parallele zu Elias Canettis Roman "Die Blendung". Diplomarbeit (type-written). Graz 1988.

31. *Die Fackel im Ohr* (note 6), p. 90. Cf. also Kristie A. Foell: Whores, Mothers and Others: Reception of Otto Weininger's *Sex and Character* in Elias Canetti's *Auto-da-fé.* In: Nancy A. Harrowitz, Barbary Hyams (eds.): Jews & Gender. Responses to Otto Weininger. Philadelphia: Temple University Press 1995, pp. 245-255, p. 245.

32. Cf. e.g. Hugo Bettauer: Die Stadt ohne Juden. Salzburg: Hannibal 1980, p. 82.

33. The word "Jud" comprises a slight nuance of contempt, which the translation ("little Jew") does not render.

34. On Fischerle as a Jew, cf. also Meili (note 19), pp. 101-109.

35. *Die Fackel im Ohr* (note 6), p. 357ff.

36. Cf. Hans Veigl (ed.): Luftmenschen spielen Theater: Jüdisches Kabarett in Wien 1890-1938. Wien: Kremayr & Scheriau 1992.

37. Pöder (note 30), pp. 70f.

38. Cf. Stieg (note 13), p. 128.

39. Ibid., p. 127.

40. Cf. Stieg (note 13).

41. On the sadistic Pfaff's presaging of nazi brutality cf. Elemér Tarján: Wirklichkeitsdarstellung in Elias Canettis Roman "Die Blendung". In: Die österreichische Nation (Salzburg) 25. 1973, pp. 50-54. This article is interesting for this observation but quite unimportant as an analysis of *Auto-da-fé.*

42. On the basically satirical character of the novel cf. e.g. Foell (note 31), passim; Scheichl (note 44).

43. I could not get hold of Kurt Pinthus: Romane aus fernen Welten (containing a review of *Die Blendung*). In: C. V. Zeitung. Blätter für Deutschtum und Judentum. March 5, 1936, Beiblatt p. 4, which would have been very interesting as a decidedly Jewish reaction to the first edition of the novel.

44. Cf. Sigurd Paul Scheichl: Der Möbelkauf. Zur Funktion eines Handlungsstrangs in der "Blendung". In: Aspetsberger, Stieg (note 7), pp. 126-142; p. 137.

45. E.g., Martin Bollacher: Elias Canetti: Die Blendung (1935/36). In: Paul Michael Lützeler (ed.): Deutsche Romane des 20. Jahrhunderts. Neue Interpretationen. Frankfurt: Athenäum 1983, pp. 237-254, does not at all mention possible Jewish implications of the novel.

46. I am grateful to Ulrich Wyss for pointing out this possible function of the English title.

47. Tarján's (note 41) reading of the book reflects this historical development.

Robert Elbaz and Leah Hadomi (essay date 1993)

SOURCE: Elbaz, Robert, and Leah Hadomi. "On Canetti's Novelistic Sign." *Orbis Litterarum* 48, no. 5 (1993): 269-80.

[*In the following essay, Elbaz and Hadomi find Canetti's novel* Auto da fé *to be an important development in the narrative progress of the twentieth-century novel.*]

Elias Canetti's novelistic performance is of paramount importance in our investigation of the productive process of narrative forms as it has evolved in the modern and post-modern novel in the aftermath of the First World War.[1] Despite the relative neglect *Auto da fé* has known from its publication in the 1930s until 1981 when the author was awarded the Nobel prize for literature, this novel proves to be a topos, a privileged and destabilizing semiotic space with regard to the evolution of the novelistic sign, a field of play for multiple and very elaborate semiotizations.

Few novels, indeed, have had such an impact on the modern receptive consciousness, for *Die Blendung* (the blinding) as the author titles it in German, presents the reader with an extremely complex fictional universe which problematizes the very relationship between text and context, story and history, signifier and signified. What is at stake here is the very possibility of the novel and, by extension of text in general to make any kind of meaning, to extract a minimal signification from the historical phenomena it purports to metaphorize. Canetti seems to be saying that the novel as a privileged tool of literary expression must perforce manifest its inability to channel historical devastation and thus, if the novel is to signify, it must incorporate the breakdown of signification.

A number of questions must be posed at the outset if we are to make sense of Canetti's novelistic practice. First and foremost what type of novel are we dealing with? To what generic subgenre can we relate it? It is evidently not a realist novel, whatever meaning we confer to the concept of "realism": the mental make-up, behaviour, ideological stance and world view of the various characters, and even their physical characteristics do not warrant the use of verismilitude as an operational concept in our apprehension of this fictional space. The very physical concreteness of the characters is put in doubt for it is very difficult to conceive of such a mixed group of twisted and crippled invalids as representatives of the social types of the phenomenal world from which they are formed.

Moreover, this novel does not seem to refer to concrete phenomena in the historical reality of the period in any immediate way; it does not even make note of the contextual events that have no doubt accompanied its production. We are by no means claiming that the novel bears no relationship to the historical reality within which it was produced;[2] we are referring here to the very complex process of metaphorical referentiality. The metaphor is so overdone in *Auto da fé* that one questions the very legitimacy of its referents. For the overdoing of the metaphor, its blatant artificiality, jeopardizes the primary intent of referentiality. The artifice, so common in the grotesque and in irony—and these are the most prevalent features of this fictional universe—tends to blur the limits of its referential objects. We will see that even the physical objects that litter this novelistic space, as semiotic structures, have a tendency to lose their respective parameters, indeed, their identities: they fuse to compose an explosive semiotic reality taking a distant though perspectival look at the socio-historical phenomena they seek to manifest. Evidently, *Auto da fé* makes its references exclusively to textual realities of the past, mostly to cultural figures from the ancient past of the Chinese and sometimes Japanese civilizations as well as Western civilization.

Peter Kien, the main protagonist in the novel, is a sinologist versed in the ancient texts of the East; his basic scholarly activity is to redeem the inner truth of each text. Yet beyond this trait in the central character, an ideological statement is made about the period, in general, and about the inability of the text, in its sterility and impotence—that Kien incorporates in a variety of ways—to textualize reality. In effect, we will claim that the main thrust of the novel is not merely to represent the material world of the 1920s and 1930s in the West, after the Realist tradition, but to problematize the very principle of representation; hence the novel's privileged position in the postmodern transgressive mode of fictional writing. In effect, then, *Auto da fé* transgresses realist representation and has recourse to very elaborate modes of metaphorization to inscribe the silencing of the period. Kien, the main protagonist, often uses silence as a communicational strategy, as the only means to deal with Other, and silence will, eventually, mean power in Kien's world.[3]

Auto da fé can also be viewed as one of the precursors of the Nouveau Roman in France. Here too we encounter some of the basic narrative ingredients of what Barthes has termed "objective literature." Much like the Robbe-Grilletian object, the objects in Canetti's world hold a privileged position on the narrative scene, often occupying its very centre. The skirt, the book, or the chess set, for example, are not simply objects at the disposal of subjects, not mere objects available to their manipulation. The subjects are often evacuated and the objects substitute for them, but—and in this Canetti differs fundamentally from the Nouveau Roman—not as pure physical presence. Canetti's object is not limited to its abstracted geometrical dimensions like the object of the Nouveau Roman; it even acquires with its narrative evolution a cosmic dimension. It eventually becomes a categorical principle of the narrative consciousness through which all of reality can be filtered—the relaying matrix to all material relations in the fictional world of the novel.

Indeed, the object often overtakes the whole of consciousness due to the subject's obsession: the internalization of the object leaves no room for any other mental activity. The object overtakes the externalized reality, superimposing itself on all phenomena covering physical and perceptual space. The skirt, for example, is at the same time an object to be touched, open, torn—in short, manipulated in various ways—and, ultimately, a cosmic object to be perceived everywhere. And the movement of the narration from the internal to the external, from the stream of consciousness to third person direct narration allows for these two dimensions of the object to interact with one another. The object is both internalized and externalized through narration to take account of its ubiquity. It is first a production of consciousness, of the twisted consciousnesses of the protagonists, but then it becomes part and parcel of material reality—a referential matrix.

Thus, the Canettian object posits at the outset a perceiving consciousness no matter what its constraining features are. Again, the object here is not a geometrical entity that can support its own abstracted existence. This world despite its hallucinatory quality is still inhabited by humans and is still reducible to these consciousnesses; the objects are still *in relation* and not totally alienated from the humans that manipulate them though the objects sometimes overtake their entire mental apparatus. From the narrative point of view the sometimes tedious overanalysis of the object is there not primarily to emphasize its physicality *per se,* but to qualify the narrative consciousness which experiences great difficulty grappling with it, for the attempt to exhaust the object through narrative repetition manifests the impotence of the text in coming to terms with it.

In order to erase the alienating dimension of the object with which the characters cannot coincide since objects are by definition separated from subjects, the object will turn into a purely mental image over which the character can exercise his property rights. Consider, for example, the connection between Kien's real library and the mental one he carries within his head. There is no doubt that this problematic and complex apprehension of the object is common to both the protagonists and the narrator. The concreteness of the object, its mimetic dimension is overtaken by its fantasmatic and absurd dimension; it hovers between being and non-being, much as the novel is caught between the representation of a senseless reality and its nullification.

The cold calculation of the Nouveau Roman—an ideological configuration as well in that the novel, according to this conception, has given up on reality and subsequently created an abstracted reality replacing the material world—is totally absent in Canetti's novel, despite its strategic distance from the historical context of the period. Canetti's novel would seem to belong to the Baroque tradition that he shares with other long neglected novelists of his acquaintance, Broch and Musil. The grotesque, the repetitive, overdoing of the narrative elements, the revelation of all the decoration and artifice pertaining to the productive process whereby the text uncovers its own doing—all these manifest the moorings of this novel in the real, albeit with the transformation and, sometimes, the total twisting and manipulation of that real.

Further, on a metatextual level, the object in Canetti's world seems to constitute an organizing/structural metaphor that is central to the productive process of the novel. These organizing/metaphoric objects make for the possibility of signification and narrative deployment in Canetti's text in that they consist of permutational structures relaying one another in a variable game of repetition much like the functioning of the centipede in Robbe-Grillet's *La Jalousie*. In this permutational game of repetition, these objects contribute to form a very complex semiotic matrix where every object, every sign reflects and refracts every other sign. The novelistic sign is actually held together through its varied permutations through the repetitive elaboration of the narrative series for each narrative instance reaffirms and, at the same time, questions the multiple manifestations of the series. Devoid of any centre or any clear-cut referent to substantiate its signification, Canetti's novel relies on the play of its signifiers.

If Canetti's novel is not representational, we may then attribute it generically to the Surrealist tradition[4] that flowered in this period throughout Europe, particularly in France with André Breton and his movement. But *Auto da fé* has little in common with, for example, Breton's *Nadja* which is there to justify the Surrealist theory of automatic writing or the foundation of any conscious activity upon an unconscious stratum, which it borrows from the Freudian tradition. No doubt, traces of a Freudian libidinous structure can be found in most characters in *Auto da fé*. However, Canetti himself acknowledges his debt to a special brand of surrealism we encounter in Kafka's writings, claiming to have read *Metamorphosis* while working on his novel. Indeed, we cannot help but identify here that bizarre dimension of Kafka's surrealism; the characters' neurotic obsessions and their fantasmatic hallucinations constitute a performative strategy allowing them to measure themselves to their respective realities. The fantasmatic makeup of their individual mentalities sometimes forces itself upon their daily ventures, thus wiping out any possible concrete moorings in the real: often the obsession dislodges and even replaces reality. In the end, the obsession is the reality. And the difference among the characters is one of dosage; each has his own exclusive *idée-fixe* which often overtakes his whole mental world leaving no room for the grasp of the material world. This is true, we would claim, even of George Kien, the protagonist's brother who, on the surface, seems to embody the category of the "normal" in the novel, for we know that he is a sworn role-player jumping from role to role while pretending to engage in genuine communication.[5]

The exchanges and conversations amount to dialogues of the deaf until the moment when the characters do wake up and see the abysmal gap separating them from their interlocutors. A model dialogue is the one between Kien and Therese regarding the will. Each genuinely believes that the other will draw up a will to answer his demands and needs: Kien believes that with the money from Therese's inheritance he will be able to buy Old Silzinger's library, thus adding four rooms to the four he already owns while Therese believes that the million comes from her husband's legacy. Thus develops the following dialogue:

> 'The books are mine!'
>
> 'What?'
>
> 'Three rooms belong to the wife, one belongs to the husband.'

'We are now speaking of eight rooms. Four additional ones—those in the next flat, I mean. I need room to house the Silzinger library. That alone contains twenty-two thousand volumes.'

'And where is the money coming from?'

Again he was tired of these hints. 'From your legacy. There is no more to be said on that score.'

'Not a penny.'

'The legacy belongs to me.'

'But I have the disposal of it.'

'A man's got to die first, he can dispose after.'

'What is the meaning of this?'

'I won't bargain!'

'Our common interest is concerned in this matter.'

'I want the rest!'

'You cannot but appreciate . . .'

'Where is the rest?'

'A wife must respect her husband.'

'And her husband steals the rest from his wife.'

'I ask a million for the acquisition of the Silzinger Library.'

'Ask, ask, ask. I want the rest. I want all of it.'

'I am the master in this house.'

'I'm the mistress.'

'I present you with an ultimatum. I demand categorically a million for the acquisition . . .'

'I want the rest. I want the rest.'

'In three seconds. I shall count up to three . . .'

'Anyone can count. I shall count too!'

> (A [*Auto da fé*] 129-130)

Only at the end of Chapter XII is the circularity of this dialogue broken. "A few moments later they had understood each other for the first time." (*A* 131). The confusion multiplies when there are more than two interlocutors involved in the exchange. After Therese, Pfaff and Kien are arrested by the police in the Theresianum, they are brought to the police station where a Tower of Babel communicational situation develops among all parties. In this exchange Kien, who thinks he is on trial, takes his own defense and speaks of his encounter with his "murdered wife" (*A* 278) and proceeds to describe in full detail how she was devoured by a bloodhound. Kien is referring, of course, to the Therese in front of him: he cannot believe his eyes—he will touch the skirt to see if she is real—for he is convinced that she died and that he might be accused of causing her death. Therese, on the other hand, believes that Kien must have murdered his first wife (who no doubt had the same skirt as hers), hidden the corpse and smuggled it bit by bit out of the house. The caretaker thinks that the professor was alluding to his own daughter whose death he brought about. "The Professor was talking about a wife, but he meant his daughter." (*A* 279) The police inspector cannot make head or tail of the story (he is also very preoccupied by his own nose which he comtemplates repeatedly in a pocket mirror) and Kien will go over his narrative obsessively until the matter is finally cleared up.

Yet despite their split personalities and their respective imprisonment in closed mental worlds, there happens to be some kind of communication among them. Kien does relate to Therese, to Fischerle, to his brother George, to Pfaff and to others; Fischerle relates to his four workers, his wife, the capitalist, etc., There is even an intense communication between George the psychiatrist and the gorilla, the presumed madman, who speaks some kind of primitive variant of an African dialect comprehensible only to himself and to his privileged nurse and slave. At certain moments Kien himself makes a lot of sense; his dialogue with the Metzger boy at the beginning of the novel and part of the exchange with his brother towards the end constitute moments (among many others) where pure lucidity is recovered. In effect, all the characters live in synchrony within their delusive mental structures and in some kind of relation with the real: though negatively, they do after all engage with one another.[6] The reader is very much aware of the gaps between them and, dephased as they may be, they do meet somewhere, at least physically, in that they partake in the mob. The mob maintains its own channels of communication regardless, as it were, of the subjectivities that compose it.

It is the mixture of these two registers which the reader finds upsetting, for we have difficulty understanding the gap between the effective order of reality of the various characters—they do move, live, exchange, consume and engage in a variety of physical activities—and the misconceptions they hold of this very ordering. Fischerle's projected trip to America, Paris and Japan (these locations are interchangeable) is an obsessional figment of his imagination yet concrete steps are taken toward the realization of his project: he buys a ticket, goes to the tailor, purchases shirts, a hat, shoes and a briefcase. The narrative leaves us with the sensation that the trip is plausible; he is about to embark and he would have reached one of his destinations had he not gone back home at the last moment, yet we know that no trip is possible given Fischerle's mental makeup. In their relations with the others all characters experience lucidity and cold calculation (especially in money matters) on the one hand and a paranoid delusion on the other.[7]

The characters do indeed move from lucidity to delusion and back as if by an act of magic, and hence the basic indeterminacy in their functioning. In the first

section of the book the hatred and sado-masochism surrounding the will are described in great detail, until that magical moment when Kien suddenly realizes, for no apparent reason, that he is all wrong and that, in effect, his wife does everything out of love for him:

> The scales fell from Kien's eyes; the hated will was forgotten. He saw her, wretched, begging for love; she wanted to seduce him, he had not seen her like this before. *He* had married her for the books, *she* loved him . . . This was love.
>
> (*A* 110)

Kien then proceeds to a whole series of rationalizations to justify this new attitude: her delicate treatment of the book *The Trousers of Herr von Bredow* was actually addressed to him; "she had wanted to help him;" her interest in a will is purely altruistic for she knows that she will die before him, given the sixteen years difference between them; "She proves her love with money . . ." because "among illiterates money is regarded as the measuring rod for all things." (*A* 110-111). And if she was interested in his bank account, it is because "she trembles fearing he may lose his money. Her own savings are too scanty to keep him above water for long" (*A* 111). She had loved him for eight years in silence and devotion which he had not noticed and "to escape her love, he will submit to her demands for his own sake." (*A* 113). Kien undergoes the same process with regard to Fischerle: suspicion and trust go together. At a certain moment he wants to dismiss this "shameless deformity" (*A* 230); at the next moment "Kien began to understand" that he had not paid him a salary and that "he abused him for his deformity."[8] (*A* 231).

This indetermination and unmotivated change of attitude is true of all the characters. Fischerle has difficulties deciding whether Kien is simply mad or a real crook and their relationship undergoes changes accordingly: "If the creature was mad, then he was generously mad; if he only pretended to be, then he was the boldest crook in the world" (*A* 224). After giving her husband a good thrashing, nearly killing him, Therese "knew how deeply she had loved him;" then "she took him up in her arms as gently as a child." (*A* 141). The capitalist says of her husband, Fischerle, that he is her only child, yet she in the end delivers his death blow.

But what remains ultimately is the delusion. It is as though the mental world exists parallel to the physical world with little connection between the two; we seem to be dealing with abstracted entities completely overtaken by their obsessions, whose physical traits and activities are there merely to support the diffusion of their ideologies. Consider, for example, Kien's physionomy in relation to his impotence. The idée-fixe, the obsession, is taken to its absurd logical extremity in a way consuming its own author much as Kien *must* go up in flames together with his world, his cosmic library, at the end of the novel. Fischerle, Kien's counterpart, is eventually consumed by *his* obsession with chess: he is ritually murdered when he goes back home to get his notebook containing the famous list of chess champions.

The combination of these two registers, of qualified reality and bizarre surreality, makes for the novel's hesitation between meaningful linear narrative development and the breakdown of all signification, thus hovering between sense and non-sense. For, minimal as it is, the plot does provide a sequence of narrative events and we do follow the gradual mental, and sometimes physical, disintegration of the characters from beginning to end. Yet all these narrative events are merely functional and teleological: inscribed in their memory is the unavoidable end to which they must lead. The genetic makeup of every event in the narrative series is quite evident right from the start for the narrative development, as Canetti himself will suggest, is basically quantitative—always more of the same.

The ultimate holocaust at the end of the novel could be appropriated by every event in the narrative series; catastrophe is ominous in every chapter. Canetti's predilection for the fragment, the micro-narrative, the vignette, underlies the fact that these subgenres constitute privileged forms of expression of the basic lack of narrative deployment so germane to his fictional universe. This stage of the embryo in the sign (abortion in the very process of production) manifests the metaphysical void inherent in the Canettian universe. The story which is the metaphorization of history in its repetitive and fragmentary structure, incorporates this primordial ontological lack. The sterile repetition of the basic narrative ingredients in the novel is inescapable and leads perforce to existential doom and formal failure. *Auto da fé* would seek to announce the death of novelistic practice as it has evolved in the West.

The narrator of the autobiographies is much aware of this inescapable oncoming doom; in the first chapter of **The Play of the Eyes**, he tells us of this unbearable experience that accompanied the writing of the novel:

> I wrote scene after scene, each stood by itself, none was connected with any other, but all ended with an immense catastrophe, which alone connected it with the others.
>
> (**The Play of the Eyes,** 5)

Thus, the scenes stand separately, each micro-narrative in its own right, bearing no connection with what precedes or follows it, the only connection being that ultimate end to which they all must lead. It is as though in attempting to deploy a narrative space the novel by definition must lead to its exhaustibility and ultimate

consumption. At the heart of Canetti's narrative event creeps nothingness: the narrative event of necessity points exclusively to its meaninglessness and death. What goes up in flames is the important representative of Western rationality together with his library—that elemental matrix that makes for the possibility of methodic rationality and signification. What goes up in flames is the discourse of Modernism and all it stands for together with the cultures of the East "for the sinologist's library included everything that was of importance to the world." (**The Play of the Eyes,** 3)

Hence the *sine qua non* absence of contextual referentiality, and hence the unicity (and uniqueness) of Canetti's novel. The novelistic sign can therefore only denote its own sterility, and one such experiment is enough to show the inability of the text to make meaning; once exhausted, there is no need to deploy any further this narrative space. Since *Auto da fé* Canetti has not returned to his novelistic practice, turning to other modes of writing that come to compensate, as it were, for the inner lack of the novel. "There was no question of my undertaking any new novel . . . My enormous undertaking had been stifled in the smoke of the burning books." (**The Play of the Eyes,** 4) The novel must fail if it is to make any meaning of the basic ontological lack of meaning. Thus signification is lost and the novelistic sign must bear the mark of its emptiness.[9]

Notes

"A" in the text refers to *Auto da fé,* New York, Stein and Day, 1964.

1. In his *Elias Canetti: Stationen zum Werk.* (Bern, Frankfurt/M: Peter Lang, 1973) Alfons-M. Bischoff sees twofold reasons for Canetti's relatively late reception and low popularity: a) reasons ensuing from the complexity of the novel itself and b) those resulting from the period. Initially, Bischoff claims, Canetti belonged to the "lost generation" arriving to the literary scene only in the aftermath of World War 2.

2. Aspetsberger, "Weltmeister der Verachtung. Zur 'Blendung'" in: A. Friedbert und Stieg G. *Blendung als Lebensform. Elias Canetti.* (Hg.), 1985 (101-125) claims there are three important events, literary and historical, that contribute to the background and are inherent in the novel: a) the popular novel by Willibald Alexis, *Die Hosen des Herrn von Bredow* (1846), and mainly the central character Brigitte von Bredow who is a kind of she-devil and after whom Therese is modelled. But Canetti complexified the character to include low middle class characteristics and, particularly, a fascist mentality. b) The influence of the crowd experience of the Justizpalast fire on July 15, 1927. c) Karl Kraus's public reaction to the events of 1927.

3. Canetti attributes an essential dimension to silence and even claims that silence is the peak of speech, that is, the blanks pertaining to any verbal chain. Indeed, "every language has its own silence." *The Human Province*, 1978, p. 17. Here, of course, silence comes to replace the verbal chain.

4. Joachim Günther in his "Die Provinz des Menschen." In: *Neue Deutsche Hefte*, 1974, H. 141, S. 177-180 suggests that Canetti's production is based on a "fantastic dialectic" which turns against reality by surrealistic means: ". . . der Erfindung surrealistischer Gegenphantasien zur Wirklichkeit." (S. 178)

5. David Roberts regards George as a foil to Peter. George, he claims, is inclined to openness, recognizes the individuality of the other, and tries to overcome the blindness caused by language. He is both artist and actor as opposed to Peter who is a fixed character. But is George indeed antithetical to Peter, his brother? To Roberts this presumed antithetical relation between the two consists of a "negative dialectic"; the brothers neutralize one another (Kopf und Welt. Elias Canettis Roman, *Die Blendung,* München: Hauser Verlag, 1975, S. 118) Diese negative Dialektik verneint die mögliche Synthese. Peter und George würden zusammen nicht den vollkommenen Menschen, den universalen Menschen ergeben, weil jeder das negative Gegenstück des andern ist."

6. For Canetti language is the defining category of human behaviour and the uniqueness of the individual is manifested by the language in use which takes the form a syntactic combination and choice of words (about 500 to a person) as well as the pitch and rhythm of the verbal expression. The combination of all these constitutes the "acoustic mask" of the individual: "Er ist im Sprechen so sehr Gestalt geworden, nach allen Seiten hin deutlich abgegrenzt, von allen übringen Menschen verschieden, wie etwas in seiner Physiomonie, die ja einmalig ist. Diese sprachliche Gestalt eines Menschen, das Gleichbleibende seines Sprechens, diese Sprache, die mit ihm entstanden ist, die er für sich allein hat, die nur mit ihm vergehen wird, nenne ich seine akustische Maske." (Canetti, *Fried* [Hg] 1962, S. 13). The first time Canetti used the expression "acoustic mask" was in 1937, in an interview with a journalist of *Der Sonntag:* ". . . denn für das wichtigste Element dramatischer Gestaltung halte ich die "akustische Maske . . ." (Quoted by Bischoff, 1973, S. 35)

7. "Im Roman *Die Blendung* geht es also fortwährend um Wunschträume und Wahnideen, um *Besitz* und *Geld.*" Mechthild Curtius, *Kritik der Verdinglichung in Canettis Roman Die Blendung,* Bonn: Bouvier, 1973, S. 12.

8. "I am not interested in grasping precisely a man I know. I am interested only in exaggerating him precisely." (*The Human Province,* 1978, p. 262). "The dissolution of the character in recent literature; the figures that our time would need are so monstrous that no one is daredevil enough to invent them." *The Human Province,* 258.

9. Peter Haselberg in his "Experimenting with the Novel," in: Michael Hulse's (trans.) *Essays in Honour of Elias Canetti* comments that: "It could be objected that this way of writing, departing so far from the psychological and so closely approaching a rhetoric of gesture, is a factor that would explode the nature of the novel. But it is less this and rather the absence of communicating human sensibilities that raises the tension to a point where it threatens to shatter the form." (pp. 298-299)

Thomas H. Falk (essay date 1993)

SOURCE: Falk, Thomas H. "Masks and Transformations: *The Wedding, Comedy of Vanity, Life-Terms.*" In *Elias Canetti*, pp. 68-83. New York: Twayne Publishers, 1993.

[*In the following essay, Falk examines Canetti's plays to determine why he considered himself to be first and foremost a dramatist.*]

"Above all else, I consider myself to be a dramatist and everything associated with dramatic work represents the nucleus of my personality."[1] This is a surprising statement if one considers only that Canetti has published just three plays. If, however, one also considers how Canetti has included parts of his novel and numerous character sketches in his public readings, for example, his statement becomes far less astonishing. In conversations, occasional interviews, and in some written statements, Canetti has mentioned—without giving titles—having written other plays, but no further information about such works is available. An examination of the three plays that were published will facilitate an understanding of his dramatic work.

The earliest adventure of a dramatic nature that Canetti describes in his autobiography was his active participation in the reading of the Haggadah at the time of Passover. As the youngest male in the family, he joined his grandfather in performing the question-and-answer ritual explaining the significance of the holiday. Canetti's first creative experience with dramatic work occurred at age six when the family moved to Manchester, England. There, in his room, he spoke to the wallpaper, making up elaborate stories and assigning specific parts to the "many dark circles in the pattern of the wallpaper" that seem "like people to me" (*TF* [*The*

Tongue Set Free], 38). When he was all alone he could become quite animated and "tried to persuade the wall-paper people to do bold deeds, and when they refused, I let them feel my scorn" (*TF,* 39). When the governess caught him in this unusual game, she tried to make him give up the "unhealthy" activity, but he would not. He merely changed the process and articulated his stories silently.

A host of other dramatic encounters in his youth could be described as preparatory work. Certainly the extensive reading of classical dramas that he shared with his mother contributed greatly to Canetti's early proclivity for dramatic literature. And shortly after World War I, when he was living in a boardinghouse in Zurich, the 14-year-old Canetti wrote his first play, "Junius Brutus," a historical tragedy in five acts of 2,298 lines of blank verse. The play, written in three months (but never published), was dedicated and solemnly presented to his mother on Christmas Day 1919. Young Elias soon realized "how miserable this work was, and that it didn't entitle me to the slightest hopes" (*TF,* 198). He clearly learned from this event, however, "the distrust that I later felt against everything I wrote down in haughtiness and self-assurance" (*TF,* 198).

A dozen years passed before Canetti wrote plays again. During this apprenticeship period, Canetti matured, he read a great deal, and he participated in events that influenced his dramatic work profoundly. Many of these encounters are described in considerable detail in the second volume of his autobiography *The Torch in My Ear,* while he reflects on other aspects of his dramatic work in the third volume, *The Play of the Eyes,* and in his notes and aphorisms, *The Human Province* and *The Secret Heart of the Clock.* While it is not possible to examine each observation that Canetti has made on dramatic literature in general and on his plays in particular, it is informative to highlight a few experiences.

Of the many playwrights Canetti read and undoubtedly also saw in performance in Vienna, three seem to have had an indelible impact on him: the greatest writer of Greek comedy, Aristophanes; the nineteenth-century Austrian master of wit and language, Johann Nestroy; and the leading satirist of the day, Karl Kraus. From each Canetti learned a great deal, and each contributed to his concept and theory of the drama.

The writings of Aristophanes (c. 448-380 B.C.) assumed an important role in Canetti's life during the last few months of his residency in Frankfurt in 1924. Indeed, he even describes this time as his "Aristophanic apprenticeship" (*TE* [*The Torch in My Ear*], 53), when he read Aristophanes' works and simultaneously observed that a very similar condition existed in his own world. The basic condition Canetti noted was "the raging plunge of money" caused by the inflation in Germany

(*TE,* 53). In those days, Canetti observed the reality of—for example—a loaf of bread costing several billion marks while the price of commodities doubled and tripled in the course of just one day. This total destruction of the structure of society was comprehensible to Canetti only through the works of Aristophanes. He points out that "the cruelty of Aristophanes' vision offered the sole possibility of holding together a world that was shivering into a thousand particles" (*TE,* 53).

From Aristophanes Canetti also learned about the structure of the comedy. An Aristophanic comedy is by no means a light and amusing drama with a typically happy ending, but rather a very serious play using the comedic for the exposition of an important and consequential topic. The typical plan for this comedy presents a protagonist who seriously undertakes some preposterous project, and the play becomes an elaboration of his success or failure. Although Aristophanes' plays do not follow a consistent pattern, structurally each play falls into two parts: one in which the preposterous project or "basic idea" is presented and debated, and the other part in which that idea is put into practice.

Canetti's own *Comedy of Vanity* follows Aristophanes' pattern: a prologue with announcement of the "basic idea" or ingenious plan conceived by a specific actor; the *prados* and *agon,* the former being a presentation by a chorus, while the latter offers a debate between the proponents and opponents of the plan; the *parabis,* which is an interlude in which the characters address the audience quite directly; numerous episodes illustrating the preposterous project; and the exodus that celebrates the successful resolution of the "basic idea." Despite the general absurdity of the situation, the characters are real as types, their verisimilitude coming from their perfectly natural behavior in rather unnatural circumstances. Canetti believes that such a drama will be successful if it can "demand the utmost from the spectator, shake him, take him, and drain him" (*TE,* 54).

Johann Nestroy (1801-1862) owed much of his esteem during Canetti's early years to one of Karl Kraus's finest literary-critical essays, "Nestroy and Posterity," a tribute read before an audience of 1500 in May 1912. Prior to that time, Nestroy was thought of merely as the author of over 80 comedies, most of them in Viennese dialect. Kraus, however, focused on Nestroy's satirical genius and the exemplary fashion in which he mirrored his times, the era of mid-nineteenth-century Biedermeier Vienna. Just as Kraus saw Nestroy as the satirist at the end of a period of decline, Kraus saw himself as the prophet of Austrian decline at the turn of the century. And likewise, Canetti stands at the conclusion of his era. What Kraus wrote about Nestroy could be said of all three writers: "The satirical artist stands at the end of a development which has forgone art. He is its product and its despairing opposite. He organizes the flight of the spirit from humanity, he concentrates on going back. After him comes the deluge."[2]

From Nestroy, Canetti also learned how the playwright can make effective use of dialects in creating characters. Even though Nestroy's individual characters speak in various Viennese dialects, they can—with the exception of only a very few words—be easily understood even today by every speaker of German. The dialects allow the playwright to create characters representing different and distinct classes, be they economic, social, political, or educational classes. This phenomenon is particularly evident in the two plays Canetti wrote in Vienna, *The Wedding* and *Comedy of Vanity.*

A third characteristic of Canetti's plays that might be attributed to Nestroy is the successful way in which various parts of the stage are used simultaneously. In contrast to the traditional convention of presenting scenes in sequence, Nestroy, in a medieval tradition, divides his stage into two or more areas for action, making it possible to simultaneously offer a particular point of view from different perspectives. Using this technique Canetti can display the views of two or more dozen characters and the audience can follow without the slightest confusion.

Karl Kraus (1874-1936) had an immeasurable effect on Canetti's dramatic work. Aside from everything else he learned at the many Kraus lectures and readings he attended, Kraus's great skill as an orator had an important influence on Canetti. Recalling his first lecture shortly after he arrived in Vienna in 1924, Canetti writes: "When he sat down and began to read, I was overwhelmed by his voice, which had something unnaturally vibrating about it, like a decelerated crowing. But this impression quickly vanished, for his voice instantly changed and kept changing incessantly, and one was very soon amazed at the variety that he was capable of" (*TE,* 70).

Kraus had founded what he called his "Theater of Poetry" (*Theater der Dichtung*), at which he gave spellbound audiences readings of the dramatic and poetic classics, above all Shakespeare, Nestroy, and Offenbach. But the most famous performances were the readings from his visionary-satirical play *The Last Days of Mankind,* a vast assemblage of scenes documenting the years of the Austrian apocalypse, 1914-1919. Canetti remembers those readings as times when Kraus "populated Vienna for me" (*TE,* 159).

As the foremost satirical gadfly of his day, Kraus was well known for the masterful way in which he could accuse his enemies and find them guilty. He merely looked closely at their writings, extracted any error however small, and then used their own writing against

them. Canetti learned from this experience at Kraus's lectures that "each individual has a linguistic shape distinguishing him from all others" (*CW* [*The Conscience of Words*] 34), an idea that he would later articulate as the "acoustic mask."

One important characteristic that Canetti shares with these three predecessors is that of taking personal responsibility for the most critical and dangerous roles. According to tradition, Aristophanes played the role of Cleon in his comedy *The Knights* because in those days no actor would have ventured to impersonate a politician. It is known that Johann Nestroy not only wrote over 80 plays but also played important roles in most of them; many provoked the ire of the censors, leading to his arrest and incarceration. In his public readings from *The Last Days of Mankind,* Kraus had reserved the role of the Grumbler for himself. Canetti writes in his autobiography that in Vienna in the 1930s he gave public readings of parts or all of *The Wedding* and *Comedy of Vanity* because no theater was prepared to stage the plays. In later years he even prepared recordings of his plays where he read every role.

From time to time Canetti has indicated that he was writing a book on his theory of the drama. Although this book has not been published, three key concepts emerge as the basis of his theory from various interviews he has given, from his notes and aphorisms, and from his essays and theoretical writings. These concepts are the acoustic mask (*akustische Maske*), the basic idea (*Grundeinfall*), and the transformation (*Verwandlung*). Although they appear in the dramatic and theoretical works of many writers, Canetti's understanding of these concepts is quite unique.

For approaching and interpreting Canetti's dramatic work, a complete understanding of the composition of the "acoustic mask" is essential. In an interview published in a supplement to the Viennese paper *Der Sontag,* 18 April 1937, Canetti articulated some of the aspects of his theory of the drama and outlined specifically how each character of his plays acquires an acoustic mask. Erich Fried includes a verbatim transcript of the interview in the introduction to the volume *Welt im Kopf* (*World in the Head*), a small collection of excerpts from Canetti's works.[3]

"The drama lives in its own peculiar way in language. One could almost say . . . the drama lives in language and, consequently, I consider the acoustic mask to be the most important element of the dramatic structure" (12). Recognizing that it is difficult to define this concept, Canetti offers an example.

> Go to a popular pub, sit at any table, and strike up an acquaintance with . . . a total stranger. To begin with you will be unable to cheer him up with several kind

sentences. However, as soon as he really starts talking—and he will like to talk; that's why he goes to this pub—you must persist in keeping quiet and listen to him intently for a few minutes. . . .

There you will now find that your new acquaintance has a very individual way of speaking. It is not enough to determine that he speaks German or he speaks a dialect, most or all people in this pub do that. No, his way of speaking is unique and should not be mistaken as being that of someone else. It has its own pitch and speed, it has its own rhythm. He changes his sentences infrequently. Certain words and expressions occur again and again. Indeed, his language is made up of only 500 words.[4] He makes do quite well—they are his 500 words. Another person, also "word-poor," speaks a different 500 words. You can, if you listened to him well, recognize him the next time by his language, without even seeing him. He has, in his speaking, become such a figure, clearly delimited on all sides, different from all people, like his physiognomy, which of course is also unique. This linguistic structure of a person, this "remaining-the-same" of his speaking, this language which has been created by him, which he has completely to himself, which will only pass away with him, this I call the acoustic mask.

(12-13)

Of course, Canetti does not intend to serve merely as an "ambling phonograph" collecting samples of speech but to use the acoustic mask with all its linguistic possibilities and limitations in his creation of each unique character in his plays. These characters also have a visual configuration when one observes their deportment and manner of walking. Once the linguistic and physical masks have been established, each character represents a particular point of view the author has assigned to them, and, consequently, they take on what might be described as a philosophical mask. In summary, the mask defines all aspects of a particular character.

Unfortunately, the elements of the acoustic mask that are based primarily on the use of specific dialects are essentially lost in the translations of the plays. In *The Wedding* and *Comedy of Vanity*, Canetti's characters speak the dialects that are found in all the various districts of old Vienna and that are peculiar to their social and economic status in that society. Such an environment does not have a good equivalent in the English-speaking world and it is impossible to adapt this aspect of the acoustic mask to another socioeconomic setting; therefore, successful translations have had to eliminate that part of the acoustic mask. One can, however, note the names assigned to places and characters as representing at least a portion of the acoustic mask. For example, one of the main characters in *The Wedding* is Oberbaurat Segenreich. His title translates as senior engineer or construction official, and his name means that he is "richly blessed." Another is Dr. Bock, the 80-year-old family physician, whose name should be translated as Dr. Stud because that is the role he plays. One can

also observe that the play takes place in a house on Gütigkeitstraße, kindness street—just another bit of Canetti's irony.

The second key concept evident in each drama is the "basic idea." Canetti insists that "every drama proceed from a completely new basic idea" (15). The play must be so novel in its plot that it presents viewers with a world they have never seen or experienced. It is insufficient for the play to represent characters that exhibit individual interpersonal relationships with other characters. The basic idea must also include a great variety of unique features so that the dramatic environment will illustrate a singular but complete event that is entirely new to the audience.

The notion of the "transformation" refers to Canetti's belief that the theater is not a place for entertainment, but rather should serve as an educational institution. The playwright and the theater are to confront the audience with a reality that results in a catharsis in the Aristotelian sense. Canetti does not seek to describe and interpret the world; he wants to present his "uncomfortable" dramas, grotesque and absurd satires, to bring about a change—a transformation—through confrontation. The reception of his plays shows that audiences are not infrequently reluctant to accept the harsh moral responsibilities that Canetti demands of them so forcefully and unrelentingly in his dramatic works.

An examination of Canetti's three plays illustrates how he executed these key concepts. The published plays are *The Wedding (Hochzeit)*, written in Vienna in the winter of 1931-32; *Comedy of Vanity (Komödie der Eitelkeit)*, also written in Vienna, in 1933-34; and *Life-Terms (Die Befristeten)*,[5] written many years later in London in 1952-53. The plays had their premieres in reverse order from their writing. *Die Befristeten* premiered in English translation as *The Numbered* on 5 November 1956 at the Playhouse Theatre, Oxford, England; its German premiere occurred at the Theater in der Josefstadt, Studiobühne, in Vienna on 17 November 1967. The other two plays premiered in 1965 at the Staatstheater in Braunschweig, Germany, *Comedy of Vanity* on 6 February and *The Wedding* on 3 November.

THE WEDDING

The Wedding has as its "basic idea" the exposition of three protagonists: greed, lasciviousness, and death. The play presents the cruel and merciless conditions of a society that seems no longer to have a moral code to live by and is now participating in a repetitive ritual leading to Armageddon. *The Wedding* is divided into two parts: a prelude in five scenes and the main act, which presents the actual wedding celebration.

The prelude serves as a brief introduction to the disparate characters residing in an apartment house on Gütigkeitstraße, all possessed by the singular goal of owning the house in which they live. At first we meet the landlady, Mrs. Gile, a shrewd old woman whose granddaughter visits every day to ask to inherit the house while hoping the old lady will soon die. Each time the grandmother's parrot hears the word *house* he repeats it three times and thereby caws the major theme of this scene and the entire play. Subsequent scenes of the prelude illustrate how other residents are trying to cheat the old woman out of her house: a pompous school teacher, a young couple, and a very crafty couple who want to purchase the house cheaply. The fifth scene takes place in the janitor's basement apartment. His wife is lying on her deathbed while he is reading the biblical story of Samson from the book of Judges; blinded Samson pulls down the house on the Philistines. This foreshadows the events of the main play.

The wedding celebrated in the main act centers on a depraved, petite-bourgeois family. The father of the bride is Mr. Blest, an engineer, who insists in his vanity that everyone acknowledge that he has built not only this solid house on the Gütigkeitstraße but also this fine family. The other members of the family and wedding party have in common greed to possess property and other people, as well as a demonic obsession with sexual excesses. The nymphomaniacal mother of the bride thinks only of copulating with the groom; the bride lusts for three friends of the family before settling down to the boredom of married life; and—representing the crudest form of sexuality—the 80-year-old family doctor, erotomaniac and pedophile Dr. Stud, brags that he has "had" all the women in the family and at the party. The bride, Christa, summarizes life in this house: upstairs the guileful landlady, downstairs a corpse, and here at this bacchanalian feast she is getting married.

Into this macabre world, Hark, an idealist, introduces a play within the play. He asks what each person would do if his or her beloved were threatened by imminent danger. In this game of illusion each person, of course, thinks only of satisfying their own greed and lust. A sudden earthquake then changes the game into reality. Now that everyone could really save the person they love, they do nothing but try to save themselves. The play closes with cruel, hateful screams that cut into silence. The parrot has the last word: "House! House! House!" (*W* [*The Wedding*], 63).

The premiere performance of *The Wedding* in 1965 at the Staatstheater in Braunschweig led to a sensational scandal followed by extensive coverage in the local and national press. The publicity resulted in the closing of the play after only seven performances and undoubtedly discouraged further stagings in the years that followed. Directed by Alexander Wagner, with stage and costumes designed by Manfred Schröter, the initial production seems to have been a faithful rendition of Canetti's text. But spectators were offended by some words, by

the way some characters were portrayed, and even by the theme, content, and/or message of the play. The day before the premiere, a Braunschweig newspaper even printed an anonymous charge suggesting that the play was pornographic and contained sexually stimulating and offensive materials. Before the next performance a host of writers and critics, from Günter Grass to Theodor Adorno, interceded on behalf of Canetti and the performance and vouched for the artistic quality and integrity of the play.

The Wedding is considered Canetti's most stageable play. It was successfully performed under the direction of Karl Paryla in 1970 in Cologne and was enthusiastically received when Canetti himself read it later that year at the Schauspielhaus in Kiel. In October 1985 the city of Vienna celebrated Canetti's eightieth birthday. As "their" Nobel Prize laureate, they made him an honorary citizen of Vienna and Hans Hollmann directed *The Wedding* at the Akademietheater with a distinguished cast. The newspaper *Frankfurter Rundschau* called the performance "Hollmann's crowning accomplishment in staging Canetti's plays."[6]

COMEDY OF VANITY

The "basic idea" of the second play from the Vienna period, *Comedy of Vanity,* is that humankind would gradually waste away if deprived of its vanity. Vanity, a characteristic quality developed to a greater or lesser extent in each person, is the basic attribute that distinguishes the individual and provides a life-sustaining force.

A government decree to eliminate vanity is imposed on the population:

> Official declaration—The Government has decided:
>
> Point One: The possession and use of mirrors is prohibited. All extant mirrors must be destroyed. All manufacture of mirrors must be stopped. If after a period of thirty days a person is found still to possess or use a mirror, he or she will be punished with ten to twelve years imprisonment. The manufacture of mirrors carries the death penalty.
>
> Point Two: The taking of pictures of humans and related beings is strictly prohibited. All extant photographs of human or related beings will be destroyed. . . .
>
> Point Three: The creation of portraits or self-portraits in oil, watercolor, charcoal, pencil or any other medium is strictly prohibited. . . . All extant portraits or self-portraits must be turned in at the nearest government agency. . . .
>
> (*CV* [*Comedy of Vanity*], 30)
>
> Point Four: All movie theaters will be closed down. All reels, originals as well as copies, will be destroyed . . .
>
> (*CV,* 21)

The consequence of not abiding by each item of the decree is, as in point one, punishment by long imprisonment or even death. A period of 30 days has been set to give people time to comply with the decree.

The play illustrates how a series of unique individuals react to the decree, first in the implementation of the law and then in living with this new restriction. There are at least two dozen distinct characters representing many acoustic masks and individual personalities. In part one of the play we see a carnival-like atmosphere in which all are gathered to destroy their pictures and mirrors, each heeding the call in their own way.

A few examples illustrate the manner in which Canetti creates his dramatic personalities. The teacher Fritz Shakee appears as a traditional enforcer of conduct, but he has a severe stuttering problem whenever he is not acting in an authoritative role. It is Shakee who reads the official decree, during which it is observed that he "has grown in size . . . and reads with a high, loud voice without stammering once" (*CV,* 29).

S. Bleiss, a photographer prior to the government declaration, has been in the business of perpetuating vanity right along. His favorite gimmick was to take pictures of poor newlyweds standing in front of his car. The couple would not only have a picture but also acquire the capital investment of a car and have the picture as proof of their new wealth.

François Fant is a coxcomb. He has stolen all his mother's mirrors to take to the carnival, where he smashes them with a ball while watching the reflection of his own image in the mirrors. Mme. Emily Fant initially appears to be simply François's doting mother, but quickly reveals that she needs the mirrors in her business so that her girls can check themselves in order to be attractive for their gentlemen customers.

Henry Breeze strolls across the stage, pontificating to his companion Leda Fresh that a self-image of good health provides the individual with a meaningful life. Encouraged by Leda, his magniloquence leads him to boast that his brilliance in talking on a higher level of consciousness makes him "appear more virile" (*CV,* 31).

In the second half of the play each of the characters has come to terms with the decree 10 years later. Fritz Shakee is now the powerful chairman of the "Group of Four," an enforcement committee of crime fighters. It has come to his attention that young girls have found a way of circumventing the government decree by looking into one another's eyes to see themselves. Fritz Shakee advocates passage of a new law under which the eyes of those young girls will be torn out if they continue their illegal practice. It turns out that Shakee is

actually married to one of these girls. In time he grows ill and despondent because he has contracted the "mirror sickness," a disease that can be cured only by looking into a mirror. When his wife illegally procures a mirror for him, Shakee is cured but his original stammering returns. Subsequently, when he tries to bury this illegal mirror, he is consumed by the "voices of stuttering choruses" (*CV,* 87).

S. Bleiss is still perpetuating vanity. "Help yourself to some happiness" (*CV,* 45) is his slogan as he goes from door to door selling time in front of a mirror at five shillings for two minutes. Although occasionally caught in this illegal venture, Bleiss survives since his crime is always also someone else's crime—the perfect black-marketeer. Unlike many other characters, Bleiss has never had a conscience to make him feel guilty. No harm comes to him during this period of prohibition.

The clever businesswoman Mme. Fant continues to indulge her son, but now she has established a "Spiegelbordell," a mirror brothel. Here almost all the characters of the play pay high prices to sit in front of mirrors and admire themselves. Henry Breeze stands before a full-length mirror in a "Luxury Cabin" making pompous and trivial pronouncements. After each proclamation he pushes a button and hears applause, but each time the applause grows weaker until there is none. Dementedly, he shouts basic truths on the condition of the world in a thundering voice as he threatens destruction of the establishment.

In the final scene most of the characters are in Mme. Fant's "Spiegelsaal," her "Hall of Mirrors." Each is confronted by and recoils from a "Thundering Voice" that summarizes their individual personality and the falseness of the mask that each has created. The carnival atmosphere that had robbed them of their individuality at the beginning of the play is transformed into an invocation and affirmation of an individual "Ich!" ("I"). All raise high a mirror or picture of themselves, but never merge into a chorus or group. The "I" of individual vanity prevails.

The premiere performance of *Comedy of Vanity* also took place at the Staatstheater in Braunschweig and was directed by Helmut Matiasek, with set and costumes designed by Manfred Schröter. The press had hailed Matiasek for "discovering" Canetti for the German theater, but their reviews of opening night were generally so negative that the run closed after only eight performances. By and large the reviewers thought highly of the play and placed the blame on the director, who had set the play historically in the period of Hitler's Germany. Matiasek created film segments and photomontages that transformed Canetti's play into a commentary on Nazism. The "mirror sickness" became the Hitler sickness, rather than a general statement on totalitarian systems. "The devices used in the staging changed the play" stated Günther Rühle[7]; that eliminated the catharsis Canetti had intended.

In Austria, **Comedy of Vanity** premiered at the Graz Schauspielhaus in October 1972 as part of the "Steirische Herbst" program (the Styrian Fall Arts Festival). The reviews of this performance were quite favorable, although they did mention that the director, Hermann Kutscher, had not fully realized the concept of the acoustic masks.

The most successful rendition of Canetti's play was the performance in Basel, Switzerland, in February 1978 under the direction of Hans Hollmann. Peter Iden's review quotes Canetti: "After all, 40 years after the *Komödie* was written it has now been performed correctly for the first time in Basel."[8] What made the Hollmann production so successful was his full comprehension of Canetti's concept of the acoustic mask and the uniqueness of the basic idea. In the 1985 *Festschrift* for Canetti, Hollmann describes how he came to understand Canetti, via work with plays by Horvath, Karl Kraus, Aristophanes and Nestroy, and honors him by revealing that he uses Canetti's concept of the acoustic mask in all of his productions.[9]

LIFE-TERMS

For the play written in London, **Life-Terms,** the "basic idea" is a portrayal of a utopian society in which people are no longer tormented by the uncertainty of when they will die. In the prologue two men are talking about the olden days (the present time) when people did not know the "*Augenblick*" (the moment) when they were to die. Their names were merely names then, rather than the numbers now used to indicate the age when death will occur. Life used to be constantly threatened by the arbitrariness of the hour of death.

Now, at birth everyone is given a locket containing their dates of birth and death and a number that serves as their name and indicates how many years they will live. Although everyone can know his or her own number, it is a crime—labeled murder—to reveal to others the information in the locket. Death has become the ultimate taboo, and to question the accuracy of the established age of one's death is the greatest crime. The Locketeer is the only person who can open the locket at the time of death to confirm the accuracy of the birth and death dates recorded there.

The play has 3 major and 20 minor characters, as well as a "Chorus of the Unequal." The minor characters have names such as the Mother 32, the Boy 70, two Young Men 28 and 88, the Professor 46, and the Boy 10. Their personality and behavior are determined entirely by the number. The Mother 32, for example, is unable to persuade her son, the Boy 70, to be cautious while playing because the son knows that nothing can hurt him—his name is 70. The Boy 10 is allowed to act like a spoiled brat because everyone knows he has only a short life. In a scene with a grandmother and granddaughter, the fairy-tale concept of living happily ever after is negated when the grandmother must remind the girl that she will not live happily ever after, but only until her "moment" (**LT** [**Life-Terms**], 120). Those with high numbers, whether men with 88 or women with 93 and 96, display a superiority and arrogance over those with low numbers; they have been ordained as higher and more valuable citizens in their society.

The major characters are Fifty, Friend, and the Locketeer. Fifty is reluctant to accept the dictatorship of the Locketeer. For many years he has suspected that the lockets were really empty and that the Locketeer was a swindler. He reveals the deception to the Friend and subsequently to the others, the masses, who follow him joyfully, bringing the downfall of the Locketeer's deceptive system. For just one moment the masses rejoice, believing that now they would live forever. With the death of the first person, however, this dream vanishes. The newly established hope for immortality, a new form of freedom, turns out to be only a freedom to die at a time not determined by the Locketeer. Now the time of death is once again unforeseeable; the uncertainty of death is even more unendurable than the certainty of a pre-established moment of death had been before. Fifty may have brought about a freedom, but the burden of this responsibility is more than he is able and willing to endure.

There are few available reviews of the premiere performance of **Die Befristeten** by the Meadow Players of the Oxford Playhouse Company on 5 November 1956, but these are very positive. The play was translated by Carol Stewart under the title of **The Numbered** and directed by Mionos Volanakis, with sets by Wilfred and Samuel Avery. The London *Times* correspondent compares Canetti's play with previous productions of works by Giraudoux and Cocteau and states: "Into this distinguished repertoire Mr. Elias Canetti's play erupts with a strangely mathematical absorption."[10] *Oxford Magazine* reports that "the writing is forceful and plain, as is the production. . . . In scene upon scene they build up the delicate web of tension, achieving with truth and economy effects which grip the mind."[11]

The German language premiere in Vienna under the direction of Friedrich Kallina was not well received. Canetti had just been honored with the 1967 Great Austrian State Prize for Literature, and from the reviews one gets the impression that the Vienna theater establishment felt obligated to give a German language performance. The correspondent from *Die Welt* thought that the production at the small Studiobühne of the Theater in der Josefstadt was "on average good" but that "the whole thing is an amiable play for the mind but not for the stage."[12]

When Hans Hollmann staged a production of *Life-Terms* at the Württembergisches Staatstheater in Stuttgart in February 1983, the press was still inclined to think it was a play for the mind. The performance was very well received, however, because of Hollmann's extraordinary ability to take this parable and make it a dramatic event. There was praise for the performers' "magnificent accomplishments as actors."[13] Although the concept of the acoustic mask is generally not applied to this play by other critics and directors, Hans Hollmann believes that it is essential and applicable for a successful production of *Life-Terms.*

CONCLUSION

There is no record of major productions of Canetti's plays in the United States. The translator of the plays, Professor Gitta Honegger, did a reading of excerpts from the plays at a meeting of the PEN American Center in New York in the mid-1980s and reports a reading of *Life-Terms* at about that time.[14]

In spite of the difficulties that a production of Canetti's plays may present, there is no reason for not staging these works. From the comments and reviews of performances in the German-speaking theaters, one has the impression that the major objection by audiences to Canetti's works is an antipathy to the philosophical and moral issues the author raises. No one seems to want to hear what this contemporary satirist has to say, just as his predecessors from Aristophanes to Kraus were repeatedly rejected by their audiences.

The concepts of the "acoustic mask" and the "basic idea" in the plays can be examined and articulated with relative ease. But the third concept, the "transformation," can only be tested when the spectator or reader fully confronts the work. Canetti has certainly addressed major issues facing humanity in the modern world: greed, power, lasciviousness, freedom, death, the depersonalization of the individual, and the creation of an inhumane mass society. Susan Sontag has quoted Canetti as saying that he set out to "grab this century by the throat,"[15] and he has done so with power and grace. Some critics have used epithets such as the "difficult" or "uncomfortable" writer in describing Canetti. Not infrequently the controversy surrounding performances of the plays is explained as a public unwilling to see itself in such a brutally honest way—their mask is revealed and they don't like what they see. They are troubled and horrified by their "transformation."

Notes

1. Interview with Elias Canetti and Friedrich Witz, 23 August 1968, Radio DRS, II. Programm, Studio Zurich. Quoted in A. M. Bischoff, *Elias Canetti—Stationen zum Werk* (Bern: Herbert Lang, 1973), 70; trans. mine.

2. Karl Kraus, "Nestroy und die Nachwelt," *Die Fackel,* nos. 349-50 (1912): 23; trans. mine.

3. Elias Canetti, *Welt im Kopf,* intro. and sel. Erich Fried (Graz: Stiasny, 1962); hereafter cited in text, all trans. mine.

4. The number "500 words" must be understood figuratively rather than literally because it would be impossible to limit anyone's speech to such a low number if one were to count each word the individual utters. Canetti undoubtedly was suggesting that the "word-poor" person's vocabulary is restricted by the small number of concepts he might discuss in such a setting. Linguists have examined this issue extensively and have concluded that "the claim that . . . some individual people . . . manage with a vocabulary of only a few hundred words . . . is mere fantasy" (Robbins Burling, *Patterns of Language* [San Diego: Academic Press, 1992], 64).

5. Elias Canetti, *Die Befristeten* (Munich: Carl Hanser, 1964); *Life-Terms,* trans. Gitta Honegger (New York: Performing Arts Journal Publications, 1983); *The Numbered,* trans. Carol Stewart (London: Calder & Boyars, 1984); hereafter cited in text as *LT.*

6. Paul Kruntorad, "Kompromißlose Texttreue," *Frankfurter Rundschau,* 1 October 1985; trans. mine.

7. Günther Rühle, "Ein Skandal in Braunschweig," *Frankfurter Allgemeine Zeitung,* 9 February 1965; trans. mine.

8. Peter Iden, "Vom Ich zum Wir und wieder zurück," *Die Zeit,* 17 February 1978; trans. mine.

9. Hans Hollmann, "Working on Canetti's Plays," in *Essays in Honor of Elias Canetti,* 240-45.

10. "Playhouse Theatre, Oxford—The Numbered," *Times* (London), 6 November 1956.

11. "The Playhouse—The Numbered by Elias Canetti," *Oxford Magazine,* n. d., p. 1.

12. egw., "Warten auf Canetti," *Die Welt,* 21 November 1967; trans. mine.

13. Siegfried Kienzle, "Der verordnete Tod," *Darmstädter Echo,* 7 February 1983; trans. mine.

14. Gitta Honegger in a letter to me dated 3 October 1989.

15. Susan Sontag, *Under the Sign of Saturn* (New York: Farrar, Straus & Giroux, 1980), 190.

John McClelland (essay date 1996)

SOURCE: McClelland, John. "The Place of Elias Canetti's *Crowds and Power* in the History of Western Social and Political Thought." *Thesis Eleven,* no. 45 (1996): 16-27.

[*In the following essay, McClelland examines sources and influences for Canetti's* Crowds and Power *to determine the book's place in the twentieth-century Western cultural landscape.*]

This somewhat ponderously Leavisite title is meant to suggest that, in the English-speaking world at least, the problem of Canetti's **Crowds and Power** is to find its place in our cultural landscape. Those of us who first read **Crowds and Power** in the early sixties will never forget the sense of bewilderment that the book caused us. We had no doubt that we had something important in our hands. It sounded a bit oracular at times, but we easily forgave this, because Canetti was offering some kind of original explanation of the great horrifying events of the twentieth century. The world wars, the rise of fascism, and especially of Nazism, the Holocaust and the threat of the nuclear holocaust, were all being interpreted in a strikingly new way. But the problem still remained of deciding what it was, in general, that Canetti was trying to say. The details of **Crowds and Power** are marvellously clear and direct, and its erudition is part of its charm, but the problem remained of deciding what all the detail added up to? Another way of putting the problem is to say that it was very difficult to decide what subject **Crowds and Power** was *part of.* What other books was it speaking to? Those of us who were reading the book in universities could easily recognise chunks of the different academic subjects as we then thought of them: anthropology, history, sociology, social psychology, political science and so on, and in general the work looked like a piece of social or political theory, but how **Crowds and Power** spoke to other social and political theories was far from clear. Where were Hegel and Marx? Where was Darwin? Machiavelli was there, in a rather eccentric way, and so was Freud, though he is treated rather dismissively. Instead of Darwin we got Pasteur, and instead of psychoanalysis we got schizophrenia. And, above all, we got crowds until they were coming out of our ears.

It was Canetti's insistence on the crowd as the fundamental explanatory category which was truly puzzling. The idea of the crowd had a mildly anachronistic tinge to it. Almost the only thing we knew or remembered about the crowd was Le Bon's *The Crowd: a Study of*

the Popular Mind, the first French edition of which had appeared way back in 1895. Specialists might have known about Freud's *Group Psychology and the Analysis of the Ego* (1921), which begins from Le Bon, but nobody knew much more than that. The received view was that crowd theory was really a dead end, and perhaps it always had been. For one thing, it relied rather too heavily on hypnotism to explain the hold that leaders of the crowd had over their followers, and there has always been a large scientific question mark hanging over hypnotism as a music hall trick. Also, crowd theory, such as it appeared to be, was regarded pre-sociological. Crowd theorists like Le Bon had used the crowd as a very broad explanatory category. There was no social phenomenon which crowd theory could not explain. Le Bon himself was an intellectual imperialist and a ruthless reductivist. He thought there was no need for separate social sciences. Anthropology, sociology, political science and economics would all be satisfactorily reduced to crowd theory. A riot, a revolution, or a family or the workings of an ordinary society, were all, at bottom, different manifestations of the behaviour of crowds. Even the word "crowds" in the plural does an injustice to the reductivist thrust of Le Bon's theory. It would be nearer the mark to say *"the* crowd" explains everything, because Le Bon is one of history's heroic simplifiers. For him, there was only really one crowd, everywhere and at all times the same.

Modern social science has developed largely as a hostile reaction to the Le Bon kind of theory. Le Bon's *The Crowd* came at the end of a scientific enterprise in which the goodness of a theory was judged according to its universality: the more it explained, the better. This view of theory looked back to the social theory which the Enlightenment had always tried to construct after the manner of what it thought was Newtonianism. A good theory was one which, like Newtonian physics, explained the workings of a huge amount of apparently disparate phenomena through a very small number of simple laws. Le Bon, despite his own hostility to most of what the Enlightenment had stood for, was in this sense much more enlightened than he knew.

This was the perspective on crowd theory which most readers of **Crowds and Power** brought back to the work in the nineteen-sixties. The theory of the crowd was simplistic. It came out of a tired old scientific paradigm, about which the only good thing that could be said was that it explained a lot of things very weakly indeed. Modern social science had domesticated the crowd by dividing up the problem of the explanation of collective behaviour between the various academically institutionalised social sciences. Surely Canetti could not be going back beyond all that to a kind of social theory which had been so comprehensively discredited. Canetti was going back beyond more recent social theory, but his reasons are complicated. Canetti suspects that crowd theory in the old Le Bon sense has not really gone away. Nor does he think that the old crowd theory of the late nineteenth and early twentieth centuries was as innovative as it so determinedly proclaimed itself to be. Canetti's view is that crowd theory, for all the touted modernity of its depth psychological bases, is not very different from an elitist justification of rule by the best which goes at least as far back as Plato's *Republic*.

What is at issue here is the nature of western political theory since the beginning. It has long been customary to regard the history of Western political thought from Plato to some more or less arbitrary date in the late nineteenth century, as being in an important sense the product of reason. Until the rise of irrationalism in the second half of the nineteenth century, political theory was supposed to be reasoned discourse between rational men. Political theory was the product of reason and it was addressed to rationality. This did not mean, of course, that it was addressed to everybody. The ancient Greek view that reason could only work properly within a narrow circle of a particular kind of men, lasted a very long time (and has not yet run its course). It was not until the Enlightenment that it began even to be possible to begin to believe that reason was some kind of generalised human birthright, shared by everybody regardless of race or gender. (How far enlightened political thinkers *really* believed this is still a moot point. Some, like Rousseau, probably did; some, like Voltaire, probably did not, but enlightened thinkers of the more radical kind certainly talked as if they believed it.) Out of enlightened optimism came the idea of the parliamentary republic, the bourgeois republic of the Marxists, which existed to make and enforce the public rationality of law. Free and rational citizens would choose representatives to make law after widespread and public discussion of the merits of pieces of legislation, and that legislation would be binding on everybody because everybody had the right and the opportunity to take part at some stage in the process by which law was made. This, or something very like it, was the basis of the republics founded after the American and French Revolutions, and it remains part of the basis on which modern liberal democracy is still supposed to rest.

This was also the idea which irrationalists like Le Bon set out to undermine, though Le Bon is only the most famous of a whole host of thinkers who ganged up on the supposed rationality of the parliamentary republic. At bottom, their argument was remarkably simple and persuasive. The new depth psychology of the second half of the nineteenth century, of which Freudianism can be seen as the apogee, coupled with a widely diffused pessimistic Darwinism, showed that men (let alone women) were hardly rational in any sense that really made sense. Not only was most of mind "unconscious", but that unconscious had never changed since the now unimaginably remote origins of human and animal life. It still takes an effort to conceive of what the new evolutionary time-scales meant to the social theories being formed during the period when evolutionism was making its way through the natural and social sciences. In the age of Newton it had still been possible to believe that the world had been created about five thousand years ago. In 1800, perfectly respectable philologists argued against their opponents that languages did not really have a history, all of them having been invented by God. Yet fifty years later, thinking men were aware that human civilized life, however defined, came at the very end of historical, prehistoric, anthropological, biological, botanical and geological time-scales, so that even to speak of "origins" as Darwin did, was to engage with phenomena so far back as to be absolutely beyond any form of human control.

The most obvious social theory to fall victim to Darwinism was what was left of the theory of the social contract, because it relied for its plausibility on the idea that, at some time in the not too distant past, a group of rational men had made an agreement to live together according to a set of rules. How could this be squared with the idea that human societies must have evolved like everything else? And how could the idea of mutual agreement between equals to abide by laws, be squared with the idea of the survival of the fittest? But social contract was not the only form of theory to be vulnerable to irrationalism, simply because the pessimistic evolutionist perspective cast a long shadow over almost every form of ordered human utterance. If human beings were driven by unconscious imperatives even now only coming to be dimly understood, then it was not very clear how the products of human reason fitted into the picture. Social and political theory became especially problematical because it dealt with questions of who was fittest to rule over whom. But, if Darwinism was true, then it was nature, not reason, which was to decide about questions of fitness. But human nature was not always red in tooth and claw. Rhetoric had always been a recognised part of the human armoury, and theory as rhetoric did square easily with the Darwinian perspective. Theory was one of the ways, and perhaps the characteristically human way, that sets of human beings dominated others. All forms of theory, then, became automatically suspect as vehicles of a human will to power, rationalisations, ideologies, residues, the fair and outward face of not very deeply buried hegemonial drives.

For those who thought like this, the history of western political and social theory was straightforwardly bogus. The whole attempt since Plato to justify forms of political obedience was to be seen as the cultural trappings of a succession of more or less successful ruling groups. Perhaps those groups had known what they were doing, or perhaps not. Whether conspiratorial or self-deluded, ruling elites had always acted as if they realised that being able to persuade the ruled that their subjection was ethically justified, was a cheap way to political power.

This irrationalist world was where crowd theory made its name. What was left when it came to be realised that men were too irrational for theory and that theory itself was necessarily bogus? What was left was a moral and political naturalism which was content to expect the worse from human nature and to work from there. Human beings were what Machiavelli in his pessimistic moments had always taken them for: greedy, stupid, self-indulgent, unwilling to make their own decisions, always willing to be deceived by spurious leaders in doubtful causes. Far from playing down the role of ideas in politics, irrationalism cried that role up. The history of western political thought and the history of western politics ran together. Ideas had been successful in the past, and could be expected to be increasingly successful in the present. Mass literacy and universal suffrage would see to that. The ultimate failure of Enlightenment lay in the dismal fact that the energising power of ideas was in inverse proportion to their truth. This perception led inexorably to a politics of pure manipulation. The crowd was out there just waiting for its leaders. Modernity, the atomistic individualism of liberal society and politics, presented the demagogue with an ideal territory in which to operate. Liberal individualism meant that the masses were faced with all kinds of life-choices which they had never had to face before, and a certain economic ruthlessness in liberal societies meant that life-choices would often have to be faced in conditions of considerable uncertainty and insecurity. This was a demagogue's dream. All he had to do was to answer as many of life's questions as possible with as few and as simple answers as possible, and the masses would rush to put power into his hands.

Of course, crowd theorists had the decency to say what a pity all this was. The only way forward, as far as they could see, was to try to find ways of making sure that the crown got the right leaders. In the age of the masses, it was up to existing elites quickly to learn the business of mass manipulation, otherwise the crowd would produce leaders of its own with very different political agendas. Hence the obsession of crowd theory of the Le Bon kind with the question of the leadership of crowds. Crowds were said to want to be dominated, in exactly the same way that it was believed, in that unenlightened age, that women wanted to be dominated. Crowds, like women, were supposed to be fickle, direction-less, mindless, yet knowing in their heart of hearts that they wanted to surrender to demagogues. The crowd would create power for its leaders compared to which the ordinary power structures of existing states were models of constitutional restraint. If a leader were to emerge from the crowd, unschooled in the manners and morals of existing elites, then there was literally no limit to what

he might ask his followers to do, and there was certainly no limit to what his followers would be prepared to do for him. The leader hypnotised his crowd, and the notorious malleability of hypnotised subjects showed that the crowd had, properly speaking, no mind of its own. To all intents and purposes, the leader's mind was the only mind the crowd had.

It is this supposed desire for leadership on the crowd's part which sticks in Canetti's craw, and which informs everything he has to say about crowds in *Crowds and Power.* Crowd theory held that the crowd craves authority; that being part of a crowd reinforces the desire for authority; that the more a society becomes a crowd society, the more the masses are likely to will down upon themselves leadership of a kind which, in its completeness, makes a mockery of the pretensions of the tyrannies of the past. To undo the leadership claims of crowd theory, Canetti has to try to disentangle the hitherto firm connection between crowds and their leaders, but he does not do this directly. He never even mentions Le Bon, and there are almost no references to hypnotic suggestion in the whole of *Crowds and Power.* Canetti is nothing if not haughty. He appears to think that the whole Le Bon tradition of crowd theory can be made to disappear. Instead, in *Crowds and Power* we get a relentlessly elaborate typology of crowds without Canetti's even mentioning the fact that crowds sometimes have leaders.

This was what was so puzzling when we first read *Crowds and Power,* though, in retrospect, we can see how Canetti upstaged us all. He *knew* that we would be looking for Le Bon, and that is why he left him out. Leaving out Le Bon, declaring him abolished, so to speak, left the way open for a view of crowds in which the crowd would be something very different from its leader's creature. Canetti develops a theory of crowds in which the tremendous variety of crowds would be stressed, and in which the crowd would be seen as a refuge from authority, and not its creator.

But there is far more to *Crowds and Power* than the dismissal of Le Bon. Le Bon's vulgarised social science was treated with considerable respect in its own day. The social science of the late nineteenth and early twentieth century that we still take seriously was either heavily influenced by Le Bon, or it spoke with a very similar voice. Le Bon has gone out of fashion, but Pareto, Mosca, Sorel and Michels are still names to be reckoned with. Out of them comes a critique of parliamentary democracy, and, by deliberate extension, of all democratic politics, which still stands, and which has been absorbed into mainstream social science as elite theory, and, as its close neighbour, the theory of mass society. The western tradition of political theory turned out to be the royal road to political sociology. The experience of mass democracy, even in its infancy, showed that nothing had really changed. Both liberalism, and its un-wanted offspring, mass democratic socialism, were both chimeras, fronts behind which the ages-old superiority of superior men operated much as before. The elitist critics of the egalitarian pretensions of both liberal democracy and democratic socialism did not doubt that the elites created in modern societies really were elites. What political thinkers had always wanted, rule by the best, turned out to be a historical law. The Iron Law of Oligarchy still worked, and perhaps worked particularly well, in the superficially hostile-seeming conditions of universal suffrage and mass socialist parties. If the Iron Law of Oligarchy worked there, then, *a fortiori,* it would work anywhere.

Canetti believes that the conditions of modernity greatly increase the scope of power for leaders. He is not especially concerned to distinguish between established leaders and demagogues, inside and outside leaders, because he thinks that distinction tends to obscure the fact that all power is exercised over numbers of people, that is, all power is power over crowds. Making a great fuss about the leaders of crowds, in the ordinary sense of mobs or potential mobs, tends to draw our attention away from the central characteristic of all power, which is that largely measurable by the numbers of people (or other things) over which it is exercised. History's great rulers, and especially its conquerors, had always been obsessed with numbers—more subjects, more slaves, more and bigger palaces and tombs, higher and higher piles of loot—but it is only in the modern world that the true scope of numbers has come to be felt. This is partly the result of the fact that there is more of everything in the modern world, and partly the result of an awareness, after Pasteur, that human beings share a world with other living things which it would be absurd even to begin to try to count. The planet is overcrowded to an extent which would have been unimaginable in a world which had never heard of microbes. The modern world is crawling with people, and so it follows that the scope of power has been widened.

Political leaders come looking for crowds. Why, exactly, do they do it? Why do people *want* power? Canetti's answer to this question is an attempt to fill an obvious gap in the western tradition of political thought. All political thought concerns itself with political power, but surprisingly little of it deals with questions about why power has always appeared to be a human good. If the desire for power is treated at all, it is either seen to be desired to do good or to do evil, where evil really means self-indulgence. Aristotle, for instance, mentions a tyrant of Syracuse who was drunk for three months to show that tyrants are happier than ordinary men, an opinion that ancient Greek political thinkers were very keen to deny. Christian political thinkers emphasised that princes have wider opportunities for doing good and evil than private men. Human sinfulness meant that

rulers would always have to be watched, and who better to watch them than mother church?

Plato, and to an extent, Machiavelli, are exceptional in taking the treatment of why men want power beyond these commonplaces. Machiavelli makes it clear that the men who cannot stay away from the power game are very exceptional types, like ancient heroes, in whose fate the gods take a special, if treacherous, interest. The Machiavellian prince must be a master of concealment, but also an adept at what Canetti calls "unmasking" others. The princes Machiavelli is interested in are those who come from nowhere, or almost from nowhere. They are bastards and adventurers who lack the traditional legitimacy of regular hereditary descent. These *arrivistes* end up, by a combination of ability and good luck, ruling over subjects who knew them as private men and who therefore know that, in the received wisdom, that the new princes are not really kings at all. Bending the knee to a pretend prince has something more than just analogously theatrical about it, because both the prince and his subject are playing parts. Each must wear the mask. The kneeling subject conceals his sense of the demeaning ridiculousness of doing obeisance to a bogus prince, and the prince conceals his own awareness of what is going through his subject's mind. Perhaps they were both rivals once for the prize of princely government, and the one who won was just lucky. The prince could be looking at a future pretender every time a courtier makes his bow, a man who is likely to kill him one day, and so it would be better for the prince to kill his potential rival right away, but that would probably mean that he would end up by having to kill everybody. This is why the power of "unmasking" is essential for the prince who is going to survive: he has to know who his real enemies are. Of course, he must conceal this himself, and with it the dreadful "anxiety of command", because subjects, like schoolboys, have an unerring eye for weakness in their masters. New princes live among false protestations of love and loyalty which they must always appear to believe, because that makes them look like real kings. The danger is always that they come to believe that they are real kings, genuinely loved by their subjects and courtiers. That would be the moment of vulnerability, the lethal failure of the power of unmasking. Already, here, we can see the beginning of one of the central parts of Canetti's theory of power, namely, that above all the *leader* wants to survive others. Like Plato, Canetti links the desire for power to a certain psychopathology. Plato thought that the only clear motive that just and rational men could have for desiring political power was self-defence. Such men would have to save themselves from the power which fell into the hands of the wicked and foolish. By the foolish he meant the crowd, and by the wicked he meant the demagogues, into whose hands the crowd was willing to press power. Demagogic tyrants, wallowing in drunken, sexual and gastronomic self-indulgence, sleep badly and dream horrifically, and before long they begin to work out the worst of their dream fantasies in waking life. Above all, they acquire a taste for blood, a master passion which can never be satisfied. Plato does not take his treatment of the psychopathology of power any further in the direction of numbers in the way Canetti will, because, as a moralist, he is mainly concerned to argue against some of the poets that, despite appearances, the tyrant who can indulge any appetite is the unhappiest of men. Besides, the essentially restricted world of the Greek polis could not provide what Canetti calls the "million magic".

It bears repeating that, these suggestive hints in Plato and Machiavelli apart, there is not much in the history of western political thought about what Canetti calls the "entrails of power". Canetti goes beyond psychology to biology to explain "power in the raw". Like Nietzsche, Canetti thinks that in its most basic form, power is the physical power of capturing and killing. Power reaches its nadir in digestion—the cannibal turns his enemies into shit, and every meat-eater is a "king in a field of corpses". A fat cannibal advertises his power to the world. Killers cannot ingest all their victims. Surviving them is enough. This is why Pasteur is so important to Canetti. It is only after Pasteur that we realise how fantastically prodigal nature is. An overwhelmingly high proportion of living organisms are not meant to survive, and it would be a disaster if they did. (We all remember from our childhood those calculations about the rate of increase of greenfly. If they were to breed at their ideal rate, and all were to survive, we would be up to our necks in greenfly in six months, and it would not be long before the surface of the earth was moving towards the sun at the speed of light.) Canetti believes that aggregations, numbers, crowds, have always been irresistible to the power-seekers, because the number of the dead that the wielder of power can survive is in principle limitless. Canetti shrewdly realises that we have always secretly wanted to be survivors, hence our sneaking admiration for the Jewish patriot-traitor, Josephus, the only survivor of the siege of Jotapata, who ended up as a pampered apologist for Roman imperialism. Each one of us asks ourselves privately: Who can blame him?

Numbers are the obvious point of contact between power and the crowd. Like its lineal ancestor, the hunting-pack and the tribe, the crowd "always wanted to be more". This, rather than its much touted viciousness, explains the destructiveness of the crowd. The destructiveness of the crowd is the crowd's way of destroying barriers to its own growth. (The crowd sets fire to things because it sees its own growth in the spread of fire in a city.) Canetti does not doubt that all of the great events of the modern world are crowd events, and, like Le Bon and with the consensus of the social sciences, he thinks of the modern age as the age of the masses. All this really means is that the numbers of everything have got bigger. Huge aggregates are, so to speak, lying around in modern societies, and the power seeker will come looking for them.

In *Crowds and Power* Canetti makes us wait for a very long time before he begins his treatment of power. It might be said that his treatment of the crowd is complete before his treatment of power begins. We have already touched on his reasons for doing this. If *Crowds and Power* can be said to have a central thrust, it is that the crowd is not, and never can be, the creation of its leaders. Hence the almost complete ban in *Crowds and Power* of the theory of hypnotic suggestion, the most obviously Hobbesian aspect of crowd theory before Canetti. Canetti wants us to believe that the crowd wants to be a crowd before it has even heard of leaders. The crowd, Canetti believes, is a refuge from everything that is irksome in ordinary life. The crowd is not mindless, just waiting to be animated by the mind of its leader. Rather, it has a mind of its own (or, to keep the distance between Canetti and Le Bon, there are many crowds with many minds). Ordinary life is lived with what Canetti calls "burdens of distance", and each one of us carries within ourselves those "stings of command" which emanate from society's sources of authority. "Burdens of distance" and "stings of command" add up to what sociologists call social structure, or the distribution of social power. Burdens of distance disappear in the crowd as people lose their fear of being touched. Strictly speaking, the physical throng does not become a crowd until this "moment of discharge", when everyone begins to feel equal. Canetti insists on the importance of the moment of discharge to emphasise his downgrading of demagogues. The demagogue may *think* that he creates the crowd, and the appearance of a demagogue may be the occasion for a crowd to form, but neither of these is what makes the crowd. It may even appear as if the crowd obeys its leader with a single will, but Canetti believes that this is only an appearance. The leader does not command the crowd *as a whole*. Rather, he communicates what he wants to one member of the crowd, and he begins to communicate it to the others. In the crowd everyone commands, and the appearance of the crowd's being commanded as a whole by its leader is simply another example of the renowned "quickness of crowds". The implication of Canetti's point is immediately clear. Mass leaders have taken theorists for a ride. Theory makes exactly the same claims for mass leaders as they make for themselves. Each cries the other up to a ridiculous extent. Crowd theory may even contribute to the success of modern demagogues by creating leadership expectations.

Canetti has no doubt that the desire for power is a kind of madness. He goes to great lengths to explicate two cases of power madness, the fourteenth century sultan of Delhi, Mohammad Tuglak, and the celebrated paranoid memoirist, Schreber. Neither was a crowd leader in the demagogic sense, Mohammad Tuglak because he succeeded to his throne legitimately, and Schreber because he exercised power over crowds only in his own head. Canetti has chosen his cases carefully. They are, in one sense, as far away from the case which really interests him, the Hitler case, because there is nothing of the rabble-rouser about either of them. However, Canetti chooses them precisely because he wants to dismantle the whole Hobbes-Le Bon tradition. The crowd did not force power on Hitler. He came looking for it. How leaders got power is really irrelevant to its nature and to its exercise. Again, it is a question of numbers. The clue comes from poor mad Schreber's *Memoirs of My Nervous Illness.* The myriad crowds Schreber produced in his head always diminished. No matter how large the crowds became, even the stars seemed to get smaller. This Canetti thinks of as an example of one of the ages-old secrets of power, the capacity to degrade. With the growth of numbers, things begin to count for less. At some point, the units become absolutely meaningless as units of value (the classic example is inflation), and as the numbers themselves grow, they too become meaningless. As leaders heap numbers upon numbers, they begin to see their followers and their enemies as degraded crowds in no real way different from the myriads of pests that the world has become familiar with since Pasteur. Pests easily come to be seen as problems of public hygiene, hence attempts at extermination, and hence genocide.

This is a remarkable perspective. Political theory since Plato, crowd theory of the Le Bon kind, and much of modern political sociology, always insist on the danger that *comes from* the crowd. Ever since the French Revolution, and especially since the Paris *commune* of 1871, the crowd's nastiness has always been put centre stage. This, in its turn, feeds on an ancient tradition of contempt for the crowd as the mob which condemned Socrates and Jesus. From the famous riots between the Blue and the Green circus factions of Justinian's Constantinople to the football hooliganism that we often see on our televisions, the crowd has been seen as the antithesis of everything a civilized society should be. Canetti singlehandedly tries to get us to see the crowd from a diametrically opposite point of view, as victims. He will have none of the typically modern stance that the crowd is up for grabs, so that modern politics becomes a race for who can get to the crowd first. The crowd has a mind of its own, according to Canetti, and it is mere travesty to claim with the consensus that, without its leader, the crowd is nothing.

Canetti's sympathy for the crowd must always be seen in the context of the history of political theory in general, and of the history of crowd theory in particular. Canetti knows perfectly well that the crowd does not always wear a pretty face. His meticulous typology of crowds allows more than enough room for history's crowd horrors: crowds waiting for public executions, for example, or crowds on the lookout for victims. Canetti's relentless typology of crowds is meant to hammer home the message that these nastier crowds are only particular types of crowds in a possible range of different crowd experience which it would take a pocket calculator exactly to put a number on. There are, in the most literal sense of the words, crowds of crowds. To take vicious and atavistic crowds as *the* crowd, and to generalise from there to a theory of "the masses" as a mindless crowd when left on their own, and a civilization-threatening mob when they find their own leaders, is itself a mindless exercise in elitist vituperation, the language of which has not changed much since the grumbling of oligarchs in ancient Thebes.

To dismantle an elitist ideology masquerading as social science is one thing, but it would be quite wrong to suppose that Canetti's own position on the crowd is simply the converse of what the crowd's theoretical enemies have had to say about it. Perhaps above all, Canetti's insistence that crowds have minds of their own means that the crowd cannot be blameless. The crowd theory of the late nineteenth and early twentieth centuries, with its emphasis on hypnotism, came very close to holding that nothing could really be the crowd's fault. There was a debate within hypnotic theory itself about whether or not anybody could be said to be genuinely impervious to hypnotic suggestion, but the debate was inconclusive. What all crowd theorists agreed about was that imperviousness to hypnotic suggestion must be very rare. Perhaps there were a few strong-minded individuals who could resist the arts of the hypnotist, and, by extension, the demagogue, but the consensus was that enough people were suggestible for the crowd to be feared as a mindless mass. If hypnotic suggestibility was an in-built human characteristic, then, so the argument ran, human beings could hardly be blamed for becoming hypnotised. Hypnotism almost always necessarily worked. There was a subsidiary debate among crowd theorists about how "deep down" hypnotic suggestibility actually went. Some thought that hypnotised subjects retained their "fundamental" moral integrity, so that they would not obey hypnotic suggestions which violated deeply moral convictions, but the consensus was that, again, this would only be true of exceptional individuals. Hypnotists, and, by extension, the leaders of crowds, could get people to do *anything,* and this seemed to be confirmed by the history of crowd atrocity. On this, history and depth psychology spoke with the same voice: crowds would do unspeakable things if asked to do them by unspeakably wicked leaders.

This is the perspective Canetti absolutely will not have. He knows that it leads to the morally banal position that all the crimes of followers are really the crimes of leaders alone, as if the suicide of a leader could wipe the slate clean. If, as Canetti asserts, crowds have minds, then there must be a sense in which they know what they are doing. Leaders know what they are doing because they have always understood power. Their form of pretence is that they are the servants of the people, or of a mystically conceived sense of destiny, or of both, but nobody should be fooled by this. Add the crowd theory view of human suggestibility to the self-exculpation of leaders, and you could end up believing that nobody is ever responsible for anything.

Canetti is a residual Kantian, despite *Auto-da-Fe.* The message of *Crowds and Power* is not despairing. Mass behaviour of the old crowd theory kind is only one form of a huge variety of available collective experience. We don't "get a taste" for authoritarian subjection in crowds with leaders. We do not want more caesarism just because caesars and their theorists say we do. Crowds are not always, or even typically, the creations of leaders. Crowds do know what they are doing. Human masses are not docile, though they can fall into the trap of thinking they are. The slaughtered millions of the twentieth century testify to that. That century, and the "million-magic" of its rulers, is not over yet. The nuclear holocaust promises leaders crowds of the dead which would have excited the envy of former tyrants like Hitler, and certainly mere tyros like Ghengis Khan. If the secret of power is the leader's survival of untold millions of diminished dead, then politicians with their fingers on the nuclear trigger have got what leaders have wanted since the world began. Leaders wear the mask of benevolence, but Canetti insists that, for our survival, it is we and not they who should cultivate the skill of unmasking.

Rousiley C. M. Maia (essay date 1996)

SOURCE: Maia, Rousiley C. M. "Elias Canetti's *Auto-da-Fé*: From the Antithesis of the Crowd-Man to the Madness of Power." *Thesis Eleven,* no. 45 (1996): 28-38.

[*In the following essay, Maia explores Canetti's crowd theory as it appears in his novel* Auto da Fé.]

Auto-da-Fe represents a new style of novel about the crowd, which incorporates aesthetically many of Canetti's theoretical concerns with crowd phenomena. In his highly introspective novel, the most interesting crowd is never the physical throng and there are just a few examples of the human crowd, in the obvious sense. However, *Auto-da-Fe* is full of crowd symbolism, which is comprehensible only in relation to the complex typology and theory of crowds Canetti develops in *Crowds and Power.* Canetti ranges very widely in *Crowds and Power* to challenge the evolutionary-atavist tradition

underpinning classical crowd theory of the Le Bon type and to provide a complete crowd theory of a new type. *Auto-da-Fe* also provides new insights into many familiar and puzzling aspects of crowd psychology, as well as its relationship with power, in an essentially original way.

A central thematic equation between *Auto-da-Fe,* is given by the comparison between Kien, the protagonist of *Auto-da-Fe,* with Daniel Paul Schreber whose book *Memoirs of My Nervous Illnesses* provides Canetti with the model case of the psychopathology of power, with which *Crowds and Power* concludes. It is possible to relate the protagonist of *Auto-da-Fe* with Paul Schreber in two ways. First, Kien is the model of the last surviving rational individual, who despises the crowd in all its representations and fiercely struggles to keep himself apart from it. Peter Kien's isolation from society, his desire to keep his ego autonomous and his ambition to impose a total control over the surrounding world, are carried to such an extreme that becomes indistinguishable from the model case of the paranoid. Secondly, Kien's frame of mind can be compared to the mind of a paranoiac ruler. Kien's notions of greatness and exclusiveness, just as Schreber's, reveal an unbridled will-to-power and a radical intolerance of others. Kien, as the prototype of a paranoiac ruler, offers the pathological example of the psychology and structure of authority and many aspects of power present in *Crowds and Power.*

Peter Kien is the very antithesis of the crowd-man. He strives to keep the boundaries of his ego intact, autonomous and permanently structured according to his self-determining will. He shields himself against any kind of influence that would invade and devour his individuality. "Distances", in the sense Canetti discusses in *Crowds and Power,* determine the protagonist's entire life. The starting point of *Crowds and Power* is the assertion of the fear of contact, "the fear of being touched", "the fear of the unknown" that characterizes the individual. "All life, so far as he knows it, is laid out in distances—the house in which he shuts himself in his property, the position he holds, the rank he desires—all these serve to create distance, to confirm and extend them" (*CP* [*Crowds and Power*] 18). The boundaries of man's personality are, in this sense, guaranteed by distance—distinctions of class, status, authority. "Men as individuals are always conscious of these distinctions they weigh heavily on them and they keep them firmly apart from one another" (*CP* 17).[1]

In *Auto-da-Fe,* the first boundary which separates the protagonist from the hurried movement of the world is established by his flat, whose door is carefully protected by the tyrannical eye of the caretaker, Pfaff. To guarantee the privacy of Kien's space, a second borderline had been drawn inside the flat to divide the rooms converted into a library, a realm destined for the scholar, from the domains of the maid, Therese. No one can gain access to Kien's windowless library. With the walls lined with books, it represents a self-contained cosmos that provides a desperately defended immutable order against the chaos of outside reality. The scholar obstinately keeps his distance from other people and retreats from all kinds of human interactions, the boundaries of the self especially guaranteed by the avoidance of conversation. Kien often refuses to answer when a question is addressed to him, and, when he speaks, his words are rarely understood. He hates noise, particularly human voices. In his morning walks, he keeps his eyes cast upwards to prevent him from seeing the few passers-by, "since he felt not the slightest desire to notice anyone, he kept his eyes lowered or raised above their heads" (*ADF* [*Auto-da-Fe*] 13).[2]

Seeking an absolute supremacy for his intellect, the protagonist also strives to separate his mind from his body. Kien does all he can to minimize the attention devoted to the necessities of his physical existence and contemplates with detachment the actions of his own body—he takes his meals at his desk and sleeps in a divan placed in his library. His physical hygiene requirements are reduced to fifteen minutes per day. Women and sex are not just neglected but considered particularly disgusting. Everything emotional, intuitive and compulsive—irrational and thus uncontrollable—is excluded. Careless about money and badly dressed, the protagonist despises all that is material. He does not even know his physical features: "If you had character it determined your outward appearance . . . He knew his face only casually from its reflection in bookshop windows. He had no mirror in his house, there was no room for it among the books" (*ADF* 13).

At the beginning of the novel, Kien appears as a kind of a thinker who rejects the everyday world, with its obvious uncertainties and delusions, for a supposed more real and more certain world of permanencies. Aspiring to transcend material existence and live platonically in the realm of ideas, the sinologist devotes himself to a routine of exacting and austere study—a rigid daily ritual that protects his solitary and silent encapsulation. His object of study—the reconstruction of ancient Chinese manuscripts—given its remoteness in historical and geographical terms, is also ideal for removing him from the present. Kien becomes a disembodied "head without a world", as the novel labels him, a living allegory of the pure intellect.

The scholar's complete unresponsiveness to environmental demands and physiological stimuli can be seen as a desire to be a truly independent individual. To forge his apparently stable individuality and preserve his "pure self-identity", Kien has to armour himself and erect impassable barriers between himself and the rest

of the world and also pay the price of instinctual renunciation. Holding himself aloft from the moods of social anguish and ignoring the pressure to accept and conform to the collective model, Kien supposed that he could keep himself apart from the crowd. Kien insists in acting individually, minimizing his social needs and biological drives and maximizing his control over them. In other words, he tries to shift the control of his behaviour from external stimuli to internal cognitive controls. "His ambition was to persist stubbornly in the same manner of existence. Not for a mere month, not for a year, but for the whole of his life, he would be true to himself" (*ADF* 13).

It is possible to say that Kien, as the last rational individual, perceives the duty to preserve his "character" in a caricature of Kantianism.[3] In order to live as a moral being, to progress from the state of "nature", in which man lives as a mere mechanism in an undifferentiated state, to one of "culture" in which man could be free and autonomous, Kien must obey the rational law of his own making, so that enlightened thought can overwhelm natural impulses and morality can become strong enough to be a "second nature". Kien supposed that thinking and believing alone, independent of society, could gain him total freedom from the behavioural prescriptions imposed by history, culture, and society. But Kien's project of self is just a caricature of Kantianism. Reason, the ability to grasp the world in rational terms, comes together with the notion of will, volition and acceptance of personal commitment, in order to form the model of the rational Kantian individual. However, instead of encountering the world with the fresh joy and courage of discovery, the audacity to know, the protagonist fearfully retreats from the world. From the outset, Kien suppresses his senses and deliberately prefers self-delusion. Kien demonstrates, in this sense, an awareness of the weakness of his self against the forces of the surrounding world, what implicitly justifies his absurd self-encapsulation. In other words, the strenuous effort to self-preservation comes from the fear of losing his "I", the fear of death and destruction.

Canetti shows in his novel the paradoxical process of individuation. The domination of man over himself and the very act of self-preservation implies a huge sacrifice of the self. Only through a constant struggle to keep the boundaries of the self intact does Kien survive. Struggle is his survival. For most of the novel, the protagonist is struggling to protect the distances which give him a sense of autonomy and support his illusion of power, but at the same time he is drawn into a terrible isolation and helpless anxiety. The struggle of Kien with the symbolic representations of the crowd which intrude into his library and progressively attack the dividing borderlines in his apartment, finally expelling him from his realm, has been analyzed.[4] While the crowd of the outside world can be watched and controlled, the crowd inside the protagonist is hidden and insidious. Kien insists in rationalizing all his drives, so that nothing poses a threat to the eyes of his mind. The rationalization of drives, represented by the transformation of instincts into reflection, does result indeed in a kind of mastery by the rational will. But this mastery is brought at the price of a crescendo of denial and prohibition on transformations. For, as becomes increasingly clear, the self that fights for external and internal security and stability cannot be safe and stable against the resistance of nature. The process through which one erects distance from inner nature through control—which enables the identity of the self—is a repeated source of fear in relation to nature, and such a fear must be controlled through the reinforcement of control, needing to dissimulate its origin in fear. The process of increasing domination by the rational subject is achieved at the price of a progressive inflation of the "second nature", the "armour" of the rational will.

For Canetti, the process of individuation, related to man's fundamental sense of isolation—in his individual body, mind and personality—induces the desire to break these limits and expand the self into a seemingly prior condition of limitless. "Man petrifies and darkens in the distances he has created. He drags at the burden of them, but cannot move. He forgets that it is self-inflicted and longs for liberation. But how, alone, can he free himself? Whatever he does, and however determined he is he will always find himself amongst others who thwart his efforts. So long as they hold *their* distances, he can never come any nearer to them" (*CP* 18). Social life is formulated in terms of distances and the exercise of power in all situations presupposes distinctions, hierarchy and inequality. Aware of the uncertain character of contemporary moral experience, Canetti recognizes that the affirmation of oneself in the social power struggle becomes the denial of others, and, both options of commanding or obeying leave a profound irritation in the self, which isolates the individual or annuls his autonomy. Canetti maintains that "only together can man free themselves from their burdens of distances; and this precisely, is what happens in a crowd" (*CP* 18). In the crowd, the hierarchical devices of social life—distinctions of class, race, rank, status, that is, patterns of authority and justifications of power—are annihiliated. All individuals *feel equal,* and there is the possibility of unity, of being together, without domination. In the crowd, Canetti claims, there is the reversal of the fear of being touched, directing the individuals toward a compact unification of bodies, dissolving the weight of individuality and the resentments of power. "In that density, where there is scarcely any space between, and body presses against body, each man is as near the other as he is to himself; and an immense feeling of relief ensues. It is for the sake of this blessed moment, when no-one is greater or better than another, that people become a crowd" (*CP* 18).

In *Auto-da-Fe* Canetti pushes the paradox of the individual's intoxication with power and the resentment caused by it to its extreme and shows the deadly end to which it can lead. The protagonist of *Auto-da-Fe* tries to represent his identity as an *a priori* structure of the human reason, remaining faithfully loyal to his determination to "be true to himself" and persist "in the same manner of existence . . . for the whole of his life" (*ADF* 13). Obsession with identity, self-preservation and distinction culminates in the will to power. What needs to be stressed here for the development of our argument is that, behind the armoured, self-preserving and rationalizing self of the protagonist, Canetti delineates a prototype of the totalitarian self. Many of Kien's attitudes recall what Canetti calls the "illness of power" and can be analyzed in the light of some aspects and elements of power discussed in *Crowds and Power* such as "judgment and condemnation", "secrecy and silence", "the prohibition of transformation", "the survivor".

First, the protagonist's sense of greatness can be related to the "ivory tower" mentality commonly attributed to the scholar. He sees himself removed from the everyday world, where those illiterate barbarians, as he calls all others, live. Secluded in his library, he preserves for himself the power of "judgment and condemnation" (*CP* 296) and shows in various disguised ways a kind of pleasure in "exalting himself by abasing others", and "relegating others to a group inferior to which he himself decided he belonged" (*CP* 296). For example, it was Kien's custom to look through the windows of every bookshop in his morning walks, "to be able to assure himself, with a kind of pleasure, that smut and trash were daily gaining ground" (*ADF* 8), while "he, himself, was the only person in his great town who possessed a library that could be taken at all seriously" (*ADF* 10).

Kien's existence is surrounded by secrecy and silence (*CP* 284-296). Kien almost never shows himself in public, he refuses to teach and never appears at celebrations or conferences, leaving his academic fellows in constant expectation. Such a voluntary withdrawal from normal scholarly relationships makes Kien's person mysterious and inaccessible, as if he were a "guardian of a treasure which is inside himself" (*CP* 294). However, Kien makes sure to send a paper "of the most estimable value for science" to every conference, ensuring that he remains a "much discussed person" (*ADF* 15-17). Kien certainly fears the subversive power of communicative interactions because of the danger they pose to the autonomous self (*CP* 375). As Canetti argues in *Crowds and Power,* questioning is an expression of power and "a forcible intrusion" into other individuals' freedom. "A man who maintains a deliberate silence does not allow others to see through him", while he "who is answering a question is forced to reveal more of himself" (*CP* 285). However, by pushing the inner armour against questioning to its extreme and re-maining a silent observer, unapproachable and aloof when his existence requires a concern with everyday matters, Kien becomes a kind of paranoiac ruler, the one "who uses every means to keep danger away from his person" (*CP* 231). Invulnerability of this kind can-not be sustained without ingenious despotism: "instead of challenging and confronting it [danger] and abiding the issue of a fight which may go against him, he seeks by circumspection and cunning to block its approach to him. He creates an empty space all round him which he can survey, and he observes and assesses every sight of approaching danger" (*CP* 231-2).

Kien is proud of his absolute unchangeableness and the faithful perseverance of his character. However, to pre-serve his character, Kien has to stop the endless flux of metamorphosis that occurs in the chaotic reality of the inner and outer world. As discussed in *Crowds and Power*, the psychopathological aspect of the "distances" that each man creates to protect his self and to keep apart from others, is that of immobility. Silence, immo-bility and isolation inhibit self-transformation:

> A man who will not speak can dissemble, but only in a rigid way, he can wear a mask, but he has to keep a firm hold of it. The fluidity of transformations is denied to him . . . People become silent when they fear trans-formation. Silence prevents them responding to occa-sions of transformation . . . Silence is motionless.
>
> (*CP* 294)

Kien's face, described as a mask, is completely fixed. "The mask is only known from outside . . . it reveals nothing of what is behind it" (*CP* 376). To maintain the stability of his world-order, and feel an absolute control and command over it, Kien needs to perpetuate a di-chotomy between a permanently structured self and a rigidly patterned world. In this sense, the mechanical regularity of Kien's daily habits can be understood as a paranoid desire to reduce the world to a constant same-ness, making it understandable, manageable and safer. The meticulous routine and his exaggerated emphasis on order serve to reduce the threatening multiplicity of existence to a structured uniformity, which accords with the designs of his omnipotent will. "A ruler wages con-tinuous warfare against spontaneous and uncontrolled transformations" (*CP* 370-3).

The ruler's sense of power, Canetti argues, depends not only on suppressing transformations in himself but also in controlling transformations in others. The "I" be-comes so important to itself that everything that is ex-ternal, "other" in relation to oneself acquires a negative value: the other is seen as hostile, dangerous, needing to be dominated. Only by banishing everybody from his life and ruling out any deviation in his hermetic library, is Kien left free to conceive himself as a "pure self";

his subjectivity can be perceived as unlimited; his rea-son can be elevated to the conception of the absolute. Denial of others is reaffirmation of oneself; but it is soon obvious that if it is carried to an extreme, it be-comes a quest for inflexible sovereignty.

For Canetti, the exposure of the "entrails of power" re-veals the hidden mechanisms of domination. Kien's sense of greatness and distinction, related to his great scholarly erudition, can be disclosed through an exami-nation of the scholar's complex relationship with his books, according to Canetti's idea of self-consumption and self-increase, analyzed in *Crowds and Power* (*CP* 107-11).[5] Since his only passion is collecting books, Kien strives to increase their number as much as pos-sible. "Books, even the bad ones, tempted him easily into making a purchase" (*ADF* 8-9; 125-6). The in-crease in books not only corroborates his feelings of su-periority but also gives him a sense of protection. The twenty-five thousand volumes of his library, roughly of equal size and similar appearance, uniformly lined up in endless rows, obeying a rigid organization, represent in Kien's mind a kind of loyal army that forms a wall around him, safe-guarding the lucidity of his mind, giv-ing him confidence, power and a sense of ontological security. Beyond the obsession to possess books, Kien seeks to "incorporate" the books into himself.[6] Wher-ever the scholar goes, he carries a minute portion of his library with him in his briefcase. It is as if he wished literally to insert the books into his body:

> He clasped it [the briefcase full of books] tightly to him in a very particular manner which assured that the greatest possible area of his body was always in con-tact with it. Even his rib could feel its presence through his cheap, thin suit. His upper arm covered the whole side of elevation, it fitted exactly. The lower portion of his arm supported the case from below. His outstretched fingers splayed out over every part of the flat surface to which they yearned.
>
> (*ADF* 9)

Kien privately excuses this excess of care because of the value of the books' contents. There is nothing more precious than his priceless volumes, by possessing their contents he can be endowed with their value as well. Because of his remarkable memory, we are assured that Kien has "absorbed" thousands of books in his head. The scholar has in his mind "a library as well provided and reliable as his actual one". "He could sit at his writing desk and sketch out a treatise down to the mi-nutest detail without turning over a single page, except in his mind" (*ADF* 17). "Incorporation" obviously fur-nishes Kien with power. Once the substance of each in-dividual book of his library is "absorbed", Kien be-comes a kind of living library, containing within him all the forces and potentialities that were dispersed (*CP* 413-474). Precisely because he is isolated, he can see himself as superior. His value is the value of what he contains and it is his duty not to allow it to escape. At this point Canetti's analysis of power and the crowd meet. Canetti's analysis of the leader's exploitative attitudes towards crowds in *Crowds and Power* is already evident in *Auto-da-Fe,* supporting the view that power feeds on crowds.[7]

The role of Kien as a despotic ruler, using his books as an army (for Canetti, a "closed crowd") in order to increase the scope of his power and to extend his dominion over others, becomes increasingly clear as his library is progressively invaded. One of the best examples occurs in the scene in which the troubled scholar transforms himself into a commander-in-chief and mobilizes his imaginary army of books into a state of war against Therese. He climbs a ladder, "his head touched the ceiling, his extended legs reached the ground, and his eyes embraced the whole united extent of the library" (*ADF* 81). Explicitly in terms of a military operation, he commands:

> Since the invasion of an alien power into our life, I have been labouring with the idea of placing our relationship on a firm foundation. Your survival is granted by treaty, but we are, I take it, sage enough not to deceive ourselves as to the danger by which, in defiance of a legal treaty, you are threatened.
>
> (*ADF* 81)

> Do not overestimate the strength of the enemy, my people! Between the letters of your pages you will crush him to death, each line is a club to batter out his brain; each letter a leaden weight to burden his feet; each binding a suit of armour to defend you from him! A thousand decoys are yours to lead him astray, a thousand nets to entangle his feet, a thousand thunderbolts to burst him asunder, O you my people, the strength, the grandeur, the wisdom of the centuries.
>
> (*ADF* 85)

The more the process of self-preservation is effected the more it increases self-alienation and domination of the self by outside people and things. When Kien is thrown out of his library his first and sole preoccupation is to acquire all the books he can. He explores every bookshop in the city and then sets out to obtain the books held in the national pawnshop, the *Theresianum.* However, instead of buying the books, he simply stores the titles in his mind. Carrying a new imaginary library in his head, he can nourish the illusion that he is still guarded by books. What seemed just a metaphorical expression regarding the phenomenal memory of the scholar comes to be taken by Kien as a concrete reality. Every night he has to unpack the books, remove them from his head and lay them on the floor of his hotel room, before sleeping.

Engulfed in the agitated, chaotic life of the outside world, a world that is without the structuring power of the intellect, the desperate need for protection becomes

more rigid and grotesque. Like Schreber's paranoia, discussed in *Crowds and Power* (*CP* 434-48), the protagonist of *Auto-da-Fe* sees threats everywhere, and becomes convinced that everything is intended to confuse his reason and destroy him. Kien interprets the world around him from his own isolated perspective, void of any empirical mechanism or verificatory interaction with external reality. Unable to make contact with anything external to the circle of his own universe, Kien becomes increasingly susceptible to the power of delusions and his persecution mania grows at the same rate. It ends up in a paranoiac process that drives him to destroy everything that he supposes is challenging his sovereignty: "The greatness they [the paranoiacs] imagine is always under attack and their notions tend also to become more and more rigid . . . When the hostile crowd gets the upper hand, these turn into delusions of persecution" (*CP* 407).

When a desire of power is carried to this extreme, Canetti implies that the dialectic between self and world is obliterated by the self acquiring absolute supremacy. The supreme subject no longer promotes a dialogue between his inner and the changing outer world but rather tries to subjugate the world by the reinforcement of his fixed ideas. The paranoiac ruler perceives his self as the centre of everything and becomes the god-like creator of a world that is nothing but the projection of his will. Behind all the multiplicity of appearances he detects only the presence of the enemy that challenges his omnipotence. The urge to unmask appearances and discover enemies "becomes a kind of tyranny": "He waits for the right moment 'to tear the mask from their faces'; behind it he finds the malevolence he knows so well in himself" (*CP* 377-8). As meticulously unraveled in *Crowds and Power,* the process of acquiring and maintaining power induces anxiety. The ruler's ability to issue commands allows him to surpass others (*CP* 303-5). However, the ruler, in his position of power is left with the threat of recoil, growing into what Canetti calls the "anxiety of command", the fear that the subordinate will one day take his revenge. "The despot lives to command and he needs to dissemble his anxiety, as he already dissembles his 'inner malevolence'" (*CP* 377). But after a lifetime of power, it can suddenly manifest itself as madness, as with certain Roman emperors (*CP* 309). Despite Kien's supposed love and sympathy for books, Kien represents a real threat to them. Throughout the novel the books are forced to serve Kien, either to enforce his notions of greatness or to defend him against the hostile crowd and "the touch of the unknown". However, once he perceives that the books are no longer ready to respond to his commands, he does not hesitate to threaten them with death by fire. In this perspective, it is finally possible to see that all that Kien or a despotic ruler really wants it to be a survivor (*CP* 227-278), "standing in an immense field of corpses". To be the last man alive, Canetti thinks, is "the deepest urge of every real seeker of power" (*CP* 443-4).

In the last chapter, "The Red Cock", Kien's final surrender to madness is a multiform expression of the crowd. In spite of being enclosed in his flat, he still feels persecuted by the representations of the crowd. The red tiger, the mythical animal form of the temptation to realise the basic impulses to liberate repressed nature, haunts him. A set of Canetti's crowd symbols—blood, the colour red, fire—appear insistently in a frenzied flux of metamorphosis. Kien's delusions are populated by images of victimized and persecuted crowds. He hears fire engines racing through the streets and sees from the attic window the reddish glow in the sky. He imagines that all books in the Theresianum are burning and desperately crying for his help. Kien also hears mobs of police and citizens knocking on his door to arrest him for the supposed murder of his wife. In his hallucinatory state, Kien sees red stains in the carpet and imagines that this constitutes criminal evidence against him that must be destroyed. The image of fire, the most powerful crowd symbol for Canetti—it "spreads rapidly, it is contagious and insatiable, it is multiple and . . . it destroys irrevocably" (*CP* 77)—comes obsessively into Kien's mind. Each new line of incoherent thought, each chain of associations returns inevitably to the same compelling idea: Fire! Fire, as the symbol of passion, of sex, of the excitement of the inexhaustible mob, stands for everything repressed by Kien. However, fire arises "from time to time and often inexplicably has . . . its own restless and violent life" (*CP* 77). From the stifling confines of the library, fire arises spontaneously. The crowd-drive, the individual's desire to dissolve himself into the mass and "become like fire, knowing no bounds" (*CP* 76) overwhelms him.

With the flames flickering before his eyes, Kien tries to return to his former peaceful world, the written world of books; but he does not manage to read a line. The letters are "dancing". He commands them to be quiet. Animated by Kien's hallucination, the letters detach themselves from the page and assault him physically, slapping, kicking and striking. The books now act as a "reversal crowd", "this damnable revolutionary mob" (*ADF* 427) are "taking their revenge on him, for the long time he has made them suffer and has gone unpunished" (*CP* 456-7). As the lines dance up and down, the letters jump out of their pages and the pages out of their book bindings, the "closed crowd" transforms itself into the "open crowd", the "stagnating crowd" into a "rhythmic crowd" (*CP* 49-62). "The books cascade off the shelves onto the floor" (*ADF* 427). Order is destroyed, power is overthrown, rationality disintegrates. Ironically, it is in his library, the artifically created cos-

mos and the refuge Kien has used against the human masses, that the books finally reveal their real grievance and turn themselves into a crowd. It is his books, once his loyal army and spiritual resource, used as a counterpoise to the threat of the despised illiterate barbarians at the gates, that finally in reversal attack him. The excess of denial and severity of repression make the unthinkable happen: Kien sets all his books on fire, plunges into the fire and joins laughing the crowd outside him, the crowd he struggled so relentlessly to evade. Kien, who manifested the paranoiac ambition to assert the total domination of the rational intellect over the world, is finally possessed by the things of this world; the dichotomy between self and world is finally obliterated. Nevertheless, Kien's suicide, in this "auto-da-fe", is ambiguous: as a defeated paranoiac despot he does not die alone, but takes with him all his troops, so that no one may enjoy the power of surviving him.

Notes

1. Elias Canetti, *Crowds and Power* [1960] (London, Victor Gollancz, 1962).

2. Canetti, *Auto-da-Fe* [1935] (London, Pan Books, 1981).

3. Canetti's first intention was to name the protagonist of *Auto-da-Fe* Kant, and the manuscript originally had the title "Kant catches fire", a title Hermann Broch dissuaded the young Canetti from using.

4. W. E. Steward, "The Role of the Crowd in Elias Canetti's Novel *Die Blendung*" (M.A., Manchester University, 1968); R. Maia, "Crowd Theory in Some Modern Fiction: Dickens, Zola and Canetti" (PhD., Nottingham University, 1992).

5. Analyzing rites, legends and ancient myths from different cultures, Canetti claims that men symbolically grow stronger by the incorporation of animals, plants and objects that are associated with strength or power (*CP* 107-12).

6. By the incorporation of the word into the self, the individual is not only elevated but he is also protected: "the paranoiac retaliates against the attack of the crowd by seeking to absorb them into himself" (*CP* 440). For an assessment of this analysis see John S. McClelland, *The Crowd and the Mob. From Plato to Canetti* (London, Unwin Hyman, 1989), pp. 293-326.

7. According to Canetti, degradation justifies power and anyone who wants to rule men soon realizes the secret of degradation: "Seizure of another body is power in the raw . . . Cannibals incorporate their captures to degrade them into excrement" (*CP* 209-10).

Simon Tyler (essay date 1996)

SOURCE: Tyler, Simon. "Homage or Parody? Elias Canetti and Otto Weininger." In *Gender and Politics in Austrian Fiction,* edited by Ritchie Robertson and Edward Timms, pp. 134-49. Edinburgh, Scotland: Edinburgh University Press, 1996.

[*In the following essay, Tyler discusses parallels between Canetti's* Auto-da-fé *and Otto Weininger's famously misogynistic 1903 tract* Sex and Character.]

Weininger's principal work, *Geschlecht und Charakter* (*Sex and Character*), received enormous interest in Austrian literary circles when it was first published in 1903, an interest heightened by the fact that Weininger committed suicide shortly after its publication in the house where Beethoven had died. This suicide is but one disturbing element in the conception and reception of this vehemently misogynist and anti-Semitic work, which Gerald Stieg has claimed to be a psychological and metaphysical prelude to National Socialism and its variants.[1] The extraordinary popularity of this work is indicated by the fact that it went through twenty-eight editions between 1903 and 1932. As Nike Wagner has shown, Karl Kraus, the man who most inspired the young Canetti, introducing him to the richness of Viennese culture, drew extensively on the writings of Weininger; and indeed, Kraus contributed greatly to Weininger's fame, although he did not agree with his anti-feminist conclusions.[2] Canetti himself acknowledges how popular discussions of Weininger's philosophy were in those circles in which he mixed during his studies at the University of Vienna throughout the 1920s: 'Other boys whom I met in this circle indulged in the arrogance of higher literature: if not Karl Kraus, then Otto Weininger or Schopenhauer. Pessimistic or misogynous utterances were especially popular . . .' and 'Otto Weininger's *Sex and Character,* though published twenty years earlier, cropped up in every discussion.'[3] Alfons M. Bischoff informs us that Canetti attended the lectures given by Hermann Swoboda, who had been a close friend of Weininger and who published an evaluation of his work, *Otto Weiningers Tod,* in 1911.[4] It is therefore clear from external evidence alone that Canetti must have had a thorough knowledge of this infamous best-selling author.

That Canetti was influenced by Weininger has already been suggested by some critics. Jacques Le Rider has alluded to the possibility of such influence, and two articles have indicated some traces of it in *Auto-da-fé,* but these articles fail to account for the positive similarities between Canetti, Weininger and Kien.[5] The religious and racial aspects of Weininger's work go beyond the scope of this essay: a comparison between Weininger's views on the Jewish character and Canetti's characterisation of Fischerle deserves separate treatment.[6] This article will compare Weininger's notion of the masculine genius and of the female with the sexual imagery, characterology and world-view presented in *Auto-da-fé* and Canetti's later works in order to show that these parallels are even closer than has been suspected. I shall also attempt to account for this influence, to set it in the context of Viennese culture and to analyse its significance for an interpretation of his presentation of women.

THE MASCULINE GENIUS

Although critics have tended to emphasise the importance of Weininger's ideas on Jews and women, his typology of the male as genius forms a large section of his writings and was considered by the young author to be an integral part of his whole philosophy. Just as Weininger prefers to circumscribe the female as an absolute negative type (W) rather than to describe actual women, so he constructs a positive type (M) as a masculine ideal. He posits a theory of universal bisexuality: every individual is constituted by a combination of both masculine and feminine characteristics. However, he claims that all men are more likely than women to display those traits characteristic of that absolute, metaphysical ideal represented by M: the masculine genius. The necessary features of this type include an extraordinary memory, clear, logical thinking and precocity.[7] Of these three qualities, memory is primary, 'the sure, most general, and most easily proved mark of a genius' (*Sex and Character,* pp. 114-15); logical thinking is the necessary precondition for memory, and precocity can retrospectively be attributed to the man whose first memory refers to an event very early on in his childhood. Hence Weininger claims that the desire and the ability to write an autobiography are signs of genius (p. 122). M, a supremely intellectual being, derives his ethics from Kant's categorical imperative and not from pragmatic, utilitarian or emotional considerations. The link Weininger thus establishes between the intellect and morality is taken to the extreme: he considers lying immoral in all circumstances because it is a betrayal of the intellect (as does Kant),[8] and even forgetfulness is considered a sin (p. 150) since '[c]onsciousness and consciousness alone is in itself moral; all unconsciousness is immoral, and all immorality is unconscious' (p. 182). As M, through logical reasoning, is an ethical being, he has a soul that harbours the desire for immortality ('Unsterblichkeitsbedürfnis'), a desire that his spiritual achievements be preserved (p. 127). The masculine genius must be able to comprehend the external world rationally by a process of assimilation while retaining the distinct unity of the self—a notion based on Leibnizian monadogy, according to which man is a discrete microcosm capable of grasping the whole of the macrocosm (pp. 169-72). He is further characterised physiognomically by sharp, distinct features, representing decisiveness and perspicacity (pp. 100-1).

The character in Canetti's works who comes nearest to this ideal is of course Peter Kien. He has a phenomenal memory, 'no less than a heaven-sent gift'.[9] His thought-patterns are always extremely clear and logical, even when he hallucinates (*Auto-da-fé*, pp. 306-7). Like Weininger, Peter was an early developer. The opening of *Auto-da-fé* presents Peter's young *alter ego*, Franz Metzger, whose enthusiasm for books and learning reminds Peter of his own youthful eagerness, comically, yet also uncannily, recalled in the episode describing the night Peter spent with a crowd of ghosts in a bookshop (pp. 13-14).

Kien was called Kant in one manuscript version of the novel, but his name was changed at Hermann Broch's request.[10] Like Kant, he claims to base his morality on the intellect, but this emphasis on the intellect is taken to extremes. For Kien, morality does not entail empathy for other individuals or social responsibility but an attempt to maximise the efficiency of his academic activities. His relationship with others—Therese and Benedikt Pfaff in the first half of the novel, and Fischerle in the second half—is founded on his own need to isolate himself from the rest of society, and in each case, books, the symbol of the intellect, are placed above human considerations. Benedikt is bribed to ensure that undesirables are removed from the house before they reach Peter's library on the top floor. Fischerle is paid to help unload books from Peter's head and, later, to rescue books from the clutches of the monsters in the Theresianum. Peter only marries Therese in order to have a supposed book-lover at hand to care for the library: 'I shall marry her! She is the heaven-sent instrument for preserving my library' (p. 47). Here, Kien is satirised by his own implied use of the dehumanising word 'instrument' to describe the woman he is about to marry, thereby transgressing Kant's ethical principle requiring that other human beings be treated as ends in themselves rather than means. Kien's resemblance to Kant and his adherence to Kantian tenets are thus shown to be superficial; he merely supports opinions that serve to justify his own asocial nature and selfish purposes.

Kien wishes to achieve immortality, not only by his publications, each of which serves as the inspiration for many other scholars' research, but also by his absurdly materialistic bequest of his 'skull with all its contents' (p. 20) to science. Peter is further described as if he is a microcosm: the windowless library on the top floor represents his own self, cut off from the world, yet its 25,000 volumes are themselves another window on the world (p. 67). And, finally, Peter is characterised by his sharp features and distinct gestures: he is tall and thin, bony and angular.

Even Peter Kien's sado-masochism can be seen, according to Weininger's world-view, not as a negative trait, but as another sign of his genius. Weininger dog-matically claims that all men of genius suffer from the strongest sexual perversions, either sadism or, more usually, masochism.[11] Kien's sadism is revealed in his vicious treatment of Franz Metzger when this nine-year-old boy returns to visit Kien's library, in his fantasising about Therese's death and in his strangling of Pfaff's canaries. His masochism is even more pronounced: when his self-transformation into stone fails to impress, he accepts Therese's physical abuse as a just punishment (p. 152), and his actions at the end of the chapter 'The Mussel Shell',[12] when he flees Therese's clutches by locking himself in the toilet, correspond to Weininger's assertion that sadomasochism in the genius is the sign of a healthy aversion to the repulsive bestiality of any sexual contact.

This brief survey of Peter's character not only demonstrates the undeniable parallels with Weininger's ideal type, but also highlights, by the tenor of the instances I have cited, that Peter is a comic figure. Canetti's absurd exaggeration of Peter's memory capacity; the fact that even his dreams and hallucinations conform to the Cartesian criteria of clarity and distinction and are devoid of emotion; the uncanny eagerness the young Peter shows for books (whereas Franz Metzger displays a healthy desire for knowledge, Peter's youthful obsession already showed signs of fantastical hallucinations); the ridiculous and vain project of bequeathing his brain to science in order to achieve immortality; his instrumentalisation of human relationships by paying others to help him maintain his condescending social isolation; his pathetic sadism and his self-deceptive masochism—all these traits indicate that Canetti is satirising the main protagonist of his novel. Canetti's satirical style requires detailed analysis beyond the scope of this essay, but his use of the ironic semi-distancing of free indirect style needs to be mentioned, as it is a technique which Canetti has commented on in several interviews and essays. The speech patterns of the 'acoustic mask' ('akustische Maske'), usually repetitive, tautologous and clichéd, reveal a character's dogmatic, obsessive and egocentric unconscious thoughts.[13] Even though Kien's thought-patterns are far more structured than those of the other characters, they still form a mask. That Kien's memory is a 'heaven-sent gift' is not an objective statement, but an example of free indirect speech as self-revealing irony; Kien's implied use of this term to describe himself is a sign of arrogance. Like his memorisation of pi, Kien's accumulation of books is an arid pursuit and the spiritual wisdom of Chinese culture is lost on him. The phrase 'skull with all its contents' indicates that Kien's own conception of knowledge is material, not spiritual—or rather physiological, as Canetti is perhaps parodying Paul Julius Möbius' revival of Gall's phrenology in *Über den physiologischen Schwachsinn des Weibes* of 1900 where brain size is linked with intelligence.

Yet this does not necessarily mean that Canetti is also satirising Weininger through Kien, implicitly condemning the whole of Weininger's philosophy to laughter. Elfriede Pöder's claim (echoed by Michel-François Demet and Gerald Stieg) that *Auto-da-fé* constitutes the definitive derisive satire of Weininger's concept of the male genius needs to be reviewed.[14] Kien is a complex figure, displaying both male and female traits: he is a satirical character not only because of the extremism of his ideas, but also because of his inability to remain true to the ascetic, masculine principles he has set himself. Kien proclaims a Kantian aversion to all lies and a love of the truth (p. 13), yet his unpleasant experience of the external world leads him to adopt, at first unconsciously, then consciously, a highly selective position towards his environment, one which carefully filters out anything which does not conform to his preconceptions: 'It is his right to apply that blindness, which protects him from the excesses of the senses to every disturbing element in his life. . . . *Esse percipi,* to be is to be perceived. What I do not perceive, does not exist. . . . Whence, with cogent logic, it was proved that Kien was in no wise deceiving himself' (p. 71). Kien exploits Berkeley's philosophy of perception, according to which reality consists solely of what is perceived, by adopting an absurdly parodistic version: he deliberately fails to perceive those aspects of the material world he does not wish to acknowledge, thus denying their reality.[15] He unconsciously reconstructs certain events that have revealed his own failings: when he does not realise that he is being asked where the Mutstrasse is until the questioner starts hitting him, he later convinces himself that he did not want to humiliate the questioner by telling him that he was already standing in the required street; when he does not recognise who is in his bed, he prefers to believe that it is his wife's murderer rather than the fearsome Therese herself; when his plan to overcome his wife's brutality by turning himself into stone fails, he persuades himself that he was only trying to fool her and to encourage her to throw him out of his own house. Kien repeatedly disparages the masses: 'barbarians' and 'illiterates' are terms he frequently uses to contrast them to his own ideal of 'culture'. Despite this, twice in the novel he becomes aware of his isolation and decides to venture among common people, to be absorbed in the crowd (pp. 122-4 and p. 173), but his belief that he has finally managed to understand another human being (Fischerle) and his plan 'to become learned in men' (p. 219) only lead to his being swindled. He even briefly adopts a philosophy of love and pity for Therese (p. 123), yet this is soon replaced by an overriding hatred for her when she again insists on his writing a will in her favour. All these examples of self-deception are satirical, admittedly, but they also suggest a deeper pathos: Kien's blindness exposes him to ex-

ploitation by others, which ultimately leads to his madness and suicide. Kien's fate, in some respects, could be seen as tragic, like Weininger's.

There are various passages in Canetti's essays, 'Aufzeichnungen' ('jottings') and autobiography that suggest that his own conception of the ideal writer comes very close to that of Weininger. What Canetti principally satirises in the character of Kien is his specialisation; although, ironically, as Canetti explains in his conversation with Joachim Schickel, Chinese philosophy (especially that of Confucius and Chuang Tzu) rejects any form of specialisation.[16] This specialisation is a failing that Weininger, like Canetti, repeatedly attacks: 'There is no such thing as a special genius, a genius for mathematics, or for music, or even for chess, but only a universal genius' (*Sex and Character,* p. 112). Indeed, Weininger explicitly attacks the specialisation of the philologist's memory (p. 115). The sort of memory Weininger considers characteristic of the genius is not that of Kien, not a memory which has been crammed with bookish study, but that of men of genius, which 'is of what they have experienced, not of what they have learned' (p. 115). A similar idea is found in one of Canetti's satirical jottings, which implicitly characterises Kien: 'What he has read serves to catch his experiences; and without reading, he doesn't experience.'[17] Canetti satirises a form of misanthropic isolationism; Weininger insists that M should become acquainted with other men.

Besides satirising specialisation in the character of Kien, Canetti overcomes its dangers in his own work by covering the diverse fields of anthropology, literary criticism, psychology, politics, cultural history and philosophy, claiming: 'My whole life is nothing but a desperate attempt to overcome the division of labour and think about everything myself, so that it comes together in a head and thus becomes one again.'[18] Similarly, Weininger stresses the dual nature of *Sex and Character,* a work combining science and idealist philosophy, emulating Nietzsche's synthesis of Schopenhauerian moral philosophy and Darwinian biology, and advocates that the ideal man alternate between the pursuit of science and that of art (*Sex and Character,* p. 108).

As I have already explained, Weininger stresses that only a true genius is capable of the desire and the ability to write an autobiography because of its demands on one's memory. Canetti has been accused by some critics (especially Eigler)[19] of glossing over the difficulties of remembering, naïvely presenting reconstruction as an immediate account of lived experience. His response was to emphasise his trust in his own extraordinary memory: 'Often it is those who think they know what one is supposed to remember who expect you to emphasise and linger on your doubt, as if the one who spells out his doubts were more truthful for that. In reality he is just weaker and preempts the doubts of others with his own.'[20] As Jacques Le Rider has shown, the emphasis on the subjectivity of memoirs and autobiographies in Vienna at the start of this century is linked to the modernist crisis of the individual and his pessimistic awareness of the failings of language in a nonrational, decadent world lacking absolute values.[21] However, Weininger wards off the possibility of this disintegration by basing a strong, stable self on an intensified cognition of one's own ego, an 'Ich-Ereignis' (*Sex and Character*, pp. 246-66); and Canetti's autobiography wards off the same danger by the power of the reminiscing subject. Weininger's emphasis on the desire for immortality complements Canetti's own campaign as the 'Todfeind' ('enemy of death'), the writer who, proud of his own personal identity, refuses to accept death in any of its forms.

Weininger also emphasises the importance of gratitude, of piety towards one's ancestors (pp. 178-9) and, like Canetti,[22] he attaches great importance to a person's name as a link to the history of one's family (p. 133). He considers the artist, the philosopher or the founder of a religion superior to men of action, who are necessarily compromised by considerations of power and materialism (p. 139)—an idea reflected throughout *Crowds and Power*. Like Kien and Weininger, Canetti shows revulsion towards man's base instincts, and he not only seems to find sexual instincts distasteful, but all bodily processes, including eating, in accordance with Weininger's analogies between the oral, laryngal and anal regions'.[23] One of his jottings asks rhetorically: Wouldn't everything be better if we had a different aperture for food and used our mouths only for words?'[24] and in his autobiography he writes of his 'emerging sensitivity on all questions of eating and getting eaten' after visiting a slaughter-house on a school trip.[25] This sensitive, anti-instinctual attitude is particularly clear in Canetti's condemnation of the excesses of decadent Berlin in the fourth part of *The Torch in My Ear*: 'The Throng of Names'.

Canetti's oft-repeated ideal of 'Verwandlung' ('metamorphosis'), which receives especial elucidation in the essay **'The Writer's Profession',**[26] bears a resemblance to Weininger's idealised conception of the perceptive processes of the genius. Weininger states that:

> To understand a man is really to be the man . . . and a man is the closer to being a genius the more men he has in his personality, and the more really and strongly he has these others within him.
>
> (*Sex and Character*, pp. 105-6)

And Canetti:

> Man must learn to *be* many men consciously and to keep them all together. This latter and far more difficult task will give him the character he imperils with his plurality.
>
> (*The Human Province*, p. 76)

If we take Weininger's above statement together with his insistence on a stable self (*Sex and Character*, p. 133), the resemblance between their views is striking: both hope to enrich their own inner life by the internalisation of other human beings' characteristics. Furthermore, both Weininger and Canetti have developed a theory of human characterology that relies on man's ability to metamorphose into an animal: Weininger writes that there are few men who do not have one or more animal faces.[27] Canetti had his own 'early childhood typology . . . based on animals', and in an interview he claimed that man is the sum of all the animals into which he has transformed himself throughout history.[28] The physical nature of this form of understanding, underlined by the anthropological, biological and zoological origins Canetti ascribes to modern forms of human interaction (especially in the chapter 'Presentiment and Transformation among the Bushmen' in *Crowds and Power*, pp. 337-42), is foreshadowed in Weininger's physiognomy, and both consider metamorphosis as an ideal: Canetti calls himself the 'keeper of metamorphoses' and Weininger writes: 'The number of different aspects that the face of a man has assumed may be taken almost as a physiognomical measure of his talent.'[29] Despite both authors' insistence on rationality, the rationality they advocate is no arid pedantry: Canetti's jottings are whimsical and bizarre like much that is to be found in Weininger, especially the sections 'Aphoristisch Gebliebenes' and 'Metaphysik' in *Über die letzten Dinge*.

Because of these parallels between Canetti's and Weininger's view of the genius, the claim that *Auto-da-fé* is an incisive satire of Weininger cannot be upheld. Kien is an ambivalent figure: many of his characteristics are not so much reminiscent of Weininger as of Canetti. The love of books (especially as physical objects) and the interest in oriental religion and philosophy are particularly striking features that both Kien and Canetti share. However, although there may be points of comparison between Peter and Canetti, there are even more parallels between George Kien's philosophy and Canetti's: both advocate 'metamorphosis', are opponents of Freud,[30] and emphasise the importance of paying attention to the non-linguistic, musical aspects (the 'acoustic mask') of one's interlocutor (*Auto-da-fé*, p. 417). Yet George is not perfect: he confesses to making a mistake in his judgement of Therese and Pfaff, whose malice he failed to appreciate because of his overly sympathetic view of other human beings, a view that excludes rational value-judgements (pp. 463-4). Canetti recognises that man is a many-peopled microcosm, but he also insists that this microcosm be kept under control; George's anarchic vision of humanity as a termites' nest is not Canetti's ideal. George and Peter should be considered complementary opposites, which is suggested by the fact that they both fail to appreciate novels, each for an opposite reason: Peter because novels disrupt the unity of the reading subject, thus undermining the basis of logical thought (p. 42), and George because novels are overly structured and rational (p. 398). So if *Auto-da-fé* does contain a positive model of genius it is that proposed by George: a combination of the characteristics of both Peter and George, of the former's intellectual rigour and the latter's expertise in human understanding; as George explains to Peter: 'Both together, a memory for feelings and a memory for facts—for that is what yours is—would make possible the universal man' (p. 436).

Weininger's masculine genius conforms closely to Canetti's ideal, proposed in the novel by George; it is an ideal which stresses the importance of logic and memory, but also of empathetic understanding, it is an ideal combining intellectual rigour with flexibility. It is the ideal of the anti-traditionalist, yet also anti-decadent Kraus, opposing both rigid dogma and disintegration. Peter is parodied for his one-sided display of the qualities of the genius, but his devotion to his studies is also a positive quality, admired by George. George himself acknowledges that he lacks 'character', and that he learns from his brother (p. 427). But what he learns only confirms that trait which both brothers already share: misogyny.

THE UNSTABLE FEMALE

According to Weininger's characterology, the female (W) is the opposite of the masculine ideal of the genius (M). She is a completely sexual being; if she ever seems otherwise, this is due to a man's influence (*Sex and Character*, p. 89). Whereas M thinks precisely and logically, W thinks in 'henids', characteristic of a stage of thinking in which emotional colouring and logical conceptualisation have not yet been distinguished (p. 100). As W cannot think logically (Weininger writes that 'she may be regarded as "logically insane"' [p. 149]), it is in her nature to be mendacious, not so much out of malice as because of an inability to distinguish truth and falsehood (p. 264). She lacks the will-power to form her own judgements, and therefore she attaches undue value to mere material possessions or diverting pursuits (pp. 201ff.). Her inability to understand the logic of Kant's categorical imperative entails that she is amoral and does not possess a soul (p. 186). Her physical features and gestures are characterised by indistinctness and curves, rather than resoluteness and lines.

Whereas Peter is an ambivalent embodiment of Weininger's masculine genius, Therese can be shown to conform to all aspects of his typology of women. Weininger establishes two contrasting pairs of female types. On the one hand: the mother and the prostitute, on the other: the hysterical woman and the shrew. The mother is defined by her desire to have children and her embeddedness in nature. As it is repeatedly stressed that Therese does not like children, a reader with a knowledge of Weininger would naturally classify her as a prostitute (which for Weininger is a psychological and physiological type, independent of social position, and not a profession). At the start of the novel, Therese conforms to the type of the hysterical woman. Despite Therese's claims to the contrary, her reiterated appeals to 'decency', she is shown to have a strong repressed sexual drive: this is revealed by the two occasions on which she faints, both of which are imbued with an intense eroticism (*Auto-da-fé*, p. 74 and p. 124), and by her obsessive condemnation of contemporary sexual mores: 'Every factory girl has to have a new blouse. I ask you, and what do they do with all their fancy stuff? Go off bathing and take it all off again. With boys, too. Whoever heard of such a thing in my time' (pp. 36-7). Her obsessive reading of personal advertisements in the newspaper (p. 64) confirms her latent correspondence with Weininger's fundamental typological trait for women: match-making, described by Weininger as 'the only positively general female characteristic' (*Sex and Character*, p. 259) because it reveals how W's sexuality destroys her personal individuality so as to encompass an obsession with sex in general. However, for W the bridal night is a turning-point (p. 91), and it proves to be so for Therese. Although Therese's bridal night ends in disaster, it is the point at which Therese is transformed from the outwardly respectable hysterical woman into the openly sexual shrew, another character type. Her failure to seduce Kien spurs her on to find another sexual partner. Just as, according to Weininger, a woman's vanity, revealed in her narcissistic use of a mirror, indicates a desire to be seduced (p. 201), so Therese, as she admires herself in a mirror, conducts an imagined erotic conversation with the shop-assistant Mr. Brute ('Herr Grob') in anticipation of her desired love-affair (*Auto-da-fé*, pp. 270-2). However, Therese does not succeed in persuading Brute to kill Kien and become her lover; instead she manages to seduce Benedikt Pfaff. Therese's seduction of this retired policeman conforms precisely to the model Weininger suggests: 'It is a noticeable fact that a policeman usually finds his sexual complement in the housemaid' (*Sex and Character*, p. 272, note).

Therese not only conforms to Weininger's concept of female pansexuality but also to that of 'logical insanity', or 'Kartoffellogik' ('potato logic') as Dieter Dissinger has described it.[31] Whereas Kien's insanity derives from logical extremism, his obstinate refusal to accept any phenomenon that does not easily fit within his precon- ceived world-view, Therese's repetitive speech patterns, her 'acoustic mask', reveal an incoherence deriving from her emotional obsessions: sex, money and power. Among the words and phrases she overuses—along with 'Excuse me', 'Potatoes already cost double', 'a real man'—is the word 'beautiful' ('schön'),[32] the over- use of which word is explicitly condemned by Wein- inger as a sign of female shamelessness.[33] Therese's speech also reveals her own mendacity; having just failed to seduce Brute by inviting him to a meal, she in- dignantly persuades herself that she is still a respectable woman and that it is all Peter's fault: 'In the streets all the men stared at her. Whose fault was it anyway? It was all her husband's fault!' (*Auto-da-fé*, pp. 101-2). The fact that Therese just as frequently lies to herself as to others proves that her mendacity is of the sort Wein- inger attributes to W, a mendacity deriving from logical confusion and heightened emotionality, rather than criminal intent (*Sex and Character*, p. 273). Therese shows no sign of remorse for her crimes, no realisation of the consequences of her suggestions: she indignantly asserts the rightfulness of her having deceived her mother into believing that she slept with the latter's boyfriend; she calmly proposes that Brute murder her husband—she would not do it herself as she is 'decent'. Therese insists that her husband draft a will, but has no intention of drafting one herself—a sign, according to Weininger, of her lack of the male desire for immortal- ity (p. 135). Canetti's description of Therese's physical appearance and movements also accords with the fe- male characteristics laid down by Weininger: in opposi- tion to Kien's sharply outlined features and gestures, Therese is characterised by her gliding gait, and a cur- vaceousness that she aims to conceal beneath her blouse and starched skirt, her armour against the external world.

Therese is not the only female character in *Auto-da-fé* who conforms to Weininger's characterisation. Fischer- le's wife, humorously known as the Capitalist, is de- voted to her husband and her regular client. She shows the same submissiveness as the gorilla's mistress (the 'secretary') and the Fishwife, whose catch-phrase 'He's all I've got in the world!' (*Augo-da-fé*, p. 223) tallies with Weininger's proposition that women's value judge- ments are always dependent on men. That this subservi- ence can lead to crime is demonstrated by George's wife, who poisons her first husband, the director of the mental asylum, so that George may take over. Anna, Pfaff's physically abused daughter, is driven by roman- tic yearning for Franz, who works as a grocer's assis- tant. Her dreams, in which he appears as a knight on horseback, could be interpreted as a sign of her pliabil- ity to male domination, a transference of her need to be dominated by her father onto the character of Franz, or,

on the other hand, as her exploitation of another man in order to escape from her family home. Her hidden sa- distic tendencies are revealed by her strange fantasis- ing:

> He [Franz] holds out the match to her and the cigarette burns. I'll burn you, she says, he's frightened. She points it at him, she touches him. Oh, he cries, my hand, that hurts! She calls: 'For love', and runs away.
>
> (p. 372)

This may at first appear a distorted interpretation of what most readers will consider a wholly sympathetic character, but Dieter Dissinger views Anna in just such a negative light, without even referring to Weininger (*Vereinzelung und Massenwahn*, p. 96). However this may be in the case of Anna, Canetti satirises all his other female characters by presenting them as represen- tatives of W: their lack of intelligence and moral aware- ness, their self-deception and their submissiveness make them appear comically absurd. Canetti presents his char- acters as Weiningerian types inasmuch as he refrains from presenting any account of individual psychologi- cal or social history. We receive no more explanation why the female characters are so egoistic and sexually obsessive than why Peter is so obsessed with sinology.

Not only do all Canetti's female characters show some correspondence with Weininger's typology, but his male characters, although they fall short of the ideal of the male genius, are all more or less misogynist. In the case of Fischerle and Pfaff this misogyny takes the form of crude slogans: Fischerle exclaims: 'A woman who isn't a whore, there's no such thing!' (*Auto-da-fé*, p. 285), and Pfaff declares: 'Women ought to be beaten to death. The whole lot of them. . . . They're all criminals.' (p. 111). Kien's misogyny displays distinct similarities to the more intellectual misogyny of Weininger. He em- phasises the sexuality of mothers: 'If a mother could be content to be nothing but a mother; but where would you find one who would be satisfied with that particular part alone? Each is a specialist first and foremost as a woman, and would make demands which an honest man of learning would not even dream of fulfilling' (pp. 12-13). He considers a woman's modesty as a cover for lasciviousness, using the punning phrase 'shame- facedness of the shameless' to characterise Therese (p. 453); similarly, Weininger writes: 'Women can give an impression of being modest because there is nothing in her to contrast with her sexuality' (*Sex and Character*, p. 200). Peter interprets figures of women in history and mythology (Cleopatra, Helen of Troy, Aphrodite, Ca- lypso, Nausicaa, Penelope, Hera, Eve, Eudoxia, Messalina) in such a way as to reveal the immorality, or amorality, hidden under the gloss of male idealisation, supporting his arguments with the names of famous mi- sogynists (Aquinas, Thomas More, Juvenal, Confucius, Buddha). This erudite misogyny is directly paralleled throughout Weininger's work; indeed the whole chapter 'Warywise Odysseus', devoted to Peter's lengthy tirade against women, resembles Weininger's list of authorities to support his claim that W does not possess a soul (pp. 186-8).

Although we must bear in mind that George is consciously attempting to cure his brother's psychosis in their discussion by pretending to agree with his rantings, there are passages in the novel indicating that he is as misogynist as his brother. George says to Peter: '. . . you don't even guess how much I owe you: my character as far as I have any, my love of learning, my way of life, my rescue from all those women . . .' (*Auto-da-fé*, p. 427), and he reaches the conclusion: 'I believe in learning more firmly every day, and every day less firmly in the indispensability of love!' (p. 433). This praise of his brother is undoubtedly tongue-in-cheek, but George does admire certain aspects of Peter's work and acknowledges what he has learnt from him: 'From it George learnt that there was a cure for the woman, more certain than poison . . .' (p. 494). We learn that George's period of womanising did not contribute to his love of women, and that he finds his wife boring in contrast to true 'characters': his patients at the asylum (p. 413). His ideal woman is one who has been transformed by the domination of a man, or rather, of a 'gorilla' (p. 436).

If as I have suggested, the positive ideal Canetti proposes in *Auto-da-fé is* that of a combination of the intellectual rigour of Peter and the empathetic understanding of George, this ideal does not seem to exclude misogyny. Peter Kien may be an eccentric misogynist, lacking self-awareness and mulishly blotting out aspects of the external world which displease him, but he is not as unambiguously antipathetic as Therese, who is deceitful, greedy, aggressive and manipulative. George conscientiously goes about his work at the mental asylum, developing his theory of psychotherapy based on empathetic understanding and a genuine concern for the mentally ill (in contrast to his assistants and predecessors who are scornful of their patients); on the other hand, his wife is aggressively ambitious and has no qualms about murdering her first husband in order to further her second husband's career. As Therese and George's wife are presented as a potential and an actual murderess, within the fictional world of the novel the Kiens' misogyny appears justified. It is true that the violence exerted within Pfaff's household demonstrates how family ties can be perverted in order to reinforce male domination, yet Therese's treatment of her mother and her brutality towards Peter, as well as George's wife's murder of her former husband, suggest that women can be just as much a source of violence as men.

Canetti's own explanations of his characterology in *Auto-da-fé* run counter to the suggestion that his char-

acterisation might be a parody of Weiningerian philosophy. As he explains in *'The First Book: Auto-da-fé'* (*The Conscience of Words,* p. 123-33), Therese is based upon a real woman, Canetti's own housekeeper in the Hagenberggasse in Hacking from 1927 to 1933 (p. 124). This shows that Canetti does not consider Therese as the projection of a misogynist's distorted mind, but as a character reflecting reality, despite the exaggeration that satire entails.

That Canetti conceived of the relationship between the sexes as one of animosity is demonstrated in the chapter 'The Double Crowd: Men and Women. The Living and the Dead' in *Crowds and Power* and by the fact that Canetti claims not to have believed in love until he saw a performance of Kleist's *Penthesilea*, a play characterised by its portrayal of a murderous sex war (*The Torch in My Ear,* p. 48). Canetti's cynicism about love is suggested in some of the jottings: 'The dungeon that love has actually prepared will turn visible only gradually' (*The Human Province,* p. 76), and other jottings are curiously misogynist in a wistful way:

> As soon as the word 'love' occurs, a woman believes anything. Men reserve the same gullibility for fighting.
>
> (*The Human Province,* p. 55)

> The stupidest women: those who come and report everything right away; to the nearest ear; it hasn't even fully happened yet.
>
> (*The Human Province,* p. 131)

Canetti explicitly compares Therese with Tolstoy's wife (*The Conscience of Words,* p. 103) and with Goya's second wife (*The Secret Heart of the Clock,* p. 135), and implicitly with Felice Bauer.[34] Similarly, Canetti paints a devastatingly satirical portrait of Alma Mahler-Werfel, formerly married to a great composer, now just to a third-rate author, and of Fritz Wotruba's wife.[35] All these women, according to Canetti, shared a lack of appreciation for the work of their talented husband or fiancé and only hindered them in the expression of their genius.

Canetti's three plays also conform in their characterisation to Weininger's typology. In *Wedding,* Leni is wholly subservient to her husband Professor Thut. Anita, despite appearances, confirms Weininger's claim that there is no genuine female modesty. Gretchen, like Therese, has to remind Max of his duties as a man in order to get what she wants. However, in this play, all the characters display the decadent characteristics associated, by Weininger, with femininity (or Jewishness): lasciviousness and materialism. This play, like Kraus' *Die demolirte Literatur,* can be interpreted as an attack on a decadently feminine society.

In *Comedy of Vanity,* the feminine characteristic of vanity is presented in an ambiguous way. On the one hand, the fact that the female characters show a stronger need to use mirrors can be considered to reinforce the Weiningerian view that women lack self-esteem; yet, in a totalitarian society in which mirrors have been banned, vanity has become a form of resistance, contrasting with the hypocrisy of Fritz Schakerl's fascistic committee meetings. However, it is a woman, Therese Kreiss, who is most susceptible to the hysteria of the mass photograph-burnings; and one of the least sympathetic characters in the play, Emilie Fant, was, Canetti says, based upon Alma Mahler-Werfel.[36]

In *The Numbered,* the three main characters, who rationally discuss the positive and negative aspects of a society in which everyone knows when he will die, are all male. Whereas the two Colleagues and the two Young Men inquire into the effects of their society's laws, the two Ladies show an interest in match-making, and the two Old Women are only too willing to exchange their official lockets for Fifty's gold ones.

However, Canetti's later works show a slighter tendency to portray women in such a negative way. In *The Voices of Marrakesh* women are shown as victims of social circumstance, not as types: in the chapter 'The woman at the grille', Canetti sympathetically describes the imprisonment of a woman, and in 'Sheherazade' he recounts the story of Ginette, enslaved in an unhappy marriage. In *Earwitness,* although the Granite-cultivator resembles Therese, the Tempted Woman Anna Pfaff, and the Paper Drunkard Kien, many of the women appear in direct contradiction to Weiningerian typology: the Narrow-smeller and the Allusive Woman are entirely ascetic, not sexual; the Man-splendid Woman, the Archeocrat and the Horse-dark Woman are proud of their independence; the Syllable-pure Woman speaks eloquently and with precision. Often it is the male characters who display those traits Weininger ascribes to women: the Misspeaker is characterised by his confused thinking, the Bequeathed Man by his submissiveness.

Yet despite this less stereotypical portrayal of women in his late fiction, Canetti's autobiography still shows signs of a Weiningerian view of women, as Friederike Eigler has pointed out.[37] Frau Weinreb has lost all sense of self-worth since the death of her husband, whose photographs she licks in fetishistic adoration (*The Torch in My Ear,* pp. 181-2); Kokoschka's portrait of Alma Mahler-Werfel is described as 'portrait of the composer's murderess' (*The Play of the Eyes,* p. 52); Canetti's cousin Laurica is portrayed as only interested in her search for a husband, and as having such a bad memory that she cannot remember Elias's having tried to murder her with an axe (*The Torch in My Ear,* pp. 94-8). The portrayal of the principal woman in the autobiography, Canetti's mother, is highly ambivalent, and would merit a detailed study. Let it here suffice to note that, just as Weininger debunks the idealisation of mother-

hood by stressing the sexual aspect of breast-feeding,[38] so Canetti emphasises the mother's desire to exercise power over her child: 'The mother's power over a young child is absolute, not only because its life depends on her, but also because she herself feels a very strong urge to exercise this power all the time' (*Crowds and Power,* p. 221).

It is, therefore, unlikely that Canetti wished to satirise Weininger in his works. If Canetti satirised a form of philosophy in his works, then it is an inflexible dogmatism—a dogmatism, however, just as typical, in Canetti's view, of Aristotle, Kant or Kraus as of Weininger. If Canetti borrowed ideas, images and terms from Weininger, then his world-view and that of Weininger must overlap. The point of intersection is a particular view of women. It should not unduly surprise us that this novel contains misogynist elements. Canetti is known not only to have read Weininger, but also Strindberg, whose laudatory obituary of Weininger, 'Idolatrie, Gynolatrie', Kraus published in the *Fackel.*[39] Some motives in the novel are suggestive of Strindberg's early anti-feminist plays, which we know Canetti's mother read eagerly, but which were initially forbidden reading for the young Elias. Laura's attempt forcibly to remove her husband from the family home in *The Father* (a play Weininger praises for its supposed thematisation of his theory of telegony or 'germinal infection' [*Sex and Character,* p. 233]) resembles Therese's actions towards Peter, and in this play, as well as in the novel, a writing-desk plays an important symbolic role, representative of Kien's and the Captain's academic pursuits. Alfred Kubin's fantasy-novel, *Die andere Seite* (The Other Side), presents femininity as a decadent threat to civilisation; and it is Kubin whom Canetti chose to illustrate the cover of the first edition of *Auto-da-fé.* Despite the opposition to Kraus that Canetti describes in **'Karl Kraus: The School of Resistance'** (*The Conscience of Words,* pp. 29-39), his attitude towards women still moves within the triangle Strindberg, Weininger, Kraus.

The disintegration of the self and of value-systems, which Canetti and Weininger hoped to arrest, is a far-reaching topic that is often thematised in Austrian literature of the early twentieth century. It is associated in Canetti's work with the conflict between the crowd and the individual, and in Weininger's with the opposition between Machian monist empiriocriticism and Neo-Kantian dualist idealism. In the battle between those acknowledging a feminisation of culture ('Jung Wien', Altenberg, Otto Gross) and those who fear the crisis of identity and loss of values such an encroachment of the feminine might cause (Schoenberg, Loos, Kraus, Wittgenstein), Canetti has ranked himself among the latter.

Notes

1. Gerald Stieg, 'Otto Weiningers "Blendung": Weininger, Karl Kraus und der Brenner-Kreis' in *Otto*

Weininger: Werk und Wirkung, ed. Jacques Le Rider and Norbert Leser (Vienna, 1984), p. 60.

2. Nike Wagner, *Geist und Geschlecht: Karl Kraus und die Erotik der Wiener Moderne* (Frankfurt, 1982).

3. Canetti, *The Torch in My Ear,* tr. Joachim Neugroschel (London, 1988), p. 77 and p. 118.

4. Alfons M. Bischoff, *Elias Canetti: Stationen zum Werk* (Frankfurt, 1973), p. 19.

5. Jacques Le Rider, *Der Fall Otto Weininger: Wurzeln des Antifeminismus und Antisemitismus* (Vienna and Munich, 1985), Elfriede Pöder, 'Spurensicherung. Otto Weininger in der "Blendung"' in *Elias Canetti: Blendung als Lebensform,* ed. Friedbert Aspetsberger and Gerald Stieg (Konigstein/Ts., 1985), pp. 57-72, and Gerald Stieg, 'Otto Weiningers "Blendung". Weininger, Karl Kraus und der Brenner-Kreis'. See also: Johannes G. Pankau, 'Korper und Geist. Das Geschlechtsverhältnis in Elias Canettis *Die Blendung*', in *Colloquia Germanica,* 23 (1990), 146-70.

6. But see: Ritchie Robertson, '"Jewish self-hatred?" The cases of Schnitzler and Canetti', in *Austrians and Jews in the Twentieth Century,* ed. Robert S. Wistrich (London, 1992), pp. 82-96.

7. See the chapters: 'Talent and Memory' (pp. 114-41) and 'Logic, Ethics and the Ego' (pp. 153-62) in Otto Weininger, *Sex and Character: Authorised Translation from the Sixth German Edition* (London and New York, 1906).

8. Cf. Kant: 'Levity, nay, even good-nature, may be its cause [i.e. of a lie], or some good end may be aimed at by it. However, the giving way to such a thing is by its bare form a crime perpetrated by man against his own person, and a meanness, making a man contemptible in his own eyes' (*The Metaphysics of Ethics,* by Immanuel Kant, tr. J. W. Semple, 3rd ed. (Edinburgh, 1871), pp. 244-5).

9. Canetti, *Auto-da-fé,* tr. C. V. Wedgwood (London, 1946), p. 210.

10. Canetti, *The Conscience of Words,* tr. Joachim Neugroschel (London, 1986), p. 232.

11. Otto Weininger, *Geschlecht und Charakter* (Vienna and Leipzig, 1903), p. 385, n. 1. This footnote is not found in the English translation.

12. The German word 'Muschel' points to the latent sexuality of this chapter. As well as meaning 'mussel', it is also a vulgar word for 'female genitals' and a colloquial Austrian term for 'toilet pan'.

13. The phrase 'akustische Maske' was used for the first time in 'Interview mit Elias Canetti: Leergegessene Bonbonnieren', in *Wiener Sonntag,* 19 April 1937.

14. Michel-François Demet, 'Blutphantasien bei Otto Weininger' in *Otto Weininger: Werk und Wirkung,* ed. Jacques Le Rider and Norber Leser (Vienna, 1984), p. 53, Gerald Stieg, 'Otto Weiningers "Blendung"', p. 61 and Elfriede Pöder, 'Spurensicherung', p. 69.

15. See David Darby, '"Esse percipi", "Sein ist Wahrgenommenwerden": perception and perspective in Berkeley and Canetti', *Neophilologus,* 75 (1991), 425-32.

16. Canetti, *Die gespaltene Zukunft: Aufsätze und Gespräche* (Munich, 1972), pp. 104-31.

17. Canetti, *The Human Province,* tr. Joachim Neugroschel (London, 1985), p. 93.

18. Ibid., p. 34.

19. Friederike Eigler, *Das autobiographische Werk von Elias Canetti* (Tübingen, 1988), pp. 63-6.

20. Canetti, *The Secret Heart of the Clock,* tr. Joel Agee (London, 1991).

21. Jacques Le Rider, *Modernity and Crises of Identity: Culture and Society in Fin-de-Siècle Vienna,* tr. Rosemary Morris (Cambridge, 1993), p. 35 and p. 40.

22. See 'Gesprach mit Joachim Schickel' in *Die gespaltene Zukunft,* pp. 104-31.

23. Weininger, *Über die letzten Dinge,* 9th edn (Vienna and Leipzig, 1930).

24. Canetti, *The Human Province,* p. 106.

25. Canetti, *The Tongue Set Free,* tr. Joachim Neugroschel (London, 1988), p. 228.

26. Canetti, *The Conscience of Words,* pp. 156-66.

27. Weininger, *Über die letzten Dinge,* p. 123.

28. Canetti, *The Tongue Set Free,* p. 150 and *Die gespaltene Zukunft,* p. 97.

29. Canetti, *The Conscience of Words,* p. 161 and Weininger, *Sex and Character,* p. 108.

30. 'He prods me to deal the decisive blow against Freud. Can I do that, since I *am* this decisive blow?' (*The Secret Heart of the Clock,* p. 53) The assistants in the asylum are satirised for their Freudian analysis of George (*Auto-da-fé,* pp. 411-12).

31. Dieter Dissinger, *Vereinzelung und Massenwahn* (Bonn, 1971), p. 107.

32. He was so beautiful, she was so beautiful, everything was beautiful . . .' (*Auto-da-fé,* p. 273). 'She was looking forward to his beautiful punishment' (ibid., p. 298).

33. Weininger, *Geschlecht und Charakter*, p. 339. Passage not found in the English translation.

34. Canetti, *Kafka's Other Trial—The Letters to Felice*, tr. Christopher Middleton (London, 1974).

35. Canetti, *The Play of the Eyes*, tr. Ralph Manheim (London, 1990), pp. 50-5.

36. Manfred Durzak, 'Die Welt ist nicht mehr so darzustellen wie in früheren Romanen', in *Gespräche über den Roman: Formbestimmungen und Analysen*, ed. Manfred Durzak (Frankfurt, 1976), pp. 96-7.

37. Friederike Eigler, *Das autobiographische Werk von Elias Canetti*, p. 189.

38. Weininger, *Geschlecht und Charakter*, p. 291. Passage not found in the English translation.

39. *Die Fackel*, 144 (1903), p. 3.

Kristie A. Foell (essay date 1997)

SOURCE: Foell, Kristie A. "July 15, 1927: The Vienna Palace of Justice Is Burned in a Mass Uprising of Viennese Workers, a Central Experience in the Life of Elias Canetti." In *Yale Companion to Jewish Writing and Thought in German Culture 1096-1996*, edited by Sander L. Gilman and Jack Zipes, pp. 464-70. New Haven: Yale University Press, 1997.

[*In the following essay, Foell explains the impact of the burning of the Vienna Palace of Justice on Canetti's thinking and works.*]

> I can still feel the indignation that came over me when I picked up the *Reichspost*; its huge headline read, "A Just Verdict." There had been shooting in Burgenland [the region of Eastern Austria bordering Hungary], workers had been killed. The court had let the murderers go free. Now the governing party's newspaper called this exoneration a "just" decision, as the headline trumpeted. . . . From every quarter of Vienna the workers marched in dense processions to the Palace of Justice, whose very name embodied injustice in their eyes. It was an entirely spontaneous reaction, I felt by my own actions just how spontaneous. I rode into the city on my bicycle and joined one of the trains of protesters.
>
> The workers, who were otherwise well-disciplined, who trusted their Social Democratic leaders and were satisfied that those leaders ran the City of Vienna in an exemplary fashion, acted on this day *without* their leaders. When they set the Palace of Justice on fire, Mayor Seitz stood in their way on a fire truck, his right fist raised on high. His gesture was ineffectual: the Palace of Justice *burned*. The police were told to shoot; there were ninety dead.

Elias Canetti's autobiographical account of this mass uprising of Viennese workers, and his own minor role in it, written some fifty years after the event, still

breathes with the outrage and excitement of the young Canetti's Communist sympathies. But far from leading to revolution and a more just society, the historical events he described had sinister implications for Austrian history and the fate of Austria's Jews. The "workers" who had been killed on January 30, 1927, were demonstrators for the Austrian Social Democratic Party (SDAPÖ); their attackers were members of the local *Frontkämpfer* organization (right-wing World War I veterans); Walter Riehl, the lawyer who successfully pleaded that the murderers acted in self-defense, was a Nazi. Although Canetti interprets the largely spontaneous protest against this verdict positively, the ensuing reaction from the political Right, and even from the more conservative Social Democrats (Karl Renner and Julius Deutsch), was not so sanguine: the "crimes" of the horde (foremost among them the destruction of property) were widely attributed to the Social Democrats' failure to educate their followers in proper party discipline, and some of the Social Democratic leaders admitted as much. Predictably, the nascent Austrian Nazi Party blamed the uprising on a "Jewish conspiracy" by the Social Democratic leadership to corrupt their loyal German followers, a ridiculous and untenable argument that would become ever more familiar in this "accelerated time" (Canetti's words). Chancellor Ignaz Seipel, a Catholic priest and political arch-conservative, seized the opportunity to call for a rollback of recently established republican rights, including the right to trial by jury and freedom of the press. The Social Democrats, unsettled, were placed on the defensive; the republic and its liberal constitution of 1920 were called into question.

Thus these events were one of the first clear signs of the end of Austria's First Republic and the coming of fascism. For that reason alone, they might be seen as central to the life of an Austrian-Jewish writer like Canetti, who would emigrate from Austria at the last possible minute (1938), never to return. For Canetti's individual, intellectual development, however, his experience of July 15 has another, though related, dimension. Canetti's central concern is the crowd, a topic to which he would devote over thirty years of study, culminating in the 1960 publication of his idiosyncratic anthropological study, *Crowds and Power*. The 1927 experience was not Canetti's first encounter with the mass, but Canetti calls this day "perhaps the most decisive day of my life since the death of my father." For it was on that day that he "realized that the crowd does not need a *leader* (*Führer*), all previous theories notwithstanding." With this seemingly simple statement, Canetti challenges not only the führer phenomenon, but also the strong-arm political conservatism that was urged by the Right in response to July 15. Not least, Canetti's claim contradicts the best-known "mass psychologist" of the day, Sigmund Freud, whose *Group Psychology and Ego Analysis* Canetti had read and rejected in 1925. So basic is the experience of the mass to Canetti that he posited a "mass drive," which he placed "next to the sex drive as its equal." Canetti objects to the reductionism inherent in Freud's theory, claiming that Freud acknowledges neither the phenomenon nor the power of crowd experiences.

Canetti's plea for the irreducibility of experience (and of art) is both his boldest contribution to twentieth-century thought and the most problematic aspect of *Crowds and Power.* In his desire not to reduce the phenomenon, Canetti often reduces his own thought to description without explanatory or methodological potential. His work is nonetheless an original and independent challenge to the truisms of twentieth-century intellectual life. Four concepts are both central and original to this study: the command and its "sting" (*Befehlsstachel*), transformation (*Verwandlung*), the survivor (*der Überlebende*), and especially his diagnosis of the structure of power. The command, according to Canetti, bears an almost physical sting that lodges itself in the person who carries out the command and remains there unchanged until he or she can discharge it by passing on an identical command to another person. Canetti's description applies especially well to hierarchical structures (such as the military) and to the parent-child relationship (Canetti shows overwhelming sympathy for the child, who receives more commands than any other member of society). Psychologists might call this operation "identification with the oppressor"; Canetti, however, resists psychologizing in favor of the mechanistic metaphor of the sting.

Much of Canetti's research for *Crowds and Power* consisted of readings in the mythology and practice of world religions, from the mightiest to the most obscure. Canetti sees transformation (or metamorphosis) as a basic element of both literature and religion, and as one of humanity's best hopes. As long as a religion allows and even enables its constituents to transform themselves, Canetti approves; this happens especially in totemistic and animistic religions in which identification with a particular animal, consultation of the animal as an oracle, and even ritual transformation into the animal are holy acts. (An ecological impulse in Canetti's work can be traced to his belief in the central role animals play in preserving the human capacity for transformation.) Once a religion has become too large, however, and ossified in its structures, it tends to regularize and limit the formation of crowds (for example, by encouraging worship together only at certain times), as well as the possibilities for transformation; here Canetti has a sharp eye for pointing out religion's complicity with power. His diagnosis is most biting when applied to the Catholic Church, whose political representatives were the leading voice against the crowd on July 15: "There has never been a state on earth capable of defending itself in so many ways against the crowd.

Compared with the Church all other rulers seem poor amateurs" (Canetti 1960, 155). Canetti sees the Church's function as postponing the experience of the "open crowd" indefinitely (that is, until the afterlife); the Church, like the Social Democratic Party in 1927, is to discipline the people and keep them from discovering one another in a revolutionary crowd capable of transforming itself and the world.

Canetti affirms the "open crowd," the free and anarchical gathering of people that enables their experience of one another and their transformation. The opposite is true of the holder of power, who regiments the masses, separates himself from them, and opposes them, making of them a collection of dead or at least immobile bodies in order to bolster his own feelings of power. This kind of control of the crowd is the opposite of transformation, and death itself is the ultimate enemy of transformation. In **"The Survivor"** (a section of *Crowds and Power* also published separately), Canetti amasses examples from world history to demonstrate the deep need of the powerful to pile up ever more corpses in order to "win" and see themselves as the sole survivor. The applicability of these ideas to the aesthetics of fascism and to the Holocaust is apparent.

Crowds and Power ends with a discussion of the similarities between the holder of power and the paranoiac (a reading of the Schreber case without Freud) and with an impassioned complaint against the survivor, the command, death, and the power it serves. But because no methodology is developed that could even pretend to offer solutions to concrete problems (as do Freud's dream analysis and his "talking cure"), the book has not had the influence Canetti might have wished for it. Social scientists view it as a literary work, whereas literary scholars at most apply its insights to Canetti's own works. Although the insights of *Crowds and Power* might fruitfully be connected to the work of Foucault, Freud, Adorno, Reich, and others, Canetti strongly resisted such comparisons. The sui generis nature of *Crowds and Power,* combined with the fact that the author held a position defiantly outside of any discipline or professional organization that might promote it, has hindered its reception.

Canetti's lasting literary reputation, sealed by his receipt of the Nobel Prize for literature in 1981, is founded on his first novel, *Die Blendung,* which was completed in 1932 and published in 1936. Translated as *Auto-da-Fé,* its title literally means "the blinding." Canetti has pointed to the relationship between his only novel and the 1927 fire by calling the novel a "fruit of the fire." Here, Canetti's central notion of the crowd overlaps with anti-Semitism and misogyny. The protagonist (really an anti-hero), Peter Kien, seems to stand apart from the crowd: an individualist and intellectual, his very name (Peter means "rock") signifies the opposite of the transformation Canetti glorifies. The character's original name, Kant, makes it clear that he stands for the Enlightenment ideal of autonomy. But his lonely scholarly aerie—a self-contained, four-room library at the top of an apartment building—is threatened by a woman and a Jew. First his housekeeper, Therese, swindles him into marriage. This in itself signifies the breakdown of his isolation, but the woman is further associated with the proletarian mass by her rudeness and lack of education, and with the symbolic idea of the mass through the metonymy of water: she wears a blue skirt and at one point "dissolves" into a stream of tears. The "rock" is always worn down by the persistence of water, and Kien is no exception: his new wife throws him out of their apartment after a bitter struggle, and he enters the real space of the mob, the street.

In a cellar bar frequented by denizens of the demimonde, Peter Kien is thrown on the mercy of a Jewish pimp and swindler, Siegfried Fischerle, who gradually acquires most of Kien's money. Fischerle is a brutal caricature of the would-be assimilated Jew: although his first name tries to signify Germanness, his hump is the physical reminder of the Jewish "nature" he cannot shed. A pseudo-intellectual who fancies that he would be a chess champion if he only had the financial backing, Fischerle gradually draws the reader into his plot to bilk Kien and flee to America. Though Fischerle spends Kien's money on a flatteringly tailored suit designed to hide the hump, it is only his brutal murder that "frees" him from the hump once and for all. Fischerle is captured by one of his "wife's" customers and slaughtered like a beast; the attacker carves off his hump, throws it in a corner, and proceeds to make love to the murdered man's wife "all night long." The connections among Jewishness, women, and prostitution all recall the misogynistic and (self-hating) anti-Semitic theory of Otto Weininger. Although Canetti clearly and prophetically saw the impossibility of Jews being accepted—with or without the "hump" of Jewishness—in mainstream Austrian society, it is less clear to what extent he himself had internalized the negativity he purges in this novel.

Peter Kien, who appears to represent the privileged sons of the haute bourgeoisie (both Karl Kraus and Canetti himself have been suggested as models), is ultimately destroyed, not by women or Jews, but by forces within himself. In a paranoiac panic, he sets fire to his own library and goes up in flames along with his priceless collection of books. Kien projects onto the external world a threat that is no longer present (Fischerle is dead, Therese safely remarried) and commits suicide to escape. The lonely scholar who—like Vienna's conservative leaders—believed himself above the plebeian mass, finally succumbs to its pull within himself. Kien's final self-immolation has also been read as an instance of homosexual panic strongly influenced by Kien's virulent misogyny, a reading supported by his lengthy Wein-

ingerian diatribe against women in the book's penultimate chapter. Whether Kien hates the mass in himself, the woman in himself, or possibly even the Jew in himself (either of which would also symbolize the mass), the mechanism and the result are the same; both rely heavily on the Freudian concept of repression, though Canetti would certainly have preferred a different terminology.

The reception of *Auto-da-Fé* was cut short by Nazism, the annexation of Austria, Canetti's own flight to England in 1938, and World War II. A second edition, appearing in 1947, also found little response; it was not until the book's third appearance in 1963 that it enjoyed extended critical reception. Canetti's two plays from his Viennese period—*The Wedding* (1932) and *Comedy of Vanity* (1934)—suffered a similar fate; both were first premiered in 1965, more than thirty years after they were written. Both plays experiment with turning the crowd into a stage character, and both are deeply pessimistic, even apocalyptic: the first ends in mass death, the second in an eruption of mass narcissism.

With a decidedly Marxist bent, *The Wedding* portrays a petty bourgeoisie that strives only for property (in the form of real estate and sexual "ownership"). The biblical story of Samson's destruction of the temple forms the play's narrative kernel; the dramatic realization relies on Canetti's theory of the acoustic mask, a technique also used in *Auto-da-Fé.* In its most extreme form, each person's acoustic mask is an immutable and limited characteristic set of words, expressions, and intonations that both reveal and mask the individual's character but do not foster communication. In this play, a parrot's obsessive repetition of the word "House" offers such an extreme version; the bird is not capable of linguistic communication, but nonetheless wears an acoustic mask that mirrors the materialism of its human surroundings.

The central premise of *Comedy of Vanity* is a government edict banning mirrors, photographs, or any other human likeness that might promote vanity. Although the content of the edict seems like an extreme interpretation of the biblical first commandment, the form in which it is carried out (a huge bonfire) reflects the book burnings in Nazi Germany shortly after Hitler's seizure of power. It is unfortunate that, like *Auto-da-Fé,* these early works were denied the full effect they might have had in their own time. (Canetti was, literally, not alone in having his literary career fatefully altered by the war. His wife, the former Veza Taubner-Calderon, whom he married in 1934, was at the time of their marriage a more successful author than her husband, having published several short stories in Vienna's *Arbeiter-Zeitung* and elsewhere, whereas Canetti had published nothing. Veza's creativity was disrupted by the flight to England, however, and she did not publish for the remainder of her life. Three of her books are now available under the name Veza Canetti.)

Canetti's third play, *The Numbered* (1952; also translated as *Life-Terms,* 1982), dramatizes Canetti's most radical philosophical position: his opposition to death. Instead of names, the characters in this play have numbers assigned by a government bureaucrat that signify the age at which they will die. Government regulation and control of death, although they do away with murder and aggression (both pointless, because death is preordained), lead to other undesirable social by-products such as the devaluation of those "destined" to die young. It is taboo to reveal one's birth date, which is engraved in a locket that holds the key to both age and life expectancy; but one citizen becomes skeptical of the entire system, breaks his locket, and discovers that it is empty, a fraud. Perhaps one may read into this taboo—breaking Canetti's wish that death itself may one day be revealed as a fraud.

The tortured history of the reception of Canetti's early works deserves further, biographically based comment, for Canetti's life story both underscores and radically questions his multiple identities as an Austrian, a bearer of German culture, a pan-European citizen, a Jew, and even a literary artist or *Dichter.* Canetti was born in Ruschuk, Bulgaria, in 1905, to Sephardic Jewish parents who had fallen in love in Vienna after being drawn together by their common love for that city's Burgtheater. Because German was the "secret language" that united his parents in love and literature, the child Elias was attracted to this language and to Vienna long before he himself experienced either. Early in his autobiography, Canetti notes that most of the Sephardic Jews he knew were still Turkish citizens and that the Ottoman Empire had treated them better than it treated Christians. Thus Canetti's earliest identity spans not only Eastern and Western Europe, but also the traditional enemy of a Europe conceived as Christian, the great Muslim empire. The Canetti family moved to Manchester, England, when Elias was five; here, he added French and English to his Spanish (Ladino), Bulgarian, Hebrew, and snippets of Turkish. Canetti did not learn German until age eight, and then under traumatic circumstances: his father's sudden and unexpected death prompted Canetti's mother to take him and his two younger brothers "back" to Vienna, where she forcibly taught him German in a period of three months. It seems likely that this powerful personal legacy played as strong a role as any cultural or literary considerations in Canetti's later unwavering loyalty to the German language while in exile.

These events are related in Canetti's three-volume autobiography, which some critics such as Sander Gilman and Dagmar Barnouw consider his finest work; this appeal seems due in equal measure to the international odyssey of the life itself and to the vivid engagement with which it is told. The three volumes—*The Tongue Set Free, The Torch in My Ear,* and *The Play of the Eyes*—offer a highly readable, but also very subjective, account of European intellectual and cultural life from 1905 to 1938. Canetti's early travels across Europe not only gave him a core identity as a pan-European, but also mirrored the cosmopolitan nature of what was Habsburg Austria, which prided itself on being a *Vielvölkerstaat,* or state of many nations. Within this "multicultural" context, however, it was always clear that German language and culture had the upper hand. It is therefore no coincidence that Canetti's mother, a member of the Jewish middle class concerned with economic and social status, would take her sons to the capital and teach them German, rather than returning to the backwater of Ruschuk. Whatever emotional considerations played a role in her decision, they were supported by strong practical incentives.

The "class distinction" between the lowly Eastern Jews and the assimilated German Jews is made palpable in numerous ways in Canetti's autobiography. The beginning of *The Tongue Set Free* fairly bursts with the child's excitement at the varied experiences his village provides him. He is proud to recite the child's question at Passover (but oddly "translates" the holiday for his readers as "Easter"). Already as a child, however, he is ashamed of a grandfather who claims he speaks seventeen languages, including some Western ones, although he has never left the Balkans. On his only visit back to his extended family in Bulgaria as an adult, Canetti experiences the East as a backward place where individuality is squelched by the demands of family, and he vents his own feelings of oppression in a misogynistic tirade against a female cousin.

Canetti's ambivalence toward his Jewish origins can be seen clearly in his relationships with two father figures who embody different aspects of Jewish heritage and identity. During the early 1930s, Canetti made a daily pilgrimage to the coffeehouse table of a man he called "Dr. Sonne" (Dr. Sun). This solitary scholar was himself an Eastern Jew whose family had lived in Przemysl, and who had published Hebrew poetry under the name Abraham ben Yitzchak. From him, Canetti learned to appreciate the riches of the Sephardic poetic tradition and above all the Hebrew Bible. Discussing Martin Buber's new translation with Dr. Sonne was, Canetti (1980) writes, "my opportunity to learn the wording [of the Prophets] in the original language. Until then, I had avoided such knowledge; it would have made me feel trapped to learn more about things so close to my roots." Whether Canetti's avoidance of things Jewish was assimilationism, self-hatred, or merely a young adult's rebellion against the limitations of tradition and provenance, it was in some measure shared by Dr. Sonne himself, who participated in a dance of denial: "He never used the word 'Jew' to refer to either me or himself" (Canetti 1980).

Another father figure, closer to the Jewish religion but far more removed from Canetti, provokes feelings of shame in the author at his loss of Jewish heritage. In *The Voices of Marrakesh,* Canetti records his impressions of a trip to Morocco in 1954. He is fascinated by the Mellah, the slum-like Jewish quarter; there, Canetti is overcome by "boundless love" for an acquaintance's father, a scholar of scripture who reads all night. Their meeting takes place in silence, because they have no language in common, and Canetti avoids a second meeting by turning down an invitation to celebrate Purim with the family: "I imagined his father's disappointment at my ignorance of the old customs. I would have done everything wrong, and I could only have said the prayers like someone who never prays. I was ashamed in the face of the old man, whom I loved." Love and distance, secret communication and silence, reverence and rejection characterize Canetti's paradoxical relationship to things Jewish and non-Western.

It is possible that the sense of shame in the above passage feeds from the guilt of a Holocaust survivor who did not take the Holocaust as an occasion to return to the beliefs and traditions of Judaism, or even to involve himself in the politics of the newly formed state of Israel. Nonetheless, Canetti's moral seriousness gains its full impetus and effect from the Holocaust. His immediate reaction to the war was a form of artistic asceticism: he abandoned his projected "Human Comedy of Madmen," which would have comprised seven novels in addition to the first, and forbade himself all literary activity until *Crowds and Power* was completed. He broke the taboo only once, for his third play. As a counterbalance to this work, in 1942 he began to keep an intellectual diary of "jottings" (*Aufzeichnungen*); these have been published in three volumes spanning fifty years. The jottings are Canetti's most spontaneous, unguarded self-revelation, because they are not structured with an eye to personal mythology as is the autobiography; this has led one scholar (Eigler) to view them as a Derridean "supplement" to the autobiography, a sort of autobiographical repressed. At the same time, the jottings are pruned into aphorisms that are carefully selected and cryptically encoded; many entries of a seemingly personal nature are phrased in the third person so that the reader never knows whether Canetti is revealing something of himself, recording the attitudes of a friend, or making a general observation about human nature.

Aside from the immediate outrage expressed in his entries from the war years, Canetti's first extended reckoning with the war occurs in two essays from 1971, published in *The Conscience of Words.* **"Hitler According to Speer,"** Canetti's response to Speer's diaries containing his monumental architectural plans for Berlin, would have become a discussion of fascist aesthetics in the hands of any other writer. But Canetti is interested in the content of this aesthetic, particularly as it concords with his findings in *Crowds and Power.* The virtuosity with which he applies his own terminology to Speer's and Hitler's plans suggests that *Crowds and Power,* however early it may have been conceived, was in its execution always guided by the phenomenon of Hitler. Speer's plans are emblems of Hitler's power, not only because of their size, but also because of their intended use in forming and maintaining the crowds on which Hitler depended. Hitler's truest subjects, however, are the masses of dead: the dead of World War I, those he had assassinated, the soldiers who would fall in his own war, and those he gassed. Canetti compares Hitler's paranoiac nature with his own discussion of the Schreber case, the conclusion of *Crowds and Power,* once more strengthening the impression that the longer work is a response to Hitler.

In the second essay, **"Dr. Hachiya's Hiroshima Diary,"** Canetti turns to the "other" holocaust. Although he elsewhere makes the threat of nuclear war the most important issue confronting the human race (in *The Sundered Future*), here Canetti is concerned with the morality of surviving a catastrophe. Canetti repeatedly distances himself culturally from the Japanese doctor, who is a Buddhist and a believer in the emperor, yet he also confesses that he has understood the Japanese better through this piece of writing than any other. No wonder, because Canetti is in the same survivor position as this doctor, who must try to cure the victims of a disease he does not understand. When the doctor pays his respects to the dead by praying for each one of them at the site of their death, the religiously skeptical Canetti seems to concur that such piety is the only way to survive with one's own dignity intact and without succumbing to the crass position of power inherent in survival. It is typical of Canetti that he does not address the question of his own survivorship directly, but displaces it onto a cultural "other."

In Canetti's penultimate volume of jottings, *Die Fliegenpein* (*The Agony of Flies*; 1992), he makes a rare first-person confession that summarizes his difficult position as a secular humanist Jewish writer: "My stubborn resistance to the Bible, which kept me away from it for decades, has to do with the fact that I never wanted to give in to my origin. . . . I didn't want to lead an intellectual life that was predetermined from the outset, I didn't want a *prescribed* intellectual life. I wanted to be surprised and overpowered again and again, and thereby gradually become a friend and connoisseur of all that is human. I could not simply accept the preponderance of the Biblical that has marked the world for so long."

Referring only obliquely to his Jewishness, Canetti seems to include the worldwide influence of Christianity under colonialism in his rejection of the biblical. He thus both claims and rejects not only Hebrew Scripture, but also the New Testament as part of his origin, and he opposes both of these narrowly scriptural traditions to a post-Enlightenment notion of humanity that Canetti always aspired to know in its entirety.

Bibliography

Elias Canetti, *Das Augenspiel: Lebensgeschichte, 1931-1937* (Munich: Hanser, 1985); Canetti, *Die Blendung* (Munich: Hanser, 1963); Canetti, *Dramen* (Munich: Hanser, 1964); Canetti, *Die Fackel im Öhr: Lebensgeschichte, 1921-1931* (Munich: Hanser, 1980); Canetti, *Die Fliegenpein: Aufzeichnungen* (Munich: Hanser, 1992); Canetti, *Das Geheimherz der Uhr: Aufzeichnungen, 1973-1985* (Munich: Hanser, 1987); Canetti, *Die gerettete Zunge: Geschichte einer Jugend* (Munich: Hanser, 1977); Canetti, *Die gespaltene Zukunft: Aufsätze und Gespräche* (Munich: Hanser, 1972); Canetti, *Das Gewissen der Worte: Essays* (Munich: Hanser, 1975); Canetti, *Masse und Macht* (Hamburg: Claassen, 1960); Canetti, *Die Provinz des Menschen: Aufzeichnungen, 1942-1972* (Munich: Hanser, 1973); Canetti, *Die Stimmen von Marrakesch* (Munich: Hanser, 1978); Veza Canetti, *Die gelbe Straße* (Munich: Hanser, 1990); V. Canetti, *Geduld bringt Rosen* (Munich: Hanser, 1992); Friederike Eigler, *Das autobiographische Werk von Elias Canetti* (Tübingen: Stauffenberg, 1988); Eigler, *Essays in Honor of Elias Canetti*, trans. Michael Hulse (New York: Farrar, Straus, Giroux, 1987); Kristie A. Foell, *Blind Reflections: Gender in Elias Canetti's "Die Blendung"* (Riverside, Calif.: Ariadne Press, 1994); Richard H. Lawson, *Understanding Elias Canetti* (Columbia: University of South Carolina Press, 1991); Barbara Meili, *Erinnerung und Vision: Der lebensgeschichtliche Hintergrund von Elias Canetti's Roman "Die Blendung"* (Bonn: Bouvier, 1985); and Gerald Stieg, *Frucht des Feuers: Canetti, Doderer, Kraus und der Justizpalastbrand* (Vienna: Edition Falter im Österreichischen Bundesverlag, 1990).

Michael Mack (essay date 1999)

SOURCE: Mack, Michael. "*Die Blendung* as a Negative Poetics: Positivism, Nihilism, Fascism." *Orbis Litterarum* 54, no. 2 (1999): 146-60.

[*In the following essay, Mack posits that Canetti proposes a negative poetics in* Die Blendung, *demonstrating what the poet should not be, which in turn leads to a better understanding of* Crowds and Power.]

In this essay I shall discuss Canetti's novel ***Die Blendung*** in relation to Canetti's poetics, which in turn influenced his friend Franz Baermann Steiner's image of the poet.[1] Peter Kien—the novel's main protagonist—embodies the positivist scholar whose rationalism consists in nihilism, which mirrors fascism, rather than opposing it. Kien's skepticism opposes Steiner's and Canetti's poetics: indeed his specialism precludes any form of radicalism and as a result it also prevents the existence of a world in which death is transcended through a belief in metamorphosis. Kien figures as an anti-type of Canetti's image of the poet, who unites knowledge and social responsibility.

Canetti's poetics originates in an examination of language: according to Canetti, in poetic language knowledge and social responsibility interpenetrate.[2] Canetti's self-depiction as a poet points to a trust in the force of language; and indeed in an interview with Joachim Schickel Canetti speaks of his "wirklich magische Beziehung zu Namen" (magical relation to language).[3] By calling himself a poet, therefore, Canetti makes it clear that he is aware of the power which his words can exert. The poet masters language, but he can also master through language. This recognition of the power of language occurs to Canetti as a young child. The first part of his autobiography ***Die Gerettete Zunge*** (***The Tongue set free***) opens with a threat: the threat of having the tongue cut out.[4] Here two spheres of power confront each other; one is physical might, the other is the transcending dimension that the tongue can set free. In this way the opening of ***Die Gerettete Zunge*** can be read as a parable, a parable of Canetti as a poet who sets great store by language, and as an intellectual who, by virtue of language's transcending force, influences social thought and practice. As an intellectual Canetti has learned from his childhood experience that those who wield physical power are most keen on eliminating the power of language which might oppose them. Canetti saw the justification of his claim to public responsibility confirmed by the rise of fascism and by the Holocaust in particular. In the novel ***Die Blendung,*** whose criticism of the positivist scholar Peter Kien will be discussed below, Canetti depicts a world which foreshadows the approach of fascism and the crimes of the Nazis.[5] Canetti emphasises that he wrote the novel under the impact of the upsurge of Nazism in an interview with Raphaël Sorin:

> Je sentais que des choses terribles se préparaient. Ce pressentiment fut confirmé lors de mon séjour à Berlin en 1928 et 1929. Je vis alors les marches et les bagarres entre les nazis et les socialistes. Mon livre est donc né dans un climat d'agitation et de fureur. Il porte en lui, sans que ce soit toujours bien caché, les marques de ces circonstances tragiques.[6]

I will show how Canetti criticises an ethically non-committed type of intellectual under the impact of the approach of Nazism. Peter Kien, the scholar who deliberately seeks isolation mirrors an atomised society that drifts towards a totalitarian mass-state in which history realises horrid fantasies, and in which rationality serves irrational ends.[7] The rationalist scholar Kien can be called a nihilist in that he devalues any form of life that has nothing to do with the abstractions of his specialist field of study. Kien's nihilism reflects the grotesque and nihilist form of representation whose signs are either empty or tend to entropy. In an important essay Robert Elbaz and Leah Hadomi show how signification in *Die Blendung* "hovers between being and non-being, much as the novel is caught between the representation of a senseless reality and its nullification."[8]

In his representation of a fragmented society and in his critique of the positivist Kien Canetti develops a negative poetics: he shows what a responsible poet should not be as well as what he should work against. This poetics paves the way to a better understanding of *Masse und Macht*. David Darby has rightly criticised scholars who use the later work (*Masse und Macht*) as an explanation of the earlier one (*Die Blendung*). Rather *Die Blendung* helps to explain Canetti's social-ethical project in *Masse und Macht,* which is, as I have argued elsewhere, a response to the Holocaust.[9] In *Masse und Macht* Canetti examines non-Western communities; as an anthropologist he stands in close proximity to Kien's scholarly discipline, sinology. *Masse und Macht* is a scholarly book, written by someone who spent years reading anthropological studies. Indeed, Canetti encourages his readers to do the same by offering them a huge bibliography. Yet Canetti transgresses conventional scholarship by both writing in a narrative manner and by avoiding specialisation.

Given that Canetti presents himself as quite 'bookish,' one might wonder why he does not employ the notion of a *poeta doctus,* rather than that of a Dichter. The reason he abstains from calling himself a poeta doctus or a social scientist perhaps lies in the fact that all these scholarly words might move him into a self-enclosed world as described in *Die Blendung.* Peter Kien represents the scholar as the anti-type of Canetti's image of the poet: if the poet is 'der Hüter der Verwandlung' (the guardian of metamorphosis),[10] if the poet makes room in his breast for all human and spiritual voices, then Kien's hermeticism and his uncommunicative attitude preclude such openness.[11] In *Die Blendung* Canetti portrays the scholar as someone who follows the derangement of his time instead of opposing it.

When they focus on his alleged powerlessness, many critics fail to see that Kien himself exercises power over his books.[12] Following this line of thinking, Jutta Paal has recently perceived a dichotomy between Peter Kien as an 'enlightened intellectual' and the other protagonists of the novel who discard the humanitarian ideals of the enlightenment. I shall show that Kien's scholarship does not represent enlightenment ideals (it is far too cut off from social concerns to do so) rather it

depicts the realisation of a positivist agenda. Kien is a madman in a world that has generally turned mad: no protagonist can be called sane, all are obsessed by an idée fixe.[13]

This *idée fixe* turns each character into an isolated world, and, as a result, they are all unable to form intimate relationships: Therese loves money which, she thinks, might be earned by marrying Peter Kien, Peter Kien, in turn only marries Therese because he is impressed by the care she apparently takes for books; Pfaff only courts his daughter and Therese in order to satisfy his sadism, and Georg Kien has nothing on his mind apart from being revered in his hospital like a god. This implies that every figure in the novel has an absolutist approach to his/her interests; they are all blind-folded by the desires for which they live; and this act of being blindfolded is well conveyed in the German title *Die Blendung*: which has etymological connections with the word blind.[14] This act of blinding has a further connotation, as the noun 'Blendung' or the verb 'blenden' are often used in connection with the blinding force of pure light: a 'Blendung' can describe the process of being blinded by the sun, and indeed Jacob and Wilhelm Grimm define 'blenden' as 'das Blenden der Sonne.'[15] Similarly the title of Canetti's novel evokes the dazzling power of the sun. Light often functions as a metaphor for enlightenment. This connection to the idea of enlightenment is also present in the original title of the novel *Kant Fängt Feuer* which suggests the end of enlightenment in fire; and in so doing it emphasises the novel's concern with the deadlock, the utter helplessness of an enlightenment that is unable to reflect critically upon its own enterprise, and which results in being an instrument for domination and reification.[16]

In *Die Blendung* light achieves the opposite of enlightenment; light, as the title makes clear, dazzles those who come in contact with it, rather than clearing up their vision. Against this background it is not surprising that Kien walls up the windows of his room: his scholarly pursuits, his positivist approach make him shy away from the light of the sun. The rationalist can only survive as nihilist. The positivist who devalues any form of material existence cannot face the sun, whose light brings out the contour of things. Walling up the windows of his study also serves as an image for the isolation to which, as discussed above, all characters of the novel fall prey. In this respect one cannot find any difference in the behaviour of Peter Kien on the one hand and his brother, Pfaff, and Therese, on the other: all take their world to be absolute. Whether it is a head without a world, or world without a head, what we encounter is a universe which is fragmented in the extreme; it is a world in which parts exist on their own and shy away from making contacts with their surroundings. It is this atomisation of society which undermines the validity of a combination of materialism and religiosity and which, as a consequence, disrupts social cohesion. Atomisation and its social consequences eventually lead to the madness of crowds.[17] As for his friend Franz Baermann Steiner, Canetti criticises individualism which paradoxically destroys individuality.[18] Steiner's analysis of atomisation in his aphorisms echoes Canetti's implicit critique of fragmentation in *Die Blendung*.

When one recalls Canetti's aim of avoiding specialisation in scholarship the inability of a scholarly intellectual to offer an alternative to a world that collapses into entropy is quite striking. Kien is a caricature of the specialist. Indeed, for him the 'truth' can only be found if the scholar ignores everything that has nothing to do with his area of research. This might have an autobiographical reference in Canetti's chemical research.[19] LaCapra's definition of positivism as being a narrowly focused discourse that "avoids or occludes the very problem of a critical theory of society and culture" fits Kien's specialist pursuits well.[20] Kien's undertaking is quite a contrast to the anthropological projects of both Canetti and F. B. Steiner, who want to have a social-ethical impact on modern Western society:

> Man nähert sich der Wahrheit, indem man sich von den Menschen abschloß. Der Alltag war ein oberflächliches Gewirr von Lügen. Soviele Passanten, soviele Lügner. Drum sah er sie gar nicht an.
>
> (*Bl* [*Die Blendung*], p. 14)

> You draw closer to the truth by shutting yourself off from mankind. Daily life was a superficial clatter of lies. Every passer-by was a liar. For that reason he never looked at them.
>
> (*AF* [*Auto-da-Fé*], p. 18)

The antithetical structure of the first sentence here mirrors Kien's way of thinking, which only allows for absolutes: drawing closer to the truth has to amount to a denial of social life; and any form of life in his own society antithetically precludes a drawing closer to the truth. This antithesis between truth, on the one hand, and ethics on the other, also indicates a deep split between spirit and concrete, physical reality. In Kien's mind there is a gap between these two entities which cannot be bridged.

This division between spirit and every-day reality leads to Kien's disgust with physical reality as such. The loss of an ethical perspective that unites different parts of society by means of a combination of knowledge and a sense of social responsibility—which finds its equivalent in the relation between truth and ethics as propounded by Hayden White—becomes a main cause of Kien's positivism.[21] Kien's positivist nihilism that does not allow for a rationality embedded in a value system and transcends the instrumental concerns of scholarly

enquiries, ironically outdoes itself in its main point of reference. David Darby has shown how Kien's repeated reference to Berkley's *Principles* undermines his own scholarly objectives. Berkley, "rather than affirming the autonomy of the individual subject's perceptions," argues "against the skepticism implicit in the reading adopted by Kien and the schoolmen."[22] Although Kien disbelieves any kind of creed that might integrate his scholarship into a societal-religious context, Kien clings to a secular religion. John Milbank's analysis of positivism as replacing religion only to "become itself religion" offers an explanation for Peter Kien's wish to figure as an *imago Christi*.[23] Kien indeed identifies with Christ, as a saviour of books rather than man. Kien as a self-perceived miracle-working figure differs from Christ only in that his martyrdom testifies exclusively to the absolutism of specialist scholarship.

Kien's secular religion results in his disgust with humanity. As a scholar who only looks for the truth, he can never look at people with whom he walks on the street. Although he actually walks with these people, he strongly desires to dissociate himself from them completely. As a consequence he mentally robs all these pedestrians of their humanity, calling them a 'mass'. A mass is primarily a quantitative term and it precludes any notion of a qualitative one, like that of humanity. This disgust with the 'masses' also implies that Kien has no interest in influencing the ethical behaviour of the public. This becomes apparent when he declares his solitude to be independent of the opinion of the 'mob':

> . . . er lebe ja allein, was der Wissenschaft nütze, sei der Menge an Wichtigkeit voraus.
>
> (*Bl*, p. 70)

> He lived alone; the service of knowledge was more important than the opinion of the mob.
>
> (*AF*, p. 77)

Kien conceives of knowledge as something which cannot be shared; that is why we never learn anything about the actual substance of his scholarship. Timms noticed this absence of any presentation of Kien's scholarly inquiries:

> Kien, as Canetti represents him has no inner life. We may be told time and again that his mind is filled with oriental erudition, but these values are never shown.

> The reference in the opening scene of the novel to the wisdom of Mencius (Mong Tse) raises expectations of an intellectual feast which are never fulfilled. This failure to give the reader access to Kien's inner life seems to me to constitute the major limitation of Canetti's novel. It is a novel about the intellect which tells us nothing about the intellect—the richness of the mind replete with scholarship or of an imagination fired by the vision of an alternative culture.[24]

In comparison to Karl Kraus, Canetti does not give a vision of China that offers an alternative to occidental shortcomings; yet one might ask whether this constitutes a failure. It would be truer to say that Canetti consciously represents Kien with this limitation in order to show the incommunicative character of this kind of scholar. If the reader learned anything of the fruits of Kien's research he/she would have the impression of someone who can engage in dialogue. Kien's solipsism is, however, one of his most striking features, and Canetti would have been inconsistent, if he had presented the scholar's imaginative, or excitingly learned inward wealth. Kien perceives any form of communication as succumbing to the lures of the "masses," while Canetti wants to have an impact on the social behaviour of the public. In contrast to Kien the scholar, Canetti the poet seeks to win the attention of a huge audience.

Canetti's preference for a non-specialist audience accounts for his all-encompassing approach as an anthropological writer. This is in fact one reason for the amazing scope of the issues and indeed of the geographical distance dealt with in *Masse und Macht*: Canetti here moves from Siberia to Africa, from Australia to the North-pole, from America to India. Not only does Canetti break down the barriers between specialised fields of scholarly research; he also bridges the gap between the physical and the intellectual which for Peter Kien remains unbridgeable. This radical difference can be seen in a key aspect of the scholarly work: in *Masse und Macht,* the human body features as a main point of departure to ground Canetti's theory of human aggression. Unlike Kien he uses the empirical evidence gathered by workers in the field, such as anthropologists and thinkers concerned with the physical character of life.

The universalist approach of Canetti as a scholar and poet sharply contrasts with Kien's specialisation in ancient China. But it even goes further than that: Kien's scholarship depends on the intellectual force of the scholar only, whereas Canetti's notion of the *Dichter* presupposes the absence of a clearly defined individuality. The scholar Peter Kien only exists when he holds on to his individuality as a positivist scientist. The poet Elias Canetti, on the other hand, only comes into being when the individual Elias Canetti falls silent. Kien, the scholar, wants to affirm his distinctive personality; Canetti, the poet opens up his personality in a chain of metamorphoses:

> Ein Dichter bin *ich* nicht: ich kann nicht schweigen. Aber viele Menschen in mir schweigen, die ich nicht kenne. Ihre Ausbrüche machen mich manchmal zum Dichter.
>
> *(Aphorismen* p. 254)

> *I* am not a poet. I cannot be silent. But many men are silent within me, whom I do not know. Their eruptions sometimes transform me into a poet.
>
> (My transl.)

Most important here is the italicised 'ich' upon whose negation the existence of Elias Canetti as *Dichter* depends. This 'ich' would be a poet as 'ich,' if it could always be silent, but, as Canetti makes clear, he cannot achieve this silence of the individual which is the prerequisite for the true poet. As it is, Canetti's *Dichtung* can only come into being when the one who writes falls asleep, and the alien voices which normally refrain from speaking, burst out into language. Only at these moments does Canetti write as a *Dichter,* and yet at these moments he clearly loses his individuality. One can perhaps best understand this notion of the poet as having lost all features belonging to the individual person who writes, when one recalls John Keats's notion of negative capability. Like Canetti's, Keats's poetics heavily relies on the concept of metamorphosis: the poet is only capable of writing poetry when he can negate his individuality and metamorphose into different figures which speak through him. In this way Keats's negative capability characterises the poet as the mere receiver of voices other than himself. Keats the poet appears as an Aeolian harp upon which the vocal pressure of his poem's protagonists play. The Romantic image of the Aeolian harp, and the Keatsian concept of negative capability greatly influenced modernist writers like T. S. Eliot. One could draw attention to James Joyce's famous words: when Joyce was in a café, he said that not he, but all the people around him actually wrote his novels; rather than being a writer, Joyce is a listener, who registers all that is given to the human in language. Canetti arranged to be buried beside James Joyce in Zürich. He similarly admired Fernando Pessoa who assumed a dozen different individualities, each having a distinctive poetic voice. There are many more references in modernist writing (Pirandello for example) in which the poet transforms into different personalities. It is against the background of this Romantic and modernist understanding of the poet that we should examine Canetti's notion of the *Dichter.* As a consequence, writing verse does not characterise a poet; rather it is his capability to undergo transformations; it is the openness which allows a multitude of voices into the heart of the writer. After the Holocaust the voices that haunt Canetti cannot be those set in tone by Keats's Aeolian harp; they need to be voices of utter darkness filled with death and all possible imaginable brutalities that has become a reality in the Nazi concentration camps.

Canetti's study of the 'masses' goes hand in hand with his listening to the voices of the victims of Nazi terror. By contrast, Kien's monoperspectival view of life results in his hatred of 'uneducated people':

> Immer und ausnahmslos nehme man sich vor den Leuten der Masse in acht . . . sie sind gefährlich, weil sie keine Bildung, also keinen Verstand haben.
>
> *(Bl,* p. 95)

. . . we must beware of these people of the masses. They are dangerous, because they have no education, which is as much as to say no understanding.

(*AF,* p. 103)

Kien's hatred of the 'masses' coincides with his refusal to have any impact on the ethical behaviour of his readership. Kien would argue that such an impact cannot be made because of the lack of education which one generally finds in the public. For Kien, lack of education means absence of learning, and with this absence of learning no understanding whatever is possible. As we will see later, Canetti the *Dichter* makes 'experience' part of his concept of education (*Bildung*). Kien, however, transposes any experience on the street into the realm of his library, and there, we suddenly see him needing the masses; we encounter a paranoid ruler, who would be unhappy without a mass-following. Canetti-scholarship has often taken Georg Kien's comment on the lack of a collective urge in his brother as an authorial commentary.[25] Georg Kien argues that intellectuals like his brother have no idea of a collective urge:

> Von der viel tieferen und eigentlichen Triebkraft der Geschichte, den Drang des Menschen, in eine höhere Tiergattung, die Masse, aufzugehen, und sich darin vollkommen zu verlieren, als hätte es nie einen Menschen gegeben, ahnten sie nichts. Denn sie waren gebildet, und Bildung ist ein Festungsgürtel des Individuums gegen die Masse in ihm selbst.

(*Bl,* p. 446)

> Of that far deeper and most special motive force of history, the desire of men to rise into a higher type of animal, into the mass, and to lose themselves in it so completely as to forget that one man ever existed, they had no idea. For they were educated men, and education is a cordon sanitaire for the individual against the mass of his own soul.

(*AF,* p. 461)

If Georg Kien knew that his brother had an idea of a mass-drive, he would have been able to anticipate the burning of the books with which the novel closes. The reader, on the other hand, learns after the first hundred pages that Peter Kien knows about the desire of losing oneself in a mass. In the chapter *Mobilisation* Kien addresses books as a kind of 'Hetzmasse' (rabble-rousing crowd); he wants to de-individualise each of them:

> Noch sind wir in der Lage, als unverletzte, geschlossene Körperschaft, einer für alle, und alle für einen, zur Abwehr zu rüsten.

(*Bl,* p. 96)

> We are still in the position of a complete and self-sufficient body, to arm ourselves in our own defence, one for all and all for one.

(*AF,* p. 104)

One for all and all for one is exactly the kind of slogan Nazis use to abolish their personality and immerse themselves in the 'all' of the crowd. The chiasmus of the 'one for all and all for one' construction stresses the lack of any distinction between the members of the crowd. Kien, who has despised the 'masses' on the street, turns into a mass-organiser within the walls of his library, and even when he angrily calls pedestrians a 'mob', he actually creates it by using the word.

However, Kien not only feels himself at one with the 'masses' of his books, he also appears as ruler who employs the sting of death as his main weapon:

> 2) die Verräter verfallen der Feme. 3) das Kommando ist zentralisiert. Ich bin oberster Kriegsherr, einziger Führer und Offizier.

> 2) The traitors will be shot out of hand. 3) That all authority is united in one man. That I am commander-in-chief, sole leader and officer in command.

'Commander-in-chief', 'sole leader' 'officer' and 'command,' all of these words are used to describe the character of the ruler in *Masse und Macht.* Kien in fact displays the disgust of 'masses' as the desire to bring these 'masses' into existence so as to be able to rule them. Ironically the books refuse to be transformed into a de-individualised 'mass': Kant, Hegel, Schopenhauer, all of them insist on their personalities.

Whereas Kien the scholar desires to create masses out of individuals, Canetti the Dichter makes room in his heart for a variety of individual voices. In order to find room for these voices the poet must have undergone experiences which opened his heart for a multitude of different lives and sentiments; and it is this kind of experience which Kien fears most. According to Canetti, the poet must have experienced how other people think as well as feel in order to be able to communicate with them, and Canetti perceives this union between scholarship and experience (which is exactly what Kien lacks) in Herodotus.[26]

In contrast to Kien's scholarship, Herodotus's learning is in Canetti's view innocent, because it wants to communicate. Whereas Kien confirms scholarship only in terms of specialisation, Herodotus subdivides different people not according to further specialist fields of knowledge; rather, he wants to open up space for different voices through the subdivision, and thanks to this experience of the 'other' he makes room in the heart of his readers who experience this otherness by reading him.

The interrelation between knowledge and social responsibility moves scholarship into the realm of ethics. This mode of poetic writing is not fictional since it is invested with the authority of empirical (experience) and scholarly (knowledge) facts. Dagmar Barnouw uses the notion 'anthropologische Phantasie' in order to convey the hybrid state of *Masse und Macht* between scholarly and imaginative writing.[27] In reading the works of Jakob Burkhardt, Canetti encounters such bodily scholarship, which also fits into his category of poetry as it allows for an infinity of voices.[28] In Jakob Burkhardt's writing, Canetti finds a bodily form of scholarship that is at the same time poetry, because it bestows new names on a reality that seemed to be isolated. A new name transforms the thing it denotes; it creates a universe that dissolves into a flux of metamorphoses. This world of transformation evokes a feeling of 'körperlicher Erweiterung'[29] (bodily expansion) in the reader; the world which this kind of scholarship inhabits is therefore bodily indeed.

As a scholar Canetti opens up the bodily experience of his readers through a chain of metamorphoses. The scholar as the guardian of metamorphoses exactly covers Canetti's definition of the Dichter as 'Hüter der Verwandlung', and it is indeed very close to that of Franz B. Steiner who calls the poet 'der einzige Hüter der Mythen aller Völker' (the only guardian of the myths of all peoples).[30] In his speech **'Der Beruf des Dichters'** (1976), Canetti refers to the myths of primitive peoples as the richest source for his notion of 'metamorphosis.' In this speech Canetti expresses his gratitude to social anthropology for having preserved the myths of 'primitive' people who have already died out or are in the process of dying out, but he contrasts the scholar who collects these myth with the poet who can bring them to life again ("Für seine Rettung [of mythical experiences] kann man der Wissenschaft nicht genug dankbar sein; seine eigentliche Bewahrung, seine Auferstehung zu unserem Leben, ist Sache der Dichter.").[31] For Canetti myths offer an immense richness of metamorphoses. This connection between myth and the ability to believe in the reality of ideas such as metamorphosis has been made in E. B. Tylor's *Primitive Culture,* a book which Canetti cites in his bibliography to *Masse und Macht* and which Steiner would have been familiar with as an anthropologist. Tylor sees the poet as a remnant of primitivism within modernity; the poet still belongs to the 'mythologic stage of thought' that characterises primitive thinking:

> A poet of our day has still much in common with the minds of uncultured tribes in the mythologic stage of thought. The rude man's imagination may be narrow, crude and repulsive, while the poet's more conscious fictions may be highly wrought into shapes of fresh artistic beauty, but both share in that sense of the reality of ideas which fortunately or unfortunately modern education has proved so powerful to destroy.[32]

Modern poet and savage alike take ideas for reality: what they cannot grasp as a reality proved by empirical test is nevertheless real, in fact, the 'primitive' does not differentiate between the empirical and the metaphysical, between the immanent and the transcendent. For the 'primitive' myths themselves are empirical. Tylor's concept of the 'mythologic stage of thought' coincides with Steiner's and Canetti's understanding of myths as grounded in empirical reality: the empirical itself is seen as the mythological.

Tylor's interpretation of the modern poet as a remnant of the 'primitive' in modern culture contributes a great deal to the understanding of Steiner's and Canetti's definition of the 'Dichter.' Canetti's 'Hüter der Verwandlung' takes ideas of metamorphosis as a reality, otherwise he would not be able to transform himself into a variety of animal and human identities. The concept of metamorphosis presupposes a union between knowledge and belief. The one who undergoes metamorphosis needs to have an image of the empirical as a fluid entity, in which bodies can flood as easily and as quickly as ideas in the mind. According to Steiner and Canetti, therefore, a mythological world presumes a perception of the empirical that is radically different from that of the modern scientific world; it has to be a perception that does not distinguish between ideas and empirical facts, instead it has to perceive the empirical as driven by ideas. Metamorphosis can only be a real force in a society which is mythical. In a mythical society knowledge has not been separated from belief. As a consequence, the Dichter as 'Hüter der Verwandlung' takes care of a mythological world that is deeply threatened by the rationalist-nihilistic world-view of modern science.[33] Interestingly, Canetti, following Tylor and Steiner, explains the link between metamorphosis and myth in *Der Beruf des Dichters*:

> Was aber neben allen spezifischen Einzelgehalten das Eigentliche der Mythen ausmacht, ist die in ihnen geübte Verwandlung. Sie ist es, durch die sich der Mensch erschaffen hat.
>
> (*GW* [*Das Gewissen der Worte*], p. 289)
>
> What, however characterises the essence of the myth—disregarding all specific singular features—is the metamorphosis which is practised in them. It is this by which man has created himself.
>
> (My transl.)

Here Canetti discusses metamorphosis as the main characteristic of a mythological world, but whereas Tylor is doubtful as to the merits of such 'primitive' state of mind (". . . fortunately or unfortunately modern education has proved so powerful to destroy") Canetti sees human identity as dependent on a mythological world in which the empirical still offers the possibility of metamorphosis.

Like Canetti, Steiner mourns the loss of what Tylor calls 'the mythologic stage of thought' and following Tylor's concept of the poet as a 'primitive', he calls the

Dichter the preserver of the myths of all peoples; of myths, that is to say, which embody a world capable of undergoing metamorphoses. 'Der einzige Hüter der Mythen aller Völker' moves the poet in fact into close proximity to the anthropologist of religion: an anthropologist of religion, who identifies with the 'primitive', undermining a modern diremption between knowledge and belief.

Canetti's poetics in many respects coincides with the anthropology of religion as advanced by F. B. Steiner.[34] In *Die Blendung* Canetti depicts the positivist scholar Kien as a representative of nihilism, which furthers the cause of fascism. Canetti's negative poetics contrasts with his image of the poet as a radical intellectual, who works for a mythological world in which knowledge and social responsibility interpenetrate. A connection between scholarship and literary modes of writing—in which myths are taken seriously—constitutes the style of *Masse und Macht.* The anthropological poetics implicit in *Masse und Macht* has its counter-image in the scholar Peter Kien of *Die Blendung.*

Notes

1. For Canetti's portrait of F. B. Steiner see: Canetti *Aufzeichnungen 1992-1993,* Zürich: Hanser 1996, pp. 17-24.

2. Interestingly Canetti characterises Steiner's poetry as the examination of words: "Dichten war für ihn ein Prüfen von Worten." (Canetti, 1996, p. 21). Similarly Steiner characterises himself as a 'prüfer' (F. B. Steiner *Eroberungen,* Heidelberg: Lamerbert Schneider, 1964, p. 50.)

3. "Gespräch mit Joachim Schickel": p. 104-131. In: Elias Canetti: *Die Gespaltene Zukunft,* München: Hanser, 1972.: p. 105.

4. See also discussions of this opening scene in: M. Barth: *Canetti versus Canetti/Identität, Macht und Masse im literarischen Werk Elias Canetti,* Frankfut a.M: P. Lang), 1994: p. 34-35, and: Hans Reiss: "The Writers Task: Some Reflections on Elias Canetti's Autobiography", in: A. Stevens (Ed.), *Elias Canetti. Londoner Symposium,* Stuttgart, 1991: pp. 45-58, p. 47.

5. Harriet Murphy depicts Canetti's novel as an self-referential aesthetic universe "devoid of concrete references" (Murphy: *Canetti and Nietzsche. Theories of Humor in Die Blendung,* New York: SUNY, 1997, p. 46). This may be true as far as the solipsism of the protagonists is concerned, but it distorts Canetti's social agenda.

6. R. Sorin "Souvenirs", in Blanc-Montmayer (Ed.) *Elias Canetti,* Paris: Édition du Centre Pompidou, 1995, pp. 51-57, p. 53.

7. R. Hartung has referred to the connection between atomisation and lack of moderation in "Fabel und Gestalt" in: *Literarische Revue* 3, 1948, pp. 341-47.

8. R. Elabaz and L. Hadomi "On Canetti's Novelistic Sign" in: *Orbis Litterarum,* Vol. 48, 1993, pp. 269-80, p. 272.

9. For a discussion of *Masse und Macht* as a response to the Holocaust see my article "'Representing the Holocaust'. Power, Death and Metamorphosis: An Examination of Elias Canetti's Use of Anthropological Sources" in *Masse und Macht.* (forthcoming in *Germanisch-Romanische Monatsschrift*).

10. E. Canetti *Das Gewissen der Worte,* Frankfurt a. M.: Fischer, 1985, p. 283.

11. For a discussion of Kien's one-sidedness see: A. Doppler: "'Der Hüter der Verwandlungen'. Canetti's Bestimmung des Dichters.": pp. 45-55. In: F. Aspertsberger and G. Stieg: *Blendung als Lebensform/Elias Canetti.* Königstein, 1985. M. Moser has argued that *Die Blendung* depicts the realisation of mad obsessions (Moser *Musil Canetti Eco Calvino. Die überholte Philosophie,* Vienna, 1986, pp. 72-73.

12. For a discussion of Kien's powerlessness see: D. Dissinger *Vereinzelung und Massenwahn,* Bonn: Bouvier, 1971, p. 185, and D. Roberts *Kopf und Welt,* München: Hanser 1975, p. 164.

13. For a discussion of the one-sidedness of all characters in the novel see: P. Russel: "The Vision of Man in Elias Canetti's *Die Blendung*" in: *German Life and Letters,* 1974: p. 24-35, and E. Timms: "Canetti, Kraus and China" in: Stevens, 1991: p. 21-31.

14. F. Kluge: *Etymologisches Wörterbuch,* Berlin, New York, 1982: p. 92.

15. Grimm: *Deutsches Wörterbuch/Zweiter Band,* Leipzig, 1860: p. 106.

16. Canetti's novel as a critique of enlightenment touches on many issues discussed in Horkheimer's and Adorno's *Dialektik der Aufklärung,* which is again a response to fascism.

17. Dissinger discusses the dialectic between individualism and the craving for an emergence in the crowd (Dissinger, 1971, p. 99).

18. For Steiner's critique of individualism see a short selection from his aphorisms: "Festellungen und Versuche", in: *Akzente,* 3, 1995, pp. 213-227.

19. Barbara Meili has pointed out coincidences between Canetti's autobiography and his only novel (Meili *Erinnerung und Vision,* Bonn: Bouvier, 1985).

20. D. LaCapra *Soundings in Critical Theory,* Ithaca: Cornell University Press, 1989, p. 13.

21. White argues for an interpenetration between truth and ethics in his essay on the Holocaust "Historical Employment and the Problem of Truth" in: Friedlander *Probing the Limits of Representation. Nazism and the 'Final Solution',* 1992, Havard U. P., pp. 22-36.

22. D. Darby *Structures of Disintegration. Narrative Strategies in Elias Canetti's 'Die Blendung'* Riverside, 1992, p. 52.

23. J. Milbank "Stories of Sacrifice: From Wellhausen to Girad" in: *Theory, Culture & Society,* Vol. 12, pp. 15-46, p. 27.

24. E. Timms: "Canetti, Kraus and China" in: Stevens, 1991, p. 28.

25. Stephan Wiesenhöfer takes Georg to be an authoritative commentator on all protagonists of the novel (S. Wiesenhöfer *Mythos zwischen Wahn Kunst. Elias Canettis Roman 'Die Blendung',* Munich: tuduv), 1987, p. 145). Recently Nicola Riedner has followed Georg's interpretation in seeing Peter Kien as separated from the masses (N. Riedner *Canetti's Fischerele. Eine Figur zwischen Masse, Macht und Blendung,* Würzburg: Könnigheusen & Neumann, 1995, p. 113. A notable exception of this absolutisation of Georg's view of his brother is Martin Bollacher (M. Bollacher "Elias Canetti: Die Blendung" in: P. M. Lützler *Deutsche Romane des 20. Jahrhunderts,* Königstein: Athenäum), 1983, pp. 237-254, p. 249.

26. For Canetti's view of Herodotus see *GZ,* [*Die gerettete Zunge*] p. 242.

27. Anthropologische Phantasie: "Canetti und Freud zum Phänomen der Masse" in: John Pattillo-Hess (Ed.) *Canettis Masse und Macht oder die Aufgabe des Gegenwärtigen Denkens,* Vienna: Bundesverlag, 1988, pp. 37-51, p. 38. For a discussion of the connection between Canetti's social responsibility and his interdisciplinary approach, see: Dagmar Barnouw "Masse, Macht und Tod im Werk von Elias Canetti" in: *Jahrbuch der Deutschen Schillergesellschaft,* 19, 1975, pp. 344-388, p. 345.

28. For Canetti's view of J. Burkhardt see *GZ,* p. 224.

29. *ibid.*

30. Steiner coined this phrase as a result of his close intellectual friendship with Canetti in the context of a commentary on his lyrical cycle *Eroberungen* (*E,* p. 125).

31. Canetti, 1985, p. 285.

32. E. B. Tylor: *Primitive Culture: Researches into the Development of Mythology, Philosophy, Religion, Art, and Custom,* Vol. 1, London, 1871: p. 284

33. In *Der Europäische Nihilismus* Heidegger has shown how much Nietzsche's nihilism is the outcome of Descarte's rationalism.

34. For a discussion of F. B. Steiner's and E. Canetti's poetics see my article "Dichter und Anthropologe: Franz Baermann Steiner's Auseinandersetzung mit dem Nationalsozialismus" in: *Mit der Ziehharmonika. Zeitschrift für Literatur des Exils und Widerstands,* Nr. 3, 1997.

Eugene Goodheart (essay date fall 2000)

SOURCE: Goodheart, Eugene. "The Power of Elias Canetti." *Partisan Review* LXVII, no. 4 (fall 2000): 613-21.

[*In the following essay, Goodheart provides an overview of themes in Canetti's works and finds that Canetti was above all a great observer of the human condition.*]

I met Elias Canetti in a café in Hampstead in 1965 while on a fellowship in London. The photo on the book jacket of a recent edition of his memoirs brings him back to me with a fidelity you rarely expect from photographs. He was stocky with a round well-fed face, a full head of hair, and a mustache. In the photo he is dressed in a three-piece suit and is seated behind a desk upon which lies a manuscript. He stares at the reader with what seems an attentive skepticism, the very picture of a cultivated European. At some point during our acquaintance, he presented me with a copy of his masterwork, *Crowds and Power* (1962), *Masse und Macht* (1960) in its original German version, the product of a thirty-five-year devotion. I dipped into the book, but never read it through until now. His other famous book is *Auto-da-fé* (1935) in which the library of its bibliophile hero, the paranoid sinologist Peter Kien, goes up in flames. Canetti would have appreciated the fate of my copy of *Crowds and Power.* It survived a fire in my own house, its cover permanently darkened by a smoke stain.

Canetti was born in 1905 in Bulgaria, the son of Sephardic parents. The vicissitudes of his family fate brought him to Vienna, Berlin, Lausanne, Zurich, and eventually to England, where he lived until his death in 1994. Fluent in several languages, he wrote exclusively in German. In addition to *Auto-da-fé* and *Crowds and Power,* he is the author of a number of plays (*Comedy of Vanity, The Numbered,* and *The Wedding,* among others), books of what he calls "jottings" (most notably, *The Human Province*) and three remarkable memoirs (*The Tongue Set Free, The Torch in My Ear,* and *The Play of the Eyes*). He has not been wanting in admirers, among whom are writers of the distinction of Iris Murdoch, John Bayley, Salman Rushdie, Susan Sontag, and George Steiner. And he was the recipient of the Nobel Prize for literature in 1981. But he has remained a singular and diffident figure without a large following who has avoided one of the great pitfalls for intellectuals and artists, celebrity.

In *The Torch in My Ear,* Canetti locates the source of his lifelong obsession with crowds in "one of those not too frequent public events that seize an entire city so profoundly that it is no longer the same afterwards." At a coffeehouse in Vienna on June 15, 1927, he reads of a "just verdict" in which a court declares those responsible for the shootings of workers in Burgenland not guilty.

> The acquittal had been termed, nay, trumpeted, as "a just verdict" in the organ of the government party. It was this mockery of any sense of justice rather than the verdict itself that triggered an enormous agitation among the workers of Vienna.

When they set fire to the Palace of Justice, the mayor of the city ordered the police to shoot, causing ninety deaths. "Fifty years have passed, and the agitation of that day is still in my bones. It is the closest thing to a revolution that I have physically experienced."

What is the effect of the event on Canetti? It is not the sense of injustice, which originally moved him, but rather the experience of the crowd in action. He descends into the streets, joins the procession, indeed "dissolves in it" and feels not "the slightest resistance to what the crowd was doing." At the same time, he says "[I was] amazed that despite my frame of mind, I was able to grasp all the concrete individual scenes taking place before my eyes." In *Crowds and Power* Canetti would provide an explanation for the irresistible attraction of the crowd. It rests on a paradox:

> There is nothing that man fears more than the touch of the unknown. . . . Man always tends to avoid physical contact with anything strange. In the dark, the fear of an unexpected touch can amount to panic. . . . It is only in a crowd that man can become free of this fear of being touched. That is the only situation in which the fear changes into its opposite. The crowd he needs is the dense crowd, in which body is pressed to body; a crowd too, whose psychical constitution is also dense, or compact, so that he no longer notices who it is that presses against him. As soon as a man has surrendered himself to the crowd, he ceases to fear its touch.

The crowd is a kind of homeopathy for a universal phobia: the fear of touch.

Canetti dissolves in the crowd and yet finds that he is able to grasp all the events taking place before his eyes. This capacity for participation and detached observation is a remarkable feature of all his work. (He would be an exception to Gustave Le Bon's view in his classic study of the crowd in which participants lose themselves in it and any sense of critical objectivity.) The moral indignation that moved Canetti to join the crowd seems to evaporate in his account of its behavior. He becomes a fiercely dispassionate observer of its sensory elements: "the excitement, the advancing, and the fluency of the movement," the dominant presence of the word fire, and then the actual fire. There is the throbbing of his head, shots fired "like whips," the avoidance of corpses, the seeming increase of the size of the corpses in the growing excitement he feels. He notes the overwhelming presence of people and then their vanishing. "Everything yielded and invisible holes open everywhere." Things tug and tear at him. He hears "something rhythmic in the air, an evil music" which elevates him. He experiences himself as a resonant wind. Images of water, fire, and air dominate the scene. Canetti was trained as a chemist, and he seems to combine a visionary poetic gift with a scientific passion for precise notation. In his account the crowd is an agent of neither good nor evil. It is an elemental force to be studied with the objectivity one might use to study the motions of matter, the actions of wolves, lions, and tigers.

Crowds and Power is an idiosyncratic work. Its extensive bibliography makes no reference to Le Bon's work, nor is there any reference to Marx or Freud, though there is a section on the paranoid Dr. Schreber, whom Freud analyzed. Canetti's typology is his own invention. Crowds can be opened or closed; they can be invisible, baiting, prohibition, reversal and feast crowds, each having its own dynamic. They are a development of the "pack," an older unit, whose main characteristic is that it cannot grow, though its "fiercest wish is to be more." Like the crowd, the pack is prolific in the forms it assumes: hunting, war, lamenting, increase. Much of the exposition has the air of apodictic assertion, which the reader can trust or resist, depending on his or her disposition to the work. An example:

> Of the four essential attributes of the crowd which we have come to know, two are only fictitious as far as the pack is concerned, though these are the two which are most strenuously desired and enacted. Hence the other two must be all the more strangely present in actuality. *Growth* and *density* are only acted; *equality* and *direction* really exist. The first thing that strikes one about the pack is its direction; equality is expressed in the fact that all are obsessed by the same goal, the sight of an animal perhaps, which they want to kill.

It is asserted, not demonstrated, that growth and density are only acted. Why is it that the pack cannot grow? And if it cannot grow, what does an *increase* pack mean? The lucidity of Canetti's prose doesn't always throw light on the motives of his thought.

In the section "On the Psychology of Eating," he writes that "the person who eats alone renounces the prestige which the process would bring him in the eyes of others." And what is the prestige of eating in public? "But when people eat together they can see other's mouths opening. Everyone can watch everyone else's teeth while his own are in action at the same time. To be without teeth is contemptible." The turn of mind here is peculiar to Canetti. I can think of more obvious reasons for eating together: the pleasures of company and conversation. It would be strange, at least for those in advanced societies, to concentrate on the masticating habits of others while eating—though one appreciates a description of those habits by a writer like Canetti or Naipaul. There are numerous passages that are idiosyncratic, if not perverse, in this manner. There are also passages that tell us what we already know without the shock of recognition.

Crowds and Power contains no thesis or doctrine. It is a work of observation and speculation from which one can infer a view of the human condition. For Canetti crowds appear everywhere and in myriad forms and are the source of power, the other major theme of the book. Power has force and violence as it cognates and is invariably destructive. Unlike Hannah Arendt, who distinguished between power as benign and force as malign, Canetti conceives of force as the actualization of power. If there is a moral bias in the work, it is against power. Much of the book is given over to ethnographic accounts of massacres of tribes by other tribes. As a non-religious, non-Christian writer, Canetti does not believe that man has fallen from grace to a condition of sin. Violence is aboriginally human and has no significant history. Canetti's anthropological perspective creates the impression of endless cycles of destruction, human and non-human. He does not share the Enlightenment view that human nature is malleable and susceptible to the influences of society, for good or evil. Destruction seems to issue from the biology that human beings share with all animal life. At times Canetti reads like a zoologist whose main subject happens to be the human species. His survey of anthropological literature only confirms the conviction that the world wars that have marked our past century were manifestations on a grand scale of what has always been true of human life everywhere. Bosnia, Kosovo, Rwanda, Somalia, Sierra Leone would find their place in a revised edition of *Crowds and Power*. They are the normal, not exceptional, events in the story that Canetti tells about human life.

World War I haunts Canetti's imagination of human destructiveness as it did his idol, Karl Kraus, the influential author of *The Last Days of Mankind* and innumerable polemics against the decadence that brought Europe to catastrophe. Canetti tells in his memoirs of the tremendous effect Kraus's lectures (he attended more than a hundred) had on him. And yet the influence of a catastrophic "moment" in history does not translate into a historical perspective on the subject. Although the emergence of democracy in the past two hundred years has focused our minds on crowds and has affected the forms they have taken and their significance, Canetti writes as if crowds have no history.

In a study of power, we expect an attention to its sublimations in politics. We learn of power relationships between chiefs and their tribes, but not of how a knowledge of those relationships can be transferred to an understanding of *political* behavior in advanced societies. Canetti brings Hobbes to mind in his vision of men at war with one another in the state of nature, but unlike Hobbes he has only the rudiments of a political imagination of possible solutions. He writes of parliamentary factions as double crowds, but the translation of one term to another seems little more than a tautology. We are told little of the dynamics of factional life in parliamentary democracies. In this respect, Canetti resembles Foucault, a writer of an altogether different character, for whom power is also pervasive and oppressive. Both writers pay little attention to its political expression and are pessimistic on the question of whether power can be resisted.

In an epilogue, Canetti suggests that the obsession with productivity in both capitalist and socialist countries might be understood as an antidote to war. "Production cannot but be peaceful. War and destruction mean decrease and thus, by definition, harm it. Here capitalism and socialism are at one, twin rivals in the same faith. For both of them production is the apple of their eye and their main concern." This ignores the "creative destruction" (Schumpeter's phrase) that characterizes advanced capitalism or for that matter war itself. Canetti here expresses the faith (not necessarily his own) in our global economy decades before its appearance. He sees parliaments "in its peaceful and regular rotation of power" as another recourse against war and destruction, anticipating current wisdom that there is an affinity between democracy and peace. And he turns to ancient Rome as an example of how "sport can replace war as a crowd phenomenon." (What would he have made of the behavior of soccer fans in his own adopted country, England?)

Canetti devotes a section to the role of the survivor as an agent of power. We should not confuse Canetti's survivor with how we commonly understand the survivor nowadays. In his exemplary embodiment, he is the person who has survived the concentration camps. He may have done so at the expense of others, but he does not pride himself on having outlived his fellow inmates. On the contrary, for the rest of his life he will bear a burden of guilt. Canetti's survivor seems close to Darwin's conscienceless victor in the struggle for existence, though Darwin is never mentioned in the book. He desires nothing less than to outlive the rest of the world. Ruler or paranoid, often both at the same time, he seeks the extermination of his subjects. Paranoia in this perspective is not so much a pathology as it is the very condition of rule and command. In Sophocles's *Antigone,* Creon's son Haimon warns his father that if he puts Antigone to death he will rule a desert. Haimon reflects the wisdom of the play that to rule one must have subjects. The ruler who remains alone on the earth ceases to be a ruler. Not so for Canetti, for whom the very idea of rule entails destruction. The survivor is not only its embodiment, he is "mankind's worst evil, its curse and perhaps its doom." Canetti wonders whether it is "possible for us to escape him, even now at its last moment." The concluding sentence of his book is a call to the disarmament of power. "If we would master power we must face command openly and boldly, and search for means to deprive it of its sting."

What then is the alternative to power? In one of his most eloquent essays, **"Kafka's Other Trial,"** Canetti finds a recourse against power in Kafka's vulnerability to his father, his lovers—indeed, to every aspect of his world. His account of Kafka's tormented relationship with Felice Bauer is so compelling and so moving that it may overcome a reader's resistance to its affirmation of powerlessness. Would we care to read *The Metamorphosis* or *The Trial* if its author had not transformed the pathos of his existence into a powerful art? Does power need always to be invidious? Shakespeare's answer is in the opening line of sonnet 132: "They that have the power to hurt and will do none." No one desires vulnerability and weakness. What we all desire—I hate to use what has become a cant word—is empowerment. Canetti admits as much when in a "jotting" in **The Human Province** he notes: "I have never heard of a person attacking power without wanting it, and the religious novelists are the worst in this respect." Hannah Arendt had a different sense of power when she understood its absence as a source of violence. Terrorism, for example, is the action of the weak, not of the strong.

Canetti's declared hostility to power may be misleading, for he is clearly attracted to it as a subject for his imagination. When he finds power in art, he admires it without reservation. Here is what he has to say about his friend, the sculptor Felix Wortruba:

> He was interested in two things and in them alone: the power of stone and the power of words, in both cases power, but in so unusual a combination of its elements that one took it as a force of nature, no more open to criticism than a storm.

It may be that when Canetti writes of stone and words, he is not thinking of power in the negative conceptual sense that informs his thinking in **Crowds and Power.**

His struggle against power is also a struggle against death, for the two are inextricably bound together in his mind. He desires immortality or longevity, if immortal-ity is unavailable, because of an insatiable curiosity about life. "The highly concrete and serious, the admitted goal of my life is to achieve immortality for men." Here he sets himself against the philosopher's creed that wisdom lies in the graceful acceptance of death. For Rilke, a poet with a philosophical gift, death is the fulfillment of life and only those with unlived lines in their bodies—and they are legion—fear it. Canetti might have accepted death if he were guaranteed the time to satisfy his desire to fully know the world. Most people don't want to die. If given a choice with the full knowledge of the prospect, few would want to live forever, especially if the promise of immortality was not accompanied by eternal youth. In his beautiful poem "Tithonus," Tennyson evokes the pathos of the goddess Aurora's lover, whom she granted immortal life, but not eternal youth.

> The woods decay, the woods decay and fall,
> The vapours weep their burthen to the ground,
> Man comes and tills the field and lies beneath,
> And after many a summer dies the swan.
> Me only cruel immortality
> Consumes; I wither slowly in thine arms . . .

But would eternal youth be sufficient? Wouldn't the boredom of a several-hundred-year existence become unbearable? Moreover, what of its consequences for new birth and new life? The virtue of a Christian conception of an afterlife is that it satisfies a desire for immortality that doesn't threaten future life on earth. And how does Canetti reconcile his view of the survivor as "mankind's worst evil" with his own desire for immortality? Although I do not share his immortal longings, I find something admirable in his stubborn refusal to submit to conventional wisdom. Risking death is a familiar experience. The risks of longevity might be worth taking, but they require a person of singular capacities.

In the memoir **The Play of the Eyes,** Canetti reproduces an exchange he had with his friend, the novelist Herman Broch. He had given Broch a copy of his manuscript, *Kant Catches Fire,* the original title of **Auto-da-fé.** Broch was struck, even scandalized by the grotesqueness of the characters in the novel. Canetti admitted that he was influenced by Gogol: "I wanted the most extreme characters at once ludicrous and horrible. I wanted the ludicrous and the horrible to be indistinguishable." And he conceded that he had a desire to terrify people, because he found everything around him terrifying. One of the terrifying characters is the protagonist, Peter Kien, a bibliophile of monstrous proportions—perhaps a parodic version of Canetti himself. The memoirs create the impression of an extremely bookish person. Like D. H. Lawrence, Canetti in his youth and young manhood was completely absorbed by his mother with whom he shared a passion for books. She had three sons, of whom Elias was the eldest, and never remarried. Whenever a suitor came on the scene and threatened the family romance, Elias made it clear to her that remarriage was out of the question. He would not allow it. His own fidelity to her turned out to be less reliable than hers to him. When women came into his life, he concealed their presence. Eventually he broke the hold that mother and son had on each other and married. His younger brother Georg took over the role of the utterly devoted son. But the bookish bond between mother and son was a permanent legacy and contributed to the kind of writer he became. One might be tempted to say that his sense of reality has been skewed by his bookishness, if it were not that he seems to be aware of the danger of living in books. The novel ends in a book burning: Canetti knows their dangerous combustible power.

There is violence enough everywhere around him, but what of the violence in Canetti himself? In his childhood, when he was not yet literate, he had tried to murder his older cousin Laurica with an ax, because she would not let him see her notebooks. The family assembled to discuss "the homicidal child."

> I could plead all I liked that Laurica tortured me bloody; the fact that I, at the age of five, had reached for the ax to kill her—indeed, the very fact that I had been able to carry the heavy ax in front of me—was incomprehensible to everyone. I think they understood that the "writing," "the script," had been so important to me; they were Jews, and "Scripture" meant a great deal to all of them, but there had to be something very bad and dangerous in me to the point of wanting to murder my playmate.

When Canetti told Broch that his lifework would be crowds, Broch responded that there was nothing to learn from a study of mass behavior. "You can't discover [its laws], because there aren't any. You'd be wasting your time. Better stick to your plays. You're a writer." Canetti had no answer, but he stuck to his guns, because it was in crowds that he could best express the violence that he found in life, in books, and in himself.

His claim to distinction does not rest on a set of original or compelling ideas. He is not a master of a particular genre, though he was the author of many plays, essays, "jottings," and a singular (in more than one sense) novel. *Crowds and Power* eludes generic definition and lacks the intellectual or scholarly substance of other works on the subject. (A recent scholarly introduction to Le Bon's work provides an extensive list of books and articles on crowds but makes no mention of Canetti's book.) His is an achievement of sensibility, which has its fulfillment in the memoirs. He is an obsessively patient observer and listener, always at an odd angle to events, alert to what is strange, weird, and frightening in his and our experience.

Dagmar Barnouw (essay date 2000)

SOURCE: Barnouw, Dagmar. "Utopian Dissent: Canetti's Dramatic Fictions." In *Critical Essays on Elias Canetti*, edited by David Darby, pp. 121-34. New York: G. K. Hall and Co., 2000.

[*In the following essay, Barnouw finds in Canetti's dramas a dystopian "dissent . . . from the utopias of the status quo."*]

1

In the twentieth century social imagination has been driven by dystopian rather than utopian energies, ostensibly because utopian possibility has receded before the "can do" of modern technology. Technocracy, however, has contributed not only to the increase of social and political problems but also to their solution. The real issue seems to be not so much the fact but the kind of creation, the various and ever-more rapid ways of change that, more than anything else, have lit up the age-old limitations of utopian models, their stasis and immutability. For the time being, utopian thought seems better served by the nonbinding reality of computer-created virtual worlds with their cheerfully mobile independence of time/space contingencies. It is no accident that almost all utopian communities since the eighteenth century have succumbed to the old utopian "corruptio pessima optimi"—a self-destruction intimately connected with these communities' sharp self-separation from the larger world.[1] Their spatial-temporal-ideological fortification and remoteness, their loquacious unanimity, their silenced contradictions ultimately turned them into dystopias.

Utopian fictions, nourished by the desire for paradisiacal origins, provided the model for this self-separation and limitation. Their radical exclusion of historical time—that is, the awareness of changing lifeworlds and lifetimes—had its source in the hope of regaining the innocence and wholeness of the beginning: the inviolability of community and the exemption from the destructive effects of time passing, finally the threat of death. Since More's *Utopia*, the elaborately constructed society on the artificial island "No-Place," Utopia has attracted the visitor/observer precisely with its radical artificiality. More's fiction was meant as a counter-projection to the economic chaos in early sixteenth-century England. As such it was conceived not as a social organism subject to temporal change but as the best possible social construct that would endure forever just as it had been planned at a certain point in time. This obvious contradiction at the core of the concept of Utopia has arguably been one of the main reasons for the fascination utopian fictions have held over the centuries. Rejecting the experiences of a shared temporal lifeworld, a shared past, the construct of utopian community is created as timeless and fully authorized—as good as, or even better than, paradise. Utopia becomes dystopia as soon as its radical constructedness becomes questionable—a process that requires a radical change in perception that eventually leads to dystopian self-destruction. It is not the visitor's different perspective that causes the breach that makes Utopia permeable to time and change. It is, rather, the insights of local dissidents trying to break out of the suprahistorical, inhumanly "perfect" construct: Zamyatin's mathematically constructed city of glass, Huxley's biochemically engineered stability defeating the fear of death, Orwell's Big-Brotherly rule by all-embracing psychological terror. The utopian dissenters' goal is the return to the contradictions, unresolvable conflicts, and contingencies of historical social experience changing in time. There are no travelers in dystopia who look at the hitherto unseen, listen to the unheard-of, and admiringly report on it. Rather, the inhabitants of utopia themselves begin to see the dystopian features of their community. Where the traveler to Utopia wishes to understand the logic of the construct offered for inspection and to reconstruct it as a whole in his narration, the dissenting inhabitant of Utopia dissects that logic and thereby removes it from representation. Dystopias are meant to be warning signals, appeals to the need for change. The more clearly they indicate that their artificiality is inherently self-destructing, the more effective they are.

Canetti's drama *Die Befristeten* (*The Numbered*), written while he was working on *Masse und Macht* (*Crowds and Power*), presents dystopia at its purest, because the construct, the new order, is revealed as a consummately planned and executed deception.[2] This is of course true for all ideological rule, all organized attempts to fit other persons into a system controlled by allegedly unchanging, unquestionable laws. The unmasking of ideologically based and constructed political rule as a lie is one of the preconditions for revealing the dystopian nature of a community. But in the dystopian society of *The Numbered,* where human temporal transformation is halted by the a priori determined duration of each individual's life, the dystopian symbiosis between ideological control and deception is at its most intimate and powerful: the deceptive state control over the subjects' life span is itself the source for the basic structures of social conduct. To Canetti, for whom the mass destruction of human life was the core experience of the twentieth century, the manipulation of lifetime in the society of *The Numbered* would indeed mean the ultimate bad place.

Like Canetti's dramas of the 1930s, *Hochzeit* (*The Wedding*) and *Komödie der Eitelkeit* (*Comedy of Vanity*), *The Numbered* is a *Lese-Drama,* a text to be read, a play for radio rather than for the stage, to be heard rather than seen. More clearly than the earlier texts, it is a also a teaching drama whose "message" suits to perfection the dystopian mode of decomposition, playing on the connection between utopian construction and dystopian self-destruction. This format does not necessarily make the text a more successful dramatic fiction, but it does make it a coherent and satisfying intellectual fiction.[3] Culled from the voices of the novel *Die Blendung* (*Auto-da-Fé*), blaring out accusations of social corruption, the two early dramas use their dystopian settings in intriguing but also problematic ways. This is partly due to the—at the time—overwhelming influence of Karl Kraus on Canetti. In his different roles as political journalist and dramatist, philosophical sociolinguist, and neo-idealist poet, and above all as a brilliantly gifted speaker who brought to life the voices of others in order to annihilate them, Kraus is powerfully present in all of Canetti's prewar texts.

Canetti celebrated this influence in later essays, emphasizing Kraus's "absolute," almost demoniacal social and political responsibility and his near fantastic ability to open his readers' and listeners' ears to the great plurality of Viennese voices.[4] But he also described here his attempts at freeing himself from the enslaving power of Kraus's "acoustic quotation" (*CW* [*The Conscience of Words*], 32) by becoming a writer himself, the author of *Auto-da-Fé*. These attempts seem to me only partially successful in the novel, and they have much to do with its grandiosely flawed composition, which is repeated, if on a minor scale, in the two dramas. The great number of "acoustic masks" recorded by means of acoustic quotation in *Auto-da-Fé* do indeed represent a stunning symbiosis of the comical and the terrible: Kraus had forced Canetti to let himself be pursued, persecuted by the voices of Vienna, drawn to them as if into an explosive microcosm of the social and political ills of the war and the postwar period. The effectiveness of the novel and the early dramas depends on a sudden defamiliarization of these voices in the acoustic masks so that their "literalness" will reveal their "horror."[5] Canetti had experienced the—to him—unique speaker Kraus as a "master of horror" who forced his listeners to join together in a "uniform and unchangeable," an "absolute" stance against war (*CW*, 33). This fact in particular was, in the older Canetti's view, the core of the irresistible attraction that Kraus exerted on the young Canetti and the overwhelming majority of young Viennese intellectuals in the years between the two world wars.[6]

Instructively, the young writer's sensation of consisting of many figures was affirmed by both the plurality of voices that Kraus enabled his listeners to distinguish and the ordering power of his sentences as judgments, particularly in his antiwar teaching drama *Die letzten Tage der Menschheit* (*The Last Days of Mankind*). Kraus, his text as he read it, was for him justice (see

CW, 137-38). He had learned from his master to select those voices from the contemporary Viennese Babel that most promptly and stunningly indicted themselves, since Kraus focused exclusively on acoustic masks in the moment of their capitulation. Quoting, he let the hunted allow themselves to be caught in the snares of their cant, and the fact of the catch itself confirmed the authority of his judgment. His enormous effect on audiences derived largely from his seemingly magical ability to pull even the most aggressive voices toward the snare that then closed on them as if with inexorable logic. In retrospect, Canetti finally understood and revolted against the superhuman effort and absolute superiority of the person who, in quoting others, became the author of the real, utterly contemptible meaning of their statements. The second volume of Canetti's autobiography, *Die Fackel im Ohr* (*The Torch in My Ear*), the title a play on the name of Kraus's influential journal *Die Fackel,* narrates the process of this revolt. Here the cruel brilliance of the master's performance of other voices is stunningly evoked in Canetti's description of the reaction of his enthralled listeners: their ecstatic aggressive laughter that mercilessly pursues all dissenters, the utopian unanimity in judging the wickedness of a corrupt world from which they were separated by light-years. It was a judgment that had itself become corrupt through the utopian exclusion and silencing of others.

This is an important insight into crucial limitations of Kraus's remarkable achievement. It is instructive that Canetti did not (wish to) apply it to his own work of the period before the Second World War, though his early texts could not deny Kraus's enduring influence. He consisted, as he said himself, of Kraus's sentences, both literally and figuratively, he had mimetically created himself in the master's image. Having listened to Kraus, he could no longer turn away from the voices reproduced by the master performer, and this hateful compulsion is reflected most clearly in the pandemonium of the voices of the novel. He may be rejecting the endless exposing of subhuman stupidity in the quotations and the inhuman perfection of the commentator who quotes them. He may understand the utopian exclusivity of the sentence that irrevocably distances the speaker from all that is stupid and wrong in contemporary social conduct. He may accuse Kraus of having built a "Great Wall of China" whose utopian perfection and impenetrability threatened to diminish and paralyze what it had been built to protect (*CW,* 35-36). The central theme of *The Torch in My Ear* is Canetti's seduction by Kraus's moral and intellectual absolutism and his gradual self-distancing from Kraus in finding his own way in *Auto-da-Fé* to the representation of the troubling reality of the 1930s. But if he wrote himself free in the novel, he did so only by showing how much and how well he had learned from Kraus. Moreover, Kraus's influence would linger on, albeit complexly transformed, in *The Numbered.*

2

When Canetti refers to the essentially dramatic nature of all his texts, he means his approach of letting others speak in their own voices.[7] He wrote *The Wedding* in the winter of 1931-1932 in response both to the social and political anxieties of these years and to Büchner's *Wozzeck.*[8] In Büchner's characters he found the same capacity for "self-denunciation" that determines the characters of *Auto-da-Fé* (*PE* [*The Play of the Eyes*], 15-18), and he was impressed by the unmediated vitality of Büchner's figures, be they victims or victimizers. The poet's justice, he argued, was not to condemn his characters; he can create their victims and show their impact on them. It seemed to him that Büchner had been successful in creating characters whose identity was not dimmed by their suffering and who yet exhibited the impact of that suffering. This is indeed a perceptive comment on a highly talented dramatist's strategies, but it has little to do with his own handling of the characters of *The Wedding* and *Comedy of Vanity.* Here, more clearly even than in *Auto-da-Fé,* he was the satirist who did not grant his figures, as did Büchner, the right to present themselves as they saw themselves, to express "the full value of the word 'I'" (*PE,* 16). The victims'—the author's—accusations stay in the foreground, always audible, and the figures remain stuck in their acoustic masks. Canetti stated in a 1937 interview with the *Wiener Sonntag* on the occasion of one of his readings from *The Wedding* that the "deeper laws of the drama" as they had become clear to him in the writing process required its structure to be derived from the spatial constellation of the characters as acoustic masks and to be as consistent and unique as the individual figures.[9] Many readers have justifiably doubted the theatrical effectiveness of the plays in view of the difficulties inherent in articulating structures of meaning through acoustic figures that are themselves—and by intention—so limited.[10] A good speaker reading the text—and by all accounts Canetti was an excellent one (Fried 15)—can help them and the structure of the play come to life by virtue of his transformative control.

Both prewar dramas are characterized by their allegorically clear contouring of antisocial speech and action and by the energy of a *Grundeinfall,* a completely new originary idea.[11] This new idea, as Canetti claimed rather grandiosely in that early interview, would "shed new light on the world as a whole," and the dramatic structure would have to derive from it, following the utopian principle of perfect construction in nowhere. The issue in *The Wedding* is the compulsion to possess objects and the concomitant exclusion of meaningful communication; in *Comedy of Vanity* it is the subject's narcissistic possession of the self that leads to destructive isolation and fragmentation. In both cases the *Grundeinfall* is overdrawn in its allegorical distinctness. In *The Wedding* the house is the most palpable presentation of the bourgeois status quo, the fetishized object at the center of everyone's wishes and desires. In *Comedy of Vanity* it is the forbidden mirror on which isolated, unauthentic characters fix their crazed desire for identity. In both cases the greed of the characters—to be in possession of objects, of themselves—is expressed by explosively inarticulate acoustic masks limited to accusations and threats. *The Wedding* reveals all social relations to be property relations: this is true no less of marital fidelity than of sexual promiscuity. The house condenses the omnipresent greed so that it becomes an icon of the craving for permanence and stability that then cannot but paralyze all human interaction. The figures' speaking, shouting past each other, comes to a climax when one of the wedding guests suggests a parlor game. As his name suggests, Horch (in Honegger's English translation, Hark) listens to and connects with other people, whereby his acoustic mask acquires more verbal range.[12] He asks everybody to come up with ideas how they would rescue the person dearest to them during an earthquake. But his appeal to the guests' humanity is at the same time an open admission—even a celebration—of lying as the core of all social communication. No reader, listener, or viewer can then be surprised when the characters' answers reveal the material and sexual greed that is fully realized when the earthquake actually happens. Their author has constructed an inhumanly perfect dystopia by having everyone's word and by leaving the dissenter nothing to say.

The dystopia of *Comedy of Vanity* is conceptually more complex and less predictable in its self-destruction. However, it shares with *The Wedding* (and *Auto-da-Fé*) the core problem of the author's excessive verbal control, which is central to the conceit of the acoustic mask. The drama's *Grundeinfall* is that the utopian taboo on all mirrors and photographs—which was intended to eradicate the antisocial vanity of the pre-utopian period—has instead intensified solipsism immeasurably. Thus more or less normal, if not particularly admirable, egocentricity has developed into pathological ego-addictiveness.[13] Very expensive brothels sell self-gratification instead of sexual intercourse by providing the forbidden experience of seeing oneself in a mirror. Casual eye contact with others has become masturbatory self-reflection. The utopian prohibition of self-images has undermined all mediation of social norms, since it has made affirmation of self-value impossible. Poor people who cannot afford the large admission fees charged by the brothels are begging for flattery in the streets. The maid Marie, presumably less corrupted by (pre-utopian) bourgeois self-presentation than other figures, laments that there are no more windowpanes to polish: they have all been replaced by frosted glass. She does not need a man in her bed, she tells the preacher; she needs a mirror in her room; she would only fight

with the man anyway. In this mirrorless society people are constantly fighting because, unable to develop self-perception, they lack perceptiveness in relation to others.

The absence of mirrors has repressed the normally intersubjective and interactive ego-development that begins with the newborn's learning to make visual contact with other people. Marie's contempt for the man who does not expect from her some attention to her looks is to be seen as positive: her acoustic mask has traits of dissent. Remaking oneself (*sich zurechtmachen*) by rearranging one's hair, applying make-up in preparation for being seen by the other person requires a glance in the mirror. Self-esteem also means both appreciating the esteem of the other person and showing this appreciation in one's self-presentation. The preacher is not interested in these connections; he works with a religious recipe against the sin of using a mirror. Presenting Marie with a mirror, he expects her to be horrified by the sinfulness of possessing it. But Marie is horrified by the consequences of what she sees in the mirror: the face that looks back at her is alien because it has developed independently of her and her relations to others, and it is therefore unacceptable. Ten years have passed without her looking at and arranging herself, without her tracing a gradual and then perceptible transformation. Marie rubs at the mirror in a rage and, finding it worse than useless now, gives it away to an old woman. She puts it to good use by charging high fees for healing the now common mirror deficiency syndrome, a sort of psychological paralysis caused by the withdrawal of self-images and the consequent lack of self-awareness and capacity for transformation.

These connections are both obvious and hidden, because none of the acoustic masks would have enough words—not to speak of language—to articulate them. Canetti again relies here too much on Kraus's symbiosis of literalness and horror, *Wörtlichkeit und Entsetzen*, which, in its complete authorial control of *Entsetzen*, disregards the potential of other speakers' *Wörtlichkeit*. The self-destruction of this society—the drama ends with a revolt of mirror-deprived individuals screaming "I" who smash all remaining mirrors and burn all images—is not brought about by dissenters able to speak intelligently about the dystopian corruption of what they had been told to see as the good (better) place. This self-destruction is too obviously the construct of its author, whose interest in its possible meanings is too limited.

The prohibition of mirrors, which is meant to weaken individual egocentricity, has not brought about the promised good (better) community but rather an extreme of social fragmentation and polarization. In their ever more rigid fixation on an increasingly hollow notion of selfhood, people have lost the ability to engage with each other as individuals and have been sucked into destructive mass-eruptions—the central theme that connects Canetti's prewar texts. Despite his unshakable belief in the theatrical effectiveness of the early dramas (see Barnouw 1996, 160-61), they have been performed very rarely. The reason given most frequently (and justifiably) is their *Kopflastigkeit,* their cerebral quality, the dominating role of conceptual patterns.[14] The novelty of the absolutely new *Grundeinfall* is too self-referential and the negativity of the grotesque characters too relentless: they could never have been—would never be—different, whatever their social environment. This is, of course, a systemic dystopian problem, but it is intensified here by the violent obviousness and rigidity of the acoustic masks that prohibit transformation. There is also a compactness of conceptual organization that can be taken apart and put together again at leisure by readers but that is not easily accessible to viewers limited by the short duration of a performance. The very weight of this compactness threatens to undermine the literalness of the *Grundeinfall*—the house and the mirror as allegories for social alienation and fragmentation—and thereby also its effectiveness as a warning signal.

3

The Numbered was not meant to work as a drama in the stricter sense. Apart perhaps from the greater immediacy of the dialogical structure, it might have worked just as well as an essay or story, were it not for Canetti's enduring preoccupation with the dramatic challenge of giving voice to others' voices. His experience of the war and of working with the materials that went into *Crowds and Power* had taught him to be appreciative of a greater variety of voices and to reproduce them accordingly. The social order of *The Numbered* is based on what is for temporal beings the most unfair, "unequal" aspect of their existence, the distribution of lifetime. At birth each is given a name that tells the number of the allotted years. Knowing the date of their death gives the Numbered a security that has eluded their pre-utopian ancestors. The new order is presented to them as the new freedom from the contingencies that plagued people in the past, since, freed from the randomness of death, they can really plan and arrange their lives as they see fit. The utopian improvement on the past turns out to be the basis of the power of the totalitarian regime under whose rule—the rule of death—intersubjective relations have been almost completely destroyed. In the prologue the reader or listener, who here takes the place of the utopian traveler, is informed that mankind's acquisition of the knowledge of "the moment" (of death) has been the greatest step forward in the history of the species. Before that people had been living in "barbarian" uncertainty, like animals more than humans. But, as the dissident Fifty comes to understand, it is the Numbered, the subjects of death,

who, knowing their "moment," resemble animals that in their innocence of death are simply subject to the laws of nature. The pre-utopian barbarians, in contrast, had been able to elude the rule of death at least temporarily by not knowing beforehand when they had to die. Together with Fifty, the protagonist of the argument that dismantles the dystopian order, we discover that in this society every command is a death sentence and every death its execution. In rituals celebrating the utopian happiness of the Numbered as the status quo of the Unequal (*die Ungleichen*), the state ideology presents their liberation from the sting of death as mediating between the rule of natural laws and the dignity of the individual. Allotting to each Numbered a death that is both anonymous and personal, this ideology systematically hides the possibility both of death sentences and of their execution.

As the dystopias of *The Wedding* and *Comedy of Vanity* referred to the explosive social and political problems of the 1930s, so the dystopia of *The Numbered* reflects the troubling implications of limited lifetime for modern societies even, particularly, at their most stable and "normal." There is no great distance between the conduct of the Numbered vis-à-vis their limited lifetime and our own. Our private taboo where death is concerned is the public taboo of the Numbered. The very fact of this taboo obscures a fuller understanding of intersubjective relations.[15] Over many decades Canetti wrote down aphoristic projections—many of them potential dramatic *Grundeinfälle*—of societies that have not abolished death but have acknowledged it as a serious social problem. Not surprisingly, some of these create their own considerable difficulties: cities, in which people live as long as they are loved; where they disappear for longer or shorter periods; where one is born old and becomes younger; where everyone has at least two ages and can be for instance simultaneously 59 and 23 years old. In 1981 he asked: "A land where *some* of the dead return. Which, and why?"[16] Common to all these projections is the perceived need to keep open for everyone the potential of transformation and not to arrest this process prematurely by accepting too easily the death of others.[17]

Canetti's concern has not been an eternal life but rather a longer and better one, taking seriously, as few writers have done, the social and political implications of the experience of death, the arch-anxiety of time passing, the arch-desire for permanence. In his view a longer life should be a better one,[18] which means, to begin with, a consistent respect for each individual life. Everyone is owed the chance to live their life as long and meaningfully as possible. This has become a new and in some ways unexpected challenge to modern societies at the end of this century when astonishing developments in medical technology that increasingly do indeed prolong life have created ever greater ethical problems. Canetti's dystopian, dissenting perspective could be useful here because it illuminates so sharply certain important aspects of these questions. One of them is the new fact that the costliness of these new treatment protocols, which then are not available to everyone who needs them, has already created a new inequality with regard to available lifetime. Canetti could not have foreseen these developments, but they are intimately connected with his plea for an understanding of the quintessentially social dimension of the experience of death. His concrete concern in his dramatic essay was the most basic aspect of that dimension from which everything follows: the connection between the enduring inertia of social relations, the constant reassertion of a status quo, and our predictably limited life span that makes us all more easily disposable—at such and such a time we will reliably be gone. Being able to take for granted a certain duration for a generation's presence and then its absence has made it much easier to plan for the future—as in *The Numbered.* Instructively, such planning is increasingly seen to be "threatened" by the increase in life expectancy and the demographics of aging populations. At the same time we accept the determinant nature of aging as a constant decrease of the individual's vitality and "market value" and have made our arrangements accordingly. The degradation and gradual decline caused by the approach of death has been a social-psychological problem much discussed in Western societies at the end of this century, but it seems to be very difficult to deal with it concretely and intelligently, other than by making it easier to die.

Canetti has done a great deal to unmask the palpable physical cruelty at the core of many of the social abstractions of the problem of death, not least in his discussion of the survivor as victor with respect to the dead in *Crowds and Power.*[19] After the completion of *The Numbered,* he recorded reflections on the repulsive satiation of the victor, his gloating contentment at being alive where others were dead. And yet it was impossible not to be a victor over every person one had known well and survived. To go on living without being (in that sense) a victor seemed to him as impossibly difficult as "the moral squaring of the circle" (*HP* [*The Human Province*], 138). The state ideology of *The Numbered* offers a solution to this challenge that cannot but reveal itself to be dystopian but that can nevertheless be related to our situation in Western societies at the end of the twentieth century. If, at a certain age, we become less willing to let it be known exactly how old we are, if we keep secret our birthdays, our age, our probable number of remaining years, so too this information has been a lifelong secret kept by the state in the society of *The Numbered.* A priest who is also a state official, the Keeper of Lockets, fastens around the neck of every newborn a capsule protected by a strong taboo that contains the date of birth and, since the number of years each individual is permitted to live is an-

nounced in the name, thereby also the date of death. This official alone is permitted to open the capsule at death and confirm its correctly predicted date. Since, with the a priori determined lifetime, the approach of death can signify a socially weaker position, the public concealment of the birthday is quite welcome and becomes internalized, a private secret. Fifty, whose time will be up very shortly, tries to share his gradual insight into the real meaning of these rituals with other members of the Numbered. At issue is their understanding the illusory nature of their freedom from the fear of death and the absolute social injustice of their inequality with respect to their life span since it is based on a random distribution—and then rigid possession—of chronological time. Like Canetti for whom he speaks here, Fifty thinks monstrous the idea that we have been made a present of life (cf. *HP,* 244). His subversive restlessness and disbelief move him to unmask the "natural law" of death. The holy "moment" of death, with its utopian significance, is in dystopian reality nothing but an execution protected and covered by the instructions of the priest who is an official of the state.

Fifty, however, encounters great difficulties when he appeals to an extra-utopian reality principle. The illusory freedom of choice within the utopian limitations occupies the social imagination of the great majority of the Numbered and thus works as a reliable support for the ruling system. Carefully controlled "indiscretions" about the remaining amount of lifetime are spread like rumors about the stock market and further isolate the members of the Numbered. The few people who understand this situation have withdrawn into resignation and do not believe that Fifty will be able to achieve anything given the deeply rooted rule of death. The unequal limitations, the arbitrarily granted allotment of years, have created a hierarchy that operates as reliably as a machine and is enacted by the chorus of the Unequal that concludes the first part of the drama. To the Keeper of Lockets's ritual question whether they like being together they answer "no," because they will be separated and are waiting for "the moment" of separation. Deprived of the fear of death, this most human reaction, they have been deprived of the equality and the bonding with others in the face of its sting. Still alive, they are already as separated as if they were dead because death here is the great unequalizer. It is consistent with the logic of this new order that the dystopians only connect as equals when urging Fifty to desist from his heretical doubting of the rule of death by natural law.

Fifty is the quintessential dissenter in this quintessential dystopia. It is true, he is coresponsible for the enduring rule of death since he has accepted the status quo for a long time. But he can also see the situation more clearly than others because he has not kept track of the number of the years he has lived. Preoccupied with living, he really does not know when exactly he is supposed to die. Above all, his not wanting to die himself means also that he does not want others to keep on dying so cooperatively. Argument by argument, he reveals first his and then every death to be the result of a death sentence passed a priori and thereby the theocratic basis of the omnipotent rule of death. Without having to lie, he can admit as well as deny to the Keeper of Lockets the fiftieth return of his birthday. Most important, he can really negotiate his "moment" with the priest who represents the power of the state. Fifty's temporary respite comes from his proving that the taboo-protected moment of death is not determined by a law of nature enacted in religious terms but by the mundane needs of theocratic rule. Exposing the utopian political control by means of religious concepts like contrition, recantation, and grace, he can himself use them strategically. The truly revolutionary aspect of his dissent is its rigorous secularism.

As with all revolutionary acts, however, destabilizing energies create their own problems, and this fact becomes part of the play's dramatic logic. When Canetti compared Fifty to Brecht's Galileo, whose new physics destabilized not just the scientific but also the social and psychological self-perception of his contemporaries, he was not only drawing attention to the cultural importance of his own new insights (*HP*, 191). He was reflecting on the fact that the disintegration of familiar order, regardless how good or bad, brings with it uncertainties and thereby a greater vulnerability to new ideological systems—utopian constructs that always already carry the seed of their own dystopian decomposition. The young dramatist did not deal with this dynamic, notwithstanding his claims made in hindsight that, an act of dissent at the time, he had understood and revealed the dystopian aspects of Kraus's utopian pursuit of verbal purity. The utopian-dystopian dynamic has been as central to twentieth-century social politics as it has been destructive, and it was not addressed in the early dramas. With all their occasional verbal brilliance and their intriguing *Grundeinfälle* that seem to touch on important issues of their time, these texts now seem curiously innocent of that period's complexities and therefore dated.

Despite its limitations as dramatic fiction **The Numbered** has aged quite well; an intricate argument that seems as cogent and valid today as it was half a century ago is well served by the very "undramatic" pace and verbal sobriety of the text. Fifty has temporarily freed himself from "his" death forced on him by the power of the utopian state. At some point in time he will die; but first he has gained human time, lifetime—like all things human a relative gain and precisely for this reason not to be despised.[20] Most of the Numbered, however, are no longer capable of this insight. Their utopian socialization has left them so isolated that they cannot use this kind of liberation intelligently. Since their own po-

tential for transformation has been so unjustly limited, they can longer see themselves in their interdependency with other persons' need for transformation. During his work on the text, Canetti reflected on the injustice of death as a death sentence inflicted a priori: "We have to be bad because we know we will die. We would be even worse if, from the very start, we knew when" (*HP*, 129). In the utopia of the Numbered, the fear of death has been muted by the religious presentation of the rule of death. Their wickedness shows itself in the inhuman indifference with which they simply accept as a law of nature what is, for conscious beings, the most unnatural thing: that there will be an end to consciousness. It turns out—logically in terms of the dramatic argument—that Fifty's most important opponent is not the Keeper of Lockets but his best, most sympathetic dialogue partner, Friend, and he—again logically—has the last word.

Friend has been open to Fifty's dissenting arguments because he has never stopped mourning his beloved sister Twelve. Under the rule of death mourning is subversive, not to be tolerated. When Fifty argues with a young woman who has just buried her child Seven that one should at least try to resist "the moment" in order to get the child more lifetime, she counters with the utopian prescriptions for motherly love that she had strictly followed. Beyond her "moment" the child is nothing but a shadow to the mother, no longer real. If the child went on living, it would no longer be her child but a ghostly witness to her crime against a society that imposes the death sentence in the case of heretical nonacceptance of death. The emotion of mourning alone signifies dissent and is punishable under the law, consequences that Friend has accepted courageously. But after Fifty's precarious victory—he broke the taboo and escaped—Friend implores him now to stop assailing the fact of death as law of nature. Fifty, however, naturally thinks and acts in cultural, that is, social terms. Instinctively, he includes others in the consequences of his revolt and logically this means here death as well as life. The precondition for not accepting death as a foregone conclusion is that everybody acknowledges the other person's right to their own life instead of death. But Friend is no longer capable of doing that. Immediately after Fifty's unmasking of "the moment" he sets off on a search for Twelve, who now might still be alive and grown into a young woman. Fifty tries in vain to keep him back, arguing that Friend ought to set her free, not continue owning her as he had tried to do when mourning her premature death. At the end of the drama Friend's decision to search for and find *his* sister is unshakable.

In Fifty's view, this in many ways understandable human desire to possess the other, reflected also in Friend's mourning more his loss of the sister than hers, was vulnerable to exploitation by the utopian rule of death. Abolishing the uncertainty regarding the time of death and thereby deadening its sting also meant numbing or, as in Friend's case, refocusing the pain of loss for the living. The utopian isolation, as Fifty has shown, negates this pain. Friend cannot understand all the implications of Fifty's dissenting view because it presents the social dimension of human life so literally. It was precisely Fifty's lack of desire to possess other people in life that enabled his insight into the social meanings of the experience of death: an indispensable insight because it makes this experience subject to human time and human measure. The underlying challenge of this and of all of Canetti's postwar texts—that we can truly share the world only if we overcome the desire to have power over others—is itself the most powerful and "unnatural" utopian desire and in that by no means harmless. Its absolutism echoes that of Kraus, if in more muted and soberly reflected form, and it has no doubt been central to Canetti's dissent, provocative and thoughtful, from the utopias of the status quo.

Notes

1. See Dagmar Barnouw, *Die versuchte Realität oder von der Möglichkeit, glücklichere Welten zu denken* (Meitingen: Corian, 1985), chaps. 1 ("Die Möglichkeit von Utopie: Wie betritt man eine andere Welt?") and 2 ("Die Realität von Utopia: Wie verhält man sich in einer anderen Welt?").

2. Translations of *Die Befristeten* have appeared under two different titles: the present essay refers to *The Numbered,* trans. Carol Stewart (London: Marion Boyars, 1984); an alternative version is found in *"Comedy of Vanity" and "Life-Terms,"* trans. Gitta Honegger (New York: PAJ Publications, 1983).

3. See Peter Iden, "Mich brennt der Tod," *Frankfurter Rundschau,* 24 August 1994; Hans Hollmann, "Erfinder der Akustischen Maske: Über Elias Canetti, den Dramatiker, Denker und Todesfeind," in *Wortmasken: Texte zu Leben und Werk von Elias Canetti,* ed. Carl Hanser Verlag (Munich: Hanser, 1995), 83-88; Wolfgang Hädecke, "Die moralische Quadratur des Zirkels: Das Todesproblem im Werk Elias Canettis," *Text und Kritik* 28, rev. ed. (1982): 27-32; and Reinhard Urbach, "Der präsumptive Todestag: Bemerkungen zu Elias Canettis *Die Befristeten,*" *Literatur und Kritik* 3 (1968): 404-8.

4. Elias Canetti, *The Conscience of Words,* trans. Joachim Neugroschel (London: Deutsch, 1979), 33-34; hereafter cited in text as *CW.*

5. Canetti identified *"literalness* and *horror"* as crucial components of the effect that Kraus achieved (*CW,* 31).

6. See Gerald Stieg, "Elias Canetti und Karl Kraus: Ein Versuch," *Modern Austrian Literature* 16, no. 3/4 (1983): 197-210.

7. Elias Canetti, "Gespräch mit Horst Bienek," *Die gespaltene Zukunft: Aufsätze und Gespräche,* Reihe Hanser 111 (Munich: Hanser, 1972), 101.

8. Elias Canetti, *The Play of the Eyes,* trans. Ralph Manheim (New York: Farrar, Straus and Giroux, 1986), 3-18; hereafter cited in text as *PE.*

9. Quoted in Erich Fried, *Elias Canetti: Welt im Kopf* (Graz: Stiasny, 1962), 14; hereafter cited in text.

10. See Dagmar Barnouw, *Elias Canetti: Zur Einführung* (Hamburg: Junius, 1996), 161; hereafter cited in text as Barnouw 1996.

11. Regarding the former, see Dagmar Barnouw, "'Noch ist das Lachen erlaubt': Dystopische Komik im Drama der Eitelkeit," *Sprache im technischen Zeitalter* 95 (1985): 200-206.

12. Elias Canetti, *The Wedding,* trans. Gitta Honegger (New York: PAJ Publications, 1986).

13. Regarding the play's *Grundeinfall,* the prohibition of mirrors, Canetti describes how, at the barber's one day, he was irritated by having to look into the mirror for the duration of the haircut but enthralled by the other customers' fascination with their own image (*PE,* 90).

14. See Peter Laemmle, "Macht und Ohnmacht des Ohrenzeugen: Zur Kategorie des Dramatischen in Canettis frühen Stücken," *Canetti lesen: Erfahrungen mit seinen Büchern,* ed. Herbert G. Göpfert (Munich: Hanser, 1975), 48. [Laemmle's essay appears in English translation elsewhere in the present volume. *Ed.*]

15. "The man who really knew what ties people together would be able to save them from death. The enigma of life is a social enigma. No one is on its track" (Elias Canetti, *The Human Province,* trans. Joachim Neugroschel [New York: Seabury, 1978], 194; hereafter cited in text as *HP*).

16. Elias Canetti, *The Secret Heart of the Clock: Notes, Aphorisms, Fragments, 1973-1985,* trans. Joel Agee (New York: Farrar, Straus and Giroux, 1989), 96; hereafter cited in text as *SHC.*

17. Canetti's stance against death has been vulnerable to many misunderstandings because of its radical originality, especially since it reflects, at the same time, a peculiarly perceptive, troubling common sense; see Barnouw 1996, 8-10, 201-17.

18. "Is everyone too good to die? One can't say that. First everyone would have to live longer" (*HP,* 48).

19. His reflections here are focused much more generally and do not refer to the guilt of the survivor common in situations of war and persecution.

20. In 1985 the 80-year-old noted: "Here he stands, looking at Death. Death approaches him, he repels it. He will not do Death the honor of taking it into account. If he finally does break down in bewilderment—he didn't bow before Death. He called it by its name, he hated it, he cast it out. He has accomplished so little, it is more than nothing" (*SHC*, 150).

Anne Fuchs (essay date 2000)

SOURCE: Fuchs, Anne. "The Dignity of Difference: Self and Other in Elias Canetti's *Voices of Marrakesh*." In *Critical Essays on Elias Canetti*, edited by David Darby, pp. 201-12. New York: G. K. Hall and Co., 2000.

[*In the following essay, Fuchs examines* Voices of Marrakesh *in the post-colonial milieu, finding that Canetti neither appropriated nor colonized his subjects.*]

For a long time Elias Canetti's **Die Stimmen von Marrakesch** (**The Voices of Marrakesh**) was considered marginal in relation to Canetti's major publications, such as **Die Blendung** (**Auto-da-Fé**) or his autobiography. The critical attention the book has received came largely from admirers of Canetti's works who praised it for its poetic quality without, however, placing the narrative in the context of current theories of travel writing.[1] This paper addresses the fallacious innocence of much of the literature on Canetti's **The Voices of Marrakesh** by reading the book with reference to several arguments central to the post-colonial debate. Canetti's journey is an exploration of the dignity of difference that neither appropriates nor colonizes the other in Orientalist terms. Scripting cultural difference, the narrative metaphorizes the repressed underside of all cultural constructs: namely, death and abjection.

Elias Canetti's **The Voices of Marrakesh** is a belated book: although Canetti accompanied an English film team on a trip to Morocco in 1954, his slim record of his Moroccan experience only appeared some 13 years later in 1967. But, as the subtitle suggests, "Aufzeichnungen nach einer Reise" (literally: notes after a journey), this belatedness is intentional: it shows that **The Voices of Marrakesh** is not conceived as a spontaneous notebook registering the traveler's immediate impressions but rather as a carefully orchestrated sequence of poetic vignettes that, according to the critic Manfred Durzak, work like Joycean epiphanies, revealing moments of metaphysical or aesthetic truth through seemingly marginal observations (Göpfert, 142).

The time lapse between the actual journey and the publication—together with the subtitle—thus highlights once more what characterizes the poeticity of Canetti's book as a whole: the voices of the title are mediated not only through the consciousness of the traveler but also through the passage of time. This built-in distance between the traveler and the narrator also creates an attitude of distance toward the world of Marrakesh on the reader's part, thus undermining the impression of presence and immediacy that is evoked by the sensual allure of the title. According to Cecile Zorach, "this unresolvable tension between the traveler's desire for immediacy . . . and his acceptance of distance results in a travel book which tells the reader relatively little about Marrakesh and very much about how Canetti sees man's position in the world at large" (Zorach, 47). In a sense this is true of all travel writing, in that travelogues—ranging from the scientific and ethnographic travel books of the eighteenth and early nineteenth centuries, the *Bildungsreise* (educational tour) à la Goethe or Karl Philipp Moritz, Laurence Sterne's *Sentimental Journey*, Johann Gottfried Seume's alternative *Spaziergang nach Syrakus* (Walk to Syracuse) to Heinrich Heine's extremely subjective *Reisebilder* (Travel-pictures), to name just a few important examples of the genre—always articulate an encounter between self and other that is premised upon the traveler's own beliefs and expectations.[2]

In Canetti's case, however, the relative absence of political, economic, and social themes—at a time when the Moroccan National Movement, the Istiklal Party, was fighting for independence (which was finally achieved in 1956)—raises the question of whether **The Voices of Marrakesh** is not just another example in Europe's long tradition of inventing the Orient as "a theatrical stage affixed to Europe."[3] In his seminal study *Orientalism: Western Conceptions of the Orient*, Edward Said argued that Orientalism was not just a field of study but rather "a *distribution* of geopolitical awareness into aesthetic, scholarly, economic, sociological, historical, and philological texts; it is an elaboration not only of a basic geographical distinction . . . but also of a whole series of 'interests'" (Said, 12). In Said's view Orientalism always promotes an essentialist difference between self and other, Europe and the Orient, and it engages in inventing an unchanging Orient that is closed off from historical change and absolutely different from the West (Said, 96). The Orientalist attitude therefore shares "with magic and with mythology the self-containing, self-reinforcing character of a closed system, in which objects are what they are *because* they are what they are, for once, for all time, for ontological reasons that no empirical material can either dislodge or alter" (Said, 70).

While Said's analysis has had a pervasive influence on the theory and history of travel writing and on the deconstruction of the white man's gaze,[4] Said's own essentialist set of premises have since been subject to considerable criticism, most notably by Robert Young and the great critic of the postcolonial condition, Homi Bhabha, with the latter arguing that Said paid inadequate attention to representation as a concept that articulates "the historical and fantasy (as the scene of desire)."[5] In the present context Bhabha is of particular interest since he highlights an ambivalence that is fundamental to colonial discourse and that is of relevance for our reading of Canetti's *The Voices of Marrakesh*: applying Freud's notion of the fetish to his analysis of colonial discourse, Bhabha defines the colonial stereotype as "a form of knowledge and identification that vacillates between what is always 'in place' and something that must be anxiously repeated."[6] On the functional level both fetish and stereotype share "the archaic affirmation of wholeness and sameness and the anxiety associated with lack and difference" (Bhabha 1994, 74).

And this brings us back to Canetti's *The Voices of Marrakesh* and the question of whether his narrative is an example of such anxious repetition of that which is already known. Or, to put it differently, does Canetti's vocabulary of "openness and concealment, of knowledge and mystery, of secrecy and curiosity" (Zorach, 56) produce the colonized as a reality "which is at once an other and yet entirely knowable and visible" (Bhabha 1994, 70)? Do we have to agree with the critic who placed Canetti in the Orientalist camp, arguing that *The Voices of Marrakesh* consists of a series of queer, bizarre, and horrific images of an abnormal Orient that is "distinct and removed from the sane and rational West"? And is it true that Canetti's Morocco aims at evoking nothing but "shock, disgust, laughter or pity" in the reader?[7]

If one studies Canetti's *The Voices of Marrakesh* only in terms of its themes and imagery, it appears to be hard to disagree with this scathing critique, since the narrative is indeed heavily peopled with decrepit animals, beggars, and veiled women; in addition, there are many metaphors of secrecy and concealment that, out of context, may suggest an Orientalist outlook on Canetti's part. However, in what follows I want to demonstrate that the book articulates a hermeneutics of otherness based on empathy and reciprocity. This hermeneutics is largely informed by a key concept in Canetti's thinking, namely that of *Verwandlung* (metamorphosis, transformation), which he developed in his anthropological study *Masse und Macht* (*Crowds and Power*) and applied to the poet in his essay **"Der Beruf des Dichters"** (**"The Writer's Profession"**).

Using anthropological studies as well as literary examples such as *The Odyssey* or Ovid's *Metamorphoses,* myths, and legends, Canetti attempts to show in *Crowds and Power* that the ability to participate with either nature or an other in an intuitive and empathic manner is a uniquely human quality.[8] In the process of civilization, however, this potential is limited and curbed by the opposite tendency toward *Erstarrung* (petrifaction), which is closely affiliated with power (*CP* [*Crowds and Power*], 377-79). Canetti analyzes history as a battle between *Verwandlung* and *Erstarrung:* he argues that in totalitarian societies the representatives of power attempt to curb and limit the human potential for *Verwandlung* because *Verwandlung* always contains the promise of change. Since history has the tendency to repress this ability, the poet, in Canetti's view, has to be a "keeper of metamorphosis," a guardian of man's most imaginative ability.[9] By virtue of creative empathy the poet breaks through those tendencies of the technocratic age that applaud petrifaction in the form of professional specialization and impose limits on the individual's horizon of expectation, rendering him or her closed to the diversity and dignity of life. Opposing the rational linearity of the technocratic age, the poet has the task of keeping alive the ability "to become *anybody and everybody,* even the smallest, the most naive, the most powerless person" (*CW* [*The Conscience of Words*], 162). He is a guardian of *Verwandlung* who imaginatively transforms himself into "every individual thing or person that lives and exists" (*CW,* 165). This is the methodological horizon of Canetti's *The Voices of Marrakesh.*

Obviously, this theory has to be placed in the romantic tradition, which Roland Barthes has attacked for its tendency to convert culture into nature. Canetti's *Verwandlung* is indeed a naturalized concept; likewise he conceives the role of the poet in highly romantic terms as an autonomous and creative subject engaged in the salvation of mankind. However, while one should be aware of the ideological implications of Canetti's romanticism, it seems to me that his theory of *Verwandlung* translates itself in *The Voices of Marrakesh* into a hermeneutics of otherness based on reciprocity. In contrast to the binary straitjacket of Said's *Orientalism* and its closed interpretation of the terrain between Orient and Occident, Canetti's concept of *Verwandlung* represents an approach to the other characterized by openness. For *Verwandlung* can never reach its telos completely; if it becomes an end in itself it reduces itself back to the petrifaction that it seeks to transcend.

The title *The Voices of Marrakesh* reflects the primacy that Canetti attaches to the nonsemantic dimension of experience. It emphasizes those prelinguistic sensual impressions that appeal to an intuitive understanding but ultimately preserve a sense of strangeness. Favoring auditory over visual impressions, Canetti thus detaches himself from the politics of ethnography and travel writing that has systematically privileged the eye as the primary agent in the discovery and colonization of the other.[10] In contrast to such visual colonization, Canetti's use of the term "voices" conjures up an image of sounds. This appeals to the aural sense, however without permitting appropriation by the language and symbolic order of the traveler. Note for instance the chapter "Storytellers and Scribes" in which Canetti captures the paralinguistic expressiveness of the narrator's public performance in the following words: "He arranged them in a rhythm that always struck me as highly personal. If he paused, what followed came out all the more forceful and exalted. I sensed the solemnity of certain words and the devious intent of others. Flattering compliments affected me as if they had been directed at myself; in perilous situations I was afraid. Everything was under control; the most powerful words flew precisely as far as the storyteller wished them to."[11] By being receptive to rhythm, tone, pitch, and gesture, the traveler feels his way into the story, without, however, understanding it. A fine balance between intuition and distance is maintained throughout.

A similar receptiveness is manifest in the traveler's approach to the tortured cries of the camels, the decrepit donkey, the repetitive calls of the beggars, the alluring babble of the madwoman, as well as the call of "the unseen" in the final chapter. Here the voice is reduced to a singular sound emitted by a little brown bundle that cannot be discerned behind a shield of cloth. Both traveler and narrator are deeply affected by this singular voice: "Only for this voice, reduced to a single sound, did I feel something akin to fear. It was at the very edge of the living; the life that engendered it consisted of nothing but that sound" (*VM* [*The Voices of Marrakesh*], 101). At the same time as interpreting this bundle as a symbol of life, Canetti voices his respect for its otherness and dignity, both of which are closely affiliated: "I was proud of the bundle because it was alive. What it thought to itself as it breathed down there, far below other people, I shall never know. The meaning of its call remained as obscure to me as its whole existence: but it was alive, and every day at the same time, there it was" (*VM*, 103). Here and in the other episodes, the traveler and narrator register the voices of Marrakesh with empathy, relating them to the dignity of all life. These voices always remain firmly in the possession of the enunciating subject and are not colonized by the outsider.

The Voices of Marrakesh thus articulates Canetti's awareness that the culture of Marrakesh is only partially accessible to him and that his encounter retains the status of sense perception even at the point of writing. Throughout the book Canetti evokes the enigmatic quality of these voices that yield an intuitive understanding, while at the same time preserving a sense of strangeness, qualities that transcend the boundaries of language: "A marvelously luminous, viscid substance is left behind in me, defying words. Is it the language I did not understand there, and that must now gradually find its translation in me? There were incidents, images, sounds, the meaning of which is only now emerging; that words neither recorded nor edited; that are beyond words, deeper and more equivocal than words" (*VM*, 23). Canetti's insistence that one must attune one's sense perceptions to a higher pitch, in order to transcend the constraints of a discursive language that is affected by power, is curiously reminiscent of Julia Kristeva's concept of the *semiotic*, the anarchic circulation of sexual energy and impulses, in short "jouissance," which antedates the distinction between subject and object and which is associated with the pre-oedipal drives and the symbiotic space shared by the mother's and child's indistinguishable bodies, all of which is eventually repressed in favor of the symbolic order, the domain of language, hierarchies, exchange, and so on. Suffice it to add that for Kristeva modern art problematizes the symbolic by liberating the unarticulated *jouissance* of the semiotic: "Art—this semiotization of the symbolic—. . . represents the flow of jouissance into language."[12] From this angle, Canetti's desire to unlearn all languages reflects his urge to escape the petrifactions of the symbolic order in favor of the archaic resonances of the semiotic state with its fluidity and pulsations. For this reason, in *The Voices of Marrakesh,* silence can speak as loudly as sounds. The silences that are written into the text are a powerful symbol of the ineffable quality of the semiotic that Canetti tries to evoke in this text. It is given a most succinct expression during the encounter with Élie Dahan's father, who, after having been introduced to Canetti, repeats the latter's full name in such a way that it appears "more substantial, more beautiful" (*VM*, 74), affecting Canetti deeply: "Awed, I remained perfectly silent. Perhaps I was also afraid of breaking the wonderful spell of the name-chanting. As a result we spent several long moments facing each other. If he only understands why I cannot speak, I thought; if my eyes could only laugh the way his do" (*VM,* 75). This aesthetically charged silence communicates a bond of intense empathy that taps into the semiotic; for this reason it can be only evoked but not interpreted through language.

On the other hand, the silence that hovers throughout the text can also point to a sense of alienation. A good example of this is to be found in the chapter "The Silent House and the Empty Rooftops," where the traveler experiences a sense of frustration at the silence and inaccessibility of the other culture. This theme is reinforced by the image of the wall prohibiting access to the private sphere, which has a mysterious allure for the traveler. For this reason he tries to catch a glimpse behind the walls and climbs onto the roof terrace where he hopes to see women in fairy tales (*VM*, 32). Feigning admiration for the mountains in the distance, he sneaks a furtive glance into the courtyard next door but is caught in the act and severely reprimanded by his friend. This scene and the ensuing dialogue between the traveler and his friend about the function of boundaries serve to parody the traveler's desire to peer behind the walls of this alien society. Canetti's irony here and elsewhere is a reminder of the limitations of the traveler who, by registering his own sense of alienation, maintains a careful equipoise between proximity and distance, empathy and frustration.

In direct contrast to the carefully guarded privacy of the houses and their inwardness is the "greater [literally: intensified] openness" (*VM,* 20) of the bazaar in the chapter "The Souks." Canetti conveys a wonderful image of the rich sensual impressions here, coupled with a semiotic reading of the trading and bartering. The bazaar is a display of abundance, craftsmanship, and dignity, human qualities that reflect the nonalienated relationship between the goods and their vendors; without labels and a fixed price, they are metonymies of the men who produce and sell them. Canetti carefully notes the proximity of the merchant to his goods, interpreting this seductive intimacy as a celebration of pride that affects the goods themselves: "There is a great deal of pride in this exhibition. They are showing what they can produce, but they are also showing how much of it there is. The effect is as if the bags themselves knew that they were wealth and were flaunting themselves in their excellence before the eyes of the passers-by. It would come as no surprise if the bags were suddenly to begin moving rhythmically, all of them together, displaying in a gaily-coloured, orgiastic dance all the seductiveness of which they were capable" (*VM,* 18-19). The image of the dancing bags evokes a carnivalesque atmosphere that highlights the communicative and symbolic function of the bazaar. Instead of describing the goods in terms of their monetary value, Canetti sees them in terms of an emotional value that is derived from the relationship between seller and buyer. Unlike shopping in capitalist societies where "any fool can go out and find what he needs" (*VM,* 21), shopping in the bazaar is a complex game. The price of each item fluctuates according to a number of variables:

> In the souks, however, the price that is named first is an unfathomable riddle. No one knows in advance what it will be, not even the merchant, because in any case there are many prices. Each one relates to a different situation, a different customer, a different day of the week. There are prices for single objects and prices for two or more together. There are prices for foreigners visiting the city for a day and prices for foreigners who have been here for three weeks. There are prices for the poor and prices for the rich, those for the poor of course being the highest.
>
> (*VM,* 21)

This passage reads like an illustration of Jean Baudrillard's observation "that an accurate theory of social objects must be based on signification rather than needs or use-value."[13] It is in line with this idea that Canetti de-

scribes the act of trading as an artful game between two parties, a communicative praxis that is as important as the outcome, that is, the agreement of a price. The price appears as a reflection of the rhetoric and arguments of the two parties:

> It is desirable that the toing and froing of negotiations should last a miniature, incident-packed eternity. The merchant is delighted at the time you take over your purchase. Arguments aimed at making the other give ground should be far-fetched, involved, emphatic, and stimulating. You can be dignified or eloquent, but you will do best to be both. Dignity is employed by both parties to show that they do not attach too much importance to either sale or purchase. Eloquence serves to soften the opponent's resolution. Some arguments merely arouse scorn; others cut to the quick. You must try everything before you surrender.
>
> (*VM,* 22)

Canetti, the tourist, is an "agent of semiotics" who interprets the bazaar in terms of a cultural praxis and a sign system (Culler, 155). Such semiotic mediation does not, however, necessarily colonize the other by appropriating it within the culture of the outsider, but in Canetti's case it is rather an exploration of the dignity of difference. An indication of this is his careful orchestration of proximity and distance throughout.

Whereas the ethnographic chapter "The Souks" offers a close-up of bazaar life and explores it in terms of a meaningful sign-system, the same semiotic approach appears to be jeopardized a little later in the chapter "The Marabout's Saliva" where the cultural distance between self and other is thematized. In a manner of speaking, this episode is a test case for Canetti's respect for the other because the chapter deals with an experience that breaks a taboo of Western culture to such an extent that it provokes disgust. Canetti describes how he watches a beggar chew something with an astounding intensity. He waits until the beggar stops chewing to see what has caused an "enjoyment, which struck me as being more conspicuous than anything I had ever seen in association with a human mouth" (*VM,* 27). When Canetti offers the beggar 20 francs, he notices to his great surprise that the beggar puts the coin in his mouth and chews it with the same delight and intensity as before. Now Canetti's sense of amazement turns into open disgust: "I tried to dissolve my disgust at this proceeding in its outlandishness. What could be filthier than money?" (*VM,* 28).

Julia Kristeva's theory of abjection in *Powers of Horror: An Essay on Abjection* provides an extremely productive horizon of interpretation for this episode, the main tenets of which I propose to outline briefly. When, for instance, a subject experiences disgust for the improper and unclean, this can often be read as a physical reaction against a "threat that seems to emanate from an exorbitant outside or inside, ejected beyond the scope of the possible, the tolerable and thinkable."[14] Since the mapping out of a "clean and proper body" is a basic condition of the subject's constitution as a speaking subject, the improper and unclean—that is, the "abject"—is banished both from the territory of individual subjectivity and the sphere of sociality. Such expulsion has nothing to do with hygiene but much to do with our sense of identity and belonging to the symbolic order. Kristeva illustrates our disgust for all transgressions that threaten our "clean and proper" body with reference to refuse and corpses: "Without makeup or masks, refuse and corpses *show me* what I permanently thrust aside in order to live. These body fluids, this defilement, this shit are what life withstands, hardly and with difficulty, on the part of death. There, I am at the border of my condition as a living being. My body extricates itself, as being alive from that border" (Kristeva 1982, 3). It seems to me that the beggar's chewing of the coin is for Canetti just such a basic violation of the body's clean and proper boundaries. His involuntary revulsion is thus less motivated by an Orientalist ideology but more by the subject's need to protect his own sense of identity and order. Looked at from this angle, Canetti's experience of repugnance is both an expression of a threat to the subject and an expression of the subject's struggle against the intolerable invasion of the abject. What is at stake in this episode for Canetti is the validity of the symbolic order and sociality as such.

At the height of his revulsion Canetti attempts to suspend his reaction in a conscious effort: "But this old man was not I; what caused me disgust gave him enjoyment, and had I not sometimes seen people kissing coins?" (*VM,* 28). Struggling for a position that recognizes the difference between self and other, he tries to reframe the episode as a ritual, the meaning of which he wants to discover. The longer he watches, however, the more clueless he feels: "The longer I looked on, the less I understood why he did it" (*VM,* 29). At this point the narrator reverses the narrative perspective and zooms in on his traveling alter ego that appears to be quite a sight for the natives: "I did not notice that people were also looking at me, and I must have presented a ridiculous spectacle. Possibly, who knows, I was even gaping open-mouthed" (*VM,* 29). Canetti's surprise at the strange beggar is matched by the native's surprise at the tourist's strange behavior. What this ironic reversal of viewpoints illustrates is the relativity of both cultures.

Eventually an orange dealer assumes the role of cultural translator and explains that the beggar is a marabout, a holy man. However, Canetti's desire for an explanation of the marabout's behavior remains unfulfilled, since the orange dealer simply adds: "'He always does that' . . . as if it had been the most natural thing in the world" (*VM,* 29). The juxtaposition of the two view-

points—namely that of the tourist who interprets the other culture in terms of an alien sign system and that of the native who sees it as his normal everyday environment—highlights once more the relativity of cultural interpretation. For the natives it is actually the tourist who is the object of curiosity: "Only now did I notice that behind every stall there were two or three pairs of eyes trained on me. The astonishing creature was myself, who stood so long uncomprehending" (*VM,* 29).

Canetti leaves, feeling strangely affected by the whole scene. A week later, when he sees the marabout again, the ritual is repeated with Canetti offering a coin, the marabout chewing, and a native who assumes the role of cultural interpreter addressing the marabout in Arabic: "'That's a marabout. He is blind. He puts the coin in his mouth to feel how much you've given him.' Then he said something to the marabout in Arabic and pointed to me. The old man, his chewing finished, had spat the coin out again. He turned to me, his face shining. He said a blessing for me, which he repeated six times. The friendliness and warmth that passed across to me as he spoke were such as I had never had a person bestow on me before" (*VM,* 30). Again it is not the meaning of the words but the nonverbal bond of empathy that makes the marabout's blessing so special for Canetti; it is a moment of *Verwandlung* that transforms the abject into the sublime. Such sublimation of abjection is the business of art.

And this leads me to the final point of my analysis. In a manner of speaking, Canetti's **The Voices of Marrakesh** is as much a book about death as about life. For death as the threatening underside of all cultural constructs is evoked throughout. But it is in the central chapter, "A Visit to the Mellah," that death becomes the central theme. The visit to the Mellah, the Jewish quarter in Marrakesh, represents the high point of Canetti's journey; this chapter and the following one on his acquaintance with the Jewish family Dahan are located at the center of the book and make up more than one-third of the narrative. The quest for a Jewish identity is therefore a latent but integral part of Canetti's narrative.

At the opening of the chapter the narrator describes the bazaar life in the Mellah, focusing this time on the diversity of the human faces that is implicitly set against the pervasive racial stereotype of a Jewish physiognomy (*VM,* 40). Yet at the same time the traveler identifies a specific quality that characterizes the group: he notices that all the Jews have a way of swiftly looking up and assessing any newcomer. Describing these looks as swift, intelligent, and guarded, Canetti then interprets them as an expression of a collective history of persecution: "They were the looks of people who are always on their guard but who, expecting hostility, do not wish to evoke it" (*VM,* 41). Canetti's walk "deeper into the Mellah" assumes an increasingly uncanny quality, culminating in his encounter with an ancient withered crone who, with her eyes fixed into the distance, walks along slowly enough to throw a curse on every living creature (*VM,* 42). When Canetti dares look at her, she feels his gaze and, turning round, "turned her gaze full on me. I hurried on; and so instinctive had been my re-action to her look that it was not for some time that I noticed how much faster I was now walking" (*VM,* 42). This uncanny encounter with this doppelgänger of death is counterbalanced by the description of a lively square, the "heart" of the Mellah. Here the traveler achieves a moment of complete identification, in Canetti's terms, of *Verwandlung:* "I did not want to leave; I had been here hundreds of years ago but I had forgotten and now it was all coming back to me. I found exhibited the same density and warmth of life as I feel in myself. I *was* the square as I stood in it. I believe I am it always" (*VM,* 45). This moment, however, cannot be sustained for long. After a visit to a Jewish school, Canetti comes across the Jewish cemetery. Here Canetti maps out a to-pography of death that is also one of fear, in Kristeva's terms "that terrifying abject referent" depriving us "of the assurance of being ourselves, that is, untouchable, unchangeable, immortal" (Kristeva 1982, 38). Unlike other cemeteries, this Jewish cemetery has the appear-ance to the visitor of a barren, threatening wasteland signifying nothing but the annihilation of all meaning: "But in that desolate cemetery of the Jews there is noth-ing. It is truth itself, a lunar landscape of death. Look-ing at it, you could not care less who lies where. You do not stoop down, you make no attempt to puzzle it out. There they all lie like rubble and you feel like scur-rying over them, quick as a jackal. It is a wilderness of dead in which nothing grows any more, the last wilder-ness, the very last wilderness of all" (*VM,* 49). This im-agery of rubble, a lunar landscape and a desert of the dead, where all meaningful individuality is annihilated, evokes the Shoah without naming it.[15] Here Canetti strips death, the latent subtext of this chapter, of its metaphysical makeup: beyond the borders of our condi-tion as living beings within the symbolic order, the sub-ject is waste. The language of fear is further intensified in the description of the beggars who inhabit this waste-land. Living not only on the margins of society, but, moreover, in this borderland of death, they are the true representatives of the abject, that terrifying nonobject that is opposed to the subject, drawing it to a place where all meaning collapses (Kristeva 1982, 2). Al-though barely existing on the borders of life, they ex-press a vitality and desire for life that the visitor experi-ences as threatening. In this context, it is hardly surprising that the visitor tries to escape when a one-legged beggar chases him on his crutches: "Like some threatening animal he came hurtling at me. In his face as it drew rapidly closer there was nothing to arouse sympathy. Like the whole figure it expressed a single, violent demand: "I'm alive! Give!" (*VM,* 50). Amid

this landscape of decay such stubborn vitality maintains the ambiguity of the abject. Rather than affirming the meaningfulness of our social constructs, the beggar's desire for life points to its opposite, the meaningless-ness of death that infects life. This phobic episode points to the repressed underside of all cultural constructs; it points, moreover, to the fact that language is, in Kriste-va's terms, our "ultimate and inseparable fetish," the fe-tish of life (Kristeva 1982, 37).

After the visit to the small synagogue in the center of the cemetery, Canetti describes another moment of *Ver-wandlung:* a frenzied crowd of beggars that surrounds and physically touches him, moves him so deeply that he loses himself in the emotion, forgetting his earlier fear (*VM,* 52). This moment of *Verwandlung* can also be read as the transformation of the abject into the sub-lime. Kristeva's observation about the writer provides a succinct and final comment here: "The writer is a pho-bic who succeeds in metaphorizing in order to keep from being frightened to death; instead he comes to life again in signs" (Kristeva 1982, 38).

Notes

1. Of the literature on *The Voices of Marrakesh,* I found the following titles useful. On the poeticity of the narrative: Herbert G. Göpfert, "Zu den *Stim-men von Marrkesch,*" in *Elias Canettis Anthro-pologie und Poetik,* ed. Stefan H. Kaszyński (Munich: Hanser, 1984), 135-50; hereafter cited in text. For a first exploration in terms of travel writ-ing: Cecile Zorach, "The Outsider Abroad: Canetti in Marrakesh," *Modern Austrian Literature* 16, no. 3-4 (1983): 47-65; hereafter cited in text. For a more recent analysis with reference to "Der fremde Blick auf das Eigene im Spannungsfeld von Sinnstiftung und Sinnentwertung": Axel G. Streussloff, *Autorschaft und Werk Elias Canettis: Subjekt, Sprache und Identität* (Würzburg: König-shausen und Neumann, 1994), 177-208. For a reading with reference to current theories of tour-ism: Anne Fuchs, "Der touristische Blick, Elias Canetti in Marrakesch: Ansätze zu einer Theorie des Tourismus" in *Reisen im Diskurs: Modelle der literarischen Fremderfahrung von den Pilgerber-tichten bis zur Postmoderne—Tagungsakten des internationalen Syposiums am University College Dublin vom 10-12. März 1994,* ed. Anne Fuchs and Theo Harden (Heidelberg: Carl Winter, 1995), 71-87.

2. For a critical reading of the construction of self and other in paradigms of travel writing from the eighteenth century, see Anne Fuchs, "Sterne's *Sen-timental Journey* and Goethe's *Italian Journey*: Two Models of the Non-Perception of Otherness," *New Comparison* 16 (1993): 25-42; Anne Fuchs, "Der Reisende und sein Geldbeutel: Zur Symbolik

des Geldes in J. G. Seume's *Spaziergang nach Syrakus*," *Euphorion* 89 (1995): 392-400; and Anne Fuchs, "'In Madrid müßten zwei Ochsen an einer Traube ziehen': Fremdverstehen in Karl Philipp Moritz' *Reisen eines Deutschen in Italien*," *Weimarer Beiträge* 44 (1998): 42-53.

3. Edward Said, *Orientalism: Western Conceptions of the Orient* (London: Penguin, 1991), 63; hereafter cited in text.

4. Cf. Mary Louise Pratt, *Imperial Eyes: Travel Writing and Transculturation* (London: Routledge, 1992); and Peter Hulme, *Colonial Encounters: Europe and the Native Caribbean, 1492-1797* (London: Routledge, 1992).

5. Robert Young, *White Mythologies: Writing History and the West* (London: Routledge, 1990), 126-40; Homi K. Bhabha, "Difference, Discrimination, Discourse of Colonialism," in *The Politics of Theory: Proceedings of the Essex Conference on the Sociology of Literature, July 1982*, ed. Francis Barker, Peter Hulme, et al. (Colchester: University of Essex Press, 1983), 200.

6. Homi K. Bhabha, "The Other Question: Stereotype, Discrimination, and the Discourse of Colonialism," in *The Location of Culture* (London: Routledge 1994), 66; hereafter cited in text as Bhabha 1994.

7. Rana Kabbani, *Europe's Myth of Orient: Devise and Rule* (Houndsmills: Macmillan, 1986), 126, 128.

8. Elias Canetti, *Crowds and Power*, trans. Carol Stewart (New York: Farrar, Straus and Giroux, 1984), 337-58; hereafter cited in text as *CP*. For a critical reading of the validity of Canetti's study in anthropological terms, see Ritchie Robertson, "Canetti as Anthropologist," in *Elias Canetti: Londoner Symposium*, ed. Adrian Stevens and Fred Wagner (Stuttgart: Hans Dieter Heinz, 1991), 131-45. [Robertson's essay is reproduced elsewhere in the present volume. *Ed.*] The poetic implications of *Verwandlung* are analyzed by Alfred Doppler, "'Der Hüter der Verwandlungen': Canettis Bestimmung des Dichters," in *Elias Canetti: Blendung als Lebensform*, ed. Friedrich Aspetsberger and Gerald Stieg (Königstein, Taunus, Germany: Athenäum, 1985), 45-56.

9. Elias Canetti, "The Writer's Profession," in *The Conscience of Words* (London: Deutsch, 1986) 160; hereafter cited in text as *CW*.

10. This has been studied by Johannes Fabian in his excellent book *Time and the Other: How Anthropology Makes Its Subject* (New York: Columbia University Press, 1983).

11. Elias Canetti, *The Voices of Marrakesh: A Record of a Visit*, trans. J. A. Underwood (New York: Farrar, Straus and Giroux, 1984), 77; hereafter cited in text as *VM*.

12. Julia Kristeva, *The Revolution in Poetic Language*, trans. Margaret Waller (New York: Columbia University Press, 1984), 80.

13. Quoted in Jonathan Culler, "The Semiotics of Tourism," in *Framing the Sign: Criticism and its Institutions* (Oxford: Basil Blackwell, 1988), 155; hereafter cited in text.

14. Julia Kristeva, *Powers of Horror: An Essay on Abjection*, trans. Leon S. Roudiez (New York: Columbia University Press, 1982), 1; hereafter cited in text as Kristeva 1982.

15. This idea is also suggested by Zorach (57).

Friederike Eigler (essay date 2000)

SOURCE: Eigler, Friederike. "'Fissures in the Monument': Reassessing Elias Canetti's Autobiographical Works." In *Critical Essays on Elias Canetti*, edited by David Darby, pp. 261-75. New York: G. K. Hall and Co., 2000.

[*In the following essay, Eigler argues against the critical notion of continuity throughout an author's canon, finding Canetti to be a thoroughly "heterogeneous" author.*]

1

In his 1976 lecture **"Der Beruf des Dichters"** (**"The Writer's Profession"**), Elias Canetti is critical of authors who write the same book over and over again.[1] Canetti himself penned, over the course of 60 years, a relatively small number of very different works: the early novel *Die Blendung* (1935; *Auto-da-Fé*), several dramas, the monumental anthropological study *Masse und Macht* (1960; *Crowds and Power*), a travelogue of his trip to Marrakesh (1968), numerous essays, a three-volume autobiography (1977-1985), and several volumes of *Aufzeichnungen*, that is, collections of notes and aphorisms.[2] Despite this heterogeneous production, which spanned a large part of the twentieth century, the reception of his works is dominated by the assumption of a homogeneous oeuvre. This applies to the earlier phase of academic and journalistic attention—following the award of the Nobel Prize to Canetti in 1981—which was predominantly laudatory in tone and affirmative in content. It also applies to the reception since the mid-1980s, when a number of scholars began critically to examine Canetti's works, arguing that its powerful means of (self-)representation are anachronistic in an era of critical examinations of the subject, the author, and language.[3] Both approaches, though resulting in opposing assessments of Canetti's works, tend to homogenize Canetti's works. One of the more recent examples is Ursula Ruppel's intriguing study *Der Tod und Canetti* (1995; *Death and Canetti*), which compares Canetti's work to a seamlessly built memorial that is hermetically sealed from the outside world.[4]

The assumption that the name of the author guarantees a certain degree of thematic continuity and stylistic consistency not only marks Canetti's critical reception but, more generally, also continues to inform a large part of literary criticism. Whenever connections between distinct works are not readily detectable, literary critics assume the role of (re)constructing continuities and consistencies. In his oft-quoted essay "What is an Author?" Michel Foucault has traced this hermeneutic activity to the biblical exegesis of Saint Jerome in the fifth century.[5] This notion of the author-function (i.e., as the guarantee of a work's coherence and unity) and the related notion of the role of literary criticism have largely survived theoretical discussions that challenge hermeneutical approaches to literature as well as unitary concepts of the author/subject.

By abandoning the assumption of an underlying continuity and coherence uniting Canetti's works, I seek to avoid what I see as two pitfalls in the critical literature: affirmative praise that confirms the presumed singularity of his oeuvre on one hand and dismissive criticism on the other. In order to explore what I contend is the heterogeneous character of Canetti's works, I look at the relationship between Canetti's three-volume autobiography and the collection of notes and aphorisms *Das Geheimherz der Uhr* (1985; *The Secret Heart of the Clock*), which he wrote during roughly the same period. While my approach challenges those critics who assume coherence throughout Canetti's work, it does not entirely discard the traditional notion of the author. Exploring discrepancies and discontinuities only makes "sense" if one continues to presume that a privileged relationship exists between the various writings of the same author. I thus suggest a revised author-function in which the name of the author remains the point of reference but is no longer seen as a guarantee for the homogeneity of the oeuvre. The approach I propose here allows not only for a careful reassessment of the heterogeneous character of Canetti's works; it also opens up new avenues of research that can look at his writings in the context of contemporary literature and thought. In the last part of this essay, for instance, I briefly examine the relationship of Canetti's works to the writings of the French philosopher Emmanuel Levinas, in particular those addressing his notion of ethics. The relationship between Levinas's ethics and Canetti's poetics cannot be fully explored in the context of this article, but I seek to locate an ethical dimension in Canetti's *Aufze-*

ichnungen that is inherent to and not separate from its poetic dimension. I thereby challenge those critics who look exclusively at Canetti's imposing rhetoric and style. But before I consider the heterogeneous aspects of his works and their relation to Levinas (parts 2 and 3), I first explore those aspects of Canetti's works that seem to suggest continuity.

Arguably, the particular sequence in which Canetti's works were published tends to support homogenizing efforts despite the heterogeneity of individual works. After the publication of *Crowds and Power* in 1960, Canetti almost exclusively published texts that either explicitly or implicitly comment on some of the main issues explored in this anthropological study. For instance, according to Canetti the main function of his 1000-page autobiography is to reconstruct the biographical circumstances within which the project of *Crowds and Power* emerged.[6] Many sections of his life story indeed comment on the genesis of his major study and on the continued pertinence of his analysis of power, crowds, death, and metamorphosis. This self-referential dimension of Canetti's works has contributed to approaches that treat Canetti's writings as an organic whole.

The four volumes of *Aufzeichnungen* published during Canetti's lifetime represent another dimension of his extensive self-commentary. The majority of notes collected in *Die Provinz des Menschen* (1973; *The Human Province*) were written during the same time as *Crowds and Power* and comment on issues related to that study; the notes in *The Secret Heart of the Clock* have accompanied the writing of his autobiography and constitute another layer of his self-commentary. In the following decade Canetti published two more collections of notes, *Die Fliegenpein* (1992; *The Agony of Flies*) and *Nachträge aus Hampstead* (1994; *Notes from Hampstead*). Neither of these two volumes is, however, a chronological continuation of the previous ones. Instead, *The Agony of Flies* includes a cross-section of notes from previous decades, and *Notes from Hampstead* includes additional texts from the years 1954-1971, the period that was already covered in *The Human Province*.

The particular sequencing of Canetti's publications and their self-referential dimension suggest continuity among his works. Like the different layers of a palimpsest, Canetti has gradually exposed various layers of his writings, always reminding the reader both of the existence of other writings that are not intended for publication and of the selective nature of the notes that he did publish (*CW* [*The Conscience of Words*], 54, 59). This carefully controlled publication process lasted until his death in 1994 and has in some ways continued even beyond his death. Canetti's daughter Johanna oversaw the posthumous publication of yet another volume of notes that Canetti had selected for publication just prior to his death.[7] It seems almost as if Canetti, who throughout his life refused to accept the finality of death, managed to guarantee his own survival in his writings by presenting them in a carefully delayed and selective manner to his readership.

Based in part on the self-referential dimension of his works, Ursula Ruppel argues that Canetti has created a body of texts sealed from contemporary social, cultural, and political concerns. As an example she mentions *Crowds and Power,* which fails to address in any direct manner the ideologies in whose name the most extreme abuse of power in this century took place, namely Communism and Fascism. Regarding the self-referential character of Canetti's entire work, Ruppel comments: "In a continuous movement, Canetti's work turns within itself and around itself. . . . This process, in which the work interprets and comments on itself, at the same time seals it hermetically from the outside. With each new text, it hardens and thickens into a monument that confronts death. A tombstone of enormous size, erected during life, in which single pieces fit together seamlessly like the square blocks of a pyramid" (Ruppel, 94, 99 [my translation]). In this categorical pronouncement, Canetti is defeated with his own analytical tools. By comparing Canetti's writings with the erection of a monumental tombstone, Ruppel evokes the imagery of death that Canetti relies on in his own analysis of the archetypical "dictator" in *Crowds and Power.* She declares Canetti, the self-declared enemy of death (*Tod-Feind*), to be an enemy of life. While I find Ruppel's analysis generally convincing, I question her assumption of continuity among Canetti's works. It is this assumption that allows her readily to relate the early novel to the autobiography, published almost half a century later, and to suggest similarities between the author and his figure of the paranoid scholar and misogynist Peter Kien in the novel *Auto-da-Fé.* Regarding Canetti's works, I maintain that the assumption of continuity obscures other important aspects of his writings. It may well be that Canetti sought to build a "perfectly smooth monument," as Ruppel argues, but my exploration in the next part of this article is of discontinuities and contradictions: the "fissures" and "cracks" that mark this written monument.

2

Similar to *The Human Province, The Secret Heart of the Clock* includes, in terms both of content and style, a broad variety of entries. Compared with the entries in *The Human Province,* those in *The Secret Heart* are generally shorter and more concise, sometimes to the point of being enigmatic, thus requiring the active involvement of the reader in the reading process.[8] There are aphorisms critically reflecting on language and prefabricated phrases, a tradition that harks back to Georg

Christoph Lichtenberg, Marie von Ebner-Eschenbach, and Karl Kraus;[9] commentaries about particular books, his own works, and the reception of the first volumes of his autobiography; observations about animals; critical observations about human behavior; and reversals of conventional patterns of thought, a figure frequently employed by Lichtenberg.[10] Many entries reflect on topics familiar to readers of Canetti's other works (e.g., crowds, power, metamorphosis, and language), but comments on death and the finality of life are *the* central topics. Yet contrary to what Ruppel's allegory of a seamless memorial suggests, the entries in *The Secret Heart* do not merely reiterate and affirm already known topics and positions. *The Secret Heart* is informed by new perspectives, probing questions, and deep skepticism concerning some of Canetti's previously well-established arguments and views. Thus *The Secret Heart* discloses some of the contradictions and disparities that Canetti's autobiography carefully obscures.

Canetti penned the entries included in *The Secret Heart* between 1973 and 1985; that is, during the same period in which he wrote and published the three volumes of his autobiography: *Die gerettete Zunge* (1977; *The Tongue Set Free*), *Die Fackel im Ohr* (1980; *The Torch in My Ear*), and *Das Augenspiel* (1985; *The Play of the Eyes*). The autobiographical narrative is set against the political and social turmoil of the early part of the twentieth century. In three volumes Canetti captures roughly 30 years of his life (1905-1937). The last volume concludes with the death of his mother and merely alludes to the political events leading to the annexation of Austria by Nazi Germany in 1938, when Canetti was forced to leave Vienna. While Vienna had been Canetti's major domicile since 1924, he had also lived in Frankfurt and Berlin, following his childhood years in Bulgaria, England, and Switzerland. These frequent moves, some of which were involuntary, do not amount to ruptures in his autobiography. Instead, the teleological organization of Canetti's autobiography renders every single event of the past meaningful.[11] In sharp contrast to most (post)modern autobiographies, Canetti's autobiography addresses the processes of writing and of recalling and interpreting earlier events only in passing.[12] The autobiography can be read as his attempt to transcend temporality and challenge death through the written word. By contrast, Canetti's aphorisms and notes include what the autobiography excludes or seeks to overcome: the irreversibility of time, the inevitability of (his own) death, the threat of global destruction—issues that undercut the seminal arguments of his life and works. To explore these discontinuous and disruptive dimensions of *The Secret Heart* further, I discuss in more detail three different types of notes: (a) socio-political entries, such as comments on current events; (b) self-referential entries, such as commentaries on the process of remembrance; and (c) self-critical entries, such as remarks that question central arguments of *Crowds and Power.*

SOCIOPOLITICAL ENTRIES

Contrary to what Ruppel's assessment of Canetti's works suggests, the five volumes of *Aufzeichnungen* do include references to contemporary social and political issues. In *The Human Province* there are comments about the aftermath of the Second World War; *The Secret Heart* includes numerous comments about torture, starvation, the threat of global destruction and the end of humanity, nuclear weapons, and the related threat of another world war in the Cold War era of the 1980s. While most of these comments refer to the state of humanity and world politics in general, there is one entry that refers to a particular event, the downing of a Korean airliner by the Soviets in 1983, which brought the superpowers to the brink of war (*SHC* [*The Secret Heart of the Clock*], 122). Seen against the backdrop of this specific reference to a particularly dangerous moment of the Cold War, the more general comments about the future of humanity increase in urgency. In the following entry Canetti reconfirms his concern about humanity while pondering the adverse effects of a fatalistic outlook: "More and more often he catches himself thinking that there is no way to save humanity. Is this an attempt to rid himself of responsibility?" (*SHC,* 25).

In *The Secret Heart* Canetti displays not only an increasing concern with worldwide political and social crises, he also expresses increasing skepticism with regard to his own role as a writer. The following note suggests the writer's complicity with contemporary humanitarian crises, while it insists that writing remains his only possible form of resistance: "While others starve, he writes. He writes while others die" (*SHC,* 89). This chiastic figure underscores an unresolvable tension between, on the one hand, the moral responsibility Canetti attributes to the writer and, on the other, those social problems that render this claim for responsibility meaningless or, at the very least, questionable. Explicit remarks about contemporary society in *The Secret Heart* are sparse but display a deep concern with the multiple threats to humankind. This dimension of the *Aufzeichnungen* stands in marked contrast to Canetti's official life story, which lacks references to contemporary societal problems and which therefore seems to have been written in a historical vacuum.

SELF-REFERENTIAL ENTRIES

Self-probing comments about the processes of remembering and writing are another dimension that distinguishes *The Secret Heart* from the autobiography, a dimension that is relevant to the questioning of the assumed homogeneity of Canetti's oeuvre. In his auto-

biography Canetti contends that remembrance and writing—the very activity of writing his life story—have the power to revitalize the past. The grand revitalization project of the autobiography seeks to ignore temporality and disruptive aspects of memory. This seemingly unshattered belief in the resurrecting power of language is probed in many entries in *The Secret Heart.* Numerous notes comment on the process of remembering, as for instance the following two: "I don't want to know what I was; I want to become what I was" (*SHC,* 58); "The paralyzing effect of reading early notebooks. It is better, it is more correct, to remember freely. The old crutches get in the way of memory [i.e., remembrance], get stuck in its spokes" (*SHC,* 54).

A close analysis of these notes sheds light on their disruptive effect vis-à-vis the autobiography. Both notes posit an opposition between the retrieval of factual information ("to know," "early notebooks") and vivid recollection ("to become," the act of remembrance). Biographical documents are seen as incompatible with the act of remembering. The accounts of the past do not assist the process of recollection. They have a "paralyzing" effect, and they interfere with the process of remembering precisely because they are fixed documents, signs of an irretrievable past. This opposition recalls Hegel's distinction between *Gedächtnis* (memory), the faculty of mechanical repetition, and *Erinnerung* (remembrance), the process of internalization (*Verinnerlichung*). According to Hegel the two realms complement one another; but the incompatibility Canetti addresses is closer to Paul de Man's reading of Hegel. De Man contends that "memory" hinders and ultimately derails any act of "remembrance."[13] In the entries quoted above, Canetti reaffirms the objective of his autobiography—to resurrect the past—but he acknowledges at the same time the impossibility of ever fully living up to this stated objective. Instead of reconfirming an unmediated access to the past that informs the autobiographical project, the notes emphasize the mediated nature of remembrance. Or, to draw once more on Ruppel's allegory: instead of sealing together the blocks of his monumental memorial, the notes draw attention to its cracks and fissures.

SELF-CRITICAL ENTRIES

Canetti's attempt to overcome or to ignore the mediated character of remembrance (and of writing)—an attempt that shapes the autobiography and that is both reaffirmed and undercut in the notes—corresponds with his lifelong unwillingness to accept death.[14] The written word, he contends, is the only way to preserve "life" beyond death and to circumvent the human inclination to dominate others. This resistance to death informs the central argument of *Crowds and Power,* namely that the finality of life is the origin of all (ab)uses of power; by seeking and abusing power, Canetti maintains, humans attempt in vain to negate or overcome the finality of life. The autobiography reconstructs and thereby reconfirms the genesis of Canetti's fight against death. His life story is from the very beginning informed by the experience of death. The first volume of his autobiography is dominated by the untimely death of Canetti's father—he died in 1912 when Canetti was seven years old—and by Canetti's refusal to accept any rational explanation for this (or any other) death.

Several notes in *The Secret Heart* refer to the life-shaping effect of this early experience of loss, as for instance: "A person who has opened himself too early to the experience of death can never turn away from it again; a wound that becomes like a lung through which one breathes" (*SHC,* 40). Through metonymic substitutions, this note evokes the image of a coexistence of life and death; life depends on the experience of death. Contrary to the autobiography, this and several other notes suggest the "productive" effect of the experience of death: "Death, which he will not tolerate, carries him" (*SHC,* 131). There are entries in *The Secret Heart* that go even further and question what is arguably Canetti's principal conviction and the founding argument of *Crowds and Power,* namely his unwillingness to accept the finality of life. For instance the following entry: "To cling to life like this—is it stinginess? When it's the life of others—is that all the more stingy? He looks for arguments against the fundamental conviction of his existence. What if that very conviction is the worst kind of slavery? Would it be easier to regard life as a gift that can be taken back? So that nothing is *part* of you, just as nothing belongs to you?" (*SHC,* 38). In this entry, the figure of reversal—which Canetti, like Lichtenberg, employs to call into question petrified patterns of language and thought—is directed against the author's own position, his lifelong fight against death. Instead of reiterating his previous arguments, Canetti turns into his own most severe critic when he considers the possibility that his rejection of death is nothing more than the self-centered and powerful attempt to hold onto life as one's property. Self-critical entries like the one quoted above can be found next to other entries that emphatically insist on the validity of his previous positions: "It's coming out. What? Something he always shied away from imagining. Is it all moving toward a declaration of love for death? . . . Renounce all the words that were the meaning and pride of his life and profess the only true faith of the church of death? It is possible, everything is possible, there is no miserable self-betrayal that did not at some time become truth; therefore, in place of the history of words, the words must stand for themselves, independent of everything after or before them" (*SHC,* 53). In this dramatic staging of a dispute with himself, Canetti seeks to annul his own (present and anticipated future) doubts. He thus assumes the role of executor of his own literary estate. Canetti, the self-declared enemy of death antici-

pates in this entry his own death and, in an attempt to determine for posterity how his works are to be read, reaffirms his lifelong resistance to the acceptance of death. In a self-ironic twist, the very assertion that the "words should speak for themselves" serves to undercut his attempt to privilege some of his views over others. As exemplified in Canetti's multiple and contradictory remarks about death and his unwillingness to accept death, *The Secret Heart* stands not only in marked contrast to *Crowds and Power* and to the autobiography (demonstrating the heterogeneity of his works), but the notes themselves are heterogeneous and defy any conclusive answers.

Both the insistence on the validity of his previous arguments and the awareness of their futility have shaped the enigmatic title *The Secret Heart of the Clock.* There are two entries that are related to the title and suggest a particular reading: "He sacrifices the clock and eludes the future" (*SHC,* 98); "Unknown to all, the secret heart of the clock" (*SHC,* 120). The first quotation can be read as imagining that temporality and, by extension, death can be overcome. The second one seems to invoke, in the combination of an organic trope (heart) and a mechanical trope (clock), both the finality of life and, at the same time, the ignorance of humans regarding the exact duration of life. Arguably, the collection of notes and aphorisms as a whole represents Canetti's confrontation with finality, his own death, and the futility of his previous efforts, issues that are carefully excluded from his autobiography. Thus, this volume of notes can be considered the "secret center" or the "heart" of the official life story.

In the notes, as one of the entries states, "he has written himself to pieces" (*SHC,* 51). The notes effectively decenter the narrative unity of the official life story, they expose the unified self presented in the autobiography as a carefully crafted construct, and they call into question language's capacity to bring the past back to life. This disruptive effect of the notes coincides with what Jacques Derrida has described as the double effect of the "supplement": the supplement is rarely a mere addition, instead it challenges or even replaces that which it ostensibly complements.[15] *The Secret Heart of the Clock* provides space for alterity and renders questionable the attempt to close off the life story in a teleological narrative.

3

It is precisely the heterogeneous character of the *Aufzeichnungen* and their decentering effect vis-à-vis the autobiography that invite their exploration in relation to the writings of Emmanuel Levinas. Levinas's approach to the question of ethics is of special interest to literary criticism, firstly because he sees the origin of language intertwined with primordial ethical behavior and secondly because Levinas posits a nonnormative notion of ethics, a notion that is in constant conflict with legal and political notions of justice. I intend to explore intersections between the works of Canetti and Levinas regarding the relationship between language and ethics. Most specifically, I argue that Levinas's ethics illuminates the relation of the aesthetic to the ethical in Canetti's notion of *Verwandlung* (metamorphosis), a notion that informs, in turn, the content and structure of Canetti's *Aufzeichnungen.*[16]

Levinas, like Canetti, is critical of the Western philosophical tradition. Levinas maintains that Western thought is marked by a pervasive search for lucidity and total comprehension that assimilates the "Other" to the "same" and ignores the irreducible alterity of human life. Yet while Canetti has entirely turned away from any established system of thought, claiming to rethink humanity from scratch in *Crowds and Power,* Levinas's critique evolves out of his continuous engagement with these philosophical traditions. In contradistinction to the primacy of ontology in Western philosophy, Levinas posits the primacy of ethics—which, in the context of this article, I can only introduce in the most schematic manner.[17]

Levinas distinguishes the "ontological Said" from the "ethical Saying." The "ontological Said" signifies the "thought of comparison, of judgement" and harks back to the "Greek tradition" of antiquity. Levinas concedes that we cannot do without this language of instrumental reason, that we have to rely on "Greek" language even when criticizing it (or when "unsaying the Said," as he terms it). The "ethical Saying," by contrast, is shaped by the Judaic tradition and specifically by the commandment "Thou shalt not kill."[18] According to Levinas, the irreducible alterity of another human being—for which he frequently employs the figure of the face—calls for our response and by the same token for our responsibility. He argues that this response to the Other's face can be considered the origin of both language and ethics (Levinas 1988, 169).

One of the childhood memories central to Canetti's autobiography literally enacts the prohibition underlying Levinas's ethics. The entire first volume, *The Tongue Set Free,* is shaped by the inscription of the primordial prohibition of killing. When the five-year-old Canetti, furious because his cousin refuses to share the secret of writing with him, intends to kill her with an ax, his outraged grandfather pronounces the absolute interdiction against committing murder.[19] Canetti presents this memory—symbolizing two principles central to Judaism, the importance of scripture and the sanctity of life—as the founding event of his life story.[20] The interdiction pronounced by the patriarchal figure in *The Tongue Set Free* visualizes in a protoreligious fashion what Levinas transforms into a universal secular prin-

ciple. He posits the Other's face, which calls for a response and for responsibility, as the primordial ethical relation.

Levinas's notion of ethics emerged against the backdrop of violence and murder as the final consequence of disrespect for the other. Continuing a secular version of the Judaic tradition, Levinas, like Canetti, refuses to assign any metaphysical meaning to death. Both consider death to be a violent rupture; ultimately any death carries with it an element of murder.[21] While *Crowds and Power* can be considered Canetti's implicit attempt to grapple with Fascism, Levinas is more explicit than Canetti in his references to recent history, namely anti-Semitism, the Second World War, and the Holocaust.[22] For instance, in *Otherwise than Being,* a study that is dedicated to the victims of National Socialism, Levinas mentions anti-Semitism as a trope for the refusal to respect and respond to the alterity of the other person. In an interview Levinas states that Auschwitz is the implicit point of reference for his attempt to develop a nonnormative ethics. The central question that emerged after the Holocaust, he maintains, is whether we can "speak of morality after the failure of morality?" (Levinas 1988, 179). In his essay "Useless Suffering," Levinas responds: "It is this attention to the Other which, across the cruelties of this century—despite these cruelties, because of these cruelties—can be affirmed as the very bond of human subjectivity, even to the point of being raised to a supreme ethical principle."[23]

In recent debates concerning the relationship of aesthetics and ethics, Klaus Scherpe, among others, has drawn on Levinas's notion of a nonnormative ethics, grounded in the response to the distinctive face of the Other. Questioning what he considers to be a false dichotomy between the aesthetic and ethical realms, Scherpe suggests a conception of art that, instead of perceiving the ethical dimension as distinct from the aesthetic (e.g., fiction with a political "message"), considers the two dimensions inseparable from one another. Literary texts that correspond to this notion of aesthetics—Scherpe mentions texts by Peter Weiss, Alfred Andersch, and Hans Magnus Enzensberger—further the awareness of the irreducible alterity of the Other and thus work against homogenization and marginalization.[24] The etymology of the term "aesthetics" underscores this ethical dimension of art: "aisthesis" means awareness or perception. What is at stake is not a moral evaluation of art but art's potential to increase our awareness of the incommensurability of the Other and the world.[25] Focusing on "aisthesis" as the intersection between the ethical and the aesthetical realms opens up a new perspective in an otherwise deadlocked debate, a perspective I find useful in discussing Canetti's poetics.[26]

The notion of *Verwandlung* is central to Canetti's anthropology and poetics. According to Canetti, the ability of the artist or the storyteller to enact and preserve by means of *Verwandlung* the multiplicity, changeability, and the specificity of human life is the only way to counter the pervasive accumulation and abuse of power.[27] The notion of *Verwandlung* rests on the potentially problematic assumption that the writing subject is able to efface the powerful aspects of authorship by assimilating itself to that which it represents.[28] Yet I argue that, within the open-ended and dialogic structure of the *Aufzeichnungen*, Canetti avoids this risk by adapting multiple and often contradictory subject positions and perspectives, and he does so by enacting multiple *Verwandlungen*. As demonstrated above, Canetti's *Aufzeichnungen* provide space for the representation of the irreducible multiplicity of the outer world as well as for the conflicted and contradictory inner world of the writing subject.

The autobiography and the long essay on Franz Kafka, **Der andere Prozeß** (1969: **Kafka's Other Trial**), represent Canetti's fascination with other humans. **Crowds and Power** and **Die Stimmen von Marrakesch** (1968; **The Voices of Marrakesh**) represent his interest in other cultures. The *Aufzeichnungen* display both—his fascination with other humans and his interest in other cultures—but they also provide space for exploring the "other" in the "self." It is in this twofold representation of alterity, I maintain, that the aesthetical realm of the notes coincides with an ethical realm. In a related sense, the author and literary critic Rudolf Hartung, who has regularly commented on Canetti's works since the 1950s, uses the term "the moral" in a review of the *Aufzeichnungen;* Hartung refers to Canetti's disregard for abstractions and his genuine respect for the concrete and the distinct aspects of "reality."[29] The ethical dimension of Canetti's *Aufzeichnungen* can be located, however, not merely on the level of content, as Hartung seems to suggest, but also on the level of style. Rhetorically the aphorisms and notes are governed by repetition and metonymic substitution, features that underscore their fragmentary and open-ended character. The autobiography, by contrast, relies heavily on metaphors and a symbolic organization of events implying a meaningful telos and closure.

The heterogeneous character of Canetti's **Aufzeichnungen** and their ethical dimension challenge those critics who simply dismiss Canetti's work as inaccessible and hermetic. Yet Ursula Ruppel, one of Canetti's strongest and most convincing critics, bases her argument concerning the hermetic character of his oeuvre in part on the role attributed to the feminine. She argues that the absence of woman and the stereotypical representation of femininity are not marginal phenomena in Canetti's works but essential aspects of his notions of life and death (Ruppel, 72-87). Canetti's desire for immortality, she contends, finds it counterpart in the virtual nonexistence of his own body in the autobiography and the explicit contempt for the mortal body that always has

feminine connotation—the most graphic example being the figure of Therese in the novel **Auto-da-Fé** (Ruppel, 74).

How, then, are women and the "feminine" represented in **The Secret Heart**? Women are for the most part strikingly absent. Canetti consistently employs the term *Mann* (man) whenever one would expect the term *Mensch* (human being). For instance: "The fragments of a man, worth so much more than he" (**SHC**, 145); "The land without brothers: no one has more than *one* child" (**SHC**, 19). Inadvertently, these notes expose the androcentric bent dominant in most of Western thought. By *explicitly* excluding women, they draw attention to the long tradition of *implicitly* excluding women, that is, the tradition of speaking of humans (*Menschen*) when in fact only men are being considered.

The few notes that explicitly refer to "woman" generally reiterate pervasive stereotypes, like the self-centered or vain woman or the woman as seductress (**SHC**, 10, 67, 136). These notes confirm the mostly stereotypical ways in which the feminine is represented in Canetti's other works.[30] Thus Canetti's representation of women reveals a blind spot in the respect for alterity that the aphorisms and notes otherwise espouse. This tendency underscores the validity of Ruppel's feminist critique of Canetti, but I do not subscribe to her wholesale dismissal of his works, a dismissal that is grounded in moral indignation. While I share her disapproval of the misogynist aspects of Canetti's writings, I find it ultimately more productive to expand Levinas's notion of ethics to the role of the critic: it would then be the "responsibility" of the critic to recognize the heterogeneity of Canetti's works in general and the heterogeneous character of the *Aufzeichungen* in particular.[31]

Notes

1. Elias Canetti, *The Conscience of Words* (London: Deutsch, 1986), 156; hereafter cited in text as *CW*.

2. In view of the unwieldiness of the English translation "notes and aphorisms," I frequently use the German term *Aufzeichnungen* in this essay.

3. The following collections of essays exemplify the two trends in the reception: the volume *Hüter der Verwandlung: Beiträge zum Werk von Elias Canetti* (Munich: Hanser, 1985), compiled by Canetti's own publisher, includes predominantly affirmative contributions (*Essays in Honor of Elias Canetti,* trans. Michael Hulse [New York: Farrar, Straus and Giroux, 1987]); and the volume *Elias Canetti: Experte der Macht,* ed. Kurt Bartsch and Gerhard Melzer (Graz: Droschl, 1985), includes several very critical contributions. [Essays by Gerhard Melzer and Bernd Witte that appear in translation in the present volume first appeared in the

collection *Elias Canetti: Experte der Macht. Ed.*] There are excellent articles in both volumes, and my overall critique of homogenizing tendencies, which mark both approaches, is not meant as a wholesale dismissal of individual articles. My critique extends to my own hermeneutic approach in *Das autobiographische Werk von Elias Canetti: Verwandlung—Identität—Machtausübung,* Stauffenburg Colloquium 7 (Tübingen: Stauffenburg, 1988), a study that displays aspects of both trends, affirmation and critical distancing; hereafter cited in text.

4. Ursula Ruppel, *Der Tod und Canetti: Essay* (Hamburg: Europäische Verlagsanstalt, 1995); hereafter cited in text.

5. Michel Foucault, "What is an Author?" trans. Josué V. Harari, in *Textual Strategies: Perspectives in Post-Structuralist Criticism,* ed. J. V. Harari (Ithaca: Cornell University Press, 1979), 141-60.

6. Elias Canetti, *The Secret Heart of the Clock: Notes, Aphorisms, Fragments, 1973-1985,* trans. Joel Agree (New York: Farrar, Straus and Giroux, 1989), 40-41; hereafter cited in text as *SHC.*

7. Elias Canetti, *Aufzeichnungen, 1992-1993* (Munich: Hanser, 1996).

8. See Ingo Seidler, "Bruchstücke einer großen Konfession: Zur Bedeutung von Canettis 'Sudelbüchern,'" *Modern Austrian Literature* 16, no. 3/4 (1983): 1-21; and Stefan H. Kaszyński, "Im Labor der Gedanken: Zur Poetik der Aufzeichungen von Elias Canetti," in *Elias Canettis Anthropologie und Poetik,* ed. Stefan H. Kaszyński (Munich: Hanser, 1984), 151-62.

9. Regarding the tradition of aphoristic writings, see Wolfgang Mieder, "'Die falschesten Redensarten haben den größten Reiz': Zu Elias Canettis Sprachaphorismen," *Der Sprachdienst* 6 (1994): 173-80.

10. Two brief examples: "If you had traveled more, you would know less" (*SHC,* 46); "Newspapers, to help you forget the previous day" (*SHC,* 48). The social critique inherent in the critique of language and in the figure of reversal is discussed by Jürgen Söring, "Die Literatur als 'Provinz des Menschen': Zu Elias Canettis Aufzeichnungen," *Deutsche Vierteljahrsschrift für Literaturwissenschaft und Geistesgeschichte* 60 (1986): 645-66; and by Thomas Lappe, *Elias Canettis Aufzeichnungen, 1942-1985: Modell und Dialog als Konstituenten einer programmatischen Utopie* (Aachen: Alano, 1989), 60.

11. In my book on Elias Canetti, I argue that the mechanisms of power Canetti analyzes in his major anthropological study *Crowds and Power* shape his extensive autobiography. Canetti's masterfully crafted life story, I maintain, is directed toward the telos of becoming a writer (specifically, the author of *Crowds and Power*) and posits the author's own written cosmos against the catastrophic events of twentieth-century history and politics. In other words, his autobiography projects both in terms of style and content an anachronistic and powerful image of a writer and his works (Eigler, 30-77). The unshattered sense of identity Canetti posits in his life story seems closer to Goethe's *Dichtung und Wahrheit* (*Poetry and Truth*) than to most twentieth-century autobiographies; cf. Robert Gould, "*Die gerettete Zunge* and *Dichtung und Wahrheit:* Hypertextuality in Autobiography and its Implications," *Seminar* 21 (1985): 79-107.

12. See Eigler, 71-77. Cf. Waltraud Wiethölter, "Sprechen—Lesen—Schreiben: Zur Funktion von Sprache und Schrift in Canettis Autobiographie," *Deutsche Vierteljahrsschrift für Literaturwissenschaft und Geistesgeschichte* 64 (1990): 168. While it is accurate, as David Darby maintains, that Canetti comments frequently on the mediated and selective character of remembrance in his autobiography, the processes of remembrance and writing are not seen as problematic; they confirm rather than threaten the identity of the writing subject (Darby, "A Literary Life: The Textuality of Elias Canetti's Autobiography," *Modern Austrian Literature* 25, no. 2 [1992]: 37-49).

13. Paul de Man, "Sign and Symbol in Hegel's *Aesthetics,*" *Critical Inquiry* 8 (1982): 761-75.

14. *The Secret Heart* includes numerous entries in which books and writing are metonymically related to life and living (for instance, *SHC,* 3, 84, 97). The metonymic relation of writing/ remembrance to life can be read in two different ways: as emphasizing the immediacy of the act of writing or, conversely, as underscoring the mediated character of life. The entries thus emphasize at the same time as they undercut Canetti's magic notion of language; that is, his attempt to overcome the difference between signifier and signified by associating language with life. The very fact that his notes insist over and over again on the revitalizing power of language and remembrance signifies the difficulty of holding on to this premodern notion of language in a postmodern age.

15. Jacques Derrida, *Of Grammatology,* trans. Gayatri C. Spivak (Baltimore: Johns Hopkins University Press, 1976), 141-64.

16. I use the German term *Verwandlung* because of the central role this particular term occupies in Canetti's writings.

17. For an introduction and overview, see Emmanuel Levinas, *Ethics and Infinity: Conversations with*

Philippe Nemo, trans. Richard A. Cohen (Pittsburgh: Duquesne University Press, 1985).

18. "The Paradox of Morality: An Interview with Emmanuel Levinas," in *The Provocation of Levinas: Rethinking the Other,* ed. Robert Bernasconi (London: Routledge, 1988), esp. 174-78; hereafter cited in text as Levinas 1988. For a more detailed elaboration of his ethics, see Levinas, *Otherwise than Being or Beyond Essence,* trans. A. Lingis, (The Hague: Nijhoff, 1981).

19. Elias Canetti: *The Tongue Set Free: Remembrance of a European Childhood,* trans. Joachim Neugroschel (New York: Seabury, 1979), 214-15.

20. Bernd Witte, "Der Erzähler als Tod-Feind: Zu Elias Canettis Autobiographie," *Text und Kritik* 28, rev. ed. (1982): 71.

21. Emmanuel Levinas, *Totality and Infinity,* trans. A. Lingis (Pittsburgh: Duquesne University Press, 1969), 236.

22. In a 1965 interview with Horst Bienek, Canetti contends that every single page of *Crowds and Power* deals with Fascism (Elias Canetti, *Die gespaltene Zukunft: Aufsätze und Gespräche,* Reihe Hanser 111 (Munich: Hanser, 1972), 98.

23. Emmanuel Levinas, "Useless Suffering," in *The Provocation of Levinas: Rethinking the Other,* ed. Robert Bernasconi (London: Routledge, 1988), 159.

24. Klaus Scherpe, "Moral im Ästhetischen: Andersch, Weiss, Enzensberger," *Weimarer Beiträge* 42 (1996): esp. 114-15.

25. Cf. Introduction, *Ethik der Ästhetik,* ed. Christoph Wulf, Dietmar Kamper, and Hans Ulrich Gumbrecht (Berlin: Akademie Verlag, 1994), xi.

26. The false dichotomy between "*engagierte Literatur*"—that is, politically or socially engaged literature that is presumed to have little aesthetic value—and "pure" art, supposedly detached from any political or social concerns continues to dominate post-1989 literary debates in Germany. The ongoing discussion of the relationship between ethics and aesthetics was provoked by questions about the complicity of East German writers in a repressive socialist state.

27. Canetti's notion of *Verwandlung* is far more complex and ambiguous than it may appear at first. According to Canetti's anthropology in *Crowds and Power, Verwandlung* is the trait that distinguishes humans from animals. On the one hand, the ability to turn into different personae has assisted humans in the subjugation of nature. On the other, Canetti refers to Ovid's *Metamorphoses* as a literal example of how *Verwandlung* has been employed to escape from violent or hostile encounters. It is this latter aspect that Canetti underscores in the poetological notion of *Verwandlung.* The writer as the "keeper of metamorphoses" (*CW,* 161) accomplishes two things: he preserves the very notion of *Verwandlung* as *the* human essence in his writings and, in doing so, he avoids becoming entangled in a society reigned by (ab)use of power. For a critical assessment of this rather idealistic notion of the writing subject, see Eigler, 90-105.

28. Canetti's anthropological study *Crowds and Power* exemplifies the risks involved in the assumption that it is possible to transcend one's own set of "prejudices" (in Hans Georg Gadamer's sense, as a given set of presuppositions): this assumption may result in a more biased or otherwise skewed representation than if one were to acknowledge the position from which one speaks.

29. Rudolf Hartung, "Ansturm gegen die Grenzen: Überlegungen zu Canetti's Aufzeichnungen aus drei Jahrzehnten," in *Elias Canetti: Ein Rezipient und sein Autor,* ed. Bernhard Albers (Aachen: Rimbaud, 1992), 124. This review first appeared in the *Süddeutsche Zeitung* (27-28 October 1973).

30. See Eigler, 175-90; Ruppel, 50-87; and Kristie A. Foell, *Blind Reflections: Gender in Elias Canetti's "Die Blendung"* (Riverside, Calif.: Ariadne, 1994).

31. This conflict between moral judgment and Levinas's call for responsibility regarding the alterity of the "Other" points to a dilemma that came to the fore in the controversy surrounding Paul de Man's wartime journalism. Jacques Derrida guarded against condemning the whole person by defending "de Man's right to differ from others and from himself" (See Derrida, *Memoirs for Paul de Man,* trans. Cecile Lindsay, Jonathan Culler, and Eduardo Cadava [New York: Columbia University Press, 1986], 50-56). Yet, as some of de Man's critics pointed out, unconditional respect for the "Other"—which according to Levinas precludes judgment—may become "irresponsible" in a broader sociopolitical sense.

Raymond L. Burt (essay date 2001)

SOURCE: Burt, Raymond L. "Autobiography as Reconciliation: The Literary Function of Elias Canetti's *Die gerettete Zunge.*" In *Modern Austrian Prose Interpretations and Insights,* edited by Paul F. Dvorak, pp. 129-49. Riverside, Calif.: Ariadne Press, 2001.

[In the following essay, Burt identifies ways in which Die gerettete Zunge *differs from later volumes of Canetti's autobiography—namely, the book's narrative and literary construct closely resembles the novel genre.]*

In 1977 Elias Canetti published *Die gerettete Zunge: Geschichte einer Jugend.* Usually this work is viewed as the first installment of his autobiographical trilogy, but there are compelling reasons to examine this work separately from the later volumes. *Die gerettete Zunge* reads like a well-constructed fictional work, not in that it resolves various plot entanglements, but in its narrative stance, its use of motifs, the poetic power of its descriptions and the development of a thematic plot. While obviously a chronological continuation of the childhood covered by *Die gerettete Zunge,* the two sequels, *Die Fackel in Ohr* and *Das Augenspiel,* exhibit stronger teleological functions due perhaps to the fact that the author of these later volumes was, as of 1981, a Nobel Prize winner. Their emphasis centers on the development of the *Dichter,* the writer, i.e., the influences behind his literary productions, *Die Blendung* (1935), *Masse und Macht* (1960), and his play *Hochzeit* (1932).

In these later volumes Canetti is invested to a greater extent in presenting a traditional literary autobiography: the presentation of the intellectual and experiential influences on his literary works, the development of his philosophical view of the world, and observations of famous persons (most notably, Karl Kraus, George Grosz, Bertolt Brecht, Alma Mahler, and Hermann Broch) with whom he came into contact. *Die gerettete Zunge,* on the other hand, may be read and interpreted profitably by a reader who is not familiar with any of Canetti's other literary accomplishments. The uniqueness of this first work is underscored by its origin. We know from an interview with Canetti that it was composed in response to a specific situation. Faced with his brother George's serious illness, Canetti sought solace for both his brother and himself by recalling their childhood.[1]

This shared childhood begins in Ruschuk, a small Bulgarian town on the Danube. As the text unfolds, the reader learns that the Canettis belonged to a community of Ladino-speaking Jews of Spanish origin in a town populated by a confusing array of ethnic groups. Grandfather Canetti was a successful merchant and patriarch of the family. Canetti's father lived beneath his shadow, until he decided to move to England. The grandfather was so opposed to the move that he publicly pronounced a curse upon his son.

At age six Canetti moved to Manchester with his parents and his two younger brothers. His father began working for his brother-in-law and the young Elias entered school. A year after their arrival, Canetti's father died suddenly one morning with no satisfactory medical explanation. The widow decides to move the family to Vienna, where they are living when the First World War breaks out. Hardships and the mother's illness cause her to relocate the family to Zurich. Two years into their new life in Switzerland, she once again falls ill. At this point the family is separated for the first time. The mother is institutionalized for treatment, and the boys are split into separate living arrangements. Elias, now fourteen, spends his time between his school and his boarding arrangement in Tiefenbrunnen. The book ends when his mother returns from her convalescence with the idea that her sixteen-year-old son needs to be exposed to the hardships of the real world, and she forces him to leave school and to move with her to Germany, where the postwar situation promises to offer a vivid exposure to reality.

The basic theme of the book revolves around the young Elias's problematic relationship to his mother, which was a reverberation of the cataclysmic effect his father's death exacted on the family. His relationship to his mother prior to this event was muted at best, but now the interpersonal dynamics shift, and the two are locked in an intense bond which has ramifications for his development as a writer. Although descriptive excursions and side episodes abound, it is this problematic situation to which the narrative consistently returns.

Die gerettete Zunge differs from most of the works covered in this volume in that it is an autobiography. The question thus arises: how different should the interpretive approach to an autobiography be from that to a novel? Up until the mid-twentieth century, the question might have been answered as follows: whereas the novel is a fictional construct developed along aesthetic guidelines, the autobiography depicts historical reality, subject perhaps to the occasional lapses in the author's memory. Just as the autobiography of a famous political or military figure might shed light on historical events, so too the autobiography of a poet could aid in the understanding of the author's literary accomplishments. Decades of critical examination of the genre have radically changed our view of autobiography vis-à-vis fictional prose. An individual autobiography may still be mined for insight into history or an artistic corpus, but as a literary genre, the autobiography is considered a close relative of the novel.

Friederike Eigler identified two major schools of thought in regard to autobiography: the hermeneutic, idealistic view and the deconstructionalist view. Among the points of contention between the two is the relationship of autobiography to fiction. While the hermeneutic view acknowledges the artistic nature of the genre and its close ties to the novel though maintaining at some level a boundary between the genres, the deconstructionalist view denies the existence of any boundaries between autobiography and fiction. Eigler observes that the two approaches tend to correspond to the two types of autobiographies, the "classical" and the "modern/postmodern."[2] The "classical" autobiography is one in which the author constructs a text in a chronologically linear flow. Its strong emphasis on the development of a distinct self appeals to the hermeneutic/idealistic critics, who value the genre for its "humanness." The "postmodern" autobiographies have a fragmented structure and cast doubt on the continuity of the self, a tendency which conforms to deconstructionalist theory. Eigler seeks the middle ground between the two approaches by acknowledging both the interpretive intention of a self-reconstructing author who lays claim to truth and the culturally dependent textual function that blurs the distinction between autobiography and fiction (29).

In the interpretation of fiction, it is misleading to identify the narrator as the voice of the author. The narrator, as any student in a first-year literature class knows, is a fictional creation of the author to the same degree as the other characters involved in the plot. On the other hand, in reading an autobiography—now that this genre has been recognized as a relative of the novel in its creative use of literary components—this same identification of author with narrator is expected. This expectation has found its most quoted source in Philip Lejeune's *Le Pacte autobiographique,* which offers a quasi-legalistic justification for the contractual acceptance of the shared identity of subject, narrator, and author.[3] Nevertheless, literary critics increasingly disavow the identification of the autobiographic narrator with the self that is portrayed in the narrative. Differences in time, life experiences, perspectives, and the vagaries of memory insure that the literary representation of one's past may reflect more on the state of the narrator than on the reality of the earlier self. In terms of literary analysis, these perspectives are expressed as two distinct planes of reality. One represents the actual life as experienced by the earlier self (the "truth," if you will), and the other is the creatively constructed interpretation of that life (the "art") as viewed by the author at the time of the autobiography's composition. The first plane can never be accurately or adequately recreated in literary form and thus the text will always be more art than truth. Thus the real question regarding autobiography is one of the quality of its artistic construction, not one of its veracity.

Following this line of thought, David Darby examines those points where the axis of the narrated self and that of the narrator are incongruent.[4] These points expose the framework of the narrative interpretation and can be used to shed light not only on the intention of the narrator, but also on the narrative strategy. By highlighting statements of the narrator, Darby documents the fact that Canetti's text is not merely a totality of recollected episodes. The narrator indicates that material was not included, and thus that selection was a conscious act. The supporting evidence he provides comes from *Die Fackel im Ohr,* but a prominent example of this admission occurs in the *Die gerettete Zunge* during a discussion of his mother's various versions of his father's death. He remembers them all and could recount them: "Perhaps some day I can write them all down com-

pletely. They would make a book, an entire book, but now I am following other trails."[5]

The inside cover of the paperback release of *Die gerettete Zunge* refers to Canetti's story of his childhood as primarily a poetic autobiography ("*in erster Linie eine poetische Autobiographie*"). This designation of "poetic" is an indication of literary quality, and yet, it is coincidentally a technical term for a subgenre which is particularly fruitful for understanding *Die gerettete Zunge.* In his book on autobiography, Richard Coe points to the fact that the first use of the term "poetic autobiography" in modern literary criticism was actually referring to a distinct literary form which he termed the "Childhood."[6] Coe offers a precise definition of the Childhood as:

> . . . an extended piece of writing, a conscious, deliberately executed literary artifact, usually in prose (and thus intimately related to the novel) but not excluding occasional experiments in verse, in which the most substantial portion of the material is directly autobiographical, and whose structure reflects step by step the development of the writer's self; beginning often, but not invariably, with the first light of consciousness, and concluding, quite specifically, with the attainment of a precise degree of maturity.
>
> (8-9)

Coe traces the rise of this genre, as it originated in the eighteenth century with the discovery of childhood and later flourished among writers of the post World War II generation.

Viewing *Die gerettete Zunge* as an example of Childhood also addresses the distinction between the narrated self and the narrator. As Coe points out: "The former self-as-child is as alien to the adult writer as to the adult reader" (1). The value of a genre designation like the Childhood is that it makes an *a priori* distinction between the narrator and the narrated self. The adult narrator and the world of the child are separated not only by distance, but also by insurmountable psychological and developmental differences. Canetti strives to place the reader in the realm of the child by structuring the narrative as a series of episodes and images seemingly organized purely by memory. This narrative strategy may conceal the fact that the narrator is consciously manipulating the text.

As befits the Childhood, Canetti begins not with a description of his birth or his lineage but with a chapter called "My Earliest Memory" (*Meine früheste Erinnerung*). The event recounted, from which the book's title is drawn, is so compelling that Waltraud Wiethölter used it as the interpretive key to the entire autobiographic trilogy. The two-year-old Elias was being carried by a young woman to a door. The door opens to reveal a smiling man who comes up to him and commands him to show him his tongue. The child obeys and the man pulls out a knife and says that he will now cut off the tongue. He moves the knife close to the tongue, then suddenly puts away the knife, saying "Not today, tomorrow" (3).[7] This frightening experience is repeated every morning. The placing of this memory at the beginning instead of the traditional birth narrative or the genealogy, signals the writer's intent to present the world from the perspective of the child, and not to offer a documented reconstruction of one's life.

The Childhood also shifts the weight of the genre considerations from the boundaries between truth and fiction to that of an individual's quest to restore the myths and poetry of an earlier lost state of being. A clue to the interpretation of *Die gerettete Zunge* can be found in its last sentence: "It is true that I, like the earliest man, came into being only by an expulsion from Paradise" (268).[8] Canetti is referring here to the idyllic Zurich period which was coming to an abrupt end; however, it also signals the end of his close, unquestioning relationship to his mother. Paradoxically, directly after his father's death Elias experienced the acceleration into adulthood at the same time that he was undergoing an extension of his childhood dependence on his mother. The end of the book documents the point in his life at which the two become increasingly estranged. In reconstructing the period of his life during which his psyche and intellectual development were inextricably bound up with his mother's strict guidance, the author may be both tracing the origins of his artistic development as well as attempting to restore his paradise lost.

In the first chapter about his life in Manchester, the narrator abruptly deviates from the chronological flow maintained throughout the work. Canetti jumps to the pivotal event in his life, the unexplained and sudden death of his father. This event immediately thrust the seven-year-old into a new role in relation to his mother. In his earliest memories, and indeed up until the death of his father, his mother played a minor role. He and his brother were under the care of nannies. He describes the regimen adhered to in Manchester, whereby the children were allowed to visit their parents on Sunday afternoons until his mother would ring the bell for the governess to fetch the children back to their room. Then suddenly, in the opening sentence of the chapter on Manchester, he states how, after the death of his father, he now sleeps in his father's bed. From the reader's point of view, this first mention of the father's death comes without warning and is a narrative strategy that transmits the shock of sudden death. This positioning at the beginning of the Manchester section also places it in direct proximity in the narrative to the grandfather's curse, which brought the Ruschuk section to a close, thus adding weight to the theory that the curse played a role in his death. It also immediately focuses on the child's new role: to prevent his mother from committing suicide during the night. At the time of his death, his father was not talking to her. The quarrel centered on her suspected infidelity. After her convalescence from an illness, she had hesitated to return to Manchester and her family. Her doctor had become infatuated with her and had declared his love. She overcame the temptation and wanted to share with her husband the story of her struggle as a sign of her love for him. He, however, did not view it that way and ceased speaking to her. He died inexplicably at the height of his anger. Canetti's memory of his father lying pale on the floor with his mother screaming "Speak to me!" assumes a deeper meaning with this revelation. His death eternalized her guilt. This is clear in her attitude toward her religion. Only two things mattered, her son being able to recite the Kaddish for his father and the Day of Atonement. Perhaps the title of the book, which should be translated "The Rescued Tongue," reflects the fact that his assumption of his father's role, as confidant and primary companion, atones for the guilt his mother experienced.

Elias was forced by his mother to fill the void left by her husband's death. Custom and circumstance would naturally demand increased familial responsibilities from him as the eldest son. However, the massive attention and demands his mother places on him effectively ended his childhood. This is demonstrated symbolically in her first words to him: "My son, you're playing, and your father is dead! You're playing, you're playing, and your father is dead! Your father is dead! Your father is dead! You're playing, and your father is dead!" (56).[9] The repetition is an indication that these words are most likely burned into his memory, and it is a testament of the violence done to his development. As the narrator has indicated, Elias remained unaware of his mother's feelings of guilt and indeed this initial reprimand, which she screamed from the window into the neighborhood until she was pulled back into the house, instills some measure of guilt in the child. From this moment on, he underwent an enforced transformation into adulthood. His mother put him through an intensive (and harsh) training in German, ostensibly to prepare him for school in Vienna, but German had been the private language of the parents, the language of their early courtship and of their discussions of literature and the theater. Now the young boy had to become her husband's replacement in the nightly discussions about literature.

The medium of the relationship was language and literature. The "rescued tongue" (Elias now speaking for his silent father) manifested itself in the emphasis on German, the language of his parents' courtship and of their artistic dreams. The language was imbued with so much power that Elias viewed it originally as a magical language, a secret cabal into which he wished to be admitted. A more detailed account of the mother's guilt in bringing about her husband's death is recounted in the third segment of the autobiography, *Das Augenspiel.* Canetti recognizes that his mother's actual transgression, of which she was unaware, was that she engaged her doctor/suitor in literary discussions in German. By doing so she had already violated the private intimacy of their marriage, regardless of any sexual infidelity on her part.

Elias's painful rebirth into his new relationship with his mother occurred during his three-month stay in Lausanne, where she subjected him to intense German instruction. After mastering the language, he embraced it as his mother tongue. It supplanted his Ladino origins to the point that his memory of his life in Ruschuk is in German, the language he then chose to express himself artistically.

In terms of his Childhood, the consequences of the child being propelled into a premature adulthood are felt in the development of his identity. The young Elias was not only subjected to her force-fed German instruction, but also to an intensive schooling in her artistic tastes. Through his evening discussions of literature, he accepted his mother's views uncritically and to such an extent that he became dependent upon her for his self-understanding. This is evident in a commentary by the narrator. "When we were alone, everything she thought, said, or did entered into me like the most natural thing in the world. I came into being from the sentences she uttered to me at such times" (125).[10] Canetti places great weight on the effect these discussions of literature had on his own development: "a good portion of me consists of them" (89).[11] When she was not talking directly to him, he eavesdropped, wanting to capture everything she said.

The intensity of his subjugation to her opinions continued even during the two years he spent apart from her at the pension in Tiefbrunnen. Although at this time in his life Elias began to exhibit signs of independence from her, such as corrupting their shared language by learning Swiss dialect and discovering authors she does not esteem, he nevertheless maintained contact by writing her all of his thoughts and composing a play dedicated to her.

The narrator recounts how grateful he was to his mother who seemingly allowed him intellectual freedom. She encouraged him to pursue all fields of knowledge equally. If we return to the image of Eden, the fruit of all trees was allowed with one exception. This intensely intimate relationship had to shun all sexuality, which it stifled with the authority of a biblical commandment. "She obstinately kept all eroticism from me, the taboo . . . remained as powerful in me as though it had been proclaimed by God himself on Mount Sinai" (163).[12] He had to follow his mother's lead and show disdain for sexuality.

In a particularly revealing incident, which is termed in the chapter heading as "The Discovery of Evil," (*Die Auffindung des Bösen*) a schoolmate told the ten-year-old Elias the facts of life in a less than delicate manner. He vehemently rejected what he heard and turned to his mother for clarification. "She, who had a clear and perfect answer for everything, she, who always made me feel that I shared the responsibility of raising the little brothers, she fell silent, silent for the first time, and remained silent so long that I grew scared" (107).[13] She asked for his trust, then she stated that the boy was lying. She explained that children come into the world "in a different way, a beautiful way."

For his part, Elias followed his mother's lead and showed disdain for the erotic awakenings of his peers and, in sharp contrast to his propensity to pursue all realms of knowledge, avoided all sexual subjects. During his years of puberty, he was the only male in a convent which had been converted into a boarding house for female students; he, nevertheless, remained ambivalent toward his enviable situation, keeping his living arrangements secret from his classmates. The power of this taboo was such that his disinterest continued throughout the years covered by *Die gerettete Zunge* and beyond his seventeenth year.

The intensity of the relationship evoked in him a jealousy toward any possible usurper of his position. His greatest nemesis in this regard entered his mother's life during her "breakdown" in Vienna. Her doctor, a university professor, began to court her affections. This temptation parallels the situation she faced shortly before the death of her husband. Uncharacteristically, his rival is not named, an unusual occurrence considering the importance young Elias places on names. This reticence might be due to discretion on Canetti's part since the doctor was married, but this event occurred over sixty years prior to its publication and would probably not stir up a scandal. A more likely explanation is that by not naming him, Canetti denies his foe the immortality of fame.

Within the narrative, the ten-year-old expressed such hatred for his rival that he reduced him to a single characteristic, his beard. "I was afraid he might someday graze me with his beard, and I would then be instantly transformed into a slave, who would have to fetch and carry for him" (119).[14] The emphasis on the beard, which is also an emphasis on manhood, could reflect the anxiety of a preadolescent competing in a realm in which he was not yet capable of understanding. In the chapter "The Beard in Lake Constance" (*Der Bart im Bodensee*), in which he triumphed over his foe, the narrator mimics the visual perception of the child watching the hated figure on the increasingly distant shore gradually shrink into nothingness.

This scene is an excellent example of the poetic quality of *Die gerettete Zunge.* In a few decisive sentences, the narrator depicts a moment of transition and transcendence in the mother/son relationship and the wife/husband relationship for which it substitutes. The mother had decided to move the family from Vienna to Switzerland due to the hardships of the war. They were aided in their departure by the professor, who accompanied them to Lindau. The departure on the boat to Switzerland represents the end of his rival's hold over his mother. After the boy watched the beard and the threat it represented fade in the distance, he turned to his mother for her reaction. In a rare gesture of physical affection, which symbolically could be meant for her husband, she stroked his hair and repeated softly over and over again the phrase: "Now, everything's fine. Now, everything's fine" (130).[15] These lines form a counterpoint to her repeated plea at the death of her husband. In the repetition of her situation, her guilt has been atoned. That this transition is linked to the death of the father may also be seen in the identification of the bearded Herr Professor with the "bane (or curse) of our life." Thus, in this scene, all three theories about the cause of the father's death; the grandfather's curse, jealousy and the rejection of war, are united.

An important characteristic of the Childhood is solitude, since the sense of aloneness and a sense of individual identity are related (Coe, 52). This, however, is not the case for Elias. His identity was violated in the attempts to fulfill the role of his father. The murderous rage Elias felt towards his rival was prompted by his fear of losing his mother, of being alone. In the chapter prior to the appearance of the professor, a man in the neighborhood leaped to his death from a window. This suicide was identical to the one he threatened to commit should his mother ever remarry, and its motivation may also have been related, for the man "had been alone and had no kin. Maybe that, she said, was why he hadn't wanted to go on living" (118).[16] His fear of solitude, of life without his special relationship to his mother, delayed him from fully developing his identity.

The next chapter, which opens the fourth section of the book, is "The Oath" (*Der Schwur*) in which Elias elicited from his mother an oath that she would never remarry. He compelled her to take this step by threatening suicide, which the narrator confirms is no idle threat. This oath was only accepted after she swore by the memory of her husband. At a later point in the narrative he refers to this as the time in which "I had virtually fought for my mother's hand and won it" (198).[17] He successfully claimed the place of his father.

The narrative structure of the book is divided into five sections corresponding to the different cities in which he spent his youth. Coe points out that the change of location in one's life is conducive to memory (17). The

more defining structure, however, are the short chapters, which often carry dual or multiple titles. The titles are more than an indication of the random pairing of topics within the chapters, as the narrator ties the two remembered events into a unity of theme, motif, intensification, or simply as a contrast of forces acting upon his development. Even chapters with one title generally have two related episodes. The pairing is a form of primitive metaphor. Placing together two events, or memories, implies a relationship. The technique mimics the action of memory, which also is known to connect two seemingly unrelated events. In the chapter "Purim. The Comet" (*Purim. Der Komet*) the narrator reflects openly on the connection between the two episodes: ". . . and since I have never thought about one event without the other, there must be some connection between them" (20).[18]

In the chapter "The Marked Man" (*Der Gezeichnete*) Canetti explicitly attributes the connection of two unrelated events to the mystery of memory. In the side garden of the house, one could escape the attention of others and enter a location of silence. In the quiet twilight one was open to "any mute event," an interesting concept for one so oriented to language. In this reclusion he spotted along the river one summer evening a ship, which appeared to him "as though I had never seen a ship, it was the only one, there was nothing outside it. Near it, there was twilight and gradual darkness" (222).[19] The ship was a vision of silent, drifting lights, reflected in the dark waters. The image resounded silently in his soul. "It . . . took possession of me, as though I had come into the orchard for the sake of that ship. I had never seen it before, but I recognized it" (222).[20] The power of this image was one which transcends the power of speech, calling forth feelings of a mystical recognition of an experience beyond the capacity of language to grasp. "I went into the house and talked to nobody; what could I have talked about?" (222).[21]

The second event in the chapter follows with a description of "a sinister figure" among his Zurich teachers. This teacher, as it turned out, bore the physical and psychological scars of a terrible tragedy. A school excursion in the mountains was ended by an avalanche, which killed many students and the only other teacher. The effects of this catastrophe on the teacher are evident in the manner in which Canetti presents him. He wore a hat to cover the "mark of Cain" of his injury. His demeanor was that of one pursued by the furies. He did not seem to exist for the present, but was internally distanced. It was an unspeakable guilt, silently respected by observers, and so he was the only teacher whom no one mimicked.

This haunting portrait is then directly tied to the image of the ship in the last statement of the chapter: "I forgot him and never thought about him again; his image resurfaced before me only with the illuminated ship" (223).[22] Memory connects the two and thus in the unspoken subconscious, the two "unspeakable" images find expression in one another. Be that as it may, the author does find the means to relate the power of the unspeakable, in his poetic tableau as well as in the fact that he offers the juxtaposition as memory provided it.

Duality occurs in symbolism as well. Notable among these is the color red. The symbolic importance of this color is immediately established in the first sentence of the book: "My earliest memory is dipped in red" (3).[23] The scene in which his tongue is threatened has red doors, floors and stairs. Rarely are other colors mentioned in the novel, so that its recurrence is striking. Red becomes the color of threat and danger. The young Elias is captivated by his mother's story of her sledding party being attacked one winter by wolves: ". . . she described the red tongues of the wolves, which had come so close that she still dreamt about them in later years" (9).[24] These wolves invaded her son's dreams after the father's wolf mask with its long, red tongue had frightened him. The mouth of hell in the Tunnel of Fun in Vienna opened red and huge, and in this instance the color evoked not only fear but also fascination with the forbidden. Red is strongly associated with eroticism, first with his infatuation with little Mary during his years in Manchester. He was so stricken by her red cheeks that he became obsessed with kissing them. In these and other examples, the color carries the dual symbolism of danger and eroticism. It should be mentioned that the importance of this color continues in his life beyond the period covered by *Die gerettete Zunge*, most notably his "revelation" which led to his work on *Masse und Macht* (as recounted in *Die Fackel im Ohr*) occurred under the red skies of Vienna.

Strings of association are the used by the narrator to show how the young Elias connected the chaotic forces around him. Like the pairing of episodes, these associations mimic in literary form the workings of the subconscious by weaving experiences and impressions into a pattern. In terms of the narrative, these associations bridge the episodic chapters and draw connections throughout the text. For example, he associated the death of his father with war. One explanation of his father's death was that he died of shock having read about the outbreak of war between Montenegro and Turkey. This rather unlikely explanation was the first one provided the young Elias and thus carried more weight than it would otherwise. The narrator states that for years he was convinced that the news of the war killed his father and from that time on he took all war "personally." Added to this image is the figure of Napoleon. The last book his father had given him was on Napoleon, a book he did not finish after his father's death. In his mind the youth had defined his disdain for his uncle by connecting him to Napoleon. Napoleon was the

bringer of war and thus a murderer (80) and his Uncle Napoleon now represented the forces that killed his father. Because his uncle also represented the utilitarian world of business, Elias's hatred of death, war, and his uncle flowed into his general aversion to the world of business.

The major theme of the book itself exhibits a duality. The mother's atonement for her guilt in the death of her husband was accomplished at the expense of her son's childhood. Elias was to be the "rescued tongue" of her husband. Inevitably, this intensified relationship set into motion the dynamics that led to the alienation of mother and son. Thus the book is centered thematically around dual reconciliation: first that of the wife/husband, then of the mother/son. The former occurs on the time-plane of the narrated self, i.e., within the plot of the narration. The latter is evident in the time-plane of the narrator. The structuring of this poetic autobiography reveals its functional role: through the interpretive art of autobiography, Canetti finds his own individual voice (his "rescued tongue") and thus makes peace with his mother.

How is this reconciliation manifested? At the beginning of the book, the narrator ends a chapter with the pronouncement that the only thing he truly hates is death, the enemy of humankind. Canetti's view of literature as a weapon against death has been the object of critical discussion,[25] yet within the pages of *Die gerettete Zunge,* the theme of the writer as an opponent of death is undeveloped. Nevertheless, this disclosure, appearing so early in the text and reverberating at the close of a chapter, carries thematic weight, and one would expect his hatred of death to unfold within the text. It does appear to do so in his reaction to his father's death: "My father's death was at the center of every world I found myself in" (58).[26] Yet both prior to this event and following it, he exhibited murderous intentions. In Ruschuk his fury against his older cousin, Laurica, let him to pursue her with an ax. During his struggles with the professor, Elias fantasized about the collapse of the balcony on which the professor was sitting. Later he threatened his mother with his own suicidal jump from the balcony if she remarries. It does not appear that Elias was engaged in the struggle against death, but the pronouncement was not from Elias, but from the narrator. As Hans Reiss stated: "He can create a world by way of language which will survive his own personal death. Thus, writing entails conquering death."[27]

An autobiography, written at the time long past his mother's death and when his brother George is threatened by illness, may serve the purpose of preserving family through literature. Gerald Stieg quotes from a *Le Monde* interview with Canetti in which the author expressly touches on this point:

> The people whom I love, my parents, my brother George, but also those whom I don't care for, will live

once again, as long as my books are read. I have an unspeakable joy, whenever I consider that they will move, speak and live independent of me.[28]

Given Canetti's view of literature as a means of combating death, the omission of his hated rival's name may be his final revenge.

From *Das Augenspiel* we know that the reconciliation with his mother as presented in *Die gerettete Zunge* did not hold, but perhaps the autobiography serves as his final recognition of his debt to his mother and his repayment of that debt. In an episode one summer, Elias became angry at his mother's obsession with having her portrait painted by a well-known artist: "He's going to paint me! I'm going to be immortal!" (173).[29] He understood this desire, but resented the fact that another person would be the one to immortalize her. She misunderstood his objections and accused him of being envious of her. "This accusation was so low and so wrong that I couldn't retort. It lamed my tongue but not my brain" (175).[30] She never sat for the painting, and Canetti, no longer with lamed tongue, achieved a more enduring and immortalizing portrait.

Notes

1. Gerald Stieg. "Betrachtungen zu Elias Canettis Autobiographie." *Zu Elias Canetti.* Ed. Manfred Durzak (Stuttgart: Ernst Klett, 1983) 160.

2. Friederike Eigler. *Das autobiographische Werk von Elias Canetti.* (Tübingen: Stauffenberg-Verlag, 1988) 15.

3. Philippe Lejeune, *Le Pacte autobiographique* (Paris: Seuil, 1975).

4. David Darby. "A Literary Life: Textuality of Elias Canetti's Autobiography." *Modern Austrian Literature* 25.2 (1992) 37-48.

5. From the English translation by Joachim Neugroschel. Elias Canetti. *The Tongue Set Free: Remembrance of a European Childhood.* (New York: The Seabury Press, 1979), 58. All quotes from this text will be indicated by the page number in parentheses. The German citations provided in the endnotes are from Elias Canetti. *Die gerettete : Geschichte einer Jugend.* (München: Carl Hanser, 1994).

   "Vielleicht kann ich sie einmal komplett niederschreiben. Es würde ein Buch daraus werden, ein ganzes Buch, und jetzt sind es andere Spuren, denen ich folge" (75).

6. Richard N. Coe. *When the Grass Was Taller: Autobiography and the Experience of Childhood.* (New Haven: Yale University Press, 1985) 2.

7. *"Heute noch nicht, morgen"* (9).

8. *"Es ist wahr, daß ich, wie der früheste Mensch, durch die Vertreibung aus dem Paradies erst entstand"* (330).

9. *"Mein Sohn, du spielst, und dein Vater ist tot! Du spielst, du spielst, und dein Vater ist tot! Dein Vater ist tot! Dein Vater ist tot! Du spielst, dein Vater ist tot!"* (72-73).

10. *"Wenn wir nur allein waren, ging alles, was sie dachte, sagte oder tat, wie die natürlichste Sache in mich ein. Aus den Sätzen, die sie mir zu solchen Zeiten sagte, bin ich entstanden"* (155).

11. *". . . ich bestehe zum guten Teil aus ihnen"* (111).

12. *"Alles Erotische enthielt sie mir hartnäckig vor, das Tabu . . . blieb so wirksam in mir, als wäre es am Berg Sinai von Gott selbst verkündigt worden"* (202).

13. *"Sie, die auf alles eine runde und klare Antwort wußte, sie, die mir immer das Gefühl gab, daß auch ich Verantwortung für die Erziehung der Kleinen hätte, sie schwieg, zum erstenmal schwieg sie, sie schwieg so lang, daß mir angst und bange wurde"* (132).

14. *"Ich fürchtete, er könne mich einmal mit dem Bart streifen und dann würde ich mich auf der Stelle in einen Sklaven verwandeln, der ihm alles zutragen müßte"* (147).

15. *"Jetzt ist alles gut. Jetzt ist alles gut"* (161).

16. *". . . sei allein gewesen und habe keine Angehörigen gehabt. Vielleicht deswegen hat er nicht mehr leben wollen"* (146).

17. *". . . in der ich sozusagen um die Hand meiner Mutter kämpfte und sie gewann"* (244).

18. *". . . da ich seither nie an das eine ohne das andere gedacht habe, muß ein Zusammenhang bestehen"* (30).

19. *". . . als hätte ich nie ein Schiff gesehen, es war das einzige, außer ihm war nichts. Neben ihm war Dämmerung und allmähliches Dunkel"* (274).

20. *"Es . . . nahm Besitz von mir, als wäre ich um seinetwillen in den Obstgarten gekommen. Ich hatte es nie zuvor gesehen, aber ich erkannte es wieder"* (274).

21. *"Ich ging ins Haus und sprach zu niemand, worüber hätte ich sprechen können"* (274).

22. *"Ich vergaß ihn und habe nie wieder an ihn gedacht, erst mit dem beleuchteten Schiff ist sein Bild wieder vor mir erschienen"* (276).

23. *"Meine früheste Erinnerung ist in Rot getaucht"* (9).

24. "*. . . sie schilderte die roten Zungen der Wölfe, die so nahe gekommen waren, daß sie noch in späteren Jahren von ihnen träumte*" (16).

25. See in particular the analysis by Hans Reiss and Dagmar Barnouw's *Elias Canetti: Zur Einführung.* Hamburg: Julius, 1996.

26. "*In Zentrum jeder Welt, in der ich mich fand, stand der Tod des Vaters*" (71).

27. Hans Reiss. "The Writer's Task: Some Reflections on Elias Canetti's Autobiography." *Elias Canetti: Londoner Symposium.* Ed. Andrian Stevens and Fred Wagner. (Stuttgart: Akademischer Verlag, 1991), 55.

28. Translated from Stieg, 159. "*Die Menschen, die ich liebte, meine Eltern, den Bruder Georg, aber auch jene, die ich nicht mochte, werden noch einmal leben, solange man mich lesen wird. Ich habe eine unsagbare Freude, wenn ich denke, dass sie sich außer mir bewegen, sprechen, leben.*"

29. "*Er wird mich malen! Ich werde unsterblich!*" (213).

30. "*Es verschlug mir noch die Rede, aber keinen Gedanken*" (216).

Additional coverage of Canetti's life and career is contained in the following sources published by Thomson Gale: *Concise Dictionary of World Literary Biography,* **Vol. 2;** *Contemporary Authors,* **Vols. 21-24R, 146;** *Contemporary Authors New Revision Series,* **Vols. 23, 61, 79;** *Contemporary Literary Criticism,* **Vols. 3, 14, 25, 75, 86;** *Contemporary World Writers,* **Ed. 2;** *Dictionary of Literary Biography,* **Vols. 85, 124;** *DISCovering Authors 3.0; Encyclopedia of World Literature in the 20th Century,* **Ed. 3;** *European Writers,* **Vol. 12;** *Literature Resource Center; Major 20th-Century Writers,* **Eds. 1, 2;** *Reference Guide to World Literature,* **Eds. 2, 3; and** *Twayne's World Authors.*

The Great Gatsby

F. Scott Fitzgerald

(Full name Francis Scott Key Fitzgerald) American novelist, short-story writer, essayist, screenwriter, and playwright.

The following entry provides criticism on Fitzgerald's *The Great Gatsby* (1925) from 1984 through 2001. For criticism on *The Great Gatsby* prior to 1984, see *TCLC*, Volume 14; For a discussion of Fitzgerald's complete career, see *TCLC*, Volumes 1 and 6; for a discussion of his novel *Tender Is the Night* (1934), see Volume 28; and for discussion of his novel *The Last Tycoon* (1941), see Volume 55.

INTRODUCTION

Critics have generally agreed that *The Great Gatsby,* published in 1925, is the crowning achievement of Fitzgerald's literary career. It evokes not only the ambiance of the jazz-age search for the American dream of wealth and happiness, but also the larger questions of fading traditional values in the face of increasing materialism and cynicism.

PLOT AND MAJOR CHARACTERS

Fitzgerald frames his plot as a story within a story, as the narrator, Nick Carraway, relates his version of Jay Gatsby's life. Nick, seeking freedom from his constricted Midwestern existence, takes a job in New York City and rents a bungalow in West Egg, Long Island, next door to the lavish mansion of the mysterious Jay Gatsby. Nick's wealthy cousin, Daisy Buchanan, and her husband Tom, invite Nick to dinner with the attractive but flighty Jordan Baker at their luxurious home on the neighboring island of East Egg. Unsettled by the Buchanans' seemingly purposeless lives, Nick returns home and notices his neighbor Gatsby staring longingly at a green light across the bay coming from the Buchanans' property. Tom later persuades Nick to accompany him to a place he calls the Valley of Ashes and introduces him to his blowsy mistress, Myrtle Wilson. Tom, Myrtle, and Nick end up at an apartment in New York, where a wild party ensues, and in a violent outburst, Tom strikes Myrtle and breaks her nose. Later in the month, Gatsby sends Nick an invitation to come to a

sumptuous party at his estate, where Nick meets his neighbor for the first time. This is the first of many parties Nick attends at the Gatsby mansion in the company of many of the rich and famous. When Gatsby later takes Nick to New York for lunch, he regales him with tales of his war medals and his Oxford education. The other guest at lunch is the notorious gangster Meyer Wolfsheim, who reportedly fixed the World Series in 1918. Nick, befuddled by Gatsby's questionable associations, is also taken aback when Jordan asks him on Gatsby's behalf to invite Daisy to lunch at Nick's bungalow. He does so even though he now knows that Daisy and Gatsby were in love prior to her marriage to Tom. The two ill-fated lovers meet, and Gatsby takes Daisy to his mansion and invites her to his next party. Daisy agrees, but when she disapproves of some of his guests, Gatsby stops entertaining altogether. He eventually tells Nick of his truly humble Midwest origins, noting that his name is really Gatz, that he did not graduate from Oxford, and that he has made his fortune in bootlegging and other nefarious ventures. One day Gatsby, the Buchanans, Jordan, and Nick drive to New York. On the way, they stop at the garage of George Wilson, husband of Myrtle, who tries to get money from Tom and announces that he and Myrtle are leaving town. At a hotel in New York, Tom accuses Gatsby of trying to steal his wife, and a fierce argument ensues. Daisy heads home with Gatsby, and shortly thereafter Tom and Jordan stop at Wilson's garage to find that Myrtle has been killed by a hit-and-run driver of a yellow car. Tom blames the death on Gatsby though the real driver at the time was Daisy, whom Gatsby seeks to protect. George Wilson, thinking Gatsby was the driver, goes to Gatsby's estate, shoots him, and then kills himself. Only Gatsby's father, who thinks his son was a great man, attends his funeral. Nick later learns that Tom had a part in Gatsby's death, having convinced Wilson that Myrtle and Gatsby were lovers. Disillusioned with the Buchanans and their ilk, Nick decides to return to the Midwest.

MAJOR THEMES

Echoes of the American Dream pervade the novel, which contrasts the supposed innocence and moral sense of the "Western" characters with the sophistication and materialism of the "Eastern" characters. Gatsby's lavish existence in the nouveau riche Long Island community of West Egg, moreover, cannot ever compensate for his lack of the more pedigreed wealth of East Egg. He remains an "innocent" in his single-minded pursuit of Daisy despite his association with underworld characters and ill-begotten money. The Valley of Ashes and the sign with the blank eyes of Dr. Eckleburg indicate a moral wasteland and an absent God—as well as the emptiness of the new commercial culture. Gatsby's pursuit of his dream takes on a mythic quality, mirroring the dream which led Americans to conquer the frontier. Gatsby's "frontier," however, is an ill-advised pursuit of a vacuous young woman not worthy of his love. Initially, Nick, the Midwestern moral arbiter, disdains Gatsby's values, but he eventually comes to see something heroic in Gatsby's vision, which reflects America's own loss of innocence in the face of the crass materialism of the 1920s.

CRITICAL RECEPTION

Early reviews of Gatsby were mixed, and relatively few copies actually had sold before Fitzgerald's death in 1940. Many critics, most notably Ernest Hemingway, were put off by the fact that Fitzgerald had been known as a writer of stories for popular magazines like The Saturday Evening Post. It was not until a revival of Fitzgerald's works in the 1950s that the novel began to attract serious criticism. For the five ensuing decades, Gatsby has continued to attract critical attention and reappraisal. Critics have praised Fitzgerald's tightly woven narrative, and many have focused on the position of the narrator, Nick Carraway, and the subjective limitations of his observations of Gatsby's saga. Although Gatsby was for many years called "a novel of the Jazz Age" (a term which Fitzgerald coined), critics have agreed that it has a much more universal meaning, not the least of which is a trenchant critique of materialist American society much like T. S. Eliot's The Waste Land. The appearance of at least four biographies in the 1990s and early 2000s is an indication that interest in Fitzgerald's novels remains unabated. Earlier critics of Gatsby emphasized biographical and cultural influences on the novel, and formalist approaches dealt with the novel's structure, point of view, symbols, use of language, and the like. By the 1980s through the early 2000s, a variety of approaches, both heavily theoretical and non-theoretical, have been evident in critics' commentaries. While many have continued to explore biographical influences or comparisons with other authors, or to use New Critical analyses, others have increasingly employed such techniques as deconstruction, feminist criticism, and discourse analysis to uncover hidden meanings in the text.

PRINCIPAL WORKS

Flappers and Philosophers (short stories) 1920
This Side of Paradise (novel) 1920
The Beautiful and Damned (novel) 1922
Tales of the Jazz Age (short stories) 1922
The Vegetable; or, From President to Postman (play) 1923
The Great Gatsby (novel) 1925
All the Sad Young Men (short stories) 1926
Tender Is the Night (novel) 1934
Taps at Reveille (short stories) 1935
The Last Tycoon (unfinished novel) 1941
The Crack-Up (essays, notebooks, and letters) 1945
Afternoon of an Author (short stories and essays) 1957
The Pat Hobby Stories (short stories) 1962
The Letters of F. Scott Fitzgerald (letters) 1963
Dear Scott/Dear Max: The Fitzgerald-Perkins Correspondence (letters) 1971
As Ever, Scott Fitz: Letters Between F. Scott Fitzgerald and His Literary Agent Harold Ober, 1919-1940 (letters) 1972
The Basil and Josephine Stories (short stories) 1973
Bits of Paradise [with Zelda Fitzgerald] (short stories) 1973
The Notebooks of F. Scott Fitzgerald (notebooks) 1978

CRITICISM

Kent Cartwright (essay date spring 1984)

SOURCE: Cartwright, Kent. "Nick Carraway as an Unreliable Narrator." *Papers on Language and Literature* 20, no. 2 (spring 1984): 218-32.

[*In the following essay, Cartwright discusses ways in which Nick Carraway is sometimes a confused or misleading narrator.*]

While I have met individuals whom I might describe as more Gatsby than Carraway, I have seldom met a critic I would so describe. As critics, we seem to cherish our disillusionment. Indeed, serious interest in **The Great Gatsby,** according to Richard Foster, was launched by a generation of neoclassical and formalist critics who tended to believe in the final, tough truth of existence imaged in the thinning possibility and thinning joy of Nick's lugubrious moral retreat. As a consequence, traditional estimates of **The Great Gatsby** have grown up around the dual assumptions that Nick speaks for his author and that the novel's mission is an essentially straightforward criticism of the American Dream.[1] Furthermore, because something about Nick's "midwesternism" seems deeply personal to Fitzgerald, critics have tended not to distinguish between either the narrator and his author or the narrator and his novel. Nick's vision, however, is not identical to Fitzgerald's, or at least to the novel's, for Nick is capable of being an unreliable narrator at moments that are crucial to the story's development. Indeed, in exactly the same ways that Nick may be a flawed character, he is also sometimes a confused, misleading, or inaccurate teller of his tale.

In the last two decades, critical acceptance of Nick's judgments has yielded to some disenchantment with the narrator and his moral actions. His detractors have described him variously (and perhaps excessively) as a defunct archpriest, panderer, prig, spiritual bankrupt, hypocrite, and "moral eunuch"—a man capable of neither assertive action nor self-knowledge.[2] Even those congenial to Carraway's views speak of his "inhibitions and lack of boldness," his failure of self-awareness, and his fear of commitment. To many readers, moreover, the hopelessness of Nick's final vision seems somehow to betray his story.[3] Part of that dissatisfaction arises from Nick's moral withdrawal to the Middle West of his past, while a related response argues that the dream lives beyond Gatsby's death and that a "gleam of hope" is left the reader at the end, a hope perhaps inspired by the very limitations of Nick's consciousness.[4]

Recent critics, that is, have begun to see Gatsby's story differently from the way Nick would have us see it. To pose such possibilities, however, is to tamper with accepted notions about the novel's integrity, for some defenders of Nick have argued that "the book makes no sense—if Carraway is repudiated."[5] Yet the limitations of Nick's character do have narrative consequences, for Nick sometimes sees only part of a meaning that a scene carries, sometimes shifts ground perplexingly, and sometimes even strains "judgments" out of inconclusive evidence. To accuse Nick of such faults might sound idiosyncratic and even churlish. After all, Nick is the novel's lone moral consciousness; only he sees the richness of meaning—the ineffable dream and its foul wake—in the events on Long Island that summer. But some readers argue that Nick's vision is "limited" and that Fitzgerald intended no simple identification either between the narrator and himself or the narrator and his reader; others have begun to discover differing, sometimes conflicting narrative "voices" in Nick.[6]

In addition, Nick develops a peculiar rigidity during the course of the novel. Concurrently, as Nick reveals a growing determination to perceive events in a fixed way, his flights of responsive imagination diminish. After chapter 6 the novel darkens. One explanation for this is that the romantic and mythic context gives way to the social and economic.[7] The darkening tone, then, proceeds in part from Nick's evolving consciousness, a staking out of his moral terrain of lost possibility. The two narrative movements are simultaneous: Nick's emerging weaknesses as a narrator parallel his progressively constricted vision, as if the truths Nick affirms are not exactly the truths of his fable. Nick's final disillusionment, that is, derives as much from his own moral dimness, his passivity, and his exaggerated gentility as it does from the facts of Gatsby's life; correspondingly, those qualities sometimes compromise the narration, altering, even from moment to moment, the response—empathy or removal, acceptance or doubt—that his telling draws from the reader. Such a view of Nick's weaknesses must challenge the traditional assumption that Nick generally doubles for Fitzgerald. It might, indeed, reveal that Nick's closing asceticism is more a preference than an imperative, that his assessment of the dream is not conclusive, and that the novel is far more open-ended than some critics have suggested.

Almost from the beginning, the narration invites readers to feel subtle distinctions between representation and explanation. This divergence is a characteristic of the novel's narrative style and is repeated variously throughout the story. The technique has the advantage of economy; it gives readers two types of impressions: one created through descriptions of places, things, and events, and another created by Nick's responses and reflections. The pattern exhibits itself, for example, in Daisy's story of the butler's nose and her comparison of Nick to an absolute rose.

> "I'll tell you a family secret," she whispered enthusiastically. "It's about the butler's nose. Do you want to hear about the butler's nose? . . . Well, he wasn't always a butler; he used to be the silver polisher for some people in New York that had a silver service for two hundred people. He had to polish it from morning till night, until finally it began to affect his nose."

> "I love to see you at my table, Nick. You remind me of a—of a rose, an absolute rose. Doesn't he?" She turned to Miss Baker for confirmation: "An absolute rose?"[8]

In the first instance, Daisy's anecdote is trivial and insipid, clearly anticlimactic to the preparation she makes; in the second her comparison is ridiculous and insincere, camouflaging her real preoccupation. But in both cases, Nick is captivated by Daisy's vibrant beauty: "For a moment the last sunshine fell with romantic affection upon her glowing face; her voice compelled me forward breathlessly as I listened" (14); "She was only extemporizing, but a stirring warmth flowed from her, as if her heart was trying to come out to you concealed in one of those breathless, thrilling words" (15). In each example, the narration creates two effects, the first through the structure of incidents—such as the thrown napkin and abrupt departure with which Daisy disposes of her interest in absolute roses—and the second through Nick's mesmerization before her shining face and the feverish modulations of her voice. But the two effects judge Daisy oppositely: the one with distance, the other with engagement. This is not to say that Nick fails to recognize that Daisy is as childish as she is womanly, rather that the response he emphasizes reveals only one-half the way the scene dramatizes her. To acknowledge such distinctions is already to put the reader at some critical remove from the narrator.

An example of Nick's inordinate responses occurs in chapter 4 during his automobile ride with Gatsby to New York (64-69). Fitzgerald's aim in this scene is to create that ambivalence fundamental to the novel by deepening our fascination with the mystery of Gatsby, even though Gatsby teeters on the edge of the ridiculous. One technique Fitzgerald employs is to preserve a kernel of actual or even metaphoric truth in each of Gatsby's falsehoods: he was educated, at least for a few months, at Oxford; he did inherit a "good deal of money" from his spiritual father, Dan Cody, though he was cheated of it; he was a genuine war hero, even if a copy of Sergeant York. Another, more subtle technique is to distance the reader from Carraway's judgment,

just as Nick is distanced from Gatsby. Through the episode we see Nick's initial, cool skepticism toppling before his sensual imagination—responses disproportionate in either extreme—which leave the reader's more balanced impressions at odds with the narrator's. Indeed, we are left reacting to Nick's reactions, a condition which not only insulates Gatsby but also evokes his power.

During the journey Fitzgerald calls our attention repeatedly to Nick's filtering lens. We begin pointedly with Nick's aesthetic intellectualism, his "disappointment" that Gatsby "had little to say" and the arch dismissal of him as "simply the proprietor of an elaborate roadhouse next door" (64). Yet juxtaposed against this wry boredom is the promise of surprise: "And then came that disconcerting ride" (65). Thus, Fitzgerald sets the drama of the scene in the dialectics of Nick's response. Nick rapidly demonstrates a repertoire of judicious responses: his strained sensitivity at Gatsby's overtness, "A little overwhelmed, I began the generalized evasions which that question deserves" (65); his fine ear for the false note as Gatsby stumbles, or chokes, over "educated at Oxford. . . . And with this doubt his whole statement fell to pieces, and I wondered if there wasn't tion deserves" (65); his fine ear for the false note as Gatsby stum-something a little sinister about him, after all" (65); and his discreet confirming of his own instincts as he asks Gatsby in what part of the Middle West he grew up and is answered "'San Francisco.'" Nick's power of lucid assessment is in full display.

Carraway's vision of Gatsby now becomes more subtle and extreme. When Gatsby recalls the "sudden extinction" of his clan, Nick responds, "For a moment I suspected that he was pulling my leg, but a glance at him convinced me otherwise" (66). Nick momentarily suspects Gatsby of an irony of which the observer is capable but the observed incapable, though Nick's glance leaves unsettled whether he thinks Gatsby means what he says or not. Gatsby's next image of himself, as a young, sad rajah in the capitals of Europe, tickles Nick with literary hilarity: "With an effort I managed to restrain my incredulous laughter. The very phrases were worn so threadbare that they evoked no image except that of a turbaned 'character' leaking sawdust at every pore as he pursued a tiger through the Bois de Boulogne" (66). Nick reacts in the full possession of his worldliness, distancing the reader with him, as he caricatures Gatsby's tale into a pastiche of incongruent cliches. And at just that moment of assurance, Nick trips unknowingly over his own learned responses. Gatsby tells his story of the Argonne Forest: "We stayed there two days and two nights, a hundred and thirty men with sixteen Lewis guns, and when the infantry came up at last they found the insignia of three German divisions among the piles of the dead. I was promoted to be a major, and every Allied government gave me a decoration—even Montenegro, little Montenegro down on the Adriatic Sea" (66).

Influenced by the absurdity of the sawdust romance, Nick dismisses Gatsby's war reminiscence: "it was like skimming hastily through a dozen magazines" (67). But Carraway misjudges. Gatsby's tale is not incredible in context: unlike the leaking rajah, its subject is realistic, its derailing local and concrete, and the whole internally consistent. It is also confirmed by Nick himself in subsequent narrative when he summarizes Gatsby's career: "He did extraordinarily well in the war. He was a captain before he went to the front, and following the Argonne battles he got his majority and the command of the divisional machine-guns" (150). Such acts of singular courage, of course, were familiar during the First World War. The narrative itself has been colored from the beginning by a sense of restless men—Nick in particular—returning from war, flushed with the adventure and thrill of combat. Nick and Gatsby had established the bond of war experience between them before they even learned each other's names (47), and the restlessness that Nick has noticed in Gatsby ("He was never quite still [64]) at the outset of their journey recalls again, like Nick's own restlessness, the agitations of the combat veteran. The Argonne Forest adventure then is not pulp fantasy in the same sense as the melancholy rajah; it is, in fact, close to Nick's own experiences and close to the texture of the novel. Nick has allowed his reactions to outrun his evidence.

Yet Carraway's opinion next does a "disconcerting" about-face. As Gatsby brandishes the medal from Montenegro, Nick begins to capitulate: "To my astonishment, the thing had an authentic look" (67). The Oxford picture completes the reversal: "Then it was all true. I saw the skins of tigers flaming in his palace on the Grand Canal; I saw him opening a chest of rubies to ease, with their crimson-lighted depths, the gnawings of his broken heart" (67). Nick's conversion is so odd that one scrutinizes for a hint of irony. There is none, nor any countervailing action either, like Nick's earlier clarifying glance. Nick's capitulation appears confirmed, furthermore, by his own "astonishment" and by Gatsby's "satisfaction" as he pockets up his trophies. Indeed, the flaming tigers' skins and the crimson-lighted chest have a familiar ring about them, recalling, for example, the blooming Mediterranean and idylls of Fifth Avenue of an earlier episode. Carraway betrays his susceptibility, much like that of which he accuses Gatsby, not only to romance but also to the fantasies of "a dozen magazines."

A culminating incident follows. When Gatsby shows a "white card from his wallet" to the motorcycle policeman, who immediately apologizes for having stopped him, Nick asks, "'What was that? . . . The picture of Oxford?'" (68). Nick's question is commonly consid-

ered sarcastic, though his habitual ambivalence makes an intentional naivete possible as well. Yet if Nick is now taking rhetorical revenge, are we to understand his vision of the Grand Canal as sarcastic, too? Or has Nick simply switched to his rationalist mode? If sarcastic, then Nick will undergo yet another sea change, since the journey ends in an affirmation of fairyland, "the city rising up across the river in white heaps and sugar lumps," where "Even Gatsby could happen, without any particular wonder" (69). Either Nick means, confusingly, sometimes more and sometimes less than what he says, or his impressionability and fastidiousness alternately swallow each other.

Nick's "judgment" of Gatsby becomes exaggerated, unstable, and finally self-compromising. The key to Nick's response, of course, is his admission that his "incredulity was submerged in fascination" (67). To whatever degree Gatsby has won Nick over, he has won him not by an appeal to evidence but by an appeal to imagination. Because of his impressionability, Nick grasps an image and decks it out with his own bright feathers. But through this submersion, Nick's belief has in some measure grown. Fascination breeds credulity. Indeed, Gatsby is such a cliché that on the flimsiest of bona fides he becomes a miracle. Fitzgerald shows Carraway increasingly convinced of Gatsby; simultaneously, he moves the reader as well, but not in unison. Because we diverge from Nick—sometimes hesitating at his reactions, sometimes moving beyond them—we feel, even as we too are compelled with fascination, a firmer objectivity. Nick's confusions, then, become values in the reader's portrait of Gatsby, making him powerful even as he is remote; plausible yet strange; possible. Thanks, curiously, to the distance Fitzgerald establishes between Nick and his reader, even Gatsby can happen here, without any particular wonder.

As the novel progresses, Nick's sense of possibility recedes. In the memorable scene when Gatsby, Daisy, and Nick tour Gatsby's house (91-97) after the two lovers have been reunited, we hear the note of doubt and disbelief echo like the faint rumble of thunder along the Sound. That counterpoint is structured, in part, into the details of the scene—the rain, the gathering darkness, the isolation of the lovers—but another part is developed by the steady commentary of the narrator. Indeed, while the scenic details are ambiguous in their import, Nick's emerging disillusionment is less so. Nick wants to suggest that for all the intensity of the moment the consummation is unreal, atavistic. But the scene we have is incomplete, perhaps contrary, evidence for his conclusion.

Just as Daisy's house is the symbol of the magical, transforming power of wealth, the tour of Gatsby's house is a ritual demonstration of his rightful entry into Daisy's world and beyond Daisy's world into a self-created beatitude of money. The tour is a set-piece, a celebration of the passage into fairyland.⁹ The three enter formally by the big posterns, the long way. Daisy murmurs enchantingly as she admires the feudal silhouette, the gardens, the odors of various flowers. The house is a castle of nascent life and incongruent riches: the Marie Antoinette music rooms and Restoration salons imminent with breathless, imagined guests, "period bedrooms swathed in rose and lavender silk and vivid with new flowers" (92). At this moment, Gatsby's life is the wild romance of the young rajah come true, and it is no wonder that Nick is on the verge of asking to see the rubies. Gatsby's shirts are the apotheosis of his wealth, part of the "youth and mystery"—like Daisy's "freshness of many clothes" (150)—that wealth imprisons. They are the riches of the East, existing only to glorify their owner, a numinous beauty so vast and so casually held that Daisy buries her face and cries, herself, in wonder. Daisy is at one with Gatsby's dream.¹⁰

And for this interlude at least, Gatsby achieves his dream of Daisy. Nick, both as participant and as narrator, realizes the immensity of this fulfillment. In the ecstasy of Daisy's presence, Gatsby has transcended his known world: "Sometimes, too, he stared around at his possessions in a dazed way, as though in her actual and astounding presence none of it was any longer real" (92). As Gatsby tries ineffectually to explain himself, Nick observes the intensity and flow of this transformation: "He had passed visibly through two states and was entering upon a third. After his embarrassment and his unreasoning joy he was consumed with wonder at her presence" (93). Nick, too, has a sense of the delicate magic of the moment. As the three of them look at the pink and golden sunset over the sea, Daisy whispers to Gatsby, "'I'd like to just get one of those pink clouds and put you in it and push you around'" (95). In the ethereal adolescence of that profession of love is its power, and Nick responds to the aura of completeness that surrounds the two lovers: "I tried to go then, but they wouldn't hear of it; perhaps my presence made them feel more satisfactorily alone" (95). The twilight falling, Nick emphasizes the removal of Gatsby and Daisy into a storybook world of their own. As "The Eve of St. Agnes" leaves its lovers suddenly long ages hence, so too Carraway leaves Gatsby and Daisy inhabiting their vision in solitude: "They had forgotten me, but Daisy glanced up and held out her hand; Gatsby didn't know me now at all. I looked once more at them and they looked at me, remotely, possessed by intense life" (97).

Countering the tone of ritual, love, and apotheosis in this episode is an undertow, a suggestion of failure and constriction, made by Nick. This judgment is more than a matter of "structural" irony; it is an awkward and personal interpretation. Of Gatsby's absorption in the thought of the green light on Daisy's dock, for example,

Nick writes: "Possibly it had occurred to him that the colossal significance of that light had now vanished forever. . . . Now it was again a green light on a dock. His count of enchanted objects had diminished by one" (94). Not only is the narrator's grammatical shift from a conditional to a declarative stance peculiar, but the comment itself is peculiar, coming from the observer who has just described a whole mansion full of objects transformed in the enchantment of the lover's presence. Daisy admiring his rooms, Daisy brushing her hair with his golden brush, Daisy sobbing into his shirts—Gatsby's count of magical objects has actually increased a thousandfold (92). Nick's reflections are not the remarks of the person who almost asks to see the rubies, but rather the more hardened and distant judgments of the man who has seen further to the ruination of Gatsby's dream. They are remarks true to Nick's developing character, but less true to the moment that Gatsby and Daisy inhabit.

Nick wants to argue that the dream is unachievable at the very moment that Gatsby is achieving it. Another such incongruent judgment comes as he leaves the lovers:

> As I went over to say good-by I saw that the expression of bewilderment had come back into Gatsby's face, as though a faint doubt had occurred to him as to the quality of his present happiness. Almost five years! There must have been moments even that afternoon when Daisy tumbled short of his dreams—not through her own fault, but because of the colossal vitality of his illusion. . . . No amount of fire or freshness can challenge what a man will store up in his ghostly heart.

> As I watched him he adjusted himself a little, visibly. His hand took hold of hers, and as she said something low in his ear he turned toward her with a rush of emotion. I think that voice held him most, with its fluctuating, feverish warmth, because it couldn't be over-dreamed—that voice was a deathless song.

[97]

Again, Nick seems to be speaking from two perspectives: the one of a man describing what he sees, the other of a man pleading, instead, his own view of life. Nick's assertion that "no amount of fire or freshness can challenge" a man's illusions argues discordantly with the "fluctuating, feverish warmth" of the voice that "couldn't be over-dreamed." Daisy's voice is as exciting and compelling as Gatsby's vision of her; her voice is, in fact, the essence of her attractiveness, and its incessant, erotic modulations are the essence of the dream. Just as Daisy's voice held Nick spellbound in chapter 1, it is commensurate also with Gatsby's capacity for wonder. Nick seems to be temporarily both "inside and outside" this scene, but the conjunction of viewpoints mystifies, as if Daisy's voice could be both overdreamed and not overdreamed. For the reader, Nick's descriptions point a different direction from his assessments.

The glory of this scene, of course, is its ambiguity about what is really won or lost, a mystery to which Nick is no master sleuth. While Nick misjudges the occasion by the measure of his own later disillusionment, Gatsby and Daisy exist inside the dream, living it.

In the novel's final chapter, a peculiar dislocation or re-orientation of the story's direction takes place which again connects Nick's personal limitations with his blurred narrative judgment. The first three sections (164-76) of the chapter deal with Gatsby's funeral. The narrator's intention is to sink Gatsby's death into anticlimax by revealing his essential irrelevance to the world in which he had seemed to be the observed of all observers and by demonstrating again the pathetic fragility of the dream which had now "broken up like glass against Tom's hard malice" (148). But the story of Gatsby's burial, ironically, turns out to be not so much about Gatsby as it is about Nick. More than in the immediately preceding chapters, Nick's judgments and responses are evident here: his feeling of responsibility toward Gatsby, his growing awareness of the callous indifference of others, his final emotional numbness.

Nick identifies Gatsby with his own progress. The chapter, in fact, is largely a probing of Nick's statement that "I found myself on Gatsby's side, and alone" (165). Nick feels an "intense personal interest" (165) and a ceremonial responsibility toward Gatsby, whose body seems to call out to him for help and companionship (166): "I wanted to get somebody for him. I wanted to go into the room where he lay and reassure him . . ." (165). On Gatsby's behalf, Nick grows in angry disillusionment at the breaches of faith by those like Daisy and Wolfsheim who should care most for Gatsby at the final hour: "I began to have a feeling of defiance, of scornful solidarity between Gatsby and me against them all" (166). Just as he takes up partial residence in his house, Nick takes up Gatsby's moral residence, becomes Gatsby's factor, seeking out for him the apparent meaning of his death. That meaning is in its abandonment. After hanging up on Klipspringer, Nick acknowledges, he "felt a certain shame for Gatsby" (170), as if embarrassed for his friend at the indifference of those who accepted his generosity. In the desolation of Gatsby's funeral Nick begins, as the canvas is rolled back, to slip into an unfeeling abstractedness: "I tried to think about Gatsby then for a moment, but he was already too far away, and I could only remember, without resentment, that Daisy hadn't sent a message or a flower" (176). Nick loses Gatsby, too, and the ceremony's diminution becomes its revelation.

The narrative perspective toward Gatsby is thus both inside and outside in an odd, sequential way. Though Nick begins as Gatsby's surrogate, he becomes the dulled consciousness of society. That external frame of reference is illustrated in Nick by the futility of his comradeship and by his own failing intimacy with Gatsby. The narrative stance toward Gatsby in death has become the opposite side of its stance toward him in life: while earlier parts of the novel witness the world from the context of Gatsby, later ones witness Gatsby from the context of an indifferent world. On the strength, and ironic failure, of Nick's very empathy, the narrative perspective reduces Gatsby's dream to ashes. The vitiated ritual of Gatsby's burial finds its emotional correlative in Nick's numbness, the tableau comprising for him life's sentence upon the dreamer and the dream. Nick's psychic depletion becomes, too, the ironic reversal of Gatsby's dazed exaltation in his reunion with Daisy, the two events parallel in their isolation, one in "intense life," the other in death.

Is Nick's judgment the same as the fable's? While Nick's numbness succeeds Gatsby's exhilaration in time, does it also succeed in value? Gatsby was a creature of magic and light, and though he used the "glitterati" of Long Island as stardust for Daisy, they were only that, as unimportant to him as he is to them. The loneliness of Gatsby's interment can only be irrelevant to the transforming power of his vision while he lived. Indeed, it is more important to Nick that Gatsby's funeral be attended than it ever could have been to Gatsby. Nick's dual perspective seems self-contradictory: the meaning that he brings to Gatsby's death from outside is inconsistent with his knowledge of Gatsby's special existence. The isolation of Gatsby's funeral cannot destroy the wonder of his life.

The centerpiece both for Nick's "intense personal interest" and for his "shame for Gatsby" is his visit to Wolfsheim, Gatsby's "closest friend" (172). Oddly, the episode resists Nick's melancholy irony. Wolfsheim's pleasant and casual gangsterism and his vision of the perfectly criminal in the perfectly patriotic and upper class render the scene comic. Nick's intention, apparently, is to show Wolfsheim as a genial sentimentalist and then to puncture his "friendship" (Gatsby's last "'goneggtion'") with his world) by revealing the facile cynicism and manipulativeness under it. For Wolfsheim will not attend the funeral, will not "'get mixed up in it'" (173): his friendship is merely conspiracy. Yet Wolfsheim also delivers some parting advice which forms a comment, in turn, upon Nick's brand of camaraderie: "'Let us learn to show our friendship for a man when he is alive and not after he is dead'" (173). Good advice—but Nick has acted out its reverse. He has been a better friend to Gatsby in death than in life, and his "interest" comes like an apology after the calamity he has watched so passively. Wolfsheim's perspective is the rejoinder to Carraway's. Just as Gatsby's dream is what ennobles him beyond Wolfsheim, so Wolfsheim's statement exposes Carraway. Nick, as he thinks to serve Gatsby in death, is really doing what he likes best: serving a form, a ceremony, a set of manners.

The problems with Nick as narrator are similar to the problems with Nick as moral center. The personal characteristics that have caused readers to distrust his moral vision are connected to the qualities that invite the reader's distrust for the accuracy of some narrative judgments: his impressionability in the car ride sequence, his confusing ambivalence during the tour of Gatsby's mansion, his self-serving proprieties surrounding the funeral. Nick's judgments, however, seem to harden in disillusionment even as the fable's ambiguities compound. Rather than the arbiter of final meanings, Nick is a contestant in the novel's internal tugging war for truth.[11] His narrative failings, in fact, recall other characters who live inside the defensive armor of their own mannerisms, pretensions, and falsehoods: Myrtle and her comic gentility; Jordan looking like a "good illustration" (178) or losing herself in the curious balancing act of her chin before a disagreeable conversation; Daisy and her "sophistication"; Tom expounding a stupid racism or swinging his forearms like a half-back along Fifth Avenue. Such masks and ploys symbolize characters who will not connect with one another or with the life around them.

Nick is the one character capable of perceiving life as Gatsby and the others live it, but he will not shake his fellows out of their defensive pretensions or their complacencies or their lies. Despite Gatsby's grand protean existence, Nick prefers to believe in the unchangeableness of the human character, or at least the unchangeableness of those careless people who smash up things and creatures. That belief is an expression of Nick's personality, for he comes to accept the loneliness and isolation of human experience, but it is not the only truth in the novel. Gatsby dies from the shallowness of Daisy, the hard malice of Tom, and his own pride and misjudgment, not from hope and wonder. Though Nick declares that "you can't repeat the past," the story neither proves nor disproves it. That is perhaps the most unsettling effect of the novel: that the myth of Gatsby survives everything—his own presumption, Tom's malice, and Nick's gloom. That is surely because the dream is as much emotion as object, as much the capacity for wonder and aesthetic contemplation as it is Daisy Buchanan. Accordingly, the dream never loses its sense of reality: the thrill of excitement and possibility in Daisy's voice convinces utterly, long after she is confirmed in triviality. Gatsby's vitality alone is the measure of his dream. That is why Nick's gradual detachment from Gatsby in death not only misrepresents the dream but is irrelevant to it.

Yet we are drawn to the narrator. Beyond the fundamental decency which Nick reveals—as he wipes the dried lather from Mr. McKee's cheek (37), or corrects Daisy's assertion that Tom is shamming about a car deal while really talking to his girlfriend (116), or erases the obscene word from Gatsby's steps (181)—his sheer, brilliant responsiveness to life sometimes redeems his passivity. That sensitivity compares for the reader, perhaps better than Gatsby's, "to one of those intricate machines that register earthquakes ten thousand miles away" (2). Images flood in upon him, touching off flights of imagination: Jordan's chin, Daisy's voice, Gatsby's smile; he perceives the subtlest social communications; he resonates with sentiment, chagrin, perplexity, and transport. Nick's imagination charms us, even more than the occasions that draw it forth. In the "unprosperous" and "bare" interior of Wilson's wretched garage, for example, Nick fantasizes "that sumptuous and romantic apartments were concealed overhead"— incredible commentary, until it turns into half-truth, for the apartments do contain a woman of "immediately perceptible vitality" and "smouldering" nerve ends (25). Again, Fifth Avenue is "so warm and soft, almost pastoral," that he "wouldn't have been surprised to see a great flock of white sheep turn the corner" (28). At the party in Washington Heights, as Catherine talks disparagingly on Monte Carlo, for Nick, "The late afternoon sky bloomed in the window for a moment like the blue honey of the Mediterranean" (34).

We feel a special affection for Nick, in part because the freshness and humor of the novel are substantially an expression of his vision. We wish him well. Our affinity with Nick is also a function of the novel's first-person point of view, a narrative perspective for which Wayne Booth's comment about *Emma* applies with equal force: "the sustained inside view leads the reader to hope for good fortune for the character with whom he travels, quite independently of the qualities revealed."[12] Together with his narrative intimacy, Nick's likeability with the audience creates (as Kenneth Burke would have it) form.[13] These two phenomena arouse expectations within the psyche of the reader that the resolution of the narrative will also bring about Nick's personal fulfillment. Some version of a positive finish—wisdom, if not joy—is implicit in the very condition of the novel, the aesthetic choices Fitzgerald has made. Part of the work's ambivalence, however, stems from Fitzgerald's undercutting of the novel's form; he defeats our expectations, for Nick loses Gatsby, misses in love, and retreats to the safe and complacent Middle West of his past. I suspect that the discomfort so many readers have felt with the novel's ending is a direct expression of this irresolution in *Gatsby*'s form, a dissonance which must reinforce our sense of Nick's limitations. The conclusion of the novel challenges any blithe acceptance of Nick—as moral arbiter, as judicious observer, as companion, as a character fully entitled to our expectations of good fortune. Indeed, Nick's charming impressionability contains the seeds of his own disablement. His imagination is the strongest part of his character, as his fantasies about entering the lives of beautiful women on Fifth Avenue suggest; but the romance of life consists more in what he rhapsodizes than in what he does. As

Nick himself observes, there is a "haunting loneliness" and "wast[e]" about such a life (57). While Nick reverberates like a tympan with felt life, he is the opposite of Gatsby, fixed, like the wall of the cave against which the shadows play.

Readers sometimes confuse the narrator of **The Great Gatsby** with its author, but the novel is far more ambiguous and morally disconcerting than the attitude that Nick would have us accept. The work represents a kind of miscegenation of forms, a romance enclosed in a novel of manners, and Nick and Gatsby seem attached as if by pulleys: as the one is more credible, the other is less so. Gatsby can be both criminal and romantic hero because the book creates for him a visionary moral standard that transcends the conventional and that his life affirms.[14] However, nothing in Nick compels our contemplation or our wonder; he lives in the image of an increasingly reductive melancholy, not of a transcending dream. While Nick has begun the novel addressing questions of judgment, he steadily reveals the infirmity of his own. Nick learns disillusionment for himself, but his unreliable assessments at several key moments distance the reader from the same inevitability. That difference, in fact, is part of the enduring fascination of Fitzgerald's employment of a first-person point of view in the novel. While Fitzgerald subverts our expectations for Nick, he does not wholly subvert the moral or emotional justice of those expectations. The possibility of fulfillment remains latent within the life of the novel despite Nick's inability to attain it. If Nick's ending betrays the story, the novel's inextinguishable sense of possibility partly restores it. Ultimately, the failure of Nick's narration is a failure of his will to believe, even in his own imagination. Too cautious to pay the price for living too long with a single dream, Nick pays the much dearer price for living too long with no dream.

Notes

1. Foster, "The Way to Read *Gatsby,*" in *Sense and Sensibility in Twentieth-Century Writing,* ed. Brom Weber (Carbondale, Ill., 1970), pp. 94-95. Cf. John W. Aldridge, "The Life of Gatsby," in *Twelve Original Essays on Great American Novels,* ed. Charles Shapiro (Detroit, 1958), p. 211; and Marius Bewley, "Scott Fitzgerald's Criticism of America," *The Sewanee Review* 62 (1954): 223.

2. Robert W. Stallman, "Gatsby and the Hole in Time," *Modern Fiction Studies,* 1, no. 4 (1955): 2-16; rpt. in *The House That James Built and Other Literary Studies* (East Lansing, Mich., 1961), pp. 131-50; Gary J. Scrimgeour, "Against *The Great Gatsby,*" *Criticism* 8 (1966): 83-85; Peter L. Hays, "Hemingway and Fitzgerald," in *Hemingway in our Time,* ed. Richard Astro and Jackson L. Benson (Corvallis, Ore., 1974), p. 96.

3. Robert Emmet Long, *The Achieving of "The Great Gatsby": F. Scott Fitzgerald, 1920-25* (Lewisburg, Pa., 1979), p. 145; Barry Gross, "Our Gatsby, Our Nick," *The Centennial Review* 14 (1970): 334-36; A. E. Elmore, "Nick Carraway's Self-Introduction," in *Fitzgerald/Hemingway Annual 1971,* ed. Matthew J. Bruccoli and C. E. Frazer Clark, Jr. (Dayton, Ohio, 1971), p. 137; Milton Hindus, *F. Scott Fitzgerald: An Introduction and Interpretation* (New York, 1968), pp. 40-41; Milton R. Stern, *The Golden Moment: The Novels of F. Scott Fitzgerald* (Urbana, Ill., 1970), p. 288; Richard D. Lehan, *F. Scott Fitzgerald and the Craft of Fiction* (Carbondale, Ill., 1966), p. 111; Foster, p. 108.

4. Lehan, p. 112; Scrimgeour, 83-84; Robert Ornstein, "Scott Fitzgerald's Fable of East and West," *College English* 18 (1956-57): 142-43; Gross, p. 339; Oliver H. Evans, "'A Sort of Moral Attention': The Narrator of *The Great Gatsby,*" in *Fitzgerald/Hemingway Annual 1971,* ed. Matthew J. Bruccoli and C. E. Frazer Clark, Jr. (Dayton, Ohio, 1971), p. 120; Robert Sklar, *F. Scott Fitzgerald: The Last Laocoön* (New York, 1967), p. 192; Sergio Perosa, *The Art of F. Scott Fitzgerald,* trans. Sergio Perosa and Charles Matz (Ann Arbor, 1965), p. 70; Ruth Betsy Tenenbaum, "'The Gray-Turning, Gold-Turning Consciousness' of Nick Carraway," in *Fitzgerald/Hemingway Annual 1975,* ed. Matthew J. Bruccoli and C. E. Frazer Clark, Jr. (Englewood, Colo., 1975), p. 54.

5. See Stern, p. 193; Scrimgeour, p. 83.

6. Evans, pp. 117-39; Tenenbaum, pp. 37-55. Cf. Hindus, pp. 40, 50; William T. Stafford, *Books Speaking to Books: A Contextual Approach to American Fiction* (Chapel Hill, N.C., 1981), pp. 43-50.

7. Sklar, p. 187. See also Richard Chase, *The American Novel and Its Tradition* (Garden City, N.Y., 1957), pp. 162-67. For a different view of the novel's change in tone see E. Fred Carlisle, "The Triple Vision of Nick Carraway," *Modern Fiction Studies* 11 (1965-66): 351-60.

8. F. Scott Fitzgerald, *The Great Gatsby* (New York, 1925), pp. 14, 15; cited hereafter in the text by page.

9. For a discussion of the fairy tale elements in *Gatsby* see Peter L. Hays, "*Gatsby,* Myth, Fairy Tale, and Legend," *Southern Folklore Quarterly* 41 (1977): 213-23.

10. Stern, p. 175, considers this effect a "slip" on the part of Fitzgerald. See also Bewley, p. 241; and Ernest H. Lockridge, Introduction, *Twentieth Century Interpretations of "The Great Gatsby": A*

Collection of Critical Essays, ed. Ernest H. Lockridge (Englewood Cliffs, N.J., 1968), p. 14.

11. See Peter Lisca, "Nick Carraway and the Imagery
of Disorder," *Twentieth Century Literature* 13
(1967): 26-27; see also Long, pp. 181-82, 214-15,
n. 8.

12. *The Rhetoric of Fiction* (Chicago, 1961), pp. 245-
46.

13. "Psychology and Form," *Counter-Statement,* 2nd
ed. (Los Altos, Calif., 1953), pp. 29-44.

14. Lawrence W. Hyman, "Moral Attitudes and the
Literary Experience," *Journal of Aesthetics and
Art Criticism* 38 (1979): 159-65.

Kenneth E. Eble (essay date 1985)

SOURCE: Eble, Kenneth E. *"The Great Gatsby* and the
Great American Novel." In *New Essays on 'The Great
Gatsby,'* edited by Matthew J. Bruccoli, pp. 79-100.
Cambridge, England: Cambridge University Press,
1985.

[*In the following essay, Eble places* Gatsby *in the tradition of the quest for an "American" literature.*]

1

In length, the book barely qualifies as a full-sized novel.
In subject, it is about an American bootlegger who nour-
ishes an adolescent dream about a golden girl he can't
have. Its plot does little more than tell us who the protagonist is and get him killed off in the end by the down-
and-out husband of the blowsy mistress of the rich brute
who has married the girl whom the hero wants but can't
have. Its manner of telling is disjointed, albeit by the
literary design of the author, and accompanied by some
seemingly casual moralizing by an omnipresent narrator
sounding suspiciously like the author and sort of occupying himself at other times by taking an interest in a
woman golfer who cheats, the only other substantial
character in the novel if we except a denizen of the underworld, the mistress's dog and friends, Gatsby's father, a bunch of assorted party goers, and one mourner.

From this perspective, the adulation **The Great Gatsby**
has received may seem totally out of proportion. For
half a century, it has held a high place among twentieth-
century novels. Its numerous reprintings around the
world and its successive presentations on film have
made Gatsby as identifiable an American figure as Huck
Finn. It has revived the twenties, set current fashions,
and provided dialogue for three generations of devoted
readers. In these respects alone, the question of its literary merits set aside, it qualifies as a great American

novel. For clearly, it has added a name to that relatively
small number of factual and fictional Americans by
which Americans know themselves and are known by
the world. And it has done so by means of a writer's
craft working within the traditional form of a long fictional narrative. If a substantial claim is to be made for
The Great Gatsby as the great American novel, it will
have to be made by a more considered examination.
What I propose here is to examine the novel's relationship to the concept of the "great American novel"; the
substance of the novel, its "great argument," as Edith
Wharton phrased it; and the novel's structure and style,
its excellence as a *literary* work, a *novel.*

John William De Forest, less than a great novelist himself, raised the question of "the great American novel"
in an essay with that specific title in 1868.[1] The literary
nationalism that spawned the concept had already been
expressing itself for at least half a century and had resulted in such documents as Joel Barlow's *Columbiad,*
Royall Tyler's *The Contrast,* and Emerson's "The
American Scholar." The novels that De Forest could
measure the concept against were not a promising lot.
Their authors are largely forgotten by now—Paulding,
Brown, Kennedy, and Simms: "ghosts," who "wrote
about ghosts, and the ghosts have vanished utterly."
Melville escaped De Forest's attention, much as *Moby-
Dick,* for all its bulk, escaped most critics' notice until
the twentieth century. Hawthorne's *The Scarlet Letter*
was there to be considered, but De Forest found the
novel, as others did also, too insubstantial, too provincial, to be either novel enough or American enough to
qualify. The novel he did single out was *Uncle Tom's
Cabin,* which had a sufficiently broad, true, and sympathetic representation of American life to make it worth
considering. De Forest was biased here by his own understandable preoccupation with the Civil War and its
aftermath, although *Uncle Tom's Cabin* deserves more
attention than it gets. Edmund Wilson has pointed out:
"It is a much more impressive work than one has ever
been allowed to suspect. The first thing that strikes one
about it is a certain eruptive force."[2]

By the time Fitzgerald began to write, seekers after the
great American novel had a much wider choice, and
since then a still wider choice. Edith Wharton's essay,
"The Great American Novel," in the *Yale Review* in
1927, expressed skepticism toward the very idea. As far
as she could determine, "The great American novel
must always be about Main Street, geographically, socially, and intellectually." This was a restriction she did
not accept, and most of her essay is about the limitations such insistence places on the novelist. Moreover,
what might be expected of American novelists when
Main Street, she argued, offered "so meagre a material
to the imagination?" Still, she pointed out Robert

Grant's *Unleavened Bread,* Frank Norris's *McTeague,* and David Graham Phillips' *Susan Lenox* as not only "great American novels," but great novels.[3]

Fifty years later, Philip Roth, writing *The Great American Novel* in name if not in fact, offered *The Scarlet Letter, Moby-Dick, Huckleberry Finn, The Ambassadors,* and *The Golden Bowl* as possibilities. To be precise, these are the choices of a "Vassar slit," presumably schooled by a modern American English department and badgered into responding to Roth's fictional Hemingway roaring: "'What about *Red Badge of Courage!* What about *Winesburg, Ohio! The Last of the Mohicans! Sister Carrie! McTeague! My Antonia! The Rise of Silas Lapham! Two Years Before the Mast! Ethan Frome! Barren Ground!* What about Booth Tarkington and Sara Orne Jewett, while you're at it? What about our minor poet Francis Scott Fitzwhat'shis name? What about Wolfe and Dos and Faulkner?'"[4]

Roth has Hemingway decide, "'It hasn't been written yet,'" and to his boast that he will write it, a seagull croaks, "Nevermore." Perhaps gulls, if not Poe, have the last word on this matter. Frank Norris said something similar about the time Fitzgerald was born: "The Great American Novel is not extinct like the Dodo, but mythical like the Hipogriff." He also said that the great American novelist was either "as extinct as the Dodo or as far in the future as the practical aeroplane," which suggests that there should be dozens of them around today. Norris had many things to say about the novel, favoring novels that were "true" and with "a purpose," and embracing both "realism" and "romance." He surmised that in his time, the great American novel must be "sectional," and yet he foresaw a unified America and American novelists reaching a "universal substratum" common to all men. By such a route, he had to admit, the idea of a distinctively "American" novel disappears when a great novelist sounds "the world-note."[5]

In his fiction—and it is well to note that he was christened Benjamin Franklin Norris,—Norris moved to the novel of epic scope that many others have in mind as requisite to the great American novel. He saw the settling of the American West as "the last great epic event in the history of civilization,"[6] as Fitzgerald also implied in *The Great Gatsby.* In this respect, Whitman had already written the great American novel, although technically it happened to be a poem, *Leaves of Grass,* rather than a novel. Whitman, as well as anyone in prose or in poetry, defined this underlying ambition for the great American novel.

The preface to the 1855 edition of *Leaves of Grass* begins with two whopping assertions, the second scarcely more defensible than the first: "The Americans of all nations at any time upon the earth have probably the fullest poetical nature. The United States themselves are

essentially the greatest poem."[7] The elaboration of these assertions, the emphasis on "the largeness of nature or the nation" needing "gigantic and generous treatment," are too familiar to need repeating. Fitzgerald expressed his awareness of Whitman's impact in an essay published in 1926 and noted for its bringing Ernest Hemingway to public attention, "How to Waste Material: A Note on My Generation": "Ever since Irving's preoccupation with the necessity for an American background, for some square miles of cleared territory on which colorful variants might presently arise, the question of material has hampered the American writer. For one Dreiser who made a single-minded and irreproachable choice there have been a dozen like Henry James who have stupid-got with worry over the matter, and yet another dozen who, blinded by the fading tale of Walt Whitman's comet, have botched their books by the insincere compulsion to write 'significantly' about America."[8]

Fitzgerald's judgment of Dreiser and James aside, his awareness of the force of Whitman's message is directly related to the idea of the great American novel and what that novel should be about. His essay describes various attempts and failures to deal with "American" materials. He cites the treatment of the American farmer, of American youth, of "American politics, business, society, science, racial problems." His point is that this search for and exploitation of American material is largely in vain: "One author goes to a midland farm for three months to obtain material for an epic of the American husbandman! Another sets off on a like errand to the Blue Ridge Mountains, a third departs with a Corona for the West Indies—one is justified in the belief that what they get hold of will weigh no more than the journalistic loot brought back by Richard Harding Davis and John Fox, Jr., twenty years ago."[9]

Fitzgerald had already made these points in various parodies of popular novels and, more directly, in a letter to Maxwell Perkins just after *The Great Gatsby* was published.[10] The letter was about Thomas Boyd's new novel, *Samuel Drummond,* which Perkins had described to Fitzgerald in terms of high praise. To Fitzgerald the novel sounded "utterly lowsy," and he sketched out a "History of the Simple Inarticulate Farmer and his Hired Man Christy" to make his point. The basic issue he raises is the same as the one in his essay: the essential weakness of novels dealing quaintly and falsely with American materials—in this instance, the earthy struggle between the American farmer and the soil—to satisfy some kind of craving for the great American novel. In both of these statements, Fitzgerald did not cite his own example from the recent past, the fact that *This Side of Paradise,* if it did not speak for all of America, was still received by the public (and promoted by Fitzgerald) as speaking for American youth.

The Beautiful and Damned, which followed in 1922, might justifiably have been regarded as trying to take in all parts of Fitzgerald's longer list, beginning with "business" and ending with "literature."

The Great Gatsby, as Fitzgerald perceived in writing it, was something different, something more consistent with and closer to Fitzgerald's wish reported by Edmund Wilson: "I want to be one of the greatest writers who have ever lived, don't you?"[11] One cannot understand Fitzgerald's work, can't come to terms with the possibility of *The Great Gatsby* being the great American novel, without responding to the naiveté, the presumptuousness, the grandiosity of that remark—as naive and presumptuous and grandiose as Whitman talking about the poetic natures of an American nation and its poets.

That sense of measuring himself against great writers persisted throughout Fitzgerald's life. The curriculum he set up for Sheilah Graham in 1939[12] was both a recapitulation of his own reading and a considered judgment of what books would best serve Sheilah Graham's beginning and his own continuing education. The novels form a diverse and respectable list, weighted toward the modern, as one might expect, and as much European as British and American. Among the various novels or parts of novels are most of those necessary to serious study of the nineteenth- and twentieth-century novel: *The Red and the Black, Vanity Fair, Bleak House, The Brothers Karamazov, Anna Karenina* and *War and Peace, Eugénie Grandet, Madame Bovary, Sister Carrie, Man's Fate,* a half-dozen or so novels by Henry James, a similar number by Hardy, Joyce's *Portrait of the Artist,* Faulkner's *Sanctuary,* and others. He prized his meeting with Joyce in 1928 and pasted the letter he received from him in his copy of *Ulysses.* The drunken serenading with which he and Ring Lardner paid their respects to Joseph Conrad is also a part of Fitzgerald lore. But there is a seriousness in this reading and literary hero worshiping that underscores Fitzgerald's conception of himself as a serious novelist. The long struggle to bring another novel into being after completing *The Great Gatsby* is not entirely to be blamed on the conditions of Fitzgerald's personal life. In part, the struggle was forced on Fitzgerald because of his ambitions to go beyond *The Great Gatsby,* to achieve that writer's goal he set forth in a letter to Scottie, "so that the thing you have to say and the way of saying it blend as one matter—as indissolubly as if they were conceived together."[13] Fitzgerald's letters to Scottie are further testimony to his seriousness as a writer. The reading he sets forth for her reaches back to *Moll Flanders* and forward to Thomas Mann's *Death in Venice.* "I wish now," he wrote to her June 12, 1940, "I'd *never* relaxed or looked back—but said at the end of

The Great Gatsby: 'I've found my line—from now on this comes first. This is my immediate duty—without this I am nothing.'"[14]

But what Fitzgerald did not emphasize, either in an offhand remark or in his written comments, was his being an American writer, a fashioner of American materials, a writer of the great American novel. To put it in a simple form, he solved the problem of what he should use for material by setting the problem aside. More precisely, he recognized that a preoccupation with what a novel should be about was probably a strike against the novel at the outset. Thus, he became free to deal as best he could with that limited substance he had, free and inadvertently American to "spin my thread from my own bowels," as Emerson said, or in Whitman's words, "launch forth, filament, filament, filament, out of itself, ever unreeling them." Or, in Fitzgerald's matter-of-fact words, "My God! It was my material, and it was all I had to deal with."[15]

What I am suggesting here is that if there is such a thing as the great American novel, it will not be because of the American-ness of what it is about. Such a novel may be, as *Moby-Dick* is, about whaling and whales and those who pursue them, much of which is American because the author is American, or as *Huckleberry Finn* is American by the same line of reasoning, or as *The Great Gatsby* is. Thus, Fitzgerald's novel is animated by and makes its impact through a writer's intensely devoted attempt to understand a portion of human experience, the personal dimensions of that experience that reach into the hearts of human beings and the contexts that always complicate and alter such personal responses. From one perspective, these contexts are indubitably American, as much so as they seem to convey the pulse beat of the urban American 1920s. But from another, they are no more American than Ithaca is Greek or *Bleak House* British. What is kept before the reader—and not setting aside the particulars by which that is made manifest—are the longings for love, wealth, power, status, for dreaming and realizing dreams and facing the realities of which dreams are compounded and by which they are compromised.

There is another side to this observation. The story of *The Great Gatsby,* both to its advantage and its disadvantage in weighing the novel's merit, is intertwined for many readers with the story of F. Scott and Zelda Fitzgerald. If one result is to question the likelihood of such a person as Fitzgerald being able to write a great novel, another is to endow the novel with something of the authenticity of the *real* story of the Fitzgeralds' gaudy but tragic lives. I further suggest that this preoccupation with "self," the fictional one focused on Gatsby, the real one lying behind the fascination that the Fitzgerald story continues to have for the American public, may be what is more American about the novel than any other aspect. Benjamin Franklin's *Autobiography* may be the original American novel, even though, like *Leaves of Grass,* it is not a novel. That aside, what followed the *Autobiography* was a succession of great American books—poems, essays, romances, novels—that were chiefly explorations of the self. Emerson's *Essays* and Thoreau's *Walden* can be added to the novels already mentioned, and to those, *Hopalong Cassidy,* on whose fly leaf Gatsby had set down his own Franklinesque resolves.

The Great Gatsby, then, is in the right American line, in regard to conceptions, implied and stated, about what should constitute the great American novel. More directly, of course, *Gatsby,* despite its brevity, illuminates the American past and present, answers the challenge of getting within its pages something of the scope and variety and dynamics of American life, the light and dark of American experience, the underside and upperside of American society. Moreover, it does so within the larger framework of human experience, invariably moving readers to the dimensions of myth that convey meaning independent of time, place, and the particulars of experience.

Robert Ornstein's "Scott Fitzgerald's Fable of East and West" is one of dozens of essays that explore the novel's symbolism, allusions, ironies, ambiguities, and mythical dimensions. Ornstein argues that Fitzgerald has created "a myth with the imaginative sweep of America's historical adventure across an untamed continent. . . . One can even say that in *The Great Gatsby* Fitzgerald adumbrated the coming tragedy of a nation grown decadent without achieving maturity." His essay, however, refuses to narrow the theme of the novel to that of the betrayal of the American dream; rather, its theme "is the unending quest after the romantic dream, which is forever betrayed in fact and yet redeemed in men's minds." Ornstein sees this theme brought out not only in terms of American experience but also in an embodiment of the romantic response to life. "Gatsby *is* great," he writes, "because his dream, however naive, gaudy, and unattainable, is one of the grand illusions of the race, which keep men from becoming too old or too wise or too cynical of their human limitations."[16] Fitzgerald dramatized that perception in a brilliant way in **"Absolution,"** originally intended as an introduction to the Gatsby story. There the crazed priest tells the young boy: "'Go and see an amusement park. . . . It's a thing like a fair, only much more glittering. . . . But don't get up close, because if you do you'll only feel the heat and the sweat and the life.'"[17] One of the prominent themes in *The Great Gatsby* is that familiar one, "All that glitters is not gold," and its corollary, "but it glitters, all the same." For much of the world and for America itself, America has been the great amusement park, holding its World's Fairs and World Series and awarding "World Championships" as events in which

most of the world never participates. What better setting for a meditation on the romantic vision and romantic disillusionment?

This dimension of *The Great Gatsby* has held a central place in the criticism of the novel since the first revival of interest in Fitzgerald shortly after his death. Prior to that time, Fitzgerald seems justified in replying to John Peale Bishop's letter about the novel: "It is about the only criticism that the book has had which has been intelligible, save a letter from Mrs. Wharton,"[18] or to Edmund Wilson: Not one of the reviews "had the slightest idea what the book was about."[19] When it was praised by such writers as T. S. Eliot, Edith Wharton, and Gertrude Stein, it was in such general terms as Eliot's "the first step that American fiction has taken since Henry James."[20] Even to such a sympathetic critic as Fitzgerald's contemporary Paul Rosenfeld, the novel was "beautifully done, breezy throughout . . . extraordinarily American, like ice cream soda with arsenic flavoring, or jazz music in a fever-dream."[21] Only Thomas Caldecott Chubb, writing in the *Forum* in 1925, perceived the book to be "a fable in the form of a realistic novel." "At once a tragedy and an extraordinarily convincing love tale and an extravaganza."[22]

Notwithstanding the restrained and ambivalent responses to the novel when it first appeared, most of the later criticism has been searching and favorable. John W. Bicknell begins with a hint dropped by Lionel Trilling that Fitzgerald's novel is a prose version of Eliot's *The Waste Land,* a poem Fitzgerald knew almost by heart. Like Conrad, Fitzgerald sees "the modern corruption in contrast to a lost rather than to an emergent ideal."[23] Bicknell's overall critical intent is to determine whether *Gatsby* is tragic or merely pessimistic. He ends by accepting Alfred Kazin's view that "in a land of promise 'failure' will always be a classic theme." Marius Bewley's essay, "Scott Fitzgerald's Criticism of America,"[24] finds more to praise in *Gatsby,* perhaps because he does not assume that tragedy is the definitive measure of a novel's greatness. He writes: "Fitzgerald—at least in this one book—is in line with the greatest masters of American prose. *The Great Gatsby* embodies a criticism of American experience—not of manners, but of a basic historic attitude to life—more radical than anything in James's own assessment of the deficiencies of his country. The theme of *Gatsby* is the withering of the American dream." Bewley's essay acknowledges that "Gatsby, the 'mythic' embodiment of the American dream, is shown to us in all his immature romanticism. His insecure grasp of social and human values, his lack of critical intelligence and self-knowledge, his blindness to the pitfalls that surround him in American society, his compulsive optimism, are realized in the text with rare assurance and understanding. And yet the very grounding of these deficiencies is Gatsby's goodness and faith in life, his compelling desire to realize all the possibilities of existence." Edwin Fussell's "Fitzgerald's Brave New World" also mentions the universality as well as the uniqueness of the American experience. "After exploring his materials to their limits, Fitzgerald knew, at his greatest moments, that he had discovered a universal pattern of desire and belief and behavior and that in it was compounded the imaginative history of modern, especially American, civilization."[25]

With respect to its serious import, its examination of both American life and lives in much of the modern Western world, *Gatsby* bears comparison with those other books that might stand as the great American novel. It does not sprawl like *Moby-Dick,* nor hover and ruminate like *The Scarlet Letter,* nor heap up its substance like any work of Dreiser. It does not hint and suggest and qualify like Henry James, nor does it have the robust, yet lyric, quality of *Huckleberry Finn.* Yet, consider some vital qualities all these novels share. Chiefly these are *Gatsby*'s moral preoccupations, as inseparable from the novel as from *Moby-Dick* or *The Scarlet Letter,* and its dramatization of innocence coming into experience, as memorably fixed in Nick Carraway and Gatsby as in Huck and Jim or Ishmael on the *Pequod.* Moreover, with the final page of the novel establishing "the old island here that flowered once for Dutch sailors' eyes" (p. 217), Fitzgerald gives the novel an amplitude that bears comparison with James's powers in *The Ambassadors* or *The American.* The persuasiveness of Fitzgerald's prose (or Keats's poetry) aside, that moment of gazing on the "fresh, green breast of the new world" must have been and may be, even "for the last time in history," "something commensurate to his capacity for wonder" (pp. 217-18).

The events following the twenties, notably a worldwide economic depression and the outbreak of another world war, may unknowingly have attuned modern readers to the serious dimensions of *Gatsby.* For it has been since World War II, and particularly in America, that the realities of living in a world of limited resources have begun to register. Throughout much of its history, America was a place of endless expanding and advancing. Without exaggerating greatly, one can place *Gatsby* with those classic statements that recall us to the fact that, as Fitzgerald came to recognize, one cannot both spend and have. Projected beyond the personal, one cannot espouse infinite progress but must accept some kind of eternal return, "boats against the current, borne back ceaselessly into the past" (p. 218).

2

All readers have been affected by Fitzgerald's style, for Fitzgerald was marvelously sensitive to the sounds and cadences of language. "For awhile after you quit Keats," he wrote, "all other poetry seems to be only whistling or humming."[26] His attraction to Conrad was due to Conrad's attention to the power of the written word, to "an unremitting never-discouraged care for the shape and ring of sentences" that aspired to "the magic suggestiveness of music—which is the art of arts."[27] Fitzgerald's sentences have movement, grace, clarity, directness when necessary, force when desired, and cadences appropriate to the mood or emotion or scene. Matched with the visual images, simile and metaphor, sentences like this emerge in profusion: "We drove over to Fifth Avenue, so warm and soft, almost pastoral, on the summer Sunday afternoon that I wouldn't have been surprised to see a great flock of white sheep turn the corner" (p. 33). "Yet high over the city our line of yellow windows must have contributed their share of human secrecy to the casual watcher in the darkening streets, and I was him too, looking up and wondering. I was within and without, simultaneously enchanted and repelled by the inexhaustible variety of life" (p. 43). "For a while these reveries provided an outlet for his imagination; they were a satisfactory hint of the unreality of reality, a promise that the rock of the world was founded securely on a fairy's wing" (p. 119). Fitzgerald's style is remarkably apt and precise, even when he is dealing with nearly ineffable matters: "He was a Son of God—a phrase which, if it means anything, means just that—and he must be about His Father's business, the service of a vast, vulgar, and meretricious beauty" (p. 118). Part of that aptness is the quality of Fitzgerald's wit, apparent in that Homeric catalog of guests that begins: "From East Egg, then, came the Chester Beckers and the Leeches, and a man named Bunsen, whom I knew at Yale, and Doctor Webster Civet . . ." and ends "All these people came to Gatsby's house in the summer" (pp. 73-6). Or the bite of such a description as: "the dim enlargement of Mrs. Wilson's mother which hovered like an ectoplasm on the wall" (p. 36).

These quotations, chosen to exemplify Fitzgerald's style, serve also to illustrate the inseparability of style and content. Major and minor characters in *Gatsby* are brilliantly created by both what Fitzgerald chooses to reveal about them and how he reveals it. Most of the preceding passages are important in creating a character and shaping a reader's perception of that character. In the first instance, that pastoral touch, seemingly a stylistic flourish, is exactly right for perceiving Tom Buchanan and Myrtle in contrast to the ash heaps surrounding Wilson's garage and the tacky apartment where Tom has been keeping her. Similarly, Nick Carraway's reflection calls a reader's attention to his being both inside and outside the main action, a vital aspect of his characterization. And speaking of Gatsby as a son of God who goes about his Father's business reverberates powerfully in one's accumulating impressions of that central character. The minor characters in the novel are created with that terse exactness that is apparent in Fitzgerald's handling of words in the novel: Meyer

Wolfsheim and his human molar cufflinks; Mr. McKee, who has "'done some nice things out on Long Island'" (p. 38); George Wilson, veiled in ashen dust; and Owl-Eyes, finding real books in Gatsby's library, but with the pages uncut.

"I think it is an honest book," Fitzgerald wrote in the introduction to the Modern Library Edition in 1934, "that is to say, that one used none of one's virtuosity to get an effect, and, to boast again, one soft-pedalled the emotional side to avoid the tears leaking from the socket of the left eye, or the large false face peering around the corner of a character's head."[28] It is this restraint, even more than the virtuosity of effects, that distinguishes Fitzgerald's style in *The Great Gatsby.* In almost all of his other fiction, the quality of the prose gives otherwise ordinary materials a polish that not only exacted high prices from popular magazines but may have hinted at more profundity than the content delivered. In *Gatsby,* straining for effect is seldom apparent. The whole novel is compactly put together, as much by repetition of images and symbols as by exposition and narrative.

The opulence associated with both Gatsby and the Buchanans is established in Chapter 1 by a physical description of the Buchanans' house and lawn: "The lawn started at the beach and ran toward the front door for a quarter of a mile, jumping over sun-dials and brick walks and burning gardens—finally when it reached the house drifting up the side in bright vines as though from the momentum of its run" (p. 8). At the end of the first chapter, the cadences change as we see Gatsby on his lawn at night: "The wind had blown off, leaving a loud, bright night, with wings beating in the trees and a persistent organ sound as the full bellows of the earth blew the frogs full of life. The silhouette of a moving cat wavered across the moonlight, and turning my head to watch it, I saw that I was not alone—fifty feet away a figure had emerged from the shadow of my neighbor's mansion and was standing with his hands in his pockets regarding the silver pepper of the stars" (p. 25). A paragraph later, Chapter 1 ends with the "single green light" (p. 26) at the end of the dock that became one of the final images in the novel. Between those two images are other descriptions of landscape and house, from the "blue gardens" after "the earth lurches away from the sun" (pp. 47-9) to the "sharp line where my ragged lawn ended and the darker, well-kept expanse of his began" (p. 99) in Chapter 5. At the end, these images accumulate: the opening of the windows at dawn, the photograph of the house that Gatsby's father shows to Nick, "cracked in the corners and dirty with many hands" (p. 207), and Carraway's last look at "that huge incoherent failure of a house. On the white steps an obscene word, scrawled by some boy with a piece of brick, stood out clearly in the moonlight, and I erased it, drawing my shoe raspingly along the stone" (p. 217).

James Joyce said of *Ulysses* that he had put in enough enigmas and puzzles to keep professors busy for centuries. *The Great Gatsby* lacks that density, but it has engaged the attention of many professors to date. Color symbolism, patterns of images, sources and analogues, ambiguities, mythical dimensions continue to be worked over. Passages of dialogue are as carefully wrought as descriptive passages. Some have become passwords of *Gatsby* cultists: "'Can't repeat the past? . . . Why of course you can!'" (p. 133) and "'Her voice is full of money'" (p. 144) and "'In any case . . . it was just personal'" (p. 182). Others are equally part of the texture of the novel, shaping character, amplifying meanings, knitting parts together: "'Is it a boy or a girl?'" Myrtle asks of the "gray old man who bore an absurd resemblance to John D. Rockefeller." "'That dog? That dog's a boy.' 'It's a bitch,' said Tom decisively. 'Here's your money. Go and buy ten more dogs with it'" (pp. 32-3). Fitzgerald also knew when to have his characters stop talking. In the draft of the novel, much of Gatsby's story is told in dialogue as he talks to Nick. It permits him to talk too much, to say, for example, before Fitzgerald excised it: "'Jay Gatsby!' he cried suddenly in a ringing voice. 'There goes the great Jay Gatsby. That's what people are going to say—wait and see.'"[29]

As with details of his style, the structure of *The Great Gatsby* has been subject to minute examination, Fitzgerald's debt to Conrad was early pointed out: "for the use of style or language to reflect theme; for the use of the modified first person narration; for the use of deliberate 'confusion' by the re-ordering of the chronology of events." Fitzgerald's use of "a series of scenes dramatizing the important events of the story and connected by brief passages of interpretation and summary" is like Henry James's "scenic method."[30] In these respects and others, *The Great Gatsby* responds, as a great American novel surely should, to the call for "newness" sounded repeatedly throughout America's literary history.

I have written at length elsewhere, as have others, about the structure of *The Great Gatsby*[31] and will not go into detail here. The facsimile of the manuscript enables any reader to study Fitzgerald's revisions, small and large. He was a careful reviser, nowhere in his work more than in *The Great Gatsby.*

In general, his revisions were devoted to solving the technical problems of presenting the story—the narrative structure—and in sharpening, trimming, amplifying descriptions, narrative, dialogue. The choice of Nick Carraway as narrator was probably not made until some jelling of the essential story took place in Fitzgerald's mind. The short stories **"Absolution"** and **"Winter Dreams"** are written in the conventional third person. The longer form in itself may have raised questions about the mode of telling; the examples of James and Conrad were at hand to suggest the use of a first-person narrator. Although that choice was in one sense a technical one, it was also a means of presenting his material "through the personal history of a young American provincial whose moral intelligence is the proper source of our understanding and whose career, in the passage from innocence to revaluation, dramatizes the possibility and mode of a moral sanction in contemporary America."[32] Such a view still seems fairly to describe Fitzgerald's intent, although a spate of criticism has pointed out the unreliability of Carraway as a narrator. The choice of narrator was related to other technical problems, chiefly that of how and when (and in what order and way in the novel) the narrator uncovers for the reader the complete story of Gatsby's past. Like other modern novels, *Gatsby* does not follow a straightforward chronology; Fitzgerald worked hard to preserve the advantages of a disjointed structure against the confusion such a method may create. One of the effects was to keep Gatsby from fully materializing, helping Fitzgerald solve the difficult problem of making a deliberately shadowy figure the central character of the novel.

It is not easy to summarize even the most important changes Fitzgerald made to achieve the structure he wanted. Suffice to say that changes and shifts of materials kept Gatsby offstage for a longer period of time than in the first version. Between his first appearance as a figure on his lawn and Nick's conversation with him in Chapter 4, the reader is exposed to Daisy, Tom, Jordan Baker, and the Wilsons, is transported through the valley of ashes and into Myrtle's Manhattan apartment, and gets a fuller glimpse of Gatsby during the first party at his house. The chief results, aside from heightening one's interest in the mysterious Gatsby, are the various juxtapositions of beauty and squalor, peace and violence, vitality and decay—in short, the intensifying of the central contrasts between the ideal and the real.

All this is accomplished in three chapters, with the material that originally comprised these chapters being rearranged in various ways. Chapter 4 extends our acquaintance with Gatsby, and Chapter 5 becomes the center of the novel. This chapter was very closely reworked, chiefly in order to give it a static quality, to approximate in the telling Gatsby's attempt to make time stand still. From that chapter on, the novel picks up speed. The real world intrudes in the guise of a reporter through whom details of Gatsby's actual past are exposed. A second party, sharper delineation of Tom Buchanan, and the second trip into Manhattan prepare the reader for the final sweep of the plot to the running down of Myrtle Wilson, "her left breast . . . swinging loose like a flap" (p. 165). "I *want* Myrtle Wilson's breast ripped off," he wrote Maxwell Perkins. "It's exactly the thing, I think, and I don't want to chop up good scenes by too much tinkering."[33]

The remaining chapters were chiefly reworked to wind down events with economy but also with measured impact. Some of Gatsby's explanations were shifted to the present tense to give them greater immediacy. The last chapter shifted attention to Nick, but still kept him linked tightly to Gatsby by means of the funeral, his talk with Gatsby's father, and those benedictory words pronounced by Owl-Eyes, "'The poor son of a bitch'" (p. 211). Nick's last encounter with Tom underscores Fitzgerald's achievement of making Carraway a vital character in his own right, a technical device that helps hold the structure together, a means of amplifying the moral and social dimensions of the novel and the way in which the story gets told. The last image of the book, the "fresh, green breast of the new world," was originally written as the conclusion of the first chapter. Now placed at the end of the novel, it enlarges even as it brings the novel to an end.

This discussion of style and structure argues for the novel's high degree of finish, surely a merit in a novel, although not necessarily what many would associate with the great American novel. The exchange between Fitzgerald and Thomas Wolfe illustrates my point. Wolfe, a great "putter-inner" of a novelist, challenges Fitzgerald's criticism of his work by citing Shakespeare, Cervantes, and Dostoevsky as "great putter-inners— greater putter-inners, in fact, than taker-outers and will be remembered for what they put in . . . as long as Monsieur Flaubert will be remembered for what he left out."[34] Wolfe's arguments are unanswerable for those who insist that a great American novel must "*boil and pour.*" By that measure, *The Great Gatsby* must fall short, for all that it has a size beyond its actual page length.

Still, one can, only half facetiously, propose that *Gatsby* is an *efficient* novel, and thereby identifiably and pleasingly American. For the time one puts into it, a great deal comes out. Even its nuances of style are not likely to be lost on American readers, for they have the laconic power of sarcasm, the brevity of the one-liner, and the directness of American speech. Its moral dimensions still touch the sense of decency and fair play, without engaging the reader in time-consuming ethical and metaphysical speculations. The novel's topicality is that of the twenties, but is not confined to that decade. The author's rhetorical flourishes are nicely spaced; the story has some action and plenty of pathos shading off into tragedy. It raises basic questions citizens of a democracy have to wrestle with: How does one recognize greatness without an established social order? How does the acquisition of power, wealth, and status accord with the professions of democratic equality? How does an idealist and an individual—both prized qualities of the American—keep himself from succumbing to the materialism of the masses or from kicking himself loose from the universe? If all this can be accomplished in a book under 200 pages and still selling for under $10 (it was priced at $2 in 1925), what could be greater and more American than that?

3

The foregoing claims may be the strongest that can be made for the stature of *The Great Gatsby* as the great American novel. A less convincing form of reasoning, but one worth addressing briefly, is to see *Gatsby* in the line of American novels of manners, novels like those of Howells and James and Edith Wharton. It is Wharton, in the essay previously mentioned, who points out that "Traditional society, with its old-established distinctions of class, its passwords, exclusions, delicate shades of language and behavior, is one of man's oldest works of art."[35] She expresses dismay that American novelists have been turned away from this material, from the novel of manners, just as James expressed to Howells his dismay that American society didn't furnish the richness and diversity that would support such novels. Nevertheless, Frank Norris saw in Howells that breadth of vision and intimate knowledge of Americans East and West that went part way toward establishing an "American school of fiction."[36] If he did not quite claim that Howells was writing the great American novel, he did call attention to Howells's efforts to establish the novel of manners as an estimable kind of American fiction.

The novel of manners in Howells's hands and in Fitzgerald's did not preclude its being a serious and socially engaged work. Gertrude Stein's letter in response to *The Great Gatsby* recognized that Fitzgerald was "creating the contemporary world much as Thackeray did his in *Pendennis* and *Vanity Fair* and this isn't a bad compliment."[37] Howells's and Fitzgerald's examinations of American society show the novel of manner's concern for moral behavior measured against social norms. In the background of both authors' work are reminders of that moralistic and idealistic strain of Americans who populated a wilderness and created its Washingtons and Lincolns. But the society each saw around him was one in which that kind of American was hard pressed to withstand the amoral and materialistic drive for power that characterized American success. The tragic hero set forth in *Gatsby* is really the American failure, failing to hold to the course of power that wins success and failing, moreover, because of the strength of idealistic illusions.

Too few readers know Howells's *The Landlord at Lion's Head,* a novel that started out as one merely about a "jay" student at Harvard but that became one of Howells's strongest social novels. Jeff Durgin, the protagonist of the story, is one more provincial who is sufficiently strong and amoral, like Gatsby, to gain power and wealth by his own shrewdness and drive and luck.

Landlord lacks the tightness and finish of *Gatsby,* but in its central theme it may be more modern and less sentimental than Fitzgerald's novel. For Durgin and his dream are not defeated, much as the many Gatsbys who pursue their driving materialistic dreams are not defeated in American life. Rather, Durgin's success at the end of that novel is the American success of power and money. The girl of Durgin's dreams turns out to be so sanctimonious as to deserve little better than the pallid artist who claims her and who, like Carraway in *Gatsby,* provides the novel's supposed moral center. Durgin ends up with the daughter of a Europeanized mother and a wealthy American father, a woman all but a dolt would prefer to Durgin's earlier choice. Like Tom Buchanan and Daisy, the Durgins seem likely to make it in the modern world, although Carraway says that they have "retreated back into their money or their vast carelessness" (p. 216) and he back to pondering his father's wisdom that "a sense of the fundamental decencies is parcelled out unequally at birth" (p. 2). A generation or two earlier than Fitzgerald, Howells, too, saw what the American dream was for most citizens: money, power, social position, and a modicum of culture. Only a "provincial squeamishness" (p. 216) in both writers caused them to question the substantiality and rightness of the materialistic dream.

I am not arguing that the novel of manners somehow provides its writers with some special claim to a novel's greatness. In fact, probably the opposite is true in regard to American writers. Mark Twain's condemnation of Jane Austen's work conveys the disrespect that assigns such novels to a distinct and lesser category. The point is, rather, that the novel of manners has an appropriateness to American writing fully as much as does the romance or tall tale. Howells and James both extended that form, achieving at their best something of what Dickens and Thackeray achieved for the British novel. Balzac and Zola can also fit into this category, as can Norris and Fitzgerald.

But categorizing a novelist's work is a folly not unlike looking for the great American novel. It matters little whether *The Great Gatsby* is the great American novel or not. It probably matters that writers, much less readers, keep such concepts before them. No reader needs an unrelieved diet of great novels, American or any other kind. Writers, on the other hand, probably do need the urging of tradition, the example of other writers and other novels and kinds of novels, and the idea of greater books than they have yet written. Even then, the novels they write will be as various as the lives they live and the thoughts they think. As there are many American writers and readers, so there are bound to be many American novels, some of them great.

Howells looked back on his career and wrote: "Mostly I suppose I have cut rather inferior window glass with it . . . perhaps hereafter when my din is done, if any one is curious to know what the noise was, it will be found to have proceeded from a small insect which was scraping about on the surface of our life and trying to get into its meaning for the sake of the other insects, larger and smaller. That is, such has been my unconscious work, consciously, I was always, as I still am, trying to fashion a piece of literature out of the life next at hand."[38] It may be enough to say of **The Great Gatsby** that F. Scott Fitzgerald achieved what he set out to do, to write "something *new,* something extraordinary and beautiful and simple + intricately patterned."[39]

Notes

1. John William De Forest, "The Great American Novel," *The Nation* 6 (1868): 27-9.

2. Edmund Wilson, *Patriotic Gore: Studies in the Literature of the American Civil War* (New York: Oxford University Press, 1962), p. 5.

3. Edith Wharton, "The Great American Novel," *Yale Review* 16 (July 1927): 646-56.

4. Philip Roth, *The Great American Novel* (New York: Holt, Rinehart and Winston, 1973), p. 33.

5. Frank Norris, *The Responsibilities of the Novelist and Other Literary Essays* (Westport, Conn: Greenwood Press, 1968), pp. 85-9.

6. Ibid., p. 61.

7. Walt Whitman, *Leaves of Grass: Comprehensive Reader's Edition,* ed. Harold W. Blodgett and Sculley Bradley (New York: New York University Press, 1965), p. 709.

8. F. Scott Fitzgerald, "How to Waste Material—A Note on My Generation," *The Bookman* 63 (May 1926): 262-5.

9. Ibid., 263.

10. *The Letters of F. Scott Fitzgerald,* ed. Andrew Turnbull (New York: Scribners, 1963), pp. 183-8.

11. Edmund Wilson, "Thoughts on Being Bibliographed," *The Princeton University Library Chronicle* 5 (February 1944): 54.

12. Sheilah Graham, *College of One* (New York: Viking Press, 1967), pp. 204-21.

13. Turnbull, ed., *Letters,* p. 11.

14. Ibid., p. 79.

15. F. Scott Fitzgerald, Introduction to *The Great Gatsby* (New York: Modern Library, 1934), p. x.

16. Robert Ornstein, "Scott Fitzgerald's Fable of East and West," *College English* 18 (December 1956): 139, 143.

17. F. Scott Fitzgerald, "Absolution," *The Stories of F. Scott Fitzgerald: A Selection of 28 Stories,* with an Introduction by Malcolm Cowley (New York: Scribners, 1951), p. 171.

18. Turnbull, ed., *Letters,* p. 358.

19. Ibid., p. 342.

20. *The Great Gatsby: A Study,* ed. Frederick J. Hoffman (New York: Scribners, 1962), p. 179.

21. *Correspondence of F. Scott Fitzgerald,* ed. Matthew J. Bruccoli and Margaret Duggan (New York: Random House, 1980), p. 171.

22. *F. Scott Fitzgerald: In His Own Time,* ed. Matthew J. Bruccoli and Margaret Duggan (Kent, Ohio: Kent State University Press, 1971): A remarkably good collection of Fitzgerald materials, including reviews of *The Great Gatsby* at the time of publication. See also G. Thomas Tanselle and Jackson R. Bryer, "*The Great Gatsby*—A Study in Literary Reputation," *Profile of F. Scott Fitzgerald,* ed. Matthew J. Bruccoli (Columbus, Ohio: Merrill, 1971), pp. 74-91.

23. John W. Bicknell, "The Waste Land of F. Scott Fitzgerald," in *F. Scott Fitzgerald: A Collection of Criticism,* ed. Kenneth Eble (New York: McGraw-Hill, 1973), pp. 67-80.

24. Tanselle and Bryer, *The Great Gatsby: A Study,* pp. 263-85.

25. Ibid., pp. 244-62.

26. Turnbull, ed., *Letters,* p. 88.

27. Joseph Conrad, "Preface to *The Nigger of the Narcissus,*" in Tanselle and Bryer, *The Great Gatsby: A Study,* pp. 59-64.

28. Fitzgerald, Introduction to *The Great Gatsby,* p. x.

29. F. Scott Fitzgerald, *A Facsimile of the Manuscript,* ed. Matthew J. Bruccoli (Washington, D.C.: Bruccoli Clark/Microcard, 1973), p. xxix.

30. James E. Miller, Jr., *The Fictional Technique of Scott Fitzgerald* (The Hague: Martinus Nijhoff, 1957), pp. 79-81.

31. Kenneth E. Eble, "The Craft of Revision: *The Great Gatsby,*" *American Literature* 26 (November 1964): 315-26.

32. Thomas Hanzo, "The Theme and the Narrator of '*The Great Gatsby,*'" *Modern Fiction Studies* 2 (Winter 1956-7): 190.

33. Turnbull, ed., *Letters,* p. 175.

34. F. Scott Fitzgerald, *The Crack-Up,* ed. Edmund Wilson (New York: New Directions, 1945), p. 314.

35. Wharton, "The Great American Novel," 652.

36. Norris, *Responsibilities of the Novelist,* pp. 193-200.

37. Fitzgerald, *The Crack-Up,* p. 308.

38. *Life in Letters of William Dean Howells,* ed. Mildred Howells, vol. II (Garden City, N.Y.: Doubleday, 1928), pp. 172-3.

39. Bruccoli and Duggan, *Correspondence,* p. 112.

Darrel Mansell (essay date December 1987)

SOURCE: Mansell, Darrel. "The *Jazz History of the World* in *The Great Gatsby.*" *English Language Notes* 25 (December 1987): 57-62.

[*In the following essay, Mansell suggests possible sources of and purposes for a reference to a jazz work in a scene of* Gatsby.]

Fitzgerald said in retrospect that his first novel had actually been not one book but three, and his second novel two. He wanted his third novel to be more coherent: more spare, economical and "intricately patterned." Indeed he wanted the new one to be "perfect."[1]

The critical consensus has been that what he produced *is* close to perfect. In **The Great Gatsby** there seem almost no loose, unworking parts—no automobile wheels lying in the ditch like the one after a Gatsby party, "unconnected to the car by any physical bond" (Chapter III). The novel is said to have "perfection of form," to be "compact," "tightly structured," to have a "tight inevitability of . . . construction," to have a "formal completeness and integrity."[2]

But there is at least one episode lying outside just about any conception of the formal integrity of the novel—one wheel lying loose in the ditch. That is the scene when the orchestra leader at the fateful party in Chapter III announces a musical work by a Mr. Vladimir Tostoff: the *Jazz History of the World.* Nick says that when the work was over

> girls were putting their heads on men's shoulders in a puppyish, convivial way, girls were swooning backward playfully into men's arms, even into groups, knowing that some one would arrest their falls. . . .[3]

What are we to think of a piece of music with such a title? Why did the work create a sensation at Carnegie Hall the previous May (as the orchestra leader says it did)? Why does he say so "with jovial condescension"? Why does the audience laugh when he says so? Surely we aren't to take a sensational piece with such a preposterous title as moving or beautiful—Nick says the

nature of the music simply eludes him. Yet the piece has a strange, mesmerizing effect on the party-goers; and, most strange of all, had in the manuscript of the novel a deeply moving effect on Nick himself. There he strives—Fitzgerald strives—for three turgid paragraphs omitted from the published novel to make us understand and feel something which seems to have taken a profound emotional hold on the author himself:

> It facinated [sic] me . . . it started out with a wierd [sic], spinning sound that seemed to come mostly from the cornets, very regular and measured and inevitable with a bell now and then that seemed to ring somewhere a great distance away. A rhythm became distinguishable after awhile in the spinning, a sort of dull beat but as soon as you'd almost made it out it disappeared. . . . The second movement was concerned with the bell only it wasn't the bell any more but a muted violin cello and two instruments I had never seen before . . . you were aware that something was trying to establish itself, to get a foothold, something soft and . . . persistent and profound and next you yourself were trying to help it, struggling, praying for it—until suddenly it was *there,* it was established rather scornfully without you and it seemed to look around with a complete self-sufficiency, as if it had been there all the time.
>
> I was curiously moved and the third part of the thing was full of even stronger emotion. I know so little about music that I can only make a story of it . . . but it wasn't really a story . . . there would be a series of interruptive notes that seemed to fall together accidentally and colored everything that came after them until before you knew it they became the theme and new discords were opposed to it outside. But what struck me particularly was that just as you'd get used to the new discord business there'd be one of the old *themes* rung in this time as a discord until you'd get a ghastly sense that it was all a cycle after all, purposeless and sardonic. . . . Whenever I think of that summer I can hear it yet.
>
> The last was weak I thought though most of the people seemed to like it best of all. It had recognizable strains of famous jazz in it—Alexander's Ragtime Band and The Darktown Strutter's Ball and recurrent hint [sic] of The Beale Street Blues.[4]

It is not impossible to make sense of this curious episode—to think of some relevance it has to the novel. Indeed almost every interpretation of the novel has a way of doing so. For instance the novel is said to be concerned with time; and the *Jazz History of the World* shows that concern in being a juxtaposition of the timeless (history) and the evanescent (jazz).[5] Or Tostoff's composition is, "amid the tossed-off names and the tossed-off identities . . . a piece of music that is itself a tossed-off debasement of the idea of history."[6] Or Gatsby himself is a kind of showman, an entrepreneur; and this "musical extravaganza" is one of his meretricious productions.[7] Or this sprawling and chaotic musical composition shows the hugeness of Gatsby's parties, their "movement, mingling, and commotion."[8] Or the composition's non-linearity, polyphony and complex rhythms are "like a buried preface, an anamorphic projection of the book's operative principle."[9] Or the composition's sensuality shows the "chaos and libertinism of Gatsby's world."[10]

There is just no consensus as to the relevance or significance of this puzzling episode. Fitzgerald himself regretted having written it: "I thought that the whole episode . . . was rotten."[11]

I think there is something of a factual, historical nature to be said about the episode. Fitzgerald liked to date his scenes by putting in them specific details his readers would associate with a particular year. Often such details have to do with music. The song "Poor Butterfly," played on a gramophone at Princeton in a scene in *This Side of Paradise,* "had been the song of that last year" (Chapter IV)—the year 1917. The song "Something Seems Tingleingleing" is described in a scene in *The Beautiful and Damned* as "the year's mellowest foxtrot" (Chapter II)—thus 1913 (from the 1913 musical *High Jinks*). In *The Great Gatsby* the orchestras in Daisy's Louisville are said to set "the rhythm of the year" with songs like the "Beale Street Blues" (Chapter VIII)—the year 1918. And "Three O'Clock in the Morning," played at one of Gatsby's parties, is a "neat, sad little waltz of that year" (Chapter VI)—the year 1922.

The *Jazz History of the World* may be just such a piece of music *dating* a scene. The orchestra leader says the piece "attracted so much attention at Carnegie Hall last May. If you read the papers you know there was a big sensation" (50). That would have been May, 1921 (the scene being the summer of 1922).

It happens that during the concert season of 1921 the great composer Richard Strauss was making a much-publicized tour of the United States conducting his own compositions with various symphony orchestras. The month of May that year would have been off-season at Carnegie Hall; but on 31 October Strauss conducted a program of his own music there. The music critic Richard Aldrich wrote next day that the hall "was filled to at least its legal capacity" to hear the celebrated composer; the audience greeted his appearance with a great roar of applause that lasted some time.[12]

Scheduled for that Carnegie Hall concert (but replaced at the last minute) had been Strauss's symphonic work *Also Sprach Zarathustra*. This piece was subsequently performed (Strauss conducting) on 15 November at the Metropolitan Opera House. A "large audience that practically filled the house" gave the concert enthusiastic appreciation (*New York Times,* 16 November 1921, 22c). Now there must be only one actual symphonic piece extant which ever became known as a history of the world like the piece played at Gatsby's party. That is

Strauss's *Zarathustra*. Its author himself described it as "an idea of the development of the human race from its origin, through the various phases of development . . ." (these words appear in the *Times* concert review cited above). Furthermore, the bell Nick makes so much of in the long description of the piece cancelled by Fitzgerald is probably the much-noted bell which peals in the *Nachtwanderlied* section of Strauss's work.

I think Fitzgerald's idea of a 1921 performance at Carnegie Hall of a composition on such an unusual, not to say bizarre, theme as the history of the world—a performance enthusiastically received and subsequently written up in the papers—grew out of these actual circumstances (Strauss's name being changed in the manuscript of the novel to Leo Epstein, then to Tostoff). I think Fitzgerald read about the concert in the papers ("If you read the papers," the orchestra leader says). Fitzgerald was in St. Paul, Minnesota, at the time, where he wrote some book reviews for the New York papers.[13] Furthermore, I think that at the time of the composition of the novel he knew *Zarathustra* itself at least vaguely from having heard it (in addition to concert performances there was at least one phonograph recording by 1924). Nick's puzzled fascination with the piece was Fitzgerald's own. Indeed *Zarathustra* celebrates the Nietzschean superman so often referred to in Fitzgerald's fiction.

What is puzzling in the *Jazz History of the World* episode may therefore be explicable more or less as follows. Fitzgerald wanted to date his scene by reference to a particular musical event of 1921 which had caught his attention: a well-publicized performance of a composition reported (in the *Times*) to have been conceived by its author as nothing less than a history of the world. Furthermore, Fitzgerald actually knew and had been arrested by Strauss's composition. He struggled unsuccessfully in the manuscript of his novel to get his fascination into Nick's remarkably long, profoundly-felt and groping attempt to describe the Epstein-Tostoff piece of music heard at Gatsby's party (by no means all of Nick's description in the manuscript applies to *Also Sprach Zarathustra*).

At the same time Fitzgerald was also trying in the scene to do something else. He wanted the piece of music in the novel to be just right for one of Gatsby's parties. Hence Strauss is transmogrified into a *jazz* history of the world. In the early twenties "jazzing" the classics was very much an issue—generally thought to be a sign of the creeping vulgarization of culture. Aldrich for instance took that position in an indignant newspaper article of 1922 ("Jazz draws the line nowhere. Nothing is safe from its devastating touch. The jazz blacksmiths . . . lay violent hands upon music that musicians have always approached with respect and . . . reverence").[14] In the manuscript even the members of the orchestra at

Mia Farrow and Bruce Dern in the 1974 film version of The Great Gatsby.

the party are themselves described as disdainful of what they are about to play: they "looked at one another and smiled as tho this was . . . a little below them. . . ."[15]

Such a piece of music at one of Gatsby's parties plays on a major theme in the novel: America's brash, energetic and meretricious vulgarization of European culture. A jazz history of the world—just right at a house where Klipspringer plays *The Love Nest* on the piano in the Marie Antoinette music room (92, 96); just right at a house which is itself an imitation of some Hotel de Ville in Normandy (5); just right in a novel where Myrtle Wilson's New York apartment is trying to summon up an image of Versailles (29).

Fitzgerald just was not successful in bringing these two ideas together: the *Jazz History of the World* as strange beauty and as the vulgarization of culture. At the last minute he threw out the former and replaced it with nothing but Nick's hasty remark, "The nature of Mr. Tostoff's composition eluded me." Then Fitzgerald went straight to the next scene as already written. The nov-

el's central figure suddenly materializes ("my eyes fell on Gatsby") as if summoned up *out* of the music to be its very embodiment—its beauty and vulgarity.

Notes

1. For Fitzgerald's comment on *This Side of Paradise* and *The Beautiful and Damned* see his letter to Maxwell Perkins, *ca.* April 16, 1924, *The Letters of F. Scott Fitzgerald,* ed. Andrew Turnbull (New York, 1963), p. 163. For Fitzgerald on wanting his new novel to be "intricately patterned" see his letter to Perkins, *ca.* July, 1922, *Correspondence of F. Scott Fitzgerald,* eds. Matthew J. Bruccoli, Margaret M. Duggan (New York, 1980), [112]. For "perfect," Fitzgerald's letter to Perkins *ca.* December 20, 1924, *Letters,* ed. Turnbull, p. 172.

2. Robert Sklar, *F. Scott Fitzgerald* (New York, 1967), p. 172 ("perfection of form"). James E. Miller, Jr., *F. Scott Fitzgerald* (New York, 1964), p. 103 ("compact"). Richard D. Lehan, *F. Scott*

Fitzgerald (Carbondale, 1966), p. 118 ("tightly structured"). Kenneth Eble, *F. Scott Fitzgerald* (New York, 1963), p. 91 ("tight inevitability . . ."). David Laird, "Hallucinations and History in *The Great Gatsby*," *South Dakota Review,* 15 No. 1 (1977), p. 19 ("formal completeness . . .").

3. *The Great Gatsby* (New York, 1953), p. 50; page references hereafter appear in parentheses in my text.

4. *F. Scott Fitzgerald, The Great Gatsby: A Facsimile of the Manuscript,* ed. Matthew J. Bruccoli (Washington, 1973), pp. 54-55.

5. Bruce Bawer, "'I Could Still Hear the Music': Jay Gatsby and the Musical Metaphor," *Notes on Modern American Literature,* 5 (1981), Item 25.

6. Milton R. Stern, *The Golden Moment* (Urbana, 1970), p. 217.

7. B. W. Wilson, "The Theatrical Motif in *The Great Gatsby*," *Fitzgerald/Hemingway Annual* (1975), p. 110.

8. Robert Emmet Long, *The Achieving of The Great Gatsby* (Lewisburg, 1979), pp. 127, 143.

9. André Le Vot, *F. Scott Fitzgerald,* trans. William Byron (New York, 1983), p. 165.

10. Gene Bluestein, *The Voice of the Folk* (Amherst, 1972), p. 119.

11. Letter to Perkins, *ca.* December 20, 1924, *Letters,* ed. Turnbull, p. 174.

12. *Concert Life in New York* (New York, 1941), p. 674.

13. See Matthew J. Bruccoli, *Some Sort of Epic Grandeur* (New York, 1981), p. 162.

14. *Concert Life,* p. 717.

15. *Facsimile,* p. 54.

Caren J. Town (essay date winter 1989)

SOURCE: Town, Caren J. "'Uncommunicable Forever': Nick's Dilemma in *The Great Gatsby*." *Texas Studies in Literature and Language* 31, no. 4 (winter 1989): 497-513.

[*In the following essay, Town deconstructs the language used by* Gatsby *narrator Nick Carraway, noting disconnections between what he says and what he actually means.*]

> From the petal's edge a line starts
> that being of steel
> infinitely fine, infinitely
> rigid penetrates
> the Milky Way
> without contact—lifting
> from it—neither hanging
> nor pushing—
>
> —William Carlos Williams, from "The Rose"

During their first meeting in **The Great Gatsby,** Daisy Fay Buchanan playfully calls her cousin (and the novel's narrator) Nick Carraway "an absolute rose." He responds:

> This was untrue. I am not even faintly like a rose. She was only extemporizing, but a stirring warmth flowed from her, as if her heart was trying to come out to you concealed in one of the breathless, thrilling words. Then suddenly she threw her napkin on the table and excused herself and went into the house.[1]

What matters to Nick here and throughout the novel, is not the veracity of what is being said, or even the words themselves, but the "heart" that is "concealed in one of the breathless, thrilling words." Words may lack the power to express objective truth, but Nick believes in their power authentically to embody emotion in metaphor and in his power therefore to be true to his story, an account of strictly emotional truth. A few pages later Nick reports:

> The instant her voice broke off, ceasing to compel my attention, my belief, I felt the basic insincerity of what she had said. It made me uneasy, as though the whole evening had been a trick of some sort to exact a contributory emotion from me. I waited, and sure enough, in a moment she looked at me with an *absolute smirk* on her lovely face, as if she had asserted her membership in a rather distinguished secret society to which she and Tom belonged.

(18; emphasis added)

The word "absolute" reappears, designating both an objective and an emotional truth: Daisy is not sincere, but she is compelling. Nick sees the insincerity but is willing to be seduced by its mode of expression, which the next line deftly confirms: "Inside the *crimson* room *bloomed* with light . . ." (emphasis added). The "absolute rose" is transformed into an "absolute smirk" that encompasses, finally, the "crimson room" blooming with light. Even though Nick makes it "absolutely" clear that he is not to be associated with that particular flower and tries to dissociate himself from Tom, Daisy, and Jordan, the rose has opened and cast its color on the *entire* company. In his attempt to establish his credibility as narrator, Nick, too, becomes tainted by the rosy tint.

Thus the "absolute" signifies the paradoxical nature of Nick's explanations of human behavior. When Nick speaks—and Gatsby's entire story is told in his words—he is never in absolute control of the story he tells. Instead, a dialectic of intention and interpretation results in patterns that finally come to dominate the novel. This web of interconnecting words and signifying relationships undercuts Nick's position as detached observer and constantly threatens to disrupt or subvert his attempts to gain distance from the characters he introduces and the situations he describes. In other words, the question is not whether Nick means what he says: Nick *means* to be reliable, but his language is unreliable, and the question becomes one of metaphorical instead of psychological reliability.[2] The effect of this trait is that Nick and the reader, from the first page of the novel, struggle for control over interpretation, engaging in an elaborate dance of acceptance and rejection of narrative authority.[3] A dance or a game: "There is not a single signified that escapes, even if recaptured, the play of signifying references that constitute language," Derrida says in his *Of Grammatology*.[4] As the rose example shows "absolutely," Nick is unable to escape the play of references that he sets in motion.[5]

The paragraph that immediately follows Daisy's exit (to confront her husband Tom about phone calls from his mistress) emphasizes the futility of Nick's belief in the transmissibility of meaning. Nick has been left alone with his new friend Jordan Baker to figure out what has just happened:

> Miss Baker and I exchanged a short glance consciously devoid of meaning. I was about to speak when she sat up alertly and said "Sh!" in a warning voice. A subdued impassioned murmur was audible in the room beyond, and Miss Baker leaned forward unashamed, trying to hear. The murmur trembled on the verge of coherence, sank down, mounted excitedly, and then ceased altogether.
>
> (15)

Daisy's voice struggles to make itself understood; it "trembled on the verge of coherence" but then was lost. As is the case with the entire novel, the meaning of particular passages promises to become clear but never does. Each phrase, each gesture, each action recorded by Nick remains as "consciously devoid of meaning" as the "subdued impassioned whisper." Jordan Baker, whose first word in the novel is "absolutely" (11), can't make sense of them either.

Daisy's voice promises but does not—or cannot—deliver; it consists of surface glitter (Gatsby will later equate it with money) and extemporaneous promises. Earlier Nick has tried to isolate its particular quality:

> It was the kind of voice that the ear follows up and down, as if each speech is an arrangement of notes that will never be played again. . . . [T]here was an excitement in her voice that men who had cared for her found difficult to forget: a singing compulsion, a whispered

"Listen," a promise that she had done gay, exciting things just a while since and that there were gay exciting things hovering in the next hour.

> (9-10)

What one hears when listening to Daisy's voice is not content but style, the "arrangement of notes." This voice carries with it a "singing compulsion," a promise of both a past and a future that is, ultimately, the goal of all effective communication. Nick hopes that his language, too, will transcend its limitations, as Daisy's conversation transcends its insubstantiality or insincerity, that it will compel its listeners with its promise. In spite of its clear desire to persuade, his voice consistently promises more than it can deliver.

Crucial to Nick's elaborate but ultimately Quixotic strategy for gaining control of his self-representation and his narrative is his attempt to win the reader's confidence, beginning on the first page of the novel.[6] First, Nick introduces himself before he introduces the rest of his characters, telling us that his father has told him that "all the people in the world haven't had the advantages [he has] had":

> In consequence, I'm inclined to reserve all judgments, a habit that has opened up many curious natures to me and also made me the victim of not a few veteran bores. The abnormal mind is quick to detect and attach itself to this quality when it appears in a normal person, and so it came about that in college I was unjustly accused of being a politician, because I was privy to the secret griefs of wild, unknown men. Most of the confidences were unsought—frequently I have feigned sleep, preoccupation, or a hostile levity when I realized by some unmistakable sign that an intimate revelation was quivering on the horizon; for the intimate revelations of young men, or at least the terms in which they express them, are usually plagiaristic and marred by obvious suppressions. Reserving judgments is a matter of infinite hope. I am still a little afraid of missing something if I forget that, as my father snobbishly suggested, and I snobbishly repeat, a sense of the fundamental decencies is parcelled out unequally at birth.

What is obvious here is that the sentences do not follow one another logically, and these ironies have often been pointed out by *Gatsby* critics.[7] The careful reader, however, is constantly asking how the ideas presented *are* related. For example, why is it "in consequence" of his having been told that all people are not equal that Nick is inclined to reserve judgments and is "made the victim" of boring confidences? There seems to be something missing here, perhaps that it suits Nick's self-definition to invite confidences. Or why does it follow, given what came before, that "reserving judgments is a matter of infinite hope"? His self-proclaimed desire to avoid conversations with "wild, unknown men" sounds more like evidence of his infinite cynicism than of his infinite hope. Or, finally, how does Nick escape the indictment heaped on other "young men" that their "intimate revelations" are "usually plagiaristic and marred by obvious suppressions"? Thus, while Nick is telling the reader one thing (that he is open minded), the logical inconsistencies are saying something entirely different (that he is not).

But the passage is doing something other than just evoking skepticism, creating simple ironies, or reflecting the incoherence of the culture out of which Nick speaks.[8] By looking closely at the language, one can see that there is a stylistic accumulation taking place, which allows the reader to reevaluate what is being said. Immediately after declaring that he is "inclined to reserve all judgments," Nick has judged those who confide in him to be "curious natures" and "veteran bores," whose minds are "abnormal." In this early passage in the novel, there is a radical injection of doubt: Nick argues for the normality of his own mind, contrasts his nature to the "curious" ones around him, and claims authenticity for his story in relation to the "plagiaristic" ones he has been told. Yet who is he arguing *with*? Surely even the most skeptical reader would not be suspicious of Nick already—we are only on page 1! The effect of Nick's pleading is to put the reader in the position of defending Nick's honor—or his sanity—a position that is crucial to the success of the narrative. For Nick's story to "work," for Gatsby to become the romantic/tragic hero that Nick intends him to be, the reader must not become suspicious of the person telling his story; he must fall under the same "singing compulsion" as do those who listen to Daisy's voice.[9]

In conflict with this bid for sympathy, however, is a linguistic pattern that emerges as the passage is read more closely. Through his use of several qualifiers ("not a few," "abnormal," "unjust," "unknown," "unsought," "unmistakable," "unequally"), Nick so qualifies himself that it becomes difficult to believe what he says *unequivocally*. The more obvious self-deprecations (his references to his snobbishness, or his lack of interest in the "intimate revelations" of his classmates) can now be seen as distractions that focus the reader's attention away from the less "obvious suppressions," from the hidden qualifications of his narrative. Nick has thus not completely succeeded in winning us over.

Derrida provides a useful metaphor to describe this process of accumulation and distraction. The genealogy of the text "is neither causality by contagion, nor the simple accumulation of layers," he says. "And if a text always gives itself a certain representation of its own roots, those roots live only by that representation, by never touching the soil, so to speak" (101). The text of **The Great Gatsby** is crisscrossed by a root system that has no fixity in the soil of absolute truth, a kind of hydroponic textuality that nevertheless searches for rootedness, for completion, for final explanations.

Thus any confidence in one's ability to distinguish between revelation and suppression in Nick's narrative can result in tripping over roots. On page 2 of the novel, Nick speaks at length, ostensibly about Gatsby's faults and merits, but he actually reveals more about himself and his own limitations.

> And, after boasting this way of my tolerance, I come to the admission that it has a limit. Conduct may be founded on the hard rock or the wet marshes, but after a certain point I don't care what it's founded on. When I came back from the East last autumn I felt that I wanted the world to be in uniform and at a sort of moral attention forever; I wanted no more riotous excursions with privileged glimpses into the human heart. Only Gatsby, the man who gave his name to this book, was exempt from my reaction—Gatsby, who represented everything for which I have an unaffected scorn. If personality is an unbroken series of successful gestures, then there was something gorgeous about him, some heightened sensitivity to the promises of life, as if he were related to one of those intricate machines that register earthquakes ten thousand miles away. This responsiveness had nothing to do with that flabby impressionability which is dignified under the name of "creative temperament"—it was an extraordinary gift for hope, a romantic readiness such as I have never found in any other person and which it is not likely I shall ever find again. No—Gatsby turned out all right in the end; it is what preyed on Gatsby, what foul dust floated in the wake of his dreams that temporarily closed out my interest in the abortive sorrows and short-winded elations of men.
>
> (2)

The same thing is happening here as in the previous passage: the reader gets only false directions and incoherent conclusions. Nick starts this passage by reminding the reader of his tolerance and then holds out a so-called admission that there are limits even to such reluctantly given tolerance, as regards human conduct. But then the "argument" turns again, with Nick saying that he wanted the world to be at "a sort of moral attention forever." However, he *also* says that Gatsby (the first mention of his name, by the way) was "exempt from [his] reaction." The reader wonders *which* of the three different reactions Nick is talking about. Was Gatsby exempt from Nick's limited tolerance, from his disregard for the foundations of conduct, or from his desire for moral attention? Then, as if this is not confusing enough, Nick utters the famous conditional phrase—"If personality is an unbroken series of successful gestures"—which is supposed to valorize Gatsby to any reader who accepts the premise. But does it? One is never completely sure if Nick believes that personality is or ought to be a series of successful gestures. And if the premise is not accepted, does that mean that Gatsby is not gorgeous after all, but something horrible, or at least something shabby? Or might it not mean that Nick's narrative is nothing more than an "unbroken series of successful gestures"? Again, as in the previous passage, Nick wants the reader to play by his rules and defend his propositions, to place hope, as he does, in reserving judgments and "romantic readiness."

Yet what Nick says he admires—Gatsby's "heightened sensitivity" and "romantic readiness"—reminds the reader of his earlier distaste for the "griefs of wild, unknown men" and qualifies the seeming praise. (Remember that these passages are only one page apart.) So when Nick comes out with the amazing "No—Gatsby turned out all right in the end," the reader wonders with whom Nick is arguing here—himself? The reader, certainly does not need to be convinced about Gatsby at this point, since he has not even seen him, watched him behave, heard his voice. But then he finds out that it is what floated in Gatsby's wake that "closed out" Nick's interest in the "abortive sorrows and short-winded elations of men." So it was not Gatsby at all (whom we did not suspect) but the characters around him (whom we have not met) whom Nick blames for Gatsby's tragedy (which we have not witnessed).[10] By the time the reader has finished the first two pages, Nick has given—or given away—the main characters, the plot, the moral, and complete directions for how to read the rest of the novel, but the reader has begun to wonder whether or not it is possible to 'get there from here.[11]

These directions seem less and less reliable as Nick continues; each story he tells about his past undercuts itself. Take, for example, his family history:

> My family have been prominent, well-to-do people in this Middle Western city for three generations. The Carraways are something of a clan, and we have a tradition that we're descended from the Dukes of Buccleuch, but the actual founder of my line was my grandfather's brother, who came here in fifty-one, sent a substitute to the Civil War, and started the wholesale hardware business that my father carries on to-day.
>
> (2-3)

The hallowed family tradition is apocryphal; Nick's family—with its merchant origins—is only a generation removed from the poverty and shabbiness of Gatsby's father. Highly ironic also is his famous assertion:

> I was rather literary in college—one year I wrote a series of very solemn and obvious editorials for the *Yale News*—and now I was going to bring back all such things into my life and become that most limited of all specialists, the "well-rounded man." This isn't just an epigram—life is much more successfully looked at from a single window, after all.
>
> (4)

The possibility of a "single window" through which to look at the world, however, has diminished significantly in the first pages of the novel; Nick's house of fiction, like Dickinson's poetry, is "more numerous of windows" and is actually a rather drafty place.

Thus reading the novel carefully involves not following Nick's directions too blindly but watching for moments when he reveals too clearly his desire to lead. Perhaps the most obvious example of this constraint occurs early in the novel when Nick describes being a newcomer to West Egg. He feels lost, he says, until a newer arrival asks him for directions, and then he comments:

> And as I walked on I was lonely no longer. I was a guide, a pathfinder, an original settler. He had casually conferred on me the freedom of the neighborhood. And so with the sunshine and the great bursts of leaves growing on the trees, just as things grow in fast movies, I had that familiar conviction that life was beginning over again with the summer.
>
> (4)

Once again, a passage *seems* to tell us something about Nick's romantic imagination: he thinks of himself as a pathfinder, an original settler. It might also be argued, less charitably, that it shows how ridiculous Nick is, since he is so quick to romanticize even the most trivial of incidents. Most important, the reader becomes like that newer arrival who has come on the scene of the novel shortly after Nick arrives but late enough so that Nick has to give directions. Nick is the map reader, movie director, creator of a clearly fictional road map filled with hidden dead ends and potholes.

A disordering pattern similar to that of the rose cycle also begins in this passage. Nick's "familiar conviction" looks forward to Jordan Baker's comment that "life starts all over again when it gets crisp in the fall" (118). The result is a confused sense of both natural and narrative time; for whom is this "familiar"? Neither version is exactly conventional; after all, the year traditionally begins with the winter solstice or with the vernal equinox. Nor do these versions conform to the action of the novel: the summer brings only heat, enervation, and hot tempers, and the fall brings no beginning either, only an ending, of his dream for Nick and of his life for Gatsby. Just as Gatsby's death is final, so is Nick's return to the Midwest a final abandonment of his illusions and his youth. Once again, the competing voices and versions have disrupted what appear to be Nick's intentions.

The conflict between initial intention and final execution is emphasized by the ongoing references to Gatsby's house. It is first described as "a factual imitation of some Hotel de Ville in Normandy, with a tower on one side, spanking new under a thin beard of raw ivy, and a marble swimming pool, and more than forty acres of lawn and garden" (5). The only thing to which this house is true is the quality of its imitation. Its history is equally problematic:

> A brewer had built it early in the "period" craze, a decade before, and there was a story that he'd agreed to pay five years' taxes on all the neighboring cottages if

the owners would have their roofs thatched with straw. Perhaps their refusal took the heart out of his plan to Found a Family—he went into immediate decline. His children sold his house with the black wreath still on the door. Americans, while occasionally willing to be serfs, have always been obstinate about being peasantry.

(89)

The story resembles Nick's family history in its unsuccessful attempt to remake the past into something more romantic. It also has at its heart a puzzling enigma: it is never clear just what the difference is between serfs and peasants, and as a result the story promises more—in terms of genealogy and moral—than it actually delivers.

This perpetual slipping away of the solidity of the romantic past and the intrusion of actual and more sordid origins is emphasized later in the novel when Gatsby, who has just asserted that it is possible to change the past, is described as "looking around him wildly, as if the past were lurking here in the shadow of his house, just out of reach of his hand" (111). It may be possible to change the past, but it is impossible to escape it.

These disruptions continue throughout the novel. Near the end Nick tries to put things into what he considers to be the proper perspective because he comes to recognize that he is in some way responsible for the chaos surrounding Gatsby's life—and death. He says, "It grew upon me that I was responsible, because no one else was interested—interested, I mean, with that intense personal interest to which everyone has some vague right at the end" (165). Nick is responsible, he says, because he became an "interested" as opposed to a detached observer. Yet notice that this interest is something to which everyone has "some vague right": what seems an intense personal involvement is only a vague connection, and Nick is no closer to explaining what happened to Gatsby, or to himself.

What the reader begins to see is that Nick is responsible because he created Gatsby, or at least a romanticized version of Gatsby, and this larger-than-life image leads to Nick's disappointment at the apparent lack of interest in Gatsby's death. In fact, Nick's most eloquent passages at the end of the novel, after Gatsby's unattended funeral, are an attempt to order the chaos that he created in his mythologizing of Gatsby, to find another way of making sense of what happened, to immortalize Gatsby. Yet the stylistic disruptions that I have described prevent the reader from feeling any sense of closure, no matter how hard Nick tries. From beginning to end, Nick's language subverts his intentions.

This responsibility is not solely Nick's, however; we all hope that language will let us make sense out of chaos, will give meaning to life, will save us from death.[12]

This hope is what Daisy's voice promised for Gatsby (as well as for Nick): "I think that voice held him most, with its fluctuating, feverish warmth, because it couldn't be over-dreamed—that voice was a deathless song" (97). The same warmth that Nick felt in Daisy's voice, the same promise, is shared by Gatsby. Because it is not real, this voice can be dreamed about endlessly; because it is insubstantial, it can never die. Yet when it actually could have saved Gatsby from death, the voice never comes:

> I have an idea that Gatsby himself didn't believe it [the phone call from Daisy] would come, and perhaps he no longer cared. If that was true he must have felt that he had lost the old warm world, paid a high price for living too long with a single dream. He must have looked up at an unfamiliar sky through frightening leaves and shivered as he found what a grotesque thing a rose is and how raw the sunlight was upon the scarcely created grass. A new world, material without being real, where poor ghosts, breathing dreams like air, drifted fortuitously about . . . like that ashen fantastic figure gliding toward him through the amorphous trees.
>
> (162)

Without Daisy's voice Gatsby's world is "material without being real," and the rose, which was "absolute" early in the novel, is now "grotesque." At Gatsby's end there is neither rose nor any voice: "I tried to think about Gatsby then for a moment, but he was already too far away, and I could only remember, without resentment, that Daisy hadn't sent a message or a flower" (176). Nick cannot depend on Daisy's "deathless song" of a voice or on roses either, but he feels compelled to find some meaning in what has happened, to find closure. He tries first to invoke geography as an explanation by recounting his annual Christmas return to the Midwest:

> I am part of that, a little solemn with the feel of those long winters, a little complacent from growing up in the Carraway house in a city where dwellings are still called through decades by a family's name. I see now that this has been a story of the West, after all—Tom and Gatsby, Daisy and Jordan and I, were all Westerners, and perhaps we possessed some deficiency in common which made us subtly unadaptable to Eastern life.
>
> (177)

Here Nick tries to claim that all the characters in the novel share some fundamental quality that both sets them apart and renders them deficient. However, the reader notices that Nick comes to this conclusion immediately after remembering his house—"where dwellings are still called through decades by a family's name." This recalls Gatsby's house, which not only has no name but also an obscure and vaguely unsavory past, as well as Nick's story of his origins, and the reader begins to suspect that Nick's frantic struggle to find common ground is a quest that is doomed to fail.

This common ground must begin to seem uncertain to Nick as well, since he next tries to invoke history as a way of unifying the novel:

> And as the moon rose higher the inessential houses began to melt away until gradually I became aware of the old island here that flowered once for Dutch sailors' eyes—a fresh, green breast of the new world. Its vanished trees, the trees that had made way for Gatsby's house, had once pandered in whispers to the last and greatest of all human dreams; for a transitory enchanted moment man must have held his breath in the presence of this continent, compelled into an aesthetic contemplation he neither understood nor desired, face to face for the last time in history with something commensurate to his capacity for wonder.
>
> (182)

Since houses have failed him in the previous passage, as they failed Gatsby earlier, Nick must now claim that they are "inessential." He then begins to speculate about the reactions of the Dutch sailors to their first view of what was to become West Egg, ascribing to them responses that are not unlike his own toward Gatsby. It would not suit Nick's purposes to paint the sailors as greedy plunderers or as exploitative conquerors; instead, they must approach the new world with "aesthetic contemplation," as artists. In order to justify his position as authoritative narrator, Nick must force both the past and the present to conform to an appreciation of beauty that is free from personal desire; the only contemplation allowed is "aesthetic." The "real," for Nick, lies not in desire or the material but in the aesthetic.

In this most lyrical passage, especially, Nick's language betrays him. The island "flowered" (evoking other flowers in this novel—roses, daisies, and myrtles—which are all tainted); it becomes a "fresh green breast" (alluding to the other breast—Myrtle's—which was ripped off); and the trees "pander in whispers" (referring to Nick's pandering for Gatsby). The reader is also transported back to the "original settler," "singing compulsion," and "absolute rose" passages, with all their ambiguity. Clearly, Nick is more "interested" in his narrative than he wants to admit.

Interested, but he remains powerless to change anything, even to set right a falsification of events. When he meets Tom for the last time, and Tom recounts his version of the accident that killed Myrtle and led to Gatsby's murder, Nick responds, "There was nothing I could say, except the one unutterable fact that it wasn't true" (180). Nick, who once saw himself as "pathfinder," now finds himself unable to correct even the most obvious and important of misinterpretations.

So, as Nick feels his distance and control slipping away from him in the last few sentences of the novel, he plays his final card and tries to implicate the reader:

> Gatsby believed in the green light, the orgiastic future that year by year recedes before us. It eluded us then, but that's no matter—tomorrow we will run faster, stretch out our arms farther. . . . And one fine morning—
>
> So we beat on, boats against the current borne back ceaselessly into the past.
>
> (182)

Nick tries to make us, his readers, feel that "we" are also caught in the same dance, that we share Nick's dream and his dilemma. We suddenly recognize that we are being inscribed in the text and forced to acknowledge that we have participated in this tragedy by listening to Nick's story. Unfortunately, the perceptive reader does not share Nick's hope that "one fine morning—" his optimism for the future, nor his nostalgic if melancholy pull toward the past. Instead, at the end of the novel, Nick's dream merges with Gatsby's dream, and Nick *and* his readers are "borne back ceaselessly into the past," the past of the novel. The chain of disconnections that has bound us up should force us to question all aspects of the narrative, including the narrator, Gatsby, and the reader's involvement with both of them. Nick has become, against his will, both lover and rival, while struggling to remain just a good friend.

In each formulation, in each attempt to reconstruct history, origin, and identity, both for himself and for Gatsby, Nick fails, not for lack of trying but for the limitations inherent in his language. Just as Gatsby, after kissing Daisy, will "never romp again like the mind of God" (112), so Nick will never be able to save Gatsby from death by explaining him:

> Through all he said, even through his appalling sentimentality, I was reminded of something—an elusive rhythm, a fragment of lost words, that I had heard somewhere a long time ago. For a moment a phrase tried to take shape in my mouth and my lips parted like a dumb man's, as though there was more struggling upon them than a wisp of startled air. But they made no sound, and what I had almost remembered was uncommunicable forever.
>
> (112)

The truth that Nick had hoped to convey becomes a "fragment of lost words," a final meaning that was "uncommunicable forever."[13]

Notes

1. F. Scott Fitzgerald, *The Great Gatsby* (New York: Scribners, 1925), 5. All subsequent references will be cited parenthetically in the text.

2. Consistently, critics have praised *The Great Gatsby* for its multiple perspectives instead of considering it flawed. Fitzgerald—unlike other novelists of the same period—is rarely called upon to decide be-

tween various means of representation; indeed, he is celebrated for combining elements of realism and romance into the same novel. But while the *novel* is praised as both a realistic representation of the 1920s and a romantic rendering of the American Dream, *Nick* is forced to be either sincere or insincere; he is very rarely permitted to be both. For to assume that Nick is both trustworthy *and* untrustworthy threatens the privileged position that allows the critic to pass moral judgment on the perspective of the novel and on the psychology of the narrator. For language to become the site of misrepresentation, regardless of the intention of either character or critic, dulls the edge—or perhaps removes the need—for critical thematizing.

I am thinking specifically of critics such as Richard Lehan, *F. Scott Fitzgerald and the Craft of Fiction* (Carbondale: Southern Illinois University Press, 1966), 122; Maxwell Geismar, "Orestes at the Ritz," in *The Last of the Provincials* (New York: Houghton Mifflin, 1943), 319; Kenneth Eble, *F. Scott Fitzgerald* (New York: Twayne, 1963), 98; F. H. Langman, "Style and Shape in *The Great Gatsby*," *Southern Review* 6 (1973): 40; and W. J. Harvey, "Theme and Texture in *The Great Gatsby*," in *Twentieth-Century Interpretations of "The Great Gatsby*," ed. Ernest Lockridge (Englewood Cliffs, N.J.: Prentice-Hall, 1968), 94. And this practice is not limited to earlier critical works; the essays in *New Essays on "The Great Gatsby"* (ed. Matthew J. Bruccoli [Cambridge: Cambridge University Press, 1985]) offer little to change the traditional formula: Nick is sincere or insincere; therefore, Fitzgerald was idealistic or cynical about America.

3. Kent Cartwright ("Nick Carraway as an Unreliable Narrator," *Papers on Language and Literature* 20 [1984]: 218-32) says we distrust Nick because his judgment is "exaggerated, unstable and finally self-compromising" (224). Nevertheless, "because we diverge from Nick—sometimes hesitating at his reactions, sometimes moving beyond them—we feel, even as we too are compelled with fascination, a firmer objectivity" (224). So lack of identification becomes a point of novelistic unification. But the novel's overall vision—meaning Fitzgerald's vision—is clouded by Nick's ambiguous narrative position; instead of being "the arbiter of final meanings, Nick is a contestant in the novel's internal tugging war for truth" (229).

4. Jacques Derrida, *Of Grammatology,* trans. Gayatri Chakravorty Spivak (Baltimore: Johns Hopkins University Press, 1974), 7. All subsequent references will be cited parenthetically in the text.

5. Mikhail Bakhtin (*The Dialogic Imagination,* ed. Michael Holquist, trans. Caryl Emerson and Michael Holquist [Austin: University of Texas Press, 1981]) also focuses attention on the multiplicity of voices and intentions in the novel. From the section called "Discourse in the Novel":

> These distinctive links and interrelationships between utterances and languages, this movement of the theme through different languages and speech types, its dispersion into the rivulets and droplets of social heteroglossia, its dialogization—this is the basic distinguishing feature of the stylistics of the novel.
>
> (263)

Any utterance is, he says, "a contradiction-ridden, tension-filled unity of two embattled tendencies in the life of language," between the "unitary" language and "social and historical" forces (272). I see these tendencies—a pulling toward and a pulling away from the desire for unity—strongly at work in *The Great Gatsby.*

6. Warwick Wadlington (*The Confidence Game in American Literature* [Princeton: Princeton University Press, 1975]) and Gary Lindberg (*The Confidence Man in American Literature* [New York: Oxford University Press, 1982]) discuss the pervasiveness of the confidence man in American novels. For Wadlington, the game of literature is a confidence game, which is made up of "problematic, ambivalent, or deceptive transactions that establish imaginative authority and renew individual identity, in both the world the writer imagines and the relationship he fashions with his reader" (ix). "Men seek and create the grounds of confidence, which is to say, mutual faith," he says, "as much to validate themselves as to control the wills of others" (6). The trickster represents the "neither-both," as opposed to "either-or" or "both-and," an "illusive fullness" that is marginal to all sectors. "The Trickster's marginal nature does not so much synthesize oppositions, as serve as a referent for them: it is what oppositions seek to capture" (19). This figure is also representative of American culture:

> In the national iconography, Americans are peddlers of assurance. The iconography was shaped early by the historical uniqueness of the experiences open to the nation, by the new Romantic faith in the self, and by the competitive energies of capitalism.
>
> (10)

Lindberg agrees with this relationship of the confidence game to America:

> [The confidence man] is a covert cultural hero for Americans. . . . It is not our official pieties that he represents but our unofficial reward sys-

tems, the strategies that we have for over two centuries allowed to succeed. He clarifies the uneasy relations between our stated ethics and our tolerated practices.

(3-4)

The confidence man, he says, "makes belief" (7). Nick can be thought of as a kind of confidence man, although he is also fooling himself.

7. Fitzgerald was also skeptical of such assertions. His narrator comments in "The Rich Boy," a story often seen as a precursor to *The Great Gatsby*:

> When I hear a man proclaiming himself an "average, honest, open fellow," I feel pretty sure that he has some definite and perhaps terrible abnormality which he has agreed to conceal—and his protestation of being average and honest and open is his way of reminding himself of his misprision.

> (*The Stories of F. Scott Fitzgerald,* ed. Malcolm Cowley [New York: Scribners, 1951], 177)

8. Ross Posnock ("'A New World, Material without Being Real': Fitzgerald's Critique of Capitalism in *The Great Gatsby*," in *Critical Essays on F. Scott Fitzgerald's "The Great Gatsby,"* ed. Scott Donaldson [Boston: G. K. Hall, 1984]: 201-13), says that Gatsby (and Nick's representation of him) "risks incoherence . . . not simply from personal defect but because he is a product of a capitalist society that Fitzgerald reveals to be profoundly incoherent" (202). But the conflict between classes does not divide the novel because Nick's "'aesthetic contemplation' abstracts Gatsby from a human world and places him in an ideal realm" (211). In sum:

> Gatsby becomes just the sort of hero that a lonely, modestly successful thirty-year-old like Nick would be likely to invent. As Nick's invention, Gatsby, in effect, is transformed into a commodity that Nick sells the reader. The object Nick provides for our consumption is a version of a perennially marketable cultural myth—the romantic hero as passive sacrificial victim.

(211)

9. In *The Resisting Reader* (Bloomington: Indiana University Press, 1977), Judith Fetterley reformulates this problem in terms of sexist cultural assumptions. The narrative structure of the novel, she says, "could be more accurately described as one of Fitzgerald's most self-conscious and most successful solutions to the problem of how to tell a story" (93). She continues:

> To accuse Nick of dishonesty in his treatment of women and Fitzgerald of carelessness in handling that dishonesty is to miss the point. Nick's dishonesty goes unrecognized by most of the novel's readers: it is not perceived as dishonest

because it is common, pervasive, and "natural" to a sexist society. *The Great Gatsby* is a dishonest book because the culture from which it derives and which it reflects is radically dishonest.

(93-94)

Fitzgerald, she says, was able to achieve his effects "by drawing on a large cultural lie which he neither recognizes as such nor makes any conscious commentary upon" (94). This lie is a double standard for men and women that goes like this: "men are legitimate subjects for romantic investment and women are not; men can support it and women cannot; Daisy must fail Gatsby but Gatsby need not fail Nick" (95). I think this too easily equates Nick, a fictional character, with Fitzgerald and diminishes what the novel reveals about Nick's struggle with self-representation and metaphor.

10. An analogy to Nick's difficulties in describing Gatsby can be seen in Derrida's discussion of the problem of naming in relation to Lévi-Strauss:

> Thus the name, especially the so-called proper name, is always caught in a chain or a system of differences. It becomes an appellation only to the extent that it may inscribe itself within a figuration. Whether it be linked by its origin to the representations of things in space or whether it remains caught in a system of phonic differences or social classifications apparently released from ordinary space, the proper-ness of the name does not escape spacing. Metaphor shapes and undermines the proper name. The literal [*propre*] meaning does not exist, its "appearance" is a necessary function—and must be analyzed as such—in the system of differences and metaphors.

(89)

The proper name, like Gatsby's made-up name, exists only in appearance; there is no inherent self that it represents. In spite of Gatsby's attempt to create a personality for himself and Nick's struggles to define that self, Gatsby—and all his name represents—is "caught in a chain or a system of differences."

11. Gary Scrimgeour ("Against *The Great Gatsby*," in *Twentieth-Century Interpretations of "The Great Gatsby,"* ed. Ernest Lockridge [Englewood Cliffs, N.J.: Prentice-Hall, 1968], 70-81) sees the problem as more one of morality than of clarity. "Carraway's honesty is a matter not of principle," he says, "but of convenience" (76). He moves from this to an assertion that Nick's assumed morality threatens the structure of the novel: "If the reader cannot accept Carraway's statements at face value, then the integrity of the technique of the novel is called in question" (77). Finally, Scrimgeour says that Nick is a "moral eunuch," which makes the

meaning of *The Great Gatsby* "much blacker than that of *Heart of Darkness*" (78).

12. For Derrida this is the predictable longing for the metaphysics of presence:

> The subordination of the trace to the full presence summed up in the logos, the humbling of writing beneath a speech dreaming its plenitude, such are the gestures required by an onto-theology determining the archeological and eschatological meaning of being as presence, as parousia, as like without difference: another name for death, historical metonymy where God's name holds death in check. That is why, if this movement begins its era in the form of Platonism, it ends in infinitist metaphysics.
>
> (71)

13. Cartwright says that part of the novel's ambivalence, "stems from Fitzgerald's undercutting of the novel's form" (231). What Fitzgerald has done is defeat traditional reader expectations both for a narrator and for an ending:

> The work represents a kind of miscegenation of forms, a romance enclosed in a novel of manners, and Nick and Gatsby seem attached as if by pulleys: as the one is more credible, the other is less so. Gatsby can be both criminal and romantic hero because the book creates for him a visionary moral standard that transcends the conventional and that his life affirms. However, nothing in Nick compels our contemplation or our wonder; he lives in the image of an increasingly reductive melancholy, not of a transcending dream.
>
> (232)

Although ultimately he capitulates to the vague cohesive power of the novel, to its "inextinguishable sense of possibility" (232), Cartwright raises the crucial questions of reader expectation and authorial intentionality. This reinforces what Bakhtin says about all novels: that they carry within them a variety of forms and constantly defeat expectations created by the structure and voices of the narrative. Cartwright's reading provides the prologue to a critique of the actual function of the novel, although he falls back on possibility (or politics, or psychology) to hold the novel together.

Richard Lehan (essay date 1990)

SOURCE: Lehan, Richard. "The Importance of the Work." In *The Great Gatsby: The Limits of Wonder,* pp. 11-15. Boston: Twayne Publishers, 1990.

[In the following essay, Lehan discusses the reasons why The Great Gatsby *is still considered a literary classic.]*

Any attempt to pinpoint the importance of a work involves a slightly circular argument. The criteria that one brings to the work establish its sense of importance, and the claim for importance then justifies the criteria. Such a necessary circularity need not, however, diminish the more obvious contexts used in establishing the worth of a literary text. Complexity and artistry, vision and technique are the values usually brought to the evaluative process. But even within these terms critics find room for disagreement. What is narratively complex and artistically accomplished to one may seem simplistic and awkward to another. So at the outset we must be aware that any discussion of the "greatness" of a work involves judgments that are both tentative and personal.

The problem of evaluation is complicated further by the fact that there are many modes of fiction: the early realism of Defoe, for example, functions differently from the comic realism of Dickens, which in turn functions differently from the romantic realism of Hugo, or the naturalism of Zola, or the mythic symbolism of Joyce. Fitzgerald began his career by writing an aesthetic novel in the tradition of the bildungsroman; moved on to write a seminaturalistic, documentary kind of novel; then under the influence of Conrad, turned to the highly wrought novel of symbolic detail, controlled by the sensibility and moral intelligence of a narrator who participates in the action. Along with the mythicsymbolism of Joyce, the stream of consciousness of Virginia Woolf, the narrative primitivism of D. H. Lawrence, this kind of novel is central to the very idea of the modern, at the same time that it functions differently—and hence must be read and evaluated differently—from the other narrative modes and the subgenres within those modes. *The Great Gatsby* is perhaps the best example of what might be called moral symbolism, and the critics who underestimate this novel tend to do so by not seeing clearly the mode in which it was written—and how successfully that mode was accomplished.

Some of these critics are also put off at the outset by Fitzgerald's reputation, which has been diminished by the short stories—many of them trivial—that he wrote for such popular journals as the *Saturday Evening Post*. Ernest Hemingway always felt superior to him on this score. That Fitzgerald diluted his craft under the urgent pressures of debt and the need for money cannot be denied. That he also wrote a dozen or so of the best short stories in the twentieth century can also not be denied. When he was in control of his craft, Fitzgerald was capable of consistently major achievements.

By 1924 Fitzgerald was in the position to write a masterwork like *Gatsby*—everything had been building toward this moment. He had served a kind of apprenticeship in the writing of his two previous novels, and he had begun to conceptualize the Gatsby novel in such short stories as **"Winter Dreams," "The Diamond as Big as the Ritz," "Absolution,"** and a bit later **"The Rich Boy."** He would never be so completely in control of his craft again, so sure of the narrative effect that he wanted to create, and in such good health that he would have the energy to work on that novel even at times to the point of exhaustion.

What Fitzgerald did in *The Great Gatsby* was to raise his central character to a mythic level, to reveal a man whose intensity of dream partook of a state of mind that embodied America itself. Gatsby is the last of the romantic heroes, whose energy and sense of commitment take him in search of his personal grail. The quest cannot be separated from the destiny of a nation—from people who came to a new world, crossed a continent, and built a nation. Such an exercise in will was not without consequence, however, for these people left behind a trail of plunder and waste—of Indians massacred, of the land and its minerals exploited, of nature pillaged. Once the frontier was exhausted, the adventurous state of mind still existed; only now the object of its contemplation was less heroic and sometimes even banal. Fitzgerald's Gatsby was a man of such heroic vision without the opportunity to find a commensurate experience for it. Once the frontier was gone, Gatsby brought his Western intensity East and found a "frontier" equivalent in the New York underworld, the world of professional gamblers, bootleggers, financial schemers, and a new breed of exploiters that the city bred differently from the land. Such a man will stand out in "respectable" company because he will lack social credentials. Novelists like Henry James, E. M. Forster, and Ford Madox Ford gave us insight into how such a highly structured world works; it turns primarily on manners, a system of decorum that those who are within the system share and that separates them from those who are outside. In this world Gatsby is a poseur, a man who fakes it, exploiting his brief contact with Oxford, his war record, and a natural physical elegance that belies his crudity of taste and his lack of a privileged knowledge of manners.

And it is this Gatsby who becomes the object of focus for Nick Carraway—a young, privileged Westerner who has also come East to try his fortune. But Nick does not have to make his own money—that was done by those who came before him, whose crude ventures are now concealed by bourgeois status. Nick's granduncle and father have settled comfortably into the business of American business, of servicing the hardware needs of the new America. Such is a diminished thing. The romantic intensity that the pioneers brought to the new world, Gatsby now brings to a beautiful but also rather superficial, self-involved, self-protecting, morally empty young woman. The power of this novel ultimately comes from the structured relationships between these narrative elements. We have two kinds of seeing in this novel: the visionary whose vision has been emptied, and a moral observer who is initially unsympathetic to what he sees in the visionary ("Gatsby . . . represented everything for which I have an unaffected scorn") but who is eventually won over by what is compelling and poignant in Gatsby's story. Nick comes to see that Gatsby's fate cannot be separated from his own or from the destiny of America—that something heroic has passed in the backwash of time; that in the era of Harding and Coolidge, the era of modern America, a crass materiality has absorbed our attention, making it a dreamer's fate to idealize what is now most hollow in an emptied past. We most often think of the visionary as one who can read the future; but the visionary is really the person who can read the past, who knows what has been used up, what has been materially exhausted and is no longer available. In this context Fitzgerald was truly a visionary.

In *The Great Gatsby* Fitzgerald tells an extremely American story, so much so that he even thought of titling it "Under the Red, White, and Blue." The sense of personal destiny in the novel gives way to a sense of national destiny and that in turn to a romantic state of mind. Fitzgerald's literary imagination was always deeply connected to the romantics; he began reading them seriously at Princeton under the influence of Professor Christian Gauss, and he brought the same intensity of romantic interest to an aesthetic tradition that spawned so many of the young disillusioned men and women that Fitzgerald made the trademark of his fiction. Such disillusionment was imbedded in the vision itself, inseparable from its workings: illusion versus reality, a transcendental ideal in conflict with an earthy materialism, the Keatsian frozen moment in contrast with time the destroyer, the romantic ideal transforming physical reality, the rose elevated beyond the garden—such was the fateful metaphysics behind a novel like *Gatsby,* a metaphysic that gave such tragic priority to the unreal that it was assured the ideal would be undone in time. But to state the problem this bluntly robs it of narrative subtlety, robs it of the greatest gift Fitzgerald brought to his novel—a style so well honed that his story takes on the intensity of a poem.

And indeed it was a poem that served among his models. In *The Great Gatsby* Fitzgerald wrote an American equivalent to *The Waste Land* and brought the same intensity of vision to the postwar, secular world of America that T. S. Eliot had brought to the world of postwar England. So many of the touches in the novel are purely Eliotic—the scene in the Washington Heights apartment where the principals talk about Mrs. Eberhardt, who "goes around looking at people's feet in their own homes" (31), or the counterscene in Daisy's mansion where it is asked, "What'll we do with ourselves this afternoon . . . and the day after that, and the next thirty years?" (118), or the scene involving Nick walking the city streets seeing both from the inside and out. Nick may start off with absolute scorn for Gatsby, but he comes to admire him both as a man and as a portent of America. Nick sees what is both pathetic and grand in the last of the American romantics, the last of the breed with an epic sense of destiny whose vision took him beyond the realm in which the rest of us live. When asked why Daisy married Tom Buchanan, Gatsby responds, "it was only personal." Such touches Fitzgerald brought to every page of *The Great Gatsby,* which radiates with its own special energy.

Fitzgerald's fiction, his conception of character, the narrative unfolding, the complexity of language—all make for a novel of unbelievable complexity. On a personal note, I can say that I have read this novel well over one hundred times, and every time I reread it, I find that I am seeing things that I had previously missed. Few novels—particularly those so seemingly simple on the surface—hold up so well and have the ability to continually surprise us. *The Great Gatsby* seems larger than the criteria that we bring to its evaluation; whatever we say about it seems never complete or satisfactory enough. It is a novel that has continually proved itself larger than its many critics, which is perhaps what we mean when we speak of it as a masterpiece. When the canon of American literature changes, the criteria we use to establish that canon change as well. Literary posterity is always a fragile thing, but challenges to the permanence of *The Great Gatsby* seem to cast more doubt on our critical criteria than they do on Fitzgerald's achievement.

Carol Wershoven (essay date 1993)

SOURCE: Wershoven, Carol. "Insatiable Girls." In *Child Brides and Intruders,* pp. 92-9. Bowling Green: Bowling Green State University Popular Press, 1993.

[*In the following essay, Wershoven notes that Daisy Buchanan is a prototypical "child bride" whose "purchase" is required by a society of commodity.*]

Undine Spragg [in Edith Wharton's *The Custom of the Country*] is only one in a series of girls whose appetite mirrors a nation's desire. In four novels that followed *The Custom of the Country*—*The Great Gatsby,* [Wharton's] *Twilight Sleep* [and Ellen Glasgow's], *The Sheltered Life* and *In This Our Life*—versions of the insatiable girl appear, and so, too, does a recognizable pattern. The desiring/desired girl stands at the center of a vortex. Around her swirl instances of failed marriages, blocked communications, social disorder and decay. Like *The Custom of the Country,* each of these four novels is set in a world of deception, where illusion and role-playing supersede reality and emotion. But a new

element appears in the pattern: a crime. In these novels, there are two shootings and two car "accidents" (hit-and-run). In each case, the innocent heroine is either the culprit or is indirectly responsible, and, in each case, society helps to cover up the deed.

These conspiracies of evasion are the logical outcomes of the crimes, as those around the heroine are her accomplices. They have created the atmosphere in which the child bride flourishes; they have, in essence, created her. And those around her perceive that she cannot be held responsible for her actions, for she embodies the pure freedom of endless choice without consequences. She is the consumer who need never pay.

She is an icon of desire and damnation. Like Undine Spragg, she is what men want, and she is full of discontent: forever attracted to a new amusement, a new toy, a new man, and forever bored, disappointed, seeking a new deal. Men strive to pay for her, and they pay twice. They work to acquire her, and they assume the responsibility of owning a delinquent child, one who smashes things and people with the petulance of a spoiled little girl.

The price of the child bride never seems to be too high. In these novels, even when the beloved child is revealed as a manipulator, betrayer, or murderer, she is carefully shielded from the consequences of her desires. This icon of longing must not be shattered, for if she is gone, what is left? Only the Valley of Ashes that created her.

In the middle of *The Great Gatsby,* Meyer Wolfsheim, who has ingeniously transformed human molars into jewelry and the dirty deal into a corporate empire, offers Nick Carraway a business connection. His offer encapsulates most of the relationships of the novel, for F. Scott Fitzgerald's book is largely about deals. Tom Buchanan has bought his wife, and Jay Gatsby wants to exercise his prior option on the merchandise. Nick, the novel's moral center, is learning to trade in stocks and bonds. Gatsby sells liquor in the guise of medicine, Tom Buchanan and George Wilson dicker over the sale of a car, Myrtle Wilson sells herself, and Meyer Wolfsheim bought the World Series.

At the center of the trading is, of course, the golden girl, or more accurately, as Michael Millgate notes, the gold and white girl. Daisy is the golden girl in the white palace, the "Daisy" with a gold center and white petals, the princess dressed in white, driving a white roadster. She is, then, the color of money but also the color of the "absence of all desire." The white palace is remote and inaccessible, Millgate says, and Daisy's white innocence is life-denying (111). Daisy wants things and people, but she feels no true sexual desire, and thus there is no space inside her that can be filled, no unfinished part of her that can be completed by another. She is a trick of blankness. Even her golden color, the color of money, is also the color of brass, the imitation. It is the color of the brass buttons on her dress the day she reunites with Gatsby, himself resplendent in a silver shirt and golden tie.

At the center of all the deals, then, is a bad bargain. Daisy is the meretricious beauty to which Gatsby consecrates his life.

It is fitting that a book about buying and selling should center on a woman who does not give full value for the money. Most trades involve some deception, or at least some illusion, on the part of buyer and/or seller. And so *The Great Gatsby* is a novel of lies, filled with open secrets, evasions, deceit, and betrayal. It begins with the open secret of Tom's infidelity and Daisy's dramatic enactment of the role of long-suffering, beautiful fool. The scenario entertains Jordan, a professional golfer who is a liar and a cheat. The first scenes introduce the keynote of deception that continues throughout. Tom lies to his mistress about his wife's refusal to divorce him; Myrtle and her sister deceive Myrtle's husband, poor George; everyone suspects Gatsby is lying about his genteel past; and a series of deceptions lead to Gatsby's murder.

As the Houyhynhms said, a lie is "the thing that is not," and this is a novel about the love of "what is not." In *The Great Gatsby,* appearances are worshipped as if they were real, things are substituted for emotions, things provoke emotion, and people become things.[1]

The central characters, Daisy and Gatsby, drift from role to role, almost as if they were searching for the most appropriate one. Daisy is first seen in an elaborate tableau of elegance and lassitude, posed on her sofa, gazing motionless at some invisible object, a figurine in a cool, lush setting. In the space of a few hours, she attempts two new roles: the injured wife and the adoring young mother. Her lover, trying to explain his past to Nick, also posits a series of roles, from which Nick can choose the one he finds most plausible: war hero of Montenegro, white hunter in the colonies, Oxford man. Daisy is drawn to Gatsby's flair for drama. As Marius Bewley notes, what Daisy likes best at Gatsby's party is the empty gesture of an actress and her director (278), slowly moving toward one another in a pantomime of love, a parody of her own slow movement back to the lover who wants to dominate her life.

And the love that supposedly binds these two is frequently represented as an uncontrollable feeling prompted by an object. Gatsby beseeches Daisy's green light in the darkness; she is where the light is, but somehow the light evokes the feeling. Daisy loses control and weeps, not on first re-encountering her lost love,

but when she sees the piles of pastel-colored shirts he flings, like tribute, into her lap. Betrayal is also revealed by a thing: George Wilson discovers his wife's adultery when he finds a jeweled dog leash in her room.

The lines dividing people, images and things become increasingly blurred. Daisy's little girl, charmingly dressed and adorably (but briefly) exhibited to Nick, seems like her mother's doll, or a prop in Daisy's drama of marital virtue wronged and affronted. Daisy's attitude towards Gatsby is most tellingly revealed in the words of passion that give the game away. Tom is certain that Daisy has been unfaithful when she lovingly compares Gatsby, so fresh and clean and beautifully dressed, to the image of a man in a shirt advertisement. There seems to be no higher tribute in this world of illusion than to compare one's beloved to an advertisement.

It is a dead world, a place dominated by a pair of eyes on a billboard, eyes that are sightless but forever peer out, looking for something. Like the eyes of Dr. Eckleburg, the innocents of the novel keep looking for something, something new and better, for they are bored with the things they have already bought. Daisy wonders what they'll do each day, and the next day, identifying the dilemma of people who can have whatever they want, as soon as they want it. Tom, too, is bored, seeking excitement first in sport, then in infidelity, seeking identity in a book of racist political philosophy. Myrtle is bored with her husband and looking for a better deal; George, too, dreams of moving to a new place where business will be better.

Gatsby, more than anyone else, is eternally hopeful, confident that one more purchase will save him. Malcolm Bradbury says Gatsby aims "to transform money into love" (65) by buying Daisy. For, as [Judith] Fetterley says, Daisy has become the embodiment of the things Gatsby has craved for so long. Her family's rich house in Alabama, where he first sees her, is "the house of romance which he can only enter through her," and she is "the ultimate object in it. It is she for whom men compete, and possessing her is the clearest sign that one has made it into that magical world" (74).

Fitzgerald's comment on his relationship to his wife Zelda is relevant to Gatsby's motives. In his notebooks, Fitzgerald discussed his marriage to Zelda, a dream fulfilled only after much frustration. Zelda had broken their engagement because Fitzgerald had no money, and she married him only after he had become rich and famous, with the publication of his first novel. Fitzgerald describes the bitter lesson learned from both denial and subsequent gratification of his longing:

> The man with the jingle of money in his pocket who married the girl a year later would always cherish an abiding distrust, an animosity, toward the leisure

class—not the conviction of the revolutionist but the smouldering hatred of a peasant. In the years since then I have never been able to stop wondering where my friends' money came from, nor to stop thinking that at one time a sort of *droit de seigneur* might have been exercised to give one of them my girl.

(Qtd. in Spindler 152)

His fear describes the plot of **The Great Gatsby,** and Spindler says the statement reveals Fitzgerald's awareness that "money was the dynamo which powered the bright lights of the leader class" (152). But the comment also reveals Fitzgerald's understanding that women are property, prizes to be won. And so his greatest character, Jay Gatsby, perceives Daisy as "that which money exists to buy," as Fetterley says. To own her "both indicates the fact of money and gives point to its possession" (74).

Fitzgerald seems to say that Daisy is the source of Gatsby's doom, that she brings him down. Critics of the novel generally agree that Daisy's destructive power is not willed or conscious, that Gatsby has simply invested too much in a property that cannot appreciate in value. Nevertheless, our general sense of Gatsby's story links his fall to his choice of the golden girl. Perhaps if he had found some other embodiment of his dreams, if he had purchased something else, his life might have been otherwise. The being who created himself, this Son of God, is incarnated, made fallible and vulnerable, when he makes the wrong consumer decision.

As Gatsby remembers it, the fatal choice is his decision to commit himself to Daisy. On that autumn night, as he and Daisy walked on a sidewalk "white with moonlight," he turned to Daisy and noticed that "the blocks of the sidewalk really formed a ladder and mounted to a secret place above the trees." The moment of choice arrives, for Gatsby can reach the secret place

> if he climbed alone, and once there he could suck on the pap of life, gulp down the incomparable milk of wonder.
>
> His heart beat faster and faster as Daisy's white face came up to his own. He knew that when he kissed this girl, and forever wed his unutterable visions to her perishable breath, his mind would never romp again like the mind of God. So he waited. . . . Then he kissed her . . . and the incarnation was complete.
>
> (112)

Gatsby has bought the definitive item; given the choice between the stars and the earth, between a secret place of endless wonder and the blank, white face of mortality with its "perishable breath," Gatsby comes down to Daisy, who must lift her face to reach him. God has been made man; anticipation, infinite promise have been reduced to a limiting realization. It seems that God has become man not by *becoming* a child, but by *loving* one.

The passage is not so straightforward. For the alternatives of Gatsby's choice are not clear. From what heights did Gatsby fall? And to what has he been reduced?

Without Daisy, Gatsby thinks, he could climb that white ladder to the sky and be safe in a solitary spot, free to suck the milk of wonder, to romp. This choice is a child's choice, a consumer choice. Gatsby perceives this secret world as a place of dependency and drift, where the maternal breast of dreams is ever-available, where he can suck the milk of wonder endlessly as he romps in innocence. To get there, he must take a white sidewalk and climb a white ladder to live on the white liquid of dreams. In a novel filled with negative images of the white princess in her white world, the world relinquished by Gatsby seems remarkably similar to the world he chooses.

Gatsby's "fall" into Daisy's perishable world is no Fortunate one. There is no moment of transition from that secret world of play to the mature world of guilt, sorrow, and perhaps redemption. If Daisy indeed brings Gatsby down, she brings him down to reality. The fallen Gatsby is not so much diminished as revealed. He has chosen Daisy not as an alternative to that playful world of wonderful white dreams, but as an embodiment of it.

As Fitzgerald points out, Gatsby makes himself, and he creates his own destiny as well. Like that first self-made man, Ben Franklin, Gatsby methodically and systematically designs his regimen of self-improvement. His diary, like Franklin's, allocates each moment of the day for one more step on the way to wealth. Gatsby learns and studies under a more modern version of the self-made man, the predator/pioneer Dan Cody. Gatsby learns to believe in his mentor's values of power, possession and control. He becomes exactly what he wanted to be—the latest incarnation of an old American dream. By Gatsby's time, the self-made man is no longer creative and inventive like Franklin, nor rapacious and atavistic, like Cody. He is polished and charming, a con man. But Gatsby's misfortune is to be the con man duped by his own yearnings.

Gatsby is brought down by his refusal to see the nature of his own dreams, and that is why he must remain faithful to Daisy until he dies. As Fetterley says, Gatsby has invested himself in Daisy (76-77), so to recognize her emptiness is to recognize his own. It is easier to remain in a world of lies, to die waiting for a call that will never come, a declaration of love from a girl who cannot love. The dream must be sustained by deception, of others and of oneself, so that identity can be sustained.

It is easier for all those in Gatsby's world to go on as they began than to confront the evil inside their dreams. When the golden girl kills, her crime must be concealed, and Gatsby, Tom, and even Nick conspire to cover up the truth. And so the novel ends as it began. It ends in falsehood, from Gatsby's lie to save Daisy, to Jordan's lie to save her pride. It ends in deception, from George Wilson's tragic mistake, to the revelation of Gatsby's real name, to the Buchanans' re-assumption of the role of united married couple.

And, most of all, it ends with a final picture of the power of money. Money can buy the innocent bride, and enough money can keep her safe in a white palace. Money can sustain the illusion that, somewhere, there is one new thing, one new pleasure or one new person that, purchased, will fill the emptiness inside. And so the story of the Buchanans ends with two more purchases, as Tom buys jewelry to adorn his new mistress, his latest acquisition. Business continues as usual.

Note

1. This blurring of polarities is very like the blurring of subject and object in *Sister Carrie*.

Works Cited

Bewley, Marius. *The Eccentric Design: Form in the Classic American Novel.* 1957. New York: Columbia UP, 1963.

Bradbury, Malcolm. *The Modern American Novel.* Oxford: Oxford UP, 1983.

Fetterley, Judith. *The Resisting Reader: A Feminist Approach to American Fiction,* 1978. Bloomington: Indiana UP, 1981.

Fitzgerald, F. Scott. *The Great Gatsby,* 1925. New York: Scribners, n.d.

Millgate, Michael. *American Social Fiction: James to Cozzens.* New York: Barnes & Noble, 1964.

Spindler, Michael. *American Literature and Social Change: William Dean Howells to Arthur Miller.* Bloomington: Indiana UP, 1983.

Ronald Berman (essay date 1994)

SOURCE: Berman, Ronald. "Contexts." In *The Great Gatsby and Modern Times,* pp. 15-37. Urbana: University of Illinois Press, 1994.

[*In the following essay, Berman discusses ideas current in America in the early part of the decade just before* Gatsby's *publication.*]

In **"Echoes of the Jazz Age,"** written in the early thirties, with a flourish Fitzgerald identified the crucial year of the preceding decade: "May one offer in exhibit the year 1922!"[1] It is the turning-point year in which *The Great Gatsby* takes place. And in the novel he makes it a point to be specific about the dating of his story. In what particular ways does the novel use its moment? Let us look at certain ideas in circulation in the summer of 1922, and in the period around it: ideas that, like that of "civilization," are referential in the text. For Tom Buchanan "civilization" is highly meaningful—and is opposed to his sense of "the modern world." Does he echo a public debate? And, is his anxiety over ideas and social situations possibly derived?

One set of anxieties can probably be discarded. In a 1921 interview Fitzgerald stated that, "except for leaving its touch of destruction here and there, I do not think the war left any real lasting effect. Why, it is almost forgotten right now."[2] Possibly to our surprise there was substantial agreement with this. Leading into the year *The Great Gatsby* takes place, on November 30, 1921, the *New Republic* states of "the new spirit" that worldwide, "improvement is spreading rapidly and is increasing in self-confidence and in positive achievement as well as in volume. It is clearly the expression of a temper radically different from that which prevailed during and after the war." Throughout 1922, the *Saturday Evening Post* showed little interest in a war that had by now receded from the memory of its readers and was no longer good copy. The *Post,* in any case, had many other quarrels to engage in, and there are good reasons for it being a magazine of choice for Tom Buchanan. In 1923, the year of the first publication of *Time,* almost nothing was said in its weekly coverage about war disillusion. The archaeologist of news will find instead that *Time* covers war debts, war finances, and armament limitations without invoking war disillusion. In the early twenties *Time* covered fiction and theater in more detail than it now does, but very little of its critical attention was devoted to books or essays about the lasting, debilitating effect of our experience in the Great War. Much attention, however, was paid by *Time,* other magazines, and by Fitzgerald to certain resentments.

On July 5, 1922, a date to remember, the *New Republic* continued its campaign of national introspection or "interpretation" (the term is from the first sentence of the first issue in 1914) of public events. There was much to interpret, beginning with the industrial war in West Virginia in which coal miners had killed nineteen strike breakers. The editors thought that these unionized miners were identical in class outlook and behavior to those who had recently beaten and tortured black migrant workers in Springfield and East St. Louis. There were troubles enough abroad: the Marines were in Haiti; Ireland was habitually regressive in politics and in culture; and in Germany Walther Rathenau had just been assassinated.[3] But, at least for the *New Republic,* foreign policy was not at this point the main issue: what mattered most in American life was the management of domestic change. There were many anxieties, and traditional kinds of explanation seemed no longer to hold. It seemed, for example, to be no longer useful to think about the relationship of Capital to Labor, or of Democrat to Republican. Politics was a waste of time. In 1922, the public duty was to reassess the aggregate of individual lives that constituted the nation and to bring to bear a new private and public sense of self. Perhaps nothing *could* be done about West Virginia until the values of a "Christian people" were asserted—and recognized. About other things much remained to be done, especially about the dual facts of too much money in circulation, and in too few hands. There was an uneasy sense of the swiftness of social change, and, even more, that it might be unmanageable. The issue of July 5 ended on an especially disquieting note, with a review of recent books on coming of age in America. Its last words were about a new cultural sense of self, about the child no longer "the subject of the parental regent, however wise." In the coming decade, it was plain to see, personal identity would be achieved through "self-direction and self-determination." The author reviewed is Rabbi Stephen S. Wise and his book *Child Versus Parent* is taken for a tract for the times. Undesired social change seems now to begin, literally, at home. Both author and reviewer believe that the growth of social character should indeed be ordered by "self-discipline" but they doubt that will happen. Fitzgerald would write in the early thirties that "the wildest of all generations" was that "which had been adolescent during the confusion of the War."[4] As for self-discipline, that had been stood on its head: the generation of children had "corrupted its elders."

There is one other thing about this issue that is of special interest to novelists: a review of *Ulysses* by Edmund Wilson. Since reading it, "the texture of other novelists seems intolerably loose and careless." *Ulysses* has invalidated traditional kinds of fiction, including, one supposes, books like ***This Side of Paradise*** and ***The Beautiful and Damned.*** New fiction will clearly have to be ironic in tone, modernist in technique. Fitzgerald dutifully read *Ulysses* and wrote to Wilson about its personal effect on him.[5] There is more to the effect of modernism on Fitzgerald that needs to be said and I will try to amplify that in later chapters.

Other magazines will of course have other concerns but they too are focused on the overriding theme of change. There is *Vanity Fair,* a publication closer than the *New Republic* to the tactical issues of Fitzgerald's fiction. *Vanity Fair* means also to be interpretative—its motto has, from the first issue in 1913, been "a record of current achievements in all the arts and a mirror of the progress and promise of American life." Its sense of "promise" resonates to Fitzgerald's themes. *Vanity Fair* was (before the advent of the *New Yorker*) the main

source for the creation of social identity through high style. It assumed that self-determination operates through consumption. One of its great themes is the acquisition of identity by conscious choice. That choice is exerted through transaction within the marketplace. The primary assumption of the marketplace of style is that we can choose what we want to be without inhibition. A secondary assumption is that diligent consumption, as thoughtful and perhaps as arduous as that of a lifetime of good works, legitimatizes our efforts. When Myrtle Wilson shops at Pennsylvania Station she is by no means being simply materialistic—she displays the care and prudence once associated with the vocation of citizenship. She understands that purchases and styles are meant not to gratify but to display the character of choice—and the choice of character.

Vanity Fair is necessarily about commodities, and its advertisements are as important as any other instructions conveyed by commercial literature. I believe that Fitzgerald took quite seriously the techniques and even the claims of advertising—he did not differentiate it from the rest of "culture" and indeed he used it to enormous advantage in a novel about people whose energies are often bent toward consumption. There are no warnings in ***The Great Gatsby*** that when we leave love for advertising or for the description of commodities we are moving from a realm of higher to lower seriousness.

Vanity Fair has a powerfully affective sequence of advertisements (nearly all illustrated, with many taking up an expensive full page) of its principal commodities, automobiles. Here they are in order of appearance in the July 1922 issue: the life-changing designs of the Chalmers Six, Oldsmobile, Wills Sainte Claire, Haynes 75, Renault, Winton, Kimball, De lage, Talbot-Duracq, Marmon, D. A. C., Mercedes, Stanley, Elgin, Dusenberg, the three-wheeled Neracar ("a new type of automotive vehicle unlike either an automobile or a motorcycle"), Ford, Le Baron, Rumpler Raindrop, Studebaker, Durant, Stutz, Pierce-Arrow, Cadillac, Sunbeam, Ballot, Packard Twin-Six, Paige, Daniels, Derham, and La Fayette. The August issue will add the Maxwell, Locomobile, Essex, and the Rolls-Royce favored by Gatsby. In relation to all advertisements and text the automobile is by far the most important commodity in the issue. It is as important a symbolic object to *Vanity Fair* as it is to ***The Great Gatsby.*** Each car has a social character to confer. Some will grant middle-class reliability. Most, however, have more extensive ambitions. The products imply consumers who are themselves "leading," "powerful," and even "perfect." These products confer "esteem," "security," "enjoyment" and, possibly more important, something not likely to be granted often by daily life, complete "satisfaction." In ***The Great Gatsby*** one of these cars will even turn out to be "triumphant."

Few of the cars on the pages of *Vanity Fair* are less elaborate than Gatsby's, which begins to seem representative rather than extreme. There are not only spare tires but cases for them; there are tools and gauges for mileage, gasoline, and oil; and logs for daily expenses. There are monograms in metal to prove ownership. There are traveling sundials. A special model of the Pierce-Arrow comes equipped with water tank and ice-box for cocktail parties; with bottles, glasses, "knives, forks, plates and other picnic paraphernalia." This model also has a Victrola and room for records to play on it. There is a built-in Kodak to memorialize its usage. The Stutz is itself interpretative, "owned and liked by men who have long since passed the Dollar Sign on the road to achievement."

Gatsby seems less idiosyncratic when a magazine of 1922 is opened. The majority of other commodities in the July issue of *Vanity Fair* are clothes *that* make the man. Advertisements of the 1990s now praise natural impulse and promise individuality within the mass. Ads of the twenties are more socially instructive. They reflect realities, not impulses. We buy underwear because of "The Question of Health." A watch is not an ornament or *jeu d'esprit* but "The Last Essential in Dress." What matters is that which allows us to be "approved" and which turns us into "ladies" and "gentlemen." B. V. D.s suggest neither sexuality nor privacy—they are what a man wears for the last perceivable stage of correctness in the club locker room. It is only natural that a considerable amount of anxiety should be generated because the marketplace is full of those who aspire to mobility but who cannot defend their origins. The marketplace of identity has to avoid the issue tackled by the great novels of social change that kept inner consciousness focused on the past. In the great line of narrative from Dickens to Lawrence and Joyce the problem is not that of achieving status but of reconciling it with one's former, inner—and true—identity. The ads of *Vanity Fair* promise a change of identity so complete that there will be no former self left to argue with.

The Vanity Fair Shopping Service undertakes "to leave the decision" about acquiring a new self through commodities "to Vanity Fair's judgment." It is a judgment much less fallible in its sense of a social self than any individual's is liable to be. There are many ads like this one in magazines of the twenties, providing instructions for those on the margins of class. The marketplace had to formulate character as well as supply demand. Fitzgerald once wrote ad copy himself and was aware of the relationship between style and status: Gatsby leaves the decision about his shirts to a man in England who sends over a "selection" of things each season. Daisy understands not only the plenum of styles but the way they reach Gatsby and what they mean to him.

The ultimate promise about acquired identity is made in *Vanity Fair* by an ad for the La Fayette: "He Who Owns

A La Fayette is envied by all who truly love fine things. Quiet, beautiful and strong, this car rules any road it travels." It should be no surprise that after Daisy tells Gatsby indirectly that she loves him, she seeks for her own objective correlative: "You resemble the advertisement of the man. . . . You know the advertisement of the man—" (93). Probably not the man in the La Fayette ad, but the man whose face is drawn a thousand times a day in the art of commercial realism, a figure perfectly achieved.[6]

But even *Vanity Fair* has second thoughts about "progress and promise." In the May 1922 issue, the omnipresent Hendrik Willem Van Loon had invoked "civilization" in a way that would reverberate throughout the decade.[7] The term will come to mean a great deal to Tom Buchanan in the spring of 1922 and to those he represents. Van Loon writes that after the war, "America has suddenly been called upon to carry forward the work of civilization." We must now provide what an exhausted Old World used to provide, "art and literature and science and music and all the other great accomplishments of the human race." Or, as Tom confusedly puts it in his redaction of profundity, "oh, science and art and all that" (14). By "art" both mean aesthetics in the service of social stasis: realistic images with moral values. But there are some redefinitions also about "the human race." Van Loon adds that civilization as we know it may well vanish, exactly as when "unknown hordes from unknown parts of Asia and Eastern Europe broke through the barriers of Rome and installed themselves amidst the ruins of the old Augustan cities." The modern equivalent of these hordes is "the latest shipment of released Ellis Islanders" who will "make a new home among the neglected residences of your own grandfathers and uncles." The issue was addressed from the other side of the aisle at exactly the same time (May 10, 1922) by the *New Republic,* which concluded that national identity would be changed no matter what people like Van Loon wanted. A "new" kind of "upstart half-breed Americans seem destined to rule the larger American cities for many years in spite of the discomfiture, the dismay and the ineffectual protests of the former ruling class." It is a good description of the political-cultural dialectic—and also of Tom Buchanan and his fears.

Harper's Monthly Magazine in the early twenties had few advertisements and showed little interest in either domestic or national policy. It was very much in the genteel tradition, concerned with manners, the fiction of sensibility, various uses of Nature, the alternatives of city and country life, and the cultural responsibilities of the enlightened middle class. More than one piece in the July 1922 issue sought to be inspirational about America. But the theme so persistent in other texts finds expression here also: we were better off before times changed. The opening essay, "What Happens to

Pioneers," is about a country once untroubled by mass migrations from Europe to America—or from South to North. It insists that before the twentieth century, ownership and working of the land themselves constituted moral character. As for the settlement of the wilderness—that had been an act of national altruism. It is bad enough that the change in population from country to city-based has wrought a change in our national character—much worse is the effect of ideas about our past. A certain nameless reviewer for the *New Republic* (clearly infected by the spirit of Veblen and of Beard) is the villain of this piece in *Harper's*. That reviewer, obviously a modern materialist with no regard for the meaning of American history, has converted "The dreaming builders" of our union, who were entirely altruistic, into "real-estate speculators, usurers, merchants, brokers," and pettifogging lawyers. The "mystic exaltation" of the Founding Fathers has been reduced to mere "pecuniary interest." Their motive for developing the wilderness is now interpreted by moderns as being only the desire to profit from it. American history, according to such new, deracinated intellectuals, *is an exact counterpart of contemporary history*. There are two main sources of resentment in this piece: that the innocent past should be so distant from the corrupt present; and that it should be judged by "modern" ideas.

The July *Harper's* ends with the "Editor's Easy Chair" in which the reader is warned that "A man's most difficult antagonist is within himself, and the same is apt to be true of nations." The specific issue is American national life perceived in terms ("anxieties," loss of "confidence," and of "balance") that are clearly not political but moral-psychological. This kind of transference is one of the great modes of periodical literature and of the entire enterprise of social commentary. There are some good reasons for the public being addressed as if it were in a continual state of moral crisis. In an age of limited government there are necessarily limited expectations. It is rare for the editorialists of the early twenties to appeal to state or federal agencies. They sermonize instead. And they persist in understanding national issues as if they *were* moral issues. This is as true of Irving Babbitt as it is of Tom Buchanan. It is as if national character were perceived as an enlarged form of individual character. Within that tradition the editor of *Harper's* looks back at the nineteenth century, and says that "the old way" of doing things "has not worked well" for us. The truth may be that twentieth-century problems are not amenable to nineteenth-century solutions. *There is an unbridgeable distance between our history and our selves.*

If we are to judge from this limited sample, public debate on the subject of true Americanism was mournful and confused. As for American "civilization," that debate was even angrier and uglier than Tom Buchanan's. The term "civilization" was everywhere in use for the expression of anxiety. It was often used as a code word meaning innocent American national character before mass immigration and Emancipation—and before the loathsome effects of modernity.

During a "polite" and "pleasant" dinner on East Egg Nick Carraway unconsciously engages a national dialectic: it takes no more than saying, "You make me feel uncivilized, Daisy" (13). Nick says that he "meant nothing in particular by this remark, but it was taken up in an unexpected way" (14). From this point on Tom Buchanan is cued to debate "civilization," and the text begins its refraction of ideas from print. As Tom says of his current favorite book, "everybody ought to read it" (14), and the implication is that ideas do in fact circulate from texts. Fitzgerald has gone to some trouble to indicate—in a very pointed communication from Nick to the reader—that an eruption has occurred that reveals underlying truths. Beneath the surface of a "pleasant" evening is resentment, even rage if we are to judge from what seems to be its displaced forms in Tom. We get from "art" and "science" to race very quickly. There is a strange parallel between this passage and another passage published a few years before, in 1919, which also moves volcanically from "art" to "civilization." William Winter's life of David Belasco complacently views the state of Broadway productions and then suddenly precipitates national resentments about the visible evidences for historical change:

> The spirit of our country is and long has been one of pagan Materialism, infecting all branches of thought, and of unscrupulous Commercialism, infecting all branches of action. Foreign elements, alien to our institutions and ideals as to our language and our thoughts,—seditious elements, ignorant, boisterous, treacherous, and dangerous—have been introduced into our population in immense quantities, interpenetrating and contaminating it in many ways: in the face of self-evident peril and of iterated warnings and protests, immigration into the United States has been permitted during the last twenty years of about 15,000,000 persons—including vast numbers of the most undesirable order. We call ourselves a civilized nation—but civility is conspicuous in our country chiefly by its absence. Gentleness is despised. Good manners are practically extinct. Public decorum is almost unknown. We are notoriously a law-contemning people. The murder rate—the *unpunished* murder rate—in our country has long been a world scandal. Mob outrage is an incident of weekly occurrence among us. Our methods of business, approved and practised, are not only unscrupulous but predatory. Every public conveyance and place of resort bears witness to the general uncouthness by innumerable signs enjoining the most elemental decency. . . . The tone of the public mind is to a woeful extent sordid, selfish, greedy. In our great cities life is largely a semi-delirious fever of vapid purpose and paltry strife, and in their public vehicles of transportation the populace—men, women, and young girls—are herded together without the remotest observance of common decency,—mauled and jammed and packed one upon

another in a manner which would not be tolerated in shipment of the helpless steer or the long-suffering swine.[8]

The suddenness of transference from "art" to "civilization" says something about the way Tom Buchanan's mind works, or fails to work. Winter clearly feels that the movement from one kind of statement about the art of theater to another kind of statement about the nature of "civilization" is appropriate *and that it makes sense.*

Daisy and Jordan make fun of Tom but they do not seriously challenge his ideas about civilization. In fact, when Daisy reveals her own ideas she says something of their sources. She has many doubts, and they come from "the most advanced people" who think that "everything's terrible anyhow" (17). We are faced in the right direction, invited to agree with those who in 1922 argue that life is unsatisfactory. Daisy's sources are cultural pessimists—there is a word for it, *Kulturpessimismus,* or the belief that modernity is without soul or public morality, and that a return to the values of the past is the only possible solution. It was a position for those opposed to the effects of democracy, in America as well as Germany. Pessimism about "civilization" was often expressed in a language strikingly similar to Tom's. In 1920 George Santayana began *Character and Opinion in the United States* with this assertion: "Civilization is perhaps approaching one of those long winters that overtake it from time to time. A flood of barbarism from below may soon level all the fair works of our Christian ancestors, as another flood two thousand years ago levelled those of the ancients."[9]

Related issues were not confined to a lunatic fringe, and they were heavily publicized by magazines and newspapers. In 1923 the celebrated *Study of American Intelligence* by McDougall and Brigham appeared, stating that "the intellectual superiority of our Nordic groups over the Alpine, Mediterranean and negro groups has been demonstrated."[10] The *New York Times* and the American Museum of Natural History agreed. Tom Buchanan would not have been perceived as a crank in the period from 1921 to 1923. He would have compared favorably with some members of Congress. He would have been understood as being under the respectable wing of the amateur anthropologists Madison Grant and Lothrop Stoddard, and of George Horace Lorimer, editor of the *Saturday Evening Post.* A modern historian observes that Grant, a notable racist, "inspired" other writers, and that he was the focus of "sympathetic comments in the editorials of such influential publications as the New York *Times* and the *Saturday Evening Post.*"[11] Grant Overton's *American Nights Entertainment* of 1923 has much to say about national figures whose ideas are assimilated by people like Tom:

> Prophecy is a very old business. It has become our habit to think of ourselves as a people without prophets; and yet there was never a time when mankind had

more seers or more interesting ones. What is H. G. Wells but a prophesier, and from whom do we receive counsel if not from Mr. Chesterton? Mr. Shaw is our Job's comforter, and George Horace Lorimer, on the editorial page of *Saturday Evening Post,* calls us to repentance. A few years ago I had the adventure of reading Madison Grant's *The Passing of the Great Race,* an impassioned proclamation of the merits of the blond Nordic race, and a lamentation over its decay. At that time such a book was in the nature of a revelation whether you gave faith to its assertions and proofs or scoffed at them. The thing that struck me was the impossibility (as it seemed to me) of any reader remaining unmoved; I thought him bound to be carried to a high pitch of enthusiastic affirmation or else roused to fierce resentment and furious denial. And so, in the event, I believe it mainly turned out. At that time, although he was the author of several books, I had not heard of Lothrop Stoddard, unless as a special writer and correspondent for magazines. It was not until April 1920, that *The Rising Tide of Color Against White World-Supremacy* was published. Even so, attention is not readily attracted to a book of this type. Many who have since read it with excitement knew nothing of the volume until, in a speech at Birmingham, Alabama, on 26 October, 1921, President Harding said: "Whoever will take the time to read and ponder Mr. Lothrop Stoddard's book on *The Rising Tide of Color . . .* must realise that our race problem here in the United States is only a phase of a race issue that the whole world confronts."[12]

According to the *Saturday Evening Post,* Stoddard's work attracted "an extraordinary amount of attention" and was recognized as "the first successful attempt to present a scientific explanation of the worldwide epidemic of unrest."[13] He was a household name, which is probably why he is encountered in Tom's household as "this man Goddard" (14) who has written "The Rise of the Coloured Empires."

In 1924 there was much political discourse over American character in Congress, and much argument in print. In a volume at least as well known as Santayana's, Irving Babbitt's *Democracy and Leadership,* the following was stated: "We are assured, indeed, that the highly heterogeneous elements that enter into our population will, like various instruments in an orchestra, merely result in a richer harmony; they will, one may reply, provided that, like an orchestra, they be properly led. Otherwise the outcome may be an unexemplified cacophony. This question of leadership is not primarily biological, but moral."[14] One admires the qualification, but the thrust of argument remains the same: pessimism over those of us who are neither Nordic nor Christian. But Babbitt was infinitely better than most on this issue: in 1925 *Reader's Digest* carried a Madison Grant piece from an earlier issue of the *Forum,* which reads as if it were designed for a Tom Buchanan who had briefly flickered into consciousness over the immigration debate. Grant's essay, "America for the Americans," argues not only against the admission into the United States of black or yellow peoples but also of Germans, inassimilable because of their guttural speech and mannerisms (the war was not adduced). During the early twenties it was widely thought that Germans were insufficiently Nordic. Grant uses the same kind of vocabulary as Tom: "our institutions are Anglo-Saxon and can be maintained by Anglo-Saxons and by other Nordic peoples in sympathy with our culture."[15]

To return to the year of the novel's events: here are two passages that may indicate what we now call intertextuality. The first is from John Higham's history of immigration. It is about a series of articles that Kenneth Roberts wrote for the *Saturday Evening Post* in 1920 and that appeared in book form under the title *Why Europe Leaves Home* in 1922. Roberts cast his findings into the framework of the Nordic theory, concluding that a continuing flood of Alpine, Mediterranean, and Semitic immigrants would inevitably produce "a hybrid race of people as worthless and futile as the good-for-nothing mongrels of Central America and Southeastern Europe."[16] The second passage, from *The Great Gatsby*, seems to be a mere interlude: "Inside, the crimson room bloomed with light. Tom and Miss Baker sat at either end of the long couch and she read aloud to him from the 'Saturday Evening Post'—the words, murmurous and uninflected, running together in a soothing tune. The lamplight, bright on his boots and dull on the autumn-leaf yellow of her hair, glinted along the paper as she turned a page with a flutter of slender muscles in her arms" (17-18).

There is action and meaning at this moment, although it would seem to be a pause in the narrative. Fitzgerald's text reminds us of the existence of other texts. The enormous, imitative enterprise of mass literacy is perceptibly within the consciousness of characters in his own text. What Tom is hearing we will never know, but we can expect that the ideas of the moment are being read to him, and that they too are soothing and uninflected. More is involved than Norman Rockwell covers.

The relationship between race and religion and culture had its critics, among them Harold Stearns, who argued against it in *Civilization in the United States* (1922). According to Stearns, "whatever else American civilization is, it is not Anglo-Saxon . . . we shall never achieve any genuine nationalistic self-consciousness as long as we allow certain financial and social minorities to persuade us that we are still an English colony."[17] But it was, by 1922, too late to sort out distinctions—the political debate over immigration from eastern and southern Europe made them easy to cloud over. Even *Civilization in the United States* had to acknowledge the current theory and its vocabulary. Other contributions, for example Geroid Robinson's essay on race, admit that "the attitude of both Northerners and Southern-

ers is somewhat coloured by the fear that the blacks will eventually overrun the country."[18] The essay of Louis Reid on small towns celebrates the "true American civilization," that is, national life before the arrival of Catholics and Jews.[19] Walter Pach, who was reasonably enlightened and has been praised as an art critic by E. H. Gombrich, found himself dependent on race and religion as determinants, arguing for an "art-instinct accumulated in a race for centuries." In the case of literature, he said that instinct belonged to "the Anglo-Saxon race."[20] Stating this was the only way he could conceive of the inherent ability of Americans to produce the cultural proofs of their existence.

The March 1, 1922, issue of the *New Republic* carried the introductory chapter of Walter Lippmann's forthcoming *Public Opinion,* and in this chapter he warned the audience "that under certain conditions men respond as powerfully to fictions as they do to realities." Fictions might be true (or false) scientific theories; they might even be "complete hallucinations"—but they were representations of the environment that determined our responses to it. Some fictions might be beneficial—useful without being accurate—but those abroad in 1922 were apt to be neither. In *Public Opinion,* Lippmann describes fictions corresponding to—identical to—the theories that Tom Buchanan raises in the first and seventh chapters of *The Great Gatsby.*[21] Lippmann's list of current fictions in "news" (he took special pains to distinguish "news" from "truth") are Tom's bugbears: ancestry and American history; race and nationality; and in particular the ideology of "Anglo-Saxons." At the heart of the Lippmann thesis is the premise that these issues, important though they may be in themselves, have become demonized by their public discussion. In both Lippmann and Fitzgerald the conveyance of ideas by print results in an intellectual tragicomedy. It is useful to see Lippmann's reaction to what Fitzgerald was to call "stale" ideas: "The more untrained a mind, the more readily it works out a theory that two things which catch its attention at the same time are causally connected. . . . In hating one thing violently, we readily associate with it as cause or effect most of the other things we hate or fear violently. They may have no more connection than smallpox and alehouses, or Relativity and Bolshevism, but they are bound together in the same emotion . . . it all culminates in the fabrication of a system of all evil, and of another which is the system of all good. Then our love of the absolute shows itself."[22] It is wise, thought-provoking, and related to one of Fitzgerald's problems in the writing of *The Great Gatsby.* Fitzgerald was no political scientist but he did need to describe the effect of political ideas upon personality and the manifestations of personality. We infer not that Tom Buchanan is either a Democrat or Republican but that within him there really is a "love of the absolute" that wants to "show itself." In essence, psychological necessity chooses belief.

H. L. Mencken agreed to a certain extent. His was eventually the most crushing rebuttal to the fiction of Anglo-Saxon civilization. Mencken's essay on the failure of Anglo-Saxon civilization (1923) was reprinted in *Prejudices: Fourth Series* (1924). But as early as 1917, in an essay on Howells, Mencken had identified what others thought was the *problem* of American democracy as its *nature*: our system worked not despite but because of "the essential conflict of forces among us."[23] In this respect Mencken was more political than either Santayana or Babbitt—and very much more political than either Pound or Eliot. The point of the 1923 essay was not only that the country needed new immigrants but that (and his essay takes on the form of a narrative) the old ones, who now called themselves natives, had failed dismally to establish any kind of "civilization" of their own. Mencken writes about the proud, vainglorious and ignorant culture-hero, or would-be culture-hero, the anxiety-ridden Anglo-Saxon whose "defeat is so palpable that it has filled him with vast alarms, and reduced him to seeking succor in grotesque and extravagant devices. In the fine arts, in the sciences and even in the more complex sorts of business the children of the later immigrants are running away from the descendants of the early settlers. . . . Of the Americans who have come into notice during the past fifty years as poets, as novelists, as critics, as painters, as sculptors and in the minor arts, less than half bear Anglo-Saxon names. . . . So in the sciences."[24] Mencken's Anglo-Saxon is constitutionally a bully, hence his many acts of aggression against social change are accompanied by "desperate efforts" of "denial and concealment." The Anglo-Saxon's "political ideas are crude and shallow. He is almost wholly devoid of esthetic feeling. The most elementary facts about the visible universe alarm him, and incite him to put them down. Educate him, make a professor of him, teach him how to express his soul, and he still remains palpably third-rate. He fears ideas almost more cravenly than he fears men. His blood, I believe, is running thin; perhaps it was not much to boast of at the start."

As Harry E. Barnes observed in the *American Mercury* in 1924, the issue was very much one of "ideas" and public opinion: Madison Grant's work on the superiority of Nordic "civilization" was itself "a literary rehash of Gobineau and Houston Stewart Chamberlain." And even Grant was "progressively debased" as his book became "widely disseminated," and decanted into Lothrop Stoddard.[25] By the time such ideas reach Tom Buchanan they exist in the form in which he states them.

The Anglo-Saxon fears the loss of his "civilization" and that fear is easily confused with conscience. He continually justifies what he does by the illusion of keeping faith with history. Mencken has created a character in a historical drama who responds to the issues of the moment and reminds us of the issues in Fitzgerald's text.

Tom seems not only to have read many texts but to originate in them. He is obsessed with acquired ideas. So much so that he expresses a great many of them in the quarrel at the Plaza at a moment when we expect other passions of body and mind. Tom is faced with his wife's lover, with the idea of love itself, but the argument over Daisy takes the form of a lecture on *Kulturbolschewismus*. Tom orates about house, home, and family; about nobodies from nowhere; and about the various abominations of "the modern world" (101). His ideas have traveled a long way from Irving Babbitt and Santayana, from Grant and Stoddard to their reification by mass media. He is so confused by ideas transmitted from mind to media that he can perceive Gatsby only as an epiphenomenon of "the modern world."[26] As for Daisy, to her embarrassment she realizes that Tom sees her only as part of the "institutions" he defends.

As if following a script written by H. L. Mencken, Tom discourses in the first chapter about the arts and sciences and "civilization" itself. He later comes to view Gatsby as a kind of problem in modern institutions. Tom is, like Mencken's satirized Anglo-Saxon, enormously alarmed by the "elementary facts about the visible universe": "pretty soon the earth's going to fall into the sun—or wait a minute—it's just the opposite—the sun's getting colder every year" (92). Fitzgerald has added to Mencken's text a kind of strategic entropy of both world and mind imagining it. When Tom begins his lecture on civilization in the first chapter the reader is tempted to write him off as a crank, which is probably the wrong thing to do. It seems logical because Tom cannot convince anyone with an independent mind of his views on history or national destiny. But there are no independent minds in his household. Daisy and Jordan do not openly disagree—in fact, they go along. They find him ridiculous but acceptable. As Jordan later says, settling differences at the Plaza, "We're all white here" (101). It would appear, by the simplest kind of extension, that there are few independent minds anywhere else.

Tom agonizes over adultery and divorce. He is alarmed into reflection over race and class. He is irrational about all those who would "throw everything overboard and have intermarriage between black and white" (101). Even a moralist must have exceptional capacities for outrage to worry about all these things. Unless, of course, his whole concept of identity were involved.[27] Part of that identity has been provided by association: the text introduces him as "Tom Buchanan of Chicago," which does more than mimic society-page seriousness. He is part of a place, and his opinions are approximations of Chicago opinions. His hometown (he and Daisy try "to settle down" (61) there after their marriage) was the most racially troubled and intolerant city in the North. Industry in the early twenties encouraged a migration of black workers from Georgia and Alabama to the factories of the Midwest. It was a cause of great concern because it raised the price of labor in the South. And, of course, the migrants ran up against a new phenomenon in American life, persecution from the side that won the Civil War. In so doing, they caused a tremendous revaluation in national life. The notorious Chicago riots were caused by confrontations over jobs, housing, and beachfront recreation. The consequence was the formation of national opinion largely in favor of racism. We recall that Tom worries in the first chapter of *The Great Gatsby* about the white race being "dominant" and keeping "control" of its civilization (both here and abroad). He was not much different from, say, the *New York Times* of July 23, 1919: "The majority of Negroes in Washington before the great war, were well-behaved . . . most of them admitted the superiority of the white race and troubles between the two races were unheard of."[28]

When Tom articulates his ideas we can see some of their likely sources and understand the allusions. But Fitzgerald's text is not a tract; it is concerned with motive as well as ideology. Idea is related to act. We recall Tom's grabbing Nick's arm, bruising Daisy, and breaking Myrtle's nose, as well as his general foaming at the mouth on the subject of marriage. Tom is three-dimensional and is equipped with a number of anxieties connected to his ideas, or to his need for ideas. For example, he seems fixated upon "I" and "we." He fears "all kinds" (81), in itself a phrase of psychological interest. He talks about "people" (who are unidentified) "sneering" at things sacred to him (101). This too seems meaningful, because the matter has been turned into psychodrama. Max Scheler's classic study of *Ressentiment,* written in the decade before *The Great Gatsby,* suggests that Fitzgerald understood the connection of idea to personality. Scheler depicts the internal language of resentment, which says to itself, "I can forgive everything, but not that you *are*—that you are *what* you are—that I am not what you are."[29] There is no textual connection, but there is a clear parallel between this mode of thought and Tom's litany about Nordic selves: "I am and you are and you are and—" (14). Tom speaks a language of absolute subjectivity. He has invested his needs in ideas, which is to say in allowable aggressions. If he is in fact a representative figure then he says much for Fitzgerald's view of the cultural moment.

We enter the narrative of *The Great Gatsby* to the description of universe, earth, hemisphere, and ocean. Throughout the story the skies will turn, with their silent commentary on the meanings we define as history. In the summer of 1922 we have been separated from the past. Given the anemic description of his family, Nick conveys that his own past has not much to recall. We gather that from the limit on his articulation of its values. He has been given the least useful of social virtues, a kind of passive toleration. It is as if all the moral energy of the nineteenth century had dwindled into good manners.

The novel begins with mention of two important events in national consciousness, the Civil War and the Great War of 1914-18. Neither holds Nick's attention for more than a moment. Hemingway was to make a career out of recollections of his war; Fitzgerald understands things differently. For him the war is a checkpoint in history, a barrier to the influence of the past. His imagination is sociological. Nick dreams neither of the past nor of the war but rather of the new agenda of the twenties—banking and credit and investment.

The postwar world is free of the past and of its institutions, but it is not free of its own false ideas. When Tom Buchanan informs Nick and the reader that "Civilization's going to pieces" (14), he has probably never said truer words. But he is of course displaying more than he describes. He echoes a vast national debate about immigration, race, science, and art. There is something seriously wrong in America—yet it may be Tom's own class and type that is responsible. He represents a group as idle and mindless as that excoriated by Carlyle in *Past and Present*. There is something wrong with the immoral pursuit of wealth by historical figures like James J. Hill—except that inherited possession seems no better. Fitzgerald's rich boys often pose as guardians of tradition and often adduce a false relationship to public values.

The more we hear about "civilization" in the text and the more we experience its style and morality the more we, like Nick Carraway, make our own withdrawal from the historical moment. History in *The Great Gatsby* can rarely be taken at face value—perhaps it is as suspect as biography. When Tom alludes to his favorite racial or geographical or class prejudices (and when Daisy plays to them) a public dialogue is refracted. The most interesting thing about that dialogue is that many of those "advanced" people who deplore civilization in America *are considerably less attractive than Tom Buchanan*. He only echoes their discourse. What matters is not the specific character (if there is any) to his ideas about "science" or "art" but his reflection of a historical moment in which their discussion is more poisonous than his own. In the summer of 1922 there will be very little use in his appealing to profound texts or Daisy appealing to the most advanced people or Nick appealing to the values of the past—or the reader appealing to a larger and more confidence-inspiring set of standards beyond those governing the action. The allusive context of the novel is meant to disturb and disorient. It is as if Fitzgerald had Balzac in mind, and, describing a milieu in which all things are permitted, made it impossible for protagonists or readers to bring to bear morals and other norms.

As for the issue of "Civilization," that was not to be adjudicated by the defenders (and inventors) of the American past. In 1924, while Fitzgerald was thinking over the story that would become *The Great Gatsby,* the

American Mercury (April 1924) had published a sardonic study of character acquired through consumption: It was richly attentive to certain kinds of ads that showed consumers "how to rise quickly" and "how to become" something other than they were.[30] It noted the increased use of phrases like "wonderful," "astounding," "amazing" and "miraculously" applied to personal change and betterment. In the marketplace of ideas personal identity was itself to become a commodity.

Notes

1. F. Scott Fitzgerald, "Echoes of the Jazz Age," in *The Crack-Up,* ed. Edmund Wilson (New York: New Directions, 1945), p. 15.

2. Frederick James Smith, "Fitzgerald, Flappers and Fame," in *The Romantic Egoists,* ed. Matthew J. Bruccoli, Scottie Fitzgerald Smith, and Joan P. Kerr (New York: Charles Scribner's Sons, 1974), p. 79.

3. The editors feared as a consequence the domination of western Europe by a "militaristic France." Peter Gay writes in *Weimar Culture* (New York: Harper & Row, 1970) that the murder of Walther Rathenau was part of the celebration of the youth culture of the twenties. According to one of Rathenau's assassins, Ernest-Walter Techow, "The younger generation" was "striving for something new, hardly dreamed of. They smelled the morning air. They gathered in themselves an energy charged with the myth of the Prussian-German past, the pressure of the present and the expectation of an unknown future" (p. 87).

4. Fitzgerald, "Echoes of the Jazz Age," p. 15.

5. In a letter to Edmund Wilson the week before the review appeared Fitzgerald admitted that Joyce had caused him to think of his own family history: "I have *Ullyses* [sic] from the Brick Row Bookshop & am starting it. I wish it was layed in America—there is something about middle-class Ireland that depresses me inordinately—I mean gives me a sort of hollow, cheerless pain. Half of my ancestors came from just such an Irish strata or perhaps a lower one. The book makes me feel appallingly naked" (*The Crack-Up,* p. 260). To use the terminology of James R. Mellow, an "invented" life might naturally proceed from these feelings, and a heightened perception of assumed identity in others.

6. "The Unspeakable Egg," a Fitzgerald story that appeared in the *Saturday Evening Post* (July 12, 1924) has the line, "he reminded her of an advertisement for a new car." Reprinted in Matthew J. Bruccoli, ed., *The Price Was High: The Last Uncollected Stories of F. Scott Fitzgerald* (New York: Harcourt Brace Jovanovich, 1979), 128.

7. For a sense of Van Loon's standing see the immensely favorable review of *The Story of Mankind* by Charles A. Beard in the December 21, 1921, issue of *The New Republic.* See also the full-page ad for Van Loon's book, with many blurbs, in the February 1, 1922, issue.

8. William Winter, *The Life of David Belasco,* 2 vols. (New York: Moffat, Yard and Company, 1918) 2:424-27. If there is a solution to Winter's problem that lies in converting art to the display of domestic virtue and history to anti-modernism:

   > If true civilization is to develop and live in our country, such conditions, such a spirit, such ideals, manners, and customs as are widely prevalent among us to-day, must utterly pass and cease. The one rational hope that they will so disappear lies in disseminating EDUCATION. . . . For that education Society must look largely to the ministry of the arts and, in particular, to the rightly conducted Theatre. . . . Few managers have been able to take or to understand that view of the Stage. David Belasco was one of them. It is because his administration of his "great office" has been, in the main, conducted in the spirit of a zealous public servant; because for many years he maintained as a public resort a beautiful theatre, diffusive of the atmosphere of a pleasant, well-ordered home, placing before the public many fine plays, superbly acted, and set upon the stage in a perfection of environment never surpassed anywhere and equalled only by a few of an earlier race of managers, of which he was the last, that David Belasco has, directly and indirectly, exerted an immense influence for good and is entitled to appreciative recognition, enduring celebration, and ever grateful remembrance.

9. George Santayana, *Character and Opinion in the United States* (New York: Doubleday, 1956), vi.

10. Cited by Geoffrey Perrett, *America in the Twenties,* (New York: Simon & Schuster, 1982), p. 79.

11. John Higham, *Strangers in the Land,* (New York: Atheneum, 1965), p. 271.

12. Grant Overton, *American Nights Entertainment* (New York: D. Appleton Company, George Doran Company, Doubleday, Page & Co., Charles Scribner's Sons, 1923), pp. 380-81. I am grateful to James R. Mellow for pointing this book out to me and copying out the passage cited.

13. Overton, *American Nights Entertainment,* pp. 382-83.

14. Irving Babbitt, *Democracy and Leadership* (Boston: Houghton Mifflin, 1924), p. 245. Henry Adams, Henry James, Santayana, Babbitt, Eliot, and Pound are like the *Kulturpessimisten* of Weimar. See the account of the battle against modernity in Walter Lacquer's *Weimar* (New York: Perigee, 1974), pp. 78f. For this side of the Atlantic there is good recent coverage in Eric Sigg's *The American T. S. Eliot* (Cambridge: Cambridge University Press, 1989), pp. 110f. Here is Sigg's ac-

count of Henry James on civilization versus immigration: "For James, ethnic pluralism jeopardized social order and cultural achievement. He assumed that America should and could produce art equal to that of Europe. He further assumed that American high culture would arise from distinctively American elements in the country's tradition, from shared assumptions about education, morality, and manners, and most important, from a common language used and preserved self-consciously. Immigrants offer James another instance of an American incongruity that is at least bathetic indecorum and at worst surrealist horror" (p. 129).

See also Samuel G. Blythe's lead article "Flux," *Saturday Evening Post,* August 19, 1922, pp. 3f. On political leadership Blythe says that "Politics in this country is now guerrilla warfare. It is not even that. It may best be compared to operations by bodies of indignant and disgusted citizens, in various parts of the country, without communication or ordered plan, getting together from sense of protest and going out and shooting in the dark, hoping they may hit something: but shooting anyhow. There is nothing coherent about our politics. There is nothing much articulate about it in its present state. The prime motive in all our demonstrations is protest. The actuating spirit is change." All things are relative: Blythe has a ferocious attack on "the increasing interference of government in private affairs." Liberals distrusted government performance; conservatives like Blythe distrusted its powers, further reasons for the constant adjuration to Americans to be more moral and more Christian.

15. Madison Grant, "America for the Americans," *Reader's Digest* (October 1925) 367-68.

16. Higham, *Strangers in the Land,* p. 273.

17. Harold E. Stearns, ed., *Civilization in the United States* (London: Jonathan Cape, 1922), vii.

18. Ibid., p. 355.

19. Ibid., p. 295.

20. Ibid., p. 228.

21. Walter Lippmann, *Public Opinion* (New York: Macmillan, 1922), pp. 317-65.

22. Ibid., pp. 154-56. See the powerful piece by Augustus Thomas, "The Print of My Remembrance, *Saturday Evening Post,* July 8, 1922, pp. 24f. Thomas apologizes for writing in a good part for a charitable Jewish physician in *As A Man Thinks,* a one-act play at the Lambs, "instead of having him ridiculed as he generally was in the theater." Thomas attributes racial hatred to the Jewish willingness to work as perceived by the more neglectful and lazy "Anglo-Saxon temperament" (94). Even

between liberals and conservatives—racism aside—the debate on cultural differences was framed in terms of the distinction between "Anglo-Saxon" and the rest.

23. H. L. Mencken, *A Mencken Chrestomathy* (New York: Vintage, 1982), p. 491.

24. Ibid., pp. 171-77.

25. See "The Drool Method in History," *American Mercury,* January 1924, pp. 31f.

26. See Perrett, *America in the Twenties,* pp. 159-60: "In 1890 there had been one divorce for every seventeen marriages; by the late twenties there was one for every six . . . novels, plays, and works of social criticism steadily derided marriage as an outmoded institution, something the modern world could well do without. There were confident predictions that marriage would die out before the end of the century."

27. I disagree with the view that American history is present in the text only to the extent that the "materialism" of "the modern American upper class" betrays our national origins. (See Kermit W. Moyer, "*The Great Gatsby*: Fitzgerald's Meditation on American History," in *Critical Essays on F. Scott Fitzgerald's The Great Gatsby,* ed. Scott Donaldson (Boston: G. K. Hall, 1984), pp. 215f. Tom is said to have a "materialist orientation" and "Daisy represents the materialism of her class." But Tom and Daisy are rarely seen evaluating things according to cost nor do they judge experience by material standards. Tom's mind is directed by texts and ideas that, far from having anything to do with materialism, are perfervid distortions of idealism.

28. Cited by Perrett in *America in the Twenties,* p. 88.

29. Max Scheler, *Ressentiment* (Glencoe: Free Press, 1961), p. 52. *Das Ressentiment* appeared in 1915.

30. "American Boobology: A Survey of Current National Advertising Campaigns," *American Mercury,* April 1924, pp. 457-58.

Bryan R. Washington (essay date 1995)

SOURCE: Washington, Bryan R. "The Daisy Chain: *The Great Gatsby* and *Daisy Miller* or the Politics of Privacy." In *The Politics of Exile: Ideology in Henry James, F. Scott Fitzgerald, and James Baldwin,* pp. 35-54. Boston: Northeastern University Press, 1995.

[*In the following essay, Washington compares Henry James's* Daisy Miller *and* Gatsby, *emphasizing the themes of racism, white cultural conservatism, and repressed homosexuality.*]

Beginning with the premise that *The Great Gatsby* revises *Daisy Miller,* the readings that I undertake in this chapter are concerned with various states of panic: sexual, racial, and social. Eve Sedgwick's theory of "homosexual panic," in other words, points toward a dense interpretive terrain extending far beyond, although always implicating, desire. As I have indicated, a repressed homosexuality undergirds "Going to Meet the Man." Moreover, it is associated with (or presented within the context of) racial discord. The idea that homosexuality and race are important for *The Great Gatsby* is hardly startling. Nick's fixation with Gatsby easily suggests flirtation, and his obsession with ethnic origins punctuates the text. But the notion that either homosexuality or race bears any relevance to James's novella may at first seem a critical anachronism.

Winterbourne, who frames the narrative, is a genteel conservator, even an enforcer. But in disciplining Daisy he responds to more than the defiant transgression of class boundaries that the time she spends with Eugenio (a courier) and Giovanelli (a questionable gentleman) represents. Published in 1878, *Daisy Miller* is not only the product of Reconstruction but also a commentary on the social (textual) implications of that era. Disembarking from the *City of Richmond,* Daisy arrives in Europe the incarnation of America after the Civil War, the unsuspecting emblem of "[c]ivilization . . . go[ne] to pieces."[1] The many references to her whiteness invite the speculation that whiteness is in serious jeopardy. But the insistence on whiteness prods blackness, in effect, into the text. Indeed, neither Winterbourne nor finally James can decide whether this new America, this Daisy, is educable, capable of understanding that, if blackness were to penetrate its discourse, James's narrative enterprise would cease to exist. Ignorant of the old textual rules, Daisy is dangerous. The threat she poses to the community of white American exiles imagined does not implicate only the potential assault of race. It also suggests the possible exposure of the homosexual underpinnings bracing not simply *Daisy Miller* but arguably all of James's texts. The effete Winterbourne, the suggestively asexual custodian of haute bourgeois conventions, is as necessary for the survival of James's genteel endeavor as the denial of blackness (or, for that matter, as Daisy herself). She, however, refuses to listen to him, refuses to be allegorized. Daisy prefers the company of comparatively manly men, who—by ushering her out of the drawing room (privileged in the text because it is so private) and through the streets to the public forum of the Roman Colosseum—quite literally put her at physical *and* social risk. His own narrative legitimacy in question, Winterbourne is almost desperate.

Equally (if less ambiguously) panicked, Nick Carraway valorizes the "Middle West"—

> not the wheat or the prairies or the lost Swede towns, but the thrilling returning trains of my youth, and the street lamps and sleigh bells in the frosty dark and the shadows of holly wreaths thrown by lighted windows on the snow. I am part of that, a little solemn with the feel of those long winters, a little complacent from growing up in the Carraway house in a city where dwellings are still called through decades by a family's name.
>
> (177)

Ethnic cohesiveness and familial continuity are exactly the values James assigns to Europe. But the most persuasive indications of *The Great Gatsby*'s Jamesianisms are realized in the figuration of Daisy Buchanan, a woman of apparently irreconcilable dualities. Fitzgerald's Daisy is both a flower of innocence with the power to rescue Nick (and by implication Gatsby as well) from a commodified world and a kind of cultural monster who betrays her creator's Romantic female ideal. As Nina Auerbach argues, "if the American Girl did not exist, James would have had to invent her as a personification of the United States. . . ."[2] Auerbach is concerned to show, and justifiably, that James's female subjects do not result from a steadfast feminism, but rather from the anticipation of a "coming 'common deluge' that threatened to drown the private and fastidious perceptions of art," thereby making it preferable to pay lip service to the rhetoric of the "new woman" rather than endure "the garbage of mass lower-class culture that surged below her."[3]

James's American girl is an invention of narrative conceived to serve a particular cultural end: to halt the displacement of the rarefied, refined, and therefore feminine aesthetic world on which his vision depended by the aggressive, anti-aesthetic, and therefore masculine world of commerce. In the sociohistorical sense, then, the female he portrays may have existed, but she by no means speaks for the whole of America—unless, of course, one assumes that the Americans who matter are white and rich. By contrast, the archetypal female whom Fitzgerald would reclaim *did* exist: she is the preoccupying force in James's most ambitious writing. The "fragment of lost words . . . uncommunicable forever" (112) is the textual past that Fitzgerald aims to recapture. Indeed, it will become clear that the critical work I draw upon, particularly in my discussion of *Daisy Miller,* is similarly invested. Lionel Trilling, William Wasserstrom, F. W. Dupee—all of whom were at their most influential in the 1950s—practiced a conservative readerly politics that contemporary critics generally revalorize.

In *Heiress of All the Ages,* William Wasserstrom sees James as the central figure in the genteel tradition, a tradition he defines as that group of texts concerned to "establish order within the human spirit and in the life of the society."[4] If, as Wasserstrom maintains, the genteel tradition strove to overcome the "vast distances of wilderness, religious disorganization, political disorder, slavery, Civil War, tenements, strikes,"[5] then the texts associated with it did so by attempting to remove themselves from them. Paradoxically, however, when the narrative scene shifts from America as such to Europe (imagined as stable) James's international fictions resonate with the tensions that made America the enemy of his narrative project. The genteel tradition saw democracy as antithetical to art. But, when it appropriated the novel—always new, always in process—as the primary vehicle of its message, it ultimately defeated itself: for the novel constitutes a democracy in and of itself. Few readers of *Daisy Miller,* however, have found solace in the dynamics of democracy animating it. F. W. Dupee, for example, considers Daisy's failure to listen to the voice of Europe intolerable, arguing that she is "a social being without a frame" who "does what she likes because she hardly knows what else to do. Her will is at once strong and weak by reason of the very indistinctness of general claims."[6] Similarly, Wasserstrom sees Daisy as "infantile," "ignorant"—a misguided innocent who "childishly throws away her life."[7]

To the extent that Daisy emblematizes the tension between America's impulse to democratize and Europe's compulsion to create hierarchies, the conflict is resolved only in her death. When Daisy sickens and dies, she is both silenced and, to invoke Bakhtin, "ennobled."[8] Wasserstrom argues that James saw the American girl as the symbol of the "dream of history," as the heiress of a society that is the "heir of all the ages. It became therefore her duty to resolve and transcend all antitheses. When she failed, the result in literature was tragic. But when she brought off the victory, she paid the nation's debt to history."[9] Ideally, then, James's American girl permits the desired union between America and Europe. Her cultural assignment: to "achieve a great marriage in which two great civilizations would be joined."[10]

"Daisy and her mama," Winterbourne insists, "haven't yet risen to that stage of—what shall I call it—culture, at which the idea of catching a count or a *marchese* begins. I believe them intellectually incapable of that conception."[11] Though in the final analysis Winterbourne dismisses Daisy as an indecipherable text ("he soon went back to live at Geneva, whence there continue to come the most contradictory accounts of his motives of sojourn: a report that he's 'studying' hard . . . —much interested in a very clever foreign lady" [74]), his investment in shielding her from the scrutiny of other, potentially more invasive readers (suitors) is considerable. Daisy's conduct with her courier, Eugenio, suggests that she regards him as more than a servant. Indeed, Mrs. Costello pronounces their relationship an "intimacy," arguing that

> there's no other name for such a relation. They treat the courier as a family friend—as a gentleman and a

scholar. I shouldn't wonder if he dines with them. Very likely they've never seen a man with such good manners, such fine clothes, so *like* a gentleman—or a scholar. . . . He probably sits with them in the garden of an evening.

> (17-18)

What is at risk here? The obvious response is that Daisy's crossing the conventional line between "mistress" and "servant" attests to her ineligibility as a genteel heroine. Which would explain Winterbourne's outrage at her ambiguously ardent relationship with Giovanelli, who on Winterbourne's terms is "a music-master or a penny-a-liner or a third-rate artist" (45). Were Giovanelli a member of the Italian nobility, were he for example Prince Amerigo of *The Golden Bowl,* then presumably he would be an appropriate suitor and a potential mate for Daisy, for America. But Daisy's transgressions implicate more than class. The emphasis on her whiteness, as I have suggested, is almost obsessive. At the beginning of the narrative she is "dressed in white muslin, with a hundred frills and flounces and knots of pale-coloured ribbon" (5). Indeed, references to her white dresses, white shoulders, white teeth crowd the text. This iterative whiteness, traditionally read as an affirmation of her virtue, is also simply—complicatedly—whiteness.

We know from *The American Scene* that James was greatly concerned that the country would never recover from the sociocultural split of the Civil War, but he also romanticized the antebellum South, which perhaps accounts for the name of the ship transporting the Millers abroad. Richmond, the capital of the Confederacy, is on the move, in transit. Why? Because white women and children must be evacuated? Implicitly, Daisy's archetypal whiteness is defined against its archetypal opposite, blackness. In short, since she blithely ignores class boundaries, would Daisy be capable of venturing further? Or, in the aftermath of the war, in the aftermath of the Emancipation, had America changed so irrevocably that anything could happen? As her conduct with Eugenio and Giovanelli invites us to speculate, Daisy would conceivably risk her own racial destruction were she permitted to pursue the implications of the social freedoms she embodies. This is what democracy does: it precipitates chaos. In James's tale, race is of course unspeakable. In ***The Great Gatsby,*** however, it dominates the discourse.

If Nick Carraway is Winterbourne unambiguously panicked, Daisy Buchanan is Daisy Miller fully recontextualized:

> "You see I think everything's terrible anyhow," she went on in a convinced way. "Everybody thinks so—the most advanced people. And I *know.* I've been everywhere and seen everything. . . . Sophisticated—God, I'm sophisticated!"

> (18)

Assuming, then, that she is to reenact the drama of American innocence, it is Daisy Buchanan's sophistication that prevents her from fulfilling, as Wasserstrom would argue, her destiny. In *The Great Gatsby* the figuration of women in general suggests an attempt to produce a suitable "heiress"—not of the ages, but to the Jamesian legacy. Daisy (murderous cosmopolite) and Jordan (innocent miller's daughter transcribed to dishonest baker's) are genteel conspirators. But Myrtle, the potentially relentless force in this gendered cultural garden, is expeditiously weeded out because she places male (textual) authority in even greater peril.

Like her namesake, Daisy Buchanan is defined by her whiteness. So is Jordan Baker:

> The only completely stationary object in the room was an enormous couch on which two young women were buoyed up as though upon an anchored balloon. They were both in white, and their dresses were rippling and fluttering as if they had just been blown back in after a short flight around the house.
>
> (8)

If these women can fly, then for Nick they are either angels or witches, saints or sinners. In short, Nick is the prisoner of his own classifications, desperately hoping that these privileged white women are the female archetypes he needs them to be and hopelessly disenchanted when they prove to be more complicated than his allegories of gender would allow.

Richard Godden suggests that Daisy has "repressed her body and cashed in her voice, . . . described as 'full of money.'"[12] For Godden, then, "the structure of Daisy's desire is economic."[13] Myrtle, on the other hand, "is described most frequently in terms of 'blood,' 'flesh,' and 'vitality.'"[14] (Her husband, Wilson, is represented as "blond," "spiritless," and "anaemic," as though his wife has drained him of his vital fluids.) But that Myrtle, in contrast to Daisy, is a woman who is entirely physical is not, as Godden maintains, a function of her lack of commitment to "the production of manners" or to the trappings of the leisure class. Her New York apartment, for example—"crowded to the doors with a set of tapestried furniture entirely too large for it, so that to move about was to stumble continually over scenes of ladies swinging in the gardens of Versailles" (29)—strives to achieve the elegance of Daisy's house on Long Island. Like everyone else in the novel, Myrtle is a bracketed figure whom Nick "reveals" to us. The woman he presents is literally Daisy in-the-flesh, ominous because of her social aspirations and because of her almost manly sexuality.

Myrtle's purchases, made en route to the apartment that Tom has procured for her, point up her ambition and her ignorance: "a copy of *Town Tattle* and a moving-picture magazine, . . . some cold cream and a small flask of perfume," and, finally, a puppy of an "indeterminate breed" (27). This, then, is a woman who has yet to learn the difference between mongrels and Airedales, between gossip magazines and the social register. In a text preoccupied with and intolerant of the racial and social hybridization of America, Myrtle's most unforgivable sin is perhaps her inability to distinguish a hybrid from a thoroughbred. Her lack of judgment applies not only to dogs but also, apparently, to men. Nick reports that Myrtle married her husband because she thought "he knew something about breeding, but," she adds, "he wasn't fit to lick my shoe" (35). But Myrtle, of course, knows nothing of breeding. The testimony of her narrow escape immediately follows her sister's narrative about an abortive affair with a Jew: "I almost married a little kike who'd been after me for years. I knew he was below me. Everybody kept saying to me: 'Lucille, that man's way below you!' But if I hadn't met Chester, he'd of got me sure" (34).

And yet, always conscious of the boundaries he transgresses, Nick too is a nativist:

> As we *crossed* [my emphasis] Blackwell's Island a limousine passed us, driven by a white chauffeur, in which sat three modish negroes [*sic*], two bucks and a girl. I laughed aloud as the yolks of their eyeballs rolled toward us in haughty rivalry.
>
> (69)

His conclusion: "Anything can happen now that we've slid over this bridge, . . . anything at all . . ." (69). Nick's is the laughter of terror, for the black men he depicts have literally passed him by. The encounter, it seems, is so disconcerting that the overtaking passengers are denied voice.

In *Modernism and the Harlem Renaissance,* Houston Baker laments Fitzgerald's failure to place "his 'pale well-dressed negro' [the black man who identifies the car that kills Myrtle] in the limousine,"[15] suggesting that had Fitzgerald done so he would have acknowledged the legitimacy of the Harlem Renaissance—the black writers of the 1920s, many of whom were indeed "pale." He would, in short, have overturned the racial stereotype of black inarticulacy upheld in the text. Moreover, the presence of "pale-skinned" blacks confirms the worst fears of those who foresee the dissolution of Anglo-Saxon supremacy. For to be pale-skinned *and* African American is to be—like Myrtle's dog—a mongrel.

Nick's reaction to the blacks in the limousine recalls Tom Buchanan's unabashed racism:

> Civilization's going to pieces. . . . I've gotten to be a terrible pessimist about things. Have you read 'The Rise of the Colored Empires' by this man God-

dard? . . . Well, it's a fine book, and everybody ought to read it. The idea is if we don't look out the white race will be—will be utterly submerged. It's all scientific stuff; it's been proved. . . . It's up to us, who are the dominant race, to watch out or these other races will have control of things.

(13)

Though Tom misidentifies the author (the reference is to Lothrop Stoddard's *Rising Tide of Color against White Supremacy,* prominently displayed in Gatsby's library), his views are corroborated in the novel as a whole. Camouflaged in the discourse of the fall of civilization or of a remembered but unattainable past, Fitzgerald's subtext, to which Tom points, encodes a darker message. As Baker argues, Tom might be "a more honestly self-conscious representation of the threat that some artists whom we call 'modern' felt in the face of a new world of science, war, technology, and imperialism. . . . What really seems under threat are not towers of civilization but rather an assumed supremacy of boorishly racist, indisputably sexist, and unbelievably wealthy Anglo-Saxon males."[16]

Myrtle's ineptitude when it comes to identifying the breed of dogs or men equates with Nick's inability to determine who Gatsby is. Nick says of his mysterious neighbor: "I knew I had discovered a man of fine breeding after I talked with him an hour. I said to myself: 'There's the kind of man you'd like to take home and introduce to your mother and sister'" (73). As I shall demonstrate, this is an intricate textual moment. Arguably, it is at this point that Nick's readiness to welcome Gatsby to the nativist family, to extend a fraternal embrace, is at its most pronounced. Given his earlier reservations about his background, Nick's renewed conviction that Gatsby is indeed a "man of fine breeding" can be read as an ethnological sigh of relief:

> I would have accepted without question the information that Gatsby sprang from the swamps of Louisiana or from the lower East Side of New York. That was comprehensible. But young men didn't—at least in my provincial inexperience I believed they didn't—drift coolly out of nowhere and buy a palace on Long Island Sound.
>
> (49)

And thus when it is finally disclosed that Jay Gatsby is Jimmy Gatz and possibly more than merely casually connected with Meyer Wolfsheim ("a small, flat-nosed Jew" with tufts of hair in his nostrils and "tiny eyes" [69-70]), why Gatsby's ambiguous ancestry, his questionable past, is intolerable to Nick begins to make sense. To say that "Jay Gatsby of West Egg, Long Island, sprang from his Platonic conception of himself" (99) is to confirm that he is the worst kind of outsider. Gatsby, unlike Daisy and Tom (Nick's distant cousins), is of no relation. He is as much a threat to the "fam-ily"—to the "Middle West," to the white cultural center—as Myrtle, the "black bucks" in the limousine, or Wolfsheim.

But complicating the deliberation over bringing Gatsby home is desire itself. Does Nick speak as a man, a woman, or both? Like Eliot's Tiresias, Nick is "within and without, simultaneously enchanted and repelled by the inexhaustible variety of life" (36)—capable, that is, of being both male and female, Jew and gentile, black and white. Insofar as *The Great Gatsby* is indebted to *The Waste Land,* its commitment to salvaging whatever is left of "civilization" (as with poem) is articulated by one "in whom the two sexes meet."[17] The androgynous Tiresias bears witness to a culture in decline. He attests to the imminent demise not only of Europe (as text) but also of its institutions (implicitly the Church) and the strictly enforced hierarchies that fostered them. The "typist home at tea time" is an outrage and a devastation precisely because she is a typist—reductio ad absurdum of Philomel.

If Nick is like Tiresias, he is also like the sexually neutral Winterbourne. When he looks at Daisy, when he "stud[ies]" her, Winterbourne's gaze is not that of a potential suitor, but instead that of a decorous cultural chaperone searching for a charge who will behave. Fitzgerald's revision of James's tale foregrounds the deeper narrative implications of her misconduct. As I have pointed out, Myrtle is Daisy's déclassé double. Just as she is socially presumptuous, she is also physically overwhelming: her clothing "stretche[s] tight over her rather wide hips," and her figure is "thickish," "faintly stout." Nick observes that "she carried her surplus flesh sensuously as some women can. Her face . . . contained no facet or gleam of beauty, but there was an immediately perceptible vitality about her as if the nerves of her body were continually smouldering" (25-26). As Nick conceives it, Myrtle's sexuality is aggressive, masculine; her body authoritative. She is a match for Tom and thus a threat to Tom, who breaks her nose. Indeed, her "smouldering" presence is so disruptive that she has to be contained, locked up in Wilson's house. And when she breaks free, shouting "Beat me! . . . Throw me down and beat me, you dirty little coward!" she runs to her death. But killing her is not enough. Her "left breast . . . swinging loose like a flap [and her] mouth . . . wide open and ripped at the corners" (138), she is also mutilated, and her sexual power (in effect) neutralized.

There is an element of misogyny at work here that further problematizes the figuration of Nick. What values are assigned to him? Does the bald revulsion at female sexuality suggest homosexual panic? If it does, then *The Great Gatsby* affirms the cliché that for homosexuals women, appetitive and predatory, are terrifying. On these homophobic terms, Myrtle is loathsome because, defined only by body, she makes it impossible for Nick to romanticize male-female relationships, to see them as anything other than base, physical exchange. On the other hand, Nick's disgust with Myrtle is conceivably Winterbourne's frustration with Daisy laid bare. The stereotypical homosexual sensibility we confront, which James's work authorizes, is one repelled by a female figure whose gross ignorance and unfailing disobedience are the enemy of manners. Myrtle (desire incarnate) and Daisy (desire disembodied) are "monstrous doubles," and thus one of them must be sacrificed. In other words, René Girard's theory of myth and ritual is in this context quite useful. For Myrtle can be read as a "surrogate victim" whose death results (or is meant to result) in the restoration of order to the community.[18]

The Great Gatsby co-opts James's figure of the hotel as a "synonym" for America's social disintegration. As James said of the Waldorf Astoria, "one is verily tempted to ask if the hotel-spirit may not just *be* the American spirit most seeking and most finding itself."[19] Indeed, in *Daisy Miller* the social critique of the hotel, which "represents the abolition of privacy and decency,"[20] is buried in the discourse of the aesthetic. Describing the rooms the Millers have taken in Rome, Daisy defers to Eugenio, who considers them the best in the city. But the aesthetic judgments of an Italian courier are in James's hierarchicized world less than worthless. "Splendid" though they may be, these rooms are nevertheless public accommodation. Giving voice to the "mysterious land of dollars and six-shooters," Daisy's brother Randolph makes it clear that the Millers are accustomed to a superabundance of gilded space: "We've got a bigger place than this. . . . It's all gold on the walls" (37). Indeed, Daisy's mother's imagination is the captive of the hostelry: "'I guess we'll go right back to the hotel,' she remarked with a confessed failure of the *larger* [my emphasis] imagination" (41). The cultural vision of Americans like these, then, is truncated. And yet the imaginative capability privileged in the text is smaller, not larger. The Millers are reproved for their attraction to the gigantic, the overstuffed, the overgilded, and the distinctly public. They are exhorted to narrow their scope, to exclude themselves from mass society—to be small.

When Daisy Buchanan decamps to her lover's house, Gatsby essentially shuts down the inn: "the whole caravansary had fallen in like a card house at the disapproval in her eyes" (114). In penetrating Gatsby's territory, then, Daisy is a potentially civilizing (privatizing) force:

> She was appalled by West Egg, this unprecedented "place" that Broadway had begotten upon a Long Island fishing village—appalled by its raw vigor that chafed under the old euphemisms and by the too obtrusive fate that herded its inhabitants along a short-cut from nothing to nothing.
>
> (108)

Gatsby's sprawling house (and by extension all that occurs there) repels because it is a phenomenon rather than a "place," an augury of things to come. It is a luxurious "roadhouse" to which all are admitted, a "factual imitation of some Hôtel de Ville in Normandy, with a tower on one side, spanking new under a thin beard of raw ivy, . . . and more than forty acres of lawn and garden" (5). The owner of this "colossal affair" is a kind of aesthetic criminal whose "art" Nick condemns—a reaction immediately undermining the reliability of a narrator who announces in the ninth line of the text that he is "inclined to reserve all judgments" (1). For, if nothing else, *The Great Gatsby* is a litany of judgments of the most reactionary sort.

In contrast to Gatsby's ersatz residence, Nick's "small eyesore" of a house is the ideologically privileged trysting place for Daisy and Gatsby. It is a model of privacy. Though, as Gatsby deduces, Nick "doesn't make much money," he is nevertheless perfectly capable of producing an afternoon tea that certifies his pedigree. Replete with lemons and lemon cakes and prepared by a female servant (unnamed, dismissed as "my Finn" [113]), the haute bourgeois tea that Nick serves to friends suggests that his house is a "home." The parvenu Gatsby, on the other hand, is host to endless caravans of visitors whom he does not know. Klipspringer, for example, is a permanent but unidentified guest—a visible indication of the social phantasmagoria Gatsby's way of life represents, as are the nightly parties themselves. Gatsby's guests are "swimmers," "wanderers," anonymous "groups [that] change more swiftly, swell with new arrivals, [and] dissolve and form in the same breath," "confident girls who . . . glide on through the seachange of . . . men pushing young girls backward in eternal graceless circles" (41, 46). Gatsby's parties play out the "Jazz History of the World," the music Nick remembers from the first party he attends. Jazz is, in Nick's eyes, the music of commerce, its syncopations and rhythms, as Theodor Adorno argues, defined by the demands of the marketplace.[21] Indiscriminate, catering to the masses, jazz, in other words, speaks for Gatsby.

Matthew Bruccoli insists that "*The Great Gatsby* provides little in the way of sociological or anthropological data,"[22] which is another way of saying that its meanings transcend their historical context. Why dehistoricize the text? To safeguard its status as a "classic"? Consider, for example, the names of some of Gatsby's guests: Blackbuck, the Poles, Da Fontano, Don S. Schwartze, Horace O'Donovan, and the Kellehers. These clearly attest to Fitzgeraldian outrage at the new America, one in which so-called ethnics are ubiquitous—in which the citizens of East Egg, who form a "dignified homogeneity" in the midst of the "many-colored, many-keyed commotion" (45, 105), must contend not only with the inhabitants of West Egg but with all of New York.

"On week-ends . . . [Gatsby's] Rolls-Royce [later characterized as "swollen . . . in its monstrous length with triumphant hat-boxes and supper-boxes, and terraced with a labyrinth of wind-shield that mirrored a dozen suns" (54)] became an omnibus, bearing parties to and from the city between nine in the morning and long past midnight, while his station wagon scampered . . . to meet *all* [my emphasis] trains" (39). And ready to welcome the masses stands Gatsby—a fraudulent feudal lord in command of a serfdom of household staff charged with keeping the whole thing going: "on Mondays eight servants, including an extra gardener, toiled all day with mops and . . . garden-shears, repairing the ravages of the night before" (39). And "every Friday five crates of oranges and lemons . . . left his back door in a pyramid of pulpless halves. There was a machine in the kitchen which could extract the juice of two hundred oranges in half an hour if a little button was pressed two hundred times by a butler's thumb" (39).

The details of Gatsby's household evoke James's Newport "white elephants," the enormous "cottages" of the summering rich that in *The American Scene* have replaced the quaint abodes James knew in his youth:

> [I]t was all so beautiful, so solitary and so "sympathetic." And that indeed has been, thanks to the "pilers-on-of gold," the fortune, the history of its beauty: that it now bristles with the villas and palaces into which the cottages have all turned, and that those monuments of pecuniary power rise thick and close, precisely, in order that their occupants may constantly remark to each other, from the windows to the "ground," and from house to house, that it *is* beautiful, it *is* solitary and sympathetic.[23]

The edifices that "rise thick and close" in Newport are in *Gatsby* faithfully reproduced: Nick's house is "squeezed between two huge places that rented for twelve or fifteen thousand a season" (5).

In *Slouching towards Bethlehem,* Joan Didion, also horrified by the crumbling of traditional values (although she attributes the erosion to the social upheaval of the 1960s), returns to James's Newport to report, quoting *The American Scene* almost verbatim, that "no aesthetic judgment could conceivably apply to the Newport of Bellevue Avenue," where "the air proclaims only the sources of money" and where "the houses [like Gatsby's] are men's houses, factories, undermined by tunnels and service railways, shot through with plumbing to collect salt water, tanks to store it, devices to collect rain water, vaults for table silver, equipment inventories of china and crystal and 'Tray cloths—fine' and 'Tray cloths—ordinary.'"[24] On these elitist terms, Gatsby's house is the quintessential male (public) bastion that presumably could be gentrified under the supervision of a woman like Daisy, whose taste Nick both endorses and replicates. The contrast, in fact, between Daisy's house and her lover's is striking: it is an architectonic utopia,

> a cheerful red-and-white Georgian Colonial mansion, overlooking the bay. The lawn started at the beach and ran toward the front door for a quarter of a mile, jumping over sun-dials and brick walks and burning gardens—finally when it reached the house drifting up the side in bright vines as though from the momentum of its run. The front was broken by a line of French windows, glowing now with reflected gold and wide open to the warm windy afternoon.
>
> (6-7)

Daisy's house is not only a model of tasteful (though conspicuous) consumption, effortlessly marrying the best of Europe with the best of America, and subtly enshrining a woman who has "been everywhere and done everything." It also embodies the natural elegance associated with Daisy Miller—as though she has finally forsaken the hotel. The Buchanan mansion is an extension of the landscape surrounding it: "The windows were ajar and gleaming white against the fresh grass outside that seemed to grow a little way into the house. A breeze blew through the room, blew curtains in at one end and out the other like pale flags, twisting them up toward the frosted wedding-cake of the ceiling, and then rippled over the wine-colored rug, making a shadow on it as wind does on the sea" (8).

Gatsby's house, by contrast, is "unnatural," not simply because of the way it imposes itself on the landscape or because of who is invited there but also because of its interior. Rather than achieving a sanctified marriage with Europe, equated in East Egg with nature itself, Gatsby's "palace" is represented as the product of a cultural rape, as a kind of bastardized museum in which visitors wander through "Marie Antoinette music-rooms and Restoration salons" (92) unable to detect an organizing logic beneath the labyrinth of exhibits. The house is so clearly designed to accommodate the public that, during a private tour with Gatsby as guide, Nick suspects that there are "guests concealed behind every couch and table, under orders to be breathlessly silent until we had passed through" (92). The most significant room, given what it says about Gatsby, is the "Merton College Library" (92)—de rigueur for a self-invented Oxford man: "we [Nick and Jordan] tried an important-looking door, and walked into a high Gothic library, panelled with carved English oak, and probably transported complete from some ruin overseas" (45). Here a "middle-aged man, with enormous owl-eyed spectacles," exclaims that the books are "absolutely real—have pages and everything. I thought they'd be a nice durable cardboard" (45-46). They are not. The pages, however, are uncut. Gatsby, as untutored as Daisy Miller, does not read: his books are merely part of the inventory.

The novel's climactic scene unfolds in the Plaza Hotel. As though guests at one of Gatsby's parties, the principal players in the text are "herded" into a single "stifling" room—their private drama acted out in what is effectively a theater. Tom and Daisy's marriage is a corporate merger. Gatsby (the Arrow Shirt man) and Daisy (whose voice itself sounds like money) are equally commodified. The reified "personal" relationships and disintegrating traditional values Nick perceives are symptomatic of a country that for him, as for Fitzgerald, has become uninhabitable. "Nowadays," Tom says, "people begin by sneering at family life and family institutions, and next they'll throw everything overboard and have intermarriage between black and white" (130). Though Nick dismisses this outburst as "impassioned gibberish" (130), as the hypocritical response of a man who has suddenly transformed himself from "libertine to prig" (131), his own view of the American dilemma bolsters Tom's.

The celebrated concluding paragraphs of **The Great Gatsby** compose a reactionary social manifesto dressed up in the romantic rhetoric of loss. But a loss of what? Of innocence? Of the promise of spiritual perfectibility that the idea of America held out to its colonizers? As Baldwin suggests in "Stranger in the Village," the answer depends on whether, ancestrally, one is a conqueror or one of the conquered. Readers who are not descended from the "Dutch sailors" invoked may wonder at Lionel Trilling's depoliticizing and still largely unquestioned assessment of a writer now unavoidable: "the root of Fitzgerald's heroism is to be found . . . in his power of love."[25]

As it turns out, Daisy was always a discursive failure. In both narratives, women are exhorted to save "America," which is to say a particular textual tradition whose values and assumptions about what a culture should properly do and be are in jeopardy. Figuring America a cultural battlefield, James advocates evacuation, manning a textual lifeboat bearing the refugee of sanctified white womanhood. Awaiting Daisy stands the ultimately ineffectual Winterbourne, whose refined (homosexual?) sensibility, whose valorization of Europe (represented as the *only* culture) is crucial to James's work as a whole. However, Daisy's baggage, the conflicts of class and race with which—from the very beginning—she is ineluctably associated, proves too heavy; thus she is disciplined, and finally punished by death.

As an illustration of the sense of urgency underscoring the discourse of white American exiles, **The Great Gatsby** is clear enough. **Tender Is the Night,** however,

to which I am about to turn, brings both Fitzgerald's social agenda and his ongoing dialogue with James into sharper focus. The opening paragraph, for example, depicting a hotel "on the pleasant shore of the French Riviera,"[26] is James's synonym for America invoked yet again. Gausse's Hôtel des Étrangers is isolated from its surroundings: bounded on all sides by mountain ranges, pine forests, "the pink and cream . . . fortifications of Cannes," and by the sea itself, where "[m]erchantmen crawled westward [i.e., to America, the land of commerce] on the horizon" (9). Inscribing a "littoral [cut off] from true Provençal France" (9) and populated by Americans as contemptible as the Buchanans, **Tender Is the Night** is a meditation on boundaries and thresholds.

Recalling James's nostalgia for the old Newport, Fitzgerald suggests that his Riviera was once a place of genteel beauty, where the "cupolas of a dozen old villas rotted like water lilies among the massed pines" (9)—was once untouched by the "pilers-on-of gold." And there are further references to James—especially to *Daisy Miller.* Geneva, Zurich, Vevey, the Swiss cities dominating the map of Daisy's European experience, are Dick Diver's familiar haunts. As with Daisy, his education begins in Switzerland, and he also hails from the same American region. Daisy is from Schenectady; Dick is from Buffalo. But in Fitzgerald's text, Switzerland is more than the backdrop for a tragicomedy of manners dramatizing the differences between Europeanized Americans and parochial patriots: it is "the true centre of the Western World" (167).

Notes

1. F. Scott Fitzgerald, *The Great Gatsby* (1925; reprint, New York: Scribner's, 1953), 13. Subsequent page references are to this edition.

2. Nina Auerbach, *Communities of Women: An Idea in Fiction* (Cambridge: Harvard University Press, 1978), 122.

3. Ibid., 116.

4. William Wasserstrom, *Heiress of All the Ages* (Minneapolis: University of Minnesota Press, 1959), ix.

5. Ibid., x.

6. F. W. Dupee, *Henry James* (1951; reprint, New York: William Morrow, 1974), 110-11.

7. Wasserstrom, *Heiress of All the Ages,* 63.

8. Bakhtin argues that discourse in the novel straddles two stylistic lines. Novels of the first type "eliminate their brute heteroglossia [the competing linguistic forces derived from everyday speech that Bakhtin maintains are unique to the novel], replacing it everywhere with a single-

imaged, 'ennobled' language." Novels of this category, then, homogenize difference. Novels of the second type, however, incorporate a multiplicity of "languages, manners, genres; . . . [they] force all exhausted and used-up, all socially and ideologically alien and distant worlds to speak for themselves in their own language and in their own style. . . ." M. M. Bakhtin, *The Dialogic Imagination,* ed. Michael Holquist, trans. Caryl Emerson and Michael Holquist (Austin: University of Texas Press, 1981), 409-10.

And yet, just as the author's intentions are dialogically linked with these languages, they are also dialogically opposed to them, thereby energizing the text with unresolved conflict. The two styles of novelistic discourse Bakhtin identifies are sometimes present within the same text, and so the reader must contend not only with heteroglossia but also with oppositional modes of discourse. Such is the case with *Daisy Miller.* Bakhtinian theory, of course, assumes a democratic reader.

9. Wasserstrom, *Heiress of All the Ages,* x.

10. Ibid., 65.

11. Henry James, *Daisy Miller,* in *Selected Fiction,* ed. Leon Edel (New York: Dutton, 1964), 61-62. Subsequent page references are to this edition.

12. Richard Godden, "Some Slight Shifts in the Manner of the Novel of Manners," in *Henry James: Fiction as History,* ed. Ian F. A. Bell (London: Vision, 1984), 162.

13. Ibid.

14. Ibid., 168.

15. Houston A. Baker, Jr., *Modernism and the Harlem Renaissance* (Chicago: University of Chicago Press, 1987), 6.

16. Ibid., 4.

17. T. S. Eliot, "Notes on 'The Waste Land,'" in *The Complete Poems and Plays: 1909-1950* (New York: Harcourt, 1971), 152.

18. René Girard, *Violence and the Sacred,* trans. Patrick Gregory (Baltimore: Johns Hopkins University Press, 1977), 95.

19. Henry James, *The American Scene,* ed. Leon Edel (1907; Bloomington: Indiana University Press, 1968), 102.

20. Virginia Fowler, *Henry James's American Girl: The Embroidery on the Canvas* (Madison: University of Wisconsin Press, 1984), 16.

21. See Theodor W. Adorno, "Jazz," in *Prisms,* trans. Samuel and Shierry Weber (1967; Cambridge: MIT Press, 1984), 121-32.

22. Matthew J. Bruccoli, introduction to *New Essays on "The Great Gatsby,"* ed. Matthew J. Bruccoli, The American Novel 2 (Cambridge: Cambridge University Press, 1985), 7.

23. James, *The American Scene,* 212.

24. Joan Didion, *Slouching towards Bethlehem* (1968; reprint, New York: Touchstone, 1979), 211-12.

25. Lionel Trilling, *The Liberal Imagination* (New York: Viking, 1950), 244.

26. F. Scott Fitzgerald, *Tender Is the Night* (1934; reprint, New York: Scribner's, 1962), 9. Subsequent page references are to this edition.

John F. Callahan (essay date fall 1996)

SOURCE: Callahan, John F. "F. Scott Fitzgerald's Evolving American Dream: The 'Pursuit of Happiness' in *Gatsby, Tender Is the Night,* and *The Last Tycoon.*" *Twentieth Century Literature* 42 (fall 1996): 374-95.

[*In the following essay, Callahan examines various manifestations of the idea of the American dream as it evolved in three Fitzgerald novels.*]

Since the first stirrings of the F. Scott Fitzgerald revival in the 1940s, readers have been fascinated by the oppositions in his work and character. Critics from several different generations have noted how Fitzgerald used his conflicts to explore the origins and fate of the American dream and the related idea of the nation.[1] The contradictions he experienced and put into fiction heighten the implications of the dream for individual lives: the promise and possibilities, violations and corruptions of those ideals of nationhood and personality "dreamed into being," as Ralph Ellison phrased it, "out of the chaos and darkness of the feudal past."[2] Fitzgerald embodied in his tissues and nervous system the fluid polarities of American experience: success and failure, illusion and disillusion, dream and nightmare.

"I did not care what it was all about," Hemingway's Jake Barnes confessed in *The Sun Also Rises.* "All I wanted to know was how to live in it."[3] Fitzgerald, who named and chronicled that brash, schizophrenic decade, was no stranger to the dissipation of values and the pursuit of sensation in the Jazz Age of the 1920s. But for all that, he strained to know what life is all about *and* how to live in it. To him, Hemingway's *it* was not simply existence and the soul's dark night of melancholia and despair. It also stood for an American reality that, combined with "an extraordinary gift for hope" and a "romantic readiness,"[4] led to the extravagant promise identified with America and the intense, devastating loss felt when the dream fails in one or another of its guises.

Face to face with his own breakdown, Fitzgerald traced his drastic change of mind and mood in his letters and *Crack-Up* pieces. From the conviction during his amazing early success in his 20s that "life was something you dominated if you were any good,"[5] Fitzgerald, at the end of his life, came to embrace "the sense that life is essentially a cheat and its conditions are those of defeat, and that the redeeming things are not 'happiness and pleasure' but the deeper satisfactions that come out of struggle."[6] Abraham Lincoln was Fitzgerald's American exemplar of this "wise and tragic sense of life" (Turnbull, *Letters* [*L*] 96). And in *The Last Tycoon* (*LT*) he associates Monroe Stahr's commitment to lead the movie industry closer to an ideal mix of art and entertainment with Lincoln's creative response to the contradictions of American democracy embodied in the Union.

Fitzgerald's invocation of Lincoln recalls the proud and humble claim he made to his daughter from Hollywood. "I don't drink," he wrote; then, as if freed from a demon's grasp, he recounted the inner civil war he fought to keep his writer's gift intact: "I am not a great man, but sometimes I think the impersonal and objective quality of my talent and the sacrifices of it, in pieces, to preserve its essential value have some sort of epic grandeur." "Some sort" he qualifies, as if preparing for the ironic, self-deflating admission in the next sentence. "Anyhow after hours I nurse myself with delusions of that sort" (*L* 62, 61). But Fitzgerald did preserve the "essential value" of his talent; the pages he left confirm that. Like Lincoln who lived only long enough to sketch out what a truly reconstructed nation might look like, Fitzgerald was defeated in his attempt to finish his last novel. Yet what he wrote is all the more poignant because, finished, *The Last Tycoon* might have recast and reformulated the intractable oppositions of *The Great Gatsby* and *Tender Is the Night*.

"The test of a first rate intelligence," Fitzgerald wrote in *The Crack-Up* (Wilson, *CU*), that posthumous collection full of his sinewy, mature, self-reliant thought, "is the ability to hold two opposed ideas in the mind at the same time and still retain the ability to function" (*CU* 69). By *function*, Fitzgerald means more than cope; he's affirming that readiness to act in the world with something approaching one's full powers—"a willingness of the heart" combined with enabling critical intelligence. Fitzgerald's fictional alter egos, Jay Gatsby and Dick Diver, lost this stance of simultaneous detachment and engagement, if they ever possessed it, for they could live in the world only with a single, consuming mission. In his life, Fitzgerald, too, had to steel himself against the tendency toward Gatsby's self-destroying romantic obsession, and like Diver, he had to wrench free from the opposed, complimentary shoals of identification and alienation in his marriage with Zelda.

After *Tender Is the Night* and before his fresh start in Hollywood in 1937, Fitzgerald reflected on his earlier search for an equilibrium of craft, reputation, and power as expressed in the literary vocation and his large personal ambition. "It seemed," he remembered,

> a romantic business to be a successful literary man— you were not ever going to be as famous as a movie star but what note you had was probably longer-lived— you were never going to have the power of a man of strong political or religious convictions but you were certainly more independent.

To the end, like the vivid, still-evolving Monroe Stahr in *The Last Tycoon,* Fitzgerald stays in motion, keeps the dialectic between life and craft going, if not to resolution—"Of course within the practice of your trade you were forever unsatisfied" (*CU* 69-70)—at least in pursuit of new and unrealized novelistic possibilities. "But I, for one, would not have chosen any other" (*CU* 69-70), he concludes, and keeps faith with his vocation by writing about craft and character in the life of a gifted movie man, whose form Fitzgerald feared might subordinate the novel, "which at my maturity was the strongest and supplest medium for conveying thought and emotion from one human being to another," to "a mechanical and communal art that, whether in the hands of Hollywood merchants or Russian idealists, was capable of rendering only the tritest thought, the most obvious emotion" (*CU* 78).

Meeting Irving Thalberg, Fitzgerald becomes more open to the craft of the movies as practiced in Hollywood. Like Fitzgerald the novelist, Monroe Stahr produces movies, not opportunistically (for the most part) but from within. There is a fluidity to Fitzgerald's conception of Stahr missing from Gatsby and his dream, so ill defined in its worldly guise, so obsessive and absolute in its fixation on Daisy; and missing also from the aspiring hubris of Dick Diver, trapped by his misguided, innocent mingling of love and vocation in his dream of personality in *Tender Is the Night.* Stahr, like the writer who created him, learns that daring to function can be a first step toward loosening the paralyzing grip of "opposed ideas."

Fitzgerald's characters, like the seismograph alluded to in *Gatsby,* register changes in his sensibility. Not that Monroe Stahr is Fitzgerald; like the others, he is a composite character. "There never was a good biography of a good novelist," Fitzgerald wrote in his notebook. "He's too many people if he's any good." Nevertheless, Fitzgerald put into Stahr's character much of the awareness he came to have in the melancholy troubled years after *Tender Is the Night.* "Life, ten years ago," he wrote in 1936, "was largely a personal matter." Without telling how that's changed but making it clear that it has, Fitzgerald confronted his present imperative:

> I must hold in balance the sense of the futility of effort and the sense of the necessity to struggle; the convic-

tion of the inevitability of failure and the determination to "succeed"—and, more than these, the contradiction between the dead hand of the past and the high intentions of the future.

(*CU* 177, 70)

To be sure, Fitzgerald did not always hold these contradictions of mind and will, memory and imagination, in equilibrium. But increasingly, as he worked on *The Last Tycoon* during his last year and a half in Hollywood, he sensed a progression from his earlier novels—enough that he strove to set a standard mingling intelligence with "a willingness of the heart." Intelligence identifies and holds in suspension "opposed ideas," but the "ability to function" in the midst of what Keats called "uncertainties, mysteries, doubts"[7] follows from that "willingness of the heart" Fitzgerald identified as a peculiarly intense American urge to do something about one's condition, to take risks for a better self, a better life, a better nation. "For example," Fitzgerald wrote, illustrating his embrace of contradiction, "one ought to be able to see that things are hopeless and still be determined to make them otherwise" (*CU* 64). So he was. And as a writer, until the end of his life, Fitzgerald linked his pursuit of craft and personality, if not any longer simply happiness—"the natural state of the sentient adult is a qualified unhappiness" (*CU* 84)—with the unfolding story of America.

Perhaps because of Fitzgerald's struggles and his paradoxical, sometimes exhilarated serenity alongside the pain and loss reflected in the diminishing hourglass of his life, in *The Last Tycoon* he was able at least to break the stalemate between previously opposed ideas. For this reason, Fitzgerald's passing before he could finish *The Last Tycoon* is an incalculable loss, only to be guessed at from the drafts he left, however much in progress, and his rich, copious notes, charts, and outlines. With Hollywood as milieu and the producer Stahr as protagonist, the American dream becomes even more identified with the urge to integrate private and public pursuits of happiness than in Fitzgerald's other novels.

In *The Last Tycoon* Fitzgerald does for the American dream what Ralph Ellison argues every serious novel does for the craft of fiction. Even as a fragment, the work extends the range of idea and phenomena associated with the dream. As a man and a writer, he became at home in that country of discipline and craft he had discovered but, later lamented, did not truly settle down in it until it was too late. As he wrote to his daughter Scottie, a student and aspiring writer at Vassar, I wish I'd said "at the end of *The Great Gatsby*: 'I've found my line—from now on this comes first. This is my immediate duty—without this I am nothing'" (*L* 79). In 1939 and 1940, *The Last Tycoon* did come first. But burdened with expenses, lacking the quick, lucrative *Saturday Evening Post* markets of his youth, lacking in

any case the "romantic readiness" to write stories with happy endings, and in sporadic, failing health, Fitzgerald had to balance his novel with other work, and eke it out in pieces. Nevertheless, he ended up a writer's writer. From that single window, he looked beyond his circumstances and saw the American dream not as a personal matter and no longer a nostalgic, romantic possibility but as a continuing defining characteristic of the American nation and its people. Far from being behind him, as Nick Carraway had claimed in *The Great Gatsby,* the dream, refigured in *The Last Tycoon,* is a recurring phenomenon in each phase, place, and guise of Fitzgerald's imagination of American experience.

The American story, Fitzgerald wrote late in life, "is the history of all aspiration—not just the American dream but the human dream. . . ."[8] The story that Fitzgerald told was his version of a dream hauntingly personal and national. "When I was your age," he wrote his daughter in 1938, "I lived with a great dream. The dream grew and I learned how to speak of it and make people listen." Like Keats, who, Fitzgerald imagined, was sustained to the end by his "hope of being among the English poets" (*CU* 81), Fitzgerald aspired to be among the novelists. But, as he confessed to his daughter in a bone-scraping passage, he compromised his artist's dream by indulging the very thing that inspired it—romantic love. Of his marriage to Zelda, he wrote in retrospect, "I was a man divided—she wanted me to work too much for *her* and not enough for my dream" (*L* 32). The imbalance Fitzgerald attributed to Zelda was also his own tension and tendency. Nevertheless, what gave his life and work such fascination was exactly that dream of mingling craft and accomplishment with love—first with Zelda, and at the end in more muted fashion with Sheilah Graham, his companion in Hollywood.

In its American guise, the dream Fitzgerald sought to realize flowed from that most elusive and original of the rights proclaimed by the Declaration of Independence. Framed as an "unalienable" right by Thomas Jefferson and espoused by the other founders of this revolutionary nation, the "pursuit of happiness" magnified the American dream into an abiding, almost sacred promise. Going back to that scripture of nationhood, it is striking to note that although Jefferson amended John Locke's "life, liberty, and property or estate" to "life, liberty, and the pursuit of happiness," neither he nor any other signatory explained or remarked in writing on the change. But naming the "pursuit of happiness" an unalienable right confirmed the newly declared American nation as an experimental, necessarily improvisational society dedicated to the principle that every human personality is sacred and inviolable. Yes, blacks, women, Native Americans, and even indentured servants were excluded, but excluded *then,* not forever. For as Lincoln was to imply in the Gettysburg Address, the Declaration's eloquent language strained toward the proposition that all persons were free, and, therefore, implicated in and responsible for the nation's destiny. And the idea and covenant of American citizenship required that all individuals make themselves up in the midst of the emerging new society. And the process of creation would be vernacular, arising from native ground, the weather, landscape, customs, habits, peoples, and values of this new world in the making.

That was and remains the promise of America. But, Fitzgerald's novels remind us, things were never this simple. And as the late Ralph Ellison, who seems closer and closer kin to Fitzgerald, put it, "a democracy more than any other system is always pregnant with its contradiction."⁹ One such contradiction unresolved by the Declaration or the ensuing Constitution, and played out since in national experience and Fitzgerald's novels, is between property and the "pursuit of happiness." Certainly, as Eugene McCarthy has noted, the third unalienable right "undoubtedly included the right to pursue property as a form of happiness, or as 'a happiness.'"¹⁰ For some the "pursuit of happiness" was simply a euphemism for property. Officially, the tension went unresolved and scarcely acknowledged until the 14th Amendment forbade the states to "deprive any person of life, liberty, or property, without due process of law." The less concrete, more elusive "pursuit of happiness" went unmentioned except by implication. Yet, for over 200 years, before and after passage of the 14th Amendment, Americans have sought to balance property's material reality with the imaginative possibilities hinted at in the phrase the "pursuit of happiness."

What if we were to read *Gatsby, Tender Is the Night,* and *The Last Tycoon* as projections of that sometime struggle, sometime alliance between property and the pursuit of happiness? As human impulses, property and the pursuit of happiness are sometimes contradictory, sometimes complementary metaphors for experience. Let property stand for the compulsion to divide the world and contain experience within fixed, arbitrary boundaries. And let the "pursuit of happiness" become imagination's embrace of the complexity, fluidity, and possibility open to human personality. In Jefferson's time, if not so strongly in Fitzgerald's or our own, the "pursuit of happiness" also implied individual responsibility for the "spirit of public happiness" that John Adams felt so strongly in the colonies, which he judged the American Revolution won almost before it began. Jefferson did not include the word *public,* but his phrase implies the individual's integration of desire with responsibility, self-fulfillment with the work of the world. In short, in this promissory initial American context, the pursuit of happiness was bound up with citizenship, and citizenship with each individual's responsibility for democracy.

The first thing to be said about Fitzgerald's novels is that these enactments of the American dream are expressed in the love affairs and worldly ambitions of Jay Gatsby, Dick Diver, and Monroe Stahr. In *The Great Gatsby (TGG), Tender Is the Night,* and *The Last Tycoon,* the matrix of the dream differs, but in each case, the hero is, like Fitzgerald, "a man divided," yet he seeks to integrate love of a woman with accomplishment in the world. Telling his story to Nick Carraway after he has lost Daisy Fay for the second and last time, Gatsby remembers that when he first met her, he felt like the latest plunderer in the line of Dan Cody, his metaphorical father, and a mythical figure who, in Fitzgerald's interpretation, "brought back to the Eastern seaboard the savage violence of the frontier brothel and saloon." Sensitive to the demarcations of background, money, and status, Gatsby

> knew he was in Daisy's house by a colossal accident. However glorious might be his future as Jay Gatsby, he was at present a penniless young man without a past, and at any moment the invisible cloak of his uniform might slip from his shoulders.

Meanwhile, "he had deliberately given Daisy a sense of security; he let her believe he was a person from much the same stratum as herself." Jay Gatsby pursues Daisy knowing that her sense of happiness and the good life depends on money and property. Nevertheless, "he took what he could get, ravenously and unscrupulously—eventually he took Daisy one still October night, took her because he had no real right to touch her hand" (*TGG* 76, 113). Ironically, Gatsby's lieutenant's uniform allows him proximity to Daisy simply as a man long enough to seduce her.

Until Gatsby makes love to Daisy, he projects little soul or feeling, only a self-absorbed passion mixed up with his urge to defy American boundaries of class, status, and money. The experience of love deeply moves and changes Gatsby, but so pervasive is the culture of material success that his new reverence and tenderness toward her are inseparable from money and possessions, and perhaps from Carraway's image of Daisy "gleaming like silver, safe and proud above the hot struggles of the poor"—Gatsby's struggles, maybe, as a boy and penniless young man in North Dakota and Minnesota. Earlier that same day in 1922, Gatsby calls Daisy's voice a voice "full of money." But his subsequent words to Carraway about that experience of love in wartime 1917, a time that obscured boundaries of class and background in favor of a seemingly all-powerful fluidity and equality, convey the mystery and tenderness of his earlier emotion. "I can't describe to you how surprised I was to find out I loved her, old sport," Gatsby tells Carraway in his sometimes too well-chosen words whose tone nonetheless carries a touch of wonder. "I even hoped for a while that she'd throw me over, but she didn't, because she was in love with me too." The more vividly Gatsby remembers, the more the tricks of his voice yield to the feeling underneath. "She thought I knew a lot because I knew different things from her. . . . Well, there I was, 'way off my ambitions, getting deeper in love every minute, and all of a sudden I didn't care" (*TGG* 114, 91, 114).

Gatsby discovers that Daisy loves him because of his different experience, not despite it as he feared. He surrenders his ambitions, as yet inchoate, unfocused, adolescent, to his intense feeling for Daisy. But their love is an interlude, happening "in the meantime, in between time." More vividly alive because of his love for Daisy, Gatsby "did extraordinarily well in the war," becoming a captain and, following the Argonne, a major given "command of the divisional machine guns" (*TGG* 72, 114). He emerges as a leader. Although his ambitions are vague, thinking of other American trajectories, a pioneering future in politics or in some other new venture, aviation, say, or advertising, might have awaited Gatsby if Daisy had stayed true to her love for him.

Instead, Daisy Fay turns fickle and self-indulgent. Desperate for Gatsby to return, impatient and petulant over his mistaken assignment to Oxford, she must have her life "shaped now, immediately—and the decision must be made by some force—of love, of money, of unquestionable practicality—that was close at hand" (*TGG* 115). Daisy's pursuit of happiness in the form of her dangerous, defiant love for Gatsby surrenders to the palpability of a safe, material, unequal propertied union with Tom Buchanan. Afterwards, on his forlorn lover's progress through the streets of Louisville, Daisy's hometown and scene of their love, Gatsby understands: To win Daisy he gathers money and property, the latter transient and garish, in the quick and illegal ways open to him—Meyer Wolfsheim and the rackets. After another interval of love inspired by the possibilities of human personality—remember, Daisy sees Gatsby's possessions for the Horatio Alger emblems that they are and responds only to the passion, will, and tenderness that lie behind them—the struggle over Daisy (and, parabolically, America) is fought on the field of property. Whose money is solid wealth, whose possessions land, oil, and the like? And whose property stays in the same hands for generations?

In *Gatsby,* sooner or later human feelings are negotiated in relation to property or some other form of material reality subject to ownership. Gatsby's wonder of discovery, Daisy's magic of "bringing out a meaning in each word that it had never had before and would never have again" (*TGG* 82), these unanticipated, intense moments of experience recede before Tom Buchanan's relentless revelation of the shady transience of Gatsby's wealth. But perhaps Gatsby, too, gives Daisy little choice between two opposed fixed ideas. When Tom Buchanan forces a showdown with Gatsby at the Plaza

Hotel, the two men turn Daisy into a prized possession to be fought over on the basis of social and economic conventions. In effect, Buchanan invokes the *droit du seigneur.* He is the lord, Gatsby the serf, Daisy the woman belonging to the vast American estate. Contending on that ground, Gatsby may well pay an emotional tithe to the poor boy from North Dakota, and again feel he has no right to touch Daisy's hand. In any case, the scene at the Plaza is an acrimonious "irritable reaching after fact or reason"[11] without love. Who can blame Daisy for withdrawing after her perspective goes unheard by both men? On this occasion, Gatsby is no more able than Buchanan to consider Daisy a woman in her own right, a unique and equal person whose voice has had the power to give the words she sings singular feeling and meaning. For each man, Daisy is a possession; for Buchanan material, for Gatsby ideal. So Daisy, the actual woman, the flawed and vulnerable human personality, flees. Held to no standard of decency or accountability by either man after her hit-and-run killing of Myrtle Wilson, she once again chooses the conventional, worldly protection of Tom Buchanan.

Gatsby's dream of love corroded to nightmare, the passion ebbs from his work, such as it is. And no wonder. His flimsy network of "gonnegtions" and sinister underworld deals in booze and bonds were all for love of Daisy. When she returns to Tom Buchanan and their leisure-class world, partly because of Gatsby's desperate bargain with the American underworld, and partly because of his narcissistic, romantic inability to comprehend her attachment to Buchanan, Gatsby is emptied of love and ambition alike. The heart and wonder are gone from him; there is no happiness to pursue. His time of love and "aesthetic contemplation" passed, Gatsby, Nick imagines, sees around him only a frightening physical landscape—"a new world, material without being real" (*TGG* 123), an American world bleaker and, for all its glut of accumulations, more insubstantial than the spare, monotonous prairie James Gatz started from in rural North Dakota. For all his romantic gifts of personality, lacking a discerning critical intelligence, Gatsby seems destined to have served that same "vast, vulgar meretricious [American] beauty" of which Dan Cody is the apotheosis (*TGG* 75).

"France was a land, England was a people, but America, having about it still that quality of the idea, was harder to utter." In this passage from **"The Swimmers,"** a 1929 story later distilled into his *Notebooks,* Fitzgerald evokes the anguished intense patriotism he finds in American faces from Abraham Lincoln's to those of the "country boys dying in the Argonne for a phrase that was empty before their bodies withered" (*CU* 197). For Fitzgerald that American "quality of the idea" finds most worthy expression in the impulse to offer the best of yourself on behalf of someone or something greater than yourself. Directed toward the world, a "willingness of the heart" intensifies the individual's feelings and experience. In *Tender Is the Night* (*TITN*) as in *Gatsby*, the dream of love and accomplishment is distorted by the values of property and possession. Like Gatsby, Dick Diver has large ambitions: ". . . to be a good psychologist—maybe to be the greatest one that ever lived."[12] Dick's colleague, the stolid Swiss, Franz Gregorovius, stops short hearing his friend's pronouncement, as did the aspiring American man of letters, Edmund Wilson, when the undergraduate Fitzgerald declared: "I want to be one of the greatest writers who have ever lived, don't you?"[13] Like Fitzgerald, Diver mingles love with ambition, though passively, almost as an afterthought: "He wanted to be loved too, if he could fit it in" (*TITN* 23).

Reminiscent of *Gatsby,* Diver's dream resides initially in a masculine world in which one man's ambition and achievement are measured against another's. But, as with Gatsby, experience changes the values implicit in Diver's equation. Stirred by professional curiosity, he meets Nicole Warren. Because of her youth and beauty, the patient becomes in Diver's eyes primarily a woman, though a woman imagined as "a scarcely saved waif of disaster bringing him the essence of a continent." To the inexperienced Diver—"only hot-cheeked girls in hot secret rooms" (*TITN* 27)—Nicole is a figure for the romantic possibility of an America that, like the "fresh green breast of the new world" whose "vanished trees . . . had made way for Gatsby's house" (*TGG* 137) is, though violated and compromised, suggestive of innocence, vitality, and possibility, and above all, still worthy of love.

So Dick Diver gambles his "pursuit of happiness" on marriage to Nicole. But his desire to be loved—"I want to be extravagantly admired again," Fitzgerald said as he was writing *Tender*—seduces him away from his scholarly writing as a psychiatrist. Once diverted from his work, he does not find happiness as curator of the leisure-class expatriate American world he and Nicole create on the Riviera, or as psychiatrist in charge of the clinic bought with Warren money, or as Nicole's husband, or, finally, "wolf-like under his sheep's clothing" a pursuer of women more in mind than in actuality. For Diver, like Gatsby, the pursuit of happiness becomes personally hollow in love, and professionally so in his work. Again, perhaps like Gatsby, only more so, Diver is more responsible than he knows for the dissolution of his dream of love and work.

For her part, Nicole, like Daisy, only more poignantly, veers between two selves. Cured, she embraces her heritage as her robber baron grandfather Warren's daughter; her white crook's eyes signify a proprietary attitude toward the world. More vividly and knowingly than before, she becomes the goddess of monopoly and dynasty described early in the novel. "For her sake

trains began their run at Chicago and traversed the round belly of the continent to California." Nicole, "as the whole system swayed and thundered onward," is, in Europe, remote product and beneficiary of her family's multinational corporate interests. Like Daisy, Nicole "has too much money"; like Gatsby, Dick Diver "can't beat that" (*TITN* 113, 311).

Yet in *Tender Is The Night,* the matter is not so simple. Marrying Nicole, Dick takes on a task demanding a heroic and perhaps a too stringent discipline and self-denial. After the most violent and threatening of Nicole's schizophrenic episodes, he realizes that "somehow [he] and Nicole had become one and equal, not opposite and complementary; she was Dick too, the drought in the marrow of his bones." Her personality reinforces rather than compensates for what is missing in him. Even more fatal for Diver's balance between husband and psychiatrist, "he could not watch her disintegrations without participating in them" (207). Underneath the historical overtones of the American dream gone terribly, incestuously, wrong, Fitzgerald explores the strained and, finally, chilling intimacy of a marriage turned inward against the autonomy and independence of each person. With slow excruciating inevitability, Diver's "willingness of the heart," so catalytic to his imagination, charm, and discipline, deserts him.

She went up to him and, putting her arm around his shoulder and touching their heads together, said:

> "Don't be sad."
>
> He looked at her coldly.
>
> "Don't touch me!" he said.
>
> (*TITN*, 319)

Diver has come so far from his former love for Nicole, "a wild submergence of soul, a dipping of all colors into an obscuring dye" (*TITN* 235), that he now recoils from her touch. The Divers are no longer man and woman to each other. In truth, the conditions and pathology sustaining the marriage are played out. Nicole is rid of her incestuous dependence on Dick, and Dick seeks to recover the independence he sacrificed as Nicole's husband, doctor, and, above all, protector.

Discipline, spirit, and imagination attenuated if not broken, Diver returns to America a stranger. With Nicole now acting as Fitzgerald's chronicler, the last news of Diver tells of the "big stack of papers on his desk that are known to be an important treatise on some medical subject, almost in process of completion." So much for his craft; as for the dream of love, he becomes "entangled with a girl who worked in a grocery store" (*TITN* 334). Homeless in spirit, Diver drifts from one lovely, lonely Finger Lakes town to another, and whatever dreams he has, he dreams in oblivion without his former promise and intensity of feeling and action.

Fitzgerald created his deepest, most realized novel out of his own predicament. His dissipation and need to write short stories for the *Saturday Evening Post* to sustain his and Zelda's standard of living seduced him away from his craft and to some extent his dream of love. Still, Fitzgerald bled out *Tender Is the Night* at La Paix—"La Paix (My God!)" (*L* 345)—in Rodgers Forge outside Baltimore. He brought his "big stack of papers" to completion. But when reviews were mixed and sales modest, also perhaps because, exhausted, he had no new novel taking shape in his mind, only the early medieval tale of Phillippe or *The Count of Darkness,* with its curiously anachronistic tilt toward Ernest Hemingway's modern code of courage, Fitzgerald sank deeper into drink and depression. Finally, as Scott Donaldson observes, Asheville, Tyron, and other North Carolina towns became suspiciously like the small towns of Diver's self-imposed exile at the end of *Tender Is the Night.*[14]

For more than three years after publication of *Tender Is the Night,* Fitzgerald continued to imitate the desolate trajectory he'd projected for Dick Diver. Everything was a struggle. Perhaps "to preach at people in some acceptable form" (*L* 63) and to show himself an unbowed Sisyphus, without the camouflage of fiction, he dove into the confessional *Crack-Up* pieces. To the chagrin of those who wished him well, and even some who did not, he wrote an even more exposed confession of faith than *Tender Is the Night.* His low point came with the appearance of "The Other Side of Paradise," a portrait of the novelist as a broken-down man and a failed writer that appeared on his fortieth birthday in the *New York Post* in September of 1936. "A writer like me must have an utter confidence, an utter faith in his star," he told the reporter. "But through a series of blows, many of them my own fault, something happened to that sense of immunity, and I lost my grip."[15] The reporter featured the empty bottles and the desolate hotel room more than Fitzgerald's words, however, and the self-inflicted blow of humiliation Fitzgerald absorbed seeing the piece in print prompted him to make an abortive gesture at suicide.

Only an offer from Hollywood less than a year later broke the pattern of waste, the spell of despair, and roused Fitzgerald from his uneasy, purgatorial hibernation. Slowly, tortuously, he came back to life as a man and a novelist. Taking another crack at Hollywood, where the "inevitable low gear of collaboration" (*CU* 78) had twice mocked his sense of artistic vocation, Fitzgerald renewed his "pursuit of happiness." His theme was another variation of the American dream. For as a place and an industry, Hollywood was at once the consequence and the purveyor of the dream, often an eager expression of the culture's lowest common denominator. Unlike his earlier moves, to the south of France to write *Gatsby* in 1924 and Baltimore to write

Tender in 1932, Fitzgerald saw going to Hollywood as a lucky last chance to recoup his fortunes. He had a screenwriter's contract; perhaps if he got himself together another novel would take shape. In the meantime, riding west on the train in July 1937, Fitzgerald welcomed the chance to pay his debts, educate Scottie, care for Zelda, and keep himself. And Hollywood also offered a fresh start. "Of all natural forces," he had written in *The Crack-Up,* "vitality is the incommunicable one" (*CU* 74). And he did not flinch from taking stock of his condition. "For over three years," he wrote his cousin Ceci, "the creative side of me has been dead as hell" (*L* 419). So, he might have added, was the side of him that lived in relationships at a high pitch of intensity.

In Hollywood almost two years, Fitzgerald pursued once more his dream of love and craft. Cherished by Sheilah Graham who had her own life and ambition, Fitzgerald felt alive enough in his pores to revive the dream of being truly among the novelists. "Look," he wrote his daughter late in October 1939 with a surge of the old vitality and self-confidence, "I have begun to write something that is maybe great." And he went on to tell her with touching understatement: "Anyhow I am alive again" (*L* 61). In the last year of his life, Fitzgerald poured into Monroe Stahr and *The Last Tycoon* the sense that life was ebbing and his resolve to pursue happiness as a writer and a man to the end. Into Stahr he put exhaustion—the sense of death in the mirror—and readiness for love—"the privilege of giving himself unselfishly to another human being," Fitzgerald's words for a love more mature than romantic. Into his new book, he put the passion to make *The Last Tycoon* "something new" that could "arouse new emotions, perhaps even a new way of looking at certain phenomena."[16] For him the "pursuit of happiness" now meant, in Francis Kroll Ring's words, "the pursuit of the limits of his craft," which she, who knew him well, notes that he felt "he had not reached."[17]

Fitzgerald did not speak directly of the dream in *The Last Tycoon* as he had in *Gatsby, Tender Is the Night,* and, with occasional bitter nostalgia, the *Crack-Up* essays. But it was there in Monroe Stahr's pursuit of private and public happiness, there with a measure of caution and maturity as well as a dangerous, consuming intensity. Monroe Stahr is both outside and inside the mold of Fitzgerald's previous heroes. Like Gatsby, Stahr is self-made, a leader of men in Hollywood as Gatsby briefly had been in France during the Great War. But Stahr's ambition and creative power fuse with the public good; he does not become a crook or a gangster to advance his ideal, romantic pursuit of happiness. Neither does he confuse love with vocation. No,

> Stahr like Lincoln was a leader carrying on a long war on many fronts; almost singlehandedly he had moved

pictures sharply forward through a decade to a point where the content of the "A productions" was wider and richer than that of the stage.

(*LT* 106)

Like Dick Diver, Stahr's mind puts him in select company, and also like Diver, Stahr is a man with a strong, specific sense of vocation. But unlike Diver, Stahr distills his passion into a sustained, disciplined appetite for his work. Stahr is also a Jew, whose identity as an American outsider is more fully, consciously felt and put to more palpable professional use than had been the case with either Gatsby or Diver.

Stahr makes it to the pinnacle in Hollywood—a world open to and largely created by Jews—by virtue of his brains, judgment, leadership, taste, and sense of craft and quality possible in the medium of film with its democratic accessibility and mass appeal. Compared to Lincoln by Fitzgerald, Stahr believes he's about to take a call from President Roosevelt in front of the woman he's just recently met and is fast coming to love. "I've talked to him before," Stahr tells Kathleen before the phone call turns out to be from an agent whose orangutan is "a dead ringer for McKinley" (*LT* 83). But Fitzgerald, always sensitive to the feel of a decade's turning points, implies parallels between Stahr's protective role in the movie industry and Roosevelt's in government. "There is no world but it has its heroes," he writes, "and Stahr was the hero." He evokes Stahr's staying power during the evolving phases of the movies, as well as in the making of an individual picture. "Most of these men had been here a long time—through the beginnings and the great upset, when sound came, and the three years of depression, he had seen that no harm came to them." Stahr was perhaps a paternal employer, as Roosevelt was a paternal, protective President. Both men preside over transitional circumstances in ways more evolutionary than revolutionary by force of character and impersonal compassionate intelligence, and by taking a personal interest in the problems of their constituencies. "The old loyalties were trembling now," Fitzgerald concludes in the passage describing Stahr mingling with those who work for him at the end of a day at the studio: "There were clay feet everywhere; but still he was their man, the last of the princes. And their greeting was a sort of low cheer as he went by" (*LT* 27).

Stahr dreams of and attains knowledge and success in Hollywood's ambiguous, often insincere world of entertainment, art, and profit, the solitary, Cartesian way. He "did his reasoning without benefit of books—and he had just managed to climb out of a thousand years of Jewry into the late eighteenth century." About the past, Fitzgerald notes that Stahr "could not bear to see it melt away" (*LT* 118). Reading this you can't help recall Fitzgerald's elegiac prose about the early promise of America "where the dark fields of the republic rolled on under the night" (*TGG* 137), or those pioneering Virginia "souls made of new earth in the forest-heavy darkness of the seventeenth century" (*TITN* 222). In a word, Fitzgerald continues, Stahr "cherished the parvenu's passionate loyalty to an imaginary past" (*LT* 118). But, having faced Stahr's and his own nostalgia, Fitzgerald invokes checks and balances against the romantic pull of the past. Stahr invents a peculiar, involuntary collaboration among the screenwriters, and his broader accomplishment as producer—"I'm the unity"—comes from his radical pragmatic courage to grasp and implement innovations. In short, Stahr is able "to retain the ability to function" amidst the contradictions of democracy and corporate power and property. Fitzgerald, too, wanted to achieve in *The Last Tycoon* what he felt he and his contemporaries so far had not done with the novel. "I want to write scenes that are frightening and inimitable,"[18] he writes in one of his notes.

Both Fitzgerald and Stahr are men whose creative powers flow more richly into the world when they are involved in a satisfying, intimate relationship with a woman. For all of Stahr's love affair with an "imaginary past," Kathleen awakens his passion for life in the present. Despite his "definite urge toward total exhaustion," when he and Kathleen touch, Stahr feels the abiding elemental world again; at the coast he comes alive to the rhythms of land and sea and sky. After he and Kathleen make love at his unfinished Malibu beach house—"It would have been good anytime, but for the first time it was much more than he had hoped or expected"—they watch countless grunion fish come to touch land "as they had come before Sir Francis Drake had nailed his plaque to the shore" (*LT* 92, 108, 152).

Stahr's love for Kathleen intensifies his confidence about his gifts and worldly aspirations in a way reminiscent of Fitzgerald. "I used to have a beautiful talent once, Baby," Fitzgerald told young Budd Schulberg during the Dartmouth Winter Carnival debacle. "It used to be wonderful feeling it was there."[19] Page by page, Fitzgerald ekes out *The Last Tycoon,* his physical stamina no longer able to keep up with his mind. Nor keep up with his will. As Frances Kroll Ring, Fitzgerald's then 20-year-old secretary tells it, he'd take a weekend off when he needed money to pay bills. With single-minded discipline fired by a desire to have the coming week free for his novel, he would plot and write a Pat Hobby story for *Esquire.*[20] But always the dream of realizing his promise as a pioneering American novelist was there, perhaps made more palpable by his love affair with Sheilah Graham and his dedication to her education, and, for that matter, to his daughter Scottie's education. The latter is especially poignant, for Scottie, of the same generation as Fitzgerald's narrator, Cecilia Brady, and his contemporary and intellectual conscience, Edmund Wilson, were Fitzgerald's two imagined readers of **The Last Tycoon,** and that connection kept him going on more than one desolate, discouraging occasion.

In the novel, Fitzgerald does not leave the connection between love and craft to speculation. While the grunion flop at their feet on the Malibu shore, Stahr and Kathleen encounter a black man who tells Stahr he "never go[es] to movies" and "never let[s his] children go" (**LT** 92). Later, at home alone, Stahr recalls the man—"He was prejudiced and wrong, and he must be shown somehow some way." The man had been reading Emerson, and for Stahr he becomes the representative responsible good citizen whose allegiance Stahr must win for his soul's sake, the movies' sake, and the sake of American culture, of which Stahr sees himself a guardian. "A picture," Stahr thinks, "many pictures, a decade of pictures, must be made to show him he was wrong." And Stahr immediately commits himself to a specific action. "[H]e submitted the borderline pictures to the Negro and found them trash. And he put back on his list a difficult picture that he had tossed to the wolves, . . . to get his way on something else. He rescued it for the Negro man" (**LT** 95). Here Stahr puts his corporate property and producer's power in service of a higher common good—democratic (e)quality. Here the "pursuit of happiness" expresses his best potential and the best of American popular culture. What's more, Stahr's responsiveness to the black man's criticism is bound up with his passionate and tender love for Kathleen. His power to act as a public man is perhaps brought to brief, occasional fullness by the experience of love and intimacy.

Yet Stahr, Fitzgerald takes pains to observe, was not born to love and intimacy. He worked hard to shape the raw materials of his personality into a sensibility capable of an intimate relationship. "Like many brilliant men, he had grown up dead cold." Looking over the way things were,

> he swept it all away, everything, as men of his type do; and then instead of being a son-of-a-bitch as most of them are, he looked around at the bareness that was left and said to himself, "*This* will never do." And so he had learned tolerance, kindness, forbearance, and even affection like lessons.
>
> (*LT* 97)

Not surprisingly, Stahr's impulses toward the private happiness of intimacy are not as natural or sure-handed as his pursuit of public happiness in the world in the form of work and power, competition and money.

For all his mingling of love and craft in what seems a mature pursuit of happiness, Stahr hesitates with Kathleen. Perhaps Fitzgerald would have changed somewhat the terms of his story; we do not know. What we do know is that Stahr waits, fatally it turns out, though he is sure in his heart and his mind. "He could have said it then, said, 'It is a new life,' for he knew it was, he knew he could not let her go now, but something else said to sleep on it as an adult, no romantic" (**LT** 115). What Stahr and Kathleen do not know is that outside forces are closing in. The man Kathleen calls "The American," who rescued her from her old life's quagmire in London, is already speeding toward Los Angeles and the marriage ceremony they've agreed to, his train hours early. If there's something hasty, even amateurish about this twist of Fitzgerald's plot, so be it. To say he might have changed it or refined the terms is to remember that he too, like Stahr, did not have the luxury of time.

In what Fitzgerald did write, Stahr says good night to Kathleen, but keeps his feelings to himself. "We'll go to the mountains tomorrow," he tells her with the public voice of the man in charge, the producer, as if that were all. For his part, Fitzgerald the novelist, unable to resist one of those asides that mark his relations with his characters, especially those he loves, reflects on Stahr's temporizing judgment: "You can suddenly blunt a quality you have lived by for twenty years" (**LT** 116).

This line does not belong entirely to Fitzgerald but to Cecelia Brady, his narrator, who also loves Stahr, and in the way of a woman, not a novelist. Here, too, Fitzgerald was breaking new and different ground from that traversed in previous novels. He gambled that this young woman, "at the moment of her telling the story, an intelligent and observant woman" (**LT** 140), could reveal Stahr's complexity as well as her own and that of Hollywood and American society in the transitional time of the Depression and the coming of the Second World War. Through Cecelia's sensibility as insider and outsider, Fitzgerald registers changes in what Ellison has called the American social hierarchy.[21] In **The Last Tycoon,** Stahr, a Jew not far from the shtetl, makes a black man his moviemaker's conscience, falls in love with an Irish immigrant, and has his story told by another woman, a young Irish American who, by virtue of her father's Hollywood money and her intelligence and grace, moves among the well-to-do on both coasts.

In Fitzgerald's fascinating, fragmentary notes and sketches for the novel's ending—three teenagers' discovery of the fallen plane and the personal effects of Stahr and other passengers—and epilogue—Stahr's lavish Hollywood funeral full of hypocrisy and intrigue—the dream fights on in life-affirming, life-denying variations. Whatever Fitzgerald might have done, we glimpse in Stahr what might unfold if the pursuit of private and public happiness were to fuse in a common responsiveness. The one transforms and intensifies the other; the self trembles, now fully alive.

Stahr, whether in conversation or the act of love with Kathleen, or in his renewed sense of aesthetic possibility in response to a black man's rejection of the movies, comes to know that his vitality depends on mingling passion and tenderness toward Kathleen with the pragmatic imagination of his producer's craft. Without one, the other falters, as Fitzgerald shows in his draft of the last episode he wrote and his notes for the novel's succeeding chapters. In the last months of his life, Fitzgerald struggled toward the same equilibrium beyond Stahr's grasp, but not his imagination, in his settled relationship with Sheilah Graham and the steadfastness with which he pursued the limits of his craft. Despite his efforts to finish *The Last Tycoon,* Fitzgerald left a fragment that is, for all its promise, as Richard Lehan put it, "a brilliantly incomplete work that has all the limitations of being a draft and thus never fully conceptualized and polished by revision, where Fitzgerald always did his best work."[22] Nevertheless, Fitzgerald's fragment is a palpable reminder, at once mocking and reassuring, about his novelist's dream and the American theme.

"So we beat on," to echo and recast *Gatsby*'s ending, not necessarily "borne back ceaselessly into the past" (*TGG* 137). For in *The Last Tycoon,* there is a fluidity and ambiguity about property and the "pursuit of happiness" missing from the social structures underlying *Gatsby* and *Tender Is the Night.* Even more than *Tender Is the Night,* in its protean state *The Last Tycoon* appears a work of ceaseless fluctuations. Unlike *Tender, Tycoon*'s unfolding and denouement were to be governed by a moral and aesthetic principle underscored in Fitzgerald's notes. ACTION IS CHARACTER, he wrote in large block letters, and they are the last words in Edmund Wilson's edition of the fragment. As Fitzgerald's notes and outlines reiterate, Monroe Stahr was to struggle until the end. He would not await his fate passively like Gatsby or, like Dick Diver, abdicate to a private corner of America. Fitzgerald imagines Stahr a player to the last, and only the ironic contemporary deus ex machina of a plane crash would interfere with his decision to call off a retaliatory murder he's arranged in sick desperation. Gatsby operates in the shadows of American violence and power; Diver becomes a sleepwalking Rip van Winkle in a time of transition, but Stahr lives in the glare never believing that "things are [entirely] hopeless." Rather, he is "determined [to the end] to make them otherwise." Such, at least, is the impression conveyed by Fitzgerald's posthumous, very much in-progress fragment of a novel.

In Stahr's case and Fitzgerald's, the choices are contingent and pragmatic rather than ideal. It is no longer the case, as Fitzgerald once believed, that "life was something you dominated if you were any good" (*CU* 69). This romantic categorical imperative is long gone from his life and burned off the pages of *The Last Tycoon.*

By 1940, life was the pursuit of equilibrium, and the dream has become an ability to put previously opposed ideas into relationship, what D. H. Lawrence, in praise of the novel, called "the trembling instability of the balance."[23] Perhaps this is why Fitzgerald, and his evolving patriot parvenu, Monroe Stahr, come to the American dream still with a "willingness of the heart." Its promise was not happiness at all, as Jefferson and Adams realized so long ago, but the pursuit of happiness. The American experiment looked toward an ideal of individuals straining for self-realization with every nerve and muscle, every thought and feeling, in order to create what Ellison identified as that "condition of being at home in the world which is called love and which we term democracy."[24] For Fitzgerald the pursuit of happiness and the American Dream were inseparable. Digging deeply into his experience and the nation's, Fitzgerald made Monroe Stahr's story and character express the complexity of American life, its contradictions and possibilities alike. "The writing gave him hope," Frances Ring remembers from Fitzgerald's last months, "that something good was happening, that he was whole again."[25]

Perhaps the sense of his powers returning prompted Fitzgerald's note to himself near the end. "I am the last of the novelists for a long time now,"[26] he wrote, and who can know what he meant? Could he have meant that he was the last of his generation to keep faith with the nineteenth-century view of the novel as a testing ground for the experiment of American culture and democracy? Could he have meant his remark as a challenge to succeeding writers to pick up where he left off in exploring the American theme? Whatever he meant, even unfinished, *The Last Tycoon* has had the effect of leading readers and writers back to Fitzgerald's work knowing, as he knew, that the story of America has an endless succession of takes, but no final script.

Notes

1. For a sense of Fitzgerald criticism over the past 4½ decades, see Jackson R. Bryer's "Four Decades of Fitzgerald Studies: The Best and the Brightest" and Sergio Perosa's "Fitzgerald Studies in the 1970s," both in *Twentieth Century Literature,* 26 (1980). Also see *Critical Essays on The Great Gatsby,* ed. Scott Donaldson, and *Critical Essays on Tender Is the Night,* ed. Milton R. Stern.

2. Ralph Ellison, *Invisible Man,* 433.

3. Ernest Hemingway, *The Sun Also Rises,* 148.

4. *The Great Gatsby,* 4. Henceforth *The Great Gatsby* will be cited in the text as *TGG.*

5. *The Crack-Up,* ed. Edmund Wilson, 69. Henceforth *The Crack-Up* will be cited in the text as *CU.*

6. Andrew Turnbull, ed., *The Letters of F. Scott Fitzgerald*, 96. Henceforth the *Letters* will be cited in the text as *L*.

7. Letter to George and Thomas Keats, 21 Dec. 1817, in Rollins, ed., 193.

8. Quoted by Andrew Turnbull in *Scott Fitzgerald*, 307.

9. Ralph Ellison, *Going to the Territory*, 251.

10. Eugene McCarthy, *Complexities and Contraries: Essays of Mild Discontent*, 112.

11. Keats, 193.

12. *Tender Is the Night*, 22. Henceforth *Tender Is the Night* will be cited in the text as *TITN*.

13. F. Scott Fitzgerald as quoted by Edmund Wilson in "Thoughts on Being Bibliographed," 54.

14. Scott Donaldson, "The Crisis of Fitzgerald's 'Crack-Up,'" 185.

15. Michel Mok, *New York Post*, 25 Sep. 1936.

16. *The Last Tycoon*, 139, 141. Henceforth *The Last Tycoon* will be cited in the text as *LT*. (Matthew J. Bruccoli, editor of *The Love of The Last Tycoon* [1993] is correct to say that Edmund Wilson assigned the title of *The Last Tycoon*. Nevertheless, Bruccoli's evidence for his title is less than convincing; thus my decision to use the 1941 Wilson edition.)

17. Letter from Frances Kroll Ring to the author.

18. F. Scott Fitzgerald's Notes as quoted by Matthew J. Bruccoli in *The Last of the Novelists: F. Scott Fitzgerald and The Last Tycoon*, 156.

19. F. Scott Fitzgerald to Budd Schulberg as quoted by Arthur Mizener in *The Far Side of Paradise*, 317.

20. Frances Kroll Ring, *Against the Current: As I Remember F. Scott Fitzgerald*, 52-55.

21. This is a recurring phrase and theme of Ellison's, found in *Shadow & Act, Going to the Territory*, and in some of his unpublished or uncollected pieces included in *Collected Essays*.

22. Richard Lehan, letter to the author.

23. D. H. Lawrence, *Phoenix: The Posthumous Papers of D. H. Lawrence*, 528.

24. Ralph Ellison, *Shadow & Act*, 105-06.

25. Frances Kroll Ring, unpublished remarks delivered at the Fitzgerald-Hemingway International Conference in 1994.

26. Bruccoli, op. cit., 156.

Works Cited

Bruccoli, Matthew J. *The Last of the Novelists: F. Scott Fitzgerald and The Last Tycoon*. Carbondale: Southern Illinois UP, 1977.

Bryer. Jackson R. "Four Decades of Fitzgerald Studies: The Best and the Brightest." *Twentieth Century Literature* 26 (1980): 247-67.

Donaldson, Scott. "The Crisis of Fitzgerald's 'Crack-Up,'" *Twentieth Century Literature* 26 (1980).

——, ed. *Critical Essays on 'The Great Gatsby.'* Boston: Hall, 1984

Ellison, Ralph. *Collected Essays of Ralph Ellison*. New York: Random, 1995.

——. *Going to the Territory*. New York: Random, 1986.

——. *Invisible Man*. New York: Random, 1952.

——. *Shadow & Act*. New York: Random, 1964.

Fitzgerald, F. Scott. *The Great Gatsby*. In *Three Novels*. New York: Scribner's, 1953.

——. *The Last Tycoon*. In *Three Novels*. New York: Scribner's, 1953.

——. *Tender Is the Night*. In *Three Novels*. New York: Scribner's, 1953.

Hemingway, Ernest. *The Sun Also Rises*. New York: Scribner's, 1926.

Keats, John. *The Letters of John Keats, 1814-21*. Ed. Edward Rollins. Vol. 1. Cambridge: Harvard UP, 1958.

Lawrence. D. H. *Phoenix: The Posthumous Papers of D. H. Lawrence*. New York: Viking, 1968.

Lehan, Richard. Letter to the author. 25 May 1995.

McCarthy, Eugene. *Complexities and Contraries: Essays of Mild Discontent*. New York: Harcourt, 1982.

Mizener, Arthur. *The Far Side of Paradise*. Boston: Houghton, 1965.

Mok, Michel. "The Other Side of Paradise." *New York Post* 25 Sep. 1936.

Perosa, Sergio. "Fitzgerald Studies in the 1970s." *Twentieth Century Literature* 26 (1980): 222-46.

Ring, Frances Kroll. *Against the Current: As I Remember F. Scott Fitzgerald*. Berkeley: Creative Arts, 1985.

——. Letter to the author. 7 Sep. 1994.

——. Unpublished remarks delivered at the Fitzgerald-Hemingway International Conference, Paris, 8 July 1994.

Stern, Milton R., ed. *Critical Essays on Tender Is the Night*. Boston: Hall, 1986.

Turnbull, Andrew, ed. *The Letters of F. Scott Fitzgerald.* New York: Scribner's, 1963.

———. *Scott Fitzgerald.* New York: Scribner's, 1962.

Wilson, Edmund, ed. *The Crack-Up.* New York: New Directions, 1965.

———. "Thoughts on Being Bibliographed," *Princeton University Library Chronicle* (Feb. 1944).

Janet Giltrow and David Stouck (essay date winter 1997)

SOURCE: Giltrow, Janet, and David Stouck. "Style as Politics in *The Great Gatsby*." *Studies in the Novel* 29, no. 4 (winter 1997): 476-90.

[*In the following essay, Giltrow and Stouck use discourse analysis to show that the novel's linguistic subtleties mask ideas of social conservatism.*]

The Great Gatsby is valued for the vividness with which it renders an historical era; perhaps more than by any other American novel written in the 1920s, we are convinced that we hear the voices of people speaking from that decade before the advent of talking motion pictures. As narrator, Nick is the medium by which those voices are heard and, as principal speaker in the text, he serves as a translator of the dreams and social ambitions of the people who surround him. But the dilemma for readers of the novel is how to interpret Nick's voice: is he genuinely critical of Gatsby's romantic imagination and the culture that informed it, or does his suave talk conceal an essentially conservative nature?

Major statements on the novel in the last twenty years identify important elements of cultural criticism in the text. Ross Posnock's Lukácsean reading, grounded in Marx's account of commodity fetishism, views Fitzgerald (and the story's narrator) as primarily a critic rather than an exponent of the American Dream; his assurance of the speaker's critical purpose is such that he can claim "the novel's account of man's relation to society . . . profoundly agrees with Marx's great discovery that it is social rather than individual consciousness that determine's man's existence" (p. 202).[1] Even Judith Fetterley, in her denunciation of the text's misogyny, allows that "certainly there is in the Carraway/Fitzgerald mind an element that is genuinely and meaningfully critical of the Gatsby imagination and that exposes rather than imitates it" (p. 99).[2] Less certain of the text's radical intent is a 'queer' reading by Edward Wasiolek who locates one of the novel's meanings in the conservatism of what he alleges to be Nick's repressed homosexuality. According to Wasiolek, Nick does not act on his intense feelings for Gatsby, but remains a voyeur, and he draws attention to a masturbatory image and rhythm in the last lines of the text ("So we beat on, boats against the current, borne back ceaselessly into the past") to suggest a regressive infantilism at the novel's center.[3] And in a deconstructionist study that negotiates the competing claims of psychoanalysis, feminism, and Marxism, Gregory S. Jay suggests in passing that Nick's identification with Gatsby belongs to that conservative order of social bonding wherein women are viewed as possessions in male power games.[4] But Jay also argues for the radical nature of the text asserting that **The Great Gatsby** is "a work of cultural criticism that enacts . . . the intellectual analysis of how the social subject can never be conceived, even *ab ovo,* as the inhabitant of a world outside commodification, exchange, spectacle, and in speculation" (pp. 164-65). Then Jay asks, concerning the moment in the text when Daisy weeps over Gatsby's shirts, does Nick reproduce the scene for us to read critically, or does he endorse Daisy's emotion—her thrill and sense of loss at both the reach and the limits of Gatsby's imagination? In other words, he asks (as if uncertain about the large claims he has made of the text's design), where does Nick stand?

In this essay we shall approach the question of critical intent and execution through an examination of the novel's style.[5] We shall use traditional accounts of English syntax to describe Fitzgerald's at sentence level, but we shall also use techniques from discourse analysis and linguistic pragmatics that will help us invesitage stylistic features that operate beyond the sentence, in the arena of language as socially situated, as utterance addressed and received both within the text and as an exchange between reader and writer. One of the major criticisms of stylistics, voiced strongly by Stanley E. Fish, is that observable formal patterns are in themselves without value, or else that stylistics assigns them value in a wholly arbitrary fashion, without regard to contexts of reception and reader expectation (p. 70).[6] Respectful of such criticisms, we point out that our analysis is inspired by advances in critical linguistics that insist that style is motivated—by context, by differentials of position, by political interest. Instead of presenting observed features of Fitzgerald's style as isolated formalities, we locate them in larger contexts, and explain how these contexts motivate the book's wordings. First we situate our findings in a consideration of mode in the novel: in the naive (or folk) romance mode as it is historically manifested in the American Dream, and in its ironic version manifested in this narrator's account of flagrant partying that convenes the tokens of social class in America. Then, after examining certain ways of speaking that adhere to the narrator's midwestern origins, we will claim that language in **The Great Gatsby** provides us with evidence for the multiple, seemingly contradictory readings of the book. We will show that alongside the expose of American material-ism—the irresponsible behaviors of the wealthy class, the corruption in business practice—there remains a conservatism, a resistance to change, and that both are evident in the book's language. In the manner of Nick's speaking, we find evidence that the critical inclination of *The Great Gatsby* is not just towards reform but to-wards restoration—restoration of a social order that has been confused and disturbed by reconfigurations of power and property, by the dishevelling forces of the age.

I

The novel's narrator, Nick Carraway, tells two stories: one about his fabulous neighbor, the other, less obvi-ously, about himself. The story he tells of Jay Gatsby, in its barest outlines, follows the pattern of romance, that reading of the individual life as an identity quest. Joseph Campbell and Northrop Frye have both de-scribed the structure of romance narrative and the tra-jectory of the hero's progression: from obscure origins he or she journeys into the unknown where an enemy, a lover, and a mentor all play crucial roles in identifying who the hero is and where he or she fits into the world. More recently, Michel Foucault defines succinctly the essence of the romance mode when he writes that the modern man is not the man who attempts to discover his personal secrets and his hidden truths; rather "he is the man who tries to invent himself," who is compelled "to face the task of producing himself" (p. 42).[7] For such an individual, writes Foucault, the high value of the present is indissociable from an eagerness "to imag-ine it otherwise than it is" (p. 41). Foucault uses the term "modern man" rather than romance hero, but his concept of modernity is not tied to an historical epoch. Rather, he suggests that modernity be considered an at-titude, a mode of relating to contemporary reality that can be found in other periods of history, consisting es-sentially of "the will to 'heroize' the present" (p. 40). Issues of identity, the nature of power and, in Fou-cault's terminology, an engagement with the Other—these all lie at the heart of the romance mode and bear on any reading of Gatsby's story.

Stretched over much of the narrative is the mystery of Gatsby's origins: rumored to be a nephew or a cousin of Kaiser Wilhelm, and claiming himself to be the scion of a wealthy, English-educated family, Gatsby, Nick learns eventually, is actually James Gatz, the son of "shiftless and unsuccessful farm people" from North Dakota (p. 104).[8] Gatsby's rejection of these humble origins is signaled by a name change, an "immigrant" surname anglicized and a formal first name made famil-iar and fashionable sounding. This reinvention begins when Gatsby is seventeen, when he leaves home and family behind and moves into a world of "reveries,"[9] where on moonlit nights "the most grotesque and fan-

tastic conceits haunted him in his bed" (p. 105). His-torically, this transformation takes place in the era when the robber barons were the model for power and suc-cess. For Gatsby, born on the margins, Daisy Fay is the embodiment of both success and the unknown; her privileged social status renders her a mysterious cyno-sure of sexual attraction, wealth, and social belonging, and when he kisses her she becomes the incarnation of his dreams and "unutterable visions" (p. 117). Nick writes that in loving her Gatsby "committed himself to the following of a grail" (p. 156); that Daisy was "[h]igh in a white palace the king's daughter, the golden girl" (p. 127). But Gatsby does not meet the test of wealth in Daisy's society (that specifically American measure of the romance quest), and he loses her to a rival suitor, Tom Buchanan. The spell Daisy casts with her voice—that "low, thrilling" siren's voice with its "singing com-pulsion" (p. 14) that "couldn't be overdreamed" (p. 101)—has been broken when Gatsby can say bluntly to Nick, "Her voice is full of money," and Nick recog-nizes that indeed its "inexhaustible charm," "the jingle of it, the cymbals' song of it" was simply that—the se-ductive power of riches (p. 127). Situated at the heart of Gatsby's story is the metanarrative central to Ameri-can culture—the deeply conservative ideology of capi-talism, the story of rags to riches, of power, love and fame achieved through personal wealth.

It is the narrator's role to discredit this myth. The story he tells of Gatsby bereft of this illusion is a story of violence, despair, and ghostliness—a fantastic dream, distorted and grotesque, like a "night scene by El Greco" (p. 185). Gatsby, he reveals, has no wise mentor to lead him on his journey; older men like Dan Cody and Meyer Wolfsheim have shown him the path of de-ceit and felony, and he follows it until one of the "ghosts . . . gliding toward him through the amorphous trees" (p. 169) takes his life. Gatsby does not emerge from his journey a hero reborn with the power to bestow boons on his fellows; Nick describes instead a wasteland, the valley of ashes, which grows while the obscure move-ments of the ash-grey men in the dumping grounds are watched over by the blinded eyes of Dr. Eckleburg. Nick tells of Gatsby's father entering the narrative not to reveal that his son was of distinguished parentage, but to offer another kind of testimony, a book and a schedule for improvement—the humble fragments of a national myth (the Ben Franklin, Horatio Alger formula) that has deluded his ambitious son.

On the level of plot then the sophisticated narrator seems to impugn the American dream, its illusions and excesses—he refers scornfully to Gatsby's "appalling sentimentality" (p. 118) and to the "foul dust" that "floated in the wake of his dreams" (p. 6). But syntacti-cally, in some of the most beautifully wrought and memorable lines of the novel, Nick Carraway demon-strates not scorn but, rather, ready sympathy for Gatsby and for those ideological presuppositions that underlie his ambitions. Nick tells Gatsby's story in what Bakhtin would describe as a lyrical style, "poetic in the narrow sense," without dialogue, the words sufficient unto themselves, "suspended from any mutual interaction with alien discourse."[10] This lyricism is accomplished grammatically in the continuation of sentences seemingly reluctant to end, sentences which go on after a syntactic core has delivered its message. Offering a profile of the narrative style Fitzgerald has given Nick, we suggest that, characteristically, the first part of the sentence, sometimes just an independent clause, does the work of the plot, moving the narrative forward in time and place and event, but a second part, often syntactically unnecessary, can go on to evoke feelings and indefinite excitements and to suggest matters that exist only in the realm of possibility and the imagination. These *sentence endings* are the site of poetic invention, which imagines the world "otherwise than it is,"[11] cultivates heightened sensation, and registers the romantic conceits and aspirations of ambition.

In Nick's way of speaking, the core of the narrative sentence establishes focus on time, place, event; drawn-out endings evoke accumulations of romantic sensitivity. Consider Nick's account of Gatsby's entry into his dream world:

> For a while these reveries provided an outlet for his imagination; they were a satisfactory hint of the unreality of reality, a promise that the rock of the world was founded securely on a fairy's wing.
>
> (p. 105)

This sentence begins, characteristically, with a time-adverbial, establishing duration and "reveries" as what is being talked about, then elaborates itself, through a second-start "they," into apposition—syntactically unnecessary, surplus, but seemingly engendered by sensitivity to words like "imagination" and "reverie." The tenuous subject of reverie and the imagination is then extended to even more tenuous matters in a "hint" and a "promise," but in the lush and improbable ending of the sentence occurs the "fairy's wing" that connects directly to the embodiment of Gatsby's dreaming, Daisy Buchanan, whose maiden name is Fay, an archaic variant of fairy. Nick hereby conveys an aura of magical destiny to Gatsby's adventure, as does the ending of another trailing sentence where Daisy is described as "gleaming like silver, safe and proud above the hot struggles of the poor" (p. 157). In this instance we glimpse something of the feudal heart of the American myth of riches.

The most evocative sentence endings are frequently constructed as elaborate appositives; they adumbrate the poetry of wealth and possessions. Nick describes in this way Gatsby's romantic excitement as a young army officer when he first views Daisy's house:

> There was a ripe mystery about it, *a hint of bedrooms more beautiful and cool than other bedrooms, of gay and radiant activities taking place through its corridors, and of romances that were not musty and laid away already in lavender, but fresh and breathing and redolent of this year's shining motor-cars and of dances whose flowers were scarcely withered.*
>
> (p. 155, emphasis added)

Everything contained in the appositive is suggestive, an elaboration of the mystery that surrounds Daisy, heightened especially by the ephemeral and transient nature of time present. Nick's own sensitivity to the passage of time is revealed in another sentence ending that evokes both the wonder and pathos of the romantic imagination:

> At the enchanted metropolitan twilight I felt a haunting loneliness sometimes, and felt it in others—*poor young clerks who loitered in front of the windows waiting until it was time for a solitary restaurant meal—young clerks in the dusk, wasting the most poignant moment of night and life.*
>
> (p. 62, emphasis added)

In these sentence endings is gathered the emotional excitement that accumulates around ambition, money, romantic love, the ripeness of the moment, and the longings and commotion they generate.

The sentence's residual momentum, or surplus, or even exorbitance, can carry across the sentence boundary, producing a variant on the appositional structure: the sentence fragment. Here Nick reflects on Gatsby's statement that Daisy's voice is "full of money" (a statement that might have just as easily thrown things into a more cynical mood):

> It was full of money—that was the inexhaustible charm that rose and fell in it, the jingle of it, the cymbals' song of it. . . . High in a white palace the king's daughter, the golden girl. . . .
>
> (p. 127, ellipses in original)

The double appositional construction—"the jingle of it, the cymbals' song of it" in apposition to "the inexhaustible charm that rose and fell in it"—here is perhaps itself inexhaustible, endlessly responding to itself: ellipsis points signify the sentence's resistance to closure, suggesting that the sentence (like the dream) has no conclusion, once this particular syntactic resource and these wordings of romance are in play (all of which seem to enable Nick to beg the question raised by the first part of the sentence—the hard fact of Daisy's wealth, a sturdy economic actuality). The abundance of this appositional surplus spills over the receding sentence boundary, its momentum sufficient to begin a new story, in a syntactic fragment, itself partly appositional, that floats free to gesture to romance in its purest form, the fairy tale of the hero striving and attaining, sights set on the transformative goal: "High in a white palace the king's daughter, the golden girl."[12] Such sentence-ending elaborations summon a virtual world of romance and possibility to attend the characters' actions and the plot's episodes, but they reveal at the same time that the myth of culture at work in the narrative is one that affirms a deeply conservative view of America—an ideology of class and property, of racial hierarchy, of women as possessions. In his reflection on Daisy's voice then, and in numerous sentences where a sharp-eyed view of events gives way to the romance of self-propogating invention, we see that Nick is both "repelled" and "enchanted" (p. 40) by Gatsby's America, that his style of speaking registers two views simultaneously.

II

That way of speaking directs us to the complexities of Fitzgerald's intention and style. In his ironic rendering of Gatsby as romance hero, Nick would appear highly critical of capitalist aspiration, but the language of this ironic narration reveals that he can be as conservative and elitist as the myths he would discredit. The tension between the naive and ironic aspects of the romance mode, between what Nick describes as Gatsby's "appalling sentimentality" (p. 118) and his own "incredulous laughter" (p. 170), would seem to describe the source of the novel's critical element.[13] But a careful examination of the language of the text reveals that Nick's irony does not always undercut the American Dream upon which Gatsby's fantastic world is founded; rather it locates Nick with the privileged denizens of the moneyed class and in a position to detach himself and look from a distance on the "foul dust" that gathers in Gatsby's wake.

Nick's ironic stance is most prominent in his representation of others' speech, as he works through the linguistic resources available for such representation, and especially as he does so on those occasions when the domains of romantic possibility and suggestion have turned sour: when he has ventured too far into the actual world occupied by Gatsby and Daisy, when the voices of others rise and collide, when he portrays himself at the afternoon get-together in Myrtle's apartment, or in Meyer Wolfsheim's company, or lingering until the end of one of Gatsby's gaudy parties.

While the wordings of naive romance evoke the ambition of the individual, the hero reconnoitering the boundaries of aspiration and seeking position and recognition within their circumference, an ironic version of the same story deflects the romantic trajectory by making audible the dissonance of the social order. Nick has an ear for these dissonances, the words and accents of daily usage, and the sociohistorical stratifications they embody. He renders these words and accents through a range of means that syntax offers for the expression in a single sentence of many voices at once: through alterations between direct and indirect reported speech; between reported speech and the naming of the speech act; between reported speech and speech simply absorbed into the narrative utterance, detectable only through what Bakhtin calls "intonational quotation marks" (p. 14, and *passim*). In every instance the sentence offers ways of entertaining the ghosts of other sentences. In its ironic dimension, cultivating the discrepancy between what is said and what is intended, *The Great Gatsby* renders not the attainment of the individual, nor the collective unity of "the republic" (*Gatsby,* p. 189), but "all the contradictory multiplicity of an epoch" (Bakhtin, p. 156), language saturated with the conditions of the historical era—"even of the hour" (Bakhtin, p. 263)—and with the rankings and calibrations of the social order: the "multiplicity of social voices and [the] wide variety of their links and interrelationships" (p. 263). Bakhtin observes (especially pp. 68-69, 76, 296) that the novelist's way of incorporating speech artefacts into narrative marks their degrees of solidarity with or distance from the narrator's point of view. In moments when Nick comes into intimate contact with brute matters, he practices speech habits of distancing, and his feeling of superiority and attitude of reserve become apparent in the differentials between the formality of his own words and the words he reports or reproduces. In the following sentence, Nick finds a delicate, arm's-length way of saying that the people in Myrtle's apartment were rapidly getting drunk: "The bottle of whiskey—a second one—was now in constant demand by all present, excepting Catherine, who 'felt just good on nothing at all'" (p. 39). Some wordings here are Nick's: "a second one" indicates his measure of excess consumption; "in constant demand by all present" converts the loud, indulgent talk of the partyers to a formal register that names that aggregate speech act as *demand*. Then, in the same sentence, words appear that are not Nick's at all, and are isolated by quotation marks: Catherine "'felt just as good on nothing at all.'" This construction tells us more than just that Catherine does not drink. As artefacts, her words come with "conditions attached" (Bakhtin, p. 75); they are words that have been attracted, as Bakhtin says, into the "orbits of certain social groups" (p. 290); words that are the alien language, their alien status being, as Bakhtin also says (pp. 278, 287), what produces art that is *not* "poetic" (or lyrical), but novelistic. Nick's way of handling Catherine's words, exposing them as artefacts of a lower social class, as not *his* way of speaking, executes his social distance from the figures he is closeted with, asserts his attitude of superiority.

As the paragraph continues, Nick reports on the partyers' plans for a meal "Tom rang for the janitor and sent him for some celebrated sandwiches that were a complete supper in themselves" (pp. 39-40)—and similarly manipulates the distance between himself and the cohort of drinkers. He tells us that the sandwiches are "celebrated"; the term at once represents a flow of talk about the sandwiches and concentrates it into a speech act the name of which comes, ironically, from a register more formal than that from which the talk itself issued. (The ironic discrepancy in speech registers could be seen as projected into the setting itself, for Tom's mistress's cramped apartment contains furniture "tapestried" with "scenes of ladies swinging in the gardens of Versailles" [p. 33].) But the relative clause that concludes the sentence appropriates the original register by identifying the sandwiches as a "complete supper in themselves," and giving a more commonplace account of the sandwiches and their advocates. In these two sentences, the narrative voice traverses the social order. Nick's formal wordings elevate him above what is a sordid scene—a drunken, adulterous, and eventually violent afternoon—while his appropriation of the language indigenous to the locale, to the eating, drinking and sexual behaviors of "certain social groups" in New York in the 1920s, imprints that alien experience in his own sentences.

Nick finds himself in such circumstances again at the end of one of Gatsby's parties. Then he calls the drunkenness a "reluctance to go home" (p. 56). Translating local arguments, he describes the evening as "rent asunder by *dissension*" (emphasis added), and the complaining of the women in raised voices as "*sympathizing* with each other" (emphasis added), in each case containing disorderly speech in elevated names of speech acts. There follows a passage whereby Nick allows us to hear the women directly, just as he previously allowed us to hear words directly from Catherine's mouth:

> "Whenever he sees I'm having a good time he wants to go home."
>
> "Never heard anything so selfish in my life."
>
> "We're always the first ones to leave."
>
> (p. 56)

Nick gives the gist of their conversation in a form of indirect reported speech as "the wives' agreement that such malevolence was beyond credibility" (p. 57). By abstracting the women's speech and introducing it in the context of Nick's abstract, educated and literary[14] speech, the narrative schematizes the ironic discrepancy between the word and its setting. From the social information concentrated in the women's direct speech, we know that they are not the kind of people who would say: "I am reluctant to go home"; "I sympathize with you"; "this malevolence is beyond credibility." Nick *is* the kind of person who talks this way, and, doing so, he reserves his advantage, imposing another speech stratum on the sociolect of others, but still leaving that sociolect to show through.

When the evening deteriorates into total confusion and disorder and Nick joins the crowd around the car wreck, he similarly distances himself with ironic wordings: "The sharp jut of a wall accounted for the detachment of the wheel which was now getting considerable attention from half a dozen curious chauffeurs" (p. 58). Now the ironic wordings achieve a conspicuous effect that perhaps has been immanent all along—an effect of high politeness. Buried in this formal statement is an account of drunk driving—somebody drove into a wall. But the formality politely suppresses agency, and very elaborately, at the cost of some linguistic effort expended to assign active-voice subject position to a non-agent ("jut of a wall") and to nominalize the only trace of the event itself (*detach* "detachment"), and thus eliminate the grammatical necessity of a doer of the action.[15] The high politeness—distancing and ironic—of this account of drunk driving is later supported by Nick's specialty, indirect speech reporting gist, the gist emanating from the speech of a social class distinct from the class of people excited by the accident. "At least half a dozen men, some of them little better off than he was, explained to [the driver] that wheel and car were no longer joined by any physical bond" (p. 60). We know that men who were "little better off" than the driver would not say "wheel and car [are] no longer joined by any physical bond." This refined gist measures the long social distance that separates Nick from the scene in which he is involved.

Especially at moments like this, when the world of romance has left him stranded in ugly confusion, Nick works most rigorously on capturing and transforming the speech of others. In so doing he asserts his social distance and superiority not only from working class people like the contemptuous butler (p. 119) or the maid that spits (p. 94), but from the fashionable society of party-goers that collect around Gatsby. By their names they are identified as the *nouveau-riche* and he stands with Gatsby, apart from them, at a distance. But at these moments, the heteroglot voices of a turbulent, unceasingly transient, contradictory social order persist in his ears. Rumor and reputation resound; notoriety and slander amplify the publicity of the newsstands; medleys of popular lyrics play over and over, and even sandwiches are "celebrated." Speech seethes with forces that Nick most acutely reports by naming a pathological speech act that echoes compulsively:

> There was the boom of a bass drum, and the voice of the orchestra leader rang out suddenly above the *echolalia* of the garden.
>
> (p. 54, emphasis added)

The utterance of the age—echolalia, dense with the disturbed sound of the historical moment—this is what Nick flees from at the end of the novel, the El Greco nightmare of history,[16] not the romantic dream of the king's daughter, "gleaming like silver, safe and proud above the hot struggles of the poor" (p. 157). In turn we too are invited—again by the style—to make a judgment, to see Nick from a distance, recognizing the political limits of his elitist stance while valuing his capacity to see and hear, and to report on the world around him, with such acuity.

III

Thus far we have examined the elaborate sentence endings which poeticize Gatsby's dream—the American myth of belonging through wealth—and we have considered Nick's ironic voice, the conservative, restraining expressions that reveal his disapproving fastidiousness and sometimes superior attitude. But beyond the voices of his social habitat, and even his refined, ironic translations of them, Nick attends to another order of experience, one that is stable, profound, original, timeless. When Nick tells his story he has returned home to the Middle West where he "wants the world to be in uniform and at a sort of moral attention forever" (p. 6). In this light of return we shall consider yet another feature of style that complicates our estimate of Nick and his judgment of the world around him.

At the beginning of his story, Nick tells us of his unusually close relationship to his father and conveys a certain pride in the Carraway clan, said to be "descended from the Dukes of Buccleuch" (p. 7). He also turns over in his mind a piece of advice from his father: "Whenever you feel like criticizing anyone . . . remember that all the people in this world haven't had the advantages that you've had" (p. 5). Nick amplifies this counsel in a snobbish generalization, claiming that "a sense of the fundamental decencies is parcelled out unequally at birth" (p. 6). Mr. Carraway's homily, his word of caution, has made a strong impression on his son. And it seems that it is the form as much as the content of the homily that impresses Nick, for, although his amplification somewhat distorts his father's intention, his speech habits can often exactly preserve the voice of the father. Despite his relative youth and his taste for partying, Nick makes a number of similar generalizations about life:

> There is no confusion like the confusion of a simple mind.
>
> (p. 131)

> No amount of fire or freshness can challenge what a man will store up in his ghostly heart.
>
> (p. 101)

> There [is] no difference between men, in intelligence or race, so profound as the difference between the sick and the well.
>
> (p. 131)

In linguistic terms such statements are maxims, that is, proverbial generalizations about human nature and human experience drawn from long reflection on the order of things. Occasionally they occur in *The Great Gatsby* as independent propositions, but more frequently they are imbedded in longer sentences, sometimes compressed into referring expressions as when Nick says that he is going to become "that most limited of all specialists, the 'well-rounded' man." Insisting on the wisdom of this paradoxical observation, he continues to generalize, adding: "This isn't just an epigram—life is much more successfully looked at from a single window, after all" (pp. 8-9). Such statements and expressions are not only general in reference ("most," "a man," "life"), they have no specific time reference, their truth being neither particular nor contingent. They are somehow above, or beside, the narrative order of events and establish in the text the speaker's recourse to an order of permanent values beyond the resounding echolalia and even its ironic representation.

Maxims also convey a speaker's claim to knowledge, his or her access to established authority and steady truths, and recognizing this, Aristotle said that while maxims were an effective tool for orators, young speakers should not use them.[17] Aristotle's advice acknowledges an incompatibility between lack of experience and wise sayings, yet Nick is very prone to thinking in maxims, despite his youth and his resolve to stay all judgments. Their incongruence draws our attention to that very divided nature of the novel's narrator who on the one hand is a heedless party-goer, imagining glamorous encounters with women in darkened doorways, but on the other hand is an apprentice in the banking and bond business and a judicious observer of human behavior. Nick describes this doubleness when he says of himself at the squalid party in Myrtle Wilson's apartment: "I was within and without, simultaneously enchanted and repelled by the inexhaustible variety of life" (p. 40). The voice of the maxim, grounded in paternal authority and wisdom, is a regulating device for Nick—solemn, stable, even magisterial—negotiating the extravagance and moral confusion of West Egg and New York, those "riotous excursions" to which he is so irresistibly drawn. For example, when trying to understand Jordan Baker's behavior early in their relationship, Nick observes that "most affectations conceal something eventually, even though they don't in the beginning" (p. 962). And reflecting on the rumor that she has cheated in a major golf tournament, he makes the sexist claim that "Dishonesty in a woman is a thing you never blame deeply" (p. 63). Nick most often speaks in this voice when under pressure; he says "I am slow thinking and full of interior rules that act as brakes on my desires" (pp. 63-64). The posture of the maxims, distributed in the text beyond particular sentences and situations, signals for the reader something regressive in Nick's character, which in turn is at work in the shaping of his narrative.

An examination of style in **The Great Gatsby** reveals strata of social and political attitudes so complex that we are perhaps no longer surprised that on the one hand Nick satirizes Tom Buchanan and his class by having him quote admiringly from the racist writer, Lothrop Stoddard ("'The Rise of the Coloured Empires' by this man Goddard" gives "scientific" evidence that "Civilization's going to pieces," says Tom [p. 17]), while on the other hand, in the novel's famous last scene, Nick tells us in romantic wordings of a Long Island that flowered once for Dutch sailor's eyes—"a fresh, green breast of the new world" (p. 189)—a pastoral and Nordic vision of America's origins that echoes directly Stoddard's ideal. Such contradictions or conflicting motivations are grounds for the interpretive perplexities that Nick's story arouses. While readers have long recognized that Nick is critical of the American scenes he describes, the focus and extent of his criticism continue to confound, as readers estimate Nick's position in the social configurations of the age: where has Fitzgerald located him? Where do Nick's interests lie?

Even as Nick's story defies the romance of wealth and status, and shows its sordid actuality, that core myth of American culture still excites a stylistic homage that sympathizes with Gatsby's aspirations. Nick can imagine the American romance; he recognizes its compelling song—a naive theme of folk consciousness, at once vulnerable and resistant to criticism. Nick's own career is not motivated by this theme—but he can hear its allure and entertain its enchantments.

Were this the sum of the novel's stylistic resources—exposé balanced by fascination—we might read Nick as a disinterested observer, sensitive to both the decadence of the age and its heady momentum, allowing each their weight. But another salient feature of his storytelling voice—his ironic representation of others' voices—begins to situate his interests, and thereby limit the scope of his critical vision. The dialogic ironies of speech locate Nick in a socially elevated position, this trick of rank or hierarchy deriving from his acute sense of social differentials—conditions that make it impossible for the naive (or folk) hero to ever really transform himself, for he will always bear the marks of his humble origins. This order of social observation secures an elite point of view, and indemnifies privileged interests.

Invoking an appreciation of social rank, these ironic gestures complicate the critical attitude of the narrative. But they might only hint at some confusion of critical intent—were it not for the voice of maxim and authority that pervades the narrative. While this voice could seem innocent or disinterested—it consults timeless principles to evaluate people's behavior—Fitzgerald shows, in his arrangements for Nick's story-telling, that this sober voice itself issues from an identifiable position in the social-order: Nick's well-placed family. Near the myth of rags-to-riches and the self-made man, endlessly replicating itself in the material imagination, there is another myth—equally conservative but more covert: the myth of a distinguished class aloof from the strivings of the marketplace, its own "rags" phase long forgotten and its riches converted to moral authority. As Fitzgerald represents it, Nick's position in the social order is not one from which visions of reform are likely to develop. In fact, social change is clearly problematic from this point of view—where change incurs consternation, and where there is more of an inclination towards restoration than towards reform.

These circumstances are embodied in Nick's voice; it is Nick's voice that reveals complications of interest that are perhaps inherent in certain traditions of American cultural criticism. In other words, style in **The Great Gatsby** is not a motionless, unitary condition, or object of afterthought, but is substance itself, incessantly shifting, forming, and engendering the novel's political and psychological complexity.

Notes

1. Ross Posnock's "'New World, Material Without Being Real': Fitzgerald's Critique of Capitalism in *The Great Gatsby*," in *Critical Essays on F. Scott Fitzgerald's "The Great Gatsby*," ed. Scott Donaldson (Boston: G. K. Hall, 1984), pp. 201-13.

2. Judith Fetterley, *The Resisting Reader: A Feminist Approach to American Fiction* (Bloomington: Indiana Univ. Press, 1978).

3. Edward Wasiolek, "The Sexual Drama of Nick and Gatsby," *The International Fiction Review* 19 (1992): 14-22. Wasiolek extends the examination of Nick's sexual ambiguiousness that was initiated by Keath Fraser in "Another Reading of *The Great Gatsby*," *English Studies in Canada* 5 (1979): 330-43.

4. Gregory S. Jay, *America the Scrivener: Deconstruction and the Subject of Literary History* (Ithaca: Cornell Univ. Press, 1990).

5. Commentaries on Fitzgerald's style have so far offered only general impressions on the subject, the most recent and worthwhile being George Garrett's essay, "Fire and Freshness: A Matter of Style in *The Great Gatsby*," ed. Matthew J. Bruccoli (New York: Cambridge Univ. Press, 1985), pp. 101-16. This essay is a response to Jackson R. Bryer's call for a focus on "the small units" of

style in Fitzgerald's writing (pp. 127-28). See Bryer's "Style as Meaning in *The Great Gatsby*: Notes Towards a New Approach," in *Critical Essays on F. Scott Fitzgerald's "The Great Gatsby"*, ed. Scott Donaldson (Boston: G. K. Hall, 1984), pp. 117-29.

6. Stanley E. Fish, "What is stylistics and why are they saying such terrible things about it?", in *Essays on Modern Stylistics*, ed. Donald C. Freeman (New York: Methuen, 1981), pp. 53-78.

7. Michel Foucault, "What is Enlightenment?", in *The Foucault Reader*, ed. Paul Rabinow (New York: Pantheon Books, 1984), pp. 32-50.

8. F. Scott Fitzgerald, *The Great Gatsby*, ed. Matthew J. Bruccoli (New York: Macmillan, 1991). All citations from the novel are taken from this authorized text.

9. In his study of the romantic hero, Joseph Campbell describes the hero's journey taking place in a world of "unfamiliar yet strangely intimate forces" wherein he must pass a series of tests before being reborn. See Campbell's *The Hero with a Thousand Faces* (New York: Pantheon Books, 1949), p. 245. (There is a thoroughgoing, if somewhat slavish, application of Campbell's description of romance to *The Great Gatsby* in Neila Seshachari's "*The Great Gatsby*: Apogee of Fitzgerald's Mythopoeia" in Donaldson, pp. 96-107). Northrop Frye characterizes this unfamiliar realm specifically as a dream world. See Frye's *The Secular Scripture: A Study of the Structure of Romance* (Cambridge: Harvard Univ. Press, 1976), p. 102. The insistence on a romantic dream state is inscribed everywhere in the text: Nick, for example, describes Gatsby's love for Daisy as driven by "the colossal vitality of his '*illusions*'" and his death as a "high price for living too long with a single *dream*" (p. 169, emphasis added).

10. M. M. Bakhtin, *The Dialogic Imagination: Four Essays*, trans. Caryl Emerson and Michael Holquist (Austin: Univ. of Texas Press, 1981).

11. Foucault, p. 41.

12. These suggestions carried in sentence endings have inspired one critic to write: "The memories of legend and fairy tale that permeate the book lift *The Great Gatsby* out of time and place as if the novel were a story celebrated for ages in song, folklore, and literature, a story deeply rooted in the psyche of the western world." See John Kuehl, "Scott Fitzgerald: Romantic and Realist," *Texas Studies in Literature and Language* 1 (1959): 413.

13. In some ironic versions of romance, what is audible in the language is the clash of warring philosophical assumptions that underpin the social order. Conrad's *Heart of Darkness* provides a striking example. At the center of that text is the story of Kurtz's self-invention in terms of Victorian philanthropy, his self-fashioning as "an emissary of pity, and science, and progress" dedicated to "weaning those ignorant millions from their horrid ways." But Marlow's ironic account of Kurtz's quest brings into play the language of another point of view that interrogates the assumptions and purposes of imperialist cultures and exposes beacons of progress to be "whited sepulchres."

14. Here we use "literary" in the sense that is developed in Bakhtin and Pierre Bourdieu (*Language and Symbolic Power*, trans. Gino Raymond and Matthew Adamson [Cambridge: Harvard Univ. Press, 1991]), and less specifically in Tony Crowley (*Standard English and the Politics of Language* [Urbana and Chicago: Univ. of Illinois Press, 1989]), that indicates forms of expression genealogically tied to formal written texts, to studied, "respectable" and prestigious utterance, in contrast to oral and often stigmatized vernaculars situated in everyday occasions. One conspicuous sign of literariness is Nick's characteristic use of words from a very sophisticated part of the lexicon: "meretricious," "adventitious," "peremptory," "vinous," "echolalia," etc.

15. In English, suppressed agency is a common resource of politeness. For example, out of respect for and deference to a distinguished but clumsy dinner guest, one could report to a server that "some wine has been spilled." Brown and Levinson's classic and comprehensive account of politeness ("Universals in Language Usage: Politeness Phenomena," in *Questions and Politeness: Strategies in Social Interaction* [Cambridge: Cambridge Univ. Press, 1978]) explains phenomena such as agentless expressions as part of larger sociolinguistic systems devoted to mitigating face-threatening acts. According to this kind of analysis, Nick's suppression of agency in a situation embarrassing to the unidentified driver is as an expression of respect a face-saving strategy. But, since Nick clearly does not estimate Gatsby's guests as deserving respect or deference, we must take another step, and recognize his politeness as ironic. Moreover, analyses of politeness such as Bourdieu's (1991) reveal politeness as the enactment not only of deference but also of domination, social superiority, and ranked distance between speaker and addressee. (So agentlessness can often serve a dominant speaker's execution of a directive speech act, as in "The door has been left open.")

16. For a comprehensive description of the "historical moment" in which the novel was written, see Ronald Berman's *The Great Gatsby and Modern Times* (Urbana and Chicago: Univ. of Illinois Press, 1994).

17. Aristotle describes the use of maxims as "suited to speakers of mature years, and to arguments on matters in which one is experienced. In a young man, uttering maxims is—like telling stories—unbecoming; and to use them in a realm where one lacks experience is stupid and boorish." See Aristotle, *The Rhetoric,* trans. Lane Cooper (Englewood Cliffs, NJ: Prentice-Hall, 1960), p. 152.

Jeffrey Hart (essay date summer 1997)

SOURCE: Hart, Jeffrey. "Fitzgerald and Hemingway in 1925-1926." *Sewanee Review* 105 (summer 1997): 369-80.

[*In the following essay, Hart examines the rivalry between Fitzgerald and Ernest Hemingway, with specific reference to* The Great Gatsby *and* The Sun Also Rises.]

My argument can be put briefly. Hemingway wrote *The Sun Also Rises* (1926) as a direct rejoinder to *The Great Gatsby* (1925): he created it as an aggressive defense of his own style against Fitzgerald's—and, derivatively, of his own view of reality. With *The Sun Also Rises* he declared almost open war against a rival whom he suddenly saw as formidable far beyond his expectations. Until *Gatsby* appeared, Hemingway had considered Fitzgerald merely a popular writer and, as a rival, a pushover.

The title *The Sun Also Rises* engages in a hostile way one of Fitzgerald's most prominent recurrent images in *Gatsby,* the romantic moon. Hemingway means to assert that the Sun, not the Moon, the earth, not the sky, constitute the essential truth of experience. This sun-moon argument includes the obvious idea that the sun stands at the center of the actual solar system while the moon merely reflects the sun—thus defining his relation to Fitzgerald. This is to say that the sun represents the major tradition in literature, the romantic moon merely reflects a subordinate one. In *The Sun Also Rises* Hemingway relentlessly pressed his war against Fitzgerald.

Fitzgerald and Hemingway both published major works in 1925. *The Great Gatsby* was released in April. Then *In Our Time* appeared in October. When Hemingway forged *In Our Time,* partly out of earlier material, he had every reason to think it a strong enough book despite its provenance and form to move him past Fitzgerald in the literary standings. And Hemingway, as we know, thought in such terms.

Fitzgerald had emerged suddenly in 1920 with *This Side of Paradise,* and his early success was part of his legend. He then wrote short stories, some of them excellent, and then finished his second novel, *The Beautiful and Damned* (1922). The stories were reprinted in two collections, *Flappers and Philosophers* and *Tales of the Jazz Age.* Fitzgerald, who was earning large sums of money from magazine publication, had a wide audience.

Hemingway played tortoise to Fitzgerald's hare. After the war he worked as a journalist and experimented with a new way of writing, also frequenting avant-garde circles in Paris. He published, almost secretly, two privately printed pamphlets, *Three Stories and Ten Poems* (July 1923; 300 copies) and then *in our time* (January 1924; 170 copies).

This minimal publication did attract enough attention in avant-garde circles for Edmund Wilson to review the two pamphlets in the influential *Dial* magazine of October 1924, and he did so with special attention to Hemingway's style, which he called "a limpid shaft into deep waters," a strikingly apt description of what Hemingway was trying to achieve, Two of the three stories in the first pamphlet and the brief vignettes that constituted the second pamphlet came forward into *In Our Time* in 1925.

Working slowly and with great discipline at his craft, Hemingway would have been justified in thinking that the 1925 edition of *In Our Time* was far superior to anything Fitzgerald thus far had written. *In Our Time* is a powerful work, not quite a novel but much more than a collection of stories; and it has multiple interconnections with Eliot's *Waste Land* (1922). To use Hemingway's lingo, this book should have knocked Fitzgerald out of the ring. Meanwhile Fitzgerald was generously promoting Hemingway as a writer and reviewed *In Our Time* with astute praise in the *Bookman* for May 1926.

In October 1925, when *In Our Time* appeared, Hemingway was no longer competing with the early works of Fitzgerald. He was competing with *The Great Gatsby,* another matter altogether. As Hemingway—like everyone else—surely noticed, *Gatsby* was an enormous advance over everything else Fitzgerald had written. Eliot, who is present in *Gatsby* in many ways, wrote that it "seems to me to be the first step that American fiction has taken since Henry James."

During that famous summer of 1925 Hemingway made his trip to Pamplona and then wrote *The Sun Also Rises* with what was, compared to his usual practice, great speed. He wrote it with Fitzgerald and *The Great Gatsby* much on his mind. His rapid composition may indicate anger and denied ambition; it surely indicates his mastery of his own style and ability to manage a longer form. Under Fitzgerald's sponsorship, Hemingway had broken with Boni and Liveright and moved to Charles Scribner's Sons and Maxwell Perkins. *The Sun Also Rises* appeared in October 1926.

In many obvious ways this novel is full of rage directed at Fitzgerald, who had shown nothing but goodwill and generosity toward Hemingway.

In *The Sun Also Rises* Robert Cohn, like Fitzgerald, has gone to Princeton—then a citadel of the WASP aristocracy. Cohn is a Jew, Fitzgerald a Catholic, and thus comparable outsiders at Princeton. Cohn's Jewishness can be read as a denigrating comment on Fitzgerald's Catholicness. Cohn tries unsuccessfully to be a gentleman, another comment directed at Fitzgerald. Fitzgerald, who was a hero-worshipper and who idolized Princeton athletes, was himself a failed football player. Cohn has had his Jewish nose flattened in the ring and thus "improved."

Cohn (read Fitzgerald) is a romantic and a bad novelist. His failure as a writer is owing to his romanticism and bad taste. He admires bad novels (*The Purple Land*) while Jake Barnes (Hemingway) knows that Turgenev has the right stuff.

Throughout the novel Cohn displays atrocious manners. Like Fitzgerald he is a sloppy drunk. He talks too much, is bad with women, and women despise him. He is "unrealistic" about women. That this was Hemingway's opinion of Fitzgerald is abundantly demonstrated in *A Moveable Feast,* as in the notorious chapter "A Matter of Measurements."

Hemingway had been befriended and promoted by Sherwood Anderson. In *The Torrents of Spring* (1925) he had launched a devastating attack on Anderson. *The Sun Also Rises* represents another such attack, this time against Fitzgerald, a much more formidable opponent.

Hemingway's attack is not only personal but also stylistic and moral. He would have framed it as moral realism versus romantic illusion.

Fitzgerald's central achievement as a writer is to use all the resources of language to capture the magnificence of the moment. In *This Side of Paradise,* he writes on the first page: "Beatrice Blaine! There was a woman!" But having said that, the very young writer must come through to show that this is so. Throughout this flawed early novel, the young writer sets himself such celebratory dares and must rise to the proof, often moving into prose poetry. Fitzgerald's prose wants to move toward and even into celebratory song.

Hemingway's prose, as the emotions it deals with grow more and more intense, moves toward total silence. At the end of *The Sun Also Rises* words fail:

"Oh, Jake," Brett said, "we could have had such a damned good time together."

"Yes," I said. "Isn't it pretty to think so."

Prose arias about Princeton, Dutch sailors, and the Riviera could not possibly live in that stylistic environment.

Gatsby provides a bravura demonstration of Fitzgerald's style and moral vision. It begins with a soggy bromide from Nick's father: "Whenever you feel like criticizing any one, just remember that all the people in this world haven't had the advantages that you've had." Nick apparently thinks so highly of this verbal legacy that he treasures it. Indeed he is rather bromidic himself as we follow him through the wild events of the story. But his gift for cliché is challenged by what happens around him, and his capacity for eloquence finally issues forth in his last great song about the Dutch sailors, the virgin American continent, and history.

No doubt what provokes this eloquence in Nick is his total experience during that strange, even visionary summer of 1922; but its most immediate source is Jay Gatsby himself. He speaks seldom, but when he does his lines are startling: "Her voice was full of money"; "Can't repeat the past? Why of course you can"; he declares also that Daisy's love for Tom Buchanan was merely "personal." At such moments Gatsby presses weirdly, magically, against ordinary expectations, even as does his half-crazy project of returning to 1917.

That Gatsby is a prince of language and can pass this power on to his demi-disciple Nick is a comment on Fitzgerald's own style. This aspect is hardly ever discussed by critics, but it is the essence of the Fitzgerald performance. He too is able to go off the charts, in scene as well as in phrase, perform in an almost crazy way, writing something zany that is also perfect, as he does, for example, in the scene in which the wheel comes off the car and the drunk can only suggest, "Put her in reverse," and "No harm in trying"; or the scene in Nick's cottage before the appearance of Daisy, when Gatsby's head tilts back the clock on the mantle and almost causes it to fall; or the old timetable on which Nick wrote the now-graying names of Gatsby's remarkable guests "that summer." Such brilliant zaniness often occurs in Fitzgerald in the smaller scale of a sentence:

> The snow of twenty-nine wasn't real snow. If you didn't want it to be snow, you just paid some money.

> "That's nothing at all. My father has a diamond bigger than the Ritz-Carlton Hotel."

> "Eatin' green peach. 'Spect to die any minute."

> There was something ineffably gorgeous somewhere that had nothing to do with God.

And dozens more. Often a single such touch redeems an otherwise mediocre magazine story. They are so striking that they gave rise to the suspicion that Fitzgerald thought of them when he was half in the bag. That his style can press up to the edges of sanity and maybe beyond Fitzgerald acknowledges in his great story "Absolution" when he gives us in Father Schwartz a visionary stylist who has slipped over the line: "Well, go and see an amusement park. . . . It's a thing like a fair, only more glittering. Go to one at night and stand a little way off from it in a dark place—under dark trees. . . . It will all just hang out there in the night like a colored balloon—like a big yellow lantern on a pole."

Nick Carraway moves from the banalities of his father into the magical world of Gatsby and his language. This central characteristic of Fitzgerald's style is Keatsian and, behind that, Shakespearian. Throughout *Hamlet* the prince says all those remarkable things while his friend Horatio remains a steady but pedestrian Senecan stoic out of Wittenberg University. But, with the death of the prince, Shakespeare gives Horatio some of the best lines in the play, far beyond anything he could articulate earlier. It is a conversion: "Goodnight, sweet prince, / May flights of angels sing thee to thy rest." So much for the Senecan stoic.

Keats, it is hardly necessary to argue, was a poet of great importance to Fitzgerald, and in *The Great Gatsby* the nightingale's song is heard only in a Keatsian moonlight.

Reading *Gatsby* in the spring of 1925, Hemingway could not have missed the large thematic role played by the moon, sailing into that novel from folklore, romantic tradition, and most immediately from Keats's *Endymion*. Gatsby himself, it has often been pointed out, seems weakened in the daylight scenes but lives much more powerfully after dark; and throughout the action he is associated with moonlight at especially important moments.

In *Endymion* the hero falls in love with Cynthia the moon goddess, and this poem has not only thematic resemblances to *Gatsby* but narrative parallels as well. The moon illumines the poem as much as it does Fitzgerald's novel.

> And lo! from opening clouds, I saw emerge
> The loveliest moon, that ever silver'd o'er
> A shell for Neptune's goblet; she did soar
> So passionately bright, my dazzled soul
> Commingling with her argent spheres did roll
> Through clear and cloudy, even when she went
> At last into a dark and vapoury tent—

When Endymion at last meets the moon goddess, she somehow brings the spirit of the moon with her to the bottom of a well as if to protect it from the violations of daylight:

> When, behold!
> A wonder fair as any I have told—
> The same bright face I tasted in my sleep,
> Smiling in the clear well. My heart did leap
> Through the cool depth.

The moon is as important in *Gatsby* as it is in *Endymion,* which Fitzgerald probably could recite from memory. The Gatsbian moon first appears in that remarkable sentence when Nick first glimpses Jay Gatsby: "The wind had blown off, leaving a loud bright night. . . . The silhouette of a moving cat wavered across the moonlight, and turning my head to watch it, I saw that I was not alone—fifty feet away a figure had emerged from the shadow of my neighbor's mansion, and was standing with his hands in his pockets regarding the silver pepper of the stars."

Gatsby, as the first chapter ends, has "stretched out his arms" toward the green light at the end of Daisy's dock. At the end of *This Side of Paradise,* the last time we see Amory Blaine, he is under the stars, stretching out his arms toward them and toward Princeton. The similarity of the postures is striking; and in his essay **"Princeton"** (1927) Fitzgerald wrote about his university in lyrical and ideal terms that could easily express the emotions of Gatsby in the scene just described.

One of Gatsby's parties ends with that amazing scene in which a wheel is broken off a car driven by the drunken driver. This is a parodic version of Gatsby himself. At the same time Gatsby is bidding farewell to his multitude of guests: "A wafer of a moon was shining over Gatsby's house, making the night fine as before, and surviving the laughter and the sound of his still glowing garden. A sudden emptiness seemed to flow now from the windows and the great doors, endowing with complete isolation the figure of the host, who stood on the porch, his hand up in a formal gesture of farewell."

In the flashback to Gatsby's boyhood in chapter 6, we learn that Jay Gatsby was born out of James Gatz under the light of the moon: "A universe of ineffable gaudiness spun itself out in his brain while the clock ticked on the wash-stand and the moon soaked with wet light his tangled clothes upon the floor. Each night he added to the pattern of his fancies." That clock ticking on the washstand recalls the clock alluded to earlier.

The moon appears again in chapter 6, but this time as a "pale, thin ray of moonlight" over one of Gatsby's parties, as Nick and Daisy stand watching a movie director slowly kiss the cheek of his star actress. The scene is a pale version of genuine romance.

Five years earlier, in 1917, when Lt. Gatsby was in love with Daisy in Louisville, "they had been walking down a street when the leaves were falling, and they came to a place where there were no trees and the side-walk was white with moonlight. They stopped here and turned toward each other." There we have the "moment," with the moon turning the sidewalk white. The leaves are falling, but the lovers are oblivious of time.

The Gatsbian moon is much more than the conventional moon of romance, and its full significance becomes clear only after Gatsby himself is dead in his swimming pool and is wreathed by the fallen leaves of autumn. Nick returns, perhaps for the last time, to the North Shore of Long Island and thinks about Gatsby. Absolutely everything in this coda is important. Nick notices "on the white steps, an obscene word scrawled by some boy with a piece of brick." Nick erases the word. (J. D. Salinger after World War II could print that but had Holden Caulfield erase it.) Then Nick wanders down to the shore and reflects: "Most of the big shore places were closed now and there were hardly any lights except the shadowy, moving glow of a ferryboat across the Sound. And as the moon rose higher the inessential houses began to melt away until I gradually became aware of the old island here that flowered once for Dutch sailors' eyes." Given the extensive preparation for this, the phrase *as the moon rose higher* is inevitable. The phrase *flowered once* reaches back to Daisy, Myrtle, the Carraways, and much else. But, though Jay Gatsby is dead, *his* moon still rises; and now Nick, no longer the child of his banal father, commences his own nightingale's song under the moon in this unexpected bravura aria.

That he is the "son" now of Gatsby is indicated by his inclusive "we" when he says that "tomorrow we . . . will stretch out our arms farther." When he had first glimpsed him, Gatsby was stretching out his own arms toward Daisy's green light, and at that point Gatsby was the son of Amory Blaine, who had stretched out his arms toward Princeton. For all the irony with which he surrounds the words "we . . . will stretch out our arms farther" at the end of *The Great Gatsby,* Fitzgerald will not give it up. It is of the essence, and it informs his style, which itself is always stretching beyond, with Fitzgerald's taking risks Hemingway could not imagine.

What we are to understand, as that moon rises over Long Island at the end of *Gatsby,* is that this end is not the end. The moon of imagination that transformed James Gatz into Jay Gatsby will continue to rise everlastingly, the imagination transforming things for better or worse according to its own quality. This is Fitzgerald's "answer" to Eliot's *Waste Land,* which he had written into this book as the Valley of Ashes and which he calls the "waste land." As against Eliot, Fitzgerald says that this moon, rising in the night sky, is a permanent force, not a force for romantic illusion. Though Gatsby mistakenly worshipped his Daisy, Fitzgerald wrote in *Gatsby* that the moon is the power of the transforming imagination.

Fitzgerald probably would not have been surprised by the prophetic grasp of *The Great Gatsby* as the transforming imagination did indeed transform the Valley of Ashes, known as Flushing Meadow. Jay Gatsby was a product of money and imagination. The New York World's Fair of 1939 and 1940 arose out of the Valley of Ashes, a landfill, as a triumph of money and imagination, its Trylon and Perisphere, designed by Wallace Harrison and André Fouilhoux, a culmination of the modernist movement in architecture and an emblem of transcendent optimism. Today, with the great fair gone, the Valley of Ashes has been once again transmogrified into the National Tennis Center, named after Louis Armstrong, a jazz musician who had no interest in tennis. Fitzgerald would have understood these startling changes completely.

Hemingway first met Fitzgerald at the Dingo Bar in the rue Delambre, Paris, in late April or early July 1925. The meeting occurred after the publication of *Gatsby* but before the publication of *In Our Time*. It seems probable that Hemingway had read *Gatsby* by the time of the meeting. However that may be, Hemingway's account of the meeting in *A Moveable Feast* is venomous at Fitzgerald's expense.

During the next summer Hemingway made his trip to Pamplona, gathering the material that would go into *The Sun Also Rises*. He completed the novel rapidly, and delivered the typescript to Maxwell Perkins at Scribner's in February 1926.

Then an episode occurred that must have been excruciating for Hemingway. By the spring of 1926 *The Sun Also Rises* was going into galley proof at Scribner's. Hemingway and his wife, Hadley, visited the Fitzgeralds at Juan-les-pins on the Riviera. The Fitzgeralds did not like their place, the Villa Paquita, and turned it over to the Hemingways. Fitzgerald read a carbon copy of the typescript of *The Sun Also Rises,* and he wrote Hemingway a long and surgically professional memorandum on the faults of the novel, which by then was in galleys in New York. Hemingway must have been appalled, but he swallowed his pride and made the changes Fitzgerald recommended, including the major cut of about the first twenty pages of the typescript, which dealt at length with Cohn. In New York the galleys had to be reworked to incorporate the changes. "I can't imagine," Fitzgerald wrote, "how you could have done these first 20 pps. so casually. You can't *play* with peoples attention."

Both the title of the novel and the epigraph from which it comes are puzzling in relation to the novel. The quotation from Ecclesiastes is about the everlastingness of the earth, which, Hemingway said, is the subject of the novel. But this is only partly true, if at all true. The novel is about ragged and painful human relationships; about transitoriness, love, and suffering; and about the courage of endurance and silence in the face of over-whelming emotion. The original title of the novel was *Fiesta,* which, with suitably ironic overtones, does seem more appropriate than the eventual title. Why Hemingway changed the title we cannot know. The one we have, however, may glance obliquely at **The Great Gatsby,** as if to say that, well, if the moon of imagination rises there, the sun of realism will rise here. The title can be seen as an assertion of moral realism (Hemingway) as against the supposed illusions of romance (Fitzgerald). We may think that as the moon rose over Gatsby's Long Island the sun will now rise triumphantly over Hemingway's Spain and in the mind of Jake.

Was there a winner in this contest that Hemingway imagined? The moon of transforming imagination did rise over Fitzgerald's Valley of Ashes, and constituted Fitzgerald's oblique answer to Eliot's *Waste Land*; but Hemingway has his own answer to Eliot. Jake Barnes is a wounded Fisher King, but there is no Grail in his blighted kingdom. With his Old Testament name, Jacob, and his residual dried-up Catholicism, and his sexual wound, Jake cannot unite himself with the pagan Brett. The old Christian-pagan Western synthesis has been shattered, and though Jake tries to pray, he cannot heal the wound in his own heart and in the heart of Western civilization. Still he does fish in that cool stream near the monastery of Roncesvalles (he cannot reach the Chapel Perilous); he does sustain the stoic code of the soldier, and he knows the power of silence. Unlike Cohn, Jake is a gentleman. He is a wounded and emotionally shattered veteran, but also a reconstructed Western man.

Furthermore Hemingway asserted his Lady Brett against Fitzgerald's Golden Girls, and she more than held her own. Such figures as Lauren Bacall, Humphrey Bogart, Edwin R. Murrow, and many other post-1920s figures would be unthinkable without Hemingway, as would the hard-bitten journalism of World War II.

After 1926 Hemingway long remained a master of the short story and wrote one more novel at the peak of his powers, *A Farewell to Arms* (1929). As a world figure Hemingway rose like the sun during the 1930s, becoming a modern Byron and a media star. Despite the gorgeous ruin of **Tender Is the Night** and whatever we make of the fragments of his Hollywood novel, **The Last Tycoon,** Fitzgerald never achieved again the near-perfection of **Gatsby.**

Hemingway seemed to forget about the power of silence, compression, and deep suggestion, becoming more and more prolix until—despite a few brilliant recoveries—he managed to achieve the verbal elephantiasis of the manuscript of *The Garden of Eden.* During the 1930s he continued his war against Fitzgerald, in-sulting him in "The Snows of Kilimanjaro," often wise-cracking about him as a writer who had passed from adolescence to senility without ever becoming an adult, and taking some nasty shots at him from the grave in *A Moveable Feast.*

And yet, in 1926, who won? In **The Great Gatsby** Fitzgerald had written an even stronger novel than *The Sun Also Rises*. He even had improved *The Sun Also Rises* with his last-minute and immensely important corrections. When Hemingway first read **The Great Gatsby** early in 1925, he may well have sensed that what Fitzgerald was doing was beyond him and been furious. Then he published *The Sun Also Rises* and proved Fitzgerald's achievement was beyond him.

Bert Bender (essay date December 1998)

SOURCE: Bender, Bert. "'His Mind Aglow': The Biological Undercurrent in Fitzgerald's *Gatsby* and Other Works." *Journal of American Studies* 32, no. 3 (December 1998): 399-420.

[*In the following essay, Bender discusses the influence of theories of evolutionary biology—including eugenics, ideas of accident and heredity, and Darwin's notions of sexual selection—on* Gatsby *and other Fitzgerald works.*]

> They talked until three, from biology to organized religion, and when Amory crept shivering into bed it was with his mind aglow . . .
>
> (Fitzgerald, *This Side of Paradise*)

Readers familiar with F. Scott Fitzgerald's early work might recall that in those years just before the Scopes trial he wrote of Victorians who "shuddered when they found what Mr. Darwin was about"; or that he joined in the fashionable comic attacks on people who could not accept their "most animal existence," describing one such character as "a hairless ape with two dozen tricks."[1] But few would guess the extent to which his interest in evolutionary biology shaped his work. He was particularly concerned with three interrelated biological problems: (1) the question of eugenics as a possible solution to civilization's many ills, (2) the linked principles of accident and heredity (as he understood these through the lens of Ernst Haeckel's biogenetic law), and (3) the revolutionary theory of sexual selection that Darwin had presented in *The Descent of Man and Selection in Relation to Sex* (1871). As I hope to show in the following pages, his concern with these issues underlies such well-known features in the Fitzgerald landscape as his insecurity in the "social hierarchy" (his sense of its "terrifying fluidity"), his emphasis on the element of time, his interest in "the musk of money," his interest in

Spengler and the naturalists, and his negative portraiture of male violence.[2] The principles of eugenics, accidental heredity, and sexual selection flow together as the prevailing undercurrent in most of Fitzgerald's work before and after *The Great Gatsby,* producing more anxiety than love from the tangled courtships of characters he deemed both beautiful and damned.

"LOVE OR EUGENICS"

By his second year at Princeton (in 1914), before he began to read the naturalists, Fitzgerald had taken in enough of the evolutionary view of life to see its relevance to the most fascinating subject for any youth of eighteen—sex. In **"Love or Eugenics"** he playfully wondered whether young men are most attracted by women of vigorous stock, with "plenty of muscle, / And Avoirdupois to spare," or by modern flappers who know the value of "good cosmetics."[3] But Fitzgerald grew a good deal more serious about the biology of sex before he left Princeton in 1917. In the scene from *This Side of Paradise* in which Amory and his friend Burne Holiday talked about biology until Amory's mind was "aglow," the two came naturally to the question that gave eugenics its pressing relevance, the idea that "The light-haired man *is* a higher type," as Burne puts it (128). When Burne (patterned on Fitzgerald's friend Henry Slater) "voluntarily attended graduate lectures in philosophy and biology" (131), he might have heard Princeton's famous Professor of Biology, Edwin G. Conklin, lecture on phylogeny (with attention to Darwin and sexual selection) and ontogeny (with emphasis on Conklin's particular interest in eugenics). Conklin published a detailed outline for the course in General Biology (*Laboratory Directions in General Biology*), and ended the section on ontogeny with this note: "All members of the class are invited, but not required, to fill out a Family Record blank, giving details of their own heredity for the use of the Committee on Eugenics."[4]

Even if Fitzgerald or Burne/Slater never read this invitation, it is clear from *This Side of Paradise* that the subject was quite palpably in the air at Princeton, no doubt heightening what Fitzgerald's biographers have described as his insecurity in the social hierarchy. Indeed, Fitzgerald was so attuned to the subject of eugenics and heredity that he included a further brief, playful scene in his next novel: a young man accused of being an "intellectual faker" responds with the challenge, "What's the fundamental principle of biology?" When his accuser guesses, "natural selection?" the young man corrects him: "Ontogony recapitulates phyllogony" (*sic, Beautiful and Damned* 153-54).

The profound social consequences of this "fundamental principle" are reflected in much of Fitzgerald's work. Articulated by Ernst Haeckel, the idea was that a spe-

cies' evolutionary development (phylogeny) is recapitulated in the individual's embryological development (ontogeny), revealing in the human embryo's gill slits, for example, our ancestral relationship with fish. But, as Stephen Jay Gould notes, "Recapitulation served as a general theory of biological determinism" with a terrible appeal to many Americans who felt the pressure of immigration from Ireland and especially southern Europe. The American paleontologist E. D. Cope "preached [it as the] doctrine of Nordic supremacy": the "inferior" groups (including "races, sexes, and classes") were arrested in development at the level of the white male's child. Just as the white embryo's development recapitulated the human descent from lower forms, so did the white *child*'s development recapitulate the development of the lower or "childlike" races (who were supposedly arrested at that stage) until, triumphantly, the white males, at least, would go on to exhibit their superiority as a race.[5]

One begins to see how the study of heredity might have appealed to Princetonians of those years, some of whom, like Fitzgerald, were so disturbed at seeing "the negroid streak creep[ing] northward to defile the nordic race" that they were overly receptive to popular and less scientific writers like Lothrop Stoddard.[6] Stoddard (cited as Goddard by Tom Buchanan in *Gatsby*) welcomed the time when "biological knowledge will have so increased" that eugenicist programs might "yield the most wonderful results"; in the meantime, he advised, "migrations of lower human types like those which have worked such havoc in the United States must be rigorously curtailed. Such migrations upset standards, sterilize better stocks, increase low types, and compromise national futures."[7] As Fitzgerald wrote to Edmund Wilson from Europe in the summer of 1921, "Raise the bars of immigration and permit only Scandinavians, Teutons, Anglo Saxons + Celts to enter" (*Letters* 47).

THE RIDDLE OF THE UNIVERSE: ACCIDENT, HEREDITY, AND SELECTION

Since Fitzgerald referred to Haeckel's "biogenetic law" and, as a reviewer, complained of another writer's "undigested Haeckel," it will be worth considering what he seems to have gathered from his own copy of Haeckel's *The Riddle of the Universe at the Close of the Nineteenth Century* (1900).[8] Although Fitzgerald's critics have never discussed it, *The Riddle of the Universe* is much more reliable in suggesting the outlines of Fitzgerald's thought than is the text most frequently cited in this regard, Oswald Spengler's *The Decline of the West* (even though it did not appear in English until 1926). In a way, the books are similar in providing different but sweeping senses of destiny: Spengler's in his advocacy of "Goethe's form-fulfillment" as destiny (rather than Darwin's causality), and Haeckel's in his closing with Goethe's lines: "By eternal laws / Of iron ruled, / Must all fulfil / The cycle of / Their destiny."[9]

But, in general, Haeckel's book does much more to bring together the two subjects about which Amory and Burne talked until their minds glowed in *This Side of Paradise*—"biology" and "organized religion." *The Riddle of the Universe* deals with many of the key biological terms that figure in Fitzgerald's work before, in, and after *Gatsby*—like *accident, egg, descended, specimen, instinct, struggle, adaptation, selection, extinction,* and the name of Darwin, himself, whom Haeckel praises as *"the Copernicus of the organic world."*[10] But Haeckel's particular attraction for Fitzgerald lay in his solution to the "riddle" of man's "place . . . in nature" by explaining the related principles of accident, heredity, and selection (62).

Of these three, Haeckel emphasizes the role of heredity, advancing it in a larger context that dispenses with the "superstition" or "primitive" religion of revelation. Yet he explains "the embryology of the soul" and calls for a "new monistic religion," "scientific" and "realistic," that will be revealed in "the wonderful temple of nature" (chs. 8 and 19; p. 382). None of this pertaining to the soul or the "new monistic religion" resembles anything that I know of in Fitzgerald, but Fitzgerald certainly seems attuned to Haeckel's criticism of primitive Christianity (which he would have especially appreciated after reading Harold Frederic's examination of it in *The Damnation of Theron Ware,* one of his favorite books); and in *Gatsby,* especially, he emphasizes the role of accident in ways that suggest that he was quite familiar with Haeckel's (and, ultimately, Darwin's) discussion of it. Haeckel, going well beyond Darwin's point about chance or accidental variation, insists that "all individual forms of existence . . . are but special transitory forms—*accidents* or *modes*—of substance": "nowhere . . . in the evolution of animals and plants do we find any trace of design, but merely the inevitable outcome of the struggle for existence, the blind controller, instead of the provident God, that effects the changes of organic forms by a mutual action of the laws of heredity and adaptation" (216, 268-69).

In *The Great Gatsby,* Fitzgerald gives us, in place of a provident God, the gazing "eyes of Doctor T. J. Eckleburg" that were set there by "some wild wag of an oculist" who "then sank down himself into eternal blindness." These are the eyes that peer out over the bleak figure of George Wilson when he is told that his wife Myrtle was killed in an "accident," and that provoke him to insist repeatedly, "God sees everything."[11] Fitzgerald's emphasis on "accident" becomes overwhelming in the closing pages of the novel, including Nick's remark that Gatsby "knew that he was in Daisy's house by a colossal accident," and most resoundingly in his last image of the dead hero afloat in his pool: "A small gust of wind that scarcely corrugated the surface was enough to disturb [the water's] accidental course with its accidental burden" (156, 170).

As a story of modern love, *Gatsby* is squarely within the tradition of American fiction that began to appropriate Darwin's theory of sexual selection immediately after *The Descent of Man,* beginning with W. D. Howells's *A Chance Acquaintance* (1873).[12] This is not to suggest that Fitzgerald had Howells particularly in mind, but he depicted Gatsby and Daisy in this way as they leave together after the confrontation between Gatsby and Tom Buchanan: "They were gone, without a word, snapped out, made accidental, isolated like ghosts even from our pity" (142). Rather than Howells, the American writers most on Fitzgerald's mind during these years were Frederic, Dreiser, Frank and Charles Norris, and Wharton—to name only a few who were quite self-consciously engaged in critiquing "love" from their various biological points of view. But, again, it would seem that the most immediate theoretical support for Fitzgerald's own critique of love was *The Riddle of the Universe,* where Haeckel refers to Darwin's theory of sexual selection. Here, writing of the "eros" or "powerful impulse that . . . leads to . . . nuptial union," Haeckel emphasizes: "the essential point in this physiological process is not the 'embrace,' as was formerly supposed, or the amorousness connected therewith; it is simply the introduction of the spermatozoa into the vagina" (138-39).

Such remarks provide the kind of biological insight into modern love that caused many characters in American fiction at around the turn of the century to question "love" and motherhood as Edna Pontellier did in *The Awakening.* Witnessing "the scene of torture" as her friend gave birth, Edna thought of her own experience in "awakening to find a little new life to which she had given being, added to the great unnumbered multitude of souls that come and go"; and she feels "a flaming, outspoken revolt against the ways of Nature" (ch. 37). In *This Side of Paradise* similar insights provoke Amory's agonizing questions, "How'll I fit in? . . . What am I for? To propagate the race?" (215). And they lead his friend Eleanor to complain of the "rotten, rotten old world" where she remains "tied to the sinking ship of future matrimony."[13] Then, voicing Fitzgerald's sense that the struggle of sexual selection is far more disturbing than what the Freudian craze had suggested in its apparent invitation to promiscuity, she remarks: "I'm hipped on Freud and all that, but it's rotten that every bit of *real* love in the world is ninety-nine per cent passion and one little soupçon of jealousy." Amory (already depressed about his purpose in life as a male) agrees that this "rather unpleasant overpowering force [is] part of the machinery under everything" (238).

Before going on to analyze what drives the "machinery" of "love" in *The Great Gatsby* (i.e., the process of sexual selection, as Fitzgerald construed it), there is a final important point—the essential point—to make about Fitzgerald's interest in *The Riddle of the Uni-*

verse. Everything is determined by the accident of heredity—"the soul-blending at the moment of conception [when] only the latent forces of the two parent souls are transmitted by the coalescence of the erotic cell-nuclei" (142). Intent on showing his theory's "far-reaching consequences" regarding "our great question" of man's place in nature, Haeckel notes that "the human ovum, like that of all other animals, is a single cell, and this tiny globular egg cell (about the 120th of an inch in diameter) has just the same characteristic appearance as that of all other viviparous organisms" (62). Thus Haeckel concludes not only that the "law of biogeny" demonstrates our heritage back through "the ape" and all the "higher vertebrates" to "our primitive fish-ancestors," but that it "destroy[s] the myth of the immortality of the soul" (65, 138). For Fitzgerald, though, Haeckel's conclusion that "each personality owes its bodily and spiritual qualities to both parents" raises questions not only about man's place in the universe, but in the social hierarchy; for it demonstrates—as "in the reigning dynasties and in old families of the nobility"—that all individuals are held "in the chain of generations" (138, 143).

For these reasons more than anything else, the imagery of eggs figures memorably in Fitzgerald's work, not only in the absolute barrier that exists between "East Egg" and "West Egg" in *The Great Gatsby,* but in such earlier works as the unsuccessful play he produced in 1923, *The Vegetable.* There, one of the characters, Doris, explains that she plans to marry a man named "Fish," and Fitzgerald heavily underscores both "Fish" and "egg." "Fish? F-i-s-h?" another character (Jerry) asks. When Doris explains that "these Fishes are very nice," he warns that she might have to live "right over his father's place of business." Doris is attracted not only by Mr. Fish's "wonderful build," but by his habit of calling her "adorable egg." Confused again, the character Jerry asks, "What does he mean by that?" and Doris explains, "Oh 'egg' is just a name people use nowadays." After Jerry asks again, "Egg?" Doris wonders, "Does your father still read the Bible?"[14] This apparently trivial exchange has its place in the play's larger plot, which tracks the vegetable-hero's failed accidental ascent to the presidency of the United States and his ultimate career as a postman. As the hero finally explains about postmen, "They not only pick 'em out—they select 'em" (134).

Even though Fitzgerald's work with the egg idea couldn't save *The Vegetable,* he did not give up on it. Before he wrote the play he had commented to Edmund Wilson that he thought Sherwood Anderson's *The Triumph of the Egg* was "a wonderful title" (**Letters** 49), and he made something much more serious of it in *Gatsby* than his readers have sensed. Aside from the East and West Egg material, he includes two other odd but meaningful scenes. In the first, sitting in the New York apartment where Tom Buchanan meets with Myrtle Wilson, Nick notes that "the only picture was an over-enlarged photograph, apparently a hen sitting on a blurred rock. Looked at from a distance however the hen resolved itself into a bonnet and the countenance of a stout old lady beamed down into the room" (33). Moments later Nick realized that it was a "dim enlargement" of Myrtle's mother that "hovered like an ectoplasm on the wall" (34). "Ectoplasm" is a succinct comment on Myrtle Wilson's place in the social and evolutionary hierarchies, its two meanings (according to the *Random House Dictionary*) being (1) "the outer portion of the cytoplasm of a cell," and (2) "the supposed emanation from the body of a medium." According to Haeckel, "the skin layer, or ectoderm, is the primitive psychic organ in the metazoa . . . the tissue-soul in its simplest form" (160).

The other "egg" scene in *The Great Gatsby* serves to gloss the well-known passage in which Tom Buchanan exclaims "violently" that "'The Rise of the Coloured Empires' by this man Goddard" shows how "Civilization's going to pieces" (17). Fitzgerald seems to discredit Tom's belief that "it's all scientific stuff; it's been proved" (17); but, through Nick's observation as he and Gatsby enter the city, Fitzgerald suggests his own anxiety about the *Rising Tide of Color.* Crossing over the Queensboro Bridge, Nick sees "a dead man" pass "in a hearse" accompanied by friends with "the tragic eyes and short upper lips of south-eastern Europe"; then "a limousine passed us, driven by a white chauffeur, in which sat three modish Negroes, two bucks and a girl. I laughed aloud as the *yolks* of their eyeballs rolled toward us in haughty rivalry" (my emphasis; 73). Nick's own anxiety is clear here when he stops laughing and thinks to himself, "Anything can happen now that we've slid over this bridge"; "Even Gatsby could happen, without any particular wonder," he concludes. But this is before Nick meets Gatsby's father, Mr. Gatz, or learns that Gatsby's "parents were shiftless and unsuccessful farm people [and that] his imagination had never really accepted them as his parents at all" (104).

Gatsby's effort to create himself—to spring "from his Platonic conception of himself"—can only fail in the biological universe that Haeckel described (104). And, if Gatsby is a true "son of God" who "must be about His Father's Business, the service of a vast, vulgar and meretricious beauty," it is in the sense that he is destined to pursue Daisy's beauty according to the laws of sexual selection.[15] This force of beauty drives many of Fitzgerald's young men, as Dexter Green is "unconsciously dictated to by his winter dreams" of Judy Jones (**"Winter Dreams," Stories** 150). Even at age eleven, Judy was "beautifully ugly as little girls are apt to be" who "are destined . . . [to] bring no end of misery to a great number of men"; "she was arrestingly beautiful . . . [and the] color and the mobility of her mouth gave a continual impression of flux, of intense life, of passionate vitality" (147, 152). "The thing . . . deep in" Dexter that compelled his response to Judy persisted until he was much older and realized that "long ago, there was something in me, but now that thing is gone. Now that thing is gone, that thing is gone" (161, 168).

By 1922 Fitzgerald had freed himself somewhat from his earlier hero's conclusion in *This Side of Paradise* that "the problem of evil" was "the problem of sex" and that "inseparably linked with evil was beauty" (280). In *The Beautiful and Damned* beauty is simply part of the "machinery under everything"—an engine of sexual selection; and Fitzgerald identifies "life" itself as "that sound out there, that ghastly reiterated female sound": "active and snarling," it moves "like a fly swarm" (*Beautiful and Damned* 150, 260). In *The Great Gatsby,* Fitzgerald anoints both Daisy and Gatsby with the power of beauty, as I will explain below; but, in both their cases, as in the "intense vitality" of Myrtle Wilson (which contains *no* "gleam of beauty"), the underlying force is simply "life" (35, 30). This is Fitzgerald's ultimate subject in *The Great Gatsby*: "the full bellows of the earth [that was blowing] the frogs full of life" at the moment on that evening in late spring when "the silhouette of a moving cat" drew Nick's eye to Gatsby for the first time (25). Later, when Nick leaves Daisy and Gatsby alone during her first visit to his house, he sees that they are "possessed by intense life" (102).

In the following section I explain how Fitzgerald dramatizes the process of sexual selection in the stories of Tom and Daisy Buchanan, Daisy and Gatsby, Myrtle and George Wilson, and Nick and Jordan Baker. But it will help at this point to sketch in the main features and implications of the tangled web of conflicted life in which all the players exist. First, everyone is subject to the anxieties that arise in the general, unending struggle for life. In Fitzgerald's presentation of the evolutionary reality everything is subject to change: accidents happen at any moment, men and women must struggle to win and then keep their mates, the "tide" of "lower" racial groups is on the rise, and civilizations themselves rise and fall. Moreover, in the individual's development through life, according to Haeckel, his or her "psychic activity" is subject to the same pattern of progress and decline. In Haeckel's five stages of "man's psychic activity," the "new-born" develops "self-consciousness," the "boy or girl" awakens to "the sexual instinct," "the youth or maiden" up to "the time of sexual intercourse" passes through "the 'idealist' period," the mature man and woman engage in "the founding of families," and then "*involution* sets in" as the "old man or woman" experience "degeneration." As Haeckel dismally concludes, "Man's psychic life runs the same evolution—upward progress, full maturity, and downward degeneration—as every other vital activity in his organization"

(146-47). Rather in this key, Nick Carraway on his thirtieth birthday looks forward to only "the promise of a decade of loneliness, a thinning list of single men to know, a thinning brief-case of enthusiasm, thinning hair." Having just witnessed the disastrous confrontation between Gatsby, Tom, and Daisy, who "loves" them both, he remarks, "So we drove on toward death through the cooling twilight" (143).

Second, in this universe of accident and change, every individual and every individual's "house" or line is fixed at the moment of conception—as in "the Carraway house," for example, "in a city where dwellings are still called through decades by a family's name" (184). And third, although people like Myrtle and Gatsby are not only free but compelled to enter the struggle of sexual selection (their only means of elevating themselves in the social and evolutionary hierarchies), they nor any other characters in Fitzgerald's fiction can break the bonds of what Haeckel calls "the chain of generations" (143). As Fitzgerald put it in **"The Unspeakable Egg"** (1924), the comic story he wrote while *Gatsby* was in press, although a young woman might have her choice of "attractive eggs" and unattractive ones, the "unspeakable egg" itself determines that even in "Umerica, a free country," there aren't really any "chauffeurs and such that marry millionaires' daughters."[16]

SEXUAL SELECTION IN *THE GREAT GATSBY*

While Fitzgerald's understanding of heredity and ontogeny seems to have originated in his informal exposure to such ideas at Princeton and his reading in *The Riddle of the Universe,* his familiarity with the theory of sexual selection probably came as much from the novelists he admired as from biologists like Conklin or Haeckel. Both of these biologists briefly discuss the "secondary sexual characters" (like "the beard of man, the antlers of the stag, the beautiful plumage of the bird of paradise") that, Haeckel remarks, "are the outcome of sexual selection" as Darwin had explained (*Riddle of the Universe* 139). For lengthier discussions of the theory of sexual selection, including courtship behavior, Fitzgerald might have turned to any number of sources, from *The Descent of Man* to Havelock Ellis's *Sexual Selection in Man* (a volume collected as part of his *Studies in the Psychology of Sex*), or Upton Sinclair's *The Book of Life* (1921). It is important to realize that, *had* he turned to these three, he would have seen distinctly different versions of the sexual reality. Ellis, for example, built on Darwin's theory but then strove to elevate the psychology of sex into the art of love and ultimately a transcendent religion in which the human's animal nature is scarcely perceptible; and Sinclair strove to emphasize the human's "supremacy over nature by his greater power to combine in groups"—as in "primitive communist society."[17] No less than the theory of natural selection, the theory of sexual selection was (and continues to be) susceptible to various interpretations, as different writers construed evolutionary theory in ways that reflected their particular points of view regarding gender, class, race, or political ideology, as well as their particular spiritual or psychological anxieties.

Whatever his sources, it is clear that Fitzgerald focused on the key principles of sexual selection that previous American novelists from Howells to Edith Wharton had depended upon in constructing their own plots of courtship and marriage. Seeing the process in general as he put it in *This Side of Paradise,* as the "rather unpleasant overpowering force that's part of the machinery under everything" (238), he emphasized the female's power to select the superior male, and the male's struggle to *be* selected. Both the male and female in Fitzgerald's fiction wield the power to attract, often through music or dance, the female through her physical beauty and the beauty of her voice, and the male through his strength or ornamental display. And like so many American novelists who had also worked with the Darwinian materials, Fitzgerald embraced Darwin's observation that civilized human beings select for wealth or social position. Also, as in Darwin and the many realist and naturalist novelists who took up his theory, the successful male is compelled to exhibit superior strength and to contest his strength with competing males in what Darwin called "the law of battle" for possession of the female. Finally, as part of a more recent development in literary interpretations of Darwin's theory, Fitzgerald was interested in (and considerably frightened by) the new woman's aggressive sexuality—her occasional desire for more than one man and her recognition that she must engage in sometimes deadly competition with other females to win her man.

Working essentially with these points in *The Great Gatsby,* then, Fitzgerald constructed a plot with a fully natural ending: Gatsby fails in his romantic quest and remains a "poor son-of-a-bitch" because he denies his genetic identity and ignores the laws of sexual selection. Moreover, while Tom Buchanan retains physical possession of Daisy, his hand covering hers in "an unmistakable air of natural intimacy," he continues in his "alert, aggressive way . . . his head moving sharply here and there, adapting itself to his restless eyes." And Nick, having exhibited much anxiety and ambivalence in his own sexual relations, having witnessed the violent, chaotic drama involving Gatsby, the Buchanans, and the Wilsons, and having realized that the most profound "difference between men . . . [is] the difference between the sick and the well"—Nick withdraws alone into the middle-west of his youth, "half sick between grotesque reality and savage frightening dreams" (183, 152, 186, 131, 154).

Fitzgerald takes his first step toward this natural ending with his epigraph. Here, carrying forward his interest in the sexual "machinery under everything" (from *This Side of Paradise*), he focuses immediately upon the essential workings of sexual selection—the male's struggle in dance or ornamental display to be selected and the female's power to select:

> Then wear the gold hat, if that will move her;
> If you can bounce high, bounce for her too,
> Till she cry "Lover, gold-hatted, high-bouncing lover,
> I must have you!"

But before Nick enters into the story of Gatsby's effort to win Daisy, he begins by referring to his own "clan's" descent and telling of his own participation in a "counter-raid" in the "Teutonic migration known as the Great War" ("the last love battle," as Fitzgerald later termed it).[18] Resulting in his feeling at "the ragged edge of the universe," Nick's war experience has made him a wounded veteran in the larger sexual struggle about which Tom Buchanan is so anxious—that "the white race will be—will be utterly submerged" in the rising tide of color, and ultimately that he stands to lose his wife to a "crazy fish" like Gatsby (7, 17, 110). If you "sit back and let Mr. Nobody from Nowhere make love to your wife," Tom complains, you might as well "throw everything overboard and have intermarriage between black and white" (137).

In his first chapter, then, Fitzgerald identifies his other main characters and sets them adrift in the fluid, evolutionary universe wherein—as Nick remarks in the famous last line—"we [all] beat on, boats against the current, borne back ceaselessly into the past" (189). Tom Buchanan, Daisy, and Gatsby all "drift" in and out of the novel as the dead Gatsby finally does in his swimming pool, where Fitzgerald surrounds him with other "poor ghosts" who "drifted fortuitously about" in this "new world" (169). Telling how by "chance" he had rented his house near the "pair of enormous eggs" in that "strangest [of] communities in North America" to which Tom and Daisy had also "drifted" (and where Daisy will joke about "accidentally" arranging Nick's marriage to Jordan Baker), Nick begins to picture a tumultuous reality of high winds and rampant growth (9, 10, 23).

The "great bursts of leaves growing . . . just as things grow in fast movies" are driven by the same cosmic force that blows the "frogs full of life" and causes the Buchanans' "lawn [to start] at the beach and [run] toward the front door for a quarter of a mile, jumping over sun-dials and brick walks in burning gardens—finally when it reached the house drifting up the side in bright vines as though from the momentum of its run" (8, 25, 11). Developing this theme, Fitzgerald writes that the "fresh grass . . . seemed to grow a little way into the [Buchanan] house," suggesting that, like all life, it emerged from the sea and is related to the life force within the Buchanan line.[19] Later in the novel Nick describes how "the Buchanans' house floated suddenly" into view (149). This household's vital force throbs in "the enormous power of [Tom's] body" with its "great pack of muscle shifting" beneath his coat; and it has produced the child about whom Nick remarks, "I suppose she talks, and—eats, and everything" (11, 21). Moreover, it is reflected in the "paternal contempt" of Tom's "gruff" voice, which seemed to say, "I'm stronger and more of a man than you are" (11). Within pages we learn of the first incident in which this dominant male, a "hulking physical specimen," uses his "cruel body" to injure each of the three women in his life (16, 11). He is responsible not only for Daisy's "black and blue" knuckle in this scene, but also for another woman's broken arm (82), and he will go on to break Myrtle Wilson's nose (41). Ultimately, Fitzgerald's point is that Tom's brutal sexual power is alive in his "house" and that it is determinant in his struggles with both George Wilson over Myrtle and with Gatsby over Daisy. By contrast, no such force resides in Gatsby's fake "ancestral home" (162). Indeed, the futility of Gatsby's romantic denial of his biological identity and the violence of sexual selection is reflected in his well-trimmed lawn (which soon grew to be as long as Nick's after Gatsby's death) and the "thin beard of raw ivy" that covers his "tower" (188, 9).

Despite Tom's brutal strength, however, neither he nor any other individual in Fitzgerald's evolutionary world can rest secure. Frequently drawing attention to Tom's prehensile power, as Darwin referred to it (the male's physical tools—secondary sexual characters—for capturing and holding the female, as in the lobster's claws), Fitzgerald notes that Tom "broke [Myrtle's] nose with his open hand," that "he put out his broad, flat hand with well-concealed dislike" when introduced to Gatsby, and finally that "his hand [fell] upon and covered" Daisy's, signaling the end of his struggle with Gatsby.[20] By contrast at this conclusive moment, Nick leaves Gatsby "with his hands in his coat pockets . . . watching over nothing" (153). Still, Fitzgerald emphasizes that in this world where "there are only the pursued, the pursuing, the busy and the tired" (85), Tom must be ever vigilant. As Nick observes in chapter one, even with *two* women, "something was making [Tom] nibble at the edge of stale ideas as if his sturdy physical egotism no longer nourished his peremptory heart," and when we see him last he continues in his "restless," "alert, aggressive way, his hands out a little from his body as if to fight off interference" (25, 186).

Also one of the "pursuing," Gatsby expresses his "restlessness" as well: "he was never quite still; there was always a tapping foot somewhere or the impatient opening and closing of a hand" (68). When told that "you can't repeat the past," he looks around "wildly, as if the past were lurking here in the shadow of his house, just

out of reach of his hand" (116-17); and, since Gatsby's past moment with Daisy is out of reach largely because of the inherent deficiency of his "house," Fitzgerald presents Gatsby in a precarious state of balance: "he was balancing himself on the dashboard of his car with that resourcefulness of movement that is so peculiarly American" (68).

For similar reasons, in chapter one Fitzgerald depicts another of his main characters, the equally unattached and restless Jordan Baker, as "the balancing girl"; she had a way of holding her "chin . . . as if she were balancing something on it which was quite likely to fall" (13). Supplementing the precariousness of her social situation as a single woman who is both pursuer and pursued is her notably androgynous nature. A "small-breasted girl with an erect carriage" who looks "like a young cadet" and whom Fitzgerald identifies as the other athlete in his group, she displays, "a flutter of slender muscles in her arms" within the same sentence that captures the bright "lamp-light [on Tom's] boots" (15, 22). As others have noted, Jordan's androgyny appeals to Nick, who "enjoyed looking at her," and seems part of Fitzgerald's effort to reveal Nick's own sexual ambivalence (15).

As Nick explains in chapter one, one of the reasons he went "east [to] learn the bond business" was to escape the rumors that he was engaged (7, 24), and during his time in the east he breaks off with two other women. With a history of being "privy to the secret griefs of wild, unknown men" whose "intimate revelation[s]" sometimes "quiver[ed] on the horizon . . . marred by obvious suppressions," Nick will go on to tell of one of his most intimate moments in the east—when he reaches out to touch Mr. McKee, the "pale feminine man from the flat below" Tom's and Myrtle's. Minutes later, Nick and McKee "groaned down in the elevator" together on the way to McKee's flat (5-6, 34, 41-42). And, immediately after the strange brief scene in which Nick stands beside McKee's bed (where "between the sheets, clad in his underwear," he shows Nick some of his photographs), Nick finds himself "half asleep in the cold lower level of the Pennsylvania Station" (42). Aside from the possible reflections of Fitzgerald's and Nick's vague homoerotic desire that others have sensed in this scene, it would seem that Fitzgerald's emphasis on "down," "below," and "lower," represent another dimension in his view of the social and evolutionary hierarchy.[21]

Further suggested by Tom's remark when meeting Nick unexpectedly at lunch, "How'd you happen to come up this far to eat?" Fitzgerald's references to *up* and *down* in regard to Nick's biological activities suggest his susceptibility to degeneracy (78). This possibility is further suggested in the uncorrected galleys, where Nick tells of having written the names of Gatsby's guests (names like Bull, Fishguard, Hammerhead, and Beluga) on an "old time-table [that was] degenerating at its folds."[22] That is, as a reference to Nick's sexual identity, the idea that he "groaned down in the elevator" suggests more than his possible moral degeneration, as someone like Max Nordau would emphasize. Rather, Jordan's androgyny and Nick's sexual ambivalence reflect on one of the darker aspects in the evolution of sex that Darwin brought to light in *The Descent of Man*: that "it has now been ascertained that at a very early embryonic period both sexes possess true male and female glands. Hence some extremely remote progenitor of the whole vertebrate kingdom appears to have been hermaphrodite or androgynous" (1: 207). Fitzgerald was certainly aware of this idea from his having read of Dr. Ledsmar's Darwinian experiment about hermaphroditism in plants (in *The Damnation of Theron Ware*), and probably from having read Haeckel's discussion of such "rudimentary structures" as "the nipple and milk-gland of the male" (265). At any rate, an important result of Fitzgerald's presentation of these possibilities in *The Great Gatsby* is that they contribute to Nick's being repelled by the chaotic nature of sex. "Half sick between grotesque reality and savage frightening dreams," he withdraws from both the brutal male force that nevertheless fascinates him in Tom Buchanan, and from "the secret griefs of wild, unknown men," though they fascinate him as well (he frequently "feigned sleep" when the "intimate revelation was quivering on the horizon" [154, 5-6]). He let one "short affair with a girl" "blow quietly away" when he was confronted with a violent male: "her brother began throwing mean looks in my direction" (61). Similarly, although he had come east to learn "the bond business," when he found himself confined with the unlovely couples Tom and Myrtle and the McKees, Nick "wanted to get out and walk eastward toward the park." But "each time [he] tried to go [he] became entangled in some wild strident argument which pulled [him] back" (40). Still a resounding Darwinian term in the early 1920s, "entangled" in this scene soon leads to the outburst of Tom's violence (when he breaks Myrtle's nose) that causes Nick to leave with the "feminine" McKee. As the scene in McKee's apartment ends, Fitzgerald suggests in the titles of the first two pictures in McKee's portfolio that Nick's underlying story has to do mostly with "Beauty and the Beast" and "Loneliness" (42).

If Tom's brutal male power represents the "beast" in Fitzgerald's imagination, Daisy's voice is the deadly instrument of beauty. At the end of *This Side of Paradise* Amory had begun "to identify evil with . . . strong phallic worship" and concluded that "inseparably linked with evil was beauty," as in "Eleanor's voice, in an old song at night . . . half rhythm, half darkness" (280). There is certainly something of Eleanor's struggle with her female nature that lingers in Daisy: as Eleanor cried, "*why* am I a girl? . . . tied to the sinking ship of future

matrimony," Daisy wept when she learned that her baby was a girl, thinking "the best thing a girl can be in this world [is] a beautiful little fool" (*Paradise* 237, *Gatsby* 21). But even as she is aware of her biological entrapment (as Hemingway would later refer to it in *A Farewell to Arms*[23]) she cannot refrain from voicing what is perhaps the most alluring appeal in American literature. Playing on Darwin's analysis of the sexual appeal of music and the voice, many writers had invested the female voice with such power, as in W. D. Howells's Lydia Blood and James's Verena Tarrant.[24] But, whatever Fitzgerald's sources for this idea (Darwin, Haeckel, or any of the many "Darwinian" novelists), no writer dramatizes it more fully. He introduces the musical theme as part of the scene of natural history wherein the grass grows up from the beach into the Buchanan "house" and a sea "breeze . . . rippled over the wine-colored rug, making a shadow on it as wind does on the sea" (12). Then Daisy began asking Nick

> questions in her low, thrilling voice. It was the kind of voice that the ear follows up and down as if each speech is an arrangement of notes that will never be played again. Her face was sad and lovely with bright things in it, bright eyes and a bright passionate mouth—but there was an excitement in her voice that men who had cared for her found difficult to forget: a singing compulsion, a whispered "Listen," a promise that she had done gay, exciting things just a while since and that there were gay, exciting things hovering in the next hour.
>
> (13-14)

In his innumerable references to Daisy's voice, Fitzgerald identifies it as the principle instrument with which she casts her spell over Gatsby, compelling his belief in the kind of love that cannot exist in Fitzgerald's view of life. As Nick notes even in this first scene, "the instant her voice broke off, ceasing to compel my attention, my belief, I felt the basic insincerity of what she had said" (22). But the "deathless song" of Daisy's "voice held" Gatsby "with its fluctuating, feverish warmth because it couldn't be over-dreamed" (101). And when Gatsby tells Nick that "her voice is full of money," Nick immediately realizes that "the inexhaustible charm that rose and fell in it [was] the cymbals' song of . . . the king's daughter, the golden girl."[25]

As Daisy consciously or unconsciously wields her irresistible power, she becomes further entangled in the web of sexual struggle. When Gatsby left for the war after their brief romance, she had "suddenly" begun to date other men, only to find that, with her "evening dress tangled among dying orchids on the floor beside her bed . . . she wanted her life shaped . . . by some force," which soon proved to be the "force . . . of Tom Buchanan" (158-59); and even when she has not only Tom but possibly Gatsby, she looks back at Gatsby's house as she leaves the party, wondering, "what would happen now in the dim incalculable hours? Perhaps some unbelievable guest would arrive, a person infinitely rare and to be marvelled at, some authentically radiant young girl who with one fresh glance at Gatsby, one moment of magical encounter, would blot out those five years of unwavering devotion" (115). She is instinctively aware of "the first law of woman"—that she is a competitor in the sexual arena, as Fitzgerald had treated this subject in 1924 in **"Diamond Dick and the First Law of Woman."** Diana **("Diamond Dick")** Dickey's "nickname survived"—"she had selected it herself"—and she lived up to it by threatening a sexual competitor with a revolver (*The Price Was High* 69). "I think you've got my man" (82), she explains; "I wasn't made for anything like love" (79). No less a hunter than this Diana, or perhaps even Hemingway's Margot Macomber, Daisy is implicated in Myrtle Wilson's "accidental" death, as Fitzgerald suggests in Nick's concern that if "Tom found out that Daisy had been driving . . . he might think he saw a connection in it—he might think anything."[26]

Gatsby himself can never conceive of such a grim possibility, for he is determined to deny his origins and wants to believe "that the rock of the world was founded securely on a fairy's wing" (105). Nor can he accept the other part of his reality, as suggested in Fitzgerald's epigraph—that he was destined to perform the lover's dance in the biological struggle to be selected. He is always acted upon by the natural laws he cannot accept, as when the "universe of ineffable gaudiness spun itself out in his brain" one night as "the clock ticked" and his "tangled clothes [lay] upon the floor"; then "an instinct toward his future glory" led him on his way, first to St. Olaf College, and finally to his second opportunity to be selected by Daisy (105). Even then, "as if he were on a wire," he seems unaware that his most effective moment comes, as Fitzgerald's epigraph and Darwin's theory suggest, when he proudly displays his ornamental attractions—the "many-colored disarray . . . [of] shirts with stripes and scrolls and plaids in coral and apple green and lavender and faint orange with monograms of Indian blue" (91, 97-98). Not too subtly invoking the Darwinian idea when he has Gatsby explain that "a man in England . . . sends over a selection of things at the beginning of each season," Fitzgerald illustrates how effective is the power of beauty in sexual selection: "'They're such beautiful shirts,' [Daisy] sobbed, her voice muffled in the thick folds . . . 'I've never seen such—such beautiful shirts before'" (97-98).

Certainly the most splendid peacock in American literature, Gatsby repeatedly wears his famous pink suit, has his man Klipspringer perform "The Love Nest" on the piano, and, in general, "deck[s] out [his illusion] with every bright feather that drifted his way" (100-01). Nothing could be gaudier to attract the female's eye for ornamental beauty unless it is perhaps the taxi cab that appeals to Myrtle Wilson: "she let four taxi cabs drive away before she selected a new one, lavender-colored with grey upholstery [in which the party] slid out from the mass of the station into the glowing sunshine" (31). The image of phallic power and beauty is evident here, as it is in "Gatsby's gorgeous car . . . [of] rich cream color, bright with nickel, swollen here and there in its monstrous length with triumphant hatboxes," and so forth (68). But as Fitzgerald suggests in the line from "Ain't We Got Fun?" ("nothing's surer / The rich get richer"), despite Gatsby's gorgeous ornamentation and phallic appeal, he is no match for Buchanan when they finally confront each other "with competitive firmness" (101, 138).

Gatsby manages moderately well in the dance, with his "graceful, conservative fox-trot" (112); and Tom reveals himself to be no more impressive at this natural feat, in which, as Fitzgerald knew in *This Side of Paradise,* people are "selected by the cut-in system at dances, which favors the survival of the fittest" (58). More restrained in this dance with Daisy than at the first raucous event that Nick attended, Gatsby conceals his instinctive sense that music and dance can be effectively combined in what Darwin called "love-antics and dances" (*Descent of Man* 2: 68). There he had requested that the orchestra play the "Jazz History of the World," and it achieved its desired effect: "girls were putting their heads on men's shoulders . . . and swooning backward . . . into men's arms" (55). The trouble is, such primitive performances tend also to arouse the combative instincts that are inherent in the struggle for reproductive success. In a passage that Fitzgerald cut from the galleys, the "Jazz History of the World" is something like H. G. Well's evolutionary *Outline of History,* providing "a weird sense that it was a preposterous cycle after all"—one "discord" after another.[27] In the novel, the scene ends with one "fight" leading to several others, and the frenzy of "dissension" and "flank attacks" subsides only when two "wives [are] lifted kicking into the night."[28]

Of course, this is the way the struggle will end in *The Great Gatsby,* with the stronger male prevailing not so much for his beauty or "love," as Gatsby might have hoped, but for the superior physical and financial strength that inheres in his "house." Other American novelists had reached similar conclusions but in different ways: some of Howells's heroes in the 1870s, for example, who prevail over rival males because women select them for their *moral* as well as financial strength; or James's Basil Ransom, who prevails over weaker males (as well as a female competitor) because of his physical and *mental* power; or Harold Frederic's Joel Stormont Thorp because of his combined "never-force" and physical and financial strength, as well as the woman's attraction to his "frank barbarism of power"; or Edith Wharton's Cobham Stilling, in her story "The Choice," because of his sheer physical strength without financial wealth (Mrs. Stilling possesses the wealth).[29]

Unlike any of these, Fitzgerald's plot is quite in accord with "the fundamental principle of biology" that he alluded to in **The Beautiful and Damned,** the "ontogenic fact" that in the "tiny globular egg cell" one is already bound within "the chain of generations" (Haeckel 63, 62, 143). Representing a different "strata" from Daisy's, Gatsby "had no real right to touch her hand"; and when she saw his "huge incoherent failure of a house," it simply fell "in like a card house at the disapproval in her eyes" (156, 188, 120). For such reasons Fitzgerald suggests in his closing paragraphs that there never has been a "new world," only the "old unknown world." The "fresh, green breast of the new world . . . pandered in whispers" to the first sailors, compelling their unwanted "aesthetic contemplation"; and beauty is still part of the "machinery under everything" that derives us toward an "orgastic future" (189). "The essential point," as Haeckel remarked, "is not the 'embrace' . . . or the amorousness connected therewith; it is simply the introduction of the spermatozoa into the vagina" (139). Thus the imagined "pap of life" at which Gatsby would "gulp down the incomparable milk of wonder" is destroyed by the "accident," and by the grotesque reality of Myrtle's "left breast . . . swinging loose like a flap" (117, 145).

Notes

1. F. Scott Fitzgerald, *This Side of Paradise* (1920; New York: Scribner's, 1970), 151; F. Scott Fitzgerald, *The Beautiful and Damned* (1922; New York: Scribner's, 1955), 415-16.

2. Discussions of these elements in Fitzgerald's life and work can be found, for example, in Jeffrey Meyers, *Scott Fitzgerald: A Biography* (New York: Harper Collins, 1994), 1-3; and James W. Tuttleton, "Seeing Slightly Red: Fitzgerald's 'May Day,'" in *The Short Stories of F. Scott Fitzgerald: New Approaches in Criticism,* ed. Jackson R. Bryer (Madison: University of Wisconsin Press, 1982), 196; in Matthew J. Bruccoli, "Preface" to *The Great Gatsby* (New York: Collier Books, 1991), xiv-xv; in Scott Donaldson, *Fool for Love: F. Scott Fitzgerald* (New York: Congdon and Weed, 1983), 99-115, quote on p. 101; in John S. Whitely, "'A Touch of Disaster': Fitzgerald, Spengler and the Decline of the West," in *Scott Fitzgerald: The Promises of Life,* ed. A. Robert Lee (New York: St. Martins, 1989) throughout his article; and in Judith Fetterly, "Who Killed Dick Diver? The Sexual Politics of *Tender is the Night,*" *Mosaic,* 17:1 (1984), 124-26.

3. Matthew J. Bruccoli and Jackson R. Bryer, eds., *F. Scott Fitzgerald In His Own Time: A Miscellany* (n.p.: Kent State University Press, 1971), 18.

4. Edwin G. Conklin, *Laboratory Directions in General Biology* (n.p., n.d., held in the Seeley G. Mudd Manuscript Library, Princeton University)

78; in his well-known book, Conklin builds toward his long last chapters on eugenics, arguing for example that "the promotion of human evolution [through eugenics] must be undertaken by society as its greatest work," and that "individual freedom must be subordinated to racial welfare" (*Heredity and Environment in the Development of Men* 6th edn [Princeton: Princeton University Press, 1929], 348-49).

5. Stephan Jay Gould, *The Mismeasure of Man* (New York: Norton, 1981), 115.

6. Letter from Fitzgerald to Edmund Wilson, dated July 1921, in *F. Scott Fitzgerald: A Life in Letters,* ed. Matthew J. Bruccoli (New York: Scribner's, 1994), 46-47.

7. Lothrop Stoddard, *The Rising Tide of Color Against White World-Supremacy* (New York: Scribner's, 1922), 309, 308.

8. The "Fitzgerald Book Lists" in the F. Scott Fitzgerald Papers at Princeton University indicate that Fitzgerald owned and had signed a copy of *The Riddle of the Universe,* but that volume is not now contained in the University's Department of Rare Books and Special Collections. These book lists include no volumes by Darwin. In his enthusiastic review of Dos Passos's *Three Soldiers,* Fitzgerald cited Owen Johnston's *The Wasted Generation* as an example of a current war story that paled by comparison, in part because "it abounded with . . . undigested Haeckel" (*In His Own Time,* 123).

9. Oswald Spengler, *The Decline of the West,* abridged edn, trans. Charles Francis Atkinson, eds. Helmut Werner and Arthur Helps (New York: Knopf, 1962), 231; Spengler definitely rejected modern evolutionary thought, criticizing the shallowness of Darwinism and referring to the "soulless and soul-killing generation of . . . Haeckel" (132); Ernst Haeckel, *The Riddle of the Universe at the Close of the Nineteenth Century* (New York: Harper, 1900), 383.

10. Some of these words and other key terms in the Darwinian lexicon (like *tangle*) are traceable in Andrew Crosland, *A Concordance to F. Scott Fitzgerald's The Great Gatsby* (Detroit: Gale, 1975); *Riddle of the Universe* 252. As Haeckel notes here, he had first referred to Darwin in this way in 1868—long before Freud's more famous remark that after Copernicus' first great blow to human narcissism (by showing that the earth is not at the center of the universe), Darwin dealt the second or *"biological"* blow by proving the human's animal nature (Sigmund Freud, *The Standard Edition of the Complete Psychological Works of Sigmund Freud,* ed. James Strachey [London: Hogarth Press and The Institute of Psycho-Analysis, 1953-74] 17, 141).

11. F. Scott Fitzgerald, *The Great Gatsby*, preface by Matthew J. Bruccoli, 27-28, 166-67.

12. For a discussion of the Darwinian elements in *A Chance Acquaintance* and other novels of courtship and marriage by Howells, see Bert Bender, *The Descent of Love: Darwin and the Theory of Sexual Selection in American Fiction, 1871-1926* (Philadelphia: University of Pennsylvania Press, 1996).

13. P. 237; another example of Fitzgerald's biological critique of sexual love and motherhood is contained in these remarks about the character Gloria in *The Beautiful and Damned*: "She knew that in her breast she had never wanted children. The reality, the earthiness, the intolerable sentiment of child-bearing, the menace to her beauty—had appalled her. She wanted to exist only as a conscious flower, prolonging and preserving itself. Her sentimentality could cling fiercely to her own illusions, but her ironic soul whispered that motherhood was also the privilege of the female baboon. So her dreams were of ghostly children only" (392-93).

14. F. Scott Fitzgerald, *The Vegetable or from President to Postman* (1923; New York: Scribner's, 1976), 25-28; it is worth recalling that when Tom Buchanan learns that Gatsby knows his wife, he complains that "these days . . . [women] meet all kinds of crazy fish" (110).

15. P. 104; as many critics have remarked, Fitzgerald's earlier story, "Absolution" (1924), represents a preliminary effort to deal with the problem of his and his characters' origins. As I would put it, Rudolph in that story exemplifies the kind of anxiety about his fixed evolutionary state that Gatsby and other characters in Fitzgerald experience. Rudolph confessed his sin "of not believing I was the son of my parents" and so imagined himself as Blatchford Sarnemington, a character who then "established dominance over him" (F. Scott Fitzgerald, *The Stories of F. Scott Fitzgerald* [New York: Scribner's, 1969] 187, 189). As Haeckel might remark of such figures as Rudolph and especially Gatsby, the "boundless presumption of conceited man has misled him into making himself 'the image of God,' claiming an 'eternal life' for his ephemeral personality, and imagining that he possesses unlimited 'freedom of will'" (15).

16. *The Price Was High: The Last Uncollected Stories of F. Scott Fitzgerald*, ed. Matthew J. Bruccoli (New York: Harcourt Brace Jovanovich, 1979) 132, 134.

17. Upton Sinclair, *The Book of Life*, 2 Vols. in 1 (Chicago: Paine, 1922), 2, 9-10.

18. Pp. 6-7; in *Tender Is the Night*, as Dick Diver surveys a battlefield on the western front, he remarks: "Why this was a love battle—there was a century

of middle-class love spent here. This was the last love battle" (*Tender Is the Night* [1934; New York: Scribner's, 1962], 68).

19. P. 12; elsewhere, in many places, Fitzgerald is far more explicit in suggesting the human link to fish and the sea. In "The Swimmers" (1929), for example, the character Henry Marston enjoys swimming and feeling like a "porpoise," and he thinks that Americans could better deal with their restlessness if they had developed "fins and wings"; he comments ironically on the American idea that we could "leave out history and the past," "inheritance or tradition" (*Bits of Paradise: 21 Uncollected Stories by F. Scott and Zelda Fitzgerald* [London: The Bodley Head, 1973], 201). Similarly, in *Tender Is the Night*, Fitzgerald remarks that "Nicole had been designed for change, for flight with money as fins and wings" (311).

20. Pp. 41, 122, 152; discussions of other writers' work with the male's prehensile power are indexed in *The Descent of Love*, where, on pp. 143 and 191, for example, I discuss Henry James's use of these materials in *The Portrait of a Lady*. In his initial discussion of this male "secondary sexual character," evolved in order for the male to gain an "advantage . . . over other individuals of the same sex and species, in exclusive relation to reproduction," Darwin writes that "when the male has found the female he sometimes absolutely requires prehensile organs to hold her" (Charles Darwin, *The Descent of Man and Selection in Relation to Sex*, 2 vols. in 1 [1871; Princeton University Press, 1981], 1, 256).

21. For other controversial but insightful studies of androgyny and homosexual possibilities in *The Great Gatsby* that have only recently emerged (especially in the scene with Nick and McKee), see Keath Fraser, "Another Reading of *The Great Gatsby*," *English Studies in Canada*, 5:3 (1979); Patricia Pacey Thornton, "Sexual Roles in *The Great Gatsby*," *English Studies in Canada*, 5:4 (1979); and Edward Wasiolek, "The Sexual Drama of Nick and Gatsby," *The International Fiction Review*, 19:1 (1992). Also in reference to Nick's evolutionary identity, consider the ironic possibilities of Gatsby's repeated way of addressing him as "old sport," as on pp. 86-87.

22. *F. Scott Fitzgerald Manuscripts III The Great Gatsby: The Revised and Rewritten Galleys*, intro. and arranged by Matthew J. Bruccoli (New York: Garland, 1990), 47.

23. Ernest Hemingway, *A Farewell to Arms* (1929; New York: Scribner's, 1932), 139, 320.

24. Discussions of Howells's, James's and other novelists' uses of Darwin's observations about the sexual appeal of music and the voice are indexed

in *The Descent of Love*. Whether Fitzgerald caught it or not, Darwin referred to Haeckel's "interesting discussion of this subject," agreeing that "women . . . possess sweeter voices than men," but concluding "that they first acquired [these] musical powers in order to attract the opposite sex" (*Descent of Man*, 2, 337).

25. P. 127; among the innumerable parallels in Fitzgerald's story of a naive male's destruction in an encounter with the sexual reality, compared with Harold Frederic's in *The Damnation of Theron Ware*, are Celia Madden's several musical performances and Theron's fascination with "Miss Madden's riches"; the "glamour" of wealth "shown upon her," the "veritable gleam of gold" (*The Damnation of Theron Ware or Illumination*, Vol. 3 of *The Harold Frederic Edition* [1896; Lincoln: University of Nebraska Press, 1985], 254). Both Fitzgerald and Frederic work with Darwin's point that human beings select for wealth and social position.

26. P. 152; in Fitzgerald's story "The Dance" (1926) another sexual struggle between women ends in murder because "all the girls are good friends . . . except when two of them are try'n to get hold of the same man" (*Bits of Paradise*, 154).

27. P. 36; something of Fitzgerald's early attraction to the evolutionary view of life is evident in the interest he showed in Wells's *Outline of History, Being a Plain History of Life and Humankind*, which, he remarked in 1920, was "Most absorbing!" (*Correspondence of F. Scott Fitzgerald*, eds. Matthew J. Bruccoli and Margaret M. Duggan [New York: Random House, 1980], 73).

28. Pp. 56-57; for similar remarks by Fitzgerald on the role of music and dance in sexual selection, see "The Dance," which is set in a small town where life's affairs and scandals "live on all tangled up with the natural ebb and flow of outward life" (*Bits of Paradise*, 140).

29. Discussions of these examples are indexed in *The Descent of Love*.

James D. Bloom (essay date spring 1999)

SOURCE: Bloom, James D. "Out of Minnesota: Mythography and Generational Poetics in the Writings of Bob Dylan and F. Scott Fitzgerald." *American Studies* 40, no. 1 (spring 1999): 5-21.

[*In the following essay, Bloom draws parallels between Fitzgerald and singer Bob Dylan's life and works, arguing that both were anti-prophets who made myths of themselves and at the same time undermined those myths.*]

AFFINITIES

"You've been through all of F. Scott Fitzgerald's books. You're very well read. It's well known." So runs a memorable line in Bob Dylan's "Ballad of a Thin Man" on his 1965 album *Highway 61 Revisited*. Not only did this song provide "an instant catchphrase for the moral, generational, and racial divisions" that, in Greil Marcus' formulation, separated the cognoscenti from the "squares" (8-9); this album also marked Dylan's controversial introduction to LP buyers of his paradigm-shifting hybrid, "folk rock." Brian Morton's 1991 novel, *The Dylanist*, describes the appeal of this watershed: "Dylan gave . . . hope: He showed that you could make your life a work of art" (91). Morton's protagonist "loved the way" Dylan "remained fluid, reinventing himself endlessly, refusing to be trapped by other people's expectations." Reflecting the pervasiveness of this appeal, Fred Goodman's social history of rock-music business declared Dylan "unquestionably the most influential artist of his generation" (96).

In view of Dylan's singular impact on his generation, his citation of Fitzgerald points to the aspiration and the achievement that place both writers among the select few, among a handful of modern writers who turned themselves into generational idols and their work into durable models. Dylan's famous 1965 breakthrough (the momentum of which persisted through his 1975 album *Desire*) clinched this icon status. The decisive point in this breakthrough occurred at the 1965 Newport Folk Festival, when Dylan scandalized fans by marrying his signature acoustic folk protest style with a seemingly more "commercial" electric rock-and-roll idiom. Ratifying this sea-change, Dylan framed this "folk-rock" assault on generic boundaries with the release of two albums, *Bringing it all Back Home* and *Highway 61 Revisited*. Fellow protest folksinger Phil Ochs' reaction to one cut on *Highway 61* illustrates this impact: "Phil, a huge fan of Dylan to begin with, was thunderstruck by this latest composition," entitled "Mr. Tambourine Man." Ochs believed that "Dylan, already being labeled a spokesperson for his generation . . . had suddenly in the course of one song, come dangerously close to becoming a generation's poet" (Schumacher 82).

Beyond such claims for Dylan as the 1960s generational poet, which invite obvious comparisons with Fitzgerald's status as a generational novelist in the 1920s—another youth-centered decade, and beyond coincidental geographical parallels—each artist's bourgeois Minnesota origins, the affinity between the two artists rests most significantly on a shared career narrative and cultural critique. Dylan's early song, "North Country Blues," a reminder of their shared Minnesota background, sums up this shared aesthetic as the discovery that "there ain't nothing here now to hold them." This poetics of unmooring lies at the heart of what

Ronald Berman characterizes as "the movement in Fitzgerald . . . toward existential heroism" (*World* 114) and the product of this movement: an art that recurrently depicts inconclusive arrivals, such as *Tender is the Night* hero Dick Diver's incessant beginnings of a "career . . . like Grant's in Galena" consisting well into middle age of "biding his time . . . in one town or another" (315), with each town-to-town movement impelled by the decision Dylan affirms in "A Hard Rain's Gonna Fall," as the decision to keep "goin' on out," the commitment reaffirmed throughout his songs, to "move on to the next hope" with "hard-eyed . . . skepticism" (Edmundson 54) in the face of whatever defeat or humiliation looms.

CAREERS

This sort of language also greeted the 1920 publication of Fitzgerald's first novel, *This Side of Paradise,* and the later turns in Fitzgerald's career that came to be regarded as betrayals by many of his fans (Mangum 3-7). *This Side of Paradise* came "to influence us profoundly," according to the publisher, autobiographer, and self-appointed generational spokesman Donald Friede. Fitzgerald "set the pattern for the mood of the day," laying a "solid foundation for the basic philosophy of the whole decade. . . . We were never the same again" (180). Favoring Dylan, English critic Michael Gray made the Fitzgerald-Dylan parallel explicit in suggesting that "there is a sense in which, more fully than Fitzgerald, Dylan created a generation" (5). Similarly, David Dunaway argues that "for the generation coming-of-age in the 1960s . . . there was no comparable . . . influence" to Dylan's. Dunaway elaborates by associating Dylan with earlier, cultural paradigm-shifters in an account recalling Fitzgerald's meteoric rise between 1920 and 1925. "Like that of Rimbaud, Dylan's recognition came impossibly fast, but being a god turns out to be a short-lived occupation." Consequently, Dylan "has spent many years of his life trying to get to where he once was. To find another writer who so thoroughly affected his time, one has to probe in history—Voltaire, Shakespeare, Dickens" (154).

Dunaway's potted history of cultural change recalls Nick Carraway's mid-novel rhapsody in *The Great Gatsby* equating the eponymous hero with "a son of God" (105) as well as his closing summary of his own "awkward unpleasant" (185) effort to return home. Dunaway's view of Dylan points to *Gatsby* as the center of Dylan's debt to Fitzgerald's legacy and underscores the lasting vitality of that legacy. Dylan's seizure of this legacy constitutes an enrichment, in contrast to the appropriations of it that became especially marked during the Reagan-era plutocracy revival—the Jay McInerney era to chroniclers of American fiction. A Gatsby-like Roaring 20s look (derived from a 1974 screen adaptation starring Robert Redford as Gatsby) briefly colored

fashion advertising in the early eighties (Hurowitz), and at the end of the decade Calvin Klein turned to *Gatsby*—along with *Madame Bovary* and *The Sun Also Rises*—to caption print-ads for a new fragrance called Obsession (Foltz), while *New York Times* columnist Anthony Lewis more solemnly devoted an entire column to the Reagan administration's uncannily Gatsby-like "emptiness" and the way it "corrupted the American Dream." Four months earlier a *Times* editorial argued that "the eighties aren't so far past the twenties" inasmuch as "Jay Gatsby would be right at home today" in the company of Michael Milken and Ivan Boesky. More recently, an Atlanta antiques shop called Gatsby's drew national media attention when it bought the auctioned belongings of convicted CIA mole Aldrich Ames.

Unlike such merchandising ventures, Dylan's citation of Fitzgerald goes beyond name-dropping and glamour-mongering. In the context of Dylan's larger body of work, his Fitzgerald line belongs to an oeuvre-saturating acknowledgement of his debt to Fitzgerald and a profitable reinvestment of that legacy. In sarcastically singling Fitzgerald out as an index of cultural arrival, a measure of cultural-capital, Dylan prompts listeners to the songs of his most influential and most conspicuously literary period, between 1964-1975, to account for Fitzgerald's endurance as artistic resource and incitement.

This affiliation extends beyond obvious biographical parallels between the two Minnesota college dropouts who grew up non-Protestant in America's Lutheran heartland before heading east to triumph as artists, to transform radically their respective media, and to become generational icons. Dylan's pursuit of this Fitzgeraldian agenda seems most evident in his refashioning of Bobby Zimmerman into Bob Dylan. This move recalls how Jimmy Gatz, also a fugitive from the Lake Superior littoral, where he fatefully rescued a grateful tycoon's yacht, began refashioning himself into Jay Gatsby. The extent to which Dylan "sprang from a Platonic conception of himself" (106) and thus the extent to which Dylan, like Fitzgerald, regards "the crafting of identity as demiurgic activity" (Weinstein 131) resonates in Martha Bayles' image of "Zimmerman hanging around every coffeehouse in Greenwich Village, playing for pennies and promoting a mythic identity as 'Bob Dylan,' a precocious drifter who had spent his youth traveling the highways and byways and learning his music directly from the folk" (210-217). This mythic identity contrasts markedly with the prosaic stability of Dylan's Hibbing, Minnesota, boyhood in "the Jewish mercantile middle class of America's Midwest" (Friedlander 136) and his brief stint at the University of Minnesota before departing for Greenwich Village in 1960.

Such transformations involve efforts to ride the zeitgeists of their respective decades—in Gatsby's becoming a sporty Anglophile bootlegger and in Dylan's becoming an indignant bohemian iconoclast. "By taking a new name," biographer Justin Kaplan notes, "an unfinished person may hope to enter into more dynamic—but not necessarily more intimate—transactions, both with the world outside and with his or her 'true soul,' the naked self." The description of Gatsby's self-transformation in chapter 6 of the novel stresses its lack of "intimacy" and the extent to which both Gatsby himself as well as his various audiences only got to regard him at a distance: as an "invention," as a "conception," as a "legend," and as "news" (103-104). This chapter also emphasizes the turbulence or "dynamism" of Gatz's metamorphosis with such verbs as "spin" and "rock" and "tangle," complemented by images of Gatsby as a master of "bracing" outdoor manual labor (104-105).

ROMANTIC READINESS

As a commentator on his own pursuit of such dynamic transactions and on the conditions shaping it, Dylan also takes on attributes of Nick Carraway, the commentator and Fitzgerald alter-ego, who records Gatsby's transformations. Like Dylan, *Gatsby* changes his name, with Carraway registering both Gatsby's "dynamic transactions" and his own repression of intimacy. In the confession that opens *Gatsby,* Carraway remembers joining in disparaging college friends' "quivering . . . revelations" with an insistence that "the world be in uniform and at a sort of moral attention forever" (6). With its refrain, "I was so much older then / I'm younger than that now," Dylan's 1964 song "My Back Pages" even more emphatically enunciates a similarly divided stance. After the singer recalls his quest for a world "at moral attention" by picturing himself "in a soldier's stance," he stresses in the last stanza his once overly vigilant antipathy to intimacy: "my noble guard stood hard when abstract threats / Too noble neglect / Deceived me into thinking I had something to protect."

Dylan's confession early in "My Back Pages" of having "dreamed / Romantic facts of musketeers / Foundationed deep somehow" pointedly aligns his persona with the most pronounced effort *Gatsby*'s narrator makes: finding or making "something gorgeous" out of "everything for which I have unaffected scorn" (6). The tension this effort produces helps account for Carraway's admittedly "rather literary" (8) voice. This voice swerves repeatedly in its account of Gatsby, sometimes displaying and sometimes chastening its own romantic excesses. In their self-satisfied version, these excesses appear as "romantic readiness" (6) and, in the censorious version, as "appalling sentimentality" (118). Such responses to Gatsby, to "the romantic speculation he inspired" (48), reflect the narrator's own susceptibilities to sentimental and romantic constructions. These surface in his early attraction to Jordan Baker, to "the way the last sunshine fell with romantic affection upon her

glowing face" (18)—an attraction for which he later fastidiously censures himself—and in the voyeuristic rhapsody his "restless eye" prompts as it "picks out the romantic women on Fifth Avenue" and follows home in "the enchanted metropolitan twilight" as "loitered" with fellow solitaries "in front of windows" (61-62). Recurrently showing Nick as a window-gazer (182, 184), Fitzgerald has him evoke and embody here the romance of voyeurism and resigned exclusion that the Japanese novelist Haruki Murakami's appreciation of Dylan locates at the core of his achievement: "His voice," which sounds "like a kid standing at the window watching the rain" (345), like the rain repeatedly filtering Nick's and the reader's closing glimpses of *Gatsby* (180-183). This romance of voyeurism abounds in Dylan's writing, though perhaps nowhere as effusively and self-reproachfully as in the 1966 *Blonde on Blonde* cut, "Visions of Johanna," which opens with the singer observing "Louise and her lover so entwined" and then tempting listeners with rumors of "the all-night girls' escapades out on the E train," only to deride, after a drawn-out harmonica interruption, his Carrawayesque alter-ego as a "little boy lost" who "takes himself so seriously" while recalling her "farewell kiss to me."

Despite the Dylan singer's projecting this voyeuristic self-regard onto an alter-ego and despite Nick's self-reassurance that "no one would ever know or disapprove" of his Romanticized voyeurism, of course both the reader or listener and retrospective narrator or singer "know," though perhaps only Fitzgerald's narrator "disapproves." While Nick's seemingly conclusive abandonment of the ambiguous metropolis for the straightforward Midwest—the "city" in the "West" where "dwellings are still called through decades by a family's name"—appears to confirm this censure, the confounding of any linear sense of arrival and departure at the end of *Gatsby* erodes the moral high ground on which Nick strives to stand, both in abandoning Eastern urban "sophistication and in reproaching his "younger and more vulnerable" (5) self.

AMERICAN TIME-SPACE

The contrast between Carraway, the decamping narrator, and Fitzgerald, his doggedly metropolitan author, also anticipates Dylan's narrative geography and the array of inconclusive arrivals and provisional departures this geography contains. One of Dylan's geographical narratives transforms an abandonment of the Midwest, which Dylan also views retrospectively and metonymically as simply "the West," into a disheartening inescapable "story of the West." "Talking New York," the very first song on Dylan's first album concerns a guitar-toting young man "ramblin' outta the wild West / Leavin' towns that" the singer claims to "love the best" as he "come into New York town." Just as his incredulity at "buildings goin' up to the sky" echoes Carraway's memorable view of "the city rising up across the river as the city seen for the first time" (73), so too Dylan's image of his West as a congeries of towns in "Talking New York" calls to mind Carraway's confession of his preference for "the bored, sprawling, swollen towns beyond the Ohio" over the "superiority" of the East (184). Dylan plays with familiar East-West "superiority/inferiority" tensions in showing the song's hero "in one of them coffee-houses" in Greenwich Village where the proprietor unwittingly affirms the narrator's western authenticity by rejecting him, telling him "You sound like a hillbilly / We want folksingers." Calling someone a "hillbilly," as Cecelia Tichi observes, encapsulates a broad historical and sociological narrative by which a monied, mannered, urban East has sought to exclude by disparagement and condescension a presumably vulgar, upstart, disruptive West (133-34). Carraway invokes this narrative with the realization that *Gatsby* "has been after all a story of the West, after all—Tom and Gatsby, Daisy and Jordan, and I were all Westerners, and perhaps we possessed some deficiency in common which made us subtly unadaptable to Eastern life" (184).

In an ironic turn at the end of "Talking New York," the singer's return to the West, his announcement that he "headed out for them western skies" becomes self-canceling, like the first ending, the autobiographical homecoming ending of Nick Carraway's own narrative. After this first ending seems to resolve Nick's own autobiographical plot, Fitzgerald shows Nick recollecting a return to New York on business about a year after Gatsby's murder. This return prompts the novel's actual conclusion, Carraway's famous transhistorical meditation, his evocation and imaginative replacement of the suburban Long Island landscape where most of *The Great Gatsby* takes place (189).

Deferred and alternative endings abound in Dylan's songs, often turning on his signature switches between guitar and harmonica self-accompaniment. More memorably, endings turn on Dylan's management of lyrics and narrative, as in "The Ballad of Frankie Lee and Judas Priest." In a false farewell reminiscent of *Gatsby,* Dylan's would-be Village folksinger in "Talkin' New York" welcomes the "western skies" to which he retreats with the phrase "Howdy, East Orange"—naming a suburban New Jersey city about ten miles from Manhattan, far closer to Times Square than even West Egg. This desire for and irreparable exile from the West surfaces comically in a single line on Dylan's next album, *Freewheelin' Bob Dylan,* in "Bob Dylan's Blues." The line,

> The Lone Ranger and Tonto
> They are ridin' down the line
> Fixin' everybody's troubles
> Everybody's 'cept mine

sardonically deprives the singer of the superior virtue and justice public mythmakers customarily attribute to the West.

In a more elegiac vein, "Bob Dylan's Dream" on Dylan's next album, situates the Dylan persona "on a train going west," a stance identical to Carraway's evoking "vivid memories" of school friends on Chicago-bound trains at the end of *Gatsby* (183). Here Dylan's narrator recollects "the first few friends I had" and the way "we longed for nothin' and were quite satisfied" in their illusion of immunity from "the world outside" and the conviction that "we could never get old." Dylan's narrator seems to buy into Gatsby's illusion that "of course you can repeat the past" (116) until midsong, when he points out that the "chances" of recovering this state "really was a million to one" and in closing merges this Gatsby stance with the chastening Carraway position that opens this exchange, the reminder that "you can't repeat the past" (116). Just as Fitzgerald lets the gap between a diminished present and an irretrievable past linger by having both Carraway and Gatsby repeat the phrase, "can't repeat the past," Dylan's recorded vocal and instrumental performance reinforces this gap. It punctuates each intimation of his diminished present by interrupting the vocal's steady guitar accompaniment with fermata harmonica solos.

Though elegiac strains in both works make time and history appear intractable, both Dylan's songs and *Gatsby* present space and geography as easily manipulated. Gatsby's striking relocation of San Francisco to a transcontinental "midwest" (67) and the drunken displacement of Biloxi to Tennessee (134) later in *Gatsby* belong to the same cartographic revisionism whereby Dylan places East Orange under "western skies." Dylan also indulges in such remapping in "Just Like Tom Thumb Blues," which sets a redundantly bilingual "Rue Morgue Avenue" in Juarez, and in "Bob Dylan's 115th Dream," which shifts the Mayflower landing to "the Bowery slums."

Dylan elaborates this Gatsbyesque move most extravagantly at the close of his 1975 ballad "Tangled Up In Blue," a trans-American odyssey like *Gatsby.* The song opens with the singer "headin' out for the East Coast" and then abandoning a "car we drove as far as we could" somewhere "out West" and then working "in the great north woods and drifting down to New Orleans." It ends with the narrator "still on the road headin' for another joint." All this map-scrambling moves, like Fitzgerald's most accomplished prose, "in two directions at once" (McInerney 26), and culminates, like *Gatsby,* in giving the last word to the narrator's sententious recognition that "the past was close behind." Thus Dylan's remembered odyssey ultimately fails, though providing much pleasure, in the form of verbal pyrotechnics, instrumental exuberance, and vocal surprise in reaching this realization. This argument between extravagance and fatalism gives narrative and descriptive credence to his closing realization that he and whomever he encountered on his odyssey "just saw" all the pursuit and evasion the song renders "from a different point of view." With the acknowledgment of this contingency, the singer achieves a Carraway-like distance on his own odyssey. This distance promises liberation from youthful parochialism, the code of the Carraway "clan," (7) or from the "illusion" that Dylan, voice dropping, associates with "all the people we used to know" at the end of "Tangled Up in Blue."

This distance also provides both writers with the same sort of rhetorical leverage by turning their residual attachment to a lost home in the West into a distant, even Olympian, vantage point for viewing Americanness *tout cort.* According to David Minter, "Fitzgerald made the history and myths of the U.S.—promises kept and betrayed—his own" (112). Dylan claims a similar agenda as the omniscient first-person narrator who tells the history of American violence in "God on Our Side," on his third album. Dylan follows Carraway in postulating the midwestern perspective as the national one: "My name it ain't nothing, my age it ain't less, the *country* I come from they call the midwest."

This critical, even jeremiadic, distance presents all of U.S. history as a fiction, a story, a collection of hegemony-making books. In the last verse of "With God on Our Side," Dylan admits that "words fill my head" rather than facts or convictions. A similar recognition informs both the self-referential epigraph to *Gatsby* and the opening paragraphs, which show the narrator mulling over his father's words, along with his subsequent timetable name-scribbling (64). Dylan's sense of reality as verbal construct appears most succinctly in "Love Minus Zero/No Limit":

> In the dime stores and bus stations
> People talk of situations
> Read books repeat quotations
> Draw conclusions on the wall.

As Carraway illustrates at the end of *Gatsby,* the advantage of such a conviction lies in the susceptibility of "reality" to revision, critique, and erasure: "an obscene word, scrawled by some boy with a piece of brick, stood out clearly in the moonlight and I erased it, drawing my shoe raspingly along the stone" (188). Central to both writers' sensibilities is the understanding that the power of erasure and revision, which rest on an appreciation of the constructedness of our verbal and ideological universes, at once provokes and disciplines romanticizing impulses.

In Dylan's songs and in *Gatsby* this preoccupation with words extends to larger verbal packages, books. Early in "With God on Our Side" Dylan sings, "the history books tell it, they tell it so well the cavalry charged and the Indians fell," while the next verse announces via poetic inversion, "the names of the heroes I was made to memorize." The penultimate verse appeals to the most canonic book of all, citing the Bible's account of Judas betraying Jesus, but it leaves an opening for the reader to step outside its ordained constructions and those of school history books, by reminding the listener, "you'll have to decide whether Judas Iscariot had God on his side." From Tom Buchanan's proto-Nazi reading recommendations in chapter one (17) to Gatsby's bookish self-fashioning as reflected in the Franklinesque plan-making that Mr. Gatz presents to the narrator before Gatsby's funeral and in the Hopalong Cassidy dime novel in which the narrator finds Gatsby's life-plan, a similar awareness of how books and words make people and peoples—or nations—pervades *Gatsby.* Fitzgerald plays on the distinctly American reverberations in the word "West" by inscribing Hopalong Cassidy, as does Dylan with recurring references to the dime-novel and Hollywood West: to the Lone Ranger, to the Cisco Kid, to cavalry-and-Indian battles.

Dylan's most conspicuous stress on the verbal and imaginative construction of America comes in "Bob Dylan's 115th Dream," which provides a critical retrospect on the familiar stock of formative discovery and settlement narratives with references and allusions that recall the "Dutch explorers" and the "New world" that "pandered" to these explorers' utopian fantasies in Carraway's closing meditation. Dylan's singer frames his announcement, "I think I'll *call* it America I *said* as we hit land" (emphasis added), with references to "riding on the Mayflower" and to "Captain Arab" (for Ahab) "saying boys forget the whale." The song closes with the narrator's abandonment of the New World, leaving "Arab stuck on some whale," out West and "married to the deputy sheriff of the jail." Dylan's dream song saves for last "the funniest thing," his final encounter with "three ships" whose captain "said his name was Columbus," to whom the singer "just said, 'Good luck.'"

Standing at once beyond and within such constructions of self and nation, both Fitzgerald's narrator and the recurring voice of Dylan's first, most influential, decade strive for and achieve a cosmopolitan perspective that takes them and their audience beyond the U.S. western substratum of their work. The cover picture of Dylan's suggestively titled 1965 album *Bringing It All Back Home* depicts the artist very much at home, viewing the album's owner from a worldly rather than a parochial vantage point. Shot in "an old Victorian mansion" along the Hudson, this mockingly Gatsbyesque "stagy cover photo" situates the performer in "a setting" that was "elegant and chic" with Dylan looking "alert and interested . . . [,] not detached as he had been on his previous albums" and projecting an "image of choice—the sophisticated Bob Dylan—the jet-setter, arbiter of taste

. . . [,] not some hayseed folksinger" (Spitz 272). The most emphatic announcement of Dylan's integrating worldliness—politics and commerce—with the imperatives of artistic expression appears in the foreground of this cover. A cover-within-a-cover picture of *Time* features President Lyndon Baines Johnson as man-of-the-year standing out in a field of competing covers, a blurred Jean Harlow magazine and a fanned-out pile of albums by blues and folk artists who influenced Dylan. The pairing here of the "respectable" history-producing *Time,* which with its ubiquitous, Big Brother-like "staring covers" threatened, according to Allen Ginsberg, to "run" every American's "emotional life" ("America"), with down-market fanzine, recalls Fitzgerald's agenda in "evoking newspapers, magazines, and their influence" in *Gatsby*: to indict the way the mass-circulation magazine "represents coerced common judgment" (Berman, *World 135; cf. Gatsby 48, 103*) or, as the *a clef* Dylan figure in Scott Spencer's novel, *Rich Man's Table,* puts it:

> What kills you is the consensus, what you read in the papers and hear on the television, it's an invisible fence of received wisdom, and government-inspected ideas, it's the conspiracy of common knowledge. Common knowledge is worse than lies. Common knowledge eats the truth and then shits it out and buries it.
>
> (236)

In the background of this album cover, holding a bent elbow over LBJ's face, a swarthy raven-haired young woman in a short-sleeved red peignoir points a cigarette at an off-white neoclassical mantle while looking defiantly at the camera. Her pose intimates stereotypically Old World worldliness, if not decadence. Evidence of Dylan's attention to pitting clichés of European sophistication and corruption against equally compelling, equally hackneyed, ideas of American innocence and ignorance surfaced comically in the utopianly titled talking blues, "I Shall Be Free," on Dylan's second album, in which the singer imagines:

> Well, my telephone rang it would not stop.
> It's President Kennedy callin' me up.
> He said, 'My friend Bob, what do we need to make
>   the country grow?'

Posing as presidential confidant, the sort of mysteriously influential role popularly imputed to Gatsby (*Gatsby* 48, 103), Dylan recalls his counsel:

> I said, 'My friend, Jack, Brigitte Bardot, Anita Ekberg, Sophia Loren.'
> (Put 'em all in the same room with Ernest Borgnine.)

A similar though subtler play on images informs the *Bringing It All Back Home* cover: In contrast to the woman's pose, Dylan faces the camera with a weary gaze, his lips on the verge of pout. He wears all muted colors and shares the foreground of the photo with a gray long-haired kitten set between his hands and staring straight at the camera and with a Cold War-style yellow and black "fallout shelter" sign turned on its side and partly blurred by the overexposure-induced circle of light that serves as an inner frame for the photo. This *mise-en-scene* seems to aim at the "continuous and cumulative effect" Lionel Trilling ascribed to Fitzgerald's *Gatsby* style, which weds "tenderness" with "a true firmness of moral judgment" (243-44).

Critique also seems to inform the topical allusiveness that textures *Gatsby*: allusions to immigration-policy controversies; to popular songs, movies, and familiar advertisements (Berman, *Modern* 19-20, 24-28, 46-48, 128). Recurring snippets from the 1920s hit song "Ain't We Got Fun," the looming image of an optician's billboard, Myrtle Wilson's utopian shopping fantasies, and Daisy Buchanan's vision of Gatsby as "you know the advertisement of the man" (125) all illustrate the extent to which consumption and mass entertainment contest Fitzgerald's narrator's opening demand for unstinting "moral attention" (6). Topicality (in the form of Bette Davis, Hitchcock's *Psycho,* James Meredith, Medgar Evers, Emmett Till, boxers Davey Moore and Hurricane Carter, hit man Joey Gallo, No-Doz caffeine pills, and pillbox hats) functions similarly throughout Dylan's songs. Often this topicality belongs to an American exceptionalist utopianism and the claims to virtue it sanctions, as in Dylan's "Gates of Eden," "The Hour that the Ship Comes In," and Dylan's answer to the labor anthem, "I Dreamed I Saw Joe Hill Last Night," "I Dreamed I Saw Augustine." In contrast to these compositions' meditative and elegiac politics, Dylan protest songs, such as "The Lonesome Death of Hattie Carol" (Edmundson 52-3) and "Masters of War," call to mind Nick Carraway's unsettling turn from "reserving all judgments" (5), the balancing of contraries and ironies and ambiguities that Fitzgerald judged the crux of genius in *The Jazz Age,* to the expressly moralizing sentence Fitzgerald has Carraway pronounce against the Buchanans at the end of *Gatsby.* Carraway states, "They were careless people, Tom and Daisy—they smashed things and creatures around them and then retreated back into their money or their vast carelessness or whatever it was that kept them together, and let other people clean up the mess they had made" (187-88). Morally charged commentary in both artists' writings seems at once to prompt and to deny hopes of social betterment.

CONCLUSION: SHARING AN IMPASSE

Both Fitzgerald's and Dylan's ambivalent stress on worldly, even topical, engagement demands a commensurate verbal style. In his reassessment of *Gatsby,* George Garret calls it a "wildly experimental novel" with a "composite style whose chief demonstrable point appears to be the inadequacy of any style (or any single means of perception or single point of view) by which to do justice to the story" (114). Dylan articulates just such an artistic credo in his early song, "Restless Farewell," which begins complaining that "the silent night is shattered by the sounds inside my mind," prompting the singer to turn back to consider "the signs," just as Carraway ponders signs in the form of a Long Island Railroad timetable and an optician's billboard. After an interruptive, contemplation-provoking harmonica break, Dylan concludes:

> I got the restless hungry feeling
> That don't mean no one no good.

He then softens this confession of malevolence with a Whitmanesque gesture, a profession of egalitarian inclusiveness:

> . . . everything I've been saying, friend,
> You could say it just as good.
> You're right from your side and I'm right from mine.
> We're both just one too many mornings and a thousand miles behind.

Dylan's rhyming here of "good" with itself hammers home the inadequacy, the inevitability of stylistic impasse, the recognition of which Garret imputes to Fitzgerald. This recognition echoes in Carraway's resignation at his failure to communicate with Tom Buchanan at the close of *Gatsby*: "I felt suddenly as though I were talking to a child" (188).

The management of such difficulty in *Gatsby* and Dylan's songs is remarkably similar. It consists of rehearsing the inadequacies Garret cites in order to overcome them, embracing stock vocabularies and tropes as a means of purging their staleness. Christopher Ricks (who treats Dylan as a legitimate heir to Fitzgerald's precursor, Keats) praised Dylan as Shakespeare's equal, citing Dylan's "intuition as to how a cliché may incite reflection, and not preclude" it ("Clichés" 61; *Keats* 98). Such an intuition surfaces in Fitzgerald's play on almost all of Tom Buchanan's global pronouncements—on the Nordic race (17), on "self-control" and in coining the cliché "Mr. Nobody From Nowhere" (137).

Fitzgerald's rendering of Wolfsheim's mawkish redundant reminiscence about the "old Metropole" rests on sustained elaboration of this intuition (74-75). While lunching with Carraway and Gatsby, Wolfsheim "brooded gloomily" under "Presbyterian nymphs"—a brutal counterpoint to the virile, Jewish, unabashedly corrupt Wolfsheim presiding over a space "filled with faces dead and gone. Filled with friends now gone forever." The redundant phrase "dead and gone" and the presiding nymphs evoke a "sentimental atmosphere"—a decidedly clichéd ambience, which Fitzgerald empties of reassuring familiarity by having Wolfsheim turn from

the cliché to a cheerful account of his friend Rosy Rosenthal's gangland-style execution at the Metropole, a turn the narrator stretches with the observation that "a succulent hash" prompted Wolfsheim to forget the "sentimental atmosphere" he had established. Fitzgerald completes this scene's alienation effect with an oxymoronic modifier, which at once stresses the inadequacy of language to depict Wolfsheim and the narrator's pleasure in trying: "he began to eat with a ferocious delicacy."

Fitzgerald also purges "sentimental atmosphere" from matters even more susceptible to sentimentalizing, from "love" itself. As Leslie Fiedler observed, "For Fitzgerald, 'love' was essentially frustration and yearning" (316). Fiedler went on to ascribe Fitzgerald's antipathy to conventional, sentimental renderings of love to the way in which Fitzgerald "identified himself with that sexual revolution which the '20's thought of as their special subject." As the voice of a successor "sexual revolution," Dylan further unpacks the sentimental discourse of romance by disclosing its unspoken sexual underside, which the phrase "four-letter-word" usually fits, most forthrightly in the refrain and title phrase of "Love is Just A Four Letter Word."

This impetus and talent for unpacking bromides and platitudes also shapes many of Dylan's rhyme-and-image sequences. The 1965 "Tombstone Blues," for example, takes "Gypsy Davey" from an old English folk ballad and has him arrive with a "blowtorch" and an assistant from the Cisco Kid TV westerns, "his faithful slave Pedro." Pedro provides a stamp collection and, with it the hoariest modern American cliché of all, a phrase right out of Dale Carnegie's best-seller—"a fantastic collection of stamps to win friends and influence. . . ." In the 1965 recording, Dylan's voice pauses at "influence," thus calling into question its grammatical status: Is "influence" here Dale Carnegie's verb, minus its predicate, or a sentence-ending noun? After this pause, Dylan swerves away from Dale Carnegie's stock phrase and substitutes the expected predicate "people" with the phrase "his uncle." This substitution reinforces the cliché-defeating switch by breaking the rhyme-pattern in the verse (camps / tramps / stamps—uncles) as Dylan does throughout "Tombstone Blues."

The force of these lines also lies in their image juxtapositions, a characteristic of Dylan's style that peaked in the late sixties on the album *Blonde on Blonde* and in such narratives on the *John Wesley Harding* album as "The Ballad of Frankie Lee and Judas Priest." In the Wolfsheim passage above, Fitzgerald presents Carraway as a student of "startling juxtapositions," the most memorable of which may be the juxtaposition of Gatsby's soft, rich billowy shirts and Daisy's stormy crying (97-98). This stress on juxtaposition in *Gatsby* anticipates Fitzgerald's famous pronouncement in *The Crack*

Up that "the test of a first-rate intelligence" is "the ability to hold to opposed ideas in the mind at the same time" (69). Just as Fitzgerald's *Gatsby* style results from the way his "sentences achieve an unhappy marriage" (Godden 80), Dylan's style in his most memorable songs rests on "awkward marriages" between melody and lyric, image and syntax (Thomson). The result in both writers' work is, in Philip Weinstein's assessment of Fitzgerald, art that "mocks both closure and exposure" (143) and writing, in Frank Kermode's verdict on Dylan, that's "tough on allegorists" (188).

Throughout American literary history such resistance to allegory and antipathy to closure has marked the aspiration and the differentia of distinctly American writing, as hallmarks of the poet Emerson famously summoned in 1844 the artist who provokes "the imagination . . . to flow and not to freeze," the antithesis of the mystic who "nails a symbol to one sense, which was true for a moment but soon becomes old and false" (322). Leading up to Emerson's account of language as "vehicular and transitive," this devaluation of belief in favor of irresolution echoes in the "transitory moment" at the center of the narrator's closing meditation in *Gatsby,* a meditation that follows from Nick's inconclusive departure from the East and from the romance he sought there.

The "un-American" "mysticism" that Emerson disparages also figures as Fitzgerald's antagonist in his rigorously ambivalent limning of Catholic priestcraft throughout his fiction. The most notable instances include Father Schwartz, whom Fitzgerald's sympathetically severe narrator leaves "muttering inarticulate and heart-broken words in **'Absolution,'**" which Matthew Bruccoli cites as *Gatsby*'s precursor (*Babylon* 150; *Gatsby* vii-ix), and the defeated "papal cross" with which Dick Diver "blessed the [Riviera] beach" he created and from which his own corrosive charm and corrupting knowledge has banished him (*Tender* 5-6, 314). Similarly acknowledging the aesthetic appeal and the cognitive dubiousness of priestcraft, Dylan's 1967 anti-allegory, "The Ballad of Frankie Lee and Judas Priest," features an unnamed pallbearer reminding listeners that "nothing is revealed" before announcing "the moral of this story, the moral of this song." This "moral" boils down to an admonition: "Don't go mistaking paradise for that home across the road"—or, as *Gatsby* instructs, that home across the bay.

These two passages chasten utopianism while warning against the sort of "revelation" sanctioned by the apocalyptic and utopian ideologies to which *Gatsby*'s eponymous hero and his Veblenian antagonist, Tom Buchanan, both subscribe. This convergence illustrates the role that Fitzgerald and Dylan share, as anti-prophets who made myths of their *selves* while in their art they undermined the very ground on which such myths rest.

Works Cited

Bayles, Martha. *Hole In Our Soul: The Loss of Beauty and Meaning in American Popular Music.* New York, 1994.

Berman, Ronald. *The Great Gatsby and Fitzgerald's World of Ideas.* Tuscaloosa, 1997.

———. *The Great Gatsby and Modern Times.* Urbana, 1994.

Dunaway, David. "No Credit Given: The Underground Bob Dylan." *Virginia Quarterly Review* 69 (Winter 1993): 149-155.

Dylan, Bob. *Lyrics, 1962-1985.* New York, 1985.

Edmundson, Mark. "Tangled Up in Truth." *Civilization* 4 (October/November 1997):50-55.

Emerson, Ralph Waldo. *Selected Writings.* Edited by William Gilman. New York, 1965.

Fiedler, Leslie. *Love and Death in the American Novel.* 1960. Rev. 1966. Briarcliff Manor, NY, 1982.

Fitzgerald, F. Scott. *Babylon Revisited and Other Stories.* New York, 1934.

———. *The Crack Up.* Edited by Edmund Wilson. New York, 1945.

———. *The Great Gatsby.* 1925. Edited by Matthew Bruccoli. New York, 1995.

———. *Tender Is the Night.* New York, 1934.

Foltz, Kim. "A New Twist for Obsession." *New York Times* (15 August 1990): D19.

Friede, Donald. *The Mechanical Angel.* New York, 1948.

Friedlander, Paul. *Rock and Roll: A Social History.* Boulder, 1996.

Garrett, George. "Fire and Freshness: A Matter of Style in *The Great Gatsby. New Essays on The Great Gatsby.* Edited by Matthew Bruccoli. New York, 1985.

Ginsberg, Allen. *Howl and Other Poems.* San Francisco, 1956.

Godden, Richard. *Fictions of Capital: The American Novel From James to Mailer.* New York, 1990.

Goodman, Fred *The Mansion on the Hill: Dylan, Young, Geffen, Springsteen and the Head-on Collision of Rock and Commerce.* New York, 1997.

Gray, Michael. *Song and Dance Man: The Art of Bob Dylan.* New York, 1972.

Hurowitz, B. "The 20's Roar Back Into Style," *Macleans* (2 August 1982): 30-33.

Kaplan, Justin. "The Naked Self and Other Problems" in Pachter, Marc. *Telling Lives: The Biographer's Art.* New York, 1979.

Kermode, Frank & Spender, Stephen. "The Metaphor at the End of the Funnel." *Esquire* (May 1972): 109-118, 188.

Lewis, Anthony. "The Great Gatsby." *New York Times* (6 August 1987): A 27.

Life Styes of the Rich and Shady. *New York Times* (7 April 1987): A24.

Mangum, Bryant. *A Fortune Yet: Money in the Art of F. Scott Fitzgerald.* New York, 1991.

Marcus, Greil. *Invisible Republic: Bob Dylan's Basement Tapes.* New York, 1997.

McInerney, Jay. "Fitzgerald Revisited." *New York Review of Books* (15 August 1991): 23-28.

Minter, David. *A Cultural History of the American Novel From Henry James to William Faulkner.* New York, 1994.

Morton, Brian. *The Dylanist.* New York, 1991.

Murakami, Haruki. *Hard-Boiled Wonderland.* Tr. Alfred Birnbaum. 1991. New York, 1993.

Ricks, Christopher. "Cliches." *The State of the Language.* Ed. Ricks & Leonard Michaels. Berkeley, 1981.

———. *Keats and Embarrassment.* London, 1974.

Schumacher. Michael. *There But For Fortune: The Life of Phil Ochs.* New York, 1997.

Spencer, Scott. *Rich Man's Table.* New York, 1998.

Spitz, Bob. *Dylan: A Biography.* New York, 1989.

Thomson, Liz. "Fighting in the Captain's Tower." *New Statesman & Society* (5 February 1992): 39-40.

Ticchi, Cecilia. *High Lonesome: The American Culture of Country Music.* Chapel Hill, 1994.

Trilling, Lionel. *The Liberal Imagination: Essays on Literature and Society.* 1950. New York, 1953.

Weinstein, Arnold. *Nobody's Home: Speech, Self, and Place in American Fiction From Hawthorne to DeLillo.* New York, 1993.

Robert Seguin (essay date winter 2000)

SOURCE: Seguin, Robert. "*Ressentiment* and the Social Poetics of *The Great Gatsby*: Fitzgerald Reads Cather." *Modern Fiction Studies* 46, no. 4 (winter 2000): 917-40.

[*In the following essay, Seguin uses the theme of "ressentiment" (loosely, the envy of the lower toward the upper classes) to explore Fitzgerald's social sensibilities in* Gatsby, *also noting similarities between Fitzgerald's novel and Willa Cather's* A Lost Lady.]

Following his bout of emotional exhaustion in the mid 1930s, F. Scott Fitzgerald came to describe what he called his "crack-up" in more than strictly personal terms. In his meditation on his depression, the crack-up expands outward in waves from Fitzgerald as individual, encompassing disparate social and cultural materials and achieving a certain allegorical intensity. At one point, the shape of Fitzgerald's psyche becomes expressive of the very curve of national history, from the bull-market twenties to the depressed thirties:

> My own happiness in the past often approached such an ecstasy that I could not share it even with the person dearest to me but I had to walk it away in quiet streets and lanes with only fragments of it to distil into little lines in books—and I think that my happiness, or talent for self-delusion or what you will, was an exception. It was not the natural thing but the unnatural— unnatural as the Boom; and my recent experience parallels the wave of despair that swept the nation when the Boom was over.
>
> (*Crack-Up* 84)

There is an extravagance to this declaration, an extravagance I want to take seriously. I will thus assume as my working hypothesis that Fitzgerald is entirely correct in this bit of analytical retrospection, and that the discontinuous sine waves of emotions and history can, in some exceptional cases, become temporarily synchronized. Indeed, the nexus mediating between the individual subject and the social ground in this passage seems principally an affective one, and in general Fitzgerald's writerly metabolism, its shape and trajectory through time, appears tied with unusual intimacy to a consistent and highly wrought emotional set. This affective matrix, as the above quote from *The Crack-Up* illustrates, is often self-consciously foregrounded as a kind of interpretive apparatus in its own right. What I wish to pursue in these pages, then, is the manner in which a particular affect can attain a deeper historical resonance, how it might furnish a singular set of conduits or relays between the facts of an individual life, a determinate set of aesthetic practices, and the specific rhythms of a given historical moment.

The social and political sources and functions of the emotions in general remain poorly understood, screened off in part by a tendency to grasp their material complexity as a matter of the individual subject as such, of one's own idiosyncratic makeup. The case of Fitzgerald prompts us, however, to explore a little further, to imagine the affective realm as one of concrete social expression, complete with precise temporal dynamics and figural embodiments which variously mediate social content and lived experience. The specific affect that I focus on here is, not happiness, but rather *ressentiment*, "resentment" in English. I retain the French to remind the reader of its Nietzschean usage, wherein it already begins to assume the form of a social-structural passion, as Nietzsche (in a politically conservative manner) positions *ressentiment* as the principal class affect—the "smouldering hatred of a peasant," as Fitzgerald would describe his own attitude toward the upper classes (*Crack-Up* 77)—directed at the putatively superior aristocracy and related titled or monied groups. While it remains an ideological maneuver to interpret progressive and egalitarian political movements in terms of envy and hatred—a move that marks *ressentiment*'s discursive translation into what Fredric Jameson has termed an ideologeme, one of the minimal units of antagonistic class discourse[1]—nonetheless *ressentiment* is real, a corrosive emotion that extends across the breadth of the class structure, the very tone of both its grim dramas of rising and falling and its petty quotidian power games alike. Such a choice of affect, one that already displays vivid social content, perhaps makes our overall task here somewhat easier, and allows us to specify at the outset that class dynamics—one of Fitzgerald's abiding interests—will be a central preoccupation in what follows.[2]

But things become complicated at once, as I suggest that what we discover in Fitzgerald is not so much *ressentiment* in its naked aspect but rather a kind of sublimated and softened form of it, its deeper energies still active but its surface manifestations, its characteristic linguistic expressions, having undergone a decided shift. Certainly the requisite familial context was in place for the early nurturing of social slights and resentments: Fitzgerald expressed lifelong shame over his déclassé upbringing and was haunted by his father's career failures, and as a child frequently prayed "that they might not have to go to the poorhouse" (Mizener 38). Though never actually in poverty, the experience of growing up on the frayed edges of more well-to-do neighborhoods marked him deeply, resulting in a lifelong sense of social unease and inculcating a kind of compensatory snobbishness. The full metamorphosis of such attitudes into an aesthetic practice occurs only with *The Great Gatsby,* and only after, I would argue, the intercession of another literary practice, that of Willa Cather's in *A Lost Lady*. It is only after Cather's literary mediation that Fitzgerald finds himself able to rewrite a certain personal history in consonance with economic and social developments, suffused with the characteristic notes of loss, of regret, of diminution—the lyrical echoes of feeling oneself to have been burned by History. Hence this essay will in a small way be a study of that rather old fashioned thing, literary influence, but in a new key, the emphasis upon affect and historical rhythm designed to aid in my larger purpose: a clearer understanding of the ultimate *social* grounds of the literary achievement that is Fitzgerald's in *The Great Gatsby*. I will begin by looking at the inter-textual currents flowing between the two writers before turning in the second part of the essay to a closer examination of *The Great Gatsby* itself.

In *The Crack-Up,* Fitzgerald invokes the voice of an unnamed woman who urges him not to think small but instead embrace his breakdown in world-historical fashion: "By God, if I ever cracked, I'd try to make the world crack with me. Listen! The world only exists through your apprehension of it, and so it's much better to say that it's not you that's cracked—it's the Grand Canyon" (74). By the end of his account, as we saw above, Fitzgerald seemed willing to entertain such an approach. In 1936, the same year that *The Crack-Up* was written, Willa Cather, in a famous remark in the headnote to *Not Under Forty*, echoed something of Fitzgerald's interlocutor: "The world broke in two in 1922 or thereabouts" (v). Here Cather grandly names a crack in the world, and while there is no clear evidence that she suffered the sort of psychic ordeal that Fitzgerald experienced, still the year 1922 was an exceptionally difficult one for her: having undergone several operations related to gastrointestinal troubles, she was in poor health for much of the year; her great love Nellie McClung moved permanently to Europe; and her novel *One of Ours* was published that fall to harsh reviews that pierced her usual stoicism and wounded her sharply. As if seeking a kind of solace or retreat, she joined the ceremonious and tradition-oriented Episcopal church that December, signaling a renewed interest in religion and the beginnings of a slow movement into the past that would increasingly mark her fiction.

The novel that Cather published after this "year of the break" was *A Lost Lady*. In it, the prairie town of Sweet Water has decidedly seen better days. The town's leading citizens, the Forresters, are facing decline: Daniel Forrester, the incorruptible railroad magnate known mainly as the Captain, has suffered business failures and a stroke, while his beautiful wife Marian begins spending too much time with dubious locals like the unpleasant Ivy Peters, a crude and ambitious young man whose principal desire is to ascend the town's social ladder and displace the Forresters. Their troubles provoke a wave of hitherto suppressed and unsuspected bouts of spite and resentment from those who no longer regard the Forresters as models of civility and citizenship, or who no longer see in them the fulfillment of their own most powerful desires. In short, the veil of social decorum in Sweet Water is tearing apart, revealing a parched and bitter social and affective landscape.

As is well known, Fitzgerald read *A Lost Lady* in 1924, while he was working on the first draft of *The Great Gatsby*. He subsequently sent a copy of *Gatsby* to Cather with a letter acknowledging a writerly debt to her and even asking her leave for his close modeling of some passages in *The Great Gatsby* on *A Lost Lady*. Critical work on the precise nature of this debt has tended to follow Fitzgerald's lead and concentrate on the question of a certain transference of style.[3] Others have pointed specifically to Fitzgerald's rendering of the first-person narrator in *The Great Gatsby*: the Nick Carraway we know today only fully emerges after Fitzgerald reads *A Lost Lady,* where there is, if not a first-person narrator, at least a limited third-person narrator who closely follows the perspective of Niel Herbert and his ambivalent fascination with the charming Marian Forrester (a relationship echoed in *The Great Gatsby*). While these stylistic and technical aspects are important, I prefer to grasp the matter of influence more in terms of an awakening or sharpening of an aesthetic or theoretical problem field. From this perspective, what comes into focus is the question of social representation, of how to narrate social and historical content, a primary concern as both Cather and Fitzgerald are equally concerned with questions of class and social structure. In particular, it is Cathers's use of affect as a means of charting social space and cultural change that Fitzgerald learned from but also altered for his own purposes: what is an aesthetic pedagogy is also, and at a certain level indistinguishably, an emotional pedagogy.

For it is indeed *ressentiment,* a searing, class-driven force, that grips Sweet Water. In addition to the hate-driven Ivy Peters, the townspeople in general are portrayed as sheer vermin whose sole purpose is to invade and bring down the Forresters' once elegant hilltop home. Even some of the wives of those "handworkers and homesteaders" who have settled the area, women who elsewhere in the Cather imaginary might merit considerable sympathy, fall prey to this bitter passion. When Marian Forrester falls ill, they have their opportunity: into the house they trounce, rooting through the closets and cellar and discovering, to their satisfaction, that in its diminished state there is really "nothing remarkable about the place at all!" (138).

Meanwhile, Niel Herbert, the young man who at first idealizes Marian only to become disillusioned with her once the household begins to decline, is himself marked as déclassé, a state that at length occasions his own bout of *ressentiment.* Niel's father has lost his property, and "there was an air of failure and defeat about his family" (30). Niel's status clearly informs his basic perspective: he can libidinally invest in the Forresters as representatives of a realm of wealth and beauty once available to him, but turns on Marian when the same fate befalls her after the death of her husband. Hence, the narrator's striking statement that "what Niel most held against Mrs. Forrester [was] that she was not willing to immolate herself, like the widow of all these great men [that is, the bourgeois pioneers], and die with the pioneer period to which she belonged" (169), can be understood as less an exaggerated expression of pain at the passing of obsolete ideals than an externalization and transference of Niel's own self-hatred, the self-hatred of the déclassé whose imaginary escape from failure has been definitively blocked.

The resemblances to *The Great Gatsby* are evident. Nick Carraway shares with Niel an ambivalent attraction to those of higher social status as well as an air of failure (Nick does not finally make it in the East and returns to the Midwest, to the bosom of his family and the hardware business). The texts also share a concern with the real or imaginary fluidity of class positions—the apparent increase in the permeability of the upper social strata. What seems absent from the parched and intolerable social world of Sweet Water is any imaginative space of escape, or at least this space is present only minimally in the figure of the Blum boys, sons of German immigrants who are clearly marked as peasants (that is, Old World types who know nothing of American democratic ways). There exists between them and Marian a natural bond of sympathy, a note of interclass harmony at odds with the rest of the novel and very different from that "smouldering anger" of which Fitzgerald spoke.

If we imagine the vocation of narrative to be the working through of the various representational possibilities inherent in a given social content, the narrative task remaining after the aesthetic and ideological work of *A Lost Lady* is a more complete envisioning of some alternative or negation of Sweet Water's social bitterness. This task was taken up not only in *The Great Gatsby* but also by Cather herself in her next novel, *The Professor's House,* published in 1925, the same year as *The Great Gatsby.* In *The Professor's House,* this effort emerges first in a more fully elaborated version of the relationship between Marian and the Blum boys. Here there is a naturally harmonious relation between the Professor, a slightly aloof man of dark Spanish aspect who is figured as an aristocrat, and his peasant opposite, the earthy German seamstress Augusta. More crucial, though, is the figure of Tom Outland, described as an orphaned "tramp boy" who roams the Southwest as a cowboy until he eventually falls in with some Jesuits who clean him up and teach him some Latin. This rudimentary education soon launches him toward a metamorphosis into a scientific genius: chemist, physicist, and a mean amateur archaeologist to boot. Still, he retains a roughhewn and naive charm that wins over any social situation, and almost everyone in the novel is or was in love with him. In short, he's a wholly implausible fantasy figure, a utopian fusion of High and Low in all the cultural and social senses of those terms, a kind of "classless" narrative register. At some level Cather's novel recognizes this very implausibility, for Tom is already dead when the narrative opens. The only extended exposure to him that we receive is in the form of an interpolated first-person account of one of his Southwest adventures.

Is not Jay Gatsby a similar wish-fulfillment figure, intensely if variously invested in by those around him? His obsessive history with Daisy begins, of course, when he steps across the threshold of her house in Louisville, traces of his impoverished class background wiped clean by the "invisible cloak" of his military uniform. Bootlegger, Oxford man, distinguished veteran, rumored murderer: the sense of implausibility drapes him like a cheap suit. Rather than registering that implausibility indirectly, at the edges of the narrative as Cather does with Outland, Fitzgerald pulls that very uncertainty wholly within the perspective of Nick Carraway, creating a figure who alternately doubts and endorses Gatsby, or who sometimes seems to do both at the same time. Perhaps more importantly, the Nick/Gatsby dyad affords Fitzgerald the opportunity of critically restaging the thematics of *ressentiment* found in *A Lost Lady*. In Cather's novel, they had been used to chart in a lucid fashion the shifting social dynamics of Sweet Water; right alongside them, however, was a persistent register of idealized romanticism, waxing nostalgic about the faded ideals of the original Western pioneers. Cather puts some efforts into keeping these domains separate, marking the romantic imaginings as belonging to the past and the various resentments as part of the contemporary moment, but at certain points, particularly in the figure of Niel Herbert, the two strains are sufficiently conjoined, suggesting a rather more interdependent and symbiotic relationship.

In *The Great Gatsby,* Fitzgerald seizes upon this more conflicted and ambivalent possibility, interweaving romanticism and *ressentiment* more intensely and in the process transforming both. Again, this is chiefly in the consciousness of Nick, where a related kind of splitting occurs. Characteristic of someone suffering from resentments of his own, Nick attributes *ressentiment* to all those around Gatsby, those who emblematize the "foul dust" that envelops and destroys him. Nick reserves for himself and Gatsby the more lyrical and romantic registers. It is the textual productivity of this conjoined affect machine that I wish to draw attention to here, one which seeks in its own fashion the eradication of the present. Fitzgerald's aesthetic practice creates a sensitive apparatus for the detection of new socio-historical content, one which has presented something of a conundrum to later critics in regards to its possible political and ideological valences. The novel has famously been taken as both a clinical exposé and a ringing affirmation of the American dream, as radical and conservative all at once. I think here of Fitzgerald's own characterization of himself in 1924 as "a pessimist, [and] a communist (with Nietzschean overtones)" (Bruccoli and Jackson 270), certainly an interesting phrase from our present perspective, implying as it does a simultaneous fealty and animus toward social hierarchy.[4] Something of this dynamic is present in Cather as well, where some hierarchical relations are destructive while others point toward an imagined self-transcendence (though

her generally conservative ideological investments are more readily limned). This works itself out in intricate ways in Fitzgerald.

In his 1932 essay **"My Lost City,"** one of several pieces collected in *The Crack-Up* which center on loss and dissipation, Fitzgerald recalls a striking moment from sometime in 1920 when *This Side of Paradise* was out and selling well, and he was on top of the world: "And lastly from that period I remember riding in a taxi one afternoon between very tall buildings under a mauve and rosy sky; I began to bawl because I had everything I wanted and knew I would never be so happy again" (29). His crying is precipitated, not by happiness itself, but via a secondary and temporally removed operation, as if Fitzgerald was at that moment imaginatively placing himself ten or twenty years in the future, a future already assumed to be diminished in comparison to that present, looking back on the moment and thereby generating what appears to be an intense regret. This recalls the stark process of inexorable declension announced at the opening of **"The Crack-Up"**: "Of course all life is a process of breaking down [. . .]" (69). It is a process that follows various paths, with distinct temporalities: some psychic blows are registered quickly, while others are more stealthy and only come to consciousness long after the fact. The latter is the form taken by Fitzgerald's trauma, as he realizes that for two years he has been an empty shell, a man merely going through the motions of living. It is in either case a peremptory affair, seemingly less a matter of inexorable Spenglerian decline—a minor interest of Fitzgerald's, and another Nietzschean motif—than of a sudden rupture, or a series of staggered, unpredictable blows. In his writing from this period he broods on such rhythms, imagining, as above, similar occurrences much earlier in his life, in what amount to dress rehearsals for the definitive crack-up in the thirties. Recalling again in **"Early Success"** the time of his first rush of good fortune, he notes that "it is a short and precious time—for when the mist rises in a few weeks, or a few months, one finds that the very best is over" (*Crack-Up* 86). Or, after a distressing visit to Princeton during that same period: "But on that day in 1920 most of the joy went out of my success" (89). First months, then weeks, now days—what takes shape in the movement of these reminiscences is a kind of vanishing point of experience, a hole slowly opening up within the frame of a (now past) present such that immediacy is hollowed out and slips rapidly out of one's grasp. The duration of experience steadily shrinks until, as in the limousine, Fitzgerald is in a sense after or beyond the moment even as he lives it, caught in a complex movement of proleptic retroactivity and its attendant affective correlatives of loss and longing.

"But one was now a professional": with this rather grim-faced assertion from **"Early Success"** Fitzgerald introduces what is in effect the counter-temporality to that more breach or rupture-oriented one just examined. The advent of this, too, occurs around 1920, when *This Side of Paradise* is due out: "While I waited for the novel to appear, the metamorphosis of amateur into professional began to take place—a sort of stitching together of your whole life into a pattern of work, so that the end of one job is automatically the beginning of another" (86). Here then is an unbroken continuum, a seamless expanse stretching to the ends of time, one whose inner logic maintains a peculiar symbiosis with the multiply-segmented breakdown line, at once a countervailing force and a kind of incitement.[5] Fitzgerald never stopped lauding what he called the "old virtues" of work and courage, but he was also perpetually bitter over the extensive amount of inferior (he thought) writing he had to do, chiefly for popular magazines, in order to maintain his notoriously extravagant lifestyle—work which he felt kept him from his real vocation as novelist. A professional, then, is not quite an artist, or not only one; rather, a professional is someone for whom every moment is at least potentially one of work, a position familiar enough to intellectual and cultural laborers whose generally privileged and satisfying work is shadowed by this disconcerting temporal structure. This is overcoded in Fitzgerald's case by his early terror of the poorhouse, suggesting that he was being oddly evasive in his characterization of that peasantlike rage which supposedly marked his feeling toward the wealthy. Setting aside the anachronism, what emerges from the poorhouse in this society is not a peasant but a proletarian; the deeper fear of this potential destiny, like some alternate life line lodged inside his actual one, colored his class metabolism. It is thus striking that the chapter of Marx's *Capital* that he perhaps knew best was the central one on the working day (that "terrible chapter," he called it [*Crack-Up* 290]). Here Marx precisely notes that, considered in the abstract, the very definition of the worker is that of a person whose every instant of lived time (minus the necessities of eating and sleeping) can be considered potential labor time. This is a "stitching together" into an infernal and inhuman continuity that resonates with Fitzgerald's own conception of his craft, constituting something like the "inner *ressentiment*" of the writing profession as such.

Signs of these competing temporalities are present throughout *The Great Gatsby*. Some of Daisy's remarks, remarkable for their simultaneous evocation of a breathless excitement and a peculiar sadness, elicit this competition: "'In two weeks it'll be the longest day of the year.' She looked at us all radiantly. 'Do you always watch for the longest day of the year and then miss it? I always watch for the longest day in the year and then miss it'" (12). This is Fitzgerald again in the taxi, in some ways a textbook lesson about the absence of presence: you move toward a future moment, one which in this case promises some particular enchantment, then

suddenly you are on the far side of it, "it" having never really taken place—or perhaps it took place without you, which might well be Nick's great fear—leaving you with only a vague regret. Or a slightly different version: "'What'll we do with ourselves this afternoon?' cried Daisy, 'and the day after that, and the next thirty years?'" (118). Here, rather than the vanishing nodal point of the longest day, we have the setting up of a sharp anticipation, then, leaping across a suddenly empty-feeling thirty years, a desolate stretch perhaps more akin to the world of the "professional." Jordan Baker catches the flavor of this: "Don't be morbid" she says at once to Daisy, at which point Daisy herself is on the verge of tears (118).

These examples rhetorically concretize and enact in miniature much of the prevailing mood of the novel as a whole, dramatizing the absent or hollow center which animates it—the invented life, the glamorous ephemera, the death in which it culminates. In them the present wavers just a little, not unlike those gaps or seams Nick perceives in Gatsby's self-presentation. These seams afford a glimpse of the dull machinery behind what Nick describes as the gorgeous "unbroken series of successful gestures" (2) that constitute Gatsby's personality. "My incredulity was submerged in fascination now," Nick says when Gatsby informs him of war decorations received from the Montenegrin government. "It was like skimming hastily through a dozen magazines" (67). This makes Gatsby a virtual parable of the modernist crisis of *Schein* or aesthetic appearance,[6] as a host of processes during this period—from painterly abstraction, to Dadaist interventions, to the increasing autonomy of narrative episodes and even of the sentence itself—threatened the aesthetic object with a collapse back into its initial raw materials: smudges of paint on canvas, black marks on a page, or (in Tolstoy's famous example of the theater) people milling about and occasionally talking on a raised platform. Indeed, Mitchell Breitwieser posits Gatsby as a kind of modernist impresario, a Long Island Le Corbusier whose enormous parties strive toward the totality itself, liquor-fueled *villes radieuses* which stand as prolegomena "to the construction of a society utterly responsive to unification by a single design" (32). But the trick can fall flat, the plan can be seen through, and those who have invested considerable time and effort participating in a particular elaboration of *Schein* can turn away in bewilderment and hostility (a hostility Nick will be quick to attribute to those around him and Gatsby). Gatsby as *Gesamtkunstwerk* thus falls short of realization and is shunned and disowned, a certain failure of aesthetic possibility being at one and the same time the allegory of the failure of a dual social and national possibility itself conceived largely in aesthetic terms. This is a persistent theme in American letters, from Hawthorne through Williams and West and beyond, and I will return below to its further implications.

There is a particular sort of excess figured in moments like Daisy's outbursts or in others like Gatsby's straight-faced offering of an anecdote of his life while seemingly doubled-up with laughter at the same time. They have in them something overwrought or histrionic, a straining to express more than is possible ("I'm p-paralyzed with happiness" [9]), or a rapid inflation and sudden deflation, like a balloon quickly filling then bursting. This excess, and there are perhaps different forms of it, is the most characteristic motif or pattern in the novel. This excess is produced when the generalized *ressentiment* of Cather and the social portrait she fashions is drawn within one centering consciousness or point of view, where it meshes with a certain expressive tonality and becomes a kind of aesthetic resource in its own right. *Ressentiment* in *A Lost Lady* already had a formal complexity to it, at once temporal and emotional: a rage directed at the present and the force of its circumstances and exigencies in the name of an imaginary past of idealized values that is at the same time the place of an original (and unrecognized) wound or insult—an intricate play of destruction and preservation. The animating irony, or even aporia, at work here is that the afflicted white bourgeois or petit bourgeois Americans of the story are precisely, as instigators of a pattern of historical modernization, the source of the wound in question. The temporality of the crack-up is, as Deleuze argues (though I think he too quickly assimilates the matter to alcoholism as such), strikingly similar, though it is wound-up more tightly and concentrated within the movement of a singularity: it is a kind of permanent past perfect (*passé composé*), a constant "I have been" in which a momentary hardness or intensity of the present ("I have . . .) invariably fades or takes flight into phantasmatic pasts (. . . been"). "It is," Deleuze says, "at once love and the loss of love, money and the loss of money, the native land and its loss" (*The Logic of Sense* 160).[7] He calls this the depressive aspect of Fitzgerald's condition, though Breitwieser, in examining the affective texture of **The Great Gatsby,** employs what strikes me as the more productive term, *melancholia*. He nicely characterizes this as an "anorexic" strategy designed to keep at bay the everyday viscousness of the Real and create a space for lyrical flights, "a chamber in which the dream *can* echo because the chamber is otherwise silent" (31). Here then is one register of the rather more sweetened form of *ressentiment* articulated by Fitzgerald seeking expression in those lyrical registers he learned so well from Keats (a lower-middle-class fellow with some fervid resentments of his own).

Melancholic, indeed, though this term risks remaining tied too closely to Fitzgerald's psychology and to a lyric embodiment. Hence it is together with those moments of "excess" that the full scope of the pattern detailed by Deleuze is played out. A certain level of excess in the novel is obvious enough: the lavishness of the parties, the Rolls Royces, the servants—the familiar trappings of Veblenesque leisure-class conspicuousness. But it extends down into individual narrative and linguistic moments in an instructive fashion. "He found her excitingly desirable," (148) says Nick of Gatsby's initial reaction to Daisy. Not just exciting, or just desirable, but both, a little adjectival whirligig that spins and chases its own tail; this marks the origin of Gatsby's dream, which might well be recast as his obsession, a form of excess in itself. Think, too, of the wonderful, Homeric list of partygoers at Gatsby's that gathers a kind of deadpan comic momentum, or the old man selling dogs "who bore an absurd resemblance to John D. Rockefeller" (27), or (the already excessively Jewish) Meyer Wolfsheim's cufflinks made of human teeth that suddenly lend him the dark aura of some cannibal chieftain. There are as well those sheep rounding the Manhattan street corner, and Myrtle Wilson's pent-up, volcanic energy. All of these examples are moments or figures that momentarily exceed what they actually are, hijacking the world of present appearances and creating a parallel track of fantasy which flees into some alternative, but indefinite, realm. So, too, with the witness to Myrtle's death, the "pale well-dressed negro," (140) whose appearance, as Breitwieser argues, exceeds narratological requirements: Why light skinned? Why well dressed? Is he too an aspirant, an outsider wanting in, not unlike Gatsby himself? We cannot know, as this figure vanishes at once, but the suggestion has been lodged. What to make, as well, of that odd and slightly notorious scene at the end of chapter 2 when Nick ends up beside Mr. McKee's bed, where the half-naked McKee shows Nick his book of photographs? An extravagant innuendo, at the very least ("keep your hands off the lever!" [38]), exceeding anything we might reasonably ascertain.

Finally, recall Gatsby's remarkable response to Nick's question about where he's from: the middle west, it turns out. What part of the middle west, asks Nick? "San Francisco" (65). Does Gatsby really think that San Francisco is in the Midwest? But this is a pointless inquiry. The sheer absurdity of the response, aside from giving it the aforementioned aspect of deadpan comedy, makes it another figure of excess, something that does not quite fit the container in which it is placed, threatening to burst things asunder. This already incredible answer of Gatsby's is in the midst of a longer and even less credible account offered of his Oxford education and his cavorting with European princes. Just as Nick seems about ready to call his bluff, Gatsby produces a photograph showing him with some other young men, holding cricket bats, with spires in the background. "Then it was all true," says Nick, "I saw the skins of tigers flaming in his palace on the Grand Canal; I saw him opening a chest of rubies to ease, with their crimson-lighted depths, the gnawings of his broken heart" (67). For the reader, however (less given to romantic leaps), the photograph does not exactly dispel all doubts: given the evident fabrications of Gatsby's tale, in what sense could it be simply "true"? What indeed is it really depicting? That is, rather than standing as some mundane arbiter of the facts of the matter, a simple registration of empirical realities, the photo instead becomes an exceedingly strange artifact, an excessive and even surrealistic object glowing with mysterious energies.

Such "excess" suggests the narrative and even rhetorical refiguration of the encounter between Fitzgerald's and Cather's particular instantiations of *ressentiment.* This stems at least in part from the very nature of *ressentiment,* which might itself be grasped as a form of excess, as it is an insistent, corrosive, and often malignant intensification of a certain class awareness, wherein what might have remained a discrete piece of social knowledge becomes an overriding passion or drive. Within the field of Fitzgerald's narrative and ideological practice, a form of splitting or fragmentation occurs, and different expressive forms of *ressentiment* crystallize. These range from Nick's snobbish asides, melancholic intimations of longing, and (one suspects) wellnigh permanently delayed gratification through to the notes and images of excess detailed above.[8] Nick's romanticism tends to carry the more palpable affective charge and does the work of deflecting felt slights and cruel deprivations into a compensatory structure of fantasy which softens the rage into something more bittersweet. The figuration of excess is generally more affectively neutral, but all of this, I think—much like Daisy's utterances—involves a temporal component that seeks the sudden inflation and distortion of the present moment, a brief placement of the present *sous rature* or under erasure, as an early Derridean protocol had it, both absent and present, an incursion of the supramundane that renders the present temptingly fungible. Together these registers work to produce the simultaneous intensification and flight of the present: moments never quite realized, events that never quite took place, desires that were never quite fulfilled—or, as Deleuze more sharply puts it, they all were and were not in the one selfsame movement. "I was within and without, simultaneously enchanted and repelled by the inexhaustible variety of life" (36), Nick muses in a formulation that nicely approaches what we are describing here.

The tension thus created stands as the very material index of the intricate and ambivalent positioning of the novel with respect to both its social ground and its exemplary place in the arc of Fitzgerald's career. Indeed, I like to imagine, in an Adornian fashion, a kind of utter subordination of the writer to his or her project, as a certain social and historical content, seeking, in the dynamism of its becoming, adequate aesthetic expression, seizes upon the accidental features of an individual life and psychology and draws them wholly within the process of its artistic self-elaboration. The artist in effect becomes a now fascinated and helpless appendage to this process—not passive, exactly, but one whose intentions and emotions themselves become transformed into so much literary raw material (what Goethe once spoke of in terms of "possession" by an aesthetic demon). It is to this social content that we can at last turn, by way of recalling that problematic of social representation that *A Lost Lady* embodied for Fitzgerald. For *A Lost Lady* is in some sense a narrative of social crisis, of rapid and debilitating social change that had implications for Cather's own aesthetic practice: in the twenties, after the world has "broken in two," she can no longer write the same sorts of novels she once did. For Fitzgerald, however, this combined social and writerly crisis takes a rather different form.

Indeed, are the 1920s not themselves conventionally imagined as a period of excess, "roaring" from one over-the-top display to the next, with Fitzgerald himself as their duly-anointed chronicler? There are important truths in these popular images, though I think that sociologically speaking things were rather more complicated and ambivalent than this. While what I referred to above as a Veblenesque social structure was still much in evidence with its ostentatiously visible ruling elites, another material force to be reckoned with was on the scene, implying a rather different logic of social and ideological relations. I refer of course to the first full implantation of a mass consumer society in America: the assembly line, the five dollar day, the invention and aggressive extension of consumer credit, and the quantum leap forward in mass communication and advertising. This is much more than certain upper- or middle-class sectors buying commodities; this is the purchase of ever more and ever cheaper industrially produced goods by ever greater numbers of the whole population (including the working classes, numerically the greatest segment).[9] This links for the first time what might be called the formalism of the profit motive—the restless, purely formal necessity for more pluses than minuses at the bottom of the accounting ledger—with consumption itself, now a formalized "more more more" en route to becoming a generalized social value for the first time (rather than a local "ethos" of this or that regional bourgeois fraction). Such a movement involves more than a simple ideology, but is a genuine material force, instantiated in practices, institutions, and social apparatuses, as well as ideologies, an excess which represents a problem for the kinds of leisure class representations of class content we normally associate with ***The Great Gatsby.*** This new sort of excess is of course nominally "democratic." Unlike the Veblenesque scenario, which vividly dramatized class hierarchies and exclusions, the dynamic of consumption—partly ideologically but also partly for real, existing regardless of whatever patterns of status differentiation it becomes enmeshed with—this dynamic presented itself as at least tendentially available to all. This play of distinction versus leveling is interestingly complicated in the text by the figure of Gatsby, who is a transitional figure in that he himself uses conspicuous consumption to challenge and open up a still older form of distinction as represented by East Egg. Even this putative antiquity is deceptive, though, since the Buchanans—Midwestern interlopers themselves—happily take their place in it, testament to the difficulties involved in trying to preserve intact boundaries of wealth, exclusivity, and "breeding" that have essentially been generated out of thin air.

More crucially still, industrial production and its attendant dynamic of mass consumption encode within their historical deployment and elaboration the ultimate suppression or shearing away of older style class content, such that we end up, as in the contemporary period, with no functional or socially resonant representations of the ruling class (pop-cultural detritus like TV's *Lifestyles of the Rich and Famous* in no way fulfilling this role). Fitzgerald's contemporaries, such as Leon Samson, an unorthodox socialist and analyst of American exceptionalism whose work deserves wider recognition, were beginning to notice this trend. "The more complete and complicated the American system becomes," Samson wrote, "the more independent it gets to be of its owners and heirs [. . .] American capital has succeeded in scaling such titanic heights that it has proletarianized even the capitalists themselves" (281-82). Samson here employs what was for him a characteristic mode of ironic overstatement, but the trend he calls attention to was genuine enough. The individualizing and leveling effects of mass consumption work over time to suppress the meaningful visibility of ruling groups, a visibility necessary for the cultural and discursive maintenance and presentation of the class character of society. I presume, of course, that ruling groups still rule; the problem, however, is with their representability, with the fashioning of a culturally credible image of this power, something beautifully allegorized in the novel in the contrast between the initial view of Tom and Daisy and our later glimpses of them. The opening is sweeping and cinematic:

> The lawn started at the beach and ran toward the front door for a quarter of a mile, jumping over sun-dials and brick walks and burning gardens—finally when it reached the house drifting up the side in bright vines as though from the momentum of its run. The front was broken by a line of French windows, glowing now with reflected gold and wide open to the warm windy evening, and Tom Buchanan in riding clothes was standing with his legs apart on the front porch.
>
> (7)

Later, however, after the accident that kills Myrtle, Nick does a little reconnaissance for Gatsby, in search of Tom and Daisy, who are now secreted away:

> I walked back along the border of the lawn, traversed the gravel softly, and tiptoed up the veranda steps. The

drawing-room curtains were open, and I saw that the room was empty. Crossing the porch where we had dined that June night three months before, I came to a small rectangle of light which I guessed was the pantry window. The blind was drawn, but I found a rift at the sill.

> Tom and Daisy were sitting opposite each other at the kitchen table [. . .].
>
> (146)

A dramatic decrease, then, in the Buchanans' visibility, an allegorical sequestering from public view whose now small-scale intimacy is itself tellingly described by Nick, who notes that "anybody would have said that they were conspiring together" (146). This is a remarkable premonition of what happens when the functionality of social groups is suppressed, a condition precisely identified by Jameson as the tendency "to dissociate the acknowledgment of the individual existence of a group from any attribution of a project that becomes registered not as a group but as a *conspiracy*" (*Postmodernism* 349). The cultural existence or presence of the economic and political agency of social classes is thus a signal casualty of our era and a development with serious social and political consequences. In the Marxian optic, of course, the very possibility of "real" politics—those that can significantly alter and improve the material well being and daily lifeworld of the broad masses of the population, indeed permitting them to undertake such a profound renovation for themselves—depends in large measure on at least some sort of tendentially dichotomizing dynamic (whose initial contours need not express themselves in strict class terms). In other words, the potential for working-class consciousness is itself dependent in part upon the perceptible reality of ruling groups.

So the excess of mass consumption is in tension with the excess of Veblen's conspicuous consumption. The latter is on the surface in *The Great Gatsby,* but I think it is the former which is at work in those more local, figurally striking moments. Such a reading is further suggested by the chief desire projected by Nick throughout the course of the story, a desire for *security*. This might be seen, for example, in his reluctance to involve himself in the uncertain play of human affairs (his "anorexic" tendency), the counterpoint to which are the moments when an unwanted public attention is turned upon him: "[Myrtle] pointed suddenly at me, and every one looked at me accusingly. I tried to show by my expression that I had played no part in her past" (35). Here the force of the Look pulls him out of his more comfortable spectatorial role; recall as well the suspicious glances of the women on the train as Nick bends to retrieve a dropped pocketbook. More crucial is the gravitational pull of that "warm center of the world" (3) represented by the Midwest of his childhood, to which his thoughts so often turn and to whose comforting embrace he has returned to write the narrative we now read. Indeed, he is now virtually as "safe and proud above the hot struggles of the poor" (150) as Daisy herself. There is perhaps an infantile and Oedipal aspect to this, but before leaving it at that Freudian level it must be noted that security is also a value projected by mass consumption. Whereas the leisure class seeks to affirm itself via the direct or indirect class humiliation of everyone else, and thus promote a certain level of social *insecurity,* mass consumption promises something else. If, as Jameson notes, "we all do want to 'master' history in whatever ways turn out to be possible" (*Postmodernism* 342), and hence seek out a certain insulation from blind historical forces, then piles of more or less available commodities offer themselves up to recently proletarianized populations as another warm center of the world, something which again is more than mere ideological trickery but is bound up with materially dense forces of attraction and appeals to deep Utopian impulses.

And so, finally, Gatsby's shirts: another very famous scene, usually taken as emblematic of the commodity-drunk twenties and the mediation of Gatsby and Daisy's relationship by these commodities. Let me instead suggest a somewhat different reading, inspired in part by Richard Godden's observation that Daisy's precise action—"she *bent* her head into the shirts and began to cry stormily" (93)—to the extent that she does not simply collapse with abandon into them, implies more consideration than is normally supposed, a kind of distance or gap between herself and the shirts (*Fictions* 86). Rather than try, as Godden does, to ascertain what is really going through Daisy's mind here,[10] I would simply observe a certain tension or *agon* between these two images, the leisureclass woman on the one hand, and on the other the pile of commodities whose very logic threatens to erase her social visibility. Allegorical tears, then, from a character whose "disappearance" will be as marked as (if, as so often with this class, rather less violent than) that of her working-class double, Myrtle Wilson.

Hence, in the end, the profound ambivalence and unique achievement of this novel, as the narrative tracks the emergence of new social content whose laws of operation will suppress the very social meaning of those images and representations from which Fitzgerald's aesthetic practice drew its initial and enduring inspiration. As in some devil's pact—though in this particular pact the two moments of charmed existence and terrible payment are coterminous—Fitzgerald's aesthetic impulses seize upon (or are exploited by) an historical dynamic that both sustains and destroys, and which portends the ultimate extinction of his writerly vocation and being. And, at some obscure level, this is at once known and fearfully cherished: getting burned by History as a kind of ecstatic self-realization. This dynamic

issues in the complex movement of splitting and sublimation of *ressentiment* that we have discussed here, with its simultaneous intensification and undermining of present reality, its vivid excess and sharp longing, its romantic nostalgia and quiet bitterness (at once love and the loss of love, money and the loss of money). These all remarkably dovetail and spiral around one another in an effort to vehiculate a dense and tense knot of social, and essentially class, relations, themselves in complicated transition. This effort to capture and portray what is in the end an historical conundrum is one that perhaps can only end in exhaustion, and indeed, from this point onward Fitzgerald's career will never be quite the same. Writing will never again come so easily to him, and will at times, as during the writing of **Tender is the Night,** become a veritable torment.

Thus it is appropriate that the novel ends (as we, and so many other commentaries on the text, also end) with Nick sprawled on Gatsby's beach, his thoughts returning to the dawn of the New World. Here we are at that moment of the break with the old world, that moment of breathless Utopian possibility when the project of "America" rises in the imagination as an essentially *aesthetic* project, something it has largely remained ever since. But with remarkable echoes of Adorno's interpretation of Odysseus's encounter with the Sirens, Fitzgerald offers a rhetorically complex version of a dialectic of myth and enlightenment. In Adorno, the aesthetic (the Sirens' song, heard only by the bound master Odysseus) and exploited labor (the oarsmen, deaf with plugged ears to the fatal temptation) split off from one another at the very outset of "western" culture.[11] Fitzgerald's Dutch sailors are themselves afforded a moment's aesthetic contemplation before the frenzied plunge into the continent which will inaugurate that very historical dynamic destined to vitiate the aesthetic dream, namely the stupendous eruption of human labor aimed at extracting as much wealth as possible: that is to say, class dynamics as such, the very ones so consistently disavowed in the dream of America and now materially masked by the advent of mass consumption. What results is a kind of spatio-temporal loop or prison, a seemingly forward movement that leads only backward: "His dream must have seemed so close that he could hardly fail to grasp it. He did not know that it was already behind him [. . .]. And so we beat on, boats against the current, borne back ceaselessly into the past" (182). Like Fitzgerald in the taxi, or Daisy awaiting the summer solstice, what is evoked here is a vanishing point in time that amounts finally to a foreclosure on the future, a condemnation to empty longing and repetition without issue. This includes both Fitzgerald's future, left now with only the insidious and changeless grind of sheer professionalism and its particular *ressentiment* (an omen of the crack-up to come), as well as our collective future as such. Here is the kernel of materialist insight that emerges from the political unconscious of this text and its serendipitous interaction with the details of Fitzgerald's writerly metabolism: no ultimate political or social future is possible without that class dynamic which **The Great Gatsby** at once dramatizes and effaces. Until such a development, a spectral "America" remains suspended in mythic brooding over the trauma of its always-failed attempts to realize itself.

Notes

1. For this discussion, see Jameson, *The Political Unconscious* 201-205.

2. Here and throughout I intend the term "class" not only in its more mainstream sense of income stratification but also and more crucially in the Marxian sense of a hierarchical organization of the labor process which affords the imposition of surplus labor and the extraction of surplus value via the production of commodities.

3. On this, see Quirk. I have written in more detail on *A Lost Lady* and *The Professor's House* in my forthcoming book, *Around Quitting Time: Work and Middle-Class Fantasy in American Fiction* (Duke UP).

4. Compare as well the following, taken from a letter Fitzgerald wrote to Max Perkins (March 5, 1922): "I'm still a socialist but sometimes I dread that things will grow worse and worse the more people nominally rule. The strong are too strong for us and the weak too weak" (Kuehl and Bryer 57).

5. For this terminology of break and segmentation, see the brief discussion of "The Crack-Up" in Deleuze and Guattari 198-200.

6. The term *Schein* comes from German idealist aesthetics, where it designates the aesthetic effect achieved by the application of some process of construction upon a given set of raw materials. Its English equivalents (aesthetic appearance or illusion, fiction) tend to suggest some truth or reality existing behind the mere appearance, an implication not present in the German original. For a useful discussion of these issues, one which also broaches the problem of modernism, see Jameson, *Late Marxism* 165-176.

7. I think that this *passé composé* can shift into a *futur antérieur* ("I will have been") from time to time, though Deleuze, with characteristic schematic rigor, attributes this latter tense exclusively to another literary alcoholic, Malcolm Lowry.

8. Though there has been much debate over his ethico-political status as narrator, I take Nick's snobbishness as a given. Not only is it announced on the first page—"as my father snobbishly sug-

gested, and I snobbishly repeat"—it is effectively performed. His father's advice, after all, concerned the need to be mindful of the disparate "advantages" available to people; it counseled, in a liberal and democratic spirit, a certain forbearance in the face of material inequality. Nick translates this into the unequal distribution of "a sense of the fundamental decencies," an altogether more vaporous and idealistic matter far more open to corruption by class attitudes. This of course leads into Nick's oft-noted belief that he "reserves judgment," when he is in fact busy judging left and right.

9. For a persuasive periodization of the full creation of consumer society, one nicely grounded in the details of economic history, see Livingston.

10. Godden suggests that Daisy momentarily recalls here the "original," uniformed and classless Gatsby she knew from Louisville; the awful distance between that earlier, innocent figure and the improbable parvenu before her sparks her tears.

11. See Horkheimer and Adorno, 33-4. I follow the widely shared feeling (by no means provable) that this astonishing rewrite of the myth, given its sheer dialectical brilliance and concentration, must be Adorno's doing, rather than that of the more prosaic Horkheimer.

Works Cited

Breitwieser, Mitchell. "*The Great Gatsby*: Grief, Jazz, and the Eye-Witness," *Arizona Quarterly* 47.3 (1991): 17-70.

Bruccoli, Matthew J. and Jackson R. Breyer, eds. *F. Scott Fitzgerald in His Own Time: A Miscellany*. Kent, OH: Kent State UP, 1972.

Cather, Willa. *A Lost Lady*. 1923. New York: Vintage, 1972.

———. *Not Under Forty*. Lincoln: U of Nebraska P, 1988.

Deleuze, Gilles. *The Logic of Sense*. Trans. Mark Lester and Charles Stivale. New York: Columbia UP, 1990.

Deleuze, Gilles and Félix Guattari. *A Thousand Plateaus*. Trans. Brian Massumi. Minneapolis: U of Minnesota P, 1987.

Fitzgerald, F. Scott. *The Crack-Up*. Ed. Edmund Wilson. New York: New Directions, 1945.

———. *The Great Gatsby*. New York: Scribner's, 1925.

Godden, Richard. *Fictions of Capital: The American Novel from James to Mailer*. Cambridge: Cambridge UP, 1990.

Horkheimer, Max and Theodor W. Adorno. *Dialectic of Enlightenment*. Trans. John Cumming. New York: Continuum, 1972.

Jameson, Fredric. *The Political Unconscious*. Ithaca: Cornell UP, 1981.

———. *Late Marxism; or, The Persistence of the Dialectic*. London: Verso, 1990.

———. *Postmodernism; or, The Cultural Logic of Late Capitalism*. Durham: Duke UP, 1990.

Kuehl, John and Jackson Bryer, eds. *Dear Scott/Dear Max: The Fitzgerald/Perkins Correspondence*. New York: Scribner's, 1971.

Livingston, James. *Pragmatism and the Political Economy of Cultural Revolution, 1850-1940*. Chapel Hill: U of North Carolina P, 1994.

Mizener, Arthur. *The Far Side of Paradise*. New York: Avon, 1974.

Quirk, Tom. "Fitzgerald and Cather: *The Great Gatsby*." *American Literature* 54 (1982): 576-91.

Samson, Leon. *The American Mind: A Study in Socio-Analysis*. New York: Cape, 1932.

Mitchell Breitwieser (essay date fall 2000)

SOURCE: Breitwieser, Mitchell. "Jazz Fractures: F. Scott Fitzgerald and Epochal Representation." *American Literary History* 12, no. 3 (fall 2000): 359-81.

[*In the following essay, Breitwieser explores ways in which Fitzgerald used the phrases "the Jazz Age" and "The Last Tycoon" to define epochs in American literary history, prefiguring the discipline which would become American studies.*]

An earlier version of this essay was presented at "History in the Making: The Future of American Literary Studies," a conference held at the University of Wisconsin at Madison in late March 1999. At the beginning of my talk, I remarked that I had grown up in Monona, a small town about five miles from the campus, and that I earned my BA from UW-Madison in 1975. Preparing for the talk, I confessed, had stirred up memories, among them my first reading of *The Great Gatsby* (1925), which powerfully evoked what F. Scott Fitzgerald called the promise of life. My students, I noted, hearing again that elusive tune I had heard 25 years before, tend to dislike, affably, my middle-aged reading, for instance my claims concerning Nick Carraway's bad faith or my preference for the centrifugal disturbances of *Tender is the Night* (1933). In the difference between my reading and theirs I see that, though Fitzgerald still interests me deeply, he has changed, or

rather, the center of his gravity has for me moved not only to the discoveries of his later fiction but also to certain facets I had not noticed in *The Great Gatsby,* where he begins to think critically about history, about race, class, region, nationality, and about how the intersections of such powers provoke, shape, and frustrate desire. Fitzgerald's writing seems to me now less an expression and celebration of pure longing than an archaeology of American desire—not the unbroken lineage from Dutch explorers to Jazz Age dreamer that Fitzgerald posited at the end of his most famous work, but a sedimentation of desires, like the layers of Troy or the layers of meanings Freud peeled away in the analysis of the symptom—"America" as a condensation, aggregate, or depository of subject-residues, rather than a mystical being. This, I would say, is where Fitzgerald parts company from Thomas Wolfe and Ernest Hemingway and keeps company with William Faulkner and Zora Neale Hurston, his historical sense laying the foundation for what would be called American studies and prefiguring some of the disciplinary transformations within literary study that were the topic of "History in the Making." To sketch out something of that prefiguration, I reflected on two terms, "the Jazz Age" and "The Last Tycoon." Since the term "Jazz Age" appears in the 1931 essay **"Echoes of the Jazz Age,"** a postmortem of the 1920s, we have in both phrases an announcement that an American epoch has ended, an implied analysis of the subjective forms that the epoch produced, and speculations concerning the forces that brought about the end. I differentiated the two terms by contrasting the melancholia that typifies endings in **The Great Gatsby** and the 1931 essay with some new ways of thinking about social and personal coherence that Fitzgerald was exploring at the time of his death in 1940.

First, then, the "Jazz Age." For Fitzgerald the term may have resonated humorously with Stone Age, Bronze Age, and Iron Age—periodizations of archaic humanity that came into use among archaeologists during the second half of the nineteenth century. If so, the irony is two-sided: first, whereas an "age" used to span centuries, the velocity of change is now such that we run through an age in 10 years or so, as long as it takes a culture-defining group of young people to follow the arc of its third decade; and second, whereas the universal plastic material that defines us used to be substance—stone, bronze, iron—it is now an intense, ungraspable cultural energy, jazz, "an arrangement of notes that will never be played again," as Nick Carraway says of Daisy Buchanan's voice (11).[1]

As fundamental material, jazz saturates the culture of its epoch, supplying people, events, and artifacts with the character by which they are most succinctly grasped. The term "Jazz Age" therefore imputes to 1920s jazz what Louis Althusser and Etienne Balibar call "expressive causality" (310), which "describe[s] the effect of the whole on the parts, but only by making the latter an 'expression' of the former, a phenomenon of its essence" (316). Althusser and Balibar's "but only" indicate their conviction that "expression" is a restrictive way to understand a society, that there are more complex and satisfying ways to think about parts and wholes, an idea, I will eventually argue, that Fitzgerald was approaching as he wrote *The Last Tycoon* (1941). But for now, let's stay with the idea of expressive causality, with, in Fitzgerald's case, a temporary national whole of which the parts are expressions, which is what makes an epoch—when the parts break away from their expressivity, become dark and single, then begin to recohere around a new core, the epoch gives way to its successor. Fitzgerald's commitment to expressive structure is especially evident in his post-Emersonian linkage between charisma and history, his belief, first, that in their alertness to the spirit of the epoch, remarkable individuals such as Jay Gatsby, Dick Diver, and Monroe Stahr are like "those intricate machines that register earthquakes ten thousand miles away" (6), and second, the belief that such harbingers will catalyze a similar spirit among those who enter the remarkable man's zone of self-display. Expressing the whole, the members of a transcendent avant-garde lead lesser persons to discover their latent character as symbols of the nation. Like his social vision, Fitzgerald's symbolist aesthetic is undergirded by his passionate theoretical commitment to the transcendent whole, his spiritual and libidinal nationalism appropriating the emotional and theoretical energies of his Roman Catholic upbringing—the essence of the nation bestows the kiss of worth on objects that then partake of its splendor by expressing it symbolically.[2] America is where the Eucharist couples with the commodity fetish, a fervent articulation of American exceptionalism that influenced such literary works as *On the Road* (1957) and *The Crying of Lot 49* (1966), and that anticipated in fiction the line of scholars from Henry Nash Smith and Charles Feidelson through Richard Slotkin to Sacvan Bercovitch. Perhaps even more than Nathaniel Hawthorne, Fitzgerald is the prose poet of what Lauren Berlant calls the "National Symbolic"—"the order of discursive practices whose reign within a national space produces, and also refers to, the 'law' in which the accident of birth within a geographic/political boundary transforms individuals into subjects of a collectively-held history. Its traditional icons, its metaphors, its heroes, its rituals, and its narratives provide an alphabet for a collective consciousness or national subjectivity; through the National Symbolic the historical nation aspires to achieve the inevitability of the status of natural law, a birthright" (20).

The symbolicity of the symbol—its character as vessel containing abstract reality or as portal opening onto wonder—supplies the symbolic thing with its vitality.

Failing that access, the thing is a mere thing, a dispirited outcome that in *The Great Gatsby* is figured as "foul dust" or ashes—devitalized remainder (6). These symbols of nonsymbolicity are extremely interesting to me, because they are the valleys where Fitzgerald, or his narrator at least, confines social life that fails to express the ideal (revulsion marking that place where insight will later appear). Insofar as a person is a living seismograph of the ideal, a pure register of abstract national content, he is truly vital, alive, luminous; insofar as he is particular—a person with projects, worries, tics, pleasures, and sorrows, all of them inflected by ethnicity, region, religion, class, gender, parental neurochemistry, and so on—he is a failure, merely particular, an outpost in which the rhythms of the capital have long since been forgotten. Determination by real circumstance and the complexity that this yields are markers of inadequacy. This is why Gatsby is great: he is always and only desirer-of-Daisy, and not desiring her as a particular woman, but desiring her for the abstract stuff that she is "full of" (94).

To exemplify the spirit of the nation is therefore to be a knight of desire, like Søren Kierkegaard's knight of virtue, for whom purity of heart is to will one thing. But what if the one thing that the symbol incarnates—the essence that makes the epoch an epoch—is not itself at one with itself, but rather fractured, internally complex? As my title suggests, this brings us back to jazz, the primal X of the decade. Jazz is mentioned most often in Chapter 3 of *The Great Gatsby,* Nick's excited account of the first party he attended across the lawn at Gatsby's: "By midnight the hilarity had increased. A celebrated tenor had sung in Italian and a notorious contralto had sung in jazz and between the numbers people were doing 'stunts' all over the garden while happy vacuous bursts of laughter rose toward the summer sky" (51). A little later,

> There was the boom of a bass drum, and the voice of the orchestra leader rang out suddenly above the echolalia of the garden.
>
> "Ladies and gentlemen," he cried. "At the request of Mr. Gatsby we are going to play for you Mr. Vladimir Tostoff's latest work which attracted so much attention at Carnegie Hall last May. If you read the papers you know there was a big sensation." He smiled with jovial condescension and added "Some sensation!" whereupon everyone laughed.
>
> "The piece is known," he concluded lustily, "as Vladimir Tostoff's Jazz History of the World."

However: "The nature of Mr. Tostoff's composition eluded me, because just as it began my eyes fell on Gatsby, standing alone on the marble steps and looking from one group to another with approving eyes" (54). This is a briefly puzzling moment—if Nick is simply distracted by Gatsby's appearance, why doesn't he say, "but I didn't hear the piece because" rather than "the nature of the piece eluded me because"? Several years ago I found the answer to this question in Fitzgerald's manuscript, which includes a long description of the "Jazz History" that was cut from the final version:

> "The piece is known," he concluded lustily, "as Les Epstien's Jazz History of the World."
>
> When he sat down all the members of the orchestra looked at one another and smiled as tho this was <u>after</u> all a little below them after all. Then the conductor raised his wand—and they <u>all</u> launched into one of the most surprising pieces of music I've ever heard in my life. It fascinated me. <u>perhaps it was the champagne</u> I've never heard it since and perhaps it was the champagne but for about fifteen minutes I don't think anyone stirred in their chairs—except to laugh now and then in a curious puzzled way when they came to the end of a movement.
>
> It started out with a weird, spinning sound that seemed to come mostly from the cornets, very regular and measured and inevitable with a bell now and then that seemed to ring somewhere a good distance away. A rythm became distinguishable after a while in the spinning, a sort of dull beat but as soon as you'd almost made it out it disappeared—until finally something happened, something tremendous, you knew that, and the spinning was all awry and one of the distant bells had come alive, it had <u>a meaning and</u> a personality somehow of its own.
>
> That was the first movement and we all laughed and looked at each other rather nervously as the second movement began. [new paragraph mark] The second movement was concerned with the bell only it wasn't the bell anymore but <u>two intrum wi</u> a muted violin cello and two instruments I had never seen before. At first there was a sort of monotony about it—a little disappointing at first as if it were just a repitition of the spinning sound but pretty soon you were aware that something was trying to establish itself, to get a foothold, something soft and persistent and profound and next you yourself were trying to help it, struggling, praying for it—until suddenly it was *there,* it was established rather scornfully without you and it <u>stayed there</u> seemed to lurk around <u>as</u> with a complete self-sufficiency as if it had been there all the time.
>
> I was curiously moved and the third part of the thing was full of an even stronger emotion. I know so little about music that I can only make a story of it—which proves I've been told that it must have been pretty low brow stuff—but it wasn't really a story. He didn't have lovely music for the prehistoric ages with tiger-howls from the trap finishing up with a strain ffrom Onward Christian Soldiers in the year two B. C. If wsn't like that at all. There would be a series of interruptive notes that seemed too fall together accidently and colored everything that came after them until before you knew it they became the theme and new discords were opposed to it outside. But what struck me particularly was that just as you'd get used to the new discord business there'd be one of the old themes rung in this time as a discord until you'd get a ghastly sense that it was all a cycle after all, purposeless and sardonic until you
>
> wanted to get up and walk out of the garden. It never stopped—after they had finished playing that movement it went on and on in everybody's head until the next one started. Whenever I think of that summer I can hear it yet.
>
> The last was weak I thought though [ ] most of the people seemed to like it best of all. It had recognizable strains of famous jazz in it—Alexander's Ragtime Band and the Darktown Strutter's Ball and recurrent hint of The Beale Street Blues. It made me restless and looking casually around my eye was caught by the straight, <u>graceful easy figure of well proportioned</u> well-made figure of Gatsby who stood alone on <u>the</u> his steps looking from one group to another with a strange eagerness in his eyes. It was as though he felt the necessity of supplying, physically at least, a perfect measure of entertainment to his guests. He seemed absolutely alone—I never seen anyone who seemed so alone.

(***The Great Gatsby: A Facsimile*** 54-56)

Startling, fascinating, ultimately dismaying, and even frightening in its manifest but inexplicable logic, the "Jazz History" seems not to express its audience, but rather to stand in sardonic or satiric relation to them, making them drop their hilarity and mutuality, and to look to one another for a reassurance that none can supply to the others. But the dismay and consequent revulsion Nick feels do not overwhelm an obvious interest: "I was curiously moved." The nature of the piece eludes him, he says, just when he seems to be about to have it in hand: it seems to have a core, but it veers off just when about to present itself. The performance does not venture into the unexpected in order to return to the domestic consolation of familiar motifs or melodies: even the return of familiar elements is uncanny and threatening, since those elements, when they recur, are embedded in a miasma that distorts them not beyond recognition, but in such a way that recognition and disorientation become the same thing. The music seems to amplify rather than to soothe the party's echolalia.

Such a contortion of the familiar world breaks out at several points in the novel, for instance in Nick's speculations concerning Gatsby's last moments: "[H]e must have felt that he had lost the old warm world, paid too high a price for living too long with a single dream. He must have looked up at an unfamiliar sky through frightening leaves and shivered as he found what a grotesque thing a rose is and how raw the sunlight was upon the scarcely created grass. A new world, material without being real, where poor ghosts, breathing dreams like air, drifted fortuitously about . . ." (169). Material, without being real: only the ideal confers real reality on material things, and lacking it they become nightmares. "[D]isruptions in the realm of the National Symbolic," according to Berlant, "create a collective sensation of almost physical vulnerability: the subject without a nation experiences his/her own mortality and vulnerability because s/he has lost control over physical space as a part of his/her inheritance" (24).

Even when the East excited me most . . . it had always a quality of distortion. West Egg especially still figures in my more fantastic dreams. I see it as a night scene by El Greco: a hundred houses, at once conventional and grotesque, crouching under a sullen, overhanging sky and a lustreless moon. In the foreground four solemn men in dress suits are walking along the sidewalk with a stretcher on which lies a drunken woman in a white evening dress. Her hand, which dangles over the side, sparkles cold with jewels. Gravely the men turn in at a house—the wrong house. But no one knows the woman's name, and no one cares.

(185)

The wonder, interest, and horror of "The Jazz History of the World" is that its distortion of the world is a deliberate human production, rather than a symptom of postepochal decay: it is an artifact, not a ruin. Nick and Fitzgerald are baffled by and irresistibly interested in what seems to them to be the enormous perversity of the act of intentionally disconnecting things from their expressivity and turning them into stranded, carefully fashioned monstrosities—terminating expression, dissevering the conduit that makes things really real, assiduously producing a residue of unique creations that only a rather total failure of attention could assign to a category such as ashes or junk. Though the excised passage does not associate such intentional distortion with African-American cultural practice, a 1926 letter thanking Carl Van Vechten for a copy of his novel *Nigger Heaven* (1926) makes the connection clearly: "[Your novel] seems, outside of its quality as a work of art, to sum up subtly and inclusively, all the *direction* of the northern nigger, or, rather, the nigger in New York. Our civilization imposed on such virgin soil takes on a new and more vivid and more poignant horror as if it had been dug out of its context and set down against an accidental and unrelated background" (Fitzgerald, *Letters* 490).[3]

Those readers who listen to jazz may have concluded that, despite the incomprehension and ethnocentric or racist revulsion, Fitzgerald realized what jazz is. Compare his account of "The Jazz History of the World," for instance, with André Hodeir's analysis of Louis Armstrong's "Butter and Egg Man," written in the 1950s about a recording from the time Fitzgerald was writing *The Great Gatsby*:

In this record, Armstrong manages to transfigure completely a theme whose vulgarity might well have overwhelmed him; and yet his chorus is only a paraphrase. The theme is not forgotten for a moment; it can always be found there, just as it was originally conceived by its little-known composer, Venable. Taking off melodically from the principal note of the first phrase, the soloist begins with a triple call that disguises, behind its apparent symmetry, subtle differences in rhythm and expressive intensity. This entry by itself is a masterpiece; it is impossible to imagine anything more sober and balanced. During the next eight bars, the para-

phrase spreads out, becoming freer and livelier. Armstrong continues to cling to the essential notes of the theme, but he leaves more of its contour to the imagination. At times he gives it an inner animation by means of intelligent syncopated repetitions, as in the case of the first note of the bridge. From measures 20 to 30, the melody bends in a chromatic descent that converges toward the theme while at the same time giving a felicitous interpretation of the underlying harmonic progression. This brings us to the culminating point of the work. Striding over the traditional pause of measures 24-25, Armstrong connects the bridge to the final section by using a short, admirably inventive phrase. Its rhythmic construction of dotted eighths and sixteenths forms a contrast with the more static context in which it is placed, and in both conception and execution it is a miracle of swing. During this brief moment, Louis seems to have foreseen what modern conceptions of rhythm would be like. In phrasing, accentuation, and the way the short note is increasingly curtailed until finally it is merely suggested (measure 25) how far removed all this is from New Orleans rhythm!

(qtd. in Hadlock 30)

Hodeir is free of the discomfort that suffuses the Fitzgerald passage, but the point is the same, which makes Fitzgerald's excised fragment—itself set adrift from the novelistic whole it would have quite significantly failed to express—one of the first perceptive reactions to jazz performance among white American writers. By contrast, Rudy Vallee's dismay seems much less alert: "Truly I have no conception of what 'jazz' is, but I believe the term should be applied . . . to the weird orchestral effects of various colored bands up in Harlem. . . . These bands have a style all their own, and at times it seems as though pandemonium had broken loose. Most of the time there is no distinguishable melody. . . . [I]t is absolutely impossible for even a musical ear to tell the name of the piece" (qtd. in Stearns 182). Though partaking of Vallee's perplexity, Fitzgerald anticipates Hodeir's understanding that jazz by design offers no reunion with the already known, but rather, by way of improvisation, disconnects the familiar from its familiarity, making it do startling things. To someone as intensely and deeply committed to a sacramental and holistic conception of art and society as Fitzgerald was at this time in his life, such created tension could only appear as a fracture, a break in the body of the work and in the body politic, an alienation shared even by so recent and influential a critic as Ted Gioia:

An aesthetics of jazz would almost be a type of non-aesthetics. Aesthetics, in principle if not in practice, focuses our attention on those attributes of a work of art which reveal the craftsmanship and careful planning of the artist. Thus the terminology of aesthetic philosophy—words such as form, symmetry, balance—emphasizes the methodical element in artistic creation. But the improviser is anything but methodical; hence these terms have only the most tangential applicability to the area of jazz. The very nature of jazz demands spontaneity; were the jazz artist to approach his music in a methodical and calculated manner, he would cease to be an improviser and become a composer. For this reason the virtues we search for in other art forms—premeditated design, balance between form and content, an overall symmetry—are largely absent in jazz. In his act of impulsive creation, the improvising musician must shape each phase separately while retaining only a vague notion of the overall pattern he is forging. Like the great chess players who, we are told, must be able to plan their attack some dozens of moves ahead, the jazz musician must constantly struggle with his opaque medium if he hopes to create a coherent musical statement. His is an art markedly unsuited for the patient and reflective.

(55)

Fitzgerald's perception of jazz performance in the excised passage might seem to be more astute than a remark in **"Echoes of the Jazz Age"**: "The word jazz in its progress toward respectability has meant first sex, then dancing, then music. It is associated with a state of nervous stimulation, not unlike that of big cities behind the lines of a war" (16). But notice that Fitzgerald does not say this is what jazz is, but rather this is what jazz has meant and what it has been associated with. He is not really departing from the insight of the excised passage, but rather changing the subject from jazz to the image of jazz in the middle-class white popular imagination. His feeling for the distinction accords with the subsequent judgment of cultural and social historians: thought of primarily in terms of its conspicuous and propulsive rhythm, jazz came to emblematize for white Americans both an erotic vitality nearly lost in an effete society (but still effective among African Americans) and the pace of postwar technological modernity. This is the image of jazz, jazz understood as energy and velocity, that is implied in the term "Jazz Age" and embodied in Gatsby, the restless, not-quite-really-white roughneck with the world's most extraordinary car. Leopold Stokowski succinctly articulated this understanding of jazz: "Jazz has come to stay because it is an expression of the times, of the breathless, energetic, superactive times in which we are living, it is useless to fight against it. . . . America's contribution to the music of the past will have the same revivifying effect as the injection of new, and in the larger sense, vulgar blood into dying aristocracy. . . . The Negro musicians of America are playing a great part in this change" (qtd. in Ogren 7).[4] Jazz could signify both primitivity and hypermodernity because in both cases it is thought of as raw energy preceding or outrunning form—a beat, rather than a conversation, a meditation, a paraphrase, or a discovery. An alternative form so radically disparate from popular performative norms as to be aesthetically unrecognizable to inexperienced listeners, jazz seems not to be form at all, only outburst.

When I talk about "real jazz" I mean to appeal only to a formal authenticity: we can, for example, say whether a poem is or is not a sonnet without recourse to mystical essentialism. The distinction between real jazz and the image of jazz became more tangled, however, when popularizers began to compose, perform, and record music that reflected the popular image of jazz. As such simulation gathers steam. the distinction between, say, the performances of the Fletcher Henderson Orchestra and what those performances are imagined to amount to is succeeded by the distinction between the Fletcher Henderson Orchestra and, say, the Paul Whiteman Orchestra, which was generally thought to be America's premiere ensemble. According to Burnett James, "Paul Whiteman, though called the 'King of Jazz,' fronted an orchestra of semi-symphonic proportions. His jazzmen had their way from time to time, but in essence only as a sideline" (15). Marshall Stearns expands this point:

> The number of prosperous dance bands at the popular level multiplied, while the jazz content remained slight. At the same time, dancing the Charleston, the Black Bottom, and the Lindy was highly popular and the bands tried to oblige by playing a little hot jazz. . . . None of these large dance bands, however, could swing as a whole. The formula consisted of importing one or two "hot" soloists, or "get-off" men, letting them take a chorus once in a while surrounded by acres of uninspired fellow musicians. "Society band leaders like Meyer Davis and Joe Moss always wanted to have at least one good jazzman in their bands," says clarinetist Tony Parenti. Bix Beiderbecke was doing this for Paul Whiteman in 1927. Beiderbecke was very well paid and his colleagues all looked up to him—the "hot" soloists were always the elite—but the frustration of being allowed to play so little, when he was hired because he could play so much, led to all kinds of personal problems and, indirectly, to the after-hours "jam session," where a musician could play his heart out.

(180)[5]

Kathy Ogren agrees with this assessment of the dance bands, especially Whiteman's:

> Whiteman, who became the "King of Jazz," saw his role as that of dignifying and legitimating jazz. He . . . explained away certain characteristics and performance practices original to the music. Whiteman warned musicians against using syncopation, which "gives a sense to the ignorant of participation in the world's scientific knowledge." But, Whiteman continued, with a sense of relief, "Syncopation no longer rules American music . . . as we use it in the United States [it] is an African inheritance . . . but to-day it is no longer a necessary thing. It has been retained much as an ornament." Whiteman's popular music became so closely identified with jazz that many Americans had no knowledge of its Afro-American origins. Whiteman himself, who disliked the association with jazz and dance music, titled his Aeolian Hall concert an "Experiment in Modern Music."

(159)

The Aeolian Hall concert is a key cultural locus for my argument: commencing with some horsing around on "Livery Stable Blues" (1917) (introduced by Whiteman as "an example of the depraved past from which modern jazz has risen" [Ogren 161]), the orchestra proceeded through Tin Pan Alley numbers such as "Yes We Have No Bananas" (1923), escalated to the debut of "Rhapsody in Blue" (1924), with George Gershwin on piano, and concluded with Edward Elgar's "Pomp and Circumstance" (1901-07). The sequence of the performance thus seems like a progression from energy to art, an effect that depends on agreeing with Whiteman's pronouncement that the structural core of jazz is an African ornament that can be sacrificed without significant loss in order to move to an aesthetic high ground. Where we might see a nonjazz orchestra equipped with a couple of jazz "stunts," whinnying trumpets, and some boosted drumming, Whiteman claimed that his music was jazz emerged from its cocoon, its inner necessity fulfilled.

Thanks to extensive advance publicity, the Aeolian Hall concert was packed—invitations had been sent to Stokowski, Fritz Kreisler, Sergei Rachmaninoff, Van Vechten, and many other prominent white New Yorkers—and the response was tumultuous (Jablonski 66-67; Stearns 165-67). The concert was performed on 12 February 1924, a couple of months before the Fitzgeralds sailed for France; their celebrity at the time was such that they may have been included on the guest list, though I have been unable to discover whether they were invited or attended. In any case, the coverage in the New York papers after the concert was so extensive that Fitzgerald could not have failed at least to hear about the occasion. I am satisfied that the Aeolian Hall concert was the prototype for "The Jazz History of the World," a lineage first suggested, as far as I can tell, by Darrell Mansell.[6] (Mansell suggests that Fitzgerald may also have been thinking of jazz-inflected works by Darius Milhaud and Igor Stravinsky.) If Fitzgerald is in fact alluding to Whiteman's hubristic and ethnically defamatory extravaganza, the allusion is rather biting: though the excised passage seems at points to describe "Rhapsody in Blue," it nonetheless alludes to, stays close to, what jazz is at its core, to what Whiteman called unnecessary ornament, a trope not far from Fitzgerald's "foul dust." The performance at Gatsby's party, therefore, were Fitzgerald to have left the excised fragment in, would have put on view a rather fabulous cultural reversal, jazz per se reviving or breaking out at the heart of an event staged to curtail jazz and to appropriate its aura, not only an overturning of Whiteman's pretension but also an exuberant betrayal of the aesthetic norms governing the book in which it would have been enclosed. Though it is as hard to say for sure what Fitzgerald listened to as it is to prove he was at the Aeolian Hall concert, I am quite sure he would have heard the real thing as well as the smooth simulacrum:

it is hard to imagine him not joining in on Van Vechten's Harlem fieldtrips, and in France Fitzgerald's friend and fellow émigré Gerald Murphy made a point of having the latest jazz records on hand—his yacht, the *Weatherbird*, took its name from an Armstrong record that he had sealed in the yacht's keel, a recording made two years after "Butter and Egg Man" (Tomkins 32, 116-17).

But if Fitzgerald heard jazz per se, his narrator nevertheless responds with aversion to what Thelonious Monk would later call jazz's ugly beauty, and the excised passage shows no awareness of the African-American motivations for jazz performance. If the serial paraphrasing that Nick hears seems to him to be a prolonged deformity or brutalization, to the performer improvisation means a kind of circumstance-based freedom, taking an element from the dominant culture, twisting it, turning it around and inside-out, seeing if it will serve ends other than the usual and familiar ones. Like experiment in general, it seeks to discover avenues of possibility through the midst of inevitability, and to do so without special worry about the survival of coherence. It is useful to recall Ralph Ellison's praise of Armstrong in the preface to *Invisible Man* (1952):

> Perhaps I like Louis Armstrong because he's made poetry out of being invisible. I think it must be because he's unaware that he is invisible. And my own grasp of invisibility aids me to understand his music. Once when I asked for a cigarette, some jokers gave me a reefer, which I lighted when I got home and sat listening to my phonograph. It was a strange evening. Invisibility, let me explain, gives one a slightly different sense of time, you're never quite on the beat. Sometimes you're ahead and sometimes behind. Instead of the swift and imperceptible flowing of time, you are aware of its nodes, those points where time stands still or from which it leaps ahead. And you slip into the breaks and look around. That's what you hear vaguely in Louis' music.

(8)

Willfully putting fidelity to the original aside, the performer liberates cultural matter, puts it into motion. Though this sort of individual departure from script seems to Nick to endanger the coherence and recognizability of the whole—to endanger the sort of expressive structure that Fitzgerald saw in his vision of American sacramentalism—in fact it adumbrates a radically different vision of cohesion, if not of wholeness in its ultimately metaphysical sense. Martin Williams explains this other vision well:

> In all its styles, jazz involves some degree of collective ensemble improvisation, and in this it differs from Western music even at those times in its history when improvisation was required. The high degree of individuality, together with the mutual respect and cooperation required in a jazz ensemble carry with them

philosophical implications that are so exciting and far-reaching that one almost hesitates to contemplate them. It is as if jazz were saying to us that not only is far greater individuality possible to man than he has so far allowed himself, but that such individuality, far from being a threat to a co-operative social structure, can actually enhance society.

(252)

My feeling that Fitzgerald came to a similar conclusion about jazz's motive brings me to **The Last Tycoon,** the novel on which he was working when he died of heart failure in 1940. Monroe Stahr, loosely based on Irving Thalberg, is Hollywood's most successful producer, dominating and organizing the ensemble of labor at his studio—drunken writers, extras, peevish celebrities, lighting men, etc.—with a firm, bluff, equable, brilliant, and self-assured demeanor that commands instant respect from all and yields successful collective enterprise. He thus recapitulates the social potency of Gatsby and Dick Diver from the preceding novels, but because he has found a young industry in a young place, his potency can exercise itself in legitimate business triumph rather than in crime, Riviera beach parties, or obsession with the daughters of old money. Because Hollywood is the last new industry and California is the geographical terminal beach for the series of longings that began with Dutch sailors staring at Long Island. Stahr is the last tycoon. He therefore culminates and closes an epoch somewhat longer than the Jazz Age, the century, more or less, from Andrew Jackson's election to the time of the novel. The commencement date is established early on in **The Last Tycoon,** when three characters enduring a long stopover during a transcontinental flight take an early-morning cab ride out to Jackson's mansion, The Hermitage. The first couple of times I read the novel this interlude seemed rather pointless, until it occurred to me that Fitzgerald meant us to see Jackson as the first tycoon—not a businessman, but a charismatic and unorthodox westerner who marshaled broad-spectrum appeal independently from established elites, creating in the process the economic domain in which the subsequent tycoons down to Stahr would flourish. From Jackson to Stahr, then, we have the Tycoon Age, with Stahr's life being the epoch's sunset, the moment when structure crumbles and the individuated pieces shed their expressivity, the luster they enjoyed while they stood firm in Stahr's light.

The novel is *very* unfinished. In what we do have, Fitzgerald launches the plot along two arcs, the thematic relations between which are not at first clear. First, Stahr is suffering the strain of overwork to the point of risking his life. Producing effective charisma is no longer an effortless or fulfilling enterprise, in part because Stahr's belief in the worth of his work, in the quality of his films, is diminished; and this subterranean slippage is aggravated by widening divisions in the stu-

dio, conspiratorial maneuverings by rivals whose crass profiteering is an index of their contempt for the movie-going public, and advancing unionization among the laborer-writers. Such splitting and fraying suggests to Stahr that, despite his titanic labors, he only has a limited number of rabbits left in his hat.

In the second plot line, Stahr meets by chance a woman named Kathleen who closely resembles his dead wife Minna, an actress, and the resemblance stirs him from his apathy into a desperate and eerie erotic pursuit that recalls Edgar Allan Poe's "Ligeia" (1838) and anticipates Alfred Hitchcock's *Vertigo* (1958): "It was Minna's face—the skin with its peculiar radiance as if phosphorus had touched it, the mouth with its warm line that never counted costs—and over all the haunting jollity that had fascinated a generation" (64). As in those texts, the generative problem is the quandary of second love. If one is destined to love some one, then the act of doing so expresses his fundamental inner truth, his profoundest self, the continuity to which all changes can be subordinated. When love is seen this way, there can be no second love—either the first or the second must have only seemed to be love—because a second love would mean that the lover had a fluid or split core, and that change can therefore be radical. Recall Gatsby's incredulity when Daisy says she loved Tom *too.* The narrative of the second beloved who reincarnates or exactly resembles the first papers over this fracture in desire and in the desiring self by allowing the supposition that the second love is the first beloved *redevivus.* But in several quite stirring and uncomfortably beautiful encounters, Stahr seems to discover Kathleen's mystery, her difference from Minna, and this discovery only deepens the attraction, without provoking any severe crisis in self-image. Relinquishing the obsessive and coercive concern with near-exact repetition that predominates in Poe and Hitchcock, Fitzgerald quickly establishes Kathleen's not-Minnaness, with wisps of abiding uncanny reminder, as if, perhaps, second love improvises on the first, "to repeat yet not recapitulate the past" (89).

It should be clear what I consider to be the deep link between the two plot lines, the opening of divisions within what had seemed to be secure wholes—between Stahr and his profession, within his professional world, within his ambition and within his desire—splinterings that Fitzgerald emblematizes as the dispersal of light-sources: "Other lights shone in Hollywood since Minna's death: in the open markets lemons and grapefruits and green apples slanted a misty glare into the street. Ahead of him the stop-signal of a car winked violet and at another crossing he watched it wink again. Everywhere floodlights raked the sky. On an empty corner two mysterious men moved a gleaming drum in pointless arcs over the heavens" (62). This dispersed glow recurs later, on a Pacific beach near a half-completed house Stahr is having built. He takes Kathleen there one night for what turns out to be one of the most frank and moving sexual encounters to be found in Fitzgerald, who is usually prudish where the act is concerned. It is both funny and touching when their postcoital barefoot stroll along the ocean brings them into a field of squirming light, dozens of sparkling, spawning grunion, shiny, sexual, fecund, an extraordinary organic improvisation on what happened just moments before in Stahr's oceanside hermitage: "It was a fine blue night. The tide was at the turn and the little silver fish rocked off shore waiting for 10:16. A few seconds after the time they came swarming in with the tide and Stahr and Kathleen stepped over them barefoot as they flicked slip-slop in the sand. A Negro man came along the shore toward them collecting the grunion quickly like twigs into two pails. They came in twos and threes and platoons and companies, relentless and exalted and scornful around the great bare feet of the intruders, as they had come before Sir Francis Drake had nailed his plaque to the boulder on the shore" (92-93).[7] In Fitzgerald's novels, African Americans commonly appear at the moment when the main characters' world is deeply disturbed, as if breaking-up is also breaking-open. Only in *The Last Tycoon,* though, is that disturbance refreshing and inexplicably inspiring—a sense of possibility perhaps enhanced by the echo between Drake's arrival in California and the transfixed gaze of the Dutch sailors at the end of *The Great Gatsby.* The man on the beach tells Stahr and Kathleen that he doesn't really come for the fish, but rather to read Emerson, a copy of which he is carrying in his shirt. His pensiveness is confirmed a moment later when, on hearing that Stahr makes movies, he remarks that he and his children don't go to the movies, "because there's no profit in it." He continues down the beach, "unaware that he had rocked an industry" by shining this harsh light on Stahr's alreadyuneasy feeling of professional worth (93).

"Now they were different people as they started back" (94). The conversation with the man on the beach and the sexual interlude with Kathleen upset the elementary articles of Stahr's self-image, his commitment to his work, and his loyalty to his desire for his wife, but these inner fractures turn out not to be premonitions of subjective decay of the kind Fitzgerald described in **"The Crack-Up"** (1935) and depicted in *Tender is the Night.* Instead, they crack Stahr open, rather than up, investing him with an intuition of life below the monolithic, frozen unities of the tycoon and romantic love systems. This post-epochal intuition runs underground while he drives Kathleen home, then surfaces. We should recognize the terms Fitzgerald uses to describe Stahr's anomalous epiphany:

> Winding down the hill he listened inside himself as if something by an unknown composer, powerful and strange and strong, was about to be played for the first time. The theme would be stated presently but because the composer was always new, he would not recognize it as the theme right away. It would come in some such guise as the auto-horns from the Technicolor boulevards below or be barely audible, a tattoo on the muffled drum of the moon. He strained to hear it, knowing only that the music was beginning, new music that he liked and did not understand. It was hard to react to what one could entirely compass—this was new and confusing, nothing one could shut off in the middle and supply the rest from an old score.

(96-97)

Lest we be ignorant of the source of such music, Fitzgerald immediately adds: "Also, and persistently, and bound up with the other, there was the Negro on the sand" (96). Without the disgust—"he liked and did not understand"—Fitzgerald returns to the insight of the excised fragment, acknowledging jazz's cultural origins and motivations, its allegiance to a future contemplated as something more interesting than the return of fulfillment.

Fitzgerald's early death strikes all the more sharply, for me at least, when I think about this new way of thinking that he was laboring so hard to convey, the series of discoveries of the real that *The Last Tycoon* would have been about—desire that is not a suburb of commodity-fetishism, labor politics, uninhibited capitalism, the self and the nation as diverse and nonselfidentical. He was on the verge of something, like Stahr's unbuilt house, permanently unbuilt.

How did he come to that continental extremity? Perhaps something of an answer lies in the difference between Emerson's "Representative Man," who *has* something, some mystical X that he bestows, and Gatsby, who has only desire, that is, who *lacks* rather than has, bestowing only a sharply focused version of others' more diffuse lacking. Gatsby apprises one that he shares an absence at the core, a vacancy that precedes the fantasms that address themselves to that vacancy—mystic nationhood, voices full of money, and fresh green breasts. If Fitzgerald found himself in the predicament Nick surmises in Gatsby, "[paying] too high a price for living too long with a single dream" (169), then he may have turned to face the constitutive deficit that the pursuit of the dream had been designed to distract him from. If the common feature of the artifacts in the American archaeological dig is longing, then perhaps the common feature of American experience is not the nation but rather the absence of the nation, temporalized as not yet. This feeling of the absence of the nation is historically produced by the deep belief that there ought to be—and that there could be—a nation, that is, a political and spiritual object that compensates for the extreme losses that typify the experience of modernity. I derive this conception of the nation as imaginary compensation from Benedict Anderson:

The extraordinary survival over thousands of years of Buddhism, Christianity or Islam in dozens of different social formations attests to their imaginative response to the overwhelming burden of human suffering—disease, mutilation, grief, age and death. Why was I born blind? Why is my best friend paralyzed? Why is my daughter retarded? . . . At the same time, in different ways, religious thought also responds to obscure intimations of immortality, generally by transforming fatality into continuity (karma, original sin, etc.). In this way, it concerns itself with the links between the dead and the yet unborn, the mystery of re-generation. Who experiences their child's conception and birth without dimly apprehending a combined connectedness, fortuity and fatality, in a language of "continuity"?

Shortly later, Anderson addresses the predicament of modernity:

[I]n Western Europe the eighteenth century marks not only the dawn of the age of nationalism but the dusk of religious modes of thought. The century of the Enlightenment, or rationalist secularism, brought with it its own modern darkness. With the ebbing of religious belief, the suffering which belief in part composed did not disappear. Disintegration of paradise: nothing makes fatality more arbitrary. Absurdity of salvation: nothing makes another style of continuity more necessary. What then was required was a secular transformation of fatality into continuity, contingency into meaning. As we shall see, few things were (are) better suited to this end than the idea of a nation. If nation-states are widely conceded to be "new" and "historical," the nations to which they give political expression always loom out of an immemorial past, and, still more important, glide into a limitless future. It is the magic of nationalism to turn chance into destiny.

(18-19)

"The nation," Homi Bhabha contends, "fills the void left in the uprooting of communities and kin, and turns that loss into the language of metaphor. Metaphor, as the etymology of the word suggests, transfers the meaning of home and belonging, across the 'middle passage,' or the central European steppes, across those distances, and cultural differences, that span the imagined community of the nation-people" (291). The US is of course one of the special cases, since its immemorial pasts are European and Native American: the past of the locale entails ethnic difference, whereas ethnic continuities are not local, that is, they connect to other nations. In large measure, Fitzgerald's reference to the Dutch sailors has seemed to many readers an attempt to say, we do have our own time immemorial now, finally, and thereby to transfigure or positivize the peculiarly originary place that lacking has occupied in the imagination of American national self-constitution. What I am proposing is that Fitzgerald may in his last years have begun to shift his focus from fantasmatic reimbursements—the green breast in all its avatars—to constitutive hunger or deficit, and to contemplate such deficit as an opportunity, rather than as an occasion for stoic resignation. If I am

right, this development would echo with Claude Lefort's notion of democracy (rather than of nation):

Power was embodied in the prince, and it therefore gave society a body. And because of this, a latent but effective knowledge of what *one* meant to *the other* existed throughout the social. This model reveals the revolutionary and unprecedented feature of democracy. The locus of power becomes an *empty place*. There is no need to dwell on the details of the institutional apparatus. The important point is that this apparatus prevents governments from appropriating power for their own ends, from incorporating it into themselves. The exercise of power is subject to the procedures of periodical redistributions. It represents the outcome of a controlled contest with permanent rules. This phenomenon implies an institutionalization of conflict. The locus of power is an empty place, it cannot be occupied—it is such that no individual and no group can be consubstantial with it—and it cannot be represented.

(17)

Gazing from a Swiss mountain, Dick Diver observes a crucial vacuum that rivals, in its transfigured sorrow, Melville's Grand Armada, a play of figurality which is not restrained by a clear distinction between the thing and its shadow: "On the centre of the lake, cooled by the piercing current of the Rhone, lay the true centre of the Western World. Upon it floated swans like boats and boats like swans, both lost in the nothingness of the heartless beauty. It was a bright day, with sun glinting on the grass beach below and the white courts of the Kursal. The figures on the courts threw no shadows" (Fitzgerald, *Tender* 147-48).[8] If the center is nothingness, then loneliness—the historical circumstance to which nationalism so ferociously and unsuccessfully responds—might come to seem mysteriously opportune, people and their things freed from the burden of symbolizing, finding their way through an epoch's ruin: "They sat on high stools and had tomato broth and hot sandwiches. It was more intimate than anything they had done, and they both felt a dangerous sort of loneliness, and felt it in each other. They shared in varied scents of the drug-store, bitter and sweet and sour, and the mystery of the waitress, with only the outer part of her hair dyed and black beneath, and, when it was over, the still life of their empty plates—a silver of potato, a sliced pickle and an olive stone" (Fitzgerald, *Love* [*The Love of the Last Tycoon*] 85).

Notes

1. All future parenthetical references to the novel will refer to Fitzgerald's *The Great Gatsby: The Authorized Text* (1991) unless noted otherwise.

2. My understanding of the connection between nationalism, symbolization, and the simplification of historical reality is heavily indebted to John F. Callahan, *The Illusions of a Nation*:

   What, in America, have been the relations between complex human personality, history, and those myths summoned to explain the facts of history? What in the national past tempts succeeding generations to evade their history and seek mythologies of fraudulent innocence/ particularly misleading, when applied to history, is the mythic mode's assumption that ongoing experience endlessly repeats past patterns of action and policy. Nevertheless, history and myth raise the same question for America: how does history rationalized subvert personality? How have dominant myths swayed consciousness away from complexity and freedom? Why have fixity, stereotype and a one-dimensional, denotative perception won out over fluidity, archetype, and personality in the round?

(3)

3. I apologize for entering the term "nigger" into print. Would that it died out from misuse. But Fitzgerald's comment concerning the "direction" of African-American culture in New York seems important to me.

4. This quotation originally appeared in Alain Locke's *The New Negro* (1925), but I found it in Ogren. Ogren's book has been extremely helpful. I am also indebted to Burton Paretti, *The Creation of Jazz* (1992); Martin Williams, *The Jazz Tradition* (1983); Samuel Charters and Leonard Kunstadt, *Jazz: A History of the New York Scene* (1962); Arnold Shaw, *The Jazz Age: Popular Music in the 1920s* (1987); Stearns; Gunther Schuller, *Early Jazz: Its Roots and Musical Development* (1968); and Gioia. I have been deeply affected by (and would like sometime to write an essay on) Sidney Bechet's autobiography, *Treat it Gentle* (1960). I am especially indebted to Richard Hadlock, both for his *Jazz Masters of the Twenties,* and for his weekly Sunday night radio show, "The Annals of Jazz," from KCSM in San Mateo, CA, also at KCSM.org on the Web.

5. I am continually surprised that an extended comparison of the careers of Beiderbecke and Fitzgerald has not been attempted, perhaps because of their different performative media. The resonances are many: in addition to death from drinking, they share an upper midwestern origin, rapid and somewhat scandalous celebrity, the pressure of coming to terms with the constraints imposed by success, and a fine strain of alluring and disturbing melancholia.

6. For a discussion of the relation between jazz and symphonic performance during this period, see Bernard Gendron, "Jamming at Le Boeuf: Jazz and the Paris Avant-Garde" (1989-90).

7. My feeling that this is for Fitzgerald a breakthrough (rather than a breakdown) moment, and that he felt it to be so, is reinforced by the presence of an item from his personal erotic code, bare feet. In a ledger he composed to help him recall his early years, Fitzgerald recalled that in August 1901, he "went to Atlantic City—where some Freudean complex refused to let him display his *feet,* so he refused to swim, concealing the real reason" (Turnbull 9). For July 1903, he writes: "There was also a boy named Arnold who went barefooted in his yard and peeled plums. Scott's freudian shame about his feet kept him from joining in" (Turnbull 11). In *This Side of Paradise* (1920), Amory Blaine is at one point the victim of a fantasmatic tormentor who leers at Blaine as if in full knowledge of Blaine's worst traits: "Then, suddenly, Amory perceived the feet, and with a rush of blood to the head he realized he was afraid. The feet were all wrong . . . with a sort of wrongness that he felt rather than knew. . . . It was like weakness in a good woman, or food on satin; one of those terrible incongruities that shake little things in the back of the brain. He wore no shoes, but, instead, a sort of half moccasin, pointed, though, like the shoes they wore in the fourteenth century, and with the little ends curling up. They were a darkish brown and his toes seemed to fill them to the end. . . . They were unutterably terrible . . . (113). The "terrible incongruity" anticipates the "Jazz History," so it is not surprising that the issue of race would surface shortly after: "The elevator was close, and the colored boy was half asleep, paled to a livid bronze. . . . Axia's beseeching voice floated down the shaft. Those feet . . . those feet . . ." (114).

8. See Callahan 82 on this passage.

Works Cited

Althusser, Louis, and Etienne Balibar. *Reading Capital.* Trans. Ben Brewster. London: New Left, 1970.

Anderson, Benedict. *Imagined Communities: Reflections on the Origin and Spread of Nationalism.* New York: Verso, 1983.

Berlant, Lauren. *The Anatomy of National Fantasy: Hawthorne, Utopia, and Everyday Life.* Chicago: U of Chicago P, 1991.

Bhabha, Homi. "DisseminNation: Time, Narrative, and the Margins of the Modern Nation." *Nation and Narration.* Ed. Homi Bhabha. London: Routledge, 1990. 291-322.

Callahan, John F. *The Illusions of a Nation: Myth and History in the Novels of F. Scott Fitzgerald.* Urbana: U of Illinois P, 1972.

Ellison, Ralph. *Invisible Man.* New York: Vintage, 1972.

Fitzgerald, F. Scott. "Echoes of the Jazz Age." *The Crack-Up.* Ed. Edmund Wilson. New York: New Directions, 1945.

————. *The Great Gatsby: The Authorized Text.* New York: Scribner's, 1991.

————. *The Great Gatsby: A Facsimile of the Manuscript.* Ed. Matthew J. Bruccoli. Washington, DC: Microcard Editions, 1973.

————. *The Letters of F. Scott Fitzgerald.* Ed. Andrew Turnbull. New York: Scribner's, 1963.

————. *The Love of the Last Tycoon.* New York: Scribner's, 1994.

————. *This Side of Paradise.* New York: Scribner's, 1986.

————. *Tender is the Night.* New York: Scribner's, 1962.

Gendron, Bernard. "Jamming at Le Boeuf: Jazz and the Paris Avant-Garde," *Discourse* 12.1 (1989-90): 3-27.

Gioia, Ted. *The Imperfect Art: Reflections on Jazz and Modern Culture.* New York: Oxford UP, 1988.

Hadlock, Richard. *Jazz Masters of the Twenties.* New York: Da Capo, 1988.

Jablonski, Edward. *Gershwin: A Biography.* Boston: Northeastern UP, 1987.

James, Burnett. *Bix Beiderbecke.* New York: A. S. Barnes, 1961.

Lefort, Claude. *Democracy and Political Theory.* Trans. David Macey. Minneapolis: U of Minnesota P, 1988.

Mansell, Darrell. "The Jazz History of the World in *The Great Gatsby.*" *English Language Notes* 25.2 (1987): 57-62.

Ogren, Kathy J. *The Jazz Revolution: Twenties America and the Meaning of Jazz.* New York: Oxford UP, 1989.

Stearns, Marshall W. *The Story of Jazz.* New York: Oxford UP, 1959.

Tomkins, Calvin. *Living Well Is the Best Revenge.* New York: Viking, 1962.

Turnbull, Andrew. *Scott Fitzgerald.* New York: Scribner's, 1962.

Williams, Martin. *The Jazz Tradition.* New York: Oxford UP, 1983.

George Monteiro (essay date fall 2000)

SOURCE: Monteiro, George. "Carraway's Complaint." *Journal of Modern Literature* 24, no. 1 (fall 2000): 161-71.

[*In the following essay, Monteiro discusses possible sources for the last passage in* Gatsby, *in which Nick muses on how Long Island might have looked to the early explorers.*]

In one of the most familiar passages in twentieth—century literature, Nick Carraway thinks back on the late Jay Gatsby, who had suffered so grievously from the hard malice of the Buchanans and their like in the inhospitable East. It begins as an elegy but turns into a lament for humankind's capacity for wonder and awe in the face of the hard truths of history. Disillusioned, sad, sentimental, this child of the Midwest looks out, through the mind's eye, across Long Island Sound and reimagines the "old island" as it must have looked four centuries earlier to the Western sailors who were but the advance guard of the adventurers, immigrants, and settlers to come. Like the psalmist who sits by the rivers of Babylon, lamenting the lost Zion, he, too, weeps for what is past and will not return. It bears repeating.

> Most of the big shore places were closed now and there were hardly any lights except the shadowy, moving glow of a ferryboat across the Sound. And as the moon rose higher the inessential houses began to melt away until gradually I became aware of the old island here that flowered once for Dutch sailors' eyes-a fresh, green breast of the new world. Its vanished trees, the trees that had made way for Gatsby's house, had once pandered in whispers to the last and greatest of all human dreams; for a transitory enchanted moment man must have held his breath in the presence of this continent, compelled into an aesthetic contemplation he neither understood nor desired, face to face for the last time in history with something commensurate to his capacity for wonder. . . . Gatsby believed in the green light, the orgastic future that year by year recedes before us. It eluded us then, but that's no matter—to-morrow we will run faster, stretch out our arms farther. . . . And one fine morning—
>
> So we beat on, boats against the current, borne back ceaselessly into the past.[1]

These final sentences of **The Great Gatsby** take on a strange and surprising significance when they are read against Fitzgerald's immediate sources for them in the literature about Columbus and the New World. Behind Nick's words and sentiments lies a vast body of Western literature on notions of a terrestrial paradise. Since Fitzgerald ties this "fresh, green breast of the new world" to a New York island that "flowered once," as Carraway imagined, for "Dutch sailors' eyes," it is possible to pin down his principal if not sole source for Nick's last rueful vision.

Washington Irving's *A History of New York, from the Beginning of the World to the End of the Dutch Dynasty,* first published in 1809 and attributed to the fictional *persona* of "Diedrich Knickerbocker," is a problem for the genre purist. While the book often mocks history and historical writing, it otherwise suits perfectly Fitzgerald's fictional imagination. For among other matters, it demonstrates how one fabulating writer confronts the stuff of history, drawing on his considerable folkloristic ability to turn historic materials into the romanticized stuff of national legend and Western myth. Irving's history describes the first look which those "honest Dutch tars" had of the New World when their ships "entered that majestic bay which at this day expands its ample bosom before the city of New York, and which had never before been visited by any European."

> The island of Manna-hatta spread wide before them, like some sweet vision of fancy or some fair creation of industrious magic. Its hills of smiling green swelled gently one above another, crowned with lofty trees of luxuriant growth, some pointing their tapering foliage towards the clouds, which were gloriously transparent, and others loaded with a verdant burden of clambering vines, bowing their branches to the earth, that was covered with flowers.[2]

Irving's description echoes earlier accounts of what the so-called "terrestrial paradise" might look like. In *Voyages and Discoveries of the Companions of Columbus* (1828), Irving places Columbus' considerations of this theme within a greater tradition of such speculation, beginning with the "Grand Oasis of Arabia," where, he writes, "exhausted travellers, after traversing the parched and sultry desert, hailed this verdant spot with rapture; they refreshed themselves under its shady bowers, and beside its cooling streams, as the crew of a tempest tost vessel repose on the shores of some green island in the deep."[3] He also summarizes St. Basilius' discourse on "Paradise":

> There the earth is always green, the flowers are ever blooming, the waters limpid and delicate; not rushing in rude and turbid torrents, but welling up in crystal fountains and winding in peaceful and silver streams. There no harsh and boisterous winds are permitted to shake and disturb the air and ravage the beauty of the groves; there prevails no melancholy nor darksome weather, no drowning rain nor pelting hail, no forked lightning nor rending and resounding thunder; no wintry pinching cold nor withering and panting summer heat, nor any thing else that can give pain or sorrow or annoyance; but all is bland and gentle and serene; a perpetual youth and joy reigns throughout all nature and nothing decays and dies.[4]

Later, in *A History of the Life and Voyages of Christopher Columbus* (1828), Irving summarizes Columbus' own thinking about the shape of the earth and the nature of the vast new world before him. "Philosophers had described it [the earth] as spherical," he wrote,

> but they knew nothing of the part of the world which he had discovered. The ancient part, known to them, he had no doubt was spherical; but he now supposed that the real form of the earth was that of a pear, one part much more elevated than the rest, and tapering upwards toward the skies. This part he supposed to be in the interior of this newly found continent, and immediately under the equator. . . . He beheld a vast world, rising, as it were, into existence before him; its nature

and extent unknown and undefined, as yet a mere region for conjecture. Every day displayed some new feature of beauty and sublimity. Island after island, whose rocks he was told were veined with gold, whose groves teemed with spices, or whose shores abounded with pearls. Interminable ranges of coast; promontory beyond promontory, stretching as far as the eye could reach; luxuriant valleys, sweeping away into a vast interior, whose distant mountains, he was told, concealed still happier lands, and realms of still greater opulence. When he looked upon all this region of golden promise, it was with the glorious conviction, that his genius had, in a manner, called it into existence; he regarded it with the triumphant eye of a discoverer.[5]

Irving's major source for Columbus' speculations, theories, and convictions were Columbus' letters reporting on his four voyages to the New World. It was in his third-voyage letter that Columbus explained that the earth was in "the form of a pear . . . or like a round ball, upon one part of which is a prominence like a woman's nipple, this protrusion being the highest and nearest the sky, situated under the equinoctial line, and at the eastern extremity of this sea."[6] So important did he think his discovery to be that he repeated it in the same letter, in pretty much the same terms, only a few sentences further on. Therefore, when he reached the island of Trinidad, he was not surprised to find "the temperature exceedingly mild; the fields and the foliage likewise were remarkably fresh and green," adding:

> all this must proceed from the extreme blandness of the temperature, which arises, as I have said, from this country being the most elevated in the world, and the nearest to the sky. On these grounds, therefore, I affirm, that the globe is not spherical, but that there is the difference in its form which I have described; the which is to be found in this hemisphere, at the point where the Indies meet the ocean, the extremity of the hemisphere being below the equinoctial line. And a great confirmation of this is, that when our Lord made the sun, the first light appeared in the first point of the east, where the most elevated point of the globe is. . . .[7]

That Fitzgerald was acquainted with Columbus' letters may be confirmed further by his account of hardships suffered on his fourth voyage. As echoed later in Fitzgerald, he writes of "currents [that] were still contrary," "currents still oppos[ing]" the progress of ships "in the worst possible condition" but "always beating against contrary winds."[8]

If the finale of ***The Great Gatsby*** owes a good deal to Washington Irving, it is curious to note that Fitzgerald's novel might have had its own small share in a later historian's rendering of Columbus' Spanish in his letter on the third voyage. Samuel Eliot Morison, finding the existing translations of Columbus' letters into English to be unsatisfactory, informs readers of his *Admiral of the Ocean Sea: A Life of Christopher Columbus* (1942) that he has made his own translations of the original Spanish. Morison renders "*de la forma de una pera . . . ó como quien tiene una pelota muy redonda, ye en un lugar della fuese como una teta de muger alli puesta*"[9] as "the earth was not round after all, but 'in the shape of a pear,' or, like a round ball 'on one part of which is placed something like a woman's breast."[10] "This breast," continues Morison, "reached nearer Heaven than the rest of the world, and on the nipple the Terrestrial Paradise was located."[11] Interestingly, the English scholar Stephen Reckert, who quotes Morison's explanation for Columbus' miscalculations, also provides his own translation of the passage from Columbus' third voyage letter, which reads in part: "I began to think this about the world: I find it is not round . . . , but the shape of a quite round pear, and in one place like a woman's breast . . . , and this nipple part is the highest and nearest to Heaven. . . ."[12]

Foreshadowing Fitzgerald's Nick Carraway, Columbus sets down his impressions on first looking at what would come to be called the New World:

> All these islands are very beautiful, and distinguished by a diversity of scenery; they are filled with a great variety of trees of immense height, and which I believe to retain their foliage in all seasons; for when I saw them they were as verdant and luxuriant as they usually are in Spain in the month of May,—some of them were blossoming, some bearing fruit, and all flourishing in the greatest perfection, according to their respective stages of growth, and the nature and quality of each. . . . The nightingale and various birds were singing in countless numbers. . . .[13]

For the dreamer, as Dick Diver learns in ***Tender Is the Night***, the nightingale of the imagination knows no spatial limitations. It has no natural habitat. But it does for Nick Carraway, of course, whose plaintive anthem evokes Columbus' vision as it is replayed for Dutch sailors, first in Irving, then in Fitzgerald. Gatsby embodies a twentieth-century version of their dream—it was William Butler Yeats's notion, it will be recalled, that man embodies truth but cannot know it—but he cannot get past the green light at the end of Daisy's dock, which has signaled from the start the absolute barrier to the realization of his dream of Daisy and the recoverable past.[14]

Of course what is problematic about Gatsby's dream is that it not only has roots in the past but that it is intended to remake the past. In short, it is temporally disoriented, for the dreams of Columbus and the others, including the Dutch sailors, are keyed to the possibilities of the future. Henry David Thoreau quotes Humboldt's words on Columbus as he first faces the New World:

> The grateful coolness of the evening air, the ethereal purity of the starry firmament, the balmy fragrance of flowers, wafted to him by the land breeze, all led him

to suppose (as we are told by Herrara, in the Decades) that he was approaching the garden of Eden, the sacred abode of our first parents. The Orinoco seemed to him one of the four rivers which, according to the venerable tradition of the ancient world, flowed from Paradise, to water and divide the surface of the earth, newly adorned with plants.[15]

Thoreau reveals his own wonderment, as he looks out over the beach at Cape Cod, that "men do not sail the sea with more expectation. Nothing remarkable was ever accomplished in a prosaic mood. The heroes and discoverers have found true more than was previously believed, only when they were expecting and dreaming of something more than their contemporaries dreamed of, or even themselves discovered," he continues, "that is, when they were in a frame of mind fitted to behold the truth." Thus, even the quixotic "expeditions for the discovery of El Dorado, and of the Fountain of Youth, led to real, if not compensatory discoveries."[16] Such quests differ from Jay Gatsby's, though, for there can be nothing compensatory when, as in his case, the risk is absolute.

Washington Irving's *History of the Life and Voyages of Christopher Columbus* also anticipates Carraway's simile connecting the egg to Columbus in the first chapter of ***The Great Gatsby***:

> Next to the countenance shown him by the king and queen, may be mentioned that of Pedro Gonzalez de Mendoza, the grand cardinal of Spain, and first subject of the realm; a man whose elevated character for piety, learning, and high prince-like qualities, gave signal value to his favours. He invited Columbus to a banquet, where he assigned him the most honourable place at table, and had him served with the ceremonials which in those punctilious times were observed towards sovereigns. At this repast is said to have occurred the well known anecdote of the egg. A shallow courtier present, impatient of the honours paid to Columbus, and meanly jealous of him as a foreigner, abruptly asked him whether he thought that, in case he had not discovered the Indias, there were not other men in Spain, who would have been capable of the enterprize? To this Columbus made no immediate reply, but, taking an egg, invited the company to make it stand upon one end. Every one attempted it, but in vain; whereupon he struck it upon the table so as to break the end, and left it standing on the broken part; illustrating in this simple manner, that when he had once shown the way to the new world, nothing was easier than to follow it.[17]

Irving then adds a footnote: "This anecdote rests on the authority of the Italian historian Benzoni. . . . It has been condemned as trivial, but the simplicity of the reproof constitutes its severity, and was characteristic of the practical sagacity of Columbus. The universal popularity of the anecdote is a proof of its merit."[18] Interestingly enough, Mary Shelley borrowed the anecdote of Columbus and the egg from the 1828 edition of Irving's *Columbus*. In her 1831 preface to *Frankenstein*, she writes:

Invention, it must be humbly admitted, does not consist in creating out of void, but out of chaos; the materials must, in the first place, be afforded: it can give form to dark, shapeless substances, but cannot bring into being the substance itself. In all matters of discovery and invention, even of those that appertain to the imagination, we are continually reminded of the story of Columbus and his egg. Invention consists in the capacity of seizing on the capabilities of a subject, and in the power of moulding and fashioning ideas suggested to it.[19]

This is not a bad explanation for what encourages Jay Gatsby to think that he can re-fashion the factual past, bringing it into line with his clear dreams and hazy ideals, much like the Dutch sailors with all time and place seemingly opening out before them. So too, Jay Gatsby, that young student of "needed inventions," succeeds in becoming both his own Dr. Frankenstein and his own creation. He is, after all, to Nick's amazement, his own best invention: the product of his Platonic conception of himself. Like Mary Shelley's monster, he is not accepted by the villagers, from whose ranks will come his murderer.

Behind Fitzgerald's story of New York and the East, however, lies still another major source, this time not for the anecdote about Columbus' triumph over his carping critics, but for the fable of failure that is the story of the two Eggs, West and East. Into the mix out of which emerged *The Great Gatsby* had gone Sherwood Anderson's "The Triumph of the Egg." Published in *The Dial* in March 1920 and collected in 1921 in a volume bearing the same title as the story, Anderson's story, from one point of view at least, offers a major criticism of that version of the American Dream promising success to those who work honestly, hard, and long, especially to those independent souls who strike out on their own into the adventurous but dangerous realm of small business.

Like *The Great Gatsby,* "The Egg" (its final title) is a first-person retrospective narrative. A son recalls his boyhood, his mother and father, his father's attempts to succeed. He meditates on the dark metaphysics of raising chickens and the darksome effects on a child of living among the daily dying of chicks and chickens. Not so mysterious diseases decimate the population, and the stupid chicken has a predilection, like a character in *Gatsby,* for running out into the road and being struck dead by passing vehicles. The chicken farm fails (compare the Uncle Sol of E. E. Cummings' poem "Nobody Loses All the Time," who, after committing suicide, finally starts a successful business, a "worm farm"), and the father starts a restaurant. But chickens and eggs are in his blood. He has a collection of monster chicks, with two heads, multiple legs, and the like, preserved in jars, and he has learned to perform tricks with eggs. Anxious to satisfy his ambition for himself

and his family (when single he had his own horse), his desperation takes a singularly American turn toward Barnumism. He will attract customers to his restaurant by exhibiting his chicken wonders and doing magic tricks that he will not hesitate to explain to his customers. The showing of his exhibits is doomed from the start. It would take a rare bird, indeed, to order a fried egg sandwich or a Western omelet as a bizarrie of chicken freaks before him suspended in preservative alcohol stare out at him.

The father on this day, to amuse and bemuse his only customer, moves anxiously and excitedly to his magic tricks. He promises to do the real trick that Columbus said he would do but did not.

> "Well," he began hesitatingly, "well, you have heard of Christopher Columbus, eh?" He seemed to be angry. "That Christopher Columbus was a cheat," he declared emphatically. "He talked of making an egg stand on its end. He talked, he did, and then he went and broke the end of the egg." My father seemed to his visitor to be beside himself at the duplicity of Christopher Columbus. He muttered and swore. He declared it was wrong to teach children that Christopher Columbus was a great man when, after all, he cheated at the critical moment. He had declared he would make an egg stand on end and then when his bluff had been called he had done a trick.[20]

The father proceeds to his trick. He will make the egg stand alone by rolling the egg between the palms of his hands, claiming that he was coaxing the electricity from the human body into the egg. When he does bring off the trick, however, his customer is not looking, and by the time the latter looks back, the egg has fallen over.

It does not seem to be far-fetched to think here of Gatsby's grand entertainments designed to attract Daisy, weekend parties that have no other meaning for Gatsby beyond that one purpose. Of course, they too fail ultimately. Nick Carraway early on foreshadows the notion of the Columbian sham that so angers the father in Anderson's story "The Egg" when he describes West Egg and East Egg, "a pair of enormous eggs, identical in contour and separated only by a courtesy bay, jut out into the most domesticated body of salt water in the Western hemisphere, the great wet barnyard of Long Island Sound. They are not perfect ovals," he continues, "—like the egg in the Columbus story, they are both crushed flat at the contact end." With Columbus on his mind, it is no wonder that Nick describes himself as "a guide, a pathfinder, an original settler."[21] For all of his Barnum-like tricks and Columbus-like antics, Gatsby will fall before the "hard malice" of others. Fitzgerald was, of course, not rewriting Anderson's story. But it might have been one of its starting points, not the least of which was the ironic, elegiac, rueful tone of its retrospective narration.[22]

Nick is carried away with his narration, his mythologizing, his defense of Gatsby the criminal with an impossibly sentimental ideal that fails to recognize both the incarnation in Daisy of the grail which he is in the quest of and the realities of the human condition, among the contingencies of which is inevitable mutability and the passage of time. The battle of East Egg and West Egg is over, and there is no winner.

The Columbus and egg story surfaces also in the William Faulkner story "The Bear." "Cass" McCaslin Edmonds presents his cousin Isaac McCaslin with a global overview of an exhausted Old World just before the New World is discovered. For a "thousand years . . . men fought over the fragments of that collapse until at last even the fragments were exhausted and men snarled over the gnawed bones of the old world's worthless evening until an accidental egg discovered to them a new hemisphere."[23] That new hemisphere provided him with opportunity, but at a cost, as Faulkner reported to the Delta Council, a Mississippi group honoring him in 1952:

> By remaining in the old world, we could have been not only secure, but even free of the need to be responsible. Instead, we chose the freedom, the liberty, the independence and the inalienable right to responsibility; almost without charts, in frail wooden ships with nothing but sails and our desire and will to be free to move them, we crossed an ocean which did not even match the charts we did have; we conquered a wilderness in order to establish a place, not to be secure in because we did not want that, we had just repudiated that, just crossed three thousand miles of dark and unknown sea to get away from that; but a place to be free in, to be independent in, to be responsible in.[24]

Yet, as "The Bear" indicates, this continent was already owned by men "while He—this Arbiter, this Architect, this Umpire—condoned—or did He? looked down and saw—or did He? Or at least did nothing: saw, and could not, or did not see; saw, and would not, or perhaps He would not see—perverse, impotent, or blind: which?"[25] Faulkner's indifferent or uncaring deity is an avatar of Fitzgerald's Dr. T. J. Eckleberg, whose vacant eyes overlook the valley of ashes on the way to Mana-hatta. So Faulkner joins the story of Columbus' egg with arguably Fitzgerald's most famous Modernist image, dropping the entire matter, in all its aspects, into heady ruminations about history and divinity in Yoknapatawpha.

Just as his use of the Columbus anecdote emerges in Faulkner's great hunting story, so Fitzgerald's sorrowful look into the past for the green light and the paradisal hopes the Dutch sailors saw in the promised land of New York shores has lived on, one imagines, in the breasts of many, each manifestation taking its own form and seeking out its own expression. One of the more striking versions of Nick Carraway's vision is wonderfully emblematic—the words of a professor of literature later turned university president and, still later, baseball commissioner:

> [Baseball] is designed to break your heart. The game begins in the spring, when everything else begins again, and it blossoms in the summer, filling the afternoons and evenings, and then as soon as the chill rains come, it stops and leaves you to face the fall alone. . . . It breaks my heart because it was meant to, because it was meant to foster in me again the illusion that there was something abiding, some pattern and some impulse that could come together to make a reality that would resist the corrosion; and because, after it had fostered again that most hungered-for illusion, the game was meant to stop, and betray precisely what it promised. Of course, there are those who learn after the first few times. They grow out of sports. And there are others who were born with the wisdom to know that nothing lasts. These are the truly tough among us, the ones who can live without illusion, or without even the hope of illusion. I am not that grown-up or up-to-date. I am a simpler creature, tied to more primitive patterns and cycles. I need to think something lasts forever, and it might as well be that state of being that is a game; it might as well be that, in a green field, in the sun.[26]

In this piece, published in the *Yale Alumni Magazine* in 1977 when he was president of the university, Bart Giamatti gives a new emphasis and a re-focused meaning to Gatsby's dreaming, and he does so in a voice that sounds a bit like Nick Carraway's. It was not inappropriate that the young Angelo Bartlett Giamatti, the author of a doctoral dissertation later published as *The Earthly Paradise and the Renaissance Epic,* had served an apprenticeship at Princeton, teaching Dante, Petrarch, and Spenser, before journeying home to New Haven. "Columbus thought he had found the blessed land across the wide waters," Giamatti had written in the *Earthly Paradise,* "and he was certainly not the last man to search."[27]

In notes toward his last novel, now known as *The Love of the Last Tycoon: A Western* (note, a "Western"), Fitzgerald has his female narrator, a young woman named Cecilia, tell of her first sight of sheep in the flesh:

> I thought of the first sheep I ever remember seeing— hundreds of them, and how our car drove suddenly into them on the back lot of the old Laemmle studio. They were unhappy about being in pictures but the men in the car with us kept saying:
>
> "Swell?"
>
> "Is that what you wanted, Dick?"
>
> "Isn't that swell?" And the man named Dick kept standing up in the car as if he were Cortez or Balboa, looking over that grey fleecy undulation. If I ever knew what picture they were in I have long forgotten.[28]

It is the narrator who refers to "Balboa or Cortez" as the one who first looks out over the Pacific Ocean. One of them is commonly accepted as the first European to do so. The narrator confesses to confusing the two Spaniards. Her confusion recalls John Keats, of course, whose poem mistakenly credits this primary experience to Cortez. The confusion in *The Love of the Last Tycoon* is not, of course, Fitzgerald's. That he introduces it into his fiction, however, suggests that he found the confusion meaningful or at least suggestive of meaning.

There are, for example, the parallels between the Spaniards (represented by Balboa and Cortez) and the Dutch sailors who first saw in wonderment the greenness of Mana-hatta. It is the wonder that each experiences at new discovery which each feels brings them together. Just as the whole of the Pacific Ocean lies before the Spanish Europeans, the whole of the North American continent lies before the Dutch Europeans. Just as Keats can imagine how Balboa (or Cortez) felt, along with his men, so too can Nick Carraway imagine how the Dutch sailors felt. But what is more important is the parallel between Keats and Carraway. Each has had to resort to a simile to define his amazement. Keats's "discovery" of Chapman's translation of Homer is like Carraway's discovery of Gatsby and his intransigent dream. Only the discovery of a new planet or the sight of a new ocean can reveal the depth and magnitude of discovering Chapman's Homer. Only the one-time awe of the Dutch sailors can reveal the depth and magnitude of Gatsby's American dream. So Carraway has to reach for a new loop in the coda to his narrative to put that narrative in its proper historical-mythic perspective.

Interestingly, the effect that Fitzgerald achieves is, in a funny way, something like that of the Dutch girl pictured on the cleanser container. Fitzgerald as author stands to Carraway as Carraway as author stands to Gatsby, while Gatsby stands to the East Egg world as, in history, the first Dutch sailors stand to the green islands before them. Keats saw in Balboa silence and in his men "wild surmise." History has told us what such "wild surmise" led to with the brutal violence and bloody conquests of Cortez. Yet the Gatsbys stay the course. They will not learn the lessons of history. If they are doomed to repeat the mistakes, they will keep the dreams (though they be violent and destructive) both alive and verdant. They shall persist if not prevail, like the boats beating against the current, doomed to fail at the last.

Of course, in Keats's time, Europe's "discovery" of the Western hemisphere was not much deplored, nor was Britain's still-expanding empire much questioned except by her rivals in empire building. For Fitzgerald, however, who would soon discover Oswald Spengler's *Decline of the West,* the discoverer's egg turned out to be the great humpty-dumpty. It could never be put back

together again any more than Gatsby could fix the past or Sherwood Anderson could abandon the hopeful mystery he cast over his "almost beautiful," single-truth grotesques.[29]

Notes

1. F. Scott Fitzgerald, *The Great Gatsby* (Scribners, 1925), pp. 217-18.

2. Washington Irving, *A History of New York, from the Beginning of the World to the End of the Dutch Dynasty* (Author's rev. ed.) (David McKay, 1891), pp. 80, 81.

3. Washington Irving, *Voyages and Discoveries of the Companions of Columbus,* ed. James W. Tuttleton (Twayne, 1986), p. 333.

4. Irving, *Voyages and Discoveries,* p. 337.

5. Washington Irving, *History of the Life and Voyages of Christopher Columbus* (G. and C. Carvill, 1828), II, 184, 187-88.

6. I quote from *Christopher Columbus: Four Voyages to the New World, Letters and Selected Documents,* ed., and trans. R. H. Major, intro. John E. Fagg (Citadel, 1992), p. 130. This is a bilingual edition of *Select Letters of Christopher Columbus, with Other Original Documents, Relating to his Four Voyages to the New World* (Hakluyt Society, 1847).

7. Fagg, *Four Voyages,* pp. 132-33.

8. Fagg, *Four Voyages,* pp. 180, 188.

9. Fagg, *Four Voyages,* p. 130.

10. Samuel Eliot Morison, *Admiral of the Ocean Sea: A Life of Christopher Columbus* (Little, Brown, 1942), p. 557.

11. Morison, *Admiral,* p. 557. In a later translation of the same passage, Morison substitutes "teat" for "breast" (*Journals and Other Documents of the Life and Voyages of Christopher Columbus,* trans., ed. Samuel Eliot Morison [Heritage Press, 1963], p. 286).

12. Stephen Reckert, *Beyond Chrysanthemums: Perspectives on Poetry East and West* (Clarendon Press, 1993), p. 179, n. 40.

13. Fagg, *Four Voyages,* p. 5.

14. In the same year that saw the publication of *The Great Gatsby,* William Carlos Williams rendered Columbus' vision: "[W]e saw the trees very green, and much water and fruits of divers kinds. . . . Bright green trees, the whole land so green that it is a pleasure to look on it. Gardens of the most beautiful trees I ever saw. . . . I walked among

the trees which was the most beautiful thing which I had ever seen" (*In the American Grain,* intro. Horace Gregory [New Directions, n.d.], pp. 25-26).

15. Henry David Thoreau, *Cape Cod,* intro. Paul Theroux (Penguin, 1987), pp. 139-40.

16. Thoreau, *Cape Cod,* pp. 139-40.

17. Irving, *Life and Voyages,* I, p. 275.

18. Irving, *Life and Voyages,* I, p. 275. See William A. Fahey, "Fitzgerald's Eggs of Columbus," *ANQ,* VIII (1995), pp. 26-27. Girolamo Benzoni's anecdote appears as an epigraph to *Columbus' Egg: New Latin American Stories on the Conquest,* ed. Nick Caistor (Faber and Faber, 1992).

19. Mary Shelley, Introduction (1831), in *Frankenstein; or, the Modern Prometheus,* Volume I of *The Novels and Selected Works of Mary Shelley,* ed. Nora Crook, intro. Betty T. Bennett (William Pickering, 1996), pp. 178-79.

20. Sherwood Anderson, "The Egg," in *The Portable Sherwood Anderson,* ed., and intro. Horace Gregory (Viking, 1949, p. 459).

21. Fitgerald, *Great Gatsby,* pp. 5-6, 4.

22. Until Anderson's "collapse" with the publication of the novel *Dark Laughter* Fitzgerald's attitude toward his work had always been laudatory. In 1923, he had reviewed the novel *Many Marriages* favorably, and even as late as 1925 he still considered Anderson, as he wrote to Maxwell Perkins, "one of the very best and finest writers in the English language today" (*The Letters of F. Scott Fitzgerald,* ed. Andrew Turnbull [Scribners, 1963], p. 187). By 1927, however, he had changed his mind. It was Hemingway who, since "Anderson's collapse," was "the best we have, I think," as he informed Mencken (*Correspondence of F. Scott Fitzgerald,* ed. Matthew J. Bruccoli and Margaret M. Duggan [Random House, 1980], p. 210).

23. William Faulkner, "The Bear," in *Go Down Moses* (Random House 1963), pp. 257-58.

24. William Faulkner, "Address to the Delta Council" (Cleveland, Mississippi, May 15, 1952), in *Essays, Speeches & Public Letters,* ed. James B. Meriwether (Random House, 1965), p. 128.

25. Faulkner, "The Bear," p. 258.

26. A. Barlett Giamatti, "The Green Fields of the Mind," in *A Great and Glorious Game: Baseball Writings of A. Bartlett Giamatti,* ed. Kenneth S. Robson, foreword by David Halberstam (Algonquin Books, 1998) pp. 7, 12-13.

27. A. Bartlett Giamatti, *The Earthly Paradise and the Renaissance Epic* (W. W. Norton, 1989), p. 4.

28. F. Scott Fitzgerald, *The Love of the Last Tycoon: A Western,* ed. Matthew J. Bruccoli (Cambridge University Press, 1993), pp. 9-10.

29. Sherwood Anderson, *Winesburg, Ohio,* intro. Glen A. Love (Oxford University Press, 1997), p. 8.

Brian Sutton (essay date fall 2000)

SOURCE: Sutton, Brian. "Fitzgerald's *The Great Gatsby.*" *Explicator* 59, no. 1 (fall 2000): 37-9.

[*In the following essay, Sutton examines the significance of a recurring image of the framing of Tom and Daisy in a frame of artificial light in* Gatsby.]

In F. Scott Fitzgerald's **The Great Gatsby,** Gatsby goes to spectacular lengths to try to achieve what Nick Carraway calls "his incorruptible dream" (155): to recapture the past by regaining Daisy Buchanan's love and getting her to tell her husband, Tom, that she never loved him (111). For much of the novel, Gatsby seems likely to succeed, not only because his efforts are so extraordinary, but because Daisy's marriage seems so miserable and corrupt that she must surely be looking for the chance to escape. But Daisy herself proves to be corrupt and thus perfectly suited for marriage with Tom, with whom she shares membership in an exclusive society from which Gatsby is barred. Whenever Fitzgerald emphasizes the resilience of Tom and Daisy's corrupt marriage, he relies on a recurring image: He portrays Tom and Daisy together, side by side, framed by a square or rectangle of artificial light.[1]

The image first occurs late in the opening chapter. Although at this point Fitzgerald hasn't yet established the possibility that Daisy might leave Tom for Gatsby, he has clearly shown how miserable Daisy seems within her marriage. When the narrator, Nick Carraway, attends a small dinner party at Tom and Daisy's mansion, Daisy publicly blames Tom for a bruise on her knuckle, suggesting physical violence (12). She calls him "a brute" and "hulking," repeating the latter word immediately after he "crossly" says he doesn't like it (12). She belittles his ideas, twice winking at Nick during Tom's comments about a book he claims to have read (13-14). Then she abruptly leaves the dinner table to retrieve Tom after he has left to answer a telephone call, evidently from his lover, Myrtle Wilson (14-16), and when Daisy is alone with Nick, she complains bitterly about her marriage and her life (17-18).

Yet the instant she finishes her complaint, Nick "felt the basic insincerity of what she had said," and a moment later she looks at Nick "with an absolute smirk on her lovely face, as if she had asserted her membership in a rather distinguished secret society to which she and

Tom belonged" (18). Therefore almost from the beginning of the novel, Fitzgerald hints that despite or perhaps because of the corruption in the marriage, Daisy is content to be married to Tom. And when Nick leaves for the night, Fitzgerald uses the square of artificial light to frame an image emphasizing Tom and Daisy's basic compatibility with one another. At their front door, they "stood side by side in a cheerful frame of light" (20). Tom and Daisy speak like a happy couple, agreeing with one another and referring to themselves as a unit:

> "We heard you were engaged to a girl out West."
>
> "That's right," corroborated Tom kindly. "We heard you were engaged."
>
> (20)

By the time we encounter the second instance of the frame of light, near the end of chapter 6, Gatsby has become Daisy's lover. Once again the image occurs at the conclusion of a party, this time one of the larger, wilder parties that Gatsby throws. Again events of the evening underscore problems in the marriage, problems that by now suggest that Daisy may indeed leave Tom and end up with Gatsby. She spends a considerable portion of the evening dancing with and talking alone to Gatsby, whereas Tom spends much of the evening pursuing a woman he has met (106-07). Besides being irritated with each other's flirtatious behavior, Daisy and Tom are both disdainful of the other's potential lover: Daisy describes the woman Tom pursues as "common but pretty" and sarcastically offers him a pencil to write down the woman's address (107). Tom describes the party as a "menagerie" and says of Gatsby, "A lot of these newly rich people are just big bootleggers, you know" (109). But this snobbishness, although expressed through bickering, ultimately unites Daisy and Tom within the "distinguished secret society" Gatsby cannot penetrate. Although Daisy defends Gatsby when Tom mocks his party, she too is "offended" and "appalled" by the party's garish, drunken-Broadway atmosphere and joins her husband in a mutual distaste for Gatsby's world. At the end of the evening, standing side by side framed in "ten square feet of light" emanating from Gatsby's front door, Tom and Daisy leave together, and Gatsby admits to Nick, "She didn't like it. [. . .] I feel far away from her" (110-11).

When at the end of chapter 7 the frame of light appears for the third and final time, it is at the close of a day in which Gatsby has forced the love triangle to its inevitable crisis. Once again he at first seems likely to succeed: Daisy's facial expression and tone of voice have made Tom sense that she loves Gatsby (119), and Daisy calls Tom "revolting" after he obliquely acknowledges having had a succession of adulterous affairs (132). But when Gatsby takes the ultimate step of asking Daisy to

tell Tom that she has never loved him, her immediate reaction makes clear that "she had never, all along, intended doing anything at all" (133) about leaving Tom. When Tom brings up the shady means by which Gatsby has made his fortune, Gatsby's chances of winning Daisy are dead, not because Daisy now finds Gatsby immoral, but because Gatsby is now firmly established as a mere social-climbing bootlegger, in contrast to Tom and Daisy who were born into wealth. When Tom learns of Gatsby's relationship with Daisy, his initial reaction is indignation that "Mr. Nobody from Nowhere" could threaten his marriage (130). And in the end, Daisy thinks much the same way Tom does, rendering Gatsby's dreams hopeless.

Although this encounter is disastrous for Gatsby, worse is to follow. Driving back to Long Island in Gatsby's car, Daisy accidentally runs over and kills Myrtle Wilson. With violence hanging in the air, Gatsby is reduced to hiding in the bushes near Tom and Daisy's house, hoping to protect Daisy in the event that, as he says to Nick, her husband "tries to bother her about that unpleasantness this afternoon" and "tries any brutality" (145). Although his concern for Daisy's safety is undoubtedly genuine, Gatsby may also hope for an outburst from Tom, because Gatsby's only remaining chance to win Daisy would be if Tom were to drive her away through violence.

But when Nick goes up to the house to "see if there's any sign of commotion" (145), he comes to "a small rectangle of light" at a window and finds Tom and Daisy framed within that light, sitting together, his hand covering hers, and Daisy nodding in agreement as he speaks (146). Once again, the artificial light frames a scene portraying Tom and Daisy as well matched, united in mutual corruption. Nick observes, "There was an unmistakable air of natural intimacy about the picture, and anybody would have said they were conspiring together" (146).

Judging from later events, perhaps Tom and Daisy were "conspiring together." Daisy evidently allows Tom to believe that Gatsby was driving when Myrtle Wilson was killed. And when Tom encounters Myrtle's husband, who is armed and deluded with grief into thinking that whoever ran over Myrtle had been her lover and had killed her deliberately, Tom directs him to Gatsby's house. Myrtle's husband then murders Gatsby and commits suicide. Thus, whereas Tom and Daisy and their marriage survive, Gatsby is killed for running over Myrtle—something Daisy did—and for being Myrtle's lover—something Tom was. It is ironic that despite the repeated imagery of Tom and Daisy together in a frame of light, in the end it is Gatsby who is framed by Tom and Daisy.

Note

1. For a contrasting analysis of this image pattern, one correlating the pattern with the novel's themes related to the American Dream and the first European explorers' encounter with the American wilderness, see Lawry.

Works Cited

Fitzgerald, F. Scott. *The Great Gatsby.* New York: Scribner's, 1925.

Lawry, J. S. "Green Light or Square of Light in *The Great Gatsby.*" *Dalhousie Review* 55 (1975): 114-32.

Chikako D. Kumamoto (essay date fall 2001)

SOURCE: Kumamoto, Chikako D. "Fitzgerald's *The Great Gatsby.*" *Explicator* 60, no. 1 (fall 2001): 37-41.

[*In the following essay, Kumamoto explores Fitzgerald's use of the "egg and chicken" metaphors as part of Gatsby's structure.*]

FITZGERALD'S *THE GREAT GATSBY*

Having moved to the suburbs of New York City, Nick Carraway makes the now-famous comparison between his neighborhood and its adjacent community: "Twenty miles from the city a pair of enormous eggs, identical in contour and separated only by a courtesy of bay, jut out into the most domesticated body of salt water in the Western Hemisphere, the great barnyard of Long Island Sound" (Fitzgerald 9).

One may inquire, however, whether Nick means the egg metaphor simply as a felicitous coincidence or as a surreptitious carrier of his narrative thesis. Among theme-clarifying studies of Fitzgerald's major images in the novel—studies by Lehan, Geismer, Johnson, Laying, Miller, and Sutton, for instance—only Kermit Moyer comments specifically on the egg-shaped setting as Fitzgerald's structural design shoring up the parallel between the novel's narrative circularity and the circular geography (45). In my essay I examine this and also investigate how Nick's seldom-critiqued "a pair of enormous eggs," as well as other heretofore unnoticed egg-inspired images in the narrative, acts as his submerged thematic signals.

Plausible meanings of egg references can be traced to two sources, the first of which is Fitzgerald's known attraction to "The Feast of Trimalchio" in Petronius's *The Satyricon.* Fitzgerald scholars document the frequent correspondence between Fitzgerald and Maxwell Perkins chronicling Fitzgerald's obsession with using Trimalchio as part of the final title, as in *Trimalchio* or

Trimalchio in West Egg, before he settled down to **The Great Gatsby.**[1] The recent Cambridge University Press publication of *Trimalchio: An Early Version of **The Great Gatsby*** also makes us privy to the history of the Trimalchio text that would eventually become **The Great Gatsby** (West xiii-xix). As Gatsby's literary antecedent, Trimalchio appears to have provided Fitzgerald with a keen awareness of the elevating effect of classical inscriptions on the Gatsby character. As Brian Way speculates, Fitzgerald must have learned from Petronius something of "the dramatic organization of such scenes [Gatsby's parties]—about the mounting rhythms that run through huge entertainment" (105-06). I argue, then, that this Trimalchio link can further intimate Fitzgerald's possible secondary awareness of the satiric suggestiveness of images of eggs and fowls underscoring Gatsby's "vast, vulgar, and meretricious" dream shared by the social-climbing Trimalchio (104).

It is in this respect that Gatsby's parties revisit Trimalchio's, where Roman celebrities and adventurers are courted with rare dishes of peahen's eggs, oriole, and other fowls:

> We, meanwhile, were still occupied with the hors d'oeuvres when a tray was carried in and set down before us. On it lay a basket, and in it a hen, carved from wood, with wings outspread as though sitting on her eggs. Then two slaves came forward and, to a loud flourish from the orchestra, began rummaging in the straw and pulling out peahen's eggs which they divided among the guests. Trimalchio gave the whole performance his closest attention. "Friends," he said, "I ordered peahen eggs to be set under that hen, but I'm half afraid they may have hatched already. Still, let's see if we can suck them." We were handed spoons [. . .] and cracked open the eggs. [. . .] I heard one of the guests, obviously a veteran of these dinners, say, "I wonder what little surprise we've got in here." So I cracked the shell with my hand and found inside a fine fat oriole, nicely seasoned with pepper.

> (Petronius 30-31)

Roman feasts like Trimalchio's were a popular social institution where the host enhanced personal status by expending great care and effort on the visual sumptuousness of the food (Donahue; D'Arms 308-20). Moreover, hen's eggs were a highly prized item in the Roman diet, and fabulous public feasts were judged incomplete without various dishes of eggs, chicken, ducks, and other fowls (Smith 551-55; Macrobius). In the notes to his translation of *The Satyricon,* William Arrowsmith explains that during the Republic peahen eggs were considered a fabulous delicacy and that an oriole (or fig eater) is a brilliantly colored bird whose habit of stuffing itself on ripe figs endeared it to Roman epicures (Petronius 192). In Petronius's Menippean pen, the egg and fowl dishes coalesce into a satiric iconography of Trimalchio's pretensions to social status and his attempts to belong to Roman patrician society. From such egg and fowl lore of antiquity, one can infer Fitzgerald's intertextual ambition to heighten the irreconcilable social gap between West Egg, with a chauffeur clad "in a uniform of robin's egg blue," and East Egg, "with a single green light" (26, 45). Like Trimalchio's, Gatsby's parties attract guests with illegal liquors, rare foods, popular entertainment, and upstart celebrities, in spite of "Tom and Daisy's aversion to them" (West xviii).[2]

Fitzgerald expands the Petronian association in chapter 7, in which Gatsby desperately clings to his dream of having what he believes to be the status of the American patrician. Fitzgerald first pays homage to his classical indebtedness by writing that "his career as Trimalchio was over" when Gatsby stops his Saturday night parties (119). He then adds a satiric bite to the egg and fowl allusions with the aid of the idiomatic meanings of "chicken" when he describes Nick's glimpse of Tom and Daisy "sitting opposite each other at the kitchen table with a plate of cold fried chicken between them and two bottles of ale [. . .] conspiring together" (152-53). By this point in the narrative, Nick has learned from Gatsby that it was Daisy who was driving the car that killed Myrtle Wilson. Lexical sources from as early as 1400 and 1630 use "chicken" to mean people who are cowardly and have lost their nerve at crucial moments, in phrases like "cherles chekyn" and "Not finding the Defendants to be Chikins, to be afraid of every cloud or kite" (Barnhart 120; Rogers 56). Another connotation of "chicken" for Fitzgerald's contemporaries was general prosperity for the masses, as in "a chicken in every pot, a car in every garage," the slogan of the Republican Party in the 1928 presidential campaign (Hurwitz 107). What better symbol of the death of normal human conscience, courage, and empathy at the heart of the narrative action than the picture of cold chicken appropriated to Tom and Daisy, paired with Nick's tiptoeing away, which renders all those colloquial meanings of chicken ironically apt? On one hand, the term "chicken" points to Daisy's panicky self-absorption in the face of her punishable crime. Most damningly, Tom's lawless, face-saving exercising of social privilege (his callous unconcern with his mistress's death) colludes with Daisy's ready renunciation of her talismanic power that has so attracted Gatsby ("Once in a while she looked up at him [Tom] and nodded in agreement"). Thus the chicken trope unmasks the cowardly Tom and Daisy's "conspiring together" to reestablish the unbreakable, unholy alliance of marriage, cash, and status—a fundamental cause of Gatsby's tragedy.

More than a show of witty conceit, "a pair of enormous eggs" and fowls are visual analogs for Fitzgerald's ironic gaze, obliquely trained on the bitter abilities of inherited rank and the magic of money to subvert genuine human connectives like love.

Notes

1. The following sources document Fitzgerald's title-naming history: West xi; Bryer and Kuehl; Turnbull 478; Bruccoli and Duggan 153.

2. James L. W. West III, the editor of the recent Cambridge edition of *Trimalchio,* notes that one of the differences between the early version and the final *The Great Gatsby* is the reader's increased awareness of "Gatsby's courting of celebrities—and Tom and Daisy's aversion to them" (xviii).

Works Cited

Barnhart, Robert K., ed. *The Barnhart Concise Dictionary of Etymology.* New York: Harper, 1995.

Bruccoli, Matthew J., and Margaret M. Duggan, eds. *Correspondence of F. Scott Fitzgerald.* New York: Random House, 1980.

Bryer, Jackson R., and John Kuehl, eds. *Dear Scott/ Dear Max.* New York: Scribner, 1971.

D'Arms, John. "The Roman Convivium and the Idea of Equality." *Sympotica: A Symposium on* The Symposition. Ed. Oswyn Murray. Oxford: Clarendon. 308-20.

Donahue, John F. "Euergetic Self-Representation and the Inscription at *Satyricon* 71.10." *Classical Philology* 94.1 (January 1994).

Fitzgerald, F. Scott. *The Great Gatsby.* Ed. Matthew J. Bruccoli. New York: Macmillan, 1992.

Geismer, Maxwell. "F. Scott Fitzgerald: Orestes at the Ritz." *The Last of the Provincials: The American Novels 1915-1925.* Boston: Houghton Mifflin, 1947. 316-20.

Hurwitz, Howard. *An Encyclopedic Dictionary of American History.* New York: Washington Square, 1970.

Johnson, Christine. "*The Great Gatsby*: The Final Vision." *Fitzgerald/Hemingway Annual* 1976: 109-15.

Laying, George W. "Fitzgerald's *The Great Gatsby.*" *Explicator* 56.2 (Winter 1998): 93-95.

Lehan, Richard D. "*The Great Gatsby.*" *F. Scott Fitzgerald and the Craft of Fiction.* Carbondale: Southern Illinois UP, 1966. 91-122.

Macrobius. "Saturnalia Convivia, III. 13: The Bill of Fare of a Great Roman Banquet. 63 BCE." *Readings in Ancient History: Illustrative Extracts from the Sources.* Ed. William Stearns Davis. Vol. 2. Boston: Allyn and Bacon, 1912-13. Available through *Ancient History Source Book,* ‹http://www.fordham.edu/halsall/ancient/macrobius-3-13.html›.

Miller, James E. "Fitzgerald's *Gatsby*: The World as Ash Heap." *The Twenties: Fiction, Poetry, Drama.* Delena: Everett/Edwards, 1975. 181-202.

Moyer, Kermit W. "*The Great Gatsby*: Fitzgerald's Meditation on American History." *Fitzgerald/Hemingway Annual,* 1972: 45-49.

Petronius, Arbiter. *The Satyricon of Petronius.* Trans. and introd. William Arrowsmith. Ann Arbor: U of Michigan P, 1959.

Rogers, James. *The Dictionary of Clichés.* New York: Ballantine, 1985.

Smith, Martin. "Ducks Eggs in Statius, 'Silvae' 4.9.30?" *Classical Quarterly* 44.2 (July-December 1994): 551-55.

Sutton, Brian. "Fitzgerald's *The Great Gatsby.*" *Explicator* 55.2 (Winter 1997): 94-95.

Turnbull, Andrew. *The Letters of F. Scott Fitzgerald.* New York: Scribner, 1963.

Way, Brian. *F. Scott Fitzgerald and the Art of Social Fiction.* London: Arnold, 1980.

West, James L. W., III, ed. *Trimalchio: An Early Version of The Great Gatsby.* By F. Scott Fitzgerald. Cambridge: Cambridge UP, 2001.

FURTHER READING

Criticism

Magistrale, Tony, and Mary Jane Dickerson. "The Language of Time in *The Great Gatsby.*" *College Literature* 16, 1 (spring 1989): 117-28.
Draws on theories of Mikhail Bakhtin to explain the juxtaposition of past and present in *Gatsby.*

Tyson, Lois. "The Romance of the Commodity: The Concellatation of Identity in F. Scott Fitzgerald's *Great Gatsby*" In *Psychological Politics of the American Dream: The Commodification of Subjectivity in Twentieth-Century American Literature,* pp. 40-62. Columbus: Ohio State University Press, 1994.
Argues that *Gatsby* is not a portrayal of an idealized yet corrupted American dream, but rather a false dream corrupted by a culture of commodity.

Weinstein, Arnold. "Fiction as Greatness: The Case of *Gatsby.*" *Novel* 19 (fall 1985): 22-38.
Attempts to define the "greatness" of *The Great Gatsby* in terms of its evocation of the power of a dream.

Additional coverage of Fitzgerald's life and career is contained in the following sources published by Thomson Gale: *American Writers; American Writers: The Classics,* **Vol. 2;** *American Writers Retrospective Supplement,* **Vol. 1;** *Authors and Artists for Young Adults,* **Vol. 24;** *Authors in the News,* **Vol. 1;** *Beacham's Encyclopedia of Popular Fiction: Biography & Resources,* **Vol. 1;** *Concise Dictionary of American Literary Biography, 1917-1929; Contemporary Authors,* **Vols. 123, 110;** *Dictionary of Literary Biography,* **Vols. 4, 9, 86, 219, 273;** *Dictionary of Literary Biography Documentary Series,* **Vols. 1, 15, 16;** *Dictionary of Literary Biography Yearbook,* **1981, 1996;** *DISCovering Authors; DISCovering Authors: British Edition; DISCovering Authors: Canadian Edition; DISCovering Authors Modules: Most-studied Authors* **and** *Novelists; DISCovering Authors 3.0; Encyclopedia of World Literature in the 20th Century,* **Ed. 3;** *Exploring Novels; Exploring Short Stories; Literature and Its Times,* **Vol. 3;** *Literature Resource Center; Major 20th-Century Writers,* **Eds. 1, 2;** *Novels for Students,* **Vols. 2, 19;** *Reference Guide to American Literature,* **Ed. 4;** *Reference Guide to Short Fiction,* **Ed. 2;** *Short Stories for Students,* **Vols. 4, 15;** *Short Story Criticism,* **Vols. 6, 31;** *Twayne's United States Authors; Twentieth-Century Literary Criticism,* **Vols. 1, 6, 14, 28, 55; and** *World Literature Criticism.*

Alfred Richard Orage
1873-1934

English journalist and literary critic.

The following entry provides criticism on Orage's works from 1926 through 1992.

INTRODUCTION

Orage's career combined economic socialism, religious mysticism and a keen desire to integrate aesthetic norms into daily life. His most important public role was as editor for fifteen years of *The New Age,* a literary journal that published many of the leading lights of the Edwardian Age—and many of those who would become important literary figures in decades to follow. Orage's fluctuating economic beliefs made him an interesting political figure but left no lasting mark. His emphasis on textual analysis in literary criticism and his persistent attention to style in his own work and that of others earned him a minor place in the history of early twentieth century letters.

BIOGRAPHICAL INFORMATION

Orage was born on January 22, 1873, in Yorkshire, England. His father died when he was one year old and his mother was forced to support the family by taking in washing. A wealthy local patron sent Orage to a teacher's college, leading him to become a schoolmaster in Leeds. Here Orage joined various intellectual and socialist groups. Orage moved to London in 1906, where he became active in the socialist Fabian Society. Orage sought to convince his fellow Fabians to pay greater attention to aesthetic concerns and, with help from friends, purchased *The New Age* periodical, turning it into a leading journal of eclectic literary style and economic beliefs. As editor he published work by such leading figures as George Bernard Shaw and Ezra Pound. Orage also published specifically socialist journalism, particularly expositions of the theory of social credit, which demanded government programs to increase workers' purchasing power so that they might be less dependent on their own labor. Orage also published essays on mysticism and his own spiritual leanings influenced much of his work. He resigned as editor in 1922 to become a disciple of the mystic Georgy Gurdjieff in France and New York. He returned to England and in 1932 founded another journal, *The New English Weekly,* which he ran much as he had *The New Age* until his death on November 5, 1934.

MAJOR WORKS

Early in his career Orage published two books interpreting the writing of Friedrich Nietzsche. In 1917 he published an economics primer, *An Alphabet of Economics,* in an attempt to gain adherents for his socialist views. But Orage was best known during his lifetime for his journalism and literary criticism. Over the fifteen years in which he edited *The New Age* and the two years he edited *The New English Weekly,* he produced hundreds of essays on economics, art and literature. Chief collections include *Readers and Writers (1917-1921)* (1922) and *The Art of Reading* (1930). Both volumes have the strengths and weaknesses of their genre. They include many engaging essays showing wit, style and at times significant depth of critical understanding, yet contain writings of such short length and journalistic intent that their lasting importance is sometimes open to question. Three posthumous collections, *Selected Essays and Critical Writings of A. R. Orage* (1935), *Political and Economic Writings* (1936) and *Orage as Critic* (1975) give further evidence of Orage's eclectic interests and journalistic style.

CRITICAL RECEPTION

Critical appraisal of Orage's writings was often intertwined with opinions on his political and social beliefs. In general, adherents to his causes found more substance and value in his works than nonbelievers, who emphasized the limitations of his chosen genre and found Orage's ideas less persuasive to those not already in agreement with the tenets of socialism. Although his writing is not considered highly relevant in modern times, Orage was quite influential among his contemporaries, including G. K. Chesterton, Ezra Pound, H. G. Wells, and Frank Swinnerton, many of whose works are still of interest in the twenty-first century.

PRINCIPAL WORKS

Consciousness: Animal, Human, and Superman (essays) 1907

CRITICISM

Waldo David Frank (essay date 1926)

SOURCE: Frank, Waldo David. "Mystery in a Sack Suit." In *Time Exposures By Searchlight,* pp. 151-56. New York: Boni and Liveright, Inc., 1926.

[*In the following excerpt from a book of portraits about cultural figures from the 1920's, Frank presents a colorful image of Orage, a man who "despises the world so well that he is at peace with it."*]

With a bird's-eye view of our City, you will have noticed for the past two years growing numbers of little knots of people scattered about town in comfortable places—very intent, largely silent. Closer, you observed that these groups consisted of editors, wives of Wall Street, professors, novelists, shingled girls, restless business men, artistic youths. Here were true intellectuals who despise Greenwich Village. Here were socially elect who looked down on Park Avenue as a gilded slum. Here indeed were men and women dry and fresh, smart and solemn, rich or merely famous—perpendicular extremes of our extremely perpendicular New York. And now if you looked still closer, you saw that they were listening with passionate concern to a man they call Orage (pronounce it precisely like the French for *storm*): and that Orage was most intempestuously sitting in an upholstered armchair, smoking a cigarette and cavalierly smiling.

He seems a proverbial schoolboy, slightly damaged by the years, yet on the whole intact—as he sits enwreathed in all those seeking brains and eager eyes. He has a hard body in a tight drab suit. He has hair like a cap drawn close upon his skull. The finger tips are yellow with tobacco. The face is gray with thought. And its prominent part is the nose. The nose is the pinnacle of Orage. Intense brow, willful jaw, keen eyes, ironic mouth—they all converge upon this proboscidean symbol of pertinence and search.

Who is he? and what is he telling the good men and ladies, that they should hearken to him—leaders though they are—with humble rapture? He is propounding a simple, matter-of-fact psychologic method. A method too simple, really, to be written down either by him or by me. So what that Method is, you'll have to find out for yourself. What it *does*—or claims to do—is nothing less than the whole and utter overturning of everything you live by. All your standards—ethical, religious. All your darlings—historical, artistic. From Æschylus to Bertie Russell, he sweeps them off the table. From Pentateuch to Theosophy, he shows them up. All the world's religions are wrong. All the good intentions are bad. All the truths are lies. All self-improvement is vain. With a most humane smile, Orage blights the claims of humaneness. With valedictory sentiment, wipes sentiment off the slate. With logic swift as a machine, he discredits logic. With courteous manner, drops spiritual bombs into the laps of ladies who adore him.

Oh, ho! you say. Another fanatic? Yes—a most cool and balanced one. Another mystifier? Yes—one whose logical gifts gained him, long years ago, the name of the most dangerous debater in all England. He may be a poisoner of traditional wells; but what sweet venom he drips. He may be a revolutionist; but can you gainsay his classical, scholarly words? Perhaps this is a sect. But if the men and women whom he draws are themselves leaders of men and women?

In London they tried to keep pace with Alfred Richard Orage, and they failed. He came to that Metropolis in 1903, from the hinterlands of Birmingham and Yorkshire. He was thirty, then, and already versed in the mysteries of Socialism, Occultism, Nietzscheanism. He had written books on such timid little subjects as *The Dionysian Spirit of the Age, Consciousness: Animal, Human, Superman, An Alphabet of Economics.* Now he started a magazine with a name similarly modest (*The New Age*) and proceeded to midwife, prune, or otherwise direct a good measure of the respectable—and some of the infamous—literary reputations of the last twenty years in England. Arnold Bennett, Katharine Mansfield, Ernest Boyd, were discoveries of Orage—and so was Michael Arlen. Between these two extremes, fill in the name of your favorite British writer and most probably you'll find, somewhere upon him, the mark of this unemphatic man. Scores and scores of volumes have been dedicated to him. London knew he was *there*. Philosophy, poetry, criticism, fiction, knew it. His own essays, signed with false initials, kept a running fire on the world—and made England heartily sick, and Orage heartily hated; and incidentally, gave to English literature a prose that ranks with Shaw's and that, for pure revolutionary thought, puts Shaw in his place as the quite proper Devil of old ladies.

Orage looks like a boy and his shoulders are sharp. They have a way of shrugging—shrugging off fads and facts and systems at a pace poor slow England could not hope to keep up with. Before she knew it, Orage had gone through Socialism and shrugged it off: Nietzscheanism and shrugged it off: had become a psychoanalyst and shrugged it off. (I don't know what effect, if any, this had on Doctor Freud but the Freudians of England awoke one morning and found they had a subtle foe in their midst.) Then, Ouspensky, Russian mystic-mathematician, came to England.

And that is why Orage's shoulders have ceased forevermore from shrugging, and why New York is gathering in eager knots, week after week, season after season, to learn the Method whereby New York, and Culture, and Mortal Life itself, may be successfully shrugged into the ash-heap, in exchange for a Consciousness possibly Mephistophelian, possibly God-like—but avowedly not human.

The Method belongs neither to Orage nor to Ouspensky, but to their Master, Gurgieff, who visited our City several years ago, leaving Orage here ever since, like a pregnancy upon us. And Gurgieff is the Greek with a Polish wife and a Russian name, who was once Prime Minister of Tibet, who has practiced all professions from highway robbery to selling carpets, who trains his neophites in the Sacred Eastern Dances with a brutal perfection that makes Diaghileff a tyro, and who—according to several men whom the world calls great—is the greatest man in the world.

This is no place for Cosmologies. My subject is Orage. Let me say merely this unto the fond who read in the worldly brilliance of certain of Orage's groups an argument against his value: Know your history of religions. There you will learn that the first followers of the Buddha were snobbish Brahmins and rich youth of Benares: and that the society ladies of that day pestered Gotama until—to be rid of them—he opened convents.

Orage believes in no convents. If you dressed him in robe and turban, he would laugh them off. He does not claim the race of Buddhas; and his one incense is the smoke of his incessant Piedmont. He talks more of Behaviorism, Astronomy and Mechanics than of what is commonly called religion. And he believes in literally nothing. *Nothing that is,* I mean. This is what makes him so detached. He knows all the scriptures from the Mahābhārata to Hart Crane, and he is detached from them all.

Even Buddha believed in the world enough to cry against it, to invent harsh disciplines to combat it. Not Orage. He despises the world so well that he is at peace with it wholly. See him by the hearth, smoking, sipping his liqueur, utterly charming his young hostess, and you will understand the superiority of his unworldiness over a mere Buddha's. Orage accepts the casual graces of the flesh, as doubtless Buddha accepted a springtime zephyr blowing in his face. Orage would no more refuse the pleasures of metropolitan New York, than a Hindu ascetic would decline a sunset.

His sensuous hospitality is the sign of his contempt. Even so, his boy face is the counterfeit of candor; and his language, which for fluent clarity has few peers in England, weaves a mist about him. Orage knows not alone the Pali Canon, but as well the Jesuits and Machiavelli. He barbs you with his words; he swathes and soothes you with his perhaps too unctuous manner—and himself glides by.

Thus, he glided from England—shrugged it quite out of his life, leaving in London Town the smoke of his adventures and the sparks of his electric passage. The Puritan Socialism of Bernard Shaw—dear Shaw who takes liquor, meat, tobacco, coffee, tea and women so seriously that he does not take 'em at all—was not for Orage. Shaw stayed on in England: Orage—who takes 'em all—has come to our wider land.

The man's life and mind is so very full of shifts that I'm justified in shifting metaphors to catch him. Thus: there is light in him, yet he has no heat. He does not push, he invades. You grow aware of him, as you might of a scentless gas when it had filled your lungs—or of a knife so edged that when it cut you, you endured no pain.

And here at last is the key which will unlock him. You recall the pin with which the great Jacques Loeb so wondrously pricked female sea-urchins into fecundity, without benefit of the male? Orage is such a fecundating pin. Neither creative nor intellectually profound, he is both since he has spent his life pricking men and women into fecundity.

This is what he did in England with Socialism, with Theosophy, with his magazine, with Freud. Until these pins grew dull. And until London grew dull. Gurgieff replenished him with sharpness. And then he came to us. Does he love us? Does he want to save our souls because he loves us? What was Loeb's sentiment toward his dear sea-urchins?

C. Hartley Grattan (review date 11 June 1930)

SOURCE: Grattan, C. Hartley. "The Mahabharata Blues." *The Nation* 130, no. 3388 (11 June 1930): 684-86.

[*In the following negative review of Orage's* The Art of Reading, *Grattan finds few ideas of lasting import despite Orage's reputation.*]

A. R. Orage has a vast reputation for profundity, and indeed is more than a literary critic in the eyes of his intimates: he is a sage. But I fail to see what it is that so interests our Columbuses of the spirit, for I can find nothing in the man except an Englishman who happens to be a fairly interesting critic. And it would be a gross bit of flattery to say that as a critic he deserves the majuscule.

This latest book of his [*The Art of Reading*] is made up of selected excerpts from literary notes originally printed in the *New Age*. It is amusingly miscellaneous, and whoever tried to get some order into the chaos did not do a very good job. In fact the book would have been just as interesting if it had not been marked off into sections, and more interesting if the labor so expended had gone into dating the excerpted passages. Fortunately Orage knows how to write, and however they are presented his remarks have point. They were, most of them, written controversially, and they still bite and sting. They make good literary paragraphs.

Of course in a book made up of paragraphs the number of ideas which the author presents is large, but with a fair degree of accuracy it may be said that Orage's principal beliefs are these: (1) that the first duty of a literary critic is that he study texts; (2) that style is the man; (3) that biography and literary gossip are a plague and a nuisance; (4) that most current literature is journalism; (5) that we have gone as far as we can with the intelligence, and what we now need is to draw upon some other human faculties for knowing; (6) that Western European literature is hopelessly dry and uninteresting and needs to be revived by contact with a radically new fecundating force, which force, in his opinion, is bound to be the "Mahabharata."

(1) No one in his right senses would deny that Mr. Orage is quite correct in insisting that the business of criticism is the study of the texts of literature. (2) In his effort to prove that style is the man Mr. Orage carries his dogma to absurd extremes, even deducing the moral character of a writer from the nature of his prose. (3) His anxiety that the text be studied leads him into an excessive depreciation of biographical fact. So far does he go in this direction that my impulse is to defend even literary gossip rather than admit the validity of Orage's strictures. (4) Calling what one doesn't happen to like "journalism" is a quite popular dodge, but so overworked as to be unimpressive, especially when one's author writes: ". . . popular writers (I mean journalists) like Zola, Bourget, Maurice Barrès, and André Gide . . ." (5) I have many times lately had occasion to say that I do not agree that intelligence has yet proved itself an incompetent instrument for solving the problems facing mankind. And certainly when the appeal is from intelligence to mysticism, true or false, one cannot but draw back with reasonably polite disdain. (6) Orage's

appeal to the "Mahabharata" as the body of literature which is to bring in a Western European renaissance leaves one pretty cold, since it is obvious that his reason for thinking so is its mystical content.

Together with these major ideas one finds in Orage a host of minor notions which are even less appealing. He makes a monotonous appeal to tradition. For instance, he writes that a "critic's principles of judgment should be the established principles of the world's literature," and on another occasion makes reference to "the established laws of literature." What are these "laws" beyond such elementary ideas as the necessity for communication, the revelation of original insight before the writer deserves the honor of praise, and others of the kind? So long as they remain undefined they are concealed blackjacks for knocking out the unsuspecting aspirant. Orage is a linguistic imperialist, holding that anything written in the so-called English language must be judged by English standards. This is a curious notion to find in a man like Orage, but it is there. At bottom every Englishman is a nationalistic patriot and most of them are imperialists. Orage talks too much about the common and vulgar (like an Englishman!) on the one hand, and the noble on the other, that is, he is a snob in his thinking and has never analyzed these terms to discover that they are survivals from a feudalistic social situation and have a distinctly snobbish connotation when used today.

Mr. Orage's reputation as a sage seems to rest on two pillars: first, his constant reference to Sanskrit writings, and, second, his devotion to "psychological exercises," whatever they may be. There is, it is alleged, an aura which hangs about him, and his mere presence plus the utterance of a few commonplace words is enough to change the course of one's life. By way of illustration I may refer the reader to Margaret Anderson's "My Thirty Years' War," pages 268-270. In any case, the point is that Mr. Orage is a pleasant fellow, well read in literature, who has a weakness for the esoteric and the vague. He makes a pretty obvious appeal to the soft spot in the American mentality, the spot that allows men like Count Keyserling to flourish in this country.

It is not at all curious, I think, that but two American critics, so far as I know, would acknowledge the influence of Mr. Orage: Gorham B. Munson and, with a chuckle in his beard, Ernest Augustus Boyd.

F. R. Leavis (review date December 1935)

SOURCE: Leavis, F. R. "The Orage Legend." *Scrutiny* 4, no. 3 (December 1935): 319.

[*In the following review, Leavis believes that given Orage's powerful influence and literary standing,* Selected Essays and Critical Writings of A. R. Orage *is disappointing for its lack of originality and critical thinking.*]

[*Selected Essays and Critical Writings of A. R. Orage*] will be opened with some eagerness by those whose acquaintance with the *New English Weekly* leaves them wondering over the legend of A. R. Orage. They will hope to find some explanation of the influence he is said to have wielded and the enormous impression he appears to have made in distinguished quarters. They will be disappointed. This selection from Orage's writings was, no doubt, undertaken as an act of piety, but it will not help to prolong his reputation. For what it exhibits to us is a mind of no distinction or force of any kind. There is a certain pontifical egotism as of a would-be Arnold Bennett, but Orage has none of the liveliness and vigour that make *Books and Persons,* Bennett's best journalism, still enjoyable. In fact, he shows here as a very poor journalist, while certainly offering no grounds for being taken seriously as a thinker or critic. He does indeed offer evidence of unusually wide reading (for a journalist), and he accosts with assurance a wide range of topics. But his air of cogency and incisiveness is not even superficially convincing; the effect is lame, limp and dull. He clearly thinks he is thinking, and as clearly doesn't know what thinking is—which, of course, is the almost inevitable result of a journalistic career, however fine the natural endowment the journalist may have started with, and however high the level at which he is supposed to work.

That Orage had some compelling personal quality we are forced, by the nature of his reputation, to conclude. Yet on the evidence of the *New English Weekly* it is difficult to see why he should have been reputed a brilliant editor, even. Was what followed on that prolonged inaugural fanfare anything but a pitiful flop? One remembers a good contributor or two, but that is all. And it appeared that Orage was ready to encourage the most brassily empty young careerist.

Perhaps you have to be a Social Crediter to appreciate him.

Samuel Hynes (essay date 1968)

SOURCE: Hynes, Samuel. "Orage and the *New Age.*" In *Edwardian Occasions: Essays on English Writing in the Early Twentieth Century,* pp. 39-47. New York: Oxford University Press, 1972.

[*In the following essay, originally published in 1968, Hynes finds that despite Orage's personal failings, he was ultimately a successful editor who published works from some of the most groundbreaking and original thinkers of the day.*]

Alfred Orage was a man who, as Shaw observed, 'did not belong to the successful world'. He was an editor who never ran a profitable paper, a socialist who backed Guild Socialism against the Fabians, an economist who preached Social Credit against the Keynesians, a literary critic who found *Ulysses* repellent and disliked the poems of Yeats, a mystic who expected the Second Coming. In thirty years of public life he never supported a winning cause, or profited from a losing one; the movements that consumed his energies are dead, and so are the journals that he edited, and the books that he wrote.

Yet when Orage died in 1934 he was remembered, and mourned, by many men more celebrated than he. The memorial number of the *New English Weekly* (of which he was the founder and first editor) included elegiac notes from Eliot, Chesterton, Shaw, A. E., Pound, Wells, Augustus John, Richard Aldington, Herbert Read, Middleton Murry, G. D. H. Cole, Frank Swinnerton, Edwin Muir, and St John Irvine, all expressing a sense of loss, and all for different reasons. Eliot praised the literary critic, A. E. the *guru,* Pound the economist; others admired Orage's brilliance as an editor, his flair for discovering talent, his prose style, his disinterestedness, his obstinacy. There is no doubt that to his contemporaries Orage was important; the question is, what importance, if any, remains?

One might say, first of all, that Orage is important as a representative of a type—the lower-middle-class provincial intellectual who turned up in considerable numbers around the beginning of this century and gave a new thrust and tone to English literary life. He belongs, that is, with Wells and Bennett and Lawrence. And he had all the characteristics of the type; he was learned but half-educated, arrogant and quick to take offence, charming but humourless, grimly serious about art and ideas ('a judge of literature cannot afford to indulge in witticisms', he said, and he never did). He was extremely susceptible to conversion, and it could be said of him, as Wells remarked of Nietzsche, that he was so constituted that to get an idea was to receive a revelation. He had many revelations, and like Wells and Lawrence he had a messianic itch to turn his revelations into dogmas. Part radical reformer and part heterodox evangelist, he helped to give Edwardian intellectual life its characteristic tone of strenuous but sombre zeal.

Orage is most representative of his type in the variety of his enthusiasms. Like many another man of his time he had gone to the two sources of Victorian values—science and liberalism—and had found them bankrupt.

> Spencer and Darwin had mechanized the world [he wrote] and carried the industrial revolution into thought. Tennyson on his lawn had prettified it and hung it with paper garlands. But nothing could conceal the fact that the new world was repellent and that *nothing* was better than the only certainty promised by it.

For a born believer like Orage, such nihilism was not in fact possible, and he turned instead to newer, less orthodox systems in search of values. In his earlier years he was a Theosophist, a Nietzschean, and a Fabian Socialist; later he tried psychoanalysis, Social Credit, and Gurdjieff's 'institute' at Fontainebleau. Some of his spiritual restlessness one must attribute to the temper of the time, but the eccentric forms in which it was expressed is a function of the type; a man like Orage, rooted neither in a traditional education nor in a fixed social role, will regard society and its ideas as infinitely revisable because he has no stake in either. And he will set few limits on the intellectual instruments that he employs to re-build society and its ideas so that they will include him.

Orage's own roots were in Yorkshire, and in poverty. His father was an improvident schoolmaster who died when his son was a year old, and his mother supported her family by taking in washing. Alfred, the clever child of the family, was encouraged by the local squire, who sent him to a teachers' training college. He became, like Lawrence, a schoolmaster, and settled in Leeds. There he joined the Theosophical Society, the Fabian Society, and a 'Plato Group', and helped to found the Leeds branch of the Independent Labour Party and the Leeds Arts Club. This is a remarkable range of intellectual activities for a provincial city in the 1890s, but for Orage it was insufficient. In 1906 he left Leeds, his teaching career, and his wife, and went up to London to become a full-time intellectual.

In London Orage entered into political activities, and became at once two kinds of socialist: he joined the Gilds Restoration League, and he re-joined the Fabian Society. His intentions as a socialist are made clear in a letter that he wrote to Wells in July 1906:

> I beg to enclose for your consideration a draft of the objects of a *Gilds Restoration League.* You have, I know, advocated at the Fabian Society and elsewhere a propaganda of Socialism among the middle classes. The main objection to Socialism which I have found amongst those classes is to its materialism. This, of course, is due to the accident that Socialism has been largely bound up with trades unionism. Which in its turn has been necessarily an economic protestant movement. Thus the real obstacle to middle class conversion to Socialism is the fear that it may involve government by trades union officials.
>
> The defect of the Trades Union movement is felt however quite as much by many Socialists as by non-Socialists. Most of the artists and craftsmen I have met are in favour of the Labour Programme on grounds of Justice but *not* on grounds of art. As explained in the enclosed draft the Arts and Crafts Movement while really as much a social reform movement as trades unionism, has nevertheless kept itself since Morris' day aloof from actual politics. And this absence of the artists and craftsmen *as* artists from the Socialist movement really accounts for the objections raised by the middle classes. The object of the proposed *Gilds Restoration League* is to bring about a union between the economic aims of

the Trades Unionists and the aesthetic aims of the craftsmen. Hitherto, the collectivist proposals have been designed solely to make economic poverty impossible; it is necessary to design them not only to make economic but also aesthetic poverty impossible. This, of course, would involve a considerable modification of the usual Collectivist formulas, on the lines, I think, sketched in your *Modern Utopia.* However, I am proposing to issue the enclosed in printed form and over a wide area during the coming autumn: and to call together all those who are interested for the purpose of discussing the best methods of procedure.

> As a member of the Fabian Society, I should have been glad to see that Society take up the present propaganda; but I am afraid the major part of the Fabians is too rigidly bound to the collectivist formulas to make such a hope practicable.

This William-Morrisy mixture of romantic medievalism and aestheticism may strike one as improbable, and as altogether incompatible with the statistical rationalism of the Fabian Society, but socialism in 1906 was a slumgullion of fads and dissensions that could accommodate any view, so long as it was unconventional. It was, Orage later recalled,

> a cult, with affiliations in directions now quite disowned—with theosophy, art and crafts, vegetarianism, the 'simple life', and almost, one might say, with the musical glasses. Morris had shed a medieval glamour over it with his stained-glass *News from Nowhere,* Edward Carpenter had put it into sandals, Cunninghame Graham had mounted it upon an Arab steed to which he was always saying a romantic farewell. Keir Hardie had clothed it in a cloth cap and a red tie. And Bernard Shaw, on behalf of the Fabian Society, had hung it with innumerable jingling epigrammatic bells—and cap. My brand of socialism was, therefore, a blend or, let us say, an anthology of all these, to which from my personal predilections and experience I added a good practical knowledge of working classes, a professional interest in economics which led me to master Marx's *Das Kapital* and an idealism fed at the source—namely Plato.

If this socialist anthology seems an odd account of a Fabian, one need only remind oneself that the society began as The Fellowship of the New Life, a front-parlour discussion group that included communists, spiritualists, psychic researchers and single taxers, and that for a long time it remained receptive to members from the queer fringes of radicalism.

Orage's conception of his role in the Fabian Society became clear very quickly; he was to be a leader of the philosophical and aesthetic wing. With his friend Holbrook Jackson he created the Fabian Arts Group, with the ostensible aim of making an appeal to 'minds that remained unmoved by the ordinary Fabian attitude', and of providing 'a platform for the discussion of the more subtle relationships of man to society which had been brought to the front in the works of such modern philosopher-artists as Nietzsche, Ibsen, Tolstoy, and

Bernard Shaw'. One might think that the Fabian leaders, faced with this frank contempt for their methods and opinions, would have discouraged Orage, but instead they encouraged him to buy a paper. In the spring of 1907 Orage and Jackson raised enough money to buy the *New Age,* a failing weekly of uncertain convictions and no circulation, and the *Fabian News* announced the birth of a new socialist journal, to be run strictly 'on Fabian Lines'. If the Fabians had paused to consider the sources of Orage's funds, they might have viewed the birth of his paper with less confidence; he had got £500 from Shaw, but the other £500 had come from a theosophical banker in the City. This curiously mixed parentage one may take as symbolical; for from birth the *New Age* was at best a bastard socialist.

The *New Age* gives Orage another kind of importance. He edited it, almost without help, for fifteen years. During those years he published a more impressive list of contributors than any other British journal: among more than 700 were Belloc, Bennett, Bierce, Brooke, Burns, Carpenter, Chesterton, Cunninghame Graham, Havelock Ellis, Ervine, Galsworthy, Gogarty, Harris, Hulme, John, Mansfield, Murry, Pound, Herbert Read, Sassoon, Shaw, Sickert, Swinnerton, Webb, Wells, West, and Zangwill; art work reproduced included drawings by Epstein, Gaudier-Brzeska, Wyndham Lewis, Sickert, and Picasso. 'Great editorship', Orage said, 'is a form of creation, and the great editor is measured by the number and quality of the writers he brings to birth—or to ripeness.' By this standard, Orage was the greatest English editor of this century; nowadays, when that title is often awarded to Ford Madox Ford for his *English Review,* it is worth noting that Ford ran his review for little more than a year, lost £5,000, and was fired, while Orage kept the *New Age* going for fifteen years with an initial investment one-fifth the size of Ford's, and resigned. Ford was brilliant, but Orage lasted.

Orage's notion of a great editor says nothing about ideas, principles, or editorial policy, and the paper that he edited had little intellectual coherence; it was, like its editor's socialism, an anthology of views. It first appeared as 'an Independent Socialist Weekly' with impeccable socialist credentials—the first issue carried letters of congratulation from Sidney Webb, Edward Pease (the Secretary of the Fabian Society), and Prince Kropotkin. But it also contained an editorial that those congratulators must have read with sinking hearts. 'Socialism as a progressive will', the editors observed,

> is neither exclusively democratic nor aristocratic, neither anarchist nor individualist. Each of the great permanent moods of human nature, as imperfectly reflected in the hierarchy of society, has its inalienable right to a place in the social pyramid.
>
> Believing that the darling object and purpose of the universal will of life is the creation of a race of supremely and progressively intelligent beings, *The New*

Age will devote itself to the serious endeavour to cooperate with the purposes of life, and to enlist in that noble service the help of serious students of the new contemplative and imaginative order.

This untidy mixture of socialism, Nietzscheanism, and mysticism is a fair expression of Orage's untidy thought, and the journal that he edited was similarly eclectic. It published, for example, the reactionary philosophical essays of T. E. Hulme as well as the heretical socialism of Wells, and found space both for Ford's support of women's suffrage and Orage's fierce opposition to it. If it had an editorial policy at all, it was simply an open-door policy. 'One used to write to *The New Age*', Belloc later recalled, 'simply because one knew it to be the only paper in which the truth with regard to our corrupt policies, or indeed with regard to any powerful evil, could be told. And when Hulme was asked why he wrote for such a radical journal, he replied simply, 'Because they'll print me'. The *New Age* may have set out to be an 'independent socialist weekly', but the emphasis was on 'independent', and one can see why the Webbs soon gave up hope of seeing it run on Fabian lines, and founded the *New Statesman* to serve that purpose.

The greatest appeal of such a farraginous chronicle was to people like Orage, provincial intellectuals in search of a faith, and it is not surprising that such people made up a substantial number of both its contributors and its readers. The regular writers—the now forgotten journalists who attended Orage's salon in the basement of the Chancery Lane ABC—were mostly, like Orage, poor intellectual outsiders. And the subscribers included people like young D. H. Lawrence, who shared the paper with the Eastwood intelligentsia and liked it more for its literature than for its politics. One may guess that it was far better read in Eastwood than in Westminster, because it meant more there; it was the voice of rebellion and liberation, not clear, perhaps, but loud.

This point of authorship and audience may in part account for the fact that the *New Age,* for all its vigour and occasional distinction, seems to have had little impact on the direction of English thought in its time. But a more important factor is that it had little direction itself. Eclecticism may stimulate, but it does not move, and the *New Age* left behind vivid impressions of its editor's personality, but no impressions of its policies.

When Orage left the journal in 1922, he left a remarkable record of achievements. He had run a weekly for fifteen years virtually without capital. He had persuaded most of the important writers of the time to write for him, and to write for nothing (Arnold Bennett, that most cash-conscious of writers, wrote a weekly piece in the *New Age* for eighteen months without payment). He had not only published Ezra Pound, but had made him into a music critic. He had encouraged many young writers, and had published the first works of a number who later made names for themselves, including Katherine Mansfield, Richard Aldington, and Middleton Murry. He had taught and demonstrated the importance of good writing, the style, as he called it, of 'brilliant common sense'. But most important, he had brought new ideas to a new audience, and had helped to redefine the English intellectual class.

Having said so much, one should note also the *New Age*'s limitations. It never published an excellent poem, rarely a good story. It opened its pages to a good deal of rubbish, simply because it was *new* rubbish. In the post-war years Orage indulged his strong mystical streak, and published the incomprehensible writings of a Serbian prophet called Mitrinović; at the same time he was giving space to Major Douglas and Social Credit, and the result was a concentrated unreadability that diminished Orage's reputation, and nearly destroyed the paper.

Orage's own contributions were sometimes examples of the brilliant common sense that he preached, and these won him the admiration of distinguished contemporaries like Chesterton, who described Orage as 'a man who wrote fine literature in the course of writing fighting journalism', and Eliot, who admired him both as a leader-writer and a critic. For Orage these elements—the literary quality, the editorial vigour, and the critical judgment—were not distinct, and his ideal writing was a prose that would combine them all. Recalling his **'Readers and Writers'** columns in the *New Age,* which he wrote weekly for seven or eight years, Orage wrote:

> My original design was to treat literary events from week to week with the continuity and policy ordinarily applied to comments on current events; that is to say, with equal seriousness and from a similarly more or less fixed point of view as regards both means and ends. This design involved of necessity a freedom of expression distinctly out of fashion . . .

When he achieved this goal, he was very good indeed, and his two books of these essays—***Readers and Writers*** and ***The Art of Reading***—do give a lively sense of the literary politics of those years. But the art of the leader-writer is a transitory one, and it is not surprising that Orage's essays are not read now; for by treating literature as current events, he had guaranteed his own swift obsolescence. But even when they were written many of his pieces must have seemed unworthy of his talents, for his doctrine of free expression encouraged vigorous writing at the expense of judgment and restraint, and he was capable of crude brutality in his criticisms, and of windy vagueness in his philosophizing. As his causes failed and his voice lost authority, he became more and more negative in his own defence, and less readable.

Orage's last years, after his resignation from the *New Age,* are puzzling and sad. He became a disciple of Gurdjieff and laboured for him for a year at Fontainebleau. Then he went to New York as Gurdjieff's representative and stayed six years, teaching and raising funds for the 'institute'. In 1931 he returned to England to found a new paper, the *New English Weekly,* which he edited until his death.

The *New English Weekly* clearly set out to be another *New Age,* and was greeted as such by the dozens of old admirers who wrote their testimonies for the first issue—A. E., Epstein, Henry Nevinson, Swinnerton, Herbert Read, Gogarty, Havelock Ellis, Eric Gill, T. Sturge Moore. These were the readers, and in most cases the writers, of Orage's first paper, and what they hoped for was more of the same. To a considerable degree they got it: Pound returned with Cantos and economic theories, Major Douglas contributed his own economic essays, A. J. Penty, from the Gild Restoration days, was still around offering alternatives to communism. But the times had changed, and so had Orage; his mind was fixed on economic issues, and economics, even in the 1930s, could not make a paper lively. He continued to demonstrate his good eye for promising young writers—one finds Walter Allen, Basil Bunting, Erskine Caldwell, Emily Hahn, Storm Jameson, Stephen Potter, and Michael Roberts in early issues—and he had improved his taste in poetry (or his advisers) remarkably, with poems by David Gascoyne, Dylan Thomas, and William Carlos Williams, but he never found a formula, or an audience, that would make the paper succeed.

Looking back over Orage's life, one can see that his need to follow was as great as his need to lead, and that his submission to Gurdjieff's beliefs and discipline was inevitable. But to the unconverted the spectacle of a strong mind capitulating is depressing, and Orage's later life seems a waste of a lively intelligence. In his memoir of Orage, Eliot remarked his 'restless desire for the absolute'; the desire one may call a strength in Orage's character, but the restlessness dissipated that strength, drove him aimlessly from faith to faith, and made his life, in the end, incoherent. 'Gurdjieff once told me', Orage said, 'that he knew my ambition. He said I wanted to be one of the "elder brothers" of the human race, but that I had not the ability it required.' That observation will do for Orage's epitaph.

Louise Welch (essay date spring 1969)

SOURCE: Welch, Louise. "A. R. Orage." *Gurdjieff International Review* 2, no. 3 (spring 1999): 1-2.

[*In the following essay, originally published in 1969, Welch details Orage's expertise in a myriad of fields while simultaneously demonstrating the esteem with which he was held by many literary figures of note.*]

The brilliant editor of the *New Age,* regarded by T. S. Eliot as London's best literary critic of his time, abandons his journal and is next heard of cleaning stables in the farmyard of a French chateau. The magnet is a then little-known Greek named Gurdjieff, called by some a mystic and by others a magician. How could that departure from his lifework be understood by the friends of Alfred Richard Orage in 1923?

"He was a man who could be both perfectly right and wholly wrong," said Eliot, "but when he was wrong one respected him all the more, as a man who was seeking the essential things. . . ."

Another *New Age* writer, Ezra Pound, said, "Orage's impersonality was his greatness, and the breadth of his mind was apparent in the speed with which he threw over a cumbrous lot of superstitions, and a certain number of fairly good ideas, for a new set of better ones."

The light thrown on the mind of Orage by his friends and critics tells us more about the essential man than such details as his birth in rural Yorkshire in January 1873 and his effect on his school teachers quite early in his life. At twelve, the excellence of his mind and his sympathetic personal qualities so impressed the county squire that he helped young Alfred to go to teachers' training college, where he swallowed, absorbed and improved upon the material he was to use for the next ten years in teaching children.

It is not surprising to learn from an old friend of Orage's that his pupils competed for his attention rather than he for theirs. The fertilizing gift, that talent of his for calling the creative impulse in others, had its effect on people of all ages.

If temperament is destiny, there was something fated in his decision to marry, when he knew that the price he would have to pay was giving up the education at Oxford that he desired and was promised. In the end, it may have been a good thing to have lost a conventional education, for that might conceivably have fettered an intelligence so original, dynamic and inquiring, a mind that abhorred fuzzy thinking and defined reason as the sum of all functions, not the sterile, unconnected activity of the head alone. "A man," Orage said, "can only think as deeply as he feels."

"To see a thing in the germ, this I call intelligence," the Irish poet, AE[1], quotes Laotze, and then remarks that Orage had such intelligence. "Almost everywhere I explored in his mind," AE says, "I found the long corridors lit." It was probably that trait more than any other that drew the subtlest and best endowed writers of the day to the *New Age,* often for little or no pay. To mention a few of them, there were Sir Herbert Read, G. K. Chesterton, Storm Jameson, Arnold Bennett, Hilaire Belloc, Edwin Muir, A. J. Penty and P. L. Travers; even Bernard Shaw congratulated himself on his good judgment in contributing some five hundred pounds to help start the publication of the *New Age.*

In trying to understand a mind so unlike his own, yet to him sympathetic, Chesterton said that Orage, whose literary style he admired, managed somehow to avoid the awful fate of looking like a literary man. He added that Orage aimed at "doing something rather than writing something . . . He was in the true sense a man of action. . . ." At the same time Chesterton regretted that English as good as Orage's might disappear into the files of the *New Age.*

Certainly the true works of Orage can not be limited to the literary. His passionate interest in cleaning up the kitchen of economics began with his eloquent advocacy of Guild Socialism, a socialism not concerned merely with improving the material lot of men but one that asked for a high quality of skill in the goods produced and for conditions allowing inner development in the producers. Later, with energy and brilliant common sense, he supported the ideas of Social Credit as put forth by Major Douglas. To those who followed the thought of Orage during this period, it is now quite evident that many of the most practical and desirable solutions recommended today by economists, mirror Orage's suggestions made in the *New Age* and the *New English Weekly* long in advance of his time.

His foresight was observable not only in economics, a field that interested and engaged him because he felt it to be the necessary ground work for a life concerned with more inclusive and essential interests—the life of art and ideas. The next powerful influence was to be the philosophy and metaphysics of the East, an influence, Orage held, that could bring a much needed renaissance of thought and feeling to the Western world. *The Bhagavad Gita* and the *Mahabharata* become, as his biographer, Philip Mairet says, "vital and permanent influences in his mental life."

But his search for truth was not restricted to Eastern teachings. He refused nothing that promised enlightenment. He studied the theories of Freud and Jung, characteristically enlarging the context by comparing them with the ideas of Thomas Aquinas, the Hermeticists and Patanjali. Of the articles Orage wrote in this connection, Mairet says, "How good they are, even now!" He tells us that Orage discussed the new psychology with a number of distinguished psychiatrists and physicians who agreed with him that a psychoanalysis might be worse than useless without a psychosynthesis. They formed a group to explore this idea.

It may have been the need for this psychosynthesis that drew Orage to the lectures of P. D. Ouspensky, who had appeared in London, and finally to Ouspensky's teacher,

G. I. Gurdjieff. As one who had investigated and practiced the soundest ideas available in the world of metaphysics, Orage's touchstone was sensitive to the truth he needed; as he said simply to his secretary, who regarded his leaving the *New Age* as the abandonment of all his work, "I am going to find God."

He was seven years with Gurdjieff, much of which he spent in the United States, where he was loved and appreciated. There, as he said, he experienced what a true brotherhood might be. When he returned to England to found the *New English Weekly,* it was his intention to make it a vehicle for important ideas—metaphysical, psychological as well as economic—including of course those of the Gurdjieff teaching he had spent so many intensive years studying. In that last period he kept a journal, some of which was published; and three essays from it are included here, in addition to the essay **"On Love,"** which he wrote after he had met Gurdjieff.[2] His comment that it was "freely adapted from the Tibetan" is, of course, Orage's way of gently leading the reader to an impersonal consideration of the ideas the essay contains—quite apart from his own preference for anonymity.

"On Love" has already become something of a classic. It will no doubt find additional literary acclaim before the end of this 'Age of Aquarius.' It has already quietly made its way into the minds and hearts of many, in the role Orage would most have wanted—as an influence in the direction of individual inner growth.

Notes

1. George W. Russell. Eds.

2. These three essays as originally published in the *Aryan Path,* along with a fourth, are included in this issue under Orage's name as "My Note Book." The essay "On Love" is much anthologized and readily available. Eds.

Tom H. Gibbons (essay date 1973)

SOURCE: Gibbons, Tom H. "Art For Evolution's Sake: Alfred Orage." In *Rooms in the Darwin Hotel: Studies in English Literary Criticism and Ideas 1880-1920,* pp. 98-126. Nedlands, Australia: University of Western Australia Press, 1973.

[*In the following essay, Gibbons charts Orage's flirtations with many radical movements of the early twentieth century: from socialism, vorticism and Fabianism to his ultimate alignment with G. I. Gurdjieff's brand of mysticism.*]

Alfred James Orage, familiarly known as Alfred *Richard* Orage, was born on 22 January 1873, at Dacre in Yorkshire. When his father died soon afterwards, the widow and her four children returned to Fenstanton, the village in Huntingdonshire from which the family originated. The family was so poor that Orage could not have continued to attend the village school without the help of the local squire, who also helped him to attend a teachers training college at Abingdon, near Oxford, during 1892 and part of 1893.

In 1893 Orage went as an elementary-school teacher to Leeds, in Yorkshire. He had been converted to socialism during his time at college, and once in Leeds helped form a local branch of the newly founded Independent Labour Party. Between 1895 and 1897 he wrote a weekly 'Bookish Causerie' for Keir Hardie's weekly socialist magazine *The Labour Leader.* In 1896 he married, and in or about the same year joined the local branch of the Theosophical Society, of which he became a leading member. In 1900 he met the young Holbrook Jackson, who introduced him to the work of Nietzsche, and in the same year the two men joined forces with the architect Arthur J. Penty to form the lively and successful Leeds Art Club.

In 1905, having taught for twelve years in Leeds, Orage resigned from his position, left his wife, and went to London. Here he stayed for a time with Arthur Penty, who had preceded him to London, and tried to live by serious journalism. During 1906 and 1907 he published articles in *The Monthly Review, The Theosophical Review* and *The Contemporary Review.* His first book, **Friedrich Nietzsche: The Dionysian Spirit of the Age,** was published in 1906. Two more books were published in 1907: **Nietzsche in Outline and Aphorism,** and **Consciousness: Animal, Human, and Superman.** The two works on Nietzsche were the first systematic introductions to Nietzsche's thought to be published in book form in England.

During these early years in London Orage also attempted to found a Gilds [*sic*] Restoration League with Arthur Penty. This venture failed, but Orage and Holbrook Jackson, who had also come to London, succeeded in founding a Fabian Arts Group. This group was intended as a rallying-ground for socialists who thought the arts of fundamental importance, and who were consequently opposed to the bureaucratic Fabian socialism of Sidney and Beatrice Webb and their supporters.

Early in 1907 Orage and Jackson bought an existing periodical called *The New Age* for £1,000, half of which was put up by George Bernard Shaw. Orage and Jackson became joint editors, but Jackson resigned after a few months as a result of disagreement over policy. Under Orage's editorship *The New Age* quickly established itself as a leading journal of political, literary and artistic debate. Established writers such as Wells and Shaw contributed free of charge, and articles by the English

Nietzscheans (J. M. Kennedy, A. M. Ludovici and Oscar Levy) appeared regularly. Always eager to encourage new talent, Orage was the first editor to publish work by Richard Aldington, F. S. Flint, Katherine Mansfield, Edwin Muir and Middleton Murry. According to one of his letters Ezra Pound owed his life to Orage's financial support.[1] Orage was also the first editor to publish the work of T. E. Hulme, and between 1912 and 1914 *The New Age* regularly reproduced cubist and vorticist paintings and drawings.

The New Age was always a journal of discussion and debate, in whose pages Orage himself often disputed with his own editorial staff. In the first three years of his editorship its policy appears to have been mainly that of providing a forum in which the many varieties of current socialist opinion could be expressed. After 1910, however, in a period of rapidly mounting social and political violence, *The New Age* became increasingly a vehicle for political and literary neo-feudalist views, and in 1912 it began to advocate guild-socialist policies editorially.

Although the outbreak of war in 1914 rendered the guild socialist movement virtually irrelevant, a National Guilds League was formed in April 1915, and *The New Age* continued as the official organ of the movement until this foundered through internal dissension in 1920. For some time before this happened, however, Orage's own interests had been turning in other directions. He had become increasingly involved in the Social Credit policies of Major C. H. Douglas, the mystical doctrines of P. D. Ouspensky, and the psychoanalytical doctrines of Freud. These changes of direction in Orage's thinking after the 1914-18 war are reflected in the changed subtitle of *The New Age*. Previously 'A Weekly Review of Politics, Literature, and Art', it became in January 1921 'A Socialist Review of Religion, Science, and Art'.

In 1922 the mystical teacher G. I. Gurdjieff arrived in London, and plans were made to found the Institute for the Harmonious Development of Man at Fontainebleau-Avon in France. In October 1922 Orage resigned from *The New Age* in order to join Gurdjieff at the Institute. In December of the following year he went to New York to lecture on the aims of the Institute, remaining in the United States in this capacity until 1930. During this period he published a series of retrospective articles entitled **'An Editor's Progress'** in *The New Age* for 1926, and two collections of his earlier weekly literary articles for *The New Age*: *Readers and Writers* (1922) and *The Art of Reading* (1930). His own contributions to *The New Age* between 1907 and 1922 had been as follows: **'Towards Socialism'** (ten articles in 1907); the mainly political **'Notes of the Week'** between 1909 and 1922; **'Unedited Opinions'** (a series of eighty-six Platonic dialogues, between 1909 and 1916); seven anti-feminist **'Tales for Men Only'** (1911, 1912, 1916); **'Readers and Writers',** a weekly article of literary reviews and comment which appeared between 1913 and 1921.

Orage returned to England in 1930, but did not resume editorship of *The New Age*. He decided to found a new periodical during the financial crisis of 1931, and *The New English Weekly* began publication in April 1932 as the organ of the Social Credit movement. Orage died in November 1934, and was succeeded as editor of *The New English Weekly* by Philip Mairet, his subsequent biographer. Among the many admiring letters on Orage published in the obituary number of *The New English Weekly* of 15 November 1934 was one by T. S. Eliot, who described him as being, during his editorship of *The New Age*, 'the best literary critic of that time in London'.

Orage's *Selected Essays and Critical Writings* were edited by Herbert Read and Denis Saurat and published posthumously in 1935. His *Political and Economic Writings* were edited by Montgomery Butchart and others, including T. S. Eliot, and published in the following year. His translation of Gurdjieff's *Meetings with Remarkable Men* was not published until 1962.

II

Socialism in the 1890s was no merely economic plan for the State-ownership of the means of production. As Orage described it in 1926 it was 'much more of a cult, with affiliations in directions now quite disowned—with theosophy, arts and crafts, vegetarianism, the "simple life," and almost . . . with the musical glasses. Morris had shed a mediaeval glamor over it with his stained-glass News from Nowhere. Edward Carpenter had put it into sandals . . .'[2]

Of these various affiliations and influences, the two most obvious in Orage's own early writings for *The Labour Leader* are those of the arts and crafts movement, and of Theosophy. As a follower of William Morris (and, behind Morris, of Carlyle and Ruskin), Orage holds the Liberal creed of commercial competition responsible for the decadence and disintegration of contemporary art and society. As a Theosophist he looks to spiritual evolution as a means of restoring wholeness to art and to social life.

Orage's unremitting campaign against social and literary decadence began in *The Labour Leader* in 1895, which was the year of Nordau's *Degeneration* and the Wilde trial. Reviewing a new American literary magazine entitled *Moods*, he writes as follows: 'America needs . . . a physician. It is down with the "yellow fever." The English "Yellow Book" has got cured just too late to stop the spread of the infection, and America has now its "Moods." The usual symptoms appear, things Weirdsley wonderful, impressionism, and weakness.'³ This decadence has not been brought about by the degenerate nature of individual artists, however, but by commercial competition:

> I do not believe in the absolute decadence and degenerateness of modern times. . . . But it is . . . only too obvious that the 'damnable commercialism which buys and sells all things' is sliming our literature and lowering for a while our standard of art. This degradation . . . is the natural outcome of the same spirit manifested in our system of economy, in science, in politics, and in life.⁴

It is commercial competition, according to Orage, which has caused some modern writers to go 'hopelessly astray . . . in the pursuit of mere commercial success', and as a consequence 'The high traditions of literature have fallen into the hands of men who betray them for thirty pieces of silver.' Although much modern literature is 'mere literary pathology, analysing, dissecting, diagnosing disease', this is the fault of the commercial system, which is itself 'an unnatural life which has brought about the conditions which our novelists describe'.⁵ Commercialism has also corrupted the standards of criticism, complains Orage in his obituary article on William Morris:

> Our system of competition, based on the degradation of the vast majority of mankind, has won us baubles which we fondly believe to be pearls of great price, but at the cost of works of priceless value, the best that human souls might do, in art, literature, craftsmanship, life, for whose loss no future age can forgive us, and for whose loss it is our shame that we can still forgive ourselves.⁶

In attacking a society based exclusively upon commercial competitiveness Orage reveals the direct influence of Morris. Elsewhere in his articles for *The Labour Leader* he reveals the Theosophical 'affiliations' of his socialism, making it clear that the sources of his guiding beliefs in Theosophy and evolution are mainly literary. Among those whom he describes as having helped to familiarize Western students with 'the "divine science" of the East' are not only Max Müller, Schopenhauer and the Theosophists, but Sir Edwin Arnold, Rudyard Kipling, the authoress Flora Steel, and, especially, Walt Whitman and Edward Carpenter.⁷

The basis of Orage's Theosophy is his belief in the concept of the universal self or world-soul, which he was to describe in 1907 as 'a perfectly similar underlying consciousness common to all living things, visible and invisible'. Orage was converted to this doctrine of the universal self by reading Edward Carpenter's *Towards Democracy* and Walt Whitman's *Leaves of Grass,* and it was Whitman who also confirmed his belief in mankind's evolutionary progress towards god-head. Whitman, says Orage, 'taught us plainly what the oldest Rig Vedas had mistily written, . . . that God himself is perfect man, and the goal of every speck of dust'.⁸

The critical applications of Orage's evolutionary mysticism are best seen in his two articles for *The Labour Leader* on Edward Carpenter's *Towards Democracy*. In the first of these he defends Carpenter's use of free verse on the grounds that it embodies the rhythms of the life which pervades the universe, and that it consequently enables the poet of democracy to integrate men more closely into the universal self to which he and they belong:

> to knit men closer with themselves and nature by expressing nature in man; to electrify and vitalise the dormant nerves which connect the heart of Nature with her outlying limbs; to express the universal in terms of humanity—this is the function of the poet of Democracy.⁹

It may not be immediately apparent that Orage is here proposing a social function for poetry: poetry creates social wholeness, knitting closer together men who have been disunified and set against each other by 'our system of competition'.

Although poetry has this extremely important function, Orage is reluctant to discuss the kind of meaning that it possesses. In his second article on Carpenter he defines poetry as 'the expression in words of the universal in man' and poetic rhythms as 'the embodiment in words of the movement of life'. These definitions are probably less important than the grounds upon which Orage justifies them. 'It will be said that these are vague phrases . . .', he comments. 'Vagueness, however, is inevitable from the very nature of great poetry; but it is the vagueness of [trying to discuss] the illimitable.'¹⁰ As will be seen in the next section of the present chapter, these views did not change when, after 1900, the thought of Nietzsche was added to the already diverse list of influences upon Orage's socialism. Great art was always to remain for Orage 'an expression of the illimitable', and though he was always a fervent advocate of great works of literature, holding them to be of the highest social importance, he was always reluctant to discuss their meaning in any detail.

Before his Nietzschean phase is discussed, it is worth remarking that the views put forward in 1896 by this twenty-three-year-old elementary-school teacher in his articles on Edward Carpenter, and published in an obscure socialist weekly, have certain basic similarities to those expressed some three years later by Arthur Symons in *The Symbolist Movement in Literature*. Orage's universal self is another name for the universal consciousness which Symons puts forward as 'the central secret of the mystics' in *The Symbolist Movement*. For both men, literature of the proper kind serves as a unifying force. 'What is Symbolism', asks Symons, 'if not an establishing of the links which hold the world together?'[11] For both men it is the *sounds* of poetry which achieve this unification by embodying the occult universal life which permeates all created things. As Orage puts it:

> if poetry is to express the 'Universal Idea', it must embody the 'Universal Idea': that is, it must be the counterpart in words of the universal in essence.

> . . . that rhythm most nearly approaches perfection which most nearly corresponds to the rhythm of life. Colour, form, and sound—all of which words may suggest—have their place also; and generally speaking the more perfect the form of poetry the more perfect its embodiment of the rhythm, colour, form, and sound of life.[12]

The difference between prose and poetry, according to Orage in the latter of these two articles, is that 'prose must have something to say, while poetry has only something to express'. Prose makes statements *about* life, in other words, while poetry embodies and expresses the universal life force itself.

III

In the third section of this chapter I discuss the ideas expressed by Orage in a number of books and articles published between 1902 and 1907, when he was responding enthusiastically to the doctrines of Nietzsche. I examine in turn Orage's highly evolutionistic views upon three inter-related topics: the coming of what Galton had called a 'highly gifted race of men', the place of this race in the socialist State of the future, and the rôle of the arts in furthering the development of this new society.

According to Holbrook Jackson it was a momentous occasion when he introduced Orage to the work of Nietzsche in the year 1900: 'did we not on that occasion build a bridge from the Orient to the Occident? You left behind you . . . a translation of the *Bhagavad Gita*; and you carried under your arm my copy of the first English version of *Thus spake Zarathustra*.'[13]

The occasion is a revealing one. It reveals of course that intelligent young Englishmen at the turn of the century were keenly interested in Indian mysticism and the thought of Nietzsche. The occasion is more neatly symbolic than at first appears, however, for the bridge was built from orient to occident and not in the reverse direction. Orage, like a number of his contemporaries, did not by any means abandon his existing beliefs under the influence of Nietzsche. Instead he adapted Nietzsche's views to a predominantly Theosophical view of things, presenting him as a mystic who was no longer consciously in sympathy with his own mysticism. No-one who really understands Nietzsche, he tells us, 'will doubt that behind all his apparent materialism there was a thoroughly mystical view of the world'.[14] On one oc-

casion he even went so far as to describe Nietzsche's doctrine of the will-to-power as 'perhaps the nearest Western approach to the intellectual formulation of *one* of the aspects of the mystical Trinity'.[15] Just as J. M. Kennedy saw Nietzsche as a second Benjamin Disraeli, so Orage (in company with Arthur Symons[16] and W. B. Yeats[17]) saw him as a second William Blake. '. . . he who has read *The Marriage of Heaven and Hell,* and grasped its significance', writes Orage, 'will have little to learn from the apostle of *Zarathustra*.'[18]

Similarly, Nietzsche's gospel of the superman was grafted by Orage onto notions of man's high evolutionary destiny which he had already derived from a variety of sources. His first mention of Nietzsche is in fact contained in an article on Lytton's *Zanoni* in *The Theosophical Review* for 1902. Here he approves of the desire of Mejnour, Zanoni's fellow magus, to create a 'mighty and numerous race' of superhuman occult adepts, even if this necessitates the sacrifice of thousands of aspirants for the sake of a single success. 'Such an ideal', writes Orage, 'can be paralleled perhaps in the work of a real man . . . Frederic Nietzsche; and the parallel is almost complete when one finds Mejnour saying of himself, "my art is to make man above mankind".'[19]

The superiority of the Nietzschean superman is not of course physical. 'Nowhere is Nietzsche to be taken less grossly than in his conception of power', writes Orage in his ***Nietzsche in Outline*** (1907). 'The men of power in his eyes are not the men of sinew and brawn, but men in whom the power of mastery over both themselves and others is greatest.'[20] Nor is the superman 'merely man writ large', he writes in his ***Friedrich Nietzsche*** (1906). 'It is probable . . . that new faculties, new modes of consciousness, will be needed, as the mystics have always declared; and that the differencing element of man and Superman will be the possession of these.'[21]

In his ***Consciousness: Animal, Human, and Superman*** (1907) he suggests that 'superman consciousness' will in fact be a continuous state of visionary ecstasy. In the course of evolution, animal consciousness has become 'folded' upon itself and produced human self-consciousness. A second evolutionary folding will by analogy produce the *ecstasis* of superconsciousness:

> superman, or . . . cosmic consciousness, is consciousness in three dimensions, or human consciousness folded upon itself . . . the typical product of [this] folding is to create another observer appearing to stand outside the human mind, as the human observer appears to stand outside the animal mind. If analogy is any guide, we may . . . say that the dominant characteristic of the superman state in relation to the human state is a standing outside, or ecstasis.[22]

In short, Orage's superman will be a mystic who has attained to a permanent condition of 'cosmic consciousness'. On balance he appears to owe less to Nietzsche than to the race of superhuman mystical adepts foreshadowed earlier for English readers by Bulwer Lytton and Madame Blavatsky.

Like his books on Nietzsche and superman consciousness, Orage's articles of 1906-07 on education, politics, and the arts and crafts movement are primarily devoted to the fostering of a new race of men of genius, to the encouragement of 'the few alone who give new significances to things'. In his two articles on education (**'Esprit de Corps in Elementary Schools'** and **'Discipline in Elementary Schools'**) he criticizes the 'appalling uniformity of schools and teachers' in State schools. In his article entitled **'Politics for Craftsmen'** he condemns the English socialist parties for their drift towards policies of State collectivism. All three articles strongly oppose standardization and social levelling, and call for measures to increase individualism. 'The hope of Europe lies in its great individuals', according to Orage, and they alone can check what he calls 'the devastations of democracy'.[23]

The socialist movement as a whole, he claims in **'Politics for Craftsmen'**, has betrayed 'the interests of artists, craftsmen and imaginative minds generally' by concentrating all its efforts on improving the economic conditions of the working class. He protests against this 'exclusive association of Socialism, which in its large sense is no less than the will to create a new order of society, with the partial and class-prejudiced ideals of the working man'.[24]

The inspiration of socialism is nothing less than the creation of a new civilization, states Orage in his series of articles entitled **'Towards Socialism'**, which appeared in *The New Age* during 1907. The improvement of purely economic conditions is no more than a preliminary to the accomplishment of this utopian task: 'Abolish poverty for us, and our men of genius will then begin their cyclopean task of building a civilisation worthy of the conquerors of titans.'[25] Great individuals are necessary to the creation of this new socialist civilization because men are led forward by such 'noble illusions' as religion, nationalism, beauty, honour and glory. These illusions are usually formed for them by the small number of men of creative imagination upon whom a civilization ultimately rests. 'Civilisation', says Orage, 'is no more than the possession by a people of individuals . . . capable of inspiring great enthusiasms, and of individuals . . . capable of being so inspired. The rest is all but leather and prunella.'[26]

In an article of 1907 entitled **'The New Romanticism'**, Orage equates these great individuals with the 'guardians', the élite class of Plato's ideal republic. Life is intolerable, he states, without some illusion to pursue, and the function of legislators is to provide the ma-

jority with a viable illusion. 'The question for legislators (I have Plato's guardians in my eye, Horatio) is which of the possible illusions is at once most necessary, most beneficent, and most enduring.'[27] Whether or not these great individuals were to constitute a definite aristocratic caste is a matter upon which Orage equivocates. In **'Politics for Craftsmen'** he rebukes the Labour Party for having no interest in a 'reconstructed society arranged in some such hierarchy of human values as Plato sketched and Mr. Wells has lately revived.' (The reference is to Wells's *A Modern Utopia,* which is governed by an aristocratic caste of so-called Samurai.) In **'Esprit de Corps in Elementary Schools'** Orage proposes 'that almost forbidden word aristocracy' as his possible alternative to the uniform and egalitarian society aimed at by the collectivists. 'Call it if you will', he says '. . . the Hierarchy. The idea at least is the same, namely the classification of children, schools, institutions, yes, the whole State, in the ancient Platonic way of iron and brass and silver and gold.'[28]

In **'Towards Socialism'** Orage appears to reverse these views, however, claiming that contemporary advocates of a new aristocracy have been misled. Mankind basically prefers 'all the horrors of freedom to the amenities of benevolent slavery', he says. 'Hence not only a hereditary aristocracy is ridiculous, inhuman, and in the long run impossible, but an aristocracy of intellect, character, or what not, as well.'[29] He makes it clear however that his ideal socialist state of the future is to be led by an evolutionary élite of noble minds. Socialism will provide increasing opportunities for the development of great creative individuals. These will command the service of the majority not by coercion, however, but by the beauty of their visionary ideas, and Orage looks forward to a 'State in which personal desire is poured out like wine in offering to the great lords of life'.[30]

That the 'great lords of life' come from *Zanoni* rather than *Zarathustra* is a point of minor interest. The major interest of Orage's élitism is twofold: it is entirely characteristic of the period 1880-1920 that evolution should be thought of as producing a new breed of men of genius, or great individuals, and it is equally characteristic that these new evolutionary notions should be used in support of proposals which were far from new, such as 'the ancient Platonic way'.

In his articles on Edward Carpenter's *Towards Democracy* Orage had claimed that poetry such as Carpenter's served a social purpose: that of bringing men closer together in socialist brotherhood. Nietzsche provided him with a quite different concept of the way in which literature might help in the creation of a new socialist civilisation, and one of the guiding principles of his criticism after he had absorbed the influence of Nietzsche may fairly be expressed in the phrase 'art for evolution's sake'. While Nietzsche modified Orage's views on the *function* of art, as will be seen, he did not however modify Orage's views on the *content* of art in the least. 'Nietzsche's main view emerges clearly enough in this form', he writes in his *Nietzsche in Outline.* '"Ecstasy as both cause and effect of all great Art."'[31]

This belief that art communicates the indefinable *ecstasis* of the visionary artist continues to be central to all Orage's affirmative criticism. In 1902, for example, reviewing Arthur Machen's *Hieroglyphics,* he agrees with Machen that 'All great art is symbolic'. Art is not concerned with the everyday world, he says, but with the spiritual world by which we are surrounded. Only the mystic knows where art and literature originate, 'for his whole life lies in the world whence literature and art have come—the world that begins where the world enclosed by the five senses ends'. It is the duty of Theosophists, whom Orage has chided for their neglect of the arts, to work for the revival of a literature which expresses these transcendental realities:

> far from having nothing to say to the literary man the Theosophist has everything to say; . . . no less than the rejuvenation of religion, is his work the restoration of its ancient lights to literature, that literature may become, as once it was, the handmaid of the Spirit sacramental in its nature, and divinely illumining for the darkling sight of men.[32]

The view of art presented in Orage's *Consciousness* is equally other-worldly. According to this book, art is one of the chief means by which an evolving mankind is made aware of its 'marvellous powers to come'. Like religion, love, nature and great men it is 'a perpetual reminder of the reality and . . . the possibility of the continuous ecstatic state', lifting us 'out of our duality into a sphere where for an instant we become one of Plato's spectators of time and existence', and in which we are 'above our human mode of consciousness, freed and released, superconscious'.[33]

As far as the *function* of art is concerned, the most important chapter in Orage's two books on Nietzsche is that on 'Willing, Valuing and Creating' in his *Nietzsche in Outline.* Here he emphasizes that artists and philosophers are uniquely important in the evolutionary process of 'becoming' which constitutes the sole *raison d'être* of the universe, for they alone are capable of creating the new imaginative values which will inspire mankind to create the superman. According to Orage's paraphrase of Nietzsche, the world as we perceive it is entirely 'an imaginative creation, the work of great creative and imaginative artists who . . . brooded upon the face of shapeless and meaningless chaos'.[34] Artists, that is, provide mankind with meaningful interpretations of the human situation, and in doing so create ideals: 'where the artist leads there the people follow; he is

the standard-bearer, the inspiring pioneer, the creator of new worlds, new values, new meanings . . .' It follows from this that art cannot be an end in itself. It has a moral value, although its morality is not that of any specific or transient moral code:

> In the sense that Art is thus the great stimulus to life, the enchanter who unfolds or creates alluring vistas, and so seduces the will to the task of the eternal becoming, Art is moral. But the morality is not that of any creed or Sinaitic tablets or transient mode of life, but of life itself. Art for Art's sake means in effect, says Nietzsche, no more than 'Devil take morality.'[35]

In the past, to continue Orage's paraphrase, the philosopher's rôle has been to test the new values created by the artist, on behalf of the human race as a whole. In the future, however, their rôles will be reversed. It is the philosopher who will create the new ends and meanings which will lead mankind towards the superman, while the artist's rôle will be to make these attractive, to 'glorify and englamour them'.

Given the concept of the superman as the goal of human progress, states Orage in his *Friedrich Nietzsche,* 'it becomes possible to estimate the values of things in specific terms'. For Orage himself it now appeared possible to judge art and ideas in terms of their evolutionary value. Far from being an incidental to human life, art was crucially important in a double sense, for by rendering attractive things which were inimical to the evolutionary process the artist might subvert life instead of enhancing it: 'Because . . . Art is the great seducer to life it may also be the great seducer to death . . . and the artist may be saviour or traitor to the race.' Orage readily accepted the Nietzschean view that 'All art . . . is either ascendant or decadent, either leads the will upwards to increase and power, or downwards to decrease and feebleness.'[36] Decadent art is that which works against evolutionary progress towards the superman, in other words, and ascendant art is whatever encourages it. Or, as Orage put it in *The New Age* during 1920, 'The test of literature is whether it gives and intensifies life or takes away and diminishes life.'[37]

One cannot complain that Orage does not think sufficiently highly of the arts, nor would one wish to quarrel with the view that works of literature, for example, can provide us with new interpretations and evaluations of human experience. As we have seen, Orage talks of the 'new ends and meanings' which philosophers are to create and artists are to make attractive. His visionary concept of great art made him always reluctant to discuss these ends and meanings in any detail, however. In his criticism for *The New Age,* to which I now turn, he continued to maintain that the meaning of great literature could not be discussed on an everyday level, stating for example that poetry is 'mystical, superrational',[38] and that 'Drama begins where reason leaves off.'[39]

IV

The fourth and fifth sections of this chapter are devoted to the increasingly polemical criticism published by Orage in *The New Age* after 1910. In the present section I discuss his attacks upon social anarchy and literary realism between 1910 and 1912, and in the section which follows I discuss his weekly articles entitled **'Readers and Writers'**, which began to appear in 1913.

There is a marked change in Orage's attitudes and tone from late 1910 onwards, whether he is discussing politics, feminism or literature. In his articles of 1907 entitled **'Towards Socialism'** he had taunted the cautious and bureaucratically minded Fabian socialists by declaring that every good socialist was a utopian. His attitudes only four years later were very different. The only remaining Conservatives, he wrote in 1911, 'are a handful of Tories . . . and a few Socialists like ourselves. All the rest have joined in the wild goose chase after "social reform", "progress", "democracy", or some equally chimerical fowl.'[40]

The increasing conservatism of Orage's attitudes and the increasingly violent tone in which he expressed them are probably best understood in the light of the major social upheavals which were taking place at the time. 'As the summer of 1914 opened', writes Paul Johnson, 'Britain was on the verge of civil war . . .'[41] The years 1910 and 1911 in Great Britain introduced a period of social anarchy which, but for the outbreak of war, would have culminated in the projected general strike of 1914. The spread of syndicalist doctrines caused an unprecedented number of industrial strikes during 1911, and a general strike was threatened for August of that year. The battle for women's suffrage intensified in violence after the riots of Black Friday (18 November 1910), while the constitutional crisis of 1911 concerning the House of Lords was followed by equally desperate political struggles over the Irish Home Rule Bill and Lloyd George's National Insurance Bill. The latter was regarded by many, including Orage and Hilaire Belloc, as an ominous move in the direction of a collectivist 'servile State'.

Orage's opinions on the suffragette movement provide a good index of his increasingly conservative attitudes during these years. In one of his **'Unedited Opinions'** of 1909 entitled **'Votes for Women'** he had spoken approvingly of female emancipation. In 1912, however, he attacked the movement as one of feminine self-contempt, declaring in the following year that the female revolt could occur only because 'the instincts have lost their unity and become anarchic'.[42]

During 1911 and 1912 Orage also published in *The New Age* six **'Tales for Men Only'**, moral fables which describe in great psychological detail the disastrous effects of female influence upon the masculine creative imagination. The structure of all six tales is basically the same, the narrator R. H. Congreve (Orage's usual pen-name) being *primus inter pares* of a group of artist-philosophers who are 'intent on creating between them a collective soul or superman'. In their evolutionary attempt to 'form a communal mind, which . . . shall constitute a new order of being in the hierarchy of intelligent creation',[43] they have found women to be their greatest obstacle. In the second of these tales, for example, the poet Freestone is warned that his poetry will inevitably deteriorate if he continues to rank his girlfriend higher than his poetic muse: 'From mythopoeia you will descend to symbolism, and if that is too obscure for the girl, down you will go to valentines.'[44]

The fourth of these tales stands out from the rest by reason of its greater satirical liveliness. Its protagonist, the political scientist Tremayne, is guilty of 'the last infirmity of noble minds . . . the ambition to cure a woman of femininity'. He unsuccessfully attempts to educate a Mrs. Foisacre, a woman whose furnishings are as 'promiscuous' as her mind and morals:

> Her room was quaintly furnished, for all the world as if relays of minor poets had each been given a cubic yard to decorate. On this wall were the deposits of the French Symbolist school—drawings of spooks and of male and female figures shaped like vegetables. On that wall were photographic reproductions of the Parthenon friezes; the high-water mark, I suspected, of some pseudo-classic youth who yearned to be strong. The floor was covered with matting, and an earthenware fountain in the midst played by means of a pump. There was a piano and a host of divans. Oh, divans, I thought. Divans! What a lollipop life we are in for! Turkish delight, scented cigarettes, lotus-land, minor poetry, spooks—and where is the guitar? There, as I live, hanging behind the door![45]

Mrs. Foisacre is also described as an embodiment of 'Maya' (the world of illusory appearances) and 'the mob'. She is clearly and revealingly intended by Orage as a complex emblem of contemporary social anarchy, sexual promiscuity, cultural disunity, and artistic decadence.

There is an equally strong change of emphasis in Orage's comments upon literature after 1910. In 1909 he had confidently announced that 'We are now standing . . . at the cradle of a second English Renaissance in Art, Literature, and the Drama.'[46] In his **'Unedited Opinions'** of 1910 he began a series of violent attacks upon the realistic novelists of the day for 'poisoning' their readers. He was not alone in voicing criticism of this kind, however, for a number of critics were complaining at this time of the 'sordid' and 'blasphemous' elements in the works of such authors as John Galsworthy, John Masefield, Eden Philpotts, Laurence Housman, and Lascelles Abercrombie. In 1912, for example, in *The Nineteenth Century and After,* the well-known English positivist Frederic Harrison attacked what he called 'The Cult of the Foul' in contemporary literature,[47] while *Degeneration* itself rose from the depths again in April 1913 after an interval of fifteen years.

In his own strong opposition to realism, as in his belief that 'all great art is symbolic', Orage is extremely close to the Arthur Symons who wrote *The Symbolist Movement in Literature.* He is equally close to Oscar Wilde, who in 'The Decay of Lying' (1891) had earlier distinguished between the 'imaginative reality' of Balzac and the 'unimaginative realism' of Zola, describing Zola's realism as 'the true decadence . . . from [which] we are now suffering'.[48] When Orage attacks realism as the product of commercialism, and rejects certain literary topics on aesthetic rather than moral grounds, he displays the influence of William Morris. Where he differs from such 'nineties men' as Wilde, Morris and the earlier Symons, and what characterizes him as a 'man of 1914', is above all the violence of his tone.

Orage announces the general grounds of his opposition to realism in his dialogue on **'Modern Novels'** (1910). He also reveals in passing two sources of his belief in neo-feudalism and occult supermen (Disraeli and Lytton respectively). Contemporary realistic novelists are so severely criticized by his reviewers for *The New Age,* he says, because they poison their readers with commonplace representations of reality. Instead of doing this, they should provide their readers with a stimulus to the noble life. 'Disraeli and Lytton are in my opinion the two English novelists who aimed highest', writes Orage, 'though I admit they fell far short in actual achievement. Their heroic characters were at least planned on the grand scale.'[49]

So strong is Orage's concern for correct evolutionary development that he will not allow literary artists to describe ugly and sordid aspects of life in order to condemn them, for even this is to run the risk of making vice attractive: 'To add to the poison-fangs of the snake its glittering fascinating eye is . . . to give it strength', he claims.[50] Nor will he even allow art to acquaint us with the worst aspects of life in order that we may face them more courageously. The purpose of art is not to involve itself with the concerns of everyday life at all, he writes, but to promote spiritual progress: 'Progress in the spiritual meaning is . . . a perpetual running away from what is generally called life. . . . How mistaken to define as the purpose of art the very contrary of the purpose of the most spiritual! Yet such as declare that art is for the purpose of bracing us for life obviously do this.'[51]

In these *New Age* dialogues, as in his earliest articles for *The Labour Leader,* Orage relates realism in literature to commercialism in society. The great artist, he

claims in **'Money-Changers in Literature',** cannot give of his best in an atmosphere poisoned by commercially minded authors who 'teach the world to measure success by circulation, to regard literature as a commodity to be advertised and boomed like pills, to despise poor artists as living out of touch with their times, to attach to literature the meretricious adjuncts of contemporary gossip, social utility, fashionable crazes, topical discussions . . .'[52]

It is consequently the duty of critics, who 'cannot be too severe', to reveal the destruction caused by these commercial authors or 'usurping demagogues'. Critics must first expose the second-rate artists who deal in pain and brutality, the nine out of ten modern artists who 'do nothing but glorify mad-houses, lock-hospitals and ugly accidents'.[53] But they must also be severe with certain genuine and dedicated artists who mistakenly believe that the subject-matter of works of art should be free from restrictions. 'With our modern ideas of liberty, universality and democracy', writes Orage, 'it is difficult for artists to remember that these ideas are not for them. They resent . . . the limitations which former artists deliberately put upon themselves; with the consequence that the most uncouth materials are to be found in modern works.' Orage criticizes the 'uncouth materials' to be found in realistic novels, not on moral grounds, but on aesthetic grounds. Against the view that it is only the literary treatment of a subject that matters, he argues that certain types of subject-matter can never be made beautiful:

> . . . I should say that disease ought never to be treated by the artist; likewise vulgar murders, rapes, adulteries, kitchen squabbles, the doings and sayings of vulgar and repellent persons, the sexual affairs of nonentities, the trivial, the base, the sordid, the mean. . . . The rejection is not primarily on moral grounds, but on aesthetic grounds. These things simply cannot be made beautiful. . . . The literary artist should no more employ his pen on them than a painter would put mud and rubbish on his palette.[54]

Orage presents his moral critique of realism as an aesthetic critique because of his reluctance to allow that literature communicates *ideas* in the everyday sense of the word, a reluctance particularly evident in his strictures upon realism in the contemporary drama. He condemns as 'mummery' the type of play in which ideas are discussed, and dismisses the notion of propagandist art as a contradiction in terms. 'The sole object of a work of art', he argues, 'is to reveal beauty and to leave that beauty to affect whom it may. Surely, it argues a small belief in beauty if we must add to it a moral or a purpose other than itself. . . . It is in the nature of all spiritual things that they are above utility.'[55] Writing in 1912 he describes genuine drama as being, like all genuine art, 'sacramental', a claim which is virtually identical with that made for symbolist works by Arthur Symons. According to Orage true drama is a 'pentecostal art', a religious ceremony which concerns and addresses man's immortal soul, and which like the Mass conveys an experience which cannot be communicated in words:

> Actions that we can rationalise, explain, forecast, determine, are actions motivated in the reasoning brain. With them drama has nothing to do, for drama is the representation of a mystery. . . . Drama begins where reason leaves off. . . . Drama is the representation and therewith the illumination of the subconscious. We are made to *feel* that we understand, though we are aware that our understanding cannot be expressed in words. Deep calleth unto deep.[56]

That our understanding of great literature cannot be expressed in words is a position which Orage continued to maintain in his **'Readers and Writers'** articles of 1913-21, to which I now turn. In these articles he continues the polemical critique of contemporary social and literary decadence which he had begun in 1910, frequently undertaking to demonstrate the decadence of contemporary literature by making what would now be called a 'practical criticism' of chosen extracts. He continues to be reluctant to discuss great works of literature in any detail, however. Their greatness is apparently subject to no such demonstration as applies in the case of decadent writing, and we must consequently rely upon Orage's assertion that certain works are supremely great. Orage's statements that the highest poetry is 'in the octave beyond the rational mind',[57] and that in Milton's prose 'The sense is nothing, but the supersense is everything',[58] remain consistent with his earliest claims that great poetry communicates 'the illimitable' and can therefore be discussed only in the most general terms.

V

Orage resumed his criticism of contemporary literature and society in his weekly **'Readers and Writers'** column, which began in *The New Age* in 1913 and continued until 1921. Extremely polemical at first, the tone of his criticism became less so after 1915, by which time the entire social and literary situation had been changed by the Great War.

Instead of discussing general issues as he had done in his dialogues of 1910-12, Orage intended in this column to discuss the particular events of each week, consistently, seriously, and with definite ends in view. In other words, his literary criticism was intended as an integral part of a much wider programme, the aim of which was to create a unified and orderly guild-socialist commonwealth in place of a society rendered in his view increasingly anarchic by the divisive Liberal creed of unrestricted commercial competition. Because weekly literary events follow no obvious pattern, as Orage later conceded, his hopes for this column were not entirely fulfilled. Nevertheless, in its strategy and its critical attitudes it possesses a consistency which is far from apparent in such published selections from it as *Readers and Writers* and *The Art of Reading.* Removed from the context of *The New Age,* moreover, its significance as part of a programme of cultural reform is also entirely lost.

As we would expect, much of Orage's criticism in **'Readers and Writers'** is directed against the commercialization of literature. He regularly indicts such manifestations of commercialism as the best-sellers of H. G. Wells and Arnold Bennett, the 'booming' of books by publishers, the critical irresponsibility of such literary journals as *The English Review* (at that time under the editorship of Austin Harrison), and the type of journalistic reviewing, such as that of the *Daily News,* which can describe a trilogy of novels by Oliver Onions as 'the highest sustained product of English literary creative genius in the present century'.[59]

Decadence continues to be another of Orage's favourite targets. Concerning that ninetyish magazine *The Gypsy,* for example, he writes: 'The association of art with luxury, of beauty with disease, of aesthetic emotion with strange and sought sensations, is the unholy union of god and ape that we have set ourselves to annul.'[60] By 'decadence' however he means much more than the eroticism of the 1890s. He claims that decadence in literature exemplifies the decadence and anarchy (and for Orage the terms are virtually interchangeable) of the entire age. Concerning a proposed study of the poet John Davidson by Frank Harris he writes, for example: 'A study of such a congeries of moods unhappily gathered in a single consciousness must be a diagnosis more of our times than of a man; and its name should not be Davidson but Anarchism.'[61]

On similar grounds he attacks a variety of allegedly interrelated targets: contemporary realist authors, for example, and such contemporary exponents of 'infantilism' and 'decadence' as the imagists, vorticists and futurists. He suggests that a connection exists between 'Imagism and Savagery, between anarchic verse and anarchic conduct, between Mr. Pound's images and Mr. Wyndham Lewis' "Blast."'[62] Of Professor Gilbert Murray he writes that his mind is 'eclectic, that is to say, it lacks unity, is anarchically tolerant of incongruities'.[63] Ezra Pound's prose-style he describes as 'a pastiche of colloquy, slang, journalism and pedantry. Of culture in Nietzche's sense of the word—a unity of style—it bears no sign'.[64] Of G. K. Chesterton and the age as a whole he writes: '. . . Mr. Chesterton, though a critic of our days, is its most complete incarnation; all styles are to be found in him save any style; all ideas save any idea; all points of view save any point of view'.[65] Examples need not be multiplied. It appears highly likely that in mounting his attack upon contemporary social and literary decadence in **'Readers**

and Writers' Orage made fuller use of what I have earlier called Bourget's formula than any other English cultural critic before or since.

In this column he continues to attack the commercially inspired book-reviewing of the day and frequently calls for severer standards of criticism. Describing contemporary critics as the worst ever known in any period of literature, he insists that it is the business of the critic to make judgements, and that these should be moralistic in intent. 'I can imagine no critic worth his office', he writes, 'who does not judge with a single eye to the upholding of the moral laws. Far from being an offence to literature, this attitude of the true critic does literature honour. It assumes that literature affects life for better or worse.'[66]

Orage's own judgements in **'Readers and Writers'** are uncompromisingly harsh, and their unusual freedom of expression brought *The New Age,* as he commented later, into 'somewhat lively disrepute'.[67] They rest, however, on two basic assumptions: that literature should have (*a*) an evolutionary function, and (*b*) a visionary content.

As he expresses it in **'Readers and Writers'**, Orage's view of the proper function of literature is that it should further evolutionary progress. The writer's duty is to lead men forward by creating noble illusions to which they will aspire. 'If poets and imaginative writers want subjects for poetry', he agrees with the French socialist philosopher Proudhon, 'let them make it out of the visions of what humanity may and ought to become.'[68] The business of the artist, he states elsewhere, is to 'forward Nature by divining her plans and manifesting what is in her mind'.[69] An evolutionistic view of the function of literature also underlies his Wildean distinction between realism of a Zolaesque kind and that 'true' or 'imaginative' realism which foretells what Nature will or might produce in the future, and thereby 'raises literature to a great art again'. In **'Readers and Writers'** Orage praises writers so unalike as Longinus, Sorel, and (time and again) the author of the great Hindu epic the *Mahabharata,* because these authors have in common the qualities of nobility and sublimity which are essential to evolutionary progress.

Orage's undeviating insistence that the proper content of literature is visionary is seen at its clearest in a statement, reprinted in his *Selected Essays and Critical Writings,* in which he concludes that art has 'nothing to do either with emotions or with ideas'. Art, he goes on to say:

> arises from the creative contemplation of the artist and arouses in the beholders a corresponding appreciative contemplation. Both artist and critic are on the super-conscious plane: the one creating symbols for its ex-

pression and the other experiencing its life in contemplation. All art thus plunges the beholder into a high state of reverie or wonder or contemplation or meditation; and that is both its nature and its purpose. We should suspect a work professing to be art when it arouses either [emotion] or thought. Unless it can still both of these inferior states, and arouse us to contemplation, it is human, all too human.[70]

This distrust of 'thought' in art and literature leads Orage to claim in **'Readers and Writers'** that the 'quasi-magical effect of certain forms of literature is independent of the ostensible content', so that in Milton's prose 'It is not what he says that matters in the least, but it is the style in which he says it. The sense is nothing, but the supersense is everything.'[71] Elsewhere Orage distinguishes between the 'common sense or matter' of literature and the 'super-sense of words, or style'.[72]

In **'Readers and Writers'** Orage often undertakes a practical criticism or detailed critical analysis of particular passages. These probably represent an effort to secure for his judgements something of the prestige attaching to the scientific method, and he does on one occasion claim that 'we ought to be able to apply a scientific stylometry to literature in general'.[73] The questionable and Bourget-like assumption behind Orage's critical analyses, however, is that an author's moral decadence is evident in the decadence of his literary style. Although Havelock Ellis had urged his readers to recognize that 'decadence is an aesthetic and not a moral conception', Orage claims to be able to perceive moral decadence 'in the very construction of a man's sentences, in his rhythm, in his syntax'.[74] In fact, whether he is analysing Meredith or the military critic of *The Times,* he devotes nearly all his attention to the rhythm of the passage which he has selected, and scarcely any to its paraphrasable meaning. He always prefers to say, not that an author's thinking is illogical or that his ideas or attitudes are morally unacceptable, but (with Bourget and Nietzsche) that his *style* is decadent. Orage's stylistic analyses thus allow him to pass moralistic judgements upon an author's work whilst ignoring the morality of the views which the work itself advances.

In his unwillingness to discuss the meaning of even a poor piece of literature Orage is being entirely consistent with his views on the nature of art as we have seen them expressed above. His other-worldly concept of art renders him extremely reluctant to concede that the meaning of any work of art, good or bad, can be adequately discussed. 'It is not without reason', says Arthur Symons in *The Symbolist Movement in Literature,* 'that we cannot analyse a perfect lyric.'[75] Here, as in a number of important respects, Orage is at one with him, claiming that the more great literature is analysed, 'the more mysteriously beautiful it becomes'.[76] I return to this and allied topics in my final chapter after making my concluding remarks upon Orage.

VI

Orage might be considered as a type-figure of the critic in the Age of Evolutionism. Evolutionistic assumptions play a dominant part in all his thinking, whether he is advocating that society be led by a new breed of men of genius or attacking literary decadence because it is contrary to desirable evolutionary tendencies. He is equally typical in using these evolutionistic assumptions as a means of restating thoroughly traditional ideas. His guild socialism is firmly rooted in the neo-mediaeval tradition of Pugin, Disraeli and Morris. Furthermore, as noted in Chapter 1, he believes that evolution is proceeding to the golden age *backwards*: 'To go back is to go forward', he writes in 1915. '. . . the rediscovery of ancient Indian culture will give us the Europe of tomorrow. Nothing else will.'[77]

He is also a characteristic figure of the period 1880-1920 in his belief in Theosophy and mysticism, those movements which, as we also saw in Chapter 1, replaced for many serious-minded people a Christian world-view apparently discredited by biblical criticism and by High Victorian scientism. Orage's visionary aesthetic, which is an important corollary of his mysticism, is also characteristic of the period. So too is his use of the prestige of science itself in carrying out his 'stylometric' critical analyses. Although I have not discussed the developing interest in psychoanalysis which is apparent in **'Readers and Writers'**, it appears characteristic of Orage and a number of his contemporaries that this new and would-be scientific development should have been quickly incorporated into a programme for achieving super-consciousness.

Orage's criticism also importantly exemplifies that shift in tone, noted in Chapter 1 and already mentioned in connection with the final phase of Arthur Symons's criticism, which appears to be an important element in the shift from symbolism to expressionism. A basic hostility to realism links Orage to Yeats and the later Symons on the one hand, and on the other hand to such *avant-garde* modernists of the next generation as Pound, Lewis and Hulme. This hostility to realism also links him to Oscar Wilde, in whose 'The Soul of Man under Socialism' and 'The Decay of Lying' are to be found a significant number of notions which Orage was later to express far more polemically. Although he decisively rejected what he called the 'yellow fever' of the nineties, Orage continued to respect Wilde for his Nietzschean view that nature imitates art, just as the vorticists continued to respect the implicit anti-realism of Pater's theories[78] and of Beardsley's practice.[79] Orage himself appears to have been instrumental in re-stating the aestheticism and the symbolism of the nineties in the new hard and assertive language of early-twentieth-century expressionism.

As John Holloway has pointed out, Orage's attack upon the commercial debasement of literature and of literary criticism anticipates attitudes which were later taken up in *The Calendar of Modern Letters* and *Scrutiny*.[80] Orage's detailed critical analyses of particular passages, to which he regarded biographical and historical information as irrelevant, anticipate in certain important respects the subsequent approach to literature of I. A. Richards and the New Critics. As an important platform for classicist and neo-feudalist views concerning literature and politics, *The New Age* from about 1910 onwards anticipates much that was to appear later in the thought of Wyndham Lewis and T. S. Eliot.

The New Age was not by any means, of course, solely a platform for views of this kind. Although Orage himself was committed to guild socialism as an editor, as a political commentator, and as a literary critic, *The New Age* was above all an arena for controversy and debate. In his rôle of severe and intolerant critic Orage fiercely condemned both futurism and imagism. In his rôle of tolerant and broad-minded editor, on the other hand, he was one of the first to publish the work of both futurist painters and imagist poets. He constantly sought and encouraged new talent; as a result of his editorial catholicity *The New Age* continues to merit our attention and admiration as without doubt the most intellectually alive and seminal periodical of its day.

Notes

1. D. D. Paige (ed.), *The Letters of Ezra Pound: 1907-1941* (New York, Harcourt Brace, 1950), p. 259.

2. *N.A.* XXXVIII, 20 (18 March 1926), p. 235.

3. *The Labour Leader* VII, 86 n.s. (30 Nov. 1895), p. 3. I have silently corrected minor printing errors in quotations from this periodical.

4. *Ibid.* VIII, 106 n.s. (11 April 1896), p. 122.

5. *Ibid.* VIII, 105 n.s. (4 April 1896), p. 114.

6. *Ibid.* VIII, 132 n.s. (10 Oct. 1896), p. 352.

7. *Ibid.* VIII, 103 n.s. (21 March 1896), p. 102; VIII, 121 n.s. (25 July 1896), p. 258.

8. *Ibid.* VIII, 127 n.s. (5 Sept. 1896), p. 308.

9. *Ibid.* VIII, 114 n.s. (6 June 1896), p. 197.

10. *Ibid.* VIII, 117 n.s. (27 June 1896), p. 218.

11. *The Symbolist Movement in Literature,* p. 146.

12. *The Labour Leader* VIII, 114 n.s. (6 June 1896), p. 197.

13. Holbrook Jackson, *Bernard Shaw: a Monograph* (London, Grant Richards, 1907), pp. 11-12.

14. A. R. Orage, *Friedrich Nietzsche: The Dionysian Spirit of the Age* (London & Edinburgh, T. N. Foulis, 1906), pp. 74-5.

15. *N.A.* XVI, 2 (12 Nov. 1914), p. 42.

16. Arthur Symons, *William Blake*, pp. 1-2.

17. W. B. Yeats, *Ideas of Good and Evil*, p. 201.

18. *Friedrich Nietzsche*, p. 12.

19. 'Readings and Re-Readings: "Zanoni"', *The Theosophical Review* XXXI, 184 (15 Dec. 1902), p. 344.

20. *Nietzsche in Outline and Aphorism* (Edinburgh & London, T. N. Foulis, 1907), p. 47.

21. *Friedrich Nietzsche*, p. 75.

22. *Consciousness: Animal, Human, and Superman* (London & Benares, Theosophical Publishing Society, 1907), p. 74.

23. 'Esprit de Corps in Elementary Schools', *The Monthly Review* XXV, 75 (Dec. 1906), p. 50. ('Discipline in Elementary Schools' appeared in *The Monthly Review* for May 1907.)

24. 'Politics for Craftsmen', *The Contemporary Review* XCI (June 1907), p. 785.

25. *N.A.* I, 23 (23 Oct. 1907), p. 362.

26. *N.A.* II, 1 (31 Oct. 1907), p. 10.

27. 'The New Romanticism', *The Theosophical Review* XL, 235 (March 1907), p. 55.

28. 'Esprit de Corps in Elementary Schools', *loc. cit.* p. 48.

29. *N.A.* II, 4 (21 Nov. 1907), p. 70.

30. *N.A.* II, 3 (14 Nov. 1907), p. 50.

31. *Nietzsche in Outline and Aphorism*, p. 66.

32. 'Readings and Re-Readings: The Mystic Valuation of Literature', *The Theosophical Review* XXXI, 185 (15 Jan. 1903), p. 430.

33. *Consciousness: Animal, Human, and Superman*, p. 83.

34. *Nietzsche in Outline and Aphorism*, p. 124.

35. *Ibid.* pp. 65-6.

36. *Ibid.* p. 61.

37. *N.A.* XXVIII, 3 (18 Nov. 1920), p. 30.

38. *N.A.* IV, 20 (11 March 1909), p. 399.

39. *N.A.* X, 16 (15 Feb. 1912), p. 371.

40. *N.A.* X, 3 (16 Nov. 1911), p. 49.

41. George Dangerfield, *The Strange Death of Liberal England* (London, McGibbon & Kee, 1966), p. 12.

42. *N.A.* XI, 17 (22 Aug. 1912), p. 388.

43. *N.A.* XI, 16 (15 Aug. 1912), pp. 373-4.

44. *N.A.* IX, 22 (28 Sept. 1911), p. 518.

45. *N.A.* XI, 4 (23 May 1912), p. 85.

46. *N.A.* IV, 19 (4 March 1909), p. 379.

47. Frederic Harrison, 'Aischro-Latreia—The Cult of the Foul', *The Nineteenth Century and After* 420 (Feb. 1912), p. 333.

48. Oscar Wilde, *Intentions* (London, Osgood McIlvaine, 1891), p. 22.

49. *N.A.* VIII, 9 (29 Dec. 1910), p. 204.

50. *N.A.* IX, 24 (12 Oct. 1911), p. 563.

51. *Ibid.*

52. *N.A.* IX, 2 (11 May 1911), p. 35.

53. *N.A.* X, 24 (11 April 1912), p. 564.

54. *N.A.* IX, 23 (5 Oct. 1911), p. 539.

55. *N.A.* IX, 24 (12 Oct. 1911), p. 562.

56. *N.A.* X, 16 (15 Feb. 1912), p. 371.

57. *N.A.* XVII, 25 (21 Oct. 1915), p. 597.

58. *N.A.* XVIII, 20 (16 March 1916), p. 470.

59. *N.A.* XIII, 17 (21 Aug. 1913), p. 486.

60. *N.A.* XVII, 6 (10 June 1915), p. 133.

61. *N.A.* XIII, 11 (10 July 1913), p. 297.

62. *N.A.* XVI, 3 (19 Nov. 1914), p. 69.

63. *N.A.* XIII, 13 (24 July 1913), p. 362.

64. *N.A.* XIII, 26 (23 Oct. 1913), p. 761.

65. *N.A.* XIV, 8 (25 Dec. 1913), p. 241.

66. *N.A.* XIII, 22 (25 Sept. 1913), p. 634.

67. A. R. Orage, *Readers and Writers (1917-1921)* (New York, Knopf, 1922), preface.

68. *N.A.* XIII, 27 (30 Oct. 1913), p. 792.

69. *N.A.* XVII, 13 (29 July 1915), p. 309.

70. A. R. Orage, *Selected Essays and Critical Writings*, ed. Herbert Read & Denis Saurat (London, Stanley Nott, 1935), pp. 152-3. The version quoted prints 'caution' for what should clearly be 'emotion'.

71. *N.A.* XVIII, 20 (16 March 1916), p. 470.

72. *N.A.* XVI, 24 (15 April 1915), p. 642.

73. *N.A.* XXI, 12 (19 July 1917), p. 267.

74. *N.A.* XVIII, 4 (25 Nov. 1915), p. 85.

75. *The Symbolist Movement in Literature,* p. 90.

76. A. R. Orage, *The Art of Reading* (New York, Farrar & Rinehart, 1930), p. 73.

77. *N.A.* XVIII, 5 (2 Dec 1915), p. 110.

78. Ezra Pound, 'Vortex', *Blast* 1 (20 June 1914), p. 154.

79. Wyndham Lewis, 'Modern Caricature and Impressionism', *Blast* 2 (July 1915), p. 79.

80. Boris Ford (ed.), *The Pelican Guide to English Literature* (Harmondsworth, Penguin Books, 1961), Vol. 7, pp. 88-9.

Alan Young (review date spring 1976)

SOURCE: Young, Alan. Review of *Orage as Critic*, edited by Wallace Martin. *Critical Quarterly* 18, no. 1 (spring 1976): 84-6.

[*In the following review of* Orage as Critic, *edited by Wallace Martin, Young praises Orage's honesty and conviction of belief in his role as a cultural critic.*]

A. R. Orage (1873-1934) wrote weekly columns for Keir Hardie's *The Labour Leader* and for his own reviews *The New Age* and *The New English Weekly.* Wallace Martin has edited a selection from this writing [*Orage as Critic*] so that we may follow Orage's opinions as they developed on a number of important questions about critical attitudes, principles and methods, literary language, and the relationship between the arts and society.

The inevitable 'bittiness' of such regular short review journalism is more than compensated for by the editor's selection and skilful arrangement of the material and by the fact that Orage's thinking was naturally, directly, and seriously stimulated by the literary and social circumstances and events of his own times.

'The duty of a reader and writer' is, he held, 'to be a contemporary among contemporaries.' The failure of the Georgian poets, for example, stemmed, in his view, chiefly from their refusal to be seriously involved in the social and political issues of their day. On the other hand, discussing the antics of Marinetti and the Futurists, he declared that 'to see deeply into one's contemporary life is to see life much as it has always been and always will be.' For Orage, these beliefs entailed a responsibility to forge a positive and discriminating attitude towards both his English contemporaries and English and European cultural traditions, creative and critical. He realised that this was likely to be a difficult and not very rewarding task in an age that lacked any sense of 'a great order of society', but he believed that the critic's primary duty during a 'characterless' age is to keep up civilised standards at all costs.

Plato and Nietzsche, or, rather, his reading of Plato much modified by his later reading of Nietzsche, were among the major intellectual influences of his young manhood. These influences, together with his earlier conversion to Socialism, led him directly into the late-Victorian and Edwardian 'radicalism' of G. B. Shaw and H. G. Wells. Like Wells, from a lower-middle-class upbringing he had progressed through the pupil-teacher route to training college. In Leeds, where he helped to organise the Independent Labour Party, he taught in an elementary school, wrote for Socialist journals, and lectured to various philosophical and other groups (including the Theosophical Society). Orage's manner retained always something of the eager schoolmaster, but there is no talking down to inferiors; rather, we have the atmosphere of the senior common room of a highly civilised and progressive institution. Not that his belief in reasonableness, balance, and commen-sense—values which Orage shared with G. E. Moore and other Edwardian philosophers—was so neutral as to lack punch. On the contrary, one of Orage's strengths was his courageous belief in the critic's need to express plainly and publicly truths which had been rigorously and honestly pursued. Passionate affirmation of the efficacy of reason (rather than Platonic or scientific rationalism), the reality of objective standards of true judgment, and human dignity and individual worth remained strong throughout his life, and it is his unaffectedly optimistic urbanity which enables us to accept even his sharpest observations without much rancour. Some dismissals of contemporary poets and attitudes might seem rash or foolish unless we remind ourselves of the strength of Orage's hatred of relativism in values. In 1916, for example, he wrote of Rupert Brooke:

> I have lately been re-reading him to discover what, perhaps, my well-known prejudice against living writers might have led me to underrate in him while he was still alive. But I confess that his somewhat pathetic death has made no difference to my judgment. Dead he is as bad a poet as he was alive.

Such a cruel judgment is excusable, perhaps, only in a critic who sincerely believed, as Orage did, that his duty was to find and to express the truth because, finally, his own opinion did not matter, because, finally, every true judgment would coincide:

> a judge—that is to say, a true judge—is he with whom everybody is compelled to agree, not because he says it, but because it is so.

If this sounds rather like the High Toryism of David Hume (and Orage, almost echoing Hume, deplored the idea that one could 'invite Tom Dick and Harry to offer their opinions as of equal value with the opinions of the cultivated') we must remember that Orage also believed that the opinions of the cultivated would eventually become those of 'common sense', that education and the concept of an educated consensus are genuinely possible.

Orage is most interesting on the moderns because his respect for their serious artistic professionalism was tempered by distrust of their intellectual arrogance, their often triumphant sense of separation from the masses. It seems a pity, perhaps, that one of the few examples of Orage's use of practical criticism given by Wallace Martin is a somewhat inept analysis of the first sentences of Joyce's *Ulysses,* an analysis which exhibits the dangers and deficiencies of the method when the containing formal structures and wider sense-units of a work are left out of the reader-critic's consideration. It might have been more interesting and useful to have had Orage's demonstration (cited by the editor as the best example of his practical criticism) of why, on the basis of an examination of his known verse, one of the Shakespeare claimants, Edward de Vere, could never have written the plays? Yet there is so much in Orage's frustrated examination of those writers he recognised and admired as the genuinely gifted writers of his age—especially Joyce, T. S. Eliot, Ezra Pound, and Wyndham Lewis—that even his struggles to understand make profound demands on our own understanding. His doubts and questions about Vorticism and *Blast,* about *vers libre,* about the post-war *Little Review,* and about the whole work and career of Ezra Pound up to 1921, for example, provide sound starting-points for a critique of literary modernism.

He valued most of all the restoration of craftsmanship and professionalism to English literary life by the moderns, and he deplored Pound's final departure from England in 1920-21 because the cultural need was mutual:

> Taken by and large, England hates men of culture until they are dead. But all the same, it is here or nowhere that the most advanced trenches of the spirit are to be found; and it is here, I believe, that the enemy will have to be defeated.

In *The New Age* as later in *The New English Weekly* Orage led his own campaign against unreason, relativism, despair, and incompetence in English letters. Much of his basic attitude (his passion for a common pursuit of true judgment) was taken up and developed by writers and critics of the next generation, and many of the questions which he debated are still current. His views about technology (of which he approved) and scientific rationalism (of which he disapproved), about the attempts to standardise English spelling and pronunciation or to make grammar a science rather than an art based on good taste (all of which he thought misguided), and many other issues are refreshingly, honestly, and plainly argued.

Wallace Martin's introduction is informative and shrewd: many readers of this book will be persuaded to read his *'The New Age' under Orage* (1967) and several, guided by his useful notes, will be stimulated to seek out and read through the files of *The New Age* itself.

Michael Coyle (essay date spring 1988)

SOURCE: Coyle, Michael. "A Profounder Didacticism: Ruskin, Orage and Pound's Perception of Social Credit." *Paideuma* 17, no. 1 (spring 1988): 7-28.

[*In the following essay, Coyle expounds upon Orage's influence in shaping both Ezra Pound's literary career and his socialist views as well as examining the restless intellectual needs of Orage's that drove him from movement to movement.*]

> Under these circumstances, no designing or any other development of beautiful art will be possible.
>
> —John Ruskin, 1859

> So long as the system of competition in the production and exchange of the means of life goes on, the degradation of the arts will go on.
>
> —William Morris, 1884

> The literature and art of today are the parallels of the economic situation of today.
>
> —A. R. Orage, 1912

> A vicious economic system has corrupted every ramification of thought.
>
> —Ezra Pound, 1934

I

Despite the impotent fury with which he pursued the topic of economic reform, Ezra Pound's writings on economics generate no more interest today than they did during his own lifetime: the same elements of his work that isolated him during the twenties and thirties continue to do so. This essay shall not attempt to make Pound's economic preoccupations attractive or to establish their "humanistic" interest; but it will propose that, far from marking him as an impassioned crank, Pound's concern to integrate economic and poetic discourse stemmed from one of the most powerful and popular traditions in English literature. In fact, one should in this instance use the word "literature," as Pound himself so often did, ironically: this tradition, which I shall call "Ruskinian," was in large part concerned to resist idealist attempts to protect and isolate the "literary," or the experience of culture, from the conditions of material civilization. I shall use the term "Ruskinian" even though this essay will attend more particularly to the subsequent figures through whom Pound seems to have absorbed Ruskin's aims and methods. Our identification of Pound's participation in this tradition will have important consequences, for it will suggest that Pound's moral failures were the result, not simply of madness or personal idiosyncrasy, but of the working out of a broad cultural heritage. This is not to excuse Pound but to observe the manner in which he kept a very literal faith with promises that may have been, as he wrote in "Mauberley," "wrong from the start."

In January of 1935, in the usually polite pages of Eliot's *The Criterion,* Pound snarled that

> Any ass can see the contradictions between the three living theories: the Corporate State, Douglas, Gesell. Or between these and the technocrats. Superficial imbeciles can see the contradiction between these systems and those of Marx or Henry George. A few dozen people see the convergence of the live systems, and can see the main currents working in Time.

Pound regarded the "perception" of "convergence" among these theories as an exceptional and beleaguered faculty. Having begun by distinguishing between "convergence" and "contradiction," Pound went on to distinguish convergence from identity:

> Even Douglas seems unaware of the profound harmony between his *economics* and fascism. I am not talking about the surface of his politics. Obviously the "harmony" does not occupy all the space in these two so different systems, but there is more of it than most people think.

It is fairly typical to find Pound claiming to discern more "profound" meanings than those apparent on the surface of things. It was less usual, however, for him so to qualify the nature of his assertion. To propose that between two ideas there may be both convergence and contradiction itself seems at once a keen insight and yet an obtuse negotiation: insightful in its perception of both generic multiplicity and the probably unwitting aptness with which it characterized much of Pound's own writing and thought; obtuse in that it had almost no chance of moving Douglas, a man more or less stolidly dedicated to the rightness of a single controlling idea. But then, by 1935, Pound had probably lost any real hope of moving Douglas—if he had ever honestly entertained such a hope. Indeed, he may primarily have seen Douglas as a kind of wedge, a way into problems which had held his imagination for some time.

The rapidity with which he "reassessed" the significance of Douglas' analysis would seem to confirm such a suspicion. It had been, in 1935, only a year since

Pound had met Odon Por, Guild Socialist cum fascist, whose critiques of capitalism had a "substantial" impact on Pound's interpretation of Douglas; it had been hardly even that long since Pound first read Silvio Gesell's *Natural Economic Order.*[1] That Pound broke ranks so quickly after fifteen years of stumping for the cause would suggest that he never "was" a doctrinaire socialcreditor. But more than this I want to propose that it was the very things that led Pound to Social-Credit that eventually led him away from it. Chief among these was his obsession with problems of "method." It was on the level of method, and not of principle, that Pound discerned Douglas' convergence with the far right. It was to the level of method that Pound referred when, with a wave of his hand, he dismissed talk about "the surface" of Douglas' economics. Pound's perception of "convergence" between Douglas and the corporate state was in other words generated by principles not immediately related to particular economic issues. It was rather an exercise of the methodological "dissociation" which Pound had absorbed from the work of Remy de Gourmont: a concern to free ideas from obfuscating associations.[2]

Douglas himself would have been little interested in the distinctions between "contradiction" and mere difference. He saw immediately the "contradiction" between his plans for economic democracy and Gesell's rightwing prescriptions. Douglas had often before been troubled by the innovations of would be allies and fellow-travelers. For example, the adoption of Social Credit in 1927 by John Hargrave's bizarre legion, the "Kibbo Kift," and the reorganization of that group six years later as "the Green Shirt movement for Social Credit" had already warned Douglas that indiscriminate attempts to broaden the base of his support would endanger doctrinal purity. While *The New Age* characteristically "saw it as a strength that Hargrave was sufficiently eclectic to have drawn 'something useful from St. Paul, Mme. Blavatsky, Charlie Chaplin, Cromwell, Lao Tze, Nietzsche, Noah and Tolstoy,'" Douglas remained, at the very least, circumspect.[3] These earlier troubles, occasioned by men with claims to some popular support, left Douglas impatient with the increasingly isolated Pound. Unimpressed by Pound's relentless efforts to improve upon his analysis, and having come to regard Pound as a nuisance, Douglas eventually repudiated their association.[4] That Pound did not reciprocate that repudiation but continued, albeit with ever increasing difficulty, to invoke Douglas' authority indicates a great deal about the combinatory nature of his thinking. This is an important recognition. It can help us to understand not only how Pound's later economic interests developed from his enthusiasm for Douglas, but also how that enthusiasm developed out of economic projects that had, by 1919 (the year of Pound's supposed conversion to Douglas' economic policies), occupied Pound for the better part of a decade.

Pound's twelve year association with *The New Age* and its editor Alfred Richard Orage constitutes one of the least understood aspects of his career. Pound's own comments about those years have not helped because, after the 1919 "conversion" for which Orage was so responsible, Pound became uneasy—even embarrassed—by his earlier ties with the Guild Socialism which Orage had sponsored throughout the previous decade. Despite his later suggestion that guild socialism was an important step towards "the corporate state," Pound came to see a contradiction between his earlier involvement with Orage and his cherished public persona as a man up-to-date on matters artistic and economic.[5] But, in uncovering connections which Pound would just as soon have left forgotten, my emphasis shall not be on locating "the origin" either of his interest in economics, or of his inclusion of economics in the *Cantos*. Rather, I shall consider Pound's relationship with Orage as a means of illuminating the broad concerns that drew Pound into the arena of economic debate and fostered his incipient combinatory procedures.

It is testimony to the thoroughness of contemporary academic efforts to treat the *Cantos* in strictly "aesthetic" terms that Pound's relations to *The New Age* have figured so slightly in accounts of his poetic development. For the years of Pound's closest association with Orage were precisely the years during which he was working through "imagism" and "vorticism" and into the *Cantos*. Orage and *The New Age* performed a vital role in enlisting Pound's participation in the broad and heterogeneous tradition of combining social and aesthetic analysis which followed from the British assimilation, in the nineteenth century, of the continental idealism of the late enlightenment. Once we recognize how Orage's journalism infected Pound's poetry it will no longer be possible to preserve the familiar pigeonhole of "Pound's economics," no longer possible to treat as marginal and symptomatic what was—perhaps rampantly so—transformative and part of a seminal post-Enlightenment tradition. That we prefer today to disjoin the poetry and the economics constitutes a significant reconstruction of Pound's work, and points up our continuing resistance to a humanist tradition which unforseeably nurtured a generation of political monsters.

Of course, Pound's handling of economic issues presents its own problems, not least because he eventually sought to combine the hitherto opposed genres of lyric and didactic essay; even William Morris, who wrote in both genres, preserved their differences. But, if the *Cantos* attempted major conceptual revisions, those were very much dependent on Victorian reconceptualizations of artistic experience. The mediation of Orage who, like Ruskin, often relied upon the periodical to pursue his ends and, like Morris, could never wholly embrace socialism because it meant the sacrifice of his medieval ideals, played for Pound a role no less important. During a period in his career that was at once both vigorous and yet tentative, Pound often followed Orage's lead in political and economic questions. As Wallace Martin has observed, Orage's most fundamental critical aim was to reconcile flamboyantly romantic claims for the autonomy of literature with Ruskinian convictions about cultural responsibility. Thus, in 1915, Orage submitted that "art includes utility, but it also transcends utility."[6] This view was by no means a platitudinous compromise; these two views of art were, in their traditional terms, irreconcilable, and Orage entered the argument by striving to transform the notion of utility. This move was not lost on Pound who, as Paul Smith has said, redefined poetry so that materiality would not distort substance. So it was that, by 1922, when holding forth to Felix Schelling that "it's all rubbish to pretend that art isn't didactic," and that "only aesthetes have pretended to the contrary," Pound expanded into one of his most provoking phrases: "Art can't offer a patent medicine. A failure to dissociate that from a profounder didacticism has led to the errors of 'aesthete's' critiques."[7]

Orage's editorial ideals, although probably not his actual example, helped shape Pound's determination to modernize his critical and journalistic style, and—ultimately—his conception of the aims and nature of poetry.[8] Orage contributed not only to the subject matter that interested Pound, but also to the manner in which he addressed those subjects. Consider, for example, Pound's attack on the conventional journalistic essay form: an attack launched in his digressive series "Pastiche: the Regional," and published by Orage in *The New Age* (29 October 1919). Pound argued that

> the newspaper criterion that "an article must run straight through from start to finish" might be attributed to the tone of this period ["the Shavo-Bennetian of English secondary literature"]; the criterion is of excellent newspaper technique; it is almost pure kindness designed not to make the reader think, but to make him accept a certain conclusion; literature and philosophy constantly diverge from this groovedness, constantly throw upon the perceptions new data, new images, which prevent the acceptance of an over facile conclusion.

Pound's alternative was what he variously called the "ideogrammic method" or "the 'new' historic sense"; that is, the method that would in the coming years characterize the writing of the *Cantos*. It is important that Pound did not regard that method as strictly "poetic": important too that, at a time when his poetry was only beginning to work out and apply that historical method (his most recent collection still only the trial poetic sequences of *Quia Pauper Amavi*: "Langue d'Oc," "Moeurs Contemporaines," and "Three Cantos"), it was already a part of his journalism. Pieces like "Pastiche" did more than talk about that method—they put it into action, employing the criticism of "newspaper technique" which I have just cited. Two months earlier, for instance, in an earlier installment of "Pastiche," Pound had written:

> The city of Beziers was burned because Simon de Montfort attacked with a small force of knights and a great troup of "ribbands," tinkers, and religious pilgrims or "croises." The tinkers broke through the walls and took possession of the rich houses and plunder; the knights drove out the tinkers in order to get the booty for themselves; the tinkers then burnt the place. The violence of the Church ultimately profited the centralization of the French monarchy.

> Richelieu destroyed Beaucaire. Montmorency was taken at the altar. Montsegur outlasted the treachery against the surrendered Albigeois, and was destroyed, I have been told, by order of Louis XIV. . . .

> Snippets of this kind build up our concept of wrong, of right, of history . . . Any historical concept and any sociological deduction from history must assemble a great number of such violently contrasted facts, if it is to be valid. It must not be a simple paradox, or a simple opposition of two terms.

I have quoted from this passage at length in order to show the procedure of "assemblage" Pound was then already exploring in his journalistic prose. The historiographical position that Pound developed in the thirties, with its insistence on the inclusion of actual written texts ("whole slabs of the record") over references such as those in the example above, was crucial. But the point is that Pound's development was not purely "poetic." Throughout the teens, Pound ventured experiments in prose that his deeply held notions about "true Helicon" still prevented him from trying in his poetry.[9] At the same time, these innovations created problems that Pound did not solve to his own satisfaction until well into the *Cantos,* if even then. It was not the mere consciousness of socio-economic issues that gradually moved Pound out of his early aestheticism, but particular ways of writing about and conceptualizing them. In this respect, Orage and *The New Age* were invaluable.

II

Ultimately, the impression of national character or national honesty is a literary impression.

—Pound, 1915

Unfortunately, the genre in which Orage chose to pursue the largest part of his life's work has for some time now been devalued, and even refused the place among the ranking "literary" genres which it had held for much of the eighteenth century. Far from being interested in Orage's influence upon the various work Pound contributed to periodicals, most critics lament that it was at all necessary for Pound to have to write for a living.

Every hour Pound spent on ephemeral journalism, so it goes, was an hour stolen from his "real"—poetic—work. It is difficult not to sympathize with this view, which has in our time become normative. Few critics today would challenge Samuel Butler's conclusion that "writing for reviews or newspapers is bad training for one who may aspire to write works of more permanent interest," any more than they would contest the insistence of Cyril Connolly that "the true function of a writer is to produce a masterpiece . . . no other task is of any importance."[10] Indeed, Orage himself paradoxically maintained that "nothing is more fatal to culture than journalism." Pound too was often sensitive about this matter, as when in 1920 he attacked what he saw as George Bernard Shaw's effort "to obscure the division between literature and journalism."[11] But Pound could also dismiss prejudice against journalism as the "airy contempt" of "the normal professional attitude" (in "For Action," April 1922); and his own definition of literature as "news that stays news," by its very defining of literature in terms of a broader and nurturing matrix, unsettles any simple opposition between the "ephemeral" and the "timeless." Even when making a case for a distinctiveness in literary writing Pound tended to do so in terms of intersecting continua; so it was that he wrote in 1935 that "literary ability is not something less than or lower than journalistic ability, it is something solider and more durable."

The "solidity" that Pound regarded as the distinguishing characteristic of "literature" came from its inclusion of economics and history: "every piece of serious literature starts with a free examination of the data." Just how much of his prose Pound believed to be "serious literature" is unclear. But the fact remains that Pound devoted to his journalistic work considerable time and energy, and did so often when there was little or no hope of remuneration. To ignore this aspect of his work is understandable enough, so long as our critical aim is to constitute the *Cantos* as an aesthetic construct removed from history. But it can hardly be justified in any effort to understand the way in which the *Cantos* includes and grows out of history, or economics, or any of its other generic constituents. For genres are themselves concrete historical practices, originating, continuing, and changing in time, and Pound's poetic development was tied ineluctably to his work in other genres. His poetic procedures took shape on the basis of their dialogic and dialectical relations with his experiments in translation, journalism, explanatory or critical prose, even in musical composition. Pound's association with Orage affords one especially rich opportunity to examine the complex intersections of these heterogeneous areas of endeavor.

Moreover, Orage's changing intellectual allegiances exhibit a pattern of accommodation and adaptation very like Pound's own. By the time that Pound met him in

1911, Orage had already been through a number of intellectual conversions. Indeed, the restlessness of his intellect was such as to suggest Pound's description of his own inability to find peace: "the mind as Ixion, unstill, ever turning"—ever denied Faustian synthesis. During the nineties Orage had found no contradiction in simultaneous participation in the Independent Labour Party and the Theosophical Society. Between 1893 and 1900 he devoted as well seven years to the study of Plato, but abruptly punctuated that study to plunge into a seven years study of Nietzsche. Here too Orage became restless, and began organizing a "Guilds Restoration League" with A. J. Penty, and founded a "Fabian Arts Group" with Holbrook Jackson, groups which renewed his commerce with the socialism of Ruskin and Morris.[12] These frequent and, one would think, jarring realignments invite the conclusion that Orage was but a trifler with ideas, too shallow for enduring convictions.

The problem with such a hypothesis is that it ignores the way Orage's different interests came together, and the fact that they never did so easily. This difficulty suggests the usefulness of a historical approach concerned precisely with the nature of Orage's "conversions," the way that his career prompted the mixing of often conflicting discourses. Orage's conversion to the scientific analysis of Major Douglas in 1918 constituted a deliberate break from the attempted synthesis of Guild Socialism, and a return to the "scientific applications" of socialism which had previously led him to break with the Fabians. His conversion three years later to the system of Gurdjieff was no "synthesis" of socialism and spiritualism, but a leaving off of attempted combinations in order to pursue what Douglas' project was unable to accommodate. Even then Orage's vacillations did not end. Ten years later he returned to London hoping to reassume his role as editor of *The New Age* and, when denied that hope, founded a new journal which he intended to pick up where he had left off a decade earlier. He called this venture *The New English Weekly,* and announced its purpose to be the continuation of his earlier struggle to win an audience for Douglas' ideas. Orage's death only two years later may well have given this last turn an unimagined finality: for according to Philip Mairet, Orage had "kept alive his interest in [Gurdjieff's teachings] and was on the point of swinging over to advocating them openly when he died."[13]

John Finlay has speculated that the "open-mindedness" which spurred Orage's incompatible enthusiasms "was probably the cause of his failure" to achieve any lasting goal: "the fact that guild socialism presented twin appeals, via economics and via morals, was not a source of strength but of weakness" (pp. 65 and 118). Finlay's attitude about discursive mixtures, which refuses the heterogeneous enthusiasms that had prevailed within *The New Age* circle, derives from his aim to make a case for Social Credit as scientific analysis. So it is that

Finlay observes that the principle origins of Orage's Guild Socialism were not in scientific economics, but in the literary-humanist tradition of "the Victorian sages." If anything, Orage's eclecticism derived from an impulse to carry the consideration of economic problems even further from the realm of the quantifiable, and so from the analytical coolness of Fabian socialism, orthodox economics, or—Orage seems to have worried—Social Credit. The lack of hard science, or hard-nosed dogmatism to which Orage's detractors have always pointed was precisely Orage's ideal. He sought even as a younger man to dislocate economic discourse from the direction which, with an ever deepening commitment, it has taken ever since.

As even more argumentative contemporaries like T. E. Hulme knew, Orage was not an indecisive man. His unwillingness to commit himself to a single program really ought in itself to be seen as a commitment, however ineffectual it may seem to us. Orage's hopes for economic reform were from the first tied to programs which sought to integrate economic and cultural discussion, and to deny any privileged status to economic discourse. On another level, Orage sought to decenter economic authority, and to put it "back" in the hands of artisans and other producers. As Finlay notes, these programs betray the impact of Orage's early excitement over the anarchist socialism of Tom Mann. But, more profoundly, Orage's attitudes embodied a deep-seated rejection of nineteenth century confidence in progress and social evolution. So it was that G. S. H. Cole, one of Orage's contributors, described Guild Socialism as a fine balance between "the spirit of solidarity" among wage earners, "and the spirit of devolution" [Finlay, p. 81].

With regard to the guild revival movement led by Orage's friend A. J. Penty, devolution meant the division of political and economic authority among the various trade-unions and guilds. By 1907, when Orage first became an advocate, the guild revival movement was already in decline—its neomedievalism having proven inadequate to the problems of post-industrialist labor. But Orage took up its standard because he saw in the guild concept an idea he wanted to salvage from the wreck of the Guilds League. That idea, as Wallace Martin has explained, was that "workers should have more control over the standards and conditions of their labor"; over the next four years Orage continued to argue for that need, maintaining as well other convictions which had implicitly informed the guild revival: that neither men nor society were perfectible, and that all men were not equally gifted.[14] Orage apparently developed Guild Socialism, without any other fixed end in mind, by selecting and appropriating congenial aspects from larger projects. He did not begin putting his platform together until 1912, leaving him but three years to work at integrating the guild concept into some politically viable program before world war imposed its own solution to the labor problem.

The result, formulated for the most part in the pages of *The New Age,* Orage and his cohorts dubbed "Guild Socialism." Historians have remembered it, when at all, with little sympathy, and few would quarrel with Samuel Hyne's description of it as an "untidy mixture" that reflected "Orage's untidy thought." Hyne's description is fair enough. And yet it was just the "untidiness," the obvious heterogeneity of Orage's economics that, I believe, most appealed to Pound. Orage's work allows us to view the very mechanisms of change, and presents us with a confluence of recognizably nineteenth and twentieth century ideals much like that we encounter with Pound. What Hynes calls an "untidy mixture," and Martin an "ingenious synthesis of political Socialism and industrial Syndicalism" might well be called both. But a description satisfied merely to emphasize its partial intersections and divergences would be more valuable still, especially since, as commentators have reminded us, Guild Socialism proved seminal only insofar as it interacted with more enduring agendas. Orage himself described English socialism of this period as

> a cult with affiliations now quite disowned—with theosophy, art and crafts, vegetarianism, the "simple life," and almost, one might say, with the musical glasses. Morris had shed a medieval glamour over it with his stained-glass *News from Nowhere,* Edward Carpenter had put it into sandals, Cunninghame Graham had mounted it upon an Arab steed to which he was always saying a romantic farewell. Keir Hardie had clothed it in a cloth cap and a red tie. And Bernard Shaw, on behalf of the Fabian Society, had hung it with innumerable jingling epigrammatic bells—and cap. My brand of socialism was, therefore, a blend or, let us say, an anthology of all these, to which [I added] my personal predilections and experience.[15]

Such was Orage as Pound met him in the fall of 1911 in the Frith Street salon where Hulme was lecturing on Bergson's concept of "the image." This was an appropriate setting, since Hulme's Frith Street group was as heterogeneous as *The New Age*: attended by artists as unlike one another as Augustus John and Wyndham Lewis, poets as unlike as John Drinkwater and Ezra Pound, playwrights and actresses, editors and critics, and even the literary executor of Oscar Wilde—a marvelous illustration of the non-conformance of history with our attempts to posit distinct periods. Within this group Orage seems to have occupied a somewhat special position. For one thing, he was editor of *The New Age,* the first and then still most prestigious socialist weekly in London. For another, although generally known for his good-will, he was nonetheless recognized to be Hulme's "most stubborn contestant." Gorham Munson even described Orage as not only "the best talker I have ever listened to," but a veritable "fisher of men."[16] One can only imagine that Pound was quick to

seek his approval, and Orage ready enough to give it; for, by that November, Pound was publishing in *The New Age.*

III

> I affirm that future art criticism will be able to tell the component of usury tolerance. How far the TOLERANCE of usury prevailed, or did not prevail when a given picture was painted.
>
> —Pound, radio speech of 1942

By January of 1912, even when writing on "technique," Pound began to show signs of commerce with Orage's Guild Socialism. Taking up the question, "what have all men in common," Pound answered "money and sex and tomorrow," and wryly observed that the first was most often called "fate," the second associated with poetry—at least ever since poetry "stopped being epic," and the third "we none of us agree on." Nevertheless, he went on,

> Every man who does his job really well has a latent respect for every other man who does *his* own job really well; this is our lasting bond; whether it be a matter of buying up all the little brass farthings in Cuba and selling them at a quarter per cent. advance, or of delivering steam engines to King Menelik across three rivers and one hundred and four ravines, . . . the man who really does the thing well, if he be pleased afterwards to talk about it, always gets his auditor's attention . . . As for the arts and their technique—technique is the means of conveying an exact impression of exactly what one means in such a way as to exhilarate.[17]

Already, although not yet consistently, Pound was mixing his considerations of poetic technique with questions of money and trade. Whether he did so as a result of Orage's example, or whether he sought Orage's company because of his own inchoate interests, the two men began to meet regularly. It was the beginning of an association that would endure until Pound left London, and even then (1921) it was in *The New Age* that he would present his axiomatic "final testament" to English culture.

It was no accident that Orage should use the literary term "anthology" to describe the combinatory nature of Edwardian socialism. His "affiliations" were not only heterogeneous but, rather than establishing links with strictly political or economic thinkers, they were also "literary" in inspiration. In citing Morris, for example, Orage focused on his utopian novels, and suggested that Morris' medievalism subsequently "colored" British socialism and taught it to envision the future through, as it were, gothic stained glass. Similarly, Orage's mention of Graham implied a view of socialism inextricably caught up in romantic ideals, which both ennobled its subject and made it untenable. And as for Shaw, Orage proposed that for all its pretensions to scientific analysis, Fabian writing too depended on literary devices, on witty epigrams delivered from a position that purported to play no active part in political struggle.

These instances underscore the extent to which the "literary" quality of Orage's politics meant, more than attractive accoutrements, a distinctive group of organizational strategies. For Orage, and for the intellectuals like Pound who—however loosely—formed *The New Age* circle, literary models informed socialist ideals, as well as many different ways of arguing for them. These models effected not only what these often zealous men saw, but how they saw. For Pound, Orage's development of such models was doubly important, involving not only clusters of ideas but also ways of joining together like and unlike in an attempt to broaden the basis of cultural critique.

In his discussion of the origins of Social Credit, Finlay acknowledges the contributions which Orage's combinatory platform made to the subsequent work of Douglas, mentioning in particular one aspect of Orage's published work:

> The development of the Guild Socialist critique on the twin basis of economics and ethics gave Orage the incentive to put out a little book of observations on economics: in which he paid tribute to the "sensible" Ruskin.
>
> [p. 77]

The book to which Finlay refers is **An Alphabet of Economics** (London: T. Fisher Unwin, 1917), and we shall consider its sketch of Ruskin as a "sensible" reformer momentarily. I want first, however, to establish its importance for Pound as a generic model. Orage's attempt to popularize certain ideas about economics was by no means unprecedented. In fact, the significance of Orage's **Alphabet** for our study derives from its participation in a generic tradition that gathered considerable momentum during the late Victorian period, as economic discourse diverged ever further from common parlance. Most of these works have since been forgotten; but to name even a few instances suffices to give a general sense of their common constituent elements. Indeed, the formula requires little discussion precisely because this genre remains as heavily trafficked today as it was a century ago (just as it continues to receive little notice from the academic genres). Restricting ourselves to the field of economics, and to earlier instances than Orage's, we might cite such books as *An Alphabet of Finance* (1877) by Simon Newcomb, *An Alphabet in Finance* (1880) by Graham McAdam, *The Alphabet of Economic Science: Elements of the Theory of Value or Worth* (1888) by Phillip Henry Wicksteed, or *The ABC of the Federal Reserve System* (1918) by E. W. Kemmerer. However little these works are now respected, they belonged to a genre or class of

writings which served the important function of disseminating difficult information and of proposing the common value of fairly elite activity.

In the first quarter of the twentieth century this genre came to be very attractive to conservative thinkers, insofar as it offered a means of opposing the popular appeal of Marxian and socialist critiques of capitalism. We can discern something of the strength of this appeal in the ease with which, by 1912, Rudyard Kipling could adapt it for his distopian story *Easy as ABC*. In 1924 Hilaire Belloc published *An Economic Guide for Young People,* a book rejoined four years later by Shaw's *The Intelligent Woman's Guide to Socialism and Capitalism* (1928). Not surprisingly, the economic turmoil of the thirties occasioned the publication of a renewed welter of such economic handbooks, among which were numerous books by social creditors known to Orage. Albert Newsome published "a glossary for the plain man" which he entitled, formulaically enough, *An Alphabet of the New Economics.* E. S. Holter competed for attention with *The ABC of Social Credit.* Philip Mariet, a frequent contributor to *The New Age* and later one of Orage's biographers, also prepared a "handbook . . . outlining Social Credit": *The Douglas Manual.* It is in the company of writings like these that we can best understand such of Pound's texts as *ABC of Economics* (1933), *ABC of Reading* (1934), *Social Credit: An Impact* (1935), or even *Guide to Kulchur* (1938) as something more than eccentric, crank departures from reason. It was not just the ideas of Social Credit that Pound took up, however incompletely, but also certain ways of presenting those ideas.

Of course, Pound's handbooks also varied significantly from more typical generic instances, substituting his "ideogrammic" presentation for the constructions of expository journalism. But Pound's attraction to techniques and generic features common among popular handbooks was not limited to his "ABC's" and "guides"; it contributed to the composition of the *Cantos.* In fact, much of Pound's work suggests a fundamental revision of the relations between expository and poetic writing, and in this development his association with Orage was highly instrumental. We must make this point carefully. Pound owed his preoccupation with the materiality of language to the likes of Browning and Swinburne; similarly, the work of Flaubert, James, or Ford had already impressed upon him what the mastery of prose could accomplish. But it was Orage, and his Ruskinian insistence that "art includes utility but it also transcends utility," that most immediately encouraged Pound's conviction that the reforming of the world and the creation of a poetry fit to meet it were integrally related activities. It is here that we should return to Finlay's notice of Ruskin's importance for Orage, since it can help us understand much about Orage's, and so about Pound's, reception of Social Credit. Finlay proposes that, in seeking to resolve the ethical contradictions inherent in contemporary economic practice,

> Orage was led to a restatement of much of the Ruskinian tradition. But he went on to add points which the prophet had not mentioned. Thus, where Ruskin attacked the senseless accumulation of profit, Orage went beyond this to attack the very notion of work. "In economics," he said, "progress means the advance towards the idea of production without labour."
>
> [Finlay, p. 78]

Finlay's account affirms that Orage held a rather different view of Ruskin than that customarily taken by contemporary literary critics.[18] Orage did not regard Ruskin as a poetic visionary but as a "sensible" man committed to badly needed reforms. This was a perspective well familiar to Orage's contemporaries: J. A. Hobson, seeking in 1898 to perpetuate Ruskin's legacy, entitled his monograph *John Ruskin, Social Reformer*; G. B. Shaw, endeavoring in 1919 to make over that legacy, called his critique *Ruskin's Politics*. Pound's few explicit allusions to Ruskin situate his importance on this same contested ground. Consider his review of Swinburne's *Letters*, published the same year as Shaw's book on Ruskin. Pound wrote that when Swinburne's publishers and friends advised him to suppress *Atalanta in Calydon* "poor old Ruskin accepted the work, and later went mad in a society that wouldn't." Pound's remark not only suggests that Ruskin went "mad" in a country incapable of appreciating Swinburne's work, but also that Ruskin went "mad" in a society blind to its own moral outrage. Continuing in this way, Pound then grouped Swinburne and Ruskin together, along with Shelley, Byron and Landor, as victims of a "Platonic res publica" that has "no place for disturbing authors." In other words, Ruskin was for Pound, as for Orage, not primarily a critic of "art" but of the culture that produced it.

We can get a sense of the use Pound made of Ruskin's work by quickly considering Ruskin's *Fors Clavigera: Letters to the Workmen and Labourers of Great Britain* (1871-1878, 1880-1884) in ways that reflect on such works of Pound's as *Section: Rock-Drill* (1955). Like *Rock-Drill*, *Fors* was a late work characterized by a keen solicitude for its author's public. The title, Ruskin insisted, was an attempt "shortly to mark my chief purpose": "fors" meant "Chance, guided by the hidden hand of fate. Clavigera meant that chance carried a club, or nail or a key." While Ruskin allowed that his title might have other connotations, he himself "interpreted" it to mean "Chance, the fate that hits the nail on the head."[19] There was a serious concern behind this apparent whimsy. What Ruskin was proposing was that even the most "chance" occurrences can be made to reveal the essential condition of an entire culture. In effect, Ruskin's thinking here and elsewhere attributed to culture a unified organic life analogous to that which

Romantic aestheticians discerned in individual works of art. This way of thinking about culture characterized Pound's work as well. His enthusiasm for Remy de Gourmont, which—because Gourmont played so crucial a role in Pound's thoughts about method—is no random example, partly derived from his perception that Gourmont shared this way of thinking: "You could . . . have said to De Gourmont anything that came into your head, you could have sent him anything you had written with a reasonable assurance that he would have known what you were driving at."[20]

Ruskin's example is evident in much of Pound's work during the years he was associated with Orage—evident even in the way that Pound sometimes handled "purely technical" problems. Pound's review "Robert Bridges' New Book" (*Poetry,* October 1915) offers an illuminating case in point. Pound took the occasion of this review to defend "vers libre" from its detractors by pointing to its use by Bridges, poet laureate and so the embodiment of orthodoxy. However, it is how Pound moved to that conclusion which is of interest here. He began by pointing out that the various kinds of vers libre, like "practically all forms of verse, date from antiquity: China and India and Greece had free verse before some forgotten Italian got stuck in the beginning of a canzone and called the fragment a sonnet." Leaping then to the immediate past, Pound built towards a climax in good Ruskinian fashion—with a loosely biblical, catalogic "and":

> And after all these things came the English exposition of 1851 and the Philadelphia Centennial, introducing cast-iron house decorations, and machine-made fretwork, and there followed a generation of men with minds like the cast-iron ornament, and they set their fretful desire upon machine like regularity.

Criticism like this may have been new to the pages of Harriet Monroe's *Poetry*, but Ruskin had established its precedent over a half-century earlier. Pound's move from technical discussion of verse form to sweeping Jeremiad was sudden and unanticipated. His "and" asserted an inevitability between hypotasized verse forms, machine-made fret-work, and fretful desires that was righteously assumed rather than rigorously argued. This piece of journalism does not mark any turning point in Pound's thinking. Pound had ceased to hesitate over regarding poets in extra-aesthetic terms well before 1919. On the contrary, it is the very fact that this was a book review which Pound wrote in haste, with no special self-scrutiny, that makes its evident assumptions of interest. Its transparency permits us to observe how Pound was already mixing aesthetic and economic discourse years before his persuasion by Douglas. Without denying Pound's own originality, we should see that his manner of mixing these discourses was Ruskinian in manner, and Oragean in focus.

IV

> Don't imagine that I think economics interesting—not as Boticelli or Picasso is interesting. But at present they are interesting as a gun muzzle aimed at one's own head is "interesting," when one can hardly see the face of the gun holder and is wholly uncertain as to his temperament and intentions.
>
> —Pound, 1921 review of Douglas' *Credit Power and Democracy*

Nevertheless, Pound's review of Bridges also points us to his single greatest point of contention with Orage. For all the Ruskinian fervor of his notions about economics and culture, Orage never much altered his early convictions about the autonomy of poetic language. He always insisted on the traditionally formal and "poetical" qualities of poetry, and in this regard too he was more like Ruskin than not. Yet, unlike Ruskin, whose sense of organic form and whose faith in his own vision permitted him expansive experiments in prose form, Orage could never discover a vehicle adequate to his needs. The periodical seemed the form most conducive to eclectic tolerance, and to his ultimately didactic purpose; but even periodical form had demonstrable limits, since it had to maintain enough consistency of orientation and texture to sell copy. In none of his periodical work did Orage ever manage long to reconcile the conflicting claims of, on the one hand, scientific socialism and its purported dependence on clear-sighted analysis, and on the other, spiritualism and its call for vision. As we have noted, Pound faced similar difficulties in his own early work, and until the twenties produced poetry that for the most part bore out Orage's romantic (and Ruskinian) prejudice that "true" poetry was above material concerns: that it was the role of poetry and art to raise the incidents of ordinary life "to sublimity" and so provide "the natural perfected, and hence robbed of its moral obligations."[21] Pound's struggle, which so intensified in the years immediately after the first world war that he created little poetry that he felt worth keeping, was to develop a poetry capable of joining analysis and vision, economics and poetry.

Orage however always exempted poetry from service in his cause. His interest was in a vigorous didactic prose, one which, in its perfection

> will be anything but a sedative after a full meal of action. It will be not only action itself, but the cause of action; and its deliberate aim will be to intensify and refine action and to raise action to the level of a fine art. Anything less than a real effect upon real people in a real world is beneath the dignity even of common prose.[22]

This was the lesson that Orage found in "the sensible Ruskin," and then, largely by example of *The New Age*, impressed upon Pound. In effect, Orage sought to collapse the aesthetic realm—not by undermining its claims for value—but by expanding it not only beyond the writing of literary genres but also beyond writing itself. This was the ultimate goal of Orage's journalism, and of his editing of *The New Age*, and it was an ambition which Pound too shared. But Pound carried the brand into the very citadel of the aesthetic realm by attempting a poetry that would "intensify and refine action." This meant something more than, as Clark Emery has proposed, putting ideas into action.[23] What Orage's phrase proposes is an aestheticization of "action" itself, a notion which executed a kind of Paterian turn within what we have been calling the Ruskinian tradition. Pound's determination to pursue these ends with poetic discourse was one with which Orage could never have felt full sympathy. To be plain, Orage's reviews of Pound's work seldom offered more than a distant and qualified approval: in separate reviews of 1918, for instance, Orage doubted Pound's critical ability, and found his "irregular metrics" to be "defective;" and as late as 1921 Orage complained that his friend "has always a ton of precept for a pound of example." Still, the poetic that eventually led Pound to extra-aesthetic aims, and to combine poetry with so many non-poetic and even non-literary genres, constituted at least in this sense an innovation upon Orage's model, or for that matter upon Ruskin's. At no point did Pound find in Orage's work consistent inspiration. Pound advocated few of Orage's interests; he was, although the Guild idea remained a positive motif in the *Cantos* up through its last fragments, never a committed partisan of Guild Socialism. But Orage's work brought to the insistence of Ford Madox Ford "that poetry should be at least as well written as prose" a new dimension of possibility.

"Social Credit" as Pound came to know it had already incorporated many elements of Orage's Guild Socialism. By 1918 the guild movement had been polarized and disabled by the contention over the proper response to the Bolshevik Revolution; the eventual dominance of radical communists within the movement shattered the equilibrium of what had always been a fragile coalition. Moderates like Orage and his closer associates soon grew unable to preserve their old influence, and so Orage's "going over" to Douglas only formalized a de facto disintegration.[24] Social Credit, however, did what Guild Socialism could never do: it offered Pound and many others a concise program. It proffered solutions to immediate international problems and did so in terms of a handful of simple precepts. By restricting its concerns it was also able to provide formulas suitable for popular consumption: formulas like the "A+B Theorem," so simple that they have since been dismissed as credos, mere articles of faith. Nevertheless, the significance of Social Credit for Pound's writing at least needs to be qualified. Pound's sense of what an economics should do, and of how it should be written, was formed prior to his earliest contacts with Douglas. While it would be an overstatement to speak of Pound's "tutelage" to Orage, it would be an oversight not to recognize the importance for his largest projects of Orage, *The New Age,* and the Ruskinian tradition. I have looked to these in order to suggest how the economic and social criticism of Orage and his circle contributed to Pound's determination to alter the nature of aesthetic norms. Pound's interaction with Orage prompted both his turn from the slopes of "true Helicon," and his attempt to produce writing that would "be not only action itself, but the cause of action." It was finally just this impulse that propelled Pound into one of the most ambitious and problematic artistic projects of the modern world. His continued insistence upon the materiality of language encouraged him to attempt radical condensations of history, while yet counting on its intelligibility. Whether Pound's confidence was justified remains a matter of concern. His attempts to develop an art that "includes utility" but also transcends it—to create "a poem including history"—clearly transformed the many kinds of texts he so included; his "radiant nodes" altered the nature of the "ideas" constantly rushing from, through and in them. Nevertheless, we should see even in these more famous formulations of Pound's vorticist manifesto the divergent claims of two distinctly different conceptions of art, by whose synthesis Pound hoped to produce at last "a profounder didacticism."

Notes

1. Pound's response to Odon Por, a Hungarian by birth and living in London when Pound met him, has been discussed by Peter Nicholls in his valuable study *Ezra Pound: Politics, Economics, and Writing* (London: Macmillan, 1984), p. 84. Silvio Gesell's *Natural Economic Order* was first published in 1911, but not translated into English until 1934.

2. For a careful and critical account of Pound's debt to Gourmont, see Richard Sieburth's *Instigations: Ezra Pound and Remy de Gourmont* (Cambridge: Harvard University Press, 1978).

3. See John L. Finlay, *Social Credit: The English Origins* (Montreal: McGill-Queen's University Press, 1972), p. 155.

4. See Douglas' "taunting epistle" to Pound, of 7 January 1936, quoted in C. David Heymann's *Ezra Pound: The Last Rower* (New York: Viking, 1976) p. 78. The distinction between Douglas' notion of "economic democracy" and the proto-fascist economics which attracted Pound is, however, not to be made easily. As critics like Finlay, Nicholls, and Leon Surette have observed, Douglas himself moved ever further to the right after his initial failures to win national attention for his ideas.

5. See, for example, Pound's letter to *The New English Weekly* for 2 July 1936. Pound's letter was in part occasioned by a letter from Gladys Bing, published in *TNEW* for 18 June—and it is interesting to note that the one part of Bing's letter that did not upset Pound was her identification of Social Credit and Fascism. Pound's response was simply to attempt the dissociation of fascism from the likes of Oswald Mosley, and align it with the "PROLETARIAN" tradition of "Guild Socialism, syndicalism, and the CORPORATE STATE."

6. Orage, in *The New Age* Vol. 18, p. 761; quoted in *The New Age Under Orage,* ed. Wallace Martin (Boston: Routledge and Kegan Paul, 1974), p. 180. Compare Orage's position with Ruskin's assertion in *The Laws of Fesole* IX. 1. (1877) that: "Art is only in her right place and office when she is subordinate to use; her duty is always to teach, though to teach pleasantly; she is shamed, not exalted, when she has only graces to display, instead of truths to declare." Pound expressed much the same idea more succinctly in *ABC of Reading* (p. 64): "Beauty is aptness of purpose."

7. Letter of 8 July, 1922, *Ezra Pound: Selected Letters 1907-1941,* ed. D. D. Paige (New York: New Directions, 1950), p. 180.

8. Sieburth has written authoritatively on Gourmont's influence upon Pound's prose style (see especially Chapter Three). The interaction of Gourmont's and Orage's examples might here be usefully compared with the twin effect of the poetic models Pound observed in Yeats and Ford. In any case, the result was, as Pound remembered in a letter to Iris Barry of July 1916 (printed in *Poetry,* September 1950), that he recognized he had "ruined" his "English prose for five years trying to write English as Tacitus wrote Latin." That false step had been initiated by Pound's admiration for some translations done by a writer who embodied "the poor damned soul of the late Walter Pater."

9. For an example of Pound's early discussions of the poetically proper, see his review of Jules Romaines' *Odes ed Prieres,* published in *Poetry,* August, 1913, p. 187-189.

10. Butler's remark is from Chapter LXXXI of *The Way of All Flesh* (1906), Connolly's from the opening of *The Unquiet Grave* (1945). With regard to Pound, the definition of "literature" was an issue that often interested him during the years of his closest associations with Orage; see, for example, "Affirmations VII" (February, 1915), or "The Pleasing Art of Poetry" (July, 1915), in *The New Age.* Such denial of absolute distinctions between literary and nonliterary writing became more pronounced as Pound moved into the *Cantos.* By 1929, in *How to Read,* Pound was willing to venture that "great literature is simply language charged with meaning to the utmost possible degree" (*Literary Essays* p. 23).

11. Pound made this charge against Shaw in two places on the same day. I have quoted from "London and Its Environs," published in the Belgian biweekly *L'Art Libre,* 1 January, 1920, a translation of which was published by Archie Henderson in *Paideuma,* Vol. 13, no. 2; see also "The Revolt of Intelligence IV," (*The New Age,* 1 January 1920). Interestingly enough, Pound's next article in *L' Art Libre* (15 January 1920), (also translated by Henderson) concluded by questioning whether "the Symbolist attitude of proud isolation [can] suffice for our generation." Pound's dismissal of Shaw's utilitarian didacticism was a necessary part of his own effort to develop one that could prove "profounder."

12. Penty, for example, paid explicit homage to Ruskin, and to Carlyle and Arnold in his Preface to *The Restoration of the Guild System* (1906). See also Wallace Martin's history of Orage's activities during these years in *The New Age Under Orage* (Manchester: Manchester University Press, 1967), which I have consulted throughout this study.

13. Mairet is quoted in Finlay, p. 65; further references to Finlay's work will be identified in the text.

14. See Martin, pp. 214-217. Incidentally, as Martin points out, the Guilds League nearly outlasted Guild Socialism, not formally dissolving until 1922.

15. Quoted in Samuel Hynes, *Edwardian Occasions* (New York: Oxford University Press, 1972), p. 42.

16. Gorham Munson, *The Awakening Twenties: A Memoir-History of a Literary Period* (Baton Rouge: Louisiana State University Press, 1985), p. 258.

17. Ezra Pound, "Technique," the fourth installment of "I Gather the Limbs of Osiris," reprinted in *Selected Prose,* pp. 32-33, but originally published in *The New Age.*

18. See, for example, Harold Bloom's introduction to *The Literary Criticism of John Ruskin,* ed. Bloom, (Gloucester: Peter Smith, 1969). Bloom is primarily interested in Ruskin "the aesthetic visionary, fascinated by the world of form and color." My point is not that Bloom and contemporary critics are wrong to be concerned with an "aesthetic" or "visionary" Ruskin, nor is it that nineteenth century responses were more interesting. Rather, in this changing response to an author of continuing importance we can recover an important perspective on an aspect of Pound's career which has come to be seen as anomalous. Pound's work resembles Ruskin's precisely to the extent that it

lends itself to both aesthetic and meliorative responses, and one of the greatest tasks facing Pound's critics at this time is to understand in more than thematic terms how he combined economic and poetic discourses.

19. Quoted in Robert Hewison, *John Ruskin: the Argument of the Eye* (Princeton: Princeton University Press, 1976), p. 180. This phrase of Ruskin's may well inspissate Pound's fulmination in *Gaudier-Brzeska: A Memoir* that "when words cease to cling close to things, kingdoms fall, empires wane and diminish. Rome went mad because it was no longer in fashion to *hit the nail on the head.* They desired orators." (p. 114) [my emphasis].

20. Quoted in Sieburth, p. 42.

21. Quoted in *Orage as Critic,* ed. Wallace Martin (London: Routledge and Kegan Paul, 1974), p. 142; the essay was originally published in *The New Age* in 1915.

22. Quoted in *Orage as Critic,* p. 195; the essay was originally published in *The New Age* in 1921 as "Perfecting English Prose."

23. Clark Emery, *Ideas Into Action: A Study of Pound's Cantos* (Coral Gables: University of Miami Press, 1958). Although I qualify Emery's conclusion here, his book has long served as an important corrective to overly formal readings of Pound's work.

24. See Finlay for a full account of how the demise of Guild Socialism effected the growth of the Social Credit movement.

Tom Steele (essay date 1990)

SOURCE: Steele, Tom. "1893-1900: Socialism and Mysticism." In *Alfred Orage and the Leeds Arts Club,* pp. 25-44. Hants, England: Scolar Press, 1990.

[*In the following essay, Steele traces the roots of Orage's early professional and literary influences in attempting to build a explanatory foundation for his later drift towards radical causes.*]

Alfred Orage was twenty when he returned to Yorkshire, the county of his birth, in the autumn of 1893. It was the first time since earliest childhood, when on the death of his father his near-penniless mother had returned with him and his sister to the family village of Fenstanton in Huntingdonshire. He had come to Leeds to take up the profession at which his father had so notably failed, schoolteaching. Orage was born in the village of Dacre about fifteen miles north of Leeds on the southern escarpment of Nidderdale. A hundred years later, the birth would have been in the shadow of the dishes of the USAF Menwith Hill listening station, where the etheric communications of all Europe could be overheard. Less than fifty years later Henry Moore would have passed through it on the way to sketch the weird wind-blown rock formations at Birmham just to the north.

Orage's father William died, having drunk his patrimony, when his son was little more than a year old, leaving his wife Sarah Anne to bring the children up as best she could.[1] Back in Fenstanton, Orage was sent to the local school where he excelled in all his subjects and at the non-conformist Sunday school he impressed his teacher, Howard Coote the local squire's son, by his quickness and intelligence. Before long Coote was giving him the run of his library where he was initiated into the high moral discourses of Ruskin, Carlyle, Matthew Arnold and William Morris. At length, through Coote's intervention, he was rescued from his class destiny as plough-boy and sent to Culham training college in Oxfordshire, where, while training to be a teacher, he taught himself the craft of editor.

Through squire Coote's patronage Orage also obtained his teaching post in Leeds. Orage was appointed by Leeds School Board on 26 October 1893, as a trained certificated assistant.[2] This was possibly to Chapel Allerton School, as John Carswell thinks, but more likely to Ellerby Lane Boys, because in May 1894, just six months later, Orage was reported as having resigned from Ellerby Lane Boys to join the staff of Leylands Mixed School.[3] Orage, however, did choose to live in the comfortable suburb of Chapel Allerton whose contrast with the stinking slums of Ellerby Lane and the Leylands could only have been shocking to the country boy.

Earlier in the century Chapel Allerton had been a semi-rural village on the north of Leeds with a reputation for good clean air. Despite the quadrupling of the village population from 1,000 in 1800 to 4,000 in the early 1870s its atmosphere was still almost bucolic, though now it was becoming a respectable suburb. Ellerby Lane, however, was on the edge of the Bank, a densely populated slum on the northern side of the river Aire in the centre of town. It housed an enormous immigrant Irish population, possibly 20,000 strong, described by an inspector some years before as 'from the wildest parts of Connaught' and in urgent need of civilizing.[4] The crowded courts and alleys where disease and pollution were widespread, were the breeding ground for socialists like Tom Maguire. As he waited for the tram to take him into town, the young schoolteacher may well have contemplated the view from Chapel Allerton into Leeds with some trepidation, for the following year, he wrote:

> The view of the town from some outlying hill is like a peep from Abraham's bosom into the abode of Dives. Here on the height the air is fresh to the lungs . . . But yonder, down there, the infernal pot is boiling, and the steam hangs like a nightmare over the city. Dantes need no Virgil to show them Hell; and Miltons need not be blind. There, night and day, thousands of chimneys are allowed to belch out their poisonous breaths to be inhaled by human lungs below.[5]

and as for the river below the Bank

> The Aire is simply a huge sewer: it has the filth of Leeds in suspension. Unlike the Jordan seven dips therein would cause, not cure leprosy . . . it has been transformed into the oily-flowing mud stream, into whose waters no fish dare venture, on whose banks no leaves can breathe, no trees may grow.

Although it was in the suburb he settled, Orage chose what he called in the same article 'a knight errantry' in the boiling pot of the slums. Both Mairet and Carswell think that he lived in the end of a stone terrace called Ingle Row, which is opposite perhaps the prettiest police station cum public library in Leeds, though this cannot be confirmed from the Ward Roles. By 1896 he had moved down into Harehills a mile or so into town, but by 1900 had moved back again to Chapel Allerton.

Like Ellerby Lane Boys, the Leylands School no longer stands. It too was in a densely populated area of Leeds close to the centre of town across the York Road from the Bank. It was just starting to receive the first wave of Eastern European Jews fleeing from the pogroms, later swelling to a population of 15,000. Jews and Irish regarded each other uneasily across the York Road, occasionally skirmishing. Orage taught there for only a year and a half. In January 1896 he joined his third school, Harehills Board School, where he taught older children, probably eleven or twelve years old in Standard VI.

In September 1896, Orage received his first annual pay rise of £5, something he apparently forgot to tell Philip Mairet who was under the impression he never earned more than his initial salary of £80 a year. He remained here for three and a half years now living with his wife Jean in a small terraced house at 86 Elford Place, little more than a hundred yards away. The school log book noted that he was absent through illness for a day and a half—only marginally more disruptive than the arrival of Barnum and Bailey's Circus in 1899, for which the school closed the entire day.[6] Here he was befriended by Cyril Arthington Pease, a fellow teacher who possessed the rare distinction of a Bachelor of Arts degree from Oxford, but, not certificated, was paid even less than Orage. From a substantial middle-class family, Pease was also an active member of the ILP. He was one of those who had joined because he could not tolerate the idea that his privileges had been acquired at the expense of the impoverishment of the many and had posed the question for himself 'How can I live without robbing someone else?'

Like Orage, he had chosen to teach in a poor working-class area. He left Leeds ten years later to found a school run on progressive lines in Letchworth Garden City, in its pioneering days, and in 1905 invited Orage to join him. But by this time Orage had his eyes on higher things and passed the opportunity over to his colleague Millie Browne (later Price). In September 1897 Orage's pay was increased by another £5 but, the record shows, he declined to join the board's annuity scheme, preferring to put his trust for the future in his own wit rather than municipal thrift.

Harehills Board School was purpose built and founded in 1891. It was designed by William Landless in the Queen Anne style with 'scroll gables, broken rooflines and tall windows'[7] deemed appropriately uplifting by the board, but still overcrowded and underequipped judging from the HMI's reports summarized in the log: 'The population of the area is increasing so rapidly that the accommodation provided in this large school only opened three years ago is already inadequate and in spite of the use of large central halls for classes some of the class rooms are constantly overcrowded.'[8] Nevertheless the inspectors praised the school's tone, discipline and instruction. But, in another unexplained move in October 1899, now on a wage of £95, Orage returned to Ellerby Lane Boys where he remained until August 1902.

His last teaching post in Leeds was at Roundhay Road Boys which he joined on 25 August 1902. Like Harehills School, a little over a quarter of a mile away beyond some of the densest back-to-back housing in Europe, the school was new and imposing. The log records him as being absent once because of his sister's illness in December 1902, once due to matters of importance detaining him in early November 1903 and for nearly two weeks in early December of that year apparently without cause.[9] In June 1903 he had also been to Amsterdam for 'Miss Shaw's funeral' for three and a half days. The following year at the same time he was also in Amsterdam for seven days for a conference, almost certainly an international theosophy conference, to which Orage was one of the English delegates. He was away on only five other occasions in the three years at the school, the only cause given being, 'neuralgia', meant he was almost certainly exhausted. On 13 March 1905 he took a morning off because of his wife's illness. The doctor apparently suspected an infectious disease but sent a certificate with Orage in the afternoon saying it was safe for him to return. He finally left the school and Leeds School Board's employ not, as is usually given, in the summer but on 22 December 1905. It was supposed to be a temporary six months' leave of absence 'in order to write a book' but he never returned.

The Leeds School Board was the second largest in the country and one of the most progressive. Compared with the voluntary schools which they replaced the 45 new schools which the Board had built since the Education Act of 1870 seemed 'veritable people's palaces . . . lighter, loftier, better ventilated, more convenient in every way'. The board had set out to transform the condition of the children of Leeds and, according to a later educationalist, 'had in truth proved themselves to be great civilising and humanising agencies' who had turned out 'children who were disciplined and drilled in the rudiments of the three Rs'.[10] The Education Act's author, W. E. Forster, who was the brother-in-law of Matthew Arnold, was the Member of Parliament for Leeds neighbouring town, Bradford, where Margaret MacMillan had recently done so much pioneering work. Orage had come to Leeds during the great educational revolution, when it was fervently hoped by liberals and progressives that education would save the nation from anarchy. How far he was ever convinced by this is difficult to know but after only a year at the chalkface, he gave eloquent voice to his disillusion:

> Education has deluded the human race: it is bringing us to the wrong millennium. It promised us liberty; it oathed us equality; it hinted at fraternity. It pointed with prophetic finger to the perfection of man: Utopia was to be reached by easy stages and short cuts. Thus it piped and we have danced ever since: and the dancing is nigh killing us . . . Men are no longer their own, they have been bought with the results of the 'self-denials' of capitalists.[11]

He may at some stage have chosen to teach standard I, the very youngest of the schoolchildren, to free himself for extra-mural intellectual, political and other pursuits. Mary Gawthorpe was of the opinion that 'Standard I certainly gave more time for reading' but she also felt that 'Orage liked to teach little children because of an innate modesty. Washing the feet of little children was the idea which persisted',[12] a sentiment echoed by Mairet, who thought that he was a highly gifted teacher and a great success with children 'following all their sayings and doings with rapt interest'.[13] Millie Browne, on the other hand, remembered his advice to her on becoming a teacher was to 'Use the cane steadily for the first month, then put it away and never take it out again'.[14] His late time-keeping put him in bad odour with the authorities who occasionally suspended his annual increments and denied him advancement. Despite this, he was popular with both children and colleagues and active in the local branch of the National Union of Teachers.

In 1894, Orage had joined the newly formed Leeds branch of the Independent Labour Party. He became a socialist, says Mairet, by hearing Tom Mann, whom he regarded as the greatest orator he had ever heard, address a rally in Sheffield. But it is likely that local socialist leaders such as Tom Maguire, who died the following year at the age of 27, were just as important. Like Mann, Maguire was also a charismatic figure who was remembered by his friend Edward Carpenter as 'daring yet cautious, a dreamer and yet a man of action'.[15] A small consumptive figure, he was a photographer's assistant who preferred poetry to party politics and died tragically of tuberculosis when his political powers were at their height.

Though small, the socialist movement in Leeds had been intensely active in the previous decade, culminating in the gas workers' strike of 1890 and Maguire was, in Carpenter's words, the 'mainspring and inspirer of the movement in Leeds'.[16] This famous victory for the socialists succeeded in breaking the hold over the local labour movement of the Liberal Party and laid the foundations for independent labour representation. E. P. Thompson went so far as to claim 'if we must have one man who played an outstanding role in opening the way for the ILP, that man was a semi-employed Leeds-Irish photographer in his late twenties—Tom Maguire'.[17] Maguire and Orage collaborated on ILP propaganda. The Fabian Society branches, which had blossomed in the early nineties, decamped wholesale, according to Alf Mattinson, into the ILP upon its formation in 1893.[18]

The significance of the strength of northern provincial radicalism inherent in the formation of the ILP cannot be underestimated. As the historian of the Christian Socialist Movement, Peter d'A Jones has suggested the London Fabians misunderstood this while the Manchester factory owner Frederick Engels saw it very clearly. He told his friend Sorge: 'The Fabians here in London are a band of careerists who have understanding enough to realise the inevitability of the social revolution, but who could not possibly entrust this tremendous task to the crude proletariat alone, and are therefore kind enough to set themselves at the head.'[19] True dynamism would come from 'the rush towards socialism in the provinces,' not from London, 'the home of cliques'. If only 'the petty private ambitions and intrigues of the London would-be great men are now held in check somewhat, and the tactics do not turn out too wrong-headed, the Independent Labour Party may succeed in detaching the masses from the Social Democratic Federation, and in the provinces, from the Fabians too, and then force unity.' A few weeks later Engels added:

> Lancashire and Yorkshire are again taking the lead in this movement too, as in the chartist movement. People like Sidney Webb, Bernard Shaw and the like, who wanted to permeate the Liberals with socialism, must now allow themselves to be permeated by the spirit of the working-men members of their own society . . . Either they remain alone, officers without soldiers, or they must go along.

By the time he came to Leeds this great wave of activism was subduing and a long-term realignment of politics was emerging in which organizational problems took precedence. Asked later to contribute to a pamphlet on why he joined the ILP, Orage was characteristically flippant, using the opportunity for a lesson in intuitionist philosophy.

> Well you see, I joined first and found out afterwards. Most people flatter themselves that they look before they leap: as a matter of fact, very few people indeed look until they have leapt; and the few who do never leap at all, and go down to the vile dust from whence they sprung, unloved, unmarried and unhung. The truth is Nature is too wise to make men too wise, and it is only in life's unimportant details, such as choosing a cigar or electing an M. P., that she allows us the chance of bungling . . . Do you suppose a young man weighs the probable results of his falling in love, or even thinks anything about its results before he falls? . . . As touch is the primary material sense, whence all the others spring, so the primary mental sense, of which thought, imagination, reason are mere modifications is Feeling. After all, you cannot be an optimist with a sluggish liver, nor a philosopher with the toothache. I joined the I. L. P. because I felt it the right thing for me to do: I continue in the I. L. P. because I know it is. The feeling, however, came first, and the reasons, in plenty, came afterwards.[20]

The ILP quickly recognized Orage's literary talents and immediately commissioned articles for a propaganda leaflet with the title of *Hypnotic Leeds,* in 1895. It was edited by the founder of the Fabian Society in Leeds in 1891, Albert Marles, and other contributors included Tom Maguire and Joseph Clayton, (from whom Orage later purchased the *New Age*). Orage's articles were heavily coded literary pieces which discoursed the matter of Leeds's slumdom and poverty through biblical and classical references in the manner of Ruskin or Arnold (as can be seen from the extracts quoted earlier). The first, 'A Study in Mud' on the evils of Leeds slums advocated a secular mission or 'true Aristocracy', who would 'build their houses and live their lives in the slums'. In the second article, 'Quixotic Energy' (very quixotically for a teacher in his first year in post) he titled at the 'payment by results' system in schools for its mechanical suppression of the child's innate creativity in favour of discipline and instruction (what D. H. Lawrence later called 'the din-din-dinning of Board Schools').[21] Orage sounded a clarion call of libertarianism in the traditionally conservative profession of teachers, which, as John Carswell perceptively notes, subsequently became a willing constituency for his writing,

> The new battalions of teachers required by the Education Act had to be sought in the schools of villages and slums for the possessing classes were neither numerous enough nor willing to see their children take up teaching on weekdays. The process was at work all over England, with immense social consequences for it had created, in three decades, a large and unprecedented social category, more than half of which consisted of women . . . here was the rank and file for womens

rights, and a public for progressive journalism on a scale never known before. The teacher training programme not only gave Orage his first career: it gave him the audience for his second.[22]

His masters on the Leeds School Board, who prided themselves on their humane approach, may well have responded to Orage's challenge for the payments by results system was indeed abolished in 1897. However the dominant purpose in the board was still that of sanitizing the new generation rather than releasing creative energies.

Orage's involvement with the socialist movement was as much because of his passion for argument as conviction by its ideas. Mairet talks of him laying down his books on a summer's evening and strolling over to the newly laid-out Hyde Park on Woodhouse Moor, where socialist orators would be arguing the point with hecklers in the crowd. Orage would quietly intervene by picking holes in the heckler's argument, lead him into self-contradiction and then in a triumph of Socratism, 'deliver judgement with clarity, wit and humour'. The socialists, of course, welcomed him with open arms and for about four years he became one of the ILP's most energetic, though not wholly reliable, activists.

He flexed his own oratorical muscles on many occasions, once to a rally of eight thousand on Hunslet Moor on May Day 1896.[23] Soon a popular lecturer and debater, he lectured a number of times to the Central ILP Club in Leeds and was entrusted with leading off for the ILP in debates against other organizations. The *Labour Leader* reported on 1 February 1896, a lecture to Halton (Leeds) ILP club was filled to utmost capacity, noting 'Socialism is making itself felt in Halton'. On 4 November he lectured at Yeadon and on 22 November chaired a meeting at which the Fabian leader and early advocate of Nietzsche, Hubert Bland, lectured on German socialism. In addition he regularly chaired the Sunday meetings of the Central ILP club.

He lectured to other ILP branches also and it seems that he often used these opportunities to develop cultural themes. At a meeting attended by Millie Browne, who thought the ILP members 'a drab uncultured lot', Orage addressed the York ILP branch on Shelley's 'Prometheus Unbound'. She appears to have been as much impressed by the speaker as the subject:

> . . . one meeting I went to was epoch making for me. A speaker was announced named A. R. Orage, and he was billed to speak on Shelley's Prometheus unbound. I listened spellbound as he read the rhythmical visionary verses, and attempted to interpret the mythological characters of the lovely but abstruse and metaphysical drama. I did not understand it at all, but I was fascinated by the lecturer. He was about twenty six at the time, nine years older than I was; tall and slender with a head noble as an Arab horse, which with his thick

dark lock of hair falling in moments of eloquence over his forehead, he rather resembled. One of his dark eyes was spotted with gold, and that side of his face showed a dark golden stain where in his youth acid had been flung at him. His mouth was full and mobile, his manner of speech was golden also.[24]

Millie Price's attraction to Orage seems to have typified that of many young women teachers.

In July 1895 Orage began his career as political columnist with the first of his regular contributions to the ILP weekly paper, the *Labour Leader*, edited by Keir Hardie. In November these became his famous column, 'A Bookish Causerie', indicating that it was not merely conventional book reviewing but an attempt to change and reform the readers' tastes and appetites. To call his contribution a 'column' is somewhat misleading since it often occupied one-third to three-quarters of a page. It represented many hours of books devoured and thousands of words written, for which he received 5 shillings a piece to add to his meagre teacher's stipend. The journalistic company he kept was uplifting as, occasionally, the same page sees an article by William Morris at his head and another by Tom Mann at his feet. He kept the words flowing for about two years but in July 1897 the last contribution made its appearance. It cannot have been anything but an enormous taxing of his energies, Quixotic or otherwise.

A second venture into political journalism was offered to Orage by an ILP shopkeeper in Holbeck, who started 'a freely distributed propaganda sheet' called *Forward* from his own resources in October 1896. Under Orage's editorship the sheet was soon enlarged and expanded to a print run of 50,000 per month and distributed citywide. The shopkeeper, D. B. Foster, who became the founding secretary of the Leeds Labour Party, later wrote:

> . . . this effort to provide Socialist propaganda for the whole city brought around me quite a number of very helpful comrades amongst whom I well remember the name of . . . Mr. A R Orage, who for some years now has been the editor of the 'New Age' as he really was of 'Forward' though my name was nominally associated with that position.[25]

Another contributor to *Forward* was the pioneer socialist and feminist, Isabella Ford, who wrote a regular women's political page called 'Up and Down the World'. From a well-established Liberal Quaker family, Miss Ford became an enthusiastic leader of the ILP and later one of the first supporters of the Leeds Arts Club, serving for a while as a committee member. Older and wiser, it is unlikely that she was affected by Orage in the same way as Millie Browne but Orage probably benefited from her company and that of her sisters Emily and Bessie at the Central ILP Club sessions in Briggate. The sisters were amongst the first members of the ILP in 1893 and brought many influential contacts into the club. Both William Morris and Peter Kropotkin had stayed at the sisters' house in Adel, as had a whole galaxy of agitators, political refugees and labour leaders. Edward Carpenter was also a regular visitor. Alf Mattinson recorded in his obituary of Bessie that during the 1890s, when the impoverished young socialists had sought the generosity of the Ford sisters,

> . . . the movement in Leeds entered on its palmiest days. Never before nor since those few years when the club radiated such activities has the Labour or Socialist cause shown the same enthusiasm, the same fighting spirit, or possessed such a galaxy of diversified talent.[26]

Isabella Ford also wrote a number of novels of industrial class struggle and the fight for women's independence during the 1890s, one of which *On the Threshold,* Orage reviewed as essentially 'a book of women for men and women' adding, 'Simple and even absent as the plot may seem, and weak in places as the style may be, there are scenes of real life among real people, touches of homely unaffected pathos, which make "On the Threshold" not only readable but re-readable'.[27]

In 1896 Orage was married to Jean Watson whom he had met when he was a student at Culham College and she an art student at the Royal College.[28] Already a theosophist, it was probably she who introduced him to the Theosophical Society. The flourishing Northern Federation headquarters was then in Harrogate where many of its national illuminati were regular visitors. Here Orage first met Annie Besant, Cyril Leadbeater and G. R. S. Mead. Though still committed to the ILP Orage was depressed by its 'materialism' and lack of vision. His own strong mystical bent could not find expression even in his causeries and so he turned to theosophy to cultivate his esoteric interests. He once again ran into Millie Browne, who recalled:

> The Theosophical Society . . . opened out an avenue of interest and friendship. Harrogate was the hub of the Northern Federation of the T. S. There quarterly meetings were held attended by such famous theosophists as Annie Besant, C. W. Leadbeater, A. P. Sinnett, G. R. S. Mead, Jinaragadasa . . . I was elated at coming into contact with so many big names—sometimes I wonder whether I am an instinctive lion hunter who knows perhaps Carlyle's Hero and Hero Worship had bred this in me. I had not much time for theosophic study, but turned to Edward for instruction. He and Orage were friends so I met ARO again and he found my mind interesting.[29]

The idealist and occultist, to say nothing of other, leanings in Orage were well fed by these meetings. Theosophy, under Besant's leadership, was also a progressive social movement and one that did not discriminate between race, creed or sex in its membership. It was one of the few societies women might happily join and contribute to more or less equally with men. Orage, however, was not content simply to listen to Millie Browne's 'lions' and soon became one. Before long he was a regular lecturer at theosophical meetings, though what he had to say often disturbed the more orthodox, particularly when it took a Nietzschean turn after 1900. Nevertheless he published a number of articles in the *Theosophical Review* and a series of his lectures given to the Theosophical Lodges of Manchester and Leeds was published by the society under the title ***Consciousness, Animal, Human, and Superman*** in 1907. He also wrote a number of children's stories for the young people's magazine *The Lotus Journal.*[30]

Almost certainly Orage was studying the classical works of eastern mysticism by the mid-nineties. Many had only recently appeared in translation, though the second edition of Annie Besant's translation of the *Bhagavad Gita,* his favoured text, had come out in 1896. Mairet's suggestion that his growing powers of oratory were now exercised less on socialist platforms than in philosophic exposition is confirmed by Stanley Pierson, who sees Orage's shift of direction as part of a cultural trend:

> During the late 90s as the Socialist movement declined, Orage became a prominent speaker on the theosophical platforms of the North . . . like Carpenter and others in the socialist movement he was blending the mysticism of the east with the evolutionary optimism of late Victorian culture to provide a new foundation for personal and social hopes.[31]

Orage's mystical temperament was in fact directly encouraged by Edward Carpenter who was, as an Oxford University Extension lecturer and socialist activist, a regular visitor to Leeds. During the 1890s he lived in a cottage in the village of Millthorpe near Sheffield where he welcomed Annie Besant, Olive Schreiner and many more figures in the New Life movement. His own writing and poetry were especially influential. *Civilisation: Its Cause and Cure* (1889) inspired Arthur Penty to write his *Restoration of the Gild System* (1906), and *Love's Coming of Age* (1896), it has been argued, deeply influenced D. H. Lawrence and formed the ideological structure of *The Rainbow* and *Women in Love.*[32] But it was his long poem *Towards Democracy* (1883) which had the greatest impact on Alfred Orage.

Orage's relationship to Carpenter began much as had Carpenter's to Walt Whitman to whom he had written in 1874, 'There are many in England to whom your writings have been as the waking up to a new day . . . (you) are the centre of a new influence'[33] and he believed the force of the new will to change was feminine, 'Yet the women will save us . . .' This feminized element in the new socialism should not be underestimated and there is no doubt that however cynically Orage's relationships with women might be viewed, he was influenced by it. For a while Carpenter was Orage's mentor. Something of this is revealed in a letter to Carpenter in February 1896.[34] The letter, addressed from 86 Elford Place, Rounday Road, Leeds, humbly hopes that Carpenter has noticed his Bookish Causerie column in the *Labour Leader* and feels that although he is unknown to Carpenter, 'I may write to you as a friend'.

> . . . you will see that I have been attempting though with much less success than I had hoped to read modern literature in the light of the new old conception you and Whitman have done so much to spread. And I want if it be in my power to go still further and more persistently into what inwardly I feel the deepest need for thousands like myself.

He goes on to say that this need is for a sure foundation for the more or less transitory intellectual, physical and ethical beliefs, and regrets the lack of unity of purpose in his *Labour Leader* pieces:

> But now with your help I would do better. Some comrades have written me asking for some notes on 'Towards Democracy' as my lover comrade and 'hers' have long felt even since we read you out in the mystic air of Perth pine woods that 'Towards Democracy' is just the book for comrades.

Orage wanted to write a series of articles which may help 'those who read to understand and those who do not understand to read' and he asked Carpenter to read his articles before they went to print. Carpenter's reply is unrecorded, though it was almost certainly affirmative and two articles on 'Towards Democracy' duly appeared in the *Labour Leader* in June 1896. Though initially it was a relationship of devout discipleship, Orage's affiliations soon shifted and the tone of reverence notable in the letter changed. By February 1897 he remarks in his Bookish Causerie, 'Carpenter without Karl Marx is useless'. Later during the early Arts Club period, 1904 or 1905, in a discussion with Holbrook Jackson on the relationship of Carpenter and Whitman, Jackson reports him as saying that Carpenter was in truth 'Mrs. Whitman'.[35] Nevertheless, Carpenter was an extremely popular lecturer at the Arts Club and was made an honorary member, along with Chesterton and Shaw, in 1905. Orage also named him in a note at the end of *Friedrich Nietzsche, the Dionysian Spirit of the Age* (1906) as one of an elite band of living authors who might be considered 'Dionysian'.

But Carpenter's influence may well, with Jean's, have turned him to the Theosophical Society in 1896, in one of his recurrent moods of despair with socialist materialism. His brand of socialism, as we have seen, was anyway strongly idealist and was now embellished with Carpenter's visionary utopianism. Carpenter was also close to Annie Besant, not only a theosophist but a pioneering socialist and feminist whose activities frequently brought her to Leeds and the West Riding. Alf Mattinson, for example, records having heard her speak

a number of times on the steps of Leeds Town Hall in the late 1880s, on freethought and socialism. On one occasion he and other Socialist Leaguers had had to rescue her from a hostile crowd who were after her 'atheist' blood.[36] More pertinent perhaps, was that Annie Besant had, on 13 May 1895, given a lecture in Leeds which could not have failed to grip the young schoolteacher's imagination: 'Man the Master of his Destiny'.

The theosophical movement had arrived in Leeds at almost the same time as Orage. The inaugural meeting of the Northern Federation of the TS was held in Leeds on 5 August 1893 with 30 members present, including G. R. S. Mead.[37] Although a regular Leeds TS lodge seems to have existed from 1895, Orage does not seem to have been a member of it. Instead he and Jean appear to have set up a mysteriously named 'Alpha Centre' and applied for admission to the Federation in May 1898.

Jean Orage represented the Alpha Centre at Northern Federation meetings until 1900, often in the company of future Arts Club founders, Arthur Hugh Lee and A. W. Waddington. The Leeds TS lodge then seems to have been refounded in 1900. A certificate on the wall of the lodge's meeting rooms (still those opened by Annie Besant in 1911) in Queens Square, Leeds, reads that it was founded on 19 September 1900. The names of the founders include Alfred and Jean Orage, W. H. Bean and Miss A. K. Kennedy (Jean's cousin), who also became founder members of the Leeds Arts Club three years later. The Federation minute books still list a 'Leeds Centre' as well as a Leeds Lodge in 1907 but it has only one member. For the moment this remains an anomaly, though the explanation may owe as much to the internal politics of TS as to Orage's unorthodox approach. His temperament was also such that he was only happy in a group he led or founded.

As his commitment to the ILP declined, so his energy for theosophy increased and by 1900 he had become a regular lecturer at Northern Federation conferences. The record shows the following list of his lectures: 3 November 1900, 'Can we afford to neglect Metaphysics?'; 11 May 1901, 'The Neglect of beauty' (to which Arthur Penty contributes); 2 November 1901, 'Thought Power its control and culture'; 10 May 1902, 'Problems of Karma'; 29 November 1902, Orage leads discussion on 'What is the Personality?'; 20/21 February 1904, 'Methods of Lodge Work'. At the next federation meeting he was minuted to give a paper on 'Animal Consciousness' (also Jean Orage to give paper on 'Metempsychosis'); 30 July 1904, 'Animal Consciousness' (Annie Besant in Chair); 11 January 1906, 'Theosophy and Modern Physical Science'; and 24 February 1906, 'Theosophical Ideas in Commercial and Professional Life'.

As a regular Leeds lodge delegate he also contributed to organizational work: 2 February 1901, when he suggested that the next meeting's discussion topic should be 'Is Happiness Brotherhood?' '(On the Neglect of beauty)' and was noted as joining in the discussion on 'Our attitude towards Christian Enquirers'. Between this date and July 1904, he was the Leeds delegate on fourteen more occasions. At the council meeting of 21 February 1903, he and Jean contributed to a discussion on 'Policy and Methods of Propaganda'. He also offered to give a range of talks to local branches on theosophical and cultural matters, including 'What is Mysticism?' 'Theory of Reincarnation', 'Man and His Bodies', 'Some Hindu Short Stories', 'Theosophy and Literature', 'Nietzsche and Ibsen', 'The Republic of Plato', 'Theosophy and Modern Psychology', 'The Future of Humanity', 'What Theosophists are aiming at', 'Animal Evolution' and 'The Power of Thought',[38] an altogether ambitious programme of grass-roots education in popular philosophy.

Two other founders of the Arts Club also joined the programme. Rev. A. H. Lee offered 'Religious Ideas of the Celtic Races', 'Psychology and Religion', 'Browning and His Message', 'Objects of the Society for Psychical Research' and 'Myers' Human Personality', while A. W. Waddington suggested 'Conventionality' and 'Mediaeval Guilds'. Waddington may also have come to theosophy along the same route as Orage. In 1896 he had been the secretary of Carpenter's Sheffield Socialist Society and had subsequently taken up New Life living with fellow architect, Arthur Penty. As Millie Price later recalled: 'A. J. Penty brought his Ruskinian ethics to cooperate with "Waddy" in producing furniture of simple, undecorated and unpolished woods, and the two furnished themselves a cottage as an example of what craftsmanship could do, and there in the country lived for a while an austere Thoreauesque kind of a life.'[39]

Orage was also elected to the English Committee of the International Congress and spoke on the international correspondence scheme. In July he was elected to the subcommittee to discuss the next international congress and at the same meeting proposed that his paper, on **'Animal Consciousness'**, which he presented to the conference on that day, with Annie Besant in the chair, be published as **'Transactions'**. ('**Animal Consciousness**' in fact became the first part of *Consciousness: Animal, Human and Superman,* published by the Theosophical Publishing Society, in 1907). He proposed for the next conference, papers on 'Art and the Arts' in order to define the value of the arts in education and to discover the relative importance and place of the arts in human life. His paper on F. H. Myers's theory of human personality which he had been lecturing on to the Leeds lodge in 1904 was published in **'Transactions'** as **'Man and Death'**.[40] Though present at the council meeting of 13 May 1905, when his friend

Waddington was elected secretary of the discussions committee, he resigned suddenly from it in August. Not surprisingly, the reason given was 'strain of overwork'.[41]

However, Millie Price revealed that it was not all metaphysics and astral bodies at the Harrogate meetings as occasionally Orage attended to more corporeal ones: hers.

> When at a Theosophical conference at Harrogate Orage suggested we should play truant for one session and take a stroll on Harlow Moor. I was thrilled with delight at contacting his exciting mind in an intimate way. For he had an exciting mind. He excited himself with brilliant speculations on the structure of the soul and the universe. The doctrines of what was then called 'Esoteric Buddhism' were the most fruitful in this respect and he devoted himself to lectures on these being daringly imaginative and convincing. His mind too was crammed with poetical literature so that I owe to him my early knowledge of Yeats, for he had seized upon my copy of the Wanderings of Oisin, purloined from Dr. O'Leary's collection, and read to my entranced ears:
>
> > Autumn is over the long leaves that love us,
> > And over the mice in the barley fields
> > Yellow the leaves of rowan above us
> > And yellow the wet, wild strawberry leaves.
>
> stressing its colour values in the words used. Craftily he read also To An Isle In The Water:—'Shy one, shy one shy one of my heart' . . .

and the rest can be guessed at, presumably in the absence of Jean Orage for whom Millie had an awed respect. She tells of many more trysts and holidays by the seaside together which, though romantic, appear to have been unconsummated. Orage, she said, called her the 'Ice Maiden'.[42]

Theosophy carried Orage through his remaining ten years in Leeds including his discovery of Nietzsche and the formation of the Arts Club . . . and provided him with a circle of friends and an audience for his experimental humanism more congenial than the ILP. He carried many of these like Lee and Waddington into the Arts Club with him and through it he reached a far wider social spectrum than was otherwise available to a schoolteacher of modest means. It was probably his rites of passage into a wealthy social group which included academics, businessmen and bankers, one of whom subsequently put up half the cash for the *New Age*. How convinced he was by theosophy, as opposed to finding it a congenial vehicle for his own ideas, is another matter.

He may have belonged to theosophy's inner esoteric section. Like W. B. Yeats and Florence Farr, both of whom later visited the Arts Club on more than one occasion, though Ellic Howe does not mention him, he might have become a magician of the Hermetic Order of the Golden Dawn, an esoteric offshoot of theosophy, formed in 1888 by Macgregor Mathers.[43] Orage was later taken up with Aleister Crowley, the beast himself, who was briefly leader of the order, and according to Beatrice Hastings, would have filled the *New Age*'s pages with his 'turgid out-pourings' had she not prevented him.[44] Ms. Hastings, a brilliant though erratic talent had herself met Orage at a theosophical meeting in London in 1906, when he had jumped up on the stage in the absence of the advertised speaker, to give an impromptu lecture, and shortly after became his lover. She wrote that after about a year,

> when Aphrodite had amused herself at our expense, I found a collection of works on sorcery. Up to this time, Orage's intimate friend was not Mr. Holbrook Jackson, who thought he was, but Mr. Aleister Crowley. . . . Well, I consigned all the books and 'Equinoxes' and sorcery designs to the dustbin.[45]

She lived with Orage for some years in London, at one time sharing their apartment, and possibly Orage himself, with Katherine Mansfield, becoming virtually co-editor of the *New Age*. When she parted company with him (later to live with Modigliani) she accused him, with her customary acrimony, of 'paranoic mystagoguery'!

Though Beatrice's account has been contested by others of the *New Age* circle, Orage told C. S. Nott some years later, that he had met Crowley when he, Orage, was acting secretary of the Society for Psychical Research in 1906. The poet, Edwin Muir, remembers Orage as having been 'a member of a magic circle which included Yeats' which James Webb, the historian of the modern occult movement, thought must have been the Golden Dawn, which had split up into quarrelling factions in 1900, with Yeats and Crowley on opposite sides of the fence. Webb also refers to a Golden Dawn temple in Bradford—there is no record of one in Leeds—but it seems unlikely that the leading theosophical lecturer of the North could have avoided coming into contact with some of its members. The temple in Bradford has recently been rediscovered and there is a short account of it in a local occultist journal. The anonymous writer notes 'There was a particularly active occult scene around this time in Yorkshire. A number of mysterious groups existed such as the Rosicrucian Fathers of Keighley . . . and the less mysterious August and Oriental Order of Light Garuda which was based in Bradford.'[46] In a more serious and sustained study Logie Barrow has shown that the West Riding had been one of the most important centres of spiritualist activity in Britain since its arrival from the USA in the mid-nineteenth century.[47] Subsequently many spiritualists joined the re-invigorated socialist movement and the ILP, imparting to it some of their own utopianism. Support for Orage's dabbling in magic might come from

the fact that his diary of engagements was so full that astral-planning was the only possible way of getting from one to the next.

Back in the real world, in 1897 he and Jean moved to an apartment at 3 Exmouth Grove, Harehills, owned appropriately enough by a Mrs. Tempest. Whether Orage was still pronouncing his name as it had been spelt in Cambridgeshire or whether his new landlady had put ideas into his head would be interesting to know. After all, as Carswell remarks, a hint of *stormy* Huguenot ancestory in one's surname has to be more impressive than something that rhymes, as Shaw used to say, with 'porridge'. Nameplaying may well have been a passing diversion for a man still attempting to construct his persona. On the Ward Role of 1898, for example, he even enters himself as *Alfred O'Rage*! Another move, in 1898, took him to 11 Rossington Place, Harehills, and then in 1899 up the hill to 36 Hawthorne Mount, Chapel Allerton, where he stayed until 1905. His final Leeds address was 33 Potternewton Road, which was where Mary Gawthorpe remembered receiving a certain corporeal communication.

As for his intellectual movements between 1898 and 1900, he was certainly not merely sinking into spiritualism. But he had given up his Bookish Causerie in 1897 and his editorship of *Forward* in 1898, when it passed into more orthodox hands, and appears not to have published any more journalism until 1902. His school work at Harehills, teaching the older children of standard VI, with classes of 50 and more was undeniably demanding, but a notebook dating from this time suggests that he was still devouring books at a great rate. He appears to have read most of George Gissing, some Henry James, Kipling, Mark Twain, R. L. Stevenson, Alexander Dumas, a range of oriental and biblical texts, romantic poets and cultural criticism. The biggest single entry is from the *Philosophical Dialogues* of the French essayist, Ernest Renan, critical of what he called 'the acid of reasoning'. One quotation Orage has copied, points forward to the Arts Club and Nietzsche: 'Endeavour to be beautiful and then do act every moment as your heart inspires you'.[48]

In the meantime he had to earn a living and became an active though not especially successful member of the National Union of Teachers. In 1898 he stood for election to the Leeds and District executive but succeeded in coming only twenty-second in the poll. The following year he did even worse, getting fewer votes and coming twenty-seventh. But in 1901 he was successful, collecting 157 votes and coming eighth in the poll. Despite this his victory was short-lived. In the following year's election although he picked up nearly 90 votes more, he and most of the other sitting members were swept off the executive in a wave of revolt.[49] A slate of candidates organized by the Direct Representation Association opposing the 1902 Education Bill carried the day. They objected to non-certified teachers being transferred to board schools as cheap labour with the merging of the voluntary sector, but Orage does not appear to have sympathized.

His involvement in the NUT may have been more motivated by its potential as a platform for his own ideas, for, in a letter to the *Leeds Teacher's Journal,* he complains about the misuse of something called the NUT 'Literary Branch' which sounds like an institution Orage himself may have thought up:

> Referring to the announcement made by the Literary branch of a series of lectures (September 1902 p. 3) may I enquire whether the original intention of the branch has been deliberately or only thoughtlessly lost sight of. From what I can remember it was the object of the branch to provide primarily opportunities for the discussion of ideas, mainly of course such ideas as are expressed in literature.[50]

His complaint was that 'the literary feature seems to have been more or less retained but the teachers and the discussion are apparently omitted'. Clearly Orage was seeking another forum for debate but unfortunately the NUT 'Literary Branch' was not destined to be it. Was it seen as a forerunner of the Arts Club? Significantly, C. W. Whitmell an unusually popular school's inspector, in 1903 gave the same lecture to the Literary Branch as he gave a couple of years later to the Arts Club: 'The Dypsichus of Clough'.

As the century drew to its close the 26-year old Orage had promoted a libertarian pedagogy more or less successfully for six years (an inspiration to A. S. Neil of Summerhill). He had held mass audiences on both socialist and theosophical platforms, had distinguished himself as a cultural critic in the *Labour Leader* and had edited a successful local socialist journal, *Forward.* A quotation copied into his notebook from Kipling revealed his feelings about that: 'Any fool can write but it takes a god-given genius to be an editor'.[51] Though he made it plain to his female colleagues he believed in free-love, he was probably married to Jean Watson and had settled in to an end-terrace house in Chapel Allerton, 36 Hawthorn Mount. His life was full of immensely promising fragments but no achievable synthesis. The means to this lay in his next chance encounter.

Notes

1. Most information on Orage's early life is from Philip Mairet, *A. R. Orage A Memoir,* Dent, London, 1936. Mairet heard it all from Orage himself, but it is not as accurate as could be desired. This is supplemented by John Carswell, *Lives and Letters,* Faber, London, 1978, which, while generally excellent, has also borrowed some of Mairet's inaccuracies.

2. Leeds School Board, Education Committee Minutes, October 1893, West Yorkshire Archives, Sheepscar, Leeds.

3. Leeds School Board, School Staff Ledgers, 1894, West Yorkshire Archives, Sheepscar, Leeds.

4. Quoted in M. A. Travis, 'The Work of the Leeds School Board' in *Researches and Studies,* The School of Education, University of Leeds, no. 8, May 1953.

5. A. R. Orage, 'A Study in Mud' in Albert T. Marles (ed.) *Hypnotic Leeds,* Leeds, 1894, p. 17.

6. Harehills Board School Log Book, Harehills Primary School, Newton Garth, Leeds, pp. 127, 145, 162.

7. Derek Linstrum, *West Yorkshire Architects and Architecture,* Lund Humphries, London, 1978, p. 260.

8. HMI's report, September 1894, Harehills Mixed Log Book, Harehills Primary School, p. 58.

9. Roundhay Road Board School Log Book, West Yorkshire Archives, Sheepscar, Leeds, pp. 447, 450, 452, 453, 455.

10. M. A. Travis, op. cit., pp. 92-93.

11. A. R. Orage, 'Quixotic Energy' in *Hypnotic Leeds,* p. 43.

12. Mary Gawthorpe, *Up Hill to Holloway,* Penobscot, Maine, 1962, p. 192.

13. Mairet, op. cit., p. 10.

14. Millie Price (née Browne), *This World's Festival,* unpublished autobiography in typescript, property of Agnes Patrick, 16 Bainbrigge Road, Leeds 6, p. 5.

15. Edward Carpenter, 'A Memoir' in Bessie Ford (ed.) *Tom Maguire: A Remembrance,* Labour Press Society, Manchester, 1895, p. x.

16. Ibid.

17. Edward Thompson, 'Homage to Tom Maguire' in A. Briggs and J. Saville (eds) *Essays in Labour History,* London, 1960, p. 279; and Tom Woodhouse, 'The Working Class' in Derek Fraser (ed.) *A History of Modern Leeds,* Manchester, 1980.

18. Alf Mattinson, *Journals,* vol. 1, p. 270, Leeds City Reference Library.

19. Peter d'A Jones, *'The Christian Socialist Revival' 1877-1914,* Princeton University Press, 1968, pp. 141-2. The letters are Engels to Sorge, 18 January 1893; Engels to Sorge, 18 March 1893 (K. Marx and F. Engels, *'Letters to Americans, 1848-1895',* New York, 1953, pp. 246-247, 249.

20. Alfred Orage in J. Clayton (ed.) *Why I Joined the Independent Labour Party Some Plain Statements,* Leeds, no date, p. 11.

21. D. H. Lawrence, 'Nottingham and the Mining Country' in *Selected Essays,* Penguin, London, 1950, p. 119. Lawrence could only have been eight years old when Orage, some seventy miles to the north, and twelve years his senior, started in post. But like Orage, he was part of that generation and social class swept into school teaching by the demands of the 1870 Education Act. Later he became an avid reader of the *New Age* and many of its opinions became his own.

22. Carswell, op. cit., p. 16.

23. *Labour Leader,* vol. VIII, no. 110, 4 May 1896, p. 155.

24. Millie Price, op. cit., pp. 83-84.

25. D. B. Foster, *Socialism and the Christ,* published by the author, Leeds, 1921, p. 31.

26. *Leeds Citizen,* 1.8.1919.

27. *Labour Leader,* 16 November 1895.

28. In a letter to Edward Carpenter, he refers to her as his 'lover-comrade' but John Carswell could find no trace of a marriage certificate in Somerset House. Nevertheless Orage was convinced he was married since he demanded a divorce from Jean in 1915, which as Roman Catholic she refused him. (Letter from Jean Orage to Holbrook Jackson dated 24 April 1915, Harry Ransome Center, University of Texas.)

29. Millie Price, op. cit., p. 86.

30. His story 'The First Men', a creation of myth, appeared in *The Lotus Journal,* August 1907, pp. 108-11 and 'The Princesses and the Gardener' in another issue.

31. Stanley Pierson, *British Socialists: the journey from fantasy to politics,* Harvard University Press, 1979, p. 193.

32. Emile Delavennay, *Edward Carpenter and D. H. Lawrence: A Study in Edwardian Transition,* Heinemann, London, 1969.

33. Edward Carpenter, letter to Walt Whitman, 12 July 1874, copy in Alf Mattinson Collection, Brotherton Library, University of Leeds.

34. Alfred Orage, letter to Edward Carpenter, 3 February 1896, Carpenter Collection, Sheffield City Library.

35. Holbrook Jackson, 'A. R. Orage: Personal Recollections', *The Windmill* (Heinemann house journal), London, 1948, p. 44.

36. Alf Mattinson, 'Journals' 1925-28, vol 1, p. 293. Leeds City Reference Library.

37. Northern Federation of the Theosophical Society Minute Book 1893-1900, held at Harrogate TS Lodge, 6 Alexandra Road, Harrogate.

38. A list of lectures offered to federation lodges recorded in the minutes of September 1903.

39. Millie Price, op. cit., p. 113.

40. *Leeds Mercury* Weekly Supplement, 13 February and 5 March 1904, reports Orage lecturing on Myers's *Human Personality* and 'Telepathy and Clairvoyance', based on Myers, calling the theory of evolution 'panaesthetic'.

41. Northern Federation TS Minute Book, 12-13 August 1905.

42. Millie Price, op. cit., p. 98.

43. Ellic Howe, *The Magicians of the Golden Dawn,* Routledge, Kegan Paul, London, 1972.

44. Beatrice Hastings, *The Old 'New Age': Orage—and others,* Blue Moon Press, London, 1936.

45. Quoted in James Webb, *The Harmonious Circle,* Thames and Hudson, London, 1980, p. 210.

46. 'The Lamp of Thoth', vol. III, no. 4 (undated), Leeds, pp. 33-35. Available from 'The Sorcerer's Apprentice', Hyde Park Corner, Leeds 6.

47. Logie Barrow, *Independent Spirits, Spiritualism and English Plebeians 1850-1910,* Routledge, Kegan Paul, London, 1986.

48. Leeds School Board, 'Daily Notes', notebook, 'VI A' handwritten on cover, no page numbers, in possession of Richard Orage.

49. *Leeds Teacher's Journal,* monthly journal of Leeds and District National Union of Teachers, January 1899, January 1900, January 1902 and January 1903, Brotherton Library, Leeds.

50. Letter dated 18 September 1902, in The *Leeds Teacher's Journal,* Oct/Nov 1902, p. 5, signed 'A. R. Orage'.

51. Notebook entitled 'Leeds School Board, Daily Notes, VI A', undated but from internal evidence not before October 1896, p. 27, in the possession of Richard Orage.

Charles Ferrall (essay date autumn 1992)

SOURCE: Ferrall, Charles. "The *New Age* and the Emergence of Reactionary Modernism Before the Great War." *Modern Fiction Studies* 38, no. 3 (autumn 1992): 653-67.

[In the following essay, Ferrall examines the New Age and Orage's role in shaping both the modernist political fervor and the debate over the cultural role of art that existed prior to World War I.]

It is well known that the *New Age* played a vital role in the dissemination of literary modernism and post-Impressionist art in Britain before the First World War. Of the three main polemicists of early modernism—T. E. Hulme, Ezra Pound and Wyndham Lewis—Hulme wrote almost exclusively for the magazine, Pound wrote a large proportion of his criticism for its pages and Lewis, who described the *New Age* in 1914 as "one of the only good papers in the country" ("Letter" 319), published some of his early stories in the paper and used its correspondence columns to lash out at his opponents, real or imagined.

But despite its lively interest in such pre-war movements as Imagism, Vorticism, Futurism, Cubism, and Expressionism, the *New Age* was a paper primarily concerned not with contemporary developments in art and literature, but with politics. Although historians of Edwardian Britain are well acquainted with the fact that the *New Age* played an important role in pre-war British politics, very little has actually been written about the paper. John Finlay, an historian of the Social Credit movement, maintains that historians have "neglected" the journal because its politics are "so hard to categorize" (83). Rather than attempting any categorization himself, Finlay concludes that "the paper was *sui generis,* a judgment which would have appealed to its editor," Alfred Orage (83). Similarly, Wallace Martin, the main literary historian of the *New Age,* attributes the paper's mercurial politics to its writers' independence from existing political parties and factions. Martin argues that the readership of "the first Socialist weekly in London" (*The New Age* 5) was comprised mainly of an "intelligentsia" with no particular class or political affiliations (*The New Age* 8). According to Martin, therefore, the *New Age* was "independent and neutral with respect to the heterogeneous collection of organizations that then constituted the political left" (*Orage as Critic* 7).

Contrary to the assumptions of Martin and other historians, I will argue that the *New Age* was not "neutral" toward the "political left" but actively hostile. Thus if there is any connection between the anti-leftist politics of the paper and the aesthetics of its modernist writers, then we need to reassess the widely held assumption that writers and artists such as Lewis and Pound only became politicized as a result of their response to the First World War. Movements such as Vorticism and Imagism were, I will argue, both part of and influenced by a larger reactionary political culture whose relationship to early modernism remains largely unexplored by literary historians.

The *New Age* was founded in the year following the landslide victory of the Liberals and their new Labour allies in the 1906 general election. Initially, Orage and the other founding editor, Holbrook Jackson, supported the new government and its progressive and radical allies; after all, both men had been members of the Fabian Society, a political movement which advocated the gradual institution of socialism by means of parliamentary legislation. But by 1911, Orage was criticising the Labour Party for its "flunkey-like dependence upon the Liberal Party" (12 Oct. 1911: 554) and calling upon "Socialists" to boycott elections (8 June 1911: 342). As well as claiming that there was very little ideological difference within parliament between the Tories, Liberals, and Labour, Orage also attacked the institution of parliamentary democracy. At the same time as he was calling for a general strike, Orage was trumpeting: "Down with the Tricolour; by which you understand that I mean the three-headed dog of Liberty, Equality and Fraternity" ("Down with the Tricolour" 489).

Orage's hatred of liberal democracy and its institutions derived partly from his antipathy toward a series of legislative reforms which became known as the "New Liberalism." Essentially, this legislation—which provided for a system of health and unemployment insurance—represented a shift by the Liberal Party away from a nineteenth century ideology of *laissez-faire* toward a position which recognized the need for the State to take a more active role in ameliorating the conditions of the working class (Hay). For those associated with the *New Age* circle, the most sustained ideological critique of the New Liberalism was to be found in Hilaire Belloc's *The Servile State,* a text first published in serial form in the *New Age.* Maurice Reckitt, a High Churchman and contributor to the paper, thirty years later wrote that "I cannot overestimate the impact of this book upon my mind, and in this I was but symptomatic of thousands of others" (107-108).

According to Belloc, the New Liberalism would produce

> a State in which the few are left in possession of the means of production while the many, who are left without such possession, remain much as they were save that they have their lives organized and regulated under those few capitalists who are responsible for the well-being of their subordinates.
>
> (26 May 1912: 77)

The significance of Belloc's argument lies in its refusal to see capitalism and the New Liberalism as ideologies in radical conflict with each other. There is a natural progression, Belloc argues, from nineteenth-century *laissez-faire* capitalism to the New Liberalism of Lloyd George and Winston Churchill to the more radical "Collectivism" or "State Socialism" of the government's radical allies. Both socialism and capitalism dispossess the ordinary man of his land and property. Consequently, these political systems are to be contrasted with the European societies of the late Middle Ages when, during the establishment of the "great landed estates" (*The Servile State* 42) the peasant was "bound in legal theory to the soil upon which he was born (*The Servile State* 47).

While such attacks were being made upon the government, a wave of unprecedented industrial unrest swept Britain, confirming for those at the *New Age* that the workers were dissatisfied with the New Liberalism. In 1907 a little more than two million work days had been lost as a result of strikes and lockouts. By 1912 this figure had jumped to a record number of forty million days (Morgan 96 and Read 16). G. D. H. Cole, an Oxford don who began contributing to the *New Age* in 1914, maintained that

> High hopes had been roused by the Liberal and Labour political victories of 1906; but after four years of Liberal government and Labour action in Parliament the workers found themselves economically worse off than before.
>
> (*Short History* 3: 69)

When combined with an ideological opposition to "State Socialism" or "Collectivism," this new industrial militancy provided the impetus for the creation, largely within the pages of the *New Age,* of a political movement called Guild Socialism. Between 1906 and 1912, according to Orage,

> The tide of Collectivism . . . was . . . too powerful to admit of even the smallest counter-current. Some experience of Collectivism in action and political methods as distinct from economic methods was necessary before the mind of the Labour movement could be turned in another direction. This was brought about by the demand of Labour to control its industry. At the same time that Syndicalism came to be discussed, a revival of trade-union activity took place, and on such a scale that it seemed to the present writers that at last the trade unions were now finally determined to form a permanent element in society.
>
> (Preface v-vi)

Like the Syndicalists, the Guild Socialists had as their goal the institution of democracy within the industrial or economic sphere. Using the Syndicalist slogan "economic power precedes political power," the Guild Socialists argued that Collectivists were only interested in a worthless "political" or parliamentary democracy. Only when the workers had seized the means of production and taken control of their own labour would political democracy mean anything. To institute this, the Guild Socialists proposed that the existing unions should be turned into autonomous industrial units each of which would have a monopoly on whatever it produced (Glass). As Cole later attested, Guild Socialism

> set out, as against both State Socialism and what was soon to be called Communism, to assert the vital importance of individual and group liberty and the need

to diffuse social responsibility among the whole people by making them as far as possible the masters of their own lives and of the conditions under which their daily work was done.

> (*A History of Socialist Thought* 246)

As an attempt to theorize the necessary conditions for a participatory democracy, it is hard to see what is politically conservative about Guild Socialism. Yet the influence of Syndicalism, which was so important for the Guild Socialists, was not always of a politically progressive kind. In the translator's introduction to Sorel's *Reflections on Violence,* which was originally published in the *New Age,* Hulme argues that Sorel "denies the essential connection" between the working class or revolutionary movement and the ideology of "democracy." Thus according to Hulme, Sorel is calling for a "revolution" to reinstate "reactionary" values. Although this "liberal" and "democratic" ideology has dominated Western culture since the Renaissance, Hulme does not specify its contemporary English representatives (*Speculations* 250-251). However, since the Syndicalism of writers such as Sorel was used by the *New Age* front as a weapon against State Socialism and Collectivism, we can assume that Hulme has the same enemies as his *New Age* and Guild Socialist colleagues. By championing Sorel, therefore, Hulme is aligning himself with the more radical elements of the union movement and attempting to theorize the ways in which the militancy of the striking workers could be harnessed for conservative purposes.

Although far less politically self-conscious before the war than Hulme, Pound duplicates many of his colleague's political ideas. Like Hulme and the Guild Socialists, Pound places his faith in the militant unions—which alone give him "faith in the future of England and a belief in her present strength"—rather than parliamentary democracy. He concludes that within the House of Commons, "the real division . . . is somewhere about the gangway, rather than a matter of left and right" ("Through Alien Eyes [III]" 300-301). And speaking through a pseudonym, Pound describes democracy as "the worst thing on the face of the earth" and calls for the abolition of the House of Commons ("On Certain Reforms" 130-131).

Among those at the *New Age,* this apparently contradictory combination of radical and conservative political ideas was in fact rather typical. Not only was the medievalism of the Guild Socialists and fellow travellers of an often extremely conservative kind (Penty), but the Guild Socialists were aligned, within the pages of the paper, with a reactionary group of writers who believed that Nietzsche would be the cure for the diseases of liberalism and democracy.[1] While advocating a return to an aristocratic society and classical culture, these writers were, nevertheless, as hostile to contemporary con-

servative institutions and ideology as their Guild Socialist allies. Anthony Ludovici, for example, argued
that the English aristocratic "stock" was "degenerate"
because it had been "breeding" with "commercial mag-
nates" and "plutocrats" since 1688 (403-407). As a consequence, the House of Lords responded to the 1911
Parliament Act, a bill designed to curb the Lords' power,
with "remarkable meekness," even assisting "its opponents in fleecing it of its legitimate rights" (31). But the
even more profound cause of contemporary degeneracy
was not capitalism but Christianity. The latter, they argued, lay at the root of all "slave" revolts. As Oscar
Levy expresses it,

> Christianity has preached for two millennium that all
> men are equal, Protestantism has taught for four centu-
> ries that everyone is his own priest, democracy has
> given for a hundred years votes and privileges to this
> priestly congregation.
>
> ("A Book" 89)

Opposing all forms of emancipatory politics, the Nietzscheans believed that a healthy society should be rigidly hierarchical, predominantly agricultural, and either
pagan or Catholic. J. M. Kennedy, one of the mainstays
of the *New Age,* even advocated an actual slave society
in which the slaves would be "trained to submit themselves as 'property' although allowed the compensatory
privilege of 'Socialistic Sunday-schools'" (*Quintessence*
101).

Most of the writing of the Nietzscheans was, to say the
least, extremely crude philosophically. For this reason
more than any other Hulme, Lewis, and Pound were
nearly always scathing in their references to them.
Hulme defended the new post-Impressionist art against
the attacks of Ludovici (*Further Speculations* 108);
Pound refers to the "Neo-Nietzschean chatter" of pre-
war London in *Mauberly;* and Lewis, in his 1915 Preface to *Tarr,* writes that

> Nietzsche's books . . . have made "aristocrats" of
> people who would otherwise have been only mild snobs
> or meddlesome prigs . . . they have made an Overman
> of every vulgarly energetic grocer in Europe. . . . The
> modern Prussian advocate of the Aristocratic and Ty-
> rannic took *everybody* into his confidence. Then he
> would coquet: he gave special prizes. *Everybody*
> couldn't be a follower of his! No: only the *minority*:
> that is the minority who read his books, which has
> steadily grown till it comprises certainly . . . the un-
> gainliest and strangest aristocratic caste any world
> could hope to see.
>
> (15)

Yet with his reference to the democracy of "energetic
grocer[s]," Lewis duplicates the kind of snobbery of
which he accuses Nietzsche's "vulgarisers." Furthermore, the character Tarr describes himself as "the new
animal; we haven't found a name for it yet. It will suc-

ceed the Superman." Although Tarr is immediately de-
flated by the reply of his companion, Anastasy—"Jean-
Jacques Rousseau. = Kiss me" (307)—his earlier
reference to "the Artist himself, a new sort of person;
the creative man" (29) is met with no such irony. Lewis
was a little more honest thirty-five years later when he
confessed that "Nietzsche was . . . the paramount influence, as was the case with so many people prior to
world war i" (*Rude Assignment* 128). Similarly, Pound's
assertion in 1914 that "The aristocracy of entail and of
title has decayed, the aristocracy of commerce is decaying, the aristocracy of the arts is ready again for its service" ("The New Sculpture" 68), if not directly inspired
by Nietzsche, was certainly typical of the kinds of artist-
as-aristocrat cant which writers such as Orage, Ludovici,
Levy, and Kennedy believed Nietzsche's philosophy
justified.

Such Nietzscheanism had more in common with the
Guild Socialists than merely an opposition to capitalism
and parliamentary democracy. For example, A. E. Ran-
dell, one of the full-time staff at the paper, argued that
the guild system was essentially "aristocratic" because
it conceived of society as an organism. There could be
no place for "liberty" and "equality" within such an
aristocratic society because the individual's exercise of
such rights would only lead toward "democratic despotism" and "anarchy" (512). Of course such conceptions
of the organic society were not the invention of the
New Age. Raymond Williams has shown how the organic model of society has been used, since the late
eighteenth century, by socialists and conservatives as
"the basis of an attack on the conditions of men in 'industrial production' . . . and on the claims of middle-
class political democracy" (140). But by the time such
a tradition culminates in the politics of the *New Age,* it
has become antithetical to any kind of liberalism. Writers such as Ramiro de Maeztu, for example, advocated
replacing the "abstract" rights of the French Revolution
with "objective rights" which would be entirely conditional upon the individual's function within a hierarchically structured social organism. Not only can there be
no formal equality among the members of such a society (such equality would cut across and transcend the
fine gradations of the social hierarchy), but there can be
little tolerance of any kind of social heterogeneity or
difference. Thus the *New Age* writers were extremely
nationalistic and, after August 1914, their support for
the war against Germany bordered on the jingoistic.

Many of the Guild Socialists and Nietzscheans seem to
have taken the organic society metaphor almost literally. Because they habitually reduced the social sphere
to the realm of biology, the *New Age* writers were usually favorably disposed toward most varieties of eugenics. Orage did attack the eugenicists for concerning
themselves with biological "Supermen" rather than with
spiritual elites and aristocracies (**"The Superman"**

107), but most of his colleagues were less discriminating. Levy, for one, claimed that Nietzsche was a greater advocate of eugenics than Francis Galton and explained that

> A believer in race is no longer a Christian in the old sense of the word. On the contrary, he that interferes with the humble, the miserable, the bungled, the botched, the feeble-minded, and their offspring is the most deadly sinner against the spirit of a religion that was invented, that stood, and still stands, for the survival of all the lower types of humanity.
>
> ("The Nietzsche Movement" 205)

Another ugly feature of the *New Age*'s politics was its anti-Semitism. Just about every issue of the paper featured anti-Semitic articles, stories, and poems of some kind. Most of this material characterizes the Jews as rootless, cosmopolitan and over-represented in finance and international capitalism. Some did argue that the economic power of the Jews was not disproportionate to their numbers (Orage, **"The Folly of Anti-Semitism"** 449), but most agreed that the Jews were an alien presence within the body politic. Orage, for example, recounts the following anecdote:

> A Jew of ancient lineage recently said to us: "I trace my descent from Benjamin; who am I that I should marry into an upstart race? If his arrogance amused us, we also admired it. We thought that we too belonged to "No mean city"; that our own race might, after all, deteriorate by intermixture; that racial destiny, whether for Jew or Gentile, was a sacred thing and best developed to final purpose in purity of blood and spirit.
>
> (**"The Folly of Anti-Semitism"** 449)

Statements by Pound before the war to the effect that artists should "be done with Jews and Jobbery" and "SPIT upon those who fawn on the JEWS for their money" (Lewis, *Blast 1* 45) were not out of place within such a cultural milieu.

For those such as Orage the social organism must not only protect itself against alien cultures but also strictly regulate its internal hierarchies. For this reason, the demands for political equality then being made by the Suffragists were strongly resisted by all the major contributors to the paper. In a symposium on Women's Suffrage conducted by the *New Age* in early 1911, Ludovici captured the spirit of this reactionary counterattack: he is, he informs the reader, "entirely in favour of women's suffrage. Truth to tell only women ought to vote; only women do vote" (Carter 6). Pound, who expressed considerable ambivalence toward the Suffragist movement (Bush 353-371), repeats this "joke" two years later when he reports that he once told an American woman who was asking for the vote that "if you really want a vote, for heaven's sake use mine. I, perhaps, will have cast the ballot for you, but that's only

the mechanical process" ("Alien Eyes IV" 324). For both Ludovici and Pound, in other words, the democratization of society is synonymous with its feminization.

The threat to social identity which such a feminization of society represents is well illustrated by Orage's series of short stories titled **"Tales for Men Only."** Most of the stories are about a small group of men who form a "circle of equals" for the discussion of metaphysics, art, and other highbrow subjects. Stricken by the "sentimentality" of a woman, one of the group's members will attempt to introduce her into the male cabal. Of course, the group cannot operate properly with an "inferior" and "alien" woman present. The situation is usually resolved by the narrator's initiation of the fallen member into some branch of mystic knowledge. The initiate is either saved, in which case he gives up all serious ties with women, or he is lost to be "submerged by the flood of sex" (**"Another Tale"** 517). Like the Nietzscheans, Orage identifies the threatening otherness of women with the forces of democracy. Although the men have formed "a circle . . . closed against the mob" (**"Another Tale"** 518), it appears to Orage's narrator that they have "only just survived the flood of sex-infatuation that has submerged Europe since the French Revolution" (**"A Tale"** 445). As his metaphors and imagery of flooding suggest, Orage believes that liberal democracies level social hierarchies and dissolve the necessary boundaries between self and other, artist and mob, male and female.

As Orage's presentation of such anti-democratic sentiments in a fictional form would suggest, the political sympathies of the *New Age* writers were often aligned with strong aesthetic preferences. Alan Robinson has demonstrated how the promotion of "classical" aesthetics by critics such as Hulme, Ludovici, and Kennedy originated in the "political polemics of 1911" (117) and was synonymous with support for the defeated Lords or for Tory and radical right politics in general. Because these critics habitually equated "artistic styles" with desirable or undesirable social structures, "romantic" art was simplistically equated with liberal politics (90).

What has not yet been fully investigated, however, is the connection, not between classical aesthetics and conservative politics, but between the rejection of realism and the kinds of politics we find in the *New Age*. The three most prominent writers in Britain before the war—H. G. Wells, George Bernard Shaw, and Arnold Bennett—were all closely aligned with the broad leftist coalition that the *New Age* dedicated itself to attacking. Since these writers were all "realists," the aesthetic stance of the *New Age* was therefore strongly anti-realist.

Interestingly, Wells, Shaw, and Bennett had initially supported the paper. Shaw, with another backer, provided £500 to launch the paper and, like Wells, contributed articles on Socialism. An ideological rift between the Socialists and the *New Age* became apparent very early when Orage orchestrated a debate at the end of 1907 between, on the one hand, Shaw and Wells and, on the other, Belloc and Chesterton on the respective merits of a centralized Socialist state versus a society of small landowners. After the exchange with Belloc and Chesterton, Wells and Shaw never again wrote for the paper. Bennett continued to write his *literary* column until 1911, when he completely broke with the *New Age* after being violently abused by J. M. Kennedy.

That an attack upon the politics of those on the left such as Shaw, Wells, and Bennett should imply opposition to certain kinds of writing was obvious to all, including Pound. Pound argued that parliamentary democracy was represented in the world of letters by "your Bennett and Wells, your shopkeepers in 'The realm of books'" ("Alien Eyes III" 300). The link between realism, Socialism, and parliamentary democracy is in fact as explicit in Pound's writing of this period as it is for any of the *New Age* writers. Referring to John Galsworthy, another politically progressive writer sympathetic to Socialism, Pound writes in 1914 that

> It suits the convenience of our rulers that we should believe in voting, in suffrage as a universal panacea for our own stupidities. As a syndicalist, somewhat atrabilious, I disbelieve vigorously in any recognition of political institutions, of the Fabian Society, John Galsworthy, and so on.

> ("Suffragettes" 254)

Orage's main criticism of the socialist realist writers was that they "reproduced" rather than "represented" the degraded conditions of modern society:

> Contemporary life is almost always vulgarising. At least it does not offer a sufficient range of stimulus to the noble life. . . . My complaint is that our modern novelists, far from contributing to the nurture of imaginative minds, poison us all with the commonplace, reflecting and dull reproductions of just such persons, conditions and circumstances as imagination seeks to avoid.

> (**"Modern Novels"** 204)

The main function of the writer, Orage argued, was to mount some kind of "resistance" to contemporary vulgarity and resurrect the "heroic" values of the past (**"Modern Novels"** 204). Instead, he lamented, contemporary artists "positively brag about their income" or, like Shaw, their "popularity" (**"Money-Changers"** 35). But except for the "classics," according to Orage, "popular literature is a contradiction in terms. . . . The value of art is inversely as the sum paid for it" (**"Money-Changers"** 35). As a consequence, art is engaged in a perpetual battle with "journalism," "advertising," and "commercialism" of any kind. But it is precisely to

these forces that Wells and Bennett have succumbed. He is "rendered speechless with disgust," Orage informs us (in his **"Readers & Writers"** column), to find Bennett "appearing simultaneously in half the rags of London" and "even more offended physiologically" by the kind of "clap-trap" and "stunts" performed by Wells for "advertisement" (12 June 1913: 178). Alternatively, the ulterior motive for such "stunts" could be a political one: in 1911, Orage writes, Shaw is "down among the propagandists" because his drama substitutes for its proper object, the "soul," the "idea" of voting "Progressive" (**"On Drama"** 58).

Although Orage and his colleagues attacked the realist aesthetics of progressive and radical writers, their response to the new art of those such as Lewis and Pound was largely ambivalent. Nevertheless, while the *New Age* writers and the modernists may have differed as to what the new art should be, their criticisms of the realist aesthetic have much in common. Hulme's Worringerian defence of the new "geometrical," "mechanical," and abstract art is in many ways Orage's critique of realist writing applied to painting and sculpture. According to Hulme,

> You have these two different kinds of art. You have first the art which is natural to you, Greek art and modern art since the Renaissance. You have other arts like the Egyptian, Indian and Byzantine, where everything tends to be angular, where curves tend to be hard and geometrical, where the representation of the human body, for example, is often entirely non-vital, and distorted to fit into stiff lines and cubical shapes of various kinds.

> (*Speculations* 82)

Thus the post-Impressionist and "primitive" artist is driven by the desire "to create a certain abstract geometrical shape, which, being durable and permanent shall be a refuge from the flux and impermanence of outside nature" (*Speculations* 86). Like Orage, Hulme assumes that the mimetic impulse in art derives from a desire to celebrate the object of representation. Hulme calls this object "nature" whereas critics such as Orage argue that the realist novel "reproduces" a world which, with its "commercialism," "yellow journalism," and "advertising," is socially constructed. However, both Hulme and Orage assume that realist art does not establish a sufficient difference between itself and that which it represents. Such a difference is a mark of the artwork's resistance and opposition to nature or capitalist society. For Orage, true art is "heroic," or different in stature from the degraded social world, whereas for Hulme the artwork's resistance to nature is measured by its abstraction. In both cases that which is outside of art is chaotic and threatening. Consequently, the art work's difference from this external world is also a form of defence. As Hulme says, art is a "refuge" from "nature."

We find, therefore, that one of the distinguishing characteristics of classical or post-Impressionist art is its asceticism. In fact, one of the most reliable indicators of a writer's political affiliations during this period is his attitude toward "sex." Writers such as Wells, according to Orage (**"Readers & Writers"**), are obsessed with "sex-love" (28 Aug. 1913: 513), whereas classicists treat the lower and degraded pleasures of the body with a suitable disdain. The eponymous hero of *Tarr,* for example, argues that

> There was only one God, and he was a man. = A woman was a lower form of life. Everything was female to begin with. A jellyish diffuseness spread itself and gaped on the beds and in the bas fonds of everything. Above a certain level of life sex disappeared, just as in highly organized sensualism sex vanishes. And, on the other hand, *everything* beneath that line was female.

(313-314)

The asceticism which derives from such grotesque misogyny, as for all the *New Age* critics, tends to be more an anxious defence against the world of the flesh than a transcendence of it:

> *Deadness* is the first condition of art. A hippopotamus' armoured hide, a turtle's shell, feathers or machinery on the one hand; *that* opposed to naked pulsing and moving of the soft inside of life, along with infinite elasticity and consciousness of movement, on the other. The second [condition] is absence of *soul,* in the sentimental human sense. The lines and masses of the statue are its soul. No restless, quick-like ego is imagined for the *inside* of it. It has no inside.

(299-300)

These are the same oppositions—flat/three-dimensional, abstract/realist, dead/vital—which Hulme uses to defend the new art. They are in turn regulated by the oppositions of art/life and male/female. Although these terms have almost mythical characteristics, Lewis and Hulme nevertheless invest "life" and "nature" with precisely the qualities which the *New Age* writers find so characteristic of liberal democracies: both are chaotic, feminine, amorphous, and fluid. Of course, we cannot simply substitute the words "liberal democracy" every time we find the terms "life" or "nature" in the work of these writers. But what I would argue is that the adversarial and elitist culture of early modernism is partly constructed in opposition to the kinds of popular or "middle-brow" culture which the *New Age* critics found so characteristic of liberal democracies.

Writing about modernist culture in general, Andreas Huyssen argues that the ways in which modernist art rejects realism in favor of abstraction, self-referentiality, experimentalism, and autonomy are not, from about the mid-nineteenth century onwards, without political implications. "Modernism constituted itself through a con-

scious strategy of exclusion," according to Huyssen, "an anxiety of contamination by its other: an increasingly consuming and engulfing mass culture" (52). Such resistance to mass culture is also a mediated form of resistance to those who consume it—the masses. If modernist art typically figures mass culture as feminine, passive, and emotional, so turn-of-the-century works such as Gustave Le Bon's *The Crowd*—sections of which Kennedy translated for the *New Age*—describe crowds as having "feminine characteristics." The modernist artist's "resistance" to the "seductive lure of mass culture" often betrays a fear of the masses which, during "this age of declining liberalism is always also a fear of woman, a fear of nature out of control, a fear of the unconscious, of sexuality, of the loss of identity and stable ego boundaries in the mass" (Huyssen 52).

The realist novels of those writers such as Wells were not "mass culture" in quite the sense that Huyssen understands that term. Nevertheless, the implicit literary agenda of the *New Age* was to draw a political division between what Kennedy describes as "the two publics— one the small artistic public, and the other the great uncultured middle-class public" (*English Literature* 202). Certainly, Kennedy's "small artistic public" was quite different from that of the Vorticists. The latter, for example, were willing to embrace experimentalism and mechanical rather than organic forms. But the Vorticist artist and Kennedy's classicist oppose very much the same thing. In "Crowd-Master" Lewis identifies himself with the police who "with distant icy contempt herd London" (94). The London crowds, which Lewis describes as a "tide" and as a band of "Suffragette Furies" (94), are being incited to war by the newspapers and advertising posters. Lewis represents the latter as a "crude distillation of 1905 to 1915: Suffragism. H. G. Wells" (95). The newly democratized masses are not only an amorphous and feminine body but also directly associated with the popular and "journalistic" writing of Wells. Lewis is clearly fascinated by this crowd just as his magazine, *Blast,* enthusiastically experiments with and assimilates the typography of contemporary newspapers and advertising. Yet the sharp lines and jagged edges which he uses in *Blast* and the paintings of this period can be seen as boundaries of a kind between the frigid world of the aesthetic and the democratic body of the public.

Unlike Lewis, Pound has a far more ambivalent attitude toward the organic world. Nevertheless, his Vorticist aesthetics have much in common with Lewis' anti-realism. Pound maintains that Vorticist art is "interested in the creative faculty as opposed to the mimetic ("Affirmations: Vorticism" 277). Using suitably phallic metaphors, Pound describes such art as "directing a certain fluid force against circumstance, as *conceiving* instead of merely reflecting and observing" ("Vorticism" 467). The "mimetic" art about which Pound writes is primarily "impressionism," whose "logical end . . . is the cinematograph" ("Vorticism" 467), and Futurism. He describes the latter as a kind of "accelerated impressionism" ("Vorticism" 461). Pound's critique of the Vorticists' adversaries, then, is essentially the same as Orage's complaints about both the contemporary novel *and* post-Impressionist art in general: both passively receive and democratically reproduce all aspects of contemporary reality.

Of course the antirealism of Pound's Vorticist criticism came after his Imagist prescription for the "direct treatment of the thing" ("A Few Don'ts" 202). Pound's insistence on the referential qualities of poetic language during his Imagist period does, obviously, conflict with his later Vorticist polemic for an antirealist, pure, autonomous art. It is not my purpose here to resolve this apparent contradiction—if in fact it can be resolved—but instead to observe that even the Imagist poetics often display the kinds of anti-democratic bias which so characterize Pound's Vorticist writing. When Pound fought with Amy Lowell over control of the Imagist movement, he wrote to her on 1 August 1914, that

> I should like the name "Imagisme" to retain some sort of a meaning. It stands, or I should like it to stand for hard, light, clear edges. I can not trust any democratized committee to maintain that standard. Some will be splay-footed and some sentimental.
>
> (*Letters* 78)

Critics usually assume that adjectives such as "hard," "light," "clear," "precise," and "accurate"—adjectives which recur obsessively in the criticism of Pound, Lewis, and Hulme—refer to only the formal aspects of the work of art. Yet such descriptive terms always imply, and are often directly contrasted to, a set of opposing adjectives: feminine, sentimental, soft, democratic, and amorphous. If the Vorticist aesthetics of Pound and Lewis are an attempt aggressively to protect art from the levelling effects of liberal democracies, then Pound intends his Imagist poetics to cut through the vulgar, commercialized culture of such a society to what he perceives as a more lasting, and usually "pagan," tradition ("Affirmations: Analysis"). The insistence by those such as Pound, Lewis, and Hulme on the "hardness" and "clear edges" of the art work can be read as a displaced expression of anxieties about the instability of social identity in a democratizing and modernizing society, a society which was perceived by those at the *New Age* as blurring "natural" social boundaries and hierarchies.

Such attempts by the reactionary modernists to preserve the purity of art have extremely ambivalent characteristics: the aesthetic sphere is at the same time both anti-democratic and oppositional. This contradictory combination of the elitist and the adversarial is the most

significant characteristic which the aesthetics of early modernism have in common with the politics of the *New Age* front. In 1911 Kennedy, for example, argues that the most prominent thinkers and artists of the past ten years have been "all Liberals, radicals or Socialists: there is not a Conservative among them" ("Tory Democracy" 54). Hulme takes an even more extreme position by maintaining that European culture since the Renaissance has been totally dominated by a radical, progressive, and liberal *Weltanschauung*. For both Kennedy and Hulme, therefore, a true conservative or reactionary must always belong to the opposition party since the dominant institutions and traditions of contemporary society are progressive and radical. The true conservative, in other words, must be a radical. Not only has democratic ideology achieved a total ascendancy but also modernity has become the dominant European tradition. The attempts by the *New Age* writers and the reactionary modernists to return to the conditions which prevailed before the French Revolution, the Renaissance, or some other cataclysmic event, mime the revolutionary characteristics of radical advocates of modernity such as the socialists. When modernity becomes a tradition, the conservative nostalgia to return to pre-modernity is revolutionary. That contradictory combination of the traditional and radical, of right-wing politics and experimental aesthetics which characterizes the culture of reactionary modernism is partly the product of a larger culture milieu exemplified by journals such as the *New Age*.

Note

1. David S. Thatcher, who has written the fullest account of the reception of Nietzsche in Britain, either ignores or condones the extremely reactionary aspects of English Nietzscheanism.

Works Cited

Belloc, Hilaire. *The Servile State*. London: Foulis, 1912.

Bush, Ronald. "Ezra Pound." *The Gender of Modernism: A Critical Anthology*. Ed. Bonnie Kime Scott. Bloomington: Indiana UP, 1989. 351-357.

Carter, Huntly, ed. "A Symposium on Women's Suffrage." *New Age* 2 Feb. 1911: 1-15.

Cole, G. D. H. *The Second International 1889-1914*. Vol. 3 of *A History of Socialist Thought*. 2nd. ed. 5 vols. London: Macmillan, 1963.

———. *A Short History of the British Working Class Movement, 1789-1927*. 3 vols. London: Allen, 1927.

Finlay, John L. *Social Credit: The English Origins*. Montreal: McGill-Queen's UP, 1972.

Glass, S. T. *The Responsible Society: The Ideas of the English Guild Socialists*. London: Longmans, 1966.

Hay, J. R. *The Origins of the Liberal Welfare Reforms, 1906-1914.* London: Macmillan, 1975.

Hulme, T. E. *Further Speculations.* Ed. Samuel Hynes. Lincoln: U of Nebraska P, 1960.

——. *Speculations.* Ed. Herbert Read. New York: Harcourt, 1924.

Huyssen, Andreas. *After the Great Divide: Modernism, Mass Culture, Postmodernism.* Bloomington: Indiana UP, 1986.

Kennedy, J. M. *English Literature, 1880-1905.* London: Swift, 1912.

——. *The Quintessence of Nietzsche.* London: Laurie, 1909.

——. "Tory Democracy: The Importance of Ideas." *New Age* 18 May 1911: 54.

Levy, Oscar. "A Book on Nietzsche." *New Age* 28 May 1914: 89.

——. "The Nietzsche Movement in England: A Retrospect, a Confession, and a Prospect (III)." *New Age* 2 Jan. 1913: 204-206.

Lewis, Wyndam. "Crowd Master." *Blast 1.* 94-102.

——. "Letter to the *New Age*." *New Age* 8 Jan. 1914: 319.

——. *Rude Assignment: An Intellectual Autobiography.* Ed. Toby Fashay. Santa Barbara: Black Sparrow, 1984.

——. *Tarr.* Ed. Paul O'Keefe. Santa Rosa: Black Sparrow, 1990.

Lewis, Wyndham, ed. *Blast 1.* Santa Barbara: Black Sparrow, 1981.

Ludovici, Anthony. *A Defence of Aristocracy: A Text Book for Tories.* Boston: Phillips, 1915.

Maeztu, Ramiro de. *Authority, Liberty and Function in the Light of the War.* London: Allen, 1916.

Martin, Wallace. Introduction. *Orage as Critic.* By Alfred Orage. Ed. Wallace Martin. London: Routledge, 1974.

——. *The New Age Under Orage: Chapters in English Cultural History.* Manchester: Manchester UP, 1967.

Morgan, Kenneth O. "Edwardian Socialism." *Edwardian England.* Ed. Donald Read. 93-111.

Orage, Alfred. "Another Tale for Men Only (III)." *New Age* 28 Sept. 1911: 517-518.

——. "The Folly of Anti-Semitism." *New Age* 14 Aug. 1913: 449-450.

——. "Notes of the Week." *New Age* 8 June 1911: 341-343.

——. "Notes of the Week." *New Age* 12 Oct. 1911: 553-556.

——. Preface. *National Guilds.* By S. G. Hobson. 3rd. ed. London: Bell, 1919.

——. "Readers and Writers." *New Age* 12 June 1913: 177-179.

——. "Readers and Writers." *New Age* 28 Aug. 1913: 513-514.

——. "A Tale for Men Only (V)." *New Age* 7 Sept. 1911: 445-446.

——. "Unedited Opinions: Down with the Tricolour." *New Age* 21 Sept. 1911: 489-490.

——. "Unedited Opinions: Modern Novels." *New Age* 29 Dec. 1910.

——. "Unedited Opinions: Money-Changers in Literature." *New Age* 11 May 1911: 35.

——. "Unedited Opinions: On Drama." *New Age* 18 May 1911: 58.

——. "Unedited Opinions: The Superman." *New Age* 1 Dec. 1910: 107.

Penty, A. J. "Restoration of the Guild System." *New Age* 4 Sept. 1914: 544-547.

Pound, Ezra. "Affirmations: Analysis of this Decade." *New Age* 11 Feb. 1915: 409-411.

——. "Affirmations (II): Vorticism." *New Age* 14 Jan. 1914: 246-247.

——. "A Few Don'ts by an Imagist." *Poetry* Mar. 1913: 200-206.

——. *Letters of Ezra Pound, 1907-1941.* Ed. D. D. Paige. New York: Harcourt, 1950.

——. "The New Sculpture." *Egoist* 16 Feb. 1914: 67-68.

——. [Herman Carl Georg Jesus Maria], "On Certain Reforms and Pass-Times." *Egoist* 1 Apr. 1914: 130-131.

——. [Bastien von Helmholtz]. "Suffragettes." *Egoist* 1 July 1914: 254-256.

——. "Through Alien Eyes (III)." 30 Jan. 1913: 300-301.

——. "Through Alien Eyes (IV)." *New Age* 6 Feb. 1913: 324.

——. "Vorticism." *Fortnightly Review* 1 Sept. 1914: 461-471.

Randall, A. E. "Views and Reviews: On Aristocracy (II)." *New Age* 11 Mar. 1915: 512-513.

Read, Donald. "Introduction: Crisis Age or Golden Age?" *Edwardian England.* Ed. Donald Read. London: Croom, 1982.

Reckitt, Maurice B. *As It Happened: An Autobiography.* London: Dent, 1936.

Robinson, Alan. *Poetry, Painting and Ideas, 1885-1914.* London: Macmillan, 1985.

Thatcher, David S. *Nietzsche in England 1890-1914.* Toronto: U of Toronto P, 1970.

Williams, Raymond. *Culture and Society 1780-1950.* London: Chatto, 1958.

FURTHER READING

Biographies

Carswell, John. "The Moon-Girl From Port Elizabeth." In *Lives and Letters: A. R. Orage, Beatrice Hastings, Katherine Mansfield, John Middleton Murry, S. S. Koteliansky,* pp. 28-51. New York: New Directions, 1978.
    A biographical examination of how Orage came to the *New Age* and its influence on the era's writers.

Kadlec, David. "Pound, *BLAST,* and Syndicalism." *ELH* 60, no. 4 (winter 1993): 1015-31.
    An evaluation of Ezra Pound's efforts in the Syndicalist movement that discusses Orage's role in guiding these struggles.

Mairet, Philip. *A. R. Orage: A Memoir.* London, England: J. M. Dent, 1936, 132 p.
    Account of Orage's life from a member of his literary circle.

Criticism

Martin, Wallace. *The New Age Under Orage: Chapters in English Cultural History.* New York: Barnes & Noble, 1967, 303 p.
    Sympathetic treatment of Orage's literary criticism and his role in fostering political and cultural activity.

Munson, Gorham. "Orage in America." In *The Awakening Twenties: A Memoir-history of a Literary Period,* pp. 253-83. Baton Rouge: Louisiana State University Press, 1985.
    Focuses on Orage's work with the mystic Gurdjieff.

Rawlinson, Andrew. "The Gurdjieff Legacy: A. R. Orage." In *The Book of Enlightened Masters: Western Teachers in Eastern Tradition,* pp. 306-08. Chicago: Open Court Publishing Company, 1997.
    Explores Gurdjieff's influence on and relationship with Orage.

Welch, Louise. "Inner Fires." In *Orage With Gurdjieff in America,* pp. 30-7. Boston: Routledge & Kegan Paul, 1982.
    Outlines the skills of Orage that enabled him to introduce people to Gurdjieff's meta-physical ideas.

Additional coverage of Orage's life and career is contained in the following sources published by Thomson Gale: *Contemporary Authors,* **Vol. 122; and** *Literature Resource Center.*

Joe Orton
1933-1967

(Full name John Kingsley Orton) English playwright, novelist, and scriptwriter.

The following entry provides criticism on Orton's works from 1965 through 2001. For further information on Orton, see *CLC,* Volumes 4, 13, and 43.

INTRODUCTION

Orton was best known for his iconoclastic plays which demonstrate the absurdity of life. The term "Ortonesque" has come into common parlance as a description of the kind of black humor his plays exhibit.

BIOGRAPHICAL INFORMATION

Orton was born on January 1, 1933, to working-class parents in Leicester. He attended the Royal Academy of Dramatic Arts in London, where he met Kenneth Halliwell, who was to become his longtime homosexual partner. Halliwell introduced Orton to the world of classical drama and encouraged his literary inclinations. Orton worked as an assistant stage manager in Ipswich before returning to London, where he collaborated with Halliwell on several novels. He and Halliwell each served short prison sentences in 1962 after they were convicted of damaging numerous library books by removing color plates to use for art work in their home. Orton's first play was broadcast on the BBC in 1964, after which he wrote a number of full-length dramas and several short ones for television. In 1967 Halliwell, depressed and envious of Orton's burgeoning success, beat Orton to death and took his own life immediately afterwards.

MAJOR WORKS

Orton's short career was marked by considerable success. He thrived in a theatrical atmosphere which had welcomed other cynics such as Harold Pinter, whose plays revolved around characters who cause tension by annoying people and disrupting their lives. Orton's first play, *The Ruffian on the Stair* (1964), is Pinteresque, with its depressive protagonist trying to avenge a history of incest with his older brother. In *Entertaining Mr.*

Sloane (1964), a murderer is blackmailed by his victim's nymphomaniac daughter and homosexual son into granting them sexual favors. *Loot* (1965) has a number of corrupt and greedy characters, along with some farcical elements which also appear in Orton's last work, *What the Butler Saw* (1969), staged after Orton's death. This play, set in a psychiatric clinic, is a parody of the work of French playwright Georges Feydeau. Orton's one-act plays, generally considered of lesser importance, were originally seen on television. *The Erpingham Camp* (1966), based on Euripides's *Bacchae,* takes place in a British holiday camp. *The Good and Faithful Servant* (1967) deals with the meaningless and cyclical life of an injured factory worker. *Funeral Games* (1968), also produced after Orton's death, is a satire on religion. A few posthumous works have appeared, such as *Head to Toe* (1971), a fantasy novel about a man who traverses a giant's body. *The Orton Diaries,* a compilation of diaries written between 1966 and 1967, was published in 1986. *Up against It* (1979)

a screenplay commissioned and later rejected for a film starring the Beatles, became the basis of a musical in the 1990s. A novel, *Between Us Girls* (1998), and two more plays, *The Visitors* (written in 1959), and *Fred and Madge* (written in 1961), were published in 1998.

CRITICAL RECEPTION

At first, the frank language, offbeat characters, and disdain for middle-class morality in Orton's plays caused shock and outrage among critics and audiences. Orton himself contributed to this controversy with pseudonymic, tongue-in-cheek reviews of his own work. In general, however, critics have praised Orton as a major talent cut off before his time. Most have written about his dark view of the world, and some have noted his debt to earlier generations of playwrights and to Pinter, his contemporary. Others have stressed the influence of his relationship with Halliwell on his work, as well as his candid treatment of homosexual themes. Critics have often agreed that Orton wrote well-structured, witty plays which provided trenchant commentary on the contemporary scene. Several book-length critical biographies of Orton added to his reputation in the 1980s and 1990s, as did several plays based on his life. Notable among these was *Diary of a Somebody,* a play by Orton's friend, diary editor, and biographer John Lahr. A film version of Lahr's biography also brought Orton's name to even more public attention.

PRINCIPAL WORKS

Entertaining Mr. Sloane (play) 1964

*The Ruffian on the Stair (play) 1964

Loot (play) 1965

*The Erpingham Camp (play) 1966

The Good and Faithful Servant (play) 1967

Funeral Games (play) 1968

Until She Screams (play) 1969

What the Butler Saw (play) 1969

Head to Toe (novel) 1971

Joe Orton: The Complete Plays (plays) 1976

Up against It: A Screenplay for the Beatles (screenplay) 1979

The Orton Diaries (diaries) 1986

Between Us Girls (novel) 1998

The Visitors and Fred and Madge (plays) 1998

*These works performed as *Crimes of Passion,* 1967.

CRITICISM

Glenn Loney (essay date November 1965)

SOURCE: Loney, Glenn. "Entertaining Mr. Loney: An Early Interview with Joe Orton." *New Theatre Quarterly* 4 (November 1988): 300-05.

[*In the following essay, a report of a 1965 interview, Loney and the playwright talk about* Entertaining Mr. Sloane, *Orton's interest in the works of Jane Austen, the genre of black comedy, Orton's brief history in the theater, and other subjects.*]

Every summer, drama teachers desert American college campuses in search of meaningful change or new experiences. Some paint their houses. Others fly off to London to see Broadway's newest hits before they arrive in New York. This has been going on for a long time now. In July 1964, as I was frantically making up my list of what to see in the West End and at Stratford, trying to cram in as many plays as possible, I found a curious photo in a Sunday arts section. It showed a pert young man in T-shirt, jeans, and tennis-shoes, casually stretched out on a bed with turned-down sheets. The wall behind him was a psychedelic riot of Old Master art images. (And not, as some who but dimly remember this photo insist, a collage of body-builders. That must have been another part of the wall.)

The caption revealed that this was a new young playwright who had recently been endorsed and encouraged by Terence Rattigan—whose own reputation was not then at its zenith. Indeed, the fledgling author had some pages of manuscript spread out on the bed, but he was looking neither at them nor at the camera. His gaze was directed stage-right, as if seeing something of which he slightly disapproved. The playwright was Joe Orton, and his new black comedy—the catchword was itself new—***Entertaining Mr. Sloane*** was to open in the West End at Wyndhams Theatre, after a successful showing at the Arts.

At that time, Dudley Sutton, either clad in black leather or out of it entirely, was something of a surprise, especially when Madge Ryan and Peter Vaughan, as sister and brother both fascinated by Mr. Sloane's boyish but sinister allure, manoeuvred for his favours. Some may remember that incarnation of ***Sloane*** as having been successful, but in fact it ran only 152 performances. It did excite a lot of comment and controversy. Who *was* this new writer? No one seemed to know very much about him.

Then, on 12 October, 1965, ***Entertaining Mr. Sloane*** opened on Broadway at the venerable Lyceum Theatre, built in 1903, and once Daniel Frohman's repertory playhouse. Alan Schneider was directing, with Sheila Hancock as the amoral sister Kath. During rehearsals, I asked Schneider if I could talk with Orton about the play. I seemed to be one of the few New York theatre journalists (or drama teachers) who liked the play, or even knew about it. Schneider was delighted and arranged a talk backstage.

Burrowing through some old files, looking for clippings about Peter Brook, I discovered the transcript I made of that interview, on 9 October 1965. It has never been published—for the production opened to scathing, outraged reviews and rapidly closed after thirteen ill-attended performances. Orton had already gone back to London. By the time I had transcribed the tape, no one wanted to hear anything about either Mr. Sloane or Mr. Orton.

I cannot remember what I expected on my way to interview Orton. The photo-image was clearly etched in my memory, it's true, as well as that of Dudley Sutton, trousers off, getting a bit of a mend from Kath. Perhaps I thought I'd find Orton in black leather, not unlike his Sloane fantasy. In fact, I wasn't quite prepared for the actuality. A very boyish Orton, his face gleaming as if it had been oiled (I think it had been) greeted me warmly. He was togged out in a trim little blue-and-white striped nautical T-shirt and tight trousers. He was charm itself; he fairly twinkled. Sloane, it appeared, was not the only sham-innocent seducer in the Orton stable.

The London production, in my memory, had attained a kind of perfection. Schneider had Americanized the play and the performances somewhat, rather to its detriment I thought. At one point, when Kath was rummaging in a drawer, she pulled out a vaginal douche and waved it around with an apparent thrill of finding an old friend again. I admired Schneider, both as a director and as a friend, but this seemed a bit cheap. Looking at *Sloane* now, I wonder why I was bothered by this.

Orton certainly wasn't. He loved that bit of business. 'Oh, that's just wonderful! I wish I'd thought of that. I ought to put it into the acting edition. Alan is a brilliant director! We don't have anybody like him in England anymore. Showy old directors we do have—but someone who will *lift* a play, bring out everything that is in a play, without imposing his own personality? We have directors like Peter Hall, who have Hamlet play in a red-and-white striped muffler. That's *obvious* direction. But Alan does the kind of direction a playwright loves. Well, I love it anyway.'

Having watched previous Schneider shows in rehearsal, and talked with some of his actors now and then, I told Orton that some complained that he didn't help them enough—that he let them work out the roles and the conflicts by themselves. Had he found this to be so with *Sloane*?

'I've complained of that with directors in England, but I have no complaint with Alan. The things he's invented? I think I would have invented them myself—if I'd thought of them. That is always the best kind of direction.'

But had Schneider cut any of the lines? Possibly to avoid shocking susceptible New York critics?

'There was one speech cut: that was all. And there were one or two lines that I altered, that an American audience wouldn't get. If they weren't important, and an American audience could "ride over" it—if it was just a typical British phrase—I left it in.'

Kath's revelation of pregnancy to her irate brother was one of these: 'I've a bun in the oven.' Not at all an American phrase, but graphic enough as Kath lifted her apron to disclose the results of a magical night with Mr. Sloane. Orton left such lines alone.

His work was just beginning to be discovered by the German theatre, and he noted with elation that *Entertaining Mr. Sloane* had been shown at the Hamburg Schauspielhaus in the august company of Shakespeare, Molière, and O'Neill. 'I was really flattered', he said. 'I've got a whole thing at home, saying something good goes on here by Molière, and something by Shakespeare, and something by O'Neill, and a slight mention of *Entertaining Mr. Sloane,* which is very amazing. Well, it's nice to be taken seriously. I mean, I'm a serious dramatist.'

I told him that when I'd seen it in London, I thought the play was terrifically funny. But I hadn't seen any deep, dark metaphors or myths in it at all. Then, the day after I'd enjoyed it at Wyndhams, I had lunch with Harold Hobson. At that time, I was doing interviews with young writers and performers for the *Christian Science Monitor,* and he was its London critic, as well as the London *Sunday Times* reviewer.

Initially, I had regarded him as conservative, if sometimes eccentric in judgement. On our first meeting, he pointed out to me that he had been often the first of the major critics to spot new playwriting talent. He it was who urged me to interview David Storey, Peter Shaffer, Arnold Wesker, and others. Now, I wondered what he'd have to say about Orton and *Sloane,* for Hobson was never indecisive about likes and dislikes. He praised it as authentic black comedy. I told Orton this.

'He's the only critic who spotted what *Sloane* was. I remember his words. His exact words were, "the *Northanger Abbey* of the theatre". This was absolutely amazing. I wrote him a letter, saying that I've always admired Jane Austen's *Juvenilia*—before she wrote

Sense and Sensibility. Northanger Abbey is of course *Juvenilia,* which she rewrote later in life. It was published after her death. I've always admired *Northanger Abbey.*

'She really is one—' Orton broke off, trying to think of a comparison. 'I can go overboard on her works', he limply concluded. 'Most people read Jane Austen—like people who read Edna Ferber, and only see the chi-chi 1890s side. *Northanger Abbey* is wonderful because it's a straight novel, and yet it has a wonderful element of Stendahl that you can appreciate. It was really very perceptive of Hobson to recognize this. I admired him for seeing what no one else saw in it.'

This was a time in British theatre when myths and ancient rituals were being recalled, not only to give added resonance to Stratford Shakespeare productions, which were already echoing with subtextual inferences, but also, for example, to give dark meaning to seemingly ordinary farm work, as in David Rudkin's then shocking *Afore Night Come.* Rudkin's debt to Fraser and *The Golden Bough* seemed clear enough. Jane Austen's influence in ***Entertaining Mr. Sloane*** was harder to detect, but once one thought about it. . . .

'You believed so much in these labourers', Orton was saying of Rudkin's play. 'Rudkin's the one person I've read that I'd give my eye-teeth to write dialogue like. But I cannot believe in the ritual murder. I can believe that these people set on somebody and beat him in a senseless fury, but I can't believe that *Golden Bough* thing.'

How ironic then was Orton's own death later to prove, when his teeming brain was smashed by the envious hammer-blows of his mentor—roommate, Kenneth Halliwell, to whom he dedicated ***Sloane.*** At once a crime of passion—and of failure and bitter disappointment—and also a kind of ritual murder. . . .

Orton continued talking about myth: 'Symbolism like that should be integrated into the play. I mean, in ***Sloane*** I am aware of the symbols of the waste-land, and of the house at the edge of the waste-land. And that the old man is the king of the waste-land, who is killed by the young man. But it doesn't matter for ***Sloane*** if you haven't read *The Golden Bough.* Whereas, in *Afore Night Come,* I think if you haven't read it, you are lost.'

We were talking only three days before ***Sloane***'s Broadway premiere. As far as Orton knew then, he had written a shocking black comedy which had had a modest West End success, which led critics to foresee an interesting future for him. Its resounding Broadway failure and aftermath he was to experience later, largely from a safe distance. On 9 October, however, Orton still thought he had written a strong, challenging comedy, and he was not ashamed that it had enjoyed some commercial recognition.

'I did get some sneers at ***Sloane*** for being a "commercial" drama. I think that's because it had a successful West End run. It's this ridiculous thing that there's some kind of intrinsic merit in failure. There's not! We all know that some good plays go on—and they fail. But so many bad plays go on. There's no merit in playing three nights in a cellar unless the play is good. You know there is an awful lot of rubbish put on for three nights in cellars, just as there is rubbish in the commercial theatre.

'I resent this thing of being considered a "commercial dramatist". Sheila Hancock was trying to cheer me up. She said, "You playwrights think people are using the word 'commercial' as a sneer." Well, they are! O'Neill, and Wilde in his day, were very commercial. And so was Barrie, and Shaw. . . .'

Orton revealed that he had been hard at work on a new play, and now it was finished. 'It's called ***Loot.*** The William Morris Agency read it. They adored it. They said it's better than ***Sloane,*** and they want to put it on. I want it to go on in America first, because I think it will be done better here. If it's done over here first, then we can correct it.'

'You see, the terrible thing in England is that the Arts Theatre is more or less finished. ***Sloane*** was about the last thing put on there. The Arts Theatre has gone down the drain. To get into the Royal Court, you have to be on a political committee, which I'm not.'

Where were the other small theatres? Joan Littlewood's theatre at Stratford East? 'She's no longer there. She had a special personality. You could disagree with everything she did—which I did very frequently. I saw her productions, and I disagreed with them, but she compelled you to go there. You couldn't *not* go.'

In the event of a success in New York for ***Sloane,*** Orton was certain that it couldn't be toured around the United States. Outside New York, he feared audiences would be actively hostile. 'There are problems with a play like ***Sloane,*** or most certainly like ***Loot.*** He sighed. '*They* just don't understand.'

Did he think that regional audiences would denounce the play? 'Well, you really wouldn't mind if they denounced it. But the thing that happens is that they say, "Well, these are totally unbelievable characters?" "I don't understand it!" "I don't like these jokes!" "I don't understand what you are making a joke about." Even if they may be living exactly the same way at home themselves. I get some weird comments. I usually mingle with the audience.'

Had he heard, as I had at Wyndhams, spectators speculating on the dirtiness of his mind?

'I think I've got just an average mind—but what happens? Right after **Sloane** came on, there was something in *News of the World* about a man and his wife sharing another woman. So I think that lesbianism is slightly more respectable than homosexuality!'

Noting that the first German production of **Loot** would be in Munich, capital of High Catholic Bavaria, Orton explained: 'Actually, it's a Catholic household, in which a death has occurred. There are some ridiculous jokes. The boy has sex with the girl underneath a picture of the Sacred Heart. And then the boy's friend says to the girl, "While Jesus is pointing to His Sacred Heart, you're pointing to yours!"'

Orton explained that, while not a Catholic himself, 'Catholicism was always a fascinating thing for me. I've always worked—when I've worked—in warehouses and things. I've always seemed to be working with Catholic Irishmen. And so, in the end, I just got a sort of thing: that I could think like they thought. And, of course, religion is an endless subject for satire and parody.

'You see, in order to be funny about morals, you must have characters who are moral. And if you want characters to be extremely moral—from an English standpoint—you must set it in a Catholic household. The Protestant household is no longer the same. Protestantism—I don't know about America—no longer exists in England. So one must have a Catholic background. Of course the obvious thing in England is an *Irish* Catholic background, somewhere in Camden Town or Kilburn. As far as I'm concerned, it's an endless subject for satire.'

I told Orton how arresting the Sunday arts photo of him had seemed.

'That was a dreadful picture! I don't know why they took that. Oh, they wanted a picture of the background, of the wall. They wanted the picture there, so they had me lying on the bed, with a sort of double chin. It looked terrible!'

I reassured him I'd seen no double chin. and the photo didn't look terrible. 'Didn't it? Well, I don't think that Rattigan thing helped. . . . Well, I'd always been writing—for years. You see, I'd written some plays, but I'd written them before the advent of *Waiting for Godot*. There were things I wanted to do, but I couldn't until the modern school appeared. You couldn't have done **Sloane** ten years ago. They were really rather strange plays. I did one that was called **Feathers**—kind of a funny title. But that is really a commercial title.

'I was trying to write for the commercial theatre. You see, this was pre-*Godot*. Well, once *Godot* came on, you could not—even if you would—write that rot any more. So I started, but I didn't think I could write anything like *Godot*. I was writing novels mostly, because I thought you could do much more interesting things in the novel at that time.

'Then I went to prison', he said. At this time, he did not elaborate. Later, in the course of an extended correspondence across the Atlantic, he quipped that he was jailed for Grand Larceny, which proved to be 'not so grand, as it turned out'.

'When I came out', Orton said, 'I wrote a full-length play. I showed it to someone whose judgement I respected. He said, "It is awful, and you seem to have lost all your talent for dialogue, having been in prison." I said, "All right", but I was rather depressed. I went away and cut it down to about a quarter of its length, and I cut out two characters. I rewrote it and titled it **The Ruffian on the Stair.**

'I sent it to the BBC because it was a one-act. The BBC accepted it. Then the friend I'd showed it to said, "Oh, you've done so many amazing things to it . . .". Well, it took about eighteen months for the BBC to decide that they were going to put it on. I was living on National Assistance, and they were getting more and more annoyed with me because I didn't get a job. I had no intention of getting a job.

'The BBC said, "What are you doing? Are you writing another play for us?" I said, "No, because you take so long." I was writing a full-length stage-play then. So they said, "Well, if you are going to do that, you do need an agent." And so they gave me the address of Margaret Ramsay, who is an excellent agent. She doesn't care about the money. If she likes you, she'll support you.

'I sent **Sloane** to her just before Christmas 1963. Immediately, in the New Year, I got a letter saying, "I don't know if it would be a full evening's entertainment." She probably wouldn't remember that now. Well, anyway, she showed it to a London manager.

'They wanted to put it on at Stratford East, originally. I was a bit dubious, because I knew that Joan Littlewood, who ran Stratford East at that time, would have ripped it apart. I mean, she would have introduced all sorts of new characters. And it probably would have been a success, but it wouldn't have been *my* play. Finally, Michael Codron said he would put it on at the Arts Theatre. And the rest you know.'

The rest, which neither of us suspected at that point, was that most of the Broadway reviewers would dislike or even hate **Entertaining Mr. Sloane.** Walter Kerr concealed any Catholic bias against the play's amorality by saying that *Sloane* was indeed a 'bizarre black comedy', but that it wasn't black enough. It was, however, more than enough for most. The *New York Times*'s Howard Taubman thought it made 'the Jukes family seem like sane, honourable folk!'

Normal Nadel, of the now-defunct *World Telegram*, insisted that *Sloane* had the 'sprightly charm of a medieval English cesspool'. Had he, all unknowing, stumbled over the doorstep of Northanger Abbey? He found it a 'macabre, decaying kind of comedy', in any case. Richard Watts thought *Sloane* 'outrageous'. CBS-TV branded *Sloane* 'sick, sick, sick'.

Soon to return to London, Joe Orton asked me to send him any reviews or comments on *Sloane* I might come across. Taubman of the *Times* later returned to the attack. When Orton received this next essay in dramatic criticism, he wrote back immediately: 'Methinks the lady doth protest too much.' Thus began a correspondence which ended shortly before Orton's unfortunate death. He asked me to comment on the German translations of *Sloane* and *Loot*—*Seid nett zu Mr. Sloane* and *Boute*—for he could not read German, but realized that *Sloane* had done well and *Loot* not so well *auf Deutsch,* with different translators. Was that the source of the trouble? It certainly seemed possible: *Sloane* in German was a marvel.

As soon as Orton discovered that I functioned as a reviewer as well as an interviewer, he wrote: 'I loved you for yourself alone; I didn't realize you were a critic.' Still smarting from critical jibes, in a later letter Orton noted that he'd just been to see Harold Pinter's *The Homecoming.* 'Very brilliant play. The best he's written. Sexual sharing takes place in that too. A girl, though. Makes it more wholesome, I suppose. I've often wondered what foreigners think of England these days. If they relate the play to life, they must imagine we live in a Medieval Cesspool.'

Our friendship was almost entirely postal, but every summer, as soon as I arrived in London, I'd phone Orton, who always insisted on giving me lunch. He wouldn't hear of my paying: 'I'm really making some money now', he'd explain. Then we'd eat and pore over his clipping-books, noting the favourable reviews and features first. For the rest, Orton would either dismiss them or explain in detail how wrong the critic was and, in any case, a fool.

But after an hour or so, Orton would begin checking the time. Once, lunching at the Arts, I suggested we continue our discussion of the impending demise of the commercial theatre while making the rounds of a special exhibition at the National Portrait Gallery.

'No, I can't. I'm sorry but I've got to get home.' And off he'd go, to Flat 4, 25 Noel Road, Islington, N1, clutching his clippings.

Suzanne McCray (essay date fall 1984)

SOURCE: McCray, Suzanne. "The Unrelenting Pessimism of Joe Orton." *Publications of the Arkansas Philological Association* 10, no. 2 (fall 1984): 37-47.

[*In the following essay, McCray discusses the cynicism of most of Orton's work, suggesting that much of it derives from Orton's own life experience.*]

> I assure you that it is possible to draw poison from the clearest of wells.
>
> Joe Orton to Glen Loney, March 25, 1966

On Jan. 2, 1967, Joe Orton, London's then most promising young playwright, who shocked, instructed, and entertained the theater-going public of the town, wrote in his diary: "In the evening P. Willes rang. . . . I told him about the [Orton's mother's] funeral. And the frenzied way my family behave. He seemed shocked. But then he thinks my plays are fantasies. He suddenly caught a glimpse of the fact that I write the truth."[1] The truth, according to Orton, seems to be that people do not feel love or hate, happiness or sorrow, for the world offers nothing to believe in. Sex is simply something to pass the time; God is reduced to Church, defeated by life but "always well-equipped to deal with Death." And the government is peopled by individuals as corrupt as those they govern. And so Orton laughs at the world that can never be redeemed. This is not farce as antidote, as Katherine Worth suggests it is, for there is no cure.[2] Neither is it, as Martin Esslin insists, the "mindless laugh . . . which amounts to no more than an idiot's giggle at his own image in a mirror."[3] Like Beckett and Pinter, Orton laughs a bitter laugh, at a world that is "a cruel and heartless place."[4]

Reared in a dingy house in Leicester, Orton grew up listening to the rantings of his ambitious but unskilled mother, who tried desperately though unsuccessfully to make their home comfortable. His mother's frustrated and financially disastrous attempts at genteel living brought bitterness and gloom to their oppressive city project house. Orton never totally escaped the dreariness that characterized his early youth. In another diary entry in 1967—years after he had moved out of the house at Fayhurst Road—Joe Orton recorded a conversation which evokes his rather dismal childhood:

> "Yes, I've discovered I look best in cheap clothes." [said Orton.] "I wonder what the significance of that is?" Oscar [Lewenstein] said. "I'm from the gutter," I said. "And don't you ever forget it because I won't."
>
> (p. 38)

And he did not forget it. The abortive attempts of his mother to better their plight made Orton doubtful that man could ever escape the tawdriness of his environment.

In his works, the drab home of his childhood takes on a sinister decay. Orton sees putrefaction everywhere from specific settings like Fayhurst Road to the world at large. He depicts spiritually and physically mutilated people, living in crumbling homes filled with broken "conveniences." In *Endgame,* Hamm tells Clove, "We breathe, we change! We lose our hair, our teeth! Our bloom! Our ideals!"[5] And so it often is with Orton characters. The bloom is gone. Ideals are nonexistent.

Orton uses impoverished settings to reflect his spiritually impoverished characters. This is the case in *The Ruffian on the Stair,* in which Mike and Joyce live in a ransacked building in an apartment, sparingly decorated with old furniture. As emotionally ransacked as their building is empty, the two never display any tender feelings—not for others as poor as themselves, not for their boarder, Wilson, not even for each other.

Similar domestic settings appear in other plays, such as *Funeral Games* and *The Good and Faithful Servant.* But the setting of *Entertaining Mr. Sloane* offers Orton's most striking reminder that most people are from the gutter. Kemp's house, the "world" of the play, is built in the center of a rubbish dump. We are meant, as Orton's readers, to suspect our entire world as a larger version of Kemp's front yard:

> Look at it out there. An eyesore. You may admire it. I don't. A woman came all the way from Woolwich yesterday. A special trip she made in order to dump a bedstead. I told her, what do you want to saddle us with your filthy mess for? Came over in a shooting brake. She was an old woman. Had her daughter with her. Fouling the countryside with their litter.

> (p. 72)

The way Kemp views the woman seems to reflect Orton's regard for society in general. The world is an eyesore, with people constantly "dumping" on one another, "fouling the countryside with their litter." Anyone who protests—Kemp, Wilson, or Erpingham—is crushed, becoming quite literally part of the refuse.

In his only novel, *Head to Toe,* Orton depicts in savage detail man's physical environment, and by so doing delivers his most direct and biting portrait of a totally corrupt society. He compares it and its ideologies to a corpse:

> The prospect of living on a corpse did not affect many people. Indeed there were those who maintained the giant was not dead. Presented with the rotting flesh and the presence of maggots where once had been pleasant acres, they spoke in terms of temporary phenomena.[6]

Orton is clearly mocking those who speak of the world in optimistic terms. The corpse cannot be revived and so the decay will necessarily continue. Only a few relatively sensitive characters like Kemp understand this. Most are inured to the corruption around them. They can live in the middle of the dump and never smell the stench. Thus Martin Esslin and John Russell Taylor's accusation that Orton's characters are hollow puppets is scarcely surprising.[7] Given the world Orton sees, such characters, must be hollow if they are to survive.

Those who do not make it, those who have not "toughened up"—the sensitive, the simple, the kind—are invariably doomed. According to Orton, good guys are lucky to finish last, lucky to finish at all. To survive one must have a wickedly quick intelligence, be able to adapt to any situation, and be completely enervated emotionally.

Mike, a survivor in *The Ruffian on the Stair,* is just such a character. The play opens with Joyce asking him about his work:

JOYCE:

> Have you got an appointment today?

MIKE:

> Yes. I'm to be at King's Cross station at eleven. I'm meeting a man in the toilet.

JOYCE:

> You always go to such interesting places.[8]

Mike goes to such interesting places because financially he is "in a bad way." In a conversation with Wilson—a stranger looking for a room—Mike says, "With the cost of living being so high, I'm greatly in need of a weekly donation from the government . . . I've filled in a form to the effect that I'm a derelict" (p. 49).

He is a derelict who will hit a man with his van for a fee (250 quid exclusive of repairs to the van) and so he makes ends meet. Like Ben and Gus, who are similarly employed in Pinter's *The Dumb Waiter,* Mike speaks euphemistically about his job. He tells Wilson, "As a matter of fact, you've kept me. I've missed an appointment. Is shall have to drop them a line an apologize for the absence" (p. 49). The real situation behind these ever so polite words is that Mike has failed to kill a man. The disparity between Mike's diction and his actual meaning is both comic and chilling. Taking what business he can, he has totally anesthetized himself to any humane feelings.

In *Entertaining Mr. Sloane* certainly no one—except Kemp, who is brutally kicked to death—displays any depth of emotion. After Sloane murders Kemp, Kemp's children, Kath and Ed, do not experience grief or outrage, but instead use the circumstances of their father's death to keep their hold on Sloane. Both Kath and Ed are vying for Sloane's sexual favors and both have the "goods" on him. As for Sloane, he is ready to go with whoever can best save him. Finally, brother and sister decide to share him—six months for Ed, six months for Kath. Sloane responds favorably to the arrangement:

SLOANE:

I'll be grateful.

ED:

Will you?

SLOANE:

Eternally.

ED:

Not eternally boy. Just a few years.

Sloane's adaptability has saved him from prison, but it will take more than that to save him from the ravages of the "few years" with Kath and Ed.

It is easy to see why, in his review of *Entertaining Mr. Sloane,* Harold Hobson wrote, "It is a vision of total evil" (Lahr, p. 168). Yes, the vision is evil, in this and all other Orton plays. The characters are either ruthlessly self-indulgent, motivated entirely by self-interest, or they are those who are victimized by the former. And even those who win out, enjoy only a fleeting victory, for it is a "cruel and heartless" world, where the words "not eternally boy" resound. Everything, everyone is disposable.

Orton makes clear the point—that people are disposable—by juxtaposing the mechanical breakdown or the destruction of material goods with the physical breakdown or destruction of individuals. In *The Ruffian on the Stair,* Wilson, the ruffian, "trashes" the stairs, and by the end of the play he, too, has been trashed. Erpingham falls through the floor to his death following the vandalizing of his camp in *The Erpingham Camp.* In *Funeral Games,* the coffins filled with rubble foreshadow the one which will later be filled with Mrs. McLeavy. In *The Good and Faithful Servant,* George Buchanan is given a toaster and clock, symbols of the company's gratitude for his fifty years of service. Both are broken. They are indeed symbols, symbols for what George has become for society—"a load of rubbish." Mrs. Vealfoy makes this clear to George when she says, "Make sure you hand in your uniform. After lunch you're free. We've no further need for you" (p. 161). Mr. Buchanan has been put out on the stoop. Eventually, he smashes the clock and toaster and dies unnoticed.

Like Beckett, Orton focuses his attention on these castaways. Also, like Beckett, Orton illustrates man's mutilated spirit by first pointing to his mutilated or decrepit body. Kath of *Entertaining Mr. Sloane* and Mrs. McLeavy of *Loot* have no teeth. Kemp is blind. Mr. McLeavy (*Loot*) and McCorquodale (*Funeral Games*) are impotent. George Buchanan, deaf and nearly blind, has lost an arm on the job. (He occasionally wears a prosthetic arm, but this frightens Edith, who imagines that he has grown a third arm.) Much like Flannery O'Conner in "Good Country People" and *Wise Blood,* Orton casts a savage eye and laughts a bitter laugh. At times, however, Orton's savagery supersedes even O'Conner's. In *Loot,* the detective Truscott asks:

TRUSCOTT:

Have you never heard of Truscott? The man who tracked the limbless girl killer. Or was that before your time?

HAL:

Who would kill a limbless girl?

TRUSCOTT:

She was the killer.

HAL:

How did she do it limbless?

TRUSCOTT:

I'm not prepared to answer that question to anyone outside the profession. We don't want a carbon copy murder on our hands.

(pp. 249-250)

The situation is, of course, absurd and so we laugh. But what is evident is that no one escapes the slicing edge of Orton's wit. He never lapses into sentimentality, for he—much like Bertolt Brecht—does not want to touch the heart of the audience, or to let them sit comfortably pitying the less fortunate:

ERPINGHAM:

Our disability bonus was won by Mr. Laurie Russell of Market Harborough. Both Laurie's legs were certified "absolutely useless" by our Resident Medical Officer. Yet he performed the Twist and the Bossa Nova to the tune specified on the entrance form.

TED:

He fell over though. Twice.

(p. 283)

Like Beckett and Brecht, Orton does not elevate the disabled, nor does he treat them euphemistically, for they are only a part of a crippled world where everyone is debilitated, if not physically then spiritually.

To this picture of the physically broken and the spiritually empty, Orton adds the mentally unhinged. Many of Orton characters have a questionable grasp of reality; but in his last and most farcical play, **What the Butler Saw,** characters like Dr. Rance have no grasp at all.

The setting of the play is a private psychiatric clinic run by Dr. Prentice, a man more interested in seducing a secretary than treating his patients. In fact, we never see a patient. We do not need to, for those running the clinic are clearly as crazed as any patient could be. When Mrs. Prentice cries, "O this is a madhouse," we laugh because of the specific and general truth of her statement. All are mad. And again we are to associate this setting—the small society of the clinic—with our own. Just as Orton mocks society's optimistic view of the world in **Head to Toe,** so he also mocks those who believe that Freudian psychiatrists can save the insane. The insane are too numerous; and unfortunately, their number includes the psychiatrists.

Even if one manages to maintain his sanity and to keep all his limbs, his plight is still not a happy one. As Orton wrote in his diary, there is still old age and death, the universal disabilities:

> Took a walk. Nobody to pick up. Only a lot of disgusting old men. I shall be a disgusting old man myself one day, I thought mournfully.
>
> (Lahr, p. 23)

There are many "disgusting" old men in his plays—Kemp, McLeavy, McCorquodale, George Buchanan. Their last years are characterized by "needles and sterile wadding." Each has had to face the "we've no more need for you." And they are all as useless and impotent as McLeavy who "couldn't propagate a row of tomatoes."

The elderly are also something to be disposed of. In **Entertaining Mr. Sloane** Kemp says, "You'd put me in a home. (Pause) Would you be tempted?" Silence follows. Of course, Kath would be tempted, for her blind, cranky father interferes, to some extent, in her sexual play with Sloane.

In **The Good and Faithful Servant,** Orton's most sympathetic treatment of the old, the Company has neatly disposed of George Buchanan, a loyal but no longer useful employee. The Company tries to assuage its conscience by forming the "Bright Hours" club. The hour George spends there, amidst wheelchairs and senile, old men and women, is anything but bright. One woman falls over and dies during the party. All the while, Mrs. Vealfoy is treating everyone like children on Romper Room: "We're going to sing in a minute. That will cure your depression, won't it? Will you join in? A jolly sing-song. All the old favorites. Don't be a spoil sport.

You'll join in, won't you?" (p. 88). Throughout the play, Mrs. Vealfoy provides cheery words and easy solutions. She makes people conform—they marry, retire, and sing according to her dictates—but she cannot cure their depressions. Nor does she really care to as long as she can make them *seem* happy.

Given Orton's world—characterized by physical and spiritual decay—one would correctly assume that death figures importantly in his plays. Only the dead are treated with more irreverence than the elderly or the disabled. Orton's plays abound with corpses and tears are not shed for any—not for Wilson, Kemp, Erpingham, Mrs. McLeavy, or Mrs. McCorquodale. The only feeling evident at all is one of relief. In **Entertaining Mr. Sloane,** Kath demonstrates her lack of concern for her father's murder by saying:

> When doctor comes he'll want to know things. Are you asking me to deceive our G. P.? He's an extremely able man. He'll notice discrepancies. And then where will we be? He'd make his report and mamma would be behind bars. I'm sure that isn't your idea. Is it?
>
> (p. 144)

Though the man she is talking baby talk to has just kicked her father to death, her sole concern is that she not be implicated in the crime.

With a composure similar to Kath's, Joyce (**The Ruffian on the Stair**) coolly devises a plan to keep Mike out of trouble, even though he has just murdered Wilson. She remains to total control until she sees that the bullet has also gone through her goldfish bowl killing her fish. Then she is heartbroken: "They're dead. Poor things. And I reared them so carefully" (p. 61). Orton skillfully juxtaposes Joyce's cavalier handling of the murdered Wilson—"I've a bit of sacking somewhere"—and this emotional outburst for the dead fish.

In **Funeral Games,** Mrs. McCorquodale's remains are regarded even more cavalierly than Wilson's. Her husband tells a friend that "her burial was done by the National Coalboard. She's under a ton of smokeless. I got it at the reduced summer rate" (p. 331). However, the corpse which is perhaps the most abused is Mrs. McLeavy's in **Loot.** She is taken out of her casket so that her son and his cohort can hide their "loot." She is then wrapped to look like a sewing dummy. (When Truscott asks, Whose mummy is this? Hal can truthfully answer, "Mine.") When Mr. McLeavy discovers what his son has done, he demands an explanation:

MCLEAVY:

Where are your tears? She was your mother.

HAL:

It's dust, Dad.

(McLeavy shakes his head in despair)

A little dust.

MᶜLᴇᴀᴠʏ:

I loved her.

Hᴀʟ:

You had her filleted without a qualm. Who could have affection for a half-empty woman?

(pp. 263-264)

When Hal speaks of the "half-empty woman," there is some question whether he is referring to his mother when she was alive or now that she is dead. Such ambiguity is appropriate, for in Orton all the men and women—young or old, alive or dead—are cold and half-empty.

Though Orton writes comedies with plots verging on the fantastic and the absurd, his indictments against man and society are serious ones. As he told Willes, "I write the truth." And the truth for the pessimistic Orton is similar to that which Bertolt Brecht voices in *The Threepenny Opera*:

There is of course no more to add
The world is poor and men are bad
We would be good instead of base
But this old world is not that kind of place.[9]

Notes

1. As quoted in John Lahr's, *Prick Up Your Ears* (New York: Knopf Pub. Co., 1978), p. 56. All future references will be included in the text.

2. Katherine Worth, *Revolutions in Modern English Drama* (London: G. Bell and Sons, 1972) p. 149.

3. Martin Esslin, "Joe Orton: The Comedy of (Ill) Manners." Included in *Contemporary English Drama*, ed. C. W. E. Bigsby (New York: Holmes and Meier Pub. Co., 1981), p. 107.

4. Joe Orton, *Radio Times*, quoted in John Lahr's introduction of the *Complete Plays* (London: Methuen, 1976), p. vii.

5. Samuel Beckett, *Endgame* (New York: Grove Press, 1958), p. 11.

6. Joe Orton, *Head to Toe* (London: Blond, 1971), p. 157.

7. See Martin Esslin, "Joe Orton: The Comedy of (Ill) Manners," p. 107; and John Russell Taylor, *The Second Wave* (New York: Hill and Wang, 1971), pp. 137-140.

8. Joe Orton, *Complete Plays,* ed. John Lahr (London: Methuen, 1976), p. 3. Quotations from this edition will be followed by page numbers in the text.

9. Bertolt Brecht, *The Threepenny Opera* (New York: Grove Press, 1964), p. 41.

Peter Walcot (essay date 1984)

SOURCE: Walcot, Peter. "An Acquired Taste: Joe Orton and the Greeks." In *Legacy of Thespis: Drama Past and Present*, Vol. 4, edited by Karelisa V. Hartigan, pp. 99-123. Lanham, Md.: University Press of America, 1984.

[*In the following essay, Walcot discusses the "Greek" character of both Orton's work and his relationship with Kenneth Halliwell.*]

I always say to myself that the theatre is the Temple of Dionysus, and not Apollo. You do the Dionysus thing on your typewriter, and then you allow a little Apollo in, just a little to shape and guide it along certain lines you may want to go along. But you can't allow Apollo in completely.[1]

The British press loves to regale its readers with lurid details of the latest sex scandal. Sex spiced with a dash of violence provides even better copy. You can imagine what a field-day the press enjoyed early in August 1967 when it reported the murder of Joe Orton by Kenneth Halliwell. Jaded palates could be titillated while, at the same time, moral indignation was triumphantly proclaimed. This was one of those rare stories which had everything: a jailbird who had achieved notoriety as the author of plays disfigured by unmitigated filth and perversity—homosexuality, fetishism, incest, rape, transvestism, nymphomania, sadism, you name it, it was all there in Orton's so-called comedies—this graduate of Her Majesty's Prison Eastchurch, Sheerness, Kent, had been bludgeoned to death in a frenzy of violence by a lover who had proceeded to compound his crime by taking an overdose of drugs. 'A fitting end', 'just retribution' was the popular verdict, and this condemnation will come as no surprise when you consider what had happened when the victim's *Loot* was presented at Bournemouth, a seaside resort in southern England distinguished, as Kemp remarks in *Loot,* by its palms but similar to Miami only inasmuch as the middle-class favor it as a retirement home: 'Bournemouth Old Ladies Shocked' shrieked a headline in the ever sedate *Times*;[2] and then there were the letters which seemed to flow unceasingly from the pen of a certain Mrs. Edna Welthorpe, such as the epistle from this champion of common decency in which she informed the readers of the *Daily Telegraph,* our stuffiest newspaper, of the nausea which she had experienced at the endless parade of mental and physical perversion offered by *Entertaining Mr. Sloane.*[3] And if someone points out that Edna Welthorpe was simply a nom-de-plume exploited by a mischievous Orton, well, this sick joke just confirms its perpetrator's total depravity. Was nothing, even little old ladies, one of whom might be brave enough to protest to the press, was nothing sacred to Joe Orton? Apparently not.

When, in the second act of *Loot,* Fay confesses to the murder of Mrs. McLeavy, that renowned detective, 'Truscott of the Yard', compliments her on her simple and direct style: 'It's a theme', he says, 'which less skilfully handled could've given offence', and that would be my own assessment of Orton's work. As for the story of the deaths of Orton and Halliwell, that I personally find infinitely more sad than sordid, but perhaps I am prejudiced, not, I trust, because my standards of morality are corrupt, but because the relationship between the older Halliwell and a Joe Orton always desperate to learn from his seemingly much better educated lover appears to me to have been very Greek in character.

Certainly it is my belief that their relationship can be demonstrated to have had for the lovers a peculiarly Greek quality. Halliwell must have known about Greek homosexuality and must have had some understanding, however uncritical, of what the Greeks of antiquity expected from love between two males. This claim may be advanced since, in the last phase of his education at Wirral Grammar School, Halliwell was a member of a British 'institution' now virtually defunct, the classical sixth-form, and he took Latin, Greek and Ancient History at his Higher School Certificate examination.[4] The following joke appears in a file of material for possible use kept by Orton:

> Greek paederasty was a noble ideal. I hope one day to see it practised in this country alongside the Christian virtues of Love Thy Neighbour and turn the other cheek.[5]

Not the best of Orton's jokes perhaps, though the last four words do carry a punch. I quote it, however, not so much as an example of Ortonesque humor but in order to substantiate my statement that Orton and Halliwell knew about Greek homosexuality, and knew about it as it was presented by an older generation of scholars whose antiseptic approach is indicated by the choice of the term 'pederasty'.[6] Orton's biographer, John Lahr, was being, I suspect, more perspicacious than he probably appreciated when he wrote of Halliwell having played midwife to his friend's talent, for such a remark recalls the person of Socrates, himself the son of a midwife, and the philosopher's assertion that he practised the same skill as his mother in the sense that he assisted at the birth of others' thoughts: 'Those who seek my company', Socrates is recorded as saying, 'have the same experience as a woman with child; they suffer the pains of labor and, by night and day, are full of distress far greater than a woman's and my art has power to bring on these pangs or to allay them'[7] A comparison of Halliwell and Socrates may be absurd to some but it might well have been much less absurd to Halliwell himself, and Orton, I am convinced, could have cheerfully seen himself performing the part of that most maverick of Socrates' followers, the irrepressible Alcibiades. Indeed I have often imagined a scene set in that stifling room in which the pair of them spent so much

of their lives together where Halliwell and Orton are reading a translation of Alcibiades' speech from Plato's *Symposium* although a little uncomfortable because of Alcibiades' unflattering description of his teacher's physical appearance, the prematurely bald Halliwell will be responding with delight to the rest, including the sexual badinage.[8]

The relationship between Halliwell and Orton was much more than a sexual relationship. To put it crudely, it was a marriage of two minds, and it is clear from entries in his diary that Orton retained to an intensely bitter end a respect for his lover's intellectual prowess that outsiders failed to comprehend.[9] Orton continued to exhibit the naïveté of the self-educated and to betray a remarkable deference when exposed to yet another display of the wisdom affected by Halliwell. I am very struck by an entry in Orton's diary dated the 26th March, 1967, a period of time when one might expect the myth of Halliwell's omniscience to have been completely shattered for Orton:

> . . . Kenneth, who read the *Observer*, tells me of the latest wayout group in America—complete sexual licence. 'It's the only way to smash the wretched civilization,' I said, making a mental note to hot-up **What The Butler Saw** when I came to re-write.
>
> 'It's like the Albigensian heresy in the 11th Century,' Kenneth said. Looked up the article in the *Encyclopedia Britannica*. Most interesting. Yes. Sex is the only way to infuriate them. Much more fucking and they'll be screaming hysterics in next to no time.[10]

What strikes me here is not so much Halliwell's parallel, clever though it may be, but the reaction of Orton, who goes scurrying off to the *Encyclopedia Britannica* so that he may expand on the tidbit of knowledge vouchsafed him by his guru. Such an episode not only defines their relationship but also their respective roles in that relationship. Both, it seems to me, are very Greek.

Let me explain. Halliwell, of course, was no scholar but would have known what we may call orthodox if somewhat old-fashioned views about the Greeks, particularly in those areas of a special interest to him. The standard book on education in the ancient world was first published in 1956, though my own copy is dated 1977. It includes a chapter headed 'Pederasty in Classical Education' and its author, the French scholar H. I. Marrou, states that,

> "Greek love" was to provide classical education with its material conditions and its method. For the men of ancient times this type of love was essentially educative. . . . For the Greeks, education meant, essentially, a profound and intimate relationship, a personal union between a young man and an elder who was at once his model, his guide and his initiator—a relationship on to which the fire of passion threw warm and turbid re-

flections. . . . Throughout Greek history the relationship between master and pupil was to remain that between a lover and his beloved: education remained in principle not so much a form of teaching, an instruction in techniques, as an expenditure of loving effort by an elder concerned to promote the growth of a younger man who was burning with the desire to respond to this love and show himself worthy of it.[11]

Marrou's language is extravagant and he depends too heavily on the evidence of philosophical texts, but he does present the popular appraisal of Greek homosexuality and its educative function: in other words, this was the picture likely to be familiar to Halliwell and it was a picture of undoubted attraction to a person of Halliwell's circumstances and proclivities. 'In Orton', Lahr comments, 'Halliwell sensed a perfect companion. He used to stroke Orton's sleek head in front of Griffin [a RADA student who also shared in Halliwell's apartment] and call him "my pussy-cat". Halliwell played the man of the world, and Orton was impressed. Halliwell tried to mould Orton into the Ideal Friend. "Halliwell was like a Svengali to John," recalls Griffin. "He took John over. It was as if he were playing God."'[12]

As their affair developed Halliwell and Orton came to share with the Greeks of antiquity a bleak philosophy of life. In Homer's *Iliad* Achilles tells Priam that Zeus has two jars, one of disasters and the other full of blessings, and from these the god allots man's fate; but whereas we would allow for three possibilities, all from the good jar, all from the bad jar or a mixture from each jar, Achilles will admit just two, a mixture of good and bad fortune or unrelieved calamity.[13] Nobody, the Greeks believed, was entitled to live a life of unalloyed happiness, and nobody is to be accounted happy until he is dead or so Herodotus' Solon informed King Croesus of Lydia and the subsequent life of that monarch proved the validity of his guest's opinion.[14] 'Christ!', McCorquodale prays in a line from *Funeral Games* deleted from the final version, 'let me die tonight. Don't tease me. I've laughed long enough.'[15] Man is the sport of fortune, Solon says; God laughs and snaps his fingers, is the Halliwell and Orton equivalent.[16] Any excess of happiness arouses the jealousy of the Greek gods and a price has to be paid. The deaths of Halliwell and Orton were preceded by their holiday in Tangier, and it was this holiday which prompted the following entry in Orton's diary:

> Kenneth and I sat talking of how happy we both felt. We'd have to pay for it. Or we'd be struck down from afar by disaster because we were, perhaps, too happy. To be young, goodlooking, healthy, famous, comparatively rich *and* happy is surely going against nature. . . . '*Crimes of Passion* will be a disaster,' Kenneth said. 'That will be the scapegoat. We must sacrifice *Crimes of Passion* in order that we may be spared disaster more intolerable.' I slept all night soundly and woke up at seven feeling as though the whole of cre-

ation was conspiring to make me happy. I hope no doom strikes.[17]

The language as well as the sentiment of the entry is Greek through and through. Several years before, the rejection of a novel elicited the following observations from Halliwell:

> Personally, I am convinced that 'what you lose on the swings, you gain on the roundabouts' and vice versa. So it would, quite frankly, not be in the logic of things for John and I to have much success in any sphere. We live much too comfortably and pleasantly in our peculiar little way.[18]

My two quotations, one from Orton and one from Halliwell, stand in stark contrast, one regretting the potential loss of happiness and the second settling for a limited happiness in preference to success. The possible failure of *Crimes of Passion* was not an ultimate disaster for Kenneth Halliwell, but then Halliwell found their cramped apartment a refuge rather than a straitjacket and success a sacrificial offering. Clearly, the relationship between Halliwell, the lover or *erastes,* and Orton, the loved one or *eromenos,* changed as Orton became a celebrity, though in June 1964, at the opening night in the West End of *Entertaining Mr. Sloane,* Halliwell when asked where he went out with Orton could jokingly, if also somewhat bitterly, answer that he didn't go out with Orton, he went in![19] By the time of the holiday in Tangier Orton was sneering at Halliwell for just wanting to be masturbated, whereas he was 'virile" in fucking boys.[20] The *eromenos* had become an *erastes* himself, a development accepted as natural and so inevitable by the Greeks but not by that student of antiquity, Kenneth Halliwell.

Orton was ripe to be instructed by a lover who fancied himself as a classical scholar. Among the books he cherished in his youth, we are told,[21] was Thomas Bulfinch's *Greek Mythology.* Bulfinch's collections of fable are still popular today with the tiro, though well over a century old. The assessment of a professional, however, will be far less charitable: thus John Peradotto describes Bulfinch as 'this mid-Victorian mythological McGuffey, modelled on Ovid's *Metamorphoses,* but Ovid moralisé, dutifully expurgated, and written in a style not likely to set their young pulses thumping . . . It tests the imagination to realize that not five years separate the publication of *The Age of fable* from *Moby Dick.*'[22] Orton's sister Leonie was read Greek mythology by her brother, while a friend from Orton's days in repertory theater speaks of being taken by surprise at the twenty-year old's knowledge of Greek gods and goddesses.[23] Under Halliwell's tutelage Orton's knowledge and interests became more refined, so much so in fact that in 1967 he made the following statement in an interview:

> I'm very conscious of what's come before. I like Lucian and the classical writers, and I suppose that's what gives my writing a difference, an old-fashioned classi-

cal education! Which I never received, but I gave myself one, reading them all in English, for I have so little Latin and less Greek.[24]

As usual with an Orton interview, the tone is mocking and Orton has his tongue firmly anchored in his cheek. Casual references reveal that Orton the man, presumably while closeted with Halliwell, read translations of dramatists such as Aristophanes and Euripides, while in a BBC interview Orton boasted an acquaintance with Sophocles. It is not my wish to belittle Orton, but I am not inclined to accept everything that he said in an interview for public consumption without collaborative evidence. I also have considerable doubts about the veracity of some of the sexual adventures recorded in his diaries. While I agree with Joyce in **The Ruffian on the Stair** that public lavatories are interesting places, my limited experience suggests that they are not quite the haunt of those whom society regards as misfits which Orton's diaries imply.[25]

I would justify my scepticism by quoting a reply given by Orton to an interviewer who asked him about his likes and dislikes:

> Well, I hate all animals with tails and my favourite play is the *Andromeda* of Euripides. I was born in Leicester 25 years ago. My father was a gardener and my mother a machinist—both are still alive and working. I failed my eleven-plus, and went to a secondary modern: after that I was sacked from various jobs for incompetence, and ended up with a two-year scholarship at RADA. Then I worked in rep for four months, but haven't been on the stage since. During the next few years I was married, divorced, operated on for acute appendicitis, photographed in the nude and arrested for larceny. Then came a six-month spell in prison.[26]

This reply contains some blatant lies: Orton was well over thirty at the time of the interview and had never been married and divorced. His reference to the *Andromeda* of Euripides is equally misleading, for though this was one of Euripides' most celebrated tragedies, it has not survived and so could not have been read by Orton. Why then did he claim the *Andromeda* as his favourite play? Was it a slip of the tongue, a mistake for a play with a similar name, say the *Alcestis*? There is a further possibility but one which might well be thought more clever than compelling and that I shall defer for the moment. All in all, it is difficult to resist the conclusion that Orton mentioned the *Andromeda* to create an impression, and that this is another lie and not a very good lie at that.

But scepticism is not the same as total disbelief, and we should return to Orton's reputed acquaintance with Sophocles. Is this supported by evidence? The knowledge of Sophocles was claimed in an interview when Orton discussed the genesis of **Entertaining Mr. Sloane**:

> I originally started with the Oedipus legend as a basis and threw it out halfway through. It gave me the germ

to start from. I got Eddie the brother and father relationship from *Oedipus at Colonnus*—the old man won't speak to his son at all.[27]

In **Entertaining Mr. Sloane** Kemp tells Sloane that he has not been on speaking terms with his son for twenty years, and Ed finds it incredible that Kemp will not speak to his only son and feels his father to be without human feelings. The *Oedipus at Colonnus* features a crucial scene between the son Polyneices and the exiled Oedipus, who will not converse with his offspring until subjected to strong pressure from his dear friend Theseus and his devoted daughter Antigone. Without the pressure from Theseus, Oedipus declares, his son would never have heard his voice.[28] The scene ends as Oedipus dismisses his son with curses ringing in his ears. The decrepit Kemp comes on stage early in Act Two of **Sloane** [**Entertaining Mr. Sloane**] carrying a stick and tapping his way to the sideboard much in the fashion of Sophocles' blind Oedipus, while Kath displays a solicitude for the Dadda which parallels Antigone's concern for her own aged parent. Both Polyneices and Ed have horrified their fathers, the former by exposing Oedipus to exile and penury and the latter—and this, of course, is pure Orton—by having been caught by Kemp 'committing some kind of felony in the bedroom'; both need their fathers, Polyneices so that he may defeat his brother Eteocles and Ed so that some papers may be signed. Polyneices approaches his father in the guise of a suppliant,[29] while in Act Two of **Sloane** when Kemp does speak to Ed in order to tell him of Sloane's threatening behavior, the roles are reversed as Kemp falls towards the ground and Oedipus' dire curses directed against his son become these words spoken to his father by Ed:

> Dad . . . What's come over you? Don't kneel to me. I forgive you. I'm the one to kneel. Pat me on the head. Pronounce a blessing. Forgive and forget, eh? I'm sorry and so are you.

Ed has a liking for the part of priest and confessor, a facet of his character a penitent Sloane is later to exploit to his advantage, and certainly in one sense, Sloane qualifies as Kath's long lost son and thereby stands in a special relationship to her brother Ed. Both plays, in other words, are about the relationship between parents and offspring, in Sophocles the relationship between Oedipus and Polyneices and Oedipus and Antigone, and in Orton the relationship between Kemp and Ed and Kemp and Kath and, I myself would add, between Sloane and both Kath and Ed. One final point: Polyneices and his brother Eteocles attempt to share the throne of Thebes on an equitable basis but fail—are we to see any link with the sharing of Sloane by Kath and Ed and if so, does the Sophoclean parallel suggest an equally unhappy outcome to the arrangement, irrespective of Ed's experience at the conference table?

A first glance, and even a second or third glance for that matter, hardly suggests any connection between the classic Oedipus myth—the murder of Laius by his son Oedipus and Oedipus' subsequent marriage to his mother and self-blinding when his parricide and incest are revealed—and Orton's *Entertaining Mr. Sloane,* unless we link together the fact that both Oedipus and Sloane are the perpetrators of unsolved killings or compare Kemp with Laius as a murdered father and perhaps with Sophocles' herdsman also, since the herdsman alone knows exactly what happened when a murder took place. Otherwise we may note in general that the setting of *Sloane* is austere, being restricted to a single room, and that the action is similarly limited, being confined to some sexual groping and the attack on Kemp, much of which is mercifully concealed behind a settee. This, coupled with the messenger type speech in which Sloane relates how he came to kill the photographer, is reminiscent of the technique of the Greek dramatists, but none of it really adds up to very much. The picture changes, however, if we consider Orton's further account of how he used the Oedipus material he knew from Sophocles, and then examine what another modern playwright has to say about his own use of comparable material. This is how Orton continued his BBC interview:

> There's no significance in the fact that I used the two Oedipuses at all, apart from the fact that it just gave me an idea and dramatists always need a plot. It doesn't really matter what you use as a plot on which to hang your dialogue and your ideas, but you must, I think, have a plot.

No one would guess that *Entertaining Mr. Sloane* owes anything to Sophocles, if it had not been for Orton's own acknowledgement of his indebtedness, just as no one would guess that *The Cocktail Party* owes anything to the *Alcestis* of Euripides, if we had not been told by its author, T. S. Eliot.[30] In a letter to Viscount Samuel Eliot again made the point that he had himself to inform others that Euripides was a source of inspiration for *The Cocktail Party*. In the same letter Eliot compared his use of Greek material with that made by the French dramatists Cocteau, Giraudoux, Anouilh and Sartre, stating that their method was in some ways diametrically the opposite of his own:

> They have retained the names of the original characters and stuck rather more closely to the plots of the original dramatists, the innovation being merely that the characters talk as if they were contemporary French people, and in some cases employ what one might call anachronistic allusions to modern life. The method that has appealed to me has been rather to take merely the situation of a Greek play as a starting-point, with wholly modern characters, and develop it according to the workings of my own mind.[31]

These two explanations of their method of employing Greek material, by Orton and by Eliot, sound, I would suggest, remarkably alike: what both dramatists took from the Greeks was a story-line, a basic plot, and on this they grafted ideas purely their own. Any attempt to set side by side Sophocles' Oedipus plays and *Entertaining Mr. Sloane* must allow for such an approach to, and such a use of, material derived from fifth-century Athenian drama.

It was Euripides and his last tragedy, the *Bacchae,* that Orton attempted to reproduce in *The Erpingham Camp.* Critics have not always been well disposed to this play, and the fact that Orton claimed it as his version of the *Bacchae* has simply given some yet another stick with which to beat its author. Not untypical is the assessment of Martin Esslin:

> The transposition of the plot into a British holiday camp—a favourite target of topical satire at the time—yields neither a contemporary reinterpretation of the theme of *The Bacchae* nor illuminating variations on its meaning: it merely lowers its social level and trivializes the plot. While Euripides deals with profound tensions in human nature, Orton is merely describing the inmates of a holiday camp getting out of hand through the incompetence of an entertainment's manager who is too inexperienced or clumsy to control the evening's floor show. Thus the Dionysus of the play, Chief Redcoat Riley, is no God, no personification of primeval forces, while its Pentheus, Erpingham, is no more than a slightly authoritarian lay-figure, given to mouthing an occasional patriotic cliché. Even in terms of mere parody the parallels are extremely feebly drawn: the raging maenads amount to hardly more than a pregnant lady, who claims that she has been insulted, and her feebly protesting husband. And Erpingham dies not under any assault by orgiastic, unchained revellers, but merely because the floorboards of his office give way so that he drops down among the dancers on the ballroom floor.[32]

For Esslin the play is 'hardly more than an extended, a rather feeble, cabaret sketch', a judgement which I find harsh to the point of being grossly unfair. At this stage I shall simply observe that the 'feebly protesting husband' goes around, according to the stage direction, 'viciously beating up' his victims and the 'pregnant lady' tells a fellow camper to get out before she kicks her dental plate to pieces—delicacy prevents me from repeating what she has to say to the camper's husband since it begins, 'Piss off . . .'

I would agree that there are problems which make it difficult for *The Erpingham Camp* to be evaluated fairly. Like so much of Orton it is very much a product of a particular decade, the sixties, and of an intensely British environment. It is set in a holiday camp of a type known only to the British and the British working class family before the advent of affluence carried all but the very poorest winging their way south to the beaches of Spain and, more recently, Florida and Miami.[33] The holiday camp was designed to offer, at minimal cost, an inclusive holiday for the whole family where every member of that family, weary parents, restless teenagers and obstreperous children, would be kept fully amused from their moment of waking, an event traditionally accompanied by some hideously cheerful greeting over the camp's intercom system, to the blissful moment when exhaustion induced sleep. You will remember, for example, how the 'kiddies' at Camp Erpingham 'were having a quick run round with Matron'. The reputation of the holiday camp with the middle-class, and it is the middle-class which frequents the theater, and with the intellectual, and it is the intellectual who becomes a drama critic, was ghastly, and even at the level of popular humor the holiday camp rivalled the mother-in-law as a source of cheap jibes. The camps were depicted as penitentiaries and their staff as warders whose main function was to foil escape; accommodation was reputed to be in poorly constructed chalets whose roofs always leaked and this in the British climate; food was reckoned to be revolting even by the standard of the British working-class cuisine; worst of all, however, was the enforced hilarity affected by the redcoats and inflicted on the holidaymakers—you had to enjoy yourself or else! Most notorious a form of entertainment was the competition like the Glamorous Granny contest or the Mother and Child contest or the Bathing Beauty contest run at Camp Erpingham, which had, moreover, its own special refinement, the disability bonus, won at the beginning of Orton's romp by Mr. Laurie Russel who, though both his legs were certified 'absolutely useless' by the resident medical officer (trained at Dachau perhaps?), performed the Twist and the Bossa Nova 'to the tune specified on the entrance form'. No less bizarre and unique, I hope, to Orton's camp was the Ugliest Woman competition nearly won by Chief Redcoat Riley and the Screaming contest, the source of the eventual riot. The British holiday camp could be a very strange place indeed.

Another problem of a rather special kind is posed by the Euripidean background of *The Erpingham Camp*. Orton's version of the *Bacchae* has been overtaken by events. Note that it was in 1966 that the play was first presented, and next consider what happened to the *Bacchae* in the last years of the sixties and the early seventies. At that period of time by far the two most popular tragedies by Euripides were his *Trojan Women* and the *Bacchae*. The former was vastly popular because in this play we are brought face to face not only with the absolute desolation of the vanquished Trojan women but also with the corruption and brutalization that a war to the death inspired in the victorious Greeks. An analogy between the war before Troy and the war in Vietnam was seductive. The *Bacchae* owed its popularity to a social and not a political revolution, the appearance of liberation cults and a growing desire to overthrow the existing order of society in favor of total freedom. John Bowen's *The Disorderly Women* makes Euripides' maenads contemporary hippies, and I shall never forget

myself a production of the *Bacchae* that I witnessed some ten years ago in which Dionysus was a thinly veiled Charles Manson. Since then I have sat in at more than one seminar when it has been argued that in the *Bacchae* Euripides is striking a blow for women's emancipation—actually I find the tragedy a poor advertisement for any women's liberation movement. But this is how we react to the *Bacchae* today, and such a reaction must diminish an appreciation of any comic treatment of its theme. And the 'philosophy' expressed in Orton's comedy, as when Riley tells Erpingham 'one flick of Fortune's wheel and you'll be brought low' or when Harrison warns Erpingham that 'your stiff-necked attitude will bring untold harm' seems trite though no triter, I should add, than many of the words of wisdom delivered in Greek tragedy.

On the positive side, it ought to be acknowledged how effectively in *The Erpingham Camp* Orton provides a substitute for the Greek chorus in the form of the songs which punctuate the text as the comedy unfolds. Music off-stage is to be heard throughout; Riley sings his Irish number as the entertainment commences; as the excitement reaches a climax Eileen gives a rendition of 'Knees-up, Mother Brown'; the besieged Erpingham and his acolytes join in the hymn 'Love Divine, All Loves Excelling'; the final stage direction reads, 'A great choir is heard singing "The Holy City"'. Precise parallels between Euripides and Orton are more numerous and closer than Esslin admits. Take the death of Erpingham: in the corresponding incident in the *Bacchae* Euripides has Pentheus also tumbling down to his death but this time as the raging women of Thebes uproot the tree from which the king has been spying on their revels. Another parallel is provided by Dionysus' destruction of Pentheus' palace in the *Bacchae*[34] and by the damage wrought on property by the impassioned campers. But a much more telling link, for it explains a scene in *The Erpingham Camp* that otherwise holds little meaning, comes when Erpingham changes his clothes for the evening, donning white tie and tails *and* a pair of corsets. This scene surely was suggested by the transvestism practised by Pentheus when he follows the advice of Dionysus and dresses in women's clothes so that he may spy on the devotees of the god.[35] Euripides lingers long over the dressing of Pentheus, and it is not difficult to see the attraction of such a scene for Orton, who as early as *The Ruffian on the Stair* has Wilson tell Joyce that he is wearing a pair of his brother's white shorts, inconvenient though they are because 'there's no fly', while in *What the Butler Saw* clothes are exchanged between the sexes with a reckless abandon. And there is also Orton's superb joke in that play when Mrs. Prentice asks her husband whether he has taken up transvestism, adding, 'I'd no idea our marriage teetered on the edge of fashion'.

But Erpingham's corset is also meant to suggest the wearing of the same garment by the 'strait-laced', the Prussian officer or Victorian gentleman, the types of person who could say with Erpingham 'my camp is a pure camp' or cover up a portrait of the Queen when getting changed. The Greek dramatist had mask as well as costume by which he might convey to the audience the essential quality of a character, but Orton was reduced to costume alone and this means of identification he used with great adroitness. Erpingham is identified as Orton's Pentheus by the clothes he puts on as much as by his statements and his behavior. But who is Orton's Dionysus? Is it really Chief Redcoat Riley with his sash and medal? Writing to Lindsay Anderson in 1964 Orton sketched the plot of what was to become *The Erpingham Camp*:

> A representative group of sturdy, honest English folk, respectably pleasuring themselves at an August Holiday Camp, find themselves subjected to the influence of an intense, demonic leader. Their conventional habits . . . are cast aside; they feel liberation; they abandon themselves under the tutelage of Don [Dionysus] to impulse.[36]

But there is no character in *The Erpingham Camp* who bears the significant name Don; there is, however, a character with the equally suggestive name of Kenny, the abbreviation for Kenneth, Halliwell's Christian name, and it is this Kenny who is the husband of a pregnant wife and it is an insult to that wife which initiates the riot; and Kenny leads the rioters and leads them wearing a costume as indicative of his role as the white tie and tails assumed for the evening of disaster by Erpingham, for Kenny is chosen as this week's 'Tarzan of the Apes' and puts on the appropriate leopard skin. My argument that the leopard skin makes Kenny Orton's Dionysus may be readily confirmed if we now turn to Orton's last comedy, *What the Butler Saw.*

In that play Sergeant Match wears a leopard-spotted dress which, as the action concludes, is torn from one shoulder when the policeman descends through the skylight by a rope ladder[37] streaming with blood. The stage directions at the end of the play are as elaborate as those for the conclusion of *The Erpingham Camp*:

> Everyone embraces one another. The skylight opens, a rope ladder is lowered and, in a great blaze of glory, SERGEANT MATCH . . . descends . . . The dying sunlight from the garden and the blaze from above gild SERGEANT MATCH. . . . They pick up their clothes and weary, bleeding, drugged and drunk, climb the rope ladder into the blazing light.

In *What the Butler Saw* Dionysus in the form of an appropriately clad Sergeant Match descends from heaven just as in the *Bacchae* the god appears as the action of the drama is completed on the roof of the stage building,[38] the *deus ex machina* of which Euripides was es-

pecially fond. And this is not the only Euripidean touch at this point of the play, for, immediately before, Nick and Geraldine are recognized as the twin offspring of the Prentices as Mrs. Prentic spots the pair of brooches she left with her children when she abandoned them. This motif, we are invariably told, derives from the *Importance of Being Earnest* and reflects the influence of Wilde, and it is true that the mother was raped on the second floor of the Station Hotel.[39] Yet it has also been remarked that here we encounter 'the classical Plautean comedy of the separated twins'[40] and behind Plautus, of course, we have Greek New Comedy and behind Greek New Comedy lurks the person of Euripides. An ancient source, for instance, claims Euripides as the origin of Menandrean recognition,[41] and an example offers confirmation: in the *Ion* of Euripides a woman, Creusa queen of Athens, who has been raped and subsequently abandoned her son, recovers the long-lost Ion when she recognizes the baby clothes in which she exposed her infant offspring and the accompanying jewelry.[42] This is not a point I wish to press but the *Ion* also concludes with a divine epiphany and earlier there has been an attempt by Creusa to kill the unknown youth who is eventually shown to be her missing son. Instead I prefer to quote an astute commentator on the play and her remark that 'the means by which Creusa proves her identity (i.e. as Ion's mother) are a combination of physical token and intimate knowledge; the guessing game form that the scene takes here is unique and has in its stage business a touch of what we would call comedy about it'.[43]

Orton liked recognition tokens; that sad play *The Good and Faithful Servant* features such a device, the ring which reveals to Buchanan that Edith is the woman he loved so many years before. *What the Butler Saw* closes with the production of another object which may be regarded as a type of recognition token, for just as Euripides' Ion produces a basket which will be found to contain proof of his birth, so Geraldine in Orton's play possesses a box which is found to contain the 'missing parts' from a larger than lifesized bronze statue of Winston Churchill, and this 'object' is so much more potent than the symbol of Churchill's cigar. Churchill's phallus reinforces Orton's Dionysiac imagery, for there could be no more characteristic an attribute of the Greek god than the phallus; a phallus, for example, is paraded by the worshippers as the Rural Dionysia is celebrated in Aristophanes' *Acharnians*.[44] The phallus in fact typifies not only Dionysus but also the performance of Old Comedy in fifth-century Athens, and the basic comic costume consisted of tights to which a leather version of the phallus was attached.[45] But the link between the conclusion of *What the Butler Saw* and Aristophanes is considerably closer, for Aristophanes had preceded Orton by well over two thousand years in holding up to ridicule Euripides' penchant for the *deus ex machina*. Both comic writers found Euripides' fondness for this piece of theater impossible to resist and both restored to parody. Take the case of Aristophanes' *Peace*, a comedy commemorating the signing of a peace treaty between Athens and Sparta after ten years of devastating war and a comedy of enduring appeal.[46] I wish to be scrupulously fair in presenting the Aristophanic evidence and so have chosen to take advantage of Albin Lesky's summary of the first half of the *Peace*, abbreviating this to some extent. After the mid-point of the play represented by the parabasis we meet the usual series of farcical scenes in which Aristophanes reveals the mad consequences of the action taken before the parabasis.

The hero of the *Peace* is a vinegrower Trygaeus who keeps a huge dung-beetle. Lesky notes:

> This creature is to serve its enterprising owner as transport to heaven, where he will ask Zeus what he has in mind for the war-weary Hellenes. Again the fanciful invention has a specific target: the ride on the dung-beetle is a parody of the *Bellerophon* of Euripides, in which the hero tried to reach heaven on his winged steed. . . . Trygaeus reaches his goal and enters into discussions with Hermes. He notes with disapproval that the gods have withdrawn into the highest aether to be away from the endless horrors of war, and Polemos (i.e. War) reigns unchecked. He has shut up the goddess of peace, Eirene, in a pit. . . . Trygaeus . . . leads the rescue of Eirene, who is pulled up from her pit by ropes. At the same moment two goddesses appear—Opora, goddess of fruitfulness, and Theoria, who stands for joy at festivals . . . they all return to earth, not by the dung-beetle on a stage flying-machine (Trygaeus and his three goddesses would have overloaded it), but by simply climbing down a route which is pointed out by Hermes with a light-hearted breaking of the dramatic illusion.'[47]

Orton had read translations of Aristophanes, and anybody who has done that knows that Aristophanes enjoyed poking fun at Euripides and his use of stage machinery. After all, Euripides appears as a character in three of the surviving comedies of Aristophanes, the *Acharnians*, in which Euripides' employment of the wheeled platform is mocked, the *Thesmophoriazusae*, and the *Frogs*. I mentioned some time ago (see p. 106) Orton's claim that his favorite play was Euripides' *Andromeda* though that tragedy has failed to survive. In making such a claim was Orton just lying in order to create an impression or did he confuse the *Andromeda* with some other play by the Athenian? Perhaps there is a third possibility though I advance it with hesitation: Did Orton know of the *Andromeda* from Aristophanes' *Thesmophoriazusae*, since Euripides' play is parodied quite mercilessly in that comedy as Euripides in the guise of Perseus comes 'flying' on stage in order to rescue his kinsman Mnesilochus?[48] But Aristophanes' most notorious reference to the *Andromeda* comes early in the *Frogs* when the god Dionysus, posing as an intellectual, tells his half-brother the brutish Heracles that

he was on a ship reading the *Andromeda* and was suddenly seized by a yearning desire:

DIONYSUS:

> And as I sat on deck, reading *Andromeda*, a sudden pang of agonizing longing shot through my heart—I was overwhelmed.

HERACLES:

> How big a pang?

DIONYSUS:

> Well, Molon-size . . .

HERACLES:

> For a woman?

DIONYSUS:

> No.

HERACLES:

> A boy?

DIONYSUS:

> No, no.

HERACLES:

> A man?

DIONYSUS:

> (*sighs*). Ooooh'.[49]

This, I guarantee, is an exchange not likely to have passed unnoticed by Orton. All this persuades me, and you too I hope, that we are justified in detecting an Aristophanic flavor at the end of ***What the Butler Saw*** and that flavor is more than a slight whiff.

Any number of general comparisons between the comic technique and the language of Aristophanes and Orton are possible, but these tend to represent the stock-in-trade of the comic dramatist, and I will be brief. Both attack the authorities and the system, Aristophanes generals, politicians, jurymen and so on, while for Orton policemen are corrupt, clergymen murderers, psychiatrists mad and so on. I have always wanted to produce an only mildly adapted version of Aristophanes' *Clouds* in which Socrates is presented as very much a fifth-century Greek equivalent of the contemporary psychiatrist, a Dr. Prentice or Dr. Rance. There is a magnificent scene in the *Clouds* when Strepsiades is ordered by Socrates to lie down on a couch and to think: there is a strictly Ortonesque note when Socrates asks if Strepsiades has got a hold of anything at all and Strepsiades replies, 'Nothing, apart from my cock in my right hand'.[50] Orton and Aristophanes share a very similar brand of humor, both verbal humor and sexually orientated humor, and both would be in agreement that comedy furnishes a much more devastating weapon than tragedy. But let me draw to a close not with a comparison or with an argument, both of which have been inflicted upon you in what I hope is an abundance, but rather with a statement of faith. While in prison Gombold, the hero of Orton's novel **Head to Toe,** is 'educated' by a fellow-prisoner, the learned Doktor von Pregnant, and study takes the place of liberty as 'days, months and years passed in one rapid and instructive course'. Before this process began, the Doktor had assumed that Gombold must be acquainted with languages but he was wrong. 'No . . . I have little Litthom and less Glook', he was informed by Gombold, who went on to add, 'I rely upon translations'. 'Well, well', observed the Doktor, 'better a translation than remain in ignorance.'[51] In my opinion the Doktor understates the case for translations, for I believe with Louis Kelly that 'western Europe owes its civilization to translators'.[52] Need I do more than quote the Bible in support of my belief that it has been translations and not texts in the original language which have shaped our intellectual and literary traditions? And so I like to think that any discussion of Orton's debt to the Greeks is of more than just academic interest, though that debt was owed to translations and another taste acquired under the influence of Kenneth Halliwell.

But I betray Orton in ending so seriously, yet I also believe that Orton is often much more serious than that dazzling dialogue of his may lead us to suspect. Go back to **The Good and Faithful Servant.** I know of no other play, whether comedy or tragedy or a mixture of both, which indicts more crushingly the demands made by society today and the rewards offered by society today. Of course, Orton defined the problem but posited no solution. Nor for that matter did Socrates. Religion provided no answer for Orton, a comment which allows me to give Orton the final word by quoting my own favorite joke from his plays. In scene six of **Funeral Games** Tessa asks McCorquodale what has happened to his wife and the following exchange ensues:

McCorquodale:

She was taken up to Heaven. In a fiery chariot. Driven by an angel.

Tessa:

What nonsense. Valerie would never accept a lift from a stranger.

Notes

1. I quote from John Lahr's, *Prick up your Ears, the Biography of Joe Orton* (London, 1978) 15, an Orton BBC interview. Anyone writing on Orton owes an immense debt to the otherwise unpublished material assembled by Lahr, who also contributes an introduction to the standard edition of Orton, *Joe Orton, the Complete Plays* (London, 1976/New York, 1977). Much briefer but especially well illustrated is an article 'The Life and Death of Joe Orton' by James Fox, published in the *Sunday Times Magazine* for the 22nd November, 1970. Critical discussion of Orton's comedies is sparse and not very helpful with the exception of Maurice Charney on *Entertaining Mr. Sloane* in *New York Literary Forum* 4, (1980) 171-178 and on *What The Butler Saw* in *Modern Drama* 25, 4, (Dec. 1982) 496-504. The series 'Contemporary Writers' includes a somewhat pretentious essay by C. W. E. Bigsby, *Joe Orton* (London and New York, 1982). I have benefited much more from the comments of two colleagues, H. M. Quinn and Professor B. R. Rees.

2. Lahr, 250.

3. Lahr, 200; cf. 136-140. For a genuinely indignant reaction to displays of violence and cruelty on the stage in the sixties, including 'the kicking to death of an old man', see Pamela Hansford Johnson, *On Iniquity* (London, 1967) 47ff.

4. Lahr, 341 n. 25; cf. 107.

5. Lahr, 313.

6. 'Homosexuality' is preferred today and discussion of the topic is no longer inhibited, as is very evident from K. J. Dover, *Greek Homosexuality* (London, 1978). A more concise account is offered by L. P. Wilkinson, *Classical Attitudes to Modern Issues* (London, 1978), 111ff. At the same time, pederasty is a more precise description of Greek homosexuality which 'typically took the form of pederasty with an adolescent junior partner and occupied a defined, and transient, phase in the masculine life-cycle' (Paul Cartledge, *Proceedings of the Cambridge Philological Society* no. 207 (1981) 17). See further George Devereux, 'Greek Pseudo-Homosexuality and the "Greek Miracle"', *Symbolae Osloenses* 42, (1967) 69-92, on 'displaced fathering' and, with reference to the relationship between Halliwell and Orton, his remark, 'the erastes was a father surrogate (educator) and the eromenos a son surrogate (pupil)', 79.

7. Plato, *Theaetetus* 151a, translated by F. M. Cornford in Edith Hamilton and Huntington Cairns (ed.), *The Collected Dialogues of Plato* (Princeton, 1963) 855-856.

8. *Symposium* 215ff.

9. Lahr, 23-24; cf. 321.

10. Lahr, 135-36.

11. *A History of Education in Antiquity* (London, paperback edition 1977) 26ff.

12. Lahr, 120.

13. *Iliad* 24, verses 527ff.

14. Herodotus 1, 30ff.

15. Lahr, 288.

16. Herodotus 1, 32, 4; Lahr, 2 and 146.

17. Lahr, 20. On 'the enviousness of fate' in ancient thought, see, for example, G. J. D. Aalders in M. J. Vermaseren (ed.), *Studies in Hellenistic Religions* (Leiden, 1979) 1-8.

18. Lahr, 123.

19. Lahr, 199.

20. Lahr, 335.

21. Lahr, 66.

22. *Classical Mythology, an Annotated Bibliographical Survey* (Urbana, 1973), 15. See also Marie Cleary, *Classical Journal* 75, (1979-80) 248-249.

23. Lahr, 87 and 119. An extensive knowledge of classical mythology is also apparent in Orton's novel *Head to Toe,* written ten years before its posthumous publication (London, 1971),

24. Lahr, 29.

25. Public lavatories are still prominent in the 'mythology' of British homosexuality and remain a source of unending humor, a factor always to be taken into account in assessing the events listed in Orton's diaries. Thus the issue of the satiric magazine *Private Eye* for the 30th July, 1982 included the following item from the *North Avon Gazette:*

> Three men, all in their 60's, were found by police committing indecent acts with each other in public toilets at Northville Road, Filton, a court heard this week. Mr. Miles described the offences as 'at the bottom end of the scale' of seriousness.

26. 'The Biter Bit, Joe Orton introduces *Entertaining Mr. Sloane* in Conversation with Simon Trussler', *Plays and Players,* August 1964, 16.

27. Lahr, 177.

28. *Oedipus at Colonus,* verses 1154ff., 1181ff. and 1348-1351.

29. *Oedipus at Colonus,* verses 1156ff., 1278 and 1285ff.

30. In the lecture 'Poetry and Drama', included in Frank Kermode (ed.), *Selected Prose of T. S. Eliot* (London, 1975), 144.

31. *Proceedings of the Classical Association* 50, (1953), 14. Eliot and Orton are not the only artists whose debt to classical sources was unrecognized

until they themselves declared it. We may also compare, for example, Wagner to whose *Die Meistersinger* Hugh Lloyd-Jones refers as follows: 'that the address of Hans Sachs at the end of the work was inspired by the conclusion of Aeschylus' *Eumenides* would have been a bold guess. But we have Wagner's own word for it is that it was so, which may remind us that the processes by which an artist's mind works upon the material which it makes use of are not always to be discovered by the light of reason' (*Blood for The Ghosts, Classical Influences in the Nineteenth and Twentieth Centuries,* London, 1982, 130).

32. *Contemporary English Drama* (Stratford-upon-Avon Studies 19, London, 1981) 103.

33. Compare James Walvin, *Beside the Seaside, a Social History of the Popular Seaside Holiday* (London, 1978), 133-135.

34. *Bacchae,* verses 1103ff. and 585ff.

35. *Bacchae,* verses 821ff. On this motif in Euripides' play, see G. S. Kirk, *The Bacchae of Euripides* (Cambridge, 1979), 93-94 (=note on verses 857-860).

36. Lahr, 338, n. 11.

37. Lahr, 329 points out the pun on the Greek word for ladder *klimax* and Rance's line, 'We're approaching what our racier novelists term "the climax"'.

38. *Bacchae,* verses 1330 ff.

39. On the similarities between the plays of Wilde and Orton, see especially Katharine J. Worth, *Revolutions in Modern English Drama* (London, 1972), 151-153.

40. Esslin, 105.

41. *Vita* lines 8-9 (Nauck). The ancient life of Euripides is translated by Mary R. Lefkowitz, *The Lives of the Greek Poets* (London, 1981), appendix 5 (= 163-169).

42. *Ion,* verses 1395ff.

43. Anne Pippin Burnett, *Ion by Euripides* (Englewood Cliffs, N.J., 1970), 118 (=note on verse 1412).

44. *Acharnians,* verses 237ff.

45. Sir Arthur Pickard-Cambridge, *The Dramatic Festivals of Athens* (Oxford, second edition 1968), 220-222.

46. Aristophanes and the contemporary theater are well discussed by G. François, 'Aristophane et le Théâtre Moderne', *L'Antiquité Classique* 40, (1971), 38-79. See also on the problem of produc-

ing Aristophanic comedy today, Constantine Trypanis, *Proceedings of the British Academy* 65, (1979), 493-496.

47. *A History of Greek Literature* (London, 1966), 436-437.

48. *Thesmophoriazusae,* verses 1010ff.

49. I quote the translation of *Frogs,* verses 52-57 by Patric Dickinson, *Aristophanes, Plays II* (Oxford, 1970), 183.

50. *Clouds,* verse 4. 'Obscene Language in Attic Comedy' is the sub-title of *The Maculate Muse* by Jeffrey Henderson (New Haven and London, 1975), a study which offers a wealth of information on sexual humor in Aristophanes.

51. *Head to Toe,* 65.

52. L. G. Kelly, *The True Interpreter, and History of Translation Theory a Practice in the West* (Blackwell, Oxford, 1949), 1.

Sybil Steinberg (review date 5 June 1987)

SOURCE: Steinberg, Sybil. Review of *Head to Toe,* by Joe Orton. *Publishers Weekly* 231, no. 22 (5 June 1987): 70.

[*In the following review, Steinberg points to the scatological, erotic, and satiric themes in* Head to Toe, *hailing Orton as an important literary talent.*]

A cross between Gulliver and Alice, Orton's unwitting hero, Gombold, begins his journey when he wanders onto the head of a giant, hundreds of miles tall. The trip of the title, and back again, takes long enough for the host-creature to age, long enough for Gombold to have assorted adventures with assorted companions. Mostly he gets into trouble running afoul of unknown conventions, a frequent experience in such an odd landscape. Here plants talk, governments are run by large, trivial-minded women, men are occupied with war and revolution and Gombold spends many years imprisoned in a privy. Gargantuan body parts contribute an oddly gruesome, mildly distasteful humor to Gombold's travels, but on the whole his journey is a grim one, leaving him as bewildered at the end as he was at the beginning of his quest. Those who know of Orton's plays, including *What the Butler Saw,* and his violent death at the hands of his male lover, will recognize familiar satiric, scatological and erotic themes in this novel, which is powered by an unflagging, risk-taking imagination and the kind of energy associated with major literary talent.

Gabriele Annan (review date 24 September 1987)

SOURCE: Annan, Gabriele. "Changeling." *New York Review of Books* 34, no. 14 (24 September 1987): 3-4.

[*In the following review, Annan touches on John Lahr's biography of Orton and its film version, as well as* The Orton Diaries *and* Head to Toe.]

"I'm inclined to think," Joe Orton wrote in his diary in March 1967, "that the main fascination of Swift (as with Dylan Thomas, Brendan Behan and many other writers and artists) is with his life. His art certainly doesn't warrant the merit attached to him." It would be ironic if this turned out to be Orton's own epitaph. Doubly ironic, because the two lumpish, lusterless sentences are exactly the kind he was training himself not to write.

Orton got his life in 1978, eleven years after his death. It was written by John Lahr and called *Prick Up Your Ears.* Now Stephen Frears has made a film of it, and Lahr has gone on to edit **The Orton Diaries,** which Orton kept during the last eight months of his life, from December 1966 to August 1967. "My work on Orton," says Lahr's introductory note, "which began back in 1970, is now over." It's been thorough. We know everything we possibly could about the thirty-four years of Orton's life; every psychological avenue has been explored, including the gloomy cul-de-sac traveled by Orton's lover Kenneth Halliwell.

Orton was born in 1933, the disgruntled eldest child of a working-class family. The Ortons were not an affectionate bunch, and they lived in Leicester—the least magical of industrial towns, not even dark and satanic. Orton left school at sixteen, got an office job, and threw himself into amateur theatricals. It was by willpower rather than acting talent that he got himself accepted, two years later, at the Royal Academy of Dramatic Art in London. There he fell in with an older, better-educated student: Halliwell. Halliwell had a lot of style. It was based on the skittish rococo novels of Ronald Firbank, who died in 1926 and has been a literary cult figure ever since. Orton's loyalty to his first literary model was perhaps excessive: he came to think that Waugh too had modeled himself on Firbank, but wasn't as good.

Halliwell and Orton became lovers and set up house together. Their acting careers failed to take off; they began jointly writing novels while living on Halliwell's money (not much) and Orton's National Assistance check. The novels didn't take off either. If they were like Orton's solo effort **Head to Toe,** posthumously published in 1971 and now reissued, then it's not hard to see why. This one is a Swiftian allegorical fantasy. It contains some daring and funny inventions, but like many allegories, it has a grip like a dead boa constrictor's. Orton and Halliwell amused themselves meanwhile by embellishing public library books with surrealist and occasionally obscene collages. The authorities traced them. They were prosecuted and given six months in jail for "willfully damaging" public property. Ironically, again, their collages are now on view at the Islington Public Library. Islington is the North London borough where Orton and Halliwell lived. Its "gentrification" was only just beginning then.

Prison undermined Halliwell's fragile emotional stability; but for Orton it provided the "short sharp shock" that Mrs. Thatcher, years later, was to advocate as the answer to juvenile crime. There is irony here too, another double one: the disgraceful, anarchic Orton with his unbridled sex life looks like the spirit of the Sixties incarnate (especially since in the film he's played by Gary Oldman, who made his name as Sid Vicious in *Sid and Nancy*). But in a sense he was a proto-Thatcherite: determined, hard-working, quick to cut his losses and other people's, and keen to make it. Not into society, though: he loathed and despised the upper and middle classes, right down to complaining that "I've never got a hard on over a middle-class kid yet." He also loathed liberals, especially liberal women.

Jail and the separation from Halliwell—they had never been apart from their meeting in 1951 to the sentence in 1962—jolted Orton's talent into operation. "Being in the nick brought detachment to my writing. I wasn't involved any more and suddenly it worked." He began to write plays. *The Ruffian on the Stair* was accepted by BBC radio. He found an agent, Peggy Ramsay, who saw the point of him, encouraged him, and pushed his work. In 1963 she got *Entertaining Mr. Sloane* put on, first at a fringe theater, then in the West End. It was a success. *Loot* followed, flopped on tour, but a second production in 1966 won the *Evening Standard* Best Play of the Year Award. *The Erpingham Camp* was televised in 1966 and staged in 1967 in a double bill with *The Ruffian on the Stair*. The Beatles' manager commissioned a film script, and Orton began on his third stage play, *What the Butler Saw*. In just over two years the dropout had become a professional, a success, almost a star, while Halliwell grew more and more unhappy, disagreeable, and withdrawn.

Orton's promiscuity was monumental, record-breaking. Halliwell brooded alone in their bed-sitter, doing the housework and the washing up. Eventually he could bear the contrast between their lives no more. He bashed in Orton's skull with nine hammer blows, then killed himself with an overdose of Nembutal. His suicide note read: "If you read his diary all will be explained K. H. P.S. Especially the latter part." Aside from reflections on writing and gobbets of observation stored up for use, Orton's diary has three main topics: cruising; his pro-

fessional life—shading off into show-biz social life—with all his triumphs gleefully recorded; and semicomical moans about how impossible Halliwell was. Leaving his diary about was the unkindest thing Orton did to Halliwell.

Their bodies lay in the room they had shared for eight years until a chauffeur called to drive Orton to a script conference at Twickenham Studios. The arrival of this uniformed figure is almost too Ortonesque: in *Entertaining Mr. Sloane* the seductive murderer is fetishistically fitted out as a chauffeur by his patron. No wonder Lahr chose the episode to make a flash-forward opening for *Prick Up Your Ears*; the film script has followed suit.

You'd think no scriptwriter of any ambition would be interested in writing it: both the scenario and the dialogue—from Orton's diaries—are perfect already. But not at all: the distinguished playwright Alan Bennett took it on. With Gary Oldman exuding plebeian charm and sharpness and looking amazingly like Orton in his photographs, the film is convincing and impossible to walk out from (unless the language shocks you, visually it's as discreet as a family lawyer; even the scene in which eight different men have each other in Orton's favorite *pissoir* is veiled in decent obscurity). Bennett has added some very funny bits of his own, mostly attached to Mr. and Mrs. Lahr, who are shown at their biographical sleuthing and played by Wallace Shawn and marvelous Lindsay Duncan. The film isn't as doggily serious as the biography, but on the other hand it doesn't quite fizz with Orton's brutal gaiety either. Doom looms, inevitably: one knows from the start what's in store for Orton.

His story is ready-made for a cautionary tale, archetypal myth, psychological case history, or period paradigm. No use it was put to would have surprised him. He was up to every literary device, stratagem, maneuver. The diaries show how assiduously and usefully he read: Shakespeare, Swift, Congreve, Wycherley, Farquhar, Sheridan, Wilde, Marie Corelli, Brecht, Camus, Genet, Beckett. He hovered watchfully and sometimes enviously over the output of contemporaries like Pinter, Stoppard, Osborne, Nichols, and David Halliwell. You couldn't catch him out by comparing his work to someone else's. He'd have thought about it already. Still, the critic Ronald Bryden coined a neat sobriquet for him: "The Oscar Wilde of Welfare State Gentility."

It's pretty and apt: Orton's dialogue is often deliberately Wildean. For instance:

PRENTICE:

  You did have a father?

GERALDINE:

  Oh, I'm sure I did. My mother was frugal in her habits, but she'd never economize unwisely.

Or:

> Despite all appearances to the contrary, Mrs. Prentice is harder to get into than the reading room at the British Museum.

But these examples are no more than clever mimicry. Orton is not really like Wilde, because Wilde was not much of a hater. He made fun of the hypocrisy of the society he chose to write about. Orton dissolved society in hydrochloric acid.

He wasn't so much the Oscar Wilde of his period as the Karl Kraus. The way people talked enraged him as it had the Austrian satirist (someone probably not on his reading list). It enraged (and delighted) Orton because, ridden with clichés, shifty euphemisms, and media-speak, current language actually revealed what it had evolved to conceal: "the foul stench" of a corrupt society.

The diaries are packed with snatches of overheard conversation, prime samples of what Lahr pinpoints as "daft pretension." At London airport Orton "heard a woman saying to her companion, 'Well, Durban is really lovely. If you choose your time.' Her companion, a fat woman with rolls of grey hair said, 'I shall bide by that decision.'" This kind of thing is right up Bennett's street, and he has got quite a number of them into his script. What the film can't do is to show how Orton worked them up, his constant preoccupation with writing and turning life into art. "It looks pretty good," he noted in his diary about a haircut he'd just had. "It appears to be quite natural whilst in actual fact being incredibly artificial. Which is a philosophy I approve of."

Another constantly repeated tenet, though not exactly an original one, was that in order to be funny, farce must be deadpan; i.e., the characters must be ordinary (Harold Wilson, not Mick Jagger, is one example) and react in a matter-of-fact way to grotesque happenings—which, in Orton's case, are usually macabre as well. In *Loot,* one of the characters plays the castanets with his dead mother's false teeth. Orton's mother died during the run. He went to Leicester for the funeral (one of the funniest sequences in the *Diaries* and the film), returned with Mrs. Orton's false teeth, handed them to the actor in *Loot,* and recorded the effect:

> "Here, I thought you'd like the originals." He said "What?" "Teeth," I said. "Whose?" he said. "My mum's," I said. He looked very sick. "You see," I said, "it's obvious that you're not thinking of the events of the play in terms of reality, if a thing affects you like that."

But in fact the episode—almost incomprehensible in the film, incidentally—shows Orton as a willful tyrant, forcing life to imitate art. And he did manage to live a life of black comedy just like the life depicted in his plays. He even had a premonition of his own, dramatically retributive end: "Took a walk. Nobody around to pick up. Only a lot of disgusting old men. I shall be a disgusting old man one day, I thought mournfully. Only I have high hopes of dying in my prime." Now and then samples of life's cruelty and pathos got into his data bank, like the old woman seen in Marks and Spencer's on Christmas Eve: "She'd bought herself a packet of jam tarts and a half of chicken. Obviously she couldn't afford anything else. How awful to be trying to celebrate when you're old and lonely."

The Beatles grieved for "all the lonely people" in their song "Eleanor Rigby." Orton wrote no laments. He romped through the caring Sixties like a malevolent changeling. There were flashes of pity, but pity went too near the bone of his own fears: "To be young, good-looking, healthy, famous, comparatively rich *and* happy is surely going against nature," he wrote during a halcyon holiday in Tangiers—where even Halliwell was happy and Arab boys queued in such numbers to be had that they had to be numbered Mohammed I, II, and III like monarchs. "I'm a believer in Original Sin," Orton wrote. "I find people profoundly bad and irresistibly funny." He also seems to have believed, like Verdi's Iago, in "*un Dio crudel.*"

The film deals in an unexpected and brilliant way with the Moroccan interlude. The Mohammeds could have piled up like passengers in a Marx Brothers' railway compartment. But instead of going for farce, Frears has choreographed a sort of poetic mime: smiling, white-clad figures process across sunlit terraces, in eloquent contrast to pale-gray Leicester and dark, rainy North London. When it comes to the show-biz milieu, though, invention fails. Perhaps Bennett and Frears were bored with the very thought of all those bars and parties. They've peopled them with standard insincere screechers in funny hats; and Vanessa Redgrave has almost too easy a time camping it up (or down: she doesn't overdo it) as Peggy Ramsay.

What is missing is the peculiar, gratuitous cruelty of this world. Fear of libel may have something to do with it. A TV producer flashes across the screen disguised behind a beard. In *Prick Up Your Ears* and the *Diaries,* this man has an important part as Orton's professional patron. "People dislike you enough already," Orton records him saying to Halliwell (who had put on an Old Etonian tie to go to a party). "Why make them more angry? I mean—it's permissible, although silly, as a foible of youth, but you—a middle-aged nonentity—it's sad and pathetic!" It would be difficult to get over that. Halliwell didn't have time to. He killed himself and Orton just over a fortnight later.

Alfred Molina's performance as Halliwell was considered far-out by some British critics. He's oddly cast: in the photographs, Orton and Halliwell look almost like twins, whereas Molina seems a foot taller and several dozen pounds heavier than Oldman. Halliwell was prematurely bald and wore a wig; the makeup department had given him total alopecia. Combined with his size and huge, liquid black eyes, it makes him look like one of Edmund Dulac's Oriental strongmen. There's nothing wrong with his acting, but the dramatic contrast between his appearance and Oldman's adds a freakish dimension: life imitating art and overdoing it.

Robert Brustein (review date 17 April 1989)

SOURCE: Brustein, Robert. "Robert Brustein on Theater." *New Republic* 200, no. 16 (17 April 1989): 34.

[*In the following excerpt from a review of two plays, Brustein comments that, in light of the shock value of contemporary entertainment, Orton's work seems less outrageous than it once did.*]

An example of [unrealized promise] is currently on view at the Manhattan Theatre Club in Joe Orton's *What the Butler Saw.* Orton, who died at 34, was notable for taking the traditional conventions of farce and burlesque and liberating their underground meanings. Sensitive to the sexual and aggressive connotations of the most inoffensive-seeming gags, and particularly fond of the comic possibilities of transvestism, he gained something of a dangerous reputation by daring to make these manifest. But an age that has experienced Camp, the Theater of the Ridiculous, Ethyl Eichelberger, and Monty Python, not to mention Richard Pryor and Eddie Murphy's *Raw,* is likely to find Orton rather tame. *What the Butler Saw* today looks like a highly carpentered, sometimes mechanical and contrived farce, full of physical action and verbal amusement but suffering a little from period fatigue.

The play takes place in a doctor's office with an inordinate number of doors. "Why are there so many doors?" the doctor is asked. "Was your house designed by a lunatic?" Actually, multiple exits are the design required by the lunatic logic of farce, but it is Orton's inspiration to set this farce in a madhouse. When the curtain rises, Dr. Prentice (Charles Keating) is asking a curvaceous job applicant (Joanne Whalley-Kilmer) to disrobe in order to determine her suitability for the position. Enter the doctor's nymphomaniac wife (Carole Shelley), accompanied by the bell boy (Bruce Norris) who tried to rape her, and followed by a policeman (Patrick Tull) looking for a phallus missing from a statue of Winston Churchill. Before long, the effort to hide the naked girl and conceal her clothes becomes the engine of the plot. Most of the funnier jokes are indebted to burlesque (She: "You put me in an impossible position." He: "No

position's impossible when you're young and healthy"). But *What the Butler Saw* is essentially a relentless farce about clothes involving transvestism and gender confusion.

The transsexual overtones of this crossdressing emerge from time to time. More often, it is treated, like the convention of Elizabethan disguise, as a case of mistaken identity, a stimulus for laughter. What is not altogether funny, however, is Orton's treatment of women. The job applicant, being certified insane, has her head shaved, gets stuffed in a straitjacket, and is brutally beaten in a scene that touches on realism. Like most cartoon characters, she shows no lasting ill effects, and after a series of mad chases, proves to be the long-lost daughter of Dr. and Mrs. Prentice in a Gilbert and Sullivan denouement full of incestuous implications. But the hidden will at work here occasionally breaks out of the comic frame into genuine misogyny.

Under John Tillinger's laissez-faire direction, the production lurches between languorous undulation and super-animation. While the rest of the mostly British cast gets by with high-velocity, deadpan deportment, that fine actor, Joseph Maher, as Dr. Rance, sometimes seems at sea amidst the general mayhem. What's most disappointing, though, is the impression left by Orton himself, who with the passage of time appears to have been assimilated by the very conventions he thought he was flouting. *What the Butler Saw* retains some vitality as a manic farce, but with the edge of danger gone, it rushes past you like a high-speed train without a destination.

John Simon (review date 18 December 1989)

SOURCE: Simon, John. "Beelzebubee." *New York* 22, no. 50 (18 December 1989): 105-07.

[*In the following excerpt from a review of several plays, Simon presents an unfavorable assessment of the stage version of* Up against It.]

Up Against It was a screenplay, the last work of Joe Orton before his lover murdered him and killed himself. The producer who bought it for a pretty penny did not make the movie (initially intended for the Beatles); whether this was because the scandal proved too great or the script too puny I cannot say. Judging from the musical Tom Ross and Todd Rundgren have fashioned from it, whatever the screenplay may be like, its sleep should not have been disturbed.

It would be hopeless to try to summarize the scattershot plot. It is a chase story involving a young hero and his two mates in the England (sort of) of the sixties. There is picaresque adventure aplenty, involving a lovely but money-hungry heroine, who dumps the hero in favor of a millionaire prison warden. There is also a bad priest, a ferocious female chief of police, a comically swooning parlormaid in love with the hero, an obese gnome of a woman prime minister, a female revolution and male counterrevolution, and characters who keep disappearing only to resurface in new and stranger guises. In short, chaos.

Joe Papp, usually so prodigal with the taxpayers' money, has stinted on this one, with cut-rate direction by Kenneth Elliott and mingy sets by B. T. Whitehill. The cast is a mixed bag, with Stephen Temperley, Alison Fraser, Roger Bart, and, in particular, the persuasively acting, singing, and British-sounding Philip Casnoff doing very nicely indeed. But several others fail to score, and Mari Nelson, a brand-new graduate of Juilliard, though pretty, might seriously consider getting reimbursed for her tuition fees. Tom Ross, of the Public Theater's staff, has wrested little sense or shape from the story (which Orton might have revised), and Rundgren has further burdened it with songs that are not intoxicating, merely toxic. . . .

Alan Sinfield (essay date summer 1990)

SOURCE: Sinfield, Alan. "Who Was Afraid of Joe Orton?" *Textual Practice* 4, no. 2 (summer 1990): 259-77.

[*In the following essay, Sinfield deals with the ways in which Orton's plays increased awareness of and toleration for homosexual culture, while at the same time limiting his audience.*]

OSCAR WILDE:

> [Secrecy] seems to be the one thing that can make modern life mysterious or marvellous to us. The commonest thing is delightful if one only hides it.[1]

JOE ORTON:

> The whole trouble with Western Society today is the lack of anything worth concealing.[2]

Joe Orton went to study at the Royal Academy for Dramatic Art in 1951, in the heyday of Terence Rattigan, Whitehall farces, religious verse-drama and Agatha Christie. The Wolfenden Report on homosexuality was still six years away, and the film *Victim* ten. Theatre was often 'queer', but it was always discreet. In the late 1950s, Orton showed no interest in the socially and politically aware plays of Osborne, Delaney, and Wesker, though they accompanied and contributed to a great increase in public discussion of homosexuality—by 1958 the Lord Chamberlain, the Crown official whose task it was to censor stage plays, was obliged to allow serious

treatment of the topic. Orton and his lover Kenneth Halliwell were conducting a more distinctive and anarchic cultural critique by redesigning the covers of library books.[3]

However, in 1963, with the mysterious menace of Pinter's plays in the ascendancy, Orton wrote *Entertaining Mr. Sloane.* In 1966 *Loot* was successfully produced—London was swinging and 'permissive' and Orton was asked to write a film script for the Beatles. He died in 1967, the year when male homosexual acts were made legal (provided there were only two people, in private, over twenty-one, and not in the armed services, the merchant navy, the prisons, Northern Ireland or Scotland). In 1968 stage censorship ended, and explicit gay plays—*Spitting Image, Fortune and Men's Eyes, Total Eclipse*—were produced in London. Plays in the London theatre in 1969 besides Orton's *What the Butler Saw* included *Boys in the Band, Oh, Calcutta!* and *Hair*; it was the year when the unprecedented resistance of gays to police harassment at the Stonewall Inn in New York's Christopher Street led to the formation of the Gay Liberation Front. So Orton's involvement in theatre spans the crucial period when the scope for homosexuals, both in British society and in the theatre, was sharply contested. This was the period when Gay Liberation became conceivable.

This article explores how Orton's plays effected quite specific negotiations of these changing opportunities for theatre and male homosexuals (in this paper I discuss men in Britain; the histories of lesbians generally and of men in other countries, though partly similar, are distinct). Orton exploited and contributed to the process through which homosexuality gradually became publicly speakable, and, as theatre audiences split and reformed, he was a focus of ideological conflict. Yet, I will argue, the terms of that conflict finally trapped Orton and limited his audience and his sexual politics, particularly in the play critics have most praised, *What the Butler Saw.* I invoke another gay play as a possible model for a gay cultural politics.

SILENCE AND THE CLOSET

Typically, from Ibsen to Christie and Rattigan, naturalistic plays disclose a danger to the social order. Often it takes the form of a socially unacceptable character—an outlaw-intruder who threatens the security of the characters and, by inference, the audience. Usually the problem is satisfactorily contained at the final curtain, though dissident authors might suggest that the disruptive intruder or misfit manifests in some ways a superior ethic or wisdom.[4] Pinter's plays reorganized this pattern. In them the sense of mysterious, ominous presence is often embodied in an intruder, though now its focus is not social propriety but an unstable compound of metaphysical vacuity and sexual challenge. Its ultimate residence may be the psyche of the threatened character. Notoriously, the danger hovers also in silences in the dialogue, pregnant now not with class disapproval but with a loosely 'existential' anxiety about emptiness and disintegration.

The outlaw-intruder pattern had obvious resonances for male homosexuals, especially of the middle and upper classes. They felt obliged to 'pass' as heterosexual, and thus themselves effected the intrusion of an 'undesirable' element into good society. They might fear the irruption of knowledge about homosexuality and hence their own exposure; further, they might themselves introduce the threatening lower-class person to whom they might be attracted (this was a common pattern and constituted the dominant concept of the homosexual liaison).[5] J. R. Ackerley remarked, almost in passing, how he and his friends were 'outcasts and criminals in the sight of the impertinent English laws'; Peter Wildeblood said in 1955 that he 'would be the first homosexual to tell what it felt like to be an exile in one's own country'.[6] Homosexuality hovered upon the edge of public visibility, defining normality against a deviation so horrific that its occurrence could scarcely be admitted.

Pinter's version of the outlaw-intruder was apposite to homosexuality at this time: both were imagined as mysterious and violent, lying in wait in the silences, explicitly nowhere but, by so much, potentially everywhere. Homosexuality might manifest itself as an overemphatic and hence potentially violent inflection in a relationship. It might even be lurking, scarcely recognized, in the psyches of 'normal' people. Most of Pinter's early plays have a homosexual inflection. There are intense male relationships in *The Birthday Party* (Goldberg and McCann; 1958), *The Dwarfs* (1960), *The Caretaker* (1960) and *The Dumb Waiter* (1960). In *The Birthday Party* Stanley resists Lulu's advances and is 'mothered' by Meg; in *The Homecoming* (1965) Lenny boasts of violent relations with women but is easily disconcerted by Ruth. It is not that these plays are 'really', 'underneath', about homosexuals; to say that would be to override the ambiguity which at the time was crucial. During those decades of discretion we should not imagine homosexuality as *there*, fully formed like a statue shrouded under a sheet until ready for exhibition. The closet (as discreet homosexuality was named when it came under scrutiny in the 1960s) did not obscure homosexuality—it created it. Freud makes a similar point when he disputes that one should expect to find 'the essence of dreams in their latent content': the important thing is the dream-*work* which produces such images.[7] Similarly, oblique homosexual representation should be studied for the *process* that constitutes it so, and for the social reasons that demand such a process.

As censorship gradually relaxed, Pinter wrote *The Collection* (1961). There is tension in the (evidently) ho-

mosexual relationship of Harry and Bill and in the marriage of Stella and James because, it emerges, there is a question whether sexual congress has occurred between Stella and Bill. Homosexuality is to be inferred from the usual stereotypical cues—the 'artistic' menage of Harry and Bill, the fact that Bill is a dress designer, and the domineering attitude of the wealthier and older Harry. Martin Esslin deduces that Bill may have wanted to sleep with Stella because he 'may have been made into a homosexual by an older man who offered him social advancement, a good job, life in a middle-class milieu'.[8] We never find out what 'actually happened', of course. The need to infer the sexuality of Harry and Bill produces an additional layer of obscurity. Customary discreet indirection about homosexuality feeds neatly into Pinter's blend of mystery and menace.

While the Chamberlain's power persisted, Pinteresque mystery was a convenient mode for handling homosexuality on the stage. In *The Trigon,* by James Broom Lynne (produced at the Arts theatre in 1963), Arthur and Basil are presented through manifest homosexual hints—as the play opens, Arthur is wearing Boy Scout uniform and playing a record of 'Dance of the Sugar-Plum Fairy'. Their intentions towards their friend Mabel are evidently half-hearted (compare Stanley and Lulu in *The Birthday Party*)—it is said that if they both addressed her 'She wouldn't know which way to turn.'[9] But there is no indication of sexual feeling, as such, between the two men. The intruder, Charles, is also mysterious—though compatible with the stereotypical notion that homosexuals gain satisfaction from breaking up other people's relationships. He expels Basil and Arthur from their flat, but it is suggested that they will be better for the self-knowledge he has produced: 'It's no good either of us thinking of Mabel. Or any other woman for that matter. We'll make plans for each other. No third party' (p. 152).

This conclusion ought to mean that Arthur and Basil come to terms with their sexual relationship, but that cannot be shown. Inexplicitness makes *The Trigon* unactable outside its time. Of course Basil and Arthur are discreet about homosexuality (if wearing a Boy Scout uniform and playing 'The Sugar-Plum Fairy' is discreet). And they may delude themselves about the chances of making it with Mabel. But there is no dramatic reason for them to be discreet when they are alone together. The reason is extra-dramatic: they are being overheard by the audience, and this makes their privacy public and subject to censorship. To the reviewer of *Theatre World* (July 1964) the characters were 'inexplicably bound together emotionally'. The mystery in this play has nothing to do with the absurdist project usually attributed to Pinter, it is simply the limits of what James Broom Lynne was allowed to say.

ENTERTAINING HOMOSEXUALITY

Entertaining Mr. Sloane followed *The Trigon* into the Arts theatre in 1964 and was published in the same volume of *Penguin Modern Plays*. The whole manner was in the air, provoked by the demands of speaking the unspeakable in the conditions of that moment. However, Orton's use of 'Pinteresque' indirect dialogue and the mysteriously powerful intruder is cunning and distinctive. He incorporates them into the action, making them required by the concerns of the characters. We understand the middle-aged Eddie to be homosexual because it is the only way of making sense of his toleration of Sloane, his interest in Sloane's physique and sex life, and his horror of heterosexuality. Eddie is indirect in his approach to Sloane because he assumes he must be cautious. Sloane evidently reads this indirection: he suggests that Eddie is 'sensitive'. But Eddie denies it, insisting, 'I seen birds all shapes and sizes and I'm most certainly not . . . um . . . sensitive' (p. 204). Sloane carefully plays Eddie along because, as Orton explained, Sloane knows the score but 'isn't going to give in until he has to'.[10]

In *Sloane* obscurity and indirection make sense *within* the action as the inhibitions of discretion. The play makes apparent the operations of the closet; it comments on the discretion of the censor and polite society, as well as being subject to it. Orton also makes sense of 'Pinteresque menace'. The attractive youth, Sloane, has killed a man who wanted to photograph him, and this danger is not merely arbitrary, metaphysical, or paranoid, but part of that experienced all the time by homosexuals. In *Serious Charge* by Philip King (1955) and *The Children's Hour* by Lillian Hellman (1934; produced at club theatres in 1950 and 1956) an attractive, dishonest and violent young person tries to ruin a plausibly homosexual adult by accusing him/her of homosexuality (the accusations are false, but suspicion is allowed to remain, humouring conventional notions about artistic, bachelor vicars and intense, unmarried lady schoolteachers). In actual life, often, homosexuals are subject to violent assault and murder. By the end of the play Sloane has killed two men, and Kath and Eddie are rash to assume that he won't kill again.

The changed use of obliquity and innuendo in Orton's plays was possible partly because, by the mid-1960s, understanding was no longer the special secret of a few. A perverse benefit from the witch-hunt against homosexual men in the early 1950s was enhanced visibility and a great increase in public discussion—provoked also by the Kinsey Report (1948). In the United States, where persecution was even more vigorous, John D'Emilio observes that 'attacks on gay men and women hastened the articulation of a homosexual identity and spread the knowledge that they existed in large numbers'.[11] Commentators have often observed that in the 1950s homosexuality came to be considered less an evil or a sin, and more a medical or psychological condition. That is true, but also, increasingly, it was discussed as *a problem*. A Church of England pamphlet was called *The Problem of Homosexuality* (1954). This was the era of the problem (juvenile delinquency, unmarried mothers, the colour bar, latch-key children . . .); and it involved an expectation that the state would encourage public discussion and then pass laws to improve matters. The Wolfenden Committee on homosexual offences (and prostitution) was set up in 1954 after a minister for home affairs declared: 'Quite clearly, this is a problem which calls for very careful consideration on the part of those responsible for the welfare of the nation.' By the end of the decade Gordon Westwood believed that his 1952 objective, of bringing 'the problem of homosexuality . . . out into the open where it can be discussed and reconsidered', had been achieved.[12] Homosexuality was no longer unspoken. When *The Killing of Sister George* by Frank Marcus was playing at Wimbledon in 1967, Orton prophesied: 'I don't suppose they'll understand what the play is about.' 'Don't you believe it,' Halliwell replied, 'They'll know very well what it's about.' Orton acknowledges: 'He was right. It became clear, from the opening scenes, that they understood and weren't amused.'[13]

They could have found out from BBC radio comedy. In 1960 Peter Burton experienced the homosexual slang 'Polari' as 'our own camp secret language with which we could confound and confuse the *naffs* (straights)'.[14] But from 1964 Polari expressions such as 'bona' (attractive), 'varda' (look at), 'omee' (man) and 'polonee' (woman) featured regularly in the dialogue of two very camp men in the Light Programme comedy series *Round the Horne*, with Orton's friend Kenneth Williams as Julian (Jules) and Hugh Paddick as Sandy. Here is a typical instance from March 1967, with the couple as journalists:

PADDICK:

Can we have five minutes of your time?

HORNE:

It depends what you want to do with them.

WILLIAMS:

Well, our editor said, Why don't you troll off to Mr Horne's lattie . . .

HORNE:

Flat or home—translator's note.

WILLIAMS:

And have a palare with him . . .[15]

For regular listeners, as well as for gays, the 'translation' would be unnecessary. Its offer was part of the joke, signifying that the private was in the process of becoming public. In 1967-8 the laws on homosexuality and stage censorship were changed. By 1969 Lou Reed was a cult hero, and by 1972 Alice Cooper and David Bowie took gender-bending into the pop charts. Unevenly, in diverse institutions, homosexuality was becoming less secret.

HE DO THE POLICE

In the heyday of Noël Coward, audiences divided according to whether they would pick up hints of homosexuality. From the mid-1960s the split was hardly over decoding competence, but around a contest as to what could be said in public. Homosexual nuances in Coward's plays either were not heard, or they were rendered tolerable by the acknowledgement (in their indirection) that such matters should not be allowed into public discourse. As homosexuality became more audible, it became the subject of explicit contest.

Some people were certainly upset. When **Sloane** was considered for television the company's legal officer thought it disgusting: 'Perfectly horrible and filthy. I don't know why we want to consider such a play.'[16] She had understood what it was about. Outside London, **Loot** provoked walk-outs—'Bournemouth Old Ladies Shocked', reported *The Times*.[17] But the shockable audience understood that homosexuality (and other such causes) were at issue. Furthermore, it was confronted by another audience, associated typically with the Royal Court theatre, that wanted to see progressive plays. In the subsidized sector of theatre especially, the left-liberal intelligentsia was winning space for its kinds of representation—to the extent that a 'taboo' subject like homosexuality was hardly challenging to the people likely to attend a production known to feature it. This audience had come to indulge what was being called 'permissiveness', and felt confirmed in their progressive stance. In 1966 Frank Parkin found between 75 and 94 per cent (depending on social class) of CND supporters agreeing that laws against homosexual acts by consenting adults should be repealed.[18] While **Sloane** was running, establishment West End producers complained fiercely about 'dirty plays'—particularly at the subsidized Royal Shakespeare Company. Their objections were used to advertise **Sloane**—so far from being a disadvantage, the scandal was played up.[19] Compare what happened when Wilde was arrested: *An Ideal Husband* and *The Importance of Being Earnest* had been attracting large audiences, but Wilde's name was taken off the hoardings and the plays soon closed.[20]

However, **Entertaining Mr. Sloane** does contain a challenge for a progressive audience (this was my experience). It resides not in the homosexuality, but in the lack of interpersonal feeling which, in the character of Sloane, produces psychopathic violence. This disappoints a left-liberal pleasure in Sloane's initially relaxed attitude to homosexuality, and frustrates a wish to see diverse kinds of sexuality justified by the affective quality of the relationship. Further, progressive plays generally presented the young person as a victim of the grown-ups (for instance, *A Taste of Honey* by Shelagh Delaney, *Five Finger Exercise* by Peter Shaffer, *Roots* and *Chips with Everything* by Arnold Wesker). In part Sloane is such a victim—at the end Kath and Eddie are able to force him into their 'family'.[21] But he is also the unsocialized hooligan whom conservatives were invoking as grounds for clamping down on all youthful self-expression. He is set up in some ways as the attractive character among the four, but kicking old men to death is carrying intergenerational conflict a bit too far.

Loot was better attuned to the liberal-progressive audience (I went with a group of fellow students—it was someone's birthday). The play is on the side of the boys, Hal and Dennis, and attacks officialdom and traditional moral attitudes. Some of the dialogue is in a discreet manner, but deployed so as to challenge hypocrisy and bogus formality ('And even the sex you were born into isn't safe from your marauding').[22] Above all, **Loot** excited the youthful left-liberal intelligentsia by its treatment of the police and the law. During the relative social harmony of the 1950s, unusually, the image of the friendly 'bobby' was relatively unchallenged (though homosexuals always had reason to distrust it). But repressive attitudes to political demonstrations from around 1960, and then to drugs, gradually shifted left-liberal opinion. In 1965, while Orton was writing **Loot,** the case of Detective Sergeant Harold Challenor came to prominence. He had arrested, beaten, and planted a brick and an iron bar on people demonstrating against the Greek monarchy (because it sponsored the fascist dictatorship in Greece). Orton, says Kenneth Williams, became 'obsessed with Challenor', and as the play was reworked the part of Inspector Truscott was developed.[23]

It is not usually stressed that Orton's critique of police malpractice goes far beyond anything previously seen in the theatre, or indeed other media.

TRUSCOTT:

(*shouting, knocking HAL to the floor*). Under any other political system I'd have you on the floor in tears!

HAL:

(*crying*). You've got me on the floor in tears.

* * *

TRUSCOTT:

And you complain you were beaten?

DENNIS:

Yes.

TRUSCOTT:

Did you tell anyone?

DENNIS:

Yes.

TRUSCOTT:

Who?

DENNIS:

The officer in charge.

TRUSCOTT:

What did he say?

DENNIS:

Nothing.

TRUSCOTT:

Why not?

DENNIS:

He was out of breath with kicking.[24]

To have such things said in public, I recall, was as exciting as the relaxed attitudes to homosexuality attributed to Hal and Dennis. In the closing moments McLeavy tells Truscott 'You're mad!' The response recalled the Challenor case: 'Nonsense, I had a check-up only yesterday' (p. 274). Orton even worked into the text Challenor's actual words, reported in court: 'You're fucking nicked, my old beauty.'[25] Hilariously, the Lord Chamberlain would not allow 'fucking'. With the repressive state apparatus starkly displayed, he was still chasing after naughty words.

Introducing *Loot,* Simon Trussler said it outrages 'every expectation of a *morally* appropriate outcome'. However, in an article Trussler remarked the difference between '*kinds* of audiences': one kind 'may understand *Loot* because they share its moral assumptions', the other will prefer Whitehall farces and 'either ignore *Loot* or hate it'.[26] For left-liberals its critique was exhilarating. McLeavy's fate does not trouble us much, for he has foolishly worshipped the authority that victimizes him. The ending of *Loot* is triumphant because it displays most completely, in Truscott's behaviour, the corruption of established power and authority. (The effect is similar in the last moments of at least two other early-1960s new-wave plays, Wesker's *Chips with Everything* and Giles Cooper's *Everything in the Garden.*) Further, the final lines propose that Hal, Dennis, and Fay should all live together. This arrangement offers to resolve unconventionally but pleasantly a tension among the three most likeable characters. In fact it is exactly the happy ending of Noël Coward's *Design for Living* (1932). But times have changed and in *Loot* the idea can no longer be welcomed innocently—'People would talk. We must keep up appearances' (p. 275). In so far as this does not repudiate the *menage à trois* as such, it is pleasing to left-liberals and, in so far as it exposes the hypocrisy of 'people' once more, it is a final blow against convention.

After difficulties in the provinces, *Loot* was a hit in London. Its success could be partly because traditionally-minded people enjoyed feeling indignant— Hal says of his father, 'His generation takes a delight in being outraged.'[27] But mainly it was because younger people were excited by it.

THE MOMENT OF ORTON

The 1960s intensified both libertarian and reactionary attitudes and their conflict was staged in the theatre. These were the circumstances that permitted Orton's notoriety. Earlier, he would not have been tolerated; later he would not be so significant (though he would be the subject of determined recuperation). We might call it the moment of Orton. The plays' prominence depended on the social atmosphere of the 1950s—which produced and talked anxiously about, but did not enact, Wolfenden. They were written to scandalize the Aunt Ednas (and remember, this 'middlebrow' follower of theatre was invented by Rattigan). But the condition of their presentation and success was the fact that discretion and the audience that assumed it were already under pressure. By making visible the structure of the closet, the plays helped to make its dismantling possible. The 1960s liberalization that helped make Orton a celebrity, therefore, also set a limit to his moment.

Orton (like most people) had difficulty seeing himself as part of a trend. He enjoyed watching audiences upset by *Loot,* and believed his 'authentic voice' was 'vulgar and offensive in the extreme to middle-class susceptibilities'.[28] He scarcely realized that they were already on the run and that there was enthusiastic support for the critique he was mounting. This is partly because he had few links with the student culture of the subsidized theatre audience and distrusted its earnestness. He had studied at the Royal Academy of Dramatic Art in the early 1950s, well before the student radicalism of the CND generation, and his attitudes to homosexuality and theatre tended to assume the milieu of Coward or Rattigan. (Osborne partly shared Orton's background, and this helps to explain his poor fit with the progressive movement he initiated. He edged back to the discreet, upper-class theatrical world of Rattigan in *Hotel in Amsterdam* (1968) and *West of Suez* (1971). Orton wanted commercial managements to present his plays. He thought Kenneth Tynan wouldn't dare include

'Until She Screams', the sketch he submitted for *Oh, Calcutta!* in 1967; but this piece had basically been written in 1960. As Simon Shepherd remarks, Orton 'had a rather inflated idea of his own shockingness: they did dare do his sketch. Orton's underestimate of the sexual "liberation" of others is a mark not just of his vanity but of his isolation.'[29]

The confusions of the moment of Orton were manifested institutionally. So vigorous was the left-liberal theatre audience that it encroached on the West End, partly through the efforts of progressive impresarios to make a distinctive space for themselves. Michael Codron and Donald Albery were looking for 'disturbing' plays, and hence keen to produce *Sloane*; Codron thought it 'might turn out to have the most exciting commercial possibilities since *The Caretaker*'.[30] By the mid-1960s the boundary between West End and subsidized theatre was blurred, and Orton was unclear about where he belonged. His *Ruffian on the Stair* and *The Erpingham Camp* were presented by the Royal Court (in 1967), and when *Loot* wasn't going well Orton doubted whether it was right for commercial theatre and thought of putting it into the Royal Court or the National.[31]

More damagingly, Orton's commercial success kept him among the older type of discreet theatre homosexual, who identified with a privileged, leisure-class outlook in which conservative attitudes to homosexuality and theatre went together and constituted an inevitable and largely desirable state of affairs.[32] They believed—rightly—that more openness would spoil their kind of accommodation to homosexuality (even as it spoiled the Orton moment). In his diaries Orton shows virtually no interest in other gay plays, or in the new 'fringe' companies, or in moves to abolish stage censorship, or even in the legalization of male homosexuality. Rattigan commented: 'Orton thought it very funny that I, of all people, should have thought his play so good.'[33] Actually, they were not so far apart, for Orton's satire depended on Rattigan's world.

WHO SAW THE BUTLER?

What the Butler Saw includes powerful satire against the oppressive constructions of medicine and psychiatry, and creates continuous gender confusion, with cross-dressing and 'inappropriate' sexual advances. But it was not too disturbing for Orton's discreet friends. They were very enthusiastic about it[34] and encouraged him to have it produced by Binkie Beaumont and Tennents, with Ralph Richardson, at the Haymarket—in other words, in the heart of traditional West End theatre. Evidently Orton thought he was setting a trap: he wanted a conventionally 'lovely' set so that 'When the curtain goes up one should feel that we're right back in the old theatre of reassurance.'[35] But Orton doesn't consider

why Beaumont should want to do the play; it is he, Orton, who was trapped. Commentators agree that the text was played without flair—it wasn't the censor (by then defunct) who would not allow Churchill's 'missing part' to be produced on stage, but Richardson, the Beaumont star.[36] The production pleased neither of the divergent audiences who were striving to claim theatre for their point of view.

Nevertheless, *What the Butler Saw* has been praised by the best commentators on Orton. Albert Hunt suggests that it 'would, presumably, have been revised and tightened had he lived', but still admires the way it destroys 'the sexual stability on which the mechanics of bedroom farce depend'.[37] Hunt adduces the description by Dr. Prentice of his wife:

> My wife is a nymphomaniac. Consequently, like the Holy Grail, she's ardently sought after by young men. I married her for her money and, upon discovering her to be penniless, I attempted to throttle her. She escaped my murderous fury and I've had to live with her malice ever since.[38]

It had been complained that if Mrs. Prentice is indeed so liberal about sex then the principal motive of the action becomes absurd—namely her husband trying to keep from her his attempt to seduce his secretary. This is the point, says Hunt: the logic of farce collapses.[39] But that logic requires the assumptions of a 1950s farce audience. By 1969 very many people no longer believed that it is important to conceal adultery, that Christian imagery is sacrosanct, even that female sexual desire is shocking and/or funny. Brian Rix, sponsor of the Whitehall farces, had remarked in 1966: 'with the more tolerant climate there now is, we could put on a farce about adultery and our audience wouldn't bat an eyelid.' And he attributed 'the more liberal attitude' partly to Royal Court plays. Orton was not unaware of the issue. In the same article he is quoted as complaining: 'A lot of farces today are still based on the preconceptions of a century ago, particularly the preoccupations about sex. But we must now accept that, for instance, people *do* have sexual relations outside marriage.'[40] Things were moving faster than he realized. Back in 1962, Giles Cooper's *Everything in the Garden* was powerful when it showed conventional middle-class people finding themselves involved in prostitution and murder and getting used to the idea. In 1969, for many people, the concern in *Butler* [*What the Butler Saw*] with adultery and nakedness was merely quaint—and the speech about Mrs. Prentice's 'nymphomania' sounded like it was straining to shock (and nothing is done with Prentice's 'murderous fury'). Progressive audiences would be disappointed at the failure to develop the homosexual theme after the initial interview between Prentice and Nick.

Simon Shepherd observes that instead of a return to order at the end of *What the Butler Saw,* incestuous desire is revealed. He believes the audience, 'like any comedy audience . . . *sees* itself to be like the characters in expecting an ending to disorder; but discovers that ending to be alien and uncomfortable. Thus trapped the audience is driven wild. The first performances succeeded: people stormed out or barracked the players.'[41] But suppose one did not find incest between consenting adults so very terrible? To be sure, the play upset some of Richardson's older admirers in the preliminary week in Brighton (I saw it there). And it was booed and jeered on the opening night in London, though this was not a naïve response but an organized campaign by the group of gallery firstnighters, followers of traditional theatre, that had already disrupted Colin Spencer's *Spitting Image* a few months previously.[42] But—my title question— who was afraid of Joe Orton? Was it important to taunt those people in 1969, especially at the price of framing **Butler** in terms they would react against? The play's title, which refers to ancient seaside machines showing 'sexy' pictures of women's knickers and suspenders for a penny, was of course meant to be ironic, but it holds Orton bound to the framework of attitudes that he wants to oppose. Furthermore, he could affront the Aunt Ednas only by failing to engage with other audiences. A different kind of farce, plucking at the susceptibilities of a sophisticated liberal audience, was just ahead in the work of Alan Acykbourn and Michael Frayn. And plays on explicit gay themes—*The Killing of Sister George, When Did You Last See My Mother?, Staircase, Spitting Image, Fortune and Men's Eyes, The Madness of Lady Bright, Total Eclipse*—had been produced in London (most of these began in 'alternative' venues; all but the last two transferred to the West End).

Jonathan Dollimore has also praised **Butler**: he calls it 'black camp', and remarks the irony, parody and pastiche, held together by 'a stylistic *blankness*'. He argues that the play insinuates 'the arbitrariness and narrowness of gender roles, and that they are socially ascribed rather than naturally given'.[43] The play is thus in the mode of Wilde who, Dollimore shows, validates the artificial, the non-natural, the insincere. Wilde thus subverts the demand for depth—for authenticity, sincerity and the natural; and these are 'dominant categories of subjectivity which keep desire in subjection'.[44] So we may see that sexual relations are not essentially thus or thus, but are based on manners, convention, custom, ideology, power. This is indeed what **Butler** does some of the time. It 'becomes a kind of orgy of cross-dressing, gender confusion and hierarchical inversion', and the dialogue calls into question the 'natural'—in circumstances where the speaker is in fact mistaken, because of cross-dressing, about the 'naturalness' of the very example he is using.[45] But even so, much of the comedy depends on believing that such attitudes are outrageous, and that, whatever their clothes, Nick is really a boy and Geraldine really a girl. I am inclined to see Orton's refusal of depth as indicating weakness

rather than strength. This is not the assured position, perhaps the arrogance, of Wilde; it is looking over its shoulder to see how Aunt Edna is responding.

There is an alternative strategy to Wilde's cultivation of artificiality, as Dollimore shows. It appropriates parts of the dominant discourse, asserting the naturalness of gay relations and seeking to use sincerity and authenticity against their usual implication. This strategy was cultivated by Radclyffe Hall and André Gide. Of course, it may be no more than a pathetic plea to be allowed to share the power of the oppressor. But, alternatively, it may seize the ideology of depth and authenticate the unorthodox. And hence it may contribute to the development of what Foucault calls 'a reverse discourse', whereby 'homosexuality begins to speak on its own behalf, to forge its own identity and culture, *often in the self-same categories by which it has been produced and marginalised,* and eventually challenges the very power structures responsible for its "creation".'[46]

This latter was in fact the main strategy of the 1960s homosexual law reform campaign[47] and, shortly after Orton's death, of Gay Liberation—to produce and believe in positive representations of homosexuality ('gay is good'; the validation of surface over depth was slightly later, stimulated by such diverse concepts as the pink economy, poststructuralism, and high-energy disco-dancing). Orton was out of step with that reforming tendency; he refused nature, depth, and sincerity at least partly because, although he felt an intuitive opposition to the prevailing sexual ideology, he had difficulty conceiving a positive view of the homosexual.[48] He was stuck, in other words, in the Orton moment.

To be sure, Orton shows an untroubled practice of homosexuality in some characters—Sloane, Hal and Dennis, perhaps Nick. But none of them is apparently *a homosexual*. The instance of that is the older, closeted Eddie in **Sloane,** and his devious exercise of power makes him unattractive. This is reminiscent of Coward who, I have argued elsewhere, validates deviant sexuality when it is part of a general bohemianism but makes his specifically homosexual characters unappealing.[49] Orton was very concerned that there should be nothing 'queer or camp or odd' about Hal and Dennis—'They must be perfectly ordinary boys who happen to be fucking each other. Nothing could be more natural.' He also objected to Eddie appearing camp.[50] This seems radical; it is against stereotypes and appropriates nature. On the other hand, 'we're all bisexual really' is the commonest evasion. Hal and Dennis are said to be indifferent to the gender of their partners ('You scatter your seed along the pavements without regard to age or sex').[51] That was an unusual and disconcerting thought; it takes the implications of cross-dressing and superficiality quite literally; it could be utopian. But it also keeps a distance from very many actual homosexuals; it was not how Orton lived, or others that he knew. At this time male homosexuals were struggling to be gay, not to be indifferent to sexual orientation. Of course, we all think we want to get away from stereotypes. However, these are not arbitrary external impositions, but are implicated in the whole construction of sexuality in the modern world; they figure, positively and negatively, in gay self-understanding. You challenge them not by jumping clear but by engaging with them.

'SPITTING IMAGE'

It may be that Dollimore's two strategies can be combined—so that the strategy of superficiality deconstructs normative assumptions about patriarchy, heterosexuality and the family, and then the strategy of sincerity asserts the claims of unorthodox sexuality. I would suggest that Caryl Churchill's *Cloud Nine* (1979) does this. So does *Spitting Image* by Colin Spencer. This was produced in 1968, when the abolition of the Lord Chamberlain's censorship function made it suddenly possible to present plays that would make sense to and for a gay audience. To be sure, homosexuals had frequented discreet plays, even regarding theatre as a specially homosexual medium, but that discretion enshrined heterosexist assumptions. *Spitting Image* is written to make best sense to a gay audience eager for its own theatre. It opened at the Hampstead Theatre Club, a suitable location for a progressive audience, and proved strong enough to gain a brief West End transfer to the Duke of York's. There, *The Times* reported, it received 'loud boos from the gallery and sustained applause from the stalls': it upset the old-fashioned moralists and energized gays and radicals.[52]

To general astonishment and fear, one partner in a male homosexual couple, Gary and Tom, conceives and bears a child (who calls them Daddy One and Daddy Two). Familiar structures are shifted onto this strange situation.

DOCTOR:

Yes, yes, any other symptoms, Mr Dart?

TOM:

Oh, just the normal ones, you know.

DOCTOR:

Normal?

TOM:

I mean, well, morning sickness in the first two months and then . . .[53]

Normality disintegrates in such a bizarre application. The relation of mother and infant is one of the strongest sites for the ideology of sincerity, nature, and depth, but its images scatter. 'It's so difficult to adjust to . . . one

gets so used to the idea of mother, like you know, on those TV commercials' (p. 33). The play misses no opportunity to get the language of patriarchy, family, and heterosexuality to entangle itself. When a girl friend tries to kiss him Gary retreats: 'It's wrong. I'm a mother . . . I can't go around kissing girls' (p. 37). The authorities want to get hold of the parent and child, and decide that their tactic should be to 'break up the family unit' (p. 35): they use the term 'family' even as they plot against Gary and Tom because they are not a family.

But also, as they struggle against hostile officials and stereotypes, the gay couple appropriate the genuine and human. A psychiatrist asks: 'and would you say that you are the active partner of this relationship?' Tom replies: 'Eh? No, not really. I mean, it comes and goes. Sometimes one thing, sometimes another' (p. 28). I recall people in the audience applauding at this repudiation—in public—of one of the heterosexual myths that aspire to organize gay sexuality. Gary and Tom are not sentimentalized—most of the time they are bickering because of the strain of the situation ('Doctor Spock says that parents often find it difficult to adjust' (p. 33)). John Russell Taylor found them 'an entirely believable married couple, living and growing together and apart. Few heterosexual plays have done this so well.'[54]

Of course, gay men were to repudiate the manoeuvre that 'tolerates' us so long as we appear to approximate to supposed heterosexual norms (though in 1968 this was a provocative claim). However, *Spitting Image* never allows the heterosexist values that it is appropriating to settle down. It both subverts the ideology of depth *and* claims it for gays. It would be difficult to say which is happening when Gary, disappointed at Tom's lesser commitment, makes an emotive speech about parenthood:

> You're all surface aren't you mate? All you think about is the kind of place we live in, your pay packet, the films, plays, dinner-parties we used to go to. That was all your whole bloody life. Haven't you ever stopped for one minute and thought that we've created a new human being, a tiny creature who looks for us for love, guidance and security, who trusts both of us absolutely?
>
> (p. 36)

It is an appeal to depth, embedded in a situation where it must be absurd. Spencer said he wanted to present both the reality of a love relationship and the responsibility of having a child, and a farcical attack on bureaucracy: 'The whole play's style had to change gear constantly.'[55]

The civil service and government assume that such offspring must be studied, hidden, and prevented:

> The confusion would be unimaginable, it would distort the whole legal system.. Think of the manpower lost in the professions and industries if these damned pansies

are always prancing off becoming mothers. . . . Homosexuals of all races, colours and creeds would suddenly be given the hope of creating offspring. And what is more likely than that the offspring themselves will have the same sexual abnormalities. The whole world would be overrun—ugh!

(pp. 33-4)

This homophobic utterance deconstructs itself by invoking the potential of what was soon to be called gay power. Indeed, it transpires, in the play, that many such children are being conceived. Daddy One responds by organizing a national movement (though Daddy Two is initially apathetic). The tactics are specifically reminiscent of the Suffragettes but also, in a stroke of inspiration, they anticipate the mass solidarity of Gay Liberation.

But don't you see? Before we were alone, utterly alone, a freakish development. Now we are stronger. . . . At first we're bound to be a deprived minority. The Government will be trying to hush the whole thing up. Well I'm not going to let it. . . .

(p. 40)

Spitting Image is organized around a biological impossibility—that is the repudiation of the conventional ideology of depth. But the ending is gloriously triumphant. Gary and Tom's offspring is not only unusually strong, intelligent and humane (he worries dreadfully about the Vietnam War), he is also able to infiltrate Downing Street at night and affect the Prime Minister's mind by auto-suggestion. As a result the law is changed, producing 'happy homosexuals' (p. 45). Daddy Two conceives. Nor is the effect limited to gays: Tom's mother is converted ('Well if the papers say it's all right, I suppose it is', p. 45), and the Prime Minister repudiates militarism. Gay Liberation correlates with peace and love generally; indeed, the genuine freeing of a major oppressed group, if it occurred, would perhaps amount to that.

Of course, the triumphant ending is even more of a fantasy than the rest—'Funny how people's attitudes have changed' (p. 45). But fantasies are important: they mark the boundaries of the plausible, and may help us to see that plausibility is a powerful social construction—dominated, of course, by patriarchy, heterosexuality, and the family. Nancy K. Miller has noted the way women writers are frequently accused of falling prey to implausibilities in their fiction. They are said to manifest sensibility, sensitivity, extravagance—'code words for feminine in our culture'—at the expense of verisimilitude. But such 'improbable' plots may be read as comments on the prevailing stories of women's lives—they manifest 'the extravagant wish for a *story* that would turn out differently'.[56] That is, the wish of women for power over their lives cannot be expressed plausibly within dominant discourses, only as fantasy. The im-

probability in *Spitting Image* is utopian, but it also alludes to that fact, and to the scale of social change that would have to occur for gays to become acceptably empowered.

Colin Spencer's play has continuing resonances for gay culture. The obvious analogue for its main situation now is the oppression of lesbian mothers, whose children are taken from them in the way that is attempted in *Spitting Image*. And the government decision to place the gay parents compulsorily in an 'enclosed colony', telling them they have 'a rare disease' (p. 39), is all too like modes of control that have been proposed for people with AIDS.

Gay men have found support in the notion that homosexuals have been creators of Art (well, it's got to be better than disc jockeys and royalty). To be sure, we can and should uncover the underlying gay significance in such work. But that very act tends to reinforce a notion that gay creativity must be covert. Decoding the work of closeted homosexual artists ought to produce a recognition of oppression, rather than a cause for celebration. Theatre has long been a site of homosexual culture, but it had always to be glimpsed through ostensibly heterosexual texts and institutions. *Spitting Image* represents a new break, because although in a public mode and a public venue, it is written not for the Aunt Ednas, but for gays. It appropriates theatre for an explicit gay culture, anticipating the Gay Sweatshop company. Other audiences are invited, but they will have the perhaps disconcerting experience—which gays have all the time—of sitting in on someone else's culture. *Spitting Image* signals the possibility of a non-closeted gay subculture.

It is through involvement in a subculture that one discovers an identity in relation to others and perhaps a basis for political commitment. A subculture creates a distinctive circle of reality, partly alternative to the dominant. There you can feel that Black is beautiful, gay is good. Such a sense of shared identity and purpose is necessary for self-preservation. However, subcultures may also return to trouble the dominant. They are formed partly by and partly in reaction to it—they redeploy its cherished values, downgrading, inverting or reapplying them, and thereby demonstrate their incoherence. Their outlaw status may exert a fascination for the dominant, focusing fantasies of freedom, vitality, even squalor. So they form points from which its repressions may become apparent, its silences audible.

Notes

1. Oscar Wilde, *The Picture of Dorian Gray* (Harmondsworth: Penguin Books, 1949), p. 10.

2. Joe Orton, *The Orton Diaries,* ed. John Lahr (London: Methuen, 1986), p. 219.

3. In 1962 Orton and Halliwell were sent to prison for stealing and damaging library books: they made cover pictures bizarre and typed in false blurbs. See John Lahr, *Prick Up Your Ears* (Harmondsworth: Penguin Books, 1980), pp. 93-105; Simon Shepherd, *Because We're Queers* (London: GMP, 1989), pp. 13-14.

4. See Alan Sinfield, 'Theatre and politics', in Malcolm Kelsall, Martin Coyle, Peter Garside and John Peck (eds), *Literature and Criticism* (London: Routledge, forthcoming); Alan Sinfield, 'Closet dramas: homosexual representation in postwar British theatre', forthcoming.

5. On the cross-class liaison, see Jeffrey Weeks, 'Discourse, desire and sexual deviance: some problems in a history of homosexuality', in Kenneth Plummer (ed.), *The Making of the Modern Homosexual* (London: Hutchinson, 1981), pp. 76-111, p. 105; Jeffrey Weeks, *Sex, Politics and Society* (London and New York: Longman, 1981), pp. 108-17; Alan Sinfield, *Literature, Politics and Culture in Postwar Britain* (Oxford: Basil Blackwell, 1989; Berkeley: California University Press, 1989), ch. 5; Sinfield, 'Closet dramas'; Sinfield, 'Private lives/public theatres: Noël Coward and the politics of homosexual representation', forthcoming.

6. J. R. Ackerley, *My Father and Myself* (London: Bodley Head, 1968), p. 120; Peter Wildeblood, *Against the Law* (London: Weidenfeld, 1955), p. 55. On the marginal, scarcely audible status of homosexuality, see Eve Kosofsky Sedgwick, 'Epistemology of the closet (I)', *Raritan*, 7 (1988), pp. 39-69; Jonathan Dollimore, 'Homophobia and sexual difference', in *Sexual Difference*, ed. Robert Young (special issue of *Oxford Literary Review*, 8, nos. 1-2; 1986), pp. 5-12; Jonathan Dollimore, 'The dominant and the deviant: a violent dialectic', *Critical Quarterly*, 28, nos. 1-2 (1986), pp. 179-92.

7. Sigmund Freud, *The Interpretation of Dreams*, trans. James Strachey (New York: Avon Books, 1970), p. 545.

8. Martin Esslin, *The Peopled Wound* (London: Methuen, 1970), p. 129. John Marshall shows the persistence into the 1960s of the distinction between inverts (effeminate, anomalies in nature) and perverts (wilfully debauched); see Marshall, 'Pansies, perverts and macho men: changing conceptions of male homosexuality', in Plummer, *The Making of the Modern Homosexual*, pp. 145-50.

9. James Broom Lynne, *The Trigon*, in John Russell Taylor (ed.), *New English Dramatists 8* (Harmondsworth: Penguin Books, 1965), p. 106.

The Creeper, by Pauline McCauley (1964), was another 'Pinteresque'/homosexual play: as in *The Servant*, for which Pinter wrote the screenplay, a leisure-class man employs a mysteriously menacing, lower-class companion (*The Creeper* also resembles *The Green Bay Tree* by Mordaunt Shairp, on which see Sinfield, 'Private lives/public theatres').

10. Lahr, *Prick Up Your Ears*, p. 178; for Sloane's awareness, see Joe Orton, *The Complete Plays* (London: Eyre Methuen, 1976), pp. 125, 135.

11. John D'Emilio, *Sexual Politics, Sexual Communities* (Chicago and London: University of Chicago Press, 1983), p. 52. On the situation in the US theatre see Kaier Curtin, *We Can Always Call Them Bulgarians* (Boston: Alyson Publications, 1987).

12. H. Montgomery Hyde, *The Other Love* (1970); (London: Mayflower, 1972), p. 238; Gordon Westwood, *A Minority* (London: Longman, 1960), p. 93, referring back to Westwood's *Society and the Homosexual* (London: Gollancz, 1952). See D. J. West, *Homosexuality*, revised edn (Harmondsworth: Penguin Books, 1960), pp. 11, 71; Jeffrey Weeks, *Coming Out: Homosexual Politics in Britain, from the Nineteenth Century to the Present* (London: Quartet, 1977), ch. 14. Plays that figured in this process included *The Green Bay Tree* by Mordaunt Shairp (1933, revived in London in 1950); *Third Person* by Andrew Rosenthal (1951); *The Immoralist* by Ruth and Augustus Goetz (1954); *South* by Julien Green (1954); *Serious Charge* by Philip King (1955); *The Prisoners of War* by J. R. Ackerley (1925, revived in 1955); *The Children's Hour* by Lillian Hellman (1934, produced in London in 1956); *The Lonesome Road* by Philip King and Robin Maugham (1957); *The Balcony* by Jean Genet (1957); *The Catalyst* by Ronald Duncan (1958); *Quaint Honour* by Roger Gellert (1958); *The Hostage* by Brendan Behan (1958), *Five Finger Exercise* by Peter Shaffer (1958). Some of these evaded censorship by being produced at the 'private' Arts theatre club (see Sinfield, 'Closet dramas').

13. Orton, *Diaries*, p. 127.

14. Peter Burton, *Parallel Lives* (London: GMP, 1985), p. 42 and pp. 38-42; Weeks, *Coming Out*, pp. 41-2.

15. Barry Took, *Laughter in the Air* (London: Robson Books, 1981), pp. 153 and 146-55.

16. Orton, *Diaries*, pp. 78-9. On decoding and Coward, see Sinfield, 'Private lives'.

17. Lahr, *Prick Up Your Ears*, pp. 250-1; see Orton, *Diaries*, p. 112.

18. Frank Parkin, *Middle Class Radicalism* (Manchester: Manchester University Press, 1968), p. 43. The figures were 94 per cent in social classes 1-2, 87 per cent in classes 3-4 and 75 per cent in classes 5-7. See Alan Sinfield, 'The theatre and its audiences', in Sinfield (ed.), *Society and Literature 1945-1970* (London: Methuen, 1983).

19. Lahr, *Prick Up Your Ears*, pp. 206-7; Shepherd, *Because We're Queers*, pp. 119-20.

20. Richard Ellmann, *Oscar Wilde* (London: Hamish Hamilton, 1987), p. 430.

21. See Shepherd, *Because We're Queers*, pp. 74-7, and his comments on the cult of The Boy, the fantasy answer to so many tensions of that time (pp. 60-4); this too was affronted by the character of Sloane. The US director had difficulty with Sloane's capricious murder of Kemp (Lahr, *Prick Up Your Ears*, p. 215).

22. Orton, *Complete Plays*, p. 200.

23. Lahr, *Prick Up Your Ears*, pp. 236-8, 255-6. Also it had been revealed shortly before that rhino whips were in use in a Sheffield police station. For another appreciation of the play from this point of view, see Albert Hunt, 'What Joe Orton saw', *New Society*, 17 April 1975, pp. 148-50.

24. Orton, *Complete Plays*, pp. 245-6; and see pp. 248, 255, 266, 271-5.

25. Orton, *Complete Plays*, p. 273; for the Lord Chamberlain's changes see Simon Trussler (ed.), *New English Dramatists 13* (Harmondsworth: Penguin Books, 1968), p. 84.

26. Trussler, introduction to *Loot*, in *New English Dramatists 13*, p. 11; Trussler, 'Farce', *Plays and Players* (June 1966), p. 72.

27. Orton, *Complete Plays*, p. 262.

28. Lahr, *Prick Up Your Ears*, p. 249; see also p. 227, and Orton, *Diaries*, pp. 75-6, 150.

29. Orton, *Diaries*, p. 91; Shepherd, *Because We're Queers*, p. 126.

30. Lahr, *Prick Up Your Ears*, p. 175.

31. Lahr, *Prick Up Your Ears*, pp. 247, 258.

32. This account is indebted to Simon Shepherd's *Because We're Queers*, especially pp. 26-8, 31, 56-8, 89, 97-8, 111. Shepherd calls the standard view of Orton as hampered and ruined by Halliwell 'The Revenge of the Closet Queens' (p. 26). I have benefited also from William A. Cohen, 'Joe Orton and the politics of subversion' (unpublished paper, University of California, Berkeley, 1989), and from the comments of Joseph Bristow, Peter Burton, William A. Cohen, Jonathan Dollimore, and Simon Shepherd.

33. Lahr, *Prick Up Your Ears*, p. 204. Rattigan put money into *Sloane*—he thought it was about a society diminished by watching television (Lahr, *Prick Up Your Ears*, p. 184). Like Rattigan, Orton was not straightforward about himself in interviews (Lahr, *Prick Up Your Ears*, p. 180; Shepherd, *Because We're Queers*, p. 86).

34. Orton, *Diaries*, pp. 249-50.

35. Orton, *Diaries*, p. 256. *Butler* was produced by Beaumont and Oscar Lewenstein at the Queen's Theatre in 1969.

36. Orton, *Diaries*, p. 256; Lahr, *Prick Up Your Ears*, pp. 330-3.

37. Hunt, 'What Joe Orton saw', p. 149.

38. Orton, *Complete Plays*, p. 368.

39. Hunt, 'What Joe Orton saw', p. 150.

40. Simon Trussler, 'Farce', *Plays and Players* (June 1966), pp. 58, 72. Orton also said: 'There's supposed to be a healthy shock, for instance, at those moments in *Loot* when an audience suddenly *stops* laughing. So if *Loot* is played as no more than farcical, it won't work' (p. 72). Orton seems to have abandoned this idea in *Butler.*

41. Shepherd, *Because We're Queers*, p. 96.

42. Orton, *Diaries*, pp. 256-7. Stanley Baxter is quoted there saying that the barracking started ten minutes after the start of the second act. I'm grateful here for a personal communication from Colin Spencer, author of *Spitting Image* (on which see below).

43. Dollimore, 'The dominant and the deviant', p. 189; and Dollimore, 'The challenge of sexuality', in Sinfield (ed.), *Society and Literature*, p. 78.

44. Jonathan Dollimore, 'Different desires: subjectivity and transgression in Wilde and Gide', *Textual Practice*, 1, 1 (1987), p. 59; see also Dollimore's *Sexuality, Transgression and Subcultures*, forthcoming.

45. Dollimore, 'The dominant and the deviant', p. 189; Orton, *Complete Plays*, p. 416.

46. Dollimore, 'The dominant and the deviant', pp. 180, 182; see also Dollimore, 'Homophobia and sexual difference', p. 8.

47. Weeks, *Coming Out*, chs. 14, 15.

48. So Shepherd, *Because We're Queers*, p. 111.

49. Sinfield, 'Private lives'.

50. Lahr, *Prick Up Your Ears*, pp. 248, pp. 187, 189.

51. Orton, *Complete Plays*, p. 244.

52. Michael Billington, *Times,* 25 October 1968, p. 8. *Spitting Image* was favourably reviewed there and by Philip French in the *New Statesman* and Hilary Spurling in the *Spectator.* But Milton Shulman's review in the *Evening Standard* was headed 'Ugh!'

53. Colin Spencer, *Spitting Image,* printed in *Plays and Players,* 16 (November, 1968), p. 28.

54. John Russell Taylor, review of *Spitting Image* in *Plays and Players,* 16 (November, 1968), p. 64.

55. Colin Spencer, interview with Peter Burton, *Transatlantic Review,* 35 (Spring 1970), p. 63. Spencer was moved partly by the attempt to gain access to his son, which was being opposed on the grounds of his homosexuality (personal communication).

56. Nancy K. Miller, 'Emphasis added: plots and plausibilities', in Elaine Showalter (ed.), *The New Feminist Criticism* (London: Virago, 1986), pp. 357, 352. See Sinfield, *Literature, Politics and Culture,* pp. 25, 225-6, 300-4.

Julian Duplain (review date 5 March 1993)

SOURCE: Duplain, Julian. Review of *Entertaining Mr. Sloane,* by Joe Orton. *Times Literary Supplement,* no. 4692 (5 March 1993): 18.

[*In the following review, Duplain points to the well-structured plot and comic timing of* Entertaining Mr. Sloane.]

"Three repulsive folk well acted": for once the tone of twee outrage about the state of British morals in the theatre was not being whipped up by Edna Welthorpe (Mrs.) or another of Joe Orton's epistolary aliases. Even as his stomach turned, a contemporary critic (for the *Daily Telegraph*) had acknowledged what a well-structured play **Entertaining Mr. Sloane** is. And it is the unwinding of a tight plot with mercenary logic that still gives an edge to the play (which was first performed in 1964), even if the comic shock of carnal scheming in suburbia has been dulled by almost three decades of television satire and social liberalization. Some lines, however, are so well written that, like Wildean aphorisms, they have taken on a life outside of their original context and it is a surprise to discover their source. When Kath longs for Sloane to be present at the birth of their baby, her brother Ed (Ian Gelder) observes, "It's enough for most children if the father is there at the conception". And a line like "You showed him the gates of hell every night—he abandoned all hope when he entered there", still gathers laughs for its urbane daring in mixing high art and smut.

Janet Dale's Kath is an outsize motherly schoolgirl, alternating between the wide-eyed stares of the highly impressionable and the pursed lips of the shocked worldly-wise who would prefer to know no more. Her front room, in Mark Bailey's design, is wallpapered with huge pink roses, the sloping flats hinting at the claustrophobic cosiness of it all. Mr. Sloane (Ben Daniels) is the orphan whom she plans to use to two ends: to replace the child she had adopted twenty years earlier, and as the lover forbidden her by Ed's "principles". As soon as Sloane has taken a room in her house, Kath moves in on him, positioning his hand on the small of her back for the first embrace, borrowing his finger as a pointer when the photograph album comes out. Well-groomed and keen to please, Sloane soon catches on and in the first act finale, on the sofa, opportunity gets the better of distaste. Soon he has discarded his jeans in favour of leather trousers (those fresh Levis were the one detail out of place in an otherwise excellent period production) and appears to have gained a good few inches of loutishness, strutting from radiogram to sofa and running the household. In Orton's world, everyone has a past and kicks out ruthlessly to get as near to the top of the heap as possible. Sloane's nemesis is Kemp (Christopher Hancock), Kath and Ed's gaga old "dada", who was witness to a nasty bit of business involving his daughter's new lodger. Kath takes a long time to realize she can corner people too, but when she does she quickly learns the benefits of pragmatism.

The director, Jeremy Sams, is best known for his musical work in the theatre, but here he has taken on a well-made play pure and simple. Ironically, the one purely musical interpolation is misjudged. A stuck record is used to imply that Kath feels a qualm about her time-share arrangement with Ed for the use of Mr. Sloane, whereas everything in the text shows she is perfectly happy playing a new, more devious game.

What Sams does do well is bring out the nastiness behind the niceties, as when Sloane thinks he has Ed's permission to rough up Kemp. Then, almost instantaneously, his anger is undercut by a brilliant burst of farce as Sloane loses his cool and goes for Kath, who juggles his suitcase across the sofa to Ed, thus preventing Sloane's departure and forcing him to face the music. Moments like that, and the demeaning comedy around Kath's dentures, prefigure Orton's later plays, **Loot** and **What The Butler Saw,** where the struggle between appearances and self-interest get completely out of control.

Ted Bain (review date May 1995)

SOURCE: Bain, Ted. Review of *Up against It,* by Joe Orton. *Theatre Journal* 47 (May 1995): 299-300.

[*In the following review of a 1994 Chicago production of* Up Against It, *Bain says that the former screenplay does not translate easily into the stage version.*]

His supposed depravity explicitly countered their good behavior, but for a few short months an odd collaboration was in the works. After Joe Orton wrote *Up Against It* in 1967 as a screenplay to showcase the Beatles, the script was returned with no explanation, though the inference might be that not all working-class artists have the same intentions in mind. Nonetheless, Chicago's Lookingglass Theatre has staged the text almost verbatim and punctuated it with original songs echoing early 1960s British rock. To an extent, the conflation of the Orton persona and that of the pop musician makes sense. Both feature the posturing of young men with a talent for expressing libidinal urgencies with a nonchalant air, an element for which the ensemble's principals find the right tone. The inverted dandyism of *Up Against It*'s trio of disaffected adventurers is ably demonstrated by Lance Baker, Douglas Hara, and Raymond Fox, whose poise serves both the wit of Orton's dialogue and the contrasting banality of the ensemble's original music and lyrics.

But ultimately the Lookingglass production founders under the live-performance weight of dozens of disconnected scenes initially conceived for film. Director Bruce Norris's well-devised commotion during each transition stresses the point that Orton was depicting social chaos, but ignores the elegant style in which the author was trying to frame his subject. Actors grab instruments and microphones from an on-stage bandstand and step back and forth between Orton's formal text and their own raucous concert acts. Descriptions of scene locations are posted on the back wall of a barren, all-purpose set. Gimmicks, such as hand-tossed paper sprinklings or manually operated cutout scenery, steal an occasional laugh. The apparent idea is to "announce" rather than enact stage directions; the result is crude theatrical artificiality.

Of course, heavy-handed artifice is consistent with Orton's vision, provided that the actors themselves grasp the superficiality of their characters' circumstances and perform indelicacy delicately. To this end, the Lookingglass actors have succeeded only partially. The young male characters display a graceful flippancy, a mark of awareness that there is nothing much at stake in the world. Devoid of beliefs, their oppositional stance is wholly performed, denoted in the manner in which they wear their affectations. Unfortunately, the other characters are played as cardboard figures, as though the uncertainties of their condition must also be meaningless. Male antagonists are reduced to the tired business of low comedians. Women are portrayed as dissembling, repulsive, or daft.

Indeed, the Lookingglass production typifies the kind of performance interpretation that has allowed Orton's plays to be popularly mistaken for the writings of a misogynist. It is understandable that the resiliency of welfare-state women in Orton's earlier plays is often misread as cloying stupidity. But I would argue that in the script of *Up Against It* gender privileges are reversed and male characters assume the more degraded position. The Lookingglass performers, however, tell a different story. Christine Dunford strongly enacts the sexual indulgences of a feral police chief who forces herself on her male captives, but also celebrates the advantages of corruption by disrobing during a vamp-striptease number that utterly contradicts her character. Heidi Stillman plays a heroine with no sentiment as though the character also has no brain. And Joy Gregory as an intrepid parlormaid, who pursues one husband and ends up with three, expresses desire with an incongruous tendency to swoon. As they appear in this production, women cannot affect trivial obsessions without actually becoming trivial, and the performance of learned female behavior amounts to little more than a bald sexist joke. Consequently, Orton's characters are denied their capacity as conscious imitators to satirize anything other than themselves.

Twenty-eight years ago, Ronald Bryden suggested in an *Observer* review the need to find an "Orton style," and it appears the need still exists. In its rousing demonstration of energy, polish, and exhibitionism, the Lookingglass ensemble shares only a sporadic and intuitive empathy with the text. One actor's program note even disclaims "The Message About Women in This Play." That very "message" was in fact invented in performance, and the blame wrongly ascribed to the author.

Susan Rusinko (essay date 1995)

SOURCE: Rusinko, Susan. "*What the Butler Saw.*" In *Joe Orton,* pp. 97-115. New York: Twayne Publishers, 1995.

[*In the following essay, Rusinko reviews previous critical opinion of* What the Butler Saw, *connecting the play with a theatrical tradition of farce and with the social unrest of the 1960s.*]

RANCE:

. . . I've published a monograph on the subject [madness]. I wrote it at the university. On the advice of my tutor. A remarkable man. Having failed to achieve madness himself he took to teaching it to others.

PRENTICE:

And were you his prize pupil?

RANCE:

There were some more able than I.

PRENTICE:

Where are they now?

RANCE:

In mental institutions.

PRENTICE:

Running them?

RANCE:

For the most part.

(Plays [Complete Plays], 386)

Had Orton lived to see the first production of *What the Butler Saw,* he might have celebrated a kind of madness in the ironies associated with the posthumous production. The play opened at the Queen's Theatre in the heart of the West End on 5 March 1969, with a cast of stars led by Sir Ralph Richardson in the role of an inspector of mental hospitals, Dr. Rance. Before his death, Orton, in a conversation with a producer, had spoken of the wonderful joke it would be to have his play produced in the "Theater of Perfection" as he dubbed the Haymarket Theatre—to him the home of the kind of middle-class entertainment enjoyed by his epistolary alias, Mrs. Edna Welthorpe. The play was indeed produced at a commercial theater. Further irony resides in the all-star cast, despite which the production failed and about which Orton had opined to the producer that, although he admired Richardson, he had doubts about his comic talent. The production proved Orton right.

In her review of the production, Hilary Spurling called attention to the discrepancy between two "implacably opposed" styles, the "old and new in violent combat"[1]—one designed never to give offence (the management of Tenants) and the other whose very existence depends on offending audience sensibilities. The clash of styles, Spurling continues, is most glaring in the performance of Richardson, who spoke his lines with "extraordinary chanting, as though the text had been delivered to him in the form of church responses" (Spurling, 344).

Another ironic touch is the abolition of the theater censorship law in 1968, prior to the production but after the death of Orton. A pattern of censoring had set in with earlier plays. During the successful production of *Loot* in 1965, Orton had particularly enjoyed talking about the censor's objection to heterosexual references while completely ignoring the "homosexual bits" (Bigsby, 48, 49). The Lord Chamberlain had also cut offensive language in *The Erpingham Camp* for its airing on television. With the passage of censorship abolition there was no official threat, but in its place came one imposed by Richardson, who insisted on the use of a cigar rather than a phallus in a big scene at the play's end.

The name of Richardson continues into yet another irony: a history of first production failures of Orton's plays. Without the financial aid provided by Rattigan,

Entertaining Mr. Sloane may not have made the transfer from the small Arts Theatre to a money-making larger West End theater. Like the first production of *Loot* (which failed in its provincial tour), *What the Butler Saw* (1969) failed because of misjudgments in both casting and directing. One lonely voice of approval was that of Frank Marcus, who commented that the farce "will live to be accepted as a comedy classic of English literature."[2] Not until 1975, when the Royal Court put on an Orton retrospective, and 1986, when the Manhattan Theater Club mounted a successful production, was Marcus's prophecy realized.

The play, agreed on generally by critics and scholars as Orton's best, is yet another parody, both in its subject matter and style. Having dealt with the hypocrisy of sexual taboos in *Entertaining Mr. Sloane,* the corruption of law enforcement in *Loot,* institutionalized entertainment in *The Erpingham Camp,* corporate paternalism in *The Good and Faithful Servant,* and religion in *Funeral Games,* Orton aimed his most devastating and hilarious wit at the new religion—psychiatry—in *What the Butler Saw.*

Literary genres are also a target of Orton's farce. Having parodied the comedy of manners in *Entertaining Mr. Sloane* and the mystery genre in *Loot,* he now turned to farce, particularly one of the oldest of farce premises—twins separated at birth who must eventually reunite with each other and their families. The single most necessary convention in this process is the disguise—one that Orton carries to dizzyingly confusing heights. The multiplicity of Orton's disguises results in the expected confusions of names and identities, teeter-totter plot complications caused by a fast-paced series of exits and entrances, the big scene, and the deus ex machina ending. The sheer multiplication of each of the plot conventions is unprecedented and gives Orton opportunity to demonstrate his subversive and witty anarchy as in no other of his farces.

In *Loot,* for example, disguises exist in the roles characters assume, such as Inspector Truscott's claim to be an inspector from the water board. Nurse Fay, as well, disguises her actions in the pieties of her Catholic religion. In both characters the disguises exist to personify institutional corruption. In *What the Butler Saw,* the disguises are physical—clothes—and they exist from the very start to propel manic actions. They propel not only Orton's satire on the corruption of authority figures but his wider inquiry into the philosophical nature of reality. The physical actions, thus, take the play far beyond the satirical thrusts of his earlier plays to metaphysical questions of identity and of man's attempts to hold in check forces of nature that call those attempts into question.

The action begins innocently enough in a mental institution in which the director, Dr. Prentice, with an irresistible proclivity for attractive secretaries, interviews an applicant, Geraldine Barclay. In answer to his questions, she can produce no father or mother, except for one important bit of biographical information: that her mother had been a chambermaid at the Station Hotel. Her stepmother, she further explains, died in an explosion in which a statue of Sir Winston Churchill was damaged, a part of which (a phallus-cum-cigar), became imbedded in her stepmother. A box that Geraldine carries contains that part and becomes the detail with which Orton in his conclusion draws together the loose ends of the play. Prentice's interview of Geraldine, whose sorry qualifications include her ability to take dictation at only 20 words a minute and her lack of mastery of the typewriter keyboard, then moves to its next stage, Prentice's request that she undergo a physical examination. Despite her request for the presence of another woman, he issues his first order to her: "Undress." It is an order that he will issue repeatedly, to Nicholas Beckett and Sergeant Match, as well as to Geraldine. In succession, he orders one pair of dressing and undressing in order to solve a problem created with the previous one.

Disguises, like the masks in Greek plays, become the order of the day, beginning with the unexpected appearance of Mrs. Prentice, from whom Prentice must hide Geraldine. His wife, nymphomaniacal in her search for sexual satisfaction, has just returned from a meeting of a lesbian club and from a night at the Station Hotel. She is followed by a hotel page, Nicholas Beckett (with whom she had spent the night), who brings with him incriminating photographs taken by the hotel manager. To Nick's comment that options on the photographs had been given to a prospective buyer, she responds with Ortonesque aplomb and wit: "When I gave myself to you the contract didn't include cinematic rights" (*Plays,* 370). Financially bereft, Nick intends to blackmail her with a request for money and for the position of secretary to Dr. Prentice, the position for which Geraldine is in the process of being interviewed. In approaching her husband about the hiring of Nick, Mrs. Prentice explains Nick's resorting to rape as the result of depression "by his failures in commerce." She then informs Geraldine that the position is no longer open.

Her intrusion on her husband's attempted affair with Geraldine forces him to begin a dazzling series of disguises and counter-disguises, the first of which involves his hiding the clothes of Geraldine, now nude behind a screen. He finds a convenient flower vase which becomes the focus of subsequent complications. In compliance with his wife's request that he hire Nick, he soon has Nick in shorts and Geraldine in Nick's uniform. Changes of dress increase at a frantic pace as one disguise only breeds the necessity for another. Even his wife, who arrives from her hotel escapade naked under her coat, must be accommodated, the only available

dress being Geraldine's. A box Nick carries contains Mrs. Prentice's costume—a wig and a leopard-spotted dress—her disguise during her visit to the Station Hotel and one that Sergeant Match will appropriately don at the conclusion of the play. Thus the clothes of Geraldine, Nick, Match, and Mrs. Prentice become the modus operandi of Orton's plot complications.

Orton parodies another of farce's oldest conventions—the doubling of a character, situation, or object. Orton uses the box Geraldine brings with her, with its contents of the missing part of Sir Winston Churchill's statue, as a plot device to begin and end the play, and he uses Nick's box, containing Mrs. Prentice's attire, as a complicating factor in that plot device. Orton begins his complications with the contents of Nick's box and concludes with that in Geraldine's. It is not enough to have one sexually mad psychiatrist, Prentice; there must be the greedy and theory-obsessed practitioner, Rance, who detects in every action a confirmation of one of his theories. There is a set of twins and not two but three detectivelike interrogators—Prentice, Rance, and the police officer, Match.

Unexpected entrances and exits, another necessary farce convention, continually create new problems for Prentice, until at one point Mrs. Prentice utters, "Doctor, doctor! The world is full of naked men running in all directions" (*Plays,* 437). When Geraldine appears in a new disguise and Nick suggests restoring normality by one more change of clothes, Prentice replies that he would have to account for the secretary and page boy (the false identities of the two young people). Reminded by Geraldine that the disguises are only disguises and that, therefore, the newly created identities do not exist, Prentice offers one of Orton's many entertaining contortions of logic: "When people who don't exist disappear the account of their departure must be convincing" (*Plays,* 419). The real madness of Prentice's circular logic, expressed in self-defense, carries its own practical function for him, even as it plays havoc with the various identities that keep changing despite his attempts to stabilize them. The changing relationship of fantasy to reality becomes a precarious balancing act as manic actions and psychiatric insanity keep pace with each other, one illusion replacing another with eye-dazzling speed.

Without any evidence except his own dogmatic beliefs, the theory-spouting Rance imposes his double-incest interpretation on the events, only, in a freakish turnabout, to have his fantasy subsequently proved to be a reality. Thus the appropriateness of the epigraph to the play—a quotation from Cyril Tourneur's *The Revenger's Tragedy*: "Surely we're all mad people, and they / Whom we think are, are not."

In a perceptive essay Katharine Worth writes of Orton's view of life as a dream turned into a nightmare, where "ideas keep turning into their opposites on his stage. It's always the clergyman who is the lecherous killer, the policeman—who starts off seeming a solid Dr. Watson figure . . . who turns out to be the most adept in corruption" (Worth, 76). In this black farce two psychologists rival each other in madness—one sexually and the other professionally—in much the same manner as the two clerics in **Funeral Games** vie for the title of chief corruptor. With psychiatry replacing religion as a source of hypocrisy in the twentieth century, Dr. Rance, inspector of mental institutions, is the maddest of all. Prentice, like the earlier McCorquodale, merely attempts to survive his initial disaster—attempts that force him to tell lies that necessitate disguises.

To Geraldine's questioning of the necessity of a physical examination for a secretarial applicant, Prentice replies that he needs to see the effect of her stepmother's death on her legs. He then reports the "febrile condition of her calves" as justification for the examination and gains her sympathy by a description of his wife's nymphomania and the resulting malice he has had to endure. She offers to cheer him up, and he, in turn, promises that she can test his new contraceptive device. To all of which she replies that she would be "delighted to help you in any way I can, doctor" (**Plays,** 368). Her off-setting innocent acquiescence is Orton's comic means of devictimizing her, thus detaching the audience emotionally, an Ortonesque hallmark rendered so effectively in the famous thrashing of Hal by Truscott in **Loot.**

This balancing act permeates the farce, with Orton's epigrammatic genius reaching such heights as in Mrs. Prentice's use of cultural clichés to justify her otherwise socially unjustifiable behavior. Like her husband who later fends off an accusation with the plea that he is a married man, Mrs. Prentice, upset at the photographs taken by the hotel manager, pleads with him, "Oh, this is scandalous. I am a married woman" (**Plays,** 370). When she notices her husband's attempt to hide Geraldine's dress, she accuses him of transvestism, in one of Orton's lethally witty attacks on contemporary mores: "I'd no idea our marriage teetered on the edge of fashion." To which, with an equally devastating freshening-up of a cliché—in this case a biblical one—Prentice responds, "Our marriage is like the peace of God—it passeth all understanding" (**Plays,** 373). Orton's epigrammatic wit is at its best in this exposure of the disjunction between language and behavior.

In yet another balancing act of style and substance, Orton pits a technical staple of farce—doors—against psychiatric insanity. Doors are especially prominent in popular Feydeau farces that Orton attended in London. He uses the farce convention here to parody itself, and, as well, to satirize psychiatric madness. When Dr. Rance, as inspector of mental institutions, appears, he is immediately suspicious of the many doors in the consulting office: "Was this house designed by a lunatic?" Pouring another whiskey, Prentice replies, "Yes, we have him here as a patient from time to time" (**Plays,** 377).

Questioning further the architectural features, Rance asks if the skylight is functional, and Prentice replies, "No. It's perfectly useless for anything—except to let light in" (**Plays,** 377). The nature of Rance's investigative techniques is apparent from the start. Every detail he observes must have some significance other than the obviously pragmatic one. Each significance then only leads to another, with one becoming more ludicrous than its predecessor.

The architectural details are soon lost in the flurry of Rance's next observation—this one more susceptible to psychiatric significance: the nude Geraldine, who Prentice, to cover up his intended indiscretion, claims is a patient. On the basis of Prentice's fabrication of her background, Rance decides immediately that she must be certified. She is the first victim in a series of Rance's instant certifications or attempted certifications. His psychiatric diagnoses of those he meets run a parallel line with the physical disguises Prentice finds himself forced to impose on others. Thus, Geraldine, Nick, and Match are doubly victimized—their identity confusions resolved only in the final disclosure scenes.

In another farcical doubling, Geraldine, having already been subjected to questioning by Prentice, undergoes interrogation by Rance. Passionately imposing his theories on her answers to his questions, he proclaims her denial of rape by her father as an automatic "yes," for that is only "elementary feminine psychology." He claims her as a textbook case: "A man beyond innocence, a girl aching for experience. He finds it difficult to reconcile his guilty secret with his spiritual convictions. . . . She seeks advice from her priest. The Church, true to her ancient traditions, counsels chastity. The result—Madness" (**Plays,** 383).

Rance has now set in motion what turns out to be a landslide of psychological clichés, turning every word he hears and every action he witnesses into a case study of his theories. When Rance exits, Prentice turns his attention to Nick in the hope of acquiring clothes for Geraldine, and the merry-go-round of costume changes commences in earnest. Ordering Nick to take off his uniform, however, only fuels his wife's accusations of transvestism. Naturalism serves Orton's parodic style, as the consulting-room screen of the doctor doubles as the requisite screen behind which disguises are shed and acquired in the standard farce.

The frenzy of complications begun with the unexpected arrivals—first of Mrs. Prentice, Nick, and then Rance—is quadrupled by that of Sergeant Match, who is there to inquire about Nick and about the missing parts of Sir Winston Churchill's statue. As the object of a possible lawsuit by the Council, with the support of the Conservative and Unionist Party, those parts are the subject of his interrogation of Nick, dressed as Geraldine. In parodic investigative jargon, he asks "her" to "produce or cause to be produced" the missing part. Not missing a beat, Orton blends the formality of investigative language with sexual innuendos in Match's reply:

NICK:

What do they look like?

MATCH:

You're claiming ignorance of the shape and structure of the objects sought?

NICK:

I'm in the dark.

MATCH:

You handled them only at night? We shall draw our own conclusions.

NICK:

I'm not the kind of girl to be mixed-up in that kind of thing. I'm an ex-member of the Brownies.

(*Plays,* 405)

Ordering yet another of the many medical examinations in the farce, he appoints Mrs. Prentice to examine her (him), since "only women are permitted to examine female suspects" (*Plays,* 406). Then, as Geraldine enters, dressed as Nick, the first act ends with Match's command: "I want a word with you, my lad" (*Plays,* 407). Geraldine is now Nick, and Nick is Geraldine. Confusions multiply furiously from this point on, until even the keenest in an Orton audience finds himself, at moments, questioning who is who.

The second act begins with Match shaking his head as Geraldine, dressed as Nick, attempts to correct his confusion with a true account of things. Like Hal in *Loot,* "he" is straightforward, but Match is only baffled by the truth. To Prentice he asserts, "This is a boy, sir. Not a Girl. If you're baffled by the difference it might be as well to approach both with caution." Prentice claims that the charge by Geraldine-dressed-as-Nick about Prentice's strange behavior is ridiculous. Claiming "I'm a married man," he leads Match into one of Orton's most choice epigrams: "Marriage excuses no one the freaks' roll-call" (*Plays,* 409). Like the Prentices earlier, Match freely offers his sentiments on marriage as a justification for his theories. "Nick's" truthful confession of her real sex, however, does not convince Match and only builds his suspicion of Prentice as pervert and madman. Match then orders yet a third examination of Geraldine.

Match follows one witty dictum with another when Prentice, faced with the likelihood of being charged with homosexuality, claims he is a heterosexual. Match responds, "I wish you wouldn't use these Chaucerian words. It's most confusing" (*Plays,* 411).

Orton's real madman in the play, however, is Rance, who turns his psychiatric gaze on Prentice and challenges him to prove the charge of molesting Match by committing the act. To vindicate himself, Prentice orders Match to undress, and Match finds himself being examined, taking medication, and eventually donning Mrs. Prentice's leopard-spotted dress.

Rance reaches psychiatric apotheosis in his conclusions about the events he has witnessed. Having proved, Holmesian style, that Prentice has done away with his secretary, Rance now anticipates literary success as a best-seller writer of melodrama:

Lunatics are melodramatic. The subtleties of drama are wasted on them. The ugly shadow of anti-Christ stalks this house. Having discovered her Father/Lover in Dr. Prentice the patient replaces him in a psychological reshuffle by that archetypal figure—the devil himself. Everything is now clear. The final chapters of my book are knitting together: incest, buggery, outrageous women and strange love—cults craving for depraved appetites. All the fashionable bric-a-brac. A beautiful but neurotic girl has influenced the doctor to sacrifice a white virgin to propitiate the dark gods of unreason.

(*Plays,* 427)

Carried away by his fantasy, Rance interrupts himself to inject an actual line of purple prose from his proposed novel: "When they broke into the evil-smelling den they found her poor body bleeding beneath the obscene and half-erect phallus" (*Plays,* 427). He concludes his monologue with a self-serving commentary on the great social rewards of his investigation:

My unbiased account of the infamous sex-killer Prentice will undoubtedly add a great deal to our understanding of such creatures. Society must be made aware of the growing menace of pornography. The whole treacherous avant-garde movement will be exposed for what it is—an instrument for inciting decent citizens to commit bizarre crimes against humanity and the state. . . . You have under your roof, my dear, one of the most remarkable lunatics of all time. We must institute a search for the corpse.

(*Plays,* 427-28)

Rance's quackery is total as he pronounces Prentice "a transvestite, fetishist, bi-sexual murderer . . . [who] displays considerable deviational overlap. We may get necrophilia too. As a sort of bonus" (*Plays,* 428).

Addressing his diagnosis to Mrs. Prentice, Rance links Prentice's "insanity with primitive religion and asks Prentice why he has turned his back on religion. Prentice declares himself a rationalist, incurring Rance's comment that he "can't be a rationalist in an irrational world. It isn't rational" (**Plays,** 428). Orton's playing around with verbal contradictions takes yet another turn in his use of the term "abnormal normality":

RANCE:

> (*to Mrs. Prentice*) His belief in normality is quite abnormal. (*to Dr. Prentice*) Was the girl killed before or after you took her clothes off?

PRENTICE:

> He wasn't a girl. He was a man.

MRS. P:

> He was wearing a dress.

PRENTICE:

> He was a man for all that.

(**Plays,** 428, 429)

Abnormality as normality or irrationality as rationality illustrate Orton's by now legendary reinvention of axiomatic usage. He spares no authority, even, as in the last quoted line, famous literary allusions that have entered common usage.

Contradictory actions match contradictory linguisms. At a point in the play where any distinctions between fantasy and reality have vanished, Nick finds himself in Sergeant Match's uniform and interrupts Rance's allegations against Prentice to announce that he has just arrested his own brother, Nicholas Beckett (himself). Like Geraldine's earlier attempts at truthfulness, his comments are pounced upon by Rance as fuel for his psychiatric theories.

A mad scene follows in which Mrs. Prentice attempts to force her husband at gunpoint to have sex with her, and, failing to do so, shoots at him. Confusion breaks loose as bodies pile up on the floor, concluding in the mutual threats by Rance and Prentice to certify each other. The madness seems total. Even the blood flowing from the injuries incurred by Nick and Match in the melee is not real to Rance, whose obsession with theorizing only hardens as events feed it. For Nick and Match, the personal consequence is bloody, and for all, the social consequence is the eventual return to the normal order of things, agreed on in the conspiracy among Prentice, Rance, and Match to keep the events out of the papers.

Orton relies on another centuries-old farce convention to unravel the secrets and restore legitimate identities: the use of a trivial object, in this case a brooch. French farceurs, as with Sardou in *A Glass of Water,* regularly used such artifices by which to move the plot or to re-

solve the confusions in their plays. Shakespeare for his purpose used the handkerchief in *Othello,* and Wilde the handbag in *The Importance of Being Earnest.* Orton's brooch had been broken in two by Mrs. Prentice, each half pinned to a twin. Geraldine and Nick are revealed to be those long-lost twins born to Dr. and Mrs. Prentice as the consequence of their premarital liaison in a cupboard at the Station Hotel. They produce their halves of the brooch given them by their mother when she had to give them up.

Rance is ecstatic as he triumphantly announces a double incest that "is even more likely to produce a best-seller than murder—and this is as it should be for love *must* bring greater joy than violence" (**Plays,** 446). Double incest—Prentice's attempted rape of his daughter and Mrs. Prentice's alleged assault by her son—is beyond even Rance's wildest hopes as a psychiatrist and as a novelist.

Orton has broken boundaries in daring to take his "happy ending" beyond that of the conventional farce. He pronounces no judgment on the violators in the double-incest situation. Indeed, the major villain, Rance, who already profits from imposing his theories on others, will only increase his profits with his lucrative novel. As in the ending of **Loot**—Truscott's conspiracy to share the loot with Hal, Dennis, and Fay—Rance, Prentice, and Match compliment each other on "uncovering a number of remarkable pecadilloes" and promise to "cooperate in keeping them out of the papers" (**Plays,** 448).

Orton's parody of the happy ending is accomplished by not one but several big scenes involving the clearing up of the disguises with the brooch-engendered revelations of the twins' identities and with a second object—the missing part of the Churchill statue. With the latter, the farce returns to its first-act mystery—the contents of Geraldine's box which held the evidence of Geraldine's stepparentage. In his use of both brooch and phallus, Orton doubles Wilde's use of one object, the famous handbag. Match's earlier request that "someone produce or cause to be produced the missing parts of Sir Winston Churchill" (**Plays,** 447) is answered by Geraldine's producing the box with which she had initially arrived for her interview. From this box Match triumphantly lifts "a section from a larger than life-sized bronze statue" (**Plays,** 447). Present at the blowing up of Churchill's statue, the only mother Geraldine had ever known had left her stepdaughter a legacy. Geraldine's assumption that the box she was given at Mrs. Barclay's funeral contained only her mother's clothes is dispelled, and she is proclaimed by Match as "the only living descendant of a woman violated by the hero of 1940" (**Plays,** 447). Orton's devilish trick is the coinciding of Geraldine's personal heritage with that of the nation. Orton's final attack on audience sensibilities occurs in Rance's declaration that blends Churchillian cigar and Ortonian phallus: "How much more inspiring if, in those dark days [World War II] we'd seen what we see now. Instead we had to be content with a cigar—the symbol falling far short, as we all realize, of the object itself" (**Plays,** 447).

Personal, national, and historical occurrences undergo a ritual sanctification in the pagan-Christian scene with which the play closes. Herculean in his leopard-spotted dress, the missing Sergeant Match appears through a skylight in "a great blaze of glory" (**Plays,** 446). The final words, however, are Rance's as all, clothed in their tattered "fig leaves," leave their Edenic frolics and follow Match up the ladder to face the world.

Orton's laughter at the corrupted order of things is complete in its purity, untouched by distracting personal revenge or sympathy with characters (however unintended) as with Wilson in **The Ruffian on the Stair,** Buchanan in **The Good and Faithful Servant,** or McLeavy in **Loot.** A dead mother's eye and false teeth (**Entertaining Mr. Sloane**) and a severed hand (**Funeral Games**) are not present to cause audience unease. The farcical mode is intact throughout. With the distance of time, even the phallus, essential to Orton's antic mode, does not induce the audience unease that accompanies the eye and teeth of earlier plays.

One minor caveat to this total detachment is the bowdlerized ending of the play, when Geraldine looks into the box and sees a cigar rather than a phallus. Even here, however, that ending is canceled by Rance's reference to her identification as an illusion of youth. Aside from the alternate ending—and one that a number of scholars see as an opening of the meaning to various approaches—the play remains uncompromised in its detachment—a feat noticeably taking shape in **The Erpingham Camp** and **Funeral Games** and perfected in **What the Butler Saw.**

Kenneth Williams, an actor in **Loot,** recalls Orton's frequent quoting of "Wilde's dictum: 'Talent is the infinite capacity for taking pains.' He took pains. Polish. Reconstruct. Give you another edition. Another page. Every word polished painstakingly until the whole structure *glitters*" (quoted in Lahr 1978, 202-203). **What the Butler Saw** is Orton's glittering structure line upon line, right up to the very last one by Rance, who parodies Adam's departure from the Garden of Eden with "Let us put on our clothes and face the world" (**Plays,** 448). It is this brilliance of detachment toward which Orton had worked since his prison days.

Wilde's influence is seen in the big revelatory scene as Orton parades characters and actions from *The Importance of Being Earnest.* He transforms Wilde's Canon Chasuble into Dr. Prentice, Miss Prism into Mrs. Prentice, Algernon and Jack into Nick and Geraldine, and the identifying handbag into a similarly functioning brooch. There is even a quick allusion to Wilde's handbag in one of Prentice's many angry retorts to his wife: "Unless you're very careful you'll find yourself in a suitcase awaiting collection" (**Plays,** 393). Orton goes far beyond Wilde, however, in his addition of the character of Rance, whose theories are now to be transformed into a money-making potboiler.

The real success of **What the Butler Saw,** however, lies in Orton's transformation of the characters and situations from earlier plays into a stylistic balancing act heretofore not realized. There are the innocents and the authority figures, both of whom Orton mocks. One character type that continues in **What the Butler Saw** is the pair of innocents who, although victims of others, manage to devictimize themselves mostly by their truth-telling. Their lineage goes back to the two brothers in **The Ruffian on the Stair,** to Hal and Dennis in **Loot,** and the twins in **The Good and Faithful Servant.** Like Hal, Nick and Geraldine attempt to tell the truth whenever an opportunity presents itself, but no one will believe them. They can do little except become caught up in the whirl of events. To the Kath-like Mrs. Prentice, Orton adds a farcical touch of dysfunctional sexuality to the nymphomania both exhibit. There are the two authorities—psychiatrists who are the new religion, Milton's new presbyters as old priests writ large. They resemble the two competitive clerics in **Funeral Games** in their hostility to each other. There is, finally, the Truscott-like Sergeant Match, whose sleuthing here serves as a compounding of the psychiatric sleuthing of Rance. Both proceed with Holmesian deductive methods to put the final touches to the solution of Orton's mysteries.

Any vestiges of Pinteresque intruders are transformed into farcical types that go beyond the satirical stereotypes of earlier plays. Rance and Match carry out their duties in a sublimely unshakable conviction of sexual and professional fantasies, totally oblivious to the realities in which the others are maneuvering their ways in and out of mistaken identities. All are victims of a sort, except for Rance, who remains at the end as he was in the beginning—untouched by events.

Unlike Orton's other plays, **What the Butler Saw** contains no murders or deaths, no personal revenge. The emphasis on revenge is transformed into one on madness. The catalyst for the transformation is the sexual energy that drives Prentice and the passion that drives the theories of Rance. The phallic instinct embraces a wide variety of sexual experiences—for instance, heterosexuality, homosexuality, transvestism, rape, incest.

Orton seems to have exorcised family figures and relationships in his earlier work, so that they do not exist as important sources for the characters anymore. His father and mother—haunting the characters of Kath and Kemp in *Entertaining Mr. Sloane,* Buchanan in *The Good and Faithful Servant,* and McLeavy in *Loot*—have vanished. Although, like Elsie and John Orton, the Prentices live separate lives, Mrs. Prentice's active engagement in sexual liaisons at the Station Hotel go far beyond the attempts of Mrs. Orton merely to make herself physically attractive. Furthermore, Mrs. Prentice's actions serve more as a farcical doubling to move the plot than as a characterization technique. Sex itself is treated only partly in the manner of a traditional farce—like a Feydeau character's bumbling to disguise the *idea* of indiscretion rather than the literal action. There is one exception—Mrs. Prentice, whose sexual escapade with Nick is not only real but also, as asserted in a comment by Rance, natural. Another autobiographical detail prominent in earlier plays—the garden and floral imagery associated with William Orton—functions only as a minor mover of the plot rather than as developer of character. Prentice tries desperately to hide incriminating evidence in a vase from which roses have to be moved repeatedly to hide a new indiscretion.

Most important, Orton has finally exorcised the personal need to offend audience sensibilities, having already done so explicitly in actions such as Ed's and Kath's sharing of Sloane or of Hal's disturbing violations of his mother's body. With all elements of his farce—real and unreal—existing in proportion to each other, his outrage still energizes the actions, but it does so in hilarious complications that grow dizzyingly from one man's—Prentice's—phallic instinct. Mechanically, the plot begins and ends with a phallus carried on stage in Geraldine's box. A symbol as old as Aristophanes' *Lysistrata,* the phallus is nature's force against destructive authority—Aristophanes' target being the insanity of war.

Orton's earlier attacks on religion, law, politics, and corporate parentalism come together in his final battle with authority. His lifelong war began in *Head to Toe,* with the character of Gombold, who learns to use words to rage correctly. Although Rance, unlike the giant, lives, his creator's verbal weaponry has hit its mark with unprecedented farcical accuracy.

Orton's attacks on Rance expose fashionably glib theories that, in the context in which they are expressed, are as mad as Rance's obsession to impose them automatically on the events he witnesses. His observations drawn from the seemingly endless changes of dress prompt him to conclude that Prentice is a pervert, "a man who mauls young boys, importunes policemen and lives on terms of intimacy with a woman who shaves twice a day" (*Plays,* 417). When Prentice informs his wife that he has given his secretary the sack, she concludes that he has killed Geraldine and put her body into a sack. Her comments lead Rance, in a series of logical leaps,

to link Prentice to primitive religions. Prentice's response to Rance's further accusations of atheism is that he is a rationalist, eliciting from Rance one of the play's most often repeated lines: "You can't be a rationalist in an irrational world. It isn't rational" (*Plays,* 428).

As Orton's spokesman for contemporary theories, Rance in his madness is endowed with financial preoccupations. He concludes with a reference to his "documentary type 'novelette'" that should reap "twelve record-breaking reprints. I'll be able to leave the service of the Commissioners and bask in the attentions of those who, like myself, find other people's iniquity puts money in their purse" (*Plays,* 424-25).

In contrast, the behavior of Prentice, at first more farcically human than psychiatrically insane, is rapidly energized into a madness of its own, swept on by the passionate intensity with which Rance leaps from personal and societal levels to anthropological significance. Rance refers at one point to "the startling ideas of Dr. Goebbels on the function of the male sexual organ" from which "we pass quite logically to white golliwogs. An attempt, in fact, to change the order of creation—homosexuality slots in here—dabbling in the black arts! The reported theft of the private parts of a well-known public figure ties in with this theory. We've phallic worship under our noses or I'm a Dutchman" (*Plays,* 424). With one brilliant structural ploy, Orton links Rance's insanity with a detail with which the play opens—the contents of the box with which Geraldine enters Prentice's office. It is this detail with which Orton resolves the complications created by Prentice and Rance.

The circularity of Orton's farcical plot remains intact and the object of his satire—psychiatric insanity—remains firmly in place to the end. Katharine Worth writes of a correspondence between the madness in Orton's play and the earnestness in Wilde's *The Importance of Being Earnest.* Both are the "root vice of the play; all the other ills are seen branching out from it" (Worth, 81). She also points out an adverse truth that she regards as the central joke of Orton's plot: that the "invented identities turn out to be after all, the true ones" (Worth, 81). As a result of the disguises foisted on them, Nick and Geraldine do turn out to be in reality closer to their invented selves than they or anyone else had imagined—all of this the result of Prentice's indiscretion, the "original sin" of the play. They experience the sexual decompartmentalization of which Orton has often spoken, as realities within fantasies and truths within lies abound in the play. The punch and counterpunch of sanity and insanity momentarily liberate even as they create the wild plot complications and eventually establish family relationships.

Worth views the farce, despite its many similarities to Wilde, to the Aldwych tradition, or to the standard French farce, as a bacchanalian dream to which an end is put by the deus ex machina but also a dream that gives both "a great id-releasing experience and a reassuring demonstration of the power of wit to control it" (Worth, 84). The darkness consists in the fantasies that underlie life, and it is the balance between these fantasies and life that results in health. Like Alice's bottle instructions—"Drink Me"—farce as antidote threatens as possible poison but ultimately frees. Worth uses as a case in point Geraldine Barclay, who never grasps Prentice's overtures as seduction attempts. Her failure to do so results in her breaking up "into a number of different selves" (Worth, 80). Transformation after transformation occurs as the secretary is hunted by Mrs. Prentice, Rance, and Match. The released spirits of secretary and hotel page, created by their changes of clothes, float freely as shapes for the "real characters to go in and out of." Their real identities as illegitimate children are the result of the freeing of the id. Orton said that his aim in *What the Butler Saw* (as in *Loot*) was to "break down all the sexual compartments people have" (quoted in Gordon, 91).

Maurice Charney has cataloged the compartments in the farce as "all possible varieties of sexual behaviour, buggery, necrophilia, exhibitionism, hermaphroditism, rape, sadomasochism, fetishism, transvestism, nymphomania and the triumphant mock-Wildean recognition scene, in which sexual fulfillment awaits the 'bleeding, drugged and drunk' characters'" (Charney, 101-102). He might have added to his list Orton's favorite id-releasor—one he proudly records in his *Diaries* and was, he claims, borrowed from *Entertaining Mr. Sloane* by Pinter in *The Homecoming*—the sharing of sexual partners.

Both Worth and Charney call attention to the parodic title of Orton's last play. Unfettered by the presence of the requisite butler, the play is about what the butler may have seen had Orton, indeed, included such a character. Worth notes that not one of the characters sees a given situation as does another, so that all free-float in their respective ways, each unrestricted by views of another. The experiences of the missing butler and the play's characters can be extended to individual members of any given audience who may experience similar liberation.

Charney brings a historical perspective to his views of Orton's farce with references to sources and analogues that begin with the play from which Orton has lifted the epigraph—Tourneur's *The Revenger's Tragedy,* one of the "most extravagant of seventeenth-century black comedies . . . a play much influenced by Shakespeare's *Hamlet*" (Charney, 98). He attributes the turning of the play, as in *Hamlet,* on the matter of the missing father, with the resulting connection with incest and other odd matters of sexual satisfaction. Beyond Tourneur and Shakespeare, there is Orton's replacement of satire with

saturnalia, which provides a "comic release from the burdens of sexual identity" (Charney, 100). This, Charney points out, reflects Orton's combination of the virtues of the old and new farce—"tumultuous sexual energy of Aristophanes, the careful intrigue plotting of Plautus" (Charney, 107). These Greek, Roman, and Renaissance characteristics coexist with the black comedy styles of Beckett, Pinter, Ionesco, Stoppard, and especially Brecht.

The specific Tourneuresque qualities identified by Charney are the "bizarre and unanticipatable shifts in tone" and the "almost hysterically rhetorical" flights, so that the designation of the play as tragedy is justified only "by certain technicalities of its endings" (Charney, 98). Those technicalities—in general the return of nighttime dreams to daytime realities and specifically the blood spilling and tattered clothing—seem at odds with the farcical tone of the rest of the play. Yet they can be seen as much more than "technicalities."

Detailed Jacobean assimilations are dealt with by William Hutchings, who asserts that it is the influence of this literary period that "supersedes [that of] all other sources and analogues." He notes, first of all, the "inherent theatricality of madness"[3] that is so much a part of Renaissance tradition, beginning with the real madness of Hieronymo in Kyd's *The Spanish Tragedy* (1586) and with the title character's feigned madness in *Hamlet* (1602). Hutchings draws a picture of the psychiatrist's office as the "modern counterpart of the Jacobean stage's Italianate court," where, "amid elaborate intrigues, disguises, and self-serving duplicities—all sorts of passions and lusts, however forbidden or illicit, flourish outside any norms of moral judgment, unrestrained by social taboos and regarded with clinical detachment by both perpetrators and authorities in charge" (Hutchings, 229). The revelations of young women to be men and men to be women are those found, respectively, in Jonson's *Epicoene* (1609) and in Beaumont and Fletcher's *Philaster* (1610) and Shakespeare's *Twelfth Night* (1602). In few periods has incest been so prevalent a dramatic theme as in the seventeenth century: John Ford's *'Tis a Pity She's a Whore* (1627), Beaumont and Fletcher's *A King and No King* (1611), and Middleton's *Women, Beware Women* (1623).

In his reference to the unsettling shift in tone in the ending of Orton's farce, Hutchings recalls a reverse shifting of tone, not unlike Orton's, in the unusually harsh punishments in Ben Jonson's *Volpone* (1605). Neither Jonson nor Orton relates to "any righting of a 'moral balance,'" nor in either is justice meted out fairly "since equally 'guilty' characters do not suffer alike" (Hutchings, 231). Hutchings refers to the asylums in Rowley and Middleton's *The Changeling* (1622)— asylums run by Alibius and Lollio much as those run by Prentice and Rance. Hutchings emphasizes Orton's insistence on the copious blood shed by Nick and Match—a detail euphemized in some productions. With bloodshed as the essence of Jacobean tragedy, Orton's insistence on it, despite the discomfiting shift in style, is in order. It is there even in *The Erpingham Camp*, a television farce with a style similar to that of *What the Butler Saw*. What makes Orton's kinships with influences different from those, for example, in the plays of Tom Stoppard are Orton's cunning concealing of them so that they unify the play "in ways that were not apparent to its earliest reviewers" and in so doing justify "the seemingly inapposite bloodshed" (Hutchings, 234). It is this inapposition that Charney dismisses and that Hutchings regards importantly as part of Orton's daring "to outrage conventional proprieties" (Hutchings, 234).

Beyond all the influences or analogues linked with Orton's plays, what places Orton's genius in a category by itself is what Leslie Smith refers to as the medieval feast of fools—the brief carnival period that preceded the restoration of order. Farce has, until Orton, assumed the rightness of that order. Orton has written his name into dramatic history by his dissension with the traditional farce ending, nowhere more hilarious and dark than in *What the Butler Saw*. In his "modern and uncompromising vision, that feast of fools, in all its grotesqueness and licence, [Orton] offers a permanent image of the human condition, not a temporary one."[4]

Orton refuses to cleanse and restore the body politic. He chooses merely to continue the status quo—reality's outrage, as he has stated. Furthermore, he has done so by writing subversively in a language that Hilary Spurling says gives the impression of being a foreign language, one that "for all its sharp intelligence and formal polish, . . . is firmly rooted in the shabby, baggy catchphrases of contemporary speech; [Orton is] almost alone among contemporary playwrights" (Spurling, 344).

One of few dissenting voices about the relative merits of *What the Butler Saw* is John Russell Taylor, who, having lauded *Entertaining Mr. Sloane* as a comedy of manners and *Loot* as a parody of the detective genre, sees *What the Butler Saw* as less successful than Orton's other plays, primarily on the basis of the absence of a norm (or a straight man) on which the very idea of farce rests. Consequently, in his view the play "soon becomes reduced to a succession of lines and happenings in a total vacuum" (Taylor, 138). Taylor then qualifies his stance as a possibly unfair one in "taking apart a play which comes to us in what we may presume to be an extremely provisional form" (Taylor, 139). Orton, having been irked by Taylor's earlier references to *Entertaining Mr. Sloane* as commercial entertainment, had he been alive, would have been even more irritated with Taylor's extension of the commercial label to *What the Butler Saw.*

In 1995 the stage history of *What the Butler Saw* came full circle, from its failed premiere at a West End the-

ater in 1969, through subsequent successes at the Royal Court Theatre in 1975 and at New York's Manhattan Theater Club in 1989, to the ultimate honor—a production at one of England's two most prestigious theaters, the Royal National Theatre. Three seasoned critics pose interesting contrasts in their evaluations, all referring to the 1969 disaster. Irving Wardle, who admitted to eating his words about 1969 yet holding reservations about 1975, now judged the first act of the 1995 production to be sublime and John Alderton's running of "the longest gag in living memory" to be a guarantee of this revival's holding "a permanent place in the Orton annals."[5] Even reluctant Benedict Nightingale, like Wardle "a *Loot* fan," seemed to look mostly for an explanation of why the "gales of laughter" ended as "blustery gusts."[6] Michael Billington, however, noted the production's (Phyllida Lloyd's) "absolute understanding of Orton's peculiar mix of verbal precision and sexual anarchy," of his "ability to depict gathering chaos with algebraic precision and Wildean finesse," and of his skill in escalating the frenzy of "authority disintegrating into panic."[7] As bedraggled characters "ascend skywards on Mark Thompson's glittering golden platform, it is as if the world of farcical mayhem has suddenly been invaded by Euripides and sixties satire has mated with *The Bacchae*." To Billington's comment one may add that the 1960s turbulences in *What the Butler Saw* reach into those of seventeenth-century Britain as well as Euripides' time, all three periods marked by social and political upheavals.

Notes

1. Hilary Spurling, "Young Master," *Spectator*, 14 March 1969, 344; hereafter cited in text.

2. Frank Marcus, *Sunday Telegraph*, 9 March 1969, n.p.

3. William Hutchings, "Joe Orton's Jacobean Assimilations in *What the Butler Saw*," in *Themes of Drama*, vol. 10, *Farce*, ed. J. Redmond (Cambridge: Cambridge University Press, 1988), 228; hereafter cited in text.

4. Leslie Smith, "Joe Orton," in *Modern British Farce* (Totowa, N.J.: Barnes & Noble, 1989), 131; hereafter cited in text.

5. Irving Wardle, *Independent*, 5 March 1995, n.p.

6. Benedict Nightingale, *Times*, 4 March 1995, 5.

7. Michael Billington, *Guardian*, 4 March 1995, 28.

Grant Stirling (essay date spring 1997)

SOURCE: Stirling, Grant. "Ortonesque/Carnivalesque: The Grotesque Realism of Joe Orton." *Journal of Dramatic Theory and Criticism* 11, no. 2 (spring 1997): 41-63.

[*In the following essay, Stirling applies theoretical standards drawn by Mikhail Bakhtin about the plays of Rabelais to those of Orton; while Orton's philosophy is more grim than Rabelais's, he uses the same kind of "grotesque realism" and carnival-like scenarios to comment on the world as he sees it, making his plays more than simply farcical.*]

> [Joe Orton's] nonconformity was carried to a much greater extent than that of Shakespeare or Cervantes, who merely disobeyed the narrow classical forms. [Orton's] images have a certain undestroyable nonofficial nature. No dogma, no authoritarianism, no narrow-minded seriousness can coexist with [Ortonesque] images; these images are opposed to all that is finished and polished, to all pomposity, to every ready-made solution in the sphere of thought and world outlook.[1]

Although Mikhail Bakhtin is commenting in this passage upon the work of Francoise Rabelais, Bakhtin's comments adopt a particular currency in the field of contemporary British drama if the name of Joe Orton is substituted for that of Rabelais. Bakhtin appears to anticipate the profound challenge and revolutionary tenor of Orton's drama: a nonconformity within the sphere of both dramatic convention and normative morality; a nonofficial anti-authoritarianism; an opposition to pomposity and the prevailing norms of thought and world outlook. But since Bakhtin views Rabelais as a quintessential revolutionary, this fortuitous accord between Orton and Rabelais would seem a small curiosity, a mere trick of name substitution, were it not for the tremendous potential of Bakhtin's study to illuminate the particular nature of Orton's drama. The preeminent concepts that emerge from Bakhtin's *Rabelais and His World*—the carnivalesque and grotesque realism—have a striking congruence with the drama of Joe Orton, and while I am not arguing that Orton's drama can be described only in terms of the carnivalesque and grotesque realism, I am suggesting that these two Bakhtinian concepts provide a conceptual vocabulary through which the combined aesthetic and political properties of Orton's drama can be concisely and precisely articulated.[2]

The Bakhtinian insight is important to an appraisal of Orton's work because even the most cursory survey of Orton criticism reveals a certain anxiety about the particular generic status of Orton's drama. Much Orton criticism tends to consider Orton's work within the context of farce. However, the critics who consider Orton as a *farceur* realize that the etymology of "farce" as "extraneous stuffing" and its consequent dramatic legacy as "light entertainment"[3] cannot adequately describe the dark and at times sinister aspects of the Ortonesque; the content of Orton's apparently farcical plays is anything but the traditional material of farce:

> Where Feydeau has flirtation, Orton has rape; where Feydeau has sexual misadventure, Orton has incest. In Feydeau sensibilities are offended, in Orton physical injuries are sustained. Feydeau's characters are driven to comic despair and momentary desperation, Orton's are driven to madness and death.[4]

In an attempt to reconcile farce and the Ortonesque, a number of critics have attempted to modify the traditional definition of farce: Charney suggests "Quotidian Farce"[5]; Bigsby argues for "Anarchic Farce"[6]; Dean proposes what might be called "Dionysian Farce."[7] Although these critics differ in how they define Ortonesque farce, they share the conviction that Orton's drama invokes the conventions of farce only to violate those conventions. Thus, they argue, Orton creates the genre of farce anew. This new Ortonesque farce is formed, in part, by the doubly transgressive elements of Orton's dramas: their dark comic vision and their undeniable political nature. Both of these elements violate the traditional definition of farce as "light entertainment designed solely to provoke laughter," and the critics who discuss Orton as a *farceur* consequently face the task that Bakhtin faces when reading Rabelais: "To be understood he requires an essential reconstruction of our entire artistic and ideological perception, the renunciation of many deeply rooted demands of literary taste, and the revision of many concepts" (Bakhtin 3).

The challenge identified by Bakhtin arrives on two complementary levels in the context of Orton's work. On the one hand, the Ortonesque demands the revision and reconstruction of *artistic* perception: the conventional definition of farce within literary criticism. On the other hand, the Ortonesque demands the revision of *ideological* perception: the normative and moral distinctions of social reality. In this way, aesthetics and politics combine to mark the unique force of the Ortonesque oeuvre, and the inextricable association of these elements within the Ortonesque places those who view Orton as a *farceur* in the awkward position of implicitly apologizing for the dramatic trope they invoke. While the valuable contributions of Dean, Bigsby, and Charney illustrate the historical legacy of farce and how Orton disrupts the apolitical nature of traditional farce, each of these critics continues to place Orton within the dramatic discourse of farce even though they all recognize that Orton is the round peg who does not fit the square hole of farce. Thus, Dean, Bigsby, and Charney appear trapped within a dramatic terminology that forces them to discuss Orton in terms of what he is not—i.e. a *farceur*—rather than in terms of what he is. This is the point at which the Bakhtinian concepts of the carnivalesque and grotesque realism offer the possibility of describing the Ortonesque in terms of what it is, rather than in terms of what it is not; that is, the Bakhtinian carnivalesque appears to provide the terminology which may more precisely describe the particular generic status of the Ortonesque, while the Bakhtinian concept of grotesque realism appears to provide the terminology which may more precisely describe the particular aesthetic of the Ortonesque. But in order to proceed, it is first necessary to briefly reiterate how Bakhtin articulates the two key terms that frame this analysis: the carnivalesque and grotesque realism.

Bakhtin bases the carnivalesque upon a somewhat idealized conception of folk culture by rooting the carnivalesque in the anarchic folk festivals of the Medieval and the Renaissance periods. During these festivals, the collective power of the common folk of society is unleashed in a quasi-Bacchanalian revel during which "all hierarchical rank, privileges, norms, and prohibitions" are suspended (Bakhtin 10). The explosion of the carnivalesque results in an open and honest communication between individuals who are now stripped of the artificial designation of social rank:

> . . . all were considered equal during carnival. Here, in the town square, a special form of free and familiar contact reigned among the people who were usually divided by the barriers of caste, profession, and age . . . such free, familiar contacts were deeply felt and formed an essential element of the carnival spirit. People were, so to speak, reborn for new, purely human relations. These truly human relations were not only a fruit of imagination or abstract thought; they were experienced. The utopian ideal and the realistic merged in this carnivalesque experience, unique of its kind.
>
> (Bakhtin 10)

The carnivalesque is thus a locus of death and rebirth that destroys the prevailing hierarchical social order while simultaneously creating a new egalitarian relation. It is important to note how, in Bakhtin's view, the carnivalesque does not operate simply through ironic inversion in which the existing social hierarchy is transposed so that the fool becomes king or *vice versa*. Rather, the carnivalesque displaces the notion of hierarchy altogether as it destroys the existing social hierarchy and generates an egalitarian arena in the wake of that destruction.[8]

This fundamental structural ambivalence is one of the defining features of the carnivalesque revel, and it is sometimes overlooked. For example, Graham Pechey argues that the radical political potential of the carnivalesque is located in the "practice of inverting social hierarchies."[9] Pechey's belief that the carnivalesque maintains a hierarchical social structure, even though an inverted hierarchical structure, directly contradicts Bakhtin's stated insistence upon the notion that, in the carnivalesque, "what is suspended first of all is hierarchical structure . . .—that is, everything resulting from socio-hierarchical inequality or any other form of inequality among people (including age)."[10] Further, Bakhtin insists that the "special type of communication" created by the carnivalesque is a direct result of "the temporary suspension, both ideal and real, of hierarchical rank" (Bakhtin 10). Thus Bakhtin clearly states that the carnivalesque does not preserve the notion of hierarchy but displaces hierarchy altogether. This non-hierarchical egalitarian ethos is echoed, though not without significant and revealing distortion, in many of Orton's barbed assertions from his dramas: "We've no

privileged class here. It's a democratic lunacy we practice";[11] "You know nothing of the law. I know nothing of the law. That makes us equal in the sight of the law";[12] "All classes are criminal today. We live in an age of equality."[13] These typically Ortonesque assertions share the egalitarian emphasis of the Bakhtinian carnivalesque, but the displacement of social hierarchy in Orton's characteristically acerbic observations illustrates the unique Ortonesque adaptation of the Bakhtinian paradigm, a unique adaptation that I will discuss in greater detail below.

The displacement of hierarchy in the carnivalesque is also significant because it carries an important implication for the consideration of literary genre. In short, any work that is described as carnivalesque can only, with great care, be considered simultaneously within the context of parody or satire. While Bakhtin acknowledges that parody and satire are related to the carnivalesque and may even be tools of the carnivalesque, he clearly indicates that modern forms of parody and satire are not identical with the carnivalesque: "We must stress, however, that the carnival is far distant from the negative and formal parody of modern times. Folk humor denies, but it revives and renews at the same time. Bare negation is completely alien to folk culture" (Bakhtin 11). Bakhtin makes this point because, in his view, the kinds of parody and satire that are exemplified by the Augustan Age of Pope and Swift—and which still exert considerable influence upon our conceptions and deployments of satire and parody today—minimize the creative regenerative pole of the carnivalesque. Consequently, both can reduce the fundamental ambivalence of the carnivalesque to bare negation or destruction (Bakhtin 62). Further, in as much as these kinds of parody and satire tend to rely upon ironic inversion for their parodic and satiric effect, each tends to preserve the very notion of hierarchy that is displaced by the Bakhtinian carnivalesque.[14] The reservation that Bakhtin expresses toward parody and satire is especially relevant to the discussion of a carnivalesque-Ortonesque because Orton's work is sometimes viewed as satiric or parodic; these views are often in tension with the Bakhtinian carnivalesque.

In the largest possible terms then, the Bakhtinian carnivalesque marks a structural paradigm that is fundamentally ambivalent: simultaneously destroying while creating; fundamentally anarchic while positing a new egalitarian order. The political implications of the carnivalesque are clearly manifest in both its hostility toward the prevailing social order and, as Bakhtin states, "'the new mode of man's relation to man [that] is elaborated'" as the result of the carnivalesque itself.[15] The possibility of this new mode of social inter-relation combines with the hostility toward prevailing social structures to reveal the revolutionary political force of the carnivalesque. However, the revolutionary force of the carnivalesque is not limited to the folk in the market-place; it also extends into the realm of aesthetics. Bakhtin notes how a particular carnivalesque aesthetic develops in conjunction with revolution that takes places among the folk:

> . . . a special idiom of forms and symbols was evolved—an extremely rich idiom that expressed the unique yet complex carnival experience of the people. This experience, opposed to all that was ready-made and completed, to all pretence at immutability, sought a dynamic expression; it demanded ever changing, playful, undefined forms. All the symbols of the carnival idiom are filled with pathos of change and renewal, with the sense of gay relativity of prevailing truths and authorities.
>
> (Bakhtin 10-11)

Bakhtin identifies this special idiom, this carnival idiom, as *grotesque realism*: the aesthetic of the carnivalesque (Bakhtin 18-19).

Grotesque realism mirrors the structural ambivalence of the carnivalesque and is a fundamentally destabilizing transgressive aesthetic. This structural ambivalence can be glimpsed in the Bakhtinian folk who form the basis of the carnivalesque tableau and who, as Michael Holquist suggests, are vulgar in their brute physicality and carnal nature while also vital in the thriving life-force that permeates their appetites and existence: "His folk are blasphemous rather than adoring, cunning rather than intelligent; they are coarse, dirty, and rampantly physical, revelling in oceans of strong drink, poods of sausage, and endless coupling of bodies."[16] The vulgar corporeal vitality of the Bakhtinian folk provides a fertile arena in which the grotesque realism of the carnivalesque can thrive; indeed, only through the vulgar vitality of the folk can grotesque realism become manifest: "The essential principle of grotesque realism is degradation, that is, the lowering of all that is high, spiritual, ideal, abstract; it is a transfer to the material level, to the sphere of earth and body in all their indissoluble unity" (Bakhtin 19-20).

This degradation of the sententious and abstract to the material realm of the body and earth is not, however, a form of ironic deflation or bathos that negates the degraded object. On the contrary, the operation of degradation within grotesque realism maintains its affirmative role by lowering the abstract to the vulgar and vital realm of the body so that the object of degradation may be recreated and renewed. For example, Bakhtin points (Bakhtin 310) to a passage from Book 1, Chapter 45 of Rabelais' *Pantagruel* in which Friar John proclaims that "The very shadow of an abbey spire is fecund." Clearly, Rabelais is playing with the phallic image of the abbey spire, and in the process, satirizing the moral depravity of the monks of the Church. But Bakhtin insists that "the form of a giant phallus, with its shadow

that impregnates women, is least of all an exaggeration of the monk's depravity" (Bakhtin 312), and thus is not simply a parodic or satiric negation of the Church and her brethren. What is bound up with the satiric negation is the positive affirmation of "Friar John—glutton and drunkard, pitilessly sober, mighty and heroic, full of inexhaustible energy, and thirsting for the new" (Bakhtin 312). This particular example of grotesque realism in Rabelais reveals the double-edge of grotesque degradation: how the abstract concept of monastic corruption and the hypocrisy of the Church is brought down to the level of the material body only to be transformed into an affirmation of the corporeal vitality of Friar John's humanity. Thus, "degradation digs a bodily grave for a new birth; it has not only a destructive, negative aspect, but also a regenerating one" (Bakhtin 21).

Bakhtin discovers a pithy image of grotesque realism that captures the ambivalent duplicity of the carnivalesque aesthetic—its negative and affirmative quality—

> In the famous Kerch terracotta collection [where] we find figurines of senile pregnant hags. Moreover, the old hags are laughing. This is a typical and very strongly expressed grotesque. It is ambivalent. It is pregnant death, a death that gives birth. There is nothing completed, nothing calm and stable in the bodies of these old hags. They combine a senile, decaying and deformed flesh with the flesh of new life, conceived but as yet unformed. Life is shown in its two-fold contradictory process; it is the epitome of incompleteness.
>
> (Bakhtin 25-26)

In the process of death—the negating degradation of the abstract concept—life is born anew—the regenerating renewal of the abstract concept. Within this image of the pregnant hag, the union of death and life mirrors both the duplicitous destruction and renewal within grotesque realism, and the structural ambivalence of the larger carnivalesque revel itself. In the Ortonesque, the renewing degradation of grotesque realism is most often displayed in Orton's lowering of all human motivations to the base level of desire: sexual and material. Once human nature is reduced to this level, the social inter-relations among people are transformed from the hypocritical banality of genteel society to the naked rapacity that is true to the Ortonesque view of humanity. In this way, the Ortonesque uses a form of grotesque realism to degrade and renew social interaction.

Within the paradigm of the carnivalesque, Bakhtin outlines a distinct genre with a distinct aesthetic that unites the complementary registers of politics and art: precisely the double register that causes the critics of Orton such problems. If, as is obvious, Orton cannot easily be accommodated within the context of farce primarily because of his dark comic vision, political edge, and patent affront to normative morality, then perhaps the Ortonesque with its attendant political and aesthetic peculiarities is more easily accommodated within the Bakhtinian paradigm. The question then becomes whether and to what extent Orton's work is structurally congruent with the Bakhtinian carnivalesque and whether and to what extent Orton's drama displays the Bakhtinian aesthetic of grotesque realism. A related question, though a less prominent one in this discussion, concerns whether and to what extent the unique Ortonesque adaptation of the Bakhtinian paradigm reflects back upon and transforms the concepts of the carnivalesque and grotesque realism.

Since Bakhtin roots the carnivalesque in the vulgar and vital folk culture that is both subject to and author of the carnivalesque revel, the possibility of an Ortonesque carnivalesque must similarly be founded in the characters who populate Orton's dramas. To a large extent, the Bakhtinian folk and the Ortonesque folk share common elements. But a few revealing distinctions emerge, particularly where the issue of vulgarity is concerned. Whereas Bakhtin portrays the folk as a vulgar but vital force whose energy motivates the larger carnivalesque revel, Orton creates characters whose vital energies drive the fanciful machinations of their respective dramas, and in a strong sense, Orton's characters are every bit as vulgar as those in a carnivalesque revel. However, the vulgarity that is displayed in the Ortonesque is often of a different kind than that outlined by Bakhtin; Orton's adaptation of the Bakhtinian concept of vulgarity is inflected in a characteristically Ortonesque fashion. Whereas the Bakhtinian folk "not only picked their nose and farted, but enjoyed doing so,"[17] Orton's most intriguing characters not only murder, rape, and blackmail, but profit from it. Thus, the vulgarity of these characters is depicted not primarily in corporeal terms, but in moral terms. Whereas the Bakhtinian aesthetic finds its most forceful expression in the material body, the Ortonesque aesthetic finds its most forceful expression in the (im)morality of its characters. However, the immorality of Orton's characters is not, in itself, a sententious abstract concept that is far removed from the realm of corporeal vitality. Although the vulgarity of Orton's folk is primarily moral, rather than corporeal, that moral vulgarity is bound up with the appetites of Orton's characters: both sexual and material appetites. In short, Orton's characters hunger for sexual gratification, or money, or power, and those appetites motivate their actions.

For example, in *Entertaining Mr. Sloane,* both Kath and her brother Ed lust after and fight over the youthful and attractive Sloane; in *Loot,* Hal, Dennis, Fay, and Truscott all desire and extort their (im)proper share of the money; in *What the Butler Saw,* the incestuous liaisons between Prentice and his daughter Geraldine, Beckett and his mother Mrs. Prentice, reveal the fundamentally unregulated nature of human passions. All

these elements combine to reveal the "animalistic, and often unsavory side of human selfishness, desires, and out-and-out lust"[18] in the Ortonesque. Orton relentlessly stresses the baseness of human motivation in his drama, and thereby reduces the essence of human interaction to the level of mutual exploitation that is motivated by the need to satiate individual appetites through selfish desire. The Ortonesque proceeds to ruthlessly strip away the patina of civility that masks what the Ortonesque views as the true nature personal motivation, but in that moment of degradation, the Ortonesque proceeds to re-create the nature of human social interaction by forging a new and essentially rapacious social matrix in which the characters thrive. This kind of degrading renewal or negating affirmation of social interaction within the Ortonesque combines with the unique vulgarity of Ortonesque characters to create part of the grotesque realism in Orton's drama.

It is interesting to note, however, that the Ortonesque concept of vulgarity extends beyond the limit of a certain (im)morality, which is related to the corporeal nature of vulgarity in Bakhtin. Orton's characters are vulgar not only because they are driven by their appetites to such egregious inequities as murder, rape, and blackmail; their vulgarity extends to the more mundane pretensions of polite society: pretensions that are primarily motivated by the lower- to middle-class situation of the characters who aspire to and pretend higher class status.

In general, the characters that populate Orton's drama are not of the genteel class of society. More often, they—like the Bakhtinian folk—are part of the disaffected mass of society who are an integral component of the larger whole, but who do not share the full measure of the benefits that society has to offer (but hypocritically refuses to bestow). In *Erpingham Camp,* Orton presents Kenny and Eileen—a lower class couple whose "love was banned" and who advocate, in an orgy of socialist good-will, "Have a bash for the pregnant woman next door!"—and Lou and Ted—a middle-class couple who met "outside the Young Conservative Club" and who measure their prosperity by the intensity of their sun-lamp. In *Entertaining Mr. Sloane,* Orton depicts the opportunistic Sloane, the sexually rapacious and pathetic Kath, and the manipulative but coy Ed, all of whom reside in an arrested housing development that is located in the midst of a municipal dump site. *Loot* presents characters who all attempt to better their financial situations through morally dubious means: Hal and Dennis through robbery and violating corpses; Fay by killing her husbands; the detective Truscott by accepting a bribe. What this abbreviated description of Orton's rogues' gallery does not reveal is the way in which each of these characters mask their nature behind a patina of civility:

> Orton was preoccupied with vulgarity in his plays. All of his most vigorous characters are vulgar in the literal

sense of the term: they pretend to a refinement, tact and gentility that they do not at all have. Their politeness consists of empty, conventionalised formulae—slogans, proverbs, advertising copy, political shibboleths, and all the other verbal junk of a liberal, democratic society.[19]

Their affectations are not only a pretence to a higher social standing, but to a higher moral standard. Of course, the Ortonesque proceeds to exploit this distance between pretence and reality, between surface and substance, thus creating the characteristic darkness and edge that unsettles so many.

While all these characters are vulgar in both a social and a moral sense, they appear to lack the fundamental ambivalence of the Bakhtinian folk. Instead, Orton's characters appear nakedly rapacious and patently immoral, immersed in a sea of self-serving currents. However, although altruism and morality are surely not present in Orton's characters, this does not exclude the possibility of their similarity to the fundamental ambivalence of the Bakhtinian folk. Orton's characters are similar to the Bakhtinian folk because just as the Bakhtinian folk are vulgar but vital, so Orton's characters possess a raw energy that allows them not merely to survive their vulgarity but thrive upon it. Orton's characters not only hide their immorality behind a pretension to civility, but they flourish on the basis of their duplicity. Consequently, the fundamental ambivalence of Orton's characters is not so much a matter of their being simultaneous embodiments of good and evil or of altruism and selfishness; their ambivalence is found in their duplicitous role as agents of death and destruction who are the surviving and thriving life-force of the drama.

The fundamental ambivalence of the characters in Orton's dramas suggests that they, like the Bakhtinian folk, form the basis of a carnivalesque tableau. And, if we follow Bakhtin's example of the terracotta pregnant hags, it is possible to see an almost direct reflection of this specific example of grotesque realism in some of the women in Orton's drama. For example, after Kath's pathetic seduction of Sloane in Act One of *Sloane,* their sexual liaison continues only to result in the pregnancy of Act Two. Kath may not be a senile hag but she is depicted as far past her sexual prime: no teeth; "fat and the crow's feet under your eyes would make you an object of terror"; "You showed him the gate of Hell every night. He abandoned Hope when he entered there"; and in a withering phrase, Ed compares Kath's pretence at sexual vitality to that of "an old tart grinding to her climax" (Orton 143). In this way, Kath's physical description, combined with her role as a cognizant Jocasta in this Oedipal relationship with Sloane, positions her squarely within the aesthetic of grotesque realism as outlined by Bakhtin. Within a decaying body and a per-

verse relationship, Kath simultaneously embodies new life through her pregnancy. A similar duplicity can be seen in Eileen of *Erpingham Camp.* While on the one hand she repeatedly proclaims "I'm in the family way!" she uses her pregnancy as the justification for physical brutality and the revolution that ensues: "He hit me! I'm an expectant mother! Hit him! Hit him!" (Orton 297). Eileen is simultaneously a locus of birth and new life and an agent of death and destruction: precisely the duplicity of grotesque realism. In addition, Fay of *Loot,* although not pregnant, embodies the possibility of new life through her repeated marriages. But that possibility is always checked by her repeated murders of her husbands. Thus Fay also conforms to the fundamentally ambivalent structure outlined by Bakhtin that marks the duplicity of grotesque realism.

In this way, the characters that populate Orton's dramatic landscape are similar to the Bakhtinian folk, although cast in a distinctly Ortonesque fashion. That is, the vulgarity and vitality of Orton's characters are displayed not only through their lower to middle class status and the pretensions to a higher social and moral standard, but through their material profit and spectacular success that rests squarely upon their morally reprehensible activities: activities which are, in turn, motivated by their vulgar corporeal appetites for sexual gratification, money or power. Orton appears to expand the range of Bakhtin's grotesque ambivalence beyond the predominantly corporeal limit established in *Rabelais and His World,* although the grotesque realism of the material body that is so strongly identified by Bakhtin is clearly displayed in some of Orton's women, and less strongly—though no less significantly—related to the immoral vulgarity of the Ortonesque conception of character. Grotesque realism in Orton's drama clearly degrades its characters by reducing their motivations to the base level of desire and appetite, but it simultaneously renews those characters by re-weaving the social fabric in which those characters thrive. Within the carnivalesque moment of Orton's drama, characters no longer must hide their true motivations behind a patina of social propriety; rather, the naked lustful rapacity that churns within each is liberated and this liberation becomes the basis for a new mode of social interaction. In this way, the Ortonesque treatment of character through grotesque realism degrades those characters in order to renew the social matrix. This is how the duplicity of the Ortonesque folk is revealed: vulgar but vital; cognizant of social propriety but disregarding social convention; destroying one social system while simultaneously constructing a new social system.

With the duplicitous Ortonesque characters at the basis of the dramatic tableau, the potential for a carnivalesque explosion is prepared. But in order to follow how that carnivalesque explosion is actualized, it is necessary to consider some issues of plot in Orton's drama. A central structural component of the carnivalesque in Bakhtin is the tension between order and disorder. As Bakhtin indicates, the carnivalesque is an irruption of disorder in an otherwise ordered social system: the presence of anarchy within hierarchy. Generally, Orton's dramas are built upon a similar plot structure, one that first establishes a particular systematic order, but then proceeds to demolish that order in an anarchic carnivalesque explosion which is, in most cases, the result of a single catalytic act. The most obvious example of this progression from ordered system to anarchic explosion can be seen in *Erpingham Camp* where the drama opens by establishing first, the respective positions of Erpingham and his minions as administrators of the camp and second, the position of Lou and Ted, Eileen and Kenny, as campers. Although Ted and Kenny are differentiated by their abbreviated argument over Labour politics (Scene Two), they are both subject to the camp administration. In this way, the social division within the camp is clearly marked and it takes no large metaphorical leap to view *The Erpingham Camp* as a model of any classist society. However, in true carnivalesque fashion, this stable social order is profoundly challenged in the wake of Ted's response to Riley's smacking Eileen (Scene Six) and even more so when Ted directly attacks Erpingham: "You've struck a figure of authority!" (Orton 303). The battle lines are drawn; the peasants are revolting.

Similarly, in *Sloane,* a certain domestic order is established through the assimilation of Sloane into Kath's house. She takes Sloane as her lover while Ed's sexual hunger for Sloane prevents him from asking Sloane to leave. This uneasy order, predicated upon a quasi-Oedipal liaison between Kath and Sloane and the unresolved homosexual attraction of Ed for Sloane, is maintained until the disruptive element of Kemp threatens to undo the arrangement by revealing Sloane's murderous past. In the wake of Sloane's murder of Kemp, this uneasy order is undone and anarchy is unleashed as Kath and Ed fight for possession of Sloane who is reduced to a sexual commodity.

In *Loot* a certain social order is established once more, but it is an order of social appearances that is predicated upon the maintenance of a relationship of knowledge and ignorance between individuals. That is, the play immediately opens with the acknowledgement of a robbery by Dennis and Hal, and action of the play primarily revolves around the complications that ensue from the attempt to maintain a patina of normality in a situation that is anything but normal. Consequently, the catalytic event that motivates the anarchy of this play actually precedes the opening of the drama, and the dramatic action presented is, arguably, the anarchic result of that event. The social order that is broken by this anarchic situation is both assumed and intimated: assumed in terms of a "conventional morality" that ostensibly disdains robbery, bribery, and the violation of corpses; intimated by the desperate bid to maintain that patina of "conventional morality" by the guilty characters within the play.

According to the Bakhtinian paradigm of the carnivalesque, what occurs as a result of the carnivalesque explosion is a direct and open relation between individuals, regardless of their social rank. In the moment of the carnivalesque explosion, hierarchical rank is demolished and all are free to communicate openly and honestly in this egalitarian arena. It seems clear that carnivalesque communication Bakhtin has in mind is a fraternal and convivial communion suffused in a spirit of mutual good-will. What Orton provides through the carnivalesque arena of his dramas is an open and honest communication that is anything but fraternal and convivial. Rather, once the artificial patina of hierarchical social convention has been stripped away through carnivalesque anarchy, the raw aggression and vulgar passions of humanity are bare for all to see. To the Ortonesque eye, the social relation that is true to humanity is hostility and blackmail: Kenny tells Erpingham, "You'll pay for this you ignorant fucker!" (Orton 307); Eileen tells Ted "Piss off you dirty middle-class prat! And take your poxy wife with you" (Orton 311); Kath extorts Sloane with a blunt "I was never subtle, Mr. Sloane . . . If you go with Eddie, I'll tell the police" (Orton 145); Ed is equally blunt in extorting his sexual reward as he threatens Sloane with "Get on the blower and call the law. We're finished" (Orton 133); and *Loot* operates almost exclusively through blackmail as Hal threatens Fay who then threatens Hal who are both in turn threatened by Truscott, but who all arrive at the equitable solution of framing the innocent widower McLeavy. The "purely human relation" that Bakhtin isolates as the immediate and real result of the carnivalesque is skewed through the Ortonesque into a naked display of the essence of human interaction: vice, lust, and greed.

The relationship between the base nature of human interaction and the nature of human communication in the Ortonesque has caught the attention of many critics who, like Charney, suggest that the vacuity of sloganeering and the pervasive media-idiom spoken by Orton's characters have a specific function in the context of the Ortonesque. Charney argues that Orton's dramas operate through the deliberate deployment of an "occulted discourse" in which the surface of language masks a deeper sinister meaning: "The stated meaning is bland, polite, innocuous, even vacuous, in order to conceal a violent, chaotic, and painful truth."[20] By way of elaborating upon Charney's remark, I would argue that language is occult only when it conforms to the polite conventions of society in the pre-carnivalesque moments of Orton's dramas. What Charney identifies as the sub-textual menace of Orton's language provides part of the edge and dark vision of the Ortonesque. However, in the carnivalesque explosion that destroys the structures upon which social convention is predicated, it appears that occulted discourse is rendered transparent; the suppressed latent content of this menacing discourse is made manifest as the characters of the drama communicate in an open and honest manner. Clearly this honest communication has nothing in common with the honest communication that Bakhtin identifies as the result of the carnivalesque explosion, nothing in common except for the fact that it is honest: Kenny can call an authority figure an ignorant fucker; Kath can use her knowledge to blackmail her man; Fay can demand a cut of the loot by openly stating her intentions. The ironic relationship between the patina of civility and the underlying hostility of Ortonesque discourse is destroyed through the carnivalesque energy of Orton's dramas. In the wake of this destruction of the social order, a new egalitarian brutality is spawned, but spawned from the undercurrents that inhabited the original social order.

If the Ortonesque is viewed in this way, the carnivalesque explosion that strips the patina of civility from the naked aggression of humanity can be characterised as an unmasking. The carnivalesque-Ortonesque unmasks the true nature of social relations as avaricious, rapacious, immoral, and rampantly sexual. Figures of social authority are unmasked as petty dictators who are no less immoral than those whom they brutally subject. Conventional morality is unmasked as a normative rule that is hypocritically flaunted by those who most stridently proclaim its propriety. Social order is unmasked as an oppressive system that perpetuates class divisions. These elements of unmasking within the Ortonesque—the tendency of Orton's dramas to expose the dark truths that are obscured by the conventions of polite society—are what has led John Lahr to label Orton as a satirist,[21] and satire is undoubtedly an element of the Ortonesque: an element that is revealed through the ubiquitous use of parody, travesty, and caricature in Orton's dramas.[22] But to limit the Ortonesque to a satiric function tends to diminish the carnivalesque potential in Orton's work, at least in the context of Bakhtin's conception of satire. As Bakhtin consistently argues, the nature of modern satire is negative, diminishing, and lacking any positive affirmative power. Although Bigsby argues that "in the latter part of his career he [Orton] developed an intensely personal form of farce—brittle, contingent, violent and deliberately subversive of social and moral structures"[23]—a form of farce that strikes me as remarkably akin to satire—Bigsby does not indicate how the Ortonesque might move beyond the negativity of satirical-farce into a positive regenerative moment that is integral to the Bakhtinian conception of the carnivalesque genre. If Orton is a satirist as Lahr explicitly suggests and as Bigsby seems to suggest through what he vaguely defines as Orton's "personal form of farce,"

then the Ortonesque appears to offer no more than a critical comment upon the hypocrisy of society; the ambivalence of both the carnivalesque structure of the plays and the ambivalent nature of the characters who populate the Ortonesque is correspondingly diminished:

> What remains is nothing but a corpse, old age deprived of pregnancy, equal to itself alone; it is alienated and torn away from the whole in which it had been linked to that other, younger link in the chain in growth and development. The result is a broken grotesque figure, the demon of fertility with phallus cut off and belly crushed.
>
> (Bakhtin 53)

In order to restore the Ortonesque phallus, Orton must be rescued from what Bakhtin suggests is the negativity of satire. The ambivalence that permeates both the structure and the characters of the Ortonesque must be recognized. However, this task is not simply accomplished given the apparently ironic endings of many of Orton's dramas.

As is often noted, Orton's dramas repeatedly present the triumph of adversity over life, the valorization of the guilty at the expense of the innocent. In order to wrest some positive regenerative element from these concluding tableaux, critics have gone to considerable lengths. Bigsby brings the big gun of Adorno to bear upon the Ortonesque and argues that "Orton becomes the ultimate critic, inviting his audience to recuperate those values ruthlessly excluded from his plays."[24] Bigsby appears to suggest, according to this peculiar logic of exclusion, that the Ortonesque must be inverted in order to wrest a conventional morality from Orton's dramas; we must read black as white, murder as love:

> As Adorno implies, the temptation is perhaps to recuperate those values so absent from the plays, to respond to the crucial absences of the text, to see Orton's characters, as Adorno saw Beckett's, as 'what human beings have become,' while 'the minimal promise of happiness they contain, which refuses to be traded for comfort, cannot be had for a price less than total dislocation, to the point of worldlessness.'[25]

In his haste to make Orton postmodern—hence the recourse to Adorno—Bigsby appears to forget momentarily that the conventional morality Adorno would supply is precisely what is scrutinized throughout the Ortonesque. However, Bigsby does partially remember himself when he asserts that "Orton is less concerned with the generation of values than with ridiculing a world committed to the chimera of meaning."[26] But if the Ortonesque is to be considered within the context of the Bakhtinian carnivalesque and is not to be limited to a satiric function of "ridiculing a world," then the Ortonesque must be concerned with the generation of values. And it seems to me that Adorno is suggesting the right place to look for the creation of those values: the audience. Orton may not portray a new regenerative value system on stage, and hence he is often viewed as a satirist. But the experience of the Ortonesque arguably plants the seeds of change in the audience, and it is within those seeds that the potential for a regenerative affirmative action is located. However, in order for the conception of a carnivalesque-Ortonesque to be valid, the scope of the theatrical event of a performance of Orton's dramatic work must be conceived of as breaking through the "fourth wall" that separates stage and audience because, strictly speaking, the carnivalesque is a revolutionary force that implicates both actor and audience by conflating the distinction between participant and spectator. Indeed, the carnivalesque cannot strictly be applied to drama *per se*:

> But the basic carnival nucleus of this culture is by no means a purely artistic form nor a spectacle and does not, generally speaking, belong to the sphere of art. It belongs to the borderline between art and life. In reality, it is life itself, but shaped according to a certain pattern of play.
>
> In fact, carnival does not know footlights, in the sense that it does not acknowledge any distinction between actors and spectators. Footlights would destroy a carnival, as the absence of footlights would destroy the theatrical performance. Carnival is not a spectacle seen by the people; they live in it, and everyone participates because its very idea embraces all the people. While carnival lasts, there is no other life outside it. During carnival time life is subject only to its laws, that is, the laws of its own freedom. It has a universal spirit; it is a special condition of the entire world, of the world's revival and renewal, in which all take part. Such is the essence of carnival, vividly felt by all its participants.

(Bakhtin 7)[27]

The Ortonesque conforms to the radically transgressive dynamic of the carnivalesque and violates the boundary between stage and audience by situating the carnivalesque event half way between actor and assembly. Orton manages to extend the scope of his dramatic event beyond the limitation of the footlights by adopting the persona and *nom de plume* of Edna Welthorpe, a prudish and outraged prig who penned numerous letters to the pages of *The Daily Telegraph* and to the offices of various dramatic institutions. In these letters, Edna Welthorpe complained about the immorality of Orton's work: "the endless parade of mental and physical perversion" in *Sloane*;[28] "the raping of children with *Mars* bars" and the "other filthy details of a sexual and psychopathic nature" in *Loot*.[29] These letters can be viewed as effectively extending the scope of Orton's dramatic activity beyond the limit of the stage footlights. The letters of Edna Welthorpe attempt to orchestrate and stimulate a certain response to the Ortonesque. This response not only fosters and directs public debate upon the nature of the Ortonesque, but also extends the assault of social morality and sociable pretension that permeates the Ortonesque into the world beyond Orton's stage. As

Lahr argues, "the stupidity behind her [Edna's] censoriousness" was a strategy that sought to expose "the visciousness behind decency" which defines society not only in Orton's drama, but also in Orton's London.

The letters of Edna Welthorpe may extend the range of Orton's dramatic activity beyond the limit of the stage, and thus help push the experience of the Ortonesque through the "fourth wall" that separates actor and assembly, but they do not, in and of themselves, provide the positive regenerative affirmation that is integral to the paradigm of the Bakhtinian carnivalesque. However, Simon Shepard argues in his "Edna's Last Stand, *Or* Joe Orton's Dialectic of Entertainment," that Orton's drama, even without the additional support of the letters of Edna Welthorpe, presents the possibility of an affirmative moment to audience members. In short, Shepard argues that Orton's drama can provoke audience members to question their complicity in the world of the Ortonesque: a world that includes not only such extreme elements as murder and rape, but more pervasive and familiar principles such as hypocrisy and deceit. Shepherd argues that Orton's drama destabilizes the viewing audience by presenting them with irreconcilable alternatives that split their sympathy between equally untenable options. For example, in Shepard's view, *The Erpingham Camp* suspends the audience between their sympathy for Eileen and Ted and their horror at the violence perpetrated by Eileen and Ted:

> Eileen has the last word: 'I'm terrified all this will affect my baby.' This is the most difficult aspect of the play. Here are 'ordinary' people, who have, like us, a respect for the family. Yet hitherto their violence has horrified us. Our laughter at the theatrical camp drives us to side with the exploited, the 'real' people, but the siding is compromised, hypocritical, eventually destructive. We have been caught in a situation where two of our deepest assumptions contradict each other. We have gone to the theatre to be entertained, uncritically. That entertainment, that form of theatre, is destroyed, violently, by those who act in the name of family.[30]

The Erpingham Camp situates the audience on the horns of a dilemma and, for those audience members who care to reflect upon the nature of their divided sympathy, can thus be profoundly unsettling. What Shepard outlines in his articles is, in rudimentary Hegelian terms, a classical opposition between thesis and antithesis. And what Shepard's implicit Hegelian schema necessarily points to is the potential for sublation. This potential sublation can be achieved only by a fundamental transformation of an individual's values, a transformation that would be unique to each individual, but which would commonly be prompted by the experience of Orton's drama. In this way, the potential moment of sublation that Shepard identifies as part of the experience of Orton's drama marks the moment in which the Ortonesque can move beyond the negative limitation of satire to the positive regenerative pole that is necessary for a carnivalesque-Ortonesque. What can be potentially regenerated in this moment is, of course, the normative ethical values that orient an individual's world view. It is important to a Bakhtinian consideration of the Ortonesque that the positive regenerative potential of Orton's work does not lapse into the didactic. The implicit invitation that Shepard uncovers in the Ortonesque neither preaches to nor forces any specific moral message upon society at large, and thus Orton avoids the moral sententiousness that "destroys the very contents of the truth which it unveils" (Bakhtin 94).

Orton's Edna Welthorpe letters and Shepard's Hegelian argument about the potential audience response to Orton's drama both point to how the Ortonesque can be viewed as breaking through the "fourth wall" that separates stage and street. The inherently social nature of the carnivalesque—its concern with the folk and with the social structures of authority and value—make it necessary that the Ortonesque participate in the social sphere beyond the limit of the footlights. Although Bakhtin's implicit segregation of the theatrical stage from the larger extra-dramatic social sphere betrays a certain formalist approach that regards literature as a hermetically sealed autonomous entity—this approach has since fallen out of favour as the relationship between various social determinants and literature is ever more intensively scrutinized—the essentially social and revolutionary nature of the carnivalesque itself reveals Bakhtin's concern with precisely those social determinants that are apparently marginalized in the actor/assembly dichotomy.

One social determinant that is sometimes factored into a consideration of the Ortonesque is Orton's sexual orientation. While Orton's homosexuality—lustfully celebrated and extensively documented in his diaries—might arguably influence his drama in any number of ways, Orton's sexual orientation also provides a strong reason not to consider the Ortonesque within the context of satire. This is because in as much as satire tends to work through ironic inversion, Orton's sexual orientation might be seen as the source of such an inverted perspective by virtue of the mistaken and offensive view that homosexuality is the deviant inversion of the heterosexual norm. If this view is adopted, the trope of inversion could become invested with a moral weight which offensively implicates Orton's sexual orientation and simultaneously valorizes heterosexuality as the normative standard. Although Maurice Charney certainly *does not* make this blunder and implicate Orton's homosexuality in this way, he does open the door for others to blunder through because Charney explicitly makes a ligature between the playwright's homosexuality and the trope of satiric inversion. Charney argues that "Orton as homosexual playwright assumes the stance of alien, outsider, critic, and satirist of *all* the values that

straight middle-class society most cherishes."[31] Further, Charney suggests that Orton makes these satiric points by means of numerous "easy reversals."[32] Based upon the premise of a ligature between Orton's gay identity and the satiric function of his texts, the logical syllogism could look like this: 1) Orton is gay; 2) Orton satirizes heterosexual morality by means of easy reversals; 3) satire by means of inversion is proper to a gay playwright such as Orton because homosexuality is the inverse of heterosexuality.

This line of argument does a disservice not only to Orton himself, but also to Orton's work. The offensive conflation of homosexuality with inversion is compounded by the oversight of the fundamental ambiguity of Orton's work that is made by invoking the trope of inversion within the context of the Ortonesque. If, however, Orton's work is viewed within the context of the carnivalesque, both dangers are alleviated. Not only does the carnivalesque adequately encompass the fundamental ambiguity of Orton's drama, but it also implicates not only Orton's homosexuality, but all sexuality—including heterosexuality—within the same ambiguous, anarchic matrix. A kind of fundamentally polymorphous perversity is much closer to the Ortonesque view of sexuality; the social strictures that individuals choose either to respect or to disregard channel that fundamentally anarchic sexuality into various socially sanctioned and condoned avenues. But no matter what the ultimate expression that sexuality takes, it is still motivated, as the Ortonesque repeatedly suggests, by a kind of joyful anarchic sexual energy and impulse. This is what Charney suggests is one of the defining features of Orton's treatment of sexuality: "There is a cheerful anarchy about all of Orton's works in which nothing can be assumed, and in which all values—including the shibboleths of sexuality—are up for grabs. This endows his work with a 'carnivalesque' quality (in Bakhtin's terms)."[33]

The greatest challenge to a consideration of Orton's work within the context of the Bakhtinian carnivalesque concerns an element that is essential both to the comedy of Joe Orton and to the carnivalesque: laughter. While Orton's work is often hilariously funny, the laughter usually associated with comedy—"gay, fanciful, recreational drollery deprived of philosophical content" (Bakhtin 12)—is not the same kind of laughter that Bakhtin identifies as being particular to the carnivalesque. In Bakhtin's view, carnival laughter has three defining characteristics; it is inclusive, self-reflexive, and ambivalent:

> Let us say a few initial words about the complex nature of carnival laughter. It is, first of all, a festive laughter. Therefore it is not an individual reaction to some 'comic' event. Carnival laughter is the laughter of all the people. Second, it is universal in its scope; it is directed at all and everyone including the carnival's par-

ticipants. The entire world is seen in its droll aspect, in its gay relativity. Third, this laughter is ambivalent: it is gay, triumphant, and at the same time mocking, deriding. It asserts and denies, it buries and revives. Such is the laughter of the carnival.

(Bakhtin 11-12)

Although it is difficult, if not impossible, to separate out the laughter that results from the audience's reaction to the "comic event" of Orton's drama and the laughter that results from the audience's recognition of their unity in the existential absurdity of the human plight, it is extremely unlikely that a performance of Orton's work could be staged in which the audience laughter would be joined with the laughter of the actors. Orton's production notes for the Royal Court run of **Ruffian on the Stair** explicitly indicate that this particular play "must be directed and acted with absolute *realism*. No 'stylization,' no 'camp'. . . . Every one of the characters must be real. None of them is ever consciously funny. Every line should be played with a desperate seriousness and complete lack of any suggestion of humour."[34] Thus the separation between stage and audience appears to be maintained, at least as far as the issue of laughter is concerned. However, the self-reflexive nature of the carnivalesque laughter could be glimpsed in those audience members who recognize elements of their own social lives in the Ortonesque tableau upon the stage. Further, the ambivalence of carnivalesque laughter could be glimpsed in those audience members who are able to resolve the dialectical tension created by Orton's drama; their laughter could thus negate their divided sympathies while affirming their new resolve.

Although the argument for the self-reflexive and the ambivalent aspects of the laughter in the Ortonesque may appear to rely unduly upon speculation about a hypothetical audience response, there can be no doubt that the Bakhtinian insistence upon the inclusive nature of carnival laughter is not fulfilled in the Ortonesque. This lack of an inclusive laughter clearly violates the definition of carnivalesque laughter within the Bakhtinian paradigm. However, it is important to remember that in arguing for the merits of a Bakhtinian approach to the Ortonesque, I do not mean simply to propose a comparative measure in which a kind of checklist is used to match up defining elements of the carnivalesque with elements of Orton's dramatic craft. The larger purpose of this discussion is to examine whether the Bakhtinian paradigm productively illuminates Orton's work.

The benefits that the Bakhtinian perspective brings to a consideration of Orton's work are multiple. Foremost among these benefits is the potential for the structural nature of the carnivalesque to provide a generic rubric that emphasizes the fundamental ambivalence which permeates Orton's drama. This ambivalence not only extends to considerations of plot—the simultaneous registers of order and disorder—but also to aspects of theme—including, but not limited to, sexuality, communication, and class. Another benefit of the Bakhtinian view of the Ortonesque is revealed in how the carnivalesque aesthetic of grotesque realism emphasizes the carnal and vulgar nature of the Ortonesque view of humanity. This grotesque realism is most clearly displayed in Orton's characteristic emphasis upon the base nature of human motivation, which is intimately wedded to the lustful nature and avaricious capacity of humanity. When the fundamental ambivalence of Orton's drama is viewed in conjunction with Orton's degraded view of humanity and the sinister aspects contained within Orton's drama, the inadequacy of the generic rubric of farce becomes apparent. But that inadequacy makes the suitability of the Bakhtinian paradigm even more apparent. When conceived of as a literary genre, the carnivalesque not only encompasses the structural ambivalence of the Ortonesque, but also the dark and disturbing content of the Ortonesque. While it is true that the specific example of the carnivalesque that Bakhtin identifies in Rabelais uses the carnivalesque and grotesque realism to affirm life and human interaction in an essentially hopeful way, the Ortonesque adaptation of the carnivalesque and grotesque realism uses the Bakhtinian tropes to a distinctly different end. That is, while the Ortonesque may operate through a carnivalesque paradigm and a specific form of grotesque realism, the Ortonesque uses grotesque realism to affirm an essentially different view of humanity: avaricious, rapacious, and rampantly sexual. In this way, the carnivalesque utilizes the Bakhtinian trope, but not the Rabelaisian message. However, this utilization of the carnivalesque paradigm is consistent with Bakhtin's assertion that his categories are primarily functional and not substantive: "Carnival celebrates the shift itself, the very process of replaceability, and not the precise item that is replaced. Carnival is, so to speak, functional and not substantive. It absolutizes nothing, but rather proclaims the joyful relativity of everything."[35] The carnivalesque and grotesque realism are forms which can easily accommodate the barbed observations of Orton, and thus it appears that Orton adopts the Bakhtinian categories more than he modifies the tropes of carnivalesque and grotesque realism.

Notes

1. Mikhail Bakhtin, *Rabelais and His World*, Hélène Iswolsky, trans. (Bloomington: Indiana UP, 1984) 2-3. All subsequent references will appear in parentheses.

2. The conceptual groundwork for the carnivalesque is outlined in Bakhtin's earlier work, *Problems of Dostoevsky's Poetics* (Minneapolis: U Minnesota P, 1984) which was first published in 1929; a second and much expanded edition was completed by

Bakhtin and published in 1963. *Rabelais and His World* was completed in the mid-1930's, but was suppressed until its publication in 1965. Given that the carnivalesque is found in Bakhtin's earlier work, I will occasionally refer to *Problems of Dostoevsky's Poetics* in this paper in order to illuminate certain aspects of the Bakhtinian carnivalesque.

3. See the following two articles: Simon Trussler, "Farce," *Plays and Players,* June 1966, 56-58 & 72. Joan F. Dean, "Joe Orton and the Redefinition of Farce," *Theatre Journal.* XXXIV: 4 (1982) 481-92.

4. C. W. E. Bigsby, *Joe Orton* (London: Methuen, 1982) 56.

5. See Maurice Charney, "Joe Orton's *Loot* as 'Quotidian Farce': The Intersection of Black Comedy and Daily Life," *Modern Drama,* XXIV: 4 (December 1981) 514-24.

6. Bigsby, *Joe Orton.*

7. Dean, "Joe Orton and the Redefinition of Farce."

8. I find it helpful to think of this carnivalization of social hierarchy in terms of Derridean deconstruction in which a hierarchical opposition—Derrida addresses the specific case of speech and writing—is simultaneously *overturned* and *displaced* by means of "a double writing"

> that *simultaneously* provokes the overturning of the hierarchy speech/writing, and the entire system attracted to it, *and* releases the dissonance of a writing within speech, thereby disorganizing the entire inherited order and invading the entire field. (Jacques Derrida, *Positions.* Alan Bass, trans.
>
> (Chicago: U of Chicago P, 1981) 42

It is important to note that Derrida stresses the simultaneity of the operation in which inversion and displacement occur concurrently. Bakhtin similarly emphasizes how the carnivalesque simultaneously combines an affirmative regenerative moment with its negating destructive quality:

> The essence of the carnivalesque is precisely to present a contradictory and double-faced fullness of life. Negation and destruction (death of the old) are included as an essential phase, inseparable from affirmation, from the birth of something new and better.
>
> (Bakhtin 62)

What the Bakhtinian carnivalesque creates in the moment that it destroys the existing social hierarchy is, of course, the egalitarian social arena of the market-place.

9. Graham Pechey, "On the Borders of Bakhtin: dialogisation, decolonisation," in *Bakhtin and Cultural Theory,* Ken Hirschkop and David Shepard, eds. (Manchester: Manchester UP, 1989) 51.

10. Mikhail Bakhtin, *Problems of Dostoevsky's Poetics,* Caryl Emerson, ed. and trans. (Minneapolis: U Minnesota P, 1984) 123.

11. Joe Orton, *What the Butler Saw, Orton: The Complete Plays* (London: Methuen, 1976) 412.

12. *Loot, Orton: The Complete Plays* 254.

13. *Funeral Games, Orton: The Complete Plays* 333. All subsequent references to Orton's work will appear in parentheses.

14. Bakhtin limits his comments to modern parody and does not consider—for obvious historical reasons—the kind of postmodern parody championed by a figure such as Linda Hutcheon. In her *A Poetics of Postmodernism: History, Theory, Fiction* (New York: Routledge, 1988), Hutcheon argues that postmodern parody must be distinguished from modern parody whose definition as "ridiculing imitation" is "rooted in eighteenth-century theories of wit" (26). For Hutcheon, postmodern parody embodies a positive, regenerative impulse that is absent from its modern antecedent: "The collective weight of parodic *practice* suggests a redefinition of parody as repetition with critical distance that allows ironic signalling of difference at the very heart of similarity" (26).

15. Krystyna Pomorska, "Foreword," *Rabelais and His World* by Mikhail Bakhtin *x.*

16. Michael Holquist, "Prologue," *Rabelais and His World* by Mikhail Bakhtin *xix.*

17. *xix.*

18. Joan F. Dean, "Joe Orton and the Redefinition of Farce" 491.

19. Charney, *Joe Orton* 126.

20. 70.

21. John Lahr, "Introduction," *Orton: The Complete Plays* by Joe Orton 7.

22. Bigsby, *Joe Orton* 61.

23. 61.

24. 70.

25. 72.

26. 72.

27. Although Bakhtin stresses the fact that carnival belongs to the people and not to literature, he acknowledges that "from the second half of the seventeenth century on, carnival almost completely ceases to be a direct source of carnivalization, ceding its place to the influence of already carnivalized literature; in this way, carnivalization be-

comes a purely literary tradition" (Bakhtin, *Problems of Dostoevsky's Poetics* 131). Obviously, the fact that Bakhtin devotes his study of carnival to the literary work of Rabelais makes it possible to discuss the carnivalesque in other literary work, such as the corpus of Joe Orton.

28. John Lahr, ed., *The Orton Diaries: Including the Correspondence of Edna Welthorpe and Others* (New York: Harper & Row Publishers, 1986) 281.

29. 287.

30. Simon Shepard, "Edna's Last Stand *Or* Joe Orton's Dialectic of Entertainment," *Renaissance and Modern Studies*, XXII (1978) 95.

31. Charney, "Orton's *Loot* as 'Quotidian Farce': The Intersection of Black Comedy and Daily Life" 517.

32. 517.

33. 517. This is the only explicit mention of the Bakhtinian carnivalesque in Orton criticism that I have been able to locate.

34. John Lahr, *Prick Up Your Ears: The Biography of Joe Orton* (New York: Knopf, 1978) 130.

35. Bakhtin, *Problems of Dostoevsky's Poetics* 125.

Jonathan Keates (review date 7 November 1998)

SOURCE: Keates, Jonathan. "The Devious Escape from Leicester." *Spectator* 281, no. 8883 (7 November 1998): 54-6.

[*In the following review, Keates comments on a posthumous novel,* Between Us Girls, *and two posthumous plays,* Fred and Madge *and* The Visitors.]

What would have become of John Kingsley Orton if his lover Kenneth Halliwell had not chosen, on 9 August 1967 at 25 Noel Road, Islington, to beat out his brains with a hammer before committing suicide? In a sense the act was, in Cavafy's famous phrase about the barbarians, 'a kind of solution', not only, for obvious reasons, to Halliwell's problems with Orton's talent and success, but to certain of those unspoken yearnings through which a particular era battens on to those whose talents sculpt its profile. The murder, coming so soon after the decriminalisation of homosexuality, destroyed forever the illusion of that apparently innocent arrangement of 'two gentlemen sharing' with which cohabiting males had generally managed to circumvent the law, ironically adding fuel to Orton's complaint in his diary that 'the whole trouble with Western society today is the lack of anything worth concealing'.

Halliwell's hammer blows transformed his victim, what was more, into an icon of blighted promise, a sort of 'Chatterton, that marvellous boy', for the Sixties, which, as a British cultural moment, never properly happened until the decade was halfway over. Whereas Orton living might have degenerated into a mere lovable gadfly, the elfin pet of those whose tails he liked to tweak, we could turn him, dead, into an indispensable component of the zeitgeist, on the basis of three or four plays which essentially rejected the era's more portentous invocations of realism in art.

Orton had no wish to romanticise the dreariness of his working-class background in a suburb of Leicester. Not surprisingly, all three of the early works now released, the novel *Between Us Girls,* completed in 1957, and the plays *Fred & Madge* and *The Visitors,* written during the ensuing four years, are blatant rejections of that species of naturalism, tinged with inevitable nostalgia, explored by dramatists, novelists and film-makers in the wake of *Look Back in Anger* and *Room at the Top.* Not for Orton the idea of exploiting, in the name of a notional integrity, the provincial dullness he had dedicated his adolescence to escaping. Each of these juvenilia constitutes instead a calculated revolt against that very same 'poverty of expectation' that Ernest Bevin had famously identified as the doom, and in some sense also the fault, of the British proletariat.

Thus the world of *Between Us Girls* seems almost laboriously removed from anything with which its creator, even after his flight from Leicester, could possibly have been familiar. Orton here purposely disobeys that injunction frequently and misleadingly given to fledgling authors, 'Write about what you know.' Sophistications, even of the borrowed kind, had arrived with Kenneth Halliwell, whom he met as a Rada student in 1951. The pair had since written a series of novels with titles such as *Lord Cucumber* and *The Mechanical Womb,* and including no less than three versions of *The Boy Hairdresser,* all of which had been rejected by publishers nervous of their queerness during a period when the unholy alliance of tabloid newspapers and authoritarian home secretaries was making its last stand against the legions of Sodom. As Orton's earliest solo venture, *Between Us Girls* was a malign augury for Halliwell of his protégé's dawning independence.

The book's plot is of the flimsiest. Susan Hope, actress wannabe, joins the chorus line at the Rainier Revuebar— 'Intimate—Sexiting—Non-stop'—featuring Countess Sirie von Blumenghast ('18 sensational poses never displayed before'). Whisked off to a dodgy engagement in Panama, Les Girls fetch up as white slaves in Madame Josefa's luxury bordello, before Susan escapes to Hollywood to become the star of a musical version of the novel about Madame de Pompadour she has been reading as the story opens.

Of the two plays, *The Visitors* seems the more coherent in its portrayal of the fusspot Mrs. Platt attempting to rally her dying father Mr. Kemp with a diet of breezy bedside cliché. The tables are turned, however, as she falls under a bus and Kemp, in rapid remission, eagerly assumes her former role. *Fred & Madge,* on the other hand, a comedy of emancipation—by means of fantasies made real—from the tedium of working-class middle age, seeks to be everything at once, absurdist à la N. F. Simpson, with touches of Pinteresque minimalism, Firbank, Coward and Pirandello.

How would we have guessed that any of these was the work of Joe Orton? *Between Us Girls,* in its lack of momentum and curious flatness of tone, makes us thankful that he forsook fiction for drama, and its atmosphere of camp cinema glitz is no more typical of the writer than its generally unremarkable passages of dialogue. The plays on the other hand are as idiosyncratically Ortonian as we could hope for. Though *Fred & Madge* seems too crudely parodic of its characters' lives, and though the ending, a riotous fantasy in which the cast, having formally announced its intentions to the audience, sets off for India, looks like theatrical suicide, *The Visitors,* for all its structural flaws, is a resonant forerunner of *Loot* or *Entertaining Mr. Sloane* in speeches such as:

> She was very well known at the time. She had a voice that could break wine-glasses. That's what they said. I often wondered if it was true. I would have asked her, but I didn't like to. Not that she would have minded. She wasn't that type. But it seemed too personal, so I didn't.

Respectfully archaeological though these publications appear, this play at least deserves a theatrical outing.

Patrick O'Connor (review date 12 February 1999)

SOURCE: O'Connor, Patrick. "Quiet at the Back." *Times Literary Supplement,* no. 5002 (12 February 1999): 19.

[*In the following review of* Between Us Girls, Fred and Madge, *and* The Visitors, *O'Connor offers a mostly favorable assessment of all three works.*]

Joe Orton kept pages of notes—words or phrases, sometimes scraps of dialogue. As he used them in his plays or stories, he would cross them off. This collage mentality pervades all his work and produces the effect of surrealism that he strove for, though it can induce irritation in the reader. Orton's is the voice from the back of the hall, at first asking pertinent questions and cracking amusing jokes. By the end of the evening, one feels like telling him to shut up.

Between Us Girls was Orton's first completed work after he had ceased to collaborate with Kenneth Halliwell, his partner and eventual murderer. Written in 1957, it is a heavy-handed spoof of romantic women's magazine stories, substituting a lurid plot involving strip-clubs, slave-traders and a Hollywood happy ending for the boy-meets-girl formula. In her introduction to this first publication, Francesca Coppa identifies references to the 1952 film *Singin' in the Rain,* and students of 1950s pulp fiction will no doubt be able to find the sources for some of the other characters and settings. For example, the narrator, Susan Hope, is an aspiring actress who takes a job in the "Rainier Revuebar". Orton's earlier novels, now lost, written in tandem with Halliwell, had drawn heavily on Ronald Firbank, and although Orton is here freeing himself from the convoluted prose they had previously attempted, one still hears the Firbankian model in the choice of names. When Susan looks at a poster for the club, its star is "Düsseldorf's own Countess Sirie von Blumen-ghast". Orton's self-conscious elocution and his search for an artistic milieu away from his drab Leicester background give Susan's prissy manners in the face of Soho and then Mexican sex-work a tingling reality. When she is dressed as a novice for her first evening in the brothel, she comments: "Señora Josefa had dressed me in something which I am not going to mention. She insisted upon my virginal quality and what I wore and the furniture in my room bordered on sacrilege."

A running joke throughout *Between Us Girls* concerns Susan's copy of a novel about Madame Pompadour called *The Divine Marquisé,* the error of the acute accent never explained or noted. Nancy Mitford's *Madame de Pompadour* had been a bestseller in 1954 and must have come to the attention of Orton and Halliwell on their frequent visits to the public library. Some future student might like to take the two books and analyse Mitford's influence on Orton; it's certainly there, especially in a dream described by Susan near the end of the story, when she marries the surly and violent hero. He is Bob Kennedy, and this is the first appearance in Orton's work of the angry, attractive character who would become most famous as Mr. Sloane. Susan sees him again: "He'd grown older and wiser and tougher and more, not less intolerant."

Fred and Madge and *The Visitors* were written in 1959 and 1961 and are more recognizably Ortonesque. Like *Between Us Girls, Fred and Madge* takes a hackneyed set of characters and sets them on a fantasy ride ending in India. In one brilliant scene, two professional "insulters" vie with each other to abuse the guests at a wedding ceremony. "We must hurt the feelings of our enemies, infuriate those we dislike", declares one of these two professors of Insult, who offer scholarships in "tactlessness, incivility, ill-breeding, blackguardism and back-biting". Fred and Madge themselves have spent their working lives in Lewis Carroll-like occupations, he rolling boulders up a slope, she straining water through sieves. *The Visitors* is set in a hospital ward and introduces Orton's favourite villainess, the nurse. This figure of authority, who reappears to more sinister effect in *Loot,* as the woman who "has practised her own form of genocide for decades", will, at the end of *What the Butler Saw,* be abused and tied up in a strait-jacket.

As early runs of Orton's later work, both these plays are full of interesting similarities and pree-choes. How they would fare on stage would depend on a director finding a style which would disguise Orton's own pleasure at finding a place for each of his one-liners. In *Fred and Madge,* he mocks Noël Coward for being "an almost perfect example of the unnatural idiot", and he parodies *Private Lives* in a chance-meeting scene. The problem with playing Orton is exactly the same as that of getting Coward right. People try far too hard to be Ortonesque, whereas what is really needed is the absolute professionalism and realism which he sets out to lampoon.

Richard Helfer (review date December 1999)

SOURCE: Helfer, Richard. "Ruining Civilization." *Lambda Book Report* 8, no. 5 (December 1999): 25-6.

[*In the following review, Helfer says that* Fred and Madge *deserves staging but is less enthusiastic about* Between Us Girls *and* The Visitors.]

Like Hemingway, Joe Orton is having a prolific posthumous career. *Between Us Girls* and *The Visitors* and *Fred and Madge* are part of a large amount of writing done before Orton's fame.

Between Us Girls is a novel from 1957. Some might be surprised to see an Orton novel, but that was how he started writing, first in collaboration with Kenneth Halliwell, his lover and eventual murderer, and then on his own. It is, or starts out as, the diary of Susan Hope, a well-read but not very bright English girl with a desire to enter show business. Orton makes much of her inability to see the seediness of the jobs offered her. She leaves a job in a shabby nightclub for what turns out to be a Mexican white-slavery ring. Escaping the slavery ring—on the second day, not before being with a client (this is Orton, after all)—she flees to Hollywood, where she becomes a star.

I think Orton might have lost interest in this as he went along—or, at least might have wanted another draft before a final version. The amount of detail lessens by the middle so that the early sections, with the least action,

take up the most room. He seems to drop the idea that we are reading a diary; and the ingenue protagonist frequently offers descriptions that show an Orton-clear eye rather than that of an innocent. Despite all that, the book is, to use a technical term, a hoot.

The plays, together in one volume, are also worthwhile, though only faintly foreshadowing the style that would make Orton famous. *The Visitors,* from 1959, is written in three "acts," but is actually a television screenplay and was optioned by the BBC. Set in a hospital, it is a much more realistic and somber Orton than we are used to, and more loosely centered, as we follow nurses and visitors from room to room. The main characters are an elderly man, evidently in the final stages of a terminal disease, and his middle-aged daughter. Orton makes it clear that her blind cheeriness and refusal to face the facts of the situation actually deprive the old man of a chance to come to terms with his life. This criticism, and the hint that she is typical of her middle-class existence, are the clearest signs of Orton in what is a well-done and affecting but not unusual work.

1961s *Fred and Madge* is also untypical, but much stronger; indeed, I think it's one of the better absurdist plays I've come across, and I wonder why someone is not producing it now. The opening is very much in an Ionesco mode, as Fred and Madge discuss the boredom of their life—Fred has a job rolling rocks uphill, and Madge works at a water-sieving plant. Even here though, the specific social comment is stronger than Ionesco, and Fred reveals a deeper underlying anger.

By the second act, Fred has left both his job and Madge; and the play leaves Ionesco for Aristophanes and Lewis Carroll, with some possible minor assistance from Thornton Wilder and a plot device from Noel Coward. Orton starts destroying more and more of late '50s British society and makes the idea of "trashing" literal by roaming London, destroying buildings by laughing at them, leading to the magnificent passage:

WEBBER:

Do you want to ruin society and civilization with your laughter?

MADGE:

Yes oh yes!

This is a current cliché, but how exhilarating to see it in the original form, when it meant something.

By the end, the play and characters float away from earthly bounds, as all leave Britain and modern society for a dream-vision India.

I recommend both of these books, not just to the Orton scholar, but to anyone who loves a good, anarchic, laugh.

William Hutchings (review date winter 2000)

SOURCE: Hutchings, William. Review of *Between Us Girls,* by Joe Orton. *World Literature Today* 74, no. 1 (winter 2000): 160.

[*In the following review, Hutchings says that* Between Us Girls *is noteworthy only as a minor addition to Orton's body of work.*]

Written in 1957 and now published for the first time over thirty years after the author's death, **Between Us Girls** is the first novel that Joe Orton wrote independently of his mentor, lover, and eventual murderer Kenneth Halliwell. Its three-part picaresque plot parodies the familiar chorus-girl-to-movie-star story line of countless film and stage extravaganzas; its narrator, Susan Hope, begins in the chorus of London's Rainier Revuebar, is transported through the White Slave Trade to a brothel in Mareposa, Mexico, soon escapes from there, and establishes herself in Hollywood, where eventually (of course) she becomes a star.

The novel is written in the form of Susan's diary, with its tone echoing *Confidential, Photoplay,* and other such then-popular magazines. Yet, as in the articles whose "teaser" titles adorned their lurid covers (and indeed, as in the old peepshow arcade machines from which the title of Orton's final play **What the Butler Saw** was derived), the "confided" content of **Between Us Girls** proves to be far less sensational than the reader might be led to expect. Although the narrative is enlivened by glimpses of exotic and erotic demimondes that were not then current in serious fiction, surprisingly little is actually "revealed": at the Soho strip club, for example, "Düsseldorf's own Countess Sirie von Blumenghast" displays her "eighteen sensational poses never seen before," but Orton's description of the Mexican brothel and the goings-on therein is surprisingly demure. There, as in Jean Genet's play *The Balcony,* unusual costumes are apparently *de rigueur* and the police are prominent among the clientele, but the rampant and exuberant sexual transgressiveness of Orton's later work is undeveloped here, with Susan often seeming as naïve as Voltaire's Candide. Intermittently, diary entries are identified by the day of the week but never the date or year, and this convention is abandoned midway through the novel; the final segments reveal Susan Hope to be considerably older than in previous sections; but if, like Defoe's Moll Flanders, she has settled down after her wilder days of youth, now comfortable at last in prosperity and/or propriety, she spares the reader any moralizing about it.

The polished phrasing that characterizes Orton's later work is only occasionally evident here: a character's attire "shone with vulgarity," and another is described as "a creature with beige-colored skin who . . . stared at me out of eyes which crawled from beneath wrinkled lids like uneasy snails." There is also evidence of his fondness for parodying popular culture: on the first page Susan has just purchased a romance novel entitled *The Divine Marquisé,* and she eventually stars in the film version of it. Accordingly, the section of **Between Us Girls** that is set in Hollywood is the most comical in the book.

Francesca Coppa's thirty-page introduction to the novel provides a useful overview of Orton's career and includes a chronology of his life. **Between Us Girls** is of interest almost solely because it is Joe Orton's, however, and any new fragment of his work will be welcomed by his many devotees, ever eager to learn more about his too-short life and literary career. Had it been by an unknown author, however, the novel would attract scant attention, in the unlikely event that it had been published at all.

Joel Greenberg (essay date spring 2001)

SOURCE: Greenberg, Joel. "Joe Orton: A High Comedy of Bad Manners." *Journal of Dramatic Theory and Criticism* 15, no. 2 (spring 2001): 133-44.

[*In the following essay, Greenberg presents an overview of several Orton plays, emphasizing the comedic shock value of Orton's style.*]

Joe Orton, dubbed 'the Oscar Wilde of Welfare State Gentility' by critic Ronald Bryden, established a new kind of theatre with just three full-length plays and less than a half dozen one-act and radio plays. That so modest a body of work altered the possibilities of stage comedy is remarkable, but that the playwright spent only three years of his life, the last three years (1964-67), in his pursuit of and mastery over a unique voice is nothing short of extraordinary.

Orton was an exemplary student, whose education came not from formal training but from his inexhaustible appetite for reading, listening to radio drama, attending theatre and eavesdropping on life on the street and in the gutter. No stranger to the works of the great Restoration playwrights or Oscar Wilde, Orton eschewed the new naturalism of writers like Osborne and Wesker, preferring the indirection and obfuscation of a comedy whose ultimate aim must be to resist the predictable in order to lacerate the audience's complacency. Between 1964, with his premiere production, **Entertaining Mr. Sloane,** and 1967, when he completed the rehearsal draft of **What the Butler Saw,** Orton struck chords of outrage and delirious glee as he perfected his unique brand of high comedy which would, in his lifetime, come to be known as 'Ortonesque.'

High Comedy begins with the playwrights of the British Restoration. What is most striking about Restoration comedy is its passionate reliance on language over action, a predilection of British theatre writing that served as Orton's chief inspiration. And what Orton most valued about the Restoration period, was that it emboldened the theatre by putting sex on the stage as it had not been presented before. Innuendo, a popular device for enlivening a scene onstage, was a principal component of Restoration comedy. And while the freedom to speak lewd and carnal thoughts aloud was unique, the event was made more potent with female characters for the first time being played by women. A sexual charge, with many scenes even suggesting the sexual act itself, was created by a perfect balance of heightened language and emphatic self-adoration.

In Orton's world, people respected the impact of a well-chosen phrase, but unlike the Restoration's focus on high society, Orton's characters were drawn from many social layers, the disenfranchised as much as the well-born.

Following the Restoration, the Comedy of Manners re-emerged with writers such as Sheridan and Wilde. The best-known and most frequently studied and performed of these playwrights' works reveal society's delight at seeing itself reflected through a mirror crystal-clear that paradoxically warps the displayed middle-class values and got away with it because his audience was exhilarated at the same time as it was offended. Orton, a keen admirer of Wilde's dexterity, noted that in *The Importance of Being Earnest,* for example, Wilde shuffled an assortment of characters whose verbal jousting could sustain a threadbare plot, because what they said was infinitely more valuable and entertaining than who they were or what they did. (*Earnest,* in fact, may be the single pre-Orton play to succeed on its epigrammatic wordsmithery alone.) And Orton, like Wilde, would, in his plays, find the key to releasing the audience by driving them almost mad with laughter. But while Orton understood and appreciated Wilde's professional mastery, borrowing heavily from him as he experimented with his own comic to-and-fro, he always believed that Wilde's attempt to closet his private life blocked rather than served him.

Precisely what it was that contributed to Orton's arsenal of contempt and outrageous mischief, and why it was the theatre that was his medium of choice, is speculative. As logical as Orton's nightmare scenarios are, his own life appears to have been an illogical blueprint for his startling career.

Orton grew up in Manchester, in a lower middle-class family, the eldest of four children. His father was ineffectual, lavishing more care on his garden than on his own family. (Except for **What the Butler Saw,** all Or-

ton's older male characters reflect elements of his father.) His mother was the family's dominant force and her unceasing efforts to reach respectable middle-class status provided Orton with material enough to create several hideous matrons in his scripts. He escaped to London where he was accepted into RADA, an experience he dismissed except for the fact that it was there he met Kenneth Halliwell, the man with whom he would spend the rest of his life. (Halliwell was also the man who would eventually murder Orton and then commit suicide.) Halliwell, for his part, tutored Orton by assigning him books to read, and together they embarked on writing a series of novels that never saw publication during their lifetimes.

In the early sixties, both men were imprisoned for defacing a number of library books, but upon his release Orton emerged transformed and playwriting had become his single obsession. Though this sudden change is impossible to explain, the imprisonment released in Orton any self-censorship or lack of worth that he may have harboured previously. Orton wrote: "Before, I had been vaguely conscious of something rotten somewhere; prison crystallized this. The old whore society lifted up her skirts, and the stench was pretty foul. Not that the actual prison treatment was bad; but it was a revelation of what really lies under the surface of our industrialized society." Further exploring how the jail experience fed into his newfound gifts, Orton stated: "Being in the nick brought detachment to my writing. I wasn't involved any more and it suddenly worked." For Orton, then, the key to his comedy, a High Comedy of Bad Manners, lay in exposing the middle-class values he had grown up to revile and the society for which he had a palpable loathing. Life in Manchester drove Orton to London; working as a young actor helped him to learn that writing was the proper focus; pre-prison life with Halliwell, sharing a cramped bedsitter and collaborating on stories that were rejected as soon as they were submitted, was replaced by a professional ascendancy and a fully liberated private life.

Entertaining Mr. Sloane, the first of Orton's plays to be produced, drew critical and public praise as much as it provoked indignation from those same constituencies. With Terrence Rattigan's influence and financial assistance, the play transferred to the West End where leading commercial producers damned its filth and argued against the right of the playwright to be in the West End at all. Orton couldn't have been happier with the hysteria attending his work and his own emerging celebrity. Not since Osborne's *Look Back in Anger* had a playwright tapped so deeply into his own time. But while Osborne's creation of the post-war generation was exposed through a naturalism of language and action, Orton's vision was both comic and unrelievedly dark. His talent for blending the commonplace with the macabre, eliciting laughter in the process, set him apart from other playwrights of his day, and his young voice showed influences of his peers, particularly Harold Pinter.

Entertaining Mr. Sloane is set in a house situated in a garbage dump. The tackiness evident in the décor and the people who inhabit the house remind us of Pinter's play, *The Birthday Party.* Tension is created through the use of non-sequiturs and disjointed pauses, much as Pinter did in his early one-act plays. (In modern drama it is, after all, Pinter and Beckett who mined the pause for its myriad theatrical possibilities.) Orton, showing the influence of Pinter before him, relies exclusively on language to fuel the action of his play. The opening scene between Sloane and Kath, the woman of the house, illustrates this:

KATH:

   This is my lounge.

SLOANE:

   Would I be able to use this room? Is it included?

KATH:

   Oh, yes.

   PAUSE

   You mustn't imagine it's always like this.

SLOANE:

   The bedroom was perfect.

KATH:

   I never showed you the toilet.

SLOANE:

   I'm sure it will be satisfactory.

   PAUSE

KATH:

   I should change them curtains. Those are the winter ones.

   The summer ones are more of a chintz.

   PAUSE.

SLOANE:

   I can't give you a decision right away.

KATH:

   I don't want to rush you.

   PAUSE

   What do you think? I'd be happy to have you.

   SILENCE

SLOANE:

   Are you married?

   PAUSE

KATH:

   I was. I had a boy . . . killed in very sad circumstances.

   PAUSE

SLOANE:

   A son?

KATH:

   Yes.

SLOANE:

   You don't look old enough.

   PAUSE

KATH:

   I don't let myself go like some of them you may have noticed.

   PAUSE

SLOANE:

   I'll take the room.

Here Orton follows the pattern so popular in the standard comedy of manners. Societal norms are debunked, one after the other, and hypocrisy is revealed as the best survival technique in a patently self-serving world. Had Orton merely broadsided conventional thinking and predictable targets, the play might have vanished or, at best, might have found a small audience to jostle. But the author's genius was that he drew upon the turmoil that so characterized the sixties in London. The era, defined by consuming self-interest, desecration of the Establishment and the icons that represent the old order, sexual revolution, interchangeable gender labels and drug culture, finds a voice with Orton. In ***Entertaining Mr. Sloane,*** the title character begins the play having murdered one man and, before the final curtain, he will murder again. He sells himself willingly and knowingly to both the brother and sister of the house, and following the murder of their father by Sloane himself, they agree to an arrangement whereby they will share the young man's sexual favours, much as parents agree to shared custody of children. By our current standards this may sound tame and almost toothless, but until Orton no one had dared to speak ideas like these with such brazen audacity, let alone on a public stage in a commercial venue.

It is important to recall that homosexuality was still illegal in England, a prison sentence the likely punishment for being 'discovered'. Orton, whose published diaries reveal an aggressive fascination with and practice of dangerous sexual encounters, exposed his private life in his professional life by including references to the sex trade and his endorsement of the liberation of self at all costs. In *Sloane* the references are by way of innuendo, but the aim is to increase sexual tension and the play's unstated mysteries, more than it is to raise a quick and easy laugh. Midway through the first act, Sloane meets Ed, the brother of the family and the man who supports Kath, his sister:

ED:

I . . . my sister was telling me about you.

PAUSE

My sister was telling me about you being an orphan, Mr. Sloane.

SLOANE:

(SMILING) Oh, yes?

ED:

Must be a rotten life for a kid. You look well on it though.

SLOANE:

Yes.

ED:

I could never get used to sleeping in cubicles. Was it a mixed home?

SLOANE:

Just boys.

ED:

Ideal. How many in a room?

SLOANE:

Eight.

ED:

Really? Same age were they? Or older?

SLOANE:

The ages varied by a year or two.

ED:

Oh well, you had compensation then.

And then later in the same scene, his sister in attendance throughout, their exchange suggests a pick-up that Orton himself might have experienced in one of his tearoom excursions:

SLOANE:

. . . yes I like a good work out now and then.

ED:

A little bodybuilder are you? I bet you are . . . do you . . .

SHYLY

Exercise regularly?

SLOANE:

As clockwork.

ED:

Good, good. Stripped?

SLOANE:

Fully.

ED:

How invigorating.

SLOANE:

And I box. I'm a bit of a boxer.

ED:

Ever done any wrestling?

SLOANE:

On occasion.

ED:

So, so.

SLOANE:

I've got a full chest. Narrow hips. My biceps are—

ED:

Do you wear leather . . . next to the skin? Leather jeans, say?

Without . . . aah . . .

SLOANE:

Pants?

ED:

The question is are you clean living? You may as well know I set great store by morals.

Two years later Orton wrote *Loot,* the play that confirmed his unique voice. Like much else in Orton's life, *Loot* had begun with a false start when the out-of-town production failed to make it into the West End, leaving Orton distraught and threatening to give up writing for the theatre forever. But a successful new production, which opened eighteen months later and in the West End, liberated the writer to do what he pleased and to write as he chose. The carefully calculated dialogue in *Entertaining Mr. Sloane,* which successfully combined

tension, mystery and double entendre to excellent effect, was surpassed with the new play's truer understanding of the stage as a physical world. An equally
dull room in *Loot* replaced the dull sitting room of the
first play, but the difference was the way in which the
room was integrated into the play's action. The setting
had grown to define the play and to make its presence
inseparable from the characters that inhabited it.

Thematically, *Loot* digs deeper and touches a more exposed social nerve. Death and the way it is acknowledged and euphemized are central to this tale of theft,
murder and government corruption. Using a detective
and suspense plot as the frame, Orton inverts traditional
stereotypes at the same time that he demolishes respectability. Without sacrificing his ear for the brittle repar-
tee of high comedy, Orton accelerates the pace and the
viciousness of characters' responses so that threatened
loss of control adds an urgency entirely absent from the
earlier play.

In the opening scene, Fay, the nurse who has attended
the late Mrs. McLeavy, interrogates Hal, the late woman's son:

FAY:

> The priest at St. Kilda's has asked me to speak to you.
>
> He says you spend your time thieving from slot ma-
> chines and deflowering the daughters of better men
> than yourself. Is this a fact?

HAL:

> Yes.

FAY:

> And even the sex you were born into is not safe from
> your marauding. Father Mac is popular for the remis-
> sion of sins, as you know. But clearing up after you is
> a full-time job. You do see his point?

HAL:

> Yes.

FAY:

> What are you going to do about this dreadful state of
> affairs?

HAL:

> I'm going abroad.

FAY:

> That will please the Fathers. Who are you going with?

HAL:

> A mate of mine.

FAY:

> Have you known him long?

HAL:

> We shared the same cradle.

FAY:

> Was that economy or malpractice?

HAL:

> We were too young then to practise, and economics
> still defeat us.

Later in the same scene, she begins to suspect Hal of
committing a bank robbery:

FAY:

> Do you know the men concerned?

HAL:

> If I had that money, I wouldn't be here. I'd go away.

FAY:

> You're going away.

HAL:

> I'd go away quicker.

FAY:

> Where would you go?

HAL:

> Spain. The playground of international crime.

FAY:

> Where are you going?

HAL:

> Portugal.

In *Loot* there is a sauciness not present in *Sloane,* an
aggressive and unapologetic assault on sensibilities.
Here, nothing is sacred and everything is violable.
Sexual favours are equated with commerce and the ambiguities of *Sloane* are replaced with flagrant expressions of sexual freedom never before presented onstage.
This is where Orton separates himself forever from any
comparison to Oscar Wilde, since in Wilde's plays there
is no intercourse between characters, except above the
neck. And Orton's unashamed approach to freedom in
liberated and promiscuous sexuality defines him as an
indelible icon of London's counter-culture generation.

Additionally, government officials, the church and the
royal family emerge in this play as among Orton's
favourite brickbats. Sgt. Truscott, the detective investi-

gating the bank robbery, arrives in disguise as a representative from the water board. In a scene that can only anticipate Monty Python, he begins to question the nurse:

TRUSCOTT:

>Good afternoon.

FAY:

>Good afternoon. Who are you?

TRUSCOTT:

>I am attached to the metropolitan water board.
>
>I'm on a fact-finding tour of the area.
>
>You'll be out of the house for some considerable time this afternoon?

FAY:

>Yes, I'm attending the funeral of my late employer.

TRUSCOTT:

>Thank you, miss. You've been a great help.
>
>LOOKING OUT THE WINDOW
>
>Who sent the large wreath that has been chosen to decorate the motor?

FAY:

>The licensee of the King of Denmark. I don't think a publican should be given pride of place.

TRUSCOTT:

>You wouldn't, miss. You had a strict upbringing.

FAY:

>How do you know?

TRUSCOTT:

>You have a crucifix. It has a dent to one side and engraved on the back the words: 'St. Mary's Convent. Gentiles Only.' It's not difficult to guess at your background from such telltale clues.

FAY:

>You're quite correct. The dent was an accident.

TRUSCOTT:

>Your first husband damaged it.

FAY:

>During a quarrel.

TRUSCOTT:

>At the end of which you shot him. The incident happened at the Hermitage Private Hotel.
>
>Right?

FAY:

>This is uncanny. You must have access to private information.

TRUSCOTT:

>My methods of deduction can be learned by anyone with a keen eye and a quick brain. When I shook your hand I felt a roughness I associate with powder burns and salt. The two together spell a gun and sea air. When found on a wedding ring only one solution is possible.

FAY:

>How do you know it happened at the Hermitage Private Hotel?

TRUSCOTT:

>That particular hotel is notorious for tragedies of this kind. I took a chance which paid off.

Loot was the winner of both the Evening Standard Award and Plays and Players Award as Best Play of 1966. This public recognition only encouraged Orton to write bolder, larger and more forceful in-your-face satire and farce that dared restrained tastes to protest. And on the basis of his new status, Orton was commissioned to write a screenplay for the Beatles, a project that was never produced because the script threatened to subvert their celebrity and public image. With scenes including drug fests and multi-party sex play, there is little reason to wonder why the project evaporated.

But there is no doubt that the success of *Loot* unleashed a creative energy of extraordinary power. In the next year, the last of his life, Orton would write *Funeral Games* and *Crimes of Passion,* an evening of two one-act plays, and his masterwork, *What the Butler Saw.* At the repeated urging of his agent, Orton also began recording a personal diary, a remarkably detailed and uncensored account of his professional, personal and sexual lives. Its posthumous publication confirms that Orton was inseparable from the plays that he wrote.

A month before he was murdered, Orton finished the final draft of *What the Butler Saw,* the play that synthesizes all that had come before. As in all past writing, he maintains his firm understanding of mannered comedy through the convulsive syntax that he applies to his characters, but in this new work, Orton reaches beyond himself again, this time bridging High Comedy with dizzying, door-slamming farce. He moves past the playful antics in *Loot,* wherein the dead mother's corpse comes and goes from an armoire to a bed and back again often ending on its head in the process, and he invents a style which aims to destroy the characters' lives as the audience looks on in shock and riotous horror. The free-for-all scenario is in the style of true farce, made the more demanding by retaining the language and the wordplay that is now rightly identified as 'Ortonesque'.

Set in a psychiatrist's clinic, the play skews the basic elements of West End comedy at its tired worst. Dr. Prentice attempts to seduce a young woman while his wife is away. She returns suddenly and all hell breaks loose as he tries to maintain the appearance of respectability. By the final curtain, the play has encompassed drug use, shootings, incest, rape, cross-dressing and fetishism, among other menu items.

In **Butler** the cut-and-thrust of epigrammatic dueling abounds, but never at the loss of mounting pace to drive the farce forward and the characters increasingly away from their place of safety. The opening scene reveals Dr. Prentice as he begins his seduction of Geraldine, the young secretary, who believes she is present for a job interview:

DR. PRENTICE:

> I'm going to ask you a few questions. Write them down. In English, please. Who was your father?
>
> Put that at the head of the page. And now the reply immediately underneath for quick reference.

GERALDINE:

> I've no idea who my father was.

DR. PRENTICE:

> I'd better be frank, Miss Barclay. I can't employ you if you're in any way miraculous. It would be contrary to established practice. You did have a father?

GERALDINE:

> Oh, I'm sure I did. My mother was frugal in her habits, but she'd never economize unwisely.

His wife having returned, and the young Geraldine now hidden behind the drapes in the same room, Dr. Prentice begins his struggle to set things right or, at the very least, to suggest that everything is as it appears on the surface. Mrs. Prentice arrives pursued by a hotel bellhop, who is blackmailing her with pornographic photos he took the previous night. Within the first ten minutes of the play's opening, then we have been introduced to the principal characters not one of whom is what he or she appears to be. An exchange between husband and wife follows, and the true depth of Orton's venom is exposed:

DR. PRENTICE:

> (addressing the bellhop) My wife said breastfeeding would spoil her shape. Though, from what I remember, it would've been improved by a little nibbling. She's an example of in-breeding among the lobelia-growing classes. A failure in eugenics, combined with a taste for alcohol and sexual intercourse, makes it most undesirable for her to become a mother.

MRS. PRENTICE:

> I hardly ever have sexual intercourse.

DR. PRENTICE:

> You were born with your legs apart. They'll send you to the grave in a Y-shaped coffin.

The wife admits that she is naked beneath her coat, takes the dress left by Geraldine and proceeds to spend the balance of the play fighting to retain her identity, and ultimately her sanity, as she sees people rushing about in various states of undress, cross-dressed and bleeding, strait-jacketed and unconscious.

And with cover-up and disguise the order of the day, Orton repeats a variation of the detective character from **Loot.** In that play, the representative of the government conducts his underhanded investigation on the pretext that he is working for the water board. In this final play, Orton inverts his earlier scheme and announces the bureaucratic outsider's true identity at the start, while he drives everyone else to madness, lying about themselves by name, by gender and by sexual preference.

Dr. Rance enters the clinic and immediately encounters a startled Prentice:

DR. RANCE:

> Good morning. Are you Dr. Prentice?

DR. PRENTICE:

> Yes. Have you an appointment?

DR. RANCE:

> No. I never make appointments. I'd like to be given details of your clinic. It's run, I understand, with the full knowledge and permission of the local hospital authorities?

DR. PRENTICE:

> Yes. But it's highly confidential. My files are never open to strangers.

DR. RANCE:

> You may speak freely in front of me. I represent Her Majesty's Government. Your immediate superiors in madness.

And the momentum, thus begun, accelerates until all identities are meaningless within existing norms, until each character has been stripped of labels that hitherto defined who they were, both in themselves and to each other. Near the end of the first act, Dr. Prentice convinces the secretary and the bellhop to switch into each other's clothes as a strategy for escaping the clinic and returning to the world outside its walls. In the second act, passing themselves off as each other without ever having met, they come face-to-face with Dr. Prentice:

NICK:

> (looking at Geraldine in his uniform) Why is he wearing my uniform?

DR. P:

> He isn't a boy. He's a girl.

GERALDINE:

> (looking at Nick in her dress) Why is she wearing my shoes?

DR. P:

> She isn't a girl, she's a boy. Oh, if I live to be ninety, I'll never again attempt sexual intercourse.

NICK:

> If we change clothes, sir, we could get things back to normal.

DR. P:

> We'd then have to account for the disappearance of my secretary and the pageboy.

GERALDINE:

> But they don't exist!

DR. P:

> When people who don't exist disappear the account of their departure must be convincing.

In a world defined by as arbitrary a measure as appearance, Orton reminds us that the balance is tenuous, at best. In theatrical terms, however, he is saving his best for the last.

The play's final moment is stunning theatre because it combines the elements of pure farce: it rushes headlong to a catharsis through laughter while it remains rooted in the Comedy of Manners that inspired Orton from the start. All of the characters are in their various states of undress, some drugged and others bleeding from gunshot wounds. Dr. Rance finally locates the missing part of Sir Winston Churchill, a plot element that was introduced early in the first act, and holding a larger than life-sized phallus aloft, to the awed expressions of the assembled company, he sighs:

DR. RANCE:

> The Great Man can once more take up his place in the High Street as an example to us all of the spirit that won the Battle of Britain. How much more inspiring if, in those dark days, we'd seen what we see now. Instead we had to be content with a cigar—the symbol falling short, as we all realize, of the object itself.

The many plots resolved, the phallus providing a benediction of theatrical redemption, the characters climb up a ladder through the clinic's skylight and into the Truth and Salvation of blinding sunlight. It is an ending rich in literary imagery and equally rich in that it achieves the height of comic completion.

Shortly before his death, Orton assessed his own strength: "I'm an acquired taste. That's a double entendre if there ever was one. Oh, the public will accept me. They've given me a licence, you see . . . I'm a success because I've taken a hatchet to them and hacked my way in . . . It's always a fight for an original writer because any original writer will always force the world to see the world his way. The people who don't want to see the world your way will always be angry." And he was right. The posthumous premiere of *Butler* was greeted with shouts of indignation through the opening night. The cries of disgust were directed at Orton's careful disregard for proprieties of all kinds. But it wasn't foul words that got to the audience, because Orton rarely resorted to expletives.

In *Head to Toe,* a novel published posthumously, he stated the belief that applied to everything he had ever written: "To be destructive, words must be irrefutable. Print was less effective than the spoken word because the blast was greater; eyes could ignore, slide past, dangerous verbs and nouns. But if you could lock the enemy into a room somewhere, and fire the sentence at them you could get a sort of seismic disturbance."

Christopher Innes (essay date 2002)

SOURCE: Innes, Christopher. "Joe Orton (1933-67): Farce as Confrontation." In *Modern British Drama: The Twentieth Century*, pp. 293-306. Cambridge, England: Cambridge University Press, 2002.

[*In the following essay, Innes discusses the farcical elements of Orton's plays, noting that his outrageous situations and characters celebrated anarchy in their depiction of the universality of the abnormal and the dishonest.*]

Farce gained fresh relevance in the 1960s with Joe Orton's explosive, but short-lived eruption onto the English stage, which paved the way for Peter Barnes (see pp. 352ff. below) and influenced Howard Brenton's first short satirical pieces at the end of the decade. Savage and irreverent, Orton caught the sexual permissiveness and growing political dissent of the time. Yet although he struck a distinctive new note, his work was also a continuation of earlier trends.

Indeed, his first major farce, *Loot* (1965), clearly echoed Ben Travers' 1928 classic, *Plunder,* in its title as well as basic elements of its plot: a nurse who cuts the family out of her patient's will; a double robbery that brings police investigation; the threat of arrest for murder, and the use of blackmail to provide a resolution. At the same time, where Travers satirically presented this frenetic criminal activity as normal, Orton exaggerated it to the point of absurdity. The nurse is not just guilty of bigamy, but wholesale massacre—which is treated by the representative of law and order as a minor aberration: 'Seven husbands in less than a decade. There's something seriously wrong with your approach to marriage'.[1] Similarly, the blackmail and bribery in Orton's play involve not just one, but all the characters, including the bereaved husband and the police inspector.

Even in Orton's last, most fully developed farce, *What the Butler Saw* (1969), there are echoes of Travers' *Rookery Nook* in a hapless husband's attempts to find a dress for a naked girl and the substitution of another, very different type of character for her. But again the situation is extended way beyond anything credible by multiplication and sexual reversals. Orton declared himself to be 'a great admirer of Ben Travers, in particular'. Even so, he rejected the bowdlerization by which farce had become socially acceptable: 'French farce goes as far as adultery, but by Ben Travers's time it was only *suspected* adultery, which turns out to have been innocuous after all'. Reacting against what he saw as having 'become a very restricted form' Orton parodied Travers' formula for farce by taking it to extremes.[2] So, while Orton was clearly working in the same tradition, he is also demolishing a recognizable type of theatre; and this iconoclasm corresponds to his overall aim, which was to be provocatively outrageous.

The first lines of Orton's earliest play, *The Ruffian on the Stair* (radio 1964, revised as part of a double bill, *Crimes of Passion* 1967), had already set the characteristic tone of his drama, with its open homosexual suggestion:

MIKE:

> . . . I'm to be at King's Cross Station at eleven. I'm meeting a man in the toilet.

JOYCE:

> You always go to such interesting places.[3]

Entertaining Mr. Sloane (1964) revolves around a competition between brother and sister for the sexual favours of an amoral youth. This already objectionable situation is milked for obscene possibilities. Not only does the frumpish middle-aged sister see the youth as her own illegitimate son, transposing carnal seduction into incest. When he beats her father to death (to avoid arrest for murdering the old man's employer) filial feeling becomes merely an excuse for the sister and her homosexual brother to blackmail each other into covering up his crime. Their awareness of each other's complicity then serves as a bargaining chip in arranging a *ménage à trois* with a vicious murderer.

This attack on traditional pieties of the family, and the denial of romantic ideals in making the seduction grotesque (the 'girl' being fat, twice the age of the youth—

and with false teeth: an Orton trademark) is made doubly offensive by the conventional surface of the play. The setting of seedy naturalism, and the use of a sentimental comedy formula for a perverse action that the characters treat as perfectly acceptable behaviour, is designed to intensify the shock effect. Instead of nastiness being relegated to the woodshed, it is uncovered beneath the ordinary living-room carpet.

As his characters declare, for Orton 'sexual licence' was 'the only way to smash the wretched civilization'; and explicitness replaces innuendo in his subsequent plays. Instead of being merely imaginary, as in *Entertaining Mr. Sloane*, in *Loot* incest is linked to necrophilia, with a son being required to strip his mother's corpse naked. What the son calls 'a Freudian nightmare' in that play then becomes an actual rape of mother by son in *What the Butler Saw.* But 'licence' on the stage is not only intended as a liberating image. Its primary function is to arouse the most violent reactions possible in the average (by definition bourgeois) audience: 'Sex is the only way to infuriate them', Orton noted when determining to 'hot up' the first draft of *What the Butler Saw*: 'Much more fucking and they'll be screaming hysterics in next to no time'.[4] At first his plays were remarkably successful in provoking such an extreme response—even if critical appreciation of their stylistic qualities had already defused their shock potential less than a decade later, turning them into 'modern classics' by the 1975 Royal Court Orton season.

In 1964 *Entertaining Mr. Sloane* was greeted with revulsion by most reviewers, and Orton contributed to the furore (under various pennames, including 'Edna Welthorpe'—borrowing Terence Rattigan's symbol of the average middle-class philistine spectator). He deliberately sought to exacerbate public outrage by attacking any acceptance of his play through writing tongue-in-cheek letters to the press: such as, 'In finding so much to praise in . . . a highly sensationalized, lurid, crude and over-dramatized picture of life at its lowest, surely your dramatic critic has taken leave of his senses'. And through 'Edna', who claimed to be 'nauseated by this endless parade of mental and physical perversion', Orton scripted the kind of audience reaction he wanted for his drama: 'Today's young playwrights [referring specifically to himself] take it upon themselves to flaunt their contempt for ordinary decent people. I hope that the ordinary decent people of this country will shortly strike back!'[5]

This wish was fulfilled when public rejection forced the first production of *Loot* in 1965 to close before it reached London—although it won the award for Best Play of the Year in 1966—and *What the Butler Saw* was greeted with booing and hisses in Brighton and at the London opening in 1969. The violence remained verbal, but the antagonism between stage and audience was comparable to the Dublin riots over Synge's *Playboy of the Western World* or Sean O'Casey's *The Plough and the Stars.* The actor playing Orton's protagonist recalled 'a guilty sense of exhilaration in fighting them [the spectators]. They really wanted to jump on the stage and kill us all.'

Orton turned farce into a weapon of class warfare: as he once remarked to an admirer, 'I'm from the gutter . . . And don't you ever forget it because I won't'.[6] The sharp incongruity between subjects like death, incest or insanity, and their comic treatment was the detonator. His humour is always deployed strategically.

The key to Orton's approach is his way of treating conventionally tragic or disgusting situations as a source of comedy. This both trivialized public standards of seriousness, and used the audience's laughter to challenge their moral principles. In *Loot,* for example, a funeral is turned into knockabout slapstick (indeed, the original title was *Funeral Games*—which Orton re-used for a 1968 TV play satirizing the church). Dumped out of her coffin to make place for stolen money, a murdered woman's body is exposed to every indignity in a running gag. Stripped naked, deprived of false teeth and glass eyes, shoved upside down in a cupboard, swathed in a mattress-cover and paraded as a dress-maker's dummy, the corpse becomes the prize in a game of hide-and-seek between her son and his undertaker-accomplice, the nurse who has murdered her and is wearing her dress, her husband whom the nurse plans to marry, and a corrupt police-inspector in disguise.

In the same way, verbal elegance is combined with scatological crudity, stylish epigrams with derisive aggression: 'Why don't you shut your mouth and give your arse a chance' (*Entertaining Mr. Sloane*); 'It's Life that defeats the Christian Church. She's always been well-equipped to deal with Death' (*Funeral Games*); 'Have you taken up transvestism? I'd no idea our marriage teetered on the edge of fashion' (*What the Butler Saw*)[7]

The contrast between presentation and subject is the key element in Orton's brand of farce. An observation about unemployed actresses discussing the penalties of old age defines his theatrical approach—'It was a very sad scene because it was played in such a cheerful way'—and he extended this approach into every aspect of performance. On one hand, his dramatic situations are a collage of recognizable clichés borrowed from B grade movies, sitcoms and popular entertainment, corresponding to his perception that 'in naturalistic plays, I couldn't make any comment on what kind of policeman Truscott is [in *Loot*], or the law, or the big general things of the Establishment'. Yet although he structured his plots as a controlled frenzy (his own term for them) in order to project an image of anarchic insanity, Orton

continually stressed the need for realism. Presenting his dead mother's dentures as 'the originals' to the shocked actor playing the son in *Loot,* he remarks 'you're not thinking of the events in the play in terms of reality, if a thing affects you like that'. Then, when the first production of the play failed, he put it down to Peter Wood directing *Loot* for laughs instead of 'perfectly seriously'. Orton's advice to the Royal Court about staging *The Ruffian on the Stair* summed up his principle of contradiction: 'The play is clearly not written naturalistically, but it must be directed and acted with absolute realism. No 'stylization', no 'camp'. No attempt to match the author's extravagance of dialogue with extravagance of direction.'[8]

At the same time, Orton's view of life, as reflected in his diaries, is curiously myopic. Politics are dismissed as irrelevant, the only positive action being: 'Reject all the values of society. And enjoy sex.'[9] His own homosexuality and promiscuity is presented as a norm, universalized by his almost exclusive focus on relationships with other homosexuals. These run the whole social gamut, from Establishment figures, through the theatrical profession, to migrant labourers, in a record of frenetic sexual activity completely divorced from sentiment. Orton's one-sided selectivity implies that the (at the time banned) homosexual subculture equals the whole of society. When recording his one foreign holiday in his diary, he presents every male in Morocco as homosexual; and the only difference between Africa and England is stated to be that the law drives this 'natural' activity underground in Britain. By extension, heterosexual impulses, and indeed any feelings for others beyond physical lust, are either duplicity or self-deception. Respectability is hypocrisy. All moral principles are fraud. The logical result of such an egoistic view was Orton's brutal murder at the hands of his homosexual companion in 1967.

The premise of the diary form as literary genre (frequently misleading) is authenticity: an impression heightened in Orton's case by the sensationalism of his early death, and by the almost immediate publication of a biography (based in turn largely on Orton's diaries) which has recently been turned into a quasi-documentary film in 1987 (the film's title of *Prick Up Your Ears* being a typical double meaning that Orton had considered as a possible play-title). This process of canonization accurately reflects its subject's self-absorption, in which his own atypical personal experience is taken as universally representative.

In Orton's diaries, life is seen as validating art; and Orton's vision is directly reflected in his plays. His dramatic figures have no characteristics other than egoism, and all moral standards are inverted. Sexual deviation is seen as the norm, killing acceptable, and 'a bang on the nose . . . human contact'. Any innocence is presented as stupidity, all authority revealed as the source of chaos; and egalitarian principles only mean that everyone is equally corrupt. The whole of society is 'a madhouse. Unusual behaviour is the order of the day . . . It's democratic lunacy we practise'; and 'All classes are criminal today. We live in an age of democracy'.[10]

This universality of the abnormal and dishonest, which Orton's dialogue proclaims, is affirmed by his characters at the end of each play. Yet there is always one innocent, who actually believes in the moral principles denied by the others, and who has to be disposed of in order to 'keep up appearances' (the typical closing line of *Loot*). In *Entertaining Mr. Sloane* the senile puritanical father is killed because he insists on informing the police that his children's love-object is a murderer. In *Funeral Games,* a distraught man searching for his vanished daughter, who lies buried under the coal in her husband's cellar, is hauled away to a lunatic asylum to avoid the discovery of a faked murder. The pattern is clearest in *Loot.* The murdered woman's husband—'a law abiding citizen' who likes 'to be of assistance to authority' and refuses to credit any 'stories which bring officialdom into disrepute'[11]—is arrested on a trumped up charge and carted off to prison where an 'accidental' death has been arranged for him, with the connivance of his son, to prevent him confessing to his priest about the crimes of the others.

Significantly, all these representatives of middle class moral standards are father figures, the conventional symbol of authority. Their removal, clearing the way for a celebration of a new (dis)order, projects the destruction of restrictive social norms that Orton hoped to achieve through his drama.

This wish-fulfilment is most obvious—and least convincing—in *The Erpingham Camp* (first staged as the second half of *Crimes of Passion,* 1967), where an isolated holiday camp/prison is presented as a microcosm of society. The immediate reference of the title is to the Butlin's Holiday Camps dotted around the coasts of England, the down-market equivalent to today's Club-Med, where working-class families had their vacation activities regimented by staff dressed in bright red jackets. It also plays off the term 'camp,' relating to over-the-top homosexual display.

In this play establishment complacency and repressive morality lead to a popular uprising, and total overthrow of the corrupt power structure. But the parody is so exaggerated that it reduces the revolution to fantasy. Erpingham, the megalomaniac and puritanical Director of this institution, dons the stock corset worn by overfed husbands of nineteenth-century French Farce beneath his white tie and formal tail-coat, topped off with a gardenia-buttonhole, in a parody of the classic scene from Brecht's *Galileo* (which has become almost a re-

curring cliché in more recent British drama). There the character of the liberal Cardinal changes as he is dressed in rigid traditionalism of papal robes—but here the clothing ceremony merely exaggerates Erpingham's cartoon-personality. He has named the camp after himself; and his symbolic status is made all-too explicit when he is hit by a bottle:

PADRE:

. . . (*White-faced*). You've struck a figure of authority!

As in Orton's other plays, the primary target is hypocrisy—blatantly represented by the clergyman's criminal seduction of teenage girls during 'evangelical forays'. It infects the revolutionaries, with their slogan of 'Have a bash, for the pregnant woman next door!' (the riot having begun with a hysterical expectant-mother's face being slapped), as well as the authorities' declaration that: 'We'll have a couple of verses of 'Love Divine All Loves Excelling', Padre. It's fire-hoses, tear-gas and the boot from then on'. But Erpingham's power is as hollow as his appearance. Faced with the outraged masses marching on his command centre, the only way of restoring order that he can think of is a farcical display of traditional moral values: organizing a pageant based on Raphael's painting of 'Pope Leo turning back the Hordes of Attila', with the girl-molesting Padre and a vulgarly promiscuous camp entertainer standing in for Holiness and Virginity. Not surprisingly this empty image of moral authority fails to halt the mob, and the camp is literally demolished.

> *The red glare of fire fills the room. Distant strains of 'La Marseillaise' are heard.*
>
> With revolutionary banners flying they stream through the mists of a bloody dawn!
>
> *There is a sound of wood and glass being smashed.*[12]

However, there is no hint of political consciousness in the insurrection. All this rhetoric is deliberately inflated. The triumph of the masses is pure anarchy. The girl and the Padre are both raped, while Erpingham's ignominious death when the floor gives way beneath him brings the instant restoration of the status quo. Since these revolutionaries have no idea what type of society they want to put in his place, the brutal camp security guard (who has been manipulating the whole uprising) takes over.

What the Butler Saw (1969) gathers all these elements together. The social microcosm here is a psychiatric clinic, where madness is exploited rather than cured, following the epigraph from *The Revenger's Tragedy*: 'Surely we're all mad people, and they / Whom we think are, are not'. Each of the characters becomes convinced that all the others are insane, despite their repeated assertions that 'There's a perfectly rational explanation for what is taking place. Keep calm. All will be well.'[13]

(As another indication of continuity in the tradition of farce, one might note that the same source has been minded by Alan Ayckbourn, although instead of taking an epigraph from Tourneur's Jacobean tragedy, Ayckbourn transposes the whole theme into a modern context. But, like Orton, he casts the singular tragic action into the multiplying mould of Farce with his 1991 double play, *The Revengers' Comedies*.)

What the Butler Saw takes off from an amalgam of stock clichés: the casting couch; seduction disguised as medical examination; a wife's unexpected return. The rapid pace, proliferating parallels and multiple reversals, create an extravagant impression of absurdity, yet in itself, each incident is completely logical. A prospective typist takes off her clothes because the lascivious doctor, whom she wants to please as her future employer, persuades her that a physical examination is necessary for anyone who wants to work in a psychiatric institution (*mens sana in corpore sano,* etc.). When this 'interview' is interrupted, the doctor's natural response is to hide her discarded clothing. And when a government medical inspector mistakes her for a patient because she is naked, the doctor is forced to support this diagnosis in order to prevent his licence being removed. Her claim to be a secretary then becomes interpreted as a delusion that justifies her being certified as insane.

At first sight the insistence by the doctor's wife that he hire a hotel pageboy to fill the post, is eccentric in the extreme—until we learn that, having copulated with her in a hotel linen cupboard the previous evening, the page boy is blackmailing her into finding him employment. And his motive for making this unlikely demand (since the boy has no secretarial qualifications whatsoever) is quite rational. He needs a hiding-place, which the clinic will provide since—having gone on to seduce a party of school-girls later in the night—he is on the run from the police for sexually molesting minors. So, when a police sergeant comes in search of the secretary, to retrieve public property (part of a demolished civic statue that she picked up and put in her handbag), it is natural for the boy to put on a dress and wig belonging to the wife, and impersonate the girl, falling in with the doctor's last-ditch plan for covering up his own unethical behaviour in order to avoid arrest. Eluding her medical custodians, the maltreated secretary then seizes on the page's discarded livery as the only available clothing in which she can escape from the institute. When the boy discovers her dressed as him, he persuades the doctor that the solution for all their problems is to drug the Sergeant in order to remove his police uniform: the only way of getting out of the clinic being for the boy to masquerade as a policeman and take the fake page (as himself) into custody. The dress he has been wear-

ing is then put on the Sergeant to preserve the 'decencies', and the Sergeant's unconscious body is hidden in the shrubbery.

This manic complexity is not only an essential part of Orton's humour. The effect of such an accelerating confusion of roles and identities discredits the logic behind it. Reason and madness merge. The doctor, who accurately protests that 'I'm not mad. It only looks that way', is forced to admit that any description of the external facts reverses all standards of normal and abnormal. The truth would only make things worse when the medical inspector comes on them disposing of the unconscious Sergeant, before the boy has had time to switch out of his female clothes. So he is introduced to the inspector as the doctor's wife since he is wearing her dress, while the supposed pageboy (the secretary) takes refuge in the doctor's embrace:

PRENTICE:

I'm not a pervert!

RANCE:

How would you describe a man who mauls young boys, importunes policemen and lives on terms of intimacy with a woman who shaves twice a day?

PRENTICE:

I'd say the man was a pervert.

RANCE:

I'm glad you're beginning to face the realities of the situation.[14]

Following this line, all the permutations of transvestism are milked for every possible sexual relationship—although, with the exception of the pageboy's offstage episode with Mrs. Prentice in the hotel, no sex actually occurs.

In this sense, as well as in the use of cliché and the hectic tempo of the action, as Orton pointed out, *What the Butler Saw* is 'a conventional form' of farce: 'one should prove that one can do it, like Picasso proved that he could paint perfectly recognisable people in his early period'. Even the title is traditional, having been used as far back as 1905 (when a comedy titled 'What the Butler Saw' was presented at Wyndham's Theatre), and comes from the most well-known type of pier-end peep-show machine: one showing a keyhole, through which a French maid could be watched stripping to her suspender-belt while a gentleman sheds his pin-stripe trousers. The sexual display is literally that: exhibitionism. It is summed up in the notorious phallic image that concludes the play, where the vital missing part of Sir Winston Churchill's larger than life-size statue (dismembered by a terrorist bomb) is held aloft as an example of the national spirit—but one that even manages to insult the veterans of the war against Hitler by reducing their motive for fighting to sublimated homosexual desire:

RANCE:

> (*With admiration*) How much more inspiring if, in those dark days, we'd seen what we see now. Instead we had to be content with a cigar—the symbol falling far short, as we all realize, of the object itself.[15]

Offering symbolic surrogates for real sex is a fair definition of pornography; and in the dialogue Orton suggests that pornography not only caters to 'depraved appetites', but provides 'an instrument for inciting decent citizens to commit bizarre crimes against humanity and the state'. As a description of the play's aims, this exemplifies the unresolved contradiction in Orton's attitude to both his audience and his use of immorality.

The attack on authority figures, ranging from the 'National Hero', Winston Churchill, to the Government Inspector, Rance, is more directly challenging. Rance's position as 'a representative of order' and 'the forces of reason' is undercut by making him the cause of the 'chaos' he condemns. The moral status of the Establishment is ridiculed by his interpretation of everything in terms of the most lurid case histories. Any exercise of power is discredited by his manic progress from issuing certificates of insanity, to pouncing with strait-jackets on everyone who comes his way, or shooting all those he considers dangerous lunatics (including the policeman). The ending is consciously Euripidean, with the bleeding Sergeant in leopard-spotted dress descending as a parodistic *deus ex machina* to liberate the exhausted and injured figures. Trapped in the security bars designed to prevent the lunatics from escaping (clearly representing the cage of morality that drives a conformist population demented by repressing sexuality), they follow him up a rope ladder *'into the blazing light'*.[16]

What this final tableau celebrates, as in Orton's previous plays, is anarchy. However, at the same time as rejecting all social restraints and conventions, Orton claims traditional justification for the sexual explicitness of his work and its flouting of taboos: 'farce originally was very close to tragedy, and differed only in the *treatment* of its themes—themes like rape, bastardy, prostitution'.[17] The ending of *What the Butler Saw* is an exact rendering of this mixture.

The ironic image of redeemed humanity ascending into a saner heaven—though actually the oppressively moral world of reality that they have been temporarily liberated from by the farce—from the madhouse of furtive sex (defined solely as rape, blackmail or gender-bending perversion), derives from the apotheosis that crowns classical Greek tragedy. And Orton combines this with

the waving of a monstrously Aristophanic phallus. Similarly, the joyful recognition scene, which immediately precedes this coda and resolves the conflicts of the plot, would be a tragic outcome in conventional moral terms. The discovery of long-lost children is the ultimate disaster (although in the play presented as the opposite), since the revelation that the pageboy and the secretary are Mrs. Prentice's illegitimate twins, fathered during a wartime blackout in the same hotel linen cupboard by the man she eventually married, is simultaneously an exposure of 'Double incest'.[18] Typically too, following through Orton's concept of traditional farce, the comic affirmation of this outcome is designed as the ultimate outrage to a middle class audience's standards.

Orton's work is also traditional in another sense. He linked his style to Sheridan, Congreve and, in particular, Oscar Wilde. In Wilde's fate he saw his own experience of being a homosexual, an outsider, and imprisonment (Orton had been given a short sentence for defacing books from a public library); and there are clear echoes of Lady Bracknell in exchanges like

PRENTICE:

> It's fascinating theory . . . Does it tie in with known facts?

RANCE:

> That need not cause us undue anxiety. Civilizations have been founded and maintained on theories which refused to obey facts.

His most effective lines echo the paradoxes of Wilde and Shaw in the use of inversion to capture unacknowledged truths, as with 'Love thy neighbour . . . The man who said that was crucified by his'.[19] The epigraph to *Loot* is taken from Shaw, while in addition to borrowing the situation of the missing dress from Ben Travers, the recognition scene of *What the Butler Saw* is lifted directly from the discovery at the end of *The Importance of Being Earnest*—although Orton travesties the Wildean resolution through exaggeration.

Indeed, the degree to which Orton was consciously extending the comic tradition becomes increasingly clear within his work. As the self-referential comments on symbolism and pornography indicate, *What the Butler Saw* parodies itself, and it does so through the pastiche of other plays. To underline the point, attention is drawn to the set as a typical artefact of farce: 'Why are there so many doors. Was the house designed by a lunatic?'; and the action is continually presented as a literary cliché: 'Isn't that a little melodramatic, doctor? . . . Lunatics *are* melodramatic. The subtleties of drama are wasted on them'; or 'We're approaching what our racier novelists term "the climax"'.[20]

Orton was equally sensitive to contemporary influences. His first play borrowed heavily from Harold Pinter, with its threatening stranger forcing his way into a woman's home (as in *The Room*, 1957) and question-and-answer interrogation (as in *The Birthday Party*, 1958). But the subliminal violence in Pinter's early comedy of menace is extended into on-stage murder, while Orton always supplies logical explanations for the Pinteresque elements of indefinable personality and reversal, in which the 'ruffian' becomes the victim. If Joyce is called Madeleine—or Sarah—in *Ruffian on the Stair* (1964, staged 1967), it is because these were her trade-names as a prostitute. A stranger's completely motiveless assault on her and attempted rape turn out to be the result of her husband Mike's activities. As an Irish hit-man, his meeting at King's Cross Station, mentioned in the opening lines, was conspiratorial (not simply lavatorial). It led to the killing of the stranger's brother/lover, whom he cannot live without—and since the stranger's religious principles forbid suicide (though not homosexual incest), his attack on her is designed to manipulate her husband into shooting him. In Orton, menace only seems arbitrary until the facts are revealed. This conjunction of absurd action with rationality, which is basic to all farce, distinguishes his approach from Pinter's; and the extent of the difference can be seen in the moralistic subtext underlying Orton's work.

Paradoxically, considering their strongly anti-moral stance, on one level Orton's farces are morality plays. For instance, *Funeral Games* and *The Erpingham Camp* both deal explicitly with cardinal moral qualities. The first was originally commissioned, as an ironic expose of Faith and Justice, for a television series on the 'Seven Deadly Virtues' (a title that indicates Shaw's continuing influence on the English dramatic scene, since it comes from the Don Juan in Hell scene of *Man and Superman*). The second was written for a companion 'Seven Deadly Sins' series, to illustrate Pride. In Orton's world, ethical principles are merely counterfeit, propaganda lies propping up an immoral society.

Where his plays are most effective is in challenging all the ways society categorizes individuals, particularly in terms of gender and sexual orientation. Moral attitudes—and in *Loot* or *The Erpingham Camp* the religion on which morality is based—are not only assaulted through the subjects he chose to dramatize, but undermined by the complexities and confusions of Farce that make the audience (as bourgeois representatives) accomplices through humour. At the same time, the fantasy elements in his work devalue its social criticism, making a negative statement even out of the imperative to attack the society that victimized him as a homosexual. Indeed, in carrying his principle of inversion to its extreme the morality—for which society apparently stands indicted in his plays—always turns out to be positive and applauded. Orton's brand of Farce is not so much subversive, as a declaration of war. It embodies the anarchy it celebrates.

Notes

1. Orton, *Complete Plays,* London, 1976, p. 215.

2. Orton, in *Plays and Players,* November 1978, p. 13.

3. *Complete Plays,* p. 32.

4. *Ibid.,* p. 209; *The Orton Diaries,* London, 1986, p. 125.

5. Letters published in *The Daily Telegraph,* reprinted in *The Orton Diaries,* p. 281.

6. *The Orton Diaries,* pp. 256, 54.

7. *Complete Plays,* pp. 74, 317-18, 373.

8. *The Orton Diaries,* pp. 232, 211, 47; Orton, 1967 letter, cited by John Lahr in the introduction to *Complete Plays,* p. 20.

9. *The Orton Diaries,* p. 251.

10. *Complete Plays,* pp. 329, 412, 333.

11. *Ibid.,* pp. 274, 216-17.

12. *Ibid.,* pp. 303, 292, 310, 314 & 315.

13. *Ibid.,* p. 383.

14. *Ibid.,* pp. 418 and 417.

15. *Complete Plays,* pp. 447, 427-28. Ignoring the fact that farce is primarily a visual medium, critical analysis of Orton's work tends to follow John Lahr in emphasizing its literary quality, picking up on the assertion in his novel (*Head to Toe,* London, 1971, pp. 148-9) that 'words were more effective than actions; in the right hands verbs and nouns could create panic'. (see Lahr, Introduction to Orton's *Complete Plays,* pp. 8-10). However true this may be of the novel, as in the closing sections of *What the Butler Saw,* it is the visual imagery that dominates Orton's plays.

16. *The Orton Diaries,* p. 242; *Complete Plays,* pp. 417 & 438, 448.

17. Orton in *Plays and Players,* November 1978, p. 13.

18. *Complete Plays,* p. 446.

19. *Ibid.,* pp. 383, 340.

20. *Ibid.,* pp. 376, 427 & 447.

FURTHER READING

Bibliography

Bigsby, C. W. E. "Selected Bibliography." In *Joe Orton*, pp. 78-9. London, England: Methuen, 1982.
    Selected list of primary and secondary works.

Biographies

Charney, Maurice. *Joe Orton.* New York: Grove Press, 1984, 145 p.

>Bio-critical study of Orton which emphasizes the subtexts of Orton's dialogue.

Lahr, John. *Prick Up Your Ears: The Biography of Joe Orton.* New York: Knopf, 1978, 302 p.

>Biography of Joe Orton.

Sheperd, Simon. *Because We're Queers: The Life and Crimes of Kenneth Halliwell and Joe Orton.* London, England: GMP, 1989, 173 p.

>Joint biography of Orton and his companion and murderer.

Criticism

Feingold, Michael. "Foreign Entanglements." *Village Voice* 41, no. 10 (5 March 1996): 69.

>Joint review of *Entertaining Mr. Sloane* and Jon Robin Baitz's *A Fair Country,* critic calls Orton's play "happy" despite its "wholly improper" characters.

Kaufman, David, and John Lahr. "Love and Death." *Horizon* 30, no. 4 (May 1987): 38-40.

>Interview with Lahr in which he discusses finding hidden facts in Orton's diaries and attempting to uncover the mystery of Orton's murder.

Medhurst, Andy. "Licensed to Cheek." *Sight and Sound,* no. 7 (October 1997): 32-5.

>A discussion of so-called Queer Wit, an archetype invented by Oscar Wilde and practiced by Orton, other playwrights, and several Hollywood actors.

Nakayama, Randall S. "Domesticating Mr. Orton." *Theatre Journal* 45, no. 2 (May 1993): 185-95.

>Discussion of the ways in which the persona presented in John Lahr's *Prick Up Your Ears* differs from the image Orton creates for himself in his diaries.

Salwak, Dale. *Interviews with Britain's Angry Young Men.* San Bernardino, Calif.: Borgo Press, 1984, 96 p.

>Interviews with some of Orton's literary contemporaries, such as Kingsley Amis, John Wain, and Colin Wilson.

Stone, Laurie. "Half-Cocked." *Village Voice* 34, no. 12 (21 March 1989): 98-100.

>Rather unfavorable review of a production of *What the Butler Saw.*

Additional coverage of Orton's life and career is contained in the following sources published by Thomson Gale: *British Writers Supplement,* **Vol. 5;** *Concise Dictionary of British Literary Biography, 1960 to Present; Contemporary Authors,* **Vol. 85-88;** *Contemporary Authors New Revision Series,* **Vols. 35, 66;** *Contemporary British Dramatists; Contemporary Literary Criticism,* **Vols. 4, 13, 43;** *Dictionary of Literary Biography,* **Vol. 13;** *DISCovering Authors Modules: Dramatists; Drama Criticism,* **Vol. 3;** *Drama for Students,* **Vols. 3, 6;** *Gay & Lesbian Literature,* **Ed. 1;** *Literature Resource Center; Major 20th-Century Writers,* **Ed. 2;** *Reference Guide to English Literature,* **Ed. 2;** *Twayne's English Authors;* **and** *World Literature and Its Times,* **Vol. 4.**

How to Use This Index

CMW = *St. James Guide to Crime & Mystery Writers*
CN = *Contemporary Novelists*
CP = *Contemporary Poets*
CPW = *Contemporary Popular Writers*
CSW = *Contemporary Southern Writers*
CWD = *Contemporary Women Dramatists*
CWP = *Contemporary Women Poets*
CWRI = *St. James Guide to Children's Writers*
CWW = *Contemporary World Writers*
DA = *DISCovering Authors*
DA3 = *DISCovering Authors 3.0*
DAB = *DISCovering Authors: British Edition*
DAC = *DISCovering Authors: Canadian Edition*
DAM = *DISCovering Authors: Modules*
   DRAM: *Dramatists Module;* ***MST:*** *Most-studied Authors Module;*
   MULT: *Multicultural Authors Module;* ***NOV:*** *Novelists Module;*
   POET: *Poets Module;* ***POP:*** *Popular Fiction and Genre Authors Module*
DFS = *Drama for Students*
DLB = *Dictionary of Literary Biography*
DLBD = *Dictionary of Literary Biography Documentary Series*
DLBY = *Dictionary of Literary Biography Yearbook*
DNFS = *Literature of Developing Nations for Students*
EFS = *Epics for Students*
EXPN = *Exploring Novels*
EXPP = *Exploring Poetry*
EXPS = *Exploring Short Stories*
EW = *European Writers*
FANT = *St. James Guide to Fantasy Writers*
FW = *Feminist Writers*
GFL = *Guide to French Literature,* Beginnings to 1789, 1798 to the Present
GLL = *Gay and Lesbian Literature*
HGG = *St. James Guide to Horror, Ghost & Gothic Writers*
HW = *Hispanic Writers*
IDFW = *International Dictionary of Films and Filmmakers: Writers and Production Artists*
IDTP = *International Dictionary of Theatre: Playwrights*
LAIT = *Literature and Its Times*
LAW = *Latin American Writers*
JRDA = *Junior DISCovering Authors*
MAICYA = *Major Authors and Illustrators for Children and Young Adults*
MAICYAS = *Major Authors and Illustrators for Children and Young Adults Supplement*
MAWW = *Modern American Women Writers*
MJW = *Modern Japanese Writers*
MTCW = *Major 20th-Century Writers*
NCFS = *Nonfiction Classics for Students*
NFS = *Novels for Students*
PAB = *Poets: American and British*
PFS = *Poetry for Students*
RGAL = *Reference Guide to American Literature*
RGEL = *Reference Guide to English Literature*
RGSF = *Reference Guide to Short Fiction*
RGWL = *Reference Guide to World Literature*
RHW = *Twentieth-Century Romance and Historical Writers*
SAAS = *Something about the Author Autobiography Series*
SATA = *Something about the Author*
SFW = *St. James Guide to Science Fiction Writers*
SSFS = *Short Stories for Students*
TCWW = *Twentieth-Century Western Writers*
WLIT = *World Literature and Its Times*
WP = *World Poets*
YABC = *Yesterday's Authors of Books for Children*
YAW = *St. James Guide to Young Adult Writers*

Literary Criticism Series
Cumulative Author Index

al-Hariri, al-Qasim ibn 'Ali Abu Muhammad al-Basri
1054-1122 .... **CMLC 63**
See also RGWL 3

Ali, Ahmed 1908-1998 .... **CLC 69**
See also CA 25-28R; CANR 15, 34; EWL 3

Ali, Tariq 1943- .... **CLC 173**
See also CA 25-28R; CANR 10, 99

Alighieri, Dante
See Dante

Allan, John B.
See Westlake, Donald E(dwin)

Allan, Sidney
See Hartmann, Sadakichi

Allan, Sydney
See Hartmann, Sadakichi

Allard, Janet .... **CLC 59**

Allen, Edward 1948- .... **CLC 59**

Allen, Fred 1894-1956 .... **TCLC 87**

Allen, Paula Gunn 1939- ..... **CLC 84; NNAL**
See also AMWS 4; CA 112; 143; CANR 63, 130; CWP; DA3; DAM MULT; DLB 175; FW; MTCW 1; RGAL 4

Allen, Roland
See Ayckbourn, Alan

Allen, Sarah A.
See Hopkins, Pauline Elizabeth

Allen, Sidney H.
See Hartmann, Sadakichi

Allen, Woody 1935- .... **CLC 16, 52, 195**
See also AAYA 10, 51; CA 33-36R; CANR 27, 38, 63, 128; DAM POP; DLB 44; MTCW 1

Allende, Isabel 1942- ... **CLC 39, 57, 97, 170; HLC 1; SSC 65; WLCS**
See also AAYA 18; CA 125; 130; CANR 51, 74, 129; CDWLB 3; CLR 99; CWW 2; DA3; DAM MULT, NOV; DLB 145; DNFS 1; EWL 3; FW; HW 1, 2; INT CA-130; LAIT 5; LAWS 1; LMFS 2; MTCW 1, 2; NCFS 1; NFS 6, 18; RGSF 2; RGWL 3; SSFS 11, 16; WLIT 1

Alleyn, Ellen
See Rossetti, Christina (Georgina)

Alleyne, Carla D. .... **CLC 65**

Allingham, Margery (Louise)
1904-1966 .... **CLC 19**
See also CA 5-8R; 25-28R; CANR 4, 58; CMW 4; DLB 77; MSW; MTCW 1, 2

Allingham, William 1824-1889 ...... **NCLC 25**
See also DLB 35; RGEL 2

Allison, Dorothy E. 1949- .... **CLC 78, 153**
See also AAYA 53; CA 140; CANR 66, 107; CSW; DA3; FW; MTCW 1; NFS 11; RGAL 4

Alloula, Malek .... **CLC 65**

Allston, Washington 1779-1843 .... **NCLC 2**
See also DLB 1, 235

Almedingen, E. M. .... **CLC 12**
See Almedingen, Martha Edith von
See also SATA 3

Almedingen, Martha Edith von 1898-1971
See Almedingen, E. M.
See also CA 1-4R; CANR 1

Almodovar, Pedro 1949(?)- .... **CLC 114; HLCS 1**
See also CA 133; CANR 72; HW 2

Almqvist, Carl Jonas Love
1793-1866 .... **NCLC 42**

al-Mutanabbi, Ahmad ibn al-Husayn Abu al-Tayyib al-Jufi al-Kindi
915-965 .... **CMLC 66**
See also RGWL 3

Alonso, Damaso 1898-1990 .... **CLC 14**
See also CA 110; 131; 130; CANR 72; DLB 108; EWL 3; HW 1, 2

Alov
See Gogol, Nikolai (Vasilyevich)

al'Sadaawi, Nawal
See El Saadawi, Nawal
See also FW

Al Siddik
See Rolfe, Frederick (William Serafino Austin Lewis Mary)
See also GLL 1; RGEL 2

Alta 1942- .... **CLC 19**
See also CA 57-60

Alter, Robert B(ernard) 1935- .... **CLC 34**
See also CA 49-52; CANR 1, 47, 100

Alther, Lisa 1944- .... **CLC 7, 41**
See also BPFB 1; CA 65-68; CAAS 30; CANR 12, 30, 51; CN 7; CSW; GLL 2; MTCW 1

Althusser, L.
See Althusser, Louis

Althusser, Louis 1918-1990 .... **CLC 106**
See also CA 131; 132; CANR 102; DLB 242

Altman, Robert 1925- .... **CLC 16, 116**
See also CA 73-76; CANR 43

Alurista .... **HLCS 1**
See Urista (Heredia), Alberto (Baltazar)
See also DLB 82; LLW 1

Alvarez, A(lfred) 1929- .... **CLC 5, 13**
See also CA 1-4R; CANR 3, 33, 63, 101; CN 7; CP 7; DLB 14, 40

Alvarez, Alejandro Rodriguez 1903-1965
See Casona, Alejandro
See also CA 131; 93-96; HW 1

Alvarez, Julia 1950- .... **CLC 93; HLCS 1**
See also AAYA 25; AMWS 7; CA 147; CANR 69, 101, 133; DA3; DLB 282; LATS 1:2; LLW 1; MTCW 1; NFS 5, 9; SATA 129; WLIT 1

Alvaro, Corrado 1896-1956 .... **TCLC 60**
See also CA 163; DLB 264; EWL 3

Amado, Jorge 1912-2001 ... **CLC 13, 40, 106; HLC 1**
See also CA 77-80; 201; CANR 35, 74; CWW 2; DAM MULT, NOV; DLB 113; EWL 3; HW 2; LAW; LAWS 1; MTCW 1, 2; RGWL 2, 3; TWA; WLIT 1

Ambler, Eric 1909-1998 .... **CLC 4, 6, 9**
See also BRWS 4; CA 9-12R; 171; CANR 7, 38, 74; CMW 4; CN 7; DLB 77; MSW; MTCW 1, 2; TEA

Ambrose, Stephen E(dward)
1936-2002 .... **CLC 145**
See also AAYA 44; CA 1-4R; 209; CANR 3, 43, 57, 83, 105; NCFS 2; SATA 40, 138

Amichai, Yehuda 1924-2000 .. **CLC 9, 22, 57, 116; PC 38**
See also CA 85-88; 189; CANR 46, 60, 99, 132; CWW 2; EWL 3; MTCW 1

Amichai, Yehudah
See Amichai, Yehuda

Amiel, Henri Frederic 1821-1881 .... **NCLC 4**
See also DLB 217

Amis, Kingsley (William)
1922-1995 ...... **CLC 1, 2, 3, 5, 8, 13, 40, 44, 129**
See also AITN 2; BPFB 1; BRWS 2; CA 9-12R; 150; CANR 8, 28, 54; CDBLB 1945-1960; CN 7; CP 7; DA; DA3; DAB; DAC; DAM MST, NOV; DLB 15, 27, 100, 139; DLBY 1996; EWL 3; HGG; INT CANR-8; MTCW 1, 2; RGEL 2; RGSF 2; SFW 4

Amis, Martin (Louis) 1949- .... **CLC 4, 9, 38, 62, 101**
See also BEST 90:3; BRWS 4; CA 65-68; CANR 8, 27, 54, 73, 95, 132; CN 7; DA3; DLB 14, 194; EWL 3; INT CANR-27; MTCW 1

Ammianus Marcellinus c. 330-c. 395 .... **CMLC 60**
See also AW 2; DLB 211

Ammons, A(rchie) R(andolph)
1926-2001 ...... **CLC 2, 3, 5, 8, 9, 25, 57, 108; PC 16**
See also AITN 1; AMWS 7; CA 9-12R; 193; CANR 6, 36, 51, 73, 107; CP 7; CSW; DAM POET; DLB 5, 165; EWL 3; MTCW 1, 2; PFS 19; RGAL 4

Amo, Tauraatua i
See Adams, Henry (Brooks)

Amory, Thomas 1691(?)-1788 .... **LC 48**
See also DLB 39

Anand, Mulk Raj 1905- .... **CLC 23, 93**
See also CA 65-68; CANR 32, 64; CN 7; DAM NOV; EWL 3; MTCW 1, 2; RGSF 2

Anatol
See Schnitzler, Arthur

Anaximander c. 611 B.C.-c. 546 B.C. .... **CMLC 22**

Anaya, Rudolfo A(lfonso) 1937- ...... **CLC 23, 148; HLC 1**
See also AAYA 20; BYA 13; CA 45-48; CAAS 4; CANR 1, 32, 51, 124; CN 7; DAM MULT, NOV; DLB 82, 206, 278; HW 1; LAIT 4; LLW 1; MTCW 1, 2; NFS 12; RGAL 4; RGSF 2; WLIT 1

Andersen, Hans Christian
1805-1875 .... **NCLC 7, 79; SSC 6, 56; WLC**
See also AAYA 57; CLR 6; DA; DA3; DAB; DAC; DAM MST, POP; EW 6; MAICYA 1, 2; RGSF 2; RGWL 2, 3; SATA 100; TWA; WCH; YABC 1

Anderson, C. Farley
See Mencken, H(enry) L(ouis); Nathan, George Jean

Anderson, Jessica (Margaret) Queale
1916- .... **CLC 37**
See also CA 9-12R; CANR 4, 62; CN 7

Anderson, Jon (Victor) 1940- .... **CLC 9**
See also CA 25-28R; CANR 20; DAM POET

Anderson, Lindsay (Gordon)
1923-1994 .... **CLC 20**
See also CA 125; 128; 146; CANR 77

Anderson, Maxwell 1888-1959 .... **TCLC 2, 144**
See also CA 105; 152; DAM DRAM; DFS 16, 20; DLB 7, 228; MTCW 2; RGAL 4

Anderson, Poul (William)
1926-2001 .... **CLC 15**
See also AAYA 5, 34; BPFB 1; BYA 6, 8, 9; CA 1-4R; 181; 199; CAAE 181; CAAS 2; CANR 2, 15, 34, 64, 110; CLR 58; DLB 8; FANT; INT CANR-15; MTCW 1, 2; SATA 90; SATA-Brief 39; SATA-Essay 106; SCFW 2; SFW 4; SUFW 1, 2

Anderson, Robert (Woodruff)
1917- .... **CLC 23**
See also AITN 1; CA 21-24R; CANR 32; DAM DRAM; DLB 7; LAIT 5

Anderson, Roberta Joan
See Mitchell, Joni

Anderson, Sherwood 1876-1941 .. **SSC 1, 46; TCLC 1, 10, 24, 123; WLC**
See also AAYA 30; AMW; AMWC 2; BPFB 1; CA 104; 121; CANR 61; CDALB 1917-1929; DA; DA3; DAB; DAC; DAM MST, NOV; DLB 4, 9, 86; DLBD 1; EWL 3; EXPS; GLL 2; MTCW 1, 2; NFS 4; RGAL 4; RGSF 2; SSFS 4, 10, 11; TUS

Andier, Pierre
See Desnos, Robert

Andouard
See Giraudoux, Jean(-Hippolyte)

Andrade, Carlos Drummond de ..... **CLC 18**
See Drummond de Andrade, Carlos
See also EWL 3; RGWL 2, 3

Andrade, Mario de .... **TCLC 43**
See de Andrade, Mario
See also EWL 3; LAW; RGWL 2, 3; WLIT 1

Andreae, Johann V(alentin)
1586-1654 .... **LC 32**
See also DLB 164

Andreas Capellanus fl. c. 1185- .... **CMLC 45**
See also DLB 208

Andreas-Salome, Lou 1861-1937 ... **TCLC 56**
See also CA 178; DLB 66

Andreev, Leonid
See Andreyev, Leonid (Nikolaevich)
See also DLB 295; EWL 3

Andress, Lesley
See Sanders, Lawrence

Andrewes, Lancelot 1555-1626 .... **LC 5**
See also DLB 151, 172

Andrews, Cicily Fairfield
See West, Rebecca

Andrews, Elton V.
See Pohl, Frederik

Andreyev, Leonid (Nikolaevich)
1871-1919 .... **TCLC 3**
See Andreev, Leonid
See also CA 104; 185

Andric, Ivo 1892-1975 .... **CLC 8; SSC 36;**
TCLC 135
See also CA 81-84; 57-60; CANR 43, 60; CDWLB 4; DLB 147; EW 11; EWL 3; MTCW 1; RGSF 2; RGWL 2, 3

Androvar
See Prado (Calvo), Pedro

Angelique, Pierre
See Bataille, Georges

Angell, Roger 1920- .... **CLC 26**
See also CA 57-60; CANR 13, 44, 70; DLB 171, 185

Angelou, Maya 1928- ... **BLC 1; CLC 12, 35,**
64, 77, 155; PC 32; WLCS
See also AAYA 7, 20; AMWS 4; BPFB 1; BW 2, 3; BYA 2; CA 65-68; CANR 19, 42, 65, 111, 133; CDALBS; CLR 53; CP 7; CPW; CSW; CWP; DA; DA3; DAB; DAC; DAM MST, MULT, POET, POP; DLB 38; EWL 3; EXPN; EXPP; LAIT 4; MAICYA 2; MAICYAS 1; MAWW; MTCW 1, 2; NCFS 2; NFS 2; PFS 2, 3; RGAL 4; SATA 49, 136; WYA; YAW

Angouleme, Marguerite d'
See de Navarre, Marguerite

Anna Comnena 1083-1153 .... **CMLC 25**

Annensky, Innokentii Fedorovich
See Annensky, Innokenty (Fyodorovich)
See also DLB 295

Annensky, Innokenty (Fyodorovich)
1856-1909 .... **TCLC 14**
See also CA 110; 155; EWL 3

Annunzio, Gabriele d'
See D'Annunzio, Gabriele

Anodos
See Coleridge, Mary E(lizabeth)

Anon, Charles Robert
See Pessoa, Fernando (Antonio Nogueira)

Anouilh, Jean (Marie Lucien Pierre)
1910-1987 . **CLC 1, 3, 8, 13, 40, 50; DC**
8, 21
See also CA 17-20R; 123; CANR 32; DAM DRAM; DFS 9, 10, 19; EW 13; EWL 3; GFL 1789 to the Present; MTCW 1, 2; RGWL 2, 3; TWA

Anselm of Canterbury
1033(?)-1109 .... **CMLC 67**
See also DLB 115

Anthony, Florence
See Ai

Anthony, John
See Ciardi, John (Anthony)

Anthony, Peter
See Shaffer, Anthony (Joshua); Shaffer, Peter (Levin)

Anthony, Piers 1934- .... **CLC 35**
See also AAYA 11, 48; BYA 7; CA 200; CAAE 200; CANR 28, 56, 73, 102, 133; CPW; DAM POP; DLB 8; FANT; MAICYA 2; MAICYAS 1; MTCW 1, 2; SAAS 22; SATA 84, 129; SATA-Essay 129; SFW 4; SUFW 1, 2; YAW

Anthony, Susan B(rownell)
1820-1906 .... **TCLC 84**
See also CA 211; FW

Antiphon c. 480 B.C.-c. 411 B.C. .. **CMLC 55**

Antoine, Marc
See Proust, (Valentin-Louis-George-Eugene) Marcel

Antoninus, Brother
See Everson, William (Oliver)

Antonioni, Michelangelo 1912- .... **CLC 20,**
144
See also CA 73-76; CANR 45, 77

Antschel, Paul 1920-1970
See Celan, Paul
See also CA 85-88; CANR 33, 61; MTCW 1; PFS 21

Anwar, Chairil 1922-1949 .... **TCLC 22**
See Chairil Anwar
See also CA 121; 219; RGWL 3

Anzaldua, Gloria (Evanjelina)
1942-2004 .... **HLCS 1**
See also CA 175; 227; CSW; CWP; DLB 122; FW; LLW 1; RGAL 4

Apess, William 1798-1839(?) .... **NCLC 73;**
NNAL
See also DAM MULT; DLB 175, 243

Apollinaire, Guillaume 1880-1918 .... **PC 7;**
TCLC 3, 8, 51
See Kostrowitzki, Wilhelm Apollinaris de
See also CA 152; DAM POET; DLB 258; EW 9; EWL 3; GFL 1789 to the Present; MTCW 1; RGWL 2, 3; TWA; WP

Apollonius of Rhodes
See Apollonius Rhodius
See also AW 1; RGWL 2, 3

Apollonius Rhodius c. 300 B.C.-c. 220
B.C. .... **CMLC 28**
See Apollonius of Rhodes
See also DLB 176

Appelfeld, Aharon 1932- ... **CLC 23, 47; SSC**
42
See also CA 112; 133; CANR 86; CWW 2; DLB 299; EWL 3; RGSF 2

Apple, Max (Isaac) 1941- .... **CLC 9, 33; SSC**
50
See also CA 81-84; CANR 19, 54; DLB 130

Appleman, Philip (Dean) 1926- .... **CLC 51**
See also CA 13-16R; CAAS 18; CANR 6, 29, 56

Appleton, Lawrence
See Lovecraft, H(oward) P(hillips)

Apteryx
See Eliot, T(homas) S(tearns)

Apuleius, (Lucius Madaurensis)
125(?)-175(?) .... **CMLC 1**
See also AW 2; CDWLB 1; DLB 211; RGWL 2, 3; SUFW

Aquin, Hubert 1929-1977 .... **CLC 15**
See also CA 105; DLB 53; EWL 3

Aquinas, Thomas 1224(?)-1274 ..... **CMLC 33**
See also DLB 115; EW 1; TWA

Aragon, Louis 1897-1982 .... **CLC 3, 22;**
TCLC 123
See also CA 69-72; 108; CANR 28, 71; DAM NOV, POET; DLB 72, 258; EW 11; EWL 3; GFL 1789 to the Present; GLL 2; LMFS 2; MTCW 1, 2; RGWL 2, 3

Arany, Janos 1817-1882 .... **NCLC 34**

Aranyos, Kakay 1847-1910
See Mikszath, Kalman

Aratus of Soli c. 315 B.C.-c. 240
B.C. .... **CMLC 64**
See also DLB 176

Arbuthnot, John 1667-1735 .... **LC 1**
See also DLB 101

Archer, Herbert Winslow
See Mencken, H(enry) L(ouis)

Archer, Jeffrey (Howard) 1940- .... **CLC 28**
See also AAYA 16; BEST 89:3; BPFB 1; CA 77-80; CANR 22, 52, 95; CPW; DA3; DAM POP; INT CANR-22

Archer, Jules 1915- .... **CLC 12**
See also CA 9-12R; CANR 6, 69; SAAS 5; SATA 4, 85

Archer, Lee
See Ellison, Harlan (Jay)

Archilochus c. 7th cent. B.C. .... **CMLC 44**
See also DLB 176

Arden, John 1930- .... **CLC 6, 13, 15**
See also BRWS 2; CA 13-16R; CAAS 4; CANR 31, 65, 67, 124; CBD; CD 5; DAM DRAM; DFS 9; DLB 13, 245; EWL 3; MTCW 1

Arenas, Reinaldo 1943-1990 .. **CLC 41; HLC**
1
See also CA 124; 128; 133; CANR 73, 106; DAM MULT; DLB 145; EWL 3; GLL 2; HW 1; LAW; LAWS 1; MTCW 1; RGSF 2; RGWL 3; WLIT 1

Arendt, Hannah 1906-1975 .... **CLC 66, 98**
See also CA 17-20R; 61-64; CANR 26, 60; DLB 242; MTCW 1, 2

Aretino, Pietro 1492-1556 .... **LC 12**
See also RGWL 2, 3

Arghezi, Tudor .... **CLC 80**
See Theodorescu, Ion N.
See also CA 167; CDWLB 4; DLB 220; EWL 3

Arguedas, Jose Maria 1911-1969 .... **CLC 10,**
18; HLCS 1; TCLC 147
See also CA 89-92; CANR 73; DLB 113; EWL 3; HW 1; LAW; RGWL 2, 3; WLIT 1

Argueta, Manlio 1936- .... **CLC 31**
See also CA 131; CANR 73; CWW 2; DLB 145; EWL 3; HW 1; RGWL 3

Arias, Ron(ald Francis) 1941- .... **HLC 1**
See also CA 131; CANR 81; DAM MULT; DLB 82; HW 1, 2; MTCW 2

Ariosto, Ludovico 1474-1533 ... **LC 6, 87; PC**
42
See also EW 2; RGWL 2, 3

Aristides
See Epstein, Joseph

Aristophanes 450 B.C.-385 B.C. .... **CMLC 4,**
51; DC 2; WLCS
See also AW 1; CDWLB 1; DA; DA3; DAB; DAC; DAM DRAM, MST; DFS 10; DLB 176; LMFS 1; RGWL 2, 3; TWA

Aristotle 384 B.C.-322 B.C. .... **CMLC 31;**
WLCS
See also AW 1; CDWLB 1; DA; DA3; DAB; DAC; DAM MST; DLB 176; RGWL 2, 3; TWA

Arlt, Roberto (Godofredo Christophersen)
1900-1942 .... **HLC 1; TCLC 29**
See also CA 123; 131; CANR 67; DAM MULT; DLB 305; EWL 3; HW 1, 2; LAW

Armah, Ayi Kwei 1939- . **BLC 1; CLC 5, 33, 136**
See also AFW; BW 1; CA 61-64; CANR 21, 64; CDWLB 3; CN 7; DAM MULT, POET; DLB 117; EWL 3; MTCW 1; WLIT 2

Armatrading, Joan 1950- .... **CLC 17**
See also CA 114; 186

Armitage, Frank
See Carpenter, John (Howard)

Armstrong, Jeannette (C.) 1948- .... **NNAL**
See also CA 149; CCA 1; CN 7; DAC; SATA 102

Arnette, Robert
See Silverberg, Robert

Arnim, Achim von (Ludwig Joachim von Arnim) 1781-1831 ..... **NCLC 5; SSC 29**
See also DLB 90

Arnim, Bettina von 1785-1859 ...... **NCLC 38, 123**
See also DLB 90; RGWL 2, 3

Arnold, Matthew 1822-1888 ..... **NCLC 6, 29, 89, 126; PC 5; WLC**
See also BRW 5; CDBLB 1832-1890; DA; DAB; DAC; DAM MST, POET; DLB 32, 57; EXPP; PAB; PFS 2; TEA; WP

Arnold, Thomas 1795-1842 .... **NCLC 18**
See also DLB 55

Arnow, Harriette (Louisa) Simpson 1908-1986 .... **CLC 2, 7, 18**
See also BPFB 1; CA 9-12R; 118; CANR 14; DLB 6; FW; MTCW 1, 2; RHW; SATA 42; SATA-Obit 47

Arouet, Francois-Marie
See Voltaire

Arp, Hans
See Arp, Jean

Arp, Jean 1887-1966 .... **CLC 5; TCLC 115**
See also CA 81-84; 25-28R; CANR 42, 77; EW 10

Arrabal
See Arrabal, Fernando

Arrabal, Fernando 1932- ... **CLC 2, 9, 18, 58**
See Arrabal (Teran), Fernando
See also CA 9-12R; CANR 15; EWL 3; LMFS 2

Arrabal (Teran), Fernando 1932-
See Arrabal, Fernando
See also CWW 2

Arreola, Juan Jose 1918-2001 .... **CLC 147; HLC 1; SSC 38**
See also CA 113; 131; 200; CANR 81; CWW 2; DAM MULT; DLB 113; DNFS 2; EWL 3; HW 1, 2; LAW; RGSF 2

Arrian c. 89(?)-c. 155(?) .... **CMLC 43**
See also DLB 176

Arrick, Fran .... **CLC 30**
See Gaberman, Judie Angell
See also BYA 6

Arrley, Richmond
See Delany, Samuel R(ay), Jr.

Artaud, Antonin (Marie Joseph) 1896-1948 .... **DC 14; TCLC 3, 36**
See also CA 104; 149; DA3; DAM DRAM; DLB 258; EW 11; EWL 3; GFL 1789 to the Present; MTCW 1, 2; RGWL 2, 3

Arthur, Ruth M(abel) 1905-1979 ..... **CLC 12**
See also CA 9-12R; 85-88; CANR 4; CWRI 5; SATA 7, 26

Artsybashev, Mikhail (Petrovich) 1878-1927 .... **TCLC 31**
See also CA 170; DLB 295

Arundel, Honor (Morfydd) 1919-1973 .... **CLC 17**
See also CA 21-22; 41-44R; CAP 2; CLR 35; CWRI 5; SATA 4; SATA-Obit 24

Arzner, Dorothy 1900-1979 .... **CLC 98**

Asch, Sholem 1880-1957 .... **TCLC 3**
See also CA 105; EWL 3; GLL 2

Ascham, Roger 1516(?)-1568 .... **LC 101**
See also DLB 236

Ash, Shalom
See Asch, Sholem

Ashbery, John (Lawrence) 1927- .. **CLC 2, 3, 4, 6, 9, 13, 15, 25, 41, 77, 125; PC 26**
See Berry, Jonas
See also AMWS 3; CA 5-8R; CANR 9, 37, 66, 102, 132; CP 7; DA3; DAM POET; DLB 5, 165; DLBY 1981; EWL 3; INT CANR-9; MTCW 1, 2; PAB; PFS 11; RGAL 4; WP

Ashdown, Clifford
See Freeman, R(ichard) Austin

Ashe, Gordon
See Creasey, John

Ashton-Warner, Sylvia (Constance) 1908-1984 .... **CLC 19**
See also CA 69-72; 112; CANR 29; MTCW 1, 2

Asimov, Isaac 1920-1992 ..... **CLC 1, 3, 9, 19, 26, 76, 92**
See also AAYA 13; BEST 90:2; BPFB 1; BYA 4, 6, 7, 9; CA 1-4R; 137; CANR 2, 19, 36, 60, 125; CLR 12, 79; CMW 4; CPW; DA3; DAM POP; DLB 8; DLBY 1992; INT CANR-19; JRDA; LAIT 5; LMFS 2; MAICYA 1, 2; MTCW 1, 2; RGAL 4; SATA 1, 26, 74; SCFW 2; SFW 4; SSFS 17; TUS; YAW

Askew, Anne 1521(?)-1546 .... **LC 81**
See also DLB 136

Assis, Joaquim Maria Machado de
See Machado de Assis, Joaquim Maria

Astell, Mary 1666-1731 .... **LC 68**
See also DLB 252; FW

Astley, Thea (Beatrice May) 1925- .. **CLC 41**
See also CA 65-68; CANR 11, 43, 78; CN 7; DLB 289; EWL 3

Astley, William 1855-1911
See Warung, Price

Aston, James
See White, T(erence) H(anbury)

Asturias, Miguel Angel 1899-1974 .... **CLC 3, 8, 13; HLC 1**
See also CA 25-28; 49-52; CANR 32; CAP 2; CDWLB 3; DA3; DAM MULT, NOV; DLB 113, 290; EWL 3; HW 1; LAW; LMFS 2; MTCW 1, 2; RGWL 2, 3; WLIT 1

Atares, Carlos Saura
See Saura (Atares), Carlos

Athanasius c. 295-c. 373 .... **CMLC 48**

Atheling, William
See Pound, Ezra (Weston Loomis)

Atheling, William, Jr.
See Blish, James (Benjamin)

Atherton, Gertrude (Franklin Horn) 1857-1948 .... **TCLC 2**
See also CA 104; 155; DLB 9, 78, 186; HGG; RGAL 4; SUFW 1; TCWW 2

Atherton, Lucius
See Masters, Edgar Lee

Atkins, Jack
See Harris, Mark

Atkinson, Kate 1951- .... **CLC 99**
See also CA 166; CANR 101; DLB 267

Attaway, William (Alexander) 1911-1986 .... **BLC 1; CLC 92**
See also BW 2, 3; CA 143; CANR 82; DAM MULT; DLB 76

Atticus
See Fleming, Ian (Lancaster); Wilson, (Thomas) Woodrow

Atwood, Margaret (Eleanor) 1939- ... **CLC 2, 3, 4, 8, 13, 15, 25, 44, 84, 135; PC 8; SSC 2, 46; WLC**
See also AAYA 12, 47; AMWS 13; BEST 89:2; BPFB 1; CA 49-52; CANR 3, 24, 33, 59, 95, 133; CN 7; CP 7; CPW; CWP; DA; DA3; DAB; DAC; DAM MST, NOV, POET; DLB 53, 251; EWL 3; EXPN; FW; INT CANR-24; LAIT 5; MTCW 1, 2; NFS 4, 12, 13, 14, 19; PFS 7; RGSF 2; SATA 50; SSFS 3, 13; TWA; WWE 1; YAW

Aubigny, Pierre d'
See Mencken, H(enry) L(ouis)

Aubin, Penelope 1685-1731(?) .... **LC 9**
See also DLB 39

Auchincloss, Louis (Stanton) 1917- .. **CLC 4, 6, 9, 18, 45; SSC 22**
See also AMWS 4; CA 1-4R; CANR 6, 29, 55, 87, 130; CN 7; DAM NOV; DLB 2, 244; DLBY 1980; EWL 3; INT CANR-29; MTCW 1; RGAL 4

Auden, W(ystan) H(ugh) 1907-1973 . **CLC 1, 2, 3, 4, 6, 9, 11, 14, 43, 123; PC 1; WLC**
See also AAYA 18; AMWS 2; BRW 7; BRWR 1; CA 9-12R; 45-48; CANR 5, 61, 105; CDBLB 1914-1945; DA; DA3; DAB; DAC; DAM DRAM, MST, POET; DLB 10, 20; EWL 3; EXPP; MTCW 1, 2; PAB; PFS 1, 3, 4, 10; TUS; WP

Audiberti, Jacques 1899-1965 .... **CLC 38**
See also CA 25-28R; DAM DRAM; EWL 3

Audubon, John James 1785-1851 . **NCLC 47**
See also ANW; DLB 248

Auel, Jean M(arie) 1936- .... **CLC 31, 107**
See also AAYA 7, 51; BEST 90:4; BPFB 1; CA 103; CANR 21, 64, 115; CPW; DA3; DAM POP; INT CANR-21; NFS 11; RHW; SATA 91

Auerbach, Erich 1892-1957 .... **TCLC 43**
See also CA 118; 155; EWL 3

Augier, Emile 1820-1889 .... **NCLC 31**
See also DLB 192; GFL 1789 to the Present

August, John
See De Voto, Bernard (Augustine)

Augustine, St. 354-430 .... **CMLC 6; WLCS**
See also DA; DA3; DAB; DAC; DAM MST; DLB 115; EW 1; RGWL 2, 3

Aunt Belinda
See Braddon, Mary Elizabeth

Aunt Weedy
See Alcott, Louisa May

Aurelius
See Bourne, Randolph S(illiman)

Aurelius, Marcus 121-180 .... **CMLC 45**
See Marcus Aurelius
See also RGWL 2, 3

Aurobindo, Sri
See Ghose, Aurabinda

Aurobindo Ghose
See Ghose, Aurabinda

Austen, Jane 1775-1817 ...... **NCLC 1, 13, 19, 33, 51, 81, 95, 119; WLC**
See also AAYA 19; BRW 4; BRWC 1; BRWR 2; BYA 3; CDBLB 1789-1832; DA; DA3; DAB; DAC; DAM MST, NOV; DLB 116; EXPN; LAIT 2; LATS 1:1; LMFS 1; NFS 1, 14, 18, 20; TEA; WLIT 3; WYAS 1

Auster, Paul 1947- .... **CLC 47, 131**
See also AMWS 12; CA 69-72; CANR 23, 52, 75, 129; CMW 4; CN 7; DA3; DLB 227; MTCW 1; SUFW 2

Austin, Frank
See Faust, Frederick (Schiller)
See also TCWW 2

MULT, POET, POP; DFS 3, 11, 16; DLB
5, 7, 16, 38; DLBD 8; EWL 3; MTCW 1,
2; PFS 9; RGAL 4; TUS; WP

Baratynsky, Evgenii Abramovich
1800-1844 .... **NCLC 103**
See also DLB 205

Barbauld, Anna Laetitia
1743-1825 .... **NCLC 50**
See also DLB 107, 109, 142, 158; RGEL 2

Barbellion, W. N. P. .... **TCLC 24**
See Cummings, Bruce F(rederick)

Barber, Benjamin R. 1939- .... **CLC 141**
See also CA 29-32R; CANR 12, 32, 64, 119

Barbera, Jack (Vincent) 1945- .... **CLC 44**
See also CA 110; CANR 45

Barbey d'Aurevilly, Jules-Amedee
1808-1889 .... **NCLC 1; SSC 17**
See also DLB 119; GFL 1789 to the Present

Barbour, John c. 1316-1395 .... **CMLC 33**
See also DLB 146

Barbusse, Henri 1873-1935 .... **TCLC 5**
See also CA 105; 154; DLB 65; EWL 3;
RGWL 2, 3

Barclay, Bill
See Moorcock, Michael (John)

Barclay, William Ewert
See Moorcock, Michael (John)

Barea, Arturo 1897-1957 .... **TCLC 14**
See also CA 111; 201

Barfoot, Joan 1946- .... **CLC 18**
See also CA 105

Barham, Richard Harris
1788-1845 .... **NCLC 77**
See also DLB 159

Baring, Maurice 1874-1945 .... **TCLC 8**
See also CA 105; 168; DLB 34; HGG

Baring-Gould, Sabine 1834-1924 ... **TCLC 88**
See also DLB 156, 190

Barker, Clive 1952- .... **CLC 52; SSC 53**
See also AAYA 10, 54; BEST 90:3; BPFB
1; CA 121; 129; CANR 71, 111, 133;
CPW; DA3; DAM POP; DLB 261; HGG;
INT CA-129; MTCW 1, 2; SUFW 2

Barker, George Granville
1913-1991 .... **CLC 8, 48**
See also CA 9-12R; 135; CANR 7, 38;
DAM POET; DLB 20; EWL 3; MTCW 1

Barker, Harley Granville
See Granville-Barker, Harley
See also DLB 10

Barker, Howard 1946- .... **CLC 37**
See also CA 102; CBD; CD 5; DLB 13,
233

Barker, Jane 1652-1732 .... **LC 42, 82**
See also DLB 39, 131

Barker, Pat(ricia) 1943- ...... **CLC 32, 94, 146**
See also BRWS 4; CA 117; 122; CANR 50,
101; CN 7; DLB 271; INT CA-122

Barlach, Ernst (Heinrich)
1870-1938 .... **TCLC 84**
See also CA 178; DLB 56, 118; EWL 3

Barlow, Joel 1754-1812 .... **NCLC 23**
See also AMWS 2; DLB 37; RGAL 4

Barnard, Mary (Ethel) 1909- .... **CLC 48**
See also CA 21-22; CAP 2

Barnes, Djuna 1892-1982 .... **CLC 3, 4, 8, 11,
29, 127; SSC 3**
See Steptoe, Lydia
See also AMWS 3; CA 9-12R; 107; CAD;
CANR 16, 55; CWD; DLB 4, 9, 45; EWL
3; GLL 1; MTCW 1, 2; RGAL 4; TUS

Barnes, Jim 1933- .... **NNAL**
See also CA 108, 175; CAAE 175; CAAS
28; DLB 175

Barnes, Julian (Patrick) 1946- . **CLC 42, 141**
See also BRWS 4; CA 102; CANR 19, 54,
115; CN 7; DAB; DLB 194; DLBY 1993;
EWL 3; MTCW 1

Barnes, Peter 1931-2004 .... **CLC 5, 56**
See also CA 65-68; CAAS 12; CANR 33,
34, 64, 113; CBD; CD 5; DFS 6; DLB
13, 233; MTCW 1

Barnes, William 1801-1886 .... **NCLC 75**
See also DLB 32

Baroja (y Nessi), Pio 1872-1956 .... **HLC 1;
TCLC 8**
See also CA 104; EW 9

Baron, David
See Pinter, Harold

Baron Corvo
See Rolfe, Frederick (William Serafino Austin Lewis Mary)

Barondess, Sue K(aufman)
1926-1977 .... **CLC 8**
See Kaufman, Sue
See also CA 1-4R; 69-72; CANR 1

Baron de Teive
See Pessoa, Fernando (Antonio Nogueira)

Baroness Von S.
See Zangwill, Israel

Barres, (Auguste-)Maurice
1862-1923 .... **TCLC 47**
See also CA 164; DLB 123; GFL 1789 to
the Present

Barreto, Afonso Henrique de Lima
See Lima Barreto, Afonso Henrique de

Barrett, Andrea 1954- .... **CLC 150**
See also CA 156; CANR 92

Barrett, Michele .... **CLC 65**

Barrett, (Roger) Syd 1946- .... **CLC 35**

Barrett, William (Christopher)
1913-1992 .... **CLC 27**
See also CA 13-16R; 139; CANR 11, 67;
INT CANR-11

Barrie, J(ames) M(atthew)
1860-1937 .... **TCLC 2**
See also BRWS 3; BYA 4, 5; CA 104; 136;
CANR 77; CDBLB 1890-1914; CLR 16;
CWRI 5; DA3; DAB; DAM DRAM; DFS
7; DLB 10, 141, 156; EWL 3; FANT;
MAICYA 1, 2; MTCW 1; SATA 100;
SUFW; WCH; WLIT 4; YABC 1

Barrington, Michael
See Moorcock, Michael (John)

Barrol, Grady
See Bograd, Larry

Barry, Mike
See Malzberg, Barry N(athaniel)

Barry, Philip 1896-1949 .... **TCLC 11**
See also CA 109; 199; DFS 9; DLB 7, 228;
RGAL 4

Bart, Andre Schwarz
See Schwarz-Bart, Andre

Barth, John (Simmons) 1930- ... **CLC 1, 2, 3,
5, 7, 9, 10, 14, 27, 51, 89; SSC 10**
See also AITN 1, 2; AMW; BPFB 1; CA
1-4R; CABS 1; CANR 5, 23, 49, 64, 113;
CN 7; DAM NOV; DLB 2, 227; EWL 3;
FANT; MTCW 1; RGAL 4; RGSF 2;
RHW; SSFS 6; TUS

Barthelme, Donald 1931-1989 ... **CLC 1, 2, 3,
5, 6, 8, 13, 23, 46, 59, 115; SSC 2, 55**
See also AMWS 4; BPFB 1; CA 21-24R;
129; CANR 20, 58; DA3; DAM NOV;
DLB 2, 234; DLBY 1980, 1989; EWL 3;
FANT; LMFS 2; MTCW 1, 2; RGAL 4;
RGSF 2; SATA 7; SATA-Obit 62; SSFS
17

Barthelme, Frederick 1943- ...... **CLC 36, 117**
See also AMWS 11; CA 114; 122; CANR
77; CN 7; CSW; DLB 244; DLBY 1985;
EWL 3; INT CA-122

Barthes, Roland (Gerard)
1915-1980 .... **CLC 24, 83; TCLC 135**
See also CA 130; 97-100; CANR 66; DLB
296; EW 13; EWL 3; GFL 1789 to the
Present; MTCW 1, 2; TWA

Bartram, William 1739-1823 .... **NCLC 145**
See also ANW; DLB 37

Barzun, Jacques (Martin) 1907- ..... **CLC 51,
145**
See also CA 61-64; CANR 22, 95

Bashevis, Isaac
See Singer, Isaac Bashevis

Bashkirtseff, Marie 1859-1884 .... **NCLC 27**

Basho, Matsuo
See Matsuo Basho
See also PFS 18; RGWL 2, 3; WP

Basil of Caesaria c. 330-379 .... **CMLC 35**

Basket, Raney
See Edgerton, Clyde (Carlyle)

Bass, Kingsley B., Jr.
See Bullins, Ed

Bass, Rick 1958- .... **CLC 79, 143; SSC 60**
See also ANW; CA 126; CANR 53, 93;
CSW; DLB 212, 275

Bassani, Giorgio 1916-2000 .... **CLC 9**
See also CA 65-68; 190; CANR 33; CWW
2; DLB 128, 177, 299; EWL 3; MTCW 1;
RGWL 2, 3

Bastian, Ann .... **CLC 70**

Bastos, Augusto (Antonio) Roa
See Roa Bastos, Augusto (Antonio)

Bataille, Georges 1897-1962 .... **CLC 29;
TCLC 155**
See also CA 101; 89-92; EWL 3

Bates, H(erbert) E(rnest)
1905-1974 .... **CLC 46; SSC 10**
See also CA 93-96; 45-48; CANR 34; DA3;
DAB; DAM POP; DLB 162, 191; EWL
3; EXPS; MTCW 1, 2; RGSF 2; SSFS 7

Bauchart
See Camus, Albert

Baudelaire, Charles 1821-1867 . **NCLC 6, 29,
55; PC 1; SSC 18; WLC**
See also DA; DA3; DAB; DAC; DAM
MST, POET; DLB 217; EW 7; GFL 1789
to the Present; LMFS 2; PFS 21; RGWL
2, 3; TWA

Baudouin, Marcel
See Peguy, Charles (Pierre)

Baudouin, Pierre
See Peguy, Charles (Pierre)

Baudrillard, Jean 1929- .... **CLC 60**
See also DLB 296

Baum, L(yman) Frank 1856-1919 .. **TCLC 7,
132**
See also AAYA 46; BYA 16; CA 108; 133;
CLR 15; CWRI 5; DLB 22; FANT; JRDA;
MAICYA 1, 2; MTCW 1, 2; NFS 13;
RGAL 4; SATA 18, 100; WCH

Baum, Louis F.
See Baum, L(yman) Frank

Baumbach, Jonathan 1933- .... **CLC 6, 23**
See also CA 13-16R; CAAS 5; CANR 12,
66; CN 7; DLBY 1980; INT CANR-12;
MTCW 1

Bausch, Richard (Carl) 1945- .... **CLC 51**
See also AMWS 7; CA 101; CAAS 14;
CANR 43, 61, 87; CSW; DLB 130

Baxter, Charles (Morley) 1947- . **CLC 45, 78**
See also CA 57-60; CANR 40, 64, 104, 133;
CPW; DAM POP; DLB 130; MTCW 2

Baxter, George Owen
See Faust, Frederick (Schiller)

Baxter, James K(eir) 1926-1972 .... **CLC 14**
See also CA 77-80; EWL 3

Baxter, John
See Hunt, E(verette) Howard, (Jr.)

Bayer, Sylvia
See Glassco, John

Baynton, Barbara 1857-1929 .... **TCLC 57**
See also DLB 230; RGSF 2

Beagle, Peter S(oyer) 1939- .... **CLC 7, 104**
See also AAYA 47; BPFB 1; BYA 9, 10, 16; CA 9-12R; CANR 4, 51, 73, 110; DA3; DLBY 1980; FANT; INT CANR-4; MTCW 1; SATA 60, 130; SUFW 1, 2; YAW

Bean, Normal
See Burroughs, Edgar Rice

Beard, Charles A(ustin)
1874-1948 .... **TCLC 15**
See also CA 115; 189; DLB 17; SATA 18

Beardsley, Aubrey 1872-1898 .... **NCLC 6**

Beattie, Ann 1947- ..... **CLC 8, 13, 18, 40, 63, 146; SSC 11**
See also AMWS 5; BEST 90:2; BPFB 1; CA 81-84; CANR 53, 73, 128; CN 7; CPW; DA3; DAM NOV, POP; DLB 218, 278; DLBY 1982; EWL 3; MTCW 1, 2; RGAL 4; RGSF 2; SSFS 9; TUS

Beattie, James 1735-1803 .... **NCLC 25**
See also DLB 109

Beauchamp, Kathleen Mansfield 1888-1923
See Mansfield, Katherine
See also CA 104; 134; DA; DA3; DAC; DAM MST; MTCW 2; TEA

Beaumarchais, Pierre-Augustin Caron de
1732-1799 .... **DC 4; LC 61**
See also DAM DRAM; DFS 14, 16; EW 4; GFL Beginnings to 1789; RGWL 2, 3

Beaumont, Francis 1584(?)-1616 .. **DC 6; LC 33**
See also BRW 2; CDBLB Before 1660; DLB 58; TEA

Beauvoir, Simone (Lucie Ernestine Marie Bertrand) de 1908-1986 .... **CLC 1, 2, 4, 8, 14, 31, 44, 50, 71, 124; SSC 35; WLC**
See also BPFB 1; CA 9-12R; 118; CANR 28, 61; DA; DA3; DAB; DAC; DAM MST, NOV; DLB 72; DLBY 1986; EW 12; EWL 3; FW; GFL 1789 to the Present; LMFS 2; MTCW 1, 2; RGSF 2; RGWL 2, 3; TWA

Becker, Carl (Lotus) 1873-1945 ..... **TCLC 63**
See also CA 157; DLB 17

Becker, Jurek 1937-1997 .... **CLC 7, 19**
See also CA 85-88; 157; CANR 60, 117; CWW 2; DLB 75, 299; EWL 3

Becker, Walter 1950- .... **CLC 26**

Beckett, Samuel (Barclay) 1906-1989 .. **CLC 1, 2, 3, 4, 6, 9, 10, 11, 14, 18, 29, 57, 59, 83; DC 22; SSC 16, 74; TCLC 145; WLC**
See also BRWC 2; BRWR 1; BRWS 1; CA 5-8R; 130; CANR 33, 61; CBD; CDBLB 1945-1960; DA; DA3; DAB; DAC; DAM DRAM, MST, NOV; DFS 2, 7, 18; DLB 13, 15, 233; DLBY 1990; EWL 3; GFL 1789 to the Present; LATS 1:2; LMFS 2; MTCW 1, 2; RGSF 2; RGWL 2, 3; SSFS 15; TEA; WLIT 4

Beckford, William 1760-1844 .... **NCLC 16**
See also BRW 3; DLB 39, 213; HGG; LMFS 1; SUFW

Beckham, Barry (Earl) 1944- .... **BLC 1**
See also BW 1; CA 29-32R; CANR 26, 62; CN 7; DAM MULT; DLB 33

Beckman, Gunnel 1910- .... **CLC 26**
See also CA 33-36R; CANR 15, 114; CLR 25; MAICYA 1, 2; SAAS 9; SATA 6

Becque, Henri 1837-1899 .... **DC 21; NCLC 3**
See also DLB 192; GFL 1789 to the Present

Becquer, Gustavo Adolfo
1836-1870 .... **HLCS 1; NCLC 106**
See also DAM MULT

Beddoes, Thomas Lovell 1803-1849 .. **DC 15; NCLC 3**
See also DLB 96

Bede c. 673-735 .... **CMLC 20**
See also DLB 146; TEA

Bedford, Denton R. 1907-(?) .... **NNAL**

Bedford, Donald F.
See Fearing, Kenneth (Flexner)

Beecher, Catharine Esther
1800-1878 .... **NCLC 30**
See also DLB 1, 243

Beecher, John 1904-1980 .... **CLC 6**
See also AITN 1; CA 5-8R; 105; CANR 8

Beer, Johann 1655-1700 .... **LC 5**
See also DLB 168

Beer, Patricia 1924- .... **CLC 58**
See also CA 61-64; 183; CANR 13, 46; CP 7; CWP; DLB 40; FW

Beerbohm, Max
See Beerbohm, (Henry) Max(imilian)

Beerbohm, (Henry) Max(imilian)
1872-1956 .... **TCLC 1, 24**
See also BRWS 2; CA 104; 154; CANR 79; DLB 34, 100; FANT

Beer-Hofmann, Richard
1866-1945 .... **TCLC 60**
See also CA 160; DLB 81

Beg, Shemus
See Stephens, James

Begiebing, Robert J(ohn) 1946- .... **CLC 70**
See also CA 122; CANR 40, 88

Begley, Louis 1933- .... **CLC 197**
See also CA 140; CANR 98; DLB 299

Behan, Brendan (Francis)
1923-1964 .... **CLC 1, 8, 11, 15, 79**
See also BRWS 2; CA 73-76; CANR 33, 121; CBD; CDBLB 1945-1960; DAM DRAM; DFS 7; DLB 13, 233; EWL 3; MTCW 1, 2

Behn, Aphra 1640(?)-1689 .. **DC 4; LC 1, 30, 42; PC 13; WLC**
See also BRWS 3; DA; DA3; DAB; DAC; DAM DRAM, MST, NOV, POET; DFS 16; DLB 39, 80, 131; FW; TEA; WLIT 3

Behrman, S(amuel) N(athaniel)
1893-1973 .... **CLC 40**
See also CA 13-16; 45-48; CAD; CAP 1; DLB 7, 44; IDFW 3; RGAL 4

Belasco, David 1853-1931 .... **TCLC 3**
See also CA 104; 168; DLB 7; RGAL 4

Belcheva, Elisaveta Lyubomirova
1893-1991 .... **CLC 10**
See Bagryana, Elisaveta

Beldone, Phil "Cheech"
See Ellison, Harlan (Jay)

Beleno
See Azuela, Mariano

Belinski, Vissarion Grigoryevich
1811-1848 .... **NCLC 5**
See also DLB 198

Belitt, Ben 1911- .... **CLC 22**
See also CA 13-16R; CAAS 4; CANR 7, 77; CP 7; DLB 5

Bell, Gertrude (Margaret Lowthian)
1868-1926 .... **TCLC 67**
See also CA 167; CANR 110; DLB 174

Bell, J. Freeman
See Zangwill, Israel

Bell, James Madison 1826-1902 .... **BLC 1; TCLC 43**
See also BW 1; CA 122; 124; DAM MULT; DLB 50

Bell, Madison Smartt 1957- ...... **CLC 41, 102**
See also AMWS 10; BPFB 1; CA 111, 183; CAAE 183; CANR 28, 54, 73; CN 7; CSW; DLB 218, 278; MTCW 1

Bell, Marvin (Hartley) 1937- .... **CLC 8, 31**
See also CA 21-24R; CAAS 14; CANR 59, 102; CP 7; DAM POET; DLB 5; MTCW 1

Bell, W. L. D.
See Mencken, H(enry) L(ouis)

Bellamy, Atwood C.
See Mencken, H(enry) L(ouis)

Bellamy, Edward 1850-1898 ..... **NCLC 4, 86, 147**
See also DLB 12; NFS 15; RGAL 4; SFW 4

Belli, Gioconda 1949- .... **HLCS 1**
See also CA 152; CWW 2; DLB 290; EWL 3; RGWL 3

Bellin, Edward J.
See Kuttner, Henry

Bello, Andres 1781-1865 .... **NCLC 131**
See also LAW

Belloc, (Joseph) Hilaire (Pierre Sebastien Rene Swanton) 1870-1953 .... **PC 24; TCLC 7, 18**
See also CA 106; 152; CWRI 5; DAM POET; DLB 19, 100, 141, 174; EWL 3; MTCW 1; SATA 112; WCH; YABC 1

Belloc, Joseph Peter Rene Hilaire
See Belloc, (Joseph) Hilaire (Pierre Sebastien Rene Swanton)

Belloc, Joseph Pierre Hilaire
See Belloc, (Joseph) Hilaire (Pierre Sebastien Rene Swanton)

Belloc, M. A.
See Lowndes, Marie Adelaide (Belloc)

Belloc-Lowndes, Mrs.
See Lowndes, Marie Adelaide (Belloc)

Bellow, Saul 1915- . **CLC 1, 2, 3, 6, 8, 10, 13, 15, 25, 33, 34, 63, 79, 190; SSC 14; WLC**
See also AITN 2; AMW; AMWC 2; AMWR 2; BEST 89:3; BPFB 1; CA 5-8R; CABS 1; CANR 29, 53, 95, 132; CDALB 1941-1968; CN 7; DA; DA3; DAB; DAC; DAM MST, NOV, POP; DLB 2, 28, 299; DLBD 3; DLBY 1982; EWL 3; MTCW 1, 2; NFS 4, 14; RGAL 4; RGSF 2; SSFS 12; TUS

Belser, Reimond Karel Maria de 1929-
See Ruysslinck, Ward
See also CA 152

Bely, Andrey .... **PC 11; TCLC 7**
See Bugayev, Boris Nikolayevich
See also DLB 295; EW 9; EWL 3; MTCW 1

Belyi, Andrei
See Bugayev, Boris Nikolayevich
See also RGWL 2, 3

Bembo, Pietro 1470-1547 .... **LC 79**
See also RGWL 2, 3

Benary, Margot
See Benary-Isbert, Margot

Benary-Isbert, Margot 1889-1979 .... **CLC 12**
See also CA 5-8R; 89-92; CANR 4, 72; CLR 12; MAICYA 1, 2; SATA 2; SATA-Obit 21

Benavente (y Martinez), Jacinto
1866-1954 .... **HLCS 1; TCLC 3**
See also CA 106; 131; CANR 81; DAM DRAM, MULT; EWL 3; GLL 2; HW 1, 2; MTCW 1, 2

Benchley, Peter (Bradford) 1940- .. **CLC 4, 8**
See also AAYA 14; AITN 2; BPFB 1; CA 17-20R; CANR 12, 35, 66, 115; CPW; DAM NOV, POP; HGG; MTCW 1, 2; SATA 3, 89

Benchley, Robert (Charles)
1889-1945 .... **TCLC 1, 55**
See also CA 105; 153; DLB 11; RGAL 4

Benda, Julien 1867-1956 .... **TCLC 60**
See also CA 120; 154; GFL 1789 to the Present

Benedict, Ruth (Fulton)
1887-1948 .... **TCLC 60**
See also CA 158; DLB 246

Benedikt, Michael 1935- .... **CLC 4, 14**
See also CA 13-16R; CANR 7; CP 7; DLB 5

Bowles, William Lisle 1762-1850 . **NCLC 103**
See also DLB 93

Box, Edgar
See Vidal, (Eugene Luther) Gore
See also GLL 1

Boyd, James 1888-1944 .... **TCLC 115**
See also CA 186; DLB 9; DLBD 16; RGAL 4; RHW

Boyd, Nancy
See Millay, Edna St. Vincent
See also GLL 1

Boyd, Thomas (Alexander)
1898-1935 .... **TCLC 111**
See also CA 111; 183; DLB 9; DLBD 16

Boyd, William 1952- .... **CLC 28, 53, 70**
See also CA 114; 120; CANR 51, 71, 131; CN 7; DLB 231

Boyesen, Hjalmar Hjorth
1848-1895 .... **NCLC 135**
See also DLB 12, 71; DLBD 13; RGAL 4

Boyle, Kay 1902-1992 .... **CLC 1, 5, 19, 58, 121; SSC 5**
See also CA 13-16R; 140; CAAS 1; CANR 29, 61, 110; DLB 4, 9, 48, 86; DLBY 1993; EWL 3; MTCW 1, 2; RGAL 4; RGSF 2; SSFS 10, 13, 14

Boyle, Mark
See Kienzle, William X(avier)

Boyle, Patrick 1905-1982 .... **CLC 19**
See also CA 127

Boyle, T. C.
See Boyle, T(homas) Coraghessan
See also AMWS 8

Boyle, T(homas) Coraghessan
1948- .... **CLC 36, 55, 90; SSC 16**
See Boyle, T. C.
See also AAYA 47; BEST 90:4; BPFB 1; CA 120; CANR 44, 76, 89, 132; CN 7; CPW; DA3; DAM POP; DLB 218, 278; DLBY 1986; EWL 3; MTCW 2; SSFS 13, 19

Boz
See Dickens, Charles (John Huffam)

Brackenridge, Hugh Henry
1748-1816 .... **NCLC 7**
See also DLB 11, 37; RGAL 4

Bradbury, Edward P.
See Moorcock, Michael (John)
See also MTCW 2

Bradbury, Malcolm (Stanley)
1932-2000 .... **CLC 32, 61**
See also CA 1-4R; CANR 1, 33, 91, 98; CN 7; DA3; DAM NOV; DLB 14, 207; EWL 3; MTCW 1, 2

Bradbury, Ray (Douglas) 1920- .... **CLC 1, 3, 10, 15, 42, 98; SSC 29, 53; WLC**
See also AAYA 15; AITN 1, 2; AMWS 4; BPFB 1; BYA 4, 5, 11; CA 1-4R; CANR 2, 30, 75, 125; CDALB 1968-1988; CN 7; CPW; DA; DA3; DAB; DAC; DAM MST, NOV, POP; DLB 2, 8; EXPN; EXPS; HGG; LAIT 3, 5; LATS 1:2; LMFS 2; MTCW 1, 2; NFS 1; RGAL 4; RGSF 2; SATA 11, 64, 123; SCFW 2; SFW 4; SSFS 1, 20; SUFW 1, 2; TUS; YAW

Braddon, Mary Elizabeth
1837-1915 .... **TCLC 111**
See also BRWS 8; CA 108; 179; CMW 4; DLB 18, 70, 156; HGG

Bradfield, Scott (Michael) 1955- .... **SSC 65**
See also CA 147; CANR 90; HGG; SUFW 2

Bradford, Gamaliel 1863-1932 .... **TCLC 36**
See also CA 160; DLB 17

Bradford, William 1590-1657 .... **LC 64**
See also DLB 24, 30; RGAL 4

Bradley, David (Henry), Jr. 1950- .... **BLC 1; CLC 23, 118**
See also BW 1, 3; CA 104; CANR 26, 81; CN 7; DAM MULT; DLB 33

Bradley, John Ed(mund, Jr.) 1958- . **CLC 55**
See also CA 139; CANR 99; CN 7; CSW

Bradley, Marion Zimmer
1930-1999 .... **CLC 30**
See Chapman, Lee; Dexter, John; Gardner, Miriam; Ives, Morgan; Rivers, Elfrida
See also AAYA 40; BPFB 1; CA 57-60; 185; CAAS 10; CANR 7, 31, 51, 75, 107; CPW; DA3; DAM POP; DLB 8; FANT; FW; MTCW 1, 2; SATA 90, 139; SATA-Obit 116; SFW 4; SUFW 2; YAW

Bradshaw, John 1933- .... **CLC 70**
See also CA 138; CANR 61

Bradstreet, Anne 1612(?)-1672 ...... **LC 4, 30; PC 10**
See also AMWS 1; CDALB 1640-1865; DA; DA3; DAC; DAM MST, POET; DLB 24; EXPP; FW; PFS 6; RGAL 4; TUS; WP

Brady, Joan 1939- .... **CLC 86**
See also CA 141

Bragg, Melvyn 1939- .... **CLC 10**
See also BEST 89:3; CA 57-60; CANR 10, 48, 89; CN 7; DLB 14, 271; RHW

Brahe, Tycho 1546-1601 .... **LC 45**
See also DLB 300

Braine, John (Gerard) 1922-1986 . **CLC 1, 3, 41**
See also CA 1-4R; 120; CANR 1, 33; CDBLB 1945-1960; DLB 15; DLBY 1986; EWL 3; MTCW 1

Braithwaite, William Stanley (Beaumont)
1878-1962 .... **BLC 1; HR 2; PC 52**
See also BW 1; CA 125; DAM MULT; DLB 50, 54

Bramah, Ernest 1868-1942 .... **TCLC 72**
See also CA 156; CMW 4; DLB 70; FANT

Brammer, William 1930(?)-1978 ...... **CLC 31**
See also CA 77-80

Brancati, Vitaliano 1907-1954 .... **TCLC 12**
See also CA 109; DLB 264; EWL 3

Brancato, Robin F(idler) 1936- .... **CLC 35**
See also AAYA 9; BYA 6; CA 69-72; CANR 11, 45; CLR 32; JRDA; MAICYA 2; MAICYAS 1; SAAS 9; SATA 97; WYA; YAW

Brand, Dionne 1953- .... **CLC 192**
See also BW 2; CA 143; CWP

Brand, Max
See Faust, Frederick (Schiller)
See also BPFB 1; TCWW 2

Brand, Millen 1906-1980 .... **CLC 7**
See also CA 21-24R; 97-100; CANR 72

Branden, Barbara .... **CLC 44**
See also CA 148

Brandes, Georg (Morris Cohen)
1842-1927 .... **TCLC 10**
See also CA 105; 189; DLB 300

Brandys, Kazimierz 1916-2000 .... **CLC 62**
See also EWL 3

Branley, Franklyn M(ansfield)
1915-2002 .... **CLC 21**
See also CA 33-36R; 207; CANR 14, 39; CLR 13; MAICYA 1, 2; SAAS 16; SATA 4, 68, 136

Brant, Beth (E.) 1941- .... **NNAL**
See also CA 144; FW

Brathwaite, Edward Kamau
1930- .... **BLCS; CLC 11; PC 56**
See also BW 2, 3; CA 25-28R; CANR 11, 26, 47, 107; CDWLB 3; CP 7; DAM POET; DLB 125; EWL 3

Brathwaite, Kamau
See Brathwaite, Edward Kamau

Brautigan, Richard (Gary)
1935-1984 .... **CLC 1, 3, 5, 9, 12, 34, 42; TCLC 133**
See also BPFB 1; CA 53-56; 113; CANR 34; DA3; DAM NOV; DLB 2, 5, 206; DLBY 1980, 1984; FANT; MTCW 1; RGAL 4; SATA 56

Brave Bird, Mary .... **NNAL**
See Crow Dog, Mary (Ellen)

Braverman, Kate 1950- .... **CLC 67**
See also CA 89-92

Brecht, (Eugen) Bertolt (Friedrich)
1898-1956 ..... **DC 3; TCLC 1, 6, 13, 35; WLC**
See also CA 104; 133; CANR 62; CDWLB 2; DA; DA3; DAB; DAC; DAM DRAM, MST; DFS 4, 5, 9; DLB 56, 124; EW 11; EWL 3; IDTP; MTCW 1, 2; RGWL 2, 3; TWA

Brecht, Eugen Berthold Friedrich
See Brecht, (Eugen) Bertolt (Friedrich)

Bremer, Fredrika 1801-1865 .... **NCLC 11**
See also DLB 254

Brennan, Christopher John
1870-1932 .... **TCLC 17**
See also CA 117; 188; DLB 230; EWL 3

Brennan, Maeve 1917-1993 ... **CLC 5; TCLC 124**
See also CA 81-84; CANR 72, 100

Brent, Linda
See Jacobs, Harriet A(nn)

Brentano, Clemens (Maria)
1778-1842 .... **NCLC 1**
See also DLB 90; RGWL 2, 3

Brent of Bin Bin
See Franklin, (Stella Maria Sarah) Miles (Lampe)

Brenton, Howard 1942- .... **CLC 31**
See also CA 69-72; CANR 33, 67; CBD; CD 5; DLB 13; MTCW 1

Breslin, James 1930-
See Breslin, Jimmy
See also CA 73-76; CANR 31, 75; DAM NOV; MTCW 1, 2

Breslin, Jimmy .... **CLC 4, 43**
See Breslin, James
See also AITN 1; DLB 185; MTCW 2

Bresson, Robert 1901(?)-1999 .... **CLC 16**
See also CA 110; 187; CANR 49

Breton, Andre 1896-1966 .. **CLC 2, 9, 15, 54; PC 15**
See also CA 19-20; 25-28R; CANR 40, 60; CAP 2; DLB 65, 258; EW 11; EWL 3; GFL 1789 to the Present; LMFS 2; MTCW 1, 2; RGWL 2, 3; TWA; WP

Breytenbach, Breyten 1939(?)- .. **CLC 23, 37, 126**
See also CA 113; 129; CANR 61, 122; CWW 2; DAM POET; DLB 225; EWL 3

Bridgers, Sue Ellen 1942- .... **CLC 26**
See also AAYA 8, 49; BYA 7, 8; CA 65-68; CANR 11, 36; CLR 18; DLB 52; JRDA; MAICYA 1, 2; SAAS 1; SATA 22, 90; SATA-Essay 109; WYA; YAW

Bridges, Robert (Seymour)
1844-1930 .... **PC 28; TCLC 1**
See also BRW 6; CA 104; 152; CDBLB 1890-1914; DAM POET; DLB 19, 98

Bridie, James .... **TCLC 3**
See Mavor, Osborne Henry
See also DLB 10; EWL 3

Brin, David 1950- .... **CLC 34**
See also AAYA 21; CA 102; CANR 24, 70, 125, 127; INT CANR-24; SATA 65; SCFW 2; SFW 4

Brink, Andre (Philippus) 1935- . **CLC 18, 36, 106**
  See also AFW; BRWS 6; CA 104; CANR 39, 62, 109, 133; CN 7; DLB 225; EWL 3; INT CA-103; LATS 1:2; MTCW 1, 2; WLIT 2

Brinsmead, H. F(ay)
  See Brinsmead, H(esba) F(ay)

Brinsmead, H. F.
  See Brinsmead, H(esba) F(ay)

Brinsmead, H(esba) F(ay) 1922- ...... **CLC 21**
  See also CA 21-24R; CANR 10; CLR 47; CWRI 5; MAICYA 1, 2; SAAS 5; SATA 18, 78

Brittain, Vera (Mary) 1893(?)-1970 . **CLC 23**
  See also CA 13-16; 25-28R; CANR 58; CAP 1; DLB 191; FW; MTCW 1, 2

Broch, Hermann 1886-1951 .... **TCLC 20**
  See also CA 117; 211; CDWLB 2; DLB 85, 124; EW 10; EWL 3; RGWL 2, 3

Brock, Rose
  See Hansen, Joseph
  See also GLL 1

Brod, Max 1884-1968 .... **TCLC 115**
  See also CA 5-8R; 25-28R; CANR 7; DLB 81; EWL 3

Brodkey, Harold (Roy) 1930-1996 .. **CLC 56; TCLC 123**
  See also CA 111; 151; CANR 71; CN 7; DLB 130

Brodsky, Iosif Alexandrovich 1940-1996
  See Brodsky, Joseph
  See also AITN 1; CA 41-44R; 151; CANR 37, 106; DA3; DAM POET; MTCW 1, 2; RGWL 2, 3

Brodsky, Joseph . **CLC 4, 6, 13, 36, 100; PC 9**
  See Brodsky, Iosif Alexandrovich
  See also AMWS 8; CWW 2; DLB 285; EWL 3; MTCW 1

Brodsky, Michael (Mark) 1948- .... **CLC 19**
  See also CA 102; CANR 18, 41, 58; DLB 244

Brodzki, Bella ed. .... **CLC 65**

Brome, Richard 1590(?)-1652 .... **LC 61**
  See also DLB 58

Bromell, Henry 1947- .... **CLC 5**
  See also CA 53-56; CANR 9, 115, 116

Bromfield, Louis (Brucker)
  1896-1956 .... **TCLC 11**
  See also CA 107; 155; DLB 4, 9, 86; RGAL 4; RHW

Broner, E(sther) M(asserman)
  1930- .... **CLC 19**
  See also CA 17-20R; CANR 8, 25, 72; CN 7; DLB 28

Bronk, William (M.) 1918-1999 .... **CLC 10**
  See also CA 89-92; 177; CANR 23; CP 7; DLB 165

Bronstein, Lev Davidovich
  See Trotsky, Leon

Bronte, Anne 1820-1849 ..... **NCLC 4, 71, 102**
  See also BRW 5; BRWR 1; DA3; DLB 21, 199; TEA

Bronte, (Patrick) Branwell
  1817-1848 .... **NCLC 109**

Bronte, Charlotte 1816-1855 ...... **NCLC 3, 8, 33, 58, 105; WLC**
  See also AAYA 17; BRW 5; BRWC 2; BRWR 1; BYA 2; CDBLB 1832-1890; DA; DA3; DAB; DAC; DAM MST, NOV; DLB 21, 159, 199; EXPN; LAIT 2; NFS 4; TEA; WLIT 4

Bronte, Emily (Jane) 1818-1848 ... **NCLC 16, 35; PC 8; WLC**
  See also AAYA 17; BPFB 1; BRW 5; BRWC 1; BRWR 1; BYA 3; CDBLB 1832-1890; DA; DA3; DAB; DAC; DAM MST, NOV, POET; DLB 21, 32, 199; EXPN; LAIT 1; TEA; WLIT 3

Brontes
  See Bronte, Anne; Bronte, Charlotte; Bronte, Emily (Jane)

Brooke, Frances 1724-1789 .... **LC 6, 48**
  See also DLB 39, 99

Brooke, Henry 1703(?)-1783 .... **LC 1**
  See also DLB 39

Brooke, Rupert (Chawner)
  1887-1915 ..... **PC 24; TCLC 2, 7; WLC**
  See also BRWS 3; CA 104; 132; CANR 61; CDBLB 1914-1945; DA; DAB; DAC; DAM MST, POET; DLB 19, 216; EXPP; GLL 2; MTCW 1, 2; PFS 7; TEA

Brooke-Haven, P.
  See Wodehouse, P(elham) G(renville)

Brooke-Rose, Christine 1926(?)- ..... **CLC 40, 184**
  See also BRWS 4; CA 13-16R; CANR 58, 118; CN 7; DLB 14, 231; EWL 3; SFW 4

Brookner, Anita 1928- .. **CLC 32, 34, 51, 136**
  See also BRWS 4; CA 114; 120; CANR 37, 56, 87, 130; CN 7; CPW; DA3; DAB; DAM POP; DLB 194; DLBY 1987; EWL 3; MTCW 1, 2; TEA

Brooks, Cleanth 1906-1994 . **CLC 24, 86, 110**
  See also CA 17-20R; 145; CANR 33, 35; CSW; DLB 63; DLBY 1994; EWL 3; INT CANR-35; MTCW 1, 2

Brooks, George
  See Baum, L(yman) Frank

Brooks, Gwendolyn (Elizabeth)
  1917-2000 ...... **BLC 1; CLC 1, 2, 4, 5, 15, 49, 125; PC 7; WLC**
  See also AAYA 20; AFAW 1, 2; AITN 1; AMWS 3; BW 2, 3; CA 1-4R; 190; CANR 1, 27, 52, 75, 132; CDALB 1941-1968; CLR 27; CP 7; CWP; DA; DA3; DAC; DAM MST, MULT, POET; DLB 5, 76, 165; EWL 3; EXPP; MAWW; MTCW 1, 2; PFS 1, 2, 4, 6; RGAL 4; SATA 6; SATA-Obit 123; TUS; WP

Brooks, Mel .... **CLC 12**
  See Kaminsky, Melvin
  See also AAYA 13, 48; DLB 26

Brooks, Peter (Preston) 1938- .... **CLC 34**
  See also CA 45-48; CANR 1, 107

Brooks, Van Wyck 1886-1963 .... **CLC 29**
  See also AMW; CA 1-4R; CANR 6; DLB 45, 63, 103; TUS

Brophy, Brigid (Antonia)
  1929-1995 .... **CLC 6, 11, 29, 105**
  See also CA 5-8R; 149; CAAS 4; CANR 25, 53; CBD; CN 7; CWD; DA3; DLB 14, 271; EWL 3; MTCW 1, 2

Brosman, Catharine Savage 1934- ..... **CLC 9**
  See also CA 61-64; CANR 21, 46

Brossard, Nicole 1943- .... **CLC 115, 169**
  See also CA 122; CAAS 16; CCA 1; CWP; CWW 2; DLB 53; EWL 3; FW; GLL 2; RGWL 3

Brother Antoninus
  See Everson, William (Oliver)

The Brothers Quay
  See Quay, Stephen; Quay, Timothy

Broughton, T(homas) Alan 1936- ..... **CLC 19**
  See also CA 45-48; CANR 2, 23, 48, 111

Broumas, Olga 1949- .... **CLC 10, 73**
  See also CA 85-88; CANR 20, 69, 110; CP 7; CWP; GLL 2

Broun, Heywood 1888-1939 .... **TCLC 104**
  See also DLB 29, 171

Brown, Alan 1950- .... **CLC 99**
  See also CA 156

Brown, Charles Brockden
  1771-1810 .... **NCLC 22, 74, 122**
  See also AMWS 1; CDALB 1640-1865; DLB 37, 59, 73; FW; HGG; LMFS 1; RGAL 4; TUS

Brown, Christy 1932-1981 .... **CLC 63**
  See also BYA 13; CA 105; 104; CANR 72; DLB 14

Brown, Claude 1937-2002 ... **BLC 1; CLC 30**
  See also AAYA 7; BW 1, 3; CA 73-76; 205; CANR 81; DAM MULT

Brown, Dee (Alexander)
  1908-2002 .... **CLC 18, 47**
  See also AAYA 30; CA 13-16R; 212; CAAS 6; CANR 11, 45, 60; CPW; CSW; DA3; DAM POP; DLBY 1980; LAIT 2; MTCW 1, 2; NCFS 5; SATA 5, 110; SATA-Obit 141; TCWW 2

Brown, George
  See Wertmueller, Lina

Brown, George Douglas
  1869-1902 .... **TCLC 28**
  See Douglas, George
  See also CA 162

Brown, George Mackay 1921-1996 ... **CLC 5, 48, 100**
  See also BRWS 6; CA 21-24R; 151; CAAS 6; CANR 12, 37, 67; CN 7; CP 7; DLB 14, 27, 139, 271; MTCW 1; RGSF 2; SATA 35

Brown, (William) Larry 1951- .... **CLC 73**
  See also CA 130; 134; CANR 117; CSW; DLB 234; INT CA-134

Brown, Moses
  See Barrett, William (Christopher)

Brown, Rita Mae 1944- .... **CLC 18, 43, 79**
  See also BPFB 1; CA 45-48; CANR 2, 11, 35, 62, 95; CN 7; CPW; CSW; DA3; DAM NOV, POP; FW; INT CANR-11; MTCW 1, 2; NFS 9; RGAL 4; TUS

Brown, Roderick (Langmere) Haig-
  See Haig-Brown, Roderick (Langmere)

Brown, Rosellen 1939- .... **CLC 32, 170**
  See also CA 77-80; CAAS 10; CANR 14, 44, 98; CN 7

Brown, Sterling Allen 1901-1989 ...... **BLC 1; CLC 1, 23, 59; HR 2; PC 55**
  See also AFAW 1, 2; BW 1, 3; CA 85-88; 127; CANR 26; DA3; DAM MULT, POET; DLB 48, 51, 63; MTCW 1, 2; RGAL 4; WP

Brown, Will
  See Ainsworth, William Harrison

Brown, William Hill 1765-1793 .... **LC 93**
  See also DLB 37

Brown, William Wells 1815-1884 ...... **BLC 1; DC 1; NCLC 2, 89**
  See also DAM MULT; DLB 3, 50, 183, 248; RGAL 4

Browne, (Clyde) Jackson 1948(?)- ... **CLC 21**
  See also CA 120

Browning, Elizabeth Barrett
  1806-1861 ... **NCLC 1, 16, 61, 66; PC 6; WLC**
  See also BRW 4; CDBLB 1832-1890; DA; DA3; DAB; DAC; DAM MST, POET; DLB 32, 199; EXPP; PAB; PFS 2, 16; TEA; WLIT 4; WP

Browning, Robert 1812-1889 . **NCLC 19, 79; PC 2, 61; WLCS**
  See also BRW 4; BRWC 2; BRWR 2; CDBLB 1832-1890; CLR 97; DA; DA3; DAB; DAC; DAM MST, POET; DLB 32, 163; EXPP; LATS 1:1; PAB; PFS 1, 15; RGEL 2; TEA; WLIT 4; WP; YABC 1

Browning, Tod 1882-1962 .... **CLC 16**
  See also CA 141; 117

Brownmiller, Susan 1935- .... **CLC 159**
  See also CA 103; CANR 35, 75; DAM NOV; FW; MTCW 1, 2

Brownson, Orestes Augustus
  1803-1876 .... **NCLC 50**
  See also DLB 1, 59, 73, 243

Author Index

Cassity, (Allen) Turner 1929- .... **CLC 6, 42**
See also CA 17-20R; 223; CAAE 223; CAAS 8; CANR 11; CSW; DLB 105

Castaneda, Carlos (Cesar Aranha)
1931(?)-1998 .... **CLC 12, 119**
See also CA 25-28R; CANR 32, 66, 105; DNFS 1; HW 1; MTCW 1

Castedo, Elena 1937- .... **CLC 65**
See also CA 132

Castedo-Ellerman, Elena
See Castedo, Elena

Castellanos, Rosario 1925-1974 .... **CLC 66; HLC 1; SSC 39, 68**
See also CA 131; 53-56; CANR 58; CDWLB 3; DAM MULT; DLB 113, 290; EWL 3; FW; HW 1; LAW; MTCW 1; RGSF 2; RGWL 2, 3

Castelvetro, Lodovico 1505-1571 .... **LC 12**

Castiglione, Baldassare 1478-1529 ...... **LC 12**
See Castiglione, Baldesar
See also LMFS 1; RGWL 2, 3

Castiglione, Baldesar
See Castiglione, Baldassare
See also EW 2

Castillo, Ana (Hernandez Del)
1953- .... **CLC 151**
See also AAYA 42; CA 131; CANR 51, 86, 128; CWP; DLB 122, 227; DNFS 2; FW; HW 1; LLW 1; PFS 21

Castle, Robert
See Hamilton, Edmond

Castro (Ruz), Fidel 1926(?)- .... **HLC 1**
See also CA 110; 129; CANR 81; DAM MULT; HW 2

Castro, Guillen de 1569-1631 .... **LC 19**

Castro, Rosalia de 1837-1885 ... **NCLC 3, 78; PC 41**
See also DAM MULT

Cather, Willa (Sibert) 1873-1947 . **SSC 2, 50; TCLC 1, 11, 31, 99, 132, 152; WLC**
See also AAYA 24; AMW; AMWC 1; AMWR 1; BPFB 1; CA 104; 128; CDALB 1865-1917; CLR 98; DA; DA3; DAB; DAC; DAM MST, NOV; DLB 9, 54, 78, 256; DLBD 1; EWL 3; EXPN; EXPS; LAIT 3; LATS 1:1; MAWW; MTCW 1, 2; NFS 2, 19; RGAL 4; RGSF 2; RHW; SATA 30; SSFS 2, 7, 16; TCWW 2; TUS

Catherine II
See Catherine the Great
See also DLB 150

Catherine the Great 1729-1796 .... **LC 69**
See Catherine II

Cato, Marcus Porcius 234 B.C.-149
B.C. .... **CMLC 21**
See Cato the Elder

Cato, Marcus Porcius, the Elder
See Cato, Marcus Porcius

Cato the Elder
See Cato, Marcus Porcius
See also DLB 211

Catton, (Charles) Bruce 1899-1978 . **CLC 35**
See also AITN 1; CA 5-8R; 81-84; CANR 7, 74; DLB 17; SATA 2; SATA-Obit 24

Catullus c. 84 B.C.-54 B.C. .... **CMLC 18**
See also AW 2; CDWLB 1; DLB 211; RGWL 2, 3

Cauldwell, Frank
See King, Francis (Henry)

Caunitz, William J. 1933-1996 .... **CLC 34**
See also BEST 89:3; CA 125; 130; 152; CANR 73; INT CA-130

Causley, Charles (Stanley)
1917-2003 .... **CLC 7**
See also CA 9-12R; 223; CANR 5, 35, 94; CLR 30; CWRI 5; DLB 27; MTCW 1; SATA 3, 66; SATA-Obit 149

Caute, (John) David 1936- .... **CLC 29**
See also CA 1-4R; CAAS 4; CANR 1, 33, 64, 120; CBD; CD 5; CN 7; DAM NOV; DLB 14, 231

Cavafy, C(onstantine) P(eter) .... **PC 36; TCLC 2, 7**
See Kavafis, Konstantinos Petrou
See also CA 148; DA3; DAM POET; EW 8; EWL 3; MTCW 1; PFS 19; RGWL 2, 3; WP

Cavalcanti, Guido c. 1250-c.
1300 .... **CMLC 54**

Cavallo, Evelyn
See Spark, Muriel (Sarah)

Cavanna, Betty .... **CLC 12**
See Harrison, Elizabeth (Allen) Cavanna
See also JRDA; MAICYA 1; SAAS 4; SATA 1, 30

Cavendish, Margaret Lucas
1623-1673 .... **LC 30**
See also DLB 131, 252, 281; RGEL 2

Caxton, William 1421(?)-1491(?) .... **LC 17**
See also DLB 170

Cayer, D. M.
See Duffy, Maureen

Cayrol, Jean 1911- .... **CLC 11**
See also CA 89-92; DLB 83; EWL 3

Cela (y Trulock), Camilo Jose
See Cela, Camilo Jose
See also CWW 2

Cela, Camilo Jose 1916-2002 .... **CLC 4, 13, 59, 122; HLC 1; SSC 71**
See Cela (y Trulock), Camilo Jose
See also BEST 90:2; CA 21-24R; 206; CAAS 10; CANR 21, 32, 76; DAM MULT; DLBY 1989; EW 13; EWL 3; HW 1; MTCW 1, 2; RGSF 2; RGWL 2, 3

Celan, Paul .... **CLC 10, 19, 53, 82; PC 10**
See Antschel, Paul
See also CDWLB 2; DLB 69; EWL 3; RGWL 2, 3

Celine, Louis-Ferdinand .. **CLC 1, 3, 4, 7, 9, 15, 47, 124**
See Destouches, Louis-Ferdinand
See also DLB 72; EW 11; EWL 3; GFL 1789 to the Present; RGWL 2, 3

Cellini, Benvenuto 1500-1571 .... **LC 7**

Cendrars, Blaise .... **CLC 18, 106**
See Sauser-Hall, Frederic
See also DLB 258; EWL 3; GFL 1789 to the Present; RGWL 2, 3; WP

Centlivre, Susanna 1669(?)-1723 .... **LC 65**
See also DLB 84; RGEL 2

Cernuda (y Bidon), Luis 1902-1963 . **CLC 54**
See also CA 131; 89-92; DAM POET; DLB 134; EWL 3; GLL 1; HW 1; RGWL 2, 3

Cervantes, Lorna Dee 1954- ..... **HLCS 1; PC 35**
See also CA 131; CANR 80; CWP; DLB 82; EXPP; HW 1; LLW 1

Cervantes (Saavedra), Miguel de
1547-1616 .... **HLCS; LC 6, 23, 93; SSC 12; WLC**
See also AAYA 56; BYA 1, 14; DA; DAB; DAC; DAM MST, NOV; EW 2; LAIT 1; LATS 1:1; LMFS 1; NFS 8; RGSF 2; RGWL 2, 3; TWA

Cesaire, Aime (Fernand) 1913- .... **BLC 1; CLC 19, 32, 112; DC 22; PC 25**
See also BW 2, 3; CA 65-68; CANR 24, 43, 81; CWW 2; DA3; DAM MULT, POET; EWL 3; GFL 1789 to the Present; MTCW 1, 2; WP

Chabon, Michael 1963- ... **CLC 55, 149; SSC 59**
See also AAYA 45; AMWS 11; CA 139; CANR 57, 96, 127; DLB 278; SATA 145

Chabrol, Claude 1930- .... **CLC 16**
See also CA 110

Chairil Anwar
See Anwar, Chairil
See also EWL 3

Challans, Mary 1905-1983
See Renault, Mary
See also CA 81-84; 111; CANR 74; DA3; MTCW 2; SATA 23; SATA-Obit 36; TEA

Challis, George
See Faust, Frederick (Schiller)
See also TCWW 2

Chambers, Aidan 1934- .... **CLC 35**
See also AAYA 27; CA 25-28R; CANR 12, 31, 58, 116; JRDA; MAICYA 1, 2; SAAS 12; SATA 1, 69, 108; WYA; YAW

Chambers, James 1948-
See Cliff, Jimmy
See also CA 124

Chambers, Jessie
See Lawrence, D(avid) H(erbert Richards)
See also GLL 1

Chambers, Robert W(illiam)
1865-1933 .... **TCLC 41**
See also CA 165; DLB 202; HGG; SATA 107; SUFW 1

Chambers, (David) Whittaker
1901-1961 .... **TCLC 129**
See also CA 89-92; DLB 303

Chamisso, Adelbert von
1781-1838 .... **NCLC 82**
See also DLB 90; RGWL 2, 3; SUFW 1

Chance, James T.
See Carpenter, John (Howard)

Chance, John T.
See Carpenter, John (Howard)

Chandler, Raymond (Thornton)
1888-1959 .... **SSC 23; TCLC 1, 7**
See also AAYA 25; AMWC 2; AMWS 4; BPFB 1; CA 104; 129; CANR 60, 107; CDALB 1929-1941; DLB 226, 253; DLBD 6; EWL 3; MSW; MTCW 1, 2; NFS 17; RGAL 4; TUS

Chang, Diana 1934- .... **AAL**
See also CWP; EXPP

Chang, Eileen 1921-1995 .... **AAL; SSC 28**
See Chang Ai-Ling; Zhang Ailing
See also CA 166

Chang, Jung 1952- .... **CLC 71**
See also CA 142

Chang Ai-Ling
See Chang, Eileen
See also EWL 3

Channing, William Ellery
1780-1842 .... **NCLC 17**
See also DLB 1, 59, 235; RGAL 4

Chao, Patricia 1955- .... **CLC 119**
See also CA 163

Chaplin, Charles Spencer
1889-1977 .... **CLC 16**
See Chaplin, Charlie
See also CA 81-84; 73-76

Chaplin, Charlie
See Chaplin, Charles Spencer
See also DLB 44

Chapman, George 1559(?)-1634 . **DC 19; LC 22**
See also BRW 1; DAM DRAM; DLB 62, 121; LMFS 1; RGEL 2

Chapman, Graham 1941-1989 .... **CLC 21**
See Monty Python
See also CA 116; 129; CANR 35, 95

Chapman, John Jay 1862-1933 .... **TCLC 7**
See also CA 104; 191

Chapman, Lee
See Bradley, Marion Zimmer
See also GLL 1

Chapman, Walker
See Silverberg, Robert

Cooper, Douglas 1960- .... **CLC 86**

Cooper, Henry St. John
See Creasey, John

Cooper, J(oan) California (?)- .... **CLC 56**
See also AAYA 12; BW 1; CA 125; CANR 55; DAM MULT; DLB 212

Cooper, James Fenimore
1789-1851 .... **NCLC 1, 27, 54**
See also AAYA 22; AMW; BPFB 1; CDALB 1640-1865; DA3; DLB 3, 183, 250, 254; LAIT 1; NFS 9; RGAL 4; SATA 19; TUS; WCH

Cooper, Susan Fenimore
1813-1894 .... **NCLC 129**
See also ANW; DLB 239, 254

Coover, Robert (Lowell) 1932- ...... **CLC 3, 7, 15, 32, 46, 87, 161; SSC 15**
See also AMWS 5; BPFB 1; CA 45-48; CANR 3, 37, 58, 115; CN 7; DAM NOV; DLB 2, 227; DLBY 1981; EWL 3; MTCW 1, 2; RGAL 4; RGSF 2

Copeland, Stewart (Armstrong)
1952- .... **CLC 26**

Copernicus, Nicolaus 1473-1543 .... **LC 45**

Coppard, A(lfred) E(dgar)
1878-1957 .... **SSC 21; TCLC 5**
See also BRWS 8; CA 114; 167; DLB 162; EWL 3; HGG; RGEL 2; RGSF 2; SUFW 1; YABC 1

Coppee, Francois 1842-1908 .... **TCLC 25**
See also CA 170; DLB 217

Coppola, Francis Ford 1939- ... **CLC 16, 126**
See also AAYA 39; CA 77-80; CANR 40, 78; DLB 44

Copway, George 1818-1869 .... **NNAL**
See also DAM MULT; DLB 175, 183

Corbiere, Tristan 1845-1875 .... **NCLC 43**
See also DLB 217; GFL 1789 to the Present

Corcoran, Barbara (Asenath)
1911- .... **CLC 17**
See also AAYA 14; CA 21-24R, 191; CAAE 191; CAAS 2; CANR 11, 28, 48; CLR 50; DLB 52; JRDA; MAICYA 2; MAIC-YAS 1; RHW; SAAS 20; SATA 3, 77; SATA-Essay 125

Cordelier, Maurice
See Giraudoux, Jean(-Hippolyte)

Corelli, Marie .... **TCLC 51**
See Mackay, Mary
See also DLB 34, 156; RGEL 2; SUFW 1

Corinna c. 225 B.C.-c. 305 B.C. .... **CMLC 72**

Corman, Cid .... **CLC 9**
See Corman, Sidney
See also CAAS 2; DLB 5, 193

Corman, Sidney 1924-2004
See Corman, Cid
See also CA 85-88; 225; CANR 44; CP 7; DAM POET

Cormier, Robert (Edmund)
1925-2000 .... **CLC 12, 30**
See also AAYA 3, 19; BYA 1, 2, 6, 8, 9; CA 1-4R; CANR 5, 23, 76, 93; CDALB 1968-1988; CLR 12, 55; DA; DAB; DAC; DAM MST, NOV; DLB 52; EXPN; INT CANR-23; JRDA; LAIT 5; MAICYA 1, 2; MTCW 1, 2; NFS 2, 18; SATA 10, 45, 83; SATA-Obit 122; WYA; YAW

Corn, Alfred (DeWitt III) 1943- .... **CLC 33**
See also CA 179; CAAE 179; CAAS 25; CANR 44; CP 7; CSW; DLB 120, 282; DLBY 1980

Corneille, Pierre 1606-1684 ... **DC 21; LC 28**
See also DAB; DAM MST; DLB 268; EW 3; GFL Beginnings to 1789; RGWL 2, 3; TWA

Cornwell, David (John Moore)
1931- .... **CLC 9, 15**
See le Carre, John
See also CA 5-8R; CANR 13, 33, 59, 107, 132; DA3; DAM POP; MTCW 1, 2

Cornwell, Patricia (Daniels) 1956- . **CLC 155**
See also AAYA 16, 56; BPFB 1; CA 134; CANR 53, 131; CMW 4; CPW; CSW; DAM POP; DLB 306; MSW; MTCW 1

Corso, (Nunzio) Gregory 1930-2001 . **CLC 1, 11; PC 33**
See also AMWS 12; BG 2; CA 5-8R; 193; CANR 41, 76, 132; CP 7; DA3; DLB 5, 16, 237; LMFS 2; MTCW 1, 2; WP

Cortazar, Julio 1914-1984 ... **CLC 2, 3, 5, 10, 13, 15, 33, 34, 92; HLC 1; SSC 7, 76**
See also BPFB 1; CA 21-24R; CANR 12, 32, 81; CDWLB 3; DA3; DAM MULT, NOV; DLB 113; EWL 3; EXPS; HW 1, 2; LAW; MTCW 1, 2; RGSF 2; RGWL 2, 3; SSFS 3, 20; TWA; WLIT 1

Cortes, Hernan 1485-1547 .... **LC 31**

Corvinus, Jakob
See Raabe, Wilhelm (Karl)

Corwin, Cecil
See Kornbluth, C(yril) M.

Cosic, Dobrica 1921- .... **CLC 14**
See also CA 122; 138; CDWLB 4; CWW 2; DLB 181; EWL 3

Costain, Thomas B(ertram)
1885-1965 .... **CLC 30**
See also BYA 3; CA 5-8R; 25-28R; DLB 9; RHW

Costantini, Humberto 1924(?)-1987 . **CLC 49**
See also CA 131; 122; EWL 3; HW 1

Costello, Elvis 1954- .... **CLC 21**
See also CA 204

Costenoble, Philostene
See Ghelderode, Michel de

Cotes, Cecil V.
See Duncan, Sara Jeannette

Cotter, Joseph Seamon Sr.
1861-1949 .... **BLC 1; TCLC 28**
See also BW 1; CA 124; DAM MULT; DLB 50

Couch, Arthur Thomas Quiller
See Quiller-Couch, Sir Arthur (Thomas)

Coulton, James
See Hansen, Joseph

Couperus, Louis (Marie Anne)
1863-1923 .... **TCLC 15**
See also CA 115; EWL 3; RGWL 2, 3

Coupland, Douglas 1961- .... **CLC 85, 133**
See also AAYA 34; CA 142; CANR 57, 90, 130; CCA 1; CPW; DAC; DAM POP

Court, Wesli
See Turco, Lewis (Putnam)

Courtenay, Bryce 1933- .... **CLC 59**
See also CA 138; CPW

Courtney, Robert
See Ellison, Harlan (Jay)

Cousteau, Jacques-Yves 1910-1997 .. **CLC 30**
See also CA 65-68; 159; CANR 15, 67; MTCW 1; SATA 38, 98

Coventry, Francis 1725-1754 .... **LC 46**

Coverdale, Miles c. 1487-1569 .... **LC 77**
See also DLB 167

Cowan, Peter (Walkinshaw)
1914-2002 .... **SSC 28**
See also CA 21-24R; CANR 9, 25, 50, 83; CN 7; DLB 260; RGSF 2

Coward, Noel (Peirce) 1899-1973 . **CLC 1, 9, 29, 51**
See also AITN 1; BRWS 2; CA 17-18; 41-44R; CANR 35, 132; CAP 2; CDBLB 1914-1945; DA3; DAM DRAM; DFS 3, 6; DLB 10, 245; EWL 3; IDFW 3, 4; MTCW 1, 2; RGEL 2; TEA

Cowley, Abraham 1618-1667 .... **LC 43**
See also BRW 2; DLB 131, 151; PAB; RGEL 2

Cowley, Malcolm 1898-1989 .... **CLC 39**
See also AMWS 2; CA 5-8R; 128; CANR 3, 55; DLB 4, 48; DLBY 1981, 1989; EWL 3; MTCW 1, 2

Cowper, William 1731-1800 ..... **NCLC 8, 94; PC 40**
See also BRW 3; DA3; DAM POET; DLB 104, 109; RGEL 2

Cox, William Trevor 1928-
See Trevor, William
See also CA 9-12R; CANR 4, 37, 55, 76, 102; DAM NOV; INT CANR-37; MTCW 1, 2; TEA

Coyne, P. J.
See Masters, Hilary

Cozzens, James Gould 1903-1978 . **CLC 1, 4, 11, 92**
See also AMW; BPFB 1; CA 9-12R; 81-84; CANR 19; CDALB 1941-1968; DLB 9, 294; DLBD 2; DLBY 1984, 1997; EWL 3; MTCW 1, 2; RGAL 4

Crabbe, George 1754-1832 .... **NCLC 26, 121**
See also BRW 3; DLB 93; RGEL 2

Crace, Jim 1946- .... **CLC 157; SSC 61**
See also CA 128; 135; CANR 55, 70, 123; CN 7; DLB 231; INT CA-135

Craddock, Charles Egbert
See Murfree, Mary Noailles

Craig, A. A.
See Anderson, Poul (William)

Craik, Mrs.
See Craik, Dinah Maria (Mulock)
See also RGEL 2

Craik, Dinah Maria (Mulock)
1826-1887 .... **NCLC 38**
See Craik, Mrs.; Mulock, Dinah Maria
See also DLB 35, 163; MAICYA 1, 2; SATA 34

Cram, Ralph Adams 1863-1942 ..... **TCLC 45**
See also CA 160

Cranch, Christopher Pearse
1813-1892 .... **NCLC 115**
See also DLB 1, 42, 243

Crane, (Harold) Hart 1899-1932 .... **PC 3; TCLC 2, 5, 80; WLC**
See also AMW; AMWR 2; CA 104; 127; CDALB 1917-1929; DA; DA3; DAB; DAC; DAM MST, POET; DLB 4, 48; EWL 3; MTCW 1, 2; RGAL 4; TUS

Crane, R(onald) S(almon)
1886-1967 .... **CLC 27**
See also CA 85-88; DLB 63

Crane, Stephen (Townley)
1871-1900 ...... **SSC 7, 56, 70; TCLC 11, 17, 32; WLC**
See also AAYA 21; AMW; AMWC 1; BPFB 1; BYA 3; CA 109; 140; CANR 84; CDALB 1865-1917; DA; DA3; DAB; DAC; DAM MST, NOV, POET; DLB 12, 54, 78; EXPN; EXPS; LAIT 2; LMFS 2; NFS 4, 20; PFS 9; RGAL 4; RGSF 2; SSFS 4; TUS; WYA; YABC 2

Cranmer, Thomas 1489-1556 .... **LC 95**
See also DLB 132, 213

Cranshaw, Stanley
See Fisher, Dorothy (Frances) Canfield

Crase, Douglas 1944- .... **CLC 58**
See also CA 106

Crashaw, Richard 1612(?)-1649 .... **LC 24**
See also BRW 2; DLB 126; PAB; RGEL 2

Cratinus c. 519 B.C.-c. 422 B.C. ... **CMLC 54**
See also LMFS 1

Craven, Margaret 1901-1980 .... **CLC 17**
See also BYA 2; CA 103; CCA 1; DAC; LAIT 5

Crawford, F(rancis) Marion
1854-1909 .... TCLC 10
See also CA 107; 168; DLB 71; HGG;
RGAL 4; SUFW 1

Crawford, Isabella Valancy
1850-1887 .... NCLC 12, 127
See also DLB 92; RGEL 2

Crayon, Geoffrey
See Irving, Washington

Creasey, John 1908-1973 .... CLC 11
See Marric, J. J.
See also CA 5-8R; 41-44R; CANR 8, 59;
CMW 4; DLB 77; MTCW 1

Crebillon, Claude Prosper Jolyot de (fils)
1707-1777 .... LC 1, 28
See also GFL Beginnings to 1789

Credo
See Creasey, John

Credo, Alvaro J. de
See Prado (Calvo), Pedro

Creeley, Robert (White) 1926- .. CLC 1, 2, 4,
8, 11, 15, 36, 78
See also AMWS 4; CA 1-4R; CAAS 10;
CANR 23, 43, 89; CP 7; DA3; DAM
POET; DLB 5, 16, 169; DLBD 17; EWL
3; MTCW 1, 2; PFS 21; RGAL 4; WP

Crevecoeur, Hector St. John de
See Crevecoeur, Michel Guillaume Jean de
See also ANW

Crevecoeur, Michel Guillaume Jean de
1735-1813 .... NCLC 105
See Crevecoeur, Hector St. John de
See also AMWS 1; DLB 37

Crevel, Rene 1900-1935 .... TCLC 112
See also GLL 2

Crews, Harry (Eugene) 1935- ..... CLC 6, 23,
49
See also AITN 1; AMWS 11; BPFB 1; CA
25-28R; CANR 20, 57; CN 7; CSW; DA3;
DLB 6, 143, 185; MTCW 1, 2; RGAL 4

Crichton, (John) Michael 1942- .... CLC 2, 6,
54, 90
See also AAYA 10, 49; AITN 2; BPFB 1;
CA 25-28R; CANR 13, 40, 54, 76, 127;
CMW 4; CN 7; CPW; DA3; DAM NOV,
POP; DLB 292; DLBY 1981; INT CANR-
13; JRDA; MTCW 1, 2; SATA 9, 88;
SFW 4; YAW

Crispin, Edmund .... CLC 22
See Montgomery, (Robert) Bruce
See also DLB 87; MSW

Cristofer, Michael 1945(?)- .... CLC 28
See also CA 110; 152; CAD; CD 5; DAM
DRAM; DFS 15; DLB 7

Criton
See Alain

Croce, Benedetto 1866-1952 .... TCLC 37
See also CA 120; 155; EW 8; EWL 3

Crockett, David 1786-1836 .... NCLC 8
See also DLB 3, 11, 183, 248

Crockett, Davy
See Crockett, David

Crofts, Freeman Wills 1879-1957 .. TCLC 55
See also CA 115; 195; CMW 4; DLB 77;
MSW

Croker, John Wilson 1780-1857 .... NCLC 10
See also DLB 110

Crommelynck, Fernand 1885-1970 .. CLC 75
See also CA 189; 89-92; EWL 3

Cromwell, Oliver 1599-1658 .... LC 43

Cronenberg, David 1943- .... CLC 143
See also CA 138; CCA 1

Cronin, A(rchibald) J(oseph)
1896-1981 .... CLC 32
See also BPFB 1; CA 1-4R; 102; CANR 5;
DLB 191; SATA 47; SATA-Obit 25

Cross, Amanda
See Heilbrun, Carolyn G(old)
See also BPFB 1; CMW; CPW; DLB 306;
MSW

Crothers, Rachel 1878-1958 .... TCLC 19
See also CA 113; 194; CAD; CWD; DLB
7, 266; RGAL 4

Croves, Hal
See Traven, B.

Crow Dog, Mary (Ellen) (?)- .... CLC 93
See Brave Bird, Mary
See also CA 154

Crowfield, Christopher
See Stowe, Harriet (Elizabeth) Beecher

Crowley, Aleister .... TCLC 7
See Crowley, Edward Alexander
See also GLL 1

Crowley, Edward Alexander 1875-1947
See Crowley, Aleister
See also CA 104; HGG

Crowley, John 1942- .... CLC 57
See also AAYA 57; BPFB 1; CA 61-64;
CANR 43, 98; DLBY 1982; FANT; SATA
65, 140; SFW 4; SUFW 2

Crowne, John 1641-1712 .... LC 104
See also DLB 80; RGEL 2

Crud
See Crumb, R(obert)

Crumarums
See Crumb, R(obert)

Crumb, R(obert) 1943- .... CLC 17
See also CA 106; CANR 107

Crumbum
See Crumb, R(obert)

Crumski
See Crumb, R(obert)

Crum the Bum
See Crumb, R(obert)

Crunk
See Crumb, R(obert)

Crustt
See Crumb, R(obert)

Crutchfield, Les
See Trumbo, Dalton

Cruz, Victor Hernandez 1949- ... HLC 1; PC
37
See also BW 2; CA 65-68; CAAS 17;
CANR 14, 32, 74, 132; CP 7; DAM
MULT, POET; DLB 41; DNFS 1; EXPP;
HW 1, 2; LLW 1; MTCW 1; PFS 16; WP

Cryer, Gretchen (Kiger) 1935- .... CLC 21
See also CA 114; 123

Csath, Geza 1887-1919 .... TCLC 13
See also CA 111

Cudlip, David R(ockwell) 1933- .... CLC 34
See also CA 177

Cullen, Countee 1903-1946 .... BLC 1; HR 2;
PC 20; TCLC 4, 37; WLCS
See also AFAW 2; AMWS 4; BW 1; CA
108; 124; CDALB 1917-1929; DA; DA3;
DAC; DAM MST, MULT, POET; DLB 4,
48, 51; EWL 3; EXPP; LMFS 2; MTCW
1, 2; PFS 3; RGAL 4; SATA 18; WP

Culleton, Beatrice 1949- .... NNAL
See also CA 120; CANR 83; DAC

Cum, R.
See Crumb, R(obert)

Cummings, Bruce F(rederick) 1889-1919
See Barbellion, W. N. P.
See also CA 123

Cummings, E(dward) E(stlin)
1894-1962 .. CLC 1, 3, 8, 12, 15, 68; PC
5; TCLC 137; WLC
See also AAYA 41; AMW; CA 73-76;
CANR 31; CDALB 1929-1941; DA;
DA3; DAB; DAC; DAM MST, POET;
DLB 4, 48; EWL 3; EXPP; MTCW 1, 2;
PAB; PFS 1, 3, 12, 13, 19; RGAL 4; TUS;
WP

Cummins, Maria Susanna
1827-1866 .... NCLC 139
See also DLB 42; YABC 1

Cunha, Euclides (Rodrigues Pimenta) da
1866-1909 .... TCLC 24
See also CA 123; 219; LAW; WLIT 1

Cunningham, E. V.
See Fast, Howard (Melvin)

Cunningham, J(ames) V(incent)
1911-1985 .... CLC 3, 31
See also CA 1-4R; 115; CANR 1, 72; DLB
5

Cunningham, Julia (Woolfolk)
1916- .... CLC 12
See also CA 9-12R; CANR 4, 19, 36; CWRI
5; JRDA; MAICYA 1, 2; SAAS 2; SATA
1, 26, 132

Cunningham, Michael 1952- .... CLC 34
See also CA 136; CANR 96; DLB 292;
GLL 2

Cunninghame Graham, R. B.
See Cunninghame Graham, Robert
(Gallnigad) Bontine

Cunninghame Graham, Robert (Gallnigad)
Bontine 1852-1936 .... TCLC 19
See Graham, R(obert) B(ontine) Cunning-
hame
See also CA 119; 184

Curnow, (Thomas) Allen (Monro)
1911-2001 .... PC 48
See also CA 69-72; 202; CANR 48, 99; CP
7; EWL 3; RGEL 2

Currie, Ellen 19(?)- .... CLC 44

Curtin, Philip
See Lowndes, Marie Adelaide (Belloc)

Curtin, Phillip
See Lowndes, Marie Adelaide (Belloc)

Curtis, Price
See Ellison, Harlan (Jay)

Cusanus, Nicolaus 1401-1464 .... LC 80
See Nicholas of Cusa

Cutrate, Joe
See Spiegelman, Art

Cynewulf c. 770- .... CMLC 23
See also DLB 146; RGEL 2

Cyrano de Bergerac, Savinien de
1619-1655 .... LC 65
See also DLB 268; GFL Beginnings to
1789; RGWL 2, 3

Cyril of Alexandria c. 375-c. 430 . CMLC 59

Czaczkes, Shmuel Yosef Halevi
See Agnon, S(hmuel) Y(osef Halevi)

Dabrowska, Maria (Szumska)
1889-1965 .... CLC 15
See also CA 106; CDWLB 4; DLB 215;
EWL 3

Dabydeen, David 1955- .... CLC 34
See also BW 1; CA 125; CANR 56, 92; CN
7; CP 7

Dacey, Philip 1939- .... CLC 51
See also CA 37-40R; CAAS 17; CANR 14,
32, 64; CP 7; DLB 105

Dafydd ap Gwilym c. 1320-c. 1380 ..... PC 56

Dagerman, Stig (Halvard)
1923-1954 .... TCLC 17
See also CA 117; 155; DLB 259; EWL 3

D'Aguiar, Fred 1960- .... CLC 145
See also CA 148; CANR 83, 101; CP 7;
DLB 157; EWL 3

Dahl, Roald 1916-1990 .... CLC 1, 6, 18, 79
See also AAYA 15; BPFB 1; BRWS 4; BYA
5; CA 1-4R; 133; CANR 6, 32, 37, 62;
CLR 1, 7, 41; CPW; DA3; DAB; DAC;
DAM MST, NOV, POP; DLB 139, 255;
HGG; JRDA; MAICYA 1, 2; MTCW 1,
2; RGSF 2; SATA 1, 26, 73; SATA-Obit
65; SSFS 4; TEA; YAW

Dahlberg, Edward 1900-1977 .. **CLC 1, 7, 14**
    See also CA 9-12R; 69-72; CANR 31, 62;
    DLB 48; MTCW 1; RGAL 4
Daitch, Susan 1954- .... **CLC 103**
    See also CA 161
Dale, Colin .... **TCLC 18**
    See Lawrence, T(homas) E(dward)
Dale, George E.
    See Asimov, Isaac
Dalton, Roque 1935-1975(?) ..... **HLCS 1; PC
36**
    See also CA 176; DLB 283; HW 2
Daly, Elizabeth 1878-1967 .... **CLC 52**
    See also CA 23-24; 25-28R; CANR 60;
    CAP 2; CMW 4
Daly, Mary 1928- .... **CLC 173**
    See also CA 25-28R; CANR 30, 62; FW;
    GLL 1; MTCW 1
Daly, Maureen 1921- .... **CLC 17**
    See also AAYA 5, 58; BYA 6; CANR 37,
    83, 108; CLR 96; JRDA; MAICYA 1, 2;
    SAAS 1; SATA 2, 129; WYA; YAW
Damas, Leon-Gontran 1912-1978 .... **CLC 84**
    See also BW 1; CA 125; 73-76; EWL 3
Dana, Richard Henry Sr.
    1787-1879 .... **NCLC 53**
Daniel, Samuel 1562(?)-1619 .... **LC 24**
    See also DLB 62; RGEL 2
Daniels, Brett
    See Adler, Renata
Dannay, Frederic 1905-1982 .... **CLC 11**
    See Queen, Ellery
    See also CA 1-4R; 107; CANR 1, 39; CMW
    4; DAM POP; DLB 137; MTCW 1
D'Annunzio, Gabriele 1863-1938 ... **TCLC 6,
40**
    See also CA 104; 155; EW 8; EWL 3;
    RGWL 2, 3; TWA
Danois, N. le
    See Gourmont, Remy(-Marie-Charles) de
Dante 1265-1321 .... **CMLC 3, 18, 39, 70; PC
21; WLCS**
    See also DA; DA3; DAB; DAC; DAM
    MST, POET; EFS 1; EW 1; LAIT 1;
    RGWL 2, 3; TWA; WP
d'Antibes, Germain
    See Simenon, Georges (Jacques Christian)
Danticat, Edwidge 1969- .... **CLC 94, 139**
    See also AAYA 29; CA 152, 192; CAAE
    192; CANR 73, 129; DNFS 1; EXPS;
    LATS 1:2; MTCW 1; SSFS 1; YAW
Danvers, Dennis 1947- .... **CLC 70**
Danziger, Paula 1944-2004 .... **CLC 21**
    See also AAYA 4, 36; BYA 6, 7, 14; CA
    112; 115; CANR 37, 132; CLR 20; JRDA;
    MAICYA 1, 2; SATA 36, 63, 102, 149;
    SATA-Brief 30; WYA; YAW
Da Ponte, Lorenzo 1749-1838 .... **NCLC 50**
Dario, Ruben 1867-1916 .... **HLC 1; PC 15;
TCLC 4**
    See also CA 131; CANR 81; DAM MULT;
    DLB 290; EWL 3; HW 1, 2; LAW;
    MTCW 1, 2; RGWL 2, 3
Darley, George 1795-1846 .... **NCLC 2**
    See also DLB 96; RGEL 2
Darrow, Clarence (Seward)
    1857-1938 .... **TCLC 81**
    See also CA 164; DLB 303
Darwin, Charles 1809-1882 .... **NCLC 57**
    See also BRWS 7; DLB 57, 166; LATS 1:1;
    RGEL 2; TEA; WLIT 4
Darwin, Erasmus 1731-1802 .... **NCLC 106**
    See also DLB 93; RGEL 2
Daryush, Elizabeth 1887-1977 ...... **CLC 6, 19**
    See also CA 49-52; CANR 3, 81; DLB 20
Das, Kamala 1934- .... **CLC 191; PC 43**
    See also CA 101; CANR 27, 59; CP 7;
    CWP; FW

Dasgupta, Surendranath
    1887-1952 .... **TCLC 81**
    See also CA 157
**Dashwood, Edmee Elizabeth Monica de la
Pasture** 1890-1943
    See Delafield, E. M.
    See also CA 119; 154
da Silva, Antonio Jose
    1705-1739 .... **NCLC 114**
Daudet, (Louis Marie) Alphonse
    1840-1897 .... **NCLC 1**
    See also DLB 123; GFL 1789 to the Present;
    RGSF 2
d'Aulnoy, Marie-Catherine c.
    1650-1705 .... **LC 100**
Daumal, Rene 1908-1944 .... **TCLC 14**
    See also CA 114; EWL 3
Davenant, William 1606-1668 .... **LC 13**
    See also DLB 58, 126; RGEL 2
Davenport, Guy (Mattison, Jr.)
    1927- .... **CLC 6, 14, 38; SSC 16**
    See also CA 33-36R; CANR 23, 73; CN 7;
    CSW; DLB 130
David, Robert
    See Nezval, Vitezslav
Davidson, Avram (James) 1923-1993
    See Queen, Ellery
    See also CA 101; 171; CANR 26; DLB 8;
    FANT; SFW 4; SUFW 1, 2
Davidson, Donald (Grady)
    1893-1968 .... **CLC 2, 13, 19**
    See also CA 5-8R; 25-28R; CANR 4, 84;
    DLB 45
Davidson, Hugh
    See Hamilton, Edmond
Davidson, John 1857-1909 .... **TCLC 24**
    See also CA 118; 217; DLB 19; RGEL 2
Davidson, Sara 1943- .... **CLC 9**
    See also CA 81-84; CANR 44, 68; DLB
    185
Davie, Donald (Alfred) 1922-1995 .... **CLC 5,
8, 10, 31; PC 29**
    See also BRWS 6; CA 1-4R; 149; CAAS 3;
    CANR 1, 44; CP 7; DLB 27; MTCW 1;
    RGEL 2
Davie, Elspeth 1919-1995 .... **SSC 52**
    See also CA 120; 126; 150; DLB 139
Davies, Ray(mond Douglas) 1944- .. **CLC 21**
    See also CA 116; 146; CANR 92
Davies, Rhys 1901-1978 .... **CLC 23**
    See also CA 9-12R; 81-84; CANR 4; DLB
    139, 191
Davies, (William) Robertson
    1913-1995 .... **CLC 2, 7, 13, 25, 42, 75,
91; WLC**
    See Marchbanks, Samuel
    See also BEST 89:2; BPFB 1; CA 33-36R;
    150; CANR 17, 42, 103; CN 7; CPW;
    DA; DA3; DAB; DAC; DAM MST, NOV,
    POP; DLB 68; EWL 3; HGG; INT CANR-
    17; MTCW 1, 2; RGEL 2; TWA
Davies, Sir John 1569-1626 .... **LC 85**
    See also DLB 172
Davies, Walter C.
    See Kornbluth, C(yril) M.
Davies, William Henry 1871-1940 ... **TCLC 5**
    See also CA 104; 179; DLB 19, 174; EWL
    3; RGEL 2
Da Vinci, Leonardo 1452-1519 ..... **LC 12, 57,
60**
    See also AAYA 40
Davis, Angela (Yvonne) 1944- .... **CLC 77**
    See also BW 2, 3; CA 57-60; CANR 10,
    81; CSW; DA3; DAM MULT; FW
Davis, B. Lynch
    See Bioy Casares, Adolfo; Borges, Jorge
    Luis

Davis, Frank Marshall 1905-1987 ...... **BLC 1**
    See also BW 2, 3; CA 125; 123; CANR 42,
    80; DAM MULT; DLB 51
Davis, Gordon
    See Hunt, E(verette) Howard, (Jr.)
Davis, H(arold) L(enoir) 1896-1960 . **CLC 49**
    See also ANW; CA 178; 89-92; DLB 9,
    206; SATA 114
Davis, Rebecca (Blaine) Harding
    1831-1910 .... **SSC 38; TCLC 6**
    See also CA 104; 179; DLB 74, 239; FW;
    NFS 14; RGAL 4; TUS
Davis, Richard Harding
    1864-1916 .... **TCLC 24**
    See also CA 114; 179; DLB 12, 23, 78, 79,
    189; DLBD 13; RGAL 4
Davison, Frank Dalby 1893-1970 ..... **CLC 15**
    See also CA 217; 116; DLB 260
Davison, Lawrence H.
    See Lawrence, D(avid) H(erbert Richards)
Davison, Peter (Hubert) 1928- .... **CLC 28**
    See also CA 9-12R; CAAS 4; CANR 3, 43,
    84; CP 7; DLB 5
Davys, Mary 1674-1732 .... **LC 1, 46**
    See also DLB 39
Dawson, (Guy) Fielding (Lewis)
    1930-2002 .... **CLC 6**
    See also CA 85-88; 202; CANR 108; DLB
    130; DLBY 2002
Dawson, Peter
    See Faust, Frederick (Schiller)
    See also TCWW 2, 2
Day, Clarence (Shepard, Jr.)
    1874-1935 .... **TCLC 25**
    See also CA 108; 199; DLB 11
Day, John 1574(?)-1640(?) .... **LC 70**
    See also DLB 62, 170; RGEL 2
Day, Thomas 1748-1789 .... **LC 1**
    See also DLB 39; YABC 1
Day Lewis, C(ecil) 1904-1972 . **CLC 1, 6, 10;
PC 11**
    See Blake, Nicholas
    See also BRWS 3; CA 13-16; 33-36R;
    CANR 34; CAP 1; CWRI 5; DAM POET;
    DLB 15, 20; EWL 3; MTCW 1, 2; RGEL
    2
Dazai Osamu .... **SSC 41; TCLC 11**
    See Tsushima, Shuji
    See also CA 164; DLB 182; EWL 3; MJW;
    RGSF 2; RGWL 2, 3; TWA
de Andrade, Carlos Drummond
    See Drummond de Andrade, Carlos
de Andrade, Mario 1892-1945
    See Andrade, Mario de
    See also CA 178; HW 2
Deane, Norman
    See Creasey, John
Deane, Seamus (Francis) 1940- ...... **CLC 122**
    See also CA 118; CANR 42
**de Beauvoir, Simone (Lucie Ernestine Marie
Bertrand)**
    See Beauvoir, Simone (Lucie Ernestine
    Marie Bertrand) de
de Beer, P.
    See Bosman, Herman Charles
de Brissac, Malcolm
    See Dickinson, Peter (Malcolm)
de Campos, Alvaro
    See Pessoa, Fernando (Antonio Nogueira)
de Chardin, Pierre Teilhard
    See Teilhard de Chardin, (Marie Joseph)
    Pierre
Dee, John 1527-1608 .... **LC 20**
    See also DLB 136, 213
Deer, Sandra 1940- .... **CLC 45**
    See also CA 186
De Ferrari, Gabriella 1941- .... **CLC 65**
    See also CA 146

de Filippo, Eduardo 1900-1984 ... **TCLC 127**
See also CA 132; 114; EWL 3; MTCW 1;
RGWL 2, 3

Defoe, Daniel 1660(?)-1731 .... **LC 1, 42, 108;
WLC**
See also AAYA 27; BRW 3; BRWR 1; BYA
4; CDBLB 1660-1789; CLR 61; DA;
DA3; DAB; DAC; DAM MST, NOV;
DLB 39, 95, 101; JRDA; LAIT 1; LMFS
1; MAICYA 1, 2; NFS 9, 13; RGEL 2;
SATA 22; TEA; WCH; WLIT 3

de Gourmont, Remy(-Marie-Charles)
See Gourmont, Remy(-Marie-Charles) de

de Gournay, Marie le Jars
1566-1645 .... **LC 98**
See also FW

de Hartog, Jan 1914-2002 .... **CLC 19**
See also CA 1-4R; 210; CANR 1; DFS 12

de Hostos, E. M.
See Hostos (y Bonilla), Eugenio Maria de

de Hostos, Eugenio M.
See Hostos (y Bonilla), Eugenio Maria de

Deighton, Len .... **CLC 4, 7, 22, 46**
See Deighton, Leonard Cyril
See also AAYA 6; BEST 89:2; BPFB 1; CD-
BLB 1960 to Present; CMW 4; CN 7;
CPW; DLB 87

Deighton, Leonard Cyril 1929-
See Deighton, Len
See also AAYA 57; CA 9-12R; CANR 19,
33, 68; DA3; DAM NOV, POP; MTCW
1, 2

Dekker, Thomas 1572(?)-1632 ..... **DC 12; LC
22**
See also CDBLB Before 1660; DAM
DRAM; DLB 62, 172; LMFS 1; RGEL 2

de Laclos, Pierre Ambroise Franois
See Laclos, Pierre Ambroise Francois

Delacroix, (Ferdinand-Victor-)Eugene
1798-1863 .... **NCLC 133**
See also EW 5

Delafield, E. M. .... **TCLC 61**
See Dashwood, Edmee Elizabeth Monica
de la Pasture
See also DLB 34; RHW

de la Mare, Walter (John)
1873-1956 . **SSC 14; TCLC 4, 53; WLC**
See also CA 163; CDBLB 1914-1945; CLR
23; CWRI 5; DA3; DAB; DAC; DAM
MST, POET; DLB 19, 153, 162, 255, 284;
EWL 3; EXPP; HGG; MAICYA 1, 2;
MTCW 1; RGEL 2; RGSF; SATA 16;
SUFW 1; TEA; WCH

de Lamartine, Alphonse (Marie Louis Prat)
See Lamartine, Alphonse (Marie Louis Prat)
de

Delaney, Franey
See O'Hara, John (Henry)

Delaney, Shelagh 1939- .... **CLC 29**
See also CA 17-20R; CANR 30, 67; CBD;
CD 5; CDBLB 1960 to Present; CWD;
DAM DRAM; DFS 7; DLB 13; MTCW 1

Delany, Martin Robison
1812-1885 .... **NCLC 93**
See also DLB 50; RGAL 4

Delany, Mary (Granville Pendarves)
1700-1788 .... **LC 12**

Delany, Samuel R(ay), Jr. 1942- .... **BLC 1;
CLC 8, 14, 38, 141**
See also AAYA 24; AFAW 2; BPFB 1; BW
2, 3; CA 81-84; CANR 27, 43, 115, 116;
CN 7; DAM MULT; DLB 8, 33; FANT;
MTCW 1, 2; RGAL 4; SATA 92; SCFW;
SFW 4; SUFW 2

De la Ramee, Marie Louise (Ouida)
1839-1908
See Ouida
See also CA 204; SATA 20

de la Roche, Mazo 1879-1961 .... **CLC 14**
See also CA 85-88; CANR 30; DLB 68;
RGEL 2; RHW; SATA 64

De La Salle, Innocent
See Hartmann, Sadakichi

de Laureamont, Comte
See Lautreamont

Delbanco, Nicholas (Franklin)
1942- .... **CLC 6, 13, 167**
See also CA 17-20R, 189; CAAE 189;
CAAS 2; CANR 29, 55, 116; DLB 6, 234

del Castillo, Michel 1933- .... **CLC 38**
See also CA 109; CANR 77

Deledda, Grazia (Cosima)
1875(?)-1936 .... **TCLC 23**
See also CA 123; 205; DLB 264; EWL 3;
RGWL 2, 3

Deleuze, Gilles 1925-1995 .... **TCLC 116**
See also DLB 296

Delgado, Abelardo (Lalo) B(arrientos)
1930-2004 .... **HLC 1**
See also CA 131; CAAS 15; CANR 90;
DAM MST, MULT; DLB 82; HW 1, 2

Delibes, Miguel .... **CLC 8, 18**
See Delibes Setien, Miguel
See also EWL 3

Delibes Setien, Miguel 1920-
See Delibes, Miguel
See also CA 45-48; CANR 1, 32; CWW 2;
HW 1; MTCW 1

DeLillo, Don 1936- ..... **CLC 8, 10, 13, 27, 39,
54, 76, 143**
See also AMWC 2; AMWS 6; BEST 89:1;
BPFB 1; CA 81-84; CANR 21, 76, 92,
133; CN 7; CPW; DA3; DAM NOV, POP;
DLB 6, 173; EWL 3; MTCW 1, 2; RGAL
4; TUS

de Lisser, H. G.
See De Lisser, H(erbert) G(eorge)
See also DLB 117

De Lisser, H(erbert) G(eorge)
1878-1944 .... **TCLC 12**
See de Lisser, H. G.
See also BW 2; CA 109; 152

Deloire, Pierre
See Peguy, Charles (Pierre)

Deloney, Thomas 1543(?)-1600 .... **LC 41**
See also DLB 167; RGEL 2

Deloria, Ella (Cara) 1889-1971(?) ..... **NNAL**
See also CA 152; DAM MULT; DLB 175

Deloria, Vine (Victor), Jr. 1933- ...... **CLC 21,
122; NNAL**
See also CA 53-56; CANR 5, 20, 48, 98;
DAM MULT; DLB 175; MTCW 1; SATA
21

del Valle-Inclan, Ramon (Maria)
See Valle-Inclan, Ramon (Maria) del

Del Vecchio, John M(ichael) 1947- .. **CLC 29**
See also CA 110; DLBD 9

de Man, Paul (Adolph Michel)
1919-1983 .... **CLC 55**
See also CA 128; 111; CANR 61; DLB 67;
MTCW 1, 2

DeMarinis, Rick 1934- .... **CLC 54**
See also CA 57-60, 184; CAAE 184; CAAS
24; CANR 9, 25, 50; DLB 218

de Maupassant, (Henri Rene Albert) Guy
See Maupassant, (Henri Rene Albert) Guy
de

Dembry, R. Emmet
See Murfree, Mary Noailles

Demby, William 1922- .... **BLC 1; CLC 53**
See also BW 1, 3; CA 81-84; CANR 81;
DAM MULT; DLB 33

de Menton, Francisco
See Chin, Frank (Chew, Jr.)

Demetrius of Phalerum c. 307
B.C.- .... **CMLC 34**

Demijohn, Thom
See Disch, Thomas M(ichael)

De Mille, James 1833-1880 .... **NCLC 123**
See also DLB 99, 251

Deming, Richard 1915-1983
See Queen, Ellery
See also CA 9-12R; CANR 3, 94; SATA 24

Democritus c. 460 B.C.-c. 370
B.C. .... **CMLC 47**

de Montaigne, Michel (Eyquem)
See Montaigne, Michel (Eyquem) de

de Montherlant, Henry (Milon)
See Montherlant, Henry (Milon) de

Demosthenes 384 B.C.-322 B.C. .... **CMLC 13**
See also AW 1; DLB 176; RGWL 2, 3

de Musset, (Louis Charles) Alfred
See Musset, (Louis Charles) Alfred de

de Natale, Francine
See Malzberg, Barry N(athaniel)

de Navarre, Marguerite 1492-1549 ..... **LC 61**
See Marguerite d'Angouleme; Marguerite
de Navarre

Denby, Edwin (Orr) 1903-1983 .... **CLC 48**
See also CA 138; 110

de Nerval, Gerard
See Nerval, Gerard de

Denham, John 1615-1669 .... **LC 73**
See also DLB 58, 126; RGEL 2

Denis, Julio
See Cortazar, Julio

Denmark, Harrison
See Zelazny, Roger (Joseph)

Dennis, John 1658-1734 .... **LC 11**
See also DLB 101; RGEL 2

Dennis, Nigel (Forbes) 1912-1989 ...... **CLC 8**
See also CA 25-28R; 129; DLB 13, 15, 233;
EWL 3; MTCW 1

Dent, Lester 1904-1959 .... **TCLC 72**
See also CA 112; 161; CMW 4; DLB 306;
SFW 4

De Palma, Brian (Russell) 1940- ...... **CLC 20**
See also CA 109

De Quincey, Thomas 1785-1859 ..... **NCLC 4,
87**
See also BRW 4; CDBLB 1789-1832; DLB
110, 144; RGEL 2

Deren, Eleanora 1908(?)-1961
See Deren, Maya
See also CA 192; 111

Deren, Maya .... **CLC 16, 102**
See Deren, Eleanora

Derleth, August (William)
1909-1971 .... **CLC 31**
See also BPFB 1; BYA 9, 10; CA 1-4R; 29-
32R; CANR 4; CMW 4; DLB 9; DLBD
17; HGG; SATA 5; SUFW 1

Der Nister 1884-1950 .... **TCLC 56**
See Nister, Der

de Routisie, Albert
See Aragon, Louis

Derrida, Jacques 1930- .... **CLC 24, 87**
See also CA 124; 127; CANR 76, 98, 133;
DLB 242; EWL 3; LMFS 2; MTCW 1;
TWA

Derry Down Derry
See Lear, Edward

Dersonnes, Jacques
See Simenon, Georges (Jacques Christian)

Desai, Anita 1937- .... **CLC 19, 37, 97, 175**
See also BRWS 5; CA 81-84; CANR 33,
53, 95, 133; CN 7; CWRI 5; DA3; DAB;
DAM NOV; DLB 271; DNFS 2; EWL 3;
FW; MTCW 1, 2; SATA 63, 126

Desai, Kiran 1971- .... **CLC 119**
See also BYA 16; CA 171; CANR 127

de Saint-Luc, Jean
  See Glassco, John
de Saint Roman, Arnaud
  See Aragon, Louis
Desbordes-Valmore, Marceline
  1786-1859 .... **NCLC 97**
  See also DLB 217
Descartes, Rene 1596-1650 .... **LC 20, 35**
  See also DLB 268; EW 3; GFL Beginnings
    to 1789
Deschamps, Eustache 1340(?)-1404 .. **LC 103**
  See also DLB 208
De Sica, Vittorio 1901(?)-1974 .... **CLC 20**
  See also CA 117
Desnos, Robert 1900-1945 .... **TCLC 22**
  See also CA 121; 151; CANR 107; DLB
    258; EWL 3; LMFS 2
Destouches, Louis-Ferdinand
  1894-1961 .... **CLC 9, 15**
  See Celine, Louis-Ferdinand
  See also CA 85-88; CANR 28; MTCW 1
de Tolignac, Gaston
  See Griffith, D(avid Lewelyn) W(ark)
Deutsch, Babette 1895-1982 .... **CLC 18**
  See also BYA 3; CA 1-4R; 108; CANR 4,
    79; DLB 45; SATA 1; SATA-Obit 33
Devenant, William 1606-1649 .... **LC 13**
Devkota, Laxmiprasad 1909-1959 . **TCLC 23**
  See also CA 123
De Voto, Bernard (Augustine)
  1897-1955 .... **TCLC 29**
  See also CA 113; 160; DLB 9, 256
De Vries, Peter 1910-1993 ..... **CLC 1, 2, 3, 7,
    10, 28, 46**
  See also CA 17-20R; 142; CANR 41; DAM
    NOV; DLB 6; DLBY 1982; MTCW 1, 2
Dewey, John 1859-1952 .... **TCLC 95**
  See also CA 114; 170; DLB 246, 270;
    RGAL 4
Dexter, John
  See Bradley, Marion Zimmer
  See also GLL 1
Dexter, Martin
  See Faust, Frederick (Schiller)
  See also TCWW 2
Dexter, Pete 1943- .... **CLC 34, 55**
  See also BEST 89:2; CA 127; 131; CANR
    129; CPW; DAM POP; INT CA-131;
    MTCW 1
Diamano, Silmang
  See Senghor, Leopold Sedar
Diamond, Neil 1941- .... **CLC 30**
  See also CA 108
Diaz del Castillo, Bernal
  1496-1584 .... **HLCS 1; LC 31**
  See also LAW
di Bassetto, Corno
  See Shaw, George Bernard
Dick, Philip K(indred) 1928-1982 ... **CLC 10,
    30, 72; SSC 57**
  See also AAYA 24; BPFB 1; BYA 11; CA
    49-52; CANR 2, 16, 132; CPW;
    DA3; DAM NOV, POP; DLB 8; MTCW
    1, 2; NFS 5; SCFW; SFW 4
Dickens, Charles (John Huffam)
  1812-1870 .... **NCLC 3, 8, 18, 26, 37, 50,
    86, 105, 113; SSC 17, 49; WLC**
  See also AAYA 23; BRW 5; BRWC 1, 2;
    BYA 1, 2, 3, 13, 14; CDBLB 1832-1890;
    CLR 95; CMW 4; DA; DA3; DAB; DAC;
    DAM MST, NOV; DLB 21, 55, 70, 159,
    166; EXPN; HGG; JRDA; LAIT 1, 2;
    LATS 1:1; LMFS 1; MAICYA 1, 2; NFS
    4, 5, 10, 14, 20; RGEL 2; RGSF 2; SATA
    15; SUFW 1; TEA; WCH; WLIT 4; WYA

Dickey, James (Lafayette)
  1923-1997 .... **CLC 1, 2, 4, 7, 10, 15, 47,
    109; PC 40; TCLC 151**
  See also AAYA 50; AITN 1, 2; AMWS 4;
    BPFB 1; CA 9-12R; 156; CABS 2; CANR
    10, 48, 61, 105; CDALB 1968-1988; CP
    7; CPW; CSW; DA3; DAM NOV, POET,
    POP; DLB 5, 193; DLBD 7; DLBY 1982,
    1993, 1996, 1997, 1998; EWL 3; INT
    CANR-10; MTCW 1, 2; NFS 9; PFS 6,
    11; RGAL 4; TUS
Dickey, William 1928-1994 .... **CLC 3, 28**
  See also CA 9-12R; 145; CANR 24, 79;
    DLB 5
Dickinson, Charles 1951- .... **CLC 49**
  See also CA 128
Dickinson, Emily (Elizabeth)
  1830-1886 ... **NCLC 21, 77; PC 1; WLC**
  See also AAYA 22; AMW; AMWR 1;
    CDALB 1865-1917; DA; DA3; DAB;
    DAC; DAM MST, POET; DLB 1, 243;
    EXPP; MAWW; PAB; PFS 1, 2, 3, 4, 5,
    6, 8, 10, 11, 13, 16; RGAL 4; SATA 29;
    TUS; WP; WYA
Dickinson, Mrs. Herbert Ward
  See Phelps, Elizabeth Stuart
Dickinson, Peter (Malcolm) 1927- .. **CLC 12,
    35**
  See also AAYA 9, 49; BYA 5; CA 41-44R;
    CANR 31, 58, 88; CLR 29; CMW 4; DLB
    87, 161, 276; JRDA; MAICYA 1, 2;
    SATA 5, 62, 95, 150; SFW 4; WYA; YAW
Dickson, Carr
  See Carr, John Dickson
Dickson, Carter
  See Carr, John Dickson
Diderot, Denis 1713-1784 .... **LC 26**
  See also EW 4; GFL Beginnings to 1789;
    LMFS 1; RGWL 2, 3
Didion, Joan 1934- . **CLC 1, 3, 8, 14, 32, 129**
  See also AITN 1; AMWS 4; CA 5-8R;
    CANR 14, 52, 76, 125; CDALB 1968-
    1988; CN 7; DA3; DAM NOV; DLB 2,
    173, 185; DLBY 1981, 1986; EWL 3;
    MAWW; MTCW 1, 2; NFS 3; RGAL 4;
    TCWW 2; TUS
Dietrich, Robert
  See Hunt, E(verette) Howard, (Jr.)
Difusa, Pati
  See Almodovar, Pedro
Dillard, Annie 1945- .... **CLC 9, 60, 115**
  See also AAYA 6, 43; AMWS 6; ANW; CA
    49-52; CANR 3, 43, 62, 90, 125; DA3;
    DAM NOV; DLB 275, 278; DLBY 1980;
    LAIT 4, 5; MTCW 1, 2; NCFS 1; RGAL
    4; SATA 10, 140; TUS
Dillard, R(ichard) H(enry) W(ilde)
  1937- .... **CLC 5**
  See also CA 21-24R; CAAS 7; CANR 10;
    CP 7; CSW; DLB 5, 244
Dillon, Eilis 1920-1994 .... **CLC 17**
  See also CA 9-12R, 182; 147; CAAE 182;
    CAAS 3; CANR 4, 38, 78; CLR 26; MAI-
    CYA 1, 2; MAICYAS 1; SATA 2, 74;
    SATA-Essay 105; SATA-Obit 83; YAW
Dimont, Penelope
  See Mortimer, Penelope (Ruth)
Dinesen, Isak ..... **CLC 10, 29, 95; SSC 7, 75**
  See Blixen, Karen (Christentze Dinesen)
  See also EW 10; EWL 3; EXPS; FW; HGG;
    LAIT 3; MTCW 1; NCFS 2; NFS 9;
    RGSF 2; RGWL 2, 3; SSFS 3, 6, 13;
    WLIT 2
Ding Ling .... **CLC 68**
  See Chiang, Pin-chin
  See also RGWL 3
Diphusa, Patty
  See Almodovar, Pedro

Disch, Thomas M(ichael) 1940- ... **CLC 7, 36**
  See Disch, Tom
  See also AAYA 17; BPFB 1; CA 21-24R;
    CAAS 4; CANR 17, 36, 54, 89; CLR 18;
    CP 7; DA3; DLB 8; HGG; MAICYA 1, 2;
    MTCW 1, 2; SAAS 15; SATA 92; SCFW;
    SFW 4; SUFW 2
Disch, Tom
  See Disch, Thomas M(ichael)
  See also DLB 282
d'Isly, Georges
  See Simenon, Georges (Jacques Christian)
Disraeli, Benjamin 1804-1881 ... **NCLC 2, 39,
    79**
  See also BRW 4; DLB 21, 55; RGEL 2
Ditcum, Steve
  See Crumb, R(obert)
Dixon, Paige
  See Corcoran, Barbara (Asenath)
Dixon, Stephen 1936- .... **CLC 52; SSC 16**
  See also AMWS 12; CA 89-92; CANR 17,
    40, 54, 91; CN 7; DLB 130
Djebar, Assia 1936- .... **CLC 182**
  See also CA 188; EWL 3; RGWL 3; WLIT
    2
Doak, Annie
  See Dillard, Annie
Dobell, Sydney Thompson
  1824-1874 .... **NCLC 43**
  See also DLB 32; RGEL 2
Doblin, Alfred .... **TCLC 13**
  See Doeblin, Alfred
  See also CDWLB 2; EWL 3; RGWL 2, 3
Dobroliubov, Nikolai Aleksandrovich
  See Dobrolyubov, Nikolai Alexandrovich
  See also DLB 277
Dobrolyubov, Nikolai Alexandrovich
  1836-1861 .... **NCLC 5**
  See Dobroliubov, Nikolai Aleksandrovich
Dobson, Austin 1840-1921 .... **TCLC 79**
  See also DLB 35, 144
Dobyns, Stephen 1941- .... **CLC 37**
  See also AMWS 13; CA 45-48; CANR 2,
    18, 99; CMW 4; CP 7
Doctorow, E(dgar) L(aurence)
  1931- .... **CLC 6, 11, 15, 18, 37, 44, 65,
    113**
  See also AAYA 22; AITN 2; AMWS 4;
    BEST 89:3; BPFB 1; CA 45-48; CANR
    2, 33, 51, 76, 97, 133; CDALB 1968-
    1988; CN 7; CPW; DA3; DAM NOV,
    POP; DLB 2, 28, 173; DLBY 1980; EWL
    3; LAIT 3; MTCW 1, 2; NFS 6; RGAL 4;
    RHW; TUS
Dodgson, Charles L(utwidge) 1832-1898
  See Carroll, Lewis
  See also CLR 2; DA; DA3; DAB; DAC;
    DAM MST, NOV, POET; MAICYA 1, 2;
    SATA 100; YABC 2
Dodsley, Robert 1703-1764 .... **LC 97**
  See also DLB 95; RGEL 2
Dodson, Owen (Vincent) 1914-1983 .. **BLC 1;
    CLC 79**
  See also BW 1; CA 65-68; 110; CANR 24;
    DAM MULT; DLB 76
Doeblin, Alfred 1878-1957 .... **TCLC 13**
  See Doblin, Alfred
  See also CA 110; 141; DLB 66
Doerr, Harriet 1910-2002 .... **CLC 34**
  See also CA 117; 122; 213; CANR 47; INT
    CA-122; LATS 1:2
Domecq, H(onorio Bustos)
  See Bioy Casares, Adolfo
Domecq, H(onorio) Bustos
  See Bioy Casares, Adolfo; Borges, Jorge
    Luis
Domini, Rey
  See Lorde, Audre (Geraldine)
  See also GLL 1

Dominique
See Proust, (Valentin-Louis-George-Eugene) Marcel

Don, A
See Stephen, Sir Leslie

Donaldson, Stephen R(eeder)
1947- .... **CLC 46, 138**
See also AAYA 36; BPFB 1; CA 89-92; CANR 13, 55, 99; CPW; DAM POP; FANT; INT CANR-13; SATA 121; SFW 4; SUFW 1, 2

Donleavy, J(ames) P(atrick) 1926- .... **CLC 1, 4, 6, 10, 45**
See also AITN 2; BPFB 1; CA 9-12R; CANR 24, 49, 62, 80, 124; CBD; CD 5; CN 7; DLB 6, 173; INT CANR-24; MTCW 1, 2; RGAL 4

Donnadieu, Marguerite
See Duras, Marguerite

Donne, John 1572-1631 ... **LC 10, 24, 91; PC 1, 43; WLC**
See also BRW 1; BRWC 1; BRWR 2; CD-BLB Before 1660; DA; DAB; DAC; DAM MST, POET; DLB 121, 151; EXPP; PAB; PFS 2, 11; RGEL 3; TEA; WLIT 3; WP

Donnell, David 1939(?)- .... **CLC 34**
See also CA 197

Donoghue, P. S.
See Hunt, E(verette) Howard, (Jr.)

Donoso (Yanez), Jose 1924-1996 ... **CLC 4, 8, 11, 32, 99; HLC 1; SSC 34; TCLC 133**
See also CA 81-84; 155; CANR 32, 73; CD-WLB 3; CWW 2; DAM MULT; DLB 113; EWL 3; HW 1, 2; LAW; LAWS 1; MTCW 1, 2; RGSF 2; WLIT 1

Donovan, John 1928-1992 .... **CLC 35**
See also AAYA 20; CA 97-100; 137; CLR 3; MAICYA 1, 2; SATA 72; SATA-Brief 29; YAW

Don Roberto
See Cunninghame Graham, Robert (Gallnigad) Bontine

Doolittle, Hilda 1886-1961 . **CLC 3, 8, 14, 31, 34, 73; PC 5; WLC**
See H. D.
See also AMWS 1; CA 97-100; CANR 35, 131; DA; DAC; DAM MST, POET; DLB 4, 45; EWL 3; FW; GLL 1; LMFS 2; MAWW; MTCW 1, 2; PFS 6; RGAL 4

Doppo, Kunikida .... **TCLC 99**
See Kunikida Doppo

Dorfman, Ariel 1942- .... **CLC 48, 77, 189; HLC 1**
See also CA 124; 130; CANR 67, 70; CWW 2; DAM MULT; DFS 4; EWL 3; HW 1, 2; INT CA-130; WLIT 1

Dorn, Edward (Merton)
1929-1999 .... **CLC 10, 18**
See also CA 93-96; 187; CANR 42, 79; CP 7; DLB 5; INT CA-93-96; WP

Dor-Ner, Zvi .... **CLC 70**

Dorris, Michael (Anthony)
1945-1997 .... **CLC 109; NNAL**
See also AAYA 20; BEST 90:1; BYA 12; CA 102; 157; CANR 19, 46, 75; CLR 58; DA3; DAM MULT, NOV; DLB 175; LAIT 5; MTCW 2; NFS 3; RGAL 4; SATA 75; SATA-Obit 94; TCWW 2; YAW

Dorris, Michael A.
See Dorris, Michael (Anthony)

Dorsan, Luc
See Simenon, Georges (Jacques Christian)

Dorsange, Jean
See Simenon, Georges (Jacques Christian)

Dorset
See Sackville, Thomas

Dos Passos, John (Roderigo)
1896-1970 ... **CLC 1, 4, 8, 11, 15, 25, 34, 82; WLC**
See also AMW; BPFB 1; CA 1-4R; 29-32R; CANR 3; CDALB 1929-1941; DA; DA3; DAB; DAC; DAM MST, NOV; DLB 4, 9, 274; DLBD 1, 15; DLBY 1996; EWL 3; MTCW 1, 2; NFS 14; RGAL 4; TUS

Dossage, Jean
See Simenon, Georges (Jacques Christian)

Dostoevsky, Fedor Mikhailovich
1821-1881 .. **NCLC 2, 7, 21, 33, 43, 119; SSC 2, 33, 44; WLC**
See Dostoevsky, Fyodor
See also AAYA 40; DA; DA3; DAB; DAC; DAM MST, NOV; EW 7; EXPN; NFS 3, 8; RGSF 2; RGWL 2, 3; SSFS 8; TWA

Dostoevsky, Fyodor
See Dostoevsky, Fedor Mikhailovich
See also DLB 238; LATS 1:1; LMFS 1, 2

Doty, M. R.
See Doty, Mark (Alan)

Doty, Mark
See Doty, Mark (Alan)

Doty, Mark (Alan) 1953(?)- .... **CLC 176; PC 53**
See also AMWS 11; CA 161, 183; CAAE 183; CANR 110

Doty, Mark A.
See Doty, Mark (Alan)

Doughty, Charles M(ontagu)
1843-1926 .... **TCLC 27**
See also CA 115; 178; DLB 19, 57, 174

Douglas, Ellen .... **CLC 73**
See Haxton, Josephine Ayres; Williamson, Ellen Douglas
See also CN 7; CSW; DLB 292

Douglas, Gavin 1475(?)-1522 .... **LC 20**
See also DLB 132; RGEL 2

Douglas, George
See Brown, George Douglas
See also RGEL 2

Douglas, Keith (Castellain)
1920-1944 .... **TCLC 40**
See also BRW 7; CA 160; DLB 27; EWL 3; PAB; RGEL 2

Douglas, Leonard
See Bradbury, Ray (Douglas)

Douglas, Michael
See Crichton, (John) Michael

Douglas, (George) Norman
1868-1952 .... **TCLC 68**
See also BRW 6; CA 119; 157; DLB 34, 195; RGEL 2

Douglas, William
See Brown, George Douglas

Douglass, Frederick 1817(?)-1895 ..... **BLC 1; NCLC 7, 55, 141; WLC**
See also AAYA 48; AFAW 1, 2; AMWC 1; AMWS 3; CDALB 1640-1865; DA; DA3; DAC; DAM MST, MULT; DLB 1, 43, 50, 79, 243; FW; LAIT 2; NCFS 2; RGAL 4; SATA 29

Dourado, (Waldomiro Freitas) Autran
1926- .... **CLC 23, 60**
See also CA 25-28R; 179; CANR 34, 81; DLB 145; HW 2

Dourado, Waldomiro Autran
See Dourado, (Waldomiro Freitas) Autran
See also CA 179

Dove, Rita (Frances) 1952- . **BLCS; CLC 50, 81; PC 6**
See also AAYA 46; AMWS 4; BW 2; CA 109; CAAS 19; CANR 27, 42, 68, 76, 97, 132; CDALBS; CP 7; CSW; CWP; DA3; DAM MULT, POET; DLB 120; EWL 3; EXPP; MTCW 1; PFS 1, 15; RGAL 4

Doveglion
See Villa, Jose Garcia

Dowell, Coleman 1925-1985 .... **CLC 60**
See also CA 25-28R; 117; CANR 10; DLB 130; GLL 2

Dowson, Ernest (Christopher)
1867-1900 .... **TCLC 4**
See also CA 105; 150; DLB 19, 135; RGEL 2

Doyle, A. Conan
See Doyle, Sir Arthur Conan

Doyle, Sir Arthur Conan
1859-1930 .... **SSC 12; TCLC 7; WLC**
See Conan Doyle, Arthur
See also AAYA 14; BRWS 2; CA 104; 122; CANR 131; CDBLB 1890-1914; CMW 4; DA; DA3; DAB; DAC; DAM MST, NOV; DLB 18, 70, 156, 178; EXPS; HGG; LAIT 2; MSW; MTCW 1, 2; RGEL 2; RGSF 2; RHW; SATA 24; SCFW 2; SFW 4; SSFS 2; TEA; WCH; WLIT 4; WYA; YAW

Doyle, Conan
See Doyle, Sir Arthur Conan

Doyle, John
See Graves, Robert (von Ranke)

Doyle, Roddy 1958(?)- .... **CLC 81, 178**
See also AAYA 14; BRWS 5; CA 143; CANR 73, 128; CN 7; DA3; DLB 194

Doyle, Sir A. Conan
See Doyle, Sir Arthur Conan

Dr. A
See Asimov, Isaac; Silverstein, Alvin; Silverstein, Virginia B(arbara Opshelor)

Drabble, Margaret 1939- ...... **CLC 2, 3, 5, 8, 10, 22, 53, 129**
See also BRWS 4; CA 13-16R; CANR 18, 35, 63, 112, 131; CDBLB 1960 to Present; CN 7; CPW; DA3; DAB; DAC; DAM MST, NOV, POP; DLB 14, 155, 231; EWL 3; FW; MTCW 1, 2; RGEL 2; SATA 48; TEA

Drakulic, Slavenka 1949- .... **CLC 173**
See also CA 144; CANR 92

Drakulic-Ilic, Slavenka
See Drakulic, Slavenka

Drapier, M. B.
See Swift, Jonathan

Drayham, James
See Mencken, H(enry) L(ouis)

Drayton, Michael 1563-1631 .... **LC 8**
See also DAM POET; DLB 121; RGEL 2

Dreadstone, Carl
See Campbell, (John) Ramsey

Dreiser, Theodore (Herman Albert)
1871-1945 .... **SSC 30; TCLC 10, 18, 35, 83; WLC**
See also AMW; AMWC 2; AMWR 2; BYA 15, 16; CA 106; 132; CDALB 1865-1917; DA; DA3; DAC; DAM MST, NOV; DLB 9, 12, 102, 137; DLBD 1; EWL 3; LAIT 2; LMFS 2; MTCW 1, 2; NFS 8, 17; RGAL 4; TUS

Drexler, Rosalyn 1926- .... **CLC 2, 6**
See also CA 81-84; CAD; CANR 68, 124; CD 5; CWD

Dreyer, Carl Theodor 1889-1968 ...... **CLC 16**
See also CA 116

Drieu la Rochelle, Pierre(-Eugene)
1893-1945 .... **TCLC 21**
See also CA 117; DLB 72; EWL 3; GFL 1789 to the Present

Drinkwater, John 1882-1937 .... **TCLC 57**
See also CA 109; 149; DLB 10, 19, 149; RGEL 2

Drop Shot
See Cable, George Washington

Droste-Hulshoff, Annette Freiin von
1797-1848 .... **NCLC 3, 133**
See also CDWLB 2; DLB 133; RGSF 2; RGWL 2, 3

Drummond, Walter
See Silverberg, Robert
Drummond, William Henry
1854-1907 .... **TCLC 25**
See also CA 160; DLB 92
Drummond de Andrade, Carlos
1902-1987 .... **CLC 18; TCLC 139**
See Andrade, Carlos Drummond de
See also CA 132; 123; LAW
Drummond of Hawthornden, William
1585-1649 .... **LC 83**
See also DLB 121, 213; RGEL 2
Drury, Allen (Stuart) 1918-1998 .... **CLC 37**
See also CA 57-60; 170; CANR 18, 52; CN
7; INT CANR-18
Dryden, John 1631-1700 ..... **DC 3; LC 3, 21;**
PC 25; WLC
See also BRW 2; CDBLB 1660-1789; DA;
DAB; DAC; DAM DRAM, MST, POET;
DLB 80, 101, 131; EXPP; IDTP; LMFS
1; RGEL 2; TEA; WLIT 3
du Bellay, Joachim 1524-1560 .... **LC 92**
See also GFL Beginnings to 1789; RGWL
2, 3
Duberman, Martin (Bauml) 1930- ..... **CLC 8**
See also CA 1-4R; CAD; CANR 2, 63; CD
5
Dubie, Norman (Evans) 1945- .... **CLC 36**
See also CA 69-72; CANR 12, 115; CP 7;
DLB 120; PFS 12
Du Bois, W(illiam) E(dward) B(urghardt)
1868-1963 ..... **BLC 1; CLC 1, 2, 13, 64,**
96; HR 2; WLC
See also AAYA 40; AFAW 1, 2; AMWC 1;
AMWS 2; BW 1, 3; CA 85-88; CANR
34, 82, 132; CDALB 1865-1917; DA;
DA3; DAC; DAM MST, MULT, NOV;
DLB 47, 50, 91, 246, 284; EWL 3; EXPP;
LAIT 2; LMFS 2; MTCW 1, 2; NCFS 1;
PFS 13; RGAL 4; SATA 42
Dubus, Andre 1936-1999 ..... **CLC 13, 36, 97;**
SSC 15
See also AMWS 7; CA 21-24R; 177; CANR
17; CN 7; CSW; DLB 130; INT CANR-
17; RGAL 4; SSFS 10
Duca Minimo
See D'Annunzio, Gabriele
Ducharme, Rejean 1941- .... **CLC 74**
See also CA 165; DLB 60
du Chatelet, Emilie 1706-1749 .... **LC 96**
Duchen, Claire .... **CLC 65**
Duclos, Charles Pinot- 1704-1772 .... **LC 1**
See also GFL Beginnings to 1789
Dudek, Louis 1918-2001 .... **CLC 11, 19**
See also CA 45-48; 215; CAAS 14; CANR
1; CP 7; DLB 88
Duerrenmatt, Friedrich 1921-1990 ... **CLC 1,**
4, 8, 11, 15, 43, 102
See Durrenmatt, Friedrich
See also CA 17-20R; CANR 33; CMW 4;
DAM DRAM; DLB 69, 124; MTCW 1, 2
Duffy, Bruce 1953(?)- .... **CLC 50**
See also CA 172
Duffy, Maureen 1933- .... **CLC 37**
See also CA 25-28R; CANR 33, 68; CBD;
CN 7; CP 7; CWD; CWP; DFS 15; DLB
14; FW; MTCW 1
Du Fu
See Tu Fu
See also RGWL 2, 3
Dugan, Alan 1923-2003 .... **CLC 2, 6**
See also CA 81-84; 220; CANR 119; CP 7;
DLB 5; PFS 10
du Gard, Roger Martin
See Martin du Gard, Roger
Duhamel, Georges 1884-1966 .... **CLC 8**
See also CA 81-84; 25-28R; CANR 35;
DLB 65; EWL 3; GFL 1789 to the
Present; MTCW 1

Dujardin, Edouard (Emile Louis)
1861-1949 .... **TCLC 13**
See also CA 109; DLB 123
Duke, Raoul
See Thompson, Hunter S(tockton)
Dulles, John Foster 1888-1959 .... **TCLC 72**
See also CA 115; 149
Dumas, Alexandre (pere)
1802-1870 .... **NCLC 11, 71; WLC**
See also AAYA 22; BYA 3; DA; DA3;
DAB; DAC; DAM MST, NOV; DLB 119,
192; EW 6; GFL 1789 to the Present;
LAIT 1, 2; NFS 14, 19; RGWL 2, 3;
SATA 18; TWA; WCH
Dumas, Alexandre (fils) 1824-1895 ...... **DC 1;**
NCLC 9
See also DLB 192; GFL 1789 to the Present;
RGWL 2, 3
Dumas, Claudine
See Malzberg, Barry N(athaniel)
Dumas, Henry L. 1934-1968 .... **CLC 6, 62**
See also BW 1; CA 85-88; DLB 41; RGAL
4
du Maurier, Daphne 1907-1989 .. **CLC 6, 11,**
59; SSC 18
See also AAYA 37; BPFB 1; BRWS 3; CA
5-8R; 128; CANR 6, 55; CMW 4; CPW;
DA3; DAB; DAC; DAM MST, NOV;
DLB 191; HGG; LAIT 3; MSW; MTCW
1, 2; NFS 12; RGEL 2; RGSF 2; RHW;
SATA 27; SATA-Obit 60; SSFS 14, 16;
TEA
Du Maurier, George 1834-1896 ..... **NCLC 86**
See also DLB 153, 178; RGEL 2
Dunbar, Paul Laurence 1872-1906 ... **BLC 1;**
PC 5; SSC 8; TCLC 2, 12; WLC
See also AFAW 1, 2; AMWS 2; BW 1, 3;
CA 104; 124; CANR 79; CDALB 1865-
1917; DA; DA3; DAC; DAM MST,
MULT, POET; DLB 50, 54, 78; EXPP;
RGAL 4; SATA 34
Dunbar, William 1460(?)-1520(?) .... **LC 20**
See also BRWS 8; DLB 132, 146; RGEL 2
Dunbar-Nelson, Alice .... **HR 2**
See Nelson, Alice Ruth Moore Dunbar
Duncan, Dora Angela
See Duncan, Isadora
Duncan, Isadora 1877(?)-1927 .... **TCLC 68**
See also CA 118; 149
Duncan, Lois 1934- .... **CLC 26**
See also AAYA 4, 34; BYA 6, 8; CA 1-4R;
CANR 2, 23, 36, 111; CLR 29; JRDA;
MAICYA 1, 2; MAICYAS 1; SAAS 2;
SATA 1, 36, 75, 133, 141; SATA-Essay
141; WYA; YAW
Duncan, Robert (Edward)
1919-1988 .... **CLC 1, 2, 4, 7, 15, 41, 55;**
PC 2
See also BG 2; CA 9-12R; 124; CANR 28,
62; DAM POET; DLB 5, 16, 193; EWL
3; MTCW 1, 2; PFS 13; RGAL 4; WP
Duncan, Sara Jeannette
1861-1922 .... **TCLC 60**
See also CA 157; DLB 92
Dunlap, William 1766-1839 .... **NCLC 2**
See also DLB 30, 37, 59; RGAL 4
Dunn, Douglas (Eaglesham) 1942- .... **CLC 6,**
40
See also CA 45-48; CANR 2, 33, 126; CP
7; DLB 40; MTCW 1
Dunn, Katherine (Karen) 1945- .... **CLC 71**
See also CA 33-36R; CANR 72; HGG;
MTCW 1
Dunn, Stephen (Elliott) 1939- .... **CLC 36**
See also AMWS 11; CA 33-36R; CANR
12, 48, 53, 105; CP 7; DLB 105; PFS 21
Dunne, Finley Peter 1867-1936 ...... **TCLC 28**
See also CA 108; 178; DLB 11, 23; RGAL
4

Dunne, John Gregory 1932-2003 ..... **CLC 28**
See also CA 25-28R; 222; CANR 14, 50;
CN 7; DLBY 1980
Dunsany, Lord .... **TCLC 2, 59**
See Dunsany, Edward John Moreton Drax
Plunkett
See also DLB 77, 153, 156, 255; FANT;
IDTP; RGEL 2; SFW 4; SUFW 1
Dunsany, Edward John Moreton Drax
Plunkett 1878-1957
See Dunsany, Lord
See also CA 104; 148; DLB 10; MTCW 1
Duns Scotus, John 1266(?)-1308 ... **CMLC 59**
See also DLB 115
du Perry, Jean
See Simenon, Georges (Jacques Christian)
Durang, Christopher (Ferdinand)
1949- .... **CLC 27, 38**
See also CA 105; CAD; CANR 50, 76, 130;
CD 5; MTCW 1
Duras, Marguerite 1914-1996 . **CLC 3, 6, 11,**
20, 34, 40, 68, 100; SSC 40
See also BPFB 1; CA 25-28R; 151; CANR
50; CWW 2; DLB 83; EWL 3; GFL 1789
to the Present; IDFW 4; MTCW 1, 2;
RGWL 2, 3; TWA
Durban, (Rosa) Pam 1947- .... **CLC 39**
See also CA 123; CANR 98; CSW
Durcan, Paul 1944- .... **CLC 43, 70**
See also CA 134; CANR 123; CP 7; DAM
POET; EWL 3
Durfey, Thomas 1653-1723 .... **LC 94**
See also DLB 80; RGEL 2
Durkheim, Emile 1858-1917 .... **TCLC 55**
Durrell, Lawrence (George)
1912-1990 ..... **CLC 1, 4, 6, 8, 13, 27, 41**
See also BPFB 1; BRWS 1; CA 9-12R; 132;
CANR 40, 77; CDBLB 1945-1960; DAM
NOV; DLB 15, 27, 204; DLBY 1990;
EWL 3; MTCW 1, 2; RGEL 2; SFW 4;
TEA
Durrenmatt, Friedrich
See Duerrenmatt, Friedrich
See also CDWLB 2; EW 13; EWL 3;
RGWL 2, 3
Dutt, Michael Madhusudan
1824-1873 .... **NCLC 118**
Dutt, Toru 1856-1877 .... **NCLC 29**
See also DLB 240
Dwight, Timothy 1752-1817 .... **NCLC 13**
See also DLB 37; RGAL 4
Dworkin, Andrea 1946- .... **CLC 43, 123**
See also CA 77-80; CAAS 21; CANR 16,
39, 76, 96; FW; GLL 1; INT CANR-16;
MTCW 1, 2
Dwyer, Deanna
See Koontz, Dean R(ay)
Dwyer, K. R.
See Koontz, Dean R(ay)
Dybek, Stuart 1942- .... **CLC 114; SSC 55**
See also CA 97-100; CANR 39; DLB 130
Dye, Richard
See De Voto, Bernard (Augustine)
Dyer, Geoff 1958- .... **CLC 149**
See also CA 125; CANR 88
Dyer, George 1755-1841 .... **NCLC 129**
See also DLB 93
Dylan, Bob 1941- .... **CLC 3, 4, 6, 12, 77; PC**
37
See also CA 41-44R; CANR 108; CP 7;
DLB 16
Dyson, John 1943- .... **CLC 70**
See also CA 144
Dzyubin, Eduard Georgievich 1895-1934
See Bagritsky, Eduard
See also CA 170
E. V. L.
See Lucas, E(dward) V(errall)

Eagleton, Terence (Francis) 1943- .. **CLC 63, 132**
See also CA 57-60; CANR 7, 23, 68, 115; DLB 242; LMFS 2; MTCW 1, 2

Eagleton, Terry
See Eagleton, Terence (Francis)

Early, Jack
See Scoppettone, Sandra
See also GLL 1

East, Michael
See West, Morris L(anglo)

Eastaway, Edward
See Thomas, (Philip) Edward

Eastlake, William (Derry)
1917-1997 .... **CLC 8**
See also CA 5-8R; 158; CAAS 1; CANR 5, 63; CN 7; DLB 6, 206; INT CANR-5; TCWW 2

Eastman, Charles A(lexander)
1858-1939 .... **NNAL; TCLC 55**
See also CA 179; CANR 91; DAM MULT; DLB 175; YABC 1

Eaton, Edith Maude 1865-1914 .... **AAL**
See Far, Sui Sin
See also CA 154; DLB 221; FW

Eaton, (Lillie) Winnifred 1875-1954 .... **AAL**
See also CA 217; DLB 221; RGAL 4

Eberhart, Richard (Ghormley)
1904- .... **CLC 3, 11, 19, 56**
See also AMW; CA 1-4R; CANR 2, 125; CDALB 1941-1968; CP 7; DAM POET; DLB 48; MTCW 1; RGAL 4

Eberstadt, Fernanda 1960- .... **CLC 39**
See also CA 136; CANR 69, 128

Echegaray (y Eizaguirre), Jose (Maria Waldo) 1832-1916 .... **HLCS 1; TCLC 4**
See also CA 104; CANR 32; EWL 3; HW 1; MTCW 1

Echeverria, (Jose) Esteban (Antonino)
1805-1851 .... **NCLC 18**
See also LAW

Echo
See Proust, (Valentin-Louis-George-Eugene) Marcel

Eckert, Allan W. 1931- .... **CLC 17**
See also AAYA 18; BYA 2; CA 13-16R; CANR 14, 45; INT CANR-14; MAICYA 2; MAICYAS 1; SAAS 21; SATA 29, 91; SATA-Brief 27

Eckhart, Meister 1260(?)-1327(?) ... **CMLC 9**
See also DLB 115; LMFS 1

Eckmar, F. R.
See de Hartog, Jan

Eco, Umberto 1932- .... **CLC 28, 60, 142**
See also BEST 90:1; BPFB 1; CA 77-80; CANR 12, 33, 55, 110, 131; CPW; CWW 2; DA3; DAM NOV, POP; DLB 196, 242; EWL 3; MSW; MTCW 1, 2; RGWL 3

Eddison, E(ric) R(ucker)
1882-1945 .... **TCLC 15**
See also CA 109; 156; DLB 255; FANT; SFW 4; SUFW 1

Eddy, Mary (Ann Morse) Baker
1821-1910 .... **TCLC 71**
See also CA 113; 174

Edel, (Joseph) Leon 1907-1997 .. **CLC 29, 34**
See also CA 1-4R; 161; CANR 1, 22, 112; DLB 103; INT CANR-22

Eden, Emily 1797-1869 .... **NCLC 10**

Edgar, David 1948- .... **CLC 42**
See also CA 57-60; CANR 12, 61, 112; CBD; CD 5; DAM DRAM; DFS 15; DLB 13, 233; MTCW 1

Edgerton, Clyde (Carlyle) 1944- ...... **CLC 39**
See also AAYA 17; CA 118; 134; CANR 64, 125; CSW; DLB 278; INT CA-134; YAW

Edgeworth, Maria 1768-1849 .... **NCLC 1, 51**
See also BRWS 3; DLB 116, 159, 163; FW; RGEL 2; SATA 21; TEA; WLIT 3

Edmonds, Paul
See Kuttner, Henry

Edmonds, Walter D(umaux)
1903-1998 .... **CLC 35**
See also BYA 2; CA 5-8R; CANR 2; CWRI 5; DLB 9; LAIT 1; MAICYA 1, 2; RHW; SAAS 4; SATA 1, 27; SATA-Obit 99

Edmondson, Wallace
See Ellison, Harlan (Jay)

Edson, Margaret 1961- .... **DC 24**
See also CA 190; DFS 13; DLB 266

Edson, Russell 1935- .... **CLC 13**
See also CA 33-36R; CANR 115; DLB 244; WP

Edwards, Bronwen Elizabeth
See Rose, Wendy

Edwards, G(erald) B(asil)
1899-1976 .... **CLC 25**
See also CA 201; 110

Edwards, Gus 1939- .... **CLC 43**
See also CA 108; INT CA-108

Edwards, Jonathan 1703-1758 .... **LC 7, 54**
See also AMW; DA; DAC; DAM MST; DLB 24, 270; RGAL 4; TUS

Edwards, Sarah Pierpont 1710-1758 .. **LC 87**
See also DLB 200

Efron, Marina Ivanovna Tsvetaeva
See Tsvetaeva (Efron), Marina (Ivanovna)

Egeria fl. 4th cent. - .... **CMLC 70**

Egoyan, Atom 1960- .... **CLC 151**
See also CA 157

Ehle, John (Marsden, Jr.) 1925- ...... **CLC 27**
See also CA 9-12R; CSW

Ehrenbourg, Ilya (Grigoryevich)
See Ehrenburg, Ilya (Grigoryevich)

Ehrenburg, Ilya (Grigoryevich)
1891-1967 .... **CLC 18, 34, 62**
See Erenburg, Il'ia Grigor'evich
See also CA 102; 25-28R; EWL 3

Ehrenburg, Ilyo (Grigoryevich)
See Ehrenburg, Ilya (Grigoryevich)

Ehrenreich, Barbara 1941- .... **CLC 110**
See also BEST 90:4; CA 73-76; CANR 16, 37, 62, 117; DLB 246; FW; MTCW 1, 2

Eich, Gunter
See Eich, Gunter
See also RGWL 2, 3

Eich, Gunter 1907-1972 .... **CLC 15**
See Eich, Gunter
See also CA 111; 93-96; DLB 69, 124; EWL 3

Eichendorff, Joseph 1788-1857 .... **NCLC 8**
See also DLB 90; RGWL 2, 3

Eigner, Larry .... **CLC 9**
See Eigner, Laurence (Joel)
See also CAAS 23; DLB 5; WP

Eigner, Laurence (Joel) 1927-1996
See Eigner, Larry
See also CA 9-12R; 151; CANR 6, 84; CP 7; DLB 193

Eilhart von Oberge c. 1140-c. 1195 .... **CMLC 67**
See also DLB 148

Einhard c. 770-840 .... **CMLC 50**
See also DLB 148

Einstein, Albert 1879-1955 .... **TCLC 65**
See also CA 121; 133; MTCW 1, 2

Eiseley, Loren
See Eiseley, Loren Corey
See also DLB 275

Eiseley, Loren Corey 1907-1977 .... **CLC 7**
See Eiseley, Loren
See also AAYA 5; ANW; CA 1-4R; 73-76; CANR 6; DLBD 17

Eisenstadt, Jill 1963- .... **CLC 50**
See also CA 140

Eisenstein, Sergei (Mikhailovich)
1898-1948 .... **TCLC 57**
See also CA 114; 149

Eisner, Simon
See Kornbluth, C(yril) M.

Ekeloef, (Bengt) Gunnar
1907-1968 .... **CLC 27; PC 23**
See Ekelof, (Bengt) Gunnar
See also CA 123; 25-28R; DAM POET

Ekelof, (Bengt) Gunnar 1907-1968
See Ekeloef, (Bengt) Gunnar
See also DLB 259; EW 12; EWL 3

Ekelund, Vilhelm 1880-1949 .... **TCLC 75**
See also CA 189; EWL 3

Ekwensi, C. O. D.
See Ekwensi, Cyprian (Odiatu Duaka)

Ekwensi, Cyprian (Odiatu Duaka)
1921- .... **BLC 1; CLC 4**
See also AFW; BW 2, 3; CA 29-32R; CANR 18, 42, 74, 125; CDWLB 3; CN 7; CWRI 5; DAM MULT; DLB 117; EWL 3; MTCW 1, 2; RGEL 2; SATA 66; WLIT 2

Elaine .... **TCLC 18**
See Leverson, Ada Esther

El Crummo
See Crumb, R(obert)

Elder, Lonne III 1931-1996 ..... **BLC 1; DC 8**
See also BW 1, 3; CA 81-84; 152; CAD; CANR 25; DAM MULT; DLB 7, 38, 44

Eleanor of Aquitaine 1122-1204 ... **CMLC 39**

Elia
See Lamb, Charles

Eliade, Mircea 1907-1986 .... **CLC 19**
See also CA 65-68; 119; CANR 30, 62; CD-WLB 4; DLB 220; EWL 3; MTCW 1; RGWL 3; SFW 4

Eliot, A. D.
See Jewett, (Theodora) Sarah Orne

Eliot, Alice
See Jewett, (Theodora) Sarah Orne

Eliot, Dan
See Silverberg, Robert

Eliot, George 1819-1880 ...... **NCLC 4, 13, 23, 41, 49, 89, 118; PC 20; SSC 72; WLC**
See Evans, Mary Ann
See also BRW 5; BRWC 1, 2; BRWR 2; CDBLB 1832-1890; CN 7; CPW; DA; DA3; DAB; DAC; DAM MST, NOV; DLB 21, 35, 55; LATS 1:1; LMFS 1; NFS 17; RGEL 2; RGSF 2; SSFS 8; TEA; WLIT 3

Eliot, John 1604-1690 .... **LC 5**
See also DLB 24

Eliot, T(homas) S(tearns)
1888-1965 ...... **CLC 1, 2, 3, 6, 9, 10, 13, 15, 24, 34, 41, 55, 57, 113; PC 5, 31; WLC**
See also AAYA 28; AMW; AMWC 1; AMWR 1; BRW 7; BRWR 2; CA 5-8R; 25-28R; CANR 41; CDALB 1929-1941; DA; DA3; DAB; DAC; DAM DRAM, MST, POET; DFS 4, 13; DLB 7, 10, 45, 63, 245; DLBY 1988; EWL 3; EXPP; LAIT 3; LATS 1:1; LMFS 2; MTCW 1, 2; NCFS 5; PAB; PFS 1, 7, 20; RGAL 4; RGEL 2; TUS; WLIT 4; WP

Elizabeth 1866-1941 .... **TCLC 41**

Elkin, Stanley L(awrence)
1930-1995 .. **CLC 4, 6, 9, 14, 27, 51, 91; SSC 12**
See also AMWS 6; BPFB 1; CA 9-12R; 148; CANR 8, 46; CN 7; CPW; DAM NOV, POP; DLB 2, 28, 218, 278; DLBY 1980; EWL 3; INT CANR-8; MTCW 1, 2; RGAL 4

Elledge, Scott .... **CLC 34**
Elliott, Don
    See Silverberg, Robert
Elliott, George P(aul) 1918-1980 .... **CLC 2**
    See also CA 1-4R; 97-100; CANR 2; DLB
    244
Elliott, Janice 1931-1995 .... **CLC 47**
    See also CA 13-16R; CANR 8, 29, 84; CN
    7; DLB 14; SATA 119
Elliott, Sumner Locke 1917-1991 ..... **CLC 38**
    See also CA 5-8R; 134; CANR 2, 21; DLB
    289
Elliott, William
    See Bradbury, Ray (Douglas)
Ellis, A. E. .... **CLC 7**
Ellis, Alice Thomas .... **CLC 40**
    See Haycraft, Anna (Margaret)
    See also DLB 194; MTCW 1
Ellis, Bret Easton 1964- ...... **CLC 39, 71, 117**
    See also AAYA 2, 43; CA 118; 123; CANR
    51, 74, 126; CN 7; CPW; DA3; DAM
    POP; DLB 292; HGG; INT CA-123;
    MTCW 1; NFS 11
Ellis, (Henry) Havelock
    1859-1939 .... **TCLC 14**
    See also CA 109; 169; DLB 190
Ellis, Landon
    See Ellison, Harlan (Jay)
Ellis, Trey 1962- .... **CLC 55**
    See also CA 146; CANR 92
Ellison, Harlan (Jay) 1934- ... **CLC 1, 13, 42,
    139; SSC 14**
    See also AAYA 29; BPFB 1; BYA 14; CA
    5-8R; CANR 5, 46, 115; CPW; DAM
    POP; DLB 8; HGG; INT CANR-5;
    MTCW 1, 2; SCFW 2; SFW 4; SSFS 13,
    14, 15; SUFW 1, 2
Ellison, Ralph (Waldo) 1914-1994 .... **BLC 1;
    CLC 1, 3, 11, 54, 86, 114; SSC 26;
    WLC**
    See also AAYA 19; AFAW 1, 2; AMWC 2;
    AMWR 2; AMWS 2; BPFB 1; BW 1, 3;
    BYA 2; CA 9-12R; 145; CANR 24, 53;
    CDALB 1941-1968; CSW; DA; DA3;
    DAB; DAC; DAM MST, MULT, NOV;
    DLB 2, 76, 227; DLBY 1994; EWL 3;
    EXPN; EXPS; LAIT 4; MTCW 1, 2;
    NCFS 3; NFS 2; RGAL 4; RGSF 2; SSFS
    1, 11; YAW
Ellmann, Lucy (Elizabeth) 1956- ..... **CLC 61**
    See also CA 128
Ellmann, Richard (David)
    1918-1987 .... **CLC 50**
    See also BEST 89:2; CA 1-4R; 122; CANR
    2, 28, 61; DLB 103; DLBY 1987; MTCW
    1, 2
Elman, Richard (Martin)
    1934-1997 .... **CLC 19**
    See also CA 17-20R; 163; CAAS 3; CANR
    47
Elron
    See Hubbard, L(afayette) Ron(ald)
El Saadawi, Nawal 1931- .... **CLC 196**
    See al'Sadaawi, Nawal; Sa'adawi, al-
    Nawal; Saadawi, Nawal El; Sa'dawi,
    Nawal al-
    See also CA 118; CAAS 11; CANR 44, 92
Eluard, Paul .... **PC 38; TCLC 7, 41**
    See Grindel, Eugene
    See also EWL 3; GFL 1789 to the Present;
    RGWL 2, 3
Elyot, Thomas 1490(?)-1546 .... **LC 11**
    See also DLB 136; RGEL 2
Elytis, Odysseus 1911-1996 .... **CLC 15, 49,
    100; PC 21**
    See Alepoudelis, Odysseus
    See also CA 102; 151; CANR 94; CWW 2;
    DAM POET; EW 13; EWL 3; MTCW 1,
    2; RGWL 2, 3

Emecheta, (Florence Onye) Buchi
    1944- .... **BLC 2; CLC 14, 48, 128**
    See also AFW; BW 2, 3; CA 81-84; CANR
    27, 81, 126; CDWLB 3; CN 7; CWRI 5;
    DA3; DAM MULT; DLB 117; EWL 3;
    FW; MTCW 1, 2; NFS 12, 14; SATA 66;
    WLIT 2
Emerson, Mary Moody
    1774-1863 .... **NCLC 66**
Emerson, Ralph Waldo 1803-1882 . **NCLC 1,
    38, 98; PC 18; WLC**
    See also AMW; ANW; CDALB 1640-1865;
    DA; DA3; DAB; DAC; DAM MST,
    POET; DLB 1, 59, 73, 183, 223, 270;
    EXPP; LAIT 2; LMFS 1; NCFS 3; PFS 4,
    17; RGAL 4; TUS; WP
Eminescu, Mihail 1850-1889 .. **NCLC 33, 131**
Empedocles 5th cent. B.C.- .... **CMLC 50**
    See also DLB 176
Empson, William 1906-1984 ... **CLC 3, 8, 19,
    33, 34**
    See also BRWS 2; CA 17-20R; 112; CANR
    31, 61; DLB 20; EWL 3; MTCW 1, 2;
    RGEL 2
Enchi, Fumiko (Ueda) 1905-1986 ..... **CLC 31**
    See Enchi Fumiko
    See also CA 129; 121; FW; MJW
Enchi Fumiko
    See Enchi, Fumiko (Ueda)
    See also DLB 182; EWL 3
Ende, Michael (Andreas Helmuth)
    1929-1995 .... **CLC 31**
    See also BYA 5; CA 118; 124; 149; CANR
    36, 110; CLR 14; DLB 75; MAICYA 1,
    2; MAICYAS 1; SATA 61, 130; SATA-
    Brief 42; SATA-Obit 86
Endo, Shusaku 1923-1996 ..... **CLC 7, 14, 19,
    54, 99; SSC 48; TCLC 152**
    See Endo Shusaku
    See also CA 29-32R; 153; CANR 21, 54,
    131; DA3; DAM NOV; MTCW 1, 2;
    RGSF 2; RGWL 2, 3
Endo Shusaku
    See Endo, Shusaku
    See also CWW 2; DLB 182; EWL 3
Engel, Marian 1933-1985 .... **CLC 36; TCLC
    137**
    See also CA 25-28R; CANR 12; DLB 53;
    FW; INT CANR-12
Engelhardt, Frederick
    See Hubbard, L(afayette) Ron(ald)
Engels, Friedrich 1820-1895 .. **NCLC 85, 114**
    See also DLB 129; LATS 1:1
Enright, D(ennis) J(oseph)
    1920-2002 .... **CLC 4, 8, 31**
    See also CA 1-4R; 211; CANR 1, 42, 83;
    CP 7; DLB 27; EWL 3; SATA 25; SATA-
    Obit 140
Enzensberger, Hans Magnus
    1929- .... **CLC 43; PC 28**
    See also CA 116; 119; CANR 103; CWW
    2; EWL 3
Ephron, Nora 1941- .... **CLC 17, 31**
    See also AAYA 35; AITN 2; CA 65-68;
    CANR 12, 39, 83
Epicurus 341 B.C.-270 B.C. .... **CMLC 21**
    See also DLB 176
Epsilon
    See Betjeman, John
Epstein, Daniel Mark 1948- .... **CLC 7**
    See also CA 49-52; CANR 2, 53, 90
Epstein, Jacob 1956- .... **CLC 19**
    See also CA 114
Epstein, Jean 1897-1953 .... **TCLC 92**
Epstein, Joseph 1937- .... **CLC 39**
    See also CA 112; 119; CANR 50, 65, 117
Epstein, Leslie 1938- .... **CLC 27**
    See also AMWS 12; CA 73-76, 215; CAAE
    215; CAAS 12; CANR 23, 69; DLB 299

Equiano, Olaudah 1745(?)-1797 . **BLC 2; LC
    16**
    See also AFAW 1, 2; CDWLB 3; DAM
    MULT; DLB 37, 50; WLIT 2
Erasmus, Desiderius 1469(?)-1536 ..... **LC 16,
    93**
    See also DLB 136; EW 2; LMFS 1; RGWL
    2, 3; TWA
Erdman, Paul E(mil) 1932- .... **CLC 25**
    See also AITN 1; CA 61-64; CANR 13, 43,
    84
Erdrich, Louise 1954- .... **CLC 39, 54, 120,
    176; NNAL; PC 52**
    See also AAYA 10, 47; AMWS 4; BEST
    89:1; BPFB 1; CA 114; CANR 41, 62,
    118; CDALBS; CN 7; CP 7; CPW; CWP;
    DA3; DAM MULT, NOV, POP; DLB 152,
    175, 206; EWL 3; EXPP; LAIT 5; LATS
    1:2; MTCW 1; NFS 5; PFS 14; RGAL 4;
    SATA 94, 141; SSFS 14; TCWW 2
Erenburg, Ilya (Grigoryevich)
    See Ehrenburg, Ilya (Grigoryevich)
Erickson, Stephen Michael 1950-
    See Erickson, Steve
    See also CA 129; SFW 4
Erickson, Steve .... **CLC 64**
    See Erickson, Stephen Michael
    See also CANR 60, 68; SUFW 2
Erickson, Walter
    See Fast, Howard (Melvin)
Ericson, Walter
    See Fast, Howard (Melvin)
Eriksson, Buntel
    See Bergman, (Ernst) Ingmar
Eriugena, John Scottus c.
    810-877 .... **CMLC 65**
    See also DLB 115
Ernaux, Annie 1940- .... **CLC 88, 184**
    See also CA 147; CANR 93; NCFS 3, 5
Erskine, John 1879-1951 .... **TCLC 84**
    See also CA 112; 159; DLB 9, 102; FANT
Eschenbach, Wolfram von
    See Wolfram von Eschenbach
    See also RGWL 3
Eseki, Bruno
    See Mphahlele, Ezekiel
Esenin, Sergei (Alexandrovich)
    1895-1925 .... **TCLC 4**
    See Yesenin, Sergey
    See also CA 104; RGWL 2, 3
Eshleman, Clayton 1935- .... **CLC 7**
    See also CA 33-36R, 212; CAAE 212;
    CAAS 6; CANR 93; CP 7; DLB 5
Espriella, Don Manuel Alvarez
    See Southey, Robert
Espriu, Salvador 1913-1985 .... **CLC 9**
    See also CA 154; 115; DLB 134; EWL 3
Espronceda, Jose de 1808-1842 ..... **NCLC 39**
Esquivel, Laura 1951(?)- ... **CLC 141; HLCS
    1**
    See also AAYA 29; CA 143; CANR 68, 113;
    DA3; DNFS 2; LAIT 3; LMFS 2; MTCW
    1; NFS 5; WLIT 1
Esse, James
    See Stephens, James
Esterbrook, Tom
    See Hubbard, L(afayette) Ron(ald)
Estleman, Loren D. 1952- .... **CLC 48**
    See also AAYA 27; CA 85-88; CANR 27,
    74; CMW 4; CPW; DA3; DAM NOV,
    POP; DLB 226; INT CANR-27; MTCW
    1, 2
Etherege, Sir George 1636-1692 . **DC 23; LC
    78**
    See also BRW 2; DAM DRAM; DLB 80;
    PAB; RGEL 2
Euclid 306 B.C.-283 B.C. .... **CMLC 25**
Eugenides, Jeffrey 1960(?)- .... **CLC 81**
    See also AAYA 51; CA 144; CANR 120

Euripides c. 484 B.C.-406 B.C. .... **CMLC 23, 51; DC 4; WLCS**
See also AW 1; CDWLB 1; DA; DA3; DAB; DAC; DAM DRAM, MST; DFS 1, 4, 6; DLB 176; LAIT 1; LMFS 1; RGWL 2, 3

Evan, Evin
See Faust, Frederick (Schiller)

Evans, Caradoc 1878-1945 ... **SSC 43; TCLC 85**
See also DLB 162

Evans, Evan
See Faust, Frederick (Schiller)
See also TCWW 2

Evans, Marian
See Eliot, George

Evans, Mary Ann
See Eliot, George
See also NFS 20

Evarts, Esther
See Benson, Sally

Everett, Percival
See Everett, Percival L.
See also CSW

Everett, Percival L. 1956- .... **CLC 57**
See Everett, Percival
See also BW 2; CA 129; CANR 94

Everson, R(onald) G(ilmour) 1903-1992 .... **CLC 27**
See also CA 17-20R; DLB 88

Everson, William (Oliver) 1912-1994 .... **CLC 1, 5, 14**
See also BG 2; CA 9-12R; 145; CANR 20; DLB 5, 16, 212; MTCW 1

Evtushenko, Evgenii Aleksandrovich
See Yevtushenko, Yevgeny (Alexandrovich)
See also CWW 2; RGWL 2, 3

Ewart, Gavin (Buchanan) 1916-1995 .... **CLC 13, 46**
See also BRWS 7; CA 89-92; 150; CANR 17, 46; CP 7; DLB 40; MTCW 1

Ewers, Hanns Heinz 1871-1943 ..... **TCLC 12**
See also CA 109; 149

Ewing, Frederick R.
See Sturgeon, Theodore (Hamilton)

Exley, Frederick (Earl) 1929-1992 .... **CLC 6, 11**
See also AITN 2; BPFB 1; CA 81-84; 138; CANR 117; DLB 143; DLBY 1981

Eynhardt, Guillermo
See Quiroga, Horacio (Sylvestre)

Ezekiel, Nissim (Moses) 1924-2004 .. **CLC 61**
See also CA 61-64; 223; CP 7; EWL 3

Ezekiel, Tish O'Dowd 1943- .... **CLC 34**
See also CA 129

Fadeev, Aleksandr Aleksandrovich
See Bulgya, Alexander Alexandrovich
See also DLB 272

Fadeev, Alexandr Alexandrovich
See Bulgya, Alexander Alexandrovich
See also EWL 3

Fadeyev, A.
See Bulgya, Alexander Alexandrovich

Fadeyev, Alexander .... **TCLC 53**
See Bulgya, Alexander Alexandrovich

Fagen, Donald 1948- .... **CLC 26**

Fainzilberg, Ilya Arnoldovich 1897-1937
See Ilf, Ilya
See also CA 120; 165

Fair, Ronald L. 1932- .... **CLC 18**
See also BW 1; CA 69-72; CANR 25; DLB 33

Fairbairn, Roger
See Carr, John Dickson

Fairbairns, Zoe (Ann) 1948- .... **CLC 32**
See also CA 103; CANR 21, 85; CN 7

Fairfield, Flora
See Alcott, Louisa May

Fairman, Paul W. 1916-1977
See Queen, Ellery
See also CA 114; SFW 4

Falco, Gian
See Papini, Giovanni

Falconer, James
See Kirkup, James

Falconer, Kenneth
See Kornbluth, C(yril) M.

Falkland, Samuel
See Heijermans, Herman

Fallaci, Oriana 1930- .... **CLC 11, 110**
See also CA 77-80; CANR 15, 58; FW; MTCW 1

Faludi, Susan 1959- .... **CLC 140**
See also CA 138; CANR 126; FW; MTCW 1; NCFS 3

Faludy, George 1913- .... **CLC 42**
See also CA 21-24R

Faludy, Gyoergy
See Faludy, George

Fanon, Frantz 1925-1961 .... **BLC 2; CLC 74**
See also BW 1; CA 116; 89-92; DAM MULT; DLB 296; LMFS 2; WLIT 2

Fanshawe, Ann 1625-1680 .... **LC 11**

Fante, John (Thomas) 1911-1983 .... **CLC 60; SSC 65**
See also AMWS 11; CA 69-72; 109; CANR 23, 104; DLB 130; DLBY 1983

Far, Sui Sin .... **SSC 62**
See Eaton, Edith Maude
See also SSFS 4

Farah, Nuruddin 1945- ...... **BLC 2; CLC 53, 137**
See also AFW; BW 2, 3; CA 106; CANR 81; CDWLB 3; CN 7; DAM MULT; DLB 125; EWL 3; WLIT 2

Fargue, Leon-Paul 1876(?)-1947 .... **TCLC 11**
See also CA 109; CANR 107; DLB 258; EWL 3

Farigoule, Louis
See Romains, Jules

Farina, Richard 1936(?)-1966 .... **CLC 9**
See also CA 81-84; 25-28R

Farley, Walter (Lorimer) 1915-1989 .... **CLC 17**
See also AAYA 58; BYA 14; CA 17-20R; CANR 8, 29, 84; DLB 22; JRDA; MAICYA 1, 2; SATA 2, 43, 132; YAW

Farmer, Philip Jose 1918- .... **CLC 1, 19**
See also AAYA 28; BPFB 1; CA 1-4R; CANR 4, 35, 111; DLB 8; MTCW 1; SATA 93; SCFW 2; SFW 4

Farquhar, George 1677-1707 .... **LC 21**
See also BRW 2; DAM DRAM; DLB 84; RGEL 2

Farrell, J(ames) G(ordon) 1935-1979 .... **CLC 6**
See also CA 73-76; 89-92; CANR 36; DLB 14, 271; MTCW 1; RGEL 2; RHW; WLIT 4

Farrell, James T(homas) 1904-1979 . **CLC 1, 4, 8, 11, 66; SSC 28**
See also AMW; BPFB 1; CA 5-8R; 89-92; CANR 9, 61; DLB 4, 9, 86; DLBD 2; EWL 3; MTCW 1, 2; RGAL 4

Farrell, Warren (Thomas) 1943- ...... **CLC 70**
See also CA 146; CANR 120

Farren, Richard J.
See Betjeman, John

Farren, Richard M.
See Betjeman, John

Fassbinder, Rainer Werner 1946-1982 .... **CLC 20**
See also CA 93-96; 106; CANR 31

Fast, Howard (Melvin) 1914-2003 .. **CLC 23, 131**
See also AAYA 16; BPFB 1; CA 1-4R, 181; 214; CAAE 181; CAAS 18; CANR 1, 33, 54, 75, 98; CMW 4; CN 7; CPW; DAM NOV; DLB 9; INT CANR-33; LATS 1:1; MTCW 1; RHW; SATA 7; SATA-Essay 107; TCWW 2; YAW

Faulcon, Robert
See Holdstock, Robert P.

Faulkner, William (Cuthbert) 1897-1962 .... **CLC 1, 3, 6, 8, 9, 11, 14, 18, 28, 52, 68; SSC 1, 35, 42; TCLC 141; WLC**
See also AAYA 7; AMW; AMWR 1; BPFB 1; BYA 5, 15; CA 81-84; CANR 33; CDALB 1929-1941; DA; DA3; DAB; DAC; DAM MST, NOV; DLB 9, 11, 44, 102; DLBD 2; DLBY 1986, 1997; EWL 3; EXPN; EXPS; LAIT 2; LATS 1:1; LMFS 2; MTCW 1, 2; NFS 4, 8, 13; RGAL 4; RGSF 2; SSFS 2, 5, 6, 12; TUS

Fauset, Jessie Redmon 1882(?)-1961 .. **BLC 2; CLC 19, 54; HR 2**
See also AFAW 2; BW 1; CA 109; CANR 83; DAM MULT; DLB 51; FW; LMFS 2; MAWW

Faust, Frederick (Schiller) 1892-1944(?) .... **TCLC 49**
See Austin, Frank; Brand, Max; Challis, George; Dawson, Peter; Dexter, Martin; Evans, Evan; Frederick, John; Frost, Frederick; Manning, David; Silver, Nicholas
See also CA 108; 152; DAM POP; DLB 256; TUS

Faust, Irvin 1924- .... **CLC 8**
See also CA 33-36R; CANR 28, 67; CN 7; DLB 2, 28, 218, 278; DLBY 1980

Faustino, Domingo 1811-1888 ...... **NCLC 123**

Fawkes, Guy
See Benchley, Robert (Charles)

Fearing, Kenneth (Flexner) 1902-1961 .... **CLC 51**
See also CA 93-96; CANR 59; CMW 4; DLB 9; RGAL 4

Fecamps, Elise
See Creasey, John

Federman, Raymond 1928- .... **CLC 6, 47**
See also CA 17-20R, 208; CAAE 208; CAAS 8; CANR 10, 43, 83, 108; CN 7; DLBY 1980

Federspiel, J(uerg) F. 1931- .... **CLC 42**
See also CA 146

Feiffer, Jules (Ralph) 1929- ...... **CLC 2, 8, 64**
See also AAYA 3; CA 17-20R; CAD; CANR 30, 59, 129; CD 5; DAM DRAM; DLB 7, 44; INT CANR-30; MTCW 1; SATA 8, 61, 111

Feige, Hermann Albert Otto Maximilian
See Traven, B.

Feinberg, David B. 1956-1994 .... **CLC 59**
See also CA 135; 147

Feinstein, Elaine 1930- .... **CLC 36**
See also CA 69-72; CAAS 1; CANR 31, 68, 121; CN 7; CP 7; CWP; DLB 14, 40; MTCW 1

Feke, Gilbert David .... **CLC 65**

Feldman, Irving (Mordecai) 1928- ..... **CLC 7**
See also CA 1-4R; CANR 1; CP 7; DLB 169

Felix-Tchicaya, Gerald
See Tchicaya, Gerald Felix

Fellini, Federico 1920-1993 .... **CLC 16, 85**
See also CA 65-68; 143; CANR 33

Felltham, Owen 1602(?)-1668 .... **LC 92**
See also DLB 126, 151

Felsen, Henry Gregor 1916-1995 ..... **CLC 17**
See also CA 1-4R; 180; CANR 1; SAAS 2;
SATA 1

Felski, Rita .... **CLC 65**

Fenno, Jack
See Calisher, Hortense

Fenollosa, Ernest (Francisco)
1853-1908 .... **TCLC 91**

Fenton, James Martin 1949- .... **CLC 32**
See also CA 102; CANR 108; CP 7; DLB
40; PFS 11

Ferber, Edna 1887-1968 .... **CLC 18, 93**
See also AITN 1; CA 5-8R; 25-28R; CANR
68, 105; DLB 9, 28, 86, 266; MTCW 1,
2; RGAL 4; RHW; SATA 7; TCWW 2

Ferdowsi, Abu'l Qasem 940-1020 . **CMLC 43**
See also RGWL 2, 3

Ferguson, Helen
See Kavan, Anna

Ferguson, Niall 1964- .... **CLC 134**
See also CA 190

Ferguson, Samuel 1810-1886 .... **NCLC 33**
See also DLB 32; RGEL 2

Fergusson, Robert 1750-1774 .... **LC 29**
See also DLB 109; RGEL 2

Ferling, Lawrence
See Ferlinghetti, Lawrence (Monsanto)

Ferlinghetti, Lawrence (Monsanto)
1919(?)- ..... **CLC 2, 6, 10, 27, 111; PC 1**
See also CA 5-8R; CANR 3, 41, 73, 125;
CDALB 1941-1968; CP 7; DA3; DAM
POET; DLB 5, 16; MTCW 1, 2; RGAL 4;
WP

Fern, Fanny
See Parton, Sara Payson Willis

Fernandez, Vicente Garcia Huidobro
See Huidobro Fernandez, Vicente Garcia

Fernandez-Armesto, Felipe .... **CLC 70**

Fernandez de Lizardi, Jose Joaquin
See Lizardi, Jose Joaquin Fernandez de

Ferre, Rosario 1938- ...... **CLC 139; HLCS 1;
SSC 36**
See also CA 131; CANR 55, 81; CWW 2;
DLB 145; EWL 3; HW 1, 2; LAWS 1;
MTCW 1; WLIT 1

Ferrer, Gabriel (Francisco Victor) Miro
See Miro (Ferrer), Gabriel (Francisco
Victor)

Ferrier, Susan (Edmonstone)
1782-1854 .... **NCLC 8**
See also DLB 116; RGEL 2

Ferrigno, Robert 1948(?)- .... **CLC 65**
See also CA 140; CANR 125

Ferron, Jacques 1921-1985 .... **CLC 94**
See also CA 117; 129; CCA 1; DAC; DLB
60; EWL 3

Feuchtwanger, Lion 1884-1958 .... **TCLC 3**
See also CA 104; 187; DLB 66; EWL 3

Feuerbach, Ludwig 1804-1872 ..... **NCLC 139**
See also DLB 133

Feuillet, Octave 1821-1890 .... **NCLC 45**
See also DLB 192

Feydeau, Georges (Leon Jules Marie)
1862-1921 .... **TCLC 22**
See also CA 113; 152; CANR 84; DAM
DRAM; DLB 192; EWL 3; GFL 1789 to
the Present; RGWL 2, 3

Fichte, Johann Gottlieb
1762-1814 .... **NCLC 62**
See also DLB 90

Ficino, Marsilio 1433-1499 .... **LC 12**
See also LMFS 1

Fiedeler, Hans
See Doeblin, Alfred

Fiedler, Leslie A(aron) 1917-2003 ..... **CLC 4,
13, 24**
See also AMWS 13; CA 9-12R; 212; CANR
7, 63; CN 7; DLB 28, 67; EWL 3; MTCW
1, 2; RGAL 4; TUS

Field, Andrew 1938- .... **CLC 44**
See also CA 97-100; CANR 25

Field, Eugene 1850-1895 .... **NCLC 3**
See also DLB 23, 42, 140; DLBD 13; MAI-
CYA 1, 2; RGAL 4; SATA 16

Field, Gans T.
See Wellman, Manly Wade

Field, Michael 1915-1971 .... **TCLC 43**
See also CA 29-32R

Field, Peter
See Hobson, Laura Z(ametkin)
See also TCWW 2

Fielding, Helen 1958- .... **CLC 146**
See also CA 172; CANR 127; DLB 231

Fielding, Henry 1707-1754 .... **LC 1, 46, 85;
WLC**
See also BRW 3; BRWR 1; CDBLB 1660-
1789; DA; DA3; DAB; DAC; DAM
DRAM, MST, NOV; DLB 39, 84, 101;
NFS 18; RGEL 2; TEA; WLIT 3

Fielding, Sarah 1710-1768 .... **LC 1, 44**
See also DLB 39; RGEL 2; TEA

Fields, W. C. 1880-1946 .... **TCLC 80**
See also DLB 44

Fierstein, Harvey (Forbes) 1954- ..... **CLC 33**
See also CA 123; 129; CAD; CD 5; CPW;
DA3; DAM DRAM, POP; DFS 6; DLB
266; GLL

Figes, Eva 1932- .... **CLC 31**
See also CA 53-56; CANR 4, 44, 83; CN 7;
DLB 14, 271; FW

Filippo, Eduardo de
See de Filippo, Eduardo

Finch, Anne 1661-1720 .... **LC 3; PC 21**
See also BRWS 9; DLB 95

Finch, Robert (Duer Claydon)
1900-1995 .... **CLC 18**
See also CA 57-60; CANR 9, 24, 49; CP 7;
DLB 88

Findley, Timothy (Irving Frederick)
1930-2002 .... **CLC 27, 102**
See also CA 25-28R; 206; CANR 12, 42,
69, 109; CCA 1; CN 7; DAC; DAM MST;
DLB 53; FANT; RHW

Fink, William
See Mencken, H(enry) L(ouis)

Firbank, Louis 1942-
See Reed, Lou
See also CA 117

Firbank, (Arthur Annesley) Ronald
1886-1926 .... **TCLC 1**
See also BRWS 2; CA 104; 177; DLB 36;
EWL 3; RGEL 2

Fish, Stanley
See Fish, Stanley Eugene

Fish, Stanley E.
See Fish, Stanley Eugene

Fish, Stanley Eugene 1938- .... **CLC 142**
See also CA 112; 132; CANR 90; DLB 67

Fisher, Dorothy (Frances) Canfield
1879-1958 .... **TCLC 87**
See also CA 114; 136; CANR 80; CLR 71,;
CWRI 5; DLB 9, 102, 284; MAICYA 1,
2; YABC 1

Fisher, M(ary) F(rances) K(ennedy)
1908-1992 .... **CLC 76, 87**
See also CA 77-80; 138; CANR 44; MTCW
1

Fisher, Roy 1930- .... **CLC 25**
See also CA 81-84; CAAS 10; CANR 16;
CP 7; DLB 40

Fisher, Rudolph 1897-1934 .... **BLC 2; HR 2;
SSC 25; TCLC 11**
See also BW 1, 3; CA 107; 124; CANR 80;
DAM MULT; DLB 51, 102

Fisher, Vardis (Alvero) 1895-1968 .... **CLC 7;
TCLC 140**
See also CA 5-8R; 25-28R; CANR 68; DLB
9, 206; RGAL 4; TCWW 2

Fiske, Tarleton
See Bloch, Robert (Albert)

Fitch, Clarke
See Sinclair, Upton (Beall)

Fitch, John IV
See Cormier, Robert (Edmund)

Fitzgerald, Captain Hugh
See Baum, L(yman) Frank

FitzGerald, Edward 1809-1883 .... **NCLC 9**
See also BRW 4; DLB 32; RGEL 2

Fitzgerald, F(rancis) Scott (Key)
1896-1940 ... **SSC 6, 31, 75; TCLC 1, 6,
14, 28, 55, 157; WLC**
See also AAYA 24; AITN 1; AMW; AMWC
2; AMWR 1; BPFB 1; CA 110; 123;
CDALB 1917-1929; DA; DA3; DAB;
DAC; DAM MST, NOV; DLB 4, 9, 86,
219, 273; DLBD 1, 15, 16; DLBY 1981,
1996; EWL 3; EXPN; EXPS; LAIT 3;
MTCW 1, 2; NFS 2, 19, 20; RGAL 4;
RGSF 2; SSFS 4, 15; TUS

Fitzgerald, Penelope 1916-2000 . **CLC 19, 51,
61, 143**
See also BRWS 5; CA 85-88; 190; CAAS
10; CANR 56, 86, 131; CN 7; DLB 14,
194; EWL 3; MTCW 2

Fitzgerald, Robert (Stuart)
1910-1985 .... **CLC 39**
See also CA 1-4R; 114; CANR 1; DLBY
1980

FitzGerald, Robert D(avid)
1902-1987 .... **CLC 19**
See also CA 17-20R; DLB 260; RGEL 2

Fitzgerald, Zelda (Sayre)
1900-1948 .... **TCLC 52**
See also AMWS 9; CA 117; 126; DLBY
1984

Flanagan, Thomas (James Bonner)
1923-2002 .... **CLC 25, 52**
See also CA 108; 206; CANR 55; CN 7;
DLBY 1980; INT CA-108; MTCW 1;
RHW

Flaubert, Gustave 1821-1880 .... **NCLC 2, 10,
19, 62, 66, 135; SSC 11, 60; WLC**
See also DA; DA3; DAB; DAC; DAM
MST, NOV; DLB 119, 301; EW 7; EXPS;
GFL 1789 to the Present; LAIT 2; LMFS
1; NFS 14; RGSF 2; RGWL 2, 3; SSFS
6; TWA

Flavius Josephus
See Josephus, Flavius

Flecker, Herman Elroy
See Flecker, (Herman) James Elroy

Flecker, (Herman) James Elroy
1884-1915 .... **TCLC 43**
See also CA 109; 150; DLB 10, 19; RGEL
2

Fleming, Ian (Lancaster) 1908-1964 . **CLC 3,
30**
See also AAYA 26; BPFB 1; CA 5-8R;
CANR 59; CDBLB 1945-1960; CMW 4;
CPW; DA3; DAM POP; DLB 87, 201;
MSW; MTCW 1, 2; RGEL 2; SATA 9;
TEA; YAW

Fleming, Thomas (James) 1927- ...... **CLC 37**
See also CA 5-8R; CANR 10, 102; INT
CANR-10; SATA 8

Fletcher, John 1579-1625 .... **DC 6; LC 33**
See also BRW 2; CDBLB Before 1660;
DLB 58; RGEL 2; TEA

Fraser, Antonia (Pakenham) 1932- . **CLC 32, 107**
See also AAYA 57; CA 85-88; CANR 44, 65, 119; CMW; DLB 276; MTCW 1, 2; SATA-Brief 32

Fraser, George MacDonald 1925- ...... **CLC 7**
See also AAYA 48; CA 45-48, 180; CAAE 180; CANR 2, 48, 74; MTCW 1; RHW

Fraser, Sylvia 1935- .... **CLC 64**
See also CA 45-48; CANR 1, 16, 60; CCA 1

Frayn, Michael 1933- . **CLC 3, 7, 31, 47, 176**
See also BRWC 2; BRWS 7; CA 5-8R; CANR 30, 69, 114, 133; CBD; CD 5; CN 7; DAM DRAM, NOV; DLB 13, 14, 194, 245; FANT; MTCW 1, 2; SFW 4

Fraze, Candida (Merrill) 1945- .... **CLC 50**
See also CA 126

Frazer, Andrew
See Marlowe, Stephen

Frazer, J(ames) G(eorge) 1854-1941 .... **TCLC 32**
See also BRWS 3; CA 118; NCFS 5

Frazer, Robert Caine
See Creasey, John

Frazer, Sir James George
See Frazer, J(ames) G(eorge)

Frazier, Charles 1950- .... **CLC 109**
See also AAYA 34; CA 161; CANR 126; CSW; DLB 292

Frazier, Ian 1951- .... **CLC 46**
See also CA 130; CANR 54, 93

Frederic, Harold 1856-1898 .... **NCLC 10**
See also AMW; DLB 12, 23; DLBD 13; RGAL 4

Frederick, John
See Faust, Frederick (Schiller)
See also TCWW 2

Frederick the Great 1712-1786 .... **LC 14**

Fredro, Aleksander 1793-1876 .... **NCLC 8**

Freeling, Nicolas 1927-2003 .... **CLC 38**
See also CA 49-52; 218; CAAS 12; CANR 1, 17, 50, 84; CMW 4; CN 7; DLB 87

Freeman, Douglas Southall 1886-1953 .... **TCLC 11**
See also CA 109; 195; DLB 17; DLBD 17

Freeman, Judith 1946- .... **CLC 55**
See also CA 148; CANR 120; DLB 256

Freeman, Mary E(leanor) Wilkins 1852-1930 .... **SSC 1, 47; TCLC 9**
See also CA 106; 177; DLB 12, 78, 221; EXPS; FW; HGG; MAWW; RGAL 4; RGSF 2; SSFS 4, 8; SUFW 1; TUS

Freeman, R(ichard) Austin 1862-1943 .... **TCLC 21**
See also CA 113; CANR 84; CMW 4; DLB 70

French, Albert 1943- .... **CLC 86**
See also BW 3; CA 167

French, Antonia
See Kureishi, Hanif

French, Marilyn 1929- .. **CLC 10, 18, 60, 177**
See also BPFB 1; CA 69-72; CANR 3, 31; CN 7; CPW; DAM DRAM, NOV, POP; FW; INT CANR-31; MTCW 1, 2

French, Paul
See Asimov, Isaac

Freneau, Philip Morin 1752-1832 .. **NCLC 1, 111**
See also AMWS 2; DLB 37, 43; RGAL 4

Freud, Sigmund 1856-1939 .... **TCLC 52**
See also CA 115; 133; CANR 69; DLB 296; EW 8; EWL 3; LATS 1:1; MTCW 1, 2; NCFS 3; TWA

Freytag, Gustav 1816-1895 .... **NCLC 109**
See also DLB 129

Friedan, Betty (Naomi) 1921- .... **CLC 74**
See also CA 65-68; CANR 18, 45, 74; DLB 246; FW; MTCW 1, 2; NCFS 5

Friedlander, Saul 1932- .... **CLC 90**
See also CA 117; 130; CANR 72

Friedman, B(ernard) H(arper) 1926- .... **CLC 7**
See also CA 1-4R; CANR 3, 48

Friedman, Bruce Jay 1930- ...... **CLC 3, 5, 56**
See also CA 9-12R; CAD; CANR 25, 52, 101; CD 5; CN 7; DLB 2, 28, 244; INT CANR-25; SSFS 18

Friel, Brian 1929- .... **CLC 5, 42, 59, 115; DC 8; SSC 76**
See also BRWS 5; CA 21-24R; CANR 33, 69, 131; CBD; CD 5; DFS 11; DLB 13; EWL 3; MTCW 1; RGEL 2; TEA

Friis-Baastad, Babbis Ellinor 1921-1970 .... **CLC 12**
See also CA 17-20R; 134; SATA 7

Frisch, Max (Rudolf) 1911-1991 ... **CLC 3, 9, 14, 18, 32, 44; TCLC 121**
See also CA 85-88; 134; CANR 32, 74; CD-WLB 2; DAM DRAM, NOV; DLB 69, 124; EW 13; EWL 3; MTCW 1, 2; RGWL 2, 3

Fromentin, Eugene (Samuel Auguste) 1820-1876 .... **NCLC 10, 125**
See also DLB 123; GFL 1789 to the Present

Frost, Frederick
See Faust, Frederick (Schiller)
See also TCWW 2

Frost, Robert (Lee) 1874-1963 .. **CLC 1, 3, 4, 9, 10, 13, 15, 26, 34, 44; PC 1, 39; WLC**
See also AAYA 21; AMW; AMWR 1; CA 89-92; CANR 33; CDALB 1917-1929; CLR 67; DA; DA3; DAB; DAC; DAM MST, POET; DLB 54, 284; DLBD 7; EWL 3; EXPP; MTCW 1, 2; PAB; PFS 1, 2, 3, 4, 5, 6, 7, 10, 13; RGAL 4; SATA 14; TUS; WP; WYA

Froude, James Anthony 1818-1894 .... **NCLC 43**
See also DLB 18, 57, 144

Froy, Herald
See Waterhouse, Keith (Spencer)

Fry, Christopher 1907- .... **CLC 2, 10, 14**
See also BRWS 3; CA 17-20R; CAAS 23; CANR 9, 30, 74, 132; CBD; CD 5; CP 7; DAM DRAM; DLB 13; EWL 3; MTCW 1, 2; RGEL 2; SATA 66; TEA

Frye, (Herman) Northrop 1912-1991 .... **CLC 24, 70**
See also CA 5-8R; 133; CANR 8, 37; DLB 67, 68, 246; EWL 3; MTCW 1, 2; RGAL 4; TWA

Fuchs, Daniel 1909-1993 .... **CLC 8, 22**
See also CA 81-84; 142; CAAS 5; CANR 40; DLB 9, 26, 28; DLBY 1993

Fuchs, Daniel 1934- .... **CLC 34**
See also CA 37-40R; CANR 14, 48

Fuentes, Carlos 1928- .. **CLC 3, 8, 10, 13, 22, 41, 60, 113; HLC 1; SSC 24; WLC**
See also AAYA 4, 45; AITN 2; BPFB 1; CA 69-72; CANR 10, 32, 68, 104; CD-WLB 3; CWW 2; DA; DA3; DAB; DAC; DAM MST, MULT, NOV; DLB 113; DNFS 2; EWL 3; HW 1, 2; LAIT 3; LATS 1:2; LAW; LAWS 1; LMFS 2; MTCW 1, 2; NFS 8; RGSF 2; RGWL 2, 3; TWA; WLIT 1

Fuentes, Gregorio Lopez y
See Lopez y Fuentes, Gregorio

Fuertes, Gloria 1918-1998 .... **PC 27**
See also CA 178, 180; DLB 108; HW 2; SATA 115

Fugard, (Harold) Athol 1932- . **CLC 5, 9, 14, 25, 40, 80; DC 3**
See also AAYA 17; AFW; CA 85-88; CANR 32, 54, 118; CD 5; DAM DRAM; DFS 3, 6, 10; DLB 225; DNFS 1, 2; EWL 3; LATS 1:2; MTCW 1; RGEL 2; WLIT 2

Fugard, Sheila 1932- .... **CLC 48**
See also CA 125

Fukuyama, Francis 1952- .... **CLC 131**
See also CA 140; CANR 72, 125

Fuller, Charles (H.), (Jr.) 1939- .... **BLC 2; CLC 25; DC 1**
See also BW 2; CA 108; 112; CAD; CANR 87; CD 5; DAM DRAM, MULT; DFS 8; DLB 38, 266; EWL 3; INT CA-112; MTCW 1

Fuller, Henry Blake 1857-1929 .... **TCLC 103**
See also CA 108; 177; DLB 12; RGAL 4

Fuller, John (Leopold) 1937- .... **CLC 62**
See also CA 21-24R; CANR 9, 44; CP 7; DLB 40

Fuller, Margaret
See Ossoli, Sarah Margaret (Fuller)
See also AMWS 2; DLB 183, 223, 239

Fuller, Roy (Broadbent) 1912-1991 ... **CLC 4, 28**
See also BRWS 7; CA 5-8R; 135; CAAS 10; CANR 53, 83; CWRI 5; DLB 15, 20; EWL 3; RGEL 2; SATA 87

Fuller, Sarah Margaret
See Ossoli, Sarah Margaret (Fuller)

Fuller, Sarah Margaret
See Ossoli, Sarah Margaret (Fuller)
See also DLB 1, 59, 73

Fulton, Alice 1952- .... **CLC 52**
See also CA 116; CANR 57, 88; CP 7; CWP; DLB 193

Furphy, Joseph 1843-1912 .... **TCLC 25**
See Collins, Tom
See also CA 163; DLB 230; EWL 3; RGEL 2

Fuson, Robert H(enderson) 1927- .... **CLC 70**
See also CA 89-92; CANR 103

Fussell, Paul 1924- .... **CLC 74**
See also BEST 90:1; CA 17-20R; CANR 8, 21, 35, 69; INT CANR-21; MTCW 1, 2

Futabatei, Shimei 1864-1909 .... **TCLC 44**
See Futabatei Shimei
See also CA 162; MJW

Futabatei Shimei
See Futabatei, Shimei
See also DLB 180; EWL 3

Futrelle, Jacques 1875-1912 .... **TCLC 19**
See also CA 113; 155; CMW 4

Gaboriau, Emile 1835-1873 .... **NCLC 14**
See also CMW 4; MSW

Gadda, Carlo Emilio 1893-1973 ...... **CLC 11; TCLC 144**
See also CA 89-92; DLB 177; EWL 3

Gaddis, William 1922-1998 ... **CLC 1, 3, 6, 8, 10, 19, 43, 86**
See also AMWS 4; BPFB 1; CA 17-20R; 172; CANR 21, 48; CN 7; DLB 2, 278; EWL 3; MTCW 1, 2; RGAL 4

Gaelique, Moruen le
See Jacob, (Cyprien-)Max

Gage, Walter
See Inge, William (Motter)

Gaiman, Neil (Richard) 1960- .... **CLC 195**
See also AAYA 19, 42; CA 133; CANR 81, 129; DLB 261; HGG; SATA 85, 146; SFW 4; SUFW 2

Gaines, Ernest J(ames) 1933- .. **BLC 2; CLC 3, 11, 18, 86, 181; SSC 68**
See also AAYA 18; AFAW 1, 2; AITN 1; BPFB 2; BW 2, 3; BYA 6; CA 9-12R; CANR 6, 24, 42, 75, 126; CDALB 1968-1988; CLR 62; CN 7; CSW; DA3; DAM MULT; DLB 2, 33, 152; DLBY 1980; EWL 3; EXPN; LAIT 5; LATS 1:2; MTCW 1, 2; NFS 5, 7, 16; RGAL 4; RGSF 2; RHW; SATA 86; SSFS 5; YAW

Gaitskill, Mary (Lawrence) 1954- .... **CLC 69**
See also CA 128; CANR 61; DLB 244

Gee, Maurice (Gough) 1931- .... **CLC 29**
See also AAYA 42; CA 97-100; CANR 67, 123; CLR 56; CN 7; CWRI 5; EWL 3; MAICYA 2; RGSF 2; SATA 46, 101

Geiogamah, Hanay 1945- .... **NNAL**
See also CA 153; DAM MULT; DLB 175

Gelbart, Larry (Simon) 1928- .... **CLC 21, 61**
See Gelbart, Larry
See also CA 73-76; CANR 45, 94

Gelbart, Larry 1928-
See Gelbart, Larry (Simon)
See also CAD; CD 5

Gelber, Jack 1932-2003 ...... **CLC 1, 6, 14, 79**
See also CA 1-4R; 216; CAD; CANR 2; DLB 7, 228

Gellhorn, Martha (Ellis)
1908-1998 .... **CLC 14, 60**
See also CA 77-80; 164; CANR 44; CN 7; DLBY 1982, 1998

Genet, Jean 1910-1986 .. **CLC 1, 2, 5, 10, 14, 44, 46; TCLC 128**
See also CA 13-16R; CANR 18; DA3; DAM DRAM; DFS 10; DLB 72; DLBY 1986; EW 13; EWL 3; GFL 1789 to the Present; GLL 1; LMFS 2; MTCW 1, 2; RGWL 2, 3; TWA

Gent, Peter 1942- .... **CLC 29**
See also AITN 1; CA 89-92; DLBY 1982

Gentile, Giovanni 1875-1944 .... **TCLC 96**
See also CA 119

Gentlewoman in New England, A
See Bradstreet, Anne

Gentlewoman in Those Parts, A
See Bradstreet, Anne

Geoffrey of Monmouth c.
1100-1155 .... **CMLC 44**
See also DLB 146; TEA

George, Jean
See George, Jean Craighead

George, Jean Craighead 1919- .... **CLC 35**
See also AAYA 8; BYA 2, 4; CA 5-8R; CANR 25; CLR 1; 80; DLB 52; JRDA; MAICYA 1, 2; SATA 2, 68, 124; WYA; YAW

George, Stefan (Anton) 1868-1933 . **TCLC 2, 14**
See also CA 104; 193; EW 8; EWL 3

Georges, Georges Martin
See Simenon, Georges (Jacques Christian)

Gerald of Wales c. 1146-c. 1223 ... **CMLC 60**

Gerhardi, William Alexander
See Gerhardie, William Alexander

Gerhardie, William Alexander
1895-1977 .... **CLC 5**
See also CA 25-28R; 73-76; CANR 18; DLB 36; RGEL 2

Gerson, Jean 1363-1429 .... **LC 77**
See also DLB 208

Gersonides 1288-1344 .... **CMLC 49**
See also DLB 115

Gerstler, Amy 1956- .... **CLC 70**
See also CA 146; CANR 99

Gertler, T. .... **CLC 34**
See also CA 116; 121

Gertsen, Aleksandr Ivanovich
See Herzen, Aleksandr Ivanovich

Ghalib .... **NCLC 39, 78**
See Ghalib, Asadullah Khan

Ghalib, Asadullah Khan 1797-1869
See Ghalib
See also DAM POET; RGWL 2, 3

Ghelderode, Michel de 1898-1962 ..... **CLC 6, 11; DC 15**
See also CA 85-88; CANR 40, 77; DAM DRAM; EW 11; EWL 3; TWA

Ghiselin, Brewster 1903-2001 .... **CLC 23**
See also CA 13-16R; CAAS 10; CANR 13; CP 7

Ghose, Aurabinda 1872-1950 .... **TCLC 63**
See Ghose, Aurobindo
See also CA 163

Ghose, Aurobindo
See Ghose, Aurabinda
See also EWL 3

Ghose, Zulfikar 1935- .... **CLC 42**
See also CA 65-68; CANR 67; CN 7; CP 7; EWL 3

Ghosh, Amitav 1956- .... **CLC 44, 153**
See also CA 147; CANR 80; CN 7; WWE 1

Giacosa, Giuseppe 1847-1906 .... **TCLC 7**
See also CA 104

Gibb, Lee
See Waterhouse, Keith (Spencer)

Gibbon, Edward 1737-1794 .... **LC 97**
See also BRW 3; DLB 104; RGEL 2

Gibbon, Lewis Grassic .... **TCLC 4**
See Mitchell, James Leslie
See also RGEL 2

Gibbons, Kaye 1960- .... **CLC 50, 88, 145**
See also AAYA 34; AMWS 10; CA 151; CANR 75, 127; CSW; DA3; DAM POP; DLB 292; MTCW 1; NFS 3; RGAL 4; SATA 117

Gibran, Kahlil 1883-1931 . **PC 9; TCLC 1, 9**
See also CA 104; 150; DA3; DAM POET, POP; EWL 3; MTCW 2

Gibran, Khalil
See Gibran, Kahlil

Gibson, William 1914- .... **CLC 23**
See also CA 9-12R; CAD 2; CANR 9, 42, 75, 125; CD 5; DA; DAB; DAC; DAM DRAM, MST; DFS 2; DLB 7; LAIT 2; MTCW 2; SATA 66; YAW

Gibson, William (Ford) 1948- ... **CLC 39, 63, 186, 192; SSC 52**
See also AAYA 12, 59; BPFB 2; CA 126; 133; CANR 52, 90, 106; CN 7; CPW; DA3; DAM POP; DLB 251; MTCW 2; SCFW 2; SFW 4

Gide, Andre (Paul Guillaume)
1869-1951 ..... **SSC 13; TCLC 5, 12, 36; WLC**
See also CA 104; 124; DA; DA3; DAB; DAC; DAM MST, NOV; DLB 65; EW 8; EWL 3; GFL 1789 to the Present; MTCW 1, 2; RGSF 2; RGWL 2, 3; TWA

Gifford, Barry (Colby) 1946- .... **CLC 34**
See also CA 65-68; CANR 9, 30, 40, 90

Gilbert, Frank
See De Voto, Bernard (Augustine)

Gilbert, W(illiam) S(chwenck)
1836-1911 .... **TCLC 3**
See also CA 104; 173; DAM DRAM, POET; RGEL 2; SATA 36

Gilbreth, Frank B(unker), Jr.
1911-2001 .... **CLC 17**
See also CA 9-12R; SATA 2

Gilchrist, Ellen (Louise) 1935- .. **CLC 34, 48, 143; SSC 14, 63**
See also BPFB 2; CA 113; 116; CANR 41, 61, 104; CN 7; CPW; CSW; DAM POP; DLB 130; EWL 3; EXPS; MTCW 1, 2; RGAL 4; RGSF 2; SSFS 9

Giles, Molly 1942- .... **CLC 39**
See also CA 126; CANR 98

Gill, Eric 1882-1940 .... **TCLC 85**
See Gill, (Arthur) Eric (Rowton Peter Joseph)

Gill, (Arthur) Eric (Rowton Peter Joseph)
1882-1940
See Gill, Eric
See also CA 120; DLB 98

Gill, Patrick
See Creasey, John

Gillette, Douglas .... **CLC 70**

Gilliam, Terry (Vance) 1940- .... **CLC 21, 141**
See Monty Python
See also AAYA 19, 59; CA 108; 113; CANR 35; INT CA-113

Gillian, Jerry
See Gilliam, Terry (Vance)

Gilliatt, Penelope (Ann Douglass)
1932-1993 .... **CLC 2, 10, 13, 53**
See also AITN 2; CA 13-16R; 141; CANR 49; DLB 14

Gilman, Charlotte (Anna) Perkins (Stetson)
1860-1935 ...... **SSC 13, 62; TCLC 9, 37, 117**
See also AMWS 11; BYA 11; CA 106; 150; DLB 221; EXPS; FW; HGG; LAIT 2; MAWW; MTCW 1; RGAL 4; RGSF 2; SFW 4; SSFS 1, 18

Gilmour, David 1946- .... **CLC 35**

Gilpin, William 1724-1804 .... **NCLC 30**

Gilray, J. D.
See Mencken, H(enry) L(ouis)

Gilroy, Frank D(aniel) 1925- .... **CLC 2**
See also CA 81-84; CAD; CANR 32, 64, 86; CD 5; DFS 17; DLB 7

Gilstrap, John 1957(?)- .... **CLC 99**
See also CA 160; CANR 101

Ginsberg, Allen 1926-1997 .... **CLC 1, 2, 3, 4, 6, 13, 36, 69, 109; PC 4, 47; TCLC 120; WLC**
See also AAYA 33; AITN 1; AMWC 1; AMWS 2; BG 2; CA 1-4R; 157; CANR 2, 41, 63, 95; CDALB 1941-1968; CP 7; DA; DA3; DAB; DAC; DAM MST, POET; DLB 5, 16, 169, 237; EWL 3; GLL 1; LMFS 2; MTCW 1, 2; PAB; PFS 5; RGAL 4; TUS; WP

Ginzburg, Eugenia .... **CLC 59**
See Ginzburg, Evgeniia

Ginzburg, Evgeniia 1904-1977
See Ginzburg, Eugenia
See also DLB 302

Ginzburg, Natalia 1916-1991 .... **CLC 5, 11, 54, 70; SSC 65; TCLC 156**
See also CA 85-88; 135; CANR 33; DFS 14; DLB 177; EW 13; EWL 3; MTCW 1, 2; RGWL 2, 3

Giono, Jean 1895-1970 .... **CLC 4, 11; TCLC 124**
See also CA 45-48; 29-32R; CANR 2, 35; DLB 72; EWL 3; GFL 1789 to the Present; MTCW 1; RGWL 2, 3

Giovanni, Nikki 1943- ... **BLC 2; CLC 2, 4, 19, 64, 117; PC 19; WLCS**
See also AAYA 22; AITN 1; BW 2, 3; CA 29-32R; CAAS 6; CANR 18, 41, 60, 91, 130; CDALBS; CLR 6, 73; CP 7; CSW; CWP; CWRI 5; DA; DA3; DAB; DAC; DAM MST, MULT, POET; DLB 5, 41; EWL 3; EXPP; INT CANR-18; MAICYA 1, 2; MTCW 1, 2; PFS 17; RGAL 4; SATA 24, 107; TUS; YAW

Giovene, Andrea 1904-1998 .... **CLC 7**
See also CA 85-88

Gippius, Zinaida (Nikolaevna) 1869-1945
See Hippius, Zinaida (Nikolaevna)
See also CA 106; 212

Giraudoux, Jean(-Hippolyte)
1882-1944 .... **TCLC 2, 7**
See also CA 104; 196; DAM DRAM; DLB 65; EW 9; EWL 3; GFL 1789 to the Present; RGWL 2, 3; TWA

Gironella, Jose Maria (Pous)
1917-2003 .... **CLC 11**
See also CA 101; 212; EWL 3; RGWL 2, 3

Gissing, George (Robert)
1857-1903 .... **SSC 37; TCLC 3, 24, 47**
See also BRW 5; CA 105; 167; DLB 18, 135, 184; RGEL 2; TEA

Gordon, Mary (Catherine) 1949- .... **CLC 13, 22, 128; SSC 59**
See also AMWS 4; BPFB 2; CA 102; CANR 44, 92; CN 7; DLB 6; DLBY 1981; FW; INT CA-102; MTCW 1
Gordon, N. J.
See Bosman, Herman Charles
Gordon, Sol 1923- .... **CLC 26**
See also CA 53-56; CANR 4; SATA 11
Gordone, Charles 1925-1995 .. **CLC 1, 4; DC 8**
See also BW 1, 3; CA 93-96; 180; 150; CAAE 180; CAD; CANR 55; DAM DRAM; DLB 7; INT CA-93-96; MTCW 1
Gore, Catherine 1800-1861 .... **NCLC 65**
See also DLB 116; RGEL 2
Gorenko, Anna Andreevna
See Akhmatova, Anna
Gorky, Maxim .... **SSC 28; TCLC 8; WLC**
See Peshkov, Alexei Maximovich
See also DAB; DFS 9; DLB 295; EW 8; EWL 3; MTCW 2; TWA
Goryan, Sirak
See Saroyan, William
Gosse, Edmund (William) 1849-1928 .... **TCLC 28**
See also CA 117; DLB 57, 144, 184; RGEL 2
Gotlieb, Phyllis (Fay Bloom) 1926- .. **CLC 18**
See also CA 13-16R; CANR 7; DLB 88, 251; SFW 4
Gottesman, S. D.
See Kornbluth, C(yril) M.; Pohl, Frederik
Gottfried von Strassburg fl. c. 1170-1215 .... **CMLC 10**
See also CDWLB 2; DLB 138; EW 1; RGWL 2, 3
Gotthelf, Jeremias 1797-1854 .... **NCLC 117**
See also DLB 133; RGWL 2, 3
Gottschalk, Laura Riding
See Jackson, Laura (Riding)
Gould, Lois 1932(?)-2002 .... **CLC 4, 10**
See also CA 77-80; 208; CANR 29; MTCW 1
Gould, Stephen Jay 1941-2002 .... **CLC 163**
See also AAYA 26; BEST 90:2; CA 77-80; 205; CANR 10, 27, 56, 75, 125; CPW; INT CANR-27; MTCW 1, 2
Gourmont, Remy(-Marie-Charles) de 1858-1915 .... **TCLC 17**
See also CA 109; 150; GFL 1789 to the Present; MTCW 2
Gournay, Marie le Jars de
See de Gournay, Marie le Jars
Govier, Katherine 1948- .... **CLC 51**
See also CA 101; CANR 18, 40, 128; CCA 1
Gower, John c. 1330-1408 .... **LC 76; PC 59**
See also BRW 1; DLB 146; RGEL 2
Goyen, (Charles) William 1915-1983 .... **CLC 5, 8, 14, 40**
See also AITN 2; CA 5-8R; 110; CANR 6, 71; DLB 2; 218; DLBY 1983; EWL 3; INT CANR-6
Goytisolo, Juan 1931- .... **CLC 5, 10, 23, 133; HLC 1**
See also CA 85-88; CANR 32, 61, 131; CWW 2; DAM MULT; EWL 3; GLL 2; HW 1, 2; MTCW 1, 2
Gozzano, Guido 1883-1916 .... **PC 10**
See also CA 154; DLB 114; EWL 3
Gozzi, (Conte) Carlo 1720-1806 .... **NCLC 23**
Grabbe, Christian Dietrich 1801-1836 .... **NCLC 2**
See also DLB 133; RGWL 2, 3
Grace, Patricia Frances 1937- .... **CLC 56**
See also CA 176; CANR 118; CN 7; EWL 3; RGSF 2

Gracian y Morales, Baltasar 1601-1658 .... **LC 15**
Gracq, Julien .... **CLC 11, 48**
See Poirier, Louis
See also CWW 2; DLB 83; GFL 1789 to the Present
Grade, Chaim 1910-1982 .... **CLC 10**
See also CA 93-96; 107; EWL 3
Graduate of Oxford, A
See Ruskin, John
Grafton, Garth
See Duncan, Sara Jeannette
Grafton, Sue 1940- .... **CLC 163**
See also AAYA 11, 49; BEST 90:3; CA 108; CANR 31, 55, 111; CMW 4; CPW; CSW; DA3; DAM POP; DLB 226; FW; MSW
Graham, John
See Phillips, David Graham
Graham, Jorie 1951- .... **CLC 48, 118; PC 59**
See also CA 111; CANR 63, 118; CP 7; CWP; DLB 120; EWL 3; PFS 10, 17
Graham, R(obert) B(ontine) Cunninghame
See Cunninghame Graham, Robert (Gallnigad) Bontine
See also DLB 98, 135, 174; RGEL 2; RGSF 2
Graham, Robert
See Haldeman, Joe (William)
Graham, Tom
See Lewis, (Harry) Sinclair
Graham, W(illiam) S(idney) 1918-1986 .... **CLC 29**
See also BRWS 7; CA 73-76; 118; DLB 20; RGEL 2
Graham, Winston (Mawdsley) 1910-2003 .... **CLC 23**
See also CA 49-52; 218; CANR 2, 22, 45, 66; CMW 4; CN 7; DLB 77; RHW
Grahame, Kenneth 1859-1932 ...... **TCLC 64, 136**
See also BYA 5; CA 108; 136; CANR 80; CLR 5; CWRI 5; DA3; DAB; DLB 34, 141, 178; FANT; MAICYA 1, 2; MTCW 2; NFS 20; RGEL 2; SATA 100; TEA; WCH; YABC 1
Granger, Darius John
See Marlowe, Stephen
Granin, Daniil 1918- .... **CLC 59**
See also DLB 302
Granovsky, Timofei Nikolaevich 1813-1855 .... **NCLC 75**
See also DLB 198
Grant, Skeeter
See Spiegelman, Art
Granville-Barker, Harley 1877-1946 .... **TCLC 2**
See Barker, Harley Granville
See also CA 104; 204; DAM DRAM; RGEL 2
Granzotto, Gianni
See Granzotto, Giovanni Battista
Granzotto, Giovanni Battista 1914-1985 .... **CLC 70**
See also CA 166
Grass, Guenter (Wilhelm) 1927- ... **CLC 1, 2, 4, 6, 11, 15, 22, 32, 49, 88; WLC**
See Grass, Gunter (Wilhelm)
See also BPFB 2; CA 13-16R; CANR 20, 75, 93, 133; CDWLB 2; DA; DA3; DAB; DAC; DAM MST, NOV; DLB 75, 124; EW 13; EWL 3; MTCW 1, 2; RGWL 2, 3; TWA
Grass, Gunter (Wilhelm)
See Grass, Guenter (Wilhelm)
See also CWW 2
Gratton, Thomas
See Hulme, T(homas) E(rnest)

Grau, Shirley Ann 1929- .... **CLC 4, 9, 146; SSC 15**
See also CA 89-92; CANR 22, 69; CN 7; CSW; DLB 2, 218; INT CA-89-92, CANR-22; MTCW 1
Gravel, Fern
See Hall, James Norman
Graver, Elizabeth 1964- .... **CLC 70**
See also CA 135; CANR 71, 129
Graves, Richard Perceval 1895-1985 .... **CLC 44**
See also CA 65-68; CANR 9, 26, 51
Graves, Robert (von Ranke) 1895-1985 .. **CLC 1, 2, 6, 11, 39, 44, 45; PC 6**
See also BPFB 2; BRW 7; BYA 4; CA 5-8R; 117; CANR 5, 36; CDBLB 1914-1945; DA3; DAB; DAC; DAM MST, POET; DLB 20, 100, 191; DLBD 18; DLBY 1985; EWL 3; LATS 1:1; MTCW 1, 2; NCFS 2; RGEL 2; RHW; SATA 45; TEA
Graves, Valerie
See Bradley, Marion Zimmer
Gray, Alasdair (James) 1934- .... **CLC 41**
See also BRWS 9; CA 126; CANR 47, 69, 106; CN 7; DLB 194, 261; HGG; INT CA-126; MTCW 1, 2; RGSF 2; SUFW 2
Gray, Amlin 1946- .... **CLC 29**
See also CA 138
Gray, Francine du Plessix 1930- ..... **CLC 22, 153**
See also BEST 90:3; CA 61-64; CAAS 2; CANR 11, 33, 75, 81; DAM NOV; INT CANR-11; MTCW 1, 2
Gray, John (Henry) 1866-1934 ...... **TCLC 19**
See also CA 119; 162; RGEL 2
Gray, Simon (James Holliday) 1936- .... **CLC 9, 14, 36**
See also AITN 1; CA 21-24R; CAAS 3; CANR 32, 69; CD 5; DLB 13; EWL 3; MTCW 1; RGEL 2
Gray, Spalding 1941-2004 .... **CLC 49, 112; DC 7**
See also CA 128; 225; CAD; CANR 74; CD 5; CPW; DAM POP; MTCW 2
Gray, Thomas 1716-1771 .... **LC 4, 40; PC 2; WLC**
See also BRW 3; CDBLB 1660-1789; DA; DA3; DAB; DAC; DAM MST; DLB 109; EXPP; PAB; PFS 9; RGEL 2; TEA; WP
Grayson, David
See Baker, Ray Stannard
Grayson, Richard (A.) 1951- .... **CLC 38**
See also CA 85-88; 210; CAAE 210; CANR 14, 31, 57; DLB 234
Greeley, Andrew M(oran) 1928- ...... **CLC 28**
See also BPFB 2; CA 5-8R; CAAS 7; CANR 7, 43, 69, 104; CMW 4; CPW; DA3; DAM POP; MTCW 1, 2
Green, Anna Katharine 1846-1935 .... **TCLC 63**
See also CA 112; 159; CMW 4; DLB 202, 221; MSW
Green, Brian
See Card, Orson Scott
Green, Hannah
See Greenberg, Joanne (Goldenberg)
Green, Hannah 1927(?)-1996 .... **CLC 3**
See also CA 73-76; CANR 59, 93; NFS 10
Green, Henry .... **CLC 2, 13, 97**
See Yorke, Henry Vincent
See also BRWS 2; CA 175; DLB 15; EWL 3; RGEL 2
Green, Julian (Hartridge) 1900-1998
See Green, Julien
See also CA 21-24R; 169; CANR 33, 87; CWW 2; DLB 4, 72; MTCW 1

Highsmith, (Mary) Patricia
1921-1995 .... **CLC 2, 4, 14, 42, 102**
See Morgan, Claire
See also AAYA 48; BRWS 5; CA 1-4R; 147;
CANR 1, 20, 48, 62, 108; CMW 4; CPW;
DA3; DAM NOV, POP; DLB 306; MSW;
MTCW 1, 2

Highwater, Jamake (Mamake)
1942(?)-2001 .... **CLC 12**
See also AAYA 7; BPFB 2; BYA 4; CA 65-
68; 199; CAAS 7; CANR 10, 34, 84; CLR
17; CWRI 5; DLB 52; DLBY 1985;
JRDA; MAICYA 1, 2; SATA 32, 69;
SATA-Brief 30

Highway, Tomson 1951- ...... **CLC 92; NNAL**
See also CA 151; CANR 75; CCA 1; CD 5;
DAC; DAM MULT; DFS 2; MTCW 2

Hijuelos, Oscar 1951- .... **CLC 65; HLC 1**
See also AAYA 25; AMWS 8; BEST 90:1;
CA 123; CANR 50, 75, 125; CPW; DA3;
DAM MULT, POP; DLB 145; HW 1, 2;
LLW 1; MTCW 2; NFS 17; RGAL 4;
WLIT 1

Hikmet, Nazim 1902(?)-1963 .... **CLC 40**
See also CA 141; 93-96; EWL 3

Hildegard von Bingen 1098-1179 . **CMLC 20**
See also DLB 148

Hildesheimer, Wolfgang 1916-1991 .. **CLC 49**
See also CA 101; 135; DLB 69, 124; EWL
3

Hill, Geoffrey (William) 1932- ...... **CLC 5, 8,**
18, 45
See also BRWS 5; CA 81-84; CANR 21,
89; CDBLB 1960 to Present; CP 7; DAM
POET; DLB 40; EWL 3; MTCW 1; RGEL
2

Hill, George Roy 1921-2002 .... **CLC 26**
See also CA 110; 122; 213

Hill, John
See Koontz, Dean R(ay)

Hill, Susan (Elizabeth) 1942- ...... **CLC 4, 113**
See also CA 33-36R; CANR 29, 69, 129;
CN 7; DAB; DAM MST, NOV; DLB 14,
139; HGG; MTCW 1; RHW

Hillard, Asa G. III .... **CLC 70**

Hillerman, Tony 1925- .... **CLC 62, 170**
See also AAYA 40; BEST 89:1; BPFB 2;
CA 29-32R; CANR 21, 42, 65, 97; CMW
4; CPW; DA3; DAM POP; DLB 206, 306;
MSW; RGAL 4; SATA 6; TCWW 2; YAW

Hillesum, Etty 1914-1943 .... **TCLC 49**
See also CA 137

Hilliard, Noel (Harvey) 1929-1996 ... **CLC 15**
See also CA 9-12R; CANR 7, 69; CN 7

Hillis, Rick 1956- .... **CLC 66**
See also CA 134

Hilton, James 1900-1954 .... **TCLC 21**
See also CA 108; 169; DLB 34, 77; FANT;
SATA 34

Hilton, Walter (?)-1396 .... **CMLC 58**
See also DLB 146; RGEL 2

Himes, Chester (Bomar) 1909-1984 .. **BLC 2;**
CLC 2, 4, 7, 18, 58, 108; TCLC 139
See also AFAW 2; BPFB 2; BW 2; CA 25-
28R; 114; CANR 22, 89; CMW 4; DAM
MULT; DLB 2, 76, 143, 226; EWL 3;
MSW; MTCW 1, 2; RGAL 4

Hinde, Thomas .... **CLC 6, 11**
See Chitty, Thomas Willes
See also EWL 3

Hine, (William) Daryl 1936- .... **CLC 15**
See also CA 1-4R; CAAS 15; CANR 1, 20;
CP 7; DLB 60

Hinkson, Katharine Tynan
See Tynan, Katharine

Hinojosa(-Smith), Rolando (R.)
1929- .... **HLC 1**
See Hinojosa-Smith, Rolando
See also CA 131; CAAS 16; CANR 62;
DAM MULT; DLB 82; HW 1, 2; LLW 1;
MTCW 2; RGAL 4

Hinton, S(usan) E(loise) 1950- .. **CLC 30, 111**
See also AAYA 2, 33; BPFB 2; BYA 2, 3;
CA 81-84; CANR 32, 62, 92, 133;
CDALBS; CLR 3, 23; CPW; DA; DA3;
DAB; DAC; DAM MST, NOV; JRDA;
LAIT 5; MAICYA 1, 2; MTCW 1, 2; NFS
5, 9, 15, 16; SATA 19, 58, 115; WYA;
YAW

Hippius, Zinaida (Nikolaevna) .... **TCLC 9**
See Gippius, Zinaida (Nikolaevna)
See also DLB 295; EWL 3

Hiraoka, Kimitake 1925-1970
See Mishima, Yukio
See also CA 97-100; 29-32R; DA3; DAM
DRAM; GLL 1; MTCW 1, 2

Hirsch, E(ric) D(onald), Jr. 1928- .... **CLC 79**
See also CA 25-28R; CANR 27, 51; DLB
67; INT CANR-27; MTCW 1

Hirsch, Edward 1950- .... **CLC 31, 50**
See also CA 104; CANR 20, 42, 102; CP 7;
DLB 120

Hitchcock, Alfred (Joseph)
1899-1980 .... **CLC 16**
See also AAYA 22; CA 159; 97-100; SATA
27; SATA-Obit 24

Hitchens, Christopher (Eric)
1949- .... **CLC 157**
See also CA 152; CANR 89

Hitler, Adolf 1889-1945 .... **TCLC 53**
See also CA 117; 147

Hoagland, Edward 1932- .... **CLC 28**
See also ANW; CA 1-4R; CANR 2, 31, 57,
107; CN 7; DLB 6; SATA 51; TCWW 2

Hoban, Russell (Conwell) 1925- ... **CLC 7, 25**
See also BPFB 2; CA 5-8R; CANR 23, 37,
66, 114; CLR 3, 69; CN 7; CWRI 5; DAM
NOV; DLB 52; FANT; MAICYA 1, 2;
MTCW 1, 2; SATA 1, 40, 78, 136; SFW
4; SUFW 2

Hobbes, Thomas 1588-1679 .... **LC 36**
See also DLB 151, 252, 281; RGEL 2

Hobbs, Perry
See Blackmur, R(ichard) P(almer)

Hobson, Laura Z(ametkin)
1900-1986 .... **CLC 7, 25**
See Field, Peter
See also BPFB 2; CA 17-20R; 118; CANR
55; DLB 28; SATA 52

Hoccleve, Thomas c. 1368-c. 1437 ...... **LC 75**
See also DLB 146; RGEL 2

Hoch, Edward D(entinger) 1930-
See Queen, Ellery
See also CA 29-32R; CANR 11, 27, 51, 97;
CMW 4; DLB 306; SFW 4

Hochhuth, Rolf 1931- .... **CLC 4, 11, 18**
See also CA 5-8R; CANR 33, 75; CWW 2;
DAM DRAM; DLB 124; EWL 3; MTCW
1, 2

Hochman, Sandra 1936- .... **CLC 3, 8**
See also CA 5-8R; DLB 5

Hochwaelder, Fritz 1911-1986 .... **CLC 36**
See Hochwalder, Fritz
See also CA 29-32R; 120; CANR 42; DAM
DRAM; MTCW 1; RGWL 3

Hochwalder, Fritz
See Hochwaelder, Fritz
See also EWL 3; RGWL 2

Hocking, Mary (Eunice) 1921- .... **CLC 13**
See also CA 101; CANR 18, 40

Hodgins, Jack 1938- .... **CLC 23**
See also CA 93-96; CN 7; DLB 60

Hodgson, William Hope
1877(?)-1918 .... **TCLC 13**
See also CA 111; 164; CMW 4; DLB 70,
153, 156, 178; HGG; MTCW 2; SFW 4;
SUFW 1

Hoeg, Peter 1957- .... **CLC 95, 156**
See also CA 151; CANR 75; CMW 4; DA3;
DLB 214; EWL 3; MTCW 2; NFS 17;
RGWL 3; SSFS 18

Hoffman, Alice 1952- .... **CLC 51**
See also AAYA 37; AMWS 10; CA 77-80;
CANR 34, 66, 100; CN 7; CPW; DAM
NOV; DLB 292; MTCW 1, 2

Hoffman, Daniel (Gerard) 1923- . **CLC 6, 13,**
23
See also CA 1-4R; CANR 4; CP 7; DLB 5

Hoffman, Eva 1945- .... **CLC 182**
See also CA 132

Hoffman, Stanley 1944- .... **CLC 5**
See also CA 77-80

Hoffman, William 1925- .... **CLC 141**
See also CA 21-24R; CANR 9, 103; CSW;
DLB 234

Hoffman, William M(oses) 1939- ..... **CLC 40**
See Hoffman, William M.
See also CA 57-60; CANR 11, 71

Hoffmann, E(rnst) T(heodor) A(madeus)
1776-1822 .... **NCLC 2; SSC 13**
See also CDWLB 2; DLB 90; EW 5; RGSF
2; RGWL 2, 3; SATA 27; SUFW 1; WCH

Hofmann, Gert 1931- .... **CLC 54**
See also CA 128; EWL 3

Hofmannsthal, Hugo von 1874-1929 ... **DC 4;**
TCLC 11
See also CA 106; 153; CDWLB 2; DAM
DRAM; DFS 17; DLB 81, 118; EW 9;
EWL 3; RGWL 2, 3

Hogan, Linda 1947- ..... **CLC 73; NNAL; PC**
35
See also AMWS 4; ANW; BYA 12; CA 120,
226; CAAE 226; CANR 45, 73, 129;
CWP; DAM MULT; DLB 175; SATA
132; TCWW 2

Hogarth, Charles
See Creasey, John

Hogarth, Emmett
See Polonsky, Abraham (Lincoln)

Hogg, James 1770-1835 .... **NCLC 4, 109**
See also DLB 93, 116, 159; HGG; RGEL 2;
SUFW 1

Holbach, Paul Henri Thiry Baron
1723-1789 .... **LC 14**

Holberg, Ludvig 1684-1754 .... **LC 6**
See also DLB 300; RGWL 2, 3

Holcroft, Thomas 1745-1809 .... **NCLC 85**
See also DLB 39, 89, 158; RGEL 2

Holden, Ursula 1921- .... **CLC 18**
See also CA 101; CAAS 8; CANR 22

Holderlin, (Johann Christian) Friedrich
1770-1843 .... **NCLC 16; PC 4**
See also CDWLB 2; DLB 90; EW 5; RGWL
2, 3

Holdstock, Robert
See Holdstock, Robert P.

Holdstock, Robert P. 1948- .... **CLC 39**
See also CA 131; CANR 81; DLB 261;
FANT; HGG; SFW 4; SUFW 2

Holinshed, Raphael fl. 1580- .... **LC 69**
See also DLB 167; RGEL 2

Holland, Isabelle (Christian)
1920-2002 .... **CLC 21**
See also AAYA 11; CA 21-24R; 205; CAAE
181; CANR 10, 25, 47; CLR 57; CWRI
5; JRDA; LAIT 4; MAICYA 1, 2; SATA
8, 70; SATA-Essay 103; SATA-Obit 132;
WYA

Holland, Marcus
See Caldwell, (Janet Miriam) Taylor
(Holland)

Hubbard, L(afayette) Ron(ald)
1911-1986 .... **CLC 43**
See also CA 77-80; 118; CANR 52; CPW;
DA3; DAM POP; FANT; MTCW 2; SFW
4

Huch, Ricarda (Octavia)
1864-1947 .... **TCLC 13**
See also CA 111; 189; DLB 66; EWL 3

Huddle, David 1942- .... **CLC 49**
See also CA 57-60; CAAS 20; CANR 89;
DLB 130

Hudson, Jeffrey
See Crichton, (John) Michael

Hudson, W(illiam) H(enry)
1841-1922 .... **TCLC 29**
See also CA 115; 190; DLB 98, 153, 174;
RGEL 2; SATA 35

Hueffer, Ford Madox
See Ford, Ford Madox

Hughart, Barry 1934- .... **CLC 39**
See also CA 137; FANT; SFW 4; SUFW 2

Hughes, Colin
See Creasey, John

Hughes, David (John) 1930- .... **CLC 48**
See also CA 116; 129; CN 7; DLB 14

Hughes, Edward James
See Hughes, Ted
See also DA3; DAM MST, POET

Hughes, (James Mercer) Langston
1902-1967 ..... **BLC 2; CLC 1, 5, 10, 15,
35, 44, 108; DC 3; HR 2; PC 1, 53;
SSC 6; WLC**
See also AAYA 12; AFAW 1, 2; AMWR 1;
AMWS 1; BW 1, 3; CA 1-4R; 25-28R;
CANR 1, 34, 82; CDALB 1929-1941;
CLR 17; DA; DA3; DAB; DAC; DAM
DRAM, MST, MULT, POET; DFS 6, 18;
DLB 4, 7, 48, 51, 86, 228; EWL 3; EXPP;
EXPS; JRDA; LAIT 3; LMFS 2; MAI-
CYA 1, 2; MTCW 1, 2; PAB; PFS 1, 3, 6,
10, 15; RGAL 4; RGSF 2; SATA 4, 33;
SSFS 4, 7; TUS; WCH; WP; YAW

Hughes, Richard (Arthur Warren)
1900-1976 .... **CLC 1, 11**
See also CA 5-8R; 65-68; CANR 4; DAM
NOV; DLB 15, 161; EWL 3; MTCW 1;
RGEL 2; SATA 8; SATA-Obit 25

Hughes, Ted 1930-1998 . **CLC 2, 4, 9, 14, 37,
119; PC 7**
See Hughes, Edward James
See also BRWC 2; BRWR 2; BRWS 1; CA
1-4R; 171; CANR 1, 33, 66, 108; CLR 3;
CP 7; DAB; DAC; DLB 40, 161; EWL 3;
EXPP; MAICYA 1, 2; MTCW 1, 2; PAB;
PFS 4, 19; RGEL 2; SATA 49; SATA-
Brief 27; SATA-Obit 107; TEA; YAW

Hugo, Richard
See Huch, Ricarda (Octavia)

Hugo, Richard F(ranklin)
1923-1982 .... **CLC 6, 18, 32**
See also AMWS 6; CA 49-52; 108; CANR
3; DAM POET; DLB 5, 206; EWL 3; PFS
17; RGAL 4

Hugo, Victor (Marie) 1802-1885 .... **NCLC 3,
10, 21; PC 17; WLC**
See also AAYA 28; DA; DA3; DAB; DAC;
DAM DRAM, MST, NOV, POET; DLB
119, 192, 217; EFS 2; EW 6; EXPN; GFL
1789 to the Present; LAIT 1, 2; NFS 5,
20; RGWL 2, 3; SATA 47; TWA

Huidobro, Vicente
See Huidobro Fernandez, Vicente Garcia
See also DLB 283; EWL 3; LAW

Huidobro Fernandez, Vicente Garcia
1893-1948 .... **TCLC 31**
See Huidobro, Vicente
See also CA 131; HW 1

Hulme, Keri 1947- .... **CLC 39, 130**
See also CA 125; CANR 69; CN 7; CP 7;
CWP; EWL 3; FW; INT CA-125

Hulme, T(homas) E(rnest)
1883-1917 .... **TCLC 21**
See also BRWS 6; CA 117; 203; DLB 19

Humboldt, Wilhelm von
1767-1835 .... **NCLC 134**
See also DLB 90

Hume, David 1711-1776 .... **LC 7, 56**
See also BRWS 3; DLB 104, 252; LMFS 1;
TEA

Humphrey, William 1924-1997 .... **CLC 45**
See also AMWS 9; CA 77-80; 160; CANR
68; CN 7; CSW; DLB 6, 212, 234, 278;
TCWW 2

Humphreys, Emyr Owen 1919- .... **CLC 47**
See also CA 5-8R; CANR 3, 24; CN 7;
DLB 15

Humphreys, Josephine 1945- ..... **CLC 34, 57**
See also CA 121; 127; CANR 97; CSW;
DLB 292; INT CA-127

Huneker, James Gibbons
1860-1921 .... **TCLC 65**
See also CA 193; DLB 71; RGAL 4

Hungerford, Hesba Fay
See Brinsmead, H(esba) F(ay)

Hungerford, Pixie
See Brinsmead, H(esba) F(ay)

Hunt, E(verette) Howard, (Jr.)
1918- .... **CLC 3**
See also AITN 1; CA 45-48; CANR 2, 47,
103; CMW 4

Hunt, Francesca
See Holland, Isabelle (Christian)

Hunt, Howard
See Hunt, E(verette) Howard, (Jr.)

Hunt, Kyle
See Creasey, John

Hunt, (James Henry) Leigh
1784-1859 .... **NCLC 1, 70**
See also DAM POET; DLB 96, 110, 144;
RGEL 2; TEA

Hunt, Marsha 1946- .... **CLC 70**
See also BW 2, 3; CA 143; CANR 79

Hunt, Violet 1866(?)-1942 .... **TCLC 53**
See also CA 184; DLB 162, 197

Hunter, E. Waldo
See Sturgeon, Theodore (Hamilton)

Hunter, Evan 1926- .... **CLC 11, 31**
See McBain, Ed
See also AAYA 39; BPFB 2; CA 5-8R;
CANR 5, 38, 62, 97; CMW 4; CN 7;
CPW; DAM POP; DLB 306; DLBY 1982;
INT CANR-5; MSW; MTCW 1; SATA
25; SFW 4

Hunter, Kristin 1931-
See Lattany, Kristin (Elaine Eggleston)
Hunter

Hunter, Mary
See Austin, Mary (Hunter)

Hunter, Mollie 1922- .... **CLC 21**
See McIlwraith, Maureen Mollie Hunter
See also AAYA 13; BYA 6; CANR 37, 78;
CLR 25; DLB 161; JRDA; MAICYA 1,
2; SAAS 7; SATA 54, 106, 139; SATA-
Essay 139; WYA; YAW

Hunter, Robert (?)-1734 .... **LC 7**

Hurston, Zora Neale 1891-1960 .... **BLC 2;
CLC 7, 30, 61; DC 12; HR 2; SSC 4;
TCLC 121, 131; WLCS**
See also AAYA 15; AFAW 1, 2; AMWS 6;
BW 1, 3; BYA 12; CA 85-88; CANR 61;
CDALBS; DA; DA3; DAC; DAM MST,
MULT, NOV; DFS 6; DLB 51, 86; EWL
3; EXPN; EXPS; FW; LAIT 3; LATS 1:1;
LMFS 2; MAWW; MTCW 1, 2; NFS 3;
RGAL 4; RGSF 2; SSFS 1, 6, 11, 19;
TUS; YAW

Husserl, E. G.
See Husserl, Edmund (Gustav Albrecht)

Husserl, Edmund (Gustav Albrecht)
1859-1938 .... **TCLC 100**
See also CA 116; 133; DLB 296

Huston, John (Marcellus)
1906-1987 .... **CLC 20**
See also CA 73-76; 123; CANR 34; DLB
26

Hustvedt, Siri 1955- .... **CLC 76**
See also CA 137

Hutten, Ulrich von 1488-1523 .... **LC 16**
See also DLB 179

Huxley, Aldous (Leonard)
1894-1963 .... **CLC 1, 3, 4, 5, 8, 11, 18,
35, 79; SSC 39; WLC**
See also AAYA 11; BPFB 2; BRW 7; CA
85-88; CANR 44, 99; CDBLB 1914-1945;
DA; DA3; DAB; DAC; DAM MST, NOV;
DLB 36, 100, 162, 195, 255; EWL 3;
EXPN; LAIT 5; LMFS 2; MTCW 1, 2;
NFS 6; RGEL 2; SATA 63; SCFW 2;
SFW 4; TEA; YAW

Huxley, T(homas) H(enry)
1825-1895 .... **NCLC 67**
See also DLB 57; TEA

Huysmans, Joris-Karl 1848-1907 ... **TCLC 7,
69**
See also CA 104; 165; DLB 123; EW 7;
GFL 1789 to the Present; LMFS 2; RGWL
2, 3

Hwang, David Henry 1957- .... **CLC 55, 196;
DC 4, 23**
See also CA 127; 132; CAD; CANR 76,
124; CD 5; DA3; DAM DRAM; DFS 11,
18; DLB 212, 228; INT CA-132; MTCW
2; RGAL 4

Hyde, Anthony 1946- .... **CLC 42**
See Chase, Nicholas
See also CA 136; CCA 1

Hyde, Margaret O(ldroyd) 1917- ..... **CLC 21**
See also CA 1-4R; CANR 1, 36; CLR 23;
JRDA; MAICYA 1, 2; SAAS 8; SATA 1,
42, 76, 139

Hynes, James 1956(?)- .... **CLC 65**
See also CA 164; CANR 105

Hypatia c. 370-415 .... **CMLC 35**

Ian, Janis 1951- .... **CLC 21**
See also CA 105; 187

Ibanez, Vicente Blasco
See Blasco Ibanez, Vicente

Ibarbourou, Juana de 1895-1979 ..... **HLCS 2**
See also DLB 290; HW 1; LAW

Ibarguengoitia, Jorge 1928-1983 ..... **CLC 37;
TCLC 148**
See also CA 124; 113; EWL 3; HW 1

Ibn Battuta, Abu Abdalla
1304-1368(?) .... **CMLC 57**
See also WLIT 2

Ibn Hazm 994-1064 .... **CMLC 64**

Ibsen, Henrik (Johan) 1828-1906 .... **DC 2;
TCLC 2, 8, 16, 37, 52; WLC**
See also AAYA 46; CA 104; 141; DA; DA3;
DAB; DAC; DAM DRAM, MST; DFS 1,
6, 8, 10, 11, 15, 16; EW 7; LAIT 2; LATS
1:1; RGWL 2, 3

Ibuse, Masuji 1898-1993 .... **CLC 22**
See Ibuse Masuji
See also CA 127; 141; MJW; RGWL 3

Ibuse Masuji
See Ibuse, Masuji
See also CWW 2; DLB 180; EWL 3

Ichikawa, Kon 1915- .... **CLC 20**
See also CA 121

Ichiyo, Higuchi 1872-1896 .... **NCLC 49**
See also MJW

Idle, Eric 1943- .... **CLC 21**
See Monty Python
See also CA 116; CANR 35, 91

James, Montague (Rhodes)
1862-1936 .... **SSC 16; TCLC 6**
See James, M. R.
See also CA 104; 203; HGG; RGEL 2;
RGSF 2; SUFW 1

James, P. D. .... **CLC 18, 46, 122**
See White, Phyllis Dorothy James
See also BEST 90:2; BPFB 2; BRWS 4;
CDBLB 1960 to Present; DLB 87, 276;
DLBD 17; MSW

James, Philip
See Moorcock, Michael (John)

James, Samuel
See Stephens, James

James, Seumas
See Stephens, James

James, Stephen
See Stephens, James

James, William 1842-1910 .... **TCLC 15, 32**
See also AMW; CA 109; 193; DLB 270,
284; NCFS 5; RGAL 4

Jameson, Anna 1794-1860 .... **NCLC 43**
See also DLB 99, 166

Jameson, Fredric (R.) 1934- .... **CLC 142**
See also CA 196; DLB 67; LMFS 2

Jami, Nur al-Din 'Abd al-Rahman
1414-1492 .... **LC 9**

Jammes, Francis 1868-1938 .... **TCLC 75**
See also CA 198; EWL 3; GFL 1789 to the
Present

Jandl, Ernst 1925-2000 .... **CLC 34**
See also CA 200; EWL 3

Janowitz, Tama 1957- .... **CLC 43, 145**
See also CA 106; CANR 52, 89, 129; CN
7; CPW; DAM POP; DLB 292

Japrisot, Sebastien 1931- .... **CLC 90**
See Rossi, Jean-Baptiste
See also CMW 4; NFS 18

Jarrell, Randall 1914-1965 .... **CLC 1, 2, 6, 9,
13, 49; PC 41**
See also AMW; BYA 5; CA 5-8R; 25-28R;
CABS 2; CANR 6, 34; CDALB 1941-
1968; CLR 6; CWRI 5; DAM POET;
DLB 48, 52; EWL 3; EXPP; MAICYA 1,
2; MTCW 1, 2; PAB; PFS 2; RGAL 4;
SATA 7

Jarry, Alfred 1873-1907 .... **SSC 20; TCLC 2,
14, 147**
See also CA 104; 153; DA3; DAM DRAM;
DFS 8; DLB 192, 258; EW 9; EWL 3;
GFL 1789 to the Present; RGWL 2, 3;
TWA

Jarvis, E. K.
See Ellison, Harlan (Jay)

Jawien, Andrzej
See John Paul II, Pope

Jaynes, Roderick
See Coen, Ethan

Jeake, Samuel, Jr.
See Aiken, Conrad (Potter)

Jean Paul 1763-1825 .... **NCLC 7**

Jefferies, (John) Richard
1848-1887 .... **NCLC 47**
See also DLB 98, 141; RGEL 2; SATA 16;
SFW 4

Jeffers, (John) Robinson 1887-1962 .. **CLC 2,
3, 11, 15, 54; PC 17; WLC**
See also AMWS 2; CA 85-88; CANR 35;
CDALB 1917-1929; DA; DAC; DAM
MST, POET; DLB 45, 212; EWL 3;
MTCW 1, 2; PAB; PFS 3, 4; RGAL 4

Jefferson, Janet
See Mencken, H(enry) L(ouis)

Jefferson, Thomas 1743-1826 .. **NCLC 11, 103**
See also AAYA 54; ANW; CDALB 1640-
1865; DA3; DLB 31, 183; LAIT 1; RGAL
4

Jeffrey, Francis 1773-1850 .... **NCLC 33**
See Francis, Lord Jeffrey

Jelakowitch, Ivan
See Heijermans, Herman

Jelinek, Elfriede 1946- .... **CLC 169**
See also CA 154; DLB 85; FW

Jellicoe, (Patricia) Ann 1927- .... **CLC 27**
See also CA 85-88; CBD; CD 5; CWD;
CWRI 5; DLB 13, 233; FW

Jelloun, Tahar ben 1944- .... **CLC 180**
See Ben Jelloun, Tahar
See also CA 162; CANR 100

Jemyma
See Holley, Marietta

Jen, Gish .... **AAL; CLC 70**
See Jen, Lillian
See also AMWC 2

Jen, Lillian 1956(?)-
See Jen, Gish
See also CA 135; CANR 89, 130

Jenkins, (John) Robin 1912- .... **CLC 52**
See also CA 1-4R; CANR 1; CN 7; DLB
14, 271

Jennings, Elizabeth (Joan)
1926-2001 .... **CLC 5, 14, 131**
See also BRWS 5; CA 61-64; 200; CAAS
5; CANR 8, 39, 66, 127; CP 7; CWP;
DLB 27; EWL 3; MTCW 1; SATA 66

Jennings, Waylon 1937- .... **CLC 21**

Jensen, Johannes V(ilhelm)
1873-1950 .... **TCLC 41**
See also CA 170; DLB 214; EWL 3; RGWL
3

Jensen, Laura (Linnea) 1948- .... **CLC 37**
See also CA 103

Jerome, Saint 345-420 .... **CMLC 30**
See also RGWL 3

Jerome, Jerome K(lapka)
1859-1927 .... **TCLC 23**
See also CA 119; 177; DLB 10, 34, 135;
RGEL 2

Jerrold, Douglas William
1803-1857 .... **NCLC 2**
See also DLB 158, 159; RGEL 2

Jewett, (Theodora) Sarah Orne
1849-1909 .... **SSC 6, 44; TCLC 1, 22**
See also AMW; AMWC 2; AMWR 2; CA
108; 127; CANR 71; DLB 12, 74, 221;
EXPS; FW; MAWW; NFS 15; RGAL 4;
RGSF 2; SATA 15; SSFS 4

Jewsbury, Geraldine (Endsor)
1812-1880 .... **NCLC 22**
See also DLB 21

Jhabvala, Ruth Prawer 1927- . **CLC 4, 8, 29,
94, 138**
See also BRWS 5; CA 1-4R; CANR 2, 29,
51, 74, 91, 128; CN 7; DAB; DAM NOV;
DLB 139, 194; EWL 3; IDFW 3, 4; INT
CANR-29; MTCW 1, 2; RGSF 2; RGWL
2; RHW; TEA

Jibran, Kahlil
See Gibran, Kahlil

Jibran, Khalil
See Gibran, Kahlil

Jiles, Paulette 1943- .... **CLC 13, 58**
See also CA 101; CANR 70, 124; CWP

Jimenez (Mantecon), Juan Ramon
1881-1958 .... **HLC 1; PC 7; TCLC 4**
See also CA 104; 131; CANR 74; DAM
MULT, POET; DLB 134; EW 9; EWL 3;
HW 1; MTCW 1, 2; RGWL 2, 3

Jimenez, Ramon
See Jimenez (Mantecon), Juan Ramon

Jimenez Mantecon, Juan
See Jimenez (Mantecon), Juan Ramon

Jin, Ha .... **CLC 109**
See Jin, Xuefei
See also CA 152; DLB 244, 292; SSFS 17

Jin, Xuefei 1956-
See Jin, Ha
See also CANR 91, 130; SSFS 17

Joel, Billy .... **CLC 26**
See Joel, William Martin

Joel, William Martin 1949-
See Joel, Billy
See also CA 108

John, Saint 10(?)-100 .... **CMLC 27, 63**

John of Salisbury c. 1115-1180 ..... **CMLC 63**

John of the Cross, St. 1542-1591 .... **LC 18**
See also RGWL 2, 3

John Paul II, Pope 1920- .... **CLC 128**
See also CA 106; 133

Johnson, B(ryan) S(tanley William)
1933-1973 .... **CLC 6, 9**
See also CA 9-12R; 53-56; CANR 9; DLB
14, 40; EWL 3; RGEL 2

Johnson, Benjamin F., of Boone
See Riley, James Whitcomb

Johnson, Charles (Richard) 1948- .... **BLC 2;
CLC 7, 51, 65, 163**
See also AFAW 2; AMWS 6; BW 2, 3; CA
116; CAAS 18; CANR 42, 66, 82, 129;
CN 7; DAM MULT; DLB 33, 278;
MTCW 2; RGAL 4; SSFS 16

Johnson, Charles S(purgeon)
1893-1956 .... **HR 3**
See also BW 1, 3; CA 125; CANR 82; DLB
51, 91

Johnson, Denis 1949- . **CLC 52, 160; SSC 56**
See also CA 117; 121; CANR 71, 99; CN
7; DLB 120

Johnson, Diane 1934- .... **CLC 5, 13, 48**
See also BPFB 2; CA 41-44R; CANR 17,
40, 62, 95; CN 7; DLBY 1980; INT
CANR-17; MTCW 1

Johnson, E. Pauline 1861-1913 .... **NNAL**
See also CA 150; DAC; DAM MULT; DLB
92, 175

Johnson, Eyvind (Olof Verner)
1900-1976 .... **CLC 14**
See also CA 73-76; 69-72; CANR 34, 101;
DLB 259; EW 12; EWL 3

Johnson, Fenton 1888-1958 .... **BLC 2**
See also BW 1; CA 118; 124; DAM MULT;
DLB 45, 50

Johnson, Georgia Douglas (Camp)
1880-1966 .... **HR 3**
See also BW 1; CA 125; DLB 51, 249; WP

Johnson, Helene 1907-1995 .... **HR 3**
See also CA 181; DLB 51; WP

Johnson, J. R.
See James, C(yril) L(ionel) R(obert)

Johnson, James Weldon 1871-1938 .. **BLC 2;
HR 3; PC 24; TCLC 3, 19**
See also AFAW 1, 2; BW 1, 3; CA 104;
125; CANR 82; CDALB 1917-1929; CLR
32; DA3; DAM MULT, POET; DLB 51;
EWL 3; EXPP; LMFS 2; MTCW 1, 2;
PFS 1; RGAL 4; SATA 31; TUS

Johnson, Joyce 1935- .... **CLC 58**
See also BG 3; CA 125; 129; CANR 102

Johnson, Judith (Emlyn) 1936- .... **CLC 7, 15**
See Sherwin, Judith Johnson
See also CA 25-28R; 153; CANR 34

Johnson, Lionel (Pigot)
1867-1902 .... **TCLC 19**
See also CA 117; 209; DLB 19; RGEL 2

Johnson, Marguerite Annie
See Angelou, Maya

Johnson, Mel
See Malzberg, Barry N(athaniel)

Johnson, Pamela Hansford
1912-1981 .... **CLC 1, 7, 27**
See also CA 1-4R; 104; CANR 2, 28; DLB
15; MTCW 1, 2; RGEL 2

Johnson, Paul (Bede) 1928- .... **CLC 147**
See also BEST 89:4; CA 17-20R; CANR
34, 62, 100

Johnson, Robert .... CLC 70

Johnson, Robert 1911(?)-1938 .... TCLC 69
See also BW 3; CA 174

Johnson, Samuel 1709-1784 .... LC 15, 52;
WLC
See also BRW 3; BRWR 1; CDBLB 1660-
1789; DA; DAB; DAC; DAM MST; DLB
39, 95, 104, 142, 213; LMFS 1; RGEL 2;
TEA

Johnson, Uwe 1934-1984 .. CLC 5, 10, 15, 40
See also CA 1-4R; 112; CANR 1, 39; CD-
WLB 2; DLB 75; EWL 3; MTCW 1;
RGWL 2, 3

Johnston, Basil H. 1929- .... NNAL
See also CA 69-72; CANR 11, 28, 66;
DAC; DAM MULT; DLB 60

Johnston, George (Benson) 1913- .... CLC 51
See also CA 1-4R; CANR 5, 20; CP 7; DLB
88

Johnston, Jennifer (Prudence)
1930- .... CLC 7, 150
See also CA 85-88; CANR 92; CN 7; DLB
14

Joinville, Jean de 1224(?)-1317 ..... CMLC 38

Jolley, (Monica) Elizabeth 1923- ..... CLC 46;
SSC 19
See also CA 127; CAAS 13; CANR 59; CN
7; EWL 3; RGSF 2

Jones, Arthur Llewellyn 1863-1947
See Machen, Arthur
See also CA 104; 179; HGG

Jones, D(ouglas) G(ordon) 1929- ..... CLC 10
See also CA 29-32R; CANR 13, 90; CP 7;
DLB 53

Jones, David (Michael) 1895-1974 .... CLC 2,
4, 7, 13, 42
See also BRW 6; BRWS 7; CA 9-12R; 53-
56; CANR 28; CDBLB 1945-1960; DLB
20, 100; EWL 3; MTCW 1; PAB; RGEL
2

Jones, David Robert 1947-
See Bowie, David
See also CA 103; CANR 104

Jones, Diana Wynne 1934- .... CLC 26
See also AAYA 12; BYA 6, 7, 9, 11, 13, 16;
CA 49-52; CANR 4, 26, 56, 120; CLR
23; DLB 161; FANT; JRDA; MAICYA 1,
2; SAAS 7; SATA 9, 70, 108; SFW 4;
SUFW 2; YAW

Jones, Edward P. 1950- .... CLC 76
See also BW 2, 3; CA 142; CANR 79; CSW

Jones, Gayl 1949- ...... BLC 2; CLC 6, 9, 131
See also AFAW 1, 2; BW 2, 3; CA 77-80;
CANR 27, 66, 122; CN 7; CSW; DA3;
DAM MULT; DLB 33, 278; MTCW 1, 2;
RGAL 4

Jones, James 1921-1977 ...... CLC 1, 3, 10, 39
See also AITN 1, 2; AMWS 11; BPFB 2;
CA 1-4R; 69-72; CANR 6; DLB 2, 143;
DLBD 17; DLBY 1998; EWL 3; MTCW
1; RGAL 4

Jones, John J.
See Lovecraft, H(oward) P(hillips)

Jones, LeRoi .... CLC 1, 2, 3, 5, 10, 14
See Baraka, Amiri
See also MTCW 2

Jones, Louis B. 1953- .... CLC 65
See also CA 141; CANR 73

Jones, Madison (Percy, Jr.) 1925- ...... CLC 4
See also CA 13-16R; CAAS 11; CANR 7,
54, 83; CN 7; CSW; DLB 152

Jones, Mervyn 1922- .... CLC 10, 52
See also CA 45-48; CAAS 5; CANR 1, 91;
CN 7; MTCW 1

Jones, Mick 1956(?)- .... CLC 30

Jones, Nettie (Pearl) 1941- .... CLC 34
See also BW 2; CA 137; CAAS 20; CANR
88

Jones, Peter 1802-1856 .... NNAL

Jones, Preston 1936-1979 .... CLC 10
See also CA 73-76; 89-92; DLB 7

Jones, Robert F(rancis) 1934-2003 .... CLC 7
See also CA 49-52; CANR 2, 61, 118

Jones, Rod 1953- .... CLC 50
See also CA 128

Jones, Terence Graham Parry
1942- .... CLC 21
See Jones, Terry; Monty Python
See also CA 112; 116; CANR 35, 93; INT
CA-116; SATA 127

Jones, Terry
See Jones, Terence Graham Parry
See also SATA 67; SATA-Brief 51

Jones, Thom (Douglas) 1945(?)- ..... CLC 81;
SSC 56
See also CA 157; CANR 88; DLB 244

Jong, Erica 1942- .... CLC 4, 6, 8, 18, 83
See also AITN 1; AMWS 5; BEST 90:2;
BPFB 2; CA 73-76; CANR 26, 52, 75,
132; CN 7; CP 7; CPW; DA3; DAM
NOV, POP; DLB 2, 5, 28, 152; FW; INT
CANR-26; MTCW 1, 2

Jonson, Ben(jamin) 1572(?)-1637 . DC 4; LC
6, 33; PC 17; WLC
See also BRW 1; BRWC 1; BRWR 1; CD-
BLB Before 1660; DA; DAB; DAC;
DAM DRAM, MST, POET; DFS 4, 10;
DLB 62, 121; LMFS 1; RGEL 2; TEA;
WLIT 3

Jordan, June (Meyer)
1936-2002 .. BLCS; CLC 5, 11, 23, 114;
PC 38
See also AAYA 2; AFAW 1, 2; BW 2, 3;
CA 33-36R; 206; CANR 25, 70, 114; CLR
10; CP 7; CWP; DAM MULT, POET;
DLB 38; GLL 2; LAIT 5; MAICYA 1, 2;
MTCW 1; SATA 4, 136; YAW

Jordan, Neil (Patrick) 1950- .... CLC 110
See also CA 124; 130; CANR 54; CN 7;
GLL 2; INT CA-130

Jordan, Pat(rick M.) 1941- .... CLC 37
See also CA 33-36R; CANR 121

Jorgensen, Ivar
See Ellison, Harlan (Jay)

Jorgenson, Ivar
See Silverberg, Robert

Joseph, George Ghevarughese .... CLC 70

Josephson, Mary
See O'Doherty, Brian

Josephus, Flavius c. 37-100 .... CMLC 13
See also AW 2; DLB 176

Josiah Allen's Wife
See Holley, Marietta

Josipovici, Gabriel (David) 1940- ...... CLC 6,
43, 153
See also CA 37-40R; 224; CAAE 224;
CAAS 8; CANR 47, 84; CN 7; DLB 14

Joubert, Joseph 1754-1824 .... NCLC 9

Jouve, Pierre Jean 1887-1976 .... CLC 47
See also CA 65-68; DLB 258; EWL 3

Jovine, Francesco 1902-1950 .... TCLC 79
See also DLB 264; EWL 3

Joyce, James (Augustine Aloysius)
1882-1941 .... DC 16; PC 22; SSC 3, 26,
44, 64; TCLC 3, 8, 16, 35, 52; WLC
See also AAYA 42; BRW 7; BRWC 1;
BRWR 1; BYA 11, 13; CA 104; 126; CD-
BLB 1914-1945; DA; DA3; DAB; DAC;
DAM MST, NOV, POET; DLB 10, 19,
36, 162, 247; EWL 3; EXPN; EXPS;
LAIT 1, 2; LMFS 1, 2; MTCW 1, 2; NFS 7;
RGSF 2; SSFS 1, 19; TEA; WLIT 4

Jozsef, Attila 1905-1937 .... TCLC 22
See also CA 116; CDWLB 4; DLB 215;
EWL 3

Juana Ines de la Cruz, Sor
1651(?)-1695 ...... HLCS 1; LC 5; PC 24
See also DLB 305; FW; LAW; RGWL 2, 3;
WLIT 1

Juana Inez de La Cruz, Sor
See Juana Ines de la Cruz, Sor

Judd, Cyril
See Kornbluth, C(yril) M.; Pohl, Frederik

Juenger, Ernst 1895-1998 .... CLC 125
See Junger, Ernst
See also CA 101; 167; CANR 21, 47, 106;
DLB 56

Julian of Norwich 1342(?)-1416(?) . LC 6, 52
See also DLB 146; LMFS 1

Julius Caesar 100 B.C.-44 B.C.
See Caesar, Julius
See also CDWLB 1; DLB 211

Junger, Ernst
See Juenger, Ernst
See also CDWLB 2; EWL 3; RGWL 2, 3

Junger, Sebastian 1962- .... CLC 109
See also AAYA 28; CA 165; CANR 130

Juniper, Alex
See Hospital, Janette Turner

Junius
See Luxemburg, Rosa

Just, Ward (Swift) 1935- .... CLC 4, 27
See also CA 25-28R; CANR 32, 87; CN 7;
INT CANR-32

Justice, Donald (Rodney)
1925-2004 .... CLC 6, 19, 102
See also AMWS 7; CA 5-8R; CANR 26,
54, 74, 121, 122; CP 7; CSW; DAM
POET; DLBY 1983; EWL 3; INT CANR-
26; MTCW 2; PFS 14

Juvenal c. 60-c. 130 .... CMLC 8
See also AW 2; CDWLB 1; DLB 211;
RGWL 2, 3

Juvenis
See Bourne, Randolph S(illiman)

K., Alice
See Knapp, Caroline

Kabakov, Sasha .... CLC 59

Kabir 1398(?)-1448(?) .... PC 56
See also RGWL 2, 3

Kacew, Romain 1914-1980
See Gary, Romain
See also CA 108; 102

Kadare, Ismail 1936- .... CLC 52, 190
See also CA 161; EWL 3; RGWL 3

Kadohata, Cynthia 1956(?)- ..... CLC 59, 122
See also CA 140; CANR 124

Kafka, Franz 1883-1924 .... SSC 5, 29, 35, 60;
TCLC 2, 6, 13, 29, 47, 53, 112; WLC
See also AAYA 31; BPFB 2; CA 105; 126;
CDWLB 2; DA; DA3; DAB; DAC; DAM
MST, NOV; DLB 81; EW 9; EWL 3;
EXPS; LATS 1:1; LMFS 2; MTCW 1, 2;
NFS 7; RGSF 2; RGWL 2, 3; SFW 4;
SSFS 3, 7, 12; TWA

Kahanovitsch, Pinkhes
See Der Nister

Kahn, Roger 1927- .... CLC 30
See also CA 25-28R; CANR 44, 69; DLB
171; SATA 37

Kain, Saul
See Sassoon, Siegfried (Lorraine)

Kaiser, Georg 1878-1945 .... TCLC 9
See also CA 106; 190; CDWLB 2; DLB
124; EWL 3; LMFS 2; RGWL 2, 3

Kaledin, Sergei .... CLC 59

Kaletski, Alexander 1946- .... CLC 39
See also CA 118; 143

Kalidasa fl. c. 400-455 .... CMLC 9; PC 22
See also RGWL 2, 3

Kallman, Chester (Simon)
1921-1975 .... CLC 2
See also CA 45-48; 53-56; CANR 3

Kaminsky, Melvin 1926-
See Brooks, Mel
See also CA 65-68; CANR 16
Kaminsky, Stuart M(elvin) 1934- ..... **CLC 59**
See also CA 73-76; CANR 29, 53, 89;
CMW 4
Kamo no Chomei 1153(?)-1216 .... **CMLC 66**
See also DLB 203
Kamo no Nagaakira
See Kamo no Chomei
Kandinsky, Wassily 1866-1944 .... **TCLC 92**
See also CA 118; 155
Kane, Francis
See Robbins, Harold
Kane, Henry 1918-
See Queen, Ellery
See also CA 156; CMW 4
Kane, Paul
See Simon, Paul (Frederick)
Kanin, Garson 1912-1999 .... **CLC 22**
See also AITN 1; CA 5-8R; 177; CAD;
CANR 7, 78; DLB 7; IDFW 3, 4
Kaniuk, Yoram 1930- .... **CLC 19**
See also CA 134; DLB 299
Kant, Immanuel 1724-1804 ..... **NCLC 27, 67**
See also DLB 94
Kantor, MacKinlay 1904-1977 .... **CLC 7**
See also CA 61-64; 73-76; CANR 60, 63;
DLB 9, 102; MTCW 2; RHW; TCWW 2
Kanze Motokiyo
See Zeami
Kaplan, David Michael 1946- .... **CLC 50**
See also CA 187
Kaplan, James 1951- .... **CLC 59**
See also CA 135; CANR 121
Karadzic, Vuk Stefanovic
1787-1864 .... **NCLC 115**
See also CDWLB 4; DLB 147
Karageorge, Michael
See Anderson, Poul (William)
Karamzin, Nikolai Mikhailovich
1766-1826 .... **NCLC 3**
See also DLB 150; RGSF 2
Karapanou, Margarita 1946- .... **CLC 13**
See also CA 101
Karinthy, Frigyes 1887-1938 .... **TCLC 47**
See also CA 170; DLB 215; EWL 3
Karl, Frederick R(obert)
1927-2004 .... **CLC 34**
See also CA 5-8R; 226; CANR 3, 44
Karr, Mary 1955- .... **CLC 188**
See also AMWS 11; CA 151; CANR 100;
NCFS 5
Kastel, Warren
See Silverberg, Robert
Kataev, Evgeny Petrovich 1903-1942
See Petrov, Evgeny
See also CA 120
Kataphusin
See Ruskin, John
Katz, Steve 1935- .... **CLC 47**
See also CA 25-28R; CAAS 14, 64; CANR
12; CN 7; DLBY 1983
Kauffman, Janet 1945- .... **CLC 42**
See also CA 117; CANR 43, 84; DLB 218;
DLBY 1986
Kaufman, Bob (Garnell) 1925-1986 . **CLC 49**
See also BG 3; BW 1; CA 41-44R; 118;
CANR 22; DLB 16, 41
Kaufman, George S. 1889-1961 ...... **CLC 38;
DC 17**
See also CA 108; 93-96; DAM DRAM;
DFS 1, 10; DLB 7; INT CA-108; MTCW
2; RGAL 4; TUS
Kaufman, Sue .... **CLC 3, 8**
See Barondess, Sue K(aufman)

Kavafis, Konstantinos Petrou 1863-1933
See Cavafy, C(onstantine) P(eter)
See also CA 104
Kavan, Anna 1901-1968 .... **CLC 5, 13, 82**
See also BRWS 7; CA 5-8R; CANR 6, 57;
DLB 255; MTCW 1; RGEL 2; SFW 4
Kavanagh, Dan
See Barnes, Julian (Patrick)
Kavanagh, Julie 1952- .... **CLC 119**
See also CA 163
Kavanagh, Patrick (Joseph)
1904-1967 .... **CLC 22; PC 33**
See also BRWS 7; CA 123; 25-28R; DLB
15, 20; EWL 3; MTCW 1; RGEL 2
Kawabata, Yasunari 1899-1972 ..... **CLC 2, 5,
9, 18, 107; SSC 17**
See Kawabata Yasunari
See also CA 93-96; 33-36R; CANR 88;
DAM MULT; MJW; MTCW 2; RGSF 2;
RGWL 2, 3
Kawabata Yasunari
See Kawabata, Yasunari
See also DLB 180; EWL 3
Kaye, M(ary) M(argaret)
1908-2004 .... **CLC 28**
See also CA 89-92; 223; CANR 24, 60, 102;
MTCW 1, 2; RHW; SATA 62; SATA-Obit
152
Kaye, Mollie
See Kaye, M(ary) M(argaret)
Kaye-Smith, Sheila 1887-1956 .... **TCLC 20**
See also CA 118; 203; DLB 36
Kaymor, Patrice Maguilene
See Senghor, Leopold Sedar
Kazakov, Iurii Pavlovich
See Kazakov, Yuri Pavlovich
See also DLB 302
Kazakov, Yuri Pavlovich 1927-1982 . **SSC 43**
See Kazakov, Iurii Pavlovich; Kazakov,
Yury
See also CA 5-8R; CANR 36; MTCW 1;
RGSF 2
Kazakov, Yury
See Kazakov, Yuri Pavlovich
See also EWL 3
Kazan, Elia 1909-2003 .... **CLC 6, 16, 63**
See also CA 21-24R; 220; CANR 32, 78
Kazantzakis, Nikos 1883(?)-1957 .... **TCLC 2,
5, 33**
See also BPFB 2; CA 105; 132; DA3; EW
9; EWL 3; MTCW 1, 2; RGWL 2, 3
Kazin, Alfred 1915-1998 ..... **CLC 34, 38, 119**
See also AMWS 8; CA 1-4R; CAAS 7;
CANR 1, 45, 79; DLB 67; EWL 3
Keane, Mary Nesta (Skrine) 1904-1996
See Keane, Molly
See also CA 108; 114; 151; CN 7; RHW
Keane, Molly .... **CLC 31**
See Keane, Mary Nesta (Skrine)
See also INT CA-114
Keates, Jonathan 1946(?)- .... **CLC 34**
See also CA 163; CANR 126
Keaton, Buster 1895-1966 .... **CLC 20**
See also CA 194
Keats, John 1795-1821 ...... **NCLC 8, 73, 121;
PC 1; WLC**
See also AAYA 58; BRW 4; BRWR 1; CD-
BLB 1789-1832; DA; DA3; DAB; DAC;
DAM MST, POET; DLB 96, 110; EXPP;
LMFS 1; PAB; PFS 1, 2, 3, 9, 17; RGEL
2; TEA; WLIT 3; WP
Keble, John 1792-1866 .... **NCLC 87**
See also DLB 32, 55; RGEL 2
Keene, Donald 1922- .... **CLC 34**
See also CA 1-4R; CANR 5, 119
Keillor, Garrison .... **CLC 40, 115**
See Keillor, Gary (Edward)
See also AAYA 2; BEST 89:3; BPFB 2;
DLBY 1987; EWL 3; SATA 58; TUS

Keillor, Gary (Edward) 1942-
See Keillor, Garrison
See also CA 111; 117; CANR 36, 59, 124;
CPW; DA3; DAM POP; MTCW 1, 2
Keith, Carlos
See Lewton, Val
Keith, Michael
See Hubbard, L(afayette) Ron(ald)
Keller, Gottfried 1819-1890 .... **NCLC 2; SSC
26**
See also CDWLB 2; DLB 129; EW; RGSF
2; RGWL 2, 3
Keller, Nora Okja 1965- .... **CLC 109**
See also CA 187
Kellerman, Jonathan 1949- .... **CLC 44**
See also AAYA 35; BEST 90:1; CA 106;
CANR 29, 51; CMW 4; CPW; DA3;
DAM POP; INT CANR-29
Kelley, William Melvin 1937- .... **CLC 22**
See also BW 1; CA 77-80; CANR 27, 83;
CN 7; DLB 33; EWL 3
Kellogg, Marjorie 1922- .... **CLC 2**
See also CA 81-84
Kellow, Kathleen
See Hibbert, Eleanor Alice Burford
Kelly, M(ilton) T(errence) 1947- ...... **CLC 55**
See also CA 97-100; CAAS 22; CANR 19,
43, 84; CN 7
Kelly, Robert 1935- .... **SSC 50**
See also CA 17-20R; CAAS 19; CANR 47;
CP 7; DLB 5, 130, 165
Kelman, James 1946- .... **CLC 58, 86**
See also BRWS 5; CA 148; CANR 85, 130;
CN 7; DLB 194; RGSF 2; WLIT 4
Kemal, Yasar
See Kemal, Yashar
See also CWW 2; EWL 3
Kemal, Yashar 1923(?)- .... **CLC 14, 29**
See also CA 89-92; CANR 44
Kemble, Fanny 1809-1893 .... **NCLC 18**
See also DLB 32
Kemelman, Harry 1908-1996 .... **CLC 2**
See also AITN 1; BPFB 2; CA 9-12R; 155;
CANR 6, 71; CMW 4; DLB 28
Kempe, Margery 1373(?)-1440(?) .. **LC 6, 56**
See also DLB 146; RGEL 2
Kempis, Thomas a 1380-1471 .... **LC 11**
Kendall, Henry 1839-1882 .... **NCLC 12**
See also DLB 230
Keneally, Thomas (Michael) 1935- ... **CLC 5,
8, 10, 14, 19, 27, 43, 117**
See also BRWS 4; CA 85-88; CANR 10,
50, 74, 130; CN 7; CPW; DA3; DAM
NOV; DLB 289, 299; EWL 3; MTCW 1,
2; NFS 17; RGEL 2; RHW
Kennedy, A(lison) L(ouise) 1965- ... **CLC 188**
See also CA 168, 213; CAAE 213; CANR
108; CD 5; CN 7; DLB 271; RGSF 2
Kennedy, Adrienne (Lita) 1931- .... **BLC 2;
CLC 66; DC 5**
See also AFAW 2; BW 2, 3; CA 103; CAAS
20; CABS 3; CANR 26, 53, 82; CD 5;
DAM MULT; DFS 9; DLB 38; FW
Kennedy, John Pendleton
1795-1870 .... **NCLC 2**
See also DLB 3, 248, 254; RGAL 4
Kennedy, Joseph Charles 1929-
See Kennedy, X. J.
See also CA 1-4R, 201; CAAE 201; CANR
4, 30, 40; CP 7; CWRI 5; MAICYA 2;
MAICYAS 1; SATA 14, 86, 130; SATA-
Essay 130
Kennedy, William 1928- ... **CLC 6, 28, 34, 53**
See also AAYA 1; AMWS 7; BPFB 2; CA
85-88; CANR 14, 31, 76; CN 7; DA3;
DAM NOV; DLB 143; DLBY 1985; EWL
3; INT CANR-31; MTCW 1, 2; SATA 57

Kirsch, Sarah 1935- .... **CLC 176**
See also CA 178; CWW 2; DLB 75; EWL 3

Kirshner, Sidney
See Kingsley, Sidney

Kis, Danilo 1935-1989 .... **CLC 57**
See also CA 109; 118; 129; CANR 61; CD-WLB 4; DLB 181; EWL 3; MTCW 1; RGSF 2; RGWL 2, 3

Kissinger, Henry A(lfred) 1923- ... **CLC 137**
See also CA 1-4R; CANR 2, 33, 66, 109; MTCW 1

Kivi, Aleksis 1834-1872 .... **NCLC 30**

Kizer, Carolyn (Ashley) 1925- ... **CLC 15, 39, 80**
See also CA 65-68; CAAS 5; CANR 24, 70; CP 7; CWP; DAM POET; DLB 5, 169; EWL 3; MTCW 2; PFS 18

Klabund 1890-1928 .... **TCLC 44**
See also CA 162; DLB 66

Klappert, Peter 1942- .... **CLC 57**
See also CA 33-36R; CSW; DLB 5

Klein, A(braham) M(oses) 1909-1972 .... **CLC 19**
See also CA 101; 37-40R; DAB; DAC; DAM MST; DLB 68; EWL 3; RGEL 2

Klein, Joe
See Klein, Joseph

Klein, Joseph 1946- .... **CLC 154**
See also CA 85-88; CANR 55

Klein, Norma 1938-1989 .... **CLC 30**
See also AAYA 2, 35; BPFB 2; BYA 6, 7, 8; CA 41-44R; 128; CANR 15, 37; CLR 2, 19; INT CANR-15; JRDA; MAICYA 1, 2; SAAS 1; SATA 7, 57; WYA; YAW

Klein, T(heodore) E(ibon) D(onald) 1947- .... **CLC 34**
See also CA 119; CANR 44, 75; HGG

Kleist, Heinrich von 1777-1811 ...... **NCLC 2, 37; SSC 22**
See also CDWLB 2; DAM DRAM; DLB 90; EW 5; RGSF 2; RGWL 2, 3

Klima, Ivan 1931- .... **CLC 56, 172**
See also CA 25-28R; CANR 17, 50, 91; CDWLB 4; CWW 2; DAM NOV; DLB 232; EWL 3; RGWL 3

Klimentev, Andrei Platonovich
See Klimentov, Andrei Platonovich

Klimentov, Andrei Platonovich 1899-1951 .... **SSC 42; TCLC 14**
See Platonov, Andrei Platonovich; Platonov, Andrey Platonovich
See also CA 108

Klinger, Friedrich Maximilian von 1752-1831 .... **NCLC 1**
See also DLB 94

Klingsor the Magician
See Hartmann, Sadakichi

Klopstock, Friedrich Gottlieb 1724-1803 .... **NCLC 11**
See also DLB 97; EW 4; RGWL 2, 3

Kluge, Alexander 1932- .... **SSC 61**
See also CA 81-84; DLB 75

Knapp, Caroline 1959-2002 .... **CLC 99**
See also CA 154; 207

Knebel, Fletcher 1911-1993 .... **CLC 14**
See also AITN 1; CA 1-4R; 140; CAAS 3; CANR 1, 36; SATA 36; SATA-Obit 75

Knickerbocker, Diedrich
See Irving, Washington

Knight, Etheridge 1931-1991 ... **BLC 2; CLC 40; PC 14**
See also BW 1, 3; CA 21-24R; 133; CANR 23, 82; DAM POET; DLB 41; MTCW 2; RGAL 4

Knight, Sarah Kemble 1666-1727 .... **LC 7**
See also DLB 24, 200

Knister, Raymond 1899-1932 .... **TCLC 56**
See also CA 186; DLB 68; RGEL 2

Knowles, John 1926-2001 ... **CLC 1, 4, 10, 26**
See also AAYA 10; AMWS 12; BPFB 2; BYA 3; CA 17-20R; 203; CANR 40, 74, 76, 132; CDALB 1968-1988; CLR 98; CN 7; DA; DAC; DAM MST, NOV; DLB 6; EXPN; MTCW 1, 2; NFS 2; RGAL 4; SATA 8, 89; SATA-Obit 134; YAW

Knox, Calvin M.
See Silverberg, Robert

Knox, John c. 1505-1572 .... **LC 37**
See also DLB 132

Knye, Cassandra
See Disch, Thomas M(ichael)

Koch, C(hristopher) J(ohn) 1932- .... **CLC 42**
See also CA 127; CANR 84; CN 7; DLB 289

Koch, Christopher
See Koch, C(hristopher) J(ohn)

Koch, Kenneth (Jay) 1925-2002 .... **CLC 5, 8, 44**
See also CA 1-4R; 207; CAD; CANR 6, 36, 57, 97, 131; CD 5; CP 7; DAM POET; DLB 5; INT CANR-36; MTCW 2; PFS 20; SATA 65; WP

Kochanowski, Jan 1530-1584 .... **LC 10**
See also RGWL 2, 3

Kock, Charles Paul de 1794-1871 . **NCLC 16**

Koda Rohan
See Koda Shigeyuki

Koda Rohan
See Koda Shigeyuki
See also DLB 180

Koda Shigeyuki 1867-1947 .... **TCLC 22**
See Koda Rohan
See also CA 121; 183

Koestler, Arthur 1905-1983 ... **CLC 1, 3, 6, 8, 15, 33**
See also BRWS 1; CA 1-4R; 109; CANR 1, 33; CDBLB 1945-1960; DLBY 1983; EWL 3; MTCW 1, 2; NFS 19; RGEL 2

Kogawa, Joy Nozomi 1935- ...... **CLC 78, 129**
See also AAYA 47; CA 101; CANR 19, 62, 126; CN 7; CWP; DAC; DAM MST, MULT; FW; MTCW 2; NFS 3; SATA 99

Kohout, Pavel 1928- .... **CLC 13**
See also CA 45-48; CANR 3

Koizumi, Yakumo
See Hearn, (Patricio) Lafcadio (Tessima Carlos)

Kolmar, Gertrud 1894-1943 .... **TCLC 40**
See also CA 167; EWL 3

Komunyakaa, Yusef 1947- .. **BLCS; CLC 86, 94; PC 51**
See also AFAW 2; AMWS 13; CA 147; CANR 83; CP 7; CSW; DLB 120; EWL 3; PFS 5, 20; RGAL 4

Konrad, George
See Konrad, Gyorgy

Konrad, Gyorgy 1933- .... **CLC 4, 10, 73**
See also CA 85-88; CANR 97; CDWLB 4; CWW 2; DLB 232; EWL 3

Konwicki, Tadeusz 1926- .... **CLC 8, 28, 54, 117**
See also CA 101; CAAS 9; CANR 39, 59; CWW 2; DLB 232; EWL 3; IDFW 3; MTCW 1

Koontz, Dean R(ay) 1945- .... **CLC 78**
See also AAYA 9, 31; BEST 89:3, 90:2; CA 108; CANR 19, 36, 52, 95; CMW 4; CPW; DA3; DAM NOV, POP; DLB 292; HGG; MTCW 1; SATA 92; SFW 4; SUFW 2; YAW

Kopernik, Mikolaj
See Copernicus, Nicolaus

Kopit, Arthur (Lee) 1937- ...... **CLC 1, 18, 33**
See also AITN 1; CA 81-84; CABS 3; CD 5; DAM DRAM; DFS 7, 14; DLB 7; MTCW 1; RGAL 4

Kopitar, Jernej (Bartholomaus) 1780-1844 .... **NCLC 117**

Kops, Bernard 1926- .... **CLC 4**
See also CA 5-8R; CANR 84; CBD; CN 7; CP 7; DLB 13

Kornbluth, C(yril) M. 1923-1958 .... **TCLC 8**
See also CA 105; 160; DLB 8; SFW 4

Korolenko, V. G.
See Korolenko, Vladimir Galaktionovich

Korolenko, Vladimir
See Korolenko, Vladimir Galaktionovich

Korolenko, Vladimir G.
See Korolenko, Vladimir Galaktionovich

Korolenko, Vladimir Galaktionovich 1853-1921 .... **TCLC 22**
See also CA 121; DLB 277

Korzybski, Alfred (Habdank Skarbek) 1879-1950 .... **TCLC 61**
See also CA 123; 160

Kosinski, Jerzy (Nikodem) 1933-1991 .... **CLC 1, 2, 3, 6, 10, 15, 53, 70**
See also AMWS 7; BPFB 2; CA 17-20R; 134; CANR 9, 46; DA3; DAM NOV; DLB 2, 299; DLBY 1982; EWL 3; HGG; MTCW 1, 2; NFS 12; RGAL 4; TUS

Kostelanetz, Richard (Cory) 1940- .. **CLC 28**
See also CA 13-16R; CAAS 8; CANR 38, 77; CN 7; CP 7

Kostrowitzki, Wilhelm Apollinaris de 1880-1918
See Apollinaire, Guillaume
See also CA 104

Kotlowitz, Robert 1924- .... **CLC 4**
See also CA 33-36R; CANR 36

Kotzebue, August (Friedrich Ferdinand) von 1761-1819 .... **NCLC 25**
See also DLB 94

Kotzwinkle, William 1938- ..... **CLC 5, 14, 35**
See also BPFB 2; CA 45-48; CANR 3, 44, 84, 129; CLR 6; DLB 173; FANT; MAICYA 1, 2; SATA 24, 70, 146; SFW 4; SUFW 2; YAW

Kowna, Stancy
See Szymborska, Wislawa

Kozol, Jonathan 1936- .... **CLC 17**
See also AAYA 46; CA 61-64; CANR 16, 45, 96

Kozoll, Michael 1940(?)- .... **CLC 35**

Kramer, Kathryn 19(?)- .... **CLC 34**

Kramer, Larry 1935- .... **CLC 42; DC 8**
See also CA 124; 126; CANR 60, 132; DAM POP; DLB 249; GLL 1

Krasicki, Ignacy 1735-1801 .... **NCLC 8**

Krasinski, Zygmunt 1812-1859 .... **NCLC 4**
See also RGWL 2, 3

Kraus, Karl 1874-1936 .... **TCLC 5**
See also CA 104; 216; DLB 118; EWL 3

Kreve (Mickevicius), Vincas 1882-1954 .... **TCLC 27**
See also CA 170; DLB 220; EWL 3

Kristeva, Julia 1941- .... **CLC 77, 140**
See also CA 154; CANR 99; DLB 242; EWL 3; FW; LMFS 2

Kristofferson, Kris 1936- .... **CLC 26**
See also CA 104

Krizanc, John 1956- .... **CLC 57**
See also CA 187

Krleza, Miroslav 1893-1981 .... **CLC 8, 114**
See also CA 97-100; 105; CANR 50; CD-WLB 4; DLB 147; EW 11; RGWL 2, 3

Kroetsch, Robert 1927- .. **CLC 5, 23, 57, 132**
See also CA 17-20R; CANR 8, 38; CCA 1; CN 7; CP 7; DAC; DAM POET; DLB 53; MTCW 1

Kroetz, Franz
See Kroetz, Franz Xaver

Kroetz, Franz Xaver 1946- .... **CLC 41**
    See also CA 130; CWW 2; EWL 3
Kroker, Arthur (W.) 1945- .... **CLC 77**
    See also CA 161
Kropotkin, Peter (Aleksieevich)
    1842-1921 .... **TCLC 36**
    See Kropotkin, Petr Alekseevich
    See also CA 119; 219
Kropotkin, Petr Alekseevich
    See Kropotkin, Peter (Aleksieevich)
    See also DLB 277
Krotkov, Yuri 1917-1981 .... **CLC 19**
    See also CA 102
Krumb
    See Crumb, R(obert)
Krumgold, Joseph (Quincy)
    1908-1980 .... **CLC 12**
    See also BYA 1, 2; CA 9-12R; 101; CANR
    7; MAICYA 1, 2; SATA 1, 48; SATA-Obit
    23; YAW
Krumwitz
    See Crumb, R(obert)
Krutch, Joseph Wood 1893-1970 ..... **CLC 24**
    See also ANW; CA 1-4R; 25-28R; CANR
    4; DLB 63, 206, 275
Krutzch, Gus
    See Eliot, T(homas) S(tearns)
Krylov, Ivan Andreevich
    1768(?)-1844 .... **NCLC 1**
    See also DLB 150
Kubin, Alfred (Leopold Isidor)
    1877-1959 .... **TCLC 23**
    See also CA 112; 149; CANR 104; DLB 81
Kubrick, Stanley 1928-1999 .... **CLC 16;
    TCLC 112**
    See also AAYA 30; CA 81-84; 177; CANR
    33; DLB 26
Kumin, Maxine (Winokur) 1925- ..... **CLC 5,
    13, 28, 164; PC 15**
    See also AITN 2; AMWS 4; ANW; CA
    1-4R; CAAS 8; CANR 1, 21, 69, 115; CP
    7; CWP; DA3; DAM POET; DLB 5;
    EWL 3; EXPP; MTCW 1, 2; PAB; PFS
    18; SATA 12
Kundera, Milan 1929- . **CLC 4, 9, 19, 32, 68,
    115, 135; SSC 24**
    See also AAYA 2; BPFB 2; CA 85-88;
    CANR 19, 52, 74; CDWLB 4; CWW 2;
    DA3; DAM NOV; DLB 232; EW 13;
    EWL 3; MTCW 1, 2; NFS 18; RGSF 2;
    RGWL 3; SSFS 10
Kunene, Mazisi (Raymond) 1930- ... **CLC 85**
    See also BW 1, 3; CA 125; CANR 81; CP
    7; DLB 117
Kung, Hans .... **CLC 130**
    See Kung, Hans
Kung, Hans 1928-
    See Kung, Hans
    See also CA 53-56; CANR 66; MTCW 1, 2
Kunikida Doppo 1869(?)-1908
    See Doppo, Kunikida
    See also DLB 180; EWL 3
Kunitz, Stanley (Jasspon) 1905- .. **CLC 6, 11,
    14, 148; PC 19**
    See also AMWS 3; CA 41-44R; CANR 26,
    57, 98; CP 7; DA3; DLB 48; INT CANR-
    26; MTCW 1, 2; PFS 11; RGAL 4
Kunze, Reiner 1933- .... **CLC 10**
    See also CA 93-96; CWW 2; DLB 75; EWL
    3
Kuprin, Aleksandr Ivanovich
    1870-1938 .... **TCLC 5**
    See Kuprin, Aleksandr Ivanovich; Kuprin,
    Alexandr Ivanovich
    See also CA 104; 182
Kuprin, Aleksandr Ivanovich
    See Kuprin, Aleksander Ivanovich
    See also DLB 295

Kuprin, Alexandr Ivanovich
    See Kuprin, Aleksander Ivanovich
    See also EWL 3
Kureishi, Hanif 1954(?)- .... **CLC 64, 135**
    See also CA 139; CANR 113; CBD; CD 5;
    CN 7; DLB 194, 245; GLL 2; IDFW 4;
    WLIT 4; WWE 1
Kurosawa, Akira 1910-1998 ..... **CLC 16, 119**
    See also AAYA 11; CA 101; 170; CANR
    46; DAM MULT
Kushner, Tony 1956(?)- .... **CLC 81; DC 10**
    See also AMWS 9; CA 144; CAD; CANR
    74, 130; CD 5; DA3; DAM DRAM; DFS
    5; DLB 228; EWL 3; GLL 1; LAIT 5;
    MTCW 2; RGAL 4
Kuttner, Henry 1915-1958 .... **TCLC 10**
    See also CA 107; 157; DLB 8; FANT;
    SCFW 2; SFW 4
Kutty, Madhavi
    See Das, Kamala
Kuzma, Greg 1944- .... **CLC 7**
    See also CA 33-36R; CANR 70
Kuzmin, Mikhail (Alekseevich)
    1872(?)-1936 .... **TCLC 40**
    See also CA 170; DLB 295; EWL 3
Kyd, Thomas 1558-1594 .... **DC 3; LC 22**
    See also BRW 1; DAM DRAM; DLB 62;
    IDTP; LMFS 1; RGEL 2; TEA; WLIT 3
Kyprianos, Iossif
    See Samarakis, Antonis
L. S.
    See Stephen, Sir Leslie
Laʒamon
    See Layamon
    See also DLB 146
Labrunie, Gerard
    See Nerval, Gerard de
La Bruyere, Jean de 1645-1696 .... **LC 17**
    See also DLB 268; EW 3; GFL Beginnings
    to 1789
Lacan, Jacques (Marie Emile)
    1901-1981 .... **CLC 75**
    See also CA 121; 104; DLB 296; EWL 3;
    TWA
Laclos, Pierre Ambroise Francois
    1741-1803 .... **NCLC 4, 87**
    See also EW 4; GFL Beginnings to 1789;
    RGWL 2, 3
Lacolere, Francois
    See Aragon, Louis
La Colere, Francois
    See Aragon, Louis
La Deshabilleuse
    See Simenon, Georges (Jacques Christian)
Lady Gregory
    See Gregory, Lady Isabella Augusta (Persse)
Lady of Quality, A
    See Bagnold, Enid
La Fayette, Marie-(Madelaine Pioche de la
    Vergne) 1634-1693 .... **LC 2**
    See Lafayette, Marie-Madeleine
    See also GFL Beginnings to 1789; RGWL
    2, 3
Lafayette, Marie-Madeleine
    See La Fayette, Marie-(Madelaine Pioche
    de la Vergne)
    See also DLB 268
Lafayette, Rene
    See Hubbard, L(afayette) Ron(ald)
La Flesche, Francis 1857(?)-1932 ...... **NNAL**
    See also CA 144; CANR 83; DLB 175
La Fontaine, Jean de 1621-1695 .... **LC 50**
    See also DLB 268; EW 3; GFL Beginnings
    to 1789; MAICYA 1, 2; RGWL 2, 3;
    SATA 18
Laforgue, Jules 1860-1887 . **NCLC 5, 53; PC
    14; SSC 20**
    See also DLB 217; EW 7; GFL 1789 to the
    Present; RGWL 2, 3

Lagerkvist, Paer (Fabian)
    1891-1974 ..... **CLC 7, 10, 13, 54; TCLC
    144**
    See Lagerkvist, Par
    See also CA 85-88; 49-52; DA3; DAM
    DRAM, NOV; MTCW 1, 2; TWA
Lagerkvist, Par .... **SSC 12**
    See Lagerkvist, Paer (Fabian)
    See also DLB 259; EW 10; EWL 3; MTCW
    2; RGSF 2; RGWL 2, 3
Lagerloef, Selma (Ottiliana Lovisa)
    1858-1940 .... **TCLC 4, 36**
    See Lagerlof, Selma (Ottiliana Lovisa)
    See also CA 108; MTCW 2; SATA 15
Lagerlof, Selma (Ottiliana Lovisa)
    See Lagerloef, Selma (Ottiliana Lovisa)
    See also CLR 7; SATA 15
La Guma, (Justin) Alex(ander)
    1925-1985 . **BLCS; CLC 19; TCLC 140**
    See also AFW; BW 1, 3; CA 49-52; 118;
    CANR 25, 81; CDWLB 3; DAM NOV;
    DLB 117, 225; EWL 3; MTCW 1, 2;
    WLIT 2; WWE 1
Laidlaw, A. K.
    See Grieve, C(hristopher) M(urray)
Lainez, Manuel Mujica
    See Mujica Lainez, Manuel
    See also HW 1
Laing, R(onald) D(avid) 1927-1989 . **CLC 95**
    See also CA 107; 129; CANR 34; MTCW 1
Laishley, Alex
    See Booth, Martin
Lamartine, Alphonse (Marie Louis Prat) de
    1790-1869 .... **NCLC 11; PC 16**
    See also DAM POET; DLB 217; GFL 1789
    to the Present; RGWL 2, 3
Lamb, Charles 1775-1834 ..... **NCLC 10, 113;
    WLC**
    See also BRW 4; CDBLB 1789-1832; DA;
    DAB; DAC; DAM MST; DLB 93, 107,
    163; RGEL 2; SATA 17; TEA
Lamb, Lady Caroline 1785-1828 ... **NCLC 38**
    See also DLB 116
Lamb, Mary Ann 1764-1847 .... **NCLC 125**
    See also DLB 163; SATA 17
Lame Deer 1903(?)-1976 .... **NNAL**
    See also CA 69-72
Lamming, George (William) 1927- ... **BLC 2;
    CLC 2, 4, 66, 144**
    See also BW 2, 3; CA 85-88; CANR 26,
    76; CDWLB 3; CN 7; DAM MULT; DLB
    125; EWL 3; MTCW 1, 2; NFS 15; RGEL
    2
L'Amour, Louis (Dearborn)
    1908-1988 .... **CLC 25, 55**
    See Burns, Tex; Mayo, Jim
    See also AAYA 16; AITN 2; BEST 89:2;
    BPFB 2; CA 1-4R; 125; CANR 3, 25, 40;
    CPW; DA3; DAM NOV, POP; DLB 206;
    DLBY 1980; MTCW 1, 2; RGAL 4
Lampedusa, Giuseppe (Tomasi) di
    .... **TCLC 13**
    See Tomasi di Lampedusa, Giuseppe
    See also CA 164; EW 11; MTCW 2; RGWL
    2, 3
Lampman, Archibald 1861-1899 ... **NCLC 25**
    See also DLB 92; RGEL 2; TWA
Lancaster, Bruce 1896-1963 .... **CLC 36**
    See also CA 9-10; CANR 70; CAP 1; SATA
    9
Lanchester, John 1962- .... **CLC 99**
    See also CA 194; DLB 267
Landau, Mark Alexandrovich
    See Aldanov, Mark (Alexandrovich)
Landau-Aldanov, Mark Alexandrovich
    See Aldanov, Mark (Alexandrovich)
Landis, Jerry
    See Simon, Paul (Frederick)

Leautaud, Paul 1872-1956 .... **TCLC 83**
See also CA 203; DLB 65; GFL 1789 to the
Present

Leavis, F(rank) R(aymond)
1895-1978 .... **CLC 24**
See also BRW 7; CA 21-24R; 77-80; CANR
44; DLB 242; EWL 3; MTCW 1, 2;
RGEL 2

Leavitt, David 1961- .... **CLC 34**
See also CA 116; 122; CANR 50, 62, 101;
CPW; DA3; DAM POP; DLB 130; GLL
1; INT CA-122; MTCW 2

Leblanc, Maurice (Marie Emile)
1864-1941 .... **TCLC 49**
See also CA 110; CMW 4

Lebowitz, Fran(ces Ann) 1951(?)- ... **CLC 11,
36**
See also CA 81-84; CANR 14, 60, 70; INT
CANR-14; MTCW 1

Lebrecht, Peter
See Tieck, (Johann) Ludwig

le Carre, John .... **CLC 3, 5, 9, 15, 28**
See Cornwell, David (John Moore)
See also AAYA 42; BEST 89:4; BPFB 2;
BRWS 2; CDBLB 1960 to Present; CMW
4; CN 7; CPW; DLB 87; EWL 3; MSW;
MTCW 2; RGEL 2; TEA

Le Clezio, J(ean) M(arie) G(ustave)
1940- .... **CLC 31, 155**
See also CA 116; 128; CWW 2; DLB 83;
EWL 3; GFL 1789 to the Present; RGSF
2

Leconte de Lisle, Charles-Marie-Rene
1818-1894 .... **NCLC 29**
See also DLB 217; EW 6; GFL 1789 to the
Present

Le Coq, Monsieur
See Simenon, Georges (Jacques Christian)

Leduc, Violette 1907-1972 .... **CLC 22**
See also CA 13-14; 33-36R; CANR 69;
CAP 1; EWL 3; GFL 1789 to the Present;
GLL 1

Ledwidge, Francis 1887(?)-1917 .... **TCLC 23**
See also CA 123; 203; DLB 20

Lee, Andrea 1953- .... **BLC 2; CLC 36**
See also BW 1, 3; CA 125; CANR 82;
DAM MULT

Lee, Andrew
See Auchincloss, Louis (Stanton)

Lee, Chang-rae 1965- .... **CLC 91**
See also CA 148; CANR 89; LATS 1:2

Lee, Don L. .... **CLC 2**
See Madhubuti, Haki R.

Lee, George W(ashington)
1894-1976 .... **BLC 2; CLC 52**
See also BW 1; CA 125; CANR 83; DAM
MULT; DLB 51

Lee, (Nelle) Harper 1926- . **CLC 12, 60, 194;
WLC**
See also AAYA 13; AMWS 8; BPFB 2;
BYA 3; CA 13-16R; CANR 51, 128;
CDALB 1941-1968; CSW; DA; DA3;
DAB; DAC; DAM MST, NOV; DLB 6;
EXPN; LAIT 3; MTCW 1, 2; NFS 2;
SATA 11; WYA; YAW

Lee, Helen Elaine 1959(?)- .... **CLC 86**
See also CA 148

Lee, John .... **CLC 70**

Lee, Julian
See Latham, Jean Lee

Lee, Larry
See Lee, Lawrence

Lee, Laurie 1914-1997 .... **CLC 90**
See also CA 77-80; 158; CANR 33, 73; CP
7; CPW; DAB; DAM POP; DLB 27;
MTCW 1; RGEL 2

Lee, Lawrence 1941-1990 .... **CLC 34**
See also CA 131; CANR 43

Lee, Li-Young 1957- .... **CLC 164; PC 24**
See also CA 153; CANR 118; CP 7; DLB
165; LMFS 2; PFS 11, 15, 17

Lee, Manfred B(ennington)
1905-1971 .... **CLC 11**
See Queen, Ellery
See also CA 1-4R; 29-32R; CANR 2; CMW
4; DLB 137

Lee, Nathaniel 1645(?)-1692 .... **LC 103**
See also DLB 80; RGEL 2

Lee, Shelton Jackson 1957(?)- .. **BLCS; CLC
105**
See Lee, Spike
See also BW 2, 3; CA 125; CANR 42;
DAM MULT

Lee, Spike
See Lee, Shelton Jackson
See also AAYA 4, 29

Lee, Stan 1922- .... **CLC 17**
See also AAYA 5, 49; CA 108; 111; CANR
129; INT CA-111

Lee, Tanith 1947- .... **CLC 46**
See also AAYA 15; CA 37-40R; CANR 53,
102; DLB 261; FANT; SATA 8, 88, 134;
SFW 4; SUFW 1, 2; YAW

Lee, Vernon .... **SSC 33; TCLC 5**
See Paget, Violet
See also DLB 57, 153, 156, 174, 178; GLL
1; SUFW 1

Lee, William
See Burroughs, William S(eward)
See also GLL 1

Lee, Willy
See Burroughs, William S(eward)
See also GLL 1

Lee-Hamilton, Eugene (Jacob)
1845-1907 .... **TCLC 22**
See also CA 117

Leet, Judith 1935- .... **CLC 11**
See also CA 187

Le Fanu, Joseph Sheridan
1814-1873 .... **NCLC 9, 58; SSC 14**
See also CMW 4; DA3; DAM POP; DLB
21; 70, 159, 178; HGG; RGEL 2; RGSF
2; SUFW 1

Leffland, Ella 1931- .... **CLC 19**
See also CA 29-32R; CANR 35, 78, 82;
DLBY 1984; INT CANR-35; SATA 65

Leger, Alexis
See Leger, (Marie-Rene Auguste) Alexis
Saint-Leger

**Leger, (Marie-Rene Auguste) Alexis
Saint-Leger** 1887-1975 .. **CLC 4, 11, 46;
PC 23**
See Perse, Saint-John; Saint-John Perse
See also CA 13-16R; 61-64; CANR 43;
DAM POET; MTCW 1

Leger, Saintleger
See Leger, (Marie-Rene Auguste) Alexis
Saint-Leger

Le Guin, Ursula K(roeber) 1929- ..... **CLC 8,
13, 22, 45, 71, 136; SSC 12, 69**
See also AAYA 9, 27; AITN 1; BPFB 2;
BYA 5, 8, 11, 14; CA 21-24R; CANR 9,
32, 52, 74, 132; CDALB 1968-1988; CLR
3, 28, 91; CN 7; CPW; DA3; DAB; DAC;
DAM MST, POP; DLB 8, 52, 256, 275;
EXPS; FANT; FW; INT CANR-32;
JRDA; LAIT 5; MAICYA 1, 2; MTCW 1,
2; NFS 6, 9; SATA 4, 52, 99, 149; SCFW;
SFW 4; SSFS 2; SUFW 1, 2; WYA; YAW

Lehmann, Rosamond (Nina)
1901-1990 .... **CLC 5**
See also CA 77-80; 131; CANR 8, 73; DLB
15; MTCW 2; RGEL 2; RHW

Leiber, Fritz (Reuter, Jr.)
1910-1992 .... **CLC 25**
See also BPFB 2; CA 45-48; 139; CANR 2,
40, 86; DLB 8; FANT; HGG; MTCW 1,
2; SATA 45; SATA-Obit 73; SCFW 2;
SFW 4; SUFW 1, 2

Leibniz, Gottfried Wilhelm von
1646-1716 .... **LC 35**
See also DLB 168

Leimbach, Martha 1963-
See Leimbach, Marti
See also CA 130

Leimbach, Marti .... **CLC 65**
See Leimbach, Martha

Leino, Eino .... **TCLC 24**
See Lonnbohm, Armas Eino Leopold
See also EWL 3

Leiris, Michel (Julien) 1901-1990 ..... **CLC 61**
See also CA 119; 128; 132; EWL 3; GFL
1789 to the Present

Leithauser, Brad 1953- .... **CLC 27**
See also CA 107; CANR 27, 81; CP 7; DLB
120, 282

le Jars de Gournay, Marie
See de Gournay, Marie le Jars

Lelchuk, Alan 1938- .... **CLC 5**
See also CA 45-48; CAAS 20; CANR 1,
70; CN 7

Lem, Stanislaw 1921- ...... **CLC 8, 15, 40, 149**
See also CA 105; CAAS 1; CANR 32;
CWW 2; MTCW 1; SCFW 2; SFW 4

Lemann, Nancy (Elise) 1956- .... **CLC 39**
See also CA 118; 136; CANR 121

Lemonnier, (Antoine Louis) Camille
1844-1913 .... **TCLC 22**
See also CA 121

Lenau, Nikolaus 1802-1850 .... **NCLC 16**

L'Engle, Madeleine (Camp Franklin)
1918- .... **CLC 12**
See also AAYA 28; AITN 2; BPFB 2; BYA
2, 4, 5, 7; CA 1-4R; CANR 3, 21, 39, 66,
107; CLR 1, 14, 57; CPW; CWRI 5; DA3;
DAM POP; DLB 52; JRDA; MAICYA 1,
2; MTCW 1, 2; SAAS 15; SATA 1, 27,
75, 128; SFW 4; WYA; YAW

Lengyel, Jozsef 1896-1975 .... **CLC 7**
See also CA 85-88; 57-60; CANR 71;
RGSF 2

Lenin 1870-1924
See Lenin, V. I.
See also CA 121; 168

Lenin, V. I. .... **TCLC 67**
See Lenin

Lennon, John (Ono) 1940-1980 .. **CLC 12, 35**
See also CA 102; SATA 114

Lennox, Charlotte Ramsay
1729(?)-1804 .... **NCLC 23, 134**
See also DLB 39; RGEL 2

Lentricchia, Frank, (Jr.) 1940- .... **CLC 34**
See also CA 25-28R; CANR 19, 106; DLB
246

Lenz, Gunter .... **CLC 65**

Lenz, Jakob Michael Reinhold
1751-1792 .... **LC 100**
See also DLB 94; RGWL 2, 3

Lenz, Siegfried 1926- .... **CLC 27; SSC 33**
See also CA 89-92; CANR 80; CWW 2;
DLB 75; EWL 3; RGSF 2; RGWL 2, 3

Leon, David
See Jacob, (Cyprien-)Max

Leonard, Elmore (John, Jr.) 1925- . **CLC 28,
34, 71, 120**
See also AAYA 22, 59; AITN 1; BEST 89:1,
90:4; BPFB 2; CA 81-84; CANR 12, 28,
53, 76, 96, 133; CMW 4; CN 7; CPW;
DA3; DAM POP; DLB 173, 226; INT
CANR-28; MSW; MTCW 1, 2; RGAL 4;
TCWW 2

Machado de Assis, Joaquim Maria
1839-1908 .... **BLC 2; HLCS 2; SSC 24; TCLC 10**
See also CA 107; 153; CANR 91; LAW; RGSF 2, 3; TWA; WLIT 1

Machaut, Guillaume de c.
1300-1377 .... **CMLC 64**
See also DLB 208

Machen, Arthur .... **SSC 20; TCLC 4**
See Jones, Arthur Llewellyn
See also CA 179; DLB 156, 178; RGEL 2; SUFW 1

Machiavelli, Niccolo 1469-1527 ... **DC 16; LC 8, 36; WLCS**
See also AAYA 58; DA; DAB; DAC; DAM MST; EW 2; LAIT 1; LMFS 1; NFS 9; RGWL 2, 3; TWA

MacInnes, Colin 1914-1976 .... **CLC 4, 23**
See also CA 69-72; 65-68; CANR 21; DLB 14; MTCW 1, 2; RGEL 2; RHW

MacInnes, Helen (Clark)
1907-1985 .... **CLC 27, 39**
See also BPFB 2; CA 1-4R; 117; CANR 1, 28, 58; CMW 4; CPW; DAM POP; DLB 87; MSW; MTCW 1, 2; SATA 22; SATA-Obit 44

Mackay, Mary 1855-1924
See Corelli, Marie
See also CA 118; 177; FANT; RHW

Mackay, Shena 1944- .... **CLC 195**
See also CA 104; CANR 88; DLB 231

Mackenzie, Compton (Edward Montague)
1883-1972 .... **CLC 18; TCLC 116**
See also CA 21-22; 37-40R; CAP 2; DLB 34, 100; RGEL 2

Mackenzie, Henry 1745-1831 .... **NCLC 41**
See also DLB 39; RGEL 2

Mackey, Nathaniel (Ernest) 1947- .... **PC 49**
See also CA 153; CANR 114; CP 7; DLB 169

MacKinnon, Catharine A. 1946- ... **CLC 181**
See also CA 128; 132; CANR 73; FW; MTCW 2

Mackintosh, Elizabeth 1896(?)-1952
See Tey, Josephine
See also CA 110; CMW 4

MacLaren, James
See Grieve, C(hristopher) M(urray)

Mac Laverty, Bernard 1942- .... **CLC 31**
See also CA 116; 118; CANR 43, 88; CN 7; DLB 267; INT CA-118; RGSF 2

MacLean, Alistair (Stuart)
1922(?)-1987 .... **CLC 3, 13, 50, 63**
See also CA 57-60; 121; CANR 28, 61; CMW 4; CPW; DAM POP; DLB 276; MTCW 1; SATA 23; SATA-Obit 50; TCWW 2

Maclean, Norman (Fitzroy)
1902-1990 .... **CLC 78; SSC 13**
See also CA 102; 132; CANR 49; CPW; DAM POP; DLB 206; TCWW 2

MacLeish, Archibald 1892-1982 ... **CLC 3, 8, 14, 68; PC 47**
See also AMW; CA 9-12R; 106; CAD; CANR 33, 63; CDALBS; DAM POET; DFS 15; DLB 4, 7, 45; DLBY 1982; EWL 3; EXPP; MTCW 1, 2; PAB; PFS 5; RGAL 4; TUS

MacLennan, (John) Hugh
1907-1990 .... **CLC 2, 14, 92**
See also CA 5-8R; 142; CANR 33; DAC; DAM MST; DLB 68; EWL 3; MTCW 1, 2; RGEL 2; TWA

MacLeod, Alistair 1936- .... **CLC 56, 165**
See also CA 123; CCA 1; DAC; DAM MST; DLB 60; MTCW 2; RGSF 2

Macleod, Fiona
See Sharp, William
See also RGEL 2; SUFW

MacNeice, (Frederick) Louis
1907-1963 .... **CLC 1, 4, 10, 53; PC 61**
See also BRW 7; CA 85-88; CANR 61; DAB; DAM POET; DLB 10, 20; EWL 3; MTCW 1, 2; RGEL 2

MacNeill, Dand
See Fraser, George MacDonald

Macpherson, James 1736-1796 .... **LC 29**
See Ossian
See also BRWS 8; DLB 109; RGEL 2

Macpherson, (Jean) Jay 1931- .... **CLC 14**
See also CA 5-8R; CANR 90; CP 7; CWP; DLB 53

Macrobius fl. 430- .... **CMLC 48**

MacShane, Frank 1927-1999 .... **CLC 39**
See also CA 9-12R; 186; CANR 3, 33; DLB 111

Macumber, Mari
See Sandoz, Mari(e Susette)

Madach, Imre 1823-1864 .... **NCLC 19**

Madden, (Jerry) David 1933- .... **CLC 5, 15**
See also CA 1-4R; CAAS 3; CANR 4, 45; CN 7; CSW; DLB 6; MTCW 1

Maddern, Al(an)
See Ellison, Harlan (Jay)

Madhubuti, Haki R. 1942- ... **BLC 2; CLC 6, 73; PC 5**
See Lee, Don L.
See also BW 2, 3; CA 73-76; CANR 24, 51, 73; CP 7; CSW; DAM MULT, POET; DLB 5, 41; DLBD 8; EWL 3; MTCW 2; RGAL 4

Madison, James 1751-1836 .... **NCLC 126**
See also DLB 37

Maepenn, Hugh
See Kuttner, Henry

Maepenn, K. H.
See Kuttner, Henry

Maeterlinck, Maurice 1862-1949 ..... **TCLC 3**
See also CA 104; 136; CANR 80; DAM DRAM; DLB 192; EW 8; EWL 3; GFL 1789 to the Present; LMFS 2; RGWL 2, 3; SATA 66; TWA

Maginn, William 1794-1842 .... **NCLC 8**
See also DLB 110, 159

Mahapatra, Jayanta 1928- .... **CLC 33**
See also CA 73-76; CAAS 9; CANR 15, 33, 66, 87; CP 7; DAM MULT

Mahfouz, Naguib (Abdel Aziz Al-Sabilgi)
1911(?)- .... **CLC 153; SSC 66**
See Mahfuz, Najib (Abdel Aziz al-Sabilgi)
See also AAYA 49; BEST 89:2; CA 128; CANR 55, 101; DA3; DAM NOV; MTCW 1, 2; RGWL 2, 3; SSFS 9

Mahfuz, Najib (Abdel Aziz al-Sabilgi)
.... **CLC 52, 55**
See Mahfouz, Naguib (Abdel Aziz Al-Sabilgi)
See also AFW; CWW 2; DLBY 1988; EWL 3; RGSF 2; WLIT 2

Mahon, Derek 1941- .... **CLC 27; PC 60**
See also BRWS 6; CA 113; 128; CANR 88; CP 7; DLB 40; EWL 3

Maiakovskii, Vladimir
See Mayakovski, Vladimir (Vladimirovich)
See also IDTP; RGWL 2, 3

Mailer, Norman (Kingsley) 1923- . **CLC 1, 2, 3, 4, 5, 8, 11, 14, 28, 39, 74, 111**
See also AAYA 31; AITN 2; AMW; AMWC 2; AMWR 2; BPFB 2; CA 9-12R; CABS 1; CANR 28, 74, 77, 130; CDALB 1968-1988; CN 7; CPW; DA; DA3; DAB; DAC; DAM MST, NOV, POP; DLB 2, 16, 28, 185, 278; DLBD 3; DLBY 1980, 1983; EWL 3; MTCW 1, 2; NFS 10; RGAL 4; TUS

Maillet, Antonine 1929- .... **CLC 54, 118**
See also CA 115; 120; CANR 46, 74, 77; CCA 1; CWW 2; DAC; DLB 60; INT CA-120; MTCW 2

Mais, Roger 1905-1955 .... **TCLC 8**
See also BW 1, 3; CA 105; 124; CANR 82; CDWLB 3; DLB 125; EWL 3; MTCW 1; RGEL 2

Maistre, Joseph 1753-1821 .... **NCLC 37**
See also GFL 1789 to the Present

Maitland, Frederic William
1850-1906 .... **TCLC 65**

Maitland, Sara (Louise) 1950- .... **CLC 49**
See also CA 69-72; CANR 13, 59; DLB 271; FW

Major, Clarence 1936- ... **BLC 2; CLC 3, 19, 48**
See also AFAW 2; BW 2, 3; CA 21-24R; CAAS 6; CANR 13, 25, 53, 82; CN 7; CP 7; CSW; DAM MULT; DLB 33; EWL 3; MSW

Major, Kevin (Gerald) 1949- .... **CLC 26**
See also AAYA 16; CA 97-100; CANR 21, 38, 112; CLR 11; DAC; DLB 60; INT CANR-21; JRDA; MAICYA 1, 2; MAIC-YAS 1; SATA 32, 82, 134; WYA; YAW

Maki, James
See Ozu, Yasujiro

Malabaila, Damiano
See Levi, Primo

Malamud, Bernard 1914-1986 .. **CLC 1, 2, 3, 5, 8, 9, 11, 18, 27, 44, 78, 85; SSC 15; TCLC 129; WLC**
See also AAYA 16; AMWS 1; BPFB 2; BYA 15; CA 5-8R; 118; CABS 1; CANR 28, 62, 114; CDALB 1941-1968; CPW; DA; DA3; DAB; DAC; DAM MST, NOV, POP; DLB 2, 28, 152; DLBY 1980, 1986; EWL 3; EXPS; LAIT 4; LATS 1:1; MTCW 1, 2; NFS 4, 9; RGAL 4; RGSF 2; SSFS 8, 13, 16; TUS

Malan, Herman
See Bosman, Herman Charles; Bosman, Herman Charles

Malaparte, Curzio 1898-1957 .... **TCLC 52**
See also DLB 264

Malcolm, Dan
See Silverberg, Robert

Malcolm X .... **BLC 2; CLC 82, 117; WLCS**
See Little, Malcolm
See also LAIT 5; NCFS 3

Malherbe, Francois de 1555-1628 .... **LC 5**
See also GFL Beginnings to 1789

Mallarme, Stephane 1842-1898 ...... **NCLC 4, 41; PC 4**
See also DAM POET; DLB 217; EW 7; GFL 1789 to the Present; LMFS 2; RGWL 2, 3; TWA

Mallet-Joris, Francoise 1930- .... **CLC 11**
See also CA 65-68; CANR 17; CWW 2; DLB 83; EWL 3; GFL 1789 to the Present

Malley, Ern
See McAuley, James Phillip

Mallon, Thomas 1951- .... **CLC 172**
See also CA 110; CANR 29, 57, 92

Mallowan, Agatha Christie
See Christie, Agatha (Mary Clarissa)

Maloff, Saul 1922- .... **CLC 5**
See also CA 33-36R

Malone, Louis
See MacNeice, (Frederick) Louis

Malone, Michael (Christopher)
1942- .... **CLC 43**
See also CA 77-80; CANR 14, 32, 57, 114

Malory, Sir Thomas 1410(?)-1471(?) . **LC 11, 88; WLCS**
See also BRW 1; BRWR 2; CDBLB Before 1660; DA; DAB; DAC; DAM MST; DLB 146; EFS 2; RGEL 2; SATA 59; SATA-Brief 33; TEA; WLIT 3

Marshall, Paule 1929- .. BLC 3; CLC 27, 72; SSC 3
See also AFAW 1, 2; AMWS 11; BPFB 2; BW 2, 3; CA 77-80; CANR 25, 73, 129; CN 7; DA3; DAM MULT; DLB 33, 157, 227; EWL 3; LATS 1:2; MTCW 1, 2; RGAL 4; SSFS 15

Marshallik
See Zangwill, Israel

Marsten, Richard
See Hunter, Evan

Marston, John 1576-1634 .... LC 33
See also BRW 2; DAM DRAM; DLB 58, 172; RGEL 2

Martel, Yann 1963- .... CLC 192
See also CA 146; CANR 114

Martha, Henry
See Harris, Mark

Marti, Jose
See Marti (y Perez), Jose (Julian)
See also DLB 290

Marti (y Perez), Jose (Julian)
1853-1895 .... HLC 2; NCLC 63
See Marti, Jose
See also DAM MULT; HW 2; LAW; RGWL 2, 3; WLIT 1

Martial c. 40-c. 104 .... CMLC 35; PC 10
See also AW 2; CDWLB 1; DLB 211; RGWL 2, 3

Martin, Ken
See Hubbard, L(afayette) Ron(ald)

Martin, Richard
See Creasey, John

Martin, Steve 1945- .... CLC 30
See also AAYA 53; CA 97-100; CANR 30, 100; DFS 19; MTCW 1

Martin, Valerie 1948- .... CLC 89
See also BEST 90:2; CA 85-88; CANR 49, 89

Martin, Violet Florence 1862-1915 .. SSC 56; TCLC 51

Martin, Webber
See Silverberg, Robert

Martindale, Patrick Victor
See White, Patrick (Victor Martindale)

Martin du Gard, Roger
1881-1958 .... TCLC 24
See also CA 118; CANR 94; DLB 65; EWL 3; GFL 1789 to the Present; RGWL 2, 3

Martineau, Harriet 1802-1876 ...... NCLC 26, 137
See also DLB 21, 55, 159, 163, 166, 190; FW; RGEL 2; YABC 2

Martines, Julia
See O'Faolain, Julia

Martinez, Enrique Gonzalez
See Gonzalez Martinez, Enrique

Martinez, Jacinto Benavente y
See Benavente (y Martinez), Jacinto

Martinez de la Rosa, Francisco de Paula
1787-1862 .... NCLC 102
See also TWA

Martinez Ruiz, Jose 1873-1967
See Azorin; Ruiz, Jose Martinez
See also CA 93-96; HW 1

Martinez Sierra, Gregorio
1881-1947 .... TCLC 6
See also CA 115; EWL 3

Martinez Sierra, Maria (de la O'LeJarraga)
1874-1974 .... TCLC 6
See also CA 115; EWL 3

Martinsen, Martin
See Follett, Ken(neth Martin)

Martinson, Harry (Edmund)
1904-1978 .... CLC 14
See also CA 77-80; CANR 34, 130; DLB 259; EWL 3

Martyn, Edward 1859-1923 .... TCLC 131
See also CA 179; DLB 10; RGEL 2

Marut, Ret
See Traven, B.

Marut, Robert
See Traven, B.

Marvell, Andrew 1621-1678 .... LC 4, 43; PC 10; WLC
See also BRW 2; BRWR 2; CDBLB 1660-1789; DA; DAB; DAC; DAM MST, POET; DLB 131; EXPP; PFS 5; RGEL 2; TEA; WP

Marx, Karl (Heinrich)
1818-1883 .... NCLC 17, 114
See also DLB 129; LATS 1:1; TWA

Masaoka, Shiki -1902 .... TCLC 18
See Masaoka, Tsunenori
See also RGWL 3

Masaoka, Tsunenori 1867-1902
See Masaoka, Shiki
See also CA 117; 191; TWA

Masefield, John (Edward)
1878-1967 .... CLC 11, 47
See also CA 19-20; 25-28R; CANR 33; CAP 2; CDBLB 1890-1914; DAM POET; DLB 10, 19, 153, 160; EWL 3; EXPP; FANT; MTCW 1, 2; PFS 5; RGEL 2; SATA 19

Maso, Carole 19(?)- .... CLC 44
See also CA 170; GLL 2; RGAL 4

Mason, Bobbie Ann 1940- ... CLC 28, 43, 82, 154; SSC 4
See also AAYA 5, 42; AMWS 8; BPFB 2; CA 53-56; CANR 11, 31, 58, 83, 125; CDALBS; CN 7; CSW; DA3; DLB 173; DLBY 1987; EWL 3; EXPS; INT CANR-31; MTCW 1, 2; NFS 4; RGAL 4; RGSF 2; SSFS 3, 8, 20; YAW

Mason, Ernst
See Pohl, Frederik

Mason, Hunni B.
See Sternheim, (William Adolf) Carl

Mason, Lee W.
See Malzberg, Barry N(athaniel)

Mason, Nick 1945- .... CLC 35

Mason, Tally
See Derleth, August (William)

Mass, Anna .... CLC 59

Mass, William
See Gibson, William

Massinger, Philip 1583-1640 .... LC 70
See also DLB 58; RGEL 2

Master Lao
See Lao Tzu

Masters, Edgar Lee 1868-1950 ...... PC 1, 36; TCLC 2, 25; WLCS
See also AMWS 1; CA 104; 133; CDALB 1865-1917; DA; DAC; DAM MST, POET; DLB 54; EWL 3; EXPP; MTCW 1, 2; RGAL 4; TUS; WP

Masters, Hilary 1928- .... CLC 48
See also CA 25-28R, 217; CAAE 217; CANR 13, 47, 97; CN 7; DLB 244

Mastrosimone, William 19(?)- .... CLC 36
See also CA 186; CAD; CD 5

Mathe, Albert
See Camus, Albert

Mather, Cotton 1663-1728 .... LC 38
See also AMWS 2; CDALB 1640-1865; DLB 24, 30, 140; RGAL 4; TUS

Mather, Increase 1639-1723 .... LC 38
See also DLB 24

Matheson, Richard (Burton) 1926- .. CLC 37
See also AAYA 31; CA 97-100; CANR 88, 99; DLB 8, 44; HGG; INT CA-97-100; SCFW 2; SFW 4; SUFW 2

Mathews, Harry 1930- .... CLC 6, 52
See also CA 21-24R; CAAS 6; CANR 18, 40, 98; CN 7

Mathews, John Joseph 1894-1979 .. CLC 84; NNAL
See also CA 19-20; 142; CANR 45; CAP 2; DAM MULT; DLB 175

Mathias, Roland (Glyn) 1915- .... CLC 45
See also CA 97-100; CANR 19, 41; CP 7; DLB 27

Matsuo Basho 1644-1694 .... LC 62; PC 3
See Basho, Matsuo
See also DAM POET; PFS 2, 7

Mattheson, Rodney
See Creasey, John

Matthews, (James) Brander
1852-1929 .... TCLC 95
See also DLB 71, 78; DLBD 13

Matthews, Greg 1949- .... CLC 45
See also CA 135

Matthews, William (Procter III)
1942-1997 .... CLC 40
See also AMWS 9; CA 29-32R; 162; CAAS 18; CANR 12, 57; CP 7; DLB 5

Matthias, John (Edward) 1941- .... CLC 9
See also CA 33-36R; CANR 56; CP 7

Matthiessen, F(rancis) O(tto)
1902-1950 .... TCLC 100
See also CA 185; DLB 63

Matthiessen, Peter 1927- ... CLC 5, 7, 11, 32, 64
See also AAYA 6, 40; AMWS 5; ANW; BEST 90:4; BPFB 2; CA 9-12R; CANR 21, 50, 73, 100; CN 7; DA3; DAM NOV; DLB 6, 173, 275; MTCW 1, 2; SATA 27

Maturin, Charles Robert
1780(?)-1824 .... NCLC 6
See also BRWS 8; DLB 178; HGG; LMFS 1; RGEL 2; SUFW

Matute (Ausejo), Ana Maria 1925- .. CLC 11
See also CA 89-92; CANR 129; CWW 2; EWL 3; MTCW 1; RGSF 2

Maugham, W. S.
See Maugham, W(illiam) Somerset

Maugham, W(illiam) Somerset
1874-1965 .. CLC 1, 11, 15, 67, 93; SSC 8; WLC
See also AAYA 55; BPFB 2; BRW 6; CA 5-8R; 25-28R; CANR 40, 127; CDBLB 1914-1945; CMW 4; DA; DA3; DAB; DAC; DAM DRAM, MST, NOV; DLB 10, 36, 77, 100, 162, 195; EWL 3; LAIT 3; MTCW 1, 2; RGEL 2; RGSF 2; SATA 54; SSFS 17

Maugham, William Somerset
See Maugham, W(illiam) Somerset

Maupassant, (Henri Rene Albert) Guy de
1850-1893 . NCLC 1, 42, 83; SSC 1, 64; WLC
See also BYA 14; DA; DA3; DAB; DAC; DAM MST; DLB 123; EW 7; EXPS; GFL 1789 to the Present; LAIT 2; LMFS 1; RGSF 2; RGWL 2, 3; SSFS 4; SUFW; TWA

Maupin, Armistead (Jones, Jr.)
1944- .... CLC 95
See also CA 125; 130; CANR 58, 101; CPW; DA3; DAM POP; DLB 278; GLL 1; INT CA-130; MTCW 2

Maurhut, Richard
See Traven, B.

Mauriac, Claude 1914-1996 .... CLC 9
See also CA 89-92; 152; CWW 2; DLB 83; EWL 3; GFL 1789 to the Present

Mauriac, Francois (Charles)
1885-1970 .... CLC 4, 9, 56; SSC 24
See also CA 25-28; CAP 2; DLB 65; EW 10; EWL 3; GFL 1789 to the Present; MTCW 1, 2; RGWL 2, 3; TWA

Mavor, Osborne Henry 1888-1951
See Bridie, James
See also CA 104

McMillan, Terry (L.) 1951- . **BLCS; CLC 50, 61, 112**
See also AAYA 21; AMWS 13; BPFB 2; BW 2, 3; CA 140; CANR 60, 104, 131; CPW; DA3; DAM MULT, NOV, POP; MTCW 2; RGAL 4; YAW

McMurtry, Larry (Jeff) 1936- .. **CLC 2, 3, 7, 11, 27, 44, 127**
See also AAYA 15; AITN 2; AMWS 5; BEST 89:2; BPFB 2; CA 5-8R; CANR 19, 43, 64, 103; CDALB 1968-1988; CN 7; CPW; CSW; DA3; DAM NOV, POP; DLB 2, 143, 256; DLBY 1980, 1987; EWL 3; MTCW 1, 2; RGAL 4; TCWW 2

McNally, T. M. 1961- .... **CLC 82**

McNally, Terrence 1939- ... **CLC 4, 7, 41, 91**
See also AMWS 13; CA 45-48; CAD; CANR 2, 56, 116; CD 5; DA3; DAM DRAM; DFS 16, 19; DLB 7, 249; EWL 3; GLL 1; MTCW 2

McNamer, Deirdre 1950- .... **CLC 70**

McNeal, Tom .... **CLC 119**

McNeile, Herman Cyril 1888-1937
See Sapper
See also CA 184; CMW 4; DLB 77

McNickle, (William) D'Arcy
1904-1977 .... **CLC 89; NNAL**
See also CA 9-12R; 85-88; CANR 5, 45; DAM MULT; DLB 175, 212; RGAL 4; SATA-Obit 22

McPhee, John (Angus) 1931- .... **CLC 36**
See also AMWS 3; ANW; BEST 90:1; CA 65-68; CANR 20, 46, 64, 69, 121; CPW; DLB 185, 275; MTCW 1, 2; TUS

McPherson, James Alan 1943- . **BLCS; CLC 19, 77**
See also BW 1, 3; CA 25-28R; CAAS 17; CANR 24, 74; CN 7; CSW; DLB 38, 244; EWL 3; MTCW 1, 2; RGAL 4; RGSF 2

McPherson, William (Alexander)
1933- .... **CLC 34**
See also CA 69-72; CANR 28; INT CANR-28

McTaggart, J. McT. Ellis
See McTaggart, John McTaggart Ellis

McTaggart, John McTaggart Ellis
1866-1925 .... **TCLC 105**
See also CA 120; DLB 262

Mead, George Herbert 1863-1931 . **TCLC 89**
See also CA 212; DLB 270

Mead, Margaret 1901-1978 .... **CLC 37**
See also AITN 1; CA 1-4R; 81-84; CANR 4; DA3; FW; MTCW 1, 2; SATA-Obit 20

Meaker, Marijane (Agnes) 1927-
See Kerr, M. E.
See also CA 107; CANR 37, 63; INT CA-107; JRDA; MAICYA 1, 2; MAICYAS 1; MTCW 1; SATA 20, 61, 99; SATA-Essay 111; YAW

Medoff, Mark (Howard) 1940- .... **CLC 6, 23**
See also AITN 1; CA 53-56; CAD; CANR 5; CD 5; DAM DRAM; DFS 4; DLB 7; INT CANR-5

Medvedev, P. N.
See Bakhtin, Mikhail Mikhailovich

Meged, Aharon
See Megged, Aharon

Meged, Aron
See Megged, Aharon

Megged, Aharon 1920- .... **CLC 9**
See also CA 49-52; CAAS 13; CANR 1; EWL 3

Mehta, Gita 1943- .... **CLC 179**
See also CA 225; DNFS 2

Mehta, Ved (Parkash) 1934- .... **CLC 37**
See also CA 1-4R, 212; CAAE 212; CANR 2, 23, 69; MTCW 1

Melanchthon, Philipp 1497-1560 .... **LC 90**
See also DLB 179

Melanter
See Blackmore, R(ichard) D(oddridge)

Meleager c. 140 B.C.-c. 70 B.C. .... **CMLC 53**

Melies, Georges 1861-1938 .... **TCLC 81**

Melikow, Loris
See Hofmannsthal, Hugo von

Melmoth, Sebastian
See Wilde, Oscar (Fingal O'Flahertie Wills)

Melo Neto, Joao Cabral de
See Cabral de Melo Neto, Joao
See also CWW 2; EWL 3

Meltzer, Milton 1915- .... **CLC 26**
See also AAYA 8, 45; BYA 2, 6; CA 13-16R; CANR 38, 92, 107; CLR 13; DLB 61; JRDA; MAICYA 1, 2; SAAS 1; SATA 1, 50, 80, 128; SATA-Essay 124; WYA; YAW

Melville, Herman 1819-1891 ..... **NCLC 3, 12, 29, 45, 49, 91, 93, 123; SSC 1, 17, 46; WLC**
See also AAYA 25; AMW; AMWR 1; CDALB 1640-1865; DA; DA3; DAB; DAC; DAM MST, NOV; DLB 3, 74, 250, 254; EXPN; EXPS; LAIT 1, 2; NFS 7, 9; RGAL 4; RGSF 2; SATA 59; SSFS 3; TUS

Members, Mark
See Powell, Anthony (Dymoke)

Membreno, Alejandro .... **CLC 59**

Menander c. 342 B.C.-c. 293 B.C. . **CMLC 9, 51; DC 3**
See also AW 1; CDWLB 1; DAM DRAM; DLB 176; LMFS 1; RGWL 2, 3

Menchu, Rigoberta 1959- .. **CLC 160; HLCS 2**
See also CA 175; DNFS 1; WLIT 1

Mencken, H(enry) L(ouis)
1880-1956 .... **TCLC 13**
See also AMW; CA 105; 125; CDALB 1917-1929; DLB 11, 29, 63, 137, 222; EWL 3; MTCW 1, 2; NCFS 4; RGAL 4; TUS

Mendelsohn, Jane 1965- .... **CLC 99**
See also CA 154; CANR 94

Menton, Francisco de
See Chin, Frank (Chew, Jr.)

Mercer, David 1928-1980 .... **CLC 5**
See also CA 9-12R; 102; CANR 23; CBD; DAM DRAM; DLB 13; MTCW 1; RGEL 2

Merchant, Paul
See Ellison, Harlan (Jay)

Meredith, George 1828-1909 .. **PC 60; TCLC 17, 43**
See also CA 117; 153; CANR 80; CDBLB 1832-1890; DAM POET; DLB 18, 35, 57, 159; RGEL 2; TEA

Meredith, William (Morris) 1919- .... **CLC 4, 13, 22, 55; PC 28**
See also CA 9-12R; CAAS 14; CANR 6, 40, 129; CP 7; DAM POET; DLB 5

Merezhkovsky, Dmitrii Sergeevich
See Merezhkovsky, Dmitry Sergeyevich
See also DLB 295

Merezhkovsky, Dmitry Sergeevich
See Merezhkovsky, Dmitry Sergeyevich
See also EWL 3

Merezhkovsky, Dmitry Sergeyevich
1865-1941 .... **TCLC 29**
See Merezhkovsky, Dmitrii Sergeevich; Merezhkovsky, Dmitry Sergeevich
See also CA 169

Merimee, Prosper 1803-1870 ... **NCLC 6, 65; SSC 7**
See also DLB 119, 192; EW 6; EXPS; GFL 1789 to the Present; RGSF 2; RGWL 2, 3; SSFS 8; SUFW

Merkin, Daphne 1954- .... **CLC 44**
See also CA 123

Merleau-Ponty, Maurice
1908-1961 .... **TCLC 156**
See also CA 114; 89-92; DLB 296; GFL 1789 to the Present

Merlin, Arthur
See Blish, James (Benjamin)

Mernissi, Fatima 1940- .... **CLC 171**
See also CA 152; FW

Merrill, James (Ingram) 1926-1995 .. **CLC 2, 3, 6, 8, 13, 18, 34, 91; PC 28**
See also AMWS 3; CA 13-16R; 147; CANR 10, 49, 63, 108; DA3; DAM POET; DLB 5, 165; DLBY 1985; EWL 3; INT CANR-10; MTCW 1, 2; PAB; RGAL 4

Merriman, Alex
See Silverberg, Robert

Merriman, Brian 1747-1805 .... **NCLC 70**

Merritt, E. B.
See Waddington, Miriam

Merton, Thomas (James)
1915-1968 . **CLC 1, 3, 11, 34, 83; PC 10**
See also AMWS 8; CA 5-8R; 25-28R; CANR 22, 53, 111, 131; DA3; DLB 48; DLBY 1981; MTCW 1, 2

Merwin, W(illiam) S(tanley) 1927- ... **CLC 1, 2, 3, 5, 8, 13, 18, 45, 88; PC 45**
See also AMWS 3; CA 13-16R; CANR 15, 51, 112; CP 7; DA3; DAM POET; DLB 5, 169; EWL 3; INT CANR-15; MTCW 1, 2; PAB; PFS 5, 15; RGAL 4

Metcalf, John 1938- .... **CLC 37; SSC 43**
See also CA 113; CN 7; DLB 60; RGSF 2; TWA

Metcalf, Suzanne
See Baum, L(yman) Frank

Mew, Charlotte (Mary) 1870-1928 .. **TCLC 8**
See also CA 105; 189; DLB 19, 135; RGEL 2

Mewshaw, Michael 1943- .... **CLC 9**
See also CA 53-56; CANR 7, 47; DLBY 1980

Meyer, Conrad Ferdinand
1825-1898 .... **NCLC 81**
See also DLB 129; EW; RGWL 2, 3

Meyer, Gustav 1868-1932
See Meyrink, Gustav
See also CA 117; 190

Meyer, June
See Jordan, June (Meyer)

Meyer, Lynn
See Slavitt, David R(ytman)

Meyers, Jeffrey 1939- .... **CLC 39**
See also CA 73-76, 186; CAAE 186; CANR 54, 102; DLB 111

Meynell, Alice (Christina Gertrude Thompson) 1847-1922 .... **TCLC 6**
See also CA 104; 177; DLB 19, 98; RGEL 2

Meyrink, Gustav .... **TCLC 21**
See Meyer, Gustav
See also DLB 81; EWL 3

Michaels, Leonard 1933-2003 ..... **CLC 6, 25; SSC 16**
See also CA 61-64; 216; CANR 21, 62, 119; CN 7; DLB 130; MTCW 1

Michaux, Henri 1899-1984 .... **CLC 8, 19**
See also CA 85-88; 114; DLB 258; EWL 3; GFL 1789 to the Present; RGWL 2, 3

Micheaux, Oscar (Devereaux)
1884-1951 .... **TCLC 76**
See also BW 3; CA 174; DLB 50; TCWW 2

Michelangelo 1475-1564 .... **LC 12**
See also AAYA 43

Michelet, Jules 1798-1874 .... **NCLC 31**
See also EW 5; GFL 1789 to the Present

Michels, Robert 1876-1936 .... **TCLC 88**
See also CA 212

Mofolo, Thomas (Mokopu)
1875(?)-1948 .... **BLC 3; TCLC 22**
See also AFW; CA 121; 153; CANR 83;
DAM MULT; DLB 225; EWL 3; MTCW
2; WLIT 2

Mohr, Nicholasa 1938- .... **CLC 12; HLC 2**
See also AAYA 8, 46; CA 49-52; CANR 1,
32, 64; CLR 22; DAM MULT; DLB 145;
HW 1, 2; JRDA; LAIT 5; LLW 1; MAI-
CYA 2; MAICYAS 1; RGAL 4; SAAS 8;
SATA 8, 97; SATA-Essay 113; WYA;
YAW

Moi, Toril 1953- .... **CLC 172**
See also CA 154; CANR 102; FW

Mojtabai, A(nn) G(race) 1938- ..... **CLC 5, 9,
15, 29**
See also CA 85-88; CANR 88

Moliere 1622-1673 ..... **DC 13; LC 10, 28, 64;
WLC**
See also DA; DA3; DAB; DAC; DAM
DRAM, MST; DFS 13, 18, 20; DLB 268;
EW 3; GFL Beginnings to 1789; LATS
1:1; RGWL 2, 3; TWA

Molin, Charles
See Mayne, William (James Carter)

Molnar, Ferenc 1878-1952 .... **TCLC 20**
See also CA 109; 153; CANR 83; CDWLB
4; DAM DRAM; DLB 215; EWL 3;
RGWL 2, 3

Momaday, N(avarre) Scott 1934- ...... **CLC 2,
19, 85, 95, 160; NNAL; PC 25; WLCS**
See also AAYA 11; AMWS 4; ANW; BPFB
2; BYA 12; CA 25-28R; CANR 14, 34,
68; CDALBS; CN 7; CPW; DA; DA3;
DAB; DAC; DAM MST, MULT, NOV,
POP; DLB 143, 175, 256; EWL 3; EXPP;
INT CANR-14; LAIT 4; LATS 1:2;
MTCW 1, 2; NFS 10; PFS 2, 11; RGAL
4; SATA 48; SATA-Brief 30; WP; YAW

Monette, Paul 1945-1995 .... **CLC 82**
See also AMWS 10; CA 139; 147; CN 7;
GLL 1

Monroe, Harriet 1860-1936 .... **TCLC 12**
See also CA 109; 204; DLB 54, 91

Monroe, Lyle
See Heinlein, Robert A(nson)

Montagu, Elizabeth 1720-1800 .... **NCLC 7,
117**
See also FW

Montagu, Mary (Pierrepont) Wortley
1689-1762 .... **LC 9, 57; PC 16**
See also DLB 95, 101; RGEL 2

Montagu, W. H.
See Coleridge, Samuel Taylor

Montague, John (Patrick) 1929- ..... **CLC 13,
46**
See also CA 9-12R; CANR 9, 69, 121; CP
7; DLB 40; EWL 3; MTCW 1; PFS 12;
RGEL 2

Montaigne, Michel (Eyquem) de
1533-1592 .... **LC 8, 105; WLC**
See also DA; DAB; DAC; DAM MST; EW
2; GFL Beginnings to 1789; LMFS 1;
RGWL 2, 3; TWA

Montale, Eugenio 1896-1981 ... **CLC 7, 9, 18;
PC 13**
See also CA 17-20R; 104; CANR 30; DLB
114; EW 11; EWL 3; MTCW 1; RGWL
2, 3; TWA

Montesquieu, Charles-Louis de Secondat
1689-1755 .... **LC 7, 69**
See also EW 3; GFL Beginnings to 1789;
TWA

Montessori, Maria 1870-1952 ...... **TCLC 103**
See also CA 115; 147

Montgomery, (Robert) Bruce 1921(?)-1978
See Crispin, Edmund
See also CA 179; 104; CMW 4

Montgomery, L(ucy) M(aud)
1874-1942 .... **TCLC 51, 140**
See also AAYA 12; BYA 1; CA 108; 137;
CLR 8, 91; DA3; DAC; DAM MST; DLB
92; DLBD 14; JRDA; MAICYA 1, 2;
MTCW 2; RGEL 2; SATA 100; TWA;
WCH; WYA; YABC 1

Montgomery, Marion H., Jr. 1925- .... **CLC 7**
See also AITN 1; CA 1-4R; CANR 3, 48;
CSW; DLB 6

Montgomery, Max
See Davenport, Guy (Mattison, Jr.)

Montherlant, Henry (Milon) de
1896-1972 .... **CLC 8, 19**
See also CA 85-88; 37-40R; DAM DRAM;
DLB 72; EW 11; EWL 3; GFL 1789 to
the Present; MTCW 1

Monty Python
See Chapman, Graham; Cleese, John
(Marwood); Gilliam, Terry (Vance); Idle,
Eric; Jones, Terence Graham Parry; Palin,
Michael (Edward)
See also AAYA 7

Moodie, Susanna (Strickland)
1803-1885 .... **NCLC 14, 113**
See also DLB 99

Moody, Hiram (F. III) 1961-
See Moody, Rick
See also CA 138; CANR 64, 112

Moody, Minerva
See Alcott, Louisa May

Moody, Rick .... **CLC 147**
See Moody, Hiram (F. III)

Moody, William Vaughan
1869-1910 .... **TCLC 105**
See also CA 110; 178; DLB 7, 54; RGAL 4

Mooney, Edward 1951-
See Mooney, Ted
See also CA 130

Mooney, Ted .... **CLC 25**
See Mooney, Edward

Moorcock, Michael (John) 1939- ...... **CLC 5,
27, 58**
See Bradbury, Edward P.
See also AAYA 26; CA 45-48; CAAS 5;
CANR 2, 17, 38, 64, 122; CN 7; DLB 14,
231; FANT; MTCW 1, 2; SATA 93;
SCFW 2; SFW 4; SUFW 1, 2

Moore, Brian 1921-1999 ... **CLC 1, 3, 5, 7, 8,
19, 32, 90**
See Bryan, Michael
See also BRWS 9; CA 1-4R; 174; CANR 1,
25, 42, 63; CCA 1; CN 7; DAB; DAC;
DAM MST; DLB 251; EWL 3; FANT;
MTCW 1, 2; RGEL 2

Moore, Edward
See Muir, Edwin
See also RGEL 2

Moore, G. E. 1873-1958 .... **TCLC 89**
See also DLB 262

Moore, George Augustus
1852-1933 .... **SSC 19; TCLC 7**
See also BRW 6; CA 104; 177; DLB 10,
18, 57, 135; EWL 3; RGEL 2; RGSF 2

Moore, Lorrie .... **CLC 39, 45, 68**
See Moore, Marie Lorena
See also AMWS 10; DLB 234; SSFS 19

Moore, Marianne (Craig)
1887-1972 .... **CLC 1, 2, 4, 8, 10, 13, 19,
47; PC 4, 49; WLCS**
See also AMW; CA 1-4R; 33-36R; CANR
3, 61; CDALB 1929-1941; DA; DA3;
DAB; DAC; DAM MST, POET; DLB 45;
DLBD 7; EWL 3; EXPP; MAWW;
MTCW 1, 2; PAB; PFS 14, 17; RGAL 4;
SATA 20; TUS; WP

Moore, Marie Lorena 1957- .... **CLC 165**
See Moore, Lorrie
See also CA 116; CANR 39, 83; CN 7; DLB
234

Moore, Thomas 1779-1852 .... **NCLC 6, 110**
See also DLB 96, 144; RGEL 2

Moorhouse, Frank 1938- .... **SSC 40**
See also CA 118; CANR 92; CN 7; DLB
289; RGSF 2

Mora, Pat(ricia) 1942- .... **HLC 2**
See also AMWS 13; CA 129; CANR 57,
81, 112; CLR 58; DAM MULT; DLB 209;
HW 1, 2; LLW 1; MAICYA 2; SATA 92,
134

Moraga, Cherrie 1952- ...... **CLC 126; DC 22**
See also CA 131; CANR 66; DAM MULT;
DLB 82, 249; FW; GLL 1; HW 1, 2; LLW
1

Morand, Paul 1888-1976 .... **CLC 41; SSC 22**
See also CA 184; 69-72; DLB 65; EWL 3

Morante, Elsa 1918-1985 .... **CLC 8, 47**
See also CA 85-88; 117; CANR 35; DLB
177; EWL 3; MTCW 1, 2; RGWL 2, 3

Moravia, Alberto .... **CLC 2, 7, 11, 27, 46;
SSC 26**
See Pincherle, Alberto
See also DLB 177; EW 12; EWL 3; MTCW
2; RGSF 2; RGWL 2, 3

More, Hannah 1745-1833 ...... **NCLC 27, 141**
See also DLB 107, 109, 116, 158; RGEL 2

More, Henry 1614-1687 .... **LC 9**
See also DLB 126, 252

More, Sir Thomas 1478(?)-1535 .... **LC 10, 32**
See also BRWC 1; BRWS 7; DLB 136, 281;
LMFS 1; RGEL 2; TEA

Moreas, Jean .... **TCLC 18**
See Papadiamantopoulos, Johannes
See also GFL 1789 to the Present

Moreton, Andrew Esq.
See Defoe, Daniel

Morgan, Berry 1919-2002 .... **CLC 6**
See also CA 49-52; 208; DLB 6

Morgan, Claire
See Highsmith, (Mary) Patricia
See also GLL 1

Morgan, Edwin (George) 1920- .... **CLC 31**
See also BRWS 9; CA 5-8R; CANR 3, 43,
90; CP 7; DLB 27

Morgan, (George) Frederick
1922-2004 .... **CLC 23**
See also CA 17-20R; 224; CANR 21; CP 7

Morgan, Harriet
See Mencken, H(enry) L(ouis)

Morgan, Jane
See Cooper, James Fenimore

Morgan, Janet 1945- .... **CLC 39**
See also CA 65-68

Morgan, Lady 1776(?)-1859 .... **NCLC 29**
See also DLB 116, 158; RGEL 2

Morgan, Robin (Evonne) 1941- .... **CLC 2**
See also CA 69-72; CANR 29, 68; FW;
GLL 2; MTCW 1; SATA 80

Morgan, Scott
See Kuttner, Henry

Morgan, Seth 1949(?)-1990 .... **CLC 65**
See also CA 185; 132

**Morgenstern, Christian (Otto Josef
Wolfgang)** 1871-1914 .... **TCLC 8**
See also CA 105; 191; EWL 3

Morgenstern, S.
See Goldman, William (W.)

Mori, Rintaro
See Mori Ogai
See also CA 110

Moricz, Zsigmond 1879-1942 .... **TCLC 33**
See also CA 165; DLB 215; EWL 3

Morike, Eduard (Friedrich)
1804-1875 .... **NCLC 10**
See also DLB 133; RGWL 2, 3

Mori Ogai 1862-1922 .... **TCLC 14**
See Ogai
See also CA 164; DLB 180; EWL 3; RGWL
3; TWA

Ngugi wa Thiong'o 1938- ... **BLC 3; CLC 36, 182**
See Ngugi, James T(hiong'o); Ngugi wa Thiong'o
See also AFW; BRWS 8; BW 2; CA 81-84; CANR 27, 58; CDWLB 3; DAM MULT, NOV; DNFS 2; MTCW 1, 2; RGEL 2; WWE 1

Niatum, Duane 1938- .... **NNAL**
See also CA 41-44R; CANR 21, 45, 83; DLB 175

Nichol, B(arrie) P(hillip) 1944-1988 . **CLC 18**
See also CA 53-56; DLB 53; SATA 66

Nicholas of Cusa 1401-1464 .... **LC 80**
See also DLB 115

Nichols, John (Treadwell) 1940- .... **CLC 38**
See also AMWS 13; CA 9-12R, 190; CAAE 190; CAAS 2; CANR 6, 70, 121; DLBY 1982; LATS 1:2; TCWW 2

Nichols, Leigh
See Koontz, Dean R(ay)

Nichols, Peter (Richard) 1927- .... **CLC 5, 36, 65**
See also CA 104; CANR 33, 86; CBD; CD 5; DLB 13, 245; MTCW 1

Nicholson, Linda ed. .... **CLC 65**

Ni Chuilleanain, Eilean 1942- .... **PC 34**
See also CA 126; CANR 53, 83; CP 7; CWP; DLB 40

Nicolas, F. R. E.
See Freeling, Nicolas

Niedecker, Lorine 1903-1970 ..... **CLC 10, 42; PC 42**
See also CA 25-28; CAP 2; DAM POET; DLB 48

Nietzsche, Friedrich (Wilhelm)
1844-1900 .... **TCLC 10, 18, 55**
See also CA 107; 121; CDWLB 2; DLB 129; EW 7; RGWL 2, 3; TWA

Nievo, Ippolito 1831-1861 .... **NCLC 22**

Nightingale, Anne Redmon 1943-
See Redmon, Anne
See also CA 103

Nightingale, Florence 1820-1910 ... **TCLC 85**
See also CA 188; DLB 166

Nijo Yoshimoto 1320-1388 .... **CMLC 49**
See also DLB 203

Nik. T. O.
See Annensky, Innokenty (Fyodorovich)

Nin, Anais 1903-1977 ..... **CLC 1, 4, 8, 11, 14, 60, 127; SSC 10**
See also AITN 2; AMWS 10; BPFB 2; CA 13-16R; 69-72; CANR 22, 53; DAM NOV, POP; DLB 2, 4, 152; EWL 3; GLL 2; MAWW; MTCW 1, 2; RGAL 4; RGSF 2

Nisbet, Robert A(lexander)
1913-1996 .... **TCLC 117**
See also CA 25-28R; 153; CANR 17; INT CANR-17

Nishida, Kitaro 1870-1945 .... **TCLC 83**

Nishiwaki, Junzaburo
See Nishiwaki, Junzaburo
See also CA 194

Nishiwaki, Junzaburo 1894-1982 .... **PC 15**
See Nishiwaki, Junzaburo; Nishiwaki Junzaburo
See also CA 194; 107; MJW; RGWL 3

Nishiwaki Junzaburo
See Nishiwaki, Junzaburo
See also EWL 3

Nissenson, Hugh 1933- .... **CLC 4, 9**
See also CA 17-20R; CANR 27, 108; CN 7; DLB 28

Nister, Der
See Der Nister
See also EWL 3

Niven, Larry .... **CLC 8**
See Niven, Laurence Van Cott
See also AAYA 27; BPFB 2; BYA 10; DLB 8; SCFW 2

Niven, Laurence Van Cott 1938-
See Niven, Larry
See also CA 21-24R, 207; CAAE 207; CAAS 12; CANR 14, 44, 66, 113; CPW; DAM POP; MTCW 1, 2; SATA 95; SFW 4

Nixon, Agnes Eckhardt 1927- .... **CLC 21**
See also CA 110

Nizan, Paul 1905-1940 .... **TCLC 40**
See also CA 161; DLB 72; EWL 3; GFL 1789 to the Present

Nkosi, Lewis 1936- .... **BLC 3; CLC 45**
See also BW 1, 3; CA 65-68; CANR 27, 81; CBD; CD 5; DAM MULT; DLB 157, 225; WWE 1

Nodier, (Jean) Charles (Emmanuel)
1780-1844 .... **NCLC 19**
See also DLB 119; GFL 1789 to the Present

Noguchi, Yone 1875-1947 .... **TCLC 80**

Nolan, Christopher 1965- .... **CLC 58**
See also CA 111; CANR 88

Noon, Jeff 1957- .... **CLC 91**
See also CA 148; CANR 83; DLB 267; SFW 4

Norden, Charles
See Durrell, Lawrence (George)

Nordhoff, Charles Bernard
1887-1947 .... **TCLC 23**
See also CA 108; 211; DLB 9; LAIT 1; RHW 1; SATA 23

Norfolk, Lawrence 1963- .... **CLC 76**
See also CA 144; CANR 85; CN 7; DLB 267

Norman, Marsha 1947- . **CLC 28, 186; DC 8**
See also CA 105; CABS 3; CAD; CANR 41, 131; CD 5; CSW; CWD; DAM DRAM; DFS 2; DLB 266; DLBY 1984; FW

Normyx
See Douglas, (George) Norman

Norris, (Benjamin) Frank(lin, Jr.)
1870-1902 .... **SSC 28; TCLC 24, 155**
See also AAYA 57; AMW; AMWC 2; BPFB 2; CA 110; 160; CDALB 1865-1917; DLB 12, 71, 186; LMFS 2; NFS 12; RGAL 4; TCWW 2; TUS

Norris, Leslie 1921- .... **CLC 14**
See also CA 11-12; CANR 14, 117; CAP 1; CP 7; DLB 27, 256

North, Andrew
See Norton, Andre

North, Anthony
See Koontz, Dean R(ay)

North, Captain George
See Stevenson, Robert Louis (Balfour)

North, Captain George
See Stevenson, Robert Louis (Balfour)

North, Milou
See Erdrich, Louise

Northrup, B. A.
See Hubbard, L(afayette) Ron(ald)

North Staffs
See Hulme, T(homas) E(rnest)

Northup, Solomon 1808-1863 ...... **NCLC 105**

Norton, Alice Mary
See Norton, Andre
See also MAICYA 1; SATA 1, 43

Norton, Andre 1912- .... **CLC 12**
See Norton, Alice Mary
See also AAYA 14; BPFB 2; BYA 4, 10, 12; CA 1-4R; CANR 68; CLR 50; DLB 8, 52; JRDA; MAICYA 2; MTCW 1; SATA 91; SUFW 1, 2; YAW

Norton, Caroline 1808-1877 .... **NCLC 47**
See also DLB 21, 159, 199

Norway, Nevil Shute 1899-1960
See Shute, Nevil
See also CA 102; 93-96; CANR 85; MTCW 2

Norwid, Cyprian Kamil
1821-1883 .... **NCLC 17**
See also RGWL 3

Nosille, Nabrah
See Ellison, Harlan (Jay)

Nossack, Hans Erich 1901-1978 .... **CLC 6**
See also CA 93-96; 85-88; DLB 69; EWL 3

Nostradamus 1503-1566 .... **LC 27**

Nosu, Chuji
See Ozu, Yasujiro

Notenburg, Eleanora (Genrikhovna) von
See Guro, Elena (Genrikhovna)

Nova, Craig 1945- .... **CLC 7, 31**
See also CA 45-48; CANR 2, 53, 127

Novak, Joseph
See Kosinski, Jerzy (Nikodem)

Novalis 1772-1801 .... **NCLC 13**
See also CDWLB 2; DLB 90; EW 5; RGWL 2, 3

Novick, Peter 1934- .... **CLC 164**
See also CA 188

Novis, Emile
See Weil, Simone (Adolphine)

Nowlan, Alden (Albert) 1933-1983 ... **CLC 15**
See also CA 9-12R; CANR 5; DAC; DAM MST; DLB 53; PFS 12

Noyes, Alfred 1880-1958 ...... **PC 27; TCLC 7**
See also CA 104; 188; DLB 20; EXPP; FANT; PFS 4; RGEL 2

Nugent, Richard Bruce 1906(?)-1987 ... **HR 3**
See also BW 1; CA 125; DLB 51; GLL 2

Nunn, Kem .... **CLC 34**
See also CA 159

Nwapa, Flora (Nwanzuruaha)
1931-1993 .... **BLCS; CLC 133**
See also BW 2; CA 143; CANR 83; CD-WLB 3; CWRI 5; DLB 125; EWL 3; WLIT 2

Nye, Robert 1939- .... **CLC 13, 42**
See also CA 33-36R; CANR 29, 67, 107; CN 7; CP 7; CWRI 5; DAM NOV; DLB 14, 271; FANT; HGG; MTCW 1; RHW; SATA 6

Nyro, Laura 1947-1997 .... **CLC 17**
See also CA 194

Oates, Joyce Carol 1938- .. **CLC 1, 2, 3, 6, 9, 11, 15, 19, 33, 52, 108, 134; SSC 6, 70; WLC**
See also AAYA 15, 52; AITN 1; AMWS 2; BEST 89:2; BPFB 2; BYA 11; CA 5-8R; CANR 25, 45, 74, 113, 129; CDALB 1968-1988; CN 7; CP 7; CPW; CWP; DA; DA3; DAB; DAC; DAM MST, NOV, POP; DLB 2, 5, 130; DLBY 1981; EWL 3; EXPS; FW; HGG; INT CANR-25; LAIT 4; MAWW; MTCW 1, 2; NFS 8; RGAL 4; RGSF 2; SSFS 17; SUFW 2; TUS

O'Brian, E. G.
See Clarke, Arthur C(harles)

O'Brian, Patrick 1914-2000 .... **CLC 152**
See also AAYA 55; CA 144; 187; CANR 74; CPW; MTCW 2; RHW

O'Brien, Darcy 1939-1998 .... **CLC 11**
See also CA 21-24R; 167; CANR 8, 59

O'Brien, Edna 1936- ..... **CLC 3, 5, 8, 13, 36, 65, 116; SSC 10**
See also BRWS 5; CA 1-4R; CANR 6, 41, 65, 102; CDBLB 1960 to Present; CN 7; DA3; DAM NOV; DLB 14, 231; EWL 3; FW; MTCW 1, 2; RGSF 2; WLIT 4

O'Brien, Fitz-James 1828-1862 ..... **NCLC 21**
See also DLB 74; RGAL 4; SUFW

Orage, A(lfred) R(ichard)
1873-1934 .... **TCLC 157**
See also CA 122

Origen c. 185-c. 254 .... **CMLC 19**

Orlovitz, Gil 1918-1973 .... **CLC 22**
See also CA 77-80; 45-48; DLB 2, 5

Orris
See Ingelow, Jean

Ortega y Gasset, Jose 1883-1955 ...... **HLC 2;**
TCLC 9
See also CA 106; 130; DAM MULT; EW 9;
EWL 3; HW 1, 2; MTCW 1, 2

Ortese, Anna Maria 1914-1998 .... **CLC 89**
See also DLB 177; EWL 3

Ortiz, Simon J(oseph) 1941- .... **CLC 45;**
NNAL; PC 17
See also AMWS 4; CA 134; CANR 69, 118;
CP 7; DAM MULT, POET; DLB 120,
175, 256; EXPP; PFS 4, 16; RGAL 4

Orton, Joe ...... **CLC 4, 13, 43; DC 3; TCLC**
157
See Orton, John Kingsley
See also BRWS 5; CBD; CDBLB 1960 to
Present; DFS 3, 6; DLB 13; GLL 1;
MTCW 2; RGEL 2; TEA; WLIT 4

Orton, John Kingsley 1933-1967
See Orton, Joe
See also CA 85-88; CANR 35, 66; DAM
DRAM; MTCW 1, 2

Orwell, George ...... **SSC 68; TCLC 2, 6, 15,**
31, 51, 128, 129; WLC
See Blair, Eric (Arthur)
See also BPFB 3; BRW 7; BYA 5; CDBLB
1945-1960; CLR 68; DLB 15, 98,
195, 255; EWL 3; EXPN; LAIT 4, 5;
LATS 1:1; NFS 3, 7; RGEL 2; SCFW 2;
SFW 4; SSFS 4; TEA; WLIT 4; YAW

Osborne, David
See Silverberg, Robert

Osborne, George
See Silverberg, Robert

Osborne, John (James) 1929-1994 .... **CLC 1,**
2, 5, 11, 45; TCLC 153; WLC
See also BRWS 1; CA 13-16R; 147; CANR
21, 56; CDBLB 1945-1960; DA; DAB;
DAC; DAM DRAM, MST; DFS 4, 19;
DLB 13; EWL 3; MTCW 1, 2; RGEL 2

Osborne, Lawrence 1958- .... **CLC 50**
See also CA 189

Osbourne, Lloyd 1868-1947 .... **TCLC 93**

Osgood, Frances Sargent
1811-1850 .... **NCLC 141**
See also DLB 250

Oshima, Nagisa 1932- .... **CLC 20**
See also CA 116; 121; CANR 78

Oskison, John Milton
1874-1947 .... **NNAL; TCLC 35**
See also CA 144; CANR 84; DAM MULT;
DLB 175

Ossian c. 3rd cent. - .... **CMLC 28**
See Macpherson, James

Ossoli, Sarah Margaret (Fuller)
1810-1850 .... **NCLC 5, 50**
See Fuller, Margaret; Fuller, Sarah Margaret
See also CDALB 1640-1865; FW; LMFS 1;
SATA 25

Ostriker, Alicia (Suskin) 1937- .... **CLC 132**
See also CA 25-28R; CAAS 24; CANR 10,
30, 62, 99; CWP; DLB 120; EXPP; PFS
19

Ostrovsky, Aleksandr Nikolaevich
See Ostrovsky, Alexander
See also DLB 277

Ostrovsky, Alexander 1823-1886 .. **NCLC 30,**
57
See Ostrovsky, Aleksandr Nikolaevich

Otero, Blas de 1916-1979 .... **CLC 11**
See also CA 89-92; DLB 134; EWL 3

O'Trigger, Sir Lucius
See Horne, Richard Henry Hengist

Otto, Rudolf 1869-1937 .... **TCLC 85**

Otto, Whitney 1955- .... **CLC 70**
See also CA 140; CANR 120

Otway, Thomas 1652-1685 ... **DC 24; LC 106**
See also DAM DRAM; DLB 80; RGEL 2

Ouida .... **TCLC 43**
See De la Ramee, Marie Louise (Ouida)
See also DLB 18, 156; RGEL 2

Ouologuem, Yambo 1940- .... **CLC 146**
See also CA 111; 176

Ousmane, Sembene 1923- ... **BLC 3; CLC 66**
See Sembene, Ousmane
See also BW 1, 3; CA 117; 125; CANR 81;
CWW 2; MTCW 1

Ovid 43 B.C.-17 .... **CMLC 7; PC 2**
See also AW 2; CDWLB 1; DA3; DAM
POET; DLB 211; RGWL 2, 3; WP

Owen, Hugh
See Faust, Frederick (Schiller)

Owen, Wilfred (Edward Salter)
1893-1918 ... **PC 19; TCLC 5, 27; WLC**
See also BRW 6; CA 104; 141; CDBLB
1914-1945; DA; DAB; DAC; DAM MST,
POET; DLB 20; EWL 3; EXPP; MTCW
2; PFS 10; RGEL 2; WLIT 4

Owens, Louis (Dean) 1948-2002 .... **NNAL**
See also CA 137, 179; 207; CAAE 179;
CAAS 24; CANR 71

Owens, Rochelle 1936- .... **CLC 8**
See also CA 17-20R; CAAS 2; CAD;
CANR 39; CD 5; CP 7; CWD; CWP

Oz, Amos 1939- ...... **CLC 5, 8, 11, 27, 33, 54;**
SSC 66
See also CA 53-56; CANR 27, 47, 65, 113;
CWW 2; DAM NOV; EWL 3; MTCW 1,
2; RGSF 2; RGWL 3

Ozick, Cynthia 1928- .... **CLC 3, 7, 28, 62,**
155; SSC 15, 60
See also AMWS 5; BEST 90:1; CA 17-20R;
CANR 23, 58, 116; CN 7; CPW; DA3;
DAM NOV, POP; DLB 28, 152, 299;
DLBY 1982; EWL 3; EXPS; INT CANR-
23; MTCW 1, 2; RGAL 4; RGSF 2; SSFS
3, 12

Ozu, Yasujiro 1903-1963 .... **CLC 16**
See also CA 112

Pabst, G. W. 1885-1967 .... **TCLC 127**

Pacheco, C.
See Pessoa, Fernando (Antonio Nogueira)

Pacheco, Jose Emilio 1939- .... **HLC 2**
See also CA 111; 131; CANR 65; CWW 2;
DAM MULT; DLB 290; EWL 3; HW 1,
2; RGSF 2

Pa Chin .... **CLC 18**
See Li Fei-kan
See also EWL 3

Pack, Robert 1929- .... **CLC 13**
See also CA 1-4R; CANR 3, 44, 82; CP 7;
DLB 5; SATA 118

Padgett, Lewis
See Kuttner, Henry

Padilla (Lorenzo), Heberto
1932-2000 .... **CLC 38**
See also AITN 1; CA 123; 131; 189; CWW
2; EWL 3; HW 1

Page, James Patrick 1944-
See Page, Jimmy
See also CA 204

Page, Jimmy 1944- .... **CLC 12**
See Page, James Patrick

Page, Louise 1955- .... **CLC 40**
See also CA 140; CANR 76; CBD; CD 5;
CWD; DLB 233

Page, P(atricia) K(athleen) 1916- ...... **CLC 7,**
18; PC 12
See Cape, Judith
See also CA 53-56; CANR 4, 22, 65; CP 7;
DAC; DAM MST; DLB 68; MTCW 1;
RGEL 2

Page, Stanton
See Fuller, Henry Blake

Page, Stanton
See Fuller, Henry Blake

Page, Thomas Nelson 1853-1922 .... **SSC 23**
See also CA 118; 177; DLB 12, 78; DLBD
13; RGAL 4

Pagels, Elaine Hiesey 1943- .... **CLC 104**
See also CA 45-48; CANR 2, 24, 51; FW;
NCFS 4

Paget, Violet 1856-1935
See Lee, Vernon
See also CA 104; 166; GLL 1; HGG

Paget-Lowe, Henry
See Lovecraft, H(oward) P(hillips)

Paglia, Camille (Anna) 1947- .... **CLC 68**
See also CA 140; CANR 72; CPW; FW;
GLL 2; MTCW 2

Paige, Richard
See Koontz, Dean R(ay)

Paine, Thomas 1737-1809 .... **NCLC 62**
See also AMWS 1; CDALB 1640-1865;
DLB 31, 43, 73, 158; LAIT 1; RGAL 4;
RGEL 2; TUS

Pakenham, Antonia
See Fraser, Antonia (Pakenham)

Palamas, Costis
See Palamas, Kostes

Palamas, Kostes 1859-1943 .... **TCLC 5**
See Palamas, Kostis
See also CA 105; 190; RGWL 2, 3

Palamas, Kostis
See Palamas, Kostes
See also EWL 3

Palazzeschi, Aldo 1885-1974 .... **CLC 11**
See also CA 89-92; 53-56; DLB 114, 264;
EWL 3

Pales Matos, Luis 1898-1959 .... **HLCS 2**
See Pales Matos, Luis
See also DLB 290; HW 1; LAW

Paley, Grace 1922- .. **CLC 4, 6, 37, 140; SSC**
8
See also AMWS 6; CA 25-28R; CANR 13,
46, 74, 118; CN 7; CPW; DA3; DAM
POP; DLB 28, 218; EWL 3; EXPS; FW;
INT CANR-13; MAWW; MTCW 1, 2;
RGAL 4; RGSF 2; SSFS 3, 20

Palin, Michael (Edward) 1943- .... **CLC 21**
See Monty Python
See also CA 107; CANR 35, 109; SATA 67

Palliser, Charles 1947- .... **CLC 65**
See also CA 136; CANR 76; CN 7

Palma, Ricardo 1833-1919 .... **TCLC 29**
See also CA 168; LAW

Pamuk, Orhan 1952- .... **CLC 185**
See also CA 142; CANR 75, 127; CWW 2

Pancake, Breece Dexter 1952-1979
See Pancake, Breece D'J
See also CA 123; 109

Pancake, Breece D'J .... **CLC 29; SSC 61**
See Pancake, Breece Dexter
See also DLB 130

Panchenko, Nikolai .... **CLC 59**

Pankhurst, Emmeline (Goulden)
1858-1928 .... **TCLC 100**
See also CA 116; FW

Panko, Rudy
See Gogol, Nikolai (Vasilyevich)

Papadiamantis, Alexandros
1851-1911 .... **TCLC 29**
See also CA 168; EWL 3

Papadiamantopoulos, Johannes 1856-1910
See Moreas, Jean
See also CA 117
Papini, Giovanni 1881-1956 .... **TCLC 22**
See also CA 121; 180; DLB 264
Paracelsus 1493-1541 .... **LC 14**
See also DLB 179
Parasol, Peter
See Stevens, Wallace
Pardo Bazan, Emilia 1851-1921 .... **SSC 30**
See also EWL 3; FW; RGSF 2; RGWL 2, 3
Pareto, Vilfredo 1848-1923 .... **TCLC 69**
See also CA 175
Paretsky, Sara 1947- .... **CLC 135**
See also AAYA 30; BEST 90:3; CA 125;
129; CANR 59, 95; CMW 4; CPW; DA3;
DAM POP; DLB 306; INT CA-129;
MSW; RGAL 4
Parfenie, Maria
See Codrescu, Andrei
Parini, Jay (Lee) 1948- .... **CLC 54, 133**
See also CA 97-100; CAAS 16; CANR 32,
87
Park, Jordan
See Kornbluth, C(yril) M.; Pohl, Frederik
Park, Robert E(zra) 1864-1944 ..... **TCLC 73**
See also CA 122; 165
Parker, Bert
See Ellison, Harlan (Jay)
Parker, Dorothy (Rothschild)
1893-1967 . **CLC 15, 68; PC 28; SSC 2;
TCLC 143**
See also AMWS 9; CA 19-20; 25-28R; CAP
2; DA3; DAM POET; DLB 11, 45, 86;
EXPP; FW; MAWW; MTCW 1, 2; PFS
18; RGAL 4; RGSF 2; TUS
Parker, Robert B(rown) 1932- .... **CLC 27**
See also AAYA 28; BEST 89:4; BPFB 3;
CA 49-52; CANR 1, 26, 52, 89, 128;
CMW 4; CPW; DAM NOV, POP; DLB
306; INT CANR-26; MSW; MTCW 1
Parkin, Frank 1940- .... **CLC 43**
See also CA 147
Parkman, Francis, Jr. 1823-1893 .. **NCLC 12**
See also AMWS 2; DLB 1, 30, 183, 186,
235; RGAL 4
Parks, Gordon (Alexander Buchanan)
1912- .... **BLC 3; CLC 1, 16**
See also AAYA 36; AITN 2; BW 2, 3; CA
41-44R; CANR 26, 66; DA3; DAM
MULT; DLB 33; MTCW 2; SATA 8, 108
Parks, Suzan-Lori 1964(?)- .... **DC 23**
See also AAYA 55; CA 201; CAD; CD 5;
CWD; RGAL 4
Parks, Tim(othy Harold) 1954- ...... **CLC 147**
See also CA 126; 131; CANR 77; DLB 231;
INT CA-131
Parmenides c. 515 B.C.-c. 450
B.C. .... **CMLC 22**
See also DLB 176
Parnell, Thomas 1679-1718 .... **LC 3**
See also DLB 95; RGEL 2
Parr, Catherine c. 1513(?)-1548 .... **LC 86**
See also DLB 136
Parra, Nicanor 1914- ... **CLC 2, 102; HLC 2;
PC 39**
See also CA 85-88; CANR 32; CWW 2;
DAM MULT; DLB 283; EWL 3; HW 1;
LAW; MTCW 1
Parra Sanojo, Ana Teresa de la
1890-1936 .... **HLCS 2**
See de la Parra, (Ana) Teresa (Sonojo)
See also LAW
Parrish, Mary Frances
See Fisher, M(ary) F(rances) K(ennedy)
Parshchikov, Aleksei 1954- .... **CLC 59**
See Parshchikov, Aleksei Maksimovich

Parshchikov, Aleksei Maksimovich
See Parshchikov, Aleksei
See also DLB 285
Parson, Professor
See Coleridge, Samuel Taylor
Parson Lot
See Kingsley, Charles
Parton, Sara Payson Willis
1811-1872 .... **NCLC 86**
See also DLB 43, 74, 239
Partridge, Anthony
See Oppenheim, E(dward) Phillips
Pascal, Blaise 1623-1662 .... **LC 35**
See also DLB 268; EW 3; GFL Beginnings
to 1789; RGWL 2, 3; TWA
Pascoli, Giovanni 1855-1912 .... **TCLC 45**
See also CA 170; EW 7; EWL 3
Pasolini, Pier Paolo 1922-1975 .. **CLC 20, 37,
106; PC 17**
See also CA 93-96; 61-64; CANR 63; DLB
128, 177; EWL 3; MTCW 1; RGWL 2, 3
Pasquini
See Silone, Ignazio
Pastan, Linda (Olenik) 1932- .... **CLC 27**
See also CA 61-64; CANR 18, 40, 61, 113;
CP 7; CSW; CWP; DAM POET; DLB 5;
PFS 8
Pasternak, Boris (Leonidovich)
1890-1960 ...... **CLC 7, 10, 18, 63; PC 6;
SSC 31; WLC**
See also BPFB 3; CA 127; 116; DA; DA3;
DAB; DAC; DAM MST, NOV, POET;
DLB 302; EW 10; MTCW 1, 2; RGSF 2;
RGWL 2, 3; TWA; WP
Patchen, Kenneth 1911-1972 .... **CLC 1, 2, 18**
See also BG 3; CA 1-4R; 33-36R; CANR
3, 35; DAM POET; DLB 16, 48; EWL 3;
MTCW 1; RGAL 4
Pater, Walter (Horatio) 1839-1894 . **NCLC 7,
90**
See also BRW 5; CDBLB 1832-1890; DLB
57, 156; RGEL 2; TEA
Paterson, A(ndrew) B(arton)
1864-1941 .... **TCLC 32**
See also CA 155; DLB 230; RGEL 2; SATA
97
Paterson, Banjo
See Paterson, A(ndrew) B(arton)
Paterson, Katherine (Womeldorf)
1932- .... **CLC 12, 30**
See also AAYA 1, 31; BYA 1, 2, 7; CA 21-
24R; CANR 28, 59, 111; CLR 7, 50;
CWRI 5; DLB 52; JRDA; LAIT 4; MAI-
CYA 1, 2; MAICYAS 1; MTCW 1; SATA
13, 53, 92, 133; WYA; YAW
Patmore, Coventry Kersey Dighton
1823-1896 .... **NCLC 9; PC 59**
See also DLB 35, 98; RGEL 2; TEA
Paton, Alan (Stewart) 1903-1988 ...... **CLC 4,
10, 25, 55, 106; WLC**
See also AAYA 26; AFW; BPFB 3; BRWS
2; BYA 1; CA 13-16; 125; CANR 22;
CAP 1; DA; DA3; DAB; DAC; DAM
MST, NOV; DLB 225; DLBD 17; EWL
3; EXPN; LAIT 4; MTCW 1, 2; NFS 3,
12; RGEL 2; SATA 11; SATA-Obit 56;
TWA; WLIT 2; WWE 1
Paton Walsh, Gillian 1937- .... **CLC 35**
See Paton Walsh, Jill; Walsh, Jill Paton
See also AAYA 11; CANR 38, 83; CLR 2,
65; DLB 161; JRDA; MAICYA 1, 2;
SAAS 3; SATA 4, 72, 109; YAW
Paton Walsh, Jill
See Paton Walsh, Gillian
See also AAYA 47; BYA 1, 8
Patterson, (Horace) Orlando (Lloyd)
1940- .... **BLCS**
See also BW 1; CA 65-68; CANR 27, 84;
CN 7

Patton, George S(mith), Jr.
1885-1945 .... **TCLC 79**
See also CA 189
Paulding, James Kirke 1778-1860 ... **NCLC 2**
See also DLB 3, 59, 74, 250; RGAL 4
Paulin, Thomas Neilson 1949-
See Paulin, Tom
See also CA 123; 128; CANR 98; CP 7
Paulin, Tom .... **CLC 37, 177**
See Paulin, Thomas Neilson
See also DLB 40
Pausanias c. 1st cent. - .... **CMLC 36**
Paustovsky, Konstantin (Georgievich)
1892-1968 .... **CLC 40**
See also CA 93-96; 25-28R; DLB 272;
EWL 3
Pavese, Cesare 1908-1950 .... **PC 13; SSC 19;
TCLC 3**
See also CA 104; 169; DLB 128, 177; EW
12; EWL 3; PFS 20; RGSF 2; RGWL 2,
3; TWA
Pavic, Milorad 1929- .... **CLC 60**
See also CA 136; CDWLB 4; CWW 2; DLB
181; EWL 3; RGWL 3
Pavlov, Ivan Petrovich 1849-1936 . **TCLC 91**
See also CA 118; 180
Pavlova, Karolina Karlovna
1807-1893 .... **NCLC 138**
See also DLB 205
Payne, Alan
See Jakes, John (William)
Paz, Gil
See Lugones, Leopoldo
Paz, Octavio 1914-1998 . **CLC 3, 4, 6, 10, 19,
51, 65, 119; HLC 2; PC 1, 48; WLC**
See also AAYA 50; CA 73-76; 165; CANR
32, 65, 104; CWW 2; DA; DA3; DAB;
DAC; DAM MST, MULT, POET; DLB
290; DLBY 1990, 1998; DNFS 1; EWL
3; HW 1, 2; LAW; LAWS 1; MTCW 1, 2;
PFS 18; RGWL 2, 3; SSFS 13; TWA;
WLIT 1
p'Bitek, Okot 1931-1982 .... **BLC 3; CLC 96;
TCLC 149**
See also AFW; BW 2, 3; CA 124; 107;
CANR 82; DAM MULT; DLB 125; EWL
3; MTCW 1, 2; RGEL 2; WLIT 2
Peacock, Molly 1947- .... **CLC 60**
See also CA 103; CAAS 21; CANR 52, 84;
CP 7; CWP; DLB 120, 282
Peacock, Thomas Love
1785-1866 .... **NCLC 22**
See also BRW 4; DLB 96, 116; RGEL 2;
RGSF 2
Peake, Mervyn 1911-1968 .... **CLC 7, 54**
See also CA 5-8R; 25-28R; CANR 3; DLB
15, 160, 255; FANT; MTCW 1; RGEL 2;
SATA 23; SFW 4
Pearce, Philippa
See Christie, Philippa
See also CA 5-8R; CANR 4, 109; CWRI 5;
FANT; MAICYA 2
Pearl, Eric
See Elman, Richard (Martin)
Pearson, T(homas) R(eid) 1956- .... **CLC 39**
See also CA 120; 130; CANR 97; CSW;
INT CA-130
Peck, Dale 1967- .... **CLC 81**
See also CA 146; CANR 72, 127; GLL 2
Peck, John (Frederick) 1941- .... **CLC 3**
See also CA 49-52; CANR 3, 100; CP 7
Peck, Richard (Wayne) 1934- .... **CLC 21**
See also AAYA 1, 24; BYA 1, 6, 8, 11; CA
85-88; CANR 19, 38, 129; CLR 15; INT
CANR-19; JRDA; MAICYA 1, 2; SAAS
2; SATA 18, 55, 97; SATA-Essay 110;
WYA; YAW

Peck, Robert Newton 1928- .... **CLC 17**
　　See also AAYA 3, 43; BYA 1, 6; CA 81-84,
　　182; CAAE 182; CANR 31, 63, 127; CLR
　　45; DA; DAC; DAM MST; JRDA; LAIT
　　3; MAICYA 1, 2; SAAS 1; SATA 21, 62,
　　111; SATA-Essay 108; WYA; YAW

Peckinpah, (David) Sam(uel)
　　1925-1984 .... **CLC 20**
　　See also CA 109; 114; CANR 82

Pedersen, Knut 1859-1952
　　See Hamsun, Knut
　　See also CA 104; 119; CANR 63; MTCW
　　1, 2

Peeslake, Gaffer
　　See Durrell, Lawrence (George)

Peguy, Charles (Pierre)
　　1873-1914 .... **TCLC 10**
　　See also CA 107; 193; DLB 258; EWL 3;
　　GFL 1789 to the Present

Peirce, Charles Sanders
　　1839-1914 .... **TCLC 81**
　　See also CA 194; DLB 270

Pellicer, Carlos 1900(?)-1977 .... **HLCS 2**
　　See also CA 153; 69-72; DLB 290; EWL 3;
　　HW 1

Pena, Ramon del Valle y
　　See Valle-Inclan, Ramon (Maria) del

Pendennis, Arthur Esquir
　　See Thackeray, William Makepeace

Penn, William 1644-1718 .... **LC 25**
　　See also DLB 24

PEPECE
　　See Prado (Calvo), Pedro

Pepys, Samuel 1633-1703 ... **LC 11, 58; WLC**
　　See also BRW 2; CDBLB 1660-1789; DA;
　　DA3; DAB; DAC; DAM MST; DLB 101,
　　213; NCFS 4; RGEL 2; TEA; WLIT 3

Percy, Thomas 1729-1811 .... **NCLC 95**
　　See also DLB 104

Percy, Walker 1916-1990 .... **CLC 2, 3, 6, 8,
　　14, 18, 47, 65**
　　See also AMWS 3; BPFB 3; CA 1-4R; 131;
　　CANR 1, 23, 64; CPW; CSW; DA3;
　　DAM NOV, POP; DLB 2; DLBY 1980,
　　1990; EWL 3; MTCW 1, 2; RGAL 4;
　　TUS

Percy, William Alexander
　　1885-1942 .... **TCLC 84**
　　See also CA 163; MTCW 2

Perec, Georges 1936-1982 .... **CLC 56, 116**
　　See also CA 141; DLB 83, 299; EWL 3;
　　GFL 1789 to the Present; RGWL 3

**Pereda (y Sanchez de Porrua), Jose Maria
　　de** 1833-1906 .... **TCLC 16**
　　See also CA 117

Pereda y Porrua, Jose Maria de
　　See Pereda (y Sanchez de Porrua), Jose
　　Maria de

Peregoy, George Weems
　　See Mencken, H(enry) L(ouis)

Perelman, S(idney) J(oseph)
　　1904-1979 .. **CLC 3, 5, 9, 15, 23, 44, 49;
　　SSC 32**
　　See also AITN 1, 2; BPFB 3; CA 73-76;
　　89-92; CANR 18; DAM DRAM; DLB 11,
　　44; MTCW 1, 2; RGAL 4

Peret, Benjamin 1899-1959 .... **PC 33; TCLC
　　20**
　　See also CA 117; 186; GFL 1789 to the
　　Present

Peretz, Isaac Leib 1851(?)-1915
　　See Peretz, Isaac Loeb
　　See also CA 201

Peretz, Isaac Loeb 1851(?)-1915 ...... **SSC 26;
　　TCLC 16**
　　See Peretz, Isaac Leib
　　See also CA 109

Peretz, Yitzkhok Leibush
　　See Peretz, Isaac Loeb

Perez Galdos, Benito 1843-1920 ..... **HLCS 2;
　　TCLC 27**
　　See Galdos, Benito Perez
　　See also CA 125; 153; EWL 3; HW 1;
　　RGWL 2, 3

Peri Rossi, Cristina 1941- .. **CLC 156; HLCS
　　2**
　　See also CA 131; CANR 59, 81; CWW 2;
　　DLB 145, 290; EWL 3; HW 1, 2

Perlata
　　See Peret, Benjamin

Perloff, Marjorie G(abrielle)
　　1931- .... **CLC 137**
　　See also CA 57-60; CANR 7, 22, 49, 104

Perrault, Charles 1628-1703 .... **LC 2, 56**
　　See also BYA 4; CLR 79; DLB 268; GFL
　　Beginnings to 1789; MAICYA 1, 2;
　　RGWL 2, 3; SATA 25; WCH

Perry, Anne 1938- .... **CLC 126**
　　See also CA 101; CANR 22, 50, 84; CMW
　　4; CN 7; CPW; DLB 276

Perry, Brighton
　　See Sherwood, Robert E(mmet)

Perse, St.-John
　　See Leger, (Marie-Rene Auguste) Alexis
　　Saint-Leger

Perse, Saint-John
　　See Leger, (Marie-Rene Auguste) Alexis
　　Saint-Leger
　　See also DLB 258; RGWL 3

Perutz, Leo(pold) 1882-1957 .... **TCLC 60**
　　See also CA 147; DLB 81

Peseenz, Tulio F.
　　See Lopez y Fuentes, Gregorio

Pesetsky, Bette 1932- .... **CLC 28**
　　See also CA 133; DLB 130

Peshkov, Alexei Maximovich 1868-1936
　　See Gorky, Maxim
　　See also CA 105; 141; CANR 83; DA;
　　DAC; DAM DRAM, MST, NOV; MTCW
　　2

Pessoa, Fernando (Antonio Nogueira)
　　1888-1935 ..... **HLC 2; PC 20; TCLC 27**
　　See also CA 125; 183; DAM MULT; DLB
　　287; EW 10; EWL 3; RGWL 2, 3; WP

Peterkin, Julia Mood 1880-1961 ...... **CLC 31**
　　See also CA 102; DLB 9

Peters, Joan K(aren) 1945- .... **CLC 39**
　　See also CA 158; CANR 109

Peters, Robert L(ouis) 1924- .... **CLC 7**
　　See also CA 13-16R; CAAS 8; CP 7; DLB
　　105

Petofi, Sandor 1823-1849 .... **NCLC 21**
　　See also RGWL 2, 3

Petrakis, Harry Mark 1923- .... **CLC 3**
　　See also CA 9-12R; CANR 4, 30, 85; CN 7

Petrarch 1304-1374 .... **CMLC 20; PC 8**
　　See also DA3; DAM POET; EW 2; LMFS
　　1; RGWL 2. 3

Petronius c. 20-66 .... **CMLC 34**
　　See also AW 2; CDWLB 1; DLB 211;
　　RGWL 2, 3

Petrov, Evgeny .... **TCLC 21**
　　See Kataev, Evgeny Petrovich

Petry, Ann (Lane) 1908-1997 .. **CLC 1, 7, 18;
　　TCLC 112**
　　See also AFAW 1, 2; BPFB 3; BW 1, 3;
　　BYA 2; CA 5-8R; 157; CAAS 6; CANR
　　4, 46; CLR 12; CN 7; DLB 76; EWL 3;
　　JRDA; LAIT 1; MAICYA 1, 2; MAIC-
　　YAS 1; MTCW 1; RGAL 4; SATA 5;
　　SATA-Obit 94; TUS

Petursson, Halligrimur 1614-1674 .... **LC 8**

Peychinovich
　　See Vazov, Ivan (Minchov)

Phaedrus c. 15 B.C.-c. 50 .... **CMLC 25**
　　See also DLB 211

Phelps (Ward), Elizabeth Stuart
　　See Phelps, Elizabeth Stuart
　　See also FW

Phelps, Elizabeth Stuart
　　1844-1911 .... **TCLC 113**
　　See Phelps (Ward), Elizabeth Stuart
　　See also DLB 74

Philips, Katherine 1632-1664 . **LC 30; PC 40**
　　See also DLB 131; RGEL 2

Philipson, Morris H. 1926- .... **CLC 53**
　　See also CA 1-4R; CANR 4

Phillips, Caryl 1958- .... **BLCS; CLC 96**
　　See also BRWS 5; BW 2; CA 141; CANR
　　63, 104; CBD; CD 5; CN 7; DA3; DAM
　　MULT; DLB 157; EWL 3; MTCW 2;
　　WLIT 4; WWE 1

Phillips, David Graham
　　1867-1911 .... **TCLC 44**
　　See also CA 108; 176; DLB 9, 12, 303;
　　RGAL 4

Phillips, Jack
　　See Sandburg, Carl (August)

Phillips, Jayne Anne 1952- .... **CLC 15, 33,
　　139; SSC 16**
　　See also AAYA 57; BPFB 3; CA 101;
　　CANR 24, 50, 96; CN 7; CSW; DLBY
　　1980; INT CANR-24; MTCW 1, 2; RGAL
　　4; RGSF 2; SSFS 4

Phillips, Richard
　　See Dick, Philip K(indred)

Phillips, Robert (Schaeffer) 1938- .... **CLC 28**
　　See also CA 17-20R; CAAS 13; CANR 8;
　　DLB 105

Phillips, Ward
　　See Lovecraft, H(oward) P(hillips)

Philostratus, Flavius c. 179-c.
　　244 .... **CMLC 62**

Piccolo, Lucio 1901-1969 .... **CLC 13**
　　See also CA 97-100; DLB 114; EWL 3

Pickthall, Marjorie L(owry) C(hristie)
　　1883-1922 .... **TCLC 21**
　　See also CA 107; DLB 92

Pico della Mirandola, Giovanni
　　1463-1494 .... **LC 15**
　　See also LMFS 1

Piercy, Marge 1936- .... **CLC 3, 6, 14, 18, 27,
　　62, 128; PC 29**
　　See also BPFB 3; CA 21-24R; 187; CAAE
　　187; CAAS 1; CANR 13, 43, 66, 111; CN
　　7; CP 7; CWP; DLB 120, 227; EXPP;
　　FW; MTCW 1, 2; PFS 9; SFW 4

Piers, Robert
　　See Anthony, Piers

Pieyre de Mandiargues, Andre 1909-1991
　　See Mandiargues, Andre Pieyre de
　　See also CA 103; 136; CANR 22, 82; EWL
　　3; GFL 1789 to the Present

Pilnyak, Boris 1894-1938 . **SSC 48; TCLC 23**
　　See Vogau, Boris Andreyevich
　　See also EWL 3

Pinchback, Eugene
　　See Toomer, Jean

Pincherle, Alberto 1907-1990 ...... **CLC 11, 18**
　　See Moravia, Alberto
　　See also CA 25-28R; 132; CANR 33, 63;
　　DAM NOV; MTCW 1

Pinckney, Darryl 1953- .... **CLC 76**
　　See also BW 2, 3; CA 143; CANR 79

Pindar 518(?) B.C.-438(?) B.C. .... **CMLC 12;
　　PC 19**
　　See also AW 1; CDWLB 1; DLB 176;
　　RGWL 2

Pineda, Cecile 1942- .... **CLC 39**
　　See also CA 118; DLB 209

Pinero, Arthur Wing 1855-1934 .... **TCLC 32**
　　See also CA 110; 153; DAM DRAM; DLB
　　10; RGEL 2

Pinero, Miguel (Antonio Gomez)
1946-1988 .... **CLC 4, 55**
See also CA 61-64; 125; CAD; CANR 29,
90; DLB 266; HW 1; LLW 1

Pinget, Robert 1919-1997 .... **CLC 7, 13, 37**
See also CA 85-88; 160; CWW 2; DLB 83;
EWL 3; GFL 1789 to the Present

Pink Floyd
See Barrett, (Roger) Syd; Gilmour, David;
Mason, Nick; Waters, Roger; Wright, Rick

Pinkney, Edward 1802-1828 .... **NCLC 31**
See also DLB 248

Pinkwater, Daniel
See Pinkwater, Daniel Manus

Pinkwater, Daniel Manus 1941- .... **CLC 35**
See also AAYA 1, 46; BYA 9; CA 29-32R;
CANR 12, 38, 89; CLR 4; CSW; FANT;
JRDA; MAICYA 1, 2; SAAS 3; SATA 8,
46, 76, 114; SFW 4; YAW

Pinkwater, Manus
See Pinkwater, Daniel Manus

Pinsky, Robert 1940- .... **CLC 9, 19, 38, 94,
121; PC 27**
See also AMWS 6; CA 29-32R; CAAS 4;
CANR 58, 97; CP 7; DA3; DAM POET;
DLBY 1982, 1998; MTCW 2; PFS 18;
RGAL 4

Pinta, Harold
See Pinter, Harold

Pinter, Harold 1930- .. **CLC 1, 3, 6, 9, 11, 15,
27, 58, 73; DC 15; WLC**
See also BRWR 1; BRWS 1; CA 5-8R;
CANR 33, 65, 112; CBD; CD 5; CDBLB
1960 to Present; DA; DA3; DAB; DAC;
DAM DRAM, MST; DFS 3, 5, 7, 14;
DLB 13; EWL 3; IDFW 3, 4; LMFS 2;
MTCW 1, 2; RGEL 2; TEA

Piozzi, Hester Lynch (Thrale)
1741-1821 .... **NCLC 57**
See also DLB 104, 142

Pirandello, Luigi 1867-1936 .. **DC 5; SSC 22;
TCLC 4, 29; WLC**
See also CA 104; 153; CANR 103; DA;
DA3; DAB; DAC; DAM DRAM, MST;
DFS 4, 9; DLB 264; EW 8; EWL 3;
MTCW 2; RGSF 2; RGWL 2, 3

Pirsig, Robert M(aynard) 1928- ... **CLC 4, 6,
73**
See also CA 53-56; CANR 42, 74; CPW 1;
DA3; DAM POP; MTCW 1, 2; SATA 39

Pisarev, Dmitrii Ivanovich
See Pisarev, Dmitry Ivanovich
See also DLB 277

Pisarev, Dmitry Ivanovich
1840-1868 .... **NCLC 25**
See also Pisarev, Dmitrii Ivanovich

Pix, Mary (Griffith) 1666-1709 .... **LC 8**
See also DLB 80

Pixerecourt, (Rene Charles) Guilbert de
1773-1844 .... **NCLC 39**
See also DLB 192; GFL 1789 to the Present

Plaatje, Sol(omon) T(shekisho)
1878-1932 .... **BLCS; TCLC 73**
See also BW 2, 3; CA 141; CANR 79; DLB
125, 225

Plaidy, Jean
See Hibbert, Eleanor Alice Burford

Planche, James Robinson
1796-1880 .... **NCLC 42**
See also RGEL 2

Plant, Robert 1948- .... **CLC 12**

Plante, David (Robert) 1940- . **CLC 7, 23, 38**
See also CA 37-40R; CANR 12, 36, 58, 82;
CN 7; DAM NOV; DLBY 1983; INT
CANR-12; MTCW 1

Plath, Sylvia 1932-1963 ..... **CLC 1, 2, 3, 5, 9,
11, 14, 17, 50, 51, 62, 111; PC 1, 37;
WLC**
See also AAYA 13; AMWR 2; AMWS 1;
BPFB 3; CA 19-20; CANR 34, 101; CAP
2; CDALB 1941-1968; DA; DA3; DAB;
DAC; DAM MST, POET; DLB 5, 6, 152;
EWL 3; EXPN; EXPP; FW; LAIT 4;
MAWW; MTCW 1, 2; NFS 1; PAB; PFS
1, 15; RGAL 4; SATA 96; TUS; WP;
YAW

Plato c. 428 B.C.-347 B.C. . **CMLC 8; WLCS**
See also AW 1; CDWLB 1; DA; DA3;
DAB; DAC; DAM MST; DLB 176; LAIT
1; LATS 1:1; RGWL 2, 3

Platonov, Andrei
See Klimentov, Andrei Platonovich

Platonov, Andrei Platonovich
See Klimentov, Andrei Platonovich
See also DLB 272

Platonov, Andrey Platonovich
See Klimentov, Andrei Platonovich
See also EWL 3

Platt, Kin 1911- .... **CLC 26**
See also AAYA 11; CA 17-20R; CANR 11;
JRDA; SAAS 17; SATA 21, 86; WYA

Plautus c. 254 B.C.-c. 184 B.C. .... **CMLC 24;
DC 6**
See also AW 1; CDWLB 1; DLB 211;
RGWL 2, 3

Plick et Plock
See Simenon, Georges (Jacques Christian)

Plieksans, Janis
See Rainis, Janis

Plimpton, George (Ames)
1927-2003 .... **CLC 36**
See also AITN 1; CA 21-24R; 224; CANR
32, 70, 103, 133; DLB 185, 241; MTCW
1, 2; SATA 10; SATA-Obit 150

Pliny the Elder c. 23-79 .... **CMLC 23**
See also DLB 211

Pliny the Younger c. 61-c. 112 ...... **CMLC 62**
See also AW 2; DLB 211

Plomer, William Charles Franklin
1903-1973 .... **CLC 4, 8**
See also AFW; CA 21-22; CANR 34; CAP
2; DLB 20, 162, 191, 225; EWL 3;
MTCW 1; RGEL 2; RGSF 2; SATA 24

Plotinus 204-270 .... **CMLC 46**
See also CDWLB 1; DLB 176

Plowman, Piers
See Kavanagh, Patrick (Joseph)

Plum, J.
See Wodehouse, P(elham) G(renville)

Plumly, Stanley (Ross) 1939- .... **CLC 33**
See also CA 108; 110; CANR 97; CP 7;
DLB 5, 193; INT CA-110

Plumpe, Friedrich Wilhelm
1888-1931 .... **TCLC 53**
See also CA 112

Plutarch c. 46-c. 120 .... **CMLC 60**
See also AW 2; CDWLB 1; DLB 176;
RGWL 2, 3; TWA

Po Chu-i 772-846 .... **CMLC 24**

Podhoretz, Norman 1930- .... **CLC 189**
See also AMWS 8; CA 9-12R; CANR 7, 78

Poe, Edgar Allan 1809-1849 ..... **NCLC 1, 16,
55, 78, 94, 97, 117; PC 1, 54; SSC 1,
22, 34, 35, 54; WLC**
See also AAYA 14; AMW; AMWC 1;
AMWR 2; BPFB 3; BYA 5, 11; CDALB
1640-1865; CMW 4; DA; DA3; DAB;
DAC; DAM MST, POET; DLB 3, 59, 73,
74, 248, 254; EXPP; EXPS; HGG; LAIT
2; LATS 1:1; LMFS 1; MSW; PAB; PFS
1, 3, 9; RGAL 4; RGSF 2; SATA 23;
SCFW 2; SFW 4; SSFS 2, 4, 7, 8, 16;
SUFW; TUS; WP; WYA

Poet of Titchfield Street, The
See Pound, Ezra (Weston Loomis)

Pohl, Frederik 1919- .... **CLC 18; SSC 25**
See also AAYA 24; CA 61-64, 188; CAAE
188; CAAS 1; CANR 11, 37, 81; CN 7;
DLB 8; INT CANR-11; MTCW 1, 2;
SATA 24; SCFW 2; SFW 4

Poirier, Louis 1910-
See Gracq, Julien
See also CA 122; 126

Poitier, Sidney 1927- .... **CLC 26**
See also BW 1; CA 117; CANR 94

Pokagon, Simon 1830-1899 .... **NNAL**
See also DAM MULT

Polanski, Roman 1933- .... **CLC 16, 178**
See also CA 77-80

Poliakoff, Stephen 1952- .... **CLC 38**
See also CA 106; CANR 116; CBD; CD 5;
DLB 13

Police, The
See Copeland, Stewart (Armstrong); Summers, Andrew James

Polidori, John William 1795-1821 . **NCLC 51**
See also DLB 116; HGG

Pollitt, Katha 1949- .... **CLC 28, 122**
See also CA 120; 122; CANR 66, 108;
MTCW 1, 2

Pollock, (Mary) Sharon 1936- .... **CLC 50**
See also CA 141; CANR 132; CD 5; CWD;
DAC; DAM DRAM, MST; DFS 3; DLB
60; FW

Pollock, Sharon 1936- .... **DC 20**

Polo, Marco 1254-1324 .... **CMLC 15**

Polonsky, Abraham (Lincoln)
1910-1999 .... **CLC 92**
See also CA 104; 187; DLB 26; INT CA-
104

Polybius c. 200 B.C.-c. 118 B.C. ... **CMLC 17**
See also AW 1; DLB 176; RGWL 2, 3

Pomerance, Bernard 1940- .... **CLC 13**
See also CA 101; CAD; CANR 49; CD 5;
DAM DRAM; DFS 9; LAIT 2

Ponge, Francis 1899-1988 .... **CLC 6, 18**
See also CA 85-88; 126; CANR 40, 86;
DAM POET; DLBY 2002; EWL 3; GFL
1789 to the Present; RGWL 2, 3

Poniatowska, Elena 1933- . **CLC 140; HLC 2**
See also CA 101; CANR 32, 66, 107; CD-
WLB 3; CWW 2; DAM MULT; DLB 113;
EWL 3; HW 1, 2; LAWS 1; WLIT 1

Pontoppidan, Henrik 1857-1943 .... **TCLC 29**
See also CA 170; DLB 300

Ponty, Maurice Merleau
See Merleau-Ponty, Maurice

Poole, Josephine .... **CLC 17**
See Helyar, Jane Penelope Josephine
See also SAAS 2; SATA 5

Popa, Vasko 1922-1991 .... **CLC 19**
See also CA 112; 148; CDWLB 4; DLB
181; EWL 3; RGWL 2, 3

Pope, Alexander 1688-1744 ...... **LC 3, 58, 60,
64; PC 26; WLC**
See also BRW 3; BRWC 1; BRWR 1; CD-
BLB 1660-1789; DA; DA3; DAB; DAC;
DAM MST, POET; DLB 95, 101, 213;
EXPP; PAB; PFS 12; RGEL 2; WLIT 3;
WP

Popov, Evgenii Anatol'evich
See Popov, Yevgeny
See also DLB 285

Popov, Yevgeny .... **CLC 59**
See Popov, Evgenii Anatol'evich

Poquelin, Jean-Baptiste
See Moliere

Porphyry c. 233-c. 305 .... **CMLC 71**

Porter, Connie (Rose) 1959(?)- .... **CLC 70**
See also BW 2, 3; CA 142; CANR 90, 109;
SATA 81, 129

Robertson, Tom
See Robertson, Thomas William
See also RGEL 2
Robeson, Kenneth
See Dent, Lester
Robinson, Edwin Arlington
1869-1935 .... **PC 1, 35; TCLC 5, 101**
See also AMW; CA 104; 133; CDALB
1865-1917; DA; DAC; DAM MST,
POET; DLB 54; EWL 3; EXPP; MTCW
1, 2; PAB; PFS 4; RGAL 4; WP
Robinson, Henry Crabb
1775-1867 .... **NCLC 15**
See also DLB 107
Robinson, Jill 1936- .... **CLC 10**
See also CA 102; CANR 120; INT CA-102
Robinson, Kim Stanley 1952- .... **CLC 34**
See also AAYA 26; CA 126; CANR 113;
CN 7; SATA 109; SCFW 2; SFW 4
Robinson, Lloyd
See Silverberg, Robert
Robinson, Marilynne 1944- ...... **CLC 25, 180**
See also CA 116; CANR 80; CN 7; DLB
206
Robinson, Mary 1758-1800 .... **NCLC 142**
See also DLB 158; FW
Robinson, Smokey .... **CLC 21**
See Robinson, William, Jr.
Robinson, William, Jr. 1940-
See Robinson, Smokey
See also CA 116
Robison, Mary 1949- .... **CLC 42, 98**
See also CA 113; 116; CANR 87; CN 7;
DLB 130; INT CA-116; RGSF 2
Rochester
See Wilmot, John
See also RGEL 2
Rod, Edouard 1857-1910 .... **TCLC 52**
Roddenberry, Eugene Wesley 1921-1991
See Roddenberry, Gene
See also CA 110; 135; CANR 37; SATA 45;
SATA-Obit 69
Roddenberry, Gene .... **CLC 17**
See Roddenberry, Eugene Wesley
See also AAYA 5; SATA-Obit 69
Rodgers, Mary 1931- .... **CLC 12**
See also BYA 5; CA 49-52; CANR 8, 55,
90; CLR 20; CWRI 5; INT CANR-8;
JRDA; MAICYA 1, 2; SATA 8, 130
Rodgers, W(illiam) R(obert)
1909-1969 .... **CLC 7**
See also CA 85-88; DLB 20; RGEL 2
Rodman, Eric
See Silverberg, Robert
Rodman, Howard 1920(?)-1985 .... **CLC 65**
See also CA 118
Rodman, Maia
See Wojciechowska, Maia (Teresa)
Rodo, Jose Enrique 1871(?)-1917 .... **HLCS 2**
See also CA 178; EWL 3; HW 2; LAW
Rodolph, Utto
See Ouologuem, Yambo
Rodriguez, Claudio 1934-1999 .... **CLC 10**
See also CA 188; DLB 134
Rodriguez, Richard 1944- .... **CLC 155; HLC 2**
See also CA 110; CANR 66, 116; DAM
MULT; DLB 82, 256; HW 1, 2; LAIT 5;
LLW 1; NCFS 3; WLIT 1
Roelvaag, O(le) E(dvart) 1876-1931
See Rolvaag, O(le) E(dvart)
See also CA 117; 171
Roethke, Theodore (Huebner)
1908-1963 .... **CLC 1, 3, 8, 11, 19, 46,
101; PC 15**
See also AMW; CA 81-84; CABS 2;
CDALB 1941-1968; DA3; DAM POET;
DLB 5, 206; EWL 3; EXPP; MTCW 1, 2;
PAB; PFS 3; RGAL 4; WP

Rogers, Carl R(ansom)
1902-1987 .... **TCLC 125**
See also CA 1-4R; 121; CANR 1, 18;
MTCW 1
Rogers, Samuel 1763-1855 .... **NCLC 69**
See also DLB 93; RGEL 2
Rogers, Thomas Hunton 1927- .... **CLC 57**
See also CA 89-92; INT CA-89-92
Rogers, Will(iam Penn Adair)
1879-1935 .... **NNAL; TCLC 8, 71**
See also CA 105; 144; DA3; DAM MULT;
DLB 11; MTCW 2
Rogin, Gilbert 1929- .... **CLC 18**
See also CA 65-68; CANR 15
Rohan, Koda
See Koda Shigeyuki
Rohlfs, Anna Katharine Green
See Green, Anna Katharine
Rohmer, Eric .... **CLC 16**
See Scherer, Jean-Marie Maurice
Rohmer, Sax .... **TCLC 28**
See Ward, Arthur Henry Sarsfield
See also DLB 70; MSW; SUFW
Roiphe, Anne (Richardson) 1935- .. **CLC 3, 9**
See also CA 89-92; CANR 45, 73; DLBY
1980; INT CA-89-92
Rojas, Fernando de 1475-1541 ... **HLCS 1, 2;
LC 23**
See also DLB 286; RGWL 2, 3
Rojas, Gonzalo 1917- .... **HLCS 2**
See also CA 178; HW 2; LAWS 1
Roland, Marie-Jeanne 1754-1793 .... **LC 98**
**Rolfe, Frederick (William Serafino Austin
Lewis Mary)** 1860-1913 .... **TCLC 12**
See Al Siddik
See also CA 107; 210; DLB 34, 156; RGEL
2
Rolland, Romain 1866-1944 .... **TCLC 23**
See also CA 118; 197; DLB 65, 284; EWL
3; GFL 1789 to the Present; RGWL 2, 3
Rolle, Richard c. 1300-c. 1349 ...... **CMLC 21**
See also DLB 146; LMFS 1; RGEL 2
Rolvaag, O(le) E(dvart) .... **TCLC 17**
See Roelvaag, O(le) E(dvart)
See also DLB 9, 212; NFS 5; RGAL 4
Romain Arnaud, Saint
See Aragon, Louis
Romains, Jules 1885-1972 .... **CLC 7**
See also CA 85-88; CANR 34; DLB 65;
EWL 3; GFL 1789 to the Present; MTCW
1
Romero, Jose Ruben 1890-1952 .... **TCLC 14**
See also CA 114; 131; EWL 3; HW 1; LAW
Ronsard, Pierre de 1524-1585 . **LC 6, 54; PC
11**
See also EW 2; GFL Beginnings to 1789;
RGWL 2, 3; TWA
Rooke, Leon 1934- .... **CLC 25, 34**
See also CA 25-28R; CANR 23, 53; CCA
1; CPW; DAM POP
Roosevelt, Franklin Delano
1882-1945 .... **TCLC 93**
See also CA 116; 173; LAIT 3
Roosevelt, Theodore 1858-1919 ..... **TCLC 69**
See also CA 115; 170; DLB 47, 186, 275
Roper, William 1498-1578 .... **LC 10**
Roquelaure, A. N.
See Rice, Anne
Rosa, Joao Guimaraes 1908-1967 ... **CLC 23;
HLCS 1**
See Guimaraes Rosa, Joao
See also CA 89-92; DLB 113; EWL 3;
WLIT 1
Rose, Wendy 1948- . **CLC 85; NNAL; PC 13**
See also CA 53-56; CANR 5, 51; CWP;
DAM MULT; DLB 175; PFS 13; RGAL
4; SATA 12
Rosen, R. D.
See Rosen, Richard (Dean)

Rosen, Richard (Dean) 1949- .... **CLC 39**
See also CA 77-80; CANR 62, 120; CMW
4; INT CANR-30
Rosenberg, Isaac 1890-1918 .... **TCLC 12**
See also BRW 6; CA 107; 188; DLB 20,
216; EWL 3; PAB; RGEL 2
Rosenblatt, Joe .... **CLC 15**
See Rosenblatt, Joseph
Rosenblatt, Joseph 1933-
See Rosenblatt, Joe
See also CA 89-92; CP 7; INT CA-89-92
Rosenfeld, Samuel
See Tzara, Tristan
Rosenstock, Sami
See Tzara, Tristan
Rosenstock, Samuel
See Tzara, Tristan
Rosenthal, M(acha) L(ouis)
1917-1996 .... **CLC 28**
See also CA 1-4R; 152; CAAS 6; CANR 4,
51; CP 7; DLB 5; SATA 59
Ross, Barnaby
See Dannay, Frederic
Ross, Bernard L.
See Follett, Ken(neth Martin)
Ross, J. H.
See Lawrence, T(homas) E(dward)
Ross, John Hume
See Lawrence, T(homas) E(dward)
Ross, Martin 1862-1915
See Martin, Violet Florence
See also DLB 135; GLL 2; RGEL 2; RGSF
2
Ross, (James) Sinclair 1908-1996 ... **CLC 13;
SSC 24**
See also CA 73-76; CANR 81; CN 7; DAC;
DAM MST; DLB 88; RGEL 2; RGSF 2;
TCWW 2
Rossetti, Christina (Georgina)
1830-1894 .... **NCLC 2, 50, 66; PC 7;
WLC**
See also AAYA 51; BRW 5; BYA 4; DA;
DA3; DAB; DAC; DAM MST, POET;
DLB 35, 163, 240; EXPP; LATS 1:1;
MAICYA 1, 2; PFS 10, 14; RGEL 2;
SATA 20; TEA; WCH
Rossetti, Dante Gabriel 1828-1882 . **NCLC 4,
77; PC 44; WLC**
See also AAYA 51; BRW 5; CDBLB 1832-
1890; DA; DAB; DAC; DAM MST,
POET; DLB 35; EXPP; RGEL 2; TEA
Rossi, Cristina Peri
See Peri Rossi, Cristina
Rossi, Jean-Baptiste 1931-2003
See Japrisot, Sebastien
See also CA 201; 215
Rossner, Judith (Perelman) 1935- . **CLC 6, 9,
29**
See also AITN 2; BEST 90:3; BPFB 3; CA
17-20R; CANR 18, 51, 73; CN 7; DLB 6;
INT CANR-18; MTCW 1, 2
Rostand, Edmond (Eugene Alexis)
1868-1918 .... **DC 10; TCLC 6, 37**
See also CA 104; 126; DA; DA3; DAB;
DAC; DAM DRAM, MST; DFS 1; DLB
192; LAIT 1; MTCW 1; RGWL 2, 3;
TWA
Roth, Henry 1906-1995 ..... **CLC 2, 6, 11, 104**
See also AMWS 9; CA 11-12; 149; CANR
38, 63; CAP 1; CN 7; DA3; DLB 28;
EWL 3; MTCW 1, 2; RGAL 4
Roth, (Moses) Joseph 1894-1939 ... **TCLC 33**
See also CA 160; DLB 85; EWL 3; RGWL
2, 3
Roth, Philip (Milton) 1933- ... **CLC 1, 2, 3, 4,
6, 9, 15, 22, 31, 47, 66, 86, 119; SSC
26; WLC**
See also AMWR 2; AMWS 3; BEST 90:3;
BPFB 3; CA 1-4R; CANR 1, 22, 36, 55,
89, 132; CDALB 1968-1988; CN 7; CPW

1; DA; DA3; DAB; DAC; DAM MST, NOV, POP; DLB 2, 28, 173; DLBY 1982; EWL 3; MTCW 1, 2; RGAL 4; RGSF 2; SSFS 12, 18; TUS

Rothenberg, Jerome 1931- .... **CLC 6, 57**
See also CA 45-48; CANR 1, 106; CP 7; DLB 5, 193

Rotter, Pat ed. .... **CLC 65**

Roumain, Jacques (Jean Baptiste) 1907-1944 .... **BLC 3; TCLC 19**
See also BW 1; CA 117; 125; DAM MULT; EWL 3

Rourke, Constance Mayfield 1885-1941 .... **TCLC 12**
See also CA 107; 200; YABC 1

Rousseau, Jean-Baptiste 1671-1741 ...... **LC 9**

Rousseau, Jean-Jacques 1712-1778 .... **LC 14, 36; WLC**
See also DA; DA3; DAB; DAC; DAM MST; EW 4; GFL Beginnings to 1789; LMFS 1; RGWL 2, 3; TWA

Roussel, Raymond 1877-1933 .... **TCLC 20**
See also CA 117; 201; EWL 3; GFL 1789 to the Present

Rovit, Earl (Herbert) 1927- .... **CLC 7**
See also CA 5-8R; CANR 12

Rowe, Elizabeth Singer 1674-1737 ..... **LC 44**
See also DLB 39, 95

Rowe, Nicholas 1674-1718 .... **LC 8**
See also DLB 84; RGEL 2

Rowlandson, Mary 1637(?)-1678 .... **LC 66**
See also DLB 24, 200; RGAL 4

Rowley, Ames Dorrance
See Lovecraft, H(oward) P(hillips)

Rowley, William 1585(?)-1626 .... **LC 100**
See also DLB 58; RGEL 2

Rowling, J(oanne) K(athleen) 1966- .... **CLC 137**
See also AAYA 34; BYA 11, 13, 14; CA 173; CANR 128; CLR 66, 80; MAICYA 2; SATA 109; SUFW 2

Rowson, Susanna Haswell 1762(?)-1824 .... **NCLC 5, 69**
See also DLB 37, 200; RGAL 4

Roy, Arundhati 1960(?)- .... **CLC 109**
See also CA 163; CANR 90, 126; DLBY 1997; EWL 3; LATS 1:2; WWE 1

Roy, Gabrielle 1909-1983 .... **CLC 10, 14**
See also CA 53-56; 110; CANR 5, 61; CCA 1; DAB; DAC; DAM MST; DLB 68; EWL 3; MTCW 1; RGWL 2, 3; SATA 104

Royko, Mike 1932-1997 .... **CLC 109**
See also CA 89-92; 157; CANR 26, 111; CPW

Rozanov, Vasilii Vasil'evich
See Rozanov, Vassili
See also DLB 295

Rozanov, Vasily Vasilyevich
See Rozanov, Vassili
See also EWL 3

Rozanov, Vassili 1856-1919 .... **TCLC 104**
See Rozanov, Vasilii Vasil'evich; Rozanov, Vasily Vasilyevich

Rozewicz, Tadeusz 1921- ...... **CLC 9, 23, 139**
See also CA 108; CANR 36, 66; CWW 2; DA3; DAM POET; DLB 232; EWL 3; MTCW 1, 2; RGWL 3

Ruark, Gibbons 1941- .... **CLC 3**
See also CA 33-36R; CAAS 23; CANR 14, 31, 57; DLB 120

Rubens, Bernice (Ruth) 1923- .... **CLC 19, 31**
See also CA 25-28R; CANR 33, 65, 128; CN 7; DLB 14, 207; MTCW 1

Rubin, Harold
See Robbins, Harold

Rudkin, (James) David 1936- .... **CLC 14**
See also CA 89-92; CBD; CD 5; DLB 13

Rudnik, Raphael 1933- .... **CLC 7**
See also CA 29-32R

Ruffian, M.
See Hasek, Jaroslav (Matej Frantisek)

Ruiz, Jose Martinez .... **CLC 11**
See Martinez Ruiz, Jose

Ruiz, Juan c. 1283-c. 1350 .... **CMLC 66**

Rukeyser, Muriel 1913-1980 . **CLC 6, 10, 15, 27; PC 12**
See also AMWS 6; CA 5-8R; 93-96; CANR 26, 60; DA3; DAM POET; DLB 48; EWL 3; FW; GLL 2; MTCW 1, 2; PFS 10; RGAL 4; SATA-Obit 22

Rule, Jane (Vance) 1931- .... **CLC 27**
See also CA 25-28R; CAAS 18; CANR 12, 87; CN 7; DLB 60; FW

Rulfo, Juan 1918-1986 .. **CLC 8, 80; HLC 2; SSC 25**
See also CA 85-88; 118; CANR 26; CDWLB 3; DAM MULT; DLB 113; EWL 3; HW 1, 2; LAW; MTCW 1, 2; RGSF 2; RGWL 2, 3; WLIT 1

Rumi, Jalal al-Din 1207-1273 ...... **CMLC 20; PC 45**
See also RGWL 2, 3; WP

Runeberg, Johan 1804-1877 .... **NCLC 41**

Runyon, (Alfred) Damon 1884(?)-1946 .... **TCLC 10**
See also CA 107; 165; DLB 11, 86, 171; MTCW 2; RGAL 4

Rush, Norman 1933- .... **CLC 44**
See also CA 121; 126; CANR 130; INT CA-126

Rushdie, (Ahmed) Salman 1947- .... **CLC 23, 31, 55, 100, 191; WLCS**
See also BEST 89:3; BPFB 3; BRWS 4; CA 108; 111; CANR 33, 56, 108, 133; CN 7; CPW 1; DA3; DAB; DAC; DAM MST, NOV, POP; DLB 194; EWL 3; FANT; INT CA-111; LATS 1:2; LMFS 2; MTCW 1, 2; RGEL 2; RGSF 2; TEA; WLIT 4; WWE 1

Rushforth, Peter (Scott) 1945- .... **CLC 19**
See also CA 101

Ruskin, John 1819-1900 .... **TCLC 63**
See also BRW 5; BYA 5; CA 114; 129; CD-BLB 1832-1890; DLB 55, 163, 190; RGEL 2; SATA 24; TEA; WCH

Russ, Joanna 1937- .... **CLC 15**
See also BPFB 3; CA 5-28R; CANR 11, 31, 65; CN 7; DLB 8; FW; GLL 1; MTCW 1; SCFW 2; SFW 4

Russ, Richard Patrick
See O'Brian, Patrick

Russell, George William 1867-1935
See A.E.; Baker, Jean H.
See also BRWS 8; CA 104; 153; CDBLB 1890-1914; DAM POET; EWL 3; RGEL 2

Russell, Jeffrey Burton 1934- .... **CLC 70**
See also CA 25-28R; CANR 11, 28, 52

Russell, (Henry) Ken(neth Alfred) 1927- .... **CLC 16**
See also CA 105

Russell, William Martin 1947-
See Russell, Willy
See also CA 164; CANR 107

Russell, Willy .... **CLC 60**
See Russell, William Martin
See also CBD; CD 5; DLB 233

Russo, Richard 1949- .... **CLC 181**
See also AMWS 12; CA 127; 133; CANR 87, 114

Rutherford, Mark .... **TCLC 25**
See White, William Hale
See also DLB 18; RGEL 2

Ruyslinck, Ward .... **CLC 14**
See Belser, Reimond Karel Maria de

Ryan, Cornelius (John) 1920-1974 ..... **CLC 7**
See also CA 69-72; 53-56; CANR 38

Ryan, Michael 1946- .... **CLC 65**
See also CA 49-52; CANR 109; DLBY 1982

Ryan, Tim
See Dent, Lester

Rybakov, Anatoli (Naumovich) 1911-1998 .... **CLC 23, 53**
See Rybakov, Anatolii (Naumovich)
See also CA 126; 135; 172; SATA 79; SATA-Obit 108

Rybakov, Anatolii (Naumovich)
See Rybakov, Anatoli (Naumovich)
See also DLB 302

Ryder, Jonathan
See Ludlum, Robert

Ryga, George 1932-1987 .... **CLC 14**
See also CA 101; 124; CANR 43, 90; CCA 1; DAC; DAM MST; DLB 60

S. H.
See Hartmann, Sadakichi

S. S.
See Sassoon, Siegfried (Lorraine)

Sa'adawi, al- Nawal
See El Saadawi, Nawal
See also AFW; EWL 3

Saadawi, Nawal El
See El Saadawi, Nawal
See also WLIT 2

Saba, Umberto 1883-1957 .... **TCLC 33**
See also CA 144; CANR 79; DLB 114; EWL 3; RGWL 2, 3

Sabatini, Rafael 1875-1950 .... **TCLC 47**
See also BPFB 3; CA 162; RHW

Sabato, Ernesto (R.) 1911- .... **CLC 10, 23; HLC 2**
See also CA 97-100; CANR 32, 65; CD-WLB 3; CWW 2; DAM MULT; DLB 145; EWL 3; HW 1, 2; LAW; MTCW 1, 2

Sa-Carneiro, Mario de 1890-1916 . **TCLC 83**
See also DLB 287; EWL 3

Sacastru, Martin
See Bioy Casares, Adolfo
See also CWW 2

Sacher-Masoch, Leopold von 1836(?)-1895 .... **NCLC 31**

Sachs, Hans 1494-1576 .... **LC 95**
See also CDWLB 2; DLB 179; RGWL 2, 3

Sachs, Marilyn (Stickle) 1927- .... **CLC 35**
See also AAYA 2; BYA 6; CA 17-20R; CANR 13, 47; CLR 2; JRDA; MAICYA 1, 2; SAAS 2; SATA 3, 68; SATA-Essay 110; WYA; YAW

Sachs, Nelly 1891-1970 .... **CLC 14, 98**
See also CA 17-18; 25-28R; CANR 87; CAP 2; EWL 3; MTCW 2; PFS 20; RGWL 2, 3

Sackler, Howard (Oliver) 1929-1982 .... **CLC 14**
See also CA 61-64; 108; CAD; CANR 30; DFS 15; DLB 7

Sacks, Oliver (Wolf) 1933- .... **CLC 67**
See also CA 53-56; CANR 28, 50, 76; CPW; DA3; INT CANR-28; MTCW 1, 2

Sackville, Thomas 1536-1608 .... **LC 98**
See also DAM DRAM; DLB 62, 132; RGEL 2

Sadakichi
See Hartmann, Sadakichi

Sa'dawi, Nawal al-
See El Saadawi, Nawal
See also CWW 2

Sade, Donatien Alphonse Francois 1740-1814 .... **NCLC 3, 47**
See also EW 4; GFL Beginnings to 1789; RGWL 2, 3

Sade, Marquis de
See Sade, Donatien Alphonse Francois

Sadoff, Ira 1945- .... **CLC 9**
See also CA 53-56; CANR 5, 21, 109; DLB 120

Saetone
See Camus, Albert

Safire, William 1929- .... **CLC 10**
See also CA 17-20R; CANR 31, 54, 91

Sagan, Carl (Edward) 1934-1996 .... **CLC 30, 112**
See also AAYA 2; CA 25-28R; 155; CANR 11, 36, 74; CPW; DA3; MTCW 1, 2; SATA 58; SATA-Obit 94

Sagan, Francoise ..... **CLC 3, 6, 9, 17, 36**
See Quoirez, Francoise
See also CWW 2; DLB 83; EWL 3; GFL 1789 to the Present; MTCW 2

Sahgal, Nayantara (Pandit) 1927- .... **CLC 41**
See also CA 9-12R; CANR 11, 88; CN 7

Said, Edward W. 1935-2003 .... **CLC 123**
See also CA 21-24R; 220; CANR 45, 74, 107, 131; DLB 67; MTCW 2

Saint, H(arry) F. 1941- .... **CLC 50**
See also CA 127

St. Aubin de Teran, Lisa 1953-
See Teran, Lisa St. Aubin de
See also CA 118; 126; CN 7; INT CA-126

Saint Birgitta of Sweden c. 1303-1373 .... **CMLC 24**

Sainte-Beuve, Charles Augustin 1804-1869 .... **NCLC 5**
See also DLB 217; EW 6; GFL 1789 to the Present

Saint-Exupery, Antoine (Jean Baptiste Marie Roger) de 1900-1944 .... **TCLC 2, 56; WLC**
See also BPFB 3; BYA 3; CA 108; 132; CLR 10; DA3; DAM NOV; DLB 72; EW 12; EWL 3; GFL 1789 to the Present; LAIT 3; MAICYA 1, 2; MTCW 1, 2; RGWL 2, 3; SATA 20; TWA

St. John, David
See Hunt, E(verette) Howard, (Jr.)

St. John, J. Hector
See Crevecoeur, Michel Guillaume Jean de

Saint-John Perse
See Leger, (Marie-Rene Auguste) Alexis Saint-Leger
See also EW 10; EWL 3; GFL 1789 to the Present; RGWL 2

Saintsbury, George (Edward Bateman) 1845-1933 .... **TCLC 31**
See also CA 160; DLB 57, 149

Sait Faik .... **TCLC 23**
See Abasiyanik, Sait Faik

Saki .... **SSC 12; TCLC 3**
See Munro, H(ector) H(ugh)
See also BRWS 6; BYA 11; LAIT 2; MTCW 2; RGEL 2; SSFS 1; SUFW

Sala, George Augustus 1828-1895 . **NCLC 46**

Saladin 1138-1193 .... **CMLC 38**

Salama, Hannu 1936- .... **CLC 18**
See also EWL 3

Salamanca, J(ack) R(ichard) 1922- .. **CLC 4, 15**
See also CA 25-28R; 193; CAAE 193

Salas, Floyd Francis 1931- .... **HLC 2**
See also CA 119; CAAS 27; CANR 44, 75, 93; DAM MULT; DLB 82; HW 1, 2; MTCW 2

Sale, J. Kirkpatrick
See Sale, Kirkpatrick

Sale, Kirkpatrick 1937- .... **CLC 68**
See also CA 13-16R; CANR 10

Salinas, Luis Omar 1937- .... **CLC 90; HLC 2**
See also AMWS 13; CA 131; CANR 81; DAM MULT; DLB 82; HW 1, 2

Salinas (y Serrano), Pedro 1891(?)-1951 .... **TCLC 17**
See also CA 117; DLB 134; EWL 3

Salinger, J(erome) D(avid) 1919- .. **CLC 1, 3, 8, 12, 55, 56, 138; SSC 2, 28, 65; WLC**
See also AAYA 2, 36; AMW; AMWC 1; BPFB 3; CA 5-8R; CANR 39, 129; CDALB 1941-1968; CLR 18; CN 7; CPW 1; DA; DA3; DAB; DAC; DAM MST, NOV, POP; DLB 2, 102, 173; EWL 3; EXPN; LAIT 4; MAICYA 1, 2; MTCW 1, 2; NFS 1; RGAL 4; RGSF 2; SATA 67; SSFS 17; TUS; WYA; YAW

Salisbury, John
See Caute, (John) David

Sallust c. 86 B.C.-35 B.C. .... **CMLC 68**
See also AW 2; CDWLB 1; DLB 211; RGWL 2, 3

Salter, James 1925- .. **CLC 7, 52, 59; SSC 58**
See also AMWS 9; CA 73-76; CANR 107; DLB 130

Saltus, Edgar (Everton) 1855-1921 . **TCLC 8**
See also CA 105; DLB 202; RGAL 4

Saltykov, Mikhail Evgrafovich 1826-1889 .... **NCLC 16**
See also DLB 238:

Saltykov-Shchedrin, N.
See Saltykov, Mikhail Evgrafovich

Samarakis, Andonis
See Samarakis, Antonis
See also EWL 3

Samarakis, Antonis 1919-2003 .... **CLC 5**
See Samarakis, Andonis
See also CA 25-28R; 224; CAAS 16; CANR 36

Sanchez, Florencio 1875-1910 .... **TCLC 37**
See also CA 153; DLB 305; EWL 3; HW 1; LAW

Sanchez, Luis Rafael 1936- .... **CLC 23**
See also CA 128; DLB 305; EWL 3; HW 1; WLIT 1

Sanchez, Sonia 1934- .... **BLC 3; CLC 5, 116; PC 9**
See also BW 2, 3; CA 33-36R; CANR 24, 49, 74, 115; CLR 18; CP 7; CSW; CWP; DA3; DAM MULT; DLB 41; DLBD 8; EWL 3; MAICYA 1, 2; MTCW 1, 2; SATA 22, 136; WP

Sancho, Ignatius 1729-1780 .... **LC 84**

Sand, George 1804-1876 ..... **NCLC 2, 42, 57; WLC**
See also DA; DA3; DAB; DAC; DAM MST, NOV; DLB 119, 192; EW 6; FW; GFL 1789 to the Present; RGWL 2, 3; TWA

Sandburg, Carl (August) 1878-1967 . **CLC 1, 4, 10, 15, 35; PC 2, 41; WLC**
See also AAYA 24; AMW; BYA 1, 3; CA 5-8R; 25-28R; CANR 35; CDALB 1865-1917; CLR 67; DA; DA3; DAB; DAC; DAM MST, POET; DLB 17, 54, 284; EWL 3; EXPP; LAIT 2; MAICYA 1, 2; MTCW 1, 2; PAB; PFS 3, 6, 12; RGAL 4; SATA 8; TUS; WCH; WP; WYA

Sandburg, Charles
See Sandburg, Carl (August)

Sandburg, Charles A.
See Sandburg, Carl (August)

Sanders, (James) Ed(ward) 1939- .... **CLC 53**
See Sanders, Edward
See also BG 3; CA 13-16R; CAAS 21; CANR 13, 44, 78; CP 7; DAM POET; DLB 16, 244

Sanders, Edward
See Sanders, (James) Ed(ward)
See also DLB 244

Sanders, Lawrence 1920-1998 .... **CLC 41**
See also BEST 89:4; BPFB 3; CA 81-84; 165; CANR 33, 62; CMW 4; CPW; DA3; DAM POP; MTCW 1

Sanders, Noah
See Blount, Roy (Alton), Jr.

Sanders, Winston P.
See Anderson, Poul (William)

Sandoz, Mari(e Susette) 1900-1966 .. **CLC 28**
See also CA 1-4R; 25-28R; CANR 17, 64; DLB 9, 212; LAIT 2; MTCW 1, 2; SATA 5; TCWW 2

Sandys, George 1578-1644 .... **LC 80**
See also DLB 24, 121

Saner, Reg(inald Anthony) 1931- .... **CLC 9**
See also CA 65-68; CP 7

Sankara 788-820 .... **CMLC 32**

Sannazaro, Jacopo 1456(?)-1530 .... **LC 8**
See also RGWL 2, 3

Sansom, William 1912-1976 . **CLC 2, 6; SSC 21**
See also CA 5-8R; 65-68; CANR 42; DAM NOV; DLB 139; EWL 3; MTCW 1; RGEL 2; RGSF 2

Santayana, George 1863-1952 .... **TCLC 40**
See also AMW; CA 115; 194; DLB 54, 71, 246, 270; DLBD 13; EWL 3; RGAL 4; TUS

Santiago, Danny .... **CLC 33**
See James, Daniel (Lewis)
See also DLB 122

Santmyer, Helen Hooven 1895-1986 .... **CLC 33; TCLC 133**
See also CA 1-4R; 118; CANR 15, 33; DLBY 1984; MTCW 1; RHW

Santoka, Taneda 1882-1940 .... **TCLC 72**

Santos, Bienvenido N(uqui) 1911-1996 ... **AAL; CLC 22; TCLC 156**
See also CA 101; 151; CANR 19, 46; DAM MULT; EWL; RGAL 4; SSFS 19

Sapir, Edward 1884-1939 .... **TCLC 108**
See also CA 211; DLB 92

Sapper .... **TCLC 44**
See McNeile, Herman Cyril

Sapphire
See Sapphire, Brenda

Sapphire, Brenda 1950- .... **CLC 99**

Sappho fl. 6th cent. B.C.- ... **CMLC 3, 67; PC 5**
See also CDWLB 1; DA3; DAM POET; DLB 176; PFS 20; RGWL 2, 3; WP

Saramago, Jose 1922- .... **CLC 119; HLCS 1**
See also CA 153; CANR 96; CWW 2; DLB 287; EWL 3; LATS 1:2

Sarduy, Severo 1937-1993 .... **CLC 6, 97; HLCS 2**
See also CA 89-92; 142; CANR 58, 81; CWW 2; DLB 113; EWL 3; HW 1, 2; LAW

Sargeson, Frank 1903-1982 .... **CLC 31**
See also CA 25-28R; 106; CANR 38, 79; EWL 3; GLL 2; RGEL 2; RGSF 2; SSFS 20

Sarmiento, Domingo Faustino 1811-1888 .... **HLCS 2**
See also LAW; WLIT 1

Sarmiento, Felix Ruben Garcia
See Dario, Ruben

Saro-Wiwa, Ken(ule Beeson) 1941-1995 .... **CLC 114**
See also BW 2; CA 142; 150; CANR 60; DLB 157

Saroyan, William 1908-1981 ... **CLC 1, 8, 10, 29, 34, 56; SSC 21; TCLC 137; WLC**
See also CA 5-8R; 103; CAD; CANR 30; CDALBS; DA; DA3; DAB; DAC; DAM DRAM, MST, NOV; DFS 17; DLB 7, 9, 86; DLBY 1981; EWL 3; LAIT 4; MTCW 1, 2; RGAL 4; RGSF 2; SATA 23; SATA-Obit 24; SSFS 14; TUS

Sarraute, Nathalie 1900-1999 .... **CLC 1, 2, 4, 8, 10, 31, 80; TCLC 145**
See also BPFB 3; CA 9-12R; 187; CANR 23, 66; CWW 2; DLB 83; EW 12; EWL 3; GFL 1789 to the Present; MTCW 1, 2; RGWL 2, 3

Sarton, (Eleanor) May 1912-1995 ..... **CLC 4,
14, 49, 91; PC 39; TCLC 120**
See also AMWS 8; CA 1-4R; 149; CANR
1, 34, 55, 116; CN 7; CP 7; DAM POET;
DLB 48; DLBY 1981; EWL 3; FW; INT
CANR-34; MTCW 1, 2; RGAL 4; SATA
36; SATA-Obit 86; TUS

Sartre, Jean-Paul 1905-1980 . **CLC 1, 4, 7, 9,
13, 18, 24, 44, 50, 52; DC 3; SSC 32;
WLC**
See also CA 9-12R; 97-100; CANR 21; DA;
DA3; DAB; DAC; DAM DRAM, MST,
NOV; DFS 5; DLB 72, 296; EW 12; EWL
3; GFL 1789 to the Present; LMFS 2;
MTCW 1, 2; RGSF 2; RGWL 2, 3; SSFS
9; TWA

Sassoon, Siegfried (Lorraine)
1886-1967 .... **CLC 36, 130; PC 12**
See also BRW 6; CA 104; CANR
36; DAB; DAM MST, NOV, POET; DLB
20, 191; DLBD 18; EWL 3; MTCW 1, 2;
PAB; RGEL 2; TEA

Satterfield, Charles
See Pohl, Frederik

Satyremont
See Peret, Benjamin

Saul, John (W. III) 1942- .... **CLC 46**
See also AAYA 10; BEST 90:4; CA 81-84;
CANR 16, 40, 81; CPW; DAM NOV,
POP; HGG; SATA 98

Saunders, Caleb
See Heinlein, Robert A(nson)

Saura (Atares), Carlos 1932-1998 .... **CLC 20**
See also CA 114; 131; CANR 79; HW 1

Sauser, Frederic Louis
See Sauser-Hall, Frederic

Sauser-Hall, Frederic 1887-1961 ...... **CLC 18**
See Cendrars, Blaise
See also CA 102; 93-96; CANR 36, 62;
MTCW 1

Saussure, Ferdinand de
1857-1913 .... **TCLC 49**
See also DLB 242

Savage, Catharine
See Brosman, Catharine Savage

Savage, Richard 1697(?)-1743 .... **LC 96**
See also DLB 95; RGEL 2

Savage, Thomas 1915-2003 .... **CLC 40**
See also CA 126; 132; 218; CAAS 15; CN
7; INT CA-132; SATA-Obit 147; TCWW
2

Savan, Glenn 1953-2003 .... **CLC 50**
See also CA 225

Sax, Robert
See Johnson, Robert

Saxo Grammaticus c. 1150-c.
1222 .... **CMLC 58**

Saxton, Robert
See Johnson, Robert

Sayers, Dorothy L(eigh) 1893-1957 . **SSC 71;
TCLC 2, 15**
See also BPFB 3; BRWS 3; CA 104; 119;
CANR 60; CDBLB 1914-1945; CMW 4;
DAM POP; DLB 10, 36, 77, 100; MSW;
MTCW 1, 2; RGEL 2; SSFS 12; TEA

Sayers, Valerie 1952- .... **CLC 50, 122**
See also CA 134; CANR 61; CSW

Sayles, John (Thomas) 1950- . **CLC 7, 10, 14**
See also CA 57-60; CANR 41, 84; DLB 44

Scammell, Michael 1935- .... **CLC 34**
See also CA 156

Scannell, Vernon 1922- .... **CLC 49**
See also CA 5-8R; CANR 8, 24, 57; CP 7;
CWRI 5; DLB 27; SATA 59

Scarlett, Susan
See Streatfeild, (Mary) Noel

Scarron 1847-1910
See Mikszath, Kalman

Schaeffer, Susan Fromberg 1941- ..... **CLC 6,
11, 22**
See also CA 49-52; CANR 18, 65; CN 7;
DLB 28, 299; MTCW 1, 2; SATA 22

Schama, Simon (Michael) 1945- ..... **CLC 150**
See also BEST 89:4; CA 105; CANR 39,
91

Schary, Jill
See Robinson, Jill

Schell, Jonathan 1943- .... **CLC 35**
See also CA 73-76; CANR 12, 117

Schelling, Friedrich Wilhelm Joseph von
1775-1854 .... **NCLC 30**
See also DLB 90

Scherer, Jean-Marie Maurice 1920-
See Rohmer, Eric
See also CA 110

Schevill, James (Erwin) 1920- .... **CLC 7**
See also CA 5-8R; CAAS 12; CAD; CD 5

Schiller, Friedrich von 1759-1805 ...... **DC 12;
NCLC 39, 69**
See also CDWLB 2; DAM DRAM; DLB
94; EW 5; RGWL 2, 3; TWA

Schisgal, Murray (Joseph) 1926- .... **CLC 6**
See also CA 21-24R; CAD; CANR 48, 86;
CD 5

Schlee, Ann 1934- .... **CLC 35**
See also CA 101; CANR 29, 88; SATA 44;
SATA-Brief 36

Schlegel, August Wilhelm von
1767-1845 .... **NCLC 15, 142**
See also DLB 94; RGWL 2, 3

Schlegel, Friedrich 1772-1829 .... **NCLC 45**
See also DLB 90; EW 5; RGWL 2, 3; TWA

Schlegel, Johann Elias (von)
1719(?)-1749 .... **LC 5**

Schleiermacher, Friedrich
1768-1834 .... **NCLC 107**
See also DLB 90

Schlesinger, Arthur M(eier), Jr.
1917- .... **CLC 84**
See also AITN 1; CA 1-4R; CANR 1, 28,
58, 105; DLB 17; INT CANR-28; MTCW
1, 2; SATA 61

Schlink, Bernhard 1944- .... **CLC 174**
See also CA 163; CANR 116

Schmidt, Arno (Otto) 1914-1979 ...... **CLC 56**
See also CA 128; 109; DLB 69; EWL 3

Schmitz, Aron Hector 1861-1928
See Svevo, Italo
See also CA 104; 122; MTCW 1

Schnackenberg, Gjertrud (Cecelia)
1953- .... **CLC 40; PC 45**
See also CA 116; CANR 100; CP 7; CWP;
DLB 120, 282; PFS 13

Schneider, Leonard Alfred 1925-1966
See Bruce, Lenny
See also CA 89-92

Schnitzler, Arthur 1862-1931 ..... **DC 17; SSC
15, 61; TCLC 4**
See also CA 104; CDWLB 2; DLB 81, 118;
EW 8; EWL 3; RGSF 2; RGWL 2, 3

Schoenberg, Arnold Franz Walter
1874-1951 .... **TCLC 75**
See also CA 109; 188

Schonberg, Arnold
See Schoenberg, Arnold Franz Walter

Schopenhauer, Arthur 1788-1860 .. **NCLC 51**
See also DLB 90; EW 5

Schor, Sandra (M.) 1932(?)-1990 ..... **CLC 65**
See also CA 132

Schorer, Mark 1908-1977 .... **CLC 9**
See also CA 5-8R; 73-76; CANR 7; DLB
103

Schrader, Paul (Joseph) 1946- .... **CLC 26**
See also CA 37-40R; CANR 41; DLB 44

Schreber, Daniel 1842-1911 .... **TCLC 123**

Schreiner, Olive (Emilie Albertina)
1855-1920 .... **TCLC 9**
See also AFW; BRWS 2; CA 105; 154;
DLB 18, 156, 190, 225; EWL 3; FW;
RGEL 2; TWA; WLIT 2; WWE 1

Schulberg, Budd (Wilson) 1914- .. **CLC 7, 48**
See also BPFB 3; CA 25-28R; CANR 19,
87; CN 7; DLB 6, 26, 28; DLBY 1981,
2001

Schulman, Arnold
See Trumbo, Dalton

Schulz, Bruno 1892-1942 .. **SSC 13; TCLC 5,
51**
See also CA 115; 123; CANR 86; CDWLB
4; DLB 215; EWL 3; MTCW 2; RGSF 2;
RGWL 2, 3

Schulz, Charles M(onroe)
1922-2000 .... **CLC 12**
See also AAYA 39; CA 9-12R; 187; CANR
6, 132; INT CANR-6; SATA 10; SATA-
Obit 118

Schumacher, E(rnst) F(riedrich)
1911-1977 .... **CLC 80**
See also CA 81-84; 73-76; CANR 34, 85

Schumann, Robert 1810-1856 ...... **NCLC 143**

Schuyler, George Samuel 1895-1977 .... **HR 3**
See also BW 2; CA 81-84; 73-76; CANR
42; DLB 29, 51

Schuyler, James Marcus 1923-1991 .. **CLC 5,
23**
See also CA 101; 134; DAM POET; DLB
5, 169; EWL 3; INT CA-101; WP

Schwartz, Delmore (David)
1913-1966 ... **CLC 2, 4, 10, 45, 87; PC 8**
See also AMWS 2; CA 17-18; 25-28R;
CANR 35; CAP 2; DLB 28, 48; EWL 3;
MTCW 1, 2; PAB; RGAL 4; TUS

Schwartz, Ernst
See Ozu, Yasujiro

Schwartz, John Burnham 1965- .... **CLC 59**
See also CA 132; CANR 116

Schwartz, Lynne Sharon 1939- .... **CLC 31**
See also CA 103; CANR 44, 89; DLB 218;
MTCW 2

Schwartz, Muriel A.
See Eliot, T(homas) S(tearns)

Schwarz-Bart, Andre 1928- .... **CLC 2, 4**
See also CA 89-92; CANR 109; DLB 299

Schwarz-Bart, Simone 1938- . **BLCS; CLC 7**
See also BW 2; CA 97-100; CANR 117;
EWL 3

Schwerner, Armand 1927-1999 .... **PC 42**
See also CA 9-12R; 179; CANR 50, 85; CP
7; DLB 165

Schwitters, Kurt (Hermann Edward Karl
Julius) 1887-1948 .... **TCLC 95**
See also CA 158

Schwob, Marcel (Mayer Andre)
1867-1905 .... **TCLC 20**
See also CA 117; 168; DLB 123; GFL 1789
to the Present

Sciascia, Leonardo 1921-1989 .. **CLC 8, 9, 41**
See also CA 85-88; 130; CANR 35; DLB
177; EWL 3; MTCW 1; RGWL 2, 3

Scoppettone, Sandra 1936- .... **CLC 26**
See Early, Jack
See also AAYA 11; BYA 8; CA 5-8R;
CANR 41, 73; GLL 1; MAICYA 2; MAI-
CYAS 1; SATA 9, 92; WYA; YAW

Scorsese, Martin 1942- .... **CLC 20, 89**
See also AAYA 38; CA 110; 114; CANR
46, 85

Scotland, Jay
See Jakes, John (William)

Scott, Duncan Campbell
1862-1947 .... **TCLC 6**
See also CA 104; 153; DAC; DLB 92;
RGEL 2

Scott, Evelyn 1893-1963 .... **CLC 43**
See also CA 104; 112; CANR 64; DLB 9, 48; RHW

Scott, F(rancis) R(eginald)
1899-1985 .... **CLC 22**
See also CA 101; 114; CANR 87; DLB 88; INT CA-101; RGEL 2

Scott, Frank
See Scott, F(rancis) R(eginald)

Scott, Joan .... **CLC 65**

Scott, Joanna 1960- .... **CLC 50**
See also CA 126; CANR 53, 92

Scott, Paul (Mark) 1920-1978 ...... **CLC 9, 60**
See also BRWS 1; CA 81-84; 77-80; CANR 33; DLB 14, 207; EWL 3; MTCW 1; RGEL 2; RHW; WWE 1

Scott, Ridley 1937- .... **CLC 183**
See also AAYA 13, 43

Scott, Sarah 1723-1795 .... **LC 44**
See also DLB 39

Scott, Sir Walter 1771-1832 .... **NCLC 15, 69, 110; PC 13; SSC 32; WLC**
See also AAYA 22; BRW 4; BYA 2; CD-BLB 1789-1832; DA; DAB; DAC; DAM MST, NOV, POET; DLB 93, 107, 116, 144, 159; HGG; LAIT 1; RGEL 2; RGSF 2; SSFS 10; SUFW 1; TEA; WLIT 3; YABC 2

Scribe, (Augustin) Eugene 1791-1861 . **DC 5; NCLC 16**
See also DAM DRAM; DLB 192; GFL 1789 to the Present; RGWL 2, 3

Scrum, R.
See Crumb, R(obert)

Scudery, Georges de 1601-1667 .... **LC 75**
See also GFL Beginnings to 1789

Scudery, Madeleine de 1607-1701 .. **LC 2, 58**
See also DLB 268; GFL Beginnings to 1789

Scum
See Crumb, R(obert)

Scumbag, Little Bobby
See Crumb, R(obert)

Seabrook, John
See Hubbard, L(afayette) Ron(ald)

Seacole, Mary Jane Grant
1805-1881 .... **NCLC 147**
See also DLB 166

Sealy, I(rwin) Allan 1951- .... **CLC 55**
See also CA 136; CN 7

Search, Alexander
See Pessoa, Fernando (Antonio Nogueira)

Sebald, W(infried) G(eorg)
1944-2001 .... **CLC 194**
See also BRWS 8; CA 159; 202; CANR 98

Sebastian, Lee
See Silverberg, Robert

Sebastian Owl
See Thompson, Hunter S(tockton)

Sebestyen, Igen
See Sebestyen, Ouida

Sebestyen, Ouida 1924- .... **CLC 30**
See also AAYA 8; BYA 7; CA 107; CANR 40, 114; CLR 17; JRDA; MAICYA 1, 2; SAAS 10; SATA 39, 140; WYA; YAW

Sebold, Alice 1963(?)- .... **CLC 193**
See also AAYA 56; CA 203

Second Duke of Buckingham
See Villiers, George

Secundus, H. Scriblerus
See Fielding, Henry

Sedges, John
See Buck, Pearl S(ydenstricker)

Sedgwick, Catharine Maria
1789-1867 .... **NCLC 19, 98**
See also DLB 1, 74, 183, 239, 243, 254; RGAL 4

Seelye, John (Douglas) 1931- .... **CLC 7**
See also CA 97-100; CANR 70; INT CA-97-100; TCWW 2

Seferiades, Giorgos Stylianou 1900-1971
See Seferis, George
See also CA 5-8R; 33-36R; CANR 5, 36; MTCW 1

Seferis, George .... **CLC 5, 11**
See Seferiades, Giorgos Stylianou
See also EW 12; EWL 3; RGWL 2, 3

Segal, Erich (Wolf) 1937- .... **CLC 3, 10**
See also BEST 89:1; BPFB 3; CA 25-28R; CANR 20, 36, 65, 113; CPW; DAM POP; DLBY 1986; INT CANR-20; MTCW 1

Seger, Bob 1945- .... **CLC 35**

Seghers, Anna .... **CLC 7**
See Radvanyi, Netty
See also CDWLB 2; DLB 69; EWL 3

Seidel, Frederick (Lewis) 1936- .... **CLC 18**
See also CA 13-16R; CANR 8, 99; CP 7; DLBY 1984

Seifert, Jaroslav 1901-1986 . **CLC 34, 44, 93; PC 47**
See also CA 127; CDWLB 4; DLB 215; EWL 3; MTCW 1, 2

Sei Shonagon c. 966-1017(?) .... **CMLC 6**

Sejour, Victor 1817-1874 .... **DC 10**
See also DLB 50

Sejour Marcou et Ferrand, Juan Victor
See Sejour, Victor

Selby, Hubert, Jr. 1928-2004 ..... **CLC 1, 2, 4, 8; SSC 20**
See also CA 13-16R; 226; CANR 33, 85; CN 7; DLB 2, 227

Selzer, Richard 1928- .... **CLC 74**
See also CA 65-68; CANR 14, 106

Sembene, Ousmane
See Ousmane, Sembene
See also AFW; EWL 3; WLIT 2

Senancour, Etienne Pivert de
1770-1846 .... **NCLC 16**
See also DLB 119; GFL 1789 to the Present

Sender, Ramon (Jose) 1902-1982 ...... **CLC 8; HLC 2; TCLC 136**
See also CA 5-8R; 105; CANR 8; DAM MULT; EWL 3; HW 1; MTCW 1; RGWL 2, 3

Seneca, Lucius Annaeus c. 4 B.C.-c. 65 .... **CMLC 6; DC 5**
See also AW 2; CDWLB 1; DAM DRAM; DLB 211; RGWL 2, 3; TWA

Senghor, Leopold Sedar 1906-2001 ... **BLC 3; CLC 54, 130; PC 25**
See also AFW; BW 2; CA 116; 125; 203; CANR 47, 74; CWW 2; DAM MULT, POET; DNFS 2; EWL 3; GFL 1789 to the Present; MTCW 1, 2; TWA

Senna, Danzy 1970- .... **CLC 119**
See also CA 169; CANR 130

Serling, (Edward) Rod(man)
1924-1975 .... **CLC 30**
See also AAYA 14; AITN 1; CA 162; 57-60; DLB 26; SFW 4

Serna, Ramon Gomez de la
See Gomez de la Serna, Ramon

Serpieres
See Guillevic, (Eugene)

Service, Robert
See Service, Robert W(illiam)
See also BYA 4; DAB; DLB 92

Service, Robert W(illiam)
1874(?)-1958 .... **TCLC 15; WLC**
See Service, Robert
See also CA 115; 140; CANR 84; DA; DAC; DAM MST, POET; PFS 10; RGEL 2; SATA 20

Seth, Vikram 1952- .... **CLC 43, 90**
See also CA 121; 127; CANR 50, 74, 131; CN 7; CP 7; DA3; DAM MULT; DLB 120, 271, 282; EWL 3; INT CA-127; MTCW 2; WWE 1

Seton, Cynthia Propper 1926-1982 .. **CLC 27**
See also CA 5-8R; 108; CANR 7

Seton, Ernest (Evan) Thompson
1860-1946 .... **TCLC 31**
See also ANW; BYA 3; CA 109; 204; CLR 59; DLB 92; DLBD 13; JRDA; SATA 18

Seton-Thompson, Ernest
See Seton, Ernest (Evan) Thompson

Settle, Mary Lee 1918- .... **CLC 19, 61**
See also BPFB 3; CA 89-92; CAAS 1; CANR 44, 87, 126; CN 7; CSW; DLB 6; INT CA-89-92

Seuphor, Michel
See Arp, Jean

Sevigne, Marie (de Rabutin-Chantal)
1626-1696 .... **LC 11**
See Sevigne, Marie de Rabutin Chantal
See also GFL Beginnings to 1789; TWA

Sevigne, Marie de Rabutin Chantal
See Sevigne, Marie (de Rabutin-Chantal)
See also DLB 268

Sewall, Samuel 1652-1730 .... **LC 38**
See also DLB 24; RGAL 4

Sexton, Anne (Harvey) 1928-1974 ..... **CLC 2, 4, 6, 8, 10, 15, 53, 123; PC 2; WLC**
See also AMWS 2; CA 1-4R; 53-56; CABS 2; CANR 3, 36; CDALB 1941-1968; DA; DA3; DAB; DAC; DAM MST, POET; DLB 5, 169; EWL 3; EXPP; FW; MAWW; MTCW 1, 2; PAB; PFS 4, 14; RGAL 4; SATA 10; TUS

Shaara, Jeff 1952- .... **CLC 119**
See also CA 163; CANR 109

Shaara, Michael (Joseph, Jr.)
1929-1988 .... **CLC 15**
See also AITN 1; BPFB 3; CA 102; 125; CANR 52, 85; DAM POP; DLBY 1983

Shackleton, C. C.
See Aldiss, Brian W(ilson)

Shacochis, Bob .... **CLC 39**
See Shacochis, Robert G.

Shacochis, Robert G. 1951-
See Shacochis, Bob
See also CA 119; 124; CANR 100; INT CA-124

Shaffer, Anthony (Joshua)
1926-2001 .... **CLC 19**
See also CA 110; 116; 200; CBD; CD 5; DAM DRAM; DFS 13; DLB 13

Shaffer, Peter (Levin) 1926- .. **CLC 5, 14, 18, 37, 60; DC 7**
See also BRWS 1; CA 25-28R; CANR 25, 47, 74, 118; CBD; CD 5; CDBLB 1960 to Present; DA3; DAB; DAM DRAM, MST; DFS 5, 13; DLB 13, 233; EWL 3; MTCW 1, 2; RGEL 2; TEA

Shakespeare, William 1564-1616 .... **WLC**
See also AAYA 35; BRW 1; CDBLB Before 1660; DA; DA3; DAB; DAC; DAM DRAM, MST, POET; DFS 20; DLB 62, 172, 263; EXPP; LAIT 1; LATS 1:1; LMFS 1; PAB; PFS 1, 2, 3, 4, 5, 8, 9; RGEL 2; TEA; WLIT 3; WP; WS; WYA

Shakey, Bernard
See Young, Neil

Shalamov, Varlam (Tikhonovich)
1907-1982 .... **CLC 18**
See also CA 129; 105; DLB 302; RGSF 2

Shamloo, Ahmad
See Shamlu, Ahmad

Shamlou, Ahmad
See Shamlu, Ahmad

Shamlu, Ahmad 1925-2000 .... **CLC 10**
See also CA 216; CWW 2

Shammas, Anton 1951- .... **CLC 55**
See also CA 199

Shandling, Arline
See Berriault, Gina

Shange, Ntozake 1948- ... **BLC 3; CLC 8, 25, 38, 74, 126; DC 3**
See also AAYA 9; AFAW 1, 2; BW 2; CA 85-88; CABS 3; CAD; CANR 27, 48, 74, 131; CD 5; CP 7; CWD; CWP; DA3; DAM DRAM, MULT; DFS 2, 11; DLB 38, 249; FW; LAIT 5; MTCW 1, 2; NFS 11; RGAL 4; YAW

Shanley, John Patrick 1950- .... **CLC 75**
See also CA 128; 133; CAD; CANR 83; CD 5

Shapcott, Thomas W(illiam) 1935- .. **CLC 38**
See also CA 69-72; CANR 49, 83, 103; CP 7; DLB 289

Shapiro, Jane 1942- .... **CLC 76**
See also CA 196

Shapiro, Karl (Jay) 1913-2000 ...... **CLC 4, 8, 15, 53; PC 25**
See also AMWS 2; CA 1-4R; 188; CAAS 6; CANR 1, 36, 66; CP 7; DLB 48; EWL 3; EXPP; MTCW 1, 2; PFS 3; RGAL 4

Sharp, William 1855-1905 .... **TCLC 39**
See Macleod, Fiona
See also CA 160; DLB 156; RGEL 2

Sharpe, Thomas Ridley 1928-
See Sharpe, Tom
See also CA 114; 122; CANR 85; INT CA-122

Sharpe, Tom .... **CLC 36**
See Sharpe, Thomas Ridley
See also CN 7; DLB 14, 231

Shatrov, Mikhail .... **CLC 59**

Shaw, Bernard
See Shaw, George Bernard
See also DLB 190

Shaw, G. Bernard
See Shaw, George Bernard

Shaw, George Bernard 1856-1950 ..... **DC 23; TCLC 3, 9, 21, 45; WLC**
See Shaw, Bernard
See also BRW 6; BRWC 1; BRWR 2; CA 104; 128; CDBLB 1914-1945; DA; DA3; DAB; DAC; DAM DRAM, MST; DFS 1, 3, 6, 11, 19; DLB 10, 57; EWL 3; LAIT 3; LATS 1:1; MTCW 1, 2; RGEL 2; TEA; WLIT 4

Shaw, Henry Wheeler 1818-1885 .. **NCLC 15**
See also DLB 11; RGAL 4

Shaw, Irwin 1913-1984 .... **CLC 7, 23, 34**
See also AITN 1; BPFB 3; CA 13-16R; 112; CANR 21; CDALB 1941-1968; CPW; DAM DRAM, POP; DLB 6, 102; DLBY 1984; MTCW 1, 21

Shaw, Robert 1927-1978 .... **CLC 5**
See also AITN 1; CA 1-4R; 81-84; CANR 4; DLB 13, 14

Shaw, T. E.
See Lawrence, T(homas) E(dward)

Shawn, Wallace 1943- .... **CLC 41**
See also CA 112; CAD; CD 5; DLB 266

Shchedrin, N.
See Saltykov, Mikhail Evgrafovich

Shea, Lisa 1953- .... **CLC 86**
See also CA 147

Sheed, Wilfrid (John Joseph) 1930- . **CLC 2, 4, 10, 53**
See also CA 65-68; CANR 30, 66; CN 7; DLB 6; MTCW 1, 2

Sheehy, Gail 1937- .... **CLC 171**
See also CA 49-52; CANR 1, 33, 55, 92; CPW; MTCW 1

Sheldon, Alice Hastings Bradley 1915(?)-1987
See Tiptree, James, Jr.
See also CA 108; 122; CANR 34; INT CA-108; MTCW 1

Sheldon, John
See Bloch, Robert (Albert)

Sheldon, Walter J(ames) 1917-1996
See Queen, Ellery
See also AITN 1; CA 25-28R; CANR 10

Shelley, Mary Wollstonecraft (Godwin) 1797-1851 ...... **NCLC 14, 59, 103; WLC**
See also AAYA 20; BPFB 3; BRW 3; BRWC 2; BRWS 3; BYA 5; CDBLB 1789-1832; DA; DA3; DAB; DAC; DAM MST, NOV; DLB 110, 116, 159, 178; EXPN; HGG; LAIT 1; LMFS 1, 2; NFS 1; RGEL 2; SATA 29; SCFW; SFW 4; TEA; WLIT 3

Shelley, Percy Bysshe 1792-1822 .. **NCLC 18, 93, 143; PC 14; WLC**
See also BRW 4; BRWR 1; CDBLB 1789-1832; DA; DA3; DAB; DAC; DAM MST, POET; DLB 96, 110, 158; EXPP; LMFS 1; PAB; PFS 2; RGEL 2; TEA; WLIT 3; WP

Shepard, Jim 1956- .... **CLC 36**
See also CA 137; CANR 59, 104; SATA 90

Shepard, Lucius 1947- .... **CLC 34**
See also CA 128; 141; CANR 81, 124; HGG; SCFW 2; SFW 4; SUFW 2

Shepard, Sam 1943- .... **CLC 4, 6, 17, 34, 41, 44, 169; DC 5**
See also AAYA 1, 58; AMWS 3; CA 69-72; CABS 3; CAD; CANR 22, 120; CD 5; DA3; DAM DRAM; DFS 3, 6, 7, 14; DLB 7, 212; EWL 3; IDFW 3, 4; MTCW 1, 2; RGAL 4

Shepherd, Michael
See Ludlum, Robert

Sherburne, Zoa (Lillian Morin) 1912-1995 .... **CLC 30**
See also AAYA 13; CA 1-4R; 176; CANR 3, 37; MAICYA 1, 2; SAAS 18; SATA 3; YAW

Sheridan, Frances 1724-1766 .... **LC 7**
See also DLB 39, 84

Sheridan, Richard Brinsley 1751-1816 .... **DC 1; NCLC 5, 91; WLC**
See also BRW 3; CDBLB 1660-1789; DA; DAB; DAC; DAM DRAM, MST; DFS 15; DLB 89; WLIT 3

Sherman, Jonathan Marc .... **CLC 55**

Sherman, Martin 1941(?)- .... **CLC 19**
See also CA 116; 123; CAD; CANR 86; CD 5; DFS 20; DLB 228; GLL 1; IDTP

Sherwin, Judith Johnson
See Johnson, Judith (Emlyn)
See also CANR 85; CP 7; CWP

Sherwood, Frances 1940- .... **CLC 81**
See also CA 146; 220; CAAE 220

Sherwood, Robert E(mmet) 1896-1955 .... **TCLC 3**
See also CA 104; 153; CANR 86; DAM DRAM; DFS 11, 15, 17; DLB 7, 26, 249; IDFW 3, 4; RGAL 4

Shestov, Lev 1866-1938 .... **TCLC 56**

Shevchenko, Taras 1814-1861 .... **NCLC 54**

Shiel, M(atthew) P(hipps) 1865-1947 .... **TCLC 8**
See Holmes, Gordon
See also CA 106; 160; DLB 153; HGG; MTCW 2; SFW 4; SUFW

Shields, Carol (Ann) 1935-2003 ...... **CLC 91, 113, 193**
See also AMWS 7; CA 81-84; 218; CANR 51, 74, 98, 133; CCA 1; CN 7; CPW; DA3; DAC; MTCW 2

Shields, David (Jonathan) 1956- ...... **CLC 97**
See also CA 124; CANR 48, 99, 112

Shiga, Naoya 1883-1971 ..... **CLC 33; SSC 23**
See Shiga Naoya
See also CA 101; 33-36R; MJW; RGWL 3

Shiga Naoya
See Shiga, Naoya
See also DLB 180; EWL 3; RGWL 3

Shilts, Randy 1951-1994 .... **CLC 85**
See also AAYA 19; CA 115; 127; 144; CANR 45; DA3; GLL 1; INT CA-127; MTCW 2

Shimazaki, Haruki 1872-1943
See Shimazaki Toson
See also CA 105; 134; CANR 84; RGWL 3

Shimazaki Toson .... **TCLC 5**
See Shimazaki, Haruki
See also DLB 180; EWL 3

Shirley, James 1596-1666 .... **LC 96**
See also DLB 58; RGEL 2

Sholokhov, Mikhail (Aleksandrovich) 1905-1984 .... **CLC 7, 15**
See also CA 101; 112; DLB 272; EWL 3; MTCW 1, 2; RGWL 2, 3; SATA-Obit 36

Shone, Patric
See Hanley, James

Showalter, Elaine 1941- .... **CLC 169**
See also CA 57-60; CANR 58, 106; DLB 67; FW; GLL 2

Shreve, Susan
See Shreve, Susan Richards

Shreve, Susan Richards 1939- .... **CLC 23**
See also CA 49-52; CAAS 5; CANR 5, 38, 69, 100; MAICYA 1, 2; SATA 46, 95, 152; SATA-Brief 41

Shue, Larry 1946-1985 .... **CLC 52**
See also CA 145; 117; DAM DRAM; DFS 7

Shu-Jen, Chou 1881-1936
See Lu Hsun
See also CA 104

Shulman, Alix Kates 1932- .... **CLC 2, 10**
See also CA 29-32R; CANR 43; FW; SATA 7

Shuster, Joe 1914-1992 .... **CLC 21**
See also AAYA 50

Shute, Nevil .... **CLC 30**
See Norway, Nevil Shute
See also BPFB 3; DLB 255; NFS 9; RHW; SFW 4

Shuttle, Penelope (Diane) 1947- .... **CLC 7**
See also CA 93-96; CANR 39, 84, 92, 108; CP 7; CWP; DLB 14, 40

Shvarts, Elena 1948- .... **PC 50**
See also CA 147

Sidhwa, Bapsy (N.) 1938- .... **CLC 168**
See also CA 108; CANR 25, 57; CN 7; FW

Sidney, Mary 1561-1621 .... **LC 19, 39**
See Sidney Herbert, Mary

Sidney, Sir Philip 1554-1586 . **LC 19, 39; PC 32**
See also BRW 1; BRWR 2; CDBLB Before 1660; DA; DA3; DAB; DAC; DAM MST, POET; DLB 167; EXPP; PAB; RGEL 2; TEA; WP

Sidney Herbert, Mary
See Sidney, Mary
See also DLB 167

Siegel, Jerome 1914-1996 .... **CLC 21**
See Siegel, Jerry
See also CA 116; 169; 151

Siegel, Jerry
See Siegel, Jerome
See also AAYA 50

Sienkiewicz, Henryk (Adam Alexander Pius) 1846-1916 .... **TCLC 3**
See also CA 104; 134; CANR 84; EWL 3; RGSF 2; RGWL 2, 3

Sierra, Gregorio Martinez
See Martinez Sierra, Gregorio
Sierra, Maria (de la O'LeJarraga) Martinez
See Martinez Sierra, Maria (de la O'LeJarraga)
Sigal, Clancy 1926- .... CLC 7
See also CA 1-4R; CANR 85; CN 7
Siger of Brabant 1240(?)-1284(?) . CMLC 69
See also DLB 115
Sigourney, Lydia H.
See Sigourney, Lydia Howard (Huntley)
See also DLB 73, 183
Sigourney, Lydia Howard (Huntley)
1791-1865 .... NCLC 21, 87
See Sigourney, Lydia H.; Sigourney, Lydia Huntley
See also DLB 1
Sigourney, Lydia Huntley
See Sigourney, Lydia Howard (Huntley)
See also DLB 42, 239, 243
Siguenza y Gongora, Carlos de
1645-1700 .... HLCS 2; LC 8
See also LAW
Sigurjonsson, Johann
See Sigurjonsson, Johann
Sigurjonsson, Johann 1880-1919 ... TCLC 27
See also CA 170; DLB 293; EWL 3
Sikelianos, Angelos 1884-1951 .... PC 29; TCLC 39
See also EWL 3; RGWL 2, 3
Silkin, Jon 1930-1997 .... CLC 2, 6, 43
See also CA 5-8R; CAAS 5; CANR 89; CP 7; DLB 27
Silko, Leslie (Marmon) 1948- .... CLC 23, 74, 114; NNAL; SSC 37, 66; WLCS
See also AAYA 14; AMWS 4; ANW; BYA 12; CA 115; 122; CANR 45, 65, 118; CN 7; CP 7; CPW 1; CWP; DA; DA3; DAC; DAM MST, MULT, POP; DLB 143, 175, 256, 275; EWL 3; EXPP; EXPS; LAIT 4; MTCW 2; NFS 4; PFS 9, 16; RGAL 4; RGSF 2; SSFS 4, 8, 10, 11
Sillanpaa, Frans Eemil 1888-1964 ... CLC 19
See also CA 129; 93-96; EWL 3; MTCW 1
Sillitoe, Alan 1928- .. CLC 1, 3, 6, 10, 19, 57, 148
See also AITN 1; BRWS 5; CA 9-12R, 191; CAAE 191; CAAS 2; CANR 8, 26, 55; CDBLB 1960 to Present; CN 7; DLB 14, 139; EWL 3; MTCW 1, 2; RGEL 2; RGSF 2; SATA 61
Silone, Ignazio 1900-1978 .... CLC 4
See also CA 25-28; 81-84; CANR 34; CAP 2; DLB 264; EW 12; EWL 3; MTCW 1; RGSF 2; RGWL 2, 3
Silone, Ignazione
See Silone, Ignazio
Silver, Joan Micklin 1935- .... CLC 20
See also CA 114; 121; INT CA-121
Silver, Nicholas
See Faust, Frederick (Schiller)
See also TCWW 2
Silverberg, Robert 1935- .... CLC 7, 140
See also AAYA 24; BPFB 3; BYA 7, 9; CA 1-4R, 186; CAAE 186; CAAS 3; CANR 1, 20, 36, 85; CLR 59; CN 7; CPW; DAM POP; DLB 8; INT CANR-20; MAICYA 1, 2; MTCW 1, 2; SATA 13, 91; SATA-Essay 104; SCFW 2; SFW 4; SUFW 2
Silverstein, Alvin 1933- .... CLC 17
See also CA 49-52; CANR 2; CLR 25; JRDA; MAICYA 1, 2; SATA 8, 69, 124
Silverstein, Shel(don Allan)
1932-1999 .... PC 49
See also AAYA 40; BW 3; CA 107; 179; CANR 47, 74, 81; CLR 5, 96; CWRI 5; JRDA; MAICYA 1, 2; MTCW 2; SATA 33, 92; SATA-Brief 27; SATA-Obit 116

Silverstein, Virginia B(arbara Opshelor)
1937- .... CLC 17
See also CA 49-52; CANR 2; CLR 25; JRDA; MAICYA 1, 2; SATA 8, 69, 124
Sim, Georges
See Simenon, Georges (Jacques Christian)
Simak, Clifford D(onald) 1904-1988 . CLC 1, 55
See also CA 1-4R; 125; CANR 1, 35; DLB 8; MTCW 1; SATA-Obit 56; SFW 4
Simenon, Georges (Jacques Christian)
1903-1989 .... CLC 1, 2, 3, 8, 18, 47
See also BPFB 3; CA 85-88; 129; CANR 35; CMW 4; DA3; DAM POP; DLB 72; DLBY 1989; EW 12; EWL 3; GFL 1789 to the Present; MSW; MTCW 1, 2; RGWL 2, 3
Simic, Charles 1938- .... CLC 6, 9, 22, 49, 68, 130
See also AMWS 8; CA 29-32R; CAAS 4; CANR 12, 33, 52, 61, 96; CP 7; DA3; DAM POET; DLB 105; MTCW 2; PFS 7; RGAL 4; WP
Simmel, Georg 1858-1918 .... TCLC 64
See also CA 157; DLB 296
Simmons, Charles (Paul) 1924- .... CLC 57
See also CA 89-92; INT CA-89-92
Simmons, Dan 1948- .... CLC 44
See also AAYA 16, 54; CA 138; CANR 53, 81, 126; CPW; DAM POP; HGG; SUFW 2
Simmons, James (Stewart Alexander)
1933- .... CLC 43
See also CA 105; CAAS 21; CP 7; DLB 40
Simms, William Gilmore
1806-1870 .... NCLC 3
See also DLB 3, 30, 59, 73, 248, 254; RGAL 4
Simon, Carly 1945- .... CLC 26
See also CA 105
Simon, Claude (Eugene Henri)
1913-1984 .... CLC 4, 9, 15, 39
See also CA 89-92; CANR 33, 117; CWW 2; DAM NOV; DLB 83; EW 13; EWL 3; GFL 1789 to the Present; MTCW 1
Simon, Myles
See Follett, Ken(neth Martin)
Simon, (Marvin) Neil 1927- ... CLC 6, 11, 31, 39, 70; DC 14
See also AAYA 32; AITN 1; AMWS 4; CA 21-24R; CANR 26, 54, 87, 126; CD 5; DA3; DAM DRAM; DFS 2, 6, 12, 18; DLB 7, 266; LAIT 4; MTCW 1, 2; RGAL 4; TUS
Simon, Paul (Frederick) 1941(?)- ..... CLC 17
See also CA 116; 153
Simonon, Paul 1956(?)- .... CLC 30
Simonson, Rick ed. .... CLC 70
Simpson, Harriette
See Arnow, Harriette (Louisa) Simpson
Simpson, Louis (Aston Marantz)
1923- .... CLC 4, 7, 9, 32, 149
See also AMWS 9; CA 1-4R; CAAS 4; CANR 1, 61; CP 7; DAM POET; DLB 5; MTCW 1, 2; PFS 7, 11, 14; RGAL 4
Simpson, Mona (Elizabeth) 1957- ... CLC 44, 146
See also CA 122; 135; CANR 68, 103; CN 7; EWL 3
Simpson, N(orman) F(rederick)
1919- .... CLC 29
See also CA 13-16R; CBD; DLB 13; RGEL 2
Sinclair, Andrew (Annandale) 1935- . CLC 2, 14
See also CA 9-12R; CAAS 5; CANR 14, 38, 91; CN 7; DLB 14; FANT; MTCW 1
Sinclair, Emil
See Hesse, Hermann

Sinclair, Iain 1943- .... CLC 76
See also CA 132; CANR 81; CP 7; HGG
Sinclair, Iain MacGregor
See Sinclair, Iain
Sinclair, Irene
See Griffith, D(avid Lewelyn) W(ark)
Sinclair, Mary Amelia St. Clair 1865(?)-1946
See Sinclair, May
See also CA 104; HGG; RHW
Sinclair, May .... TCLC 3, 11
See Sinclair, Mary Amelia St. Clair
See also CA 166; DLB 36, 135; EWL 3; RGEL 2; SUFW
Sinclair, Roy
See Griffith, D(avid Lewelyn) W(ark)
Sinclair, Upton (Beall) 1878-1968 ..... CLC 1, 11, 15, 63; WLC
See also AMWS 5; BPFB 3; BYA 2; CA 5-8R; 25-28R; CANR 7; CDALB 1929-1941; DA; DA3; DAB; DAC; DAM MST, NOV; DLB 9; EWL 3; INT CANR-7; LAIT 3; MTCW 1, 2; NFS 6; RGAL 4; SATA 9; TUS; YAW
Singe, (Edmund) J(ohn) M(illington)
1871-1909 .... WLC
Singer, Isaac
See Singer, Isaac Bashevis
Singer, Isaac Bashevis 1904-1991 .. CLC 1, 3, 6, 9, 11, 15, 23, 38, 69, 111; SSC 3, 53; WLC
See also AAYA 32; AITN 1, 2; AMW; AMWR 2; BPFB 3; BYA 1, 4; CA 1-4R; 134; CANR 1, 39, 106; CDALB 1941-1968; CLR 1; CWRI 5; DA; DA3; DAB; DAC; DAM MST, NOV; DLB 6, 28, 52, 278; DLBY 1991; EWL 3; EXPS; HGG; JRDA; LAIT 3; MAICYA 1, 2; MTCW 1, 2; RGAL 4; RGSF 2; SATA 3, 27; SATA-Obit 68; SSFS 2, 12, 16; TUS; TWA
Singer, Israel Joshua 1893-1944 .... TCLC 33
See also CA 169; EWL 3
Singh, Khushwant 1915- .... CLC 11
See also CA 9-12R; CAAS 9; CANR 6, 84; CN 7; EWL 3; RGEL 2
Singleton, Ann
See Benedict, Ruth (Fulton)
Singleton, John 1968(?)- .... CLC 156
See also AAYA 50; BW 2, 3; CA 138; CANR 67, 82; DAM MULT
Siniavskii, Andrei
See Sinyavsky, Andrei (Donatevich)
See also CWW 2
Sinjohn, John
See Galsworthy, John
Sinyavsky, Andrei (Donatevich)
1925-1997 .... CLC 8
See Siniavskii, Andrei; Sinyavsky, Andrey Donatovich; Tertz, Abram
See also CA 85-88; 159
Sinyavsky, Andrey Donatovich
See Sinyavsky, Andrei (Donatevich)
See also EWL 3
Sirin, V.
See Nabokov, Vladimir (Vladimirovich)
Sissman, L(ouis) E(dward)
1928-1976 .... CLC 9, 18
See also CA 21-24R; 65-68; CANR 13; DLB 5
Sisson, C(harles) H(ubert)
1914-2003 .... CLC 8
See also CA 1-4R; 220; CAAS 3; CANR 3, 48, 84; CP 7; DLB 27
Sitting Bull 1831(?)-1890 .... NNAL
See also DA3; DAM MULT
Sitwell, Dame Edith 1887-1964 ..... CLC 2, 9, 67; PC 3
See also BRW 7; CA 9-12R; CANR 35; CDBLB 1945-1960; DAM POET; DLB 20; EWL 3; MTCW 1, 2; RGEL 2; TEA

Siwaarmill, H. P.
See Sharp, William
Sjoewall, Maj 1935- .... **CLC 7**
See Sjowall, Maj
See also CA 65-68; CANR 73
Sjowall, Maj
See Sjowall, Maj
See also BPFB 3; CMW 4; MSW
Skelton, John 1460(?)-1529 ..... **LC 71; PC 25**
See also BRW 1; DLB 136; RGEL 2
Skelton, Robin 1925-1997 .... **CLC 13**
See Zuk, Georges
See also AITN 2; CA 5-8R; 160; CAAS 5;
CANR 28, 89; CCA 1; CP 7; DLB 27, 53
Skolimowski, Jerzy 1938- .... **CLC 20**
See also CA 128
Skram, Amalie (Bertha)
1847-1905 .... **TCLC 25**
See also CA 165
Skvorecky, Josef (Vaclav) 1924- ...... **CLC 15,
39, 69, 152**
See also CA 61-64; CAAS 1; CANR 10,
34, 63, 108; CDWLB 4; CWW 2; DA3;
DAC; DAM NOV; DLB 232; EWL 3;
MTCW 1, 2
Slade, Bernard .... **CLC 11, 46**
See Newbound, Bernard Slade
See also CAAS 9; CCA 1; DLB 53
Slaughter, Carolyn 1946- .... **CLC 56**
See also CA 85-88; CANR 85; CN 7
Slaughter, Frank G(ill) 1908-2001 ... **CLC 29**
See also AITN 2; CA 5-8R; 197; CANR 5,
85; INT CANR-5; RHW
Slavitt, David R(ytman) 1935- ..... **CLC 5, 14**
See also CA 21-24R; CAAS 3; CANR 41,
83; CP 7; DLB 5, 6
Slesinger, Tess 1905-1945 .... **TCLC 10**
See also CA 107; 199; DLB 102
Slessor, Kenneth 1901-1971 .... **CLC 14**
See also CA 102; 89-92; DLB 260; RGEL
2
Slowacki, Juliusz 1809-1849 .... **NCLC 15**
See also RGWL 3
Smart, Christopher 1722-1771 . **LC 3; PC 13**
See also DAM POET; DLB 109; RGEL 2
Smart, Elizabeth 1913-1986 .... **CLC 54**
See also CA 81-84; 118; DLB 88
Smiley, Jane (Graves) 1949- ...... **CLC 53, 76,
144**
See also AMWS 6; BPFB 3; CA 104;
CANR 30, 50, 74, 96; CN 7; CPW 1;
DA3; DAM POP; DLB 227, 234; EWL 3;
INT CANR-30; SSFS 19
Smith, A(rthur) J(ames) M(arshall)
1902-1980 .... **CLC 15**
See also CA 1-4R; 102; CANR 4; DAC;
DLB 88; RGEL 2
Smith, Adam 1723(?)-1790 .... **LC 36**
See also DLB 104, 252; RGEL 2
Smith, Alexander 1829-1867 .... **NCLC 59**
See also DLB 32, 55
Smith, Anna Deavere 1950- .... **CLC 86**
See also CA 133; CANR 103; CD 5; DFS 2
Smith, Betty (Wehner) 1904-1972 .... **CLC 19**
See also BPFB 3; BYA 3; CA 5-8R; 33-
36R; DLBY 1982; LAIT 3; RGAL 4;
SATA 6
Smith, Charlotte (Turner)
1749-1806 .... **NCLC 23, 115**
See also DLB 39, 109; RGEL 2; TEA
Smith, Clark Ashton 1893-1961 .... **CLC 43**
See also CA 143; CANR 81; FANT; HGG;
MTCW 2; SCFW 2; SFW 4; SUFW
Smith, Dave .... **CLC 22, 42**
See Smith, David (Jeddie)
See also CAAS 7; DLB 5

Smith, David (Jeddie) 1942-
See Smith, Dave
See also CA 49-52; CANR 1, 59, 120; CP
7; CSW; DAM POET
Smith, Florence Margaret 1902-1971
See Smith, Stevie
See also CA 17-18; 29-32R; CANR 35;
CAP 2; DAM POET; MTCW 1, 2; TEA
Smith, Iain Crichton 1928-1998 .... **CLC 64**
See also BRWS 9; CA 21-24R; 171; CN 7;
CP 7; DLB 40, 139; RGSF 2
Smith, John 1580(?)-1631 .... **LC 9**
See also DLB 24, 30; TUS
Smith, Johnston
See Crane, Stephen (Townley)
Smith, Joseph, Jr. 1805-1844 .... **NCLC 53**
Smith, Lee 1944- .... **CLC 25, 73**
See also CA 114; 119; CANR 46, 118;
CSW; DLB 143; DLBY 1983; EWL 3;
INT CA-119; RGAL 4
Smith, Martin
See Smith, Martin Cruz
Smith, Martin Cruz 1942- .. **CLC 25; NNAL**
See also BEST 89:4; BPFB 3; CA 85-88;
CANR 6, 23, 43, 65, 119; CMW 4; CPW;
DAM MULT, POP; HGG; INT CANR-
23; MTCW 2; RGAL 4
Smith, Patti 1946- .... **CLC 12**
See also CA 93-96; CANR 63
Smith, Pauline (Urmson)
1882-1959 .... **TCLC 25**
See also DLB 225; EWL 3
Smith, Rosamond
See Oates, Joyce Carol
Smith, Sheila Kaye
See Kaye-Smith, Sheila
Smith, Stevie .... **CLC 3, 8, 25, 44; PC 12**
See Smith, Florence Margaret
See also BRWS 2; DLB 20; EWL 3; MTCW
2; PAB; PFS 3; RGEL 2
Smith, Wilbur (Addison) 1933- .... **CLC 33**
See also CA 13-16R; CANR 7, 46, 66;
CPW; MTCW 1, 2
Smith, William Jay 1918- .... **CLC 6**
See also AMWS 13; CA 5-8R; CANR 44,
106; CP 7; CSW; CWRI 5; DLB 5; MAI-
CYA 1, 2; SAAS 22; SATA 2, 68
Smith, Woodrow Wilson
See Kuttner, Henry
Smith, Zadie 1976- .... **CLC 158**
See also AAYA 50; CA 193
Smolenskin, Peretz 1842-1885 .... **NCLC 30**
Smollett, Tobias (George) 1721-1771 ... **LC 2,
46**
See also BRW 3; CDBLB 1660-1789; DLB
39, 104; RGEL 2; TEA
Snodgrass, W(illiam) D(e Witt)
1926- .... **CLC 2, 6, 10, 18, 68**
See also AMWS 6; CA 1-4R; CANR 6, 36,
65, 85; CP 7; DAM POET; DLB 5;
MTCW 1, 2; RGAL 4
Snorri Sturluson 1179-1241 .... **CMLC 56**
See also RGWL 2, 3
Snow, C(harles) P(ercy) 1905-1980 ... **CLC 1,
4, 6, 9, 13, 19**
See also BRW 7; CA 5-8R; 101; CANR 28;
CDBLB 1945-1960; DAM NOV; DLB 15,
77; DLBD 17; EWL 3; MTCW 1, 2;
RGEL 2; TEA
Snow, Frances Compton
See Adams, Henry (Brooks)
Snyder, Gary (Sherman) 1930- . **CLC 1, 2, 5,
9, 32, 120; PC 21**
See also AMWS 8; ANW; BG 3; CA 17-
20R; CANR 30, 60, 125; CP 7; DA3;
DAM POET; DLB 5, 16, 165, 212, 237,
275; EWL 3; MTCW 2; PFS 9, 19; RGAL
4; WP

Snyder, Zilpha Keatley 1927- .... **CLC 17**
See also AAYA 15; BYA 1; CA 9-12R;
CANR 38; CLR 31; JRDA; MAICYA 1,
2; SAAS 2; SATA 1, 28, 75, 110; SATA-
Essay 112; YAW
Soares, Bernardo
See Pessoa, Fernando (Antonio Nogueira)
Sobh, A.
See Shamlu, Ahmad
Sobh, Alef
See Shamlu, Ahmad
Sobol, Joshua 1939- .... **CLC 60**
See Sobol, Yehoshua
See also CA 200
Sobol, Yehoshua 1939-
See Sobol, Joshua
Socrates 470 B.C.-399 B.C. .... **CMLC 27**
Soderberg, Hjalmar 1869-1941 ...... **TCLC 39**
See also DLB 259; EWL 3; RGSF 2
Soderbergh, Steven 1963- .... **CLC 154**
See also AAYA 43
Sodergran, Edith (Irene) 1892-1923
See Soedergran, Edith (Irene)
See also CA 202; DLB 259; EW 11; EWL
3; RGWL 2, 3
Soedergran, Edith (Irene)
1892-1923 .... **TCLC 31**
See Sodergran, Edith (Irene)
Softly, Edgar
See Lovecraft, H(oward) P(hillips)
Softly, Edward
See Lovecraft, H(oward) P(hillips)
Sokolov, Alexander V(sevolodovich) 1943-
See Sokolov, Sasha
See also CA 73-76
Sokolov, Raymond 1941- .... **CLC 7**
See also CA 85-88
Sokolov, Sasha .... **CLC 59**
See Sokolov, Alexander V(sevolodovich)
See also CWW 2; DLB 285; EWL 3; RGWL
2, 3
Solo, Jay
See Ellison, Harlan (Jay)
Sologub, Fyodor .... **TCLC 9**
See Teternikov, Fyodor Kuzmich
See also EWL 3
Solomons, Ikey Esquir
See Thackeray, William Makepeace
Solomos, Dionysios 1798-1857 .... **NCLC 15**
Solwoska, Mara
See French, Marilyn
Solzhenitsyn, Aleksandr I(sayevich)
1918- .. **CLC 1, 2, 4, 7, 9, 10, 18, 26, 34,
78, 134; SSC 32; WLC**
See Solzhenitsyn, Aleksandr Isaevich
See also AAYA 49; AITN 1; BPFB 3; CA
69-72; CANR 40, 65, 116; DA; DA3;
DAB; DAC; DAM MST, NOV; DLB 302;
EW 13; EXPS; LAIT 4; MTCW 1, 2; NFS
6; RGSF 2; RGWL 2, 3; SSFS 9; TWA
Solzhenitsyn, Aleksandr Isaevich
See Solzhenitsyn, Aleksandr I(sayevich)
See also CWW 2; EWL 3
Somers, Jane
See Lessing, Doris (May)
Somerville, Edith Oenone
1858-1949 .... **SSC 56; TCLC 51**
See also CA 196; DLB 135; RGEL 2; RGSF
2
Somerville & Ross
See Martin, Violet Florence; Somerville,
Edith Oenone
Sommer, Scott 1951- .... **CLC 25**
See also CA 106
Sommers, Christina Hoff 1950- ...... **CLC 197**
See also CA 153; CANR 95

Stark, Richard
See Westlake, Donald E(dwin)

Staunton, Schuyler
See Baum, L(yman) Frank

Stead, Christina (Ellen) 1902-1983 ... CLC 2, 5, 8, 32, 80
See also BRWS 4; CA 13-16R; 109; CANR 33, 40; DLB 260; EWL 3; FW; MTCW 1, 2; RGEL 2; RGSF 2; WWE 1

Stead, William Thomas
1849-1912 .... TCLC 48
See also CA 167

Stebnitsky, M.
See Leskov, Nikolai (Semyonovich)

Steele, Sir Richard 1672-1729 .... LC 18
See also BRW 3; CDBLB 1660-1789; DLB 84, 101; RGEL 2; WLIT 3

Steele, Timothy (Reid) 1948- .... CLC 45
See also CA 93-96; CANR 16, 50, 92; CP 7; DLB 120, 282

Steffens, (Joseph) Lincoln
1866-1936 .... TCLC 20
See also CA 117; 198; DLB 303

Stegner, Wallace (Earle) 1909-1993 .. CLC 9, 49, 81; SSC 27
See also AITN 1; AMWS 4; ANW; BEST 90:3; BPFB 3; CA 1-4R; 141; CAAS 9; CANR 1, 21, 46; DAM NOV; DLB 9, 206, 275; DLBY 1993; EWL 3; MTCW 1, 2; RGAL 4; TCWW 2; TUS

Stein, Gertrude 1874-1946 .... DC 19; PC 18; SSC 42; TCLC 1, 6, 28, 48; WLC
See also AMW; AMWC 2; CA 104; 132; CANR 108; CDALB 1917-1929; DA; DA3; DAB; DAC; DAM MST, NOV; POET; DLB 4, 54, 86, 228; DLBD 15; EWL 3; EXPS; GLL 1; MAWW; MTCW 1, 2; NCFS 4; RGAL 4; RGSF 2; SSFS 5; TUS; WP

Steinbeck, John (Ernst) 1902-1968 ... CLC 1, 5, 9, 13, 21, 34, 45, 75, 124; SSC 11, 37; TCLC 135; WLC
See also AAYA 12; AMW; BPFB 3; BYA 2, 3, 13; CA 1-4R; 25-28R; CANR 1, 35; CDALB 1929-1941; DA; DA3; DAB; DAC; DAM DRAM, MST, NOV; DLB 7, 9, 212, 275; DLBD 2; EWL 3; EXPS; LAIT 3; MTCW 1; NFS 1, 5, 7, 17, 19; RGAL 4; RGSF 2; RHW; SATA 9; SSFS 3, 6; TCWW 2; TUS; WYA; YAW

Steinem, Gloria 1934- .... CLC 63
See also CA 53-56; CANR 28, 51; DLB 246; FW; MTCW 1, 2

Steiner, George 1929- .... CLC 24
See also CA 73-76; CANR 31, 67, 108; DAM NOV; DLB 67, 299; EWL 3; MTCW 1, 2; SATA 62

Steiner, K. Leslie
See Delany, Samuel R(ay), Jr.

Steiner, Rudolf 1861-1925 .... TCLC 13
See also CA 107

Stendhal 1783-1842 .. NCLC 23, 46; SSC 27; WLC
See also DA; DA3; DAB; DAC; DAM MST, NOV; DLB 119; EW 5; GFL 1789 to the Present; RGWL 2, 3; TWA

Stephen, Adeline Virginia
See Woolf, (Adeline) Virginia

Stephen, Sir Leslie 1832-1904 .... TCLC 23
See also BRW 5; CA 123; DLB 57, 144, 190

Stephen, Sir Leslie
See Stephen, Sir Leslie

Stephen, Virginia
See Woolf, (Adeline) Virginia

Stephens, James 1882(?)-1950 .... SSC 50; TCLC 4
See also CA 104; 192; DLB 19, 153, 162; EWL 3; FANT; RGEL 2; SUFW

Stephens, Reed
See Donaldson, Stephen R(eeder)

Steptoe, Lydia
See Barnes, Djuna
See also GLL 1

Sterchi, Beat 1949- .... CLC 65
See also CA 203

Sterling, Brett
See Bradbury, Ray (Douglas); Hamilton, Edmond

Sterling, Bruce 1954- .... CLC 72
See also CA 119; CANR 44; SCFW 2; SFW 4

Sterling, George 1869-1926 .... TCLC 20
See also CA 117; 165; DLB 54

Stern, Gerald 1925- .... CLC 40, 100
See also AMWS 9; CA 81-84; CANR 28, 94; CP 7; DLB 105; RGAL 4

Stern, Richard (Gustave) 1928- ... CLC 4, 39
See also CA 1-4R; CANR 1, 25, 52, 120; CN 7; DLB 218; DLBY 1987; INT CANR-25

Sternberg, Josef von 1894-1969 .... CLC 20
See also CA 81-84

Sterne, Laurence 1713-1768 .... LC 2, 48; WLC
See also BRW 3; BRWC 1; CDBLB 1660-1789; DA; DAB; DAC; DAM MST, NOV; DLB 39; RGEL 2; TEA

Sternheim, (William Adolf) Carl
1878-1942 .... TCLC 8
See also CA 105; 193; DLB 56, 118; EWL 3; RGWL 2, 3

Stevens, Mark 1951- .... CLC 34
See also CA 122

Stevens, Wallace 1879-1955 . PC 6; TCLC 3, 12, 45; WLC
See also AMW; AMWR 1; CA 104; 124; CDALB 1929-1941; DA; DA3; DAB; DAC; DAM MST, POET; DLB 54; EWL 3; EXPP; MTCW 1, 2; PAB; PFS 13, 16; RGAL 4; TUS; WP

Stevenson, Anne (Katharine) 1933- .. CLC 7, 33
See also BRWS 6; CA 17-20R; CAAS 9; CANR 9, 33, 123; CP 7; CWP; DLB 40; MTCW 1; RHW

Stevenson, Robert Louis (Balfour)
1850-1894 ...... NCLC 5, 14, 63; SSC 11, 51; WLC
See also AAYA 24; BPFB 3; BRW 5; BRWC 1; BRWR 1; BYA 1, 2, 4, 13; CD-BLB 1890-1914; CLR 10, 11; DA; DA3; DAB; DAC; DAM MST, NOV; DLB 18, 57, 141, 156, 174; DLBD 13; HGG; JRDA; LAIT 1, 3; MAICYA 1, 2; NFS 11, 20; RGEL 2; RGSF 2; SATA 100; SUFW; TEA; WCH; WLIT 4; WYA; YABC 2; YAW

Stewart, J(ohn) I(nnes) M(ackintosh)
1906-1994 .... CLC 7, 14, 32
See Innes, Michael
See also CA 85-88; 147; CAAS 3; CANR 47; CMW 4; MTCW 1, 2

Stewart, Mary (Florence Elinor)
1916- .... CLC 7, 35, 117
See also AAYA 29; BPFB 3; CA 1-4R; CANR 1, 59, 130; CMW 4; CPW; DAB; FANT; RHW; SATA 12; YAW

Stewart, Mary Rainbow
See Stewart, Mary (Florence Elinor)

Stifle, June
See Campbell, Maria

Stifter, Adalbert 1805-1868 .. NCLC 41; SSC 28
See also CDWLB 2; DLB 133; RGSF 2; RGWL 2, 3

Still, James 1906-2001 .... CLC 49
See also CA 65-68; 195; CAAS 17; CANR 10, 26; CSW; DLB 9; DLBY 01; SATA 29; SATA-Obit 127

Sting 1951-
See Sumner, Gordon Matthew
See also CA 167

Stirling, Arthur
See Sinclair, Upton (Beall)

Stitt, Milan 1941- .... CLC 29
See also CA 69-72

Stockton, Francis Richard 1834-1902
See Stockton, Frank R.
See also CA 108; 137; MAICYA 1, 2; SATA 44; SFW 4

Stockton, Frank R. .... TCLC 47
See Stockton, Francis Richard
See also BYA 4, 13; DLB 42, 74; DLBD 13; EXPS; SATA-Brief 32; SSFS 3; SUFW; WCH

Stoddard, Charles
See Kuttner, Henry

Stoker, Abraham 1847-1912
See Stoker, Bram
See also CA 105; 150; DA; DA3; DAC; DAM MST, NOV; HGG; SATA 29

Stoker, Bram . SSC 62; TCLC 8, 144; WLC
See Stoker, Abraham
See also AAYA 23; BPFB 3; BRWS 3; BYA 5; CDBLB 1890-1914; DAB; DLB 304; LATS 1:1; NFS 18; RGEL 2; SUFW; TEA; WLIT 4

Stolz, Mary (Slattery) 1920- .... CLC 12
See also AAYA 8; AITN 1; CA 5-8R; CANR 13, 41, 112; JRDA; MAICYA 1, 2; SAAS 3; SATA 10, 71, 133; YAW

Stone, Irving 1903-1989 .... CLC 7
See also AITN 1; BPFB 3; CA 1-4R; 129; CAAS 3; CANR 1, 23; CPW; DA3; DAM POP; INT CANR-23; MTCW 1, 2; RHW; SATA 3; SATA-Obit 64

Stone, Oliver (William) 1946- .... CLC 73
See also AAYA 15; CA 110; CANR 55, 125

Stone, Robert (Anthony) 1937- ... CLC 5, 23, 42, 175
See also AMWS 5; BPFB 3; CA 85-88; CANR 23, 66, 95; CN 7; DLB 152; EWL 3; INT CANR-23; MTCW 1

Stone, Ruth 1915- .... PC 53
See also CA 45-48; CANR 2, 91; CP 7; CSW; DLB 105; PFS 19

Stone, Zachary
See Follett, Ken(neth Martin)

Stoppard, Tom 1937- ... CLC 1, 3, 4, 5, 8, 15, 29, 34, 63, 91; DC 6; WLC
See also BRWC 1; BRWR 2; BRWS 1; CA 81-84; CANR 39, 67, 125; CBD; CD 5; CDBLB 1960 to Present; DA; DA3; DAB; DAC; DAM DRAM, MST; DFS 2, 5, 8, 11, 13, 16; DLB 13, 233; DLBY 1985; EWL 3; LATS 1:2; MTCW 1, 2; RGEL 2; TEA; WLIT 4

Storey, David (Malcolm) 1933- . CLC 2, 4, 5, 8
See also BRWS 1; CA 81-84; CANR 36; CBD; CD 5; CN 7; DAM DRAM; DLB 13, 14, 207, 245; EWL 3; MTCW 1; RGEL 2

Storm, Hyemeyohsts 1935- ... CLC 3; NNAL
See also CA 81-84; CANR 45; DAM MULT

Storm, (Hans) Theodor (Woldsen)
1817-1888 .... NCLC 1; SSC 27
See also CDWLB 2; DLB 129; EW; RGSF 2; RGWL 2, 3

Storni, Alfonsina 1892-1938 . HLC 2; PC 33; TCLC 5
See also CA 104; 131; DAM MULT; DLB 283; HW 1; LAW

Stoughton, William 1631-1701 .... LC 38
See also DLB 24

Stout, Rex (Todhunter) 1886-1975 ..... **CLC 3**
   See also AITN 2; BPFB 3; CA 61-64;
   CANR 71; CMW 4; DLB 306; MSW;
   RGAL 4

Stow, (Julian) Randolph 1935- ... **CLC 23, 48**
   See also CA 13-16R; CANR 33; CN 7;
   DLB 260; MTCW 1; RGEL 2

Stowe, Harriet (Elizabeth) Beecher
   1811-1896 .... **NCLC 3, 50, 133; WLC**
   See also AAYA 53; AMWS 1; CDALB
   1865-1917; DA; DA3; DAB; DAC; DAM
   MST, NOV; DLB 1, 12, 42, 74, 189, 239,
   243; EXPN; JRDA; LAIT 2; MAICYA 1,
   2; NFS 6; RGAL 4; TUS; YABC 1

Strabo c. 64 B.C.-c. 25 .... **CMLC 37**
   See also DLB 176

Strachey, (Giles) Lytton
   1880-1932 .... **TCLC 12**
   See also BRWS 2; CA 110; 178; DLB 149;
   DLBD 10; EWL 3; MTCW 2; NCFS 4

Stramm, August 1874-1915 .... **PC 50**
   See also CA 195; EWL 3

Strand, Mark 1934- .... **CLC 6, 18, 41, 71**
   See also AMWS 4; CA 21-24R; CANR 40,
   65, 100; CP 7; DAM POET; DLB 5; EWL
   3; PAB; PFS 9, 18; RGAL 4; SATA 41

Stratton-Porter, Gene(va Grace) 1863-1924
   See Porter, Gene(va Grace) Stratton
   See also ANW; CA 137; CLR 87; DLB 221;
   DLBD 14; MAICYA 1, 2; SATA 15

Straub, Peter (Francis) 1943- ... **CLC 28, 107**
   See also BEST 89:1; BPFB 3; CA 85-88;
   CANR 28, 65, 109; CPW; DAM POP;
   DLBY 1984; HGG; MTCW 1, 2; SUFW
   2

Strauss, Botho 1944- .... **CLC 22**
   See also CA 157; CWW 2; DLB 124

Strauss, Leo 1899-1973 .... **TCLC 141**
   See also CA 101; 45-48; CANR 122

Streatfeild, (Mary) Noel
   1897(?)-1986 .... **CLC 21**
   See also CA 81-84; 120; CANR 31; CLR
   17, 83; CWRI 5; DLB 160; MAICYA 1,
   2; SATA 20; SATA-Obit 48

Stribling, T(homas) S(igismund)
   1881-1965 .... **CLC 23**
   See also CA 189; 107; CMW 4; DLB 9;
   RGAL 4

Strindberg, (Johan) August
   1849-1912 ... **DC 18; TCLC 1, 8, 21, 47;
   WLC**
   See also CA 104; 135; DA; DA3; DAB;
   DAC; DAM DRAM, MST; DFS 4, 9;
   DLB 259; EW 7; EWL 3; IDTP; LMFS
   2; MTCW 2; RGWL 2, 3; TWA

Stringer, Arthur 1874-1950 .... **TCLC 37**
   See also CA 161; DLB 92

Stringer, David
   See Roberts, Keith (John Kingston)

Stroheim, Erich von 1885-1957 ..... **TCLC 71**

Strugatskii, Arkadii (Natanovich)
   1925-1991 .... **CLC 27**
   See Strugatsky, Arkadii Natanovich
   See also CA 106; 135; SFW 4

Strugatskii, Boris (Natanovich)
   1933- .... **CLC 27**
   See Strugatsky, Boris (Natanovich)
   See also CA 106; SFW 4

Strugatsky, Arkadii Natanovich
   See Strugatskii, Arkadii (Natanovich)
   See also DLB 302

Strugatsky, Boris (Natanovich)
   See Strugatskii, Boris (Natanovich)
   See also DLB 302

Strummer, Joe 1953(?)- .... **CLC 30**

Strunk, William, Jr. 1869-1946 ...... **TCLC 92**
   See also CA 118; 164; NCFS 5

Stryk, Lucien 1924- .... **PC 27**
   See also CA 13-16R; CANR 10, 28, 55,
   110; CP 7

Stuart, Don A.
   See Campbell, John W(ood, Jr.)

Stuart, Ian
   See MacLean, Alistair (Stuart)

Stuart, Jesse (Hilton) 1906-1984 ... **CLC 1, 8,
   11, 14, 34; SSC 31**
   See also CA 5-8R; 112; CANR 31; DLB 9,
   48, 102; DLBY 1984; SATA 2; SATA-
   Obit 36

Stubblefield, Sally
   See Trumbo, Dalton

Sturgeon, Theodore (Hamilton)
   1918-1985 .... **CLC 22, 39**
   See Queen, Ellery
   See also AAYA 51; BPFB 3; BYA 9, 10;
   CA 81-84; 116; CANR 32, 103; DLB 8;
   DLBY 1985; HGG; MTCW 1, 2; SCFW;
   SFW 4; SUFW

Sturges, Preston 1898-1959 .... **TCLC 48**
   See also CA 114; 149; DLB 26

Styron, William 1925- .... **CLC 1, 3, 5, 11, 15,
   60; SSC 25**
   See also AMW; AMWC 2; BEST 90:4;
   BPFB 3; CA 5-8R; CANR 6, 33, 74, 126;
   CDALB 1968-1988; CN 7; CPW; CSW;
   DA3; DAM NOV, POP; DLB 2, 143, 299;
   DLBY 1980; EWL 3; INT CANR-6;
   LAIT 2; MTCW 1, 2; NCFS 1; RGAL 4;
   RHW; TUS

Su, Chien 1884-1918
   See Su Man-shu
   See also CA 123

Suarez Lynch, B.
   See Bioy Casares, Adolfo; Borges, Jorge
   Luis

Suassuna, Ariano Vilar 1927- .... **HLCS 1**
   See also CA 178; HW 2; LAW

Suckert, Kurt Erich
   See Malaparte, Curzio

Suckling, Sir John 1609-1642 . **LC 75; PC 30**
   See also BRW 2; DAM POET; DLB 58,
   126; EXPP; PAB; RGEL 2

Suckow, Ruth 1892-1960 .... **SSC 18**
   See also CA 193; 113; DLB 9, 102; RGAL
   4; TCWW 2

Sudermann, Hermann 1857-1928 .. **TCLC 15**
   See also CA 107; 201; DLB 118

Sue, Eugene 1804-1857 .... **NCLC 1**
   See also DLB 119

Sueskind, Patrick 1949- .... **CLC 44, 182**
   See Suskind, Patrick

Suetonius c. 70-c. 130 .... **CMLC 60**
   See also AW 2; DLB 211; RGWL 2, 3

Sukenick, Ronald 1932-2004 ..... **CLC 3, 4, 6,
   48**
   See also CA 25-28R; 209; CAAE 209;
   CAAS 8; CANR 32, 89; CN 7; DLB 173;
   DLBY 1981

Suknaski, Andrew 1942- .... **CLC 19**
   See also CA 101; CP 7; DLB 53

Sullivan, Vernon
   See Vian, Boris

Sully Prudhomme, Rene-Francois-Armand
   1839-1907 .... **TCLC 31**
   See also GFL 1789 to the Present

Su Man-shu .... **TCLC 24**
   See Su, Chien
   See also EWL 3

Sumarokov, Aleksandr Petrovich
   1717-1777 .... **LC 104**
   See also DLB 150

Summerforest, Ivy B.
   See Kirkup, James

Summers, Andrew James 1942- .... **CLC 26**

Summers, Andy
   See Summers, Andrew James

Summers, Hollis (Spurgeon, Jr.)
   1916- .... **CLC 10**
   See also CA 5-8R; CANR 3; DLB 6

**Summers, (Alphonsus Joseph-Mary
   Augustus) Montague**
   1880-1948 .... **TCLC 16**
   See also CA 118; 163

Sumner, Gordon Matthew .... **CLC 26**
   See Police, The; Sting

Sun Tzu c. 400 B.C.-c. 320 B.C. ... **CMLC 56**

Surrey, Henry Howard 1517-1574 ...... **PC 59**
   See also BRW 1; RGEL 2

Surtees, Robert Smith 1805-1864 .. **NCLC 14**
   See also DLB 21; RGEL 2

Susann, Jacqueline 1921-1974 .... **CLC 3**
   See also AITN 1; BPFB 3; CA 65-68; 53-
   56; MTCW 1, 2

Su Shi
   See Su Shih
   See also RGWL 2, 3

Su Shih 1036-1101 .... **CMLC 15**
   See Su Shi

Suskind, Patrick .... **CLC 182**
   See Sueskind, Patrick
   See also BPFB 3; CA 145; CWW 2

Sutcliff, Rosemary 1920-1992 .... **CLC 26**
   See also AAYA 10; BYA 1, 4; CA 5-8R;
   139; CANR 37; CLR 1, 37; CPW; DAB;
   DAC; DAM MST, POP; JRDA; LATS
   1:1; MAICYA 1, 2; MAICYAS 1; RHW;
   SATA 6, 44, 78; SATA-Obit 73; WYA;
   YAW

Sutro, Alfred 1863-1933 .... **TCLC 6**
   See also CA 105; 185; DLB 10; RGEL 2

Sutton, Henry
   See Slavitt, David R(ytman)

Suzuki, D. T.
   See Suzuki, Daisetz Teitaro

Suzuki, Daisetz T.
   See Suzuki, Daisetz Teitaro

Suzuki, Daisetz Teitaro
   1870-1966 .... **TCLC 109**
   See also CA 121; 111; MTCW 1, 2

Suzuki, Teitaro
   See Suzuki, Daisetz Teitaro

Svevo, Italo .... **SSC 25; TCLC 2, 35**
   See Schmitz, Aron Hector
   See also DLB 264; EW 8; EWL 3; RGWL
   2, 3

Swados, Elizabeth (A.) 1951- .... **CLC 12**
   See also CA 97-100; CANR 49; INT CA-
   97-100

Swados, Harvey 1920-1972 .... **CLC 5**
   See also CA 5-8R; 37-40R; CANR 6; DLB
   2

Swan, Gladys 1934- .... **CLC 69**
   See also CA 101; CANR 17, 39

Swanson, Logan
   See Matheson, Richard (Burton)

Swarthout, Glendon (Fred)
   1918-1992 .... **CLC 35**
   See also AAYA 55; CA 1-4R; 139; CANR
   1, 47; LAIT 5; SATA 26; TCWW 2; YAW

Swedenborg, Emanuel 1688-1772 ..... **LC 105**

Sweet, Sarah C.
   See Jewett, (Theodora) Sarah Orne

Swenson, May 1919-1989 ...... **CLC 4, 14, 61,
   106; PC 14**
   See also AMWS 4; CA 5-8R; 130; CANR
   36, 61, 131; DA; DAB; DAC; DAM MST,
   POET; DLB 5; EXPP; GLL 2; MTCW 1,
   2; PFS 16; SATA 15; WP

Swift, Augustus
   See Lovecraft, H(oward) P(hillips)

Swift, Graham (Colin) 1949- ...... **CLC 41, 88**
   See also BRWC 2; BRWS 5; CA 117; 122;
   CANR 46, 71, 128; CN 7; DLB 194;
   MTCW 2; NFS 18; RGSF 2

Swift, Jonathan 1667-1745 ..... **LC 1, 42, 101; PC 9; WLC**
See also AAYA 41; BRW 3; BRWC 1; BRWR 1; BYA 5, 14; CDBLB 1660-1789; CLR 53; DA; DA3; DAB; DAC; DAM MST, NOV, POET; DLB 39, 95, 101; EXPN; LAIT 1; NFS 6; RGEL 2; SATA 19; TEA; WCH; WLIT 3

Swinburne, Algernon Charles 1837-1909 ... **PC 24; TCLC 8, 36; WLC**
See also BRW 5; CA 105; 140; CDBLB 1832-1890; DA; DA3; DAB; DAC; DAM MST, POET; DLB 35, 57; PAB; RGEL 2; TEA

Swinfen, Ann .... **CLC 34**
See also CA 202

Swinnerton, Frank Arthur 1884-1982 .... **CLC 31**
See also CA 108; DLB 34

Swithen, John
See King, Stephen (Edwin)

Sylvia
See Ashton-Warner, Sylvia (Constance)

Symmes, Robert Edward
See Duncan, Robert (Edward)

Symonds, John Addington 1840-1893 .... **NCLC 34**
See also DLB 57, 144

Symons, Arthur 1865-1945 .... **TCLC 11**
See also CA 107; 189; DLB 19, 57, 149; RGEL 2

Symons, Julian (Gustave) 1912-1994 .... **CLC 2, 14, 32**
See also CA 49-52; 147; CAAS 3; CANR 3, 33, 59; CMW 4; DLB 87, 155; DLBY 1992; MSW; MTCW 1

Synge, (Edmund) J(ohn) M(illington) 1871-1909 .... **DC 2; TCLC 6, 37**
See also BRW 6; BRWR 1; CA 104; 141; CDBLB 1890-1914; DAM DRAM; DFS 18; DLB 10, 19; EWL 3; RGEL 2; TEA; WLIT 4

Syruc, J.
See Milosz, Czeslaw

Szirtes, George 1948- .... **CLC 46; PC 51**
See also CA 109; CANR 27, 61, 117; CP 7

Szymborska, Wislawa 1923- ... **CLC 99, 190; PC 44**
See also CA 154; CANR 91, 133; CDWLB 4; CWP; CWW 2; DA3; DLB 232; DLBY 1996; EWL 3; MTCW 2; PFS 15; RGWL 3

T. O., Nik
See Annensky, Innokenty (Fyodorovich)

Tabori, George 1914- .... **CLC 19**
See also CA 49-52; CANR 4, 69; CBD; CD 5; DLB 245

Tacitus c. 55-c. 117 .... **CMLC 56**
See also AW 2; CDWLB 1; DLB 211; RGWL 2, 3

Tagore, Rabindranath 1861-1941 .... **PC 8; SSC 48; TCLC 3, 53**
See also CA 104; 120; DA3; DAM DRAM, POET; EWL 3; MTCW 1, 2; PFS 18; RGEL 2; RGSF 2; RGWL 2, 3; TWA

Taine, Hippolyte Adolphe 1828-1893 .... **NCLC 15**
See also EW 7; GFL 1789 to the Present

Talayesva, Don C. 1890-(?) .... **NNAL**

Talese, Gay 1932- .... **CLC 37**
See also AITN 1; CA 1-4R; CANR 9, 58; DLB 185; INT CANR-9; MTCW 1, 2

Tallent, Elizabeth (Ann) 1954- .... **CLC 45**
See also CA 117; CANR 72; DLB 130

Tallmountain, Mary 1918-1997 .... **NNAL**
See also CA 146; 161; DLB 193

Tally, Ted 1952- .... **CLC 42**
See also CA 120; 124; CAD; CANR 125; CD 5; INT CA-124

Talvik, Heiti 1904-1947 .... **TCLC 87**
See also EWL 3

Tamayo y Baus, Manuel 1829-1898 .... **NCLC 1**

Tammsaare, A(nton) H(ansen) 1878-1940 .... **TCLC 27**
See also CA 164; CDWLB 4; DLB 220; EWL 3

Tam'si, Tchicaya U
See Tchicaya, Gerald Felix

Tan, Amy (Ruth) 1952- . **AAL; CLC 59, 120, 151**
See also AAYA 9, 48; AMWS 10; BEST 89:3; BPFB 3; CA 136; CANR 54, 105, 132; CDALBS; CN 7; CPW 1; DA3; DAM MULT, NOV, POP; DLB 173; EXPN; FW; LAIT 3, 5; MTCW 2; NFS 1, 13, 16; RGAL 4; SATA 75; SSFS 9; YAW

Tandem, Felix
See Spitteler, Carl (Friedrich Georg)

Tanizaki, Jun'ichiro 1886-1965 ... **CLC 8, 14, 28; SSC 21**
See Tanizaki Jun'ichiro
See also CA 93-96; 25-28R; MJW; MTCW 2; RGSF 2; RGWL 2

Tanizaki Jun'ichiro
See Tanizaki, Jun'ichiro
See also DLB 180; EWL 3

Tanner, William
See Amis, Kingsley (William)

Tao Lao
See Storni, Alfonsina

Tapahonso, Luci 1953- .... **NNAL**
See also CA 145; CANR 72, 127; DLB 175

Tarantino, Quentin (Jerome) 1963- .... **CLC 125**
See also AAYA 58; CA 171; CANR 125

Tarassoff, Lev
See Troyat, Henri

Tarbell, Ida M(inerva) 1857-1944 . **TCLC 40**
See also CA 122; 181; DLB 47

Tarkington, (Newton) Booth 1869-1946 .... **TCLC 9**
See also BPFB 3; BYA 3; CA 110; 143; CWRI 5; DLB 9, 102; MTCW 2; RGAL 4; SATA 17

Tarkovskii, Andrei Arsen'evich
See Tarkovsky, Andrei (Arsenyevich)

Tarkovsky, Andrei (Arsenyevich) 1932-1986 .... **CLC 75**
See also CA 127

Tartt, Donna 1963- .... **CLC 76**
See also AAYA 56; CA 142

Tasso, Torquato 1544-1595 .... **LC 5, 94**
See also EFS 2; EW 2; RGWL 2, 3

Tate, (John Orley) Allen 1899-1979 .. **CLC 2, 4, 6, 9, 11, 14, 24; PC 50**
See also AMW; CA 5-8R; 85-88; CANR 32, 108; DLB 4, 45, 63; DLBD 17; EWL 3; MTCW 1, 2; RGAL 4; RHW

Tate, Ellalice
See Hibbert, Eleanor Alice Burford

Tate, James (Vincent) 1943- ..... **CLC 2, 6, 25**
See also CA 21-24R; CANR 29, 57, 114; CP 7; DLB 5, 169; EWL 3; PFS 10, 15; RGAL 4; WP

Tauler, Johannes c. 1300-1361 ...... **CMLC 37**
See also DLB 179; LMFS 1

Tavel, Ronald 1940- .... **CLC 6**
See also CA 21-24R; CAD; CANR 33; CD 5

Taviani, Paolo 1931- .... **CLC 70**
See also CA 153

Taylor, Bayard 1825-1878 .... **NCLC 89**
See also DLB 3, 189, 250, 254; RGAL 4

Taylor, C(ecil) P(hilip) 1929-1981 .... **CLC 27**
See also CA 25-28R; 105; CANR 47; CBD

Taylor, Edward 1642(?)-1729 .... **LC 11**
See also AMW; DA; DAB; DAC; DAM MST, POET; DLB 24; EXPP; RGAL 4; TUS

Taylor, Eleanor Ross 1920- .... **CLC 5**
See also CA 81-84; CANR 70

Taylor, Elizabeth 1932-1975 ..... **CLC 2, 4, 29**
See also CA 13-16R; CANR 9, 70; DLB 139; MTCW 1; RGEL 2; SATA 13

Taylor, Frederick Winslow 1856-1915 .... **TCLC 76**
See also CA 188

Taylor, Henry (Splawn) 1942- .... **CLC 44**
See also CA 33-36R; CAAS 7; CANR 31; CP 7; DLB 5; PFS 10

Taylor, Kamala (Purnaiya) 1924-2004
See Markandaya, Kamala
See also CA 77-80; 227; NFS 13

Taylor, Mildred D(elois) 1943- .... **CLC 21**
See also AAYA 10, 47; BW 1; BYA 3, 8; CA 85-88; CANR 25, 115; CLR 9, 59, 90; CSW; DLB 52; JRDA; LAIT 3; MAICYA 1, 2; SAAS 5; SATA 135; WYA; YAW

Taylor, Peter (Hillsman) 1917-1994 .. **CLC 1, 4, 18, 37, 44, 50, 71; SSC 10**
See also AMWS 5; BPFB 3; CA 13-16R; 147; CANR 9, 50; CSW; DLB 218, 278; DLBY 1981, 1994; EWL 3; EXPS; INT CANR-9; MTCW 1, 2; RGSF 2; SSFS 9; TUS

Taylor, Robert Lewis 1912-1998 .... **CLC 14**
See also CA 1-4R; 170; CANR 3, 64; SATA 10

Tchekhov, Anton
See Chekhov, Anton (Pavlovich)

Tchicaya, Gerald Felix 1931-1988 .. **CLC 101**
See Tchicaya U Tam'si
See also CA 129; 125; CANR 81

Tchicaya U Tam'si
See Tchicaya, Gerald Felix
See also EWL 3

Teasdale, Sara 1884-1933 .... **PC 31; TCLC 4**
See also CA 104; 163; DLB 45; GLL 1; PFS 14; RGAL 4; SATA 32; TUS

Tecumseh 1768-1813 .... **NNAL**
See also DAM MULT

Tegner, Esaias 1782-1846 .... **NCLC 2**

Teilhard de Chardin, (Marie Joseph) Pierre 1881-1955 .... **TCLC 9**
See also CA 105; 210; GFL 1789 to the Present

Temple, Ann
See Mortimer, Penelope (Ruth)

Tennant, Emma (Christina) 1937- .. **CLC 13, 52**
See also BRWS 9; CA 65-68; CAAS 9; CANR 10, 38, 59, 88; CN 7; DLB 14; EWL 3; SFW 4

Tenneshaw, S. M.
See Silverberg, Robert

Tenney, Tabitha Gilman 1762-1837 .... **NCLC 122**
See also DLB 37, 200

Tennyson, Alfred 1809-1892 ... **NCLC 30, 65, 115; PC 6; WLC**
See also AAYA 50; BRW 4; CDBLB 1832-1890; DA; DA3; DAB; DAC; DAM MST, POET; DLB 32; EXPP; PAB; PFS 1, 2, 4, 11, 15, 19; RGEL 2; TEA; WLIT 4; WP

Teran, Lisa St. Aubin de .... **CLC 36**
See St. Aubin de Teran, Lisa

Terence c. 184 B.C.-c. 159 B.C. ... **CMLC 14; DC 7**
See also AW 1; CDWLB 1; DLB 211; RGWL 2, 3; TWA

Teresa de Jesus, St. 1515-1582 .... **LC 18**
Terkel, Louis 1912-
See Terkel, Studs
See also CA 57-60; CANR 18, 45, 67, 132;
DA3; MTCW 1, 2
Terkel, Studs .... **CLC 38**
See Terkel, Louis
See also AAYA 32; AITN 1; MTCW 2; TUS
Terry, C. V.
See Slaughter, Frank G(ill)
Terry, Megan 1932- .... **CLC 19; DC 13**
See also CA 77-80; CABS 3; CAD; CANR
43; CD 5; CWD; DFS 18; DLB 7, 249;
GLL 2
Tertullian c. 155-c. 245 .... **CMLC 29**
Tertz, Abram
See Sinyavsky, Andrei (Donatevich)
See also RGSF 2
Tesich, Steve 1943(?)-1996 .... **CLC 40, 69**
See also CA 105; 152; CAD; DLBY 1983
Tesla, Nikola 1856-1943 .... **TCLC 88**
Teternikov, Fyodor Kuzmich 1863-1927
See Sologub, Fyodor
See also CA 104
Tevis, Walter 1928-1984 .... **CLC 42**
See also CA 113; SFW 4
Tey, Josephine .... **TCLC 14**
See Mackintosh, Elizabeth
See also DLB 77; MSW
Thackeray, William Makepeace
1811-1863 .... **NCLC 5, 14, 22, 43; WLC**
See also BRW 5; BRWC 2; CDBLB 1832-
1890; DA; DA3; DAB; DAC; DAM MST,
NOV; DLB 21, 55, 159, 163; NFS 13;
RGEL 2; SATA 23; TEA; WLIT 3
Thakura, Ravindranatha
See Tagore, Rabindranath
Thames, C. H.
See Marlowe, Stephen
Tharoor, Shashi 1956- .... **CLC 70**
See also CA 141; CANR 91; CN 7
Thelwell, Michael Miles 1939- .... **CLC 22**
See also BW 2; CA 101
Theobald, Lewis, Jr.
See Lovecraft, H(oward) P(hillips)
Theocritus c. 310 B.C.- .... **CMLC 45**
See also AW 1; DLB 176; RGWL 2, 3
Theodorescu, Ion N. 1880-1967
See Arghezi, Tudor
See also CA 116
Theriault, Yves 1915-1983 .... **CLC 79**
See also CA 102; CCA 1; DAC; DAM
MST; DLB 88; EWL 3
Theroux, Alexander (Louis) 1939- .... **CLC 2,
25**
See also CA 85-88; CANR 20, 63; CN 7
Theroux, Paul (Edward) 1941- ..... **CLC 5, 8,
11, 15, 28, 46**
See also AAYA 28; AMWS 8; BEST 89:4;
BPFB 3; CA 33-36R; CANR 20, 45, 74,
133; CDALBS; CN 7; CPW 1; DA3;
DAM POP; DLB 2, 218; EWL 3; HGG;
MTCW 1, 2; RGAL 4; SATA 44, 109;
TUS
Thesen, Sharon 1946- .... **CLC 56**
See also CA 163; CANR 125; CP 7; CWP
Thespis fl. 6th cent. B.C.- .... **CMLC 51**
See also LMFS 1
Thevenin, Denis
See Duhamel, Georges
Thibault, Jacques Anatole Francois
1844-1924
See France, Anatole
See also CA 106; 127; DA3; DAM NOV;
MTCW 1, 2; TWA
Thiele, Colin (Milton) 1920- .... **CLC 17**
See also CA 29-32R; CANR 12, 28, 53,
105; CLR 27; DLB 289; MAICYA 1, 2;
SAAS 2; SATA 14, 72, 125; YAW

Thistlethwaite, Bel
See Wetherald, Agnes Ethelwyn
Thomas, Audrey (Callahan) 1935- .... **CLC 7,
13, 37, 107; SSC 20**
See also AITN 2; CA 21-24R; CAAS 19;
CANR 36, 58; CN 7; DLB 60; MTCW 1;
RGSF 2
Thomas, Augustus 1857-1934 .... **TCLC 97**
Thomas, D(onald) M(ichael) 1935- . **CLC 13,
22, 31, 132**
See also BPFB 3; BRWS 4; CA 61-64;
CAAS 11; CANR 17, 45, 75; CDBLB
1960 to Present; CN 7; CP 7; DA3; DLB
40, 207, 299; HGG; INT CANR-17;
MTCW 1, 2; SFW 4
Thomas, Dylan (Marlais) 1914-1953 .... **PC 2,
52; SSC 3, 44; TCLC 1, 8, 45, 105;
WLC**
See also AAYA 45; BRWS 1; CA 104; 120;
CANR 65; CDBLB 1945-1960; DA; DA3;
DAB; DAC; DAM DRAM, MST, POET;
DLB 13, 20, 139; EWL 3; EXPP; LAIT
3; MTCW 1, 2; PAB; PFS 1, 3, 8; RGEL
2; RGSF 2; SATA 60; TEA; WLIT 4; WP
Thomas, (Philip) Edward 1878-1917 . **PC 53;
TCLC 10**
See also BRW 6; BRWS 3; CA 106; 153;
DAM POET; DLB 19, 98, 156, 216; EWL
3; PAB; RGEL 2
Thomas, Joyce Carol 1938- .... **CLC 35**
See also AAYA 12, 54; BW 2, 3; CA 113;
116; CANR 48, 114; CLR 19; DLB 33;
INT CA-116; JRDA; MAICYA 1, 2;
MTCW 1, 2; SAAS 7; SATA 40, 78, 123,
137; SATA-Essay 137; WYA; YAW
Thomas, Lewis 1913-1993 .... **CLC 35**
See also ANW; CA 85-88; 143; CANR 38,
60; DLB 275; MTCW 1, 2
Thomas, M. Carey 1857-1935 .... **TCLC 89**
See also FW
Thomas, Paul
See Mann, (Paul) Thomas
Thomas, Piri 1928- .... **CLC 17; HLCS 2**
See also CA 73-76; HW 1; LLW 1
Thomas, R(onald) S(tuart)
1913-2000 .... **CLC 6, 13, 48**
See also CA 89-92; 189; CAAS 4; CANR
30; CDBLB 1960 to Present; CP 7; DAB;
DAM POET; DLB 27; EWL 3; MTCW 1;
RGEL 2
Thomas, Ross (Elmore) 1926-1995 .. **CLC 39**
See also CA 33-36R; 150; CANR 22, 63;
CMW 4
Thompson, Francis (Joseph)
1859-1907 .... **TCLC 4**
See also BRW 5; CA 104; 189; CDBLB
1890-1914; DLB 19; RGEL 2; TEA
Thompson, Francis Clegg
See Mencken, H(enry) L(ouis)
Thompson, Hunter S(tockton)
1937(?)- .... **CLC 9, 17, 40, 104**
See also AAYA 45; BEST 89:1; BPFB 3;
CA 17-20R; CANR 23, 46, 74, 77, 111,
133; CPW; CSW; DA3; DAM POP; DLB
185; MTCW 1, 2; TUS
Thompson, James Myers
See Thompson, Jim (Myers)
Thompson, Jim (Myers)
1906-1977(?) .... **CLC 69**
See also BPFB 3; CA 140; CMW 4; CPW;
DLB 226; MSW
Thompson, Judith .... **CLC 39**
See also CWD
Thomson, James 1700-1748 .... **LC 16, 29, 40**
See also BRWS 3; DAM POET; DLB 95;
RGEL 2
Thomson, James 1834-1882 .... **NCLC 18**
See also DAM POET; DLB 35; RGEL 2

Thoreau, Henry David 1817-1862 .. **NCLC 7,
21, 61, 138; PC 30; WLC**
See also AAYA 42; AMW; ANW; BYA 3;
CDALB 1640-1865; DA; DA3; DAB;
DAC; DAM MST; DLB 1, 183, 223, 270,
298; LAIT 2; LMFS 1; NCFS 3; RGAL
4; TUS
Thorndike, E. L.
See Thorndike, Edward L(ee)
Thorndike, Edward L(ee)
1874-1949 .... **TCLC 107**
See also CA 121
Thornton, Hall
See Silverberg, Robert
Thorpe, Adam 1956- .... **CLC 176**
See also CA 129; CANR 92; DLB 231
Thubron, Colin (Gerald Dryden)
1939- .... **CLC 163**
See also CA 25-28R; CANR 12, 29, 59, 95;
CN 7; DLB 204, 231
Thucydides c. 455 B.C.-c. 395
B.C. .... **CMLC 17**
See also AW 1; DLB 176; RGWL 2, 3
Thumboo, Edwin Nadason 1933- .... **PC 30**
See also CA 194
Thurber, James (Grover)
1894-1961 .. **CLC 5, 11, 25, 125; SSC 1,
47**
See also AAYA 56; AMWS 1; BPFB 3;
BYA 5; CA 73-76; CANR 17, 39; CDALB
1929-1941; CWRI 5; DA; DA3; DAB;
DAC; DAM DRAM, MST, NOV; DLB 4,
11, 22, 102; EWL 3; EXPS; FANT; LAIT
3; MAICYA 1, 2; MTCW 1, 2; RGAL 4;
RGSF 2; SATA 13; SSFS 1, 10, 19;
SUFW; TUS
Thurman, Wallace (Henry)
1902-1934 .... **BLC 3; HR 3; TCLC 6**
See also BW 1, 3; CA 104; 124; CANR 81;
DAM MULT; DLB 51
Tibullus c. 54 B.C.-c. 18 B.C. .... **CMLC 36**
See also AW 2; DLB 211; RGWL 2, 3
Ticheburn, Cheviot
See Ainsworth, William Harrison
Tieck, (Johann) Ludwig
1773-1853 .... **NCLC 5, 46; SSC 31**
See also CDWLB 2; DLB 90; EW 5; IDTP;
RGSF 2; RGWL 2, 3; SUFW
Tiger, Derry
See Ellison, Harlan (Jay)
Tilghman, Christopher 1946- .... **CLC 65**
See also CA 159; CSW; DLB 244
Tillich, Paul (Johannes)
1886-1965 .... **CLC 131**
See also CA 5-8R; 25-28R; CANR 33;
MTCW 1, 2
Tillinghast, Richard (Williford)
1940- .... **CLC 29**
See also CA 29-32R; CAAS 23; CANR 26,
51, 96; CP 7; CSW
Timrod, Henry 1828-1867 .... **NCLC 25**
See also DLB 3, 248; RGAL 4
Tindall, Gillian (Elizabeth) 1938- ...... **CLC 7**
See also CA 21-24R; CANR 11, 65, 107;
CN 7
Tiptree, James, Jr. .... **CLC 48, 50**
See Sheldon, Alice Hastings Bradley
See also DLB 8; SCFW 2; SFW 4
Tirone Smith, Mary-Ann 1944- .... **CLC 39**
See also CA 118; 136; CANR 113; SATA
143
Tirso de Molina 1580(?)-1648 .... **DC 13;
HLCS 2; LC 73**
See also RGWL 2, 3
Titmarsh, Michael Angelo
See Thackeray, William Makepeace

Tocqueville, Alexis (Charles Henri Maurice Clerel Comte) de 1805-1859 .. NCLC 7, 63
See also EW 6; GFL 1789 to the Present; TWA

Toer, Pramoedya Ananta 1925- ...... CLC 186
See also CA 197; RGWL 3

Toffler, Alvin 1928- .... CLC 168
See also CA 13-16R; CANR 15, 46, 67; CPW; DAM POP; MTCW 1, 2

Toibin, Colm
See Toibin, Colm
See also DLB 271

Toibin, Colm 1955- .... CLC 162
See Toibin, Colm
See also CA 142; CANR 81

Tolkien, J(ohn) R(onald) R(euel) 1892-1973 .... CLC 1, 2, 3, 8, 12, 38; TCLC 137; WLC
See also AAYA 10; AITN 1; BPFB 3; BRWC 2; BRWS 2; CA 17-18; 45-48; CANR 36; CAP 2; CDBLB 1914-1945; CLR 56; CPW 1; CWRI 5; DA; DA3; DAB; DAC; DAM MST, NOV, POP; DLB 15, 160, 255; EFS 2; EWL 3; FANT; JRDA; LAIT 1; LATS 1:2; LMFS 2; MAICYA 1, 2; MTCW 1, 2; NFS 8; RGEL 2; SATA 2, 32, 100; SATA-Obit 24; SFW 4; SUFW; TEA; WCH; WYA; YAW

Toller, Ernst 1893-1939 .... TCLC 10
See also CA 107; 186; DLB 124; EWL 3; RGWL 2, 3

Tolson, M. B.
See Tolson, Melvin B(eaunorus)

Tolson, Melvin B(eaunorus) 1898(?)-1966 .... BLC 3; CLC 36, 105
See also AFAW 1, 2; BW 1, 3; CA 124; 89-92; CANR 80; DAM MULT, POET; DLB 48, 76; RGAL 4

Tolstoi, Aleksei Nikolaevich
See Tolstoy, Alexey Nikolaevich

Tolstoi, Lev
See Tolstoy, Leo (Nikolaevich)
See also RGSF 2; RGWL 2, 3

Tolstoy, Aleksei Nikolaevich
See Tolstoy, Alexey Nikolaevich
See also DLB 272

Tolstoy, Alexey Nikolaevich 1882-1945 .... TCLC 18
See Tolstoy, Aleksei Nikolaevich
See also CA 107; 158; EWL 3; SFW 4

Tolstoy, Leo (Nikolaevich) 1828-1910 . SSC 9, 30, 45, 54; TCLC 4, 11, 17, 28, 44, 79; WLC
See Tolstoi, Lev
See also AAYA 56; CA 104; 123; DA; DA3; DAB; DAC; DAM MST, NOV; DLB 238; EFS 2; EW 7; EXPS; IDTP; LAIT 2; LATS 1:1; LMFS 1; NFS 10; SATA 26; SSFS 5; TWA

Tolstoy, Count Leo
See Tolstoy, Leo (Nikolaevich)

Tomalin, Claire 1933- .... CLC 166
See also CA 89-92; CANR 52, 88; DLB 155

Tomasi di Lampedusa, Giuseppe 1896-1957
See Lampedusa, Giuseppe (Tomasi) di
See also CA 111; DLB 177; EWL 3

Tomlin, Lily .... CLC 17
See Tomlin, Mary Jean

Tomlin, Mary Jean 1939(?)-
See Tomlin, Lily
See also CA 117

Tomline, F. Latour
See Gilbert, W(illiam) S(chwenck)

Tomlinson, (Alfred) Charles 1927- .... CLC 2, 4, 6, 13, 45; PC 17
See also CA 5-8R; CANR 33; CP 7; DAM POET; DLB 40

Tomlinson, H(enry) M(ajor) 1873-1958 .... TCLC 71
See also CA 118; 161; DLB 36, 100, 195

Tonna, Charlotte Elizabeth 1790-1846 .... NCLC 135
See also DLB 163

Tonson, Jacob fl. 1655(?)-1736 .... LC 86
See also DLB 170

Toole, John Kennedy 1937-1969 ..... CLC 19, 64
See also BPFB 3; CA 104; DLBY 1981; MTCW 2

Toomer, Eugene
See Toomer, Jean

Toomer, Eugene Pinchback
See Toomer, Jean

Toomer, Jean 1894-1967 .. BLC 3; CLC 1, 4, 13, 22; HR 3; PC 7; SSC 1, 45; WLCS
See also AFAW 1, 2; AMWS 3, 9; BW 1; CA 85-88; CDALB 1917-1929; DA3; DAM MULT; DLB 45, 51; EWL 3; EXPP; EXPS; LMFS 2; MTCW 1, 2; NFS 11; RGAL 4; RGSF 2; SSFS 5

Toomer, Nathan Jean
See Toomer, Jean

Toomer, Nathan Pinchback
See Toomer, Jean

Torley, Luke
See Blish, James (Benjamin)

Tornimparte, Alessandra
See Ginzburg, Natalia

Torre, Raoul della
See Mencken, H(enry) L(ouis)

Torrence, Ridgely 1874-1950 .... TCLC 97
See also DLB 54, 249

Torrey, E(dwin) Fuller 1937- .... CLC 34
See also CA 119; CANR 71

Torsvan, Ben Traven
See Traven, B.

Torsvan, Benno Traven
See Traven, B.

Torsvan, Berick Traven
See Traven, B.

Torsvan, Berwick Traven
See Traven, B.

Torsvan, Bruno Traven
See Traven, B.

Torsvan, Traven
See Traven, B.

Tourneur, Cyril 1575(?)-1626 .... LC 66
See also BRW 2; DAM DRAM; DLB 58; RGEL 2

Tournier, Michel (Edouard) 1924- .... CLC 6, 23, 36, 95
See also CA 49-52; CANR 3, 36, 74; CWW 2; DLB 83; EWL 3; GFL 1789 to the Present; MTCW 1, 2; SATA 23

Tournimparte, Alessandra
See Ginzburg, Natalia

Towers, Ivar
See Kornbluth, C(yril) M.

Towne, Robert (Burton) 1936(?)- ..... CLC 87
See also CA 108; DLB 44; IDFW 3, 4

Townsend, Sue .... CLC 61
See Townsend, Susan Lilian
See also AAYA 28; CA 119; 127; CANR 65, 107; CBD; CD 5; CPW; CWD; DAB; DAC; DAM MST; DLB 271; INT CA-127; SATA 55, 93; SATA-Brief 48; YAW

Townsend, Susan Lilian 1946-
See Townsend, Sue

Townshend, Pete
See Townshend, Peter (Dennis Blandford)

Townshend, Peter (Dennis Blandford) 1945- .... CLC 17, 42
See also CA 107

Tozzi, Federigo 1883-1920 .... TCLC 31
See also CA 160; CANR 110; DLB 264; EWL 3

Tracy, Don(ald Fiske) 1905-1970(?)
See Queen, Ellery
See also CA 1-4R; 176; CANR 2

Trafford, F. G.
See Riddell, Charlotte

Traherne, Thomas 1637(?)-1674 .... LC 99
See also BRW 2; DLB 131; PAB; RGEL 2

Traill, Catharine Parr 1802-1899 .. NCLC 31
See also DLB 99

Trakl, Georg 1887-1914 .... PC 20; TCLC 5
See also CA 104; 165; EW 10; EWL 3; LMFS 2; MTCW 2; RGWL 2, 3

Tranquilli, Secondino
See Silone, Ignazio

Transtroemer, Tomas Gosta
See Transtromer, Tomas (Goesta)

Transtromer, Tomas (Gosta)
See Transtromer, Tomas (Goesta)
See also CWW 2

Transtromer, Tomas (Goesta) 1931- .... CLC 52, 65
See Transtromer, Tomas (Gosta)
See also CA 117; 129; CAAS 17; CANR 115; DAM POET; DLB 257; EWL 3; PFS 21

Transtromer, Tomas Gosta
See Transtromer, Tomas (Goesta)

Traven, B. 1882(?)-1969 .... CLC 8, 11
See also CA 19-20; 25-28R; CAP 2; DLB 9, 56; EWL 3; MTCW 1; RGAL 4

Trediakovsky, Vasilii Kirillovich 1703-1769 .... LC 68
See also DLB 150

Treitel, Jonathan 1959- .... CLC 70
See also CA 210; DLB 267

Trelawny, Edward John 1792-1881 .... NCLC 85
See also DLB 110, 116, 144

Tremain, Rose 1943- .... CLC 42
See also CA 97-100; CANR 44, 95; CN 7; DLB 14, 271; RGSF 2; RHW

Tremblay, Michel 1942- .... CLC 29, 102
See also CA 116; 128; CCA 1; CWW 2; DAC; DAM MST; DLB 60; EWL 3; GLL 1; MTCW 1, 2

Trevanian .... CLC 29
See Whitaker, Rod(ney)

Trevor, Glen
See Hilton, James

Trevor, William .. CLC 7, 9, 14, 25, 71, 116; SSC 21, 58
See Cox, William Trevor
See also BRWS 4; CBD; CD 5; CN 7; DLB 14, 139; EWL 3; LATS 1:2; MTCW 2; RGEL 2; RGSF 2; SSFS 10

Trifonov, Iurii (Valentinovich)
See Trifonov, Yuri (Valentinovich)
See also DLB 302; RGWL 2, 3

Trifonov, Yuri (Valentinovich) 1925-1981 .... CLC 45
See Trifonov, Iurii (Valentinovich); Trifonov, Yury Valentinovich
See also CA 126; 103; MTCW 1

Trifonov, Yury Valentinovich
See Trifonov, Yuri (Valentinovich)
See also EWL 3

Trilling, Diana (Rubin) 1905-1996 . CLC 129
See also CA 5-8R; 154; CANR 10, 46; INT CANR-10; MTCW 1, 2

Trilling, Lionel 1905-1975 ..... CLC 9, 11, 24; SSC 75
See also AMWS 3; CA 9-12R; 61-64; CANR 10, 105; DLB 28, 63; EWL 3; INT CANR-10; MTCW 1, 2; RGAL 4; TUS

Trimball, W. H.
See Mencken, H(enry) L(ouis)

Tristan
See Gomez de la Serna, Ramon
Tristram
See Housman, A(lfred) E(dward)
Trogdon, William (Lewis) 1939-
See Heat-Moon, William Least
See also CA 115; 119; CANR 47, 89; CPW;
INT CA-119
Trollope, Anthony 1815-1882 .... NCLC 6, 33,
101; SSC 28; WLC
See also BRW 5; CDBLB 1832-1890; DA;
DA3; DAB; DAC; DAM MST, NOV;
DLB 21, 57, 159; RGEL 2; RGSF 2;
SATA 22
Trollope, Frances 1779-1863 .... NCLC 30
See also DLB 21, 166
Trollope, Joanna 1943- .... CLC 186
See also CA 101; CANR 58, 95; CPW;
DLB 207; RHW
Trotsky, Leon 1879-1940 .... TCLC 22
See also CA 118; 167
Trotter (Cockburn), Catharine
1679-1749 .... LC 8
See also DLB 84, 252
Trotter, Wilfred 1872-1939 .... TCLC 97
Trout, Kilgore
See Farmer, Philip Jose
Trow, George W. S. 1943- .... CLC 52
See also CA 126; CANR 91
Troyat, Henri 1911- .... CLC 23
See also CA 45-48; CANR 2, 33, 67, 117;
GFL 1789 to the Present; MTCW 1
Trudeau, G(arretson) B(eekman) 1948-
See Trudeau, Garry B.
See also CA 81-84; CANR 31; SATA 35
Trudeau, Garry B. .... CLC 12
See Trudeau, G(arretson) B(eekman)
See also AAYA 10; AITN 2
Truffaut, Francois 1932-1984 ... CLC 20, 101
See also CA 81-84; 113; CANR 34
Trumbo, Dalton 1905-1976 .... CLC 19
See also CA 21-24R; 69-72; CANR 10;
DLB 26; IDFW 3, 4; YAW
Trumbull, John 1750-1831 .... NCLC 30
See also DLB 31; RGAL 4
Trundlett, Helen B.
See Eliot, T(homas) S(tearns)
Truth, Sojourner 1797(?)-1883 ...... NCLC 94
See also DLB 239; FW; LAIT 2
Tryon, Thomas 1926-1991 .... CLC 3, 11
See also AITN 1; BPFB 3; CA 29-32R; 135;
CANR 32, 77; CPW; DA3; DAM POP;
HGG; MTCW 1
Tryon, Tom
See Tryon, Thomas
Ts'ao Hsueh-ch'in 1715(?)-1763 .... LC 1
Tsushima, Shuji 1909-1948
See Dazai Osamu
See also CA 107
Tsvetaeva (Efron), Marina (Ivanovna)
1892-1941 .... PC 14; TCLC 7, 35
See also CA 104; 128; CANR 73; DLB 295;
EW 11; MTCW 1, 2; RGWL 2, 3
Tuck, Lily 1938- .... CLC 70
See also CA 139; CANR 90
Tu Fu 712-770 .... PC 9
See Du Fu
See also DAM MULT; TWA; WP
Tunis, John R(oberts) 1889-1975 ..... CLC 12
See also BYA 1; CA 61-64; CANR 62; DLB
22, 171; JRDA; MAICYA 1, 2; SATA 37;
SATA-Brief 30; YAW
Tuohy, Frank .... CLC 37
See Tuohy, John Francis
See also DLB 14, 139
Tuohy, John Francis 1925-
See Tuohy, Frank
See also CA 5-8R; 178; CANR 3, 47; CN 7

Turco, Lewis (Putnam) 1934- ..... CLC 11, 63
See also CA 13-16R; CAAS 22; CANR 24,
51; CP 7; DLBY 1984
Turgenev, Ivan (Sergeevich)
1818-1883 ..... DC 7; NCLC 21, 37, 122;
SSC 7, 57; WLC
See also AAYA 58; DA; DAB; DAC; DAM
MST, NOV; DLB 238, 284; EW
6; LATS 1:1; NFS 16; RGSF 2; RGWL 2,
3; TWA
Turgot, Anne-Robert-Jacques
1727-1781 .... LC 26
Turner, Frederick 1943- .... CLC 48
See also CA 73-76, 227; CAAE 227; CAAS
10; CANR 12, 30, 56; DLB 40, 282
Turton, James
See Crace, Jim
Tutu, Desmond M(pilo) 1931- .. BLC 3; CLC
80
See also BW 1, 3; CA 125; CANR 67, 81;
DAM MULT
Tutuola, Amos 1920-1997 ..... BLC 3; CLC 5,
14, 29
See also AFW; BW 2, 3; CA 9-12R; 159;
CANR 27, 66; CDWLB 3; CN 7; DA3;
DAM MULT; DLB 125; DNFS 2; EWL
3; MTCW 1, 2; RGEL 2; WLIT 2
Twain, Mark .. SSC 34; TCLC 6, 12, 19, 36,
48, 59; WLC
See Clemens, Samuel Langhorne
See also AAYA 20; AMW; AMWC 1; BPFB
3; BYA 2, 3, 11, 14; CLR 58, 60, 66; DLB
11; EXPN; EXPS; FANT; LAIT 2; NCFS
4; NFS 1, 6; RGAL 4; RGSF 2; SFW 4;
SSFS 1, 7; SUFW; TUS; WCH; WYA;
YAW
Tyler, Anne 1941- . CLC 7, 11, 18, 28, 44, 59,
103
See also AAYA 18; AMWS 4; BEST 89:1;
BPFB 3; BYA 12; CA 9-12R; CANR 11,
33, 53, 109, 132; CDALBS; CN 7; CPW;
CSW; DAM NOV, POP; DLB 6, 143;
DLBY 1982; EWL 3; EXPN; LATS 1:2;
MAWW; MTCW 1, 2; NFS 2, 7, 10;
RGAL 4; SATA 7, 90; SSFS 17; TUS;
YAW
Tyler, Royall 1757-1826 .... NCLC 3
See also DLB 37; RGAL 4
Tynan, Katharine 1861-1931 .... TCLC 3
See also CA 104; 167; DLB 153, 240; FW
Tyndale, William c. 1484-1536 .... LC 103
See also DLB 132
Tyutchev, Fyodor 1803-1873 .... NCLC 34
Tzara, Tristan 1896-1963 ..... CLC 47; PC 27
See also CA 153; 89-92; DAM POET; EWL
3; MTCW 2
Uchida, Yoshiko 1921-1992 .... AAL
See also AAYA 16; BYA 2, 3; CA 13-16R;
139; CANR 6, 22, 47, 61; CDALBS; CLR
6, 56; CWRI 5; JRDA; MAICYA 1, 2;
MTCW 1, 2; SAAS 1; SATA 1, 53; SATA-
Obit 72
Udall, Nicholas 1504-1556 .... LC 84
See also DLB 62; RGEL 2
Ueda Akinari 1734-1809 .... NCLC 131
Uhry, Alfred 1936- .... CLC 55
See also CA 127; 133; CAD; CANR 112;
CD 5; CSW; DA3; DAM DRAM, POP;
DFS 11, 15; INT CA-133
Ulf, Haerved
See Strindberg, (Johan) August
Ulf, Harved
See Strindberg, (Johan) August
Ulibarri, Sabine R(eyes)
1919-2003 .... CLC 83; HLCS 2
See also CA 131; 214; CANR 81; DAM
MULT; DLB 82; HW 1, 2; RGSF 2

Unamuno (y Jugo), Miguel de
1864-1936 .. HLC 2; SSC 11, 69; TCLC
2, 9, 148
See also CA 104; 131; CANR 81; DAM
MULT, NOV; DLB 108; EW 8; EWL 3;
HW 1, 2; MTCW 1, 2; RGSF 2; RGWL
2, 3; SSFS 20; TWA
Uncle Shelby
See Silverstein, Shel(don Allan)
Undercliffe, Errol
See Campbell, (John) Ramsey
Underwood, Miles
See Glassco, John
Undset, Sigrid 1882-1949 ..... TCLC 3; WLC
See also CA 104; 129; DA; DA3; DAB;
DAC; DAM MST, NOV; DLB 293; EW
9; EWL 3; FW; MTCW 1, 2; RGWL 2, 3
Ungaretti, Giuseppe 1888-1970 ... CLC 7, 11,
15; PC 57
See also CA 19-20; 25-28R; CAP 2; DLB
114; EW 10; EWL 3; PFS 20; RGWL 2,
3
Unger, Douglas 1952- .... CLC 34
See also CA 130; CANR 94
Unsworth, Barry (Forster) 1930- .... CLC 76,
127
See also BRWS 7; CA 25-28R; CANR 30,
54, 125; CN 7; DLB 194
Updike, John (Hoyer) 1932- . CLC 1, 2, 3, 5,
7, 9, 13, 15, 23, 34, 43, 70, 139; SSC 13,
27; WLC
See also AAYA 36; AMW; AMWC 1;
AMWR 1; BPFB 3; BYA 12; CA 1-4R;
CABS 1; CANR 4, 33, 51, 94, 133;
CDALB 1968-1988; CN 7; CP 7; CPW 1;
DA; DA3; DAB; DAC; DAM MST, NOV,
POET, POP; DLB 2, 5, 143, 218, 227;
DLBD 3; DLBY 1980, 1982, 1997; EWL
3; EXPP; HGG; MTCW 1, 2; NFS 12;
RGAL 4; RGSF 2; SSFS 3, 19; TUS
Upshaw, Margaret Mitchell
See Mitchell, Margaret (Munnerlyn)
Upton, Mark
See Sanders, Lawrence
Upward, Allen 1863-1926 .... TCLC 85
See also CA 117; 187; DLB 36
Urdang, Constance (Henriette)
1922-1996 .... CLC 47
See also CA 21-24R; CANR 9, 24; CP 7;
CWP
Uriel, Henry
See Faust, Frederick (Schiller)
Uris, Leon (Marcus) 1924-2003 ... CLC 7, 32
See also AITN 1, 2; BEST 89:2; BPFB 3;
CA 1-4R; 217; CANR 1, 40, 65, 123; CN
7; CPW 1; DA3; DAM NOV, POP;
MTCW 1, 2; SATA 49; SATA-Obit 146
Urista (Heredia), Alberto (Baltazar)
1947- .... HLCS 1; PC 34
See Alurista
See also CA 45-48, 182; CANR 2, 32; HW
1
Urmuz
See Codrescu, Andrei
Urquhart, Guy
See McAlmon, Robert (Menzies)
Urquhart, Jane 1949- .... CLC 90
See also CA 113; CANR 32, 68, 116; CCA
1; DAC
Usigli, Rodolfo 1905-1979 .... HLCS 1
See also CA 131; DLB 305; EWL 3; HW 1;
LAW
Ustinov, Peter (Alexander)
1921-2004 .... CLC 1
See also AITN 1; CA 13-16R; 225; CANR
25, 51; CBD; CD 5; DLB 13; MTCW 2
U Tam'si, Gerald Felix Tchicaya
See Tchicaya, Gerald Felix

Viereck, Peter (Robert Edwin)
1916- .... **CLC 4; PC 27**
See also CA 1-4R; CANR 1, 47; CP 7; DLB
5; PFS 9, 14

Vigny, Alfred (Victor) de
1797-1863 .... **NCLC 7, 102; PC 26**
See also DAM POET; DLB 119, 192, 217;
EW 5; GFL 1789 to the Present; RGWL
2, 3

Vilakazi, Benedict Wallet
1906-1947 .... **TCLC 37**
See also CA 168

Villa, Jose Garcia 1914-1997 .... **AAL; PC 22**
See also CA 25-28R; CANR 12, 118; EWL
3; EXPP

Villa, Jose Garcia 1914-1997
See Villa, Jose Garcia

Villarreal, Jose Antonio 1924- .... **HLC 2**
See also CA 133; CANR 93; DAM MULT;
DLB 82; HW 1; LAIT 4; RGAL 4

Villaurrutia, Xavier 1903-1950 ...... **TCLC 80**
See also CA 192; EWL 3; HW 1; LAW

Villaverde, Cirilo 1812-1894 .... **NCLC 121**
See also LAW

Villehardouin, Geoffroi de
1150(?)-1218(?) .... **CMLC 38**

Villiers, George 1628-1687 .... **LC 107**
See also DLB 80; RGEL 2

Villiers de l'Isle Adam, Jean Marie Mathias
Philippe Auguste 1838-1889 ... **NCLC 3;**
SSC 14
See also DLB 123, 192; GFL 1789 to the
Present; RGSF 2

Villon, Francois 1431-1463(?) . **LC 62; PC 13**
See also DLB 208; EW 2; RGWL 2, 3;
TWA

Vine, Barbara .... **CLC 50**
See Rendell, Ruth (Barbara)
See also BEST 90:4

Vinge, Joan (Carol) D(ennison)
1948- .... **CLC 30; SSC 24**
See also AAYA 32; BPFB 3; CA 93-96;
CANR 72; SATA 36, 113; SFW 4; YAW

Viola, Herman J(oseph) 1938- .... **CLC 70**
See also CA 61-64; CANR 8, 23, 48, 91;
SATA 126

Violis, G.
See Simenon, Georges (Jacques Christian)

Viramontes, Helena Maria 1954- .... **HLCS 2**
See also CA 159; DLB 122; HW 2; LLW 1

Virgil
See Vergil
See also CDWLB 1; DLB 211; LAIT 1;
RGWL 2, 3; WP

Visconti, Luchino 1906-1976 .... **CLC 16**
See also CA 81-84; 65-68; CANR 39

Vitry, Jacques de
See Jacques de Vitry

Vittorini, Elio 1908-1966 .... **CLC 6, 9, 14**
See also CA 133; 25-28R; DLB 264; EW
12; EWL 3; RGWL 2, 3

Vivekananda, Swami 1863-1902 .... **TCLC 88**

Vizenor, Gerald Robert 1934- .... **CLC 103;**
NNAL
See also CA 13-16R, 205; CAAE 205;
CAAS 22; CANR 5, 21, 44, 67; DAM
MULT; DLB 175, 227; MTCW 2; TCWW
2

Vizinczey, Stephen 1933- .... **CLC 40**
See also CA 128; CCA 1; INT CA-128

Vliet, R(ussell) G(ordon)
1929-1984 .... **CLC 22**
See also CA 37-40R; 112; CANR 18

Vogau, Boris Andreyevich 1894-1938
See Pilnyak, Boris
See also CA 123; 218

Vogel, Paula A(nne) 1951- ... **CLC 76; DC 19**
See also CA 108; CAD; CANR 119; CD 5;
CWD; DFS 14; RGAL 4

Voigt, Cynthia 1942- .... **CLC 30**
See also AAYA 3, 30; BYA 1, 3, 6, 7, 8;
CA 106; CANR 18, 37, 40, 94; CLR 13,
48; INT CANR-18; JRDA; LAIT 5; MAI-
CYA 1, 2; MAICYAS 1; SATA 48, 79,
116; SATA-Brief 33; WYA; YAW

Voigt, Ellen Bryant 1943- .... **CLC 54**
See also CA 69-72; CANR 11, 29, 55, 115;
CP 7; CSW; CWP; DLB 120

Voinovich, Vladimir (Nikolaevich)
1932- .... **CLC 10, 49, 147**
See also CA 81-84; CAAS 12; CANR 33,
67; CWW 2; DLB 302; MTCW 1

Vollmann, William T. 1959- .... **CLC 89**
See also CA 134; CANR 67, 116; CPW;
DA3; DAM NOV, POP; MTCW 2

Voloshinov, V. N.
See Bakhtin, Mikhail Mikhailovich

Voltaire 1694-1778 .... **LC 14, 79; SSC 12;**
WLC
See also BYA 13; DA; DA3; DAB; DAC;
DAM DRAM, MST, NOV; EW 4; GFL Begin-
nings to 1789; LATS 1:1; LMFS 1; NFS
7; RGWL 2, 3; TWA

von Aschendrof, Baron Ignatz
See Ford, Ford Madox

von Chamisso, Adelbert
See Chamisso, Adelbert von

von Daeniken, Erich 1935- .... **CLC 30**
See also AITN 1; CA 37-40R; CANR 17,
44

von Daniken, Erich
See von Daeniken, Erich

von Hartmann, Eduard
1842-1906 .... **TCLC 96**

von Hayek, Friedrich August
See Hayek, F(riedrich) A(ugust von)

von Heidenstam, (Carl Gustaf) Verner
See Heidenstam, (Carl Gustaf) Verner von

von Heyse, Paul (Johann Ludwig)
See Heyse, Paul (Johann Ludwig von)

von Hofmannsthal, Hugo
See Hofmannsthal, Hugo von

von Horvath, Odon
See von Horvath, Odon

von Horvath, Odon
See von Horvath, Odon

von Horvath, Odon 1901-1938 .... **TCLC 45**
See von Horvath, Oedoen
See also CA 118; 194; DLB 85, 124; RGWL
2, 3

von Horvath, Oedoen
See von Horvath, Odon
See also CA 184

von Kleist, Heinrich
See Kleist, Heinrich von

von Liliencron, (Friedrich Adolf Axel)
Detlev
See Liliencron, (Friedrich Adolf Axel) De-
tlev von

Vonnegut, Kurt, Jr. 1922- . **CLC 1, 2, 3, 4, 5,**
8, 12, 22, 40, 60, 111; SSC 8; WLC
See also AAYA 6, 44; AITN 1; AMWS 2;
BEST 90:4; BPFB 3; BYA 3, 14; CA
1-4R; CANR 1, 25, 49, 75, 92; CDALB
1968-1988; CN 7; CPW 1; DA; DA3;
DAB; DAC; DAM MST, NOV, POP;
DLB 2, 8, 152; DLBD 3; DLBY 1980;
EWL 3; EXPN; EXPS; LAIT 4; LMFS 2;
MTCW 1, 2; NFS 3; RGAL 4; SCFW;
SFW 4; SSFS 5; TUS; YAW

Von Rachen, Kurt
See Hubbard, L(afayette) Ron(ald)

von Rezzori (d'Arezzo), Gregor
See Rezzori (d'Arezzo), Gregor von

von Sternberg, Josef
See Sternberg, Josef von

Vorster, Gordon 1924- .... **CLC 34**
See also CA 133

Vosce, Trudie
See Ozick, Cynthia

Voznesensky, Andrei (Andreievich)
1933- .... **CLC 1, 15, 57**
See Voznesensky, Andrey
See also CA 89-92; CANR 37; CWW 2;
DAM POET; MTCW 1

Voznesensky, Andrey
See Voznesensky, Andrei (Andreievich)
See also EWL 3

Wace, Robert c. 1100-c. 1175 .... **CMLC 55**
See also DLB 146

Waddington, Miriam 1917-2004 .... **CLC 28**
See also CA 21-24R; 225; CANR 12, 30;
CCA 1; CP 7; DLB 68

Wagman, Fredrica 1937- .... **CLC 7**
See also CA 97-100; INT CA-97-100

Wagner, Linda W.
See Wagner-Martin, Linda (C.)

Wagner, Linda Welshimer
See Wagner-Martin, Linda (C.)

Wagner, Richard 1813-1883 ..... **NCLC 9, 119**
See also DLB 129; EW 6

Wagner-Martin, Linda (C.) 1936- .... **CLC 50**
See also CA 159

Wagoner, David (Russell) 1926- .... **CLC 3, 5,**
15; PC 33
See also AMWS 9; CA 1-4R; CAAS 3;
CANR 2, 71; CN 7; CP 7; DLB 5, 256;
SATA 14; TCWW 2

Wah, Fred(erick James) 1939- .... **CLC 44**
See also CA 107; 141; CP 7; DLB 60

Wahloo, Per 1926-1975 .... **CLC 7**
See also BPFB 3; CA 61-64; CANR 73;
CMW 4; MSW

Wahloo, Peter
See Wahloo, Per

Wain, John (Barrington) 1925-1994 . **CLC 2,**
11, 15, 46
See also CA 5-8R; 145; CAAS 4; CANR
23, 54; CDBLB 1960 to Present; DLB 15,
27, 139, 155; EWL 3; MTCW 1, 2

Wajda, Andrzej 1926- .... **CLC 16**
See also CA 102

Wakefield, Dan 1932- .... **CLC 7**
See also CA 21-24R, 211; CAAE 211;
CAAS 7; CN 7

Wakefield, Herbert Russell
1888-1965 .... **TCLC 120**
See also CA 5-8R; CANR 77; HGG; SUFW

Wakoski, Diane 1937- ...... **CLC 2, 4, 7, 9, 11,**
40; PC 15
See also CA 13-16R, 216; CAAE 216;
CAAS 1; CANR 9, 60, 106; CP 7; CWP;
DAM POET; DLB 5; INT CANR-9;
MTCW 2

Wakoski-Sherbell, Diane
See Wakoski, Diane

Walcott, Derek (Alton) 1930- ... **BLC 3; CLC**
2, 4, 9, 14, 25, 42, 67, 76, 160; DC 7;
PC 46
See also BW 2; CA 89-92; CANR 26, 47,
75, 80, 130; CBD; CD 5; CDWLB 3; CP
7; DA3; DAB; DAC; DAM MST, MULT,
POET; DLB 117; DLBY 1981; DNFS 1;
EFS 1; EWL 3; LMFS 2; MTCW 1, 2;
PFS 6; RGEL 2; TWA; WWE 1

Waldman, Anne (Lesley) 1945- .... **CLC 7**
See also BG 3; CA 37-40R; CAAS 17;
CANR 34, 69, 116; CP 7; CWP; DLB 16

Waldo, E. Hunter
See Sturgeon, Theodore (Hamilton)

Waldo, Edward Hamilton
See Sturgeon, Theodore (Hamilton)

Walker, Alice (Malsenior) 1944- .... **BLC 3;**
  CLC 5, 6, 9, 19, 27, 46, 58, 103, 167;
  PC 30; SSC 5; WLCS
  See also AAYA 3, 33; AFAW 1, 2; AMWS
    3; BEST 89:4; BPFB 3; BW 2, 3; CA 37-
    40R; CANR 9, 27, 49, 66, 82, 131;
    CDALB 1968-1988; CN 7; CPW; CSW;
    DA; DA3; DAB; DAC; DAM MST,
    MULT, NOV, POET, POP; DLB 6, 33,
    143; EWL 3; EXPN; EXPS; FW; INT
    CANR-27; LAIT 3; MAWW; MTCW 1,
    2; NFS 5; RGAL 4; RGSF 2; SATA 31;
    SSFS 2, 11; TUS; YAW
Walker, David Harry 1911-1992 ...... **CLC 14**
  See also CA 1-4R; 137; CANR 1; CWRI 5;
    SATA 8; SATA-Obit 71
Walker, Edward Joseph 1934-2004
  See Walker, Ted
  See also CA 21-24R; 226; CANR 12, 28,
    53; CP 7
Walker, George F. 1947- .... **CLC 44, 61**
  See also CA 103; CANR 21, 43, 59; CD 5;
    DAB; DAC; DAM MST; DLB 60
Walker, Joseph A. 1935- .... **CLC 19**
  See also BW 1, 3; CA 89-92; CAD; CANR
    26; CD 5; DAM DRAM, MST; DFS 12;
    DLB 38
Walker, Margaret (Abigail)
  1915-1998 .... **BLC; CLC 1, 6; PC 20;**
  TCLC 129
  See also AFAW 1, 2; BW 2, 3; CA 73-76;
    172; CANR 26, 54, 76; CN 7; CP 7;
    CSW; DAM MULT; DLB 76, 152; EXPP;
    FW; MTCW 1, 2; RGAL 4; RHW
Walker, Ted .... **CLC 13**
  See Walker, Edward Joseph
  See also DLB 40
Wallace, David Foster 1962- ... **CLC 50, 114;**
  SSC 68
  See also AAYA 50; AMWS 10; CA 132;
    CANR 59, 133; DA3; MTCW 2
Wallace, Dexter
  See Masters, Edgar Lee
Wallace, (Richard Horatio) Edgar
  1875-1932 .... **TCLC 57**
  See also CA 115; 218; CMW 4; DLB 70;
    MSW; RGEL 2
Wallace, Irving 1916-1990 .... **CLC 7, 13**
  See also AITN 1; BPFB 3; CA 1-4R; 132;
    CAAS 1; CANR 1, 27; CPW; DAM NOV,
    POP; INT CANR-27; MTCW 1, 2
Wallant, Edward Lewis 1926-1962 ... **CLC 5,**
  10
  See also CA 1-4R; CANR 22; DLB 2, 28,
    143, 299; EWL 3; MTCW 1, 2; RGAL 4
Wallas, Graham 1858-1932 .... **TCLC 91**
Waller, Edmund 1606-1687 .... **LC 86**
  See also BRW 2; DAM POET; DLB 126;
    PAB; RGEL 2
Walley, Byron
  See Card, Orson Scott
Walpole, Horace 1717-1797 .... **LC 2, 49**
  See also BRW 3; DLB 39, 104, 213; HGG;
    LMFS 1; RGEL 2; SUFW 1; TEA
Walpole, Hugh (Seymour)
  1884-1941 .... **TCLC 5**
  See also CA 104; 165; DLB 34; HGG;
    MTCW 2; RGEL 2; RHW
Walrond, Eric (Derwent) 1898-1966 .... **HR 3**
  See also BW 1; CA 125; DLB 51
Walser, Martin 1927- .... **CLC 27, 183**
  See also CA 57-60; CANR 8, 46; CWW 2;
    DLB 75, 124; EWL 3
Walser, Robert 1878-1956 ..... **SSC 20; TCLC**
  18
  See also CA 118; 165; CANR 100; DLB
    66; EWL 3
Walsh, Gillian Paton
  See Paton Walsh, Gillian

Walsh, Jill Paton .... **CLC 35**
  See Paton Walsh, Gillian
  See also CLR 2, 65; WYA
Walter, Villiam Christian
  See Andersen, Hans Christian
Walther von der Vogelweide c.
  1170-1228 .... **CMLC 56**
Walton, Izaak 1593-1683 .... **LC 72**
  See also BRW 2; CDBLB Before 1660;
    DLB 151, 213; RGEL 2
Wambaugh, Joseph (Aloysius), Jr.
  1937- .... **CLC 3, 18**
  See also AITN 1; BEST 89:3; BPFB 3; CA
    33-36R; CANR 42, 65, 115; CMW 4;
    CPW 1; DA3; DAM NOV, POP; DLB 6;
    DLBY 1983; MSW; MTCW 1, 2
Wang Wei 699(?)-761(?) .... **PC 18**
  See also TWA
Warburton, William 1698-1779 .... **LC 97**
  See also DLB 104
Ward, Arthur Henry Sarsfield 1883-1959
  See Rohmer, Sax
  See also CA 108; 173; CMW 4; HGG
Ward, Douglas Turner 1930- .... **CLC 19**
  See also BW 1; CA 81-84; CAD; CANR
    27; CD 5; DLB 7, 38
Ward, E. D.
  See Lucas, E(dward) V(errall)
Ward, Mrs. Humphry 1851-1920
  See Ward, Mary Augusta
  See also RGEL 2
Ward, Mary Augusta 1851-1920 ... **TCLC 55**
  See Ward, Mrs. Humphry
  See also DLB 18
Ward, Peter
  See Faust, Frederick (Schiller)
Warhol, Andy 1928(?)-1987 .... **CLC 20**
  See also AAYA 12; BEST 89:4; CA 89-92;
    121; CANR 34
Warner, Francis (Robert le Plastrier)
  1937- .... **CLC 14**
  See also CA 53-56; CANR 11
Warner, Marina 1946- .... **CLC 59**
  See also CA 65-68; CANR 21, 55, 118; CN
    7; DLB 194
Warner, Rex (Ernest) 1905-1986 ...... **CLC 45**
  See also CA 89-92; 119; DLB 15; RGEL 2;
    RHW
Warner, Susan (Bogert)
  1819-1885 .... **NCLC 31, 146**
  See also DLB 3, 42, 239, 250, 254
Warner, Sylvia (Constance) Ashton
  See Ashton-Warner, Sylvia (Constance)
Warner, Sylvia Townsend
  1893-1978 .. **CLC 7, 19; SSC 23; TCLC**
  131
  See also BRWS 7; CA 61-64; 77-80; CANR
    16, 60, 104; DLB 34, 139; EWL 3; FANT;
    FW; MTCW 1, 2; RGEL 2; RGSF 2;
    RHW
Warren, Mercy Otis 1728-1814 ..... **NCLC 13**
  See also DLB 31, 200; RGAL 4; TUS
Warren, Robert Penn 1905-1989 .. **CLC 1, 4,**
  6, 8, 10, 13, 18, 39, 53, 59; PC 37; SSC
  4, 58; WLC
  See also AITN 1; AMW; AMWC 2; BPFB
    3; BYA 1; CA 13-16R; 129; CANR 10,
    47; CDALB 1968-1988; DA; DA3; DAB;
    DAC; DAM MST, NOV, POET; DLB 2,
    48, 152; DLBY 1980, 1989; EWL 3; INT
    CANR-10; MTCW 1, 2; NFS 13; RGAL
    4; RGSF 2; RHW; SATA 46; SATA-Obit
    63; SSFS 8; TUS
Warrigal, Jack
  See Furphy, Joseph
Warshofsky, Isaac
  See Singer, Isaac Bashevis

Warton, Joseph 1722-1800 .... **NCLC 118**
  See also DLB 104, 109; RGEL 2
Warton, Thomas 1728-1790 .... **LC 15, 82**
  See also DAM POET; DLB 104, 109;
    RGEL 2
Waruk, Kona
  See Harris, (Theodore) Wilson
Warung, Price .... **TCLC 45**
  See Astley, William
  See also DLB 230; RGEL 2
Warwick, Jarvis
  See Garner, Hugh
  See also CCA 1
Washington, Alex
  See Harris, Mark
Washington, Booker T(aliaferro)
  1856-1915 .... **BLC 3; TCLC 10**
  See also BW 1; CA 114; 125; DA3; DAM
    MULT; LAIT 2; RGAL 4; SATA 28
Washington, George 1732-1799 .... **LC 25**
  See also DLB 31
Wassermann, (Karl) Jakob
  1873-1934 .... **TCLC 6**
  See also CA 104; 163; DLB 66; EWL 3
Wasserstein, Wendy 1950- ... **CLC 32, 59, 90,**
  183; DC 4
  See also CA 121; 129; CABS 3; CAD;
    CANR 53, 75, 128; CD 5; CWD; DA3;
    DAM DRAM; DFS 5, 17; DLB 228;
    EWL 3; FW; INT CA-129; MTCW 2;
    SATA 94
Waterhouse, Keith (Spencer) 1929- . **CLC 47**
  See also CA 5-8R; CANR 38, 67, 109;
    CBD; CN 7; DLB 13, 15; MTCW 1, 2
Waters, Frank (Joseph) 1902-1995 .. **CLC 88**
  See also CA 5-8R; 149; CAAS 13; CANR
    3, 18, 63, 121; DLB 212; DLBY 1986;
    RGAL 4; TCWW 2
Waters, Mary C. .... **CLC 70**
Waters, Roger 1944- .... **CLC 35**
Watkins, Frances Ellen
  See Harper, Frances Ellen Watkins
Watkins, Gerrold
  See Malzberg, Barry N(athaniel)
Watkins, Gloria Jean 1952(?)- .... **CLC 94**
  See also BW 2; CA 143; CANR 87, 126;
    DLB 246; MTCW 2; SATA 115
Watkins, Paul 1964- .... **CLC 55**
  See also CA 132; CANR 62, 98
Watkins, Vernon Phillips
  1906-1967 .... **CLC 43**
  See also CA 9-10; 25-28R; CAP 1; DLB
    20; EWL 3; RGEL 2
Watson, Irving S.
  See Mencken, H(enry) L(ouis)
Watson, John H.
  See Farmer, Philip Jose
Watson, Richard F.
  See Silverberg, Robert
Watts, Ephraim
  See Horne, Richard Henry Hengist
Watts, Isaac 1674-1748 .... **LC 98**
  See also DLB 95; RGEL 2; SATA 52
Waugh, Auberon (Alexander)
  1939-2001 .... **CLC 7**
  See also CA 45-48; 192; CANR 6, 22, 92;
    DLB 14, 194
Waugh, Evelyn (Arthur St. John)
  1903-1966 .. **CLC 1, 3, 8, 13, 19, 27, 44,**
  107; SSC 41; WLC
  See also BPFB 3; BRW 7; CA 85-88; 25-
    28R; CANR 22; CDBLB 1914-1945; DA;
    DA3; DAB; DAC; DAM MST, NOV,
    POP; DLB 15, 162, 195; EWL 3; MTCW
    1, 2; NFS 13, 17; RGEL 2; RGSF 2; TEA;
    WLIT 4
Waugh, Harriet 1944- .... **CLC 6**
  See also CA 85-88; CANR 22

Author Index

Ways, C. R.
See Blount, Roy (Alton), Jr.
Waystaff, Simon
See Swift, Jonathan
Webb, Beatrice (Martha Potter)
1858-1943 .... **TCLC 22**
See also CA 117; 162; DLB 190; FW
Webb, Charles (Richard) 1939- .... **CLC 7**
See also CA 25-28R; CANR 114
Webb, Frank J. .... **NCLC 143**
See also DLB 50
Webb, James H(enry), Jr. 1946- ...... **CLC 22**
See also CA 81-84
Webb, Mary Gladys (Meredith)
1881-1927 .... **TCLC 24**
See also CA 182; 123; DLB 34; FW
Webb, Mrs. Sidney
See Webb, Beatrice (Martha Potter)
Webb, Phyllis 1927- .... **CLC 18**
See also CA 104; CANR 23; CCA 1; CP 7;
CWP; DLB 53
Webb, Sidney (James) 1859-1947 .. **TCLC 22**
See also CA 117; 163; DLB 190
Webber, Andrew Lloyd .... **CLC 21**
See Lloyd Webber, Andrew
See also DFS 7
Weber, Lenora Mattingly
1895-1971 .... **CLC 12**
See also CA 19-20; 29-32R; CAP 1; SATA
2; SATA-Obit 26
Weber, Max 1864-1920 .... **TCLC 69**
See also CA 109; 189; DLB 296
Webster, John 1580(?)-1634(?) ...... **DC 2; LC
33, 84; WLC**
See also BRW 2; CDBLB Before 1660; DA;
DAB; DAC; DAM DRAM, MST; DFS
17, 19; DLB 58; IDTP; RGEL 2; WLIT 3
Webster, Noah 1758-1843 .... **NCLC 30**
See also DLB 1, 37, 42, 43, 73, 243
Wedekind, (Benjamin) Frank(lin)
1864-1918 .... **TCLC 7**
See also CA 104; 153; CANR 121, 122;
CDWLB 2; DAM DRAM; DLB 118; EW
8; EWL 3; LMFS 2; RGWL 2, 3
Wehr, Demaris .... **CLC 65**
Weidman, Jerome 1913-1998 .... **CLC 7**
See also AITN 2; CA 1-4R; 171; CAD;
CANR 1; DLB 28
Weil, Simone (Adolphine)
1909-1943 .... **TCLC 23**
See also CA 117; 159; EW 12; EWL 3; FW;
GFL 1789 to the Present; MTCW 2
Weininger, Otto 1880-1903 .... **TCLC 84**
Weinstein, Nathan
See West, Nathanael
Weinstein, Nathan von Wallenstein
See West, Nathanael
Weir, Peter (Lindsay) 1944- .... **CLC 20**
See also CA 113; 123
Weiss, Peter (Ulrich) 1916-1982 .. **CLC 3, 15,
51; TCLC 152**
See also CA 45-48; 106; CANR 3; DAM
DRAM; DFS 3; DLB 69, 124; EWL 3;
RGWL 2, 3
Weiss, Theodore (Russell)
1916-2003 .... **CLC 3, 8, 14**
See also CA 9-12R; 189; 216; CAAE 189;
CAAS 2; CANR 46, 94; CP 7; DLB 5
Welch, (Maurice) Denton
1915-1948 .... **TCLC 22**
See also BRWS 8, 9; CA 121; 148; RGEL
2
Welch, James (Phillip) 1940-2003 ..... **CLC 6,
14, 52; NNAL**
See also CA 85-88; 219; CANR 42, 66, 107;
CN 7; CP 7; CPW; DAM MULT, POP;
DLB 175, 256; LATS 1:1; RGAL 4;
TCWW 2

Weldon, Fay 1931- . **CLC 6, 9, 11, 19, 36, 59,
122**
See also BRWS 4; CA 21-24R; CANR 16,
46, 63, 97; CDBLB 1960 to Present; CN
7; CPW; DAM POP; DLB 14, 194; EWL
3; FW; HGG; INT CANR-16; MTCW 1,
2; RGEL 2; RGSF 2
Wellek, Rene 1903-1995 .... **CLC 28**
See also CA 5-8R; 150; CAAS 7; CANR 8;
DLB 63; EWL 3; INT CANR-8
Weller, Michael 1942- .... **CLC 10, 53**
See also CA 85-88; CAD; CD 5
Weller, Paul 1958- .... **CLC 26**
Wellershoff, Dieter 1925- .... **CLC 46**
See also CA 89-92; CANR 16, 37
Welles, (George) Orson 1915-1985 .. **CLC 20,
80**
See also AAYA 40; CA 93-96; 117
Wellman, John McDowell 1945-
See Wellman, Mac
See also CA 166; CD 5
Wellman, Mac .... **CLC 65**
See Wellman, John McDowell; Wellman,
John McDowell
See also CAD; RGAL 4
Wellman, Manly Wade 1903-1986 ... **CLC 49**
See also CA 1-4R; 118; CANR 6, 16, 44;
FANT; SATA 6; SATA-Obit 47; SFW 4;
SUFW
Wells, Carolyn 1869(?)-1942 .... **TCLC 35**
See also CA 113; 185; CMW 4; DLB 11
Wells, H(erbert) G(eorge) 1866-1946 . **SSC 6,
70; TCLC 6, 12, 19, 133; WLC**
See also AAYA 18; BPFB 3; BRW 6; CA
110; 121; CDBLB 1914-1945; CLR 64;
DA; DA3; DAB; DAC; DAM MST, NOV;
DLB 34, 70, 156, 178; EWL 3; EXPS;
HGG; LAIT 3; LMFS 2; MTCW 1, 2;
NFS 17, 20; RGEL 2; RGSF 2; SATA 20;
SCFW; SFW 4; SSFS 3; SUFW; TEA;
WCH; WLIT 4; YAW
Wells, Rosemary 1943- .... **CLC 12**
See also AAYA 13; BYA 7, 8; CA 85-88;
CANR 48, 120; CLR 16, 69; CWRI 5;
MAICYA 1, 2; SAAS 1; SATA 18, 69,
114; YAW
Wells-Barnett, Ida B(ell)
1862-1931 .... **TCLC 125**
See also CA 182; DLB 23, 221
Welsh, Irvine 1958- .... **CLC 144**
See also CA 173; DLB 271
Welty, Eudora (Alice) 1909-2001 .. **CLC 1, 2,
5, 14, 22, 33, 105; SSC 1, 27, 51; WLC**
See also AAYA 48; AMW; AMWR 1; BPFB
3; CA 9-12R; 199; CABS 1; CANR 32,
65, 128; CDALB 1941-1968; CN 7; CSW;
DA; DA3; DAB; DAC; DAM MST, NOV;
DLB 2, 102, 143; DLBD 12; DLBY 1987,
2001; EWL 3; EXPS; HGG; LAIT 3;
MAWW; MTCW 1, 2; NFS 13, 15; RGAL
4; RGSF 2; RHW; SSFS 2, 10; TUS
Wen I-to 1899-1946 .... **TCLC 28**
See also EWL 3
Wentworth, Robert
See Hamilton, Edmond
Werfel, Franz (Viktor) 1890-1945 ... **TCLC 8**
See also CA 104; 161; DLB 81, 124; EWL
3; RGWL 2, 3
Wergeland, Henrik Arnold
1808-1845 .... **NCLC 5**
Wersba, Barbara 1932- .... **CLC 30**
See also AAYA 2, 30; BYA 6, 12, 13; CA
29-32R, 182; CAAE 182; CANR 16, 38;
CLR 3, 78; DLB 52; JRDA; MAICYA 1,
2; SAAS 2; SATA 1, 58; SATA-Essay 103;
WYA; YAW
Wertmueller, Lina 1928- .... **CLC 16**
See also CA 97-100; CANR 39, 78

Wescott, Glenway 1901-1987 .. **CLC 13; SSC
35**
See also CA 13-16R; 121; CANR 23, 70;
DLB 4, 9, 102; RGAL 4
Wesker, Arnold 1932- .... **CLC 3, 5, 42**
See also CA 1-4R; CAAS 7; CANR 1, 33;
CBD; CD 5; CDBLB 1960 to Present;
DAB; DAM DRAM; DLB 13; EWL 3;
MTCW 1; RGEL 2; TEA
Wesley, John 1703-1791 .... **LC 88**
See also DLB 104
Wesley, Richard (Errol) 1945- .... **CLC 7**
See also BW 1; CA 57-60; CAD; CANR
27; CD 5; DLB 38
Wessel, Johan Herman 1742-1785 .... **LC 7**
See also DLB 300
West, Anthony (Panther)
1914-1987 .... **CLC 50**
See also CA 45-48; 124; CANR 3, 19; DLB
15
West, C. P.
See Wodehouse, P(elham) G(renville)
West, Cornel (Ronald) 1953- .... **BLCS; CLC
134**
See also CA 144; CANR 91; DLB 246
West, Delno C(loyde), Jr. 1936- .... **CLC 70**
See also CA 57-60
West, Dorothy 1907-1998 .. **HR 3; TCLC 108**
See also BW 2; CA 143; 169; DLB 76
West, (Mary) Jessamyn 1902-1984 ... **CLC 7,
17**
See also CA 9-12R; 112; CANR 27; DLB
6; DLBY 1984; MTCW 1, 2; RGAL 4;
RHW; SATA-Obit 37; TCWW 2; TUS;
YAW
West, Morris
See West, Morris L(anglo)
See also DLB 289
West, Morris L(anglo) 1916-1999 ..... **CLC 6,
33**
See West, Morris
See also BPFB 3; CA 5-8R; 187; CANR
24, 49, 64; CN 7; CPW; MTCW 1, 2
West, Nathanael 1903-1940 .. **SSC 16; TCLC
1, 14, 44**
See also AMW; AMWR 2; BPFB 3; CA
104; 125; CDALB 1929-1941; DA3; DLB
4, 9, 28; EWL 3; MTCW 1, 2; NFS 16;
RGAL 4; TUS
West, Owen
See Koontz, Dean R(ay)
West, Paul 1930- .... **CLC 7, 14, 96**
See also CA 13-16R; CAAS 7; CANR 22,
53, 76, 89; CN 7; DLB 14; INT CANR-
22; MTCW 2
West, Rebecca 1892-1983 ... **CLC 7, 9, 31, 50**
See also BPFB 3; BRWS 3; CA 5-8R; 109;
CANR 19; DLB 36; DLBY 1983; EWL
3; FW; MTCW 1, 2; NCFS 4; RGEL 2;
TEA
Westall, Robert (Atkinson)
1929-1993 .... **CLC 17**
See also AAYA 12; BYA 2, 6, 7, 8, 9, 15;
CA 69-72; 141; CANR 18, 68; CLR 13;
FANT; JRDA; MAICYA 1, 2; MAICYAS
1; SATA 23, 69; SATA-Obit 75; WYA;
YAW
Westermarck, Edward 1862-1939 . **TCLC 87**
Westlake, Donald E(dwin) 1933- . **CLC 7, 33**
See also BPFB 3; CA 17-20R; CAAS 13;
CANR 16, 44, 65, 94; CMW 4; CPW;
DAM POP; INT CANR-16; MSW;
MTCW 2
Westmacott, Mary
See Christie, Agatha (Mary Clarissa)
Weston, Allen
See Norton, Andre
Wetcheek, J. L.
See Feuchtwanger, Lion

Williams, Charles
See Collier, James Lincoln
Williams, Charles (Walter Stansby)
1886-1945 .... TCLC 1, 11
See also BRWS 9; CA 104; 163; DLB 100, 153, 255; FANT; RGEL 2; SUFW 1
Williams, Ella Gwendolen Rees
See Rhys, Jean
Williams, (George) Emlyn
1905-1987 .... CLC 15
See also CA 104; 123; CANR 36; DAM DRAM; DLB 10, 77; IDTP; MTCW 1
Williams, Hank 1923-1953 .... TCLC 81
See Williams, Hiram King
Williams, Helen Maria
1761-1827 .... NCLC 135
See also DLB 158
Williams, Hiram Hank
See Williams, Hank
Williams, Hiram King
See Williams, Hank
See also CA 188
Williams, Hugo (Mordaunt) 1942- ... CLC 42
See also CA 17-20R; CANR 45, 119; CP 7; DLB 40
Williams, J. Walker
See Wodehouse, P(elham) G(renville)
Williams, John A(lfred) 1925- . BLC 3; CLC 5, 13
See also AFAW 2; BW 2, 3; CA 53-56, 195; CAAE 195; CAAS 3; CANR 6, 26, 51, 118; CN 7; CSW; DAM MULT; DLB 2, 33; EWL 3; INT CANR-6; RGAL 4; SFW 4
Williams, Jonathan (Chamberlain)
1929- .... CLC 13
See also CA 9-12R; CAAS 12; CANR 8, 108; CP 7; DLB 5
Williams, Joy 1944- .... CLC 31
See also CA 41-44R; CANR 22, 48, 97
Williams, Norman 1952- .... CLC 39
See also CA 118
Williams, Sherley Anne 1944-1999 ... BLC 3; CLC 89
See also AFAW 2; BW 2, 3; CA 73-76; 185; CANR 25, 82; DAM MULT; POET; DLB 41; INT CANR-25; SATA 78; SATA-Obit 116
Williams, Shirley
See Williams, Sherley Anne
Williams, Tennessee 1911-1983 . CLC 1, 2, 5, 7, 8, 11, 15, 19, 30, 39, 45, 71, 111; DC 4; WLC
See also AAYA 31; AITN 1, 2; AMW; AMWC 1; CA 5-8R; 108; CABS 3; CAD; CANR 31, 132; CDALB 1941-1968; DA; DA3; DAB; DAC; DAM DRAM, MST; DFS 17; DLB 7; DLBD 4; DLBY 1983; EWL 3; GLL 1; LAIT 4; LATS 1:2; MTCW 1, 2; RGAL 4; TUS
Williams, Thomas (Alonzo)
1926-1990 .... CLC 14
See also CA 1-4R; 132; CANR 2
Williams, William C.
See Williams, William Carlos
Williams, William Carlos
1883-1963 .... CLC 1, 2, 5, 9, 13, 22, 42, 67; PC 7; SSC 31
See also AAYA 46; AMW; AMWR 1; CA 89-92; CANR 34; CDALB 1917-1929; DA; DA3; DAB; DAC; DAM MST, POET; DLB 4, 16, 54, 86; EWL 3; EXPP; MTCW 1, 2; NCFS 4; PAB; PFS 1, 6, 11; RGAL 4; RGSF 2; TUS; WP
Williamson, David (Keith) 1942- ..... CLC 56
See also CA 103; CANR 41; CD 5; DLB 289

Williamson, Ellen Douglas 1905-1984
See Douglas, Ellen
See also CA 17-20R; 114; CANR 39
Williamson, Jack .... CLC 29
See Williamson, John Stewart
See also CAAS 8; DLB 8; SCFW 2
Williamson, John Stewart 1908-
See Williamson, Jack
See also CA 17-20R; CANR 23, 70; SFW 4
Willie, Frederick
See Lovecraft, H(oward) P(hillips)
Willingham, Calder (Baynard, Jr.)
1922-1995 .... CLC 5, 51
See also CA 5-8R; 147; CANR 3; CSW; DLB 2, 44; IDFW 3, 4; MTCW 1
Willis, Charles
See Clarke, Arthur C(harles)
Willy
See Colette, (Sidonie-Gabrielle)
Willy, Colette
See Colette, (Sidonie-Gabrielle)
See also GLL 1
Wilmot, John 1647-1680 .... LC 75
See Rochester
See also BRW 2; DLB 131; PAB
Wilson, A(ndrew) N(orman) 1950- .. CLC 33
See also BRWS 6; CA 112; 122; CN 7; DLB 14, 155, 194; MTCW 2
Wilson, Angus (Frank Johnstone)
1913-1991 . CLC 2, 3, 5, 25, 34; SSC 21
See also BRWS 1; CA 5-8R; 134; CANR 21; DLB 15, 139, 155; EWL 3; MTCW 1, 2; RGEL 2; RGSF 2
Wilson, August 1945- ... BLC 3; CLC 39, 50, 63, 118; DC 2; WLCS
See also AAYA 16; AFAW 2; AMWS 8; BW 2, 3; CA 115; 122; CAD; CANR 42, 54, 76, 128; CD 5; DA; DA3; DAB; DAC; DAM DRAM, MULT; DFS 3, 7, 15, 17; DLB 228; EWL 3; LAIT 4; LATS 1:2; MTCW 1, 2; RGAL 4
Wilson, Brian 1942- .... CLC 12
Wilson, Colin 1931- .... CLC 3, 14
See also CA 1-4R; CAAS 5; CANR 1, 22, 33, 77; CMW 4; CN 7; DLB 14, 194; HGG; MTCW 1; SFW 4
Wilson, Dirk
See Pohl, Frederik
Wilson, Edmund 1895-1972 .. CLC 1, 2, 3, 8, 24
See also AMW; CA 1-4R; 37-40R; CANR 1, 46, 110; DLB 63; EWL 3; MTCW 1, 2; RGAL 4; TUS
Wilson, Ethel Davis (Bryant)
1888(?)-1980 .... CLC 13
See also CA 102; DAC; DAM POET; DLB 68; MTCW 1; RGEL 2
Wilson, Harriet
See Wilson, Harriet E. Adams
See also DLB 239
Wilson, Harriet E.
See Wilson, Harriet E. Adams
See also DLB 243
Wilson, Harriet E. Adams
1827(?)-1863(?) .... BLC 3; NCLC 78
See Wilson, Harriet; Wilson, Harriet E.
See also DAM MULT; DLB 50
Wilson, John 1785-1854 .... NCLC 5
Wilson, John (Anthony) Burgess 1917-1993
See Burgess, Anthony
See also CA 1-4R; 143; CANR 2, 46; DA3; DAC; DAM NOV; MTCW 1, 2; NFS 15; TEA
Wilson, Lanford 1937- .. CLC 7, 14, 36, 197; DC 19
See also CA 17-20R; CABS 3; CAD; CANR 45, 96; CD 5; DAM DRAM; DFS 4, 9, 12, 16, 20; DLB 7; EWL 3; TUS

Wilson, Robert M. 1941- .... CLC 7, 9
See also CA 49-52; CAD; CANR 2, 41; CD 5; MTCW 1
Wilson, Robert McLiam 1964- .... CLC 59
See also CA 132; DLB 267
Wilson, Sloan 1920-2003 .... CLC 32
See also CA 1-4R; 216; CANR 1, 44; CN 7
Wilson, Snoo 1948- .... CLC 33
See also CA 69-72; CBD; CD 5
Wilson, William S(mith) 1932- .... CLC 49
See also CA 81-84
Wilson, (Thomas) Woodrow
1856-1924 .... TCLC 79
See also CA 166; DLB 47
Wilson and Warnke eds. .... CLC 65
Winchilsea, Anne (Kingsmill) Finch
1661-1720
See Finch, Anne
See also RGEL 2
Windham, Basil
See Wodehouse, P(elham) G(renville)
Wingrove, David (John) 1954- .... CLC 68
See also CA 133; SFW 4
Winnemucca, Sarah 1844-1891 .... NCLC 79; NNAL
See also DAM MULT; DLB 175; RGAL 4
Winstanley, Gerrard 1609-1676 .... LC 52
Wintergreen, Jane
See Duncan, Sara Jeannette
Winters, Janet Lewis .... CLC 41
See Lewis, Janet
See also DLBY 1987
Winters, (Arthur) Yvor 1900-1968 .... CLC 4, 8, 32
See also AMWS 2; CA 11-12; 25-28R; CAP 1; DLB 48; EWL 3; MTCW 1; RGAL 4
Winterson, Jeanette 1959- .... CLC 64, 158
See also BRWS 4; CA 136; CANR 58, 116; CN 7; CPW; DA3; DAM POP; DLB 207, 261; FANT; FW; GLL 1; MTCW 2; RHW
Winthrop, John 1588-1649 .... LC 31, 107
See also DLB 24, 30
Wirth, Louis 1897-1952 .... TCLC 92
See also CA 210
Wiseman, Frederick 1930- .... CLC 20
See also CA 159
Wister, Owen 1860-1938 .... TCLC 21
See also BPFB 3; CA 108; 162; DLB 9, 78, 186; RGAL 4; SATA 62; TCWW 2
Wither, George 1588-1667 .... LC 96
See also DLB 121; RGEL 2
Witkacy
See Witkiewicz, Stanislaw Ignacy
Witkiewicz, Stanislaw Ignacy
1885-1939 .... TCLC 8
See also CA 105; 162; CDWLB 4; DLB 215; EW 10; EWL 3; RGWL 2, 3; SFW 4
Wittgenstein, Ludwig (Josef Johann)
1889-1951 .... TCLC 59
See also CA 113; 164; DLB 262; MTCW 2
Wittig, Monique 1935(?)-2003 .... CLC 22
See also CA 116; 135; 212; CWW 2; DLB 83; EWL 3; FW; GLL 1
Wittlin, Jozef 1896-1976 .... CLC 25
See also CA 49-52; 65-68; CANR 3; EWL 3
Wodehouse, P(elham) G(renville)
1881-1975 . CLC 1, 2, 5, 10, 22; SSC 2; TCLC 108
See also AITN 2; BRWS 3; CA 45-48; 57-60; CANR 3, 33; CDBLB 1914-1945; CPW 1; DA3; DAB; DAC; DAM NOV; DLB 34, 162; EWL 3; MTCW 1, 2; RGEL 2; RGSF 2; SATA 22; SSFS 10
Woiwode, L.
See Woiwode, Larry (Alfred)
Woiwode, Larry (Alfred) 1941- ... CLC 6, 10
See also CA 73-76; CANR 16, 94; CN 7; DLB 6; INT CANR-16

Yeats, William Butler 1865-1939 . **PC 20, 51; TCLC 1, 11, 18, 31, 93, 116; WLC**
See also AAYA 48; BRW 6; BRWR 1; CA 104; 127; CANR 45; CDBLB 1890-1914; DA; DA3; DAB; DAC; DAM DRAM, MST, POET; DLB 10, 19, 98, 156; EWL 3; EXPP; MTCW 1, 2; NCFS 3; PAB; PFS 1, 2, 5, 7, 13, 15; RGEL 2; TEA; WLIT 4; WP

Yehoshua, A(braham) B. 1936- .. **CLC 13, 31**
See also CA 33-36R; CANR 43, 90; CWW 2; EWL 3; RGSF 2; RGWL 3

Yellow Bird
See Ridge, John Rollin

Yep, Laurence Michael 1948- .... **CLC 35**
See also AAYA 5, 31; BYA 7; CA 49-52; CANR 1, 46, 92; CLR 3, 17, 54; DLB 52; FANT; JRDA; MAICYA 1, 2; MAICYAS 1; SATA 7, 69, 123; WYA; YAW

Yerby, Frank G(arvin) 1916-1991 ..... **BLC 3; CLC 1, 7, 22**
See also BPFB 3; BW 1, 3; CA 9-12R; 136; CANR 16, 52; DAM MULT; DLB 76; INT CANR-16; MTCW 1; RGAL 4; RHW

Yesenin, Sergei Alexandrovich
See Esenin, Sergei (Alexandrovich)

Yesenin, Sergey
See Esenin, Sergei (Alexandrovich)
See also EWL 3

Yevtushenko, Yevgeny (Alexandrovich)
1933- ...... **CLC 1, 3, 13, 26, 51, 126; PC 40**
See Evtushenko, Evgenii Aleksandrovich
See also CA 81-84; CANR 33, 54; DAM POET; EWL 3; MTCW 1

Yezierska, Anzia 1885(?)-1970 .... **CLC 46**
See also CA 126; 89-92; DLB 28, 221; FW; MTCW 1; RGAL 4; SSFS 15

Yglesias, Helen 1915- .... **CLC 7, 22**
See also CA 37-40R; CAAS 20; CANR 15, 65, 95; CN 7; INT CANR-15; MTCW 1

Yokomitsu, Riichi 1898-1947 .... **TCLC 47**
See also CA 170; EWL 3

Yonge, Charlotte (Mary)
1823-1901 .... **TCLC 48**
See also CA 109; 163; DLB 18, 163; RGEL 2; SATA 17; WCH

York, Jeremy
See Creasey, John

York, Simon
See Heinlein, Robert A(nson)

Yorke, Henry Vincent 1905-1974 ..... **CLC 13**
See Green, Henry
See also CA 85-88; 49-52

Yosano Akiko 1878-1942 .... **PC 11; TCLC 59**
See also CA 161; EWL 3; RGWL 3

Yoshimoto, Banana .... **CLC 84**
See Yoshimoto, Mahoko
See also AAYA 50; NFS 7

Yoshimoto, Mahoko 1964-
See Yoshimoto, Banana
See also CA 144; CANR 98; SSFS 16

Young, Al(bert James) 1939- ... **BLC 3; CLC 19**
See also BW 2, 3; CA 29-32R; CANR 26, 65, 109; CN 7; CP 7; DAM MULT; DLB 33

Young, Andrew (John) 1885-1971 ...... **CLC 5**
See also CA 5-8R; CANR 7, 29; RGEL 2

Young, Collier
See Bloch, Robert (Albert)

Young, Edward 1683-1765 .... **LC 3, 40**
See also DLB 95; RGEL 2

Young, Marguerite (Vivian)
1909-1995 .... **CLC 82**
See also CA 13-16; 150; CAP 1; CN 7

Young, Neil 1945- .... **CLC 17**
See also CA 110; CCA 1

Young Bear, Ray A. 1950- ... **CLC 94; NNAL**
See also CA 146; DAM MULT; DLB 175

Yourcenar, Marguerite 1903-1987 ... **CLC 19, 38, 50, 87**
See also BPFB 3; CA 69-72; CANR 23, 60, 93; DAM NOV; DLB 72; DLBY 1988; EW 12; EWL 3; GFL 1789 to the Present; GLL 1; MTCW 1, 2; RGWL 2, 3

Yuan, Chu 340(?) B.C.-278(?)
B.C. .... **CMLC 36**

Yurick, Sol 1925- .... **CLC 6**
See also CA 13-16R; CANR 25; CN 7

Zabolotsky, Nikolai Alekseevich
1903-1958 .... **TCLC 52**
See Zabolotsky, Nikolay Alekseevich
See also CA 116; 164

Zabolotsky, Nikolay Alekseevich
See Zabolotsky, Nikolai Alekseevich
See also EWL 3

Zagajewski, Adam 1945- .... **PC 27**
See also CA 186; DLB 232; EWL 3

Zalygin, Sergei -2000 .... **CLC 59**

Zalygin, Sergei (Pavlovich)
1913-2000 .... **CLC 59**
See also DLB 302

Zamiatin, Evgenii
See Zamyatin, Evgeny Ivanovich
See also RGSF 2; RGWL 2, 3

Zamiatin, Evgenii Ivanovich
See Zamyatin, Evgeny Ivanovich
See also DLB 272

Zamiatin, Yevgenii
See Zamyatin, Evgeny Ivanovich

Zamora, Bernice (B. Ortiz) 1938- .. **CLC 89; HLC 2**
See also CA 151; CANR 80; DAM MULT; DLB 82; HW 1, 2

Zamyatin, Evgeny Ivanovich
1884-1937 .... **TCLC 8, 37**
See Zamiatin, Evgenii; Zamiatin, Evgenii Ivanovich; Zamyatin, Yevgeny Ivanovich
See also CA 105; 166; EW 10; SFW 4

Zamyatin, Yevgeny Ivanovich
See Zamyatin, Evgeny Ivanovich
See also EWL 3

Zangwill, Israel 1864-1926 ... **SSC 44; TCLC 16**
See also CA 109; 167; CMW 4; DLB 10, 135, 197; RGEL 2

Zappa, Francis Vincent, Jr. 1940-1993
See Zappa, Frank
See also CA 108; 143; CANR 57

Zappa, Frank .... **CLC 17**
See Zappa, Francis Vincent, Jr.

Zaturenska, Marya 1902-1982 ..... **CLC 6, 11**
See also CA 13-16R; 105; CANR 22

Zayas y Sotomayor, Maria de 1590-c. 1661 .... **LC 102**
See also RGSF 2

Zeami 1363-1443 .... **DC 7; LC 86**
See also DLB 203; RGWL 2, 3

Zelazny, Roger (Joseph) 1937-1995 . **CLC 21**
See also AAYA 7; BPFB 3; CA 21-24R; 148; CANR 26, 60; CN 7; DLB 8; FANT; MTCW 1, 2; SATA 57; SATA-Brief 39; SCFW; SFW 4; SUFW 1, 2

Zhang Ailing 1920(?)-1995
See Chang, Eileen
See also CWW 2; RGSF 2

Zhdanov, Andrei Alexandrovich
1896-1948 .... **TCLC 18**
See also CA 117; 167

Zhukovsky, Vasilii Andreevich
See Zhukovsky, Vasily (Andreevich)
See also DLB 205

Zhukovsky, Vasily (Andreevich)
1783-1852 .... **NCLC 35**
See Zhukovsky, Vasilii Andreevich

Ziegenhagen, Eric .... **CLC 55**

Zimmer, Jill Schary
See Robinson, Jill

Zimmerman, Robert
See Dylan, Bob

Zindel, Paul 1936-2003 ...... **CLC 6, 26; DC 5**
See also AAYA 2, 37; BYA 2, 3, 8, 11, 14; CA 73-76; 213; CAD; CANR 31, 65, 108; CD 5; CDALBS; CLR 3, 45, 85; DA; DA3; DAB; DAC; DAM DRAM, MST, NOV; DFS 12; DLB 7, 52; JRDA; LAIT 5; MAICYA 1, 2; MTCW 1, 2; NFS 14; SATA 16, 58, 102; SATA-Obit 142; WYA; YAW

Zinov'Ev, A. A.
See Zinoviev, Alexander (Aleksandrovich)

Zinov'ev, Aleksandr (Aleksandrovich)
See Zinoviev, Alexander (Aleksandrovich)
See also DLB 302

Zinoviev, Alexander (Aleksandrovich)
1922- .... **CLC 19**
See Zinov'ev, Aleksandr (Aleksandrovich)
See also CA 116; 133; CAAS 10

Zizek, Slavoj 1949- .... **CLC 188**
See also CA 201

Zoilus
See Lovecraft, H(oward) P(hillips)

Zola, Emile (Edouard Charles Antoine)
1840-1902 ...... **TCLC 1, 6, 21, 41; WLC**
See also CA 104; 138; DA; DA3; DAB; DAC; DAM MST, NOV; DLB 123; EW 7; GFL 1789 to the Present; IDTP; LMFS 1, 2; RGWL 2; TWA

Zoline, Pamela 1941- .... **CLC 62**
See also CA 161; SFW 4

Zoroaster 628(?) B.C.-551(?)
B.C. .... **CMLC 40**

Zorrilla y Moral, Jose 1817-1893 .... **NCLC 6**

Zoshchenko, Mikhail (Mikhailovich)
1895-1958 .... **SSC 15; TCLC 15**
See also CA 115; 160; EWL 3; RGSF 2; RGWL 3

Zuckmayer, Carl 1896-1977 .... **CLC 18**
See also CA 69-72; DLB 56, 124; EWL 3; RGWL 2, 3

Zuk, Georges
See Skelton, Robin
See also CCA 1

Zukofsky, Louis 1904-1978 ... **CLC 1, 2, 4, 7, 11, 18; PC 11**
See also AMWS 3; CA 9-12R; 77-80; CANR 39; DAM POET; DLB 5, 165; EWL 3; MTCW 1; RGAL 4

Zweig, Paul 1935-1984 .... **CLC 34, 42**
See also CA 85-88; 113

Zweig, Stefan 1881-1942 .... **TCLC 17**
See also CA 112; 170; DLB 81, 118; EWL 3

Zwingli, Huldreich 1484-1531 .... **LC 37**
See also DLB 179

Literary Criticism Series
Cumulative Topic Index

This index lists all topic entries in Gale's *Children's Literature Review* (CLR), *Classical and Medieval Literature Criticism* (CMLC), *Contemporary Literary Criticism* (CLC), *Drama Criticism* (DC), *Literature Criticism from 1400 to 1800* (LC), *Nineteenth-Century Literature Criticism* (NCLC), *Short Story Criticism* (SSC), and *Twentieth-Century Literary Criticism* (TCLC). The index also lists topic entries in the Gale Critical Companion Collection, which includes the following publications: *The Beat Generation* (BG), and *Harlem Renaissance* (HR).

Topic Index

fiction into film: comparative essays, 200-23

Finance and Money as Represented in Nineteenth-Century Literature NCLC 76: 1-69
historical perspectives, 2-20
the image of money, 20-37
the dangers of money, 37-50
women and money, 50-69

Folklore and Literature TCLC 86: 116-293
overviews and general studies, 118-144
Native American literature, 144-67
African-American literature, 167-238
folklore and the American West, 238-57
modern and postmodern literature, 257-91

Food in Literature TCLC 114: 1-133
food and children's literature, 2-14
food as a literary device, 14-32
rituals involving food, 33-45
food and social and ethnic identity, 45-90
women's relationship with food, 91-132

Food in Nineteenth-Century Literature NCLC 108: 134-288
overviews, 136-74
food and social class, 174-85
food and gender, 185-219
food and love, 219-31
food and sex, 231-48
eating disorders, 248-70
vegetarians, carnivores, and cannibals, 270-87

French Drama in the Age of Louis XIV LC 28: 94-185
overview, 95-127
tragedy, 127-46
comedy, 146-66
tragicomedy, 166-84

French Enlightenment LC 14: 81-145
the question of definition, 82-9
le siècle des lumières, 89-94
women and the salons, 94-105
censorship, 105-15
the philosophy of reason, 115-31
influence and legacy, 131-44

French New Novel TCLC 98: 158-234
overviews and general studies, 158-92
influences, 192-213
themes, 213-33

French Realism NCLC 52: 136-216
origins and definitions, 137-70
issues and influence, 170-98
realism and representation, 198-215

French Revolution and English Literature NCLC 40: 96-195
history and theory, 96-123
romantic poetry, 123-50
the novel, 150-81
drama, 181-92
children's literature, 192-5

French Symbolist Poetry NCLC 144: 1-107
overviews, 2-14
Symbolist aesthetics, 14-47
the Symbolist lyric, 47-60
history and influence, 60-105

Futurism, Italian TCLC 42: 269-354
principles and formative influences, 271-9
manifestos, 279-88
literature, 288-303
theater, 303-19
art, 320-30
music, 330-6
architecture, 336-9
and politics, 339-46
reputation and significance, 346-51

Gaelic Revival See Irish Literary Renaissance

Gates, Henry Louis, Jr., and African-American Literary Criticism CLC 65: 361-405

Gay and Lesbian Literature CLC 76: 416-39

Gay and Lesbian Literature See also Contemporary Gay and Lesbian Literature

Generation of 1898 Short Fiction SSC 75: 182-287
overviews and general studies, 182-210
major short story writers of the Generation of 1898, 210-86
Azorín, 210-16
Emilia Pardo Bazán, 216-34
Vicente Blasco Ibáñez, 234-36
Gabriel Miró, 236-43
Miguel de Unamuno, 243-68
Ramon del Valle-Inclán, 268-86

German Exile Literature TCLC 30: 1-58
the writer and the Nazi state, 1-10
definition of, 10-4
life in exile, 14-32
surveys, 32-50
Austrian literature in exile, 50-2
German publishing in the United States, 52-7

German Expressionism TCLC 34: 74-160
history and major figures, 76-85
aesthetic theories, 85-109
drama, 109-26
poetry, 126-38
film, 138-42
painting, 142-7
music, 147-53
and politics, 153-8

The Ghost Story SSC 58: 1-142
overviews and general studies, 1-21
the ghost story in American literature, 21-49
the ghost story in Asian literature, 49-53
the ghost story in European and English literature, 54-89
major figures, 89-141

The Gilded Age NCLC 84: 169-271
popular themes, 170-90
Realism, 190-208
Aestheticism, 208-26
socio-political concerns, 226-70

***Glasnost* and Contemporary Soviet Literature** CLC 59: 355-97

Gothic Drama NCLC 132: 95-198
overviews, 97-125
sociopolitical contexts, 125-58
Gothic playwrights, 158-97

Gothic Novel NCLC 28: 328-402
development and major works, 328-34
definitions, 334-50
themes and techniques, 350-78
in America, 378-85
in Scotland, 385-91
influence and legacy, 391-400

The Governess in Nineteenth-Century Literature NCLC 104: 1-131
overviews and general studies, 3-28
social roles and economic conditions, 28-86
fictional governesses, 86-131

The Grail Theme in Twentieth-Century Literature TCLC 142: 1-89
overviews and general studies, 2-20
major works, 20-89

Graphic Narratives CLC 86: 405-32
history and overviews, 406-21
the "Classics Illustrated" series, 421-2
reviews of recent works, 422-32

Graphic Novels CLC 177: 163-299
overviews and general studies, 165-198
critical readings of major works, 198-286
reviews of recent graphic novels, 286-299

Graveyard Poets LC 67: 131-212
origins and development, 131-52
major figures, 152-75
major works, 175-212

Greek Historiography CMLC 17: 1-49

Greek Mythology CMLC 26: 193-320
overviews and general studies, 194-209
origins and development of Greek mythology, 209-29
cosmogonies and divinities in Greek mythology, 229-54
heroes and heroines in Greek mythology, 254-80
women in Greek mythology, 280-320

Greek Theater CMLC 51: 1-58
criticism, 2-58

Hard-Boiled Fiction TCLC 118: 1-109
overviews and general studies, 2-39
major authors, 39-76
women and hard-boiled fiction, 76-109

The Harlem Renaissance HR 1: 1-563
overviews and general studies of the Harlem Renaissance, 1-137
primary sources, 3-12
overviews, 12-38
background and sources of the Harlem Renaissance, 38-56
the New Negro aesthetic, 56-91
patrons, promoters, and the New York Public Library, 91-121
women of the Harlem Renaissance, 121-37
social, economic, and political factors that influenced the Harlem Renaissance, 139-240
primary sources, 141-53
overviews, 153-87
social and economic factors, 187-213
Black intellectual and political thought, 213-40
publishing and periodicals during the Harlem Renaissance, 243-339
primary sources, 246-52
overviews, 252-68
African American writers and mainstream publishers, 268-91
anthologies: *The New Negro* and others, 291-309
African American periodicals and the Harlem Renaissance, 309-39
performing arts during the Harlem Renaissance, 341-465
primary sources, 343-48
overviews, 348-64
drama of the Harlem Renaissance, 364-92
influence of music on Harlem Renaissance writing, 437-65
visual arts during the Harlem Renaissance, 467-563
primary sources, 470-71
overviews, 471-517
painters, 517-36
sculptors, 536-58
photographers, 558-63

Harlem Renaissance TCLC 26: 49-125
principal issues and figures, 50-67
the literature and its audience, 67-74
theme and technique in poetry, fiction, and drama, 74-115
and American society, 115-21
achievement and influence, 121-2

Havel, Václav, Playwright and President CLC 65: 406-63

Topic Index

Topic Index

AMERICAN

Adams, Andy **56**
Adams, Brooks **80**
Adams, Henry (Brooks) **4, 52**
Addams, Jane **76**
Agee, James (Rufus) **1, 19**
Aldrich, Bess (Genevra) Streeter **125**
Allen, Fred **87**
Anderson, Maxwell **2, 144**
Anderson, Sherwood **1, 10, 24, 123**
Anthony, Susan B(rownell) **84**
Atherton, Gertrude (Franklin Horn) **2**
Austin, Mary (Hunter) **25**
Baker, Ray Stannard **47**
Baker, Carlos (Heard) **119**
Bambara, Toni Cade **116**
Barry, Philip **11**
Baum, L(yman) Frank **7, 132**
Beard, Charles A(ustin) **15**
Becker, Carl (Lotus) **63**
Belasco, David **3**
Bell, James Madison **43**
Benchley, Robert (Charles) **1, 55**
Benedict, Ruth (Fulton) **60**
Benét, Stephen Vincent **7**
Benét, William Rose **28**
Bettelheim, Bruno **143**
Bierce, Ambrose (Gwinett) **1, 7, 44**
Biggers, Earl Derr **65**
Bishop, Elizabeth **121**
Bishop, John Peale **103**
Black Elk **33**
Boas, Franz **56**
Bodenheim, Maxwell **44**
Bok, Edward W. **101**
Bourne, Randolph S(illiman) **16**
Boyd, James **115**
Boyd, Thomas (Alexander) **111**
Bradford, Gamaliel **36**
Brautigan, Richard **133**
Brennan, Christopher John **17**
Brennan, Maeve **124**
Brodkey, Harold (Roy) **123**
Bromfield, Louis (Brucker) **11**
Broun, Heywood **104**
Bryan, William Jennings **99**
Burroughs, Edgar Rice **2, 32**
Burroughs, William S(eward) **121**
Cabell, James Branch **6**
Cable, George Washington **4**
Cahan, Abraham **71**
Caldwell, Erskine (Preston) **117**
Campbell, Joseph **140**
Cardozo, Benjamin N(athan) **65**
Carnegie, Dale **53**
Cather, Willa (Sibert) **1, 11, 31, 99, 132, 152**
Chambers, Robert W(illiam) **41**
Chambers, (David) Whittaker **129**
Chandler, Raymond (Thornton) **1, 7**
Chapman, John Jay **7**
Chase, Mary Ellen **124**
Chesnutt, Charles W(addell) **5, 39**

Childress, Alice **116**
Chopin, Katherine **5, 14, 127**
Cobb, Irvin S(hrewsbury) **77**
Coffin, Robert P(eter) Tristram **95**
Cohan, George M(ichael) **60**
Comstock, Anthony **13**
Cotter, Joseph Seamon Sr. **28**
Cram, Ralph Adams **45**
Crane, (Harold) Hart **2, 5, 80**
Crane, Stephen (Townley) **11, 17, 32**
Crawford, F(rancis) Marion **10**
Crothers, Rachel **19**
Cullen, Countée **4, 37**
Cummings, E. E. **137**
Darrow, Clarence (Seward) **81**
Davis, Rebecca (Blaine) Harding **6**
Davis, Richard Harding **24**
Day, Clarence (Shepard Jr.) **25**
Dent, Lester **72**
De Voto, Bernard (Augustine) **29**
Dewey, John **95**
Dickey, James **151**
Dreiser, Theodore (Herman Albert) **10, 18, 35, 83**
Dulles, John Foster **72**
Dunbar, Paul Laurence **2, 12**
Duncan, Isadora **68**
Dunne, Finley Peter **28**
Eastman, Charles A(lexander) **55**
Eddy, Mary (Ann Morse) Baker **71**
Einstein, Albert **65**
Erskine, John **84**
Faulkner, William **141**
Faust, Frederick (Schiller) **49**
Fenollosa, Ernest (Francisco) **91**
Fields, W. C. **80**
Fisher, Dorothy (Frances) Canfield **87**
Fisher, Rudolph **11**
Fisher, Vardis **140**
Fitzgerald, F(rancis) Scott (Key) **1, 6, 14, 28, 55, 157**
Fitzgerald, Zelda (Sayre) **52**
Fletcher, John Gould **35**
Foote, Mary Hallock **108**
Ford, Henry **73**
Forten, Charlotte L. **16**
Freeman, Douglas Southall **11**
Freeman, Mary E(leanor) Wilkins **9**
Fuller, Henry Blake **103**
Futrelle, Jacques **19**
Gale, Zona **7**
Garland, (Hannibal) Hamlin **3**
Gilman, Charlotte (Anna) Perkins (Stetson) **9, 37, 117**
Ginsberg, Allen **120**
Glasgow, Ellen (Anderson Gholson) **2, 7**
Glaspell, Susan **55**
Goldman, Emma **13**
Green, Anna Katharine **63**
Grey, Zane **6**
Griffith, D(avid) Lewelyn W(ark) **68**
Griggs, Sutton (Elbert) **77**
Guest, Edgar A(lbert) **95**

Guiney, Louise Imogen **41**
Haley, Alex **147**
Hall, James Norman **23**
Handy, W(illiam) C(hristopher) **97**
Harper, Frances Ellen Watkins **14**
Harris, Joel Chandler **2**
Harte, (Francis) Bret(t) **1, 25**
Hartmann, Sadakichi **73**
Hatteras, Owen **18**
Hawthorne, Julian **25**
Hearn, (Patricio) Lafcadio (Tessima Carlos) **9**
Hecht, Ben **101**
Heller, Joseph **131, 151**
Hellman, Lillian (Florence) **119**
Hemingway, Ernest (Miller) **115**
Henry, O. **1, 19**
Hergesheimer, Joseph **11**
Heyward, (Edwin) DuBose **59**
Higginson, Thomas Wentworth **36**
Himes, Chester **139**
Holley, Marietta **99**
Holly, Buddy **65**
Holmes, Oliver Wendell Jr. **77**
Hopkins, Pauline Elizabeth **28**
Horney, Karen (Clementine Theodore Danielsen) **71**
Howard, Robert E(rvin) **8**
Howe, Julia Ward **21**
Howells, William Dean **7, 17, 41**
Huneker, James Gibbons **65**
Hurston, Zora Neale **121, 131**
Ince, Thomas H. **89**
James, Henry **2, 11, 24, 40, 47, 64**
James, William **15, 32**
Jewett, (Theodora) Sarah Orne **1, 22**
Johnson, James Weldon **3, 19**
Johnson, Robert **69**
Kerouac, Jack **117**
Kinsey, Alfred C(harles) **91**
Kirk, Russell (Amos) **119**
Kornbluth, C(yril) M. **8**
Korzybski, Alfred (Habdank Skarbek) **61**
Kubrick, Stanley **112**
Kuttner, Henry **10**
Lardner, Ring(gold) W(ilmer) **2, 14**
Lewis, (Harry) Sinclair **4, 13, 23, 39**
Lewisohn, Ludwig **19**
Lewton, Val **76**
Lindsay, (Nicholas) Vachel **17**
Locke, Alain (Le Roy) **43**
Lockridge, Ross (Franklin) Jr. **111**
London, Jack **9, 15, 39**
Lovecraft, H(oward) P(hillips) **4, 22**
Lowell, Amy **1, 8**
Malamud, Bernard **129**
Mankiewicz, Herman (Jacob) **85**
March, William **96**
Markham, Edwin **47**
Marquis, Don(ald Robert Perry) **7**
Masters, Edgar Lee **2, 25**
Matthews, (James) Brander **95**
Matthiessen, F(rancis) O(tto) **100**
McAlmon, Robert (Menzies) **97**

477

Nationality Index

MEXICAN

Azuela, Mariano **3**
Gamboa, Federico **36**
Garro, Elena **153**
Gonzalez Martinez, Enrique **72**
Ibargüengoitia, Jorge **148**
Nervo, (Jose) Amado (Ruiz de) **11**
Reyes, Alfonso **33**
Romero, José Rubén **14**
Villaurrutia, Xavier **80**

NEPALI

Devkota, Laxmiprasad **23**

NEW ZEALANDER

Mander, (Mary) Jane **31**

NICARAGUAN

Darío, Rubén **4**

NORWEGIAN

Bjoernson, Bjoernstjerne (Martinius) **7, 37**
Bojer, Johan **64**
Grieg, (Johan) Nordahl (Brun) **10**
Hamsun, Knut **151**
Ibsen, Henrik (Johan) **2, 8, 16, 37, 52**
Kielland, Alexander Lange **5**
Lie, Jonas (Lauritz Idemil) **5**
Obstfelder, Sigbjoern **23**
Skram, Amalie (Bertha) **25**
Undset, Sigrid **3**

PAKISTANI

Iqbal, Muhammad **28**

PERUVIAN

Arguedas, José María **147**
Palma, Ricardo **29**
Vallejo, César (Abraham) **3, 56**

POLISH

Asch, Sholem **3**
Borowski, Tadeusz **9**
Conrad, Joseph **1, 6, 13, 25, 43, 57**
Peretz, Isaac Loeb **16**
Prus, Boleslaw **48**
Przybyszewski, Stanislaw **36**
Reymont, Wladyslaw (Stanislaw) **5**
Schulz, Bruno **5, 51**
Sienkiewicz, Henryk (Adam Alexander Pius) **3**
Singer, Israel Joshua **33**
Witkiewicz, Stanislaw Ignacy **8**

PORTUGUESE

Pessoa, Fernando (António Nogueira) **27**
Sa-Carniero, Mario de **83**

PUERTO RICAN

Hostos (y Bonilla), Eugenio Maria de **24**

ROMANIAN

Bacovia, George **24**
Caragiale, Ion Luca **76**
Rebreanu, Liviu **28**

RUSSIAN

Aldanov, Mark (Alexandrovich) **23**
Andreyev, Leonid (Nikolaevich) **3**
Annensky, Innokenty (Fyodorovich) **14**
Artsybashev, Mikhail (Petrovich) **31**
Babel, Isaak (Emmanuilovich) **2, 13**
Bagritsky, Eduard **60**
Balmont, Konstantin (Dmitriyevich) **11**
Bely, Andrey **7**

Berdyaev, Nikolai (Aleksandrovich) **67**
Bergelson, David **81**
Blok, Alexander (Alexandrovich) **5**
Bryusov, Valery Yakovlevich **10**
Bulgakov, Mikhail (Afanas'evich) **2, 16**
Bulgya, Alexander Alexandrovich **53**
Bunin, Ivan Alexeyevich **6**
Chekhov, Anton (Pavlovich) **3, 10, 31, 55, 96**
Der Nister **56**
Eisenstein, Sergei (Mikhailovich) **57**
Esenin, Sergei (Alexandrovich) **4**
Fadeyev, Alexander **53**
Gladkov, Fyodor (Vasilyevich) **27**
Gumilev, Nikolai (Stepanovich) **60**
Gurdjieff, G(eorgei) I(vanovich) **71**
Guro, Elena **56**
Hippius, Zinaida **9**
Ilf, Ilya **21**
Ivanov, Vyacheslav Ivanovich **33**
Kandinsky, Wassily **92**
Khlebnikov, Velimir **20**
Khodasevich, Vladislav (Felitsianovich) **15**
Klimentov, Andrei Platonovich **14**
Korolenko, Vladimir Galaktionovich **22**
Kropotkin, Peter (Aleksieevich) **36**
Kuprin, Aleksander Ivanovich **5**
Kuzmin, Mikhail **40**
Lenin, V. I. **67**
Mandelstam, Osip (Emilievich) **2, 6**
Mayakovski, Vladimir (Vladimirovich) **4, 18**
Merezhkovsky, Dmitry Sergeyevich **29**
Nabokov, Vladimir (Vladimirovich) **108**
Olesha, Yuri **136**
Pavlov, Ivan Petrovich **91**
Petrov, Evgeny **21**
Pilnyak, Boris **23**
Prishvin, Mikhail **75**
Remizov, Aleksei (Mikhailovich) **27**
Rozanov, Vassili **104**
Shestov, Lev **56**
Sologub, Fyodor **9**
Stalin, Joseph **92**
Tolstoy, Alexey Nikolaevich **18**
Tolstoy, Leo (Nikolaevich) **4, 11, 17, 28, 44, 79**
Trotsky, Leon **22**
Tsvetaeva (Efron), Marina (Ivanovna) **7, 35**
Zabolotsky, Nikolai Alekseevich **52**
Zamyatin, Evgeny Ivanovich **8, 37**
Zhdanov, Andrei Alexandrovich **18**
Zoshchenko, Mikhail (Mikhailovich) **15**

SCOTTISH

Barrie, J(ames) M(atthew) **2**
Brown, George Douglas **28**
Buchan, John **41**
Cunninghame Graham, Robert (Gallnigad) Bontine **19**
Davidson, John **24**
Doyle, Arthur Conan **7**
Frazer, J(ames) G(eorge) **32**
Lang, Andrew **16**
MacDonald, George **9, 113**
Muir, Edwin **2, 87**
Murray, James Augustus Henry **117**
Sharp, William **39**
Tey, Josephine **14**

SLOVENIAN

Cankar, Ivan **105**

SOUTH AFRICAN

Bosman, Herman Charles **49**
Campbell, (Ignatius) Roy (Dunnachie) **5**
La Guma, Alex **140**
Mqhayi, S(amuel) E(dward) K(rune Loliwe) **25**
Plaatje, Sol(omon) T(shekisho) **73**
Schreiner, Olive (Emilie Albertina) **9**

Smith, Pauline (Urmson) **25**
Vilakazi, Benedict Wallet **37**

SPANISH

Alas (y Urena), Leopoldo (Enrique Garcia) **29**
Aleixandre, Vicente **113**
Barea, Arturo **14**
Baroja (y Nessi), Pio **8**
Benavente (y Martinez), Jacinto **3**
Blasco Ibáñez, Vicente **12**
Echegaray (y Eizaguirre), Jose (Maria Waldo) **4**
García Lorca, Federico **1, 7, 49**
Jiménez (Mantecón), Juan Ramón **4**
Machado (y Ruiz), Antonio **3**
Martinez Sierra, Gregorio **6**
Martinez Sierra, Maria (de la O'LeJarraga) **6**
Miro (Ferrer), Gabriel (Francisco Victor) **5**
Onetti, Juan Carlos **131**
Ortega y Gasset, José **9**
Pereda (y Sanchez de Porrua), Jose Maria de **16**
Pérez Galdós, Benito **27**
Ramoacn y Cajal, Santiago **93**
Salinas (y Serrano), Pedro **17**
Sender, Ramón **136**
Unamuno (y Jugo), Miguel de **2, 9, 148**
Valera y Alcala-Galiano, Juan **10**
Valle-Inclán, Ramón (Maria) del **5**

SWEDISH

Bengtsson, Frans (Gunnar) **48**
Dagerman, Stig (Halvard) **17**
Ekelund, Vilhelm **75**
Heidenstam, (Carl Gustaf) Verner von **5**
Key, Ellen (Karolina Sofia) **65**
Lagerkvist, Pär **144**
Lagerloef, Selma (Ottiliana Lovisa) **4, 36**
Söderberg, Hjalmar **39**
Strindberg, (Johan) August **1, 8, 21, 47**
Weiss, Peter **152**

SWISS

Canetti, Elias **157**
Frisch, Max (Rudolf) **121**
Hesse, Herman **148**
Ramuz, Charles-Ferdinand **33**
Rod, Edouard **52**
Saussure, Ferdinand de **49**
Spitteler, Carl (Friedrich Georg) **12**
Walser, Robert **18**

SYRIAN

Gibran, Kahlil **1, 9**

TURKISH

Sait Faik **23**

UKRAINIAN

Aleichem, Sholom **1, 35**
Bialik, Chaim Nachman **25**

UGANDAN

p'Bitek, Okot **149**

URUGUAYAN

Quiroga, Horacio (Sylvestre) **20**
Sánchez, Florencio **37**

WELSH

Davies, William Henry **5**
Evans, Caradoc **85**
Lewis, Alun **3**
Thomas, Dylan (Marlais) **1, 8, 45, 105**

YUGOSLAVIAN

Andrić, Ivo **135**

TCLC-157 Title Index

ISBN 0-7876-8911-4

90000